elements of psychology

second edition

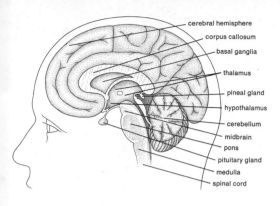

cerebral hemisphere
corpus callosum
basal ganglia
thalamus
pineal gland
hypothalamus
cerebellum
midbrain
pons
pituitary gland
medulla
spinal cord

Page 80, Figure 4.4

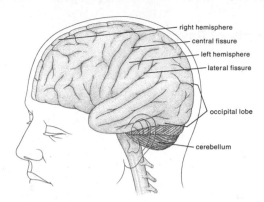

right hemisphere
central fissure
left hemisphere
lateral fissure
occipital lobe
cerebellum

Page 80, Figure 4.5

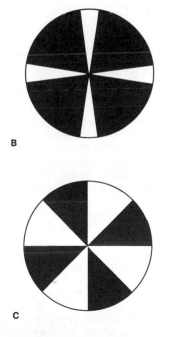

B

C

Page 167, Box 28

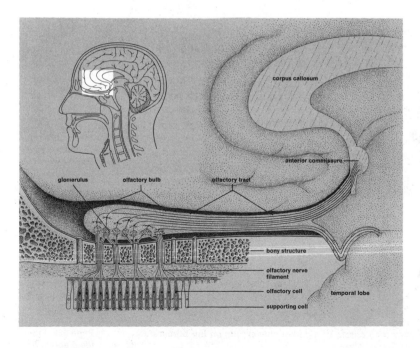

corpus callosum
anterior commissure
glomerulus
olfactory bulb
olfactory tract
bony structure
olfactory nerve filament
olfactory cell
supporting cell
temporal lobe

Page 276, Figure 18.2

Elements of Psychology

First Printing, Second Edition, March 1969

Errata

Page 35, Figure 1.6 *Caption, line 5 should read:* at right and are collected from the several vials at left

Page 76, Figure 4.2 *Caption, line 14 should read:* also (f). The inrush of the sodium (c and f) causes the

Page 233, Figure 15.1 *Caption: Numbered paragraph 1 should read:* 1. An object in the visual field is reversed both horizontally and vertically when projected on the retina: The right part of the object (the point of the arrow) is projected on the left half of the retina; the left part of the object is projected on the right half of the retina; and the object as a whole is projected upside down. *Numbered paragraph 3 should read:* 3. In the diagram the eye is focused directly on the "T" of the word "OUT." Therefore part of the "U" falls on the blind spot where there are no retinal cells (see p. 237).

Page 242, Figure 15.5 *Credit:* G. Wald and P. K. Brown, "Human Rhodopsin," *Science,* 127 (1958), p. 222.

Page 250, Figure 16.1 *Caption, line 12 should read:* (indicated by colors of a darker shade) falls on the bottoms

Page 251, Figure 16.1 *The part of the figure under the*

label: projection on left retina *belongs under the label:* projection on right retina *and vice versa.*

Page 301, Figure 20.1 *Credit line should read:* Courtesy Professor Norman Guttman.

Page 319, Box 58 *Lower graph, key should be transposed so that the solid line designates* meaningful words *and the dashed line designates* nonsense syllables.

Page 505, Box 113 *The following line should appear after the first line of the fourth paragraph:* these investigators, they found, not only that the youngest infants preferred the least complex check-

Page 607, Figure 37.5 *Description under the photo at the lower left should read:* chronic stress effects *rather than* counter stress effects.

Page 622 *In the centered equation under the heading:* Standard Deviation, a Σ should precede the d^2 of the numerator.

Page 639, Figure 38.15 *Caption, the last line should read:* tained sample is 19.5 and the σ_m is 1.97.

Page 688, Figure 41.3 *Part of the key which appears within the diagram has been omitted: a solid line should designate Negro scores; a dashed line should designate white scor*

Elements of Psychology

David Krech and Richard S. Crutchfield
University of California, Berkeley

Norman Livson
California State College, Hayward

**With the collaboration of A. Robert Rollin
and William A. Wilson, Jr.**
University of Connecticut

Alfred A. Knopf, New York, 1969

THIS IS A BORZOI BOOK

Published by Alfred A. Knopf, Inc.

First Printing

Library of Congress Catalog Card Number: 68–13168

Manufactured in the United States of America.

First published, 1958. Reprinted eleven times.
Second Edition revised, reset, and printed from new plates, 1969.

to those who would
gladly teach and gladly learn

preface to
the first edition

The preface of a book usually turns out to be the most pleasant chapter to write. This is not only because, in the inverted and realistic logic of book-making, it is the last chapter which needs to be written, but primarily because it is the one chapter where the authors can make explicit their debt to the many people who have helped make the book possible.

We cannot hope to name all who deserve our thanks, but we can, at the very least, indicate those of our friends and colleagues who contributed well beyond the normal call of friendship and good will.

Of course no book is completely the work of the authors whose names are listed on the title page, and the unnamed authors of this book, as is true of any scientific enterprise, are legion. First among these are the research workers in psychology and the cognate sciences upon whose findings we have attempted to build a systematic approach to the science of human behavior. Since this book is not only a presentation of a body of scientific knowledge and speculation, but is also a teaching instrument, it reflects, we hope, all that we have learned from our students—at Swarthmore College, Bryn Mawr College, Mount Holyoke College, Harvard University, the University of Oslo, the University of Colorado, and the University of California—where we have been privileged to teach and to share with these students the adventure of examining anew, every year, what man has learned about man.

Most immediately, we are indebted to several friends who have read and criticized the first draft of the manuscript incorporated in this book. Among them is Professor Leo Postman who carefully and painstakingly went over large sections of our manuscript, especially those dealing with perception and learning, and whose helpful criticism has not only saved us from a number of errors, but whose sound scholarship has helped make this book so much the better. Professor Mark R. Rosenzweig has read, and made suggestions relating to, the chapters on physiology and neurology, and has been most generous in helping to design the anatomical illustrations used in those chapters. Professor Edwin E. Ghiselli, through his rare combination of a basic familiarity with the "pure" science of psychology and a mastery of industrial psychology, has made many valuable suggestions which we have not hesitated to incorporate. Professors Paul H. Mussen and John P. McKee have reviewed in a critical and sympathetic manner our chapters on child development, and we have profited from their reviews. Professor

Rheem F. Jarrett has gone over our chapter on statistics, and has made several contributions to it. Professor Hans Wallach read and made a number of helpful comments on our chapters on perception, as did Professor Mason Haire, whose interest and kind enthusiasm have encouraged us greatly. And finally, as have so many others, we have profited from the wisdom and encouragement of Professor Robert B. MacLeod.

We have attempted to present in this book an effective teaching instrument. If we have been successful, a large part of the credit properly belongs to the illustrators and draftsmen who strove to put a number of our notions into interesting, clear, and pleasing graphic form. Mr. Walter Schwarz, the scientific illustrator, has shown infinite patience, a perceptive intelligence, and his usual high order of skill in his execution of the anatomical drawings. Mr. Wolfgang Lederer helped us by his imaginative capacity to translate the "write-ups" of experimental procedure into charming and clear illustrations, and Mrs. Katherine Eardley, who is responsible for the charts, graphs, and some of the line drawings of the book, has always been a friend and colleague upon whose patience, talent, and imagination we have drawn liberally. Mr. Herbert Kling, technician of our laboratory, has done yeoman's service in his able photographic and reproductive work.

Miss Jean Pierce was responsible for typing the many, many versions of our manuscript. Her interest, skill, and intelligence made her not only our typist, but our first critical reader and editor. She has helped enormously. Finally, it is with gratitude that we acknowledge our indebtedness to Dr. Ray Ginger, Editor of the College Department of Alfred A. Knopf, Inc., whose careful and sensitive readings improved both how we have had our say, and, at many points, what we have had to say.

We have been most fortunate in the generosity of many individuals who have made available to us original figures, photographs, and manuscripts: Professors Wilder Penfield, Heinrich Klüver, Donald B. Lindsley, Raúl Hernández-Peón, and Per Saugstad.

We wish also to express our most sincere appreciation to the following journals, publishers, and individuals who have granted permission to reproduce tables, figures, illustrations, and excerpts:

American Journal of Psychology
American Philosophical Society
American Psychological Association
Appleton-Century-Crofts, Inc.
Archives of Psychology
Mrs. Madison Bentley
British Journal of Psychology
Dodd, Mead & Co.
Dover Publications, Inc.
Genetic Psychology Monographs
Ginn & Company
Harper & Brothers
Henry Holt & Co., Inc.
Houghton Mifflin Company
Journal of Comparative Psychology
Journal of Electroencephalography and
   Clinical Neurophysiology
Journal of Experimental Psychology
Journal of General Psychology
Journal of Genetic Psychology
Journal of Speech and Hearing Disorders
Liveright Publishing Corp.
The Macmillan Co.

McGraw-Hill Book Co.
W. W. Norton & Company, Inc.
Perception Demonstration Center of
   Princeton University
Princeton University Press
Psychological Monographs
Psychological Review
Science
Scientific American
Scientific Publishing Company
The Technology Press
University of California Press
University of Chicago Press
University of Wichita Press
D. Van Nostrand Co., Inc.
The Viking Press, Inc.
John Wiley & Sons, Inc.
Yale University Press

David Krech / Richard S. Crutchfield
Berkeley, California
September, 1957

preface to
the second edition

Eleven years have gone by since the publication of the first edition of this book. It is a long time as revisions go and even a longer time as psychology goes these days.

This new edition is a thoroughgoing revision, as it had to be to transmit to the reader the changing structure and substance of our science. (As one index of this change, about half our references are new in this edition.) Where the essential framework of what we originally had to say has proved durable, we have been content to check our facts and update our documentation. Where particular areas have undergone significant growth in theory and in data, reflecting intensive research, we have enlarged and revised our treatment in an attempt to encompass this growth. Finally, there has been substantial response to the questioning, criticisms, and suggestions from dozens of colleagues and hundreds of students who have "talked back" to us throughout the past decade. The collection of letters from students remains a particularly precious possession. Our primary debt, however, is to the research workers in psychology. Because psychology has established or increased fruitful bonds with a variety of other disciplines during the last decade, we gratefully extend our thanks to the workers in these vineyards as well.

Readers of the first edition will notice some new varieties on the vine. There is far greater attention in this revision to the broad area of personality development, with attendant new emphases on mental disorders and the psychotherapies. Our treatment of motivation and emotion has been extended. Instrumental learning and conditioning have also been treated in somewhat greater detail. The section on language has been enriched by data and formulations from the relatively young field of developmental psycholinguistics. We have also sought to incorporate some of the more exciting recent findings of the renascent physiological psychology. Throughout the text the reader will find an intensified developmental focus. What remains unchanged is our faith that the diverse phenomena of human behavior and experience can still be usefully viewed and understood within a single, relatively coherent framework. Reaching and stretching, sometimes perhaps too far, we have continually attempted to see unity of principle and interrelation of function within the wide world of psychological events.

Turning out a textbook is not a one-man, or even a five-man, operation. Inevitably, as we have already indicated, we have been helped by many of our colleagues, whose counsel, asked or unasked, has been freely given. We cannot begin to name them, nor are we certain that they would like us to do so. But, to confirm our rule by two exceptions, we do acknowledge and appreciate the substantial efforts of Professor Egerton Ballachey, which have contributed most importantly to our social-psychology units; and we must mention the help of Florine Livson, whose expertise in personality theory and clinical psychology has left its mark on this book.

We have been particularly fortunate to have available for this revision the excellent services of two of our original illustrators, permitting us again to thank Mrs. Katherine Eardley for new charts and graphs and Mr. Walter Schwarz for revisions and additions to his initial set of anatomical drawings. Several able and patient ladies have stood by us through the shifting winds of too many manuscript drafts. Let us honor them: Ann Brixner, Elizabeth Csiki, Susan Goldhaber, Margaret Heick, Carolyn Kehrli, Nancy McDougald, and Nancy Polin.

Susan Thatcher deserves a separate paragraph—and much more. Typing the final manuscript (with generous if unscheduled editorial asides), handling copyright matters, collating and preparing an 800-item list of references—for all these things and many others we have no doubt forgotten, we are profoundly grateful to her.

Estelle Whelan and Elaine Rosenberg, of Alfred A. Knopf, have been our editors in this enterprise—a difficult task that they have performed with skill, creativity, and graciousness. For all this, and more, we thank them.

David Krech / Richard S. Crutchfield / Norman Livson
Berkeley, California
A. Robert Rollin / William A. Wilson, Jr.
Storrs, Connecticut
January, 1969

to the reader

In this book we have tried to fulfill two objectives. Our first purpose was to organize the various facts, observations, theories, and speculations of psychology in an attempt to uncover whatever inherent harmony may exist within the data of psychology. To this end, the Introduction provides a preview of the book and is intended to facilitate the integration and understanding of the details in the fifty units.

We have also attempted to create an effective teaching instrument. To further this objective we have introduced several devices intended to aid the reader in his study of the material. Among these devices are the grouping of the contents of the book into relatively short units, the overview that introduces each unit, the Boxes, and the glossary at the end of each unit, and annotated suggested readings at the end of each major part.

We have chosen to cast the material of psychology into units rather than into chapters for several reasons. We wanted to break away from the Procrustean practice of forcing into chapters of approximately equal size topics that vary greatly in the length of treatment they need. By ending discussions on any topic when no more is to be said, we have also saved ourselves the embarrassment of marriages of inconvenience between ill-mated topics joined together to fulfill arbitrary chapter page quotas. The result is, we feel, more natural units—hence the name—that permit more succinct and focused discussions in fewer words. The use of units should prove less distracting to the student; at the same time the instructor is offered a bonus in flexibility. Units, we have found, are more easily shifted about. An unwanted topic is more easily disposed of by deleting the entire unit. The instructor should thus be able to tailor the book to his own course needs. We have cross-referenced extensively so that the fabric of a course plan should remain whole under any permutation of units.

The Boxes contain material of various types. Some of the Boxes supplement the main discussion in the text; some contain further illustrative material; some provide the reader with an opportunity to carry out his own demonstration experiments; but most of them present research evidence for the generalizations stated in the text.

The last may be of particular interest. No science is sounder than its research, and, if the reader of this book is to achieve a *critical understanding* of the science of psychology, he must become familiar not only with the "conclusions" of psychology but also with the research behind these generalizations. This knowledge will enable him to understand the conclusions better and to evaluate them critically. The Boxes present enough detail to acquaint the reader with the reasoning, methods, and difficulties of research in psychology. We have also provided the reference for each study described, thus enabling him to go to the original source, should any study attract his special interest.

Almost every book in science contains two types of material that a student is expected to master: generalizations and specific information. To aid the student we have provided two types of "summaries." Some of the general principles that merit repetition and emphasis are summarized in the overviews, which the reader is urged to study when he begins a unit and also when he finishes it.

The more detailed information has been summarized at the end of each unit in the glossaries. Because the specific concepts and information of any science are summarized by its technical language, definitions of technical terms are important. Each term in the glossaries is described in some detail, so that the student will be aided in his review of the concept covered by the particular term.

The General Glossary repeats each term in the unit glossaries, without a definition but with an index to the page on which the definition may be found. This General Glossary should be a good tool for reviewing the entire book.

We hope that these various devices will help the students at either end of the log.

contents

boxes

elements of psychology

contents

introduction:
the study of man

Psychology brings to itself a number of special problems that rarely, if ever, plague other areas of scientific inquiry. Probably the reason is that psychology studies man, and man is much more likely to have strong convictions about himself than about any other natural phenomenon in his world. "Breathes there a man with soul so dead who never to himself has said"—and believed—that he knows "what makes people tick?" Barring a few unreflective souls, each of us, in the course of living, almost inevitably evolves a more or less articulate set of notions about the nature of man.

Few of us would be presumptuous enough to attempt, untutored and on our own, to provide explanations of gravity, exploding stars, or chemical reactions. More of us might embark upon explanations of historical events, of political change, and of economic trends—but, confronted by an approved "expert" who possesses appropriate academic credentials, we would usually defer to his superior knowledge and experience. Not so in psychology. In this field we encounter, with some justification, the argument that all men live and grow in human societies and that, in the process, much that is

true is learned about psychological phenomena. Proverbs and homilies abound that lay claim to the understanding and explanation of human behavior. Literature of all forms has never shied away from psychological interpretation—nor have politicians, theologians, philosophers, artists, doctors, and businessmen.

Faced with this array of opinion on matters psychological, the psychologist has a double responsibility; he must lay to rest wrong beliefs and at the same time replace them with what, at the moment, he feels are the right ones. The mythology that has grown up around human behavior is seemingly endless, so that some of the things we shall discuss in this book may contradict highly cherished, long-held, and even altogether incompatible sets of beliefs. Thus, both "Clothes make the man" and "You can't make a silk purse out of a sow's ear" have considerable truth in them, but it is up to psychological investigation to establish the degree to which, and under what circumstances, external factors can determine and change personality and under what circumstances genetic factors underlying personality override environmental forces.

Much of "popular psychology" is true. For example: We all know that children, human and animal, form close attachments to their parents and, quite early in life, gain an awareness of their "own kind." But in such "obvious" truths as this the psychologist finds a whole host of challenging problems. For example, when and under what circumstances do these close attachments form (see Box 1, p. 4)?

Psychology, more than other sciences, is also afflicted with a number of taboo topics—"dark corners" that the psychologist, perhaps as much as the layman, is reluctant to illuminate. A valuable book, entitled appropriately enough *Taboo Topics* (Farberow, 1966), enumerates and discusses a number of admittedly important research areas within psychology that, to a lesser or greater extent, are researched with probably less vigor than they deserve and that seem to elicit from the scientific community something more than the usual and desirable degree of criticism. Among these topics are human sexual behavior (particularly homosexuality), suicide (and the subject of death in general), and the study of religious experience. Parapsychological phenomena—more commonly known as ESP or mental telepathy—also are typically assigned to this outlaw status (see Box 2, p. 6).

This ruling out of certain problems as legitimate concerns for psychological research is a dangerous practice, particularly when important human phenomena are involved. Fortunately, many of these taboos are beginning to yield to irresistible human curiosity, and psychology is fast approaching the fulfillment of its inescapable credo: Nothing that is human is alien to the Compleat Psychologist.

The Strategy and Plan of This Book

In studying man, the psychologist resorts to a convenient bit of scientific fiction. He knows perfectly well that a person is a "whole" organism. He knows that he cannot study man in a piecemeal fashion without losing the unity of

Box 1

A Moment of Imprinting, A Lifetime of Loyalty

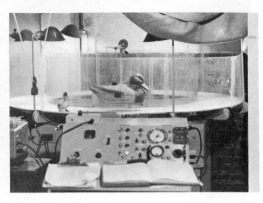

Imprinting is a curious form of early learning that, for many species, appears to play a key role in the formation of strong attachments of the very young. Perhaps the most distinctive feature of imprinting is its tendency to occur very early in life and within rather narrow age limits known as the "critical period." Specifically, an animal is imprinted when, on the basis of brief exposure to a particular object during its critical period, it thereafter behaves toward that object in a number of ways that seem to indicate a deep and enduring attachment to it (Box 10, p. 62 suggests that imprinting may occur before birth).

Some evidence for imprinting has been found in dogs, sheep, guinea pigs, even buffalo. But imprinting finds its most clear-cut expression in birds of various species. Perhaps the most popular species for work in imprinting is the mallard duckling, and a good deal of our knowledge of the imprinting process in this bird comes from the research of Eckhard Hess, a psychologist at The University of Chicago. On the basis of a number of experiments, Hess has demonstrated that a duckling becomes imprinted upon an object (usually a wooden decoy of a male mallard) after following that object for a short time—ten minutes can be enough time for imprinting to take place (see photograph). This imprinting is most easily achieved at about fourteen hours after hatching but can occur—with decreasing ease—through the first day or two of life. Thereafter, perhaps because the duckling has by that time developed a fear of new and strange objects, imprinting is difficult if not impossible. Once imprinted on an object, the duckling tends to follow that object, even under discouraging circumstances or in the presence of a more "natural" object of its affection; for example, it will remain loyal to the male decoy and resist the attractions of a live female mallard.

Not all objects are equally qualified for imprinting. Some animals imprint only upon members of their own species or upon closely related ones; others can range more widely in imprintability; thus, ducklings and other birds have been successfully imprinted on human beings. One factor that has been shown to affect "attractiveness" of an imprinting object is its general perceptual liveliness. Working with baby chicks, P. H. Klopfer and J. P. Hailman found that the chicks were much more likely to follow a visually striking mallard-duck decoy (yellow, covered with multicolored patches and stripes) than to follow a plain white one. Chicks that were initially exposed, during the critical period, to the plain decoy subsequently tended to follow the vividly colored decoy rather than the plain one.

The process of imprinting—once regarded as a rather unitary one in which the young animal defined its "mother," discovered its "own kind," and identified the target of its later sexual advance —is beginning to appear somewhat more complex. F. Schutz, working in the laboratory of Konrad Lorenz—a German zoologist and naturalist who has made many contributions to the understanding of imprinting and similar phenomena—has reported that ducks of various species show somewhat different critical periods for different aspects of a general imprinting process. Their primary attachment to a "mother" occurs first and quite early, but not until five or six weeks of age does the duckling "identify" with its species. If the duckling is exposed to one species for the first three weeks of life and then to another species, the latter species is chosen for mating when sexual maturity is achieved.

A question that has not yet been answered is whether or not anything like imprinting takes place in human infants. A baby certainly does develop, somewhere about six months of age, an unmistakable and discriminating attachment to the person, usually the mother, who takes care of him, and some psychologists have suggested that these six months define the critical period for humans. This view is supported by the fact that babies also begin to show fear of strangers at about this age, and such fear responses may signal the end of the critical period. Although this hypothesis merits—and is obtaining—research attention, we must beware making too easy a translation of this sort. All species do develop attachments and a sense of their "own kind," however, and this process does seem to occur later for more slowly developing species. This fact makes adaptive sense, as imprinting—if it is to occur—should have a critical period well within the time during which the infant remains dependent. The result would be to ensure that, barring the intervention of manipulative psychologists, every animal would be in the presence of its own species during its critical period. Otherwise, the rambling lamb might choose a casually encountered wolf as its mother, with obvious and strikingly maladaptive consequences.

E. H. HESS. 1964. Imprinting in Birds, *Science*, 146, 1128–39.
P. H. KLOPFER and J. P. HAILMAN. 1964. Perceptual Preferences and Imprinting in Chicks, *Science*, 145, 1333–4.
F. SCHUTZ. 1965. Sexuelle Prägung bei Anatiden, *Z. Tierpsychol.*, 22, 50–103.
Photo courtesy E. H. Hess, The University of Chicago.

Box 2

A Censored Sense?

One of the most prominent researchers in the field of extrasensory perception (ESP)—and one who has tried to have psychology keep an "open mind" on this controversial phenomenon—is Gardner Murphy of the Menninger Foundation. In his assessment of the reasons for the status of ESP and of the whole field of *parapsychology* as a "taboo topic," he begins with a telling anecdote. He relates the incident of a scientist who, prior to the turn of the century, presented before a meeting of the British Association for the Advancement of Science some new experimental findings concerning ESP or, as it was then commonly called, "mental telepathy." Hermann Ludwig Ferdinand von Helmholtz, one of the principal scientific figures of the day, was present at the meeting and is reported to have declared, "Neither the testimony of all the members of the British Association for the Advancement of Science, nor my own testimony from what my own eyes recorded, could convince me of telepathy, since it is manifestly impossible."

A reaction of this sort is as common today as it was decades ago. Experimental work in the area continues but is carried on by relatively few investigators and generally under a cloud of suspicion, if not outright derision. Why is this so? There are many reasons—some perhaps irrational but others well rooted in sound scientific skepticism. The notion of "thought transference" has been historically assigned to (and welcomed into) the realm of the "occult" or "supernatural." Scientists are loath to risk the accusation that they are taking "black magic" seriously. The fact that there are relatively few scientists in this field leaves room for shoddy work and even fakery. And the occasional dramatic exposé has reinforced the suspicion of all efforts to investigate these phenomena.

The crux of the scientist's objection to this research area is indicated by its very name—"extrasensory perception"—a term that implies that perception occurs without known receptor structures and processes. The implied lack of a physical basis for ESP is emphasized by other alleged phenomena of parapsychology: clairvoyance (the ability to perceive future events) and psychokinesis (the ability to move objects through thought alone). The argument, as Helmholtz said, is that the events claimed by parapsychology are "impossible" because they require us to abandon a keystone of all scientific thought: that all events must ultimately have some material basis that can be observed and measured and that can find a place within our physicalistic notion of the nature of reality.

Quite possibly a physical basis for ESP and other similar phenomena will eventually be discovered; if and when it is, scientists will gladly reverse their present verdict of incredibility. Some of

the man he is describing. But he also knows that he cannot achieve any understanding of man unless he proceeds *as if* man *could* be studied piecemeal. He has no choice, for man-as-a-whole is just too big a piece for any scientist to handle with the instruments and concepts now available. This bit of scientific fiction has proved to be profitable, not only for psychology but for all sciences. Taking a whole, breaking it down into parts, and studying each part intensively constitute a common method of science. It is the method of *analysis*.

In studying man, then, we break down our inquiry into five different parts. We analyze first the operation of *hereditary mechanisms* and their interaction with environmental fac-

the more ardent proponents of ESP deny that it need have a physical basis and assert that it is indeed "extra"-sensory. Most, however, acknowledge that a physical basis should be sought but meanwhile are determined to continue collecting data on something for which our present knowledge provides no explanation.

One study, by T. D. Duane and T. Behrendt, ophthalmologists at the Jefferson Medical College, may indicate the existence of an ESP-like phenomenon in *some* identical twins. Starting with the fact that closing one's eyes elicits an alpha rhythm in the EEG (electroencephalographic or "brain wave") patterns emanating from the cortex (see Unit 36, p. 567), these investigators recorded the EEGs from both members of sets of male identical twins, when only one twin actually closed his eyes occasionally in the course of an experimental session. For two of fifteen pairs of twins, they found that eye closure in either one of the twins instantly generated alpha rhythm patterns in *both*, despite the fact that the twins were physically isolated from one another. This occurrence was not merely an occasional coincidence but was detected in every instance of eye closure over several experimental sessions. This consistent simultaneity of eye closure never occurred for the other thirteen pairs of twins, nor did it occur when unrelated individuals were paired in the experimental situation. This finding seems to reduce the likelihood that some mechanical artifact in the testing situation was responsible for the "transmission" apparently found in the two pairs of twins. Furthermore, it does not seem likely that the results could be explained by bias in the evaluations of the EEG records. These evaluations were made "blindly"—that is, the experimenters did not know the identity of a given record when they made their evaluation.

Do these data imply that identical twins are inevitably "in contact" with each other? Certainly not, because only two of fifteen pairs showed the phenomenon. Did these two pairs differ in any way from the others? The investigators report that the successful pairs were quite at ease in the testing situation, whereas the unsuccessful ones were generally anxious and apprehensive. Does ESP perhaps work only with genetically identical individuals under conditions of minimal emotional distraction? The investigators do not draw this conclusion; they raise it only as a question for future research. Research on any problem must proceed in this way: by asking questions, making observations, then posing newly raised questions on the basis of results.

Science no doubt has come up with many wrong answers in the course of its history, and it will continue to do so. Continual experimentation, however, provides the ready and reliable remedy for error. Wrong answers there may be, but *verboten* questions there cannot be if psychology is ever to complete its study of man.

G. MURPHY. 1966. Parapsychology, in N. L. FARBEROW, ed., *Taboo Topics* (New York: Atherton).

T. D. DUANE and T. BEHRENDT. 1965. Extrasensory Electroencephalographic Induction Between Identical Twins, *Science*, 150, 367.

T. D. DUANE. 1965. Personal communication.

tors in order to determine the course of his *growth and development*. Then we turn to the study of his *perceptions*—how he sees, hears, smells, tastes, and feels the world about him. We next examine man as he attempts to *adapt* to the demands made upon him—how he solves problems, learns, remembers, and forgets. Then we concern ourselves with the *motives* and *emotions* of man—his needs, desires, aspirations, fears, and loves. Finally, we consider man as a unique and whole individual—we look into his *abilities* and *personality* and his *social relations* with other men.

But what the psychologist tears asunder, he also seeks to join together. He uses not only the method of analysis but also the method of *synthesis;* he puts the analyzed parts together to recreate an abstracted but scientifically useful facsimile of the original whole. As we progress through this book, we shall attempt such synthesis from time to time.

To aid in this task, it will be helpful to get an overview of the entire "plot" of the book and of some of the major principles of each part. In this way we may be able to see more clearly how the findings in each section of the book fit in with those of the other sections. We shall therefore present now a brief synopsis of what we are to be concerned with in the succeeding pages—the study of man.

Part One: Origins, Growth, and Development

The child is father of the man. To understand how the unique individual that is man develops, we trace him from his very beginnings. We first consider the process of conception and the mechanisms by which the genetic endowments of the parents combine to determine the hereditary base upon which the individual must build. We find here the first clues to the understanding of the two great generalizations that can be made about living creatures: Like breeds like, and each individual is unique.

Since the behavior of the organism is always limited and directed by its anatomy and physiology, the psychologist's study of the behavior of the child has gone hand in hand with his study of the biological growth of the child. Out of these studies, conducted in several complementary ways, have come a number of developmental principles relating function (behavior) to structure. These principles tell the story of the development of the human being in terms of integrated changes in structure and function. And we find that in general the story is also one of gradual, systematic unfolding of more and more complex systems. Adolescence, however, with its culmination in sexual maturity, seems to represent a sort of "turning point" in this otherwise relatively smooth developmental

sequence. Developmental features of young adulthood and then the "middle years" are next examined; finally, we turn to the special problems and challenges of aging.

All of this, and everything that follows, implies of course the essential role of the brain and nervous system in behavior. We take up, therefore, the basic facts about the structure and function of man's nervous system to conclude Part One.

Part Two: Perception

Each man lives in his own world. His world is what he experiences—what he perceives, feels, thinks about, and imagines. And what he perceives, feels, thinks about, and imagines depends upon the physical and social environments in which he lives and upon his own biological nature, particularly the way his brain and nervous system work. His world is his own, and different from the worlds of others, because his brain and nervous system and his physical and social environments are not exactly like anyone else's.

How the person behaves depends upon this idiosyncratic world that is peculiarly his own. To understand his behavior we must first ask, What is the specific nature of his world? Our first step, therefore, is to describe the worlds of men as they perceive them.

Perception and the Stimulus

Perception depends, in the first instance, upon the characteristics of the physical stimulus—light waves, sound waves, physical displacement, chemical particles, heat radiation. Thus light waves of a certain frequency will normally evoke in us the sensation of red; light waves of other frequencies will normally evoke other color sensations. A great deal of information is now available that relates the nature of the physical stimulus to the nature of the resulting sensation. And recent work has indicated that we (or at least some of the lower animals) may even be able to sense radiant energy for which no known sense organ exists (see Box 3, p. 10)!

But these relations between physical energies and perception, measured by a variety of psychophysical methods and expressed in so-called "psychophysical laws," are not simple one-to-one relationships between single stimuli and single percepts. Stimuli rarely occur singly (as in a single pinpoint of light) but mostly occur in company with a host of other stimuli. Somehow, out of this myriad of stimuli, a perception results that can best be described as organized or patterned. We therefore concern ourselves with the crucial problem of organization. Several generalizations describing this patterning have been suggested from laboratory studies. These generalizations help us to describe how the person perceives order in complex stimulus situations so that his perceptions reflect the realities of the external environment and at the same time permit him to attend to and emphasize those aspects of the environment that are biologically important for him. We explore such problems as the perception of depth or distance (for which no direct receptors exist) and the facts and determinants of the perceptual constancies (an object looks much the same under varying stimulus conditions).

Perception and Psychological State

A person's perception of physical stimuli is modulated by his immediate and temporary states of need, emotion, and "mental set." The thirsty man, the frightened man, and the hunter may perceive the same set of stimuli very differently. The more enduring characteristics of the person, such as his personality and his store of experiences, can also help to determine his perception. In this connection we examine some generalizations that, it is hoped, will lead eventually to laws relating perception to personality and to prior learning.

Perception and Physiology

A complex sequence of events occurs between the moment a stimulus impinges on the eye, the ear, the nose, or any receptor, and the eventual arrival of a neural signal in the brain.

The story of these physiological processes that underlie perception is far from complete. Yet the parts of the story we already know help us to account for many of the complex relationships between stimulus patterns and perceptual responses discovered in the psychologist's laboratory. For example, the receptors themselves are capable of a great deal of integration of stimuli. The receptors and the brain are constantly in action; they do not wait passively to be activated by outside stimuli. Stimuli do not fall on a "quiet" recording instrument or on isolated parts of a system. The nervous system is so constructed and so operates that perception is determined by the integrated pattern of activities going on in large parts of the brain—not solely in that part of the brain that receives the messages from the receptors in the first place. Much of the action in the brain is not represented in awareness. New evidence suggests, however, that at least some aspects of "unconscious" brain functioning are under voluntary control (see Box 4, p. 12).

Part Three: Adaptive Behavior

Man is not only a perceiving animal—perceiving his immediate environment. Man must also find food, shelter, and safety. To do so, he must solve problems, learn, remember, think, and acquire skills.

This third part of the book is concerned with an examination of such adaptive behavior. We find that we cannot understand problem solving without making extensive use of the perceptual principles we have already examined, but we must also anticipate our later discussion (in Part Four) of motivational and emotional prin-

Box 3

An X-Ray Sense

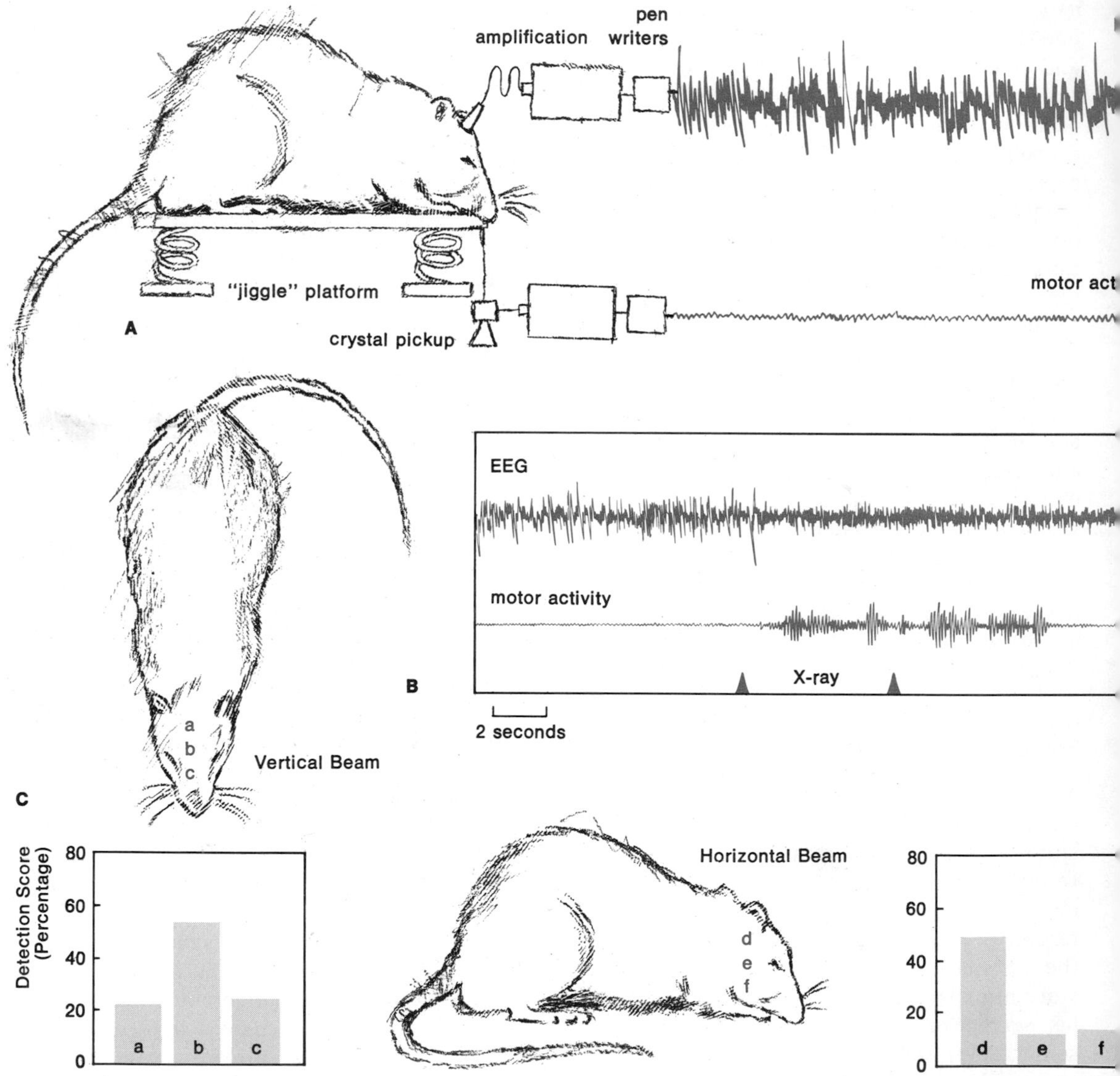

amplification

pen writers

"jiggle" platform

A

crystal pickup

motor act

B

EEG

motor activity

X-ray

2 seconds

C

Vertical Beam

a
b
c

Detection Score (Percentage)

80
60
40
20
0

a b c

Horizontal Beam

d
e
f

80
60
40
20
0

d e f

Well ahead of its competitors (among them, ESP) to qualify as a "new dimension of mind" is the apparent ability, at least of rats, to detect minute amounts of ionizing radiation. Beginning with some early research by the psychologist John Garcia, working at Massachusetts General Hospital in Boston, a team of investigators has been accumulating some impressive experimental evidence that makes a strong case for the existence of such a "radiation" sense. Using radiation as weak as 50 milliroentgens (about the same strength as that used for human chest X-rays), they have demonstrated the rat's ability to detect very rapidly (within 0.2 seconds) such low-dose radiation.

Among the responses that clearly show the immediate effect of this radiation are a tendency to increased motor activity and to a change in electroencephalographic (EEG or "brain wave") rhythms (for more on the latter, see Unit 36, p. 567). Both these responses may be measured in the same experimental apparatus (see Figure A). The rat is "wired up" for measurement of his EEGs with electrodes permanently implanted in its skull. The animal is placed upon a "jiggle" platform, so that its slightest movements can be detected. The electrical impulses generated by both EEGs and "jiggling" are amplified and then activate a pen writer, which produces visible continuous records of these responses.

Figure B is a typical record of an X-ray detection experiment conducted with a rat that was asleep at the beginning of the experiment. The left side of each record is characteristic of sleeping—minimal movement of the platform and high-amplitude sweeps of the "alpha" rhythm. Approximately one second after the onset of the X-ray, a shift in the EEG and an increase in motor activity are clearly observable. In short, the animal has been aroused—as evinced by the electrophysiological activity in his brain and by his gross muscular movements. For this arousal to have occurred, the rat —by some mechanism—must have sensed the radiant energy. Also and not surprisingly—if we are willing to assume that some kind of sensory receptor is involved—more intense irradiation increases the arousal response, although, as is true with other senses, repeated exposure results in "adaptation," a reduction in the frequency and vigor of the arousal reaction.

But what is the receptor mechanism for X-rays, if indeed there is such a sense? Figure C illustrates an ingenious experiment that helps to localize the area in which such receptors might someday be found. The detection response occurred when the rat stopped drinking water from the tube, the animal having previously been trained to stop drinking when irradiated—it was shocked if it did not stop drinking. With vertical X-ray beams directed, respectively, at regions a, b, and c, the stop in drinking is most immediate when radiation passes downward through the head in region b. Now, with horizontal beams striking the head at different levels, region d (toward the top) is clearly most sensitive. When one examines the region in which vertical b and horizontal d intrsect, it is found that it contains, most prominently, the olfactory bulbs—receptors for odors. For a number of reasons, however, it seems unlikely that radiation sensitivity reduces to the sense of smell.

Perhaps only the rat has this "sixth sense" and man cannot detect low-level radiation as easily. If so, then one may speculate that in the radioactive rubble remaining after World War III the rat will inherit the earth, for only he will be able to detect—and avoid—the fatal radiations.

B. H. FEDER, J. GARCIA, N. A. BUCHWALD, and R. A. KOELLING. 1964. Detection of Minute Doses of Ionizing Radiation. Paper read at the VII Symposium Neuroradiologicum, New York, September.
J. GARCIA, N. A. BUCHWALD, B. H. FEDER, R. A. KOELLING, and L. TEDROW. 1964. Sensitivity of the Head to X-Ray, *Science*, 144, 1470–2. Figure C adapted courtesy J. Garcia, Harvard University Medical School; copyright 1964 by the American Association for the Advancement of Science.
Figure B adapted from C. D. Hull, *et al.*, 1965, Role of the Olfactory System in Arousal to X-Ray, *Nature*, 205, 627, by permission. Figures A and B courtesy J. Garcia, Harvard University Medical School.

Box 4

Conditioned Introspection

A recently developed method for the study of human consciousness promises to open a new frontier of psychology. Combining methods of instrumental conditioning (see Unit 20, p. 301) and electrophysiology, psychologist Joe Kamiya has been training subjects to discern and control their brain activity. In 1958, while at The University of Chicago, he found that subjects could learn to discern the "inner feel" of the occurrence of alpha rhythms in their own electroencephalograms (EEGs or "brain waves").

The alpha rhythm is an irregularly recurring train of electrical oscillations (eight to twelve cycles per second) generated by the human brain and detectable through the scalp by surface electrodes. The trains vary in duration from a fraction of a second to several seconds, usually becoming more persistent when the eyes are closed and the subject is allowed to relax. Drowsiness and sleep, however, lead to disappearance of the rhythm. Without special training we are not aware of any spontaneous fluctuations in consciousness that may be related to the rapid, irregular recurrences of alpha (many times per minute). (EEGs are more fully discussed in Unit 36, p. 567.)

The training procedure Kamiya used in his Chicago experiments was to have his subject (who had been informed about the nature of the alpha rhythm) make a guess, whenever a bell sounded, whether he was at the time in an "A state" (presence of the alpha rhythm) or in a "B state" (absence of alpha). The bell was sounded two to six times per minute—half the time it was sounded when the subject was generating alpha rhythms and half the time when he was not. The subject was required to keep his eyes closed throughout the training trials. After each guess he was told whether or not he had guessed correctly.

In two to ten sessions of sixty trials each, many (but not all) subjects began to choose correctly which of the two states they were in *significantly more often than sheer guessing would have*

ciples. For, as we describe adaptive behavior and examine the conditions under which it proceeds, we see that problem solving is initiated in response to needs, is guided by perceptions, and often ends in an intense emotional experience. The relationship between adaptive behavior and motives and emotions is both intimate and complex. Indeed, it appears that the very process of problem solving is itself an expression of a basic motive. We frequently behave as if the solution of a problem were a reward in itself. And it even appears that some lower animals share this motive with man (for an experimental demonstration of this point, see Box 5, p. 14).

Adaptive behavior encompasses an overwhelming variety of different kinds of problems: discovering a cure for cancer, memorizing a list of history dates, designing a bridge, learning the route from home to school, investigating the neurological basis of thought, driving a car, learning to read and write, or recalling one's exact whereabouts at 10 P.M. on Friday, September 17.

achieved. Some could not easily find words to describe how they discerned the two states. Many subjects reported, however, that the presence of any sort of visual image was associated with the "B state."

In a later series of experiments conducted at the University of California Medical Center in San Francisco, Kamiya found that subjects could be taught to *control* the states associated with alpha rhythms. In his experiments, he devised an electronic system that would deliver a steady audible tone whenever an alpha train was detected by the electronic system via electrodes attached to the subject's scalp and that would stop the tone immediately upon the disappearance of the alpha. In short, the subject received auditory information signaling the state of his EEG. The subject was encouraged to try to discover ways to increase (or decrease) the proportion of time that the tone would be present. Within one to six sessions of about one hour each, most subjects achieved clear differences in performance between trials for increasing the tone and trials for decreasing the tone. Verbal reports on effective methods for *decreasing* the duration of the tone (and therefore the alpha rhythm) usually involved the use of visual imagery (for example, seeing faces or familiar objects). Because in these series the subjects' eyes were closed throughout, any "seeing" could occur only in the "mind's eye."

Reports on how to *increase* the duration of the tone were more diffuse, vague, and ethereal. "Calmness," "singleness of attention," "relaxation," "submitting to the tone," and "serenity" were expressions for this state frequently heard from the subjects.

Subjects who had had long practice in *meditation* (Zen and yoga) were especially efficient in increasing the duration of the alpha train.

These experiments suggest that some of the more elusive psychological properties of human life—those having to do with subjective experience—may be approachable with new techniques. Perhaps "expanding consciousness" will then come to be a relatively simple learning process. If it does—for better or for worse—the aura of mysticism currently associated with the phrase will inevitably disappear.

J. KAMIYA. 1967. Conditioned Introspection. Paper read at the Institute of Personality Assessment and Research, University of California, Berkeley.

J. STOYVA and J. KAMIYA. 1968. Electrophysiological Studies of Dreaming as the Prototype of a New Strategy in the Study of Consciousness, *Psychol. Rev.*, 75, 192–205.

Some of this adaptive behavior can be called "conditioning"; some, "learning"; some, "thinking"; some, "creative problem solving." Intertwined with all these behavior types, serving and even guiding their course, is man's language.

Conditioning and Learning

Many of the problems to be solved in our daily lives require nothing more than doing again what we have learned to do in the past—at times in a rather automatic and simplified manner, at other times in a flexible and responsive way. We are here dealing with conditioning or with simpler forms of learning. Involved are such vitally important processes as habit formation, memorizing, and skill acquisition. The nature and functions of language are of special interest, and we devote a considerable part of our discussion to the acquisition of language—the characteristic that differentiates man most clearly from all other creatures.

Box 5

Monkeys Solve a Problem for Its Own Sake

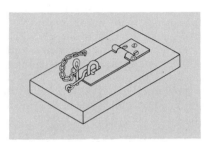

H. Harlow at the University of Wisconsin has shown that, even for monkeys, the solution of a problem may carry its own reward. He used the puzzle shown in the drawing. The pin and hook had to be opened in that order before the hasp could be raised.

In one experiment four rhesus monkeys, group A, had the assembled puzzle in their home cages for twelve days. Four group-B animals also had the puzzle, but the pin and hook were unassembled, and the hasp was raised. They could become familiar with the already opened puzzle, but there was nothing to solve. From time to time the puzzles in the A cages were checked and reassembled if they had been opened. On days thirteen and fourteen all eight monkeys were given the assembled puzzle for five five-minute periods.

In these tests the A monkeys opened the puzzle thirty-one times (see photograph), averaging less than thirty seconds per solution. The B monkeys opened the puzzle only four times, and the *best* score was sixty seconds. The A monkeys had learned to solve the puzzle during the first twelve days and had learned *without any reward from the experimenter*.

The A monkeys were then given additional tests one at a time. While the animal watched, a raisin was placed in a box, and the assembled puzzle was attached to the box so as to lock it. Then the monkey was released. Now the failures increased strikingly! And a new *kind* of error appeared. In the previous tests, without reward, the monkeys *never* touched the hasp first; with the food reward, they *always* erred by attacking (literally) the hasp first. The monkeys, when they had the raisin "in mind," could not restrain themselves from a direct attack.

"Personal involvement" and a highly desired reward may sometimes be bad for problem solving!

H. HARLOW. 1950. Learning Motivated by a Manipulation Drive, *J. Exper. Psychol.*, 40, 228–34. Figure adapted by permission.
Photo by Sponholz.

Creative Problem Solving

Creative problem solving refers to adaptive behavior in which a person produces something new and original as he attempts to cope with the problems facing him. We study, for example, how man goes about the business of explaining the events he sees about him, predicting events to come, and inventing or creating objects of utilitarian and aesthetic value. Experimental work in psychology is beginning to help us to understand these creative aspects of behavior. We find that there seem to be three basic determinants of creative problem solving: first, the nature of the problem, the circumstances under which the problem is presented, and the resulting stimulus pattern that confronts the person; second, the nature of the person's previously acquired knowledge (some of which, "badly" acquired, can inhibit creativity); and, third, the personality structure of the problem solver. The laboratory findings on these determinants point to ways of improving our own efforts at creative problem solving.

Adaptive Behavior and Physiology

Learning, even of the simplest kind and in the simplest organisms, is related, of course, to processes in some parts of the nervous system. More complex adaptive behavior depends upon the presence and effective functioning of the cerebral cortex, and different parts of the cortex contribute in different ways to various aspects of learning, remembering, and problem solving.

Only quite recently have we begun to discover something about the physiological changes in the nervous system that accompany the course of adaptive behavior. For example, it appears from psychophysiological evidence that memory has at least two stages: a short-term, quickly fading process during which the experience is initially stored; and a long-term set of mechanisms—involving physical, chemical, and physiological changes—contributing to the storage and availability of learned material over considerable periods of time.

Part Four: Motivation and Emotion

The fourth main section of the book takes up the important problems of motivation and emotion.

Patterns of Motives

The nature of man's motives has concerned people over many centuries. As different cultures have held different conceptions of human nature, so have their views of human motivation changed. Man has been regarded as a passive pawn of the fates or the gods, as a machine, as an animal, as a product of society, as a rational being, as an irrational creature. And with each of these different conceptions the story of man's motives has been rewritten. The modern synthesis of all these views provides a wide variety of specific motives. Some order can be made out of this variety by viewing all man's motives in terms of two general types of behavior: behavior directed at avoiding deficits, deprivations, threats, and disruptions; and behavior concerned with maximizing gratifications and enriching experience. Man's motives, in other words, do not consist only of seeking food when hungry, safety when frightened, shelter when cold; they also include the search for positive goals and varied stimulation. Fortunately, man is driven to explore and discover even when he is momentarily sated and secure; he seeks uncertainty, though not more than his adaptive capacities permit him to cope with effectively.

Arousal of Motives

Arousal of active states of motivation comes about through changes within the body of the organism, through changes in the physical and social environments of the individual, and through the "thoughts" of the person. The nature of the action is in part determined by the strength of the motive as well as by the nature of its goal. Too little motivation and too much may be equally harmful. An intensely desired reward may actually disrupt adjustive behavior; at the same time, insufficient motivation can be equally maladaptive.

Emotional Experience

It is difficult and perhaps not even useful to make a clear distinction between motives and emotions. The two grow hand in hand throughout development; for one thing, as our motives become more complex and differentiated, so do our emotional experiences. And, physiologically, they bear an intimate relation to each other.

Physiology of Motives and Emotions

Recent research has begun to give us a new understanding of how physiological processes relate to motivation and emotion. Instead of demonstrating, as past evidence seemed to indicate, that motivational and emotional states are dependent upon the "gut" responses of the organism—the reactions of his viscera, his glands, and so on—current research clearly indicates that the initiation and control of motives and emotions come from within the brain itself. Emotional and motivated behavior results both from visceral and from cortical factors. Both the "gut" and the brain are involved. This fact is another illustration of one of the major themes of this book: Most of man's behavior is integrated behavior.

Part Five: The Individual

In the first four sections we study the development of man as a developing biological organism, then man the perceiver, man the problem solver, and man the needful. But, as we said in the beginning, this division is merely one of convenience. There is in truth only one individual—the individual who perceives and thinks and strives. In the final section of the book we turn our attention to man the individual.

When we see a group of people, we are struck by the compelling fact of individual differences. The individual is unique. His pattern of perceptions, motives, emotions, and adaptive behavior is like no one else's.

Measurement

In order to make a scientific study of the extent and causes of individual differences among men, we must be able to measure these differences. The study of statistics permits us to acquire the techniques for such measurements. We examine the rationale of some of the fundamental statistical methods, like those involved in determining averages, variability of scores within a group, and the degree of relationship among different measurements.

As we study the theory and techniques of measurement, we find that we can never measure anything with perfect accuracy—whether the length of a table, the personality of a patient in a mental hospital, or the political attitudes of a group of voters. We also discover, however, that, although the values we obtain from our measurements are only estimates or approximations of the truth, nevertheless we can state the degree of probability that our estimates are within some specified distance from the truth. And we thus learn why the scientist must be content with "probable truth" rather than with absolute truth.

The Abilities of Man

Having learned how to measure individual differences among men (and the caution with which all measurements must be regarded), we turn to the study of the facts and theories concerning such differences. Men differ in many kinds of abilities—for example, mechanical, musical, and artistic abilities. All these abilities have been measured, but perhaps the most important characteristic in which men differ is intelligence. We find that, although much progress has been made in the measurement of intelligence, we are still not certain about many basic questions concerning it. Is it a single capacity of the person, or is it a cluster or grouping of many different capacities? Is intellectual ability mainly inherited, or is it mainly acquired through training and education after birth? What is the course of development of mental ability with age? How stable and predictable is an individual's intelligence over time? We examine all these questions.

The distribution of intelligence varies widely from the feeble-minded to the genius. Numerous studies seek to determine whether different groups or kinds of people are more intelligent than others. Differences in intelligence among different racial and national groups, and between groups differing in social class, have therefore been investigated. The evidence suggests that, as measured by current intelligence tests, there are consistent differences among such groups in average intelligence. But the interpretation of these differences is very difficult. For one thing, tests are characteristically more "fair" to one group than to another; in other words, they are often culturally biased. So also are educational opportunities and other factors that affect intellectual development. At the present time we can therefore only conclude that these differences result from hereditary and biological differences and also from differences of opportunity and environment among the groups tested.

Personality

There are numerous measurable patterns of individuality or personality. In trying to account for these different patterns, many theories of personality have been developed. In reviewing some of the major theories, we find that each includes to some degree the chief principles of perception, learning, and motivation, together with the principles of growth and development

of the child. It is here that we begin to see that a complete theory of personality will have to encompass all the principles we have encountered in the first four sections. It is in personality theory, perhaps, that the psychologist will most fully accomplish his task of synthesis.

One of the major questions discussed by all theories of personality is how the person handles emotional and motivational conflicts. Different people meet internal conflict in different ways, and it becomes clear that the methods of "defensive reaction" adopted by a person are consistent with his over-all personality. We also examine the more extreme incapacitating consequences of conflict as found in neuroses and psychoses. To do so helps us to assess some of the problems of mental illness and some of the various therapeutic methods that have been developed to treat them.

The Individual in Society

From the moment of birth man is surrounded by other people, and it is therefore clear that his social environment helps shape his development. Indeed, many problems of adjustment come from his relations to his society. But society is not something independent of the individual, a huge "impersonal" force that pushes man around. Society and its rules and regulations are human products—created by man and changeable by him. Therefore we end this book with a look at the individual in society.

An important factor in a person's social functioning is his "social perception," that is, how he perceives other people and groups, how he perceives such social institutions as the church, the state, and the economic structure and such social events as political campaigns, mob action, war, and religious services. We find that the principles of the perception of physical stimuli (studied in Part Two) help us to understand many of the more complex phenomena of "social perception."

We shall also find that how a person perceives another person helps to determine how he will feel about him; and, conversely, how a person feels about another will help to determine how he perceives him. This cause-and-effect circle helps us to understand the persistence of racial, national, and religious prejudice—or, more broadly, the persistence of pervasive social attitudes. Social attitudes are complex phenomena. They involve factors of motivation, emotion, adaptive behavior, and personality patterning as well as perceptual factors.

Finally, we examine some of the problems the person faces as a member in good standing of a social group—a family, club, school, or nation. The individual is frequently confronted with a difficult problem when he seeks to pre-serve his personal integrity and independence while also maintaining his prescribed duties, functions, responsibilities, and loyalties to his group. This is but one aspect of a major problem—perhaps the central question toward which the study of man is directed: As man is a social animal and cannot live alone, how can the liberty of the individual be maximized and the creativity of the person released through his relation with his society? An understanding of the elements of psychology, insofar as they are helpful in understanding the behavior of man, provides the beginnings of an answer to this question—perhaps the crucial question of our time.

Suggestions for Further Reading

BORING, E. G. 1950. *A History of Experimental Psychology*. 2nd ed. New York: Appleton.

    The experimental and theoretical beginnings from which modern psychology has evolved.

HYMAN, R. 1964. Paperback. *Nature of Psychological Inquiry*. Englewood Cliffs, N.J.: Prentice-Hall.

    A stimulating analysis of the processes involved in scientific investigation. Focusing on the philosophy rather than on the specific techniques of psychological inquiry, the author discusses "getting ideas, gathering facts, organizing and summarizing the findings, interpreting the data, and communicating the results."

JAMES, W. 1950. Paperback. *Principles of Psychology*. New York: Dover. Originally published 1890.

    This classic book, written by the major founder of American psychology, may still be read with profit by all students of psychology. By no means confined to the topics of Part One, it qualifies as a useful supplement to the whole of any introductory textbook.

MILLER, G. A. 1964. *The Science of Mental Life*. New York: Harper.

    A personalized and provocative treatment of selected important topics for the beginning psychology student.

MISIAK, H., and V. S. SEXTON. 1967. *History of Psychology: An Overview*. New York: Grune & Stratton.

    A good reference for "current" history, together with helpful discussions of the state of psychology country by country.

POSTMAN, L., ed. 1962. *Psychology in the Making*. New York: Knopf.

    The historical roots and current status of lively and controversial topics in psychology are presented in this set of highly readable essays.

part one

origins, growth, and development

UNIT 1

heredity and environment

overview / The evolution of life forms from the simplest organisms to man has involved an increasing complexity of structure and in general a greatly expanded flexibility for adaptation to a wide range of environmental challenges. The process of evolution, roughly speaking, has as its fundamental governing mechanism the phenomenon of natural selection. Species more able to adapt to changed environmental demands tend to survive; within species, those individuals best able to cope with these demands are more likely to remain alive and to procreate, thus passing on their particular genetic endowments.

At conception, a human individual starts off with one particular combination, among an almost infinite number of possible combinations, of twenty-three chromosomes from each parent so that, with the exception of identical twins, no two individuals have the same genetic base. The genes that make up the chromosomes determine very many human physical characteristics and even (at least in part) some psychological traits. The general rule is one of multiple determiners, that is, a given characteristic is under the control of a great number of separate genes.

The expression of genetic determinants, however, is substantially influenced by environmental factors from the moment of conception onward; intrauterine conditions affect development of the embryo and fetus, and environmental influences on maturation and development become even greater after birth.

The nature-nurture issue—the relative influence of genetic and environmental factors—continues to invite lively inquiry. We no longer seek the *one* factor responsible for a given characteristic; rather we speak of relative contributions from the two and, more importantly, admit to their interaction throughout development. In experimental behavior genetics, selective-breeding experiments with animals are providing insights on the nature-nurture question for behavioral as well as for physical characteristics. At the human level, studies of blood kin—twins, siblings, parents, and children—are beginning to provide comparable information regarding genetic and environmental determinants of behavior, particularly with respect to intelligence and personality.

In the beginnings of animal life on earth, simplicity of physical structure and an extremely narrow range of function were the rule. Yet, as we stressed in our Introduction, the hallmark of mankind is its enormous diversity. The permissible range of variation for many of man's characteristics is so very broad that we rarely know where the limits actually lie. On the need for oxygen there is a limiting level and we know it: A few minutes of total deprivation, and a man is dead. But what of the limits on human intelligence, on human skills, on human feelings and experience? Here it is only the uninformed or the arrogant who dare specify how far man can go. We need only contrast our lives today with those of people living a few decades ago to see how quickly the impossible becomes the commonplace in man's achievement and behavior. Or we can glance now at the lives of men throughout the world and immediately confront the seemingly endless variation among human societies in how the "average man" feels, thinks, and acts.

Certainly, man has come a long way, not only from his animal ancestors, but also from his own origin as a distinct species. He has not only come up in the world, but, in the sense of increasing diversity, he has also done a lot of moving sideways. When all men hunted for their food, all men were more alike. But as functions proliferated so did the kinds of men. The key to man's diversity is the key to the evolution of life forms—adaptation to environment. In evolution those new species that were able to adapt to the environmental conditions of their time were able to survive, reproduce, and—for a time—flourish. If conditions remain the same, then a species should forever endure. But conditions do change. Even if cataclysmic changes in the physical environment, an Ice Age for example, did not occur, less dramatic but nevertheless potent modifications in what is required to stay alive are inevitable. A once abundant natural food supply becomes depleted through consumption and at an increasing rate as the species thrives and multiplies; a new species comes upon the world scene and is predator to the earlier one or competes for its food supply.

Who survives? *Within* a species, those individuals who are best able to adapt to the new conditions of life: the strong, when strength can save the day; the fleet, when escape means survival; the intelligent, when intelligence can discover a solution to the new environmental problem. Thus the species continues, although its average characteristics change to reflect the increasing dominance of now this quality and now that quality. *Among* species, those that have sufficient individuals that can adapt will survive. Thus, raise the temperature of a lake, and some trout and some frogs (those that can best tolerate increased heat) will survive and reproduce; future generations in this lake will have increasingly high proportions of individuals able to tolerate warmer water. But drain the lake, and, as no trout can survive aridity, the whole trout species becomes extinct. Some frogs, however, may jump to survive as a species in another nearby lake. In short, adaptability is the inexorable *sine qua non* for survival. Species, as well as their individual members, cannot evade this law of life.

Judged by this standard, man is today preeminent. His ability as a species to adapt to new conditions, and through his technology even to change the conditions themselves, has no near rival. Fish swim, birds fly, and animals roam the land; man does all three. What is more, he is to be found living and thriving among ice floes, in dense jungle, in scorching desert, and—perhaps most impressive of all—in the concrete-

and-steel cities he has created. He has broader limits than other species on the ranges of temperature, aridity, altitude, and food sources within which he can survive and function effectively. But we must consider man's extensive adaptability as separable into two components: what a *man* can do and what *men* can do. Or, put another way, man is doubly blessed—in the range of environments to which a given man can learn to adapt and in the diversity of his kind. Each man has his limits, and they are necessarily narrower than those of his species. Sea-level dwellers, even after rigorous training, can rarely climb the highest mountain, yet the Sherpas of the Himalayas live and work comfortably at such altitudes.

Thus, what one man cannot do, or learn to do, his distant brother often can—and it is in such differences among mankind that its viability as a species and its hope for survival lies. As we said at the outset, we do not yet know the limits on what any one man can become, nor certainly on what mankind can become, given the full expression of the potential of the species for variation among its individual members. But we do know something about how a man comes to be what he is and how he comes to be different from his fellows. In a terse cliché, individual men are what they are because of their particular heredity and environment. We shall start with the first of these—heredity.

Hereditary Mechanisms

In sketching our portrait of man as an evolving species of enormous diversity and adaptability, we have so far totally ignored the mechanisms by which successive generations of mankind are linked one to the other. This link is obviously crucial, for without it the Darwinian story of evolution lacks its essential thread of continuity. What does it matter that the more adaptive members of a species tend to survive and to procreate if their progeny do not inherit the critical adaptive characteristics of the parents?

The picture of hereditary transmission, as it has been unveiled so far, is not described by the simple formula, "Like father, like son." The facts of the genetic mechanism demand that there be not only resemblances between parents and offspring, but also differences.

The Individual Begins

Individuality begins when a *sperm cell* from the father penetrates the wall of an *ovum* (or egg) from the mother and fertilizes it. Each sperm cell contains within it twenty-three *chromosomes*, the "carriers of heredity." This sperm derives from a germ cell in the father. Each mature germ cell of the father has twenty-three *pairs* of chromosomes, or a total of forty-six—the normal number of chromosomes found in all human cells (see Figure 1.1.).

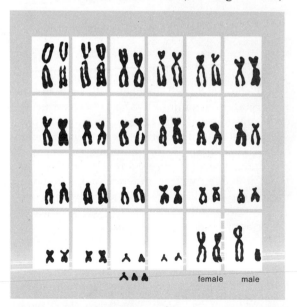

Figure 1.1. Paired human chromosomes. The first twenty-two pairs are found in both men and women. The last pair is X-X for a woman or X-Y for a man. Occasionally, instead of the normal two chromosomes found in pair 21 there occur three chromosomes (as shown in the colored margin). When this occurs the individual suffers from a condition known as trisomy-21 mental deficiency.
Courtesy of Margery W. Shaw, M.D., Department of Human Genetics, The University of Michigan, Ann Arbor, Michigan, and The Upjohn Company, Kalamazoo, Michigan.

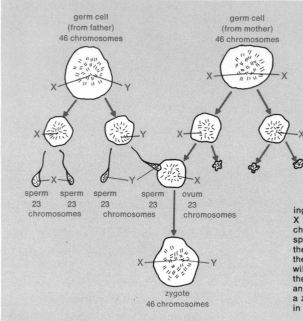

germ cell
(from father)
46 chromosomes

germ cell
(from mother)
46 chromosomes

X — Y

X — X

X

Y

X

X

sperm
23
chromosomes

sperm
23

sperm
23
chromosomes

sperm
23

ovum
23
chromosomes

X — X

Y

X

X — Y

zygote
46 chromosomes

Figure 1.2. Relations between the mature parental germ cells and the zygote. Each mature germ cell of both the father and mother (top of illustration) has the full number of chromosomes (twenty-three pairs, or forty-six chromosomes). When these germ cells reach full maturity, they undergo division and become ova (for the female) and sperm (for the male). Typically, only one of the ova is fully developed and can be fertilized; the others are shrunken and not functional.

During such division the chromosomes are assorted so that each sperm (and ovum) has only one member of each pair, that is, twenty-three chromosomes. When one sperm enters through the cell body of one ovum, a zygote is formed, and the zygote, of course, will have the full forty-six chromosomes. From the zygote a new organism develops.

One pair of the chromosomes is of a special kind—consisting of the X and Y chromosomes. The mature *male* cell has one X and one Y chromosome; the mature *female* cell has two X chromosomes. When the mature male germ cell divides into sperm, one of the resulting sperm receives the X and the other the Y. Each ovum, of course, receives an X. If the sperm with the Y chromosome happens to unite with the ovum, the zygote will have an X-Y pair (as in the illustration); if the sperm with the X chromosome fertilizes the ovum, then the zygote will have an X-X pair. A zygote with an X-Y pair will develop into a male; a zygote with an X-X pair will develop into a female. The zygote in the illustration will thus develop into a male.

When the germ cell reaches full maturity it undergoes division into two sperm cells. During such division, half the chromosomes go to one sperm and half to the other sperm. *Which* member of each pair of chromosomes goes to the particular sperm is purely a *random* matter. As there are twenty-three different pairs of chromosomes, the number of genetically *different* sperm that a single human male can produce is 2^{23}, or approximately 8 million.

In a similar manner, ova develop by division of mature germ cells in the mother. And following the same reasoning as above, a single human female can also produce approximately 8 million genetically different ova.

Thus, when the sperm penetrates the ovum the resulting *zygote* has its full complement of twenty-three pairs of chromosomes, one of each pair coming from the father and the other from the mother (see Figure 1.2.). In a single mating, therefore, any one of the 8 million different chromosome patterns of the sperm might combine with any of the 8 million different chromosome patterns of the ovum to form a single zygote. This means that the particular zygote that a particular father and a particular mother will produce is one of more than 60 trillion different possible ones.

Relatives Are the Same and Different

Chromosomes are the carriers of heredity only in the "transportation" sense. Each chromosome bears many sets of deoxyribose nucleic acid (DNA) molecules. These sets of DNA molecules are called *genes*. And it is the genes that are the determiners of inherited characteristics. The genes do not always stay put in their own chromosomes. There is a phenomenon known as *crossing-over*, which refers to the fact that occasionally, when the mature germ cell divides, one segment of a chromosome will break off and be exchanged with a corresponding segment from a homologous chromosome (see Figure 1.3.). The fact that chromosomes can exchange genes increases tremendously the already astronomically large number of genetically different zygotes that can be produced from human matings. The number of possible combinations of chromosomes in the zygote is practically infinite, and our reproductive system practically guarantees that, except in the case of identical twins who develop from a single zygote, no two brothers or sisters can ever be genetically the same. Put more generally, it is extremely unlikely (barring identical twins) that there are now or have ever been in the vast sea of humanity two people with the same genetic make-up. Heredity means individual differences.

On the other hand, no matter which combination of the chromosomes ends up in the zygote, nothing can be there that was not contributed by one of the parents. For example, if both parents have only genes for brown eyes, then no combination of their sperm and ova can produce blue-eyed offspring. In this sense, there is a definite limit to the individual differences possible in a family. For this reason, the offspring of a single set of parents will necessarily be more alike on the average than will unrelated individuals. Heredity also means similarity.

Identical Twins Because they are genetically identical, *identical twins* are of great interest to the psychologist concerned with the problem of heredity. How do identical twins come about?

The zygote multiplies by division. It first divides into two daughter cells, each of which is a complete and faithful replica of the other. We have seen that the single zygote has within it the full complement of chromosomes. This means that each daughter cell has within it the potentialities of becoming a complete individual. In most cases, however, this cell division does not mean cell separation. The two cells remain as parts of a single organism. If the two cells remain together, each one divides and subdivides until the 10 trillion cells of a human being have been formed (see Box 6, p. 26). As the number of cells increases, the mass of subdivided cells begins to become differentiated into bone cells, nerve cells, skin cells, and so forth. The *embryo*, which at first resembles an expanding ball, begins to take shape, and the first suggestions of a head, eyes, trunk, and limbs appear; eventually, it develops (at about six to eight weeks after conception) into the more differentiated *fetus*.

In some instances, however, the first two daughter cells do not stay together but actually separate. Now, they can develop into two separate individuals, through the division process occurring separately in the two daughter cells. Indeed, this actual separation can continue, so

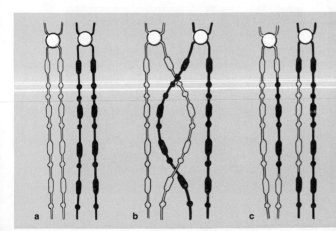

a   b   c

Figure 1.3. At one period of development of the mature germ cell, the two members of a pair of chromosomes (see a) approach each other and become intimately intertwined (see b). During this period one section of one chromosome may be exchanged with a corresponding section of the other chromosome, so that when the pair is separated again (see c) we have a recombination of genes in the two chromosomes (compare a and c). This phenomenon is called the "crossing-over of genes."

Box 6
Out of One, Many
—DNA and RNA

deoxyribose	large ball
phosphate	green ball
cytosine	small white ball
guanine	large white ball
adenine	large light green ball
thymine	small light green ball

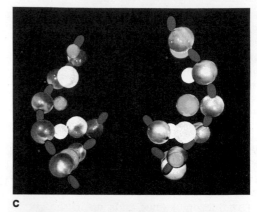

C

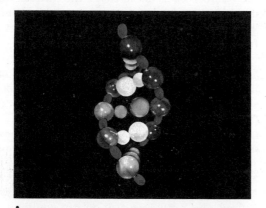

A

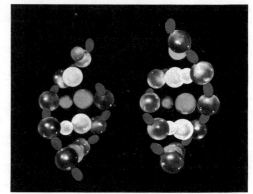

D

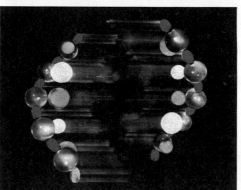

B

E

Until 1953 scientists could say only that "in some way" the full complement of forty-six chromosomes found in the fertilized ovum—the first cell of human life—was duplicated in the trillions of cells that eventually constitute a human organism. Furthermore, there was equal mystery concerning the process by which the genetic information carried within these chromosomes guided the development of the innumerable structures constituting a developed individual. But in that year three scientists—an American (J. D. Watson) and two Englishmen (F. H. C. Crick and M. H. F. Wilkins)—deduced the molecular structure of a chemical substance that is in all genetic material; this achievement quickened the pace of research that contributes to an understanding of the growth of living things and won for them the 1962 Nobel Prize in Medicine and Physiology. That substance is DNA (deoxyribose nucleic acid), and its discovery lies at the heart of the new science of molecular biology.

Watson and Crick proposed nothing less than that a chemical mechanism accounts for the storing of genetic information and for its transfer, in identical form, from cell to cell in the development of an individual organism. Very roughly, DNA is a molecule composed of two "ladders" intertwined with each other around a single, common axis. When a cell divides, the two ladders of the DNA molecule it contains come apart; each ladder then duplicates itself, so that each of the two new cells contains a complete DNA molecule identical with the one in the "parent" cell. Futhermore, the "rungs" of the ladders are composed of four chemical substances, which can be paired in specific ways, and this four-letter "alphabet" seems capable of storing or "coding" the full genetic endowment of an individual. The sequence of five photographs illustrates the DNA molecule in the process of duplication. From a resting state (A) the DNA fiber separates (B), and new complementary ladders swing into place (C, D). Each of the two completed DNA fibers (E) contains one-half the original fiber. Subsequent research has established the existence of other molecules, similar to DNA and to one another. They are the RNA molecules (ribonucleic acid). One of them, *messenger* RNA, is synthesized by the DNA molecule, which itself remains in the nucleus of the cell. It then carries the information to the "protein factories" of the body. The second, *transfer* RNA, is responsible for the transfer of the raw materials that form the protein structures constituting the organism and for the assembly of these "building blocks" according to the specifications contained in the DNA blueprint. In this way, with differing arrangements dictated by the particular code present in the DNA molecule, the trillions of cells in a human being are formed, and a human life is created from a single fertilized ovum.

It is no discredit to the magnificent research currently emerging from molecular-biology laboratories to caution the reader that, despite this work, the "secret of life" is still a long way from complete disclosure. Geneticists know that the DNA-RNA story is not the whole story. The fact that a DNA molecule cannot *exactly* duplicate itself in a test tube but requires the environment of a living organism to do so is enough to make us suspect that more remains to be told. Perhaps a fair assessment at this time is the opinion of the biologist George Gaylord Simpson, who asserts that ". . . nothing that has so far been learned about DNA has helped significantly to understand the nature of man or of any other whole organism. It certainly is necessary for such understanding to examine what is inherited, how it is expressed in the developing individual, how it evolves in populations, and so on. Up to now the triumphs of DNA research have had virtually no effect on our understanding of those subjects. In due course molecular biology will undoubtedly become more firmly connected with the biology of whole organisms and with evolution, and then it will become of greater concern for those more interested in the nature of man than in the nature of molecules."

G. G. SIMPSON. 1966. The Biological Nature of Man, *Science*, 152, 472–8. Photos courtesy Margery Shaw, M.D., Department of Human Genetics, The University of Michigan, Ann Arbor, Michigan, and the Upjohn Company, Kalamazoo, Michigan.

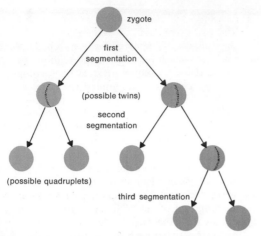

zygote

first
segmentation

(possible twins)

second
segmentation

(possible quadruplets)

third segmentation

Figure 1.4. This figure is a diagram of the process by which identical multiple births may occur. If the zygote, during the first cell division, does not segment, only one child will develop. If, at the first division, actual segmentation takes place, so that there are now two zygotes, and if no further actual separation occurs, then identical twins will develop. If, however, at the first cell division of these two identical zygotes, another separation takes place, there is the possibility of more than two identical children. The figure shows the process up to the point at which *identical quintuplets* become possible.

that three or four or more individuals can develop (see Figure 1.4.). These individuals are known as "identical twins," "identical triplets," and so on, because, as can readily be seen, they have developed from the same zygote and therefore must be genetically identical.

Fraternal Twins The mother may sometimes produce more than one functional ovum at a time. If she produces two and each is fertilized (by two different sperm, of course), then genetically the twins are different individuals no more similar than any set of brothers or sisters. They are known as *fraternal twins*.

According to available statistics, twins occur in the United States about once in eighty-six births. Identical twins are rarer than fraternal twins, amounting to about one-third of all twins. It seems fairly clear that the likelihood of giving birth to twins is hereditarily determined to a considerable extent. Thus, twinning

is found more often in some families than in others and more often even in some races than in others. The age of the parents at the time of conception seems also to be important. Older fathers, regardless of the age of the mother, are more apt to conceive twins than are younger fathers. Women in their thirties are also more likely to give birth to twins than are women of any other age.

Unlike-sex twins are obviously fraternal twins, but if both individuals are of the same sex it is by no means easy to determine whether they are identical or fraternal. External appearance is an unreliable indicator, for, although identical twins of course look alike, so do many fraternal twins of the same sex. (For a situation in which this very difficulty in distinguishing between identical and fraternal twins is a crucial advantage in research on "heredity versus environment" problems, see the Freedman-Keller study reported in Unit 44, p. 732.)

There are a great many criteria for distinguishing between fraternal and identical twins. Three of the several possible tests to be met before we can assume that a pair of like-sex twins is identical are, first, that the two children must have the same blood type; second, that they must have similar (but not identical) fingerprints; and, third, that they must show identical kinds of various serum proteins that are genetically determined. There does exist a foolproof test as to whether twins are identical or not, but this test is not generally applied to human beings. It is known that only genetically identical individuals can undergo successful skin transplantation. If the skin from one twin is transplanted to the skin of the other and if the transplanted skin "takes" and continues to grow in the host twin, then we have conclusive evidence that the donor twin and the host twin are genetically identical.

Multiple Determiners

We have said that genes are the determiners of inherited traits or characteristics (for example, eye color, hair structure, body length). But this does not mean that one gene is responsible for each trait. Actually, any one gene, although producing only one substance, does produce a multitude of effects, and each trait is determined by the interaction of many factors from several genes—often from genes found in separate chromosomes. The multifactorial determination of traits is, as we shall see, of major importance in understanding the inheritance of abilities in man.

Perhaps the simplest illustration of multiple determination is found in the interplay between dominant and recessive genes. Every gene in any one chromosome has its corresponding partner in the paired chromosome. Thus gene A in chromosome 1 will have gene a in chromosome 1', gene B will have its partner b, and so on. The two members of any pair may have opposite influences in determining a particular trait. For example, one of the sets of genes that plays an important part in determining the color of the eyes may be found in the following pairs for different individuals: AA, aa, or Aa. In the first (AA), either gene is such as to produce brown eyes. As both genes are the same, the person is said to be *homozygous* for these genes. He will have brown eyes, and so must all his progeny.

In the second combination, aa, we again have a homozygous state. Now both genes make for blue eyes. Therefore the individual will have blue eyes, and if his mate is also homozygous for blue eyes, all their progeny will be blue-eyed.

In the third combination, A tends to produce brown eyes; a, on the other hand, tends to produce blue eyes. Genetically, the individual is a mixture of determiners for brown eyes and blue eyes. Such a person is said to be *heterozygous* for these genes. But A is dominant over a (it "suppresses" the expression of a), and therefore the person will develop brown eyes. But he continues to carry within his germ cells the a genes. Now suppose an Aa father and an Aa mother (both of whom must have brown eyes)

mate. Any of the progeny who receive both an a from the father and an a from the mother, that is, aa, will have blue eyes, even though both parents were brown-eyed (see Box 7, for a partial list of dominant and recessive characteristics in man).

But we must emphasize again that very few traits are determined by single sets of genes. We must consider that, for most human traits, "dominance" and "recessiveness" can be only

---

Box 7
Dominance
and Recessiveness

The following table lists some of the dominant and recessive characters in human inheritance. Note that the "dominant" trait is not always the "desirable" one, as, for example, in fused fingers or limb dwarfing.

Dominant Characters	*Recessive Characters*
Curly hair	Straight hair
Dark hair	Light or red hair
Brown eyes	Blue eyes
Normal coloring	Albinism
Fused fingers or toes	Normal fingers and toes
Supernumerary digits	Normal number
Fingers lacking one joint	Normal length
Double-jointedness	Normal joints
Limb dwarfing	Normal proportion
Immunity to poison ivy	Susceptibility to poison ivy
Normal sight	Night blindness
Normal hair	Baldness
Normal color vision	Color blindness
Normal blood	Hemophilia
Normal hearing	Deaf-mutism

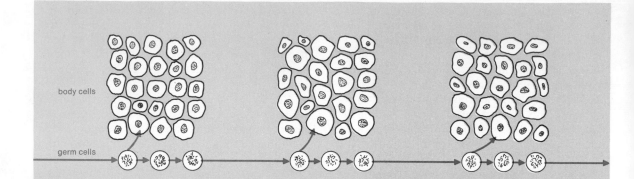

Figure 1.5. This figure diagrammatically represents the continuity of germ cells and indicates "what is inherited." Each human being starts as a fertilized germ cell—a zygote. The zygote, through the process of cell division (mitosis), gives rise to two kinds of cells: the somatic cells and the germ cells. The somatic (body) cells soon change and become specialized—as nerve cells, muscle cells, skin cells, and so on; the final result is a complete and mature person. (Each of the rectangular groups of cells in the illustration represents a person.) The cells in the line of descent of germ cells do not change in any important respect. They continue to reproduce germ cells. A sperm descendant of the original zygote combines with the ovum of a female organism to start another zygote and thus another person. It is the germ cell that "runs in a family," not the somatic cells. If he has progeny, they are "descendants" of his germ cells only. The germ cells alone can claim "immortality." No matter what happens to the body cells during the life of the father or mother, *such changes cannot be transmitted to the offspring*. The athlete who develops his muscles (body cells) during his lifetime cannot transmit his well-developed muscles to his son. The mother who learns to appreciate art during her pregnancy (thus changing her nervous system—body cells) cannot transmit a love for art to her daughter.

The *biological* inheritance that you can transmit to your children has already been determined by your parents. No program of "right living" can change that.

relative terms, for they have their all-or-none effect only when a trait is determined by one gene pair. Because psychological traits, as the term is commonly understood, typically involve multiple determination by many sets of genes, it is highly unlikely that such traits will exhibit clear-cut dominant-recessive properties. This is not to say, however, that a single gene pair may not exert a profound influence upon the psychological characteristics of an individual. Certain psychologically pervasive characteristics have a relatively simple genetic basis. For example, a type of mental deficiency called "trisomy-21" (previously known as "Mongolism") seems to be caused by the presence of an extra, forty-seventh, chromosome (Ford, *et al.*, 1959).

One point that should be immediately clear from our discussion of dominance and reces-

siveness is that the person's *phenotype* (his observable characteristics) is only a partial manifestation of his *genotype*—the gene pool he possesses and can transmit to his offspring. Yet another layer of complexity is added when we consider that each chromosome of the organism, perhaps even each gene in the zygote, influences the whole body. And each part of the process is influenced by all the others. Genetics teaches us the same lesson as does psychology —the individual is a complex interrelated unity of parts.

The Continuity of Man

The inherited characteristics that are produced by genes are passed along unchanged, with relatively rare exceptions, from one generation to another. The rare exceptions occur when genes themselves are changed through some "chemical accident" or through stimulation by such radiant energies as X-rays and cosmic rays. These genetic changes we call *mutations*, and they have been used to account for evolutionary changes in organisms.

However, the psychological experiences of an individual cannot be passed on to his progeny by heredity. The only things that are passed on are the genes, and they remain unchanged by life experiences (see Figure 1.5.). Not only is man an integrated unity; he is also—except as he is transformed by bombardment of cosmic rays, X-rays, and fallouts from hydrogen bombs —a continuous unity.

Environment

Each fertilized egg, then, carries within it hereditary determinants from the father and the mother, and each zygote almost surely differs from all other zygotes at the very moment of conception. These differences become magnified and more easily detectable as an individual grows in his mother's womb, as he is born, and as he enters into the activities of the outside world. The continuous unity that is man is an ever changing one.

These changes, however, do not take place in a biological organism suspended in a vacuum. From the very moment of fertilization, through the development of the zygote, the embryo, and the fetus, the organism is immersed in an environment that is unique to him. Just as it is nearly certain that each zygote differs from all other zygotes, we can assert with equal confidence that the environment of each zygote differs from that of every other zygote.

We have known for a long time that the conditions prevailing in the zygote's environment—the uterus—can have profound effects upon the physical development of the organism. Our knowledge of some of the conditions that interfere with normal development is extensive, and we are continually learning more about this subject. By now, all physicians and most mothers know that German measles around the third month of pregnancy can interfere seriously with the course of growth *in utero* and lead to defective offspring. Certain commonly used drugs, some antibiotics for example, have been shown to have enduring effects on the developing organism. The tragic results of taking the drug thalidomide during pregnancy—gross physical deformities in the child—have alerted us all to the by now obvious facts that the uterus is indeed a relevant environment and that the embryo, and later the fetus, does not grow and develop in a vacuum during the forty weeks of pregnancy. As more research focuses upon the effects of various externally controllable conditions in the uterus during pregnancy, we shall be better able to avoid, or to treat, conditions that are, in the broad sense, "toxic" to normal development.

But of late we have come to know something quite new about the influence of the zygote's environment, something that to many seems most surprising. It is the increasing evidence that the later *behavior* of the organism is affected by the prenatal environment. Such effects are perhaps surprising because they seem to confirm, in a very general sense, some of the "old wives' tales." Psychologists have *not* found that assiduous concert going during pregnancy leads to musically gifted offspring, but they have found, for example, that emotional upset during pregnancy can affect the emotional characteristics of offspring (see Box 8, p. 32; also see Box 10, p. 62).

Perhaps the main lesson to be learned from findings of this sort is that, as soon as the individual is conceived, he is open to environmental effects.

Environment becomes a much more important determinant of behavior after birth, and this fact may arise either from the lesser susceptibility of the organism to "outside" forces *in utero* or from the smaller range of variation

Box 8
Prenatal Influences
on Offspring

W. R. Thompson at Wesleyan University has tested the hypothesis that emotional upset undergone by female rats during pregnancy can affect the emotional characteristics of the offspring.

Thompson trained five female rats in a double-compartment shuttlebox first to expect strong shock at the sound of a buzzer and then to avoid the shock by opening a door between the compartments and running through to the safe side. When the rats had learned this lesson, they were mated. As soon as they became pregnant, they were exposed to the buzzer three times every day in the shock side of the shuttlebox, but with the shock turned off and the door to the safe side locked. This procedure was continued until the females gave birth to their pups. During pregnancy, the mother rats were thus exposed to an anxiety-arousing situation, but their accustomed means to escape was blocked. Thompson's assumption was that this exposure would generate strong "free-floating" anxiety in the pregnant females and that any resulting endocrine changes would be transmitted via the blood stream to the fetuses. Will this anxiety create emotional offspring?

The emotionality of the offspring (there were thirty of them) was measured by two tests given at 30 to 40 and at 130 to 140 days of age and compared with results for thirty offspring of control animals who had not been subjected to this stress. In test A, the offspring of the experimental and control animals were placed in a large open area for three daily sessions of ten minutes each, and their activity was measured on the assumption that, the more timid or emotional the animal, the less the activity in an open area. In test B, emotionality was measured by the time elapsing before the rat left the home cage to reach food at the end of an alley leading from the cage. For this test the animals were first deprived of food for twenty-four hours. Both these tests (especially test A, which is sometimes called the "open field" test) are used fairly commonly to measure emotionality in rats.

The results are shown in the table. It is clear that the offspring of the experimental animals differ strikingly from offspring of the control animals. Furthermore, it appears that these differences persist, to a great extent, into adulthood.

possible in the uterine environment. Whatever the case, it is clear that we have two broad sets of factors that contribute to the distinctions among organisms: heredity and environment. And both play their roles—sometimes separately, sometimes interacting with each other —from the very moment of conception.

Formulation of the Nature-Nurture Problem

The recognition that our behavioral traits result from the interaction of heredity and environment has changed the formulation of the na-ture-nurture problem. We no longer speak of the nature-nurture controversy (heredity versus environment). The questions we ask assume, at the very outset, that both heredity and environment are involved. The three major questions of concern to research workers in the field are, first, what proportion of the variation in any given trait is determined by heredity and what proportion by environment? second, what is the specific nature of the genetic mechanism responsible for the inheritance of behavior tendencies or traits? and, third, how much difference can variations in the environment make in traits that are partly determined by heredity?

	TEST A *Amount of Activity* *(Distance Moved)*	TEST B *Time to Leave Home Cage* *(Minutes)*
Tests given at age 30 to 40 days		
Experimental	86.0	14.9
Control	134.5	5.2
Tests given at age 130 to 140 days		
Experimental	114.5	4.8
Control	162.3	2.1

Although these differences are statistically reliable, there is some ambiguity regarding their cause. It is possible that the buzzer was strong enough to act on the fetuses directly rather than indirectly by causing release of hormones in the mother. For this reason Thompson concludes cautiously, ". . . there are some grounds for supposing that prenatal maternal anxiety does actually increase the emotionality of offspring."

Later research with mice supports Thompson's findings and makes his conclusion less tentative. Recent research, however, introduces some complications into the finding that prenatal stress in the mother leads to greater emotionality in her offspring. J. C. DeFries (1964), for example, finds that there are important strain differences in this effect; that is, the effects of the stress are different depending upon the particular strain or breed of mouse that is tested. Even further, not only the genotype of the mother but also that of the still-fetal child is a factor. Clearly, then, broad generalizations of these findings to all species are, to say the least, highly risky, and research will have to discover the precise mechanisms involved in the operation of prenatal influences before we can say more.

Whatever the mechanism may finally be shown to be, however, it seems that *differences in the prenatal environments of the rats make for differences in later behavior.*

W. R. THOMPSON. 1957. Influence of Prenatal Maternal Anxiety on Emotionality in Young Rats, *Science,* 125, 698–9. Table adapted by permission of the American Association for the Advancement of Science.
J. C. DEFRIES. 1964. Prenatal Maternal Stress in Mice: Differential Effects on Behavior, *J. Hered.,* 55, 289–95.

With regard to the first question, one point should be made quite clear. When we discuss the relative importance of heredity and environment as they affect a given trait, we necessarily are speaking of the *average* contribution of each factor in a population living in a particular environment. Let us elaborate on this point. Within a given *individual* the relative importance of heredity or environment can be very far from the average value. Thus, whatever we know regarding this value with respect, say, to intelligence is utterly irrelevant to an individual who is unfortunate enough to possess the single extra chromosome that has been found to be responsible for the severe mental retardation known as "trisomy-21." Here, heredity plays a massive dominant role, and the child is doomed to be intellectually defective. Yet, even aside from such extreme cases, it is clear that hereditary intellectual endowment, as well as intelligence-stimulating environments, varies enormously in the general population, so that, *for a given person,* we are unable to say to what extent his intellectual attainment is attributable to heredity, on the one hand, and to environment, on the other.

Furthermore, it is extremely rare that we can pinpoint, as in the case of trisomy-21, the exact genetic element that is responsible for a given behavioral outcome, particularly in man. Our inability to do so does not preclude experimental investigation of the genetic influence upon various behavioral phenomena, as we shall see in the discussion of behavior genetics that follows.

The answer to the third question is implicit in our discussion up to now. Again, we must caution that whatever result we obtain can apply only to a certain population of organisms *in general*. Take the realm of personality as a broad example. Without going into the details of what we know concerning the influence of heredity upon various personality traits (this topic is discussed in Unit 44), we can safely say that the potential influence of environmental variation on a given facet of personality depends heavily upon the hereditary base on which this variation impinges. Thus, as we shall see in Unit 47, the interaction between an inherited potential to develop schizophrenia and the environmental forces that can prevent or promote the emergence of this disorder is crucial. Lacking the supposed hereditary susceptibility, even the worst of psychological environments will not result in a schizophrenic breakdown. But, given the genetic potential, some people will become schizophrenic, and others will not, depending upon the stress present in their environments. Thus, when we speak of genetic influences on behavior, it is critical to remember that, apart from a relatively few hereditary defects like trisomy-21, we cannot speak of an hereditary characteristic in the all-or-none sense. By and large, genetic factors are predisposing factors so that any behavioral outcome is necessarily a varying blend of what is "given" and the environmental forces that have operated upon it. The organism's inheritance at times may set limits—often quite broad ones—on how widely a trait can range but only very rarely determines its precise nature.

This theme of continual interaction between nature and nurture, with its almost inevitable

guarantee against a rigid link between genes and behavior, is a fortunate, and even an indispensable, aspect of man's development as an individual and as a species. Most changes that have been observed in the nature of man's life on earth through recorded history are the outcome more of extraordinary environmental modifications than of genetic factors. As the geneticist Dobzhansky (1967) has observed:

"The preponderance of cultural over biological evolution will continue or increase in the foreseeable future. We would not wish this to be otherwise: adaptation to environment by culture is more rapid and efficient than biological adaptation. Moreover, control of the cultural evolution is achievable probably more easily than control of the biological evolution."

This is not to assume that man has ceased to evolve biologically and that all cultural evolution builds upon the same distribution of genotypes as existed at man's beginnings. Even if no other factors were operative, the simple fact that each new set of parents throughout time represents a potential for new and unique genetic combination would ensure continuing biological change. The relation of genetic potential to expressed behavior poses seemingly endless problems, and the field of "behavior genetics" has undertaken their investigation.

Experimental Behavior Genetics

The field of experimental behavior genetics, though now a very active one, has a rather short history. The first extensive experiment was that of Tryon, who initiated his now classic *selective breeding* experiment with rats in 1927.

Selective breeding consists of mating animals that display certain traits in a very high or very low degree, selecting from among their offspring those that express the trait in a similar high or low degree, and then breeding those offspring. If the trait is regulated by heredity, continued selection for a number of generations will result in a strain that breeds more or less true for that trait.

Tryon's results were clear: Bright maze-learners breed bright progeny; dull maze-learners breed dull progeny (see Box 9, p. 36). Many other experimenters have corroborated Tryon's results and have even gone him one better. Selective breeding for behavioral traits is by no means confined to maze learning or to the single species rats. Since the original work, experiments of this sort have been carried out on a large number of infrahuman species, among them insects, guinea pigs, mice, chickens, and dogs. Intelligence, or learning ability, variously defined, remained a popular trait in these breeding experiments, but emotionality and activity level have also come in for considerable attention. Other characteristics that have been shown to be at least somewhat susceptible to selective breeding include social dominance, aggression, sexual vigor, and even liking for alcohol. Even the geneticists' favorite experimental animal, the fruit fly (*Drosophila*), has been used for the study of behavioral genetics. For example, it has been successfully bred for strength of attraction to light (Hirsch & Boudreau, 1958; Hadler, 1964). The same species has also been shown to have a substantial genetic basis for "geotaxis," the tendency to fly with or against gravitational pull (see Figure 1.6.).

One of the most impressive and extensive investigations in mammalian behavior genetics is reported by Scott and Fuller (1965). Their main theme is the social behavior, broadly defined, of dogs. In a study lasting more than a dozen years they carefully observed the behavior of "purebred" and "crossbred" dogs of five breeds, selected in part for their characteristic behavioral differences: African Basenjis, beagles, cocker spaniels, fox terriers, and Shetland sheepdogs. These dogs, about 500 of them, were tested at various times over their first year of life in about thirty standardized situations designed to elicit data on such characteristics as emotional reactivity, trainability, and problem-solving skills. By comparing the performances of the "purebreds" with those of the "crossbreds" of various kinds and degrees, Scott and Fuller were often able to detect the genetic bases of various behavioral traits existing among the five kinds of dogs studied.

Aside from its many contributions to the science of behavior genetics, the Scott and Fuller study has had some eminently practical "side effects." Trainers of guide dogs for the blind have made extensive use of these findings and have thereby been able to improve vastly

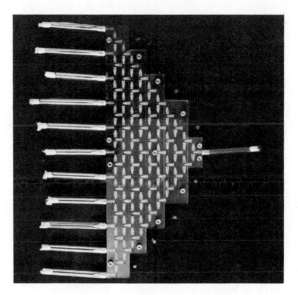

Figure 1.6. This vertical ten-unit plastic maze facing a fluorescent tube (not shown here) is an apparatus to measure geotaxis in *Drosophila*. Squads of fruit flies (*Drosophila*) are introduced to the maze through the vial at left and are collected from the several vials at right. *erratum* The flies are induced to go through the maze by the light, to which they are attracted, and by a pervasive odor of food. Successive selected breeding of flies that tend to crawl either upward or downward as they pass through the maze results eventually in two strains of fruit fly, one tending to oppose gravitational pull and one tending to go with gravity.
J. Hirsch, "Behavior Genetics and Individuality Understood," *Science*, 142, 1436–42; Copyright 1963 by the American Association for the Advancement of Science; reprinted by permission.

their success at selecting and training such animals. One report (Pfaffenberger, 1963) notes that in the middle 1940s (before the Scott and Fuller results were available) less than 10 per cent of the dogs, already selected from breeds known to be relatively trainable, completed their "course" successfully. By 1960, in large part because of the lessons learned from the Scott and Fuller study, 90 per cent of the dogs "graduated," despite some stiffening of the requirements for an acceptable guide dog.

The general picture in animal behavior genetics is one of rapid progress. But what of man?

Human Behavior Genetics

Selective breeding of humans is, for obvious reasons, not the experimental method of choice in this area. Rather, psychologists and others have had to turn to comparisons of abilities and behavior among identical and fraternal twins, among brothers and sisters, and among parents and their children. In other words, family resemblances in various traits and abilities have been investigated. One immediately apparent difficulty with this general approach is that families not only are linked genetically but also typically share the same environments over long periods. For this reason, instances of twins reared in different homes and children placed for adoption and reared by foster parents have been seized upon for research purposes in the field of human behavioral genetics.

Most of the investigations in this area have to do with the extent of the genetic contributions to intelligence, and these findings are more appropriately presented in the context of our general discussion of the sources of variation in mental ability (see Unit 41). The heritability of various emotional, temperamental, and emotional traits has fairly recently also become a topic of considerable research, and, again, we defer presentation of specific findings to the broader treatment of determinants of individual differences in personality (see Unit 44).

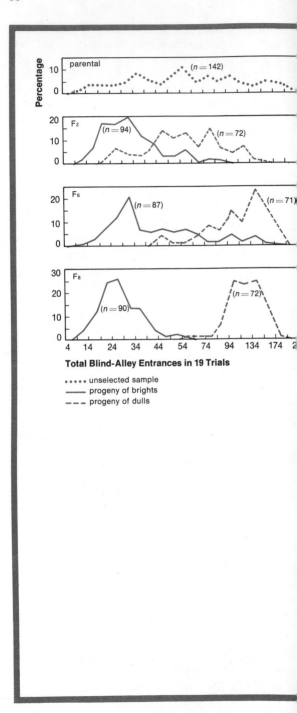

Total Blind-Alley Entrances in 19 Trials

..... unselected sample
——— progeny of brights
- - - progeny of dulls

Box 9

Inheritance of Learning Ability

The purpose of R. C. Tryon's experiment at the University of California was to establish, by selective breeding, a line of maze-bright and a line of maze-dull rats.

Tryon started with a "parental" generation of 142 male and female rats. Each animal was run for nineteen trials through a seventeen-unit maze. The brightest animals made a total of approximately fourteen errors in learning the maze, the dullest about 174. The bright females were then mated with the bright males, the dull females with the dull males; the other animals were discarded. Then the offspring of these matings were tested on the same maze. On the basis of their performance, the brightest rats within each of the bright litters were mated, and the dullest within each of the dullest litters were mated. This testing and selective breeding procedure was followed for eighteen generations. The results are summarized in the distribution curves of the figure, which shows the errors made by the parental group, the third generation (F_2), the seventh generation (F_6), and the ninth generation (F_8). With successive generations the two strains of rats pulled apart, until by the F_8 generation the dullest of the bright rats were about as bright as or brighter than the brightest of the dull rats.

Rigorous environmental controls were employed in this experiment. All animals were given identical care. In some cases, indeed, a dull mother would be given the pups of a bright mother to raise, and a bright mother would be given the pups of a dull mother. This mixing was intended to rule out the possibility of different "maternal care" as an environmental factor. The maze was highly reliable, and the errors were scored automatically by an electrical recorder, so as to eliminate any possible "unconscious bias" of the experimenter in scoring the rats.

A number of years later, L. V. Searle, working in Tryon's laboratory, tested the two strains on various other learning tests. He did not find that the "bright" were bright on everything or the "dulls" altogether dull. Instead, the rats from each strain showed different *patterns* of abilities. Here we have evidence indicating that Tryon's strains were not *generally* bright and *generally* dull.

No matter how the question of the generality of the learning ability of Tryon's two strains will eventually be answered—and more research is still being done on this question—the minimal conclusion is clear: *Some kinds of learning ability can be inherited.*

R. C. TRYON. 1940. Genetic Differences in Maze Learning in Rats, in National Society for the Study of Education, *The Thirty-ninth Yearbook* (Bloomington, Ill.: Public School Publishing Co.). Figure adapted by permission of National Society for the Study of Education.

L. V. SEARLE. 1949. The Organization of Hereditary Maze-Brightness and Maze-Dullness, *Genet. Psychol. Monogr.*, 39, 279–325.

Glossary

chromosomes Threadlike bodies of different sizes and shapes appearing in like pairs, found within animal cell bodies. Normal human cells seem to contain twenty-three pairs of chromosomes each, or a total of forty-six chromosomes. Chromosomes carry the genes.

crossing-over of genes Refers to the fact that one segment of a chromosome may break off and be exchanged with a corresponding segment from the paired chromosome. Genes thus do not always "stay put" in their original chromosomes.

embryo A young animal during the early stages within its mother's body. For man the term "embryo" is used to describe the developing individual up to the end of the seventh week after conception.

fetus Refers to the young of an animal in the womb, especially in its later stages.

fraternal twins Two individuals who have developed from *two different* fertilized ova (zygotes). They are to be contrasted with "identical twins." Fraternal twins may be both male, both female, or one of each. Fraternal twins are no more genetically similar than are any two brothers or sisters.

gene A stretch of DNA in the chromosome that codes for production of a specific part of a protein. The gene, as it reacts with the environment and other genes, is a factor in determining the hereditary traits and structures of the developing individual.

genotype The genetic potential that an individual possesses and can in part transmit to his offspring. This potential may be only partially expressed in his phenotype.

heterozygous state The state in which the individual has a pair of genes that *differ* in their effects on any one hereditary trait, for example, one dominant and one recessive gene (A, a).

homozygous state The state in which the individual has a pair of genes that are *identical* in their effects on any one hereditary trait, for example, two dominant genes (A, A) or two recessive genes (a, a).

identical twins Two complete individuals who have developed from *one* segmented fertilized ovum (zygote). They are to be contrasted with "fraternal twins." Identical twins are therefore *genetically* identical and are of great interest to the psychologist who is concerned with the problem of the hereditary factors in behavior.

mutation A change in genes that causes a sudden departure from the parent type, as when an individual is found to carry a gene that neither of his parents had.

ovum (egg) The female germ (or reproductive) cell produced by the ovaries. The ovum contains within it *one* member of each pair of chromosomes from the mother, or a total of twenty-three chromosomes. After fertilization by the sperm the ovum can develop into a new individual.

phenotype The observable characteristics of an individual that are only partial manifestations of his genetic potential, or genotype.

selective breeding A technique used in experimental genetics. It consists of mating animals that display certain traits and selecting for breeding from among their offspring those that express the trait. If the trait is regulated by heredity, continued selection for a number of generations may result in a strain that breeds true for that trait.

sperm The male germ (or reproductive) cell produced by the testes. The sperm carries within it *one* member of each pair of chromosomes from the father, or a total of twenty-three chromosomes.

zygote The fertilized ovum, or the cell produced by the union of an ovum and a sperm. The normal human zygote contains twenty-three complete pairs of chromosomes (or forty-six chromosomes), one member of each pair coming from the ovum, the other from the sperm.

UNIT 2

human development: issues and methods of study

overview / Because human development is characterized by almost continuous change, both as we grow toward maturity and as we age, the study of psychology is in very large part a developmental undertaking. Development is typically a gradual and continuous process, but relatively abrupt upsurges and declines in both structure and function can be observed outwardly, although they indeed are merely visible expressions of an actually continuous underlying developmental process. Genetic factors, for example, often must await the culmination of gradual maturational changes before they become expressed and observable.

Developmental rates vary considerably among individuals in most characteristics, as do the times at which various developmental milestones are reached. Furthermore, "ceilings," or mature levels of development, show substantial individual differences. Development also frequently involves increased differentiation, in addition to simple quantitative growth; at times this differentiation process results in progression through a sequence of qualitatively distinct stages of maturity. These various parameters of the developmental process can be combined and condensed to a relatively few models of the developmental process, which can serve to describe the course of growth for many human characteristics.

There are three primary methods for the study of human development: cross-sectional, retrospective, and longitudinal. Each can provide data on age changes in a given characteristic throughout development, and each possesses certain advantages and shortcomings.

In a very real sense almost all the field of psychology might properly be classed under the rubric "growth and development." No matter which of the conventional topics of psychology we consider—perception, learning, motivation and emotion, intelligence, personality, or social behavior—it inevitably raises certain essentially developmental questions. These questions stem from the undeniable fact that all psychological characteristics appear qualitatively quite different in the newborn infant than in the fully matured adult, so that some process of growth and development must intervene. What does an infant perceive of the world about him, and what is the course of growth of the perceptual function from its rudimentary beginnings at birth to its highly efficient state in the adult? What can a baby learn, how does he "learn to learn" more effectively as he grows older, and when and through what means does he come to achieve the impressive learning abilities of the average adult? At the start of life, are the motives that drive the infant's behavior "adult" motives, and are his emotional reactions to his environment as rich and as varied as our own? We can go on: Is "personality" the same in the infant, in the preschool child, in the adolescent, in the adult? If not, what accounts for whatever continuity is found, and what factors are responsible for personality change? When and how do the social-behavior patterns of the normal adult develop? We hardly expect or find what can be called truly "social" behavior in the newborn, not to mention the highly articulated social beliefs and attitudes of the mature adult. Add to these questions those related to the opposite end of the developmental process—the changes in each of these functions as the adult begins to age—and we have spanned the full course of human life without ever abandoning the developmental orientation.

The Study of Development

Thus all is change, at least in the psychology of man. Aside from the continuing interplay of nature and nurture discussed earlier (Unit 1), there is the obvious change in each of us from day to day. This change takes place as new experiences impinge upon and modify the "psychological self," which is each of us at any given moment—a "self" derived from what we are, genetically and constitutionally, and all that we have up until that moment seen and learned and felt. This "self" is therefore in a continual process of re-creation, yet, except for rare, stressful moments when "time is out of joint" and we are simply "not ourselves," we and others have little difficulty conceiving of a single, ongoing person. This part-fact, part-illusion makes the study of psychology possible. Let us explain.

What psychology typically does, and what we shall for the most part do in this text, is to freeze the individual at a point in time. An infant is an infant, a child is a child, and an adult is an adult—at least for the purposes of most scientific psychological investigations. Rarely does the experimental psychologist observe a given individual on more than one occasion. What is more, the psychologist must treat various psychological functions of people separately, and, even further, the psychologist's research most often attends to the behavior that occurs *on the average* in any given circumstance, with only occasional glances at behavioral differences among persons. Through this battery of simplifying devices the psychologist becomes able to begin the study of perception, learning, and so forth, as they describe and explain the behavior of the "average man." We can even relate the developmental histories of each of these functions by comparing the results of investigations of the same phenomenon among different age groups. (The rare exception to this strategy is the longitudinal method, to be discussed later, in which the same persons are studied repeatedly throughout their life spans.)

Our task in the present unit is a relatively modest one. Primarily, we intend only a consideration of some general issues intrinsic to the study of growth and development and brief ov-

erviews of a few selected phenomena that are important to one or another of the major developmental periods.

The Developmental Process

Perhaps we can best begin by pointing out that the terms "growth" and "development," though technically distinguishable, are essentially synonymous for our purposes. Strictly speaking, "growth" refers to an increase in magnitude—in bodily size, in muscular strength, in intellectual ability, or even in social poise. Not all development is growth in this sense, for, with increasing age, certain characteristics do in fact decrease. Certain motor reflexes present at birth and in infancy rapidly disappear, for example, and even certain organs, like the thymus gland (see Figure 3.6., p. 59), shrink and atrophy after adolescence. The more general term is "development," which may be broadly defined as referring to any sequential and continuous process of change, both quantitative and qualitative, in any physical structure or function and in any aspect of behavior or psychological functioning.

"Change" is sometimes understood to connote gradualness, the notion that what exists at time 2 is only a bit different from what was there at time 1. For many physical and behavioral characteristics this notion is indeed valid; our growth in height is made up of infinitesimal increments. Yet there are innumerable exceptions to this kind of change. As we shall see often throughout this text, certain psychological phenomena show very abrupt transitions. A meaningless conglomeration of blotches is instantly transformed into a perceptually meaningful picture; a totally "impossible" problem is solved in what seems an instantaneous flash of insight. Sometimes, of course, what appears to be abrupt and discontinuous is the result of other "invisible" processes that may have proceeded gradually. The blinding insight may be the end product of a continuing evaluation of evidence and a testing of hypotheses.

So it is with many aspects of human develop-ment. The attainment of menarche, or first menstruation, is for the adolescent girl an abrupt event, yet we know that it is the result of a host of gradual physiological changes that necessarily must achieve certain developmental changes before the event can take place. So with learning to read at school or, for that matter, the acquiring of any skill. For long periods, training and practice seem to lead to little if any improvement, but then, with apparent abruptness, words become meaningful and bicycles become ridable. Sometimes the course of development goes on for so long a time at "invisible" levels that it is difficult to relate cause and effect, much less to assume that some continuous underlying state or process has been involved.

Hereditary characteristics also often convey a sense of developmental discontinuity. As we have seen, an individual's genetic make-up is fully determined at the moment of conception, yet the physical or behavioral expression of these built-in potentials is not usually evident until some considerable time after birth. But, nevertheless, development according to the blueprint set down by genes proceeds continuously and sequentially, even though visible manifestations may be delayed until some considerably later time in the life of the organism. For example, although the height of an infant at birth is somewhat predictable from the height of his parents, the parent-child correlations continue to increase as the child develops and are much higher in adolescence (Livson, McNeill, & Thomas, 1962).

Intelligence, which is to a considerable extent hereditary, also exhibits this apparent "delayed action" effect. As Honzik (1963) has shown, significant parent-child resemblance in intelligence does not occur until about age three in girls and age five in boys, reflecting the generally faster maturation rate of females. (We shall see later on, in Box 142, p. 676, further details of this study.) The "delayed action" of genetic mechanisms is in fact based upon an ongoing process of physical maturation.

The important point to remember is that

developmental determinants or antecedents of any given behavior never operate "at a distance," magically bridging a chasm in time. At any point in a person's life there necessarily exists some current representation of each developmental process. Whatever can influence our behavior and experience at a particular moment—whether nature or nurture, genes or early childhood events—can do so, in theory and in practice, only because these developmental determinants have some real, current existence in the organism. This assumption is inescapable, a necessary reality for the scientific study of all aspects of human development.

Parameters of Development

All developmental processes can be described by a relatively small number of parameters, that is, characteristics of the process that vary and that define the particular course of development taken by a particular developmental process. These parameters may be quickly summarized as follows.

Rate of Development   This term refers simply to the rate of change in a given characteristic with time. This rate need not be—and in fact rarely is—constant throughout the entire period of development. Regarding height as an example, growth is extremely rapid within the first year or two of life, then slows down to a relatively moderate rate, only to experience an abrupt spurt sometime in the adolescent years. And, typically with height and most other characteristics, the developmental rate tapers off as the individual approaches maturity with respect to a given function.

Timing   Not all characteristics begin to develop, at least observably, at birth but get started at different times and reach mature levels at different times. The ability to walk is one such example, and even language development can be so classified. These two timing points are not necessarily related; the individual may be a "late starter" but is thereby not necessarily later than others in completing the developmental process. Whether or not he "catches up" is of course a function of rate of growth.

Ceiling   Quite apart from when a development begins and is completed and quite apart from its rate during the process, the parameter of the "ceiling" marks the culmination of development for a particular function. Thus, to take an obvious example, we all eventually attain different heights, and these mature heights are quite independent of the previous course of our growth curves. The same can be said to be true of intellectual development—some children are "slow starters" in the educational process, but their ultimate achievement level will not necessarily be lower.

Differentiation and Stages of Development   Certain parameters of development—*differentiation* and *stages of development*—cannot be cast in simple quantitative terms. They are essentially qualitative aspects of developmental change. Instead of speaking of a single measurable (therefore quantitative) characteristic, we must deal here with fundamental changes in the nature of the behavior exhibited by the developing organism. Intellectual or cognitive development is a prime example of this apparent noncontinuous feature of development, and the reader is referred to the discussion of Jean Piaget's elaborate scheme of developmental stages, which encompasses intelligence and thinking and even language development (see Unit 25). The achievement of sexual maturity is another example of a qualitative change in the course of a developmental process, and, although such changes in the quality of the characteristic are relatively rare in human development, they nevertheless often reflect fundamental modifications in the nature of the individual.

Models of Developmental Variation

These few parameters can be employed to construct different models of development, and with only a few such models we can encompass a large number of physical and psychological developmental processes. Loevinger (1966) has done just this, and our presentation is largely drawn from her proposals (see Figure 2.1.). Model I refers to developmental processes in which all persons ultimately attain the same ceiling, starting at the same time but proceeding at different rates. Bone development is a prime example of this kind of process; gradual ossification of the epiphyses (the regions lying between adjacent bones) is a continual phenomenon, beginning at the start of life and proceeding at different rates until the epiphyses are closed and the skeletal structure therefore reaches its mature state. Various motor skills, ranging from becoming toilet-trained to being able to walk effectively, show much the same pattern. If we ignore for the moment certain variations in starting time and ultimate level of ability, even such more complex skills as speech, reading, and writing can be included within this pattern.

Model II portrays a varying rate of development of a characteristic that differs in ceiling, or ultimate level. Here, perhaps intelligence is the best example, for mental development does proceed at different paces, does reach different final levels, and—most important—does seem to level off, no matter what the ceiling value, at about the same age (sometime during adolescence). This characterization is somewhat oversimplified, but it is true that, at least as measured by conventional tests, persons seem to reach their "mature" levels of intellectual ability at approximately the same time.

Model III is difficult to illustrate by a pure example: It includes processes in which society prescribes a fixed rate of progression but allows variation in terminal levels. One's educational career would illustrate this model, as, by and large, advancement from grade to grade goes according to a rather fixed schedule, but individuals do drop out at various points along the way. Verbal ability to some extent follows this model, at least in its earliest stage, where children show much the same increase in their vocabularies over a period of years, only to have some children level off at certain points while others go on to different higher ones. Even acquiring the social graces follows along in much this way; certain such rudimentary skills and amenities as properly manipulating knife and fork or saying "please" and "thank you" develop at about the same rate, but some children eventually reach higher than others in their levels of social skill and grace.

Model IV is the only one in which the assumption of an enduring ceiling level is discarded. To some extent, many of the characteristics we have been discussing show some decrease from peak level with time, but it is usually minor. Intelligence provides particularly illuminating data for this case. True, general intelligence reaches a certain level and stays there, barring relatively rare cases involving senile decay. But if we look at different aspects of intelligence (they are fully discussed in Unit 40), we find that some intellectual abilities follow Model II, whereas others are best described by Model IV. For the former model, we have such abilities as vocabulary and infor-

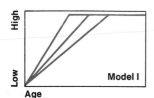 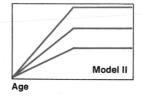 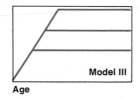 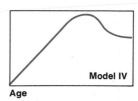

Figure 2.1. Models of the developmental process.
J. Loevinger, "Models and Measures of Developmental Variation," *Annals of the New York Academy of Sciences*, 134 (1966), 585–90; adapted by permission.

mation. They do not decrease with age, and, indeed, there is some evidence that this sort of intelligence actually increases as we grow older, especially among those who were initially quite gifted (Bayley & Oden, 1955). Other intellectual and cognitive functions, however, decay markedly as we advance in age. They include performances that require a certain cognitive flexibility, an ability to solve novel and complex problems rapidly. For example, the ability to "solve" an incomplete picture (see Figure 10.7., p. 153) reaches its peak in adolescence or early adulthood and then begins an inexorable decline (Horn & Cattell, 1966). Livson (1962) has found that persons in their seventies and eighties, even those who have remained intellectually alert and active, are almost totally unable to "make sense" of such incomplete pictures; they see collections of unrelated blobs but not coherent and meaningful objects. Cattell (1963) has made a distinction between intelligence-test items that show no age decline (he sees them as measuring "crystallized intelligence") and those that decay, often quite rapidly, with advancing age (measuring "fluid intelligence").

These models are, of course, simplifications gleaned from a survey and conceptualization of very many quite different developmental processes. There are possible variations on these models, and there are wholly new ones that have some relevance but have not been discussed. Our purpose in presenting the few we have is only to alert the reader to the fact that development is not a unitary, general process but is instead one that can follow many routes.

Alternate Methods of Studying Development

The necessary (but for certain questions insufficient) requirement for a developmental investigation is simply that we have measures of the characteristic under study at a number of different ages spotted throughout the span of its development. We can measure in a number of ways: First, at a given time we can measure groups of individuals varying in age; second, we can measure individuals at a certain age but obtain information on previous ages through the subjects' reports; third, we can measure the same individuals at various ages as they develop. The first of these methods is called *cross-sectional studies*, the second *retrospective studies*, and the last *longitudinal studies*. We shall consider what can and what cannot be reliably discovered by each.

Cross-Sectional Studies

Most data currently available on physical and psychological development are obtained by this method. The investigator, at a given point in time, collects data on a particular characteristic from children, adolescents, young adults, and so on; computes the average values; and then plots these values to yield a developmental curve. This method is certainly a convenient one and, for many purposes, is quite adequate. It can and does accurately portray average trends, except for characteristics that are subject to *secular change*, that is, to change with time (not age) as a function of environmental factors of one sort or another.

Secular change is not an insignificant factor in mapping the developmental trends of such psychological characteristics as intelligence or such physical characteristics as height. For example, Jones and Conrad (1933) tested the intelligences of almost all persons living in a small New England town in order to discover the age trends in a number of different aspects of intellectual ability. One of their main findings anticipated the Horn and Cattell result previously noted, in that performance on tests involving information declined with age at a far slower rate than did those involving speed of problem solving. But one factor that tended to exaggerate the general developmental decline in intelligence arose from a secular change, that is, the fact that, on the average, the older the person living in this town, the less formal schooling he had had. Because at least some aspects of intellectual performance are enhanced by formal schooling, it follows that at least some of the obtained difference between older and younger subjects in this study was due to a secular change in educational opportunity.

Height shows the same effect. For some time it has been widely assumed that height, which reaches mature levels sometime in late adolescence or in the early twenties, begins to *decrease* somewhat later on, perhaps in the fifties or sixties. Damon (1965) marshals the evidence on this question from his own research and that of others and reaches the conclusion that this apparent developmental decline in height may to a very large extent be due to a secular change; that is, the fact that mature adult height has been increasing for many decades. For example, in a recent study men whose average age was over eighty were 2.4 inches shorter than a group of men in their twenties. Do these data indicate that there is a shrinkage in stature of more than two inches occurring in the course of six decades of mature adulthood? By no means. Combining a number of reports of secular change in height spanning this same period, Damon comes to the conclusion that *all* of the apparent developmental decline in height could be attributable to the simple fact that men born more recently end up taller than those born several decades ago. To focus on but one short period within this sixty-year span, studies have shown that the average soldier in World War I was approximately three-quarters of an inch shorter than his counterpart in World War II. In the fifteen-year period following World War II, one study (Karpinos, 1961) reports an average increase in adult stature of about 0.5 inches. Taken together, a large number of studies of secular increase in height permit the very rough conclusion that adult males born in a given decade are about one-third inch taller than those born ten years earlier, a figure probably sufficient to account for the originally reported 2.4-inch decline in height from age twenty to age sixty.

This is not to deny that there is indeed some small degree of body shrinkage with advanced age, which shows in certain bodily characteristics and in certain individuals. The point to be made here is that secular change in a given characteristic can distort its apparent developmental trend when the data used are derived from cross-sectional studies. What are our alternatives?

Retrospective Studies

Quite simply, the essential design of this form of developmental investigation is that current measurements are compared with *recalled* values for such measurements, going back to various previous points in time. With data on a given characteristic on the same individual at several ages, we could describe developmental processes free of the errors inherent in secular change. Logically, this method should work; psychologically, it does not. Human memory is just too fallible. Data supporting this indictment necessarily come from longitudinal studies, for it is only by contrasting recalled data from an earlier age with data actually obtained from the individual at that age that the validity of recalled data can be determined. There have been a number of studies of this sort, and they are unanimous in their finding of substantial errors of recall, even when the information requested would seem to be of a highly memorable nature and when only a relatively short period of time intervened between the actual event and the moment of recall.

A pioneer study on this question, and one that focuses upon presumably "memorable" events, is by Pyles, Stolz, and Macfarlane (1935). They compared mothers' reports on items relating to pregnancy, birth, and early development for 252 children with the true data on these events ascertained at the time of their occurrence. These mothers' reports were obtained when the children were twenty-one months of age, and so, in the case of some of the recalled items, like the infant's weight at age twelve months, less than a year had elapsed between the events and their recall. In the case of this particular item, to take one example, the average error of recall (ignoring whether the mother tended to over- or underestimate her baby's weight) was approximately nineteen ounces—and at a time when average infant weight was only twenty-three pounds. Perhaps more startling is the comparison between the actual duration of the mother's labor (8.6 hours, on the average) and its average error of recall (3.5 hours), a 41 per cent error. Other items showed equally unreliable reporting. There was little more than chance correspondence between mothers' reports of their physical health during pregnancy and their actual health, as established from physicians' records. The occurrence of illness in the infant during its first year of life was somewhat better reported, but thirty mothers whose children had suffered relatively severe illnesses at some point during this period reported, when the child was twenty-one months of age, *no illnesses at all.*

When we move on to consider such more equivocal events as the child-rearing practices of the mother throughout the first few years of life and when we increase the interval of recall, retrospection is shown to be even more untrustworthy. Robbins (1963) reports from a longitudinal study in which data were collected on actual infant behavior at three-month intervals during the first year and six-month intervals thereafter. When the children were three years old, parents were asked to recall a number of child behaviors and child-rearing practices. Over-all accuracy was low, although mothers were somewhat less in error than were fathers. Robbins summarizes her findings as follows:

"Parents were quite inaccurate in their memory of details about child-rearing practices and early developmental progress, in spite of the frequent rehearsal of these data due to their participation in the longitudinal study, and in spite of the relatively young age of the children. Inaccuracies were greatest for items dealing with the age of weaning and toilet training, the occurrence of thumbsucking, and demand feeding. *Inaccuracies tended to be in the direction of the recommendations of experts in child-rearing, especially on the part of the mothers.*" (italics added)

The last sentence is important, for it points to at least one important determinant of retrospective inaccuracy—a bias toward reporting things as "better" than they actually were. This distortion is a real one, in the sense that the parents were, for the most part, not deliberately lying in order to make a more favorable impression; an earlier study of these same parents found very substantial agreement between actual observations of the children and their parents' *concurrent* reports (Chess, *et al.*, 1960). Apparently, recall must fade and memories become more ambiguous before what we may wish to remember is transformed into what we honestly do remember and report.

In light of this evidence, and there is considerably more that we have not reported, the very least the reader can come away with is a healthy skepticism. The many psychological investigations that present provocative relations between later personality characteristics of children and various aspects of their early child rearing and family atmosphere and of their early personality traits, as reported by parents and by the now adult children themselves after an elapsed interval of ten, fifteen, or more years are to be doubted. Yet interest in such questions as the consistency of various psychological characteristics throughout development and the influence of early experience on adult abilities and personality is mounting. Longitudinal studies of these questions can provide reliable answers.

Longitudinal Studies

As we have noted before, the essential feature of a longitudinal study is that it observes and measures the same group of individuals repeatedly over the period of development being investigated. This method, aside from avoiding hazards of the cross-sectional and retrospective methods, is also the *only possible* method for certain kinds of questions. As Kodlin and Thompson (1958), in their thorough appraisal of the longitudinal method, have pointed out:

"The longitudinal approach is the *only* approach which gives a complete description of the growth phenomenon. . . . The cross-sectional approach never can satisfy the objective of a study which requires the measurement of the change in a trait through time on a given individual. This means that when the objective of the growth study is to arrive at predictions of individual growth, generally, or, to establish the correlation between measurements obtained at successive ages, it is necessary to employ the longitudinal approach."

In other words, even if secular change were not a problem, cross-sectional studies can yield only *group* averages, not *individual* development curves. Such individual records are necessary if we are to find out about the variation in the rate of change among individuals for a given characteristic over a certain period. Cross-sectional studies can tell us as well as longitudinal studies that, for example, boys greatly increase their rate of growth at adolescence. Both types of studies can tell us that boys on the average experience their most rapid growth sometime between their thirteenth and fifteenth birthdays and that the amount grown during that two-year interval is, again on the average, a little more than three inches. But only a longitudinal study can tell us that some boys undergo their periods of most rapid growth as early as age ten, others as late as age seventeen (Nicolson & Hanley, 1953); indeed, the actual increase in height during this two-year period of most rapid growth, whenever it occurs, is considerably more than three inches, and inspection of individual growth records demonstrates that it can be as much as twelve inches.

Not only does longitudinal study provide us with our only access to directly measurable individual developmental changes, but it is also the only avenue to prediction of the future from the past. Whether psychologists are attempting to predict height, intelligence, emotional adjustment, or adult occupational achievement, such predictions require that we obtain measures on the individuals whose behavior is being predicted at two points in time at least.

For many reasons, longitudinal studies of development are rare, although they have recently begun to increase in number. A recent survey of such studies, those that span at least substantial periods of development between birth and adulthood, lists only ten projects (Kagan, 1964). Aside from the obvious need for money and patience in the conduct of such studies, there are other pitfalls that make them risky, though nonetheless invaluable, undertakings. We can list a few of these problems: First, there is *sample attrition*. With increasing duration of the study, subjects are lost for a variety of reasons. Some die, some move from the community, some refuse to cooperate, some no longer can participate because of illness. Second, there is *repeated measurement*. There is always the risk that continual study of individuals may affect the course of their development or at least the validity of some of the measures obtained. Subjects in longitudinal studies are typically seen annually and even more often during periods of rapid development, so that the repeated observation, interviewing, and testing may influence the data obtained. This phenomenon is perhaps most easily seen in the case of intelligence testing; it is known that frequent retesting, particularly with the same instrument, tends to increase test scores. Third, there is *time-limited generality*. Secular change troubles longitudinal research, but in a different way than in cross-sectional study. The point to bear in mind is that a longitudinal study investigates the development of persons born at a particular time and whose development spans a particular segment of real time. What is discovered concerning, say, the influence of parental disciplinary practices in the 1940s upon the development of conscience in now adult children conceivably may not hold for a sample of children born today. Historical events and cultural change may alter the social and psychological context in which children develop, so that a parental practice that led to one effect decades ago may lead to quite another if it is used now. Wars, economic upheavals, changes in educational quality and standards—all these factors may affect the applicability of a relationship obtained in a decades-old longitudinal study to the development of today's children.

Glossary

cross-sectional studies A method for developmental investigation in which developmental trends are based upon comparisons of groups who differ in age at a given time.

differentiation In growth studies, the gradual narrowing down of behavior from a massive, simultaneous pattern of many responses to several more limited and independently controlled responses.

longitudinal studies A method for developmental investigations in which the same individuals provide data directly on at least two (and usually several) occasions in the course of their development.

retrospective studies A method for developmental investigations in which recalled data are employed.

secular change Average change in a characteristic that takes place over successive generations, rather than changes that occur in the course of an individual's development.

stages of development Developmental periods, usually following a progressive sequence, that on an observable level represent qualitative changes in either structure or function.

UNIT 3

the human organism: growth and development

overview / The child is not merely a miniature adult; rather he differs qualitatively and quantitatively from an adult in many of his physical characteristics and behavioral potentials. The period of growth and development begins at birth (actually at conception) and continues through adolescence, with most rapid changes occurring shortly after birth and during the few years before puberty. Early development is primarily cephalocaudal (head-to-foot) and proximodistal (center-to-periphery), facts reflected in differing rates of growth in various physical organs and behavioral skills.

Behavioral development during the early years reflects both physical maturation through growth and differentiation and the cumulative effects of training, learning, and general experience. These two influences generally interact, although with insufficient maturation the effects of experience may be lost on the "unready" organism. Differentiation is the hallmark of the early developmental process, with gross patterns of reactivity gradually being transformed into more articulated and discriminating behavioral action.

Adolescence is a highly variable period, both with regard to physical change and behavior development, that intervenes between childhood and adulthood. Aside from the difficulty of defining this period for a given individual (various characteristics vary considerably with a person in the times that they attain mature status), differences among individuals are truly enormous, permitting variations of several years in the onset and duration of many adolescent maturation tasks. Although adolescence is initiated by, and largely under the control of, physiological events, there are important behavioral factors involved, particularly with respect to the end of adolescence. Not only are individual differences in rate of physical maturation responsible for profound psychological effects, but, more generally, cultural variation in the definitions of adolescence and the demands for the attainment of full adult status have substantial developmental consequences.

The adult years, extending from entrance into adulthood through old age, are a little-studied period of development. They are, however, "developmental," in the sense that change occurs throughout this span of life as marriage, child rearing, and vocational choice and achievement generate a continual flux in environmental demands. By and large, many of the assumed tragic points of relinquishment and decline have, through research, been found either not to exist, in a psychological sense, or even to bring with them new satisfactions. Menopause, retirement, the "empty nest" left by departing grown children—all these points are not inevitably deteriorative events but rather, especially if physical health is maintained, times of greater freedom and opportunity.

As we have seen in Unit 2, the study of human development may follow alternate routes, each beset with certain problems. It is through sensibly evaluating and employing the results of studies of all types that psychology has achieved some understanding of the course of growth and development. Developmental findings are presented at various places in the book, related to discussions of the various main aspects involved in the study of psychology. In this unit we shall attempt only a brief preview of some of these results, while placing our major emphasis on a process that is, strictly speaking, not psychological, yet provides a necessary foundation for the study of man's development. We refer to the physical growth and development of the human organism.

Development in Infancy and Childhood

The behavior of an organism is always limited and directed by its anatomical structure, neurological organization, and biochemical composition. The study of the behavior of growing children has therefore gone hand in hand with the study of the growth, development, and maturation of the child's body. We must recognize that the child is *not* an adult in miniature; the child is a different biological organism from the adult. His skeletal structure is differently proportioned, his nervous system is different,

his hormonal and biochemical make-up are different. And these differences are significant enough to prevent our generalizing from the behavior of the adult to the behavior of the child. Out of the studies of the differences have come several developmental principles relating function to structure.

Over-All Growth Rates

Data on the over-all bodily growth rate of man have been accumulating for many years, and the general shape of the physical growth curve of man is well established. The over-all mental growth rate has also been studied, and comparison between bodily and mental growth is now possible.

The two simplest measures of over-all bodily growth in man are total height and total weight. These measures tell similar stories. Figure 3.1. depicts the growth of man as represented by total height. The most rapid changes —those occurring during the prenatal period, from conception to birth—are not indicated in the figure. Immediately after birth the growth rate continues to be rapid, more so than at any other time after birth. Sometime during the second year of life the child has attained one-half his adult height. Toward the end of "childhood" at about age eleven there is, as we have seen, another spurt of growth that lasts into the adolescent years. After puberty, the rate of growth slows down considerably until the final height is reached. Then comes a fairly stable period, after which there may begin an actual slight shrinking in over-all height and body size—senescence has begun to set in.

As longitudinal data have shown us, there are large individual variations from this average picture, in terms of both the age at which puberty is reached and the maximum growth attained. Some girls reach their adult height by the time they are fourteen years old, some boys not until they are twenty-two or twenty-three years old.

There have been profound secular changes in the rate of physical maturation, all pointing toward a substantial and apparently continuing shortening in the time required to reach mature adult status. Pearson and Lee (1903), studying English boys and girls who reached maturity at about the turn of the century, reported that males did not achieve their full height until age twenty-eight, females not until age twenty-five. Age of attaining menarche, a critical milestone in sexual maturation, has also shown a remarkable shift in the last hundred years or so (see Figure 3.2.). Most recent evidence suggests that the trend is continuing; data from a variety of sources place the average age of

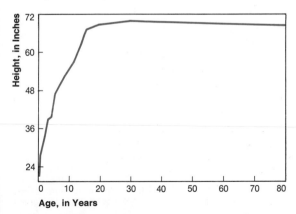

Figure 3.1. Average growth in height of American males from birth to eighty years of age.
N. Bayley, "Development and Maturation," in H. Helson, ed., *Theoretical Foundations of Psychology;* Copyright 1951 by D. Van Nostrand Company, Inc.; adapted by permission.

menarche, at least in certain areas, at twelve or even earlier.

Figure 3.3. tells the story of the growth of man and other animals in terms of total weight. The periods between conception and birth and that immediately after birth again show the most rapid increase. Then, for human beings, there is a long juvenile period (from about three to twelve) when weight accumulates rather slowly. With puberty, when growth in height has begun to taper off, growth in weight again increases and continues at a fairly rapid rate until maturity is reached. The chart does not go beyond the age of twenty-four, the current outside limit for the period of physical growth. After the beginning of decline in our physical powers (about twenty-five years or so), there is an increasing tendency to corpulence, but this increase in weight indicates senescence rather than growth. It may be due to the hormonal changes of the body that accompany decline in physical powers.

In comparing man with other animals, two conspicuous points stand out: First, for human beings the pubertal age has a special significance in weight growth. With the beginning of puberty, the rate of weight gain shows a definite change. From that point on the difference between man and other animals, as far as the shape of the growth curve is concerned, disappears. Second, although other species go through a juvenile period corresponding to man's, the length of this period in animals is relatively insignificant compared to that of man. Man's long juvenile period makes the human family unique among all animals. The human family is the only one in which there is the simultaneous presence of dependent offspring of *different* ages. This fact has important consequences for the personality development of the child and the adult.

Differential Growth Rates

An over-all growth rate is the sum of several quite different growth rates. The different parts

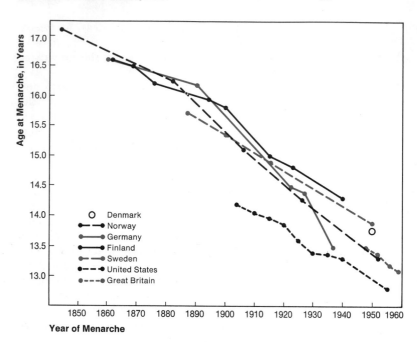

Figure 3.2. Secular changes in age of menarche for seven Western countries.
J. M. Tanner, *Growth at Adolescence*, 2nd ed. (1962); adapted by permission of Blackwell Scientific Publications, Ltd.

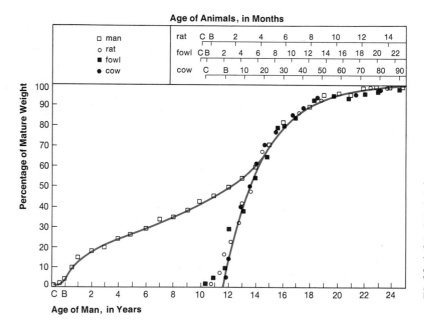

Figure 3.3. An equivalence chart of the growth in weight for man and three other species. The curves have been so adjusted as to make the age of maturity coincide for all animals (see the data at the top of the chart). The letter C represents the point of conception, B the point of birth.
W. J. Robbins, *et al., Growth* (1928); adapted by permission of Yale University Press.

of the body do not grow at the same speed. The head, the trunk, and the legs, for example, lengthen at different times and at different rates. Some of the organs of the body grow very rapidly at first, then slow down; others start off slowly, then accelerate. In some instances, one part of a single organ (for example, the brain) matures faster than another part of the same organ.

Because of these differences in rates of growth and varying times of maturation of parts, it might be expected that psychological development would also progress at differential rates; for example, some capacities would appear before others and some emotions would precede other emotions. We shall see that such is indeed the case.

Developmental Direction   One of the most striking characteristics of the growing human body is the change in the form and proportions of its various parts. Look at Figures 3.4. and 3.5. At two months after conception you were about 50 per cent head. At birth you were 25 per cent head and the rest evenly divided between trunk and legs. Eventually, you have developed into the "average" adult, whose length is 50 per cent legs, about one-third trunk, and only about

12–14 per cent head (see Figure 3.4.). (Here again we must make allowances for individual differences. Look around you at your neighbors.)

These changes come about through very different growth rates for the different parts of the body. The head starts growing at a very rapid rate almost immediately after conception. By the time the baby is born, the head has already achieved more than 60 per cent of its adult size (see Figure 3.5.). The trunk is next in growth rate, and by the end of the second year it has reached a point halfway to its final length. During the second year, the legs and arms begin to grow in earnest, reaching the 50 per cent point at about the fourth year. This progressive growth—first the head, then the trunk, then the legs—has been designated by the term *cephalocaudal* (head-to-foot).

While the body has been growing in length, it has also been growing in a *proximodistal direction*, that is, from the central part out to the peripheral part. For example, the trunk and shoulders develop first, and then the arms, fingers, and toes begin their real growth.

Correlated with these physical growth directions, the sensorimotor behavior of the infant also shows a head-to-foot and center-to-pe-

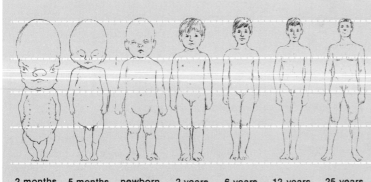

2 months   5 months   newborn   2 years   6 years   12 years   25 years
(fetal)

Figure 3.4. Changes in form and proportion of the human body during the fetal period and the postnatal period up to maturity.
W. J. Robbins, *et al.*, *Growth* (1928); adapted by permission of Yale University Press.

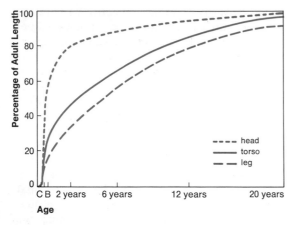

Figure 3.5. Differential growth of the human head, torso, and legs from conception to maturity. C stands for conception, B for birth.

riphery development. Nursing is the earliest and best-organized behavior in the neonate. It is, of course, primarily localized in the head. The "normal" infant shows the following sequence of *sensorimotor development:*

4 weeks—control of eye movements; ability to follow an object visually, and so forth
16 weeks—ability to balance head
28 weeks—ability to use the hands for grasping and manipulating objects
40 weeks—control of the trunk, enabling the child to sit and crawl
52 weeks—control of the legs and feet, enabling the child to stand and cruise about

A. GHESELL and C. S. AMATRUDA. 1947. *Developmental Diagnosis* (New York: Hoeber).

It is clear that we have here a cephalocaudal direction of development.

A recent comparative study of motor development, contrasting infants born in the 1960s with those born almost thirty years earlier, finds—as have many studies—the same developmental sequence and very little, if any, secular change in average age of occurrence of various motor skills within the first year (Bayley, 1965). There is, however, some suggestion of a slight acceleration in development in the later-born sample in the second year of life.

In the development of locomotion and move-

ment the proximodistal direction is also apparent. At first the child's purposeful movements stem from the shoulder and pelvic girdles. Later in infancy, movements appear at the elbows, wrists, knees, and ankles. For example, in reaching for something, the infant first moves his shoulders and elbows toward the object, and only later does he begin to use his wrists and fingers.

Differences Among Organs Not only do the chief divisions of the body (head, trunk, and limbs) show variable growth rates, but so also do the different organs within the body. Furthermore, the different parts within the individual organ grow at different rates. A consideration of both these differential growth patterns—among organs and within organs—will lead us to other important developmental principles.

The various organs of man can be grouped into four different growth types as shown in Figure 3.6. The genital organs show a positive acceleration: very slow growth during childhood and then extremely rapid acceleration at puberty. The opposite is true of the brain and its parts. Here we have a negatively accelerated growth curve, with rapid growth during the first six years of life and then a sharp slowing down. The lymphoid group shows a growth reversal, increasing very rapidly at first, then actually decreasing in size. Finally, the "general" type shows an S-shaped curve—starting and ending with rapid growth periods separated by a long period of very little gain.

Differences Within Organs Different parts of some of the endocrine glands (especially of the pituitary) develop at different rates. Perhaps the most interesting and important example of differential growths within a single organ is provided by the cerebral cortex.

At birth the cortex has all the neural cells it is ever going to have. As the body grows, however, certain changes occur in the brain. Among them are changes in the size and chemical composition of the nerve cells and in the length and state of development of the nerve fibers. These changes occur at different rates for different areas of the cortex. For example, the pyramidal Betz cells (important for motor control) are more advanced in over-all development than is any other type of cell in the cortex from birth to the age of six months. During the first six months of life the circumference, length, structural compactness, and protective covering of the nerve fibers in the primary motor and sensory areas are far advanced over the fibers in the rest of the brain. Only later do the other areas of the brain develop to the mature level (see Figure 3.7.).

Although the human infant is born with a brain, it is thus a brain whose parts and functions mature at different rates (see Figure 3.8. for an illustration of the gradual development of the alpha rhythm in the brain). The sensory and motor areas can begin to function rela-

tively early, and simple conditioning may be possible, but the association areas (presumably those importantly involved in complex perception and problem solving) are just not ready to go to work until some later time. Recent evidence, reviewed in Unit 29, p. 468, indicates that brain growth is significantly influenced, at least in animals, by early experience.

Maturation and Learning

The story of bodily growth suggests that the development of behavior will show a successive unfolding of functions and capacities as their underlying bodily structures develop. If we were to ask, therefore, why the behavior of the older child is much more complex than that of the infant, we could not merely answer "learning" or "experience." The recognition of this point has led to the following *maturation-*

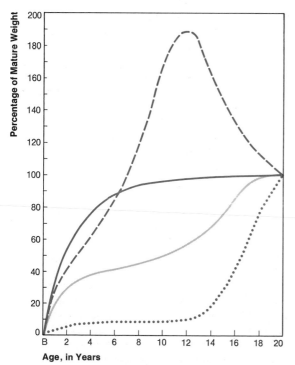

Figure 3.6. Curves showing growth rates of the four major categories of organs or tissue types in the human body. Examples of each category are listed.
R. E. Scammon, "The Measurement of the Body in Childhood," in J. A. Harris, *et al., The Measurement of Man;* Copyright 1930 by University of Minnesota; adapted by permission of University of Minnesota Press.

– – Lymphoid Type
thymus, lymph nodes, intestinal lymphoid masses

—— Neural Type
brain and its parts, spinal cord, and so on

—— General Type
respiratory and digestive organs, kidneys, musculature as a whole, skeleton as a whole

••••Genital Type
testis, ovary, uterine tube, prostate, seminal vesicles

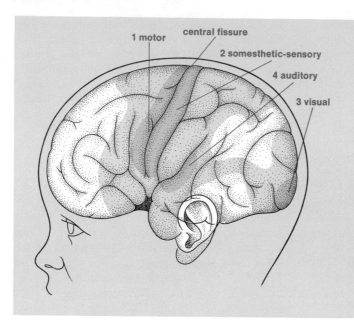

Figure 3.7. The differential rate of development of a child's cortex. This map is based on the histological examination (during autopsy) of newborn and infant brains. Some nine different measures of nerve-cell and -fiber maturation have been used in arriving at this picture. The darkest shading represents the highest stage of development. The first area to mature is thus the motor area, the second the somesthetic-sensory area, the third the visual area, the fourth the auditory area. Next come the areas surrounding these primary sensory and motor areas. The areas shown in white are the last to mature. Based on data from Conel, 1952.

learning principle: The development of behavior reflects *maturation* through growth, as well as the cumulative effects of learning through experience.

We have a good illustration of this principle in the development of the child's learning ability itself. Learning ability, in general, increases relatively gradually with age, although the work of Jean Piaget (Unit 25) suggests qualitative changes in what principles can be learned, which *do* seem to mark relatively discontinuous transitions throughout mental development. Nevertheless when we compare the newborn with even the three-month-old infant, striking differences appear.

Neonate Learning There have been many attempts to study learning in the first week or two of life. The simplest conditioning tasks have been used. For example, Marquis (1931) attempted to condition the sucking responses of infants to the sound of a buzzer, and Wickens and Wickens (1940) tried to train the infant to withdraw his foot (in order to escape an electric shock) whenever a buzzer sounded (see Unit 19 for a description of conditioning procedures). Of the many attempts to establish conditioning, only that of Marquis showed any success. The best other experimenters have been able to do is to get occasional indications of conditioning in the human infant, and these results were extremely erratic and unstable. But species may differ (see Box 10, p. 62).

When we recall that the cortex of the neonate is quite undeveloped and that we do not even have clear evidence that his cortical cells can conduct impulses at all, the "stupidity" of the newborn becomes understandable. The most impatient of parents have to wait for growth. Furthermore, we must remember that as the child grows older his cortex first becomes a motor cortex, then a motor-sensory one, and only later do the various association areas mature.

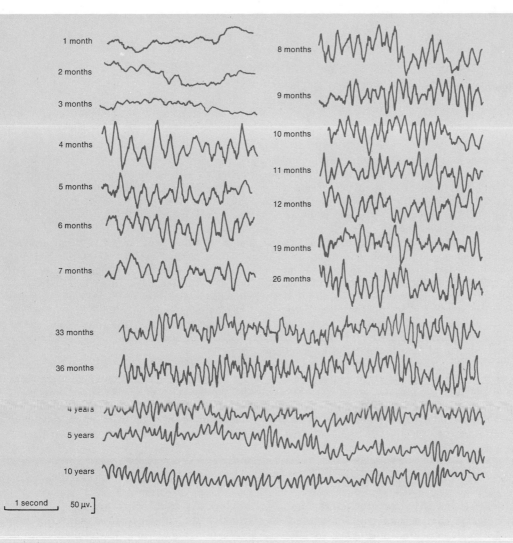

Figure 3.8. Records showing the development of the alpha rhythm (taken from the occipital area) in a boy from one month to ten years of age. For the first three months no uniform pattern appears. About the fourth month a persistent rhythm begins to develop (about three per second), and by the end of the first year the rhythm increases to about six per second. From that point on there is a slow increase in rhythm until about the age of ten or twelve years, at which time it reaches the adult frequency of ten per second. These records were taken by the psychologist D. B. Lindsley from his son.

D. B. Lindsley, "Discussion," in L. A. Jeffress, ed., *Cerebral Mechanisms in Behavior* (1951); adapted by permission of John Wiley & Sons, Inc.

Box 10

Haven't I Heard You
Somewhere Before?

As we saw earlier (Box 1, p. 4), many animals show the curious phenomenon of "imprinting" —the tendency in later behavior to recognize, be attracted to, and to follow physically an object to which it has been exposed earlier during a particular "critical period." For chicks, the critical period—the relatively short time after birth during which the animal can be easily imprinted—is early on the first day of life. The procedure is more likely to be successful if the imprinting object emits some sort of sound.

In a recent experiment, J. B. Grier, S. A. Counter, and W. M. Shearer of Northern Illinois University raised the possibility that imprinting could occur before birth. First, it was established that embryonic chicks were sensitive to sound before hatching; they did so by observing that chick embryos, removed from their shells sometime between four and eighteen days after conception, consistently showed some reaction to sound (through twitching or some other movement) from the twelfth day onward. Next, they exposed fifteen eggs to continuous sound stimulation from day twelve to day eighteen, a time shortly before hatching is normally expected. The sound consisted of a series of one-second beeps alternating with one-second periods of silence. Another batch of twenty eggs was allowed to mature quietly in an incubator.

Within a few hours after hatching, these chicks were all exposed to a test situation in which they were placed in the center of a circular table, about three feet in diameter, and were alternately exposed to the prenatal sound (to which only the experimental groups had previously been exposed) and to another, novel sound of the same general characteristics but of considerably higher pitch. These sounds were emitted, alternately, from one of two speakers situated at opposite ends

Readiness for Training The maturation-learning principle suggests that certain training should not be undertaken until the child is specifically ready for it. Pushing the child too far ahead of his maturation level may under some circumstances impose harmful stresses and strains on the child, not to mention the parent and teacher (see p. 395). But even if one were willing to pay this price, the educational objectives might still not be reached or reached only with great inefficiency of time and effort (see Box 11, p. 65).

It might therefore be thought that the child psychologist could draw up a list of the ages at which the child becomes ready for different kinds of training and that this list could be used to guide both parents and teacher. Some lists have been attempted, but there are two major considerations that limit the applicability of such *readiness* guides.

First, from the moment the ovum is fertilized until the time of death, the individual lives in a constantly changing environment, whether it is the fluid bathing the embryo in its mother's womb, the noises and cooings surrounding the baby in its cradle, or the welter

of the table, and each sound presentation lasted for forty-five seconds. The distance moved by the newborn chicks of the experimental (prenatal sound) and control (prenatal quiet) groups from the center of the table toward the speaker was measured on each trial. The following data give the average distances that each group moved toward the two different sounds in all trials.

Distance (Inches) Moved

	Prenatal Sound	*Novel Sound*
Experimental group	9.9	4.7
Control group	5.4	5.3

Clearly, the experimental chicks moved farther toward the sound that they had presumably experienced prenatally than toward the novel sound; the difference is statistically highly significant, that is, not a chance result. The control chicks, in contrast, showed an almost identical response to both sounds. Furthermore, the control-group data indicate that the two sounds were "naturally" equally attractive, assuring that the experimenters had not chosen, by chance, a particularly appealing sound for prenatal stimulation.

In a subsequent experiment, chicks that had been exposed to the prenatal sound were tested in a "following" situation. They were again placed at the center of the table, and a child's pull-toy model chicken was slowly moved across the table in front of them. On two occasions the toy was silent, on two other occasions a small speaker on the back of the toy chicken emitted the novel sound, and on two other occasions the prenatal sound came from the speaker. (The order in which these different occasions occurred was randomly mixed to ensure that each situation took place at various points in the series of six "passes.") The outcome of this procedure provides further impressive evidence for the hypothesis of prenatal auditory imprinting. Expressed in terms of the average amount of time (in seconds) that the chicks spend following the toy chicken under each of the conditions, the results are no sound, 5.4; novel sound, 10.1; prenatal sound, 15.2. Again, the differences are highly significant.

J. B. GRIER, S. A. COUNTER, and W. M. SHEARER. 1967. Prenatal Auditory Imprinting in Chickens, *Science*, 155, 1692–3.

of stimuli bombarding the child as soon as he begins to sit up and take notice. Although some performances develop despite restricted stimulation, the amount and kinds of general stimulation may affect some of the "innate" growth factors. For example, there are some data to suggest that the continued transmission of impulses through the nervous system speeds up the maturation of the nerve fibers. In other words, although learning may not be very effective until maturation has taken place, the very attempt to learn and the stimulation of the child in that attempt may speed up the maturation process. The animal data on anatomical and biochemical modifications of the cortex caused by early experience strongly support this presumption (see Unit 29).

Second, there are large individual differences in maturation rates. This statement holds true whether we use such measures as body weight or length, bone structure development, and the onset of puberty—or the more subtle measures of sensitivity to various emotional, social, and "intellectual" situations (see Figure 3.9.). The maturation-learning principle, as a guide to the educational program for a child, must be ap-

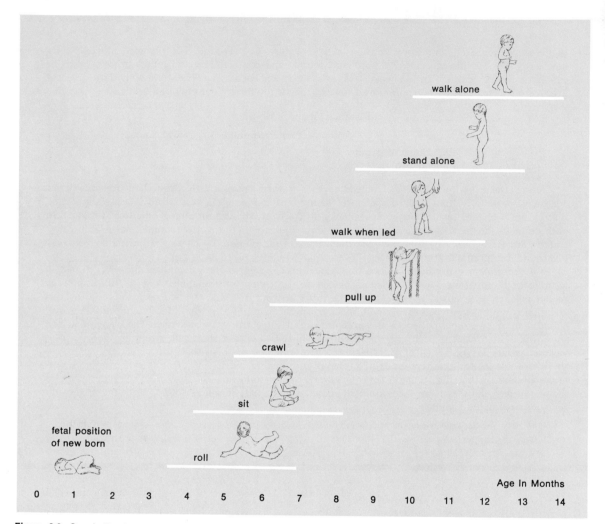

walk alone

stand alone

walk when led

pull up

crawl

sit

fetal position
of new born

roll

Age In Months

| 0 | 1 | 2 | 3 | 4 | 5 | 6 | 7 | 8 | 9 | 10 | 11 | 12 | 13 | 14 |

Figure 3.9. One indication of the extent of individual differences in maturation rate is seen in the development of walking. Although the *order* in which children progress from one stage to another is similar, the *age* at which the different stages are reached varies greatly. Shown here are the age *zones* within which 95 per cent of a group of 215 infants studied at a well-baby clinic in Rochester, Minnesota, reached the various stages of performance. In general, there was more than a four-month spread for any one stage. For example, some children were able to stand alone at about eight and a half months; others were not able to stand alone until thirteen months. (Data from Aldrich & Nerval, 1946.)

plied with full allowance for such individual differences. From various sources, it can be estimated that when a first-grade teacher meets her class of youngsters, all about six years of age, she is in fact confronted with an array of children who, on various abilities, in fact vary in "readiness" from ages three to eleven. It is not only that children differ in their *general* levels of "readiness"; rather, within a single child there may be a variation of several years in "readiness," depending upon the particular aspects of learning considered.

Box 11

Maturation, Ladder Climbing, Language Development

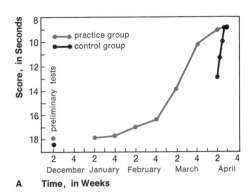

A   **Time, in Weeks**

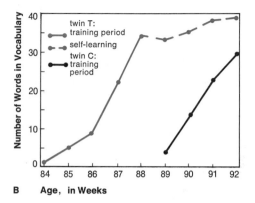

B   **Age, in Weeks**

The maturation-learning principle has been tested on various forms of behavior, from locomotion skills to the learning of language. Figure A is taken from a study by J. R. Hilgard at the Merrill-Palmer nursery school with twenty-eight-month-old children, of whom eight were trained for twelve weeks on climbing up and down a three-step ladder two and one-half feet high, and eight others were not. Both groups earned equivalent scores on a preliminary test. The untrained group, after *one* week of practice, caught up with the twelve-week-trained group. As far as this skill is concerned, "premature" practice shows considerable waste. (The "score in seconds" is the average time taken to climb up and down the ladder.)

L. C. Strayer at Yale University compared the effectiveness of vocabulary training at two different maturation periods, using the "co-twin control" method. One of a pair of identical twins is given training, and the other is reserved as a control, thus ensuring that both subjects are genetically identical and therefore, it is assumed, equally mature (see Figure B).

The subjects were identical twin sisters, T and C, eighty-four weeks of age. T was given intensive vocabulary training for five weeks, while C lived in an isolated "nonverbal" environment in which her attendants carefully avoided speaking in her presence. Then C was given a four-week training period, and T was returned to a normal language environment of other children and adults.

Among the results were the following: First, C's learning rate was faster; after an equal amount of training (four weeks), she had a larger vocabulary than did T; second, in a picture-pointing test, C, by the end of four weeks, was making *no* errors, whereas T could not pass a single test after five weeks of training; third, T's vocabulary continued to increase after training was discontinued, and therefore it was several months before C caught up with T.

"Premature" learning is not efficient, but neither is it always entirely wasted.

J. R. HILGARD. 1932. Learning and Maturation in Pre-school Children, *J. Genet. Psychol.*, 41, 36–56. Figure A adapted by permission of The Journal Press.

L. C. STRAYER, 1930. Language and Growth, *Genet. Psychol. Monogr.*, 8, No. 3. Figure B adapted by permission of The Journal Press.

Differentiation of Structure and Function

As the major parts of the body, its organs and its systems, develop, greater and greater precision of function within any one system becomes possible. For example, at first the entire upper half of the child's body—starting with the shoulder region and involving the arms, hands, and fingers—moves spasmodically and excitedly toward a desired object. With development, more and more limited movements are called forth until finally only the fingers—or even only one finger—may languidly and surely stretch out to retrieve the object.

This gradual "narrowing down" or differentiation of behavior from a massive, all-inclusive pattern to several precise, limited, and relatively independent ones has been observed at all levels of analysis. It summarizes the difference between the behavior of the neonate stage and that of early childhood. It is apparent in the growth of motor skills and in the development of the emotional life of the child. The same story is repeated again and again: From a large general pattern, several specialized ones are split off or differentiated.

Differentiation and the Neonate This principle is readily seen in the developmental history of the neonate. Although the neonate has some quite specific reflexes and response patterns, it can be described as a "generalized organism." Any one of a large number of different kinds of stimuli can call forth the neonate's responses, and its responses are rarely localized in any one part of the body or muscle group. As the neonate becomes an infant, there is progressively less and less involvement of the organism in response to any given stimulus. For example, Pratt (1937) has shown that circulatory and respiratory responses that can originally be released by several types of stimuli acting upon different sensory organs become more "discriminating," to the point at which only a relatively few and quite specific stimuli are effective. These early specialized movements

of the infant derive from, and are definitely related to, the preceding massive ones. This observation has led to the suggestion that the generalized active fetus is the one who most quickly develops the finer specialized movements when he becomes an infant (see Box 12, p. 67).

Activity level is a characteristic of the organism that shows unusual promise as a fundamental biological-behavioral characteristic. As we saw in Unit 1, it appears to possess at least some genetic basis. What is more, activity level seems to be a relatively persistent human trait, at least in the earlier years of development. Even within the first few days of life, when the neonate is a generally disorganized and unpredictable creature, its activity level represents one of its few consistent behavioral features (Bell, 1960; Kessen, *et al.*, 1961). This consistency extends through the first two years of life, according to Thomas, *et al.* (1964), and activity level observed during this early period significantly predicts this same aspect of behavior throughout childhood (Escalona & Heider, 1959; Kagan & Moss, 1962). The importance of activity level is not solely an outcome of its apparent developmental consistency, although that fact alone would draw one's attention to the usual changeability of most aspects of human behavior as seen over the developmental span. What makes this phenomenon potentially arresting is the mass of evidence that points to infantile stimulation as an important determinant of later resistance to stress, cortical growth, intellectual development, and need for later environmental interaction. If, as Schaffer (1966) proposes, a high "natural" activity level serves as a form of self-stimulation, then these various and quite pervasive consequences of early stimulation level themselves become tied to an innate characteristic of the organism—its built-in activity level.

Individual Differences in Development

Behavior does not always show a constant progression in complexity or integration. There

UNIT

seem to be lapses in development and even apparent regressions. For example, physical development is usually retarded during periods of famine (as in wartime), but, typically, the child quickly "catches up" with his developmental course once normal diet is restored. In addition there are tremendous individual differences in growth and development, some children showing a much longer preadolescent period than other children, which, at least in part, arises from genetic factors. Furthermore, skeletal, hormonal, and other developmental statuses do not always correspond to chronological age, a fact that may make difficulties for both parent and child.

People expect, for example, that a certain height and body build will go along with a correspondingly developed maturity of interests and emotions. The child who is larger than the average ten-year-old is expected to be more mature than the average ten-year-old. And, when he behaves like a typical ten-year-old or shows the muscular coordination typical of a ten-year-old, the observer may feel that the child is "backward" or "awkward." The child who is retarded (as against the average) in his body growth or emotional maturity may also run up against adjustment problems. In part, they may arise from the fact that he differs from his schoolmates and does not live up to the expectations of his teachers and the adults surrounding him. But the story is more complicated (see p. 735).

The Adolescent Period

The period of growth and development known as *adolescence* is variously defined, but most often it refers to the rather long period between childhood and mature adulthood, during which there are both quantitative and qualitative changes in various characteristics of the organism. We have suggested earlier that adolescence shows a continuing trend toward earlier beginnings and earlier attainment of adult status, and this fact, combined with the enor-

---

Box 12

Predicting Behavior Development from Fetal Movements

T. W. Richards and H. Newberg of the Fels Foundation at Antioch College have reported that the movements of the fetus in the uterus foretell its rate of behavioral development after birth.

At one-week intervals, during the last two months of pregnancy, each of twelve women recorded every fetal movement she felt over a five-hour period. From these records each fetus received a "fetal-movement score" in terms of the average number of minutes it was active per ten-minute period.

Six months after birth the babies were tested on the Gesell schedule of behavioral development, consisting of tasks like dropping an object into a cup, sitting alone, looking for a fallen object, and so on. The results showed a positive correlation (about .65) between fetal-movement score and performance on the Gesell schedule. For example, the babies who passed the test of dropping an object into a cup had earned a fetal-movement score of 5.76; those who failed had a score of 3.31. Those who passed the "sit alone" test had earned a fetal-movement score of 4.88; those who failed had a score of 2.90.

The investigators suggest the following interpretation: The movements felt by the mother indicate the level of development of the generalized behavior of the fetus. Out of this generalized behavior are differentiated the various precise motor movements of infancy. Therefore, the more advanced the organism is in the development of his *generalized* behavior, the sooner his *precise* motor movements become differentiated.

T. W. RICHARDS and H. NEWBERG. 1938. Studies in Fetal Behavior, *Child Develpm.,* 9, 79–86.

mous range of individual differences in rate of development in physical growth, sexual maturation, and so on, foredooms any attempt to define the age range that encompasses adolescence. Depending on which sex we are referring to and which facet of development is under discussion, the adolescent phase can start as early as age eight (the beginnings of breast development in early maturing girls) to as late as age twenty (the achievement of skeletal and sexual maturity, as well as adult stature, in late maturing boys). Keeping in mind that, on the average, girls are approximately two years earlier than boys in the various facets of adolescent development and that, within each sex, individuals may differ by several years, we can provide a rough timetable for when a number of developmental landmarks are reached: First, sexual maturity, as measured by a number of indicators (breast development and menarche in girls, pubic and other hair growth in both sexes), is reached sometime between ages twelve and sixteen in girls and between ages thirteen and eighteen in boys. Second, skeletal maturity is achieved between ages thirteen and nineteen in girls and between ages fourteen and twenty in boys.

Adolescence, in a physical sense, is under the control of physiological (largely hormonal) factors, and, as these factors are more or less easily measurable, it is not too difficult to define the onset and conclusion of adolescence. (Unit 36 presents some aspects of sexual maturation.) But adolescence is also a psychological phenomenon, and here we encounter differing expectations and criteria for escaping from childhood status and eventually attaining adult status. Subcultures vary widely, not only in different countries but also among different ethnic and socioeconomic groups in our own country, as to when they are willing to define an individual as no longer a child and finally as an adult. Cultural influence lays far more emphasis on the transition from adolescence to adulthood; thus the "end of adolescence" is primarily a psychological phenomenon.

Psychological End of Adolescence

The beginnings of adolescence, then, can be easily defined in physiological terms. But when does adolescence end? Here physiological measures are not very helpful. Once puberty is achieved, the last major physiological growth change has taken place, and from now on the person continues along a fairly smooth curve to the culmination of his growth. Presumably adolescence ends when the person achieves "psychological maturity" and puts away childish things to take on the responsibilities and attitudes of adulthood. Although everyone might accept this definition, it is not very useful, for we have no certain way of knowing what "psychological maturity" is or how to measure it. By general agreement the early twenties have been set aside as the terminal point for adolescence, as the "maturity" point. But this choice is quite arbitrary and varies considerably from society to society.

There are several reasons why any period set aside as the end of adolescence must be arbitrary. In the first place, here, as elsewhere, there are wide individual differences. In the second place, "psychological maturity" cannot be a unitary event. A person may mature in one respect much more rapidly than in others, and no doubt some of us go through life without ever maturing in some areas. But more important than these reasons—or perhaps underlying these reasons—is the influence of the cultural pattern.

Maturity and Culture

We all live under the confines of the cultural pattern specific to our part of the world, our national boundaries, our socioeconomic class, our religious congregation, and our familial group. Each of these groupings establishes its own rules of the game, its own demands and expectations for its members.

Perhaps the most important psychological characteristics of the adolescent are an awaken-

ing of primary sexual interest accompanied by an ability to do something about it and a desire to achieve status as an adult among adults. And it is at both these points that the culture within which the adolescent lives becomes important.

If the culture permits the adolescent to recognize his awakened sexual urges and, further, has worked out some satisfactory way of dealing with these urges, then one set of adolescent problems is considerably mitigated. If, in addition, the culture allows the adolescent to exercise responsibility early and to assume the role of the adult, the maturity of the adolescent is hastened. On the other hand, if the culture handles these two needs of the adolescent in a confused and frequently contradictory way, then emotional conflict may result and maturity be delayed.

The Adult Years

Considering current estimates of life expectancy, there are still fifty years or more to go after the adolescent has been ushered across the threshold into adulthood. We shall have little to say about psychological development during this extensive period, for the most part because truly developmental studies of change during this time span are few and far between. A lot is known concerning almost all aspects of adult behavior, for adults have frequently served as subjects in cross-sectional studies. Courtship behavior, occupational and vocational choice and achievement, marriage, parenthood, retirement—all these psychosocial events have been studied by psychologists, sociologists, and others. But they have been typically studies at a single point in time and, as such, are primarily descriptive. We thus know relatively little concerning the course of development, say, in marital adjustment or occupational achievement in the same group of individuals over any substantial time span during adulthood. We know even less concerning the antecedents in childhood and adolescence of these aspects of adult behavior.

The picture, however, is not quite as dark as depicted in this brief discussion, and, more important, the prospects are bright. Some current longitudinal studies are continuing, and, with time, they may tell us something of the early determinants of adult life styles and of the routes traveled to reach various adult outcomes. And within the adult span itself there have been some investigations of psychological changes in the same groups of persons over time. Perhaps foremost among these investigations is a collection of related studies, entitled *Personality in Middle and Later Life* (Neugarten & Associates, 1964), which has questioned a number of "common-sense" assumptions concerning this period and yielded some new and unexpected insights. For example, this and some other studies would seem to have dispelled the at least implicit assumption that personality does not change once maturity has been reached. For instance, Neugarten found that, during the latter half of life, men tend to become more nurturant and women more assertive. But, although certain traits do show some modification, a general result from a number of studies is that certain basic and underlying characteristics like "ego strength"—essentially the ability to see the world realistically, to cope with it adaptively, and to derive satisfaction from living in it—do seem to persist well into old age. Allied to this finding is the hypothesis that many so-called "age changes," whether they be in fundamental personality structure, intellectual ability, or other aspects of behavior, are in reality functions of true physical debilitation, rather than age per se. In other words, as long as the individual, no matter what his age, remains essentially healthy physically, he will remain much the same person, psychologically speaking, that he has always been.

Some of the "bugaboos" of aging, as far as research now can tell, turn out to be neither necessarily dramatic nor universally unfortunate events. The menopause not only fails to signal the end of "womanhood," but quite frequently it is a relatively ignored and even welcome event. Retirement, similarly, may have been overemphasized as a dreaded occurrence. For many individuals this event is not a burden but a goal attained. For men, particularly, retirement and aging in general provide an opportunity for the satisfaction of needs not satisfied during earlier years. For some, the goal is passivity, and retirement and old age bring relief from burdensome obligations; for others, the reward is more time to pursue interests necessarily neglected during younger, working years. Growing old may even bring about increased self-acceptance as a man comes to terms with his life goals and achievements (Reichard, *et al.*, 1962). A more pervasive process, hypothesized to occur with increased age, is that of "disengagement," a tendency to reduce responsibilities and social commitments —as parent, as worker, even as wife or husband —with a consequent easing of some of the strains of living, providing for some an avenue toward comfortable and satisfying later years (Cumming & Henry, 1961).

These few comments on the psychology of the adult years are obviously only the briefest of overviews. Their intent is to round out our story of the developmental life span, and, this done, we can embark on the systematic consideration of the various aspects of man's behavior that constitute the remainder of this book.

Glossary

adolescence Refers to the age between puberty and adulthood. Although the beginning of adolescence can be set quite accurately (as it is defined by the specific physiological criterion of sexual maturity), the terminal point of adolescence can only be approximated, for there is no sharp differentiation between adolescence and adulthood.

cephalocaudal direction Refers to the progressive growth of the body parts from the head end to the legs, characteristic of the developing human being. From the Greek word *kephale* (head) and the Latin word *cauda* (tail), from head to tail.

maturation Refers to the progressive or successive unfolding of various bodily and mental functions and capacities as their underlying bodily structures develop through the normal growth process.

maturation-learning principle The generalization that the development of behavior shows the effects of interaction between maturational and learning processes.

proximodistal direction Refers to the progressive growth of the body parts from the central to the peripheral or terminal parts, a direction of growth characteristic of the developing human being. The shoulders thus develop first, then the arms, then the hands and fingers.

puberty Refers to the earliest age at which a person is capable of procreating offspring. The term *pubescence* refers to the achievement of sexual maturity.

"readiness" A concept that states that particular learning achievements are best worked toward if one waits until the child is "ready," physiologically and psychologically, to profit from training in the given ability.

sensorimotor development The development of behavior showing coordination between perception and action, for example, the ability to direct the hand to the point in space where an object is visually perceived.

UNIT 4

the nervous system

overview / Physiological psychology is the study of the anatomical structures and physiological processes that are related to psychological events. It will involve us to a large extent in an investigation of the nervous system.

The neuron is the basic unit of the nervous system. Stimulation of a neuron causes an electrical change to take place at the point stimulated; this electrical change, the nerve impulse, is transmitted all along the length of the neuron. Each of the "terminals" at the end of a neuron comes into close contact with another neuron. The passage of an impulse along a neuron causes the release at the terminals of a chemical that tends to stimulate the *next* neuron to produce an impulse.

In this way an impulse produced in a sensory cell can transmit activity to many other nerve cells and may finally involve motor neurons that will stimulate a muscle into activity. Impulses thus provoked have this influence in conjunction with all the neural activity already present, as well as with that produced by other, concurrent sensory stimuli.

The central nervous system is made up of the brain and the spinal cord. Although these structures always work as an integrated system, we can usefully distinguish various subparts of the brain and study their functions. Studies of this kind disclose that the quality of the different senses depends upon the part of the cortex to which the sensory nerves are connected.

When we consider the structures and processes that determine the activity of a living organism, we find ourselves concerned in large part with the nervous system—the brain, the spinal cord, and the nerves. In order to appreciate as fully as possible the advances that have been made in understanding the role of bodily structures in experience and behavior, we have to know something about how the nervous system works. It will be helpful to begin by considering a single nerve cell—the "unit" of the nervous system—and then see if the activity of the total structure may be understood in terms of the activity of such elements.

The Nerve Cell

As with all living matter, the cell is considered the unit of organization of the nervous system. In the human body there are 10 billion nerve cells (or *neurons*), which differ widely in their shape, size, and activity. Nevertheless, there are basic similarities among nerve cells (see Figure 4.1.), and all nerve cells share many features with other cells of the body. Each contains a *nucleus*, in which are found the complex substances that carry the genetic messages that determine the nature of the cell and of the activity it will display. The nucleus is embedded within a *cell body;* here the many chemical processes take place that make up the respiration and metabolism of the cell. The outer portion of the entire cell is called the *cell membrane.* One gets a more accurate picture of the membrane if he realizes that it has a "thickness" and is actively involved in the chemical reactions to be discussed; it is not an inert "skin" whose only role is to maintain the physical shape of the cell.

Conduction of the Nerve Impulse

The important distinctive features of nerve cells depend upon a specialized development of the cell membrane. All cells "respond" to stimulation of the cell membrane by some change in shape or in chemical or electrical activity. The nerve cell has a unique characteristic in that certain forms of electrical or chemical stimulation of the cell membrane will produce a change in the membrane in portions of the cell far removed from the site of stimulation and in that this form of stimulation-produced change can take place rapidly, reliably, and without injury to the cell.

The structure of the nerve cell takes advantage of this characteristic: Most nerve cells have one or more long extensions (*processes*) that make it possible for a stimulus activating one part of the cell to produce a response some distance away. When we note further that the response of one nerve cell can stimulate another into activity, we can see how the nervous system carries out one of the major roles, that of *conduction* of information within the organism.

There is one region of the nerve-cell membrane that is particularly sensitive to stimulation (from the outside world, from a receptor cell, or from another nerve cell) and that in the intact organism is more likely than any other region to be exposed to such stimulation. It is called the *dendritic zone* or *dendritic surface;* in many neurons it includes the membrane around the cell body proper, as well as the surface of some relatively short thick processes called *dendrites.* The other major portion of the neuron is a long thin process called the *axon:* In the functioning organism the axon of a cell is stimulated into action by prior activity within the dendritic zone. By virtue of its length the axon manages to carry the activity to a relatively distant part of the organism, where it may stimulate yet another nerve cell or possibly a muscle or gland cell.

The transmission of activity along a neuron consists of a sequence of electrochemical events, with each point of the neuron becoming active in turn. In the *resting state* (before the neuron is stimulated) the cell membrane serves to maintain a difference in the concentration of certain chemicals between the interior of the cell and the body fluids that surround it. The most important aspect of this difference results from the fact that positively charged sodium ions are kept out of the cell and thus the outside of the cell is electrically positive, as shown in Figure 4.2. When the cell is stimulated, the membrane temporarily "breaks down" at the point of stimulation and lets the positive ions rush into the cell. The result of stimulation is therefore an electrical change that can be measured as an increase in negativity in the region of stimulation. This electrical change is the "activity" of the neuron that we have been talking about; it makes up the *nerve impulse*. We still must explore, how-

ever, how the impulse that is produced at one point on the neuron can produce similar activity farther along the neuron.

The key to understanding how the nervous impulse is propagated along the cell membrane comes when we learn that one way to stimulate the membrane to let through the sodium ions at a given point is to change the electrical charge at that spot. A fairly small shift toward the negative will cause the membrane to give way. A small negative shift will thus evoke within the neuron membrane chemical processes of its own, which lead to the larger negative shift—the impulse proper. The final point in the explanation involves the knowledge that, when an actual impulse is produced at one

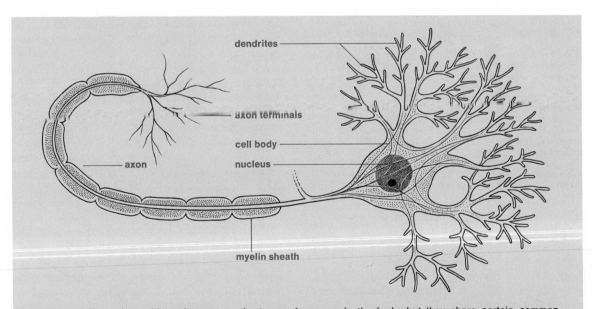

dendrites

axon terminals

cell body

nucleus

axon

myelin sheath

Figure 4.1. There is a wide variety among the types of neurons in the body, but they share certain common features, which are illustrated in this diagram. Incoming impulses from other neurons impinge upon the *dendritic zone* here made up of the membrane of the dendrites and the *cell body*. The resulting electrical changes in this region may stimulate activity that sweeps along the *axon*, in turn producing or influencing responses in the dendritic zones of the neurons with which the *axon terminals* "connect." Note also the *myelin sheath*, a segmented fatty covering of the axon, which accounts for the white color characteristic of tracts and nerves.

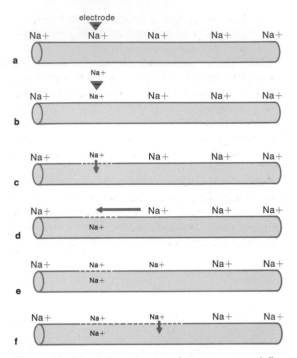

electrode

a Na+ Na+ Na+ Na+ Na+

b Na+ Na+ Na+ Na+ Na+

c Na+ Na+ Na+ Na+ Na+

d Na+ Na+ Na+ Na+
Na+

e Na+ Na+ Na+ Na+ Na+
Na+

f Na+ Na+ Na+ Na+ Na+
Na+

Figure 4.2. Stimulation of one point on an axon influences activity at adjacent points as well. Here (a) a negatively charged electrode is applied to the neuron and (b) "removes" some of the positively charged sodium (Na+) from the membrane. This removal has the effect of "breaking down" the membrane at that point (c), so that the remainder of the excess sodium can enter the cell. Sodium from the next region of the surface moves over to fill the electrochemical "vacuum" thus created (d). Now, however, the resulting reduction (e) of the electrical charge in this neighboring region produces a similar disruption of the membrane, permitting the remaining extra sodium to enter there also (e). The inrush of the sodium (c and e) causes the relative increase in negativity on the outside of the neuron that makes up the nerve impulse proper. The last three steps (d, e, and f) are repeated, with successive pairs of points, all along the length of the axon; the nerve impulse has been transmitted.

erratum

point on the neuron surface, it has electrical effects that spread somewhat beyond that point.

Now we can see the full story. An effective stimulus at one point on the neuron causes an impulse to be emitted. This impulse is measured as a local "large" (about 120 millivolts) negative shift in the electrical charge on the

exterior of the membrane. Such a change influences nearby points, producing smaller increases in negativity in such regions. The small increase in negativity provokes an impulse in these neighboring regions, an impulse that in turn spreads to the next points, and so on down the length of the neuron. The neuron has "fired."

If the original stimulus that is applied to the axon is too small, the sequence of events we have described will not be carried out. The membrane will not break down, and therefore there will be no inrush of sodium and no effective stimulation of the neighboring regions of the axon. The critical size of the stimulus necessary for production of the nerve impulse is called the *threshold of the neuron*. If the stimulus is greater than the threshold value, a nerve impulse will of course be produced, but it is important to note that the size of the impulse will not depend upon the amount by which the stimulus exceeds the threshold. If the cell fires at all, it fires with the maximum intensity possible at the moment. This rule is called the *all-or-none law* of nervous conduction.

The all-or-none nature of the impulse can be understood by remembering that the response of the axon depends upon the initial inequality of the concentration of sodium ions on the two sides of the cell membrane and involves the reduction of this inequality as the sodium moves into the cell. The size of the response depends upon the size of this inequality and not upon the size of the stimulus that provokes its reduction.

After the neuron has fired, there must be some way for the sodium to be expelled from the cell and for the membrane to regain its role as the guardian of the electrochemical imbalance (otherwise each neuron could be used only one time!). Not much is known about exactly how this expulsion occurs, but it is known that the passage of the impulse and these recovery processes take a definite period of time. During a part of this time the neuron cannot be fired again or can be fired only if a much larger stimulus is used. This time is called the *refractory period* of the cell.

Interaction Among Nerve Cells

Neurons act in systems—not alone; we must consider how one neuron can produce activity in another so that the latter will succeed it in a pattern of activity. The end of an axon branches into several small twigs, each of which ends in a small swelling. These *axon terminals* bring the end of one neuron close to the membrane of the dendritic zone of another neuron but separated from it by a space about .00002 centimeters wide. The place at which two neurons come so close together is called a *synapse* and is shown in Figure 4.3. Within each terminal there are small spherical spaces, called *synaptic vesicles*. It is believed that the passage of an impulse down the axon causes the release into the synaptic space of a chemical stored in these vesicles. This chemical quickly crosses the synapse and acts as a stimulant to the dendritic zone of the next cell. This dendritic zone may then elaborate an impulse in its axon, which will pass down the axon membrane as the nerve impulse of the second cell. The chemical that crosses the synaptic space is called a *transmitter substance* because of its role in carrying the message through the nervous system. The transmitter substance emitted at any one time is soon destroyed by enzymes found at the synapse.

Our story is still lacking a beginning and an end. How is the "first" neuron activated—that is, how do external stimuli in the real world start up activity in the nervous system? This question deserves a separate answer for each of the various sensory systems, but in general it can be said that the *sensory neuron* receives a chemical or electrical change that initiates its impulse, either directly from the external stimulus or from a specialized receptor cell in the sense organ. Finally, at the other end of the chain of activity, transmitter substances secreted by the axon terminals of each *motor*

neuron move across a space similar to that of a synapse to provoke activity in the muscle or glandular cell that it innervates.

More complexity must be added to the picture. The nervous system does not consist of a group of simple direct pathways, each beginning with one sensory neuron continuing through a chain of neurons to end up at one motor neuron. The axon terminals of one neuron bring it in contact with the dendritic zones of many other nerve cells, and many thousands of axons may terminate on the dendritic zone of a single nerve cell. In this fashion, the activity in one neuron may affect the activity in many other cells and indirectly can affect potentially all the other nerve cells in the body.

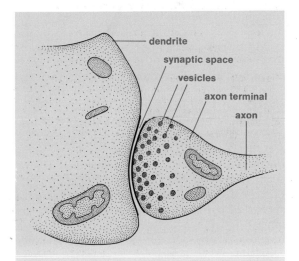

Figure 4.3. The "synapse" is the region of interaction of the end of an axon with the membrane of the succeeding neuron. The axon terminal does not quite reach the dendritic membrane, however. A nerve impulse in the axon will cause some of the vesicles to discharge their contents into the synaptic space. These vesicles contain a transmitter substance, which will diffuse across to the dendritic surface, where it may stimulate the second neuron. Also pictured are some of the many other structures within most cells; these structures take part in the metabolism and other vital functions of the cell.

If a single impulse within a neuron caused the production of an impulse in every cell with which it was connected, we would soon have all the cells in the nervous system firing as rapidly as possible. There are two reasons why this does not happen.

Remember, first, that each neuron has a threshold. The amount of stimulation that reaches the dendritic zone must exceed a certain amount before an active impulse will be established. As the amount of stimulation that results from the release of transmitter substance by one nerve impulse is almost never enough to "fire" the next neuron, a response will usually mean that the neuron's dendritic surface is receiving input from the axons of several other cells, all at approximately the same time.

Second, it must be noted that there are some transmitter substances that are "inhibitory." Such a substance, when released into the synaptic space, acts to *offset* the influences of the excitatory transmitter, so that an extra amount of excitatory transmitter will be necessary to fire the succeeding neuron in the presence of an inhibitory transmitter.

These features—the complexity of neural interconnection, the existence of a threshold, and the presence of inhibitory effects—allow the nervous system to do more than simply conduct activity (and metaphorically, information) from one point to another. The nervous system also integrates, or as some say "computes," for the activity of any cell will be a function of the activity of many, many other cells.

The Ever-Active Nervous System

In Units 15–18 we shall discuss the ways in which a stimulus causes a change in activity in the nervous system, and we shall describe the parts of the nervous system that are affected by a given stimulus. As we explore these problems, it is simplest to assume, almost without realizing that we are doing so, that the nerve cells (in the receptors and in the brain) are completely inactive until a stimulus comes along. According to this view, the sleeping or resting person is completely passive, his brain inert. A stimulus then "stimulates," producing some activity in certain specific parts of this quiescent, waiting structure. These tacit assumptions make our task seem simpler, but we must constantly bear in mind the fact that they are wrong in several important ways.

In the first place, nerve cells are *not completely* passive and inactive in the resting individual. All cells show some "spontaneous" nerve impulses, which occur without known external cause; and some large groups of cells are maintained in organized activity even when there is no specific stimulus present. Some cells "fire" more when they are not stimulated and actually reduce their rates of activity when a stimulus is given; some brain cells are more active during sleep than in the waking state.

Therefore it is more correct to think of a stimulus as changing the pattern of activity in the nervous system, rather than as instigating it. With this point in mind, it is easy to see that a stimulus will have *widespread effects* throughout the brain. Its immediate influence may be on one part of the system, but, from the complex pattern of activity thus produced, consequences will follow for many other parts of the ongoing activity.

We also might remind ourselves here of an obvious fact—no organism receives a "single stimulus" at any time. There will always be an enormous *complex of stimuli* present at any moment, each of which will have an effect upon the pattern of activity we have been describing. Finally, it must be noted that the active nervous system is so constructed that in itself it provides some *control over the amount of influence* that a stimulus will have upon the system, adding still another level of complexity to our problem of studying the physiological bases of experience and behavior.

Ten Billion Nerve Cells

The *brain* and the *spinal cord* together form the *central nervous system*. The *nerves* connect the central nervous system with various *sensory* and *motor* structures throughout the body and make up the *peripheral nervous system*.

The Central Nervous System

The brain can be divided into many different structures; we shall describe some of the major ones and for the present give only some general impression of their functions. Of course, such divisions are somewhat arbitrary, as the total consists of complexly interconnecting neurons and each part has potential connections with all others.

Observation of the central nervous system shows certain major kinds of structures. There are regions that are constructed of concentrations of cell bodies; such areas are often called *nuclei* (not to be confused with the nuclei of individual cells). An enveloping layer with a similar concentration of cell bodies is found covering some parts of the brain; it is called a *cortex*. Much of the rest of the brain and spinal cord consist of *tracts*, large groups of axons coursing together, connecting between various nuclei and between different regions of cortex.

The Brain

Early in embryological development, the brain shows three major divisions from front to back, which are called *forebrain, midbrain,* and *hindbrain*. Each gives rise to many specific parts, and further development changes greatly the external appearance of the brain; but even in the mature human we refer to these major subdivisions in describing the important structures of the brain.

Within the forebrain we must mention the *cerebrum,* the *thalamus,* and the *hypothalamus* (see Figure 4.4.). The cerebrum develops as an outgrowth from near the front end of the forebrain, and as there are two such enlargements—one on each side—they are referred to as *cerebral hemispheres* (see Figure 4.5.). On the exterior of the hemisphere there is a layer of cortex approximately one-fourth of a centimeter thick. The cerebral cortex is essential to many of the most important aspects of the complex functions of man. We shall refer to it several times in subsequent units as we examine its role in experience and behavior. Within the hemispheres are several large nuclei, known collectively as the *basal ganglia,* which are part of a neural system involved in the control of fine movement. The neurons whose cell bodies are concentrated in the cerebral cortex and the basal ganglia contribute many of their axons to the large mass of intermingled tracts that make up much of the interior (the white matter) of the hemisphere. The tracts that run from one hemisphere across to the other one are known as *commissures;* the most prominent is called the *corpus callosum*. We shall note later what happens when the commissures are cut and one side of the brain does not know what the other side is doing.

Thalamus and hypothalamus are each collective names for groups of individual nuclei. The cells of the different thalamic nuclei send fibers to different areas of the cerebral cortex. Many of the thalamic nuclei receive fibers from sensory receptors and thus serve as way stations on pathways of the incoming sensory information. Most of the sensory routes shown in Figure 4.6. are carrying messages that will pass through thalamic nuclei before going to the cerebral cortex. The *lateral geniculate body* and the *medial geniculate body* are thalamic nuclei involved in vision and audition respectively.

Several of the hypothalamic nuclei have been intensively studied. The functions of these structures differ, but one frequent finding is that they are involved in the control of emotion and motivation and related behavior. We shall find, for example, that electrical stimulation of some parts of the hypothalamus seems to be pleasant and that destruction of another part

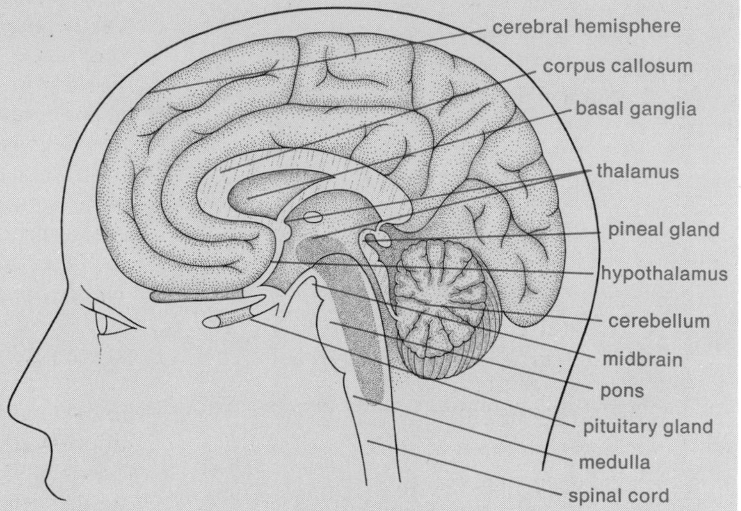

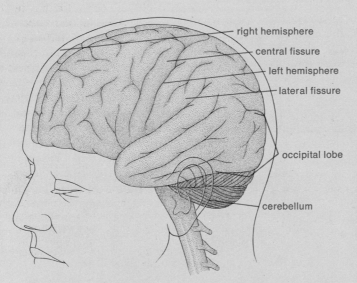

Figure 4.4. Many of the major structures of the human brain can be seen on its medial surface. The lines on the cerebral hemisphere represent folds in the cerebral cortex. Note that most of the structures pictured here would be cut in order to prepare a view like this one: The corpus callosum, for example, is made up of fibers running into and out of the plane of the page and connecting the two hemispheres.

cerebral hemisphere
corpus callosum
basal ganglia
thalamus
pineal gland
hypothalamus
cerebellum
midbrain
pons
pituitary gland
medulla
spinal cord

right hemisphere
central fissure
left hemisphere
lateral fissure

occipital lobe

cerebellum

Figure 4.5. Side view of the brain. This view shows the general geography of the surface of the cerebrum and some of its major landmarks. Note the heavily convoluted nature of the cortical surface and the deep fissures that divide the cortex into a number of areas. Both cerebral hemispheres are divided into four major portions, called "lobes," each of which contains cortex and underlying white matter.

makes an animal eat much more than he did previously. In Unit 37 we shall discuss the *limbic system,* an interconnected group of cortical and subcortical structures that is related anatomically to the hypothalamus and serves similar functions.

The midbrain includes a large part of a structure called the *reticular formation.* We shall discuss in Unit 16 the way in which the reticular formation gives rise to impulses that help to control the level of arousal or alertness of parts of the central nervous system, particularly the cerebral cortex.

The *cerebellum* is part of the hindbrain. It has a cortex much like the cerebrum and has many connections to the cerebral cortex, the basal ganglia, and the spinal cord. It plays a role in regulating and coordinating motor activity. In appearance the *pons* is a very prominent part of the hindbrain; here we can consider it simply as a way station for tracts running between the cerebrum and the cerebellum.

The *medulla* is the most posterior part of the brain; in its appearance and function it resembles to some extent the spinal cord, into which it blends. There are nuclei here that play an essential part in the control of such vital processes as respiration.

All the brain structures except the cerebral hemispheres and the cerebellum are referred to collectively as the *brain stem,* as they appear to form a stalk from which the cerebrum and cerebellum have sprouted.

The spinal cord is the continuation of the central nervous system down the back. Throughout its length there is a core made up largely of cell bodies, covered with fiber tracts carrying sensory and motor impulses between the rest of the body and the brain.

The Peripheral Nervous System

A nerve is a large group of neurons (or, more precisely, axons) running together to carry impulses between the central nervous system and some other part of the body. There is a series of *spinal nerves* up and down the spinal cord, which carry sensory impulses from the skin, joints, and internal organs of the trunk and limbs and motor impulses to the muscles and glands of the same parts of the body. There are also twelve pairs of *cranial nerves;* they carry neural messages to the brain directly. Several of them are shown in Figure 4.6., for the sensory pathways from the specialized receptor organs (nose, for example), as well as the skin of the face, make use of cranial nerves.

The "Specific Energies of Nerves" Doctrine

In Part Two we shall examine in turn the many different kinds of sensations we experience— visual, auditory, olfactory, gustatory, cutaneous, and so forth. We now face the question of the neural basis for these *qualitative* differences in our experience. How can the brain tell the difference between, say, a light and a sound on the basis of the neural impulses it receives?

Three possible solutions to this important problem were considered by the German physiologist Müller in the early 1800s. Müller rejected the possibility that it is the receptor cells that determine the qualities of perception, pointing out that if a sensory nerve is stimulated directly (for example, by electricity), the resulting experience is exactly the same as if its receptor had been stimulated. He then offered the following two explanations:

"(1) Either the nerves themselves may communicate impressions different in quality to the sensorium [the brain], which in every instance remains the same; or (2) the vibrations of the nervous principle [the nerve impulses] may in every nerve be the same and yet give rise to the perception of different sensations in the sensorium, owing to the parts of the latter with which the nerves are connected having different properties."

Müller believed it was impossible to prove either position at the time he was writing, but he favored the first, that is to say, that nerves of the different senses send special messages

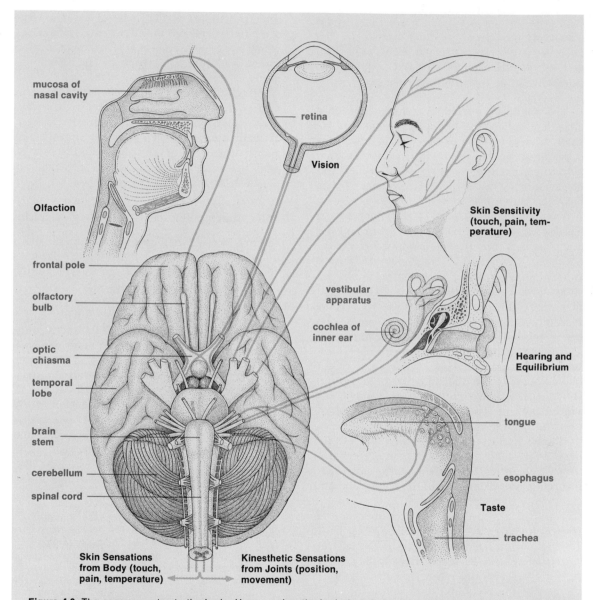

Figure 4.6. The sensory routes to the brain. Here we view the brain from beneath, in order to see clearly the routes over which neural messages travel from our sense receptors into the brain. Although our sensory system and brain are bilaterally symmetrical (we have two eyes, two sensory areas for smell, two ears), this diagram shows only one route for each of the types of sensory organ.

    Note that the nerves that carry neural messages from the eyes, nose, tongue, ears, face, and vestibular apparatus go directly to the brain, that is, not via the spinal cord. The nerves that carry impulses from the skin, muscles, and joints of the rest of the body enter the brain via connections in the spinal cord.

signaling the type of sensation. In fact he titled his discussion "The Doctrine of the Specific Energies of Nerves." An apparent difficulty with this position is that, as far as we now know, neural impulses are all alike. We have no physical or chemical test that can tell us whether a nervous impulse is signaling a visual message or an auditory message and so forth.

On the other hand, we now find support for the second position. We shall see that senses have special cortical projection areas—"reception centers" or terminal areas for their neural impulses in the cortex (Figure 4.7. depicts the sensory projection areas that can be seen from the side of the head). We shall also discover that direct stimulation of a cortical *sensory area* will produce the appropriate sensation. For example, stimulation of the occipital areas by an electrical current applied directly to the brain will result in the sensation of light (see Box 46, p. 253). Thus, it is *neither* the receptor cells *nor* their connections to the cortex that are crucial; it is the place in the cortex that is stimu-

lated that determines which sensory modality we shall experience. When the auditory sensory area of the cortex is thrown into action, we experience sound; when the visual area is activated, we experience light.

All of this discussion suggests that the quality of the different senses depends upon the place in the cortex to which the sensory nerves are connected. (If the pattern of impulses provoked by an orange light arrived at the taste area of the cortex, we would not experience an orange light; we would probably experience some sort of taste.) Much of the rest of the brain will be active also, but the distinctive part of the activity will be that aroused by stimulation of a certain sensory area in the cortex. There is "sensory localization" in the cortex.

The Neural Control of Behavior

The behavior of an individual at any instant is a product of the muscle and gland cells that are active, and the responses of the muscles and

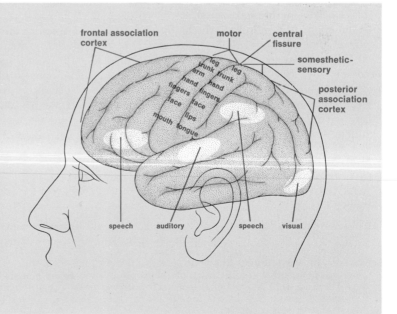

Figure 4.7. Sensory representation on the cortex. When looking down on the cortex, we can distinguish three major sensory areas. They are the areas of the cortex in which the nerve fibers from the body's various sense organs terminate. The three areas are the visual area, the auditory area, and the somesthetic-sensory area. The last area lies directly behind the central fissure. Note that the fibers from the hands and fingers along with those from the face, lips, and tongue occupy the major portion of this area.

This figure, showing the *terminal areas* of the sensory routes, should be studied in conjunction with Figure 4.6., which shows the sensory routes as they *enter* the brain. The leg and trunk areas have relatively little representation in the cortex.

frontal association cortex

motor

central fissure

somesthetic-sensory

posterior association cortex

leg trunk arm trunk leg
hand hand
fingers fingers
face face lips
mouth tongue

speech   auditory   speech   visual

glands are determined in turn by the activity of the nervous system. Although the total pattern of nervous-system activity will influence the resulting responses, all these influences can affect behavior only through their control of impulses in the motor nerves.

One major control of the spinal motor nerves is exerted by way of the *pyramidal-tract system*. It consists of neurons with cell bodies in the cerebral cortex and axons that run down through lower parts of the brain into the spinal cord, where they enter into synapses with neurons of the motor nerves. Many of the cell bodies of the pyramidal-tract neurons are found in one region of the cerebral cortex called the *motor area* (see Figure 28.2., p. 451).

There is, in addition, the *extrapyramidal system*. It also originates with neurons in the cerebral cortex, but these cells do not affect the motor nerves directly. They synapse with neurons in the basal ganglia, the midbrain, and neighboring regions, and the axons of these latter cells travel on down the spinal cord to help control the motor neurons.

It is generally believed that the neural impulses of the pyramidal system control skilled movements, determining which discrete responses will be made; the extrapyramidal system is involved in the control of posture and grosser rhythmic movements, such as those used in locomotion. Fibers from the cerebellum affect both of these systems by synapses with their cortical and subcortical neurons and add influences that appear to be necessary if the movements are to be smooth and well coordinated.

Physiological Psychology

In subsequent units we shall discuss specific aspects of the psychological processes involved in mental activity and behavior. In some of these units we shall be especially concerned with the anatomical structures and physiological processes that are related to the psychological events and shall make extensive use of the material presented in the present unit.

The facts to be disclosed from the study of the physiological bases of psychology and those that come from study of the psychological processes themselves must be consistent with one another. Psychological observations should help us in discovering physiological truths, and vice versa.

Physiological psychology—research into the nature of the physiological processes and anatomical structures underlying psychological activity—has increased more in recent years than has research in most other fields of psychology. Much of our information is new, and quite possibly some of what we think we know will later prove to be wrong. This description, however, applies to other areas of research as well and generally indicates a healthy state of affairs—a time of activity, exploration, new discoveries, and change—and an exciting time in which to be a student of the science.

Glossary

all-or-none law A term referring to the fact that every nerve impulse has the maximum intensity that the cell can produce at that time. The intensity of the stimulus that initiates the firing has no effect upon the intensity of the impulse.

axon The long, thin process of a neuron. The nerve impulse is produced on the membrane of the axon and travels along its length.

axon terminal One of the small branches into which the end of each axon divides. An axon terminal comes close to the dendritic zone of another cell to form a synapse.

basal ganglia A group of structures deep within the cerebrum. They are composed mostly of nerve-cell bodies and are part of a neural system that helps control motor responses.

brain The part of the central nervous system encased in the skull (or cranium). It is made up of many different structures, which work together to control behavior partly under the influence of incoming sensory impulses.

brain stem All the brain except the cerebral hemispheres and the cerebellum. It is so named because of its similarity to a stalk from which the cerebrum and cerebellum have grown.

cell body The large rounded part of a nerve cell, as opposed to the axon and dendrites. Most of the chemical reactions that make up the life processes of the cell take place here.

cell membrane The outer covering of any body cell, including a nerve cell. Through it must pass the substances that enter to participate in the chemical reactions of the cell.

central nervous system The portion of the nervous system made up of the brain and the spinal cord.

cerebellum A portion of the hindbrain situated (in humans) just beneath the posterior portions of the cerebrum. It is connected with the spinal cord and the cerebral hemispheres and has a cortex, as does the cerebrum. The cerebellum plays an important role in the coordination of muscular activity.

cerebral hemispheres, cerebrum The largest part of the human brain, which develops as two symmetrical protruding pouches (hemispheres) from the forebrain. There is an exterior cortex and an inner structure of white matter consisting of interlaced nerve tracts, in which are embedded the basal ganglia.

commissure A nerve tract crossing from one side of the brain to the other, interconnecting symmetrical points.

corpus callosum The most prominent commissure of the forebrain.

cortex The outer part of an organ; specifically a surface layer in the nervous system in which nerve-cell bodies are concentrated. Thus we have the cerebral cortex and the cerebellar cortex making up the folded outer part of the cerebrum and the cerebellum, respectively.

dendrites The relatively short and thick processes of a nerve cell, which provide a major part of the dendritic zone of the cell membrane.

dendritic zone The region of the nerve-cell membrane that is specialized for the receipt of stimulation, either from an external stimulus, a receptor cell, or another nerve cell. Sufficient stimulation of the dendritic zone will lead to the production of a nerve impulse in the axon.

extrapyramidal system A motor system that originates in the cerebral cortex, synapses in the basal ganglia, midbrain, and neighboring regions and ends upon the motor neurons of the spinal cord. It controls postural mechanisms and gross movements.

forebrain The most anterior of the three major embryological divisions of the brain. The cerebrum, the thalamus, and the hypothalamus develop from the forebrain.

hindbrain The most posterior of the embryological divisions of the brain, from which develop the cerebellum, pons, and medulla.

hypothalamus A forebrain structure, composed of several different nuclei, located at the base of the brain, below the thalamus. It forms part of many neural systems concerned with the control of emotional and motivational experience and behavior.

medulla The lowest part of the hindbrain, continuous with the spinal cord. Many of the cranial nerves arise or end here. Many important reflex functions (breathing and so on) are under the control of nerve cells of the medulla.

midbrain The middle (from front to back) of the three embryological divisions of the brain. Only a relatively small portion of the mature brain develops from the midbrain, but included in this portion is much of the reticular formation.

motor area of cortex A strip of the cerebral cortex lying just in front of the central fissure. Many of the neurons of the pyramidal and extrapyramidal systems originate here.

motor neuron; motor fiber A neuron, or nerve fiber, carrying nerve impulses from the brain or spinal cord to a muscle or gland. A group of such fibers running together forms a motor nerve.

nerve A bundle of axons running together in the peripheral nervous system; it may consist of all sensory fibers, all motor fibers, or a mixture of the two. A **cranial nerve** joins the central nervous system by way of the brain; a **spinal nerve** connects with the central nervous system somewhere along the length of the spinal cord.

nerve impulse The electrochemical change at the nerve-cell membrane that constitutes the activity of the cell. It results from a movement of electrically charged particles (ions) across the membrane.

neuron A nerve cell. The structural and functional unit of the nervous system.

nucleus 1. A structure within any cell, including a nerve cell. The nucleus carries the genetic information of the cell and thus controls the reproduction of the cell as well as the chemical activities that take place elsewhere in the cell body. 2. Any portion of the central nervous system, other than a cortex, in which nerve-cell bodies are concentrated. The basal ganglia are nuclei; the hypothalamus and the thalamus are each made up of many nuclei.

peripheral nervous system The motor and sensory nerves, which carry nerve impulses from the sense organs to the central nervous system and from the central nervous system to the muscles and glands of the body.

physiological psychology Study of the body parts (anatomy) and body functions (physiology) that are related to psychological events. All of the organism is involved, but attention is usually focused primarily upon the nervous system.

process Anatomically, a fiber or extension of a nerve cell, an axon or dendrite.

pyramidal-tract system A system of neurons originating in the motor area and other regions of the cortex and ending upon the motor neurons of the spinal cord. It controls the production of skilled, discrete movements.

refractory period A short period during and immediately following the passage of a nerve impulse along an axon. In the first part (the absolute refractory period), it is impossible to produce a second nerve impulse in the neuron. In the remaining part (the relative refractory period), a new impulse can be obtained but it takes a stronger stimulus (that is, the threshold of the cell is higher).

sensory area of cortex Any area in the cerebral cortex that is a major reception area for nerve impulses from a sensory receptor.

sensory neuron; sensory fiber A neuron, or nerve fiber, carrying impulses from a sensory receptor to the brain or spinal cord. A group of sensory fibers running together form a sensory nerve.

"specific energies of nerves" doctrine The name given to the theory formulated by Johannes Müller about 1825 that the differences in qualities of perception are determined either by differ-

ences in the messages carried by different sensory nerves or by the different areas of the cortex into which the sensory nerves lead. The weight of modern evidence has made us accept the latter possibility.

spinal cord The part of the central nervous system encased in the backbone. It serves as a pathway for the conduction of sensory impulses to the brain from the trunk and limbs and of motor impulses from the brain to the muscles and glands. In addition, many motor impulses originate here, directly under the control of the incoming sensory impulses.

synapse The place at which an axon terminal of one neuron comes close to the dendritic zone of another neuron. Activity in the first neuron can influence activity in the next one by the passage of a transmitter substance across the synaptic space.

synaptic vesicles Small round spaces in axon terminals in which transmitter substances are apparently stored before their release into the synaptic space.

thalamus A forebrain structure, composed of several different nuclei, located between the cerebral hemispheres. It receives input from sensory nerves and sends impulses to many regions of the cerebral cortex, including the sensory areas.

threshold of a neuron The minimal intensity of a stimulus required to produce a nerve impulse.

tract A group of nerve fibers (axons) running together within the central nervous system.

transmitter substance A chemical that is released at the axon terminal of a neuron and travels across the synaptic space to affect the dendritic zone of the next neuron. The transmitter may tend to produce a nerve impulse in the next neuron, in which case it is said to be excitatory. If it tends to prevent an impulse in the next neuron, it is called inhibitory.

Suggestions for Further Reading

Heredity and Environment

BROADHURST, D. L. 1963. *The Science of Animal Behavior*. Baltimore: Penguin.

A readable survey of research findings from laboratory and field observation on both innate and learned animal behavior.

HIRSCH, J. (ed.). 1967. *Behavior Genetic Analysis*. New York: McGraw-Hill.

A thorough discussion of the evidence for genetic influence in the psychological characteristics of men and animals, and the methods employed in its search.

STERN, C. 1960. *Principles of Human Genetics*. 2nd ed. San Francisco: Freeman.

A well-written, authoritative, and comprehensive book. It starts at the beginning and makes no assumptions about previous study in the field by the reader. An excellent introduction to human genetics.

Development

FRIEDENBERG, E. Z. 1959. Paperback. *The Vanishing Adolescent*. New York: Dell.

An insightful analysis of the role and plight of the adolescent in today's society.

HOFFMAN, M. L., and L. W. HOFFMAN (eds.). 1964. *Review of Child Development Research*. New York: Russell Sage.

First of an excellent series of volumes summarizing recent theory and research on a wide range of developmental topics.

LANDRETH, C. 1967. *Early Childhood*. New York: Knopf.

A lucid and comprehensive textbook dealing with the early years of human development.

MUSSEN, P. H. (ed.). 1969. *Carmichael's Manual of Child Psychology*. 3rd ed. New York: Wiley.

A standard reference book for research methods and results in child development.

TANNER, J. M. 1962. *Growth at Adolescence*. Oxford: Blackwell.

A thorough summary of the physical and physiological changes that mark human adolescence and of the factors that contribute to the vast individual differences in the timing of these changes.

The Nervous System

NETTER, F. H. 1953. *The CIBA Collection of Medical Illustrations, Vol. I: Nervous System*. Summit, N.J.: CIBA Pharmaceutical Products.

A collection of excellent color drawings of the nervous system, with descriptive legends and short discussions of function.

THOMPSON, R. F. 1967. *Foundations of Physiological Psychology*. New York: Harper.

A first-class textbook, thorough and up to date. It includes a useful discussion of the methods used in research on the anatomy and physiology of the nervous system and their relation to experience and behavior.

part two
perception

UNIT 5

the worlds we perceive

overview / The first step in the study of perception is to describe our immediate experience of the physical world in which we live. Our world is a spatial world containing many different objects, each with a variety of attributes. These perceptual attributes do not necessarily correspond exactly with the physical dimensions and properties of the object. The attributes may vary widely, depending upon the entire stimulus context in which they occur. Thus, the apparent size or shape or color of an object depends partly upon its immediate surroundings. At the same time, there is also a tendency toward the preservation of constancy in the perceived size, shape, and color of an object despite radical changes in its location, illumination, etc.

The relation of the object to the total organization of which it is a part is a crucial determinant of how it is perceived. The perceived structure sometimes coincides with, and at other times violates, the nature of the physical structure.

Movement and change, which are dynamic properties, give life to the static world of objects and are the essential features of what we call events and happenings. Joining these influences to bring us closer to the living realities of our perceived worlds are the expressive and affective properties we see in objects and events, attributes just as "real" psychologically as size and color. Such expressive and affective properties include sensuous and aesthetic attributes of perceived "causality" and "power."

Finally, and indispensably, there is continuous interaction among the different impressions received from the various senses, which leads to a unified perceptual experience of objects and events.

How a person behaves depends largely on how he perceives the world about him. For this reason many psychologists believe that the understanding of man begins with the study of perception.

This study—what and how man sees, hears, smells, and feels—is an ancient and honorable part of scientific inquiry. It has attracted the attention of physicists, physiologists, neurologists, and psychologists. Each of these groups has contributed much to our understanding of perceptual phenomena, and in the succeeding units of Part Two we shall examine their contributions. Before looking at the evidence from the experimental laboratories in any detail, however, we must begin our study of perception with a careful description of what people do see, hear, smell, and feel.

Our first step, in other words, is to describe our worlds as we perceive them: We must describe what is most familiar to each person—his own world of immediate experience. Because it is so familiar, the description may at first seem stale and commonplace. Yet we shall soon find, as we take a fresh look at our own worlds and compare them with descriptions by other people of theirs, that we are in for some surprises. Things that we have long taken for granted will appear in a new light, the "obvious explanation" will no longer do, and unexpected questions will arise. This first step toward the study of perception—this kind of description of one's immediate experience (technically known as *phenomenology*)—clearly does not give us an explanation but serves only as a starting point for an investigation.

We shall look first at the "simplest" kind of perception, the perception of physical objects and events. As we do so, we shall soon see why the study of perception raises so many basic questions concerning our understanding of human behavior and why it has aroused the imagination and wonder of many scientists. In this unit we shall attempt only an overview; later units will fill in the details.

Space and Objects

We humans live in a three-dimensional space and find it hard to imagine a world without this spatial character. In our very biological make-up we are basically spatial animals. Our eyes and ears are adapted to the task of bringing us information about distant parts of our physical environment; for this reason they are often referred to as "distance receptors." We are remarkably mobile animals, moving about quite freely in space. Our brains appear to have a "natural" tendency to construct space, even on the basis of stimulation that is not fully spatial. Many patterns of visual stimuli that fall on the flat, two-dimensional retinas of our eyes somehow enable us to experience three-dimensional space.

This space is inhabited by objects that are located in specific places in it, are separable from their surroundings, and possess various perceptual properties that distinguish them from other objects. Some of these perceptual properties are simple, for example, size, shape, texture, color; others are complex.

Size

Objects differ in perceived size from a minuscule, barely perceptible grain of dust to those that cover the entire visual field. A striking fact is that the perceived size of an object does not

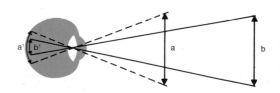

Figure 5.1. The diagram shows that two objects of the same size cast retinal images inversely proportional in size to their distances from the eye, a′ being exactly twice b′.

depend solely upon the size of the image it casts on the retina. A man standing ten feet away seems to be approximately the same height as when he is standing twenty feet away, even though the first image on the eye is twice the physical size of the second (see Figure 5.1.). The brain somehow "takes account" of the difference in distances and preserves the size constancy of the object.

Conversely, as we shall see later when we discuss the experimental investigation of size perception, at a fixed distance an object will not always appear to be the same size. The contexts in which objects of equal size appear make them seem quite different in size, as demonstrated in Figure 5.2.

Shape

Objects may be of fairly simple shapes (a ball, a book) or of more complex shapes (a typewriter, a tree, a human figure). There are almost limitless ways in which perceived shapes may be classified, for example, by circularity, angularity, elongation, symmetry, complexity, and so forth. Of a single "species" of shape—for instance, a triangular shape—there can be any number of variations; there can be an infinite number of geometrically different individual triangles, all of which we recognize as "triangles" at the same time that we see differences among them. Furthermore, there can be almost endless subtler variations of shape within a single common theme, as witness the eternal preoccupation of painters with the female nude.

Just as there is size constancy, in that identical objects at different distances from the observer may appear to be the same size, there is also shape constancy, in that an object may appear to have the same shape, even when the angle from which it is viewed changes radically. Dinner plates on the table appear round, despite the fact that, because of the level at which the diners are seated, the images of the plates on the retinas of their eyes are not circles but ellipses of varying fatness and thinness. Somehow the brain takes into account the angle of viewing.

But here again, as in the perception of size, constancy is not always the rule. Look at the slightly lopsided circular figure in Figure 5.3., as it lies on the background of striped lines. You may be surprised to discover, if you make the test, that it is actually a perfect geometric circle. Perceived shape, like perceived size, is influenced by its immediate surroundings.

Texture

Objects also differ perceptually in texture. Their surfaces may appear rough or smooth, even or uneven, coarse or fine. They may be

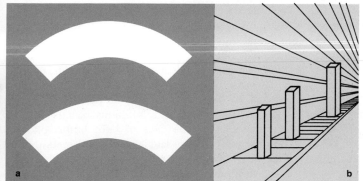

Figure 5.2. Two illusions of size. In a, the lower figure appears larger than the upper figure, although both are the same size; in b, the three posts are all the same height.

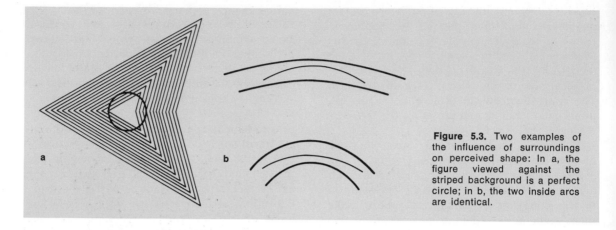

Figure 5.3. Two examples of the influence of surroundings on perceived shape: In a, the figure viewed against the striped background is a perfect circle; in b, the two inside arcs are identical.

perceived as shiny, scratchy, slippery, scaly, silky. As we shall presently note, associated closely with textures is a host of more complex properties—expressive and aesthetic—and therefore the endless permutations and combinations of textural qualities help to provide livelihoods for the clothes designer, the interior decorator, the artist, and others.

Color

The world of color is almost a world in itself. Objects vary in brightness, from the whitest snow in full sunlight to the blackest velvet in darkness; they vary in hue—red, green, yellow, blue, violet, and all the intermediate shades; they vary in saturation, from the most washed-out, dilute color to the most intensely concentrated color.

These "standard" three dimensions of color, which we treat in detail in Unit 7, are familiar to everyone, but alone they are far from telling the whole story. A fresh look at the colors around us will reveal other color qualities that relate to the "mode of appearance." All reds of the same hue, brightness, and saturation do not look alike. Under usual conditions of viewing, the colors of objects appear to be relatively solid and opaque and localized at or on the ob-

ject's surface. Such colors are known as *surface colors*. When viewed through an aperture that eliminates the contours of the object, the color may have a clearly different mode of appearance; it may be less opaque, less clearly localized, filmier in character. Such colors are known as *film colors*. Under other special circumstances—for example, viewing the blue sky, a colored haze, or a translucent colored liquid—the color seems to fill the whole space; it seems to be neither opaque nor filmy. Such colors are called *volume colors*. A striking illustration of how these different color qualities are dependent upon the precise conditions of viewing is given in Box 13, p. 95: The same physical color may be made to appear successively as volume color, film color, and surface color.

Another quality of some colors is luminosity. A red stoplight is luminous; it glows, appears to give off light, in a manner entirely different from a painted red surface. Our first inclination is to say that this luminous appearance is caused by the physical act of light emission. That is, we say it looks luminous because it *is* luminous, as in the case of light bulbs, phosphorescence of the sea, and similar instances. But this explanation will not do. Some objects look luminous even though they do not emit light but simply reflect it, as in the case of the moon. Conversely, the moon may not look luminous under certain circumstances (see Box 14, p. 96).

Smells, Tastes, Feels, and Sounds

The perceptual properties we have mentioned are largely visual in character; these properties naturally occur to us first, for we are primarily "visual animals." But the objects we perceive have important attributes pertaining to the other senses.

Objects smell fragrant, spicy, acrid, pinelike, or rotten; or they may be odorless. Objects may taste sweet, bitter, sour, or salty. Or they may seem to blend these tastes in various ways.

Objects feel different from one another when we touch and handle them. There are many textures, as we described earlier; also there are properties of lightness or heaviness, warmth or coldness, hardness or softness, brittleness or elasticity, and so on—as well as all degrees and combinations of these properties.

Objects have different sounds. The electric fan whirs, the siren shrieks, the clock ticks, the fire crackles. Sounds vary in several basic dimensions; the most familiar are loudness, pitch, and timbre. Loudness may range from a pin drop to an atomic blast; pitch from that of the bass drum to the flute's tweet; timbre from the pure tone of the tuning fork to the rich mixture of overtones in a chord of a string quartet.

Relations of Parts and Wholes

That an object is perceived as an object at all demonstrates that we perceive relationships. The whole object is seen as an organized entity, distinguishable from its surroundings, because its parts are somehow perceptually related to form the whole. Certain parts "belong" together with other parts to make the whole; the various perceived relationships among the wheels, fenders, hood, body, and top are an essential aspect of the perception of the automobile. At one and

the same time we perceive the whole car and many of its constituent parts. Our attention may shift, of course, and as a result certain parts may be perceptually more outstanding than others; or our attention may even become so narrowly focused on a single part that the

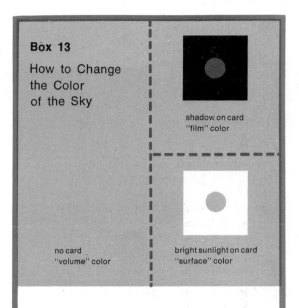

Box 13

How to Change the Color of the Sky

shadow on card
"film" color

no card
"volume" color

bright sunlight on card
"surface" color

First, look at the deep-blue sky in the late afternoon with your back to the sun, observing the quality of the blue color. Then take a piece of white cardboard with a small hole cut in it, and look at the same sky through the hole, holding the card so that it is in *shadow*. Finally, hold the card so that *bright sunlight* falls on it, and look again at the sky through the hole.

You will note that, though the sky color is the same blue hue under these three conditions of viewing, the *quality* of the color is entirely different, varying from "volume" color to "film" color to "surface" color, as a function of the immediate visual surroundings of the patch of sky observed.

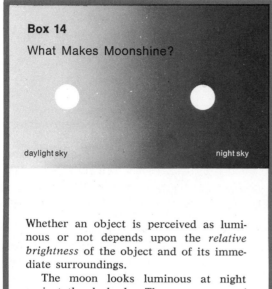

Box 14

What Makes Moonshine?

daylight sky — night sky

Whether an object is perceived as luminous or not depends upon the *relative brightness* of the object and of its immediate surroundings.

The moon looks luminous at night against the dark sky. The *same moon of identical brightness*, when viewed against the bright daylight sky, appears to be nonluminous and an opaque white in color.

All cases in which an object looks luminous are explained by the same general principle of "interaction" of brightnesses of the object and its surroundings.

perception of other parts and of the car as a whole may momentarily disappear.

The particular manner in which the parts are perceived in relation to one another in forming the whole is technically referred to as the perceived *structure* of the object. Perceived structure frequently corresponds closely with the actual physical structure of the environment. As you look at your desk, you may see a pencil, a paper clip, and a book lying side by side on the blotter. You see each as separate from the others. Its parts belong only to itself and not to the other objects; the eraser of the pencil touches the book, but you see it not as part of the book but as part of the pencil.

On the other hand, the perceived structure of

an object may not correspond with the actual structure of the physical environment. We may see "objects" that are not there. Everyone has had the experience of lying in a darkened room and seeing a frightening intruder in silhouette, only to discover that this perceived "object" was actually produced by the accidental grouping of the arm of a chair, the jamb of a door, and the sleeve of a coat hanging on the wall.

Every object is perceived to have parts, and the object itself may also be perceived as part of a still larger whole. These part-whole relations may extend indefinitely in both directions: Parts may be further differentiated into perceived subparts; wholes may be further grouped into larger perceived wholes.

In later units we shall examine the questions of how perception of the structure of objects comes about and of why the perception sometimes coincides with and at other times violates the nature of the physical structure.

Dynamic Properties: Movement and Change

Our "static" description of the perceived world up to this point has ignored Heraclitus' cry "Flux, flux, all is flux!" for we have said nothing yet about our perception of the movement and change of objects and events. Change is universal in human experience.

Movement

In our world things move, and they move in different directions, at different speeds, with different accelerations, and in various manners—smoothly, jerkily, rhythmically. We may see the object moving; or we may simply hear it, as when a car goes by outside on the street; or we may feel it, as when a spider runs across one's arm.

The physical conditions arousing the perception of movement can be specified in considerable detail, as we shall see in later units. Here we need emphasize only that, although sometimes the basis of the perceived movement is actual physical movement in the environment (the car actually drives by; the spider actually runs on one's skin), in other instances perceived movement occurs for other reasons. For instance, the moon often seems to move rapidly behind clouds, yet we know that the moon is "at rest" and that it is the clouds that are actually moving. When the train stops after a passenger has been staring at the moving landscape for a time, he still sees the landscape moving slowly forward; this illusion of movement is so compelling that he may believe that the train is actually sliding slowly backward. Moving pictures "move" as convincingly as anyone could desire, yet they consist only of a rapid succession of still pictures.

Change

Movement is one form of change, and change is a significant perceptual attribute of our world. In fact, we literally cannot see any object if, in a certain special sense, it does not move at all (see p. 234). We may perceive change in the location of an object, or in a change in its structure, or in its various qualities of size, shape, color, and sound. Usually we can readily identify the nature of the perceived change: The room is suddenly plunged into darkness, the balloon expands, the glass shatters. But sometimes we are aware of change without being able to specify its concrete nature. A girl we know looks "different" to us now—her appearance has changed; at first we cannot tell why, and only later do we realize that her hairdo is new.

These examples of perceived change arise from real change in the environment. But there may be striking cases of perceived change without corresponding physical change. Look steadily at the center of Figure 5.4. At first you may see a dotted Maltese cross lying on a cross-hatched background; after a while a marked change suddenly occurs: Now you see a propeller-like cross, and what was previously the "figure" is now the background. With continued

inspection you will see it again as you did before, and the fluctuations of this ambiguous object will persist as long as you look at it. No change whatever has taken place in the physical stimulus; the basis of the perceived change lies entirely in the functioning of the nervous system (see Box 28, p. 167, for some of the factors that influence these fluctuations).

Objects may undergo pronounced perceptual changes without losing their identities as the same objects. In fact, it is just this retention of identity that makes the perception of change possible, for change is a property involving a comparison between what the object was and what the same object is now.

This fact points to a distinction between perception of change and change of perception. We have been talking about the former; the change itself is the experienced fact. The latter refers to something quite different, the case in which the person's perception has changed but he does not perceive the change (refer to Box 21, p. 139, for a surprising demonstration of this kind of change).

Changes in perception, as we shall see, are most central to the process of learning, to productive thinking, to the shaping of attitudes and values, to the development of personality.

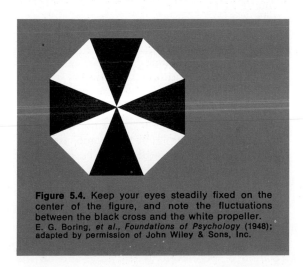

Figure 5.4. Keep your eyes steadily fixed on the center of the figure, and note the fluctuations between the black cross and the white propeller.
E. G. Boring, *et al., Foundations of Psychology* (1948); adapted by permission of John Wiley & Sons, Inc.

Time

Time is a crucial dimension of our perceived worlds. The qualities of objects and events are often perceived in relation to the ever-present background of time. The time background is often remote and of little or no perceptual consequence; at other times it is more prominent, and it may even be the most outstanding feature of a situation.

We perceive time in two quite different ways, as background and as "figure." As background, time serves as a dimension in terms of which events can be organized together. Tap with your pencil, making successive pairs of taps with very short intervals between the two taps of each pair and with somewhat longer intervals between the pairs. You will perceive a structuring of successive sounds, a pattern of pairs separated by intervals, quite analogous to the perception of pairs of dots laid out spatially on a piece of paper.

If you greatly lengthen the interval between the taps, making it, say, ten seconds, a quite different phenomenon occurs. The structural connection between the taps is weakened; we find ourselves waiting for the next tap and in so doing become aware of the passage, or flow, of time.

This time flow has perceived properties of its own, especially of fastness or slowness of flow: "Time flies," "time drags," "time stands still." And it may involve impressions of "pressure" or "remorselessness," which are examples of the kinds of expressive qualities of our perceived worlds that will be discussed later.

Perceived time is not the same as real or chronological (clock) time. The same interval of actual clock time may be perceived as long or short in duration, as slow or fast in flow, depending upon other aspects of the over-all situation. To the condemned man the hour before execution may seem to pass in a flash; to the man in a sinking boat the hour before rescue may seem interminable. Facts bearing on the relation of perceived to real time and on the conditions under which we may achieve highly accurate time judgments will be discussed in Unit 14, p. 228.

Perception of Physical Events

Our description of the perceived world has dealt mainly with objects and relations among objects. This is an appropriate place to look at the perception of physical events, for movement and change are inherent aspects of the perception of events. Happenings—movements and changes—constitute events.

Structure of Events

Perceived events, like objects, have structure and location in space and time. Take the following simple example of how we perceive a physical event. We stand in the forest beside a pond. Suddenly the wind begins to blow, and, as it blows harder and harder, the branch of a tree overhanging the pond begins to sway back and forth. Some leaves come loose, fall into the water, and float. Then a small twig breaks off and plummets into the water, which splashes and sends a series of concentric ripples out to the edges of the pond. As they go along, the ripples carry the bobbing leaves up and down. The ripples subside, the surface of the pond smooths out, the wind ceases, and the event is over.

We see that this whole episodic event has a beginning and an end; and it has a structure, in the sense that we see one set of happenings, followed by another set, which in turn is followed by others, and so on. Each part of the whole event has its distinctive perceived qualities—like the whine of the wind and its feel on the face; the pattern of sway of the branches; the size, shape, and speed of the ripples.

As in the case of physical objects, parts of the whole event can often be perceptually differentiated into still smaller subparts. Thus, we observe the flutter of a particular leaf. And conversely, the event we described may be perceived as only part of a still larger event; it may be merely the first part of a day-long storm that violently agitates the whole forest.

The parts of events are related in specific ways to one another; this set of relationships constitutes the perceived structure of the event. The twig breaks off and drops before the water splashes, not the reverse. Events are quite typically perceived as having this kind of "logical" structure, in that one happening leads to another in a way that appears "sensible" and "fitting."

To be sure, many perceived events do not have this "logical" appearance. Sometimes we see a variety of things happening close together in time and in space that do not seem to "make sense"; one thing does not appear to connect in an orderly fashion with another. It is such disarrayed events that we may perceive as sheer "confusion" and chaos. This perception does not necessarily mean, of course, that the actual physical event is lacking in regularity and order; it simply means that the person fails, for whatever reason, to perceive in it any form of regularity and order.

Conversely, perceiving a "logical" structure in an event is no guarantee that the actual event has it. The continued good health of gambling houses attests to this point; the purely random sequence of winning numbers in a session of roulette will often be perceived by the confirmed bettor who plays by an elaborate "system" as having some form of regularity and predictable order. A paranoid person suffering delusions of persecution may construct an elaborate "logical" perception of a threatening event that is, in fact, based entirely upon an accidental grouping of unrelated happenings. The "logic" *is* logical, however, in the sense that, given the "facts" as perceived, we would draw the same conclusion as the paranoid. His facts are wrong, not his reasoning.

Properly speaking, of course, there is no real physical event, merely a continuous flow of physical happenings. That we do tend to perceive such a sequence of physical happenings as a unified event, an episode with a beginning and an end, depends on the fact that certain physical happenings serve as distinguishing landmarks. What we take to be the landmarks depends both on the actual decisive changes in physical stimulus that make certain features "stand out" in our perception and on our "mental set," which disposes us to see particular things as important. When we discuss the principles of perceptual organization (Units 10 and 11), we shall see some of the determinants of the way in which we break up the continuous stream of physical happenings into perceived events.

The perception of events—how, out of a continuous stream of physical happenings, we perceive a unified event—is an extremely important problem. A sequence of physical happenings may be organized into events in different ways by different people; as a result there may be radical differences in their reactions to the physical happenings. For example, one person may perceive the sound at night of a tree against the house, followed by a footfall on the porch, as a unified event: A burglar is trying to break in. Another may perceive the same two happenings as parts of two entirely separate events: the wind blowing the tree, the neighbor coming to visit.

Expressive and Affective Properties

As we have so far described the world we perceive, despite all the sizes, shapes, colors, sounds, textures, movements, and changes, it seems somewhat "flat." Missing are the rich expressive attributes of things that provide the real "life" of our experienced worlds. To remedy this serious omission, let us look again at the ways in which we perceive objects and events, but this time let us broaden our description to include more complex and subtle properties.

A certain red color, for instance, may be experienced, not only in terms of a given hue, brightness, and saturation, but also as "warm," "lively," "advancing." A certain blue may be seen as "cold" and "receding." An elm tree may be perceived as "graceful," an oak as "sturdy." The material of one coat is a checked pattern that looks "jumpy"; another pattern looks "quiet."

In the perception of music, as a case *par excellence*, such expressive and affective properties are irresistible. One of the things we perceive most quickly in a musical piece is whether it is "plaintive," "gay," "somber," "powerful," or a complex combination of these and numerous other qualities. The major and minor modes (or "moods") have strikingly different qualities for us, depending entirely upon the particular pattern of notes in each scale.

Qualities like those just mentioned are often referred to technically as *physiognomic properties;* the term is derived from the expressive qualities exhibited on the face—the physiognomy—of a person. It is to be emphasized that such perceptual properties—for example, "gracefulness" of the elm tree—are seen immediately in the object, just as size and shape are and just as much.

There may often be close agreement among perceivers about the specific physiognomic properties they see in the object. Look at the two drawings in Figure 5.5. One is named "takete," the other "maluma." Decide which you think is which before reading the legend below the figure.

Aesthetic Qualities

Perceived properties of beauty and ugliness are especially noteworthy among these expressive qualities. The person perceives many objects in his surroundings as beautiful or as ugly and apprehends the aesthetic quality as something directly possessed by the object, not as something he subjectively adds. He looks at a strikingly beautiful woman and in describing her promptly mentions her beauty, perhaps be-

fore he mentions her height, coloring, and other simple physical attributes. Only by assuming a deliberate, "hard-boiled," analytical attitude in viewing her may he partly succeed in suppressing the idea of her beauty.

He may indeed be prepared to grant that to some other "benighted" person she may not appear to be beautiful, especially to someone from a culture other than his own that stresses different criteria of beauty. But this possibility does not in the least make her look less beautiful to him. He may admit that he knows little about "beauty," but he knows what he likes.

Power Qualities

Objects are perceived as doing things or as having the power to do things to other objects.

Figure 5.5. When told that one of these figures is named "takete" and the other "maluma," almost everyone chooses "maluma" for the upper figure and "takete" for the lower. The consistency among people in pairing these drawings and words, both of which are unfamiliar and meaningless, argues that the visual appearance of the figures and the sounds of the words share certain common physiognomic properties.
W. Köhler, *Gestalt Psychology;* Copyright 1947 Liveright Publishing Corp., Copyright © 1956 Liveright Publishing Corp.; adapted by permission.

One object is seen as "striking" another, as "chasing" or "leading" another, or as "attracting" or "threatening" another. Such perceived aspects are referred to as "power qualities." To the perceiver they are an inalienable part of the immediate appearance of an object, not simply an intellectual interpretation that he adds. The violent sea pounding heavily at the small boat is immediately perceived as having such power qualities. So is the gigantic black cloud that hangs "threateningly" over the hilltop.

A billiard ball rolls across the table and strikes another ball, which in turn moves. In observing this event, we perceive the first ball as "causing" the movement of the second; we do not see a mere sequence of neutral, unrelated events. Such perceived "causality" is the most important of the power qualities; it enters into our perceptions of virtually every event. Complex events may be perceived as organized primarily in terms of "this caused that" (see Box 45, p. 226, for proof that these elusive qualities can be studied experimentally).

Perceived "causality" may not faithfully mirror real causation. Many philosophers have completely denied the logical existence of causation, asserting that things are merely "correlated" with other things, not "caused" by them. But this logical view does not seem to affect the way we perceive phenomena; we may agree that there is no such thing as "causation," but things still look to us as though they cause other things to happen. Later on we shall learn that whether or not "causality" is perceived in a given situation depends upon the particular arrangement of the physical stimulus events.

Perception of Demands

We are all familiar with the "insistent" quality of some intense stimuli, for example, the loud, penetrating shrill of a telephone or a brightly flashing light. Such stimuli are deliberately utilized by the advertiser and others as attention-getting devices and warning signals, and they are chosen just because they possess this imperious ability to "demand" or "require" our attention.

We are dealing here with a power quality of an object, not as it is perceived to influence other objects in the field, but as it is perceived to affect us. Not only may we perceive certain objects as "demanding" or "repelling" in relation to other objects, but we may also see them as "demanding" or "repelling" in relation to ourselves. A woman may look particularly "inviting" when a man is sexually aroused; the ground may seem to "pull" us down when we stand on a high building; a fatty meat may "repel" when we are sated.

We are coming here to a very important problem of psychology—the problem of motivation: why and how we are pushed and pulled into various actions by our environments. When we take up the problems of motivation in later units, we shall find that these perceptual power qualities of objects in our world play a vital role in governing our actions, for it is largely with respect to perceived attractions and repulsions of objects that our motivated behavior is organized.

Identifying Objects

Objects are, of course, perceived as identifiable things. This particular object is perceived as more than a "something" of a certain size, shape, color, and movement; it is a "hippopotamus." The identity is perceived as "there" in the object, as are its other qualities.

The perception of identity is intimately bound up with all the other simple and complex perceptual qualities we have already reviewed. The "hippopotamusness" of the object is inseparable from its "lumbering but graceful move-

Box 15

International Physiognomic
Properties

Listed here are five common English synonym-antonym pairs, expressing simple qualities. In parallel columns are given the Chinese, Czech, and Hindi translations.

Can you correctly match the foreign words with the English? Try it by guessing which word, *tuń* or *k'uài*, means "sharp" and which "blunt." Do the same for Czech and Hindi and for the remaining English pairs.

The first word in the English pair is sometimes the top word in a foreign list and sometimes the bottom, so that you cannot judge from position.

Do not read what follows the list until you have made all your guesses.

English	*Chinese*		*Czech*		*Hindi*	
1. sharp-*blunt*	70	tuń	83	tupy	83	gothil
		k'uài		špičatý		tez
2. *bright*-dark	90	liang	77	svetly	90	chamakdar
		ań		tmavý		dhundhala
3. *bad*-good	64	huai	57	zlý	31	kharab
		haǒ		hodný		achha
4. soft-*hard*	83	kāng	96	tvrdý	64	sakht
		joú		měkký		narm
5. *sweet*-sour	51	t'ién	25	sladký	70	mitha
		suān		kyselý		khatta

The correct answers are indicated by the italicized word of the English pair, which corresponds with the *top* of the foreign pair in each case. That is, "blunt" is *tuń, tupy, gothil;* "bright" is *liang, svetly,* and *chamakdar;* and so forth.

The number preceding each foreign pair is the percentage of eighty-six Harvard and Radcliffe students who made the correct match in a study by R. W. Brown, A. H. Black, and A. E. Horowitz involving twenty-one such English pairs.

The over-all percentage of correct matches for the twenty-one pairs was 62 per cent for the Chinese, 62 per cent for the Czech, and 61 per cent for the Hindi. The chance level of guessing would be 50 per cent, so it is clear that, even when entirely ignorant of a language, a person can do better than chance in recognizing the meanings of words expressive of very simple qualities. Although Chinese is *not* an Indo-European language as is English, the percentage of correct matches was as high for it as for Czech and Hindi, which are Indo-European languages. Presumably this correlation is possible because of common physiognomic qualities in the *meaning* and in the *sound* of the word in the development of language.

But note that some of the pairs are matched correctly by almost everyone, whereas others are matched at a level only slightly above chance and still others are guesses predominantly in the *wrong* direction. We must conclude that common physiognomic qualities account for only some of the relations of meanings to sounds of words.

R. W. BROWN, A. H. BLACK, and A. E. HOROWITZ. 1955. Phonetic Symbolism in Natural Languages, *J. Abnorm. Soc. Psychol.*, 50, 388–93. Table adapted by permission of American Psychological Association.

ment," its "calm humorousness," its "open-mouthed peanut-invitingness."

Obviously, perceptions of identity vary widely, depending upon the context in which the object is perceived and the past experience of the person.

Words

The meaning of the passage you have just read is given by the words printed on the page. The words have come to convey meanings through complex processes of learning (to be discussed later) that permit us to identify each word and to know what it signifies.

Yet at the same time we must not ignore the striking physiognomic characteristics that words as physical stimuli often do have. We are familiar with onomatopoeia, the property of words that sound like what they mean: the "babbling" brook, the "swishing" skirt, the "clattering" feet. It has been suggested that in the evolution of language certain words came to represent certain things just because the sounds were similar. Box 15, p. 102, presents an interesting experiment (which you can try on yourself and on your friends) that demonstrates the physiognomic properties of words.

Unity of the Senses

The perception of objects is not completely dependent upon the particular sensory avenue through which they are apprehended, whether this avenue is the sense of vision, hearing, touch, and so on. For more than one sense is typically involved in perceiving objects, and the senses cooperate with and supplement one another. The taste of a food depends greatly upon the joint operation of taste and smell receptors; that is why food is "tasteless" when one has a stopped-up nose.

Several senses may agree on a perceptual attribute. An object may be located identically in space through the eyes, ears, and hands. It may be seen moving, heard moving, and felt moving. Sometimes the senses cooperate and agree despite discrepancies in the physical situation. When watching the moving-picture screen, we hear the voices come right from the moving lips, although the sound actually originates in loudspeakers.

There will be ample demonstration in Unit 9 of interactions within and among the senses. But before we can speak of results of studies in perception, we must know something of the methods employed (see Unit 6).

Glossary

film color A color that when seen through an aperture tends to appear less clearly localized and more filmy. One of the modes of appearance of color, along with surface color and volume color.

phenomenology The scientific study of immediate experience, in which the person seeks to give a detailed (and naïve) description of the way things look to him.

physiognomic properties The expressive qualities perceived in an object. They include aesthetic properties, affective properties, and the like.

structure The particular manner in which the parts of an object are perceived in relation to one another in forming the whole. This perceived structure may or may not correspond to the physical structure of the object.

surface color Color that is perceived as relatively opaque and localized at or on the object's surface. One of the modes of appearance of color, along with film color and volume color.

volume color Color that appears to fill an entire volume of space; it is neither opaque nor filmy. One of the modes of appearance of color, along with film color and surface color.

UNIT 6

psychophysics

overview / The stimulus is the physical energy that excites receptors and leads to perceptual experience. The study of the relationships between characteristics of such experience and those of the physical stimulus is called psychophysics.

The organism is not sensitive to all parts of the possible range of physical energies. An important psychophysical problem is the determination for a given organism of that point in the scale of intensity of the physical stimulus that separates seeing from not seeing, hearing from not hearing, tasting from not tasting, etc. This point is called the absolute threshold. There are several different ways that this threshold can be determined. Such measurement techniques are called psychophysical methods. Two basic psychophysical methods are the method of limits and the method of constant stimuli. The threshold obtained depends partly upon the particular method used, which is true of measurement everywhere in psychology. Thresholds measured on various occasions will differ also depending upon the physical and psychological conditions of the organism and the conditions of the environment.

That amount of difference in physical energy just large enough to make a "just noticeable difference" perceptually is called the differential threshold. As in the case of the absolute threshold, the value of the differential threshold varies widely, depending upon the nature of the stimulus and the state of the organism. Most importantly, it has a different value for each level of absolute magnitude of the stimulus; for example, the differential threshold for a dim light is not the same as for a bright light. Within limits, the differential threshold tends to approximate a constant fraction of the stimulus intensity, a mathematical formulation known as Weber's Law.

Our perceived worlds are made up of sights, sounds, smells, and feels, and a first scientific question is how these different sensory experiences are related to the different physical energies that arouse them. The study of these relationships is called *psychophysics*. The physical energies that surround us take many forms —radiant, vibratory, chemical, thermal, mechanical—and they vary in intensity as well as in kind. These forms of physical energy are our only direct links with the physical world of things and events. And our senses, which receive and respond to these energies, set the boundaries on what we can learn first hand about the physical world. But man has extended his understanding even to phenomena not accessible through direct sensory experience. This achievement is a tribute to man's thought and reasoning and to other higher-order mental processes. By reasoning, by experiment, and by the invention of ingenious instruments, man extends the scope of his comprehension beyond the limitations imposed by his senses. No matter how detailed and complete his knowledge of, for example, cosmic rays may be, however, he will never "know" them in the experiential sense, just as the blind man can never "know" color and the deaf man can never "know" music. This fact points to the finite, precisely definable, and relatively fragile foundation of direct sensory experience upon which the awesome complexity of man's total store of knowledge must build.

That psychophysics inaugurated experimental psychology (about 100 years ago) is probably not an historical accident. We can see that psychophysics, as the bridge between the physical world and human experience, presents the most obvious starting point for the scientific study of man. When for the first time men like the physicist Helmholtz (1821–1894) sought to determine empirically the systematic relationships between measurable aspects of physical energies and measurable attributes of sensory experience, the method was new but not

the problem. The connection between the two "separate worlds," physical and mental, was— and still is—a classical philosophical issue. Before turning to the facts of psychophysics, we must clarify a number of terms.

The Stimulus

Physical energy that can excite a sense organ (for example, the eye, the ear) and thus produce an effect on the organism is called a *stimulus*. If the energy does not produce an effect, it is not properly called a stimulus.

We must, however, distinguish stimulus from *stimulus object*. A red ball is placed ten feet in front of a child's eyes; it may be called the stimulus object. It may be objectively described in terms of its physical size, shape, color. It is an object in the environment that is the source of the stimulus.

The visual stimulus corresponding to this stimulus object is the pattern of physical light energies that, emanating from the ball, strike the retina of the eye. The stimulus object and the stimulus are not the same. As the light leaves the ball and passes through intervening space, its intensity is reduced, and it may be mixed with other light—depending, for example, on the general illumination of the room. Different eyes (for example, the nearsighted, the farsighted, those with 20/20 vision) focus the light rays in different ways, thus producing different patterns of light on the retinas of different observers of the same red ball. We see then that there are various physical reasons why a given stimulus object can give rise to an almost unlimited variety of different stimuli on the receptor surface.

The converse is also true, that the very same stimulus on the receptor surface can be produced by very different stimulus objects. The retina receives a given pattern of light stimuli, and it can make no difference to the retina how these stimuli have been produced. Although a chair may not be physically present in the en-

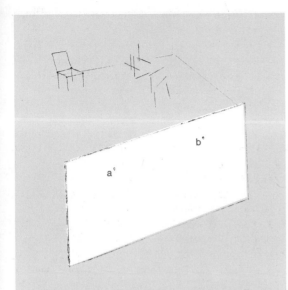

Figure 6.1. An observer looks with one eye through peephole a. The stimulus object on the left, seen from a, is a chair constructed out of lengths of string. The observer sees a "chair." Then he looks through peephole b. The pieces of string on the right, seen from b, are placed so that the image they cast on the eye is *identical* with the image cast by the other object. Here too the observer sees a "chair," although this stimulus-object differs greatly from the first. (After Kilpatrick, 1952.)

vironment, if the exact pattern of light is produced on the retina that would have been produced by looking at an actual chair, a "chair" will be perceived (see Figure 6.1.). For a perception of an object when *no* stimulus object is present, see Box 16, p. 108.

Measuring the Psychophysical Relationship

Psychophysics has not only a qualitative side (which energies result in which attributes of experience?) but also a quantitative side (how much energy results in how intense the attribute?). We shall now turn to the quantitative questions of the absolute and differential thresholds.

The Absolute Threshold

The organism is not sensitive to all parts of the possible range of physical energies. Some lights are too dim to see, some sounds too low to hear, some pressures too light to feel. An important psychological problem is the determination for a given organism of that point in the scale of the intensity of the physical stimulus that separates seeing from not seeing, hearing from not hearing, tasting from not tasting. This point is called the *absolute threshold.*

The threshold is not a single sharp dividing line but a zone in which the physical energies sometimes have an effect and sometimes do not. A sound wave whose intensity is below the threshold zone cannot be heard. If we gradually increase its intensity, it will enter the threshold zone, where it can sometimes be heard; as we make it more intense, it will be heard more often, and, as we make it still more intense, it will be heard all the time. What shall we call the threshold? Is it the lowest point at which the sound is ever heard? Or is it the lowest point at which the sound never fails to be heard? The former may be of interest to a soundproofing engineer; the latter is critical information for the siren designer.

In order to establish a universal standard, psychologists have agreed that the absolute threshold will arbitrarily be taken as that intensity of the physical stimulus that is perceived *half the time.* There are several different ways that this threshold can be determined. Such measurement techniques are called *psychophysical methods* (see Box 17, p. 110).

Measured under the best possible conditions, the absolute thresholds for various stimuli are amazingly low, which means, of course, that the sensitivity of the organism to that energy is very great. For example, it has been estimated that the physical energy equivalent to one pin dropping one inch, if converted to light energy and apportioned equally, would be sufficient to stimulate every one of the more than 5 billion human eyes on earth!

Box 16

The Phantom Limb

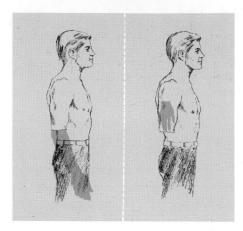

After a person has suffered the amputation of an arm or a leg, he may continue to feel that the limb is still there. He may feel itching in it; he may feel that he can still move it and may even momentarily forget that it is gone and try to use it.

Adults almost universally experience "phantom limbs" in cases of amputation. Sometimes these experiences are of brief duration, and sometimes they endure throughout the rest of the person's life. They often undergo gradual change in their perceived character. For example, D. Katz has reported that a phantom hand may gradually shrink and move up into the stump, so that finally it is experienced as a small hand embedded there. He has also observed, "If an amputee walks up to a wall, the phantom limb seems to go through it . . . the law of impermeability of matter does not seem to hold."

M. L. Simmel has extensively and imaginatively investigated this unusual phenomenon. Her main hypothesis is that phantoms represent the persistence, after amputation, of a previously learned "body schema." This view that phantoms can be experienced only for body parts that the person has had time to "learn" leads to several interesting and testable predictions. For one thing, as Simmel asks, "Are there phantoms for body parts that were never experienced because they were absent from birth?" Simmel's work and the work of others have clearly established that phantoms do *not* exist for congenitally missing limbs.

This finding, however, does not necessarily imply that learning, in the usual sense of the term, is involved in acquiring a body schema. Perhaps if a limb has *ever* been present, if only very briefly at birth, then its amputation will result in a phantom. Simmel argues otherwise, maintaining that only gradually, over a long period of experiencing movement and touch sensations in the limb, does its schema become sufficiently stable for it to be "missed" after amputation. From this reasoning, it would follow that, the later the age at which the limb is lost, the more frequent will be the phantoms. The place to look, then, is at the phantom-limb experiences of persons who have undergone amputation at different ages.

Age at Amputation	Cases	Percentage of Phantoms
Less than 2 years	10	20
2–4 years	14	25
4–6 years	13	61
6–8 years	20	75
8–10 years	19	100
10–20 years	41	100

The table summarizes Simmel's data on the experience of phantoms for more than 100 individuals whose amputations occurred sometime between early childhood and twenty years of age. Some of these cases were culled from published medical reports, but, for most of them, Simmel conducted careful interviews with the amputees and, in the case of children, with their parents as well. The developmental trend in the frequency of phantoms following amputation is clear: They gradually increase from the earliest age, and, by age eight, amputation always leads to phantom experiences. Simmel notes that perceptual and cognitive development in children shows much the same age trend, and, from this parallel, she suggests that acquiring a body schema is an instance of a relatively complex learning achievement.

Another line of evidence supports and elaborates this learned-body-schema interpretation of phantoms. Working with leprosy patients, Simmel finds that no phantoms are experienced when the parts of the body (mainly fingers and toes) have gradually disappeared through absorption. This absorption process is very slow, often extending for ten years or more, and is generally painless. When remnants of the absorbed digits are amputated, however, phantoms almost always occur afterward. Let Simmel present an interpretation of these findings in her own words.

"[During absorption] the schema can keep in step with physical reality through gradual small changes that parallel the physical alterations of the body. As a consequence, phantoms do not appear. By contrast, amputation produces a sudden alteration of physical reality at a speed at which the schema cannot change, and the persistence of the schema gives rise to the phantom experience."

In broader learning terms, whenever we have not been able to learn new adaptations to new situations, we must make do with the old ways of perceiving and reacting.

We can see from this example that the study of such fortunately rare abnormal phenomena can tell us something about normal psychological processes. Man is one, even in his most deviant forms, and a common set of principles must describe all human behavior.

D. KATZ. 1950. *Gestalt Psychology* (New York: Ronald).
M. L. SIMMEL. 1966. Developmental Aspects of the Body Scheme, *Child Develpm.*, 37, 83–95. Table adapted by permission; © 1966 by The Society for Research in Child Development, Inc.

Box 17   The Psychophysical Methods

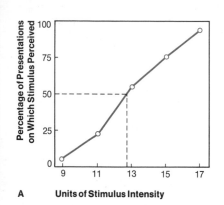

A   **Units of Stimulus Intensity**

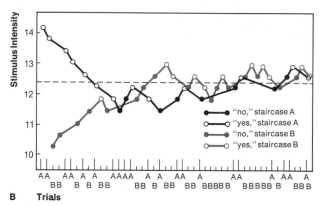

B   **Trials**

Thresholds can be determined by several different methods. Two basic methods are described here.

THE METHOD OF LIMITS. Starting with a stimulus intensity known to be well below threshold, the experimenter gradually increases the intensity until that point is reached at which the subject reports that he perceives the stimulus. Then, starting with an intensity well above threshold, the experimenter gradually decreases the intensity until that point is reached at which the subject no longer reports that he perceives the stimulus. Such ascending and descending series are alternated until a sufficient number of estimates of the "limits" have been obtained.

Stimulus Intensity (Arbitrary Units)

7	No			No		No		
8	No			No		No		
9	No			No		No		
10	No			No		No	No	10.5
11	No		No		No		No	Yes	
12	No	12.5	Yes	11.5	No	11.5	No	Yes	
13	Yes		Yes		Yes		Yes	12.5 Yes	
14			Yes		No	14.5		Yes	
15			Yes		Yes			Yes	
16			Yes		Yes			Yes	
17			Yes		Yes			Yes	
18			Yes		Yes			Yes	
19			Yes		Yes			Yes	

This method is illustrated in the table, which shows three ascending and three descending series of judgments. "No" means that the stimulus was not perceived, "yes" that it was. The horizontal bar in each column indicates the stimulus intensity of that "limit" in which there is a transition from perceiving to not perceiving or vice versa.

Note that there is variation among the series in the limits obtained. They range from 10.5 to 14.5. The threshold is computed as the average of all these obtained limits, which proves to' be 12.2.

THE METHOD OF CONSTANT STIMULI. A limited set of stimuli (usually five to eight) that range in intensity are chosen by the experimenter, on the basis of rough exploration, so that they will bracket the range of intensity from the point at which the stimulus will rarely be perceived to the point at which it will almost always be perceived. Each of the stimuli is presented for judgment a large number of times (perhaps 100) in random order. The subject is to report whether or not he perceives the stimulus. The threshold is computed to be that stimulus intensity that results in a perception of the stimulus *about 50 per cent of the time.*

The method is illustrated here by the same threshold problem used in our discussion of the method of limits (see Figure A). First, it was determined roughly that the threshold was in the vicinity of an intensity of thirteen units. Five stimuli were then prepared, varying in equal steps from nine to seventeen units. Each of the five stimuli was presented 100 times. The graph shows the percentage of times each was perceived and the percentage of times it was not perceived out of the 100 presentations.

The dotted lines show that the threshold value at which the stimulus is perceived 50 per cent of the time is about 12.8. The threshold value need not be one of the actual stimuli presented during the series; in fact it very rarely is. Here the stimulus intensity corresponding to the 50 per cent point is determined by interpolation. To interpolate we assume a certain shape of the curve between the actually measured points; in this case the simplest assumption—a straight line—was made.

There are some drawbacks to these methods. In the method of limits the progression of stimulus intensity is regular, so that the subject's expectations may distort his perception. The method of constant stimuli avoids this risk by presenting stimuli in random order but, in doing so, sacrifices efficiency. Because we do not discover the individual's threshold until all measurements are completed, it is necessary, as we have noted, to use stimulus intensities that bracket almost all possible threshold values, and therefore many superfluous readings are taken.

Tom N. Cornsweet's (1962) random, double-staircase method is designed to combine the advantages of the two earlier methods and avoids their deficiencies. This method is really nothing more than two concurrent but separate applications of the method of limits. The crucial point is that any given trial may be part of one series or the other, so that the subject cannot guess whether the stimulus is gradually increasing or decreasing. We thus have the advantage of ruling out biasing expectations (the advantage of the method of constant stimuli), and, because the direction of stimulus change is reversed each time the threshold is reached (as in the method of limits), few trials are wasted because they are far from the threshold value.

Figure B (adapted from Cornsweet) illustrates the random, double-staircase method for the same threshold problem. One way of computing the threshold in this psychophysical method is to average all the stimuli presented after the staircases have converged. In our present data, the value is 12.4.

Note that the threshold values as determined by the three methods are not identical (12.2, 12.8, 12.4). This fact has two implications: First, it indicates the complexity of psychological measurement of even the simplest functions; second, it indicates that the psychophysical method used reflects differences in the complex factors determining the threshold. Here we clearly see that the outcome of psychological measurement is always relative to the particular method used, which is true of measurement everywhere in science.

T. N. CORNSWEET. 1962. The Staircase-Method in Psychophysics, *Amer. J. Psychol.*, 75, 485–91. Figure B adapted by permission.

Thresholds measured on various occasions will differ depending upon the physical and psychological conditions of the organism and the conditions of the environment. When determining the threshold of sensitivity to light, for example, not only is there the obvious need for the person's eyes to be focused on the stimulus object, but also he must be mentally focused if his maximum sensitivity is to be determined. If he is thinking about something else or if he is being simultaneously bombarded by other stimuli (as in a noisy room), his visual threshold will be raised. Although these effects have always been known and often demonstrated experimentally, only very recently has some understanding of the physiological mechanisms involved been achieved (see, for example, Unit 16, p. 255). A relative inability to focus attention, at least in response to verbal instruction, may in part account for the generally higher thresholds characteristic of infants and young children.

The Differential Threshold

We are concerned not only with absolute sensitivity to physical energies but also with sensitivity to the differences in intensity of the energies. The individual may look at two light bulbs simultaneously or first at one and then at the other, or he may look at a single bulb whose intensity is gradually changing. In each case there is the question of whether or not he is able to perceive a difference in the lights. If we start with two lights, very slightly different in intensity, the person will be unable to detect a difference. As the intensity of one of the lights increases, he will sometimes be able to see a difference and sometimes not; and, when the difference is large enough, he will always be able to see the difference. That amount of difference in physical energy just large enough to make a "just noticeable difference" perceptually (usually abbreviated j.n.d.) is called the *differential threshold*. Here again, the convention is to take as the differential threshold that stimulus difference that will be perceived *half*

Box 18

Poor Taste and Good Pitch

The following illustrative Weber fractions [1] have been taken from the work of various investigators. For each stimulus dimension, the absolute level of stimulus intensity at which the Weber fraction was determined is indicated. These values are *minimal* values, obtained under optimal conditions of judgment.

Pitch (at 2,000 cycles per second)	1/333
Deep pressure (at 400 grams)	1/77
Visual brightness (at 1,000 photons)	1/62
Lifted weights (at 300 grams)	1/53
Loudness (at 100 decibels, 1,000 cycles per second)	1/11
Smell of rubber (at 200 olfacties)	1/10
Skin pressure (at 5 grams per square millimeter)	1/7
Taste, saline (at 3 moles per liter)	1/5

The remarkable range in sensitivities of the various senses is well demonstrated; it is about seventyfold—from pitch, in which a difference of as little as *one-third of 1 per cent* can be detected, to taste, in which there must be a difference of about 20 per cent before it can be detected.

[1] Listed in E. G. BORING, H. S. LANGFELD, and H. P. WELD, eds. 1948. *Foundations of Psychology* (New York: Wiley).

---

the time. The psychophysical methods for such determination are similar to those described in Box 17, p. 110.

As in the case of the absolute threshold, the value of the differential threshold varies widely, depending upon the nature of the stimulus and the state of the organism. Most important, it has a different value for each level of absolute magnitude of the stimulus. For example, the differential threshold for a dim light is not the same as that for a bright light.

This latter fact would seem to imply that we would have to compute the differential threshold separately for every physical intensity. But a very surprising fact was discovered early in the history of psychophysics that simplified the problem enormously: Within limits, the differential threshold tends to approximate a constant fraction of the stimulus intensity.

Suppose, for example, that the differential threshold for a weight of 50 pounds is 1 pound; that is, a weight must be at least 51 pounds to be perceived as heavier. It will then turn out that the differential threshold for a weight of 100 pounds is *2* pounds; that is, for 100 pounds the next heavier weight that can just be perceived as heavier will be 102 pounds. And for a 150-pound weight, the next heavier weight that can be discriminated will prove to be 153 pounds. In each case the differential threshold is the *same* fraction of the stimulus weight: 1/50 = 2/100 = 3/150 = .02 This value of .02 tells us that we must add 2 per cent of the original weight before we can tell that it is heavier. Knowing the constant fraction, we can thus closely estimate what the differential threshold will be for any magnitude of stimulus weight.

The increment needed to produce a j.n.d. is relative to the intensity of the original stimulus. We make use of this fact in many everyday actions. Less caution is needed in adding a spice to a highly seasoned than to a delicately seasoned dish. We hesitate less in bringing an uninvited guest to a very large party than we do to a small intimate party. Even aesthetic judgments show this effect. For example, the striking beauty benefits less from the dedicated attention of hairdresser, make-up expert, and other beauticians than does her less fortunately endowed sister.

Weber's Law

The facts we have been discussing were first made explicit by the physiologist Weber in 1834, and the mathematical formulation is called *Weber's Law:*

$$\frac{\Delta I}{I} = k.$$

I is the intensity of the stimulus, ΔI is the differential threshold, and *k* is a constant fraction for the given type of physical energy.

The constant fraction must, of course, be determined by actual measurement for each type of stimulus. As we might expect, there are enormous differences in the fractions for different senses and attributes. Shown in Box 18, p. 112, are some representative Weber fractions.

There is a limitation on Weber's Law. Although the law holds fairly well for the middle ranges, at the extremes (for example, when a light is very bright or very dim), the Weber fractions may deviate widely from the constant value.

Glossary

absolute threshold The minimal intensity of a physical stimulus required to stimulate the organism.

differential threshold The minimal difference in intensities of two stimuli that can be perceived.

psychophysical methods Methods for the determination of absolute and differential thresholds, including the method of constant stimuli and the method of limits.

psychophysics The study of the relationships between the attributes of different sensory experiences and the characteristics of the physical stimuli producing them.

stimulus Physical energy that excites a receptor and produces an effect on the organism.

stimulus object The object in the environment that is the source of the energies that serve as a stimulus.

Weber's Law The principle that the minimal perceptible difference in intensity of two stimuli (ΔI) is a constant fraction (*k*) of the absolute level of the stimuli (*I*). Formulated as

$$\frac{\Delta I}{I} = k.$$

The constant fraction differs for each given type of stimulus. The law does not hold at the extremes of the stimulus range.

UNIT 7

stimuli for vision and hearing

overview / The physical stimuli for vision are radiant energies from a very narrow region of the full range of electromagnetic waves. The hue of a color depends on the wave length of the light; its brightness upon light intensity. Saturation refers to the purity of a color—the more mixed the light waves, the lower the saturation of the resultant color. Color mixture follows fairly simple laws, but mixing light is quite different from mixing paint; the former involves the combining of light waves and the latter involves the subtracting of light waves.

The sensitivity of the eye to light waves varies with wave length and intensity, with the eye's state of adaptation resulting from previous stimulation, and with the region of the retina stimulated. Colors are seen best in the foveal region and are not seen at all in the extreme periphery of the retina. Two principal forms of partial color blindness are deuteranopia and protanopia, both having to do with deficiencies in the perception of red and green. Visual acuity—the ability to distinguish stimuli very close to each other—varies, depending upon retinal region, amount of illumination, degree of contrast between object and background, and the presence or absence of defects in the visual mechanisms.

Variations in air pressure at the eardrum result in the experience of sound. Pitch is due mainly to the frequency of the sound wave—the greater the frequency the higher the pitch. Loudness varies primarily with the amplitude of the sound waves. When sound waves of different characteristics are mixed, we experience more complex sound qualities like timbre, overtones, consonance, and dissonance (which, at the extreme, is noise).

Auditory sensitivity, like visual sensitivity, is restricted to certain bands of energy and depends, among other factors, on the intensity and frequency of sound waves.

The universe is full of radiant energy in the form of electromagnetic waves. These waves vary greatly in length, from cosmic rays of a few trillionths of an inch to radio waves of many miles. Some of these waves are the physical stimuli for vision.

The Physical Stimuli for Vision

The stimuli for vision are electromagnetic waves that fall on the eyes. Of the whole range of these waves, only a tiny fraction (called "light waves") are capable of producing a visual experience (see Color Plate 1). Above and below this "visible spectrum" there is no visual impression. Within this visible range the physical characteristics of the light waves are closely related to the principal dimensions of our perception of color—*hue, brightness,* and *saturation.*

Hue

The wave lengths of light that give rise to different hues are shown in **Color Plate 1**. Wave lengths of about 700 millimicrons (a millimicron, symbolized by mμ, is one-billionth of a meter) are seen as red light; those of about 400 millimicrons are seen as violet light. Each of the other hues of the spectrum has its own wave length, which is located somewhere between these two extremes.

There is a way in which we can experience this progression of colors in nature. When sunlight passes through a prism, it fans out into the familiar color spectrum that ranges from red through violet (as shown in Color Plate 1). The rainbow is a common example; sunlight is refracted by passing through rain drops, which serve as prisms.

If we reverse the process and recombine the various spectral colors of the rainbow, we once again have white sunlight. White light, therefore has no single wave length that produces it, and the same is true of some other important colors.

Certain colors—red, yellow, green, and blue —are often called *primary colors* in a psychological analysis of color. This "primary" quality is entirely a perceptual phenomenon; there is nothing whatever distinctive in the continuum of physical wave lengths of light at the points corresponding to these primary colors. From an analysis of the way in which people describe differences between colored lights, however, Weckroth (1960) finds that "redness," "blueness," and "greenness" seem to be the primary dimensions used in color judgments. The relation between such suggested primary colors in experience and the way in which the receptors and brain work in color perception is discussed in Unit 15.

Brightness

Any given hue, for example, red, can vary in brightness. Brightness corresponds closely with the intensity of the light energies. With greater intensity the colors are brighter, approaching white; with lesser intensities the colors are darker, approaching black.

Saturation

A color of a given hue and a given brightness may also look more or less saturated. That is, it may look richer and more concentrated or paler, more dilute, and more washed out. We can recognize the phenomenon easily by gradually diluting a rich blue watercolor paint with water, turning it into paler and paler tints of blue until no blue at all is discernible. We would then have a completely desaturated color or what we call an "achromatic" color. The continuum of grays, from white through middle gray to black, are the achromatic colors.

Desaturation of hues is produced by mixing light of different wave lengths. The greater the number of different wave lengths, the less the saturation.

The most highly saturated hues are those of

a middle level of brightness. As we go toward brighter colors or toward darker colors, the maximal saturation that can be attained is less and less, until, on reaching white or black, saturation is zero.

Color Mixture

The light that strikes the eye is very rarely of a single wave length; almost always it is a mixture of many wave lengths, because illumination on objects is mainly from light sources like the sun, which emit light waves of various lengths. Only under exceptional laboratory conditions, in which there is careful filtering, are we likely to deal with pure light of a given single wave length.

It is a striking fact that we do not and cannot analyze a light mixture into its component parts simply by looking at it. We see only the single color that results from the mixture.

Rules of Color Mixture There are specific rules by which we can mix colors and predict the resulting hue, brightness, and saturation. One of the most useful pieces of apparatus for laboratory study of color mixture is the color wheel (see Figure 7.1.).

1. Two hues mixed in equal amounts will result in a new hue lying on the visible spectrum exactly halfway between the two; if two hues are mixed in unequal amounts, the new hue will be proportionately closer to the more plentiful component.
2. The brightness of the resultant color will be the average of the brightness of the two component colors.
3. The saturation of a mixed color will be less than the average of the saturations of the component colors.
4. Every color has its own *complementary color;* when the two are mixed together in equal amounts, the resultant is an achromatic gray. For example, a properly chosen red and green (with wave lengths of about 640 and 490, respectively) will, when mixed on a color wheel, lose all color. The same is true of a yellow and a blue.

If the sequence of colors of the visible spectrum can be arranged in a circle so that the two colors that form a complementary pair lie exactly opposite one another, the arrangement is called a "color circle" (see Color Plate 2).

These rules for mixture apply not only for two but also for any number of colors. For example, a mixture of three colors lying equidistant from one another on the color circle also results in a gray.

All hues can be obtained by mixing only three initial colors. For instance, the three primary colors, red, green, and blue, when mixed in proper proportions, can give any desired color. If we simply add white and black to our three chromatic ingredients, we can obtain colors of any desired hue, brightness, and saturation.

Mixing Light versus Mixing Paint The reader may have detected a contradiction between what has been said about color mixture and his own experiences in mixing colors from a paint box. Yellow and blue, we have said, are comple-

Figure 7.1. A color wheel for mixing colors. Disks of colored paper are cut and assembled on the wheel, overlapping so that different-sized angular sectors of each color are exposed. When the wheel is rotated rapidly, a completely mixed color is seen instead of the separate component colors. The mixtures can readily be varied by changing the size of angular sectors of the two or more component colors.

mentaries and, when mixed equally, yield a gray. But we have all mixed yellow and blue paint to get green. Furthermore, by mixing all the paints of the palette, we get a dirty black, not the white we specified earlier. What is the discrepancy? The answer is simple, but first it is necessary to examine the manner in which the color of objects is perceived.

The Color of Objects   The perceived color of an object depends upon the light waves that are reflected or emitted from its surface. The differences in physical constitution of objects determine, among other things, how the objects will absorb and reflect light. A highly polished surface like a mirror reflects most of the light falling on it; snow reflects a great deal of light; soil reflects less and coal still less.

Objects also differ in the degrees to which they selectively reflect or absorb light of different wave lengths. Of all the light waves falling on an object, some will be more fully absorbed than others. Red paint in sunlight will absorb most wave lengths except those around 600 millimicrons, which correspond to "red" light; what is reflected from the paint and what strikes the eye of the viewer is therefore mainly "red" light, and he sees the paint as red. White paint reflects all wave lengths and absorbs none; it is perceived as white. Black paint absorbs almost all wave lengths and reflects almost none.

The perceived hue of an object thus depends upon two factors: first, the wave lengths of the light illuminating it and, second, the wave lengths of the light it reflects. If the illumination falling on a "red" painted object contains no "red" wave lengths, the object will appear achromatic.

Combining and Subtracting Light Waves   We can now readily account for the difference in results when we mix lights and when we mix paints. When we mix lights we are combining light waves. For example, when we spin yellow

and blue segments together on a color wheel (see Figure 7.1.), our eye is stimulated by *both* "yellow" light and "blue" light, and the result is gray. On the other hand, when we mix paints, we are subtracting light waves, in that we are mixing pigments each of which absorbs different light waves. The resulting pigment mixture absorbs a greater variety of light waves and reflects fewer than each component pigment alone. Mixing yellow and blue paints yields a green color, not gray, because the yellow pigment absorbs the extreme blue and the blue pigment absorbs the extreme yellow and only the green remains to be reflected.

Visual Sensitivity and Acuity

Sensitivity of the eye to light varies with the intensity of the wave length of light, with the state of the eye, with the point stimulated on the eye, and with other factors.

Sensitivity to Intensity   We have already noted that under optimal conditions the smallest intensity of light that the eye can detect is amazingly low. One of the optimal conditions is that the eye be dark-adapted (see p. 240). The longer a person sits in a dark room, the more sensitive his eyes become to light. Sensitivity to intensity also is a function of the wave lengths of the light. For example, light of a wave length around 500 $m\mu$ is more easily seen than light of other wave lengths.

Sensitivity to intensity is dependent upon the part of the retina stimulated. The most sensitive part lies slightly to one side of the fovea, which is the name given to the very center of the retina (see Figure 15.1., p. 233).

There is one especially interesting anomaly in the sensitivity of different parts of the retina. One part is completely blind. When you do the demonstration in Figure 7.2., you will discover this blindness, which you may not have suspected.

green

sun

green

blue-green

green

. (See p. 121.)
nore, Md.

ay paper over
ver while con-
9.)

e to the cross

oughout. (See

Sensitivity to Wave Length Sensitivity to wave length is by no means the same as sensitivity to intensity. In general, there is much greater ability to detect that there is light than to specify its color. At any given wave length, there is thus a zone of intensities within which we can see light but not color (see Figure 7.3.).

In a gradually darkening garden at twilight, the colors of flowers may begin to look different from their colors during the day. During the day the reds and yellows are far brighter than the greens and blues; at twilight, the greens and blues are relatively brighter. As darkness becomes more complete, the reds and yellows may completely disappear, long before the shorter-wave-length colors do. A red rose may look black, while the leaves are still clearly green. This shift in sensitivity is known as the *Purkinje effect* (see Figure 7.4.).

As with brightness, sensitivity to hue varies tremendously from place to place on the retina. Colors are seen best in the foveal region. They are not seen at all in the extreme periphery; everyone is "color blind" at the edge of his visual field. You can easily demonstrate this fact by fixating a point in front of you and slowly moving a colored pencil at arm's length from far to the side of your head, where you cannot see it, toward the front of your head. You will notice that you can detect the pencil moving into your visual field long before you can detect its color. Furthermore, if the pencil is half yellow and half red, you will see the yellow much sooner than the red.

Color Blindness In rare instances a person may be *totally* color blind (a state of affairs not at all uncommon among some lower animals). That is, he has no experience of differences of hue. His world is portrayed not in Technicolor but in varying shades of white, gray, and black.

Much more commonly *color blindness* is partial. The two types of partial color blindness that occur most frequently are deuteranopia and protanopia. The first involves an inability to perceive the difference between red and green; the second involves this same inability plus a weakness in sensitivity to the red end of the spectrum.

What does a partially color-blind person see? According to a recent review of what is known about human color vision (Wald, 1964), both deuteranopes and protanopes see only two hues in the spectrum, blue and yellow. Which is seen depends upon the wave length of the color stimulus. If the wave length is from the long (red) end of the spectrum, then yellow is the color perceived, whether the stimulus is actually red, orange, yellow, or greenish. If it is from the short (violet) end, the partially color-blind subject sees blue, though the stimulus is actually violet, blue, or greenish blue. In a rather narrow wave-length band, somewhere around 500 mμ (a bluish green), no color at all is seen, and the stimulus appears to be white or gray.

Tritanopia, a form of partial color blindness in which blue and yellow are confused, is a much rarer condition. Because it is so rare, we

Figure 7.2. Hold the book at arm's length, close your left eye, and gaze steadily at the dot. Then slowly bring the book toward you. You will find a place at which the circle completely disappears. It happens because, from that distance, the image of the circle is falling on an insensitive part of the retina known as the *blind spot.* Now bring the book even closer to your face, and the circle will reappear. There is, of course, a similar blind spot on the other eye.

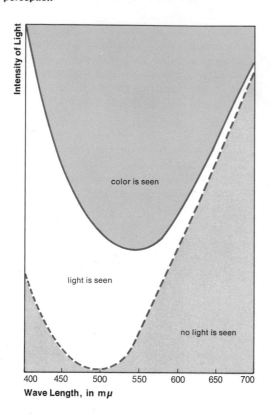

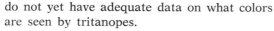

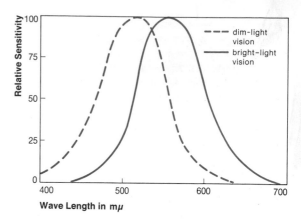

Figure 7.4. Two curves showing the relative sensitivity to various wave lengths for bright-light vision and for dim-light vision. The curves are plotted as percentages of maximal sensitivity. For example, in bright light the eye is most sensitive to wave lengths around 550 (a greenish-yellow hue), in dim light to wave lengths around 500 (a green hue).

◄ **Figure 7.3.** A chart showing the sensitivity of the human eye to light of different wave lengths. The broken curve shows the minimal intensities required at each wave length for achromatic *light* to be seen. The solid curve shows the minimal intensities required at each wave length for *color* to be seen.

do not yet have adequate data on what colors are seen by tritanopes.

Although we all have some experience of a world without color, as in the case of black-and-white movies, television, and reproductions of paintings, it is not easy to grasp what it means to be truly color blind. A person who is totally and congenitally color blind not only has no color experience now but also has no available memory or imagery of color, because he has *never* had color experience. He must make do with a pallid "language" of color names. He may seem to talk about colors in the same way others do, even though his conception of the absent colors is based only on guesses from what others say.

We are often unaware that a person with whom we associate is color blind, and sometimes he himself is unaware of it. Our world is

so constructed that we can get along fairly well without color discrimination. The color-blind driver stops even though he cannot see the redness of the traffic light, because he is able to discriminate the usual brightness difference between the green and red lights and because he remembers that the red is above the green. In coping with our physical worlds, people with sensory defects can often make use of analogous "vicarious" routes to obtain information.

The exceptions to this rule make for dramatic demonstrations. The color-blind person may dress in outlandish color combinations until he learns by rote which garment should go with which. He may make fatal errors in recognizing signals when he pilots an aircraft. He may fail to recognize a familiar figure because perception of its identity depends on distinguishing the color similarities of certain of its elements. This possibility is the basis of the diagnostic tests of color blindness (see Color Plate 3).

The color-blind person can occasionally turn the tables on the person with normal vision. Some camouflages used in wartime depend for their effect on color patterns that break up the normal contours of the object being disguised. They may indeed fool the person who sees color, but they may not fool the color-blind person.

Visual Acuity When we talk about people having "good" or "poor" vision, it is usually *visual acuity* we are referring to—their ability to differentiate small stimulus differences in the size and shape of objects.

The conventional eye chart exposes letters or other figures of varying sizes at a standard distance from the viewer. His acuity is measured in terms of his successful identification of the figures and is commonly expressed as relative to average vision. Thus 20/20 vision signifies that the viewer is able to identify stimuli at twenty feet that the average person also identifies at twenty feet. And 20/40 vision signifies that he must be as close as twenty feet to identify what average vision can identify at forty feet. For more accurate determinations of visual acuity in the laboratory, other methods are used.

Degree of acuity depends upon many factors. First, acuity becomes increasingly poor as the stimulus moves away from the center of the retina (see Figure 7.5.), except for the detection of movement, which improves (for a possible physiological basis, see Unit 15). Second, acuity improves with higher illumination. Third, acuity is higher when the contrast between the object and its background is greater; it is lower when light of high intensity (glare) shines close to the direct line of vision. Fourth, defects of the eye may affect visual acuity in various ways. For example, in conditions of nearsightedness and farsightedness, objects clearly discriminated at one distance may be

fuzzy and unclear at other distances. The reason for nearsightedness and farsightedness lies in the manner in which the eyeball adjusts or fails to adjust in focusing on an object (as we shall see in Unit 15, p. 232).

The Physical Stimuli for Sound

When a physical object is set into regular vibration (a violin string plucked, a tuning fork struck), the vibrations produce periodic compressions (increased pressure) and rarefactions (decreased pressure) of the surrounding air. These periodic compressions and rarefactions, *sound waves*, are transmitted through the air in all directions. Their impact on the eardrum is the stimulus for the hearing of sound.

It is convenient to plot the periodic compressions and rarefactions of the sound waves in graphic form (see Figure 7.6.). The two main characteristics of sound waves are frequency and amplitude. The faster the object vibrates,

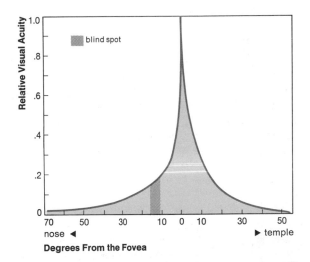

Figure 7.5. This diagram shows the varying levels of visual acuity at different places on the retina. Acuity at the fovea is maximal; it drops sharply as the stimulus moves away from the fovea toward the periphery of the retina. At the blind spot, of course, there is zero acuity.

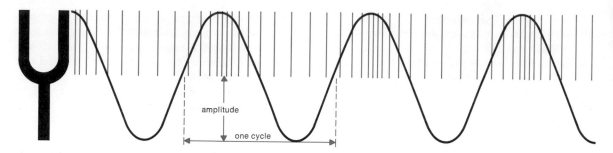

Figure 7.6. The successive compressions and rarefactions of air particles produced by the vibration of a tuning fork. The curve corresponds to these sound waves. The amplitude, or height, of the wave indicates the degree of compression or rarefaction of the air particles. The frequency of sound waves is the number of cycles passing a given point per second.

the greater the number of periodic compressions of the air per second. This number is known as the *frequency* of the sound wave, measured in cycles per second (c.p.s.). The more forcible the vibrations (for instance, the harder the tuning folk is struck), the greater the energy transmitted in the air compressions and the greater the *amplitude* of the sound wave.

The frequency of sound waves emitted by a vibrating object remains the same as they travel through the air. The sound waves from a given tuning fork have the same frequency whether nearby or far away. But the amplitude of a sound wave decreases as it travels away from the tuning fork.

Pitch

Our world is full of sounds that vary in *pitch* all the way from the deepest tone to the highest tone. The rising wail of a siren provides a helpful illustration of variations in pitch and of the stimuli that cause the variations. The sound of the siren is made by directing a jet of air against a revolving disk that has a row of holes around its periphery. As the disk moves, the air escapes through the holes in separate puffs. The faster the disk turns, the greater the rate of puffs and the higher the pitch of the siren. The pitch thus varies with the frequency of

sound waves: Low-pitched sounds are evoked by low frequencies (few puffs per second) and high-pitched sounds by high frequencies (many puffs per second). As Figure 7.7. indicates, however, the relation between pitch and frequency is not a straight line. Furthermore, pitch turns out to be determined not only by the frequency of the sound waves but also by their amplitude: The pitch of low-frequency tones drops as the amplitude increases.

Loudness

Loudness of sound varies primarily with the amplitude of the sound waves. But frequency, too, plays a role. Two tones of equal amplitude but different frequency will not be perceived as identical in loudness. Within the usual range of speech, for example, the higher the frequency, the lower the intensity required to reach absolute threshold, a fact related to the use of high-pitched sound sources (for example, a whistle) that are designed to attract attention.

Complex Attributes and Wave Mixture

Most of what we have discussed about auditory experiences up to this point pertains to the perception of *pure tones*. Pure tones are produced by a regularly vibrating object like a tuning fork, which emits waves of a single frequency. Pure tones are rare. Almost always in our physical environment sound waves are mixtures of waves of different frequencies. The sound of a violin string is much more complex than that of a tuning fork, and the sound of an entire orchestra is still more complex. The complexity may come about because the characteristics of the sound source are such as to emit mixed waves; a violin, for instance, emits not only a basic set of wave frequencies from the vibration of a string but also a large number of other related frequencies—for example, from the vibration of the wood. The sound may also be complex because there are several independent sound sources emitting waves simultaneously. No matter where the waves come from, they strike the eardrum together and are necessarily mixed there.

The consequences of different forms of wave mixture in auditory experience will now be examined.

Timbre and Overtones The tone of a tuning fork is thin compared with the full, rich tone of a cello. This attribute of tonal quality is usually referred to as "timbre." It is differences in timbre that enable us to distinguish readily among identical notes played on a violin, a piano, and a flute. Timbre is difficult to analyze, and all that we shall say here about the psychophysical relationship is that the greater the complexity of mixture of physical sound waves, the richer the timbre.

A perceptive listener can detect tones of higher pitches along with the pitch of the fundamental tone when a musical instrument is played. These tones are called *overtones*. They are based on concrete properties of the physical stimulus, as described in Figure 7.8.

Differentiation and Masking of Tones If a person is simultaneously stimulated by two tones of different wave frequencies—for instance, 1,200 and 1,700 cycles per second—he may be able to pick out each of these tones. The ease with which he can differentiate them will depend upon the degree of separation and the "harmony" of the two tones. It will also depend in an interesting way on their relative loudness.

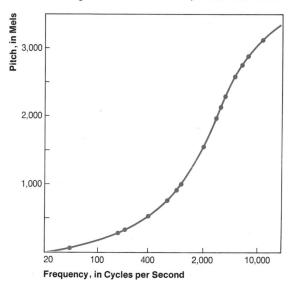

Figure 7.7. This graph shows the relation of pitch to frequency of sound waves.

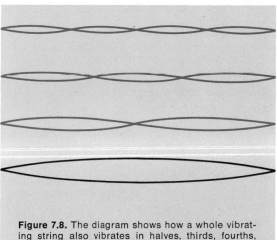

Figure 7.8. The diagram shows how a whole vibrating string also vibrates in halves, thirds, fourths, and so on. Each vibrating part produces its own set of waves of higher frequencies, resulting in overtones, which are multiples of the fundamental tone.

If the lower tone is made considerably louder than the higher tone, it tends to pre-empt attention. As the loudness difference becomes even greater, the higher tone may completely disappear, so that only the lower tone is heard. This phenomenon is called *masking*.

Dissonance and Consonance An extremely important attribute of our auditory world is the impression of consonance or of dissonance that tonal combinations can give. *Consonance* is the quality of harmony, smoothness, or unity of a combination of tones, often experienced as agreeable. *Dissonance* is the reverse, a quality of disharmony, ill-fittingness, and lack of unity of a combination of tones, often experienced as disagreeable.

A person will usually have little difficulty in sorting out tonal combinations on the basis of their consonance and dissonance, and he is likely to do it consistently on different occasions. Furthermore, many other people will agree closely with his judgments. But there is clear evidence from comparisons of musical judgments in different cultures that there is a great deal of latitude in the way the consonance or dissonance of a specific tonal combination may be perceived. And people may change their own perceptions of consonance and dissonance with experience and with musical training.

Despite these personal and cultural factors, consonance and dissonance are to a considerable degree determined by the pattern of the physical stimulus. If we make up a tonal combination of wave frequencies of 256, 512, 768, and 1,024 cycles per second, most people will hear it as high in consonance. Note that the frequencies are all simple multiples of the lowest frequency, as are overtones.

On the other hand, if we combine the following unrelated frequencies—105, 173, 251, 497, 582—the effect is highly likely to be perceived as dissonant. The general rule therefore seems to be that consonance tends to relate closely to certain mathematical regularities—and dissonance to irregularities—of relations among the frequencies mixed.

Noise Noise can be understood as dissonance carried to an extreme. The physical stimulus for noise is a complex mixture of wave frequencies that bear no simple numerical relation to one another. A mixture of sound waves that includes almost *all* the frequencies is sometimes technically referred to as *white noise* because it is roughly analogous to white light, which includes all wave lengths.

Auditory Sensitivity

Of the whole range of frequencies of physical sound waves, only a certain band is capable of

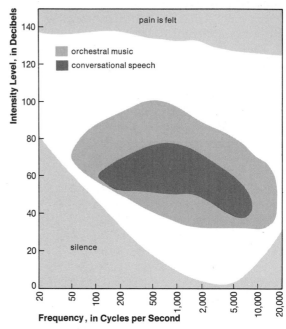

Figure 7.9. The auditory area, showing how perception of sound is a function of both intensity and frequency of sound waves. The lower curve shows the minimal intensities required at each frequency in order to hear sound. Above the upper curve the intensities are so great that they produce a painful sensation. Between the two curves is the area of hearing. Also shown are the approximate areas of conversational speech and of orchestral music.

producing sensations of sound. In man, for instance, the lowest frequency that can be heard is about 20 cycles per second, whereas the highest is about 20,000 cycles per second. Above and below these limits there is silence—silence, that is, for man, though not for all species.

Auditory sensitivity is a complex function of intensity and frequency. Figure 7.9. shows how an "auditory area" can be plotted within which all normal hearing occurs.

Discrimination of Pitch and Loudness The discriminations of differences in pitch and loudness are interrelated. For instance, the ability to detect small differences in the loudness of two tones depends partly upon their frequencies.

Even general states of the organism seem to affect these discriminations. Cohen and Fine (1961), for example, find that sleep deprivation reduces sensitivity for pitch differences and to a lesser extent for loudness differences. These effects start after thirty-two hours of wakefulness, reach a maximum at forty-eight hours, but then, paradoxically, become less up to ninety-six hours of total sleeplessness. In this instance, at least, the common-sense expectation that the organism becomes generally less sensitive with increasing fatigue is not wholly supported.

Glossary

amplitude The amount of energy carried by a sound wave. It is closely related to experienced loudness.

brightness A dimension of visual experience varying from white to black. It is closely correlated with intensity of the light waves.

color blindness A defect in sensitivity to hue. Total color blindness is very rare. There are two kinds of partial color blindness. Deuteranopia is partial color blindness involving inability to distinguish red and green. Protanopia is partial color blindness involving inability to distinguish red from green plus a weakness in sensitivity to the red end of the spectrum.

complementary colors Colors that lie exactly opposite each other on the color circle and that, when mixed in equal proportions, produce an achromatic gray—for example, red and green, yellow and blue.

consonance The quality of harmony, smoothness, or unity of a combination of tones, often experienced as agreeable.

dissonance A quality of disharmony, ill-fittingness, and lack of unity of a combination of tones, often experienced as disagreeable; the opposite of consonance.

frequency The number of periodic compressions occurring in a sound wave, measured in cycles per second (c.p.s.).

hue The color of an object—for example, blue, red, yellow, green.

masking The effect of one stimulus in reducing the experience of other stimuli presented simultaneously.

overtones Partial tones in a complex sound that have higher pitches than the fundamental tone.

pitch The attribute of tones in terms of which they may be described as high or low. This attribute is closely related to frequency of the sound waves.

primary colors The colors red, yellow, green, and blue, which appear to the observer to be "pure" rather than "mixtures" of other colors.

pure tones Tones produced by simple sound waves of a single frequency like those produced by a tuning fork.

Purkinje effect The shift in relative brightness of colors at the two ends of the spectrum as illumination decreases—for example, the greater relative brightness of reds and yellows in daylight and of blues and greens at twilight.

saturation The degree of concentration or dilution of the hue of a color.

sound waves Periodic compressions and rarefactions of the air, which, striking the ear, produce sounds. Sound waves have certain frequencies and amplitudes.

visual acuity The ability to differentiate visually small details of size and shape of objects.

white noise A complex mixture of sound waves of all frequencies, analogous to white light, which is a mixture of all wave lengths of light.

UNIT 8

stimuli for the chemical and somesthetic senses

overview / Taste and smell are intimately related; both have chemical substances as their physical stimuli, and they typically interact with one another. The basic tastes are sweet, sour, bitter, and salty. Substances of extremely different chemical make-up can evoke much the same sensation. Also, substances that chemically are very similar often taste quite different. Individuals vary widely in both their absolute and their differential gustatory thresholds.

Basic smell attributes are more difficult to identify. Many classification systems for the bewildering array of odors have been proposed but with only partial success. Absolute sensitivity to olfactory stimuli is extraordinarily high, but differential sensitivity is relatively poor.

Although it is convenient to classify skin sensations as touch, pain, heat, and cold (each of which occurs in numerous receptive spots scattered irregularly over the surface of the body), the relation of receptor to experience is not a simple one. Also, more complex experiences like itching involve an interaction among these basic sensations. Interaction among skin receptors almost always occurs; "pure" experiences of a single attribute are rare. Some spots on the skin are sensitive to warmth and others to cold. If a very hot stimulus is applied to a cold spot a sensation of "paradoxical cold" may result. A thermal stimulus feels hot or cold depending on whether it is above or below the skin temperature.

Kinesthetic sensations arise from movements of the body, whereas vestibular sensations depend on the spatial orientation of the body. Both sensations depend upon the stimulation of receptors located inside the body; both help to keep track of body posture and are critical cues for guiding our movements.

The *chemical senses* include the intimately related senses of taste and smell, whereas the *somesthetic senses* encompass sensations both from external skin receptors and from receptors inside the body.

Chemical Senses

The senses of taste and smell are classified together not only because the physical stimuli for both are chemical substances but also because they so frequently combine in producing unified perceptual experiences. Although a large part of the taste of a particular food results directly from gustatory (taste) stimuli, much, and perhaps most, of the flavor depends upon olfactory (smell) stimulation. The tastelessness of even our favorite dishes when we have bad colds is primarily because of the blocking of olfactory stimuli—we therefore fail to detect distinctive aromas.

Taste

Almost any substance that dissolves when placed on the tongue or in contact with other parts of the mouth and throat causes a rather complex taste sensation. It has proved possible, however, to identify the basic components of taste and to find chemical substances that will elicit these separate attributes. The attributes (and their chemical stimuli) are sweet (sugar), sour (hydrochloric acid), bitter (quinine), and salty (table salt).

When we seek to identify the precise chemical structure that accounts for a given attribute, we are confronted with a problem yet unsolved. Substances of extremely different chemical make-up can evoke much the same sensation. Sugar and saccharin are examples; at very high concentrations, however, a difference shows up because of the bitterness of saccharin. Also, substances that chemically are very similar often taste quite different.

People vary widely in both their absolute and their differential gustatory thresholds. Generally speaking, bitterness is most easily detected; sweetness, sourness, and saltiness are less easily detected, in the order given. Women show somewhat lower thresholds for sweet and salty tastes (although pregnancy raises the sweetness threshold); men are more able to detect traces of sourness. The order for differential sensitivity is quite different: sour, salty, sweet, and bitter. A bitter stimulus is thus detected at the lowest concentration of all taste stimuli, yet a larger relative change in intensity is necessary to notice any difference in this attribute. It is easy to speculate on the adaptive significance of these threshold differences. As bitterness is frequently associated with harmful substances, it is desirable to detect its presence; a low absolute threshold for bitterness therefore has adaptive value.

In addition to the question of sensitivity to the four taste components, there is the issue of taste preferences. Here again individual differences are considerable, but a general statement can be attempted. Sweet stimuli are rarely judged unpleasant. Sour and salty stimuli are most pleasant at very moderate intensities but even at these intensities do not approach the level of acceptance usually achieved by sweetness. Bitter stimuli are at best just tolerable when at very low concentrations; when more intense, they are almost universally unpleasant.

All this seems a far cry from the apparently infinite spectrum of flavors that we can experience in our everyday lives; a first trip to a foreign restaurant immediately attests to the wide range of possible taste experiences. But this diversity does prove analyzable, and research has not only furthered our understanding of the gustatory mechanisms (see Unit 18, p. 272) but also, for better or for worse, has made possible the manufacture of more or less convincing synthetic food flavors. Such flavors also make use of olfactory stimuli, which, as we noted earlier, are of enormous importance in the experience of tasting.

Smell

The adequate stimuli for sensations of smell are gaseous particles that are brought into contact with receptors in the upper cavity of the nose. Liquid, incidentally, may not serve as a stimulus. In one classical study, the intrepid investigator filled his nasal cavity with eau de cologne and found that he could not smell it!

The bewildering array of odors that can be experienced requires that some attempt be made to classify them; many systems have been suggested but with only partial success. One such classification scheme, in which reasonable quantification of component intensity for a given odor is possible, comes from Crocker and Hendersen (1927). Only four basic odors are used: fragrant, acidic, burnt, and caprylic (something like the smell of a sweaty dog). To locate a particular odor in this scheme it is compared to a set of standard chemical substances, each of which helps to define one of the components. The intensity of each component is rated (on a scale from 0 to 8). For example, acetic acid is classified as 3803—moderately fragrant (3), extremely acidic (8), not at all burnt (0), and somewhat caprylic (3).

Our sensitivity to olfactory stimuli is extraordinary; absolute thresholds have been estimated at one ten-thousandth of absolute taste thresholds. Differential sensitivity, however, is relatively poor; the Weber fraction averages about 1/3, compared to about 1/5 for taste, but there are exceptions (see Box 18, p. 112). There are very wide individual differences in both kinds of thresholds and, perhaps more than for any other sense, large changes within a given individual. Olfactory acuity varies during the day, depending in part on hunger; after meals the threshold rises. With pregnancy, sensitivity to odors decreases, contrary to folklore; but, though the threshold is higher, apparently there is heightened affective reactivity. Once an odor is detected, it is experienced as more unpleasant.

As with taste, difficulties have been en-

countered in trying to relate odor experiences to specifiable chemical structures of gaseous stimuli. We can only conclude that this scientific task is yet to be accomplished. In Unit 18, p. 275, we shall see some of the reasons why the task is difficult and why, perhaps, it cannot be performed.

Somesthetic Senses

Most of the psychophysical work on the somesthetic senses has been with the skin senses. It is convenient to subdivide the skin senses as follows: pressure, pain, warmth, and cold. As we shall see, these traditional categories of experience are by no means related simply to specialized receptors for each quality. This division has been encouraged by the search for, and alleged discovery of, specialized receptors for these sensations. But at the same time it tends to neglect some of the very common experiences of "itch," "ache," and "tickle." Relatively little research has yet been carried out on these complex attributes of our skin senses. These attributes cannot easily be classed as variants of pressure, pain, temperature, and kinesthetic sensations; they seem to be complex qualities resulting from patterning of pain, pressure, and thermal stimuli.

Stimulation of the skin by mechanical pressures and thermal energies reveals that it is by no means a uniform receptor. Specific parts of the skin are sensitive to some kinds of stimuli and insensitive to others. Box 19, p. 130, shows how the sensitivity of the skin is mapped.

Pressure Sensation

Objects that are forced against the skin produce sensations of pressure. Various qualitative as well as quantitative changes in sensation occur as the force increases, varying from the faintest feeling of touch to the utmost painful pressure. A mapping of the body's pressure spots indicates that the points sensitive to pressure are distributed very unevenly on the

Box 19

Mapping Spots on the Skin

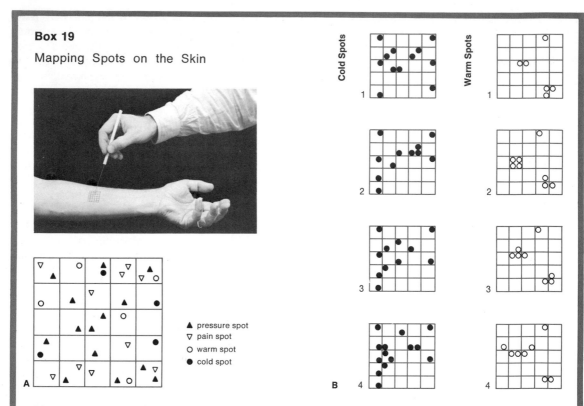

▲ pressure spot
▽ pain spot
○ warm spot
● cold spot

A   B

Almost simultaneously (1883–1885) three physiologists—Blix in Sweden, Goldscheider in Germany, and Donaldson in America—discovered that there are different "spots" on the skin that are sensitive to stimuli for pressure, pain, warmth, and cold. This occurrence is a striking instance of *independent* scientific discovery.

Having stamped a grid of fine inked lines on a given part of the skin, the experimenter can determine the exact location of these spots by applying a fine hair, a needle, a heated rod, or the like and by asking the subject to report the resulting sensation (see photograph). The results of such a mapping study on a small area of the skin are shown in Figure A.

On repeated mappings, do the spots stay in the same place, or do they seem to "migrate"? K. M. Dallenbach studied this problem by mapping warm and cold spots on the same grid on the skin for four successive days, with the results shown in Figure B.

Apparently there is a considerable degree of consistency in the location of spots, yet it is far from perfect. Perhaps the problem is in the technical difficulties of the mapping operation, perhaps in the fact that the threshold of sensitivity of the spots varies from time to time. If great care is taken to locate especially sensitive spots, they may prove very dependable on repeated stimulation. One investigator located thirty-six cold spots with great care and found that only two of them ever failed to give the cold sensation.

K. M. DALLENBACH. 1927. The Temperature Spots and End Organs, *Amer. J. Psychol.*, 39, 417. Figures adapted by permission.

body surfaces; more of them are located toward the extremities of the body.

Pain Sensation

The skin may be injured or subjected to extremes of physical energies in many ways, for example, by cutting, piercing, or burning and by the application of heat, certain chemical agents, or electrical current. All these procedures produce the experience of pain. As in the case of pressure, there are certain spots on the skin where stimuli are not effective. Here, too, mapping studies have shown that different parts of the body vary appreciably in the density of pain spots. For instance, though the tip of the nose has very many temperature and touch spots, it has relatively few pain spots.

In contrast to most of the other senses that are fairly well developed in man at birth and are often functional even in the fetus, pain has a relatively high threshold during fetal life and at birth. Such insensitivity seems biologically adaptive because it implies a sensory barrier that shields the newborn from some of the stresses of the birth process. This insensitivity rapidly dissipates. In the first four days of life there is already a sharp lowering of the pain threshold (Lipsitt & Levy, 1959).

Temperature Sensation

The stimuli for temperature sensations are thermal energies, whose intensities vary continuously, of course, along a simple scale of physical heat. But our sensory experiences do not vary along a similar intensity scale. Our temperature experiences distinguish warmth from coolness, coolness from cold, heat from warmth. And these experiences are qualitatively, not just quantitatively, different.

Cold and Warm Spots Some spots on the skin are sensitive to warmth and others to cold. Some, according to recent research, are sensitive to both. If a very hot stimulus is applied

to a cold spot, a sensation of cold may be felt; this phenomenon is known as *paradoxical cold*. The opposite phenomenon of paradoxical warmth (a sensation of warmth produced by applying a very cold stimulus to a warm spot) is less well substantiated.

Physiological Zero Whether a thermal stimulus will evoke a temperature sensation depends upon the relation of the temperature of the stimulus to the temperature of the skin. This skin temperature is called the *physiological zero*. Stimuli hotter than the physiological zero will produce sensations of warmth; stimuli that are colder will produce sensations of cold; those close to the physiological zero will produce no temperature sensations. The physiological zero changes with changes in the temperature of the environment and varies for different parts of the body. A stimulus of a given temperature can therefore evoke either a hot or a cold sensation. For example, after one immerses the left hand in ice water and the right hand in hot water for a while, the skin temperatures of the two hands will be markedly different. If he now puts both hands into the same lukewarm water, the water will simultaneously feel cool to the right hand and warm to the left.

Stimulus Mixture Extremes of heat and cold also produce pain. The fact that pain accompanies both extreme cold and extreme heat may account for the difficulty in discriminating between them.

A striking demonstration that a sensory quality can be evoked by mixtures of stimuli that each stimulus by itself could not evoke is the experience of heat that comes from the simultaneous application of warm and cold stimuli (see Figure 8.1.). Again we see the importance of interaction effects.

Internal Bodily Senses

Pains, aches, spasms, and a whole host of vague and ill-defined "organic" sensations come

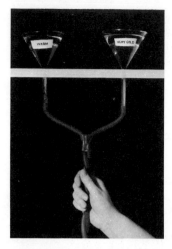

Figure 8.1. Warm water and very cold water are circulated separately through the twisted tubes grasped in the subject's hand. The combined impression he receives is of *heat.*

from organs and tissues of the body and constitute the second type of somesthetic sensation. By and large, such deep-lying sensations have not been the subject of intensive psychological investigation. As compared with those for most other senses, the physical stimuli for these sensations are hard to get at for study.

There are, however, two classes of bodily sensations that have been carefully studied. These are the *kinesthetic sensations,* which pertain to movements of the body structure, and *vestibular sensations,* which pertain to the orientation of the body in space.

Kinesthetic Sensations

Kinesthesis (literally "movement sensitivity") is one of our most basic senses. It provides information on the movements of bodily structures. The physical stimuli for kinesthetic sensations are mechanical forces that affect receptors in the muscles, tendons, and joints of the body. As the muscles function and move parts of the body, various patterns of pressures on these receptors provide the essential information for guiding motor action. As we shall see in later units, there is a great deal of interaction between such kinesthetic sensations and other aspects of our perceptual experiences; for example, the perception of visual

distance involves, among other things, a complex synthesis of information from the retinas and from the movement of the muscles of the eyeballs. Furthermore, the patterning of kinesthetic sensations plays a critical role in learning motor skills.

Kinesthetic Defect We are normally unappreciative of the role of kinesthetic sensations in our behavior, but their importance is dramatically underlined in cases in which they are missing. Patients who have neurological diseases in which kinesthetic sensations from the legs are permanently lost will shuffle as they walk, carefully looking down at their feet. Having no kinesthetic information about what the leg muscles are doing, they substitute visual information. Without such visual guidance of their actions, they would be unable to walk.

Vestibular Sensations

In addition to perceiving movements of parts of the body, we can also perceive the movement and orientation of the body as a whole. We are aware of being tilted, whirled, shaken. The stimuli for these sensations are accelerative movements of fluid in the vestibules of the inner ear. For this reason they are called "vestibular sensations" (see Unit 18, p. 280, for a description of their physiological functioning). These structures develop very rapidly in fetal life; they are well formed in the human fetus by two months.

If one's body is suddenly tilted from the vertical, the vestibular fluids are displaced by centrifugal force, and sensations of tilt occur. If he is whirled rapidly about, the fluids are displaced in another fashion, and sensations of spin are evoked. If his body is suddenly jerked in a linear direction, as in an elevator, the fluid displacement evokes a sensation of movement in that direction. These sensations of tilt; spin, and jerk often occur at the same time in a pattern of complex body-movement perceptions.

It is important to note that acceleration or deceleration (that is, *change* of rate of movement) of the vestibular system is the critical physical stimulus. Movement at a uniform speed, no matter how fast, is not a stimulus. We sit in an airplane flying smoothly at the speed of sound and have no sensation of forward movement; we are unaware of our movement in space as the earth whirls us about because its speed remains constant. But when the speed of movement is suddenly increased or decreased, or the direction abruptly changed, the vestibular sensations are aroused.

Because the receptors in the vestibules of the inner ear send neural impulses to the stomach, a side effect of such movement sensations may be the feelings of inner distress that occur in motion sickness (for example, seasickness).

Glossary

chemical senses The senses of taste and smell, both of which are stimulated by chemical substances and which frequently interact to produce a single, unified perceptual experience.

kinesthetic sensations Sensations arising from body movement and muscular strain evoked by mechanical forces affecting receptors in the muscles, tendons, and joints.

paradoxical cold A sensation of cold evoked when a very hot stimulus is applied to a cold spot on the skin.

physiological zero The temperature of the skin. Stimuli hotter than the physiological zero produce sensations of warmth; stimuli that are colder produce sensations of cold. The physiological zero varies as a function of the temperature both of the environment and of the body.

somesthetic senses These senses include sensations from external skin receptors and from internal bodily receptors.

vestibular sensations The sense of balance and of movement. The stimuli for these sensations are accelerative movements of fluids in the semicircular canals of the inner ear.

learning
and interaction
in the senses

overview / Our ability to detect stimuli and differences among them in any of the senses can be modified by learning and is thus not determined exclusively by the sensitivity of receptors and the qualities of the impinging physical stimuli. Sensory experience is also enormously dependent on a wide variety of interactive effects; these effects occur within a single receptor, among different receptors for a single sense, and across different senses. Some of these interactions derive from differences in the timing of sensory stimulation, some from differences in the spatial location of receptors, and some from the over-all patterning of incoming stimulation. Because such interaction is the typical rather than the isolated occurrence in experience arising from physical stimuli, the traditional distinction between sensation and perception may be seriously questioned.

Until now we have spoken of sensory thresholds as "givens" of the organism, although varying at birth and in rate of development. By implication, the wide individual differences in sensitivity among adults has been ascribed to constitutional factors, that is, to properties of the physical organism. Both common experience and scientific research suggest that this account may not be adequate.

Learning in Sensory Discrimination

Some psychologists believe that the ability to make sensory discriminations is determined to a measurable degree by learning. To take one example, not only do perceptions of tonal dissonance change with musical training, but also, as we have all noticed, the ability to recognize a composition, to "pick out" a melody, even to "hear more" of the subtleties of an orchestral performance improves with practice. The gourmet, the tea taster, the wine connoisseur—each with his unusual ability to discriminate minute variations in the physical stimulus—has eaten, sipped, and drunk before, and perhaps more than most of us. What is crucial, however, is that in the process each has been exposed to a

Box 20 "Seeing" with Your Ears

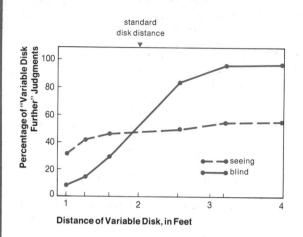

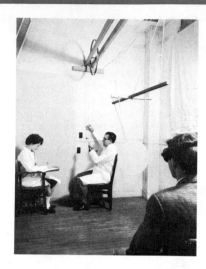

The mystery of how the totally blind person can readily detect and avoid obstacles as he moves around in space has long interested man. An early and favorite explanation was that the blind person develops an uncanny sensitivity to currents of air that strike his face and that such cues provide "facial vision," which enables him to avoid obstacles.

At Cornell University, K. M. Dallenbach and his collaborators carried out a series of studies to determine the basis of perception of obstacles by the blind. Testing both blind and seeing subjects under various experimental conditions, the experimenters were able to eliminate one by one the possible cues for detecting obstacles without vision. For example, when the touch sensitivity of the face to "air currents" was eliminated by covering the head with a felt veil and hat, the subjects could still walk up to a wall and signal correctly just before running into it. Touch sensitivity is thus clearly not necessary to the performance. As a second step, the ears were plugged so that auditory cues were eliminated. Under these conditions, no subjects were able to avoid running into the wall. Auditory cues are clearly essential. This point was further demonstrated in an ingenious way by having the *experimenter* walk toward the obstacle carrying a microphone that was connected with headphones worn by the subject, who sat in a soundproof room. The subject could hear the auditory stimuli impinging on the experimenter as the experimenter approached the obstacle. Under these conditions the subject was able to tell when the experimenter came close to the obstacle—thoroughly convincing evidence that auditory cues are the essential ones.

Just as bats flying in total darkness guide themselves by hearing the reflections of the high-pitched sounds they emit, humans can apparently also be guided by a similar kind of "sonar." Other animals also demonstrate this ability. The bottlenose dolphin (or porpoise) emits underwater rhythmic bursts of sound that enable it to avoid obstacles and to locate food. Certain species of whales and nocturnal birds also seem to employ a "sonar" system; they emit sounds whose echoes, as they bounce off objects, guide their movements.

Later research has attempted to determine the accuracy that humans can achieve with such cues. W. N. Kellogg conducted a series of experiments that compared the performance of blind subjects with that of normally sighted subjects in a number of situations. In one of them, the subject (blind, or sighted but blindfolded) made judgments of the relative distance of a plywood disk, one foot in diameter, which was presented successively in two positions: a standard position (two feet from the subject) and a position that varied in distance from one to four feet (see photograph). The subjects, both blind and sighted, were encouraged to make any sounds they wished to provide echoes and were permitted to move their heads and bodies as they chose. Some subjects spoke, often repeating the same word rhythmically; others snapped their fingers, clicked their tongues, whistled, and even sang. The blind subjects chose to bob their heads from side to side, presumably having learned that they could thereby increase the highly useful binaural cues for distance perception (see p. 192).

The chart, adapted from Kellogg's report, gives the combined results from two blind and two normally sighted subjects in this experiment. The judgments of the blind subjects show a clear tendency to vary with the objective distance between the standard and the variable disks. At each of the six test positions they were highly accurate. In contrast, the sighted subjects were never above chance in their performance. The better of the two blind subjects was able to detect a difference in the distance of the disk when it moved as little as four inches either way from its standard two-foot distance. This ability represents a Weber fraction (see p. 113) of 1/6, still considerably less accurate than the fraction of 1/40 for sighted persons using both eyes but somewhat *better* than the distance discrimination usually found for monocular vision.

In other experiments, Kellogg has found that his blind subjects can also discriminate texture differences. They reported that the echoes from hard and soft surfaces simply "sounded different." This cue was sufficient to permit them to distinguish, for example, between a metal-covered disk and a velvet-covered disk with an accuracy of 99.5 per cent. Perhaps more remarkable (and certainly more difficult to explain) is their ability to achieve 86.5 per cent accuracy in distinguishing between velvet and denim. Blindfolded normal subjects were totally unable to discriminate texture differences.

In Kellogg's size-discrimination experiments (varying the size of the disk but maintaining a constant distance), the blind subjects showed somewhat less accuracy than they had attained in distance discrimination. Kellogg suspects that this change may have been caused by certain apparatus deficiencies, and, indeed, later work by C. E. Rice and S. H. Feinstein seems to bear him out. These investigators tested four blind subjects on size discrimination with more refined instruments (but also with subjects who had more previous practice in the experimental situation) and report a Weber fraction of 1/14 for the best performance.

These fascinating phenomena raise numerous theoretical questions, which are currently being investigated. Blind persons vary tremendously in their "sonar" ability; what accounts for these differences? Does training increase this ability? If so, why? And what kind of training is best? What are the cues responsible for this ability? It seems clear that they are auditory, but what attributes of sound are relevant? Loudness? Pitch? Some research has indicated that reflected sounds of very high frequency (10,000 cycles or more per second) work best. This finding has led to ongoing work on developing an instrument that could easily be carried around by the blind person and that would continuously emit high-frequency sounds. This instrument should be a considerable improvement on the "tap-tap" of the white cane.

Clearly, theory and practice are intimately linked in these ventures, as in much of psychological research.

M. SUPA, M. COTZIN, and K. M. DALLENBACH. 1944. Facial Vision: The Perception of Obstacles by the Blind, *Amer. J. Psychol.*, 57, 133–83.

P. WORCHEL and K. M. DALLENBACH. 1947. Facial Vision: Perception of Obstacles by the Deaf-Blind, *Amer. J. Psychol.*, 60, 502–53.

W. N. KELLOGG. 1962. Sonar System of the Blind, *Science*, 137, 399–404. Figures adapted by permission; copyright 1962 by the American Association for the Advancement of Science.

C. E. RICE and S. H. FEINSTEIN. 1965. Sonar System in the Blind: Size Discrimination, *Science*, 148, 1107–8.

wider and more complex variety of stimulus patterns and has attended more closely to them (see Box 20, p. 136) than the average consumer has. He has learned to discriminate. Of course, such sensory experts may have some advantage in biological endowment. Still, "practice makes perfect" is a generally accurate axiom of perceptual discrimination. In one investigation a subject was able to identify reliably fifty distinct colors among the Munsell color chips (a standard array of colors covering the visual spectrum) after five months of practice. Initially, he could distinguish only sixteen colors (Hanes & Rhoades, 1959). The fact of perceptual learning, as this process is called, is well established, and its interpretation is a currently lively theoretical issue.

Interaction in Sensory Experience

The effects of various stimuli for a given sense interact in producing a unified experience, and for this reason we speak of patterns of physical stimuli.

The patterns of physical stimuli are both spatial and temporal. The spatial patterns come about because of simultaneous stimulation of various parts of a specific receptor, for example, the retina of the eye or the skin of the body. Temporal patterns result from the sequence of stimuli falling on a given part. A further step still, and we shall take it later on, is a consideration of the interactions among different senses and even with nonsensory processes in the organism.

Temporal Interaction

At any receptor point there is a temporal succession of stimuli. The interactions occurring from the successive stimuli can be seen in temporal summation, fusion, and adaptation.

Temporal Summation The longer the duration of a light of subthreshold intensity, the greater the probability that it will become an effective

stimulus. Apparently the effect of each momentary stimulation is not entirely independent of the stimulations that have just occurred at that receptor "point." There is, instead, a kind of summation effect over time, which we call *temporal summation*. The basis of this summation is presumably some form of "lag" in the receptor mechanism. That is, the receptor continues to act even after the first stimulus is removed. The effects of the second stimulus are thus "added to" the aftereffects of the first.

Careful quantitative studies of temporal summation have been made, involving measurements of the reaction to various durations and intensities of light stimuli on the retina. These studies have led to the formulation that, within limits, the effectiveness of a stimulus near the threshold is the product of intensity and duration. This formulation is known as the *Bunsen-Roscoe Law*. It asserts that a higher intensity for a short exposure may be equal to a lower intensity for a longer exposure. In other words, what counts is the total amount of light during the interval.

Flicker and Fusion The fact that the sensation initiated by a stimulus continues after the stimulus has ceased is demonstrated by the *flicker* and *fusion* phenomena. If we turn a light on and off at intervals of one second, the observer sees a sequence of light and dark intervals. If we then shorten the on-off intervals, the light begins to flicker. Interestingly, the rate of flicker does not correspond to the stimulus-alternation frequency. It stays about the same (about twenty per second) even when the light-dark alternation occurs at much lower or at much higher rates. If the intervals are still shorter, the flicker disappears, and a continuous light is seen. We call this process "fusion." Obviously, the aftereffect of each separate stimulus lasts long enough to bridge the interval until the next stimulus occurs. We encounter the phenomenon repeatedly in our everyday life. The movies give us the undeniable impression of continuous, unbroken stimula-

tion, yet we know that what is exposed to our eyes is an intermittent series of still photographs and short intervals of darkness.

Critical Flicker Frequency The rate of alternation of light and dark at which flicker disappears and fusion occurs is known as the *critical flicker frequency* (c.f.f.). Like any threshold value, it varies widely, depending upon the specific character of the stimulating conditions and of the states of the observer. For example, the c.f.f. is higher when the intensity difference between light and dark is greater; the brightness of the surrounding environment is also a factor. Flicker is very rarely seen, however, when the stimulus alternates as frequently as sixty times per second; this accounts for the lack of flicker in electric lights operating on standard 60-cycle-per-second current.

Attempts have even been made to relate the c.f.f. to personality variables, but to date results are only suggestive. One study shows that flyers retired from combat because of anxiety reactions have lower thresholds (fusion occurs at lower frequencies) than do normal air-crew members (Krugman, 1947).

Sensory Adaptation

There is another extremely important type of temporal interaction in which a succession of identical stimuli falling on the same receptor "point" leads to a decrease in the effectiveness of the later stimuli. This type of temporal interaction is known as *sensory adaptation*. (Its physiological basis will be discussed in Unit 15, p. 240.) The effect occurs in all senses. Some striking examples will now be given.

Visual Adaptation You can readily demonstrate the marked amount of dilution of a yellow color that occurs as a consequence of fairly short continuous exposures (see Box 21). We can make similar demonstrations for any hue.

There is also pronounced adaptation to brightness of the visual stimuli. A white or a black surface that one looks at continuously begins to look grayish. And the most impressive of all visual-adaptation effects is found in what are called light adaptation and dark adaptation. The former is illustrated by our

Box 21

Unnoticed Change in Perception

Using the yellow rectangle shown in Color Plate 4, immediately preceding page 119, you can demonstrate for yourself a convincing instance of a change in perception that occurs without your awareness. Take a piece of gray paper, and place it over the right half of the yellow rectangle so that the fixation mark is just visible.

Then stare steadily right at the fixation mark, being *careful not to shift your eyes from it*, for a period of one minute. At the end of the minute remove the gray cover from the yellow rectangle, *continuing without interruption to look at the fixation mark.*

If you are like most people, you will observe, when the cover is removed, that the yellow on the left side appears dilute and "washed out" compared with the yellow on the right. What has happened is that, during the continuous look at the left side, the perceived color slowly lost its original saturation. Yet most people *are not at all aware of this gradual change as it occurs* and only realize how pronounced it is when they see the washed-out yellow beside the unaffected bright yellow on the right after the cover is removed. Perception can change without our perceiving the change!

The *reason* for the gradual dilution of the color with continued exposure will be discussed on p. 241.

common experience in entering a darkened theater from the bright sunlight; at first we cannot see objects, then after a time we see them very easily. In the continuous sunlight the eye had become light-adapted, that is, it had become relatively less sensitive to light stimuli. After some time in the darkness the eye becomes dark-adapted and recovers. Now, on leaving the theater, we encounter a different difficulty; the sunlight is so bright that it hurts our eyes and we are "blinded" for a few moments. In this example we have another illustration of the fact that a dark-adapted eye is much more sensitive to light than is a light-adapted eye.

The *visual afterimage* is an interesting instance of adaptation phenomena. For a demonstration of this type of image, see Box 22, p. 141.

Auditory Adaptation The ear is notably less subject to sensory adaptation than the eye and other sense receptors. Even prolonged exposure to a continuous sound of ordinary intensity

shows little effect. But when we move into more intense continuous sounds, like the high-pitched machinery sound that the factory worker may be exposed to, adaptation does occur, and there is a marked loss of auditory sensitivity.

Figure 9.1. shows the results of an experiment in which a high-intensity "white noise," which contains all the frequencies in about equal amounts, was continuously experienced. There were marked adaptation effects, which gradually disappeared from five minutes to four days after cessation of the sound. There were also substantial differences in sensitivity loss for different wave frequencies; sensitivity to high tones was much more affected than was sensitivity to low tones.

Adaptation in Taste and Smell Everyday experience testifies that adaptation occurs in the chemical senses. Many an oversalted dish is the penalty for the cook's prolonged "sampling" during preparation; the salt threshold gradually increases with continual testing, so that when the "just right" point is finally reached for the (adapted) cook, the salt concentration for the unadapted guests—and for the cook later on—can be painfully above threshold. In smell, sensory adaptation usually has a more benign effect; enforced exposure to unpleasant odors is a common mishap, and the speed with which we become blissfully unaware of the offending stimulus is a fortunate asset of the human organism. In both senses, we adapt at different speeds to the separate smell or taste components of a given mixture. This fact accounts for changes in the quality of the perception that often accompany the gradual decrease in its intensity; a heady perfume not only seems more subtle with prolonged exposure but also may change in character.

Adaptation in the Skin Senses A modest pressure against the skin will soon not be noticed. For instance, in one study (Von Frey & Goldman, 1915) a pressure stimulus was continu-

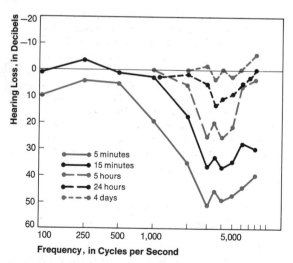

Figure 9.1. Curves showing auditory adaptation to *white noise* (a complete mixture of sound waves of all frequencies). Note that the loss is greatest at the higher frequencies and that it is less the longer the time interval after exposure to the stimulus.
L. Postman and J. P. Egan, *Experimental Psychology* (1949); adapted by permission of Harper & Row Publishers.

Box 22

Afterimages

Stare steadily at the numeral on the sail in the figure for one minute. Then look at a plain light surface like a wall or a sheet of paper. You may be surprised to see the sailboat projected there. And more surprising is the fact that the black and white areas are reversed. This image is known as a *negative afterimage*. It is called an "afterimage" because it is a sensation persisting after the original stimulus has been removed. It is called "negative" because the brightness relationships are reversed.

Negative afterimages are found with hue as well as with brightness. Turn to Color Plate 5, immediately preceding page 119. Fixate the cross in the center of the left figure for about thirty seconds; then transfer your gaze to the cross in the gray square. You will see clear colors in the locations of the four colored patches of the original stimulus, but the colors will now be the *complementaries* of the original hues.

There are also *positive afterimages*. If you look for a moment at a whirling bright light and then close your eyes, you will see the image of the path of the light persisting for some time. The image is positive, in that it appears in the same brightness relationships as did the original stimulus.

What is even more fascinating is that negative afterimages can be seen without the perception of prior positive images. G. Sperling (1960) has demonstrated this phenomenon in a number of visual situations. In one experiment a dollar bill is exposed with a bright flash so briefly that the dollar bill is not seen. But, when the subject then looks at a less brightly illuminated screen, the *pink* "greenback"—its negative afterimage—is clearly perceived on the screen.

The explanation of afterimages must lie in the fact that the nervous system continues to be aroused for some time after a stimulus has been withdrawn. Why the afterimage should often be the *negative* of the original stimulus is a fascinating question having to do with the adaptation of the visual nervous system to light (see Unit 15, p. 241).

It should be noted that afterimage phenomena are by no means restricted solely to vision. There are also auditory afterimages and various tactual afterimages, like the persistent feeling of pressure on the skin after a pressure stimulus has been withdrawn.

G. SPERLING. 1960. Negative Afterimage Without Prior Positive Image, *Science*, 131, 1613–4.

ously applied at one point on the skin, and its effectiveness was compared with that of similar pressures applied at various points of initially comparable sensitivity. In three seconds the effect of the first stimulus had dropped to less than one quarter of the initial value.

As compared with adaptation to pressure, adaptation to pain stimuli is slow. It is difficult to maintain a continuous, unchanging pain stimulus; for one thing, because of body movement in response to the pain, new pain "spots" are stimulated. This fact is perhaps the reason that we seem to note little or no adaptation to the sensory pains we experience in daily life.

Adaptation to thermal stimuli is a matter of common observation. The uncomfortably hot bath water soon becomes bearable; the cold lake into which we plunge soon does not seem cold. In the case of extremely hot and extremely cold stimuli, however, adaptation does not seem to occur or occurs only very slowly.

Spatial Interaction

Some of our receptor organs consist of a large number of separate sensitive "points" spread out on the receptor surface. The retina of the eye, containing many light-sensitive cells, is the most important example. The skin of the body is another example. Just as there is highly significant temporal interaction of stimuli, there is also highly significant spatial interaction, which occurs among the separate sensitive "points" on the receptor surface. Such interaction is exhibited in a number of different ways—spatial summation, irradiation, and spatial fusion.

Spatial Summation Whether or not a light is seen depends not only on the intensity of the light but also on the number of retinal points stimulated. The effects of light waves falling on different points of the retina seem to be additive. This phenomenon is known as *spatial summation*. The basis of this and other forms of spatial interaction lies in the fact that physi-

ologically there are connections among the various receptor "points" (see Unit 15, p. 243).

Spatial summation phenomena seem to be different for tactile stimuli. For one thing, two adjacent subthreshold pressures do not sum to yield a tactile sensation. For another thing, the simultaneous application of above-threshold pressures at two nearby points *reduces* the sensitivity of the surrounding skin area (Yai, 1959–1960).

Irradiation That spatial "spreading" of effect occurs in the retina is suggested by another phenomenon known as *irradiation*. For example, a white square on a black background appears slightly larger than a black square of equal size on a white background. It seems that the retinal excitation by the white area "spills over" to some extent into the surrounding retinal areas.

Spatial Fusion There is in spatial interaction an analogue of temporal fusion. The nature of the perception of different visual stimuli falling on the retina depends upon their spatial proximity. This face can be demonstrated by looking at textile threads of various colors woven into a pattern. When viewed close up, the separate colors can be readily distinguished. Viewed at a middle distance, an interplay of colors occurs that gives the material a "sparkle," a "liveliness," that is not apparent either when the colors are unfused or when they are completely fused. At a sufficient distance, the separate colors completely disappear, and fusion is seen.

Seurat (1859–1891), the French Neo-Impressionist painter, invented the technique called "pointillism," in which, instead of mixing paints in the traditional way on the palette or canvas, he applied single dots of color over the entire canvas. This method relies upon spatial fusion by the eye to give the desired color mixtures and produces a kind of visual "liveliness," rarely found in other paintings, when viewed at some distance.

Békésy (1964) has recently demonstrated

spatial fusion in taste but with the interesting qualification that not all taste qualities can fuse with one another. In an experiment that involved stimulating the two sides of the tongue simultaneously, each side with a different taste stimulus, he found that, with certain pairs of stimuli, the fused sensation was experienced in the middle of the tongue but that, with other pairs, the two sensations remained spatially separated. To the four basic taste attributes (sweet, sour, bitter, salty) Békésy added warmth and cold in his experiment. Each of these six stimuli was paired with each of the others over a series of trials, during which the subjects were asked to report whether a single fused sensation (in the middle of the tongue) was experienced or two distinctive sensations (one on either side). His results: Warm, bitter, and sweet stimuli interact with one another to yield a fused sensation; so do cold, sour, and salty stimuli. There is no blending of stimuli between these groups; for example, sweet and salty stimuli are experienced as separate sensations on opposite sides of the tongue (see Figure 9.2.). These findings suggest a "duplexity" theory of taste; that is, two different types of receptors (analogous, perhaps, to rods and cones in vision) may be involved in taste perception.

Contrast

Sensory adaptation, an effect of temporal interaction, and spatial interaction are the bases for certain striking phenomena in which the perceived differences in intensity or quality among stimuli are accentuated. These phenomena are called *successive contrast* and *simultaneous contrast*.

Successive Contrast After the eye has been exposed for some time to a bright stimulus, a darker stimulus will look unusually dark. This phenomenon is called *successive contrast*. The opposite is also true; a bright stimulus following a dark one will look unusually bright. There

is also chromatic contrast. After one stares for a while at a red surface, a green surface appears much greener than usual. Although perhaps our most noticeable examples of successive contrast are in vision, it is found in all the senses, for instance, in taste: An orange tastes sour after sugar, but sweet after lemon.

Simultaneous Contrast Look at the gray squares in Figure 9.3. It is hard for most observers to see them as the same gray, yet they are. A given gray is lighter in dark surroundings and darker in light surroundings. This effect is known as *simultaneous contrast*.

Similar contrast effects are found with other properties of color like hue and saturation. If two small squares of identical gray paper are compared when one is placed on a large red field and the other on a large green field, the first gray square looks distinctly greenish and the other distinctly reddish.

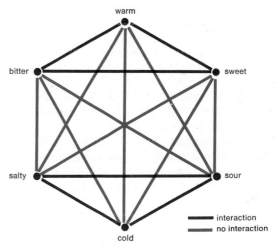

Figure 9.2. A graphic representation of the duplexity theory of taste, showing the six different sensations that can be experienced on the tongue. The stimuli that melt together into a common sensation when presented simultaneously are interconnected with black lines, indicating that they have something in common with one another. Stimuli connected with green lines can be presented to the two sides of the tongue simultaneously without showing any interaction at all.
G. von Békésy, "Duplexity Theory of Taste," *Science*, 145, 834–35; Copyright 1964 by the American Association for the Advancement of Science; adapted by permission.

Figure 9.3. A demonstration of brightness contrast. The squares are cut from identical gray paper.

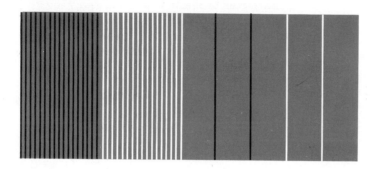

Figure 9.4. A demonstration of the failure of brightness contrast. Here the effect is reversed; the gray field surrounding the black lines seems darker. The background "takes on" the characteristics of the superimposed lines, suggesting that irradiation may be occurring. This effect is stronger when the lines are more closely spaced, so that the average distance of points in the gray field from the lines is less.
H. Helson and F. H. Rohles, Jr., "A Quantitative Study of Reversal of Classical Lightness-Contrast," *American Journal of Psychology*, 72 (1959), 530–38; adapted by permission.

The *degree* of contrast is in large measure determined by the relationships existing between the area and its surroundings. For example, the larger the difference in intensity of the area and its surroundings or the larger the relative size of the surrounding field, the greater the contrast. But we are still far from a complete understanding of the phenomena of contrast. Note, for example, the surprising "failure" of usual contrast effects in Figure 9.4. (see also Color Plate 6 immediately preceding p. 119).

Interaction Among Different Senses

So far, in speaking of temporal and spatial interaction, we have discussed these effects only as they occur within a given sensory system. One tone masks another; one odor masks another. But masking, or at least a significant increase in threshold, can also come about from simultaneous exposure to stimuli in *different* sense modalities. Perhaps it is to reduce masking that we often close our eyes when straining to hear a faint sound. Benjamin (1955–1956) has demonstrated that a painful stimulus raises thresholds for visual, auditory, tactile, and temperature sensations. Box 23, p. 145, illustrates how this effect can be happily reversed.

In our everyday perceptions the senses typically cooperate with and supplement one another. We commented earlier on the fact that flavor depends upon the joint operation of taste and smell receptors. The texture of food (a tactile sensation) is also important; steak and its poor relation, hamburger, are not likely to be confused. The usual product of a multisense stimulus pattern is a more complex and therefore a richer experience. Each sense contributes its own version of an occurrence in the physical world, each qualitatively different, yet usually blending into a coherent and unified single impression. Thus an object may look large, sound large, feel large, and perhaps even smell large. The eyes, ears, and hands typically also agree on its location in space.

Box 23

As Easy as Pulling Teeth

A dramatic example of an intersensory effect—masking of perception in one sense by stimulation of another—is the apparent effectiveness of sound in reducing experienced pain in dental operations (audio analgesia). W. J. Gardner, J. C. R. Licklider, and A. Z. Weisz report that, for 65 per cent of patients who previously required nitrous oxide or a local anesthetic, pain was completely eliminated by the judicious combination of music and noise. Here is how it is done. The patient wears headphones, through which some soothing stereophonic music is heard. As the operation (typically, tooth extraction) begins, the patient is provided with a control box that enables him to introduce a fairly loud noise, "like a waterfall," through the headphones. As soon as he feels or is afraid he will feel the slightest pain, he can adjust the volume of the sound to quite high levels in order to mask the pain. The music is itself masked by the noise, and the report asserts that "the main function of the music is to relax the patient" and that "for most patients, the noise is the main agent, the one that drowns out the pain."

The investigators discuss several factors that may contribute to this effect. The first is the most direct but difficult to explain; many patients simply report that the noise immediately shuts out the pain. Also, the unnerving sound of dental machinery, for example the dental drill, is no longer heard. Some patients emphasize that trying to follow the melody as it is dimly heard over the noise diverts their attention. Others stress the importance of having some measure of control in the situation, a factor that reduces their anxiety and therefore the pain felt. For any given patient a different combination of several of these factors is probably responsible for successfully suppressing pain. The authors do suggest a physiological mechanism to account for the effect; this mechanism involves an inhibitory interaction of the auditory and pain systems in the reticular formation and lower thalamus (see Unit 16, p. 256).

A skeptical exception to the notion that true cross-sensory masking occurs in audio analgesia has been made by S. Carlin, *et al.* Their procedure was to apply an electric current to a tooth and to have the subject (not a patient) report when he first felt a "tingle." No background music was employed, and the control of the volume of the sound (a steady tone) was not in the hands of the subject. Under these conditions, sound failed to raise the "tingle threshold," even when explicit suggestion that it would do so was employed by the experimenters. As they themselves point out, however, the situation differs in many respects from that of the classic warm-blooded dental patient, a point that the empathic reader will have noticed. Perhaps the most critical difference is that intensities near threshold were employed in the Carlin study, not the violently above-threshold pain stimuli of tooth extraction. Aside from the anxiety differences involved in the two situations, there is even the possibility that the neural pathways (and therefore the possible inhibitory mechanisms) differ for stimuli of such greatly differing intensities.

These authors, it must be said, in no sense question the effectiveness of audio analgesia in dentistry. Recent work has shown that it is useful for other operations as well. Now to discover a comparable boon for the deaf man with the bad tooth—perhaps a dazzling, multicolor, and chaotic Cinerama production will do the job for him.

W. J. GARDNER, J. C. R. LICKLIDER, and A. Z. WEISZ. 1960. Suppression of Pain by Sound, *Science*, 132, 32–3.
S. CARLIN, W. D. WARD, A. GERSHEN, and R. INGRAHAM. 1962. Sound Stimulation and Its Effect on Dental Sensation Threshold, *Science*, 138, 1258–9.

Box 24

Synesthesia

The most common form of synesthesia is *color hearing,* in which a vivid color image is evoked by a sound, for example a musical note. The tone-color relationships are not identical for different persons, but there are certain general uniformities; for example, bass notes result in darker colors, treble notes in lighter colors.

For a given individual the relationships of tones and colors may be systematic and fairly permanent. H. S. Langfeld studied one person's synesthesia over a seven-year interval with results as shown in the list.

Musical Note	Color Sensation on First Study	Color Sensation Seven Years Later
c	red	red
db	purple	lavender
d	violet	violet
eb	soft blue	thick blue
e	golden yellow	sunlight
f	pink	pink, apple blossoms
f♯	green blue	blue green
gb	greener blue	greener blue
g	clear blue	clear sky blue
a	cold yellow	clear yellow, hard, not warm
bb	orange	verges on orange
b	very brilliant coppery	very brilliant coppery

Another investigator (T. H. Howells) succeeded in artificially "conditioning" such color hearing. He presented a low tone accompanied by a red light and a high tone accompanied by a green light 5,000 times each to eight subjects. After this "conditioning" period, he presented relatively unsaturated colors, pale but still readily recognizable as reddish or greenish. If the *high* tone (previously associated with green) was given with the pale reddish hue, subjects frequently reported it as *greenish;* if the *low* tone was given with the pale greenish hue, it was often seen as *reddish.*

As a further step, two of the subjects were instructed to mix red and green on a color wheel until they achieved a neutral gray. When the high tone was sounded continuously during the color-mixing task, the subjects tended to put in *more red and less green* than were normally required for a neutral gray. Conversely, when the low tone was sounded continuously, they tended to put in more green and less red. Hearing the tone had served as an equivalent of color in the mixing task!

H. S. LANGFELD. 1914. Note on a Case of Chromaesthesia, *Psychol. Bull.,* 11, 113–4. Table adapted by permission of American Psychological Association.

T. H. HOWELLS. 1944. The Experimental Development of Color-Tone Synesthesia, *J. Exper. Psychol.,* 34, 87–103.

Of course, each of the various sensory domains has its unique and distinctive qualities. Visual experience is not likely to be confused with auditory experience, or smell with touch. There are surprising interactions of the senses in *synesthesia,* however, in which stimulation of one kind of sense receptor produces experiences also in a different sense domain (see Box 24).

Sensation versus Perception

An analysis of perception that helps us to describe the cooperative unity of the senses was first offered by the Gestalt psychologists. They were impressed by the remoteness of simple sensory attributes, as we have analyzed them in this unit, from the full-bodied perceptions we typically experience. Gibson (1963) makes this same point in the following words:

"The variables of sensory discrimination are radically different from the variables of perceptual discrimination. The former are said to be dimensions like quality, intensity, extensity, and duration, dimensions of hue, brightness, and saturation, of pitch, loudness, and timbre, of pressure, warm, cold, and pain. The latter are dimensions of the environment, the variables of events and those of surfaces, places, objects, of other animals, and even of symbols. Perception involves meaning; sensation does not. To see a patch of color is not to see an object, nor is seeing the form of a color the same as seeing the shape of an object. To see a darker patch is not to see a shadow on a surface. . . . To have a salty taste is not to taste salt, and to have a certain olfactory impression is not to smell, say, a mint julep. To feel an impression on the skin is not to feel an object. . . . To feel a local pain is not to feel the pricking of a needle. To feel warmth on one's skin is not to feel the sun on one's skin, and to feel cold is not to feel the coldness of the weather."

Gibson argues that our experiences are never determined by a stimulus but by stimulus *objects*, and that different senses provide essentially the same information; for example, we see and feel the same box.

Thus, man seems so constructed that the items of information he collects about his environment through his various sense organs usually work together to provide him with a highly accurate picture of the world. It is as easy to regard the unified and cooperative action of the senses as an inevitable outcome of evolutionary pressures for adaptation as it is difficult to conceive of a world in which this action of the senses does not hold true. Some psychologists have lived in such a peculiar world, with surprising results (see Box 41, p. 204).

Glossary

Bunsen-Roscoe Law The generalization that states that, within limits, the effectiveness of a visual stimulus near the threshold is a product of the intensity and duration of the stimulus.

critical flicker frequency (c.f.f.) The frequency of intermittent light flashes necessary to eliminate flicker and produce fusion.

flicker The visual phenomenon produced by certain rates of intermittent flashing on and off of a stimulus.

fusion The visual phenomenon in which a series of successive stimuli produce a continuous, uniform sensation, as in the case of a rapidly flashing light or a mixture of colors on a color wheel.

irradiation The tendency for the retinal stimulation in a given area to spread slightly into the surroundings. For example, a white square on a black background appears larger than does a black square of equal size on a white background.

sensory adaptation A form of temporal interaction in which immediately prior stimulation of a receptor modifies the effectiveness of later stimuli.

simultaneous contrast The tendency for the color of one area to accentuate the complementary color of a neighboring area. The effect is found both with hue and with brightness.

spatial summation The summative effect of separate stimuli spread over space. Thus, light intensities too weak to be seen when falling on a small retinal area can be seen when falling on a larger area.

successive contrast The tendency for the exposure to one color to cause the accentuation of the complementary color in that same area thereafter. The effect is found both with hue and with brightness.

synesthesia A type of perceptual experience in which stimulation of one kind of sense receptor results in sensations in a completely different sense domain, for example, when a musical sound produces the sensation of a blue color.

temporal summation The phenomenon in which a subthreshold stimulus, when continuously applied, may summate its effect to produce a response.

visual afterimage The sensation that follows removal of the external light stimulus. The positive afterimage has the same colors as the original percept; the negative afterimage has the opposite colors from those of the original percept.

UNIT 1

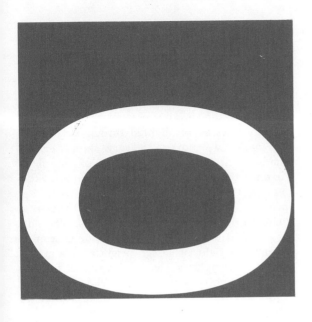

perceptual
differentiation
and grouping

overview / Through a process of assimilation we tend in perception to minimize small stimulus differences, seeing as homogeneous stimulus patterns in which such physical differences exist. A reverse process, called contrast, takes over when the differences exceed a certain level, and we then perceive differences as greater than they actually are. Both processes serve perceptual differentiation; one leads to homogeneity *within* parts of the pattern, the other to accentuating differences *between* parts.

Typically, one or more parts of a pattern are "figure," standing out from the remaining perceptually subordinated areas, which are referred to as "ground." A number of factors determine which parts of a pattern are seen as figure and which as ground.

When there are several figures present, they may be perceptually grouped according to their proximity to one another; according to their similarity in shape, color, and so forth; according to the influences of the principles of good form. These grouping principles at times cooperate to define what is figural in a stimulus pattern; at other times they compete with one another. Their relative influence is also to some degree a function of one's past perceptual experience.

A given perceptual organization is largely determined by the *relationships* among its various parts or elements, so that its basic form may be retained and recognized despite changes in the individual elements themselves. This perceptual function is called "transposition." But just as the whole percept is a function of the arrangement of its parts, the perception of the parts is also affected by the total organization. This part-whole principle asserts that we necessarily perceive objects and events in relation to their context, or frame of reference. When this context includes previous experiences and judgments, we say that a perception is influenced by a learned adaptation level.

Any stimulus pattern may give rise to a multitude of perceptual organizations. The perceiver apparently does not have to intend the particular form of organization or to be aware of how it occurs. Perceptual organization occurs spontaneously. It usually takes place without conscious direction and with greater speed and sureness than "rational" thought permits, although conscious thought and deliberate intention can play an important role.

Our problem now is to describe the principles of perceptual organization—how it comes about and how it changes. In discussing the principles of perceptual organization, we shall draw our examples almost exclusively from visual perception, which most clearly and dramatically illustrates these principles. We assume, however, that these principles generally hold for all the senses.

Differentiation of the Perceptual Field

Let us begin with one such visual example. A man is seated with his head inside a large hollow hemisphere (see Figure 10.1.). Its inner surface is smooth, unmarked, and evenly illuminated by a moderate light in such a way that the stimulation on his eyes is entirely uniform. What does he see?

Laboratory demonstrations of this kind show that he sees only a uniform light "mist" filling an endless space. He cannot tell how far away the surface of the sphere is; in fact, he perceives no surface at all. When the eye receives uniform stimulation, the result is thus complete lack of perceptual differentiation. There are no objects in such a field, not even distinguishable regions. Such homogeneity is the simplest possible perceptual experience.

When the illumination is made considerably brighter, so that the very fine "grain" of the inner surface of the sphere approaches the threshold of visual acuity, there is at once a perceptual transformation. Now our observer sees the surface, and it appears to be localized in space a short distance in front of him. But

the surface itself appears entirely uniform and without detail.

We proceed to another change in the situation. The illumination of the surface now varies from dark to light and from left to right across the field. Despite this gradient from darker to brighter in the stimulus pattern, the field is still perceived as evenly lighted throughout.

Finally, we impose a very faint vertical shadow line through the middle of this field. At once there is a sudden perceptual transformation. A vertical boundary, or *contour*, appears in the middle of the field, and the total field divides into two different parts: The half of the field to the left of the contour is seen as a uniform field of lesser brightness, and the half to the right is seen as a uniform field of greater brightness (see Figure 10.2.).

In this simple laboratory demonstration we observe that, as a result of gradual systematic

Figure 10.1 An experimental method for investigating the perceptual effect of uniform stimulation in the visual field. The inner surface of the hemisphere is completely unmarked and homogeneous. The level of illumination can be varied.

changes in the physical stimulus pattern, there is a progression from simple to more complex levels of perceptual differentiation, which vary from a field consisting of a completely undifferentiated single quality ("a lightish mist"), through a field containing a single homogeneous surface without structure, and finally to a field divided into two parts. Let us turn now to a more careful consideration of this sequence of events; particularly, let us see what accounts for the final differentiation into two parts.

Assimilation

We start with the striking fact that, at the intermediate stage (b in Figure 10.2.), the visual field still looks homogeneous despite a considerable degree of variation in the intensities of the light stimuli at various points on the retina. This tendency toward maximal uniformity and lack of differentiation in perception is known as *assimilation*. Note that assimilation of the type observed here cannot be explained in terms of small, below-threshold stimulus differences on the retina. We are talking about large stimulus differences, which under other circumstances can be readily perceived. If the darker and lighter extremes of the field were placed side by side, our observer would have no difficulty in perceiving them as different. When the difference between any two *adjacent* points in the field is below threshold, however, over-all homogeneity is produced, even though the differences between points farther apart are well above threshold. We perceive a single level of brightness, which is an average of the light intensities on the whole retina.

Contrast

Let us turn to the third stage of our demonstration (c in Figure 10.2.). When we introduce a boundary or contour into the middle of the field, two discrete and contrasting areas are perceived. Assimilation still occurs within each area separately. Each semicircle is perceived with its own level of uniform brightness. The

level of uniform brightness within each area again is an average of the light intensities within it; therefore a sharp difference in brightness is produced just at the dividing line, or contour, between the two parts. The perceived difference between two immediately adjacent points lying on different sides of the boundary is thus maximized. Despite a continuous gradient of change in the stimulus pattern, we perceive two discrete and contrasting parts.

This phenomenon of perceiving a difference as greater than that called for by the stimulus intensities is known as *contrast*. We have already encountered examples of it in the form of sensory contrast (see p. 143). Contrast means an accentuation of differences and is, like assimilation, a basic phenomenon in a great many psychological processes beside perception.

In Figure 10.3. we have a simple but compelling demonstration of the important role that a contour can play in emphasizing the contrast effect. The contrast effects from the black and white areas would ordinarily make the neutral gray of the ring brighter on the left side and

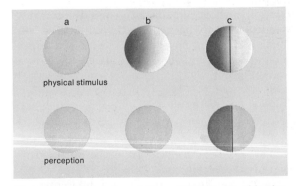

Figure 10.2. The upper circles represent the objective illumination conditions on the inner surface of the hemisphere shown in Figure 10.1. The corresponding lower circles represent the individual's perception of each of these physical stimulus conditions. In a, the homogeneous physical field looks homogeneous. In b, despite the gradient of intensity across the field, the field still looks homogeneous. In c, a faint vertical line in the middle of the hemisphere produces a perception of two different fields, each homogeneous within itself but different in apparent level of illumination.

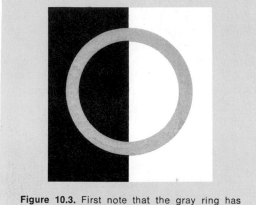

Figure 10.3. First note that the gray ring has a uniform brightness. Now place a long thin object like a pencil along the vertical line so as to divide the ring into halves. What is the apparent brightness of each half of the ring now? For an explanation of this phenomenon, see p. 151–2.

darker on the right. But because the ring is seen as a single entity, we perceive a neutral gray throughout the ring as the contrast effects are minimized.

But when we introduce a contour that separates the whole ring into two parts, the contrast tendencies can be expressed in full. The left half of the ring now appears to be a uniform lighter gray and the other half a uniform darker gray.

Figure and Ground

As we look at the parts of any differentiated field, we notice that invariably one part stands out in a distinctive way from the others. This part is technically called the *figure;* the rest is called the *ground.* Figure-ground differentiation is the simplest and most primitive form of perceptual organization. This phenomenon seems to be present at the very beginnings of visual perception. Newborn infants can follow an object (figure) with their eyes as it moves across a more homogeneous ground (see Box 40, p. 203 for more on this subject).

The perceptual properties of figure and ground differ. The figure tends to be better defined, better localized, more solid, and more integrated, whereas the ground appears to be less well structured, more indefinite. The figure appears to lie in front of or upon the ground, and the ground appears to extend continuously in an unbroken fashion behind the figure. The figure appears to be more the center of attention in the field than does the ground (see Figure 10.4.). Under certain circumstances, figure and ground fluctuate, a phenomenon known as "reversible figures" (see p. 166).

Contour If we are to distinguish a figure at all, usually there must be a contour that separates figure from ground. This contour is clearly perceived as "belonging" to the figure rather than to the ground, even though it is actually a physical boundary common to both. The function of the contour is to provide a distinctive shape to the figure. Strikingly, as figure-ground reversal occurs, the contour shifts from one figure to the other, and the appearance of the contour thus changes markedly. The identical physical contour looks entirely different in the two patterns shown in Figure 10.5.; it defines the shapes of the two figures. It is this shifting quality of contour that makes the visual assembling of parts sometimes difficult, as in the pieces of a jigsaw puzzle, which though sharing an identical contour look very different and are not easily matched.

A figure may sometimes be seen even when the physical contours do not completely define it (see Figures 10.6. and 10.7.).

Closure These examples bring to our attention a general tendency for certain figures to be so organized that they are complete or closed rather than incomplete. This tendency is known technically as *closure* and occurs in two quite different situations: first, when the resulting closed figure is "good" (Figure 10.6.), and, second, when it is familiar and meaningful (Figure 10.7.).

Livson (1968) has found a relation between this second kind of closure and age. The ability to recognize simple meaningful objects from incomplete representations of them increases with age, reaching a maximum at about adolescence. As early as the twenties this ability begins to wane, by forty it is distinctly worse, and it is almost totally absent in otherwise perfectly able and alert people in their seventies and eighties. Figure 10.7b., for example, is rarely recognized by the aged group but is quite easy for adolescent subjects.

Which Will Be Figure? Among the factors that determine which part of a stimulus pattern will tend to be figure and which part ground are the sizes, locations, and shapes of the two areas. Other things being equal, the smaller area and the more enclosed area tend to be seen as figure. And, other things being equal, the more regular area tends to be seen as figure (see Figure 10.8.). The area of greater stimulus intensity is not necessarily favored as figure; a dark

Figure 10.4. A simple example of figure and ground.

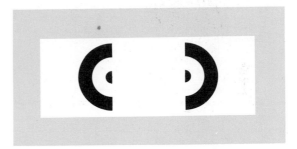

Figure 10.6. Do you see the white square? If you do, it appears to be a figure resting on top of the black oval figure, which appears to extend continuously beneath. Note that the white square can be seen, even though there are no physical contours completely defining it.

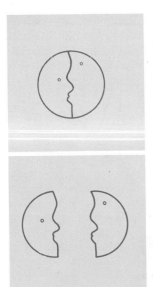

Figure 10.5. With continued inspection of the ambiguous drawing at the top, there is fluctuation of figure and ground, so that sometimes the left face is seen and sometimes the right face. The appearance of the common contour between the two faces changes completely, depending upon which figure it momentarily defines. This difference in its appearance is more easily studied when the faces are presented separately. R. Schafer and G. Murphy, "The Role of Autism in a Visual Figure-Ground Relationship," *Journal of Experimental Psychology*, 32 (1943), 335–43; adapted by permission of the American Psychological Association.

a   b

Figure 10.7. Incomplete pictures. *What are they?* Figure a is almost always seen as dog by age three. Figure b is almost always seen as a crouching man, a sprinter, and the like by age fifteen; it is almost never seen as a meaningful object at age three. L. L. Thurstone, *A Factorial Study of Perception;* Copyright 1944 by The University of Chicago; adapted by permission.

Figure 10.8. This drawing tends to be perceived as wavy white stripes on a green background rather than as green stripes on a white background, even though the total areas of white and green are equal. The reason seems to be that the white stripes are regular in width, whereas the green stripes are irregular. W. Metzger, *Gesetze des Sehens* (1953); adapted by permission of Dr. Waldemar Kramer, Frankfurt. From collection of Professor Melvin Calvin.

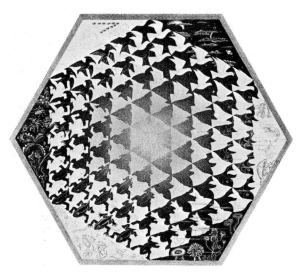

Figure 10.9. Start at any point on the periphery of the design, and you will see a meaningful pattern, for example, the frog, as figure. Move your eyes in either direction around the periphery, and, suddenly, the former figure pattern will become ground for a new meaningful figure. The effect is caused by the gradual blurring of the initially meaningful object, coupled with increase of detail—and meaningfulness—of the emerging figure. By permission of M. C. Escher.

area may be seen as figure on a light ground, and a similar light area may be seen as figure on a dark ground.

All manner of "personal" factors having to do with the perceiver's motivation and past experience also play an important role in determining figure and ground; in general, the more "meaningful" pattern is likely to be seen as figure. For an impressive demonstration of this principle in action, see Figure 10.9.; for an example of its occasional failure, see Figure 10.10. Then look at Figure 10.11.

The Universality of Figure and Ground Figure-ground differentiation probably characterizes all perceptual experience, including audition, touch, smell, and so on. For instance, if there is a continuous tone of a constant pitch or loudness, we hear a brief tone as a "figure" on the "ground" of the continuous tone. A tiny pebble in one's shoe may be perceived as a "figure" against the uniform pressure of the foot on the sole.

Everyday perception rarely involves a single figure-ground pattern; typically, several figures share a common ground. Also typically, individual figures tend to be perceived as clustering together in various groupings. An analysis of the factors determining the organization of single figures into groups of figures, or what we

Figure 10.10. What is this figure? If you cannot tell after prolonged inspection, turn to Figure 10.11.
W. Brown and H. G. Gilhousen, *College Psychology*; Copyright 1949, 1950 by Prentice-Hall, Inc., Englewood Cliffs, N.J.; adapted by permission.

call "perceptual grouping," will take us a step closer to an understanding of typical everyday perception.

Perceptual Grouping

The experimental study of the organized nature of perception was initiated primarily by a group of German psychologists in the early part of this century. Their approach has become known as *Gestalt* (the German word for "form") psychology. Max Wertheimer, one of the founders of *Gestalt psychology*, was responsible for the formulation of "grouping principles." For the most part these principles were supported by demonstrations like those illustrated in Figure 10.12.

Grouping by Proximity

Stimuli that are in closer proximity have a greater tendency to be grouped. The proximity may be spatial (as illustrated in Figure 10.12a.). Or it may be temporal: Of a series of tapping sounds occurring at irregular intervals, those that come close together in time tend to be grouped. Stimuli grouped by proximity need not all be of the same sensory mode. For example, if we hear a loud sound and see a bright light simultaneously, we tend to perceive them as belonging together, as parts of the same event. (For a curious example of the role of temporal proximity in the perception of causality, see Box 45, p. 226). Although proximity is usually defined as physical closeness, there is evidence that phenomenal or experienced proximity is the critical factor. Rock and Brosgole (1964) succeeded in separating experimentally the two factors (using a visual-illusion technique) and found that stimuli that "looked" closer (but actually were not) were grouped together, whereas stimuli that were physically closer to one another (but did not "look" closer) were not organized into groups.

Grouping by Similarity

Stimuli that are more similar to one another have a greater tendency to be grouped. Similarity means likeness in physical attributes like intensity, color, size, weight, odor, and so forth. When stimuli differ only on a single dimension, as they do in Figure 10.12b., it is easy to predict the resulting perceptual organization—horizontal lines. But, when several dimensions vary, we can rarely predict what will be seen.

Grouping by Good Form

Other things being equal, stimuli that form a *good figure* will have a tendency to be grouped. This formulation is very general, intended to embrace a number of more specific variants of the theme, traditionally classified as follows.

1. *Good Continuation:* The tendency for elements to go with others in such a way as to permit the continuation of a line, a curve, or a movement in the direction that has already been established (see Figure 10.12c.).
2. *Symmetry:* The favoring of that grouping that will lead to symmetrical or balanced as against asymmetrical wholes. It can perhaps be regarded as a form of similarity because the two halves of a symmetrical figure are exact mirror images of each other.
3. *Closure:* The grouping of elements in such a way as to make for a more closed or more complete whole figure.
4. *Common Fate:* The favoring of the grouping of those elements that move or change in a common direction, as distinguished from those having other directions of movement or change in the field. This principle, which is essentially an extension to moving objects of grouping by similarity, is an important choreographic tool. Particularly when many dancers are involved, our tendency to group those who follow parallel paths (or those who execute the same limb movements) transforms potential chaos into a fascinating and complex procession of organized movement.

A basic difficulty of this grouping principle centers on the meaning of the crucial phrase

Box 25

How to Measure "Goodness"

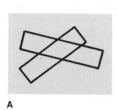

A

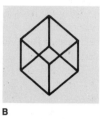

B

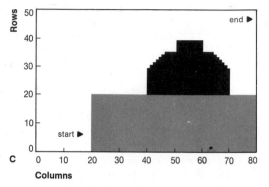

C

Two psychologists, working independently, hit upon very much the same general principle for measuring "goodness" of a figure by a yardstick equally applicable to the several varieties of good form. As put by J. E. Hochberg, the principle is as follows: The less the amount of information needed to define a given perceptual organization as compared to alternative organizations, the more likely it is that that organization will be perceived. A symmetrical grouping is thus fully defined by describing one-half the figure in detail and then stating that the rest of the figure is simply the mirror image of the described half. A closed circle can be more quickly defined than can an open one for which the location and extent of the gap must be specified. Or take one of Hochberg's examples, in which seeing the pattern as two intersecting rectangles permits a more succinct description than describing the alternate percept—five separate irregular figures (see Figure A). Hochberg contents himself with using a few quite rough indexes of the amount of information necessary to define a given figure, for example, numbers of lines, angles, and points of intersection. But these indexes are able to predict which organization of a reversible figure will be seen more frequently (see Figure B), and confirm that the more frequently perceived cube requires fewer descriptive items than does the alternate two-dimensional percept.

F. Attneave has developed a much more precise and general information-measurement technique and defines the "goodness" of a figure as the predictability of the total pattern from partial information. He does not work with reversible figures but chooses rather to determine the "goodness" of

"good figure." How can we know which configuration of stimuli is "better" than another? Clearly we have need of measurable criteria for figural goodness that avoid circularity. Otherwise we would find ourselves asserting that grouping tends toward good form and that good form is that which gets grouped. We have

such criteria in the case of simple stimulus patterns. Relative symmetry can be measured objectively; so can the extent of incompleteness of a simple figure, as well as the change in direction and similarity of movement paths. But for more complex cases we find ourselves caught in circularity, and then the general prin-

Could this be a pun?

single figures, one at a time. It should be clear, however, that, by measuring each of the alternate percepts of a reversible figure separately, we should be able to predict which would predominate in perception when combined.

How does Attneave measure "goodness"? The subject is given a sheet of graph paper composed of 4,000 tiny squares (fifty rows by eighty columns). His task is to guess whether the color of each successive square is black, white, or gray. The experimenter has in mind what the completed figure will look like (see Figure C).

Without knowing what the completed figure will be, the subject starts by guessing the square in the lower left corner. When he has correctly identified the color, he moves on to guess the next square to the right. He continues this process to the end of the row and then starts at the left end of the next row above. In this manner he successively guesses each of the 4,000 squares.

On the average, Attneave's subjects made only fifteen to twenty wrong guesses for the entire figure. How was this score possible? The answer is that the figure was deliberately designed so that knowledge of parts of the figure was sufficient to enable the subject to make fairly valid predictions about the remainder of the figure. This purpose was accomplished by making all the white squares contiguous with one another and by doing the same with the black squares and with the gray squares. Furthermore, the contours separating the white, black, and gray areas are simple and regular. Where the figure tapers, it tapers in a regular way. And it has symmetry; after exploring one side, it is easy to predict the other side. The subject, having thus discovered that the first few squares are white, continues to guess white, and he is correct until he hits the gray contour at column 20. After one or two errors, he then continues to guess gray. On the next row above, he tends to repeat the pattern of the first row.

This technique can be applied to any pattern of whatever complexity, even to three-dimensional figures, with a slight change in method and a three-dimensional recording form. A photograph of a person could thus be measured for "goodness," and we could predict the obvious result that the number of errors would vary with the subject's familiarity with the person in the photograph. This technique gives us the key that permits "familiarity" to enter as a legitimate member of the family of good-form grouping principles discussed in the text; just as we can predict the total figure once we know it is circular, we can fill in the image of the person once we know who he is. In each case relatively little information is required to define the figure; therefore both are "good" and would win out in a grouping competition against alternate patterns of, say, a zigzag line or a stranger's photograph.

J. E. HOCHBERG and E. MCALISTER. 1953. A Quantitative Approach to Figural Goodness, *J. Exp. Psychol.*, 46, 361–4. Figures A and B adapted by permission of American Psychological Association.
F. ATTNEAVE. 1954. Some Informational Aspects of Visual Perception, *Psychol. Rev.*, 61, 183–93. Figure C adapted by permission of American Psychological Association.

ciple becomes a scientifically meaningless notion. Nonetheless some psychologists find that figural "goodness" is a useful descriptive term, and some experimental work has been done— and some theoretical progress made—toward an objective definition of "good figure" (see Box 25).

These various grouping tendencies can be regarded as simplifying a stimulus pattern, as assisting us in "making sense" of the pattern with minimum effort—or at least with minimum information. The "good figure," determined by whatever principle or method of measurement, is the simple and predictable one, so that grouping according to this general organizational principle represents an efficient and adaptive mechanism in our perceptual world.

Competition and Cooperation in Grouping

In every stimulus pattern the elements have some degree of proximity, some degree of similarity, and some degree to which they fit "good form." In every stimulus pattern, therefore, all the kinds of grouping tendencies are at work simultaneously. They differ in strength and in the direction of organization toward which they point. Sometimes they work in the same direction, and sometimes they are pitted against one another. For example, Figure 10.12a. can be seen as horizontal rows if the dots in alternate rows are made extremely bright. In other words, the organization of Figure 10.12b. can be achieved even when the proximity relations of Figure 10.12a. hold. Figure 10.13. illustrates another way to overcome the effects of proximity.

A special application of the competition-of-grouping tendencies is found in the art of camouflage and in the protective coloration and marking of animals in their natural surroundings. Camouflage takes advantage of factors like "good continuation" and "closure" to mask other configurations. A simple illustration is seen in Figure 10.14.

Figure 10.11.

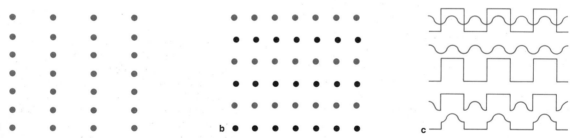

Figure 10.12. Examples of grouping. In a, the dots are perceived in vertical columns because their spatial proximity is greater in the vertical than in the horizontal direction. In b, where proximity is equal, the rows are perceived as horizontal because of grouping by similarity. In c, the principle of good continuation results in seeing the upper figure as consisting of the two parts shown immediately below, even though logically it might just as well be composed of the two parts shown at the very bottom.
M. Wertheimer, "Untersuchungen zur Lehre von der Gestalt," *Psychologische Forschung*, 4 (1923), 301–50; adapted by permission of Springer-Verlag.

Figure 10.13. An example of the competition between grouping by proximity and grouping by closure. The seven lines on the left tend to fall "naturally" into three pairs and one isolate by virtue of proximity relations. But the same lines (repeated on the right), with the addition of the short horizontal lines, tend to be grouped by closure with the more distant partners, overriding the influence of proximity.

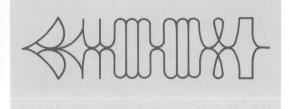

Figure 10.14. If, after studying this figure for a while, you have not seen what it is, try covering the lower half of the figure.

The Effects of Learning

The question of the relative contributions of innate predispositions and of learning to perceptual experience has a long history (see Hochberg, 1962). An illustration of the kinds of data obtained in research on this question is found in Rush's (1937) investigation of the principle of proximity. According to Rush, perceptual grouping by proximity is certainly effective by age six and no less so then a decade later. But, compared with good continuation or similarity, proximity gradually decreases in influence during this period. From these data we might conclude that proximity is the more primitive factor and that we gradually learn the usefulness of grouping according to similarity and good continuation.

Perhaps the safest general statement in light of present evidence is that at least some organizational tendencies are innate but that they are differentially strengthened or weakened in relation to one another, with the cumulative experiences of normal development.

Properties of Wholes and Parts

Grouping processes organize the parts of a stimulus pattern, but, as we move one step further to consider the properties of a total

Box 26

Experiments in Transposition

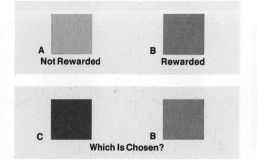

The subject is taught to choose the medium-gray card B in preference to the light-gray card A by regularly finding a reward behind B. The cards are randomly switched in position so that he cannot learn simply to choose right or left. What happens when card B is presented for the first time with a new card C, a *darker* gray?

Card C is chosen. Apparently the subject has learned to choose the card that is *relatively* the darker—that is, B over A. Therefore, when B and C are presented, C is chosen because it is darker than B, *even though* B has been regularly rewarded. The brightness relationship is "transposed" along the scale of different grays.

Studies giving essentially similar results have been made with chickens, rats, monkeys, and children and on other dimensions like size and shape.

Box 27

Adaptation Level

H. Helson has advanced a theory that a person makes a judgment of the magnitude of any stimulus attribute, like size, weight, or loudness, by establishing a sort of subjective or personal scale on which the stimuli are judged. He calls the neutral or medium point of such a scale the "adaptation level." Stimulus values above the adaptation level are perceived as "large," "heavy," "loud," and so on, and those below it are perceived as "small," "light," "soft," and so on.

According to Helson's view, first presented in 1947, the adaptation level is determined by pooling the values of all the stimuli in the judgment series. It represents the "centering" of the perceiver with respect to the range of stimuli confronting him. This pooling is not merely simple averaging; the adaptation level is therefore not the same as the arithmetic mean of the stimulus values in the series. For example, in a weight series ranging from 200 to 400 grams, the adaptation level is usually found to be about 250 grams—weights less than 250 grams are judged "light," and weights more than 250 grams are judged "heavy."

The adaptation level constantly changes as a function of all the stimuli that are acting upon the person at the moment and that have acted upon him in the past. A single extreme stimulus lying far outside the range of values of the rest of the series may have a profound effect in shifting the adaptation level in its direction. For example, in one study the adaptation level of a series of weights ranging from 400 to 600 grams was found to be 475 grams, but, when a weight of 900 grams was introduced a single time, the adaptation level rose to 550 grams.

The mathematical formulation Helson derived to permit quantitative predictions of adaptation level on the basis of the distribution of stimuli has proved able to account for a wide variety of

perception, additional processes come into operation. A particular organization of the whole can be maintained despite changes in the properties of its parts. This phenomenon is known as *transposition* of form. For example, kidney beans or pennies, arranged in square patterns, will be seen as equally "good" squares. The quality of "squareness" is common to both these stimulus patterns.

There are many examples of transposition of form. A melody is recognized as the same when played higher or lower in the scale, provided that the relations among the notes remain the same. For experiments on transposition of a brightness relation in animals and children, see Box 26, p. 159. A much more familiar example is a photograph, which looks the same whether it is wallet size or greatly

judgmental data. In a recent major restatement of his theory, Helson spells out the applicability of adaptation-level theory to such diverse areas as motivation, thinking, and personality. One interesting extension comes from D. Rethlingshafer and E. D. Hinckley. When asked by these investigators to judge ages on a scale from very young to very old, ten-year-olds designated age thirty-six as "in the middle"—neither old nor young. Adults in their early twenties set the "middle" at age forty-two; those in their seventies set it at age fifty-two. This shift in what is regarded as middle age is not surprising, but the accuracy of the mathematical predictions (made by assuming the pooled average of all *past* stimuli to be estimated by one's own age) certainly is; the predicted values are 36.3, 41.2, and 49. It is clear, however, that the pooling of stimuli in establishing the adaptation level does not occur "automatically," without regard for factors of perceptual organization. Through appropriate changes in the person's perception of the situation, the same series of stimuli may result in different adaptation levels.

In an experiment by D. R. Brown, the adaptation level for a series of weights ranging from 80 to 144 grams was first determined. Then he introduced into the series an additional extreme weight of 242 grams. As Helson would predict, the effect of this one extreme stimulus was to raise substantially the adaptation level. But Brown then made a crucial experimental variation. The experiment was repeated in every detail except that this time the extreme weight was a tray, also weighing 242 grams, which the subject was casually asked to move out of the way. As a result, he lifted the same extreme weight but without regarding it as part of the judgment series. The results clearly showed that, under these conditions, when this heavy weight was perceived as an irrelevant tray rather than as part of the stimulus series, it had no effect on raising the adaptation level.

The inference is that the tray was regarded as "something else," not that the subject was unaware of having lifted it. Later work suggests that it is not necessary to pay active attention to a stimulus in order for it to affect the adaptation level. What seems important, then, is that only stimuli that are perceived as belonging to the same group of stimuli participate in determining the adaptation level for that group.

H. HELSON. 1947. Adaptation-Level as a Frame of Reference for Prediction of Psychophysical Data, *Amer. J. Psychol.*, 60, 1–29.

H. HELSON. 1964. *Adaptation-Level Theory* (New York: Harper).

D. RETHLINGSHAFER and E. D. HINCKLEY. 1963. Influence of Judge's Characteristics Upon the Adaptation Level, *Amer. J. Psychol.*, 76, 16–123.

D. R. BROWN. 1953. Stimulus Similarity and the Anchoring of Subjective Scales, *Amer. J. Psychol.*, 66, 199–214.

enlarged to adorn a mantelpiece. In this example it is immediately evident that the spatial *relations* among the various part-figures in the photograph are perfectly preserved despite the size change.

Though the form of the whole is determined by the pattern of relations among the constituent elements, it is also true that the whole is in some ways perceived differently, depending upon the individual elements. A square composed of four dots is certainly not perceived as exactly the same square as one made up of four connected lines or of four pressure points on the skin. A transposed melody may readily be recognized as the same melody, but it may also be recognized as in a different range of pitch or intensity or as played on a different instrument.

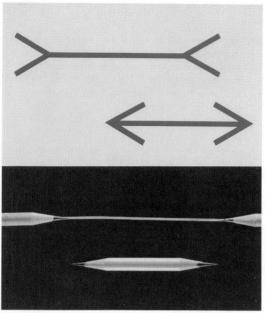

Figure 10.15. The classical Müller-Lyer illusion (with a photographic interpretation). The two horizontal lines, actually of the same length, appear unequal because of the arrowheads.
Fundamental Photographs

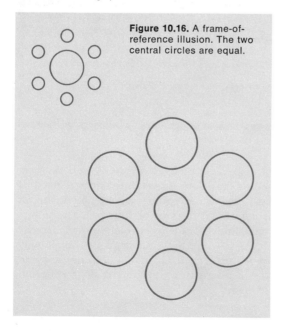

Figure 10.16. A frame-of-reference illusion. The two central circles are equal.

Just as the properties of wholes are somewhat dependent upon the nature of their constituent elements, the properties of parts are dependent upon the nature of the whole. An example is the Müller-Lyer illusion, in which a line looks longer or shorter depending upon whether it is part of the open or the closed arrowhead figure (see Figure 10.15.).

We shall find repeatedly in later parts of this book that the part-whole principle generally applies in the more complex psychological functions, for example, in solving problems and in stereotyped thinking about other persons. When discussed in this broader context, such an effect on perception is usually referred to as one's *frame of reference.*

Frame of Reference

The part-whole principle has often been discussed in connection with the concept of frame of reference. In our judgment of the perceptual properties of things, we typically make use of a standard or a framework that serves as a reference against which a particular property is judged. When we ask how big an object is, the sizes of other objects with which it is grouped may serve as a standard. Two equal circles may seem very different in size, depending upon the sizes of other circles surrounding them (see Figure 10.16.).

In our examples the frame of reference was given by the whole perceptual configuration immediately present. But there may also be temporal configurations of stimuli that serve as a frame of reference for the judgment of properties of objects.

If the person is exposed to a series of stimuli of a particular kind, each successive stimulus will to some extent be judged in relation to the whole series already experienced. Such phenomena have sometimes been experimentally studied in connection with the concept of *adaptation level,* as formulated by Helson (see Box 27, p. 160).

Glossary

adaptation level The subjective level established by a person as a standard for making judgments, derived from a "pooling" or "averaging" of a series of similar stimuli he has experienced. For example, what is regarded as a neutral weight will be determined by the other weights that he has lifted; weights above it will be judged "heavy" and those below it "light."

assimilation The tendency for the difference in intensities of adjacent parts of a field to be minimized in perception. Often these differences, even though above the threshold, are not seen at all. The effect is opposite to that observed in contrast phenomena, in which differences are maximized.

closure The tendency for certain figures to be so perceived that they seem complete or closed rather than incomplete or unclosed. For example, a circle with a tiny gap may be seen as a complete unbroken circle.

contour A line of demarcation separating one part of a perceptual field from adjacent parts. It is perceived as "belonging" to the figure and provides the figure's distinctive shape. Nevertheless, contour and figure are not identical, for the very same physical contour looks entirely different in two different figures.

contrast The phenomenon of perceiving a difference as greater than that physically present in the stimulus pattern.

figure The part of the perceptual field that stands out on the background of the remainder of the field.

frame of reference The standard or framework that serves as a reference against which a particular perceptual property is judged. For example, the apparent angle of objects in a room is partly determined by the angle of the surrounding walls. The frame-of-reference effect can be seen as an instance of the part-whole principle.

Gestalt psychology An approach to the experimental study of the organized nature of perception, initiated by a group of German psychologists, including Wertheimer, Koffka, and Köhler. *Gestalt* is the German word for "form."

good figure The characteristic of a certain stimulus pattern that has qualities of good continuation, symmetry, closure, unity, and so forth. The so-called "law of grouping by good figure" states that perceptual grouping of elements will be favored in the direction of forming a good figure.

ground The part of the perceptual field that serves as background for the figure. It appears to be less clearly structured than the figure and less the focus of attention.

transposition The recognition that a stimulus pattern is the same as another stimulus pattern, even though the elements are different. This recognition is based on maintaining an identical relationship among the stimuli in the two patterns, for instance, the transposition of a melody on the keyboard.

UNIT 1

changes
in perceptual
organization

overview / Once established, a percept may undergo modification. This may take place without change in the stimulus pattern, as with reversible figures. Prolonged exposure to a stimulus also often leads to an apparently spontaneous perceptual change, the result perhaps of a process of physiological satiation. Satiation is studied through figural aftereffect phenomena.

With actual stimulus changes, changes in the percept tend to be economical and to occur most easily in weakly organized aspects of the stimulus pattern. They tend to happen suddenly and often involve "creative solutions."

Perceptual organization depends heavily upon the set of the perceiver. Sets are determined mainly by prior experience and by the perceiver's needs, emotions, attitudes, and values. Set, in part, exerts its influence upon perception by affecting attention.

Whatever is in the focus of attention is the clearest and most differentiated percept in the field. Attention continuously shifts, inasmuch as there is a gradual "satiation" of any prolonged percept, and there is a limit to the span of what a single focus of attention can take in. With divided attention, perceptual discrimination is poorer. Attention can be either voluntary or involuntary; the latter results from certain attention-demanding properties of the stimulus itself. These properties may be classified as psychophysical (a loud sound), set-related (hunger), or "collative" (referring, usually, to a contrast between expected and presented stimuli).

Despite the number of factors capable of modifying perceptual organization, perception is in fact characteristically stable and conveys an accurate view of the real world. When it fails in this function, most often a weak structure in the stimulus pattern is the reason.

Up to this point we have been chiefly concerned with the factors that determine the establishment of a perceptual organization. But, of course, a percept once established can undergo change. Some changes in perception occur even though the stimulus pattern remains constant; others occur with changes in the stimulus pattern.

Changes With Constant Stimulus Pattern

We have already become acquainted with instances of "spontaneous oscillation" occurring between two alternate figures against the same ground. Such *reversible figures* provide a convenient avenue for an examination of perceptual change.

Figure 11.1. shows two classical examples of reversible figures, the Necker cube and the reversible staircase. Casual inspection for just a few moments should lead to perception of the two alternate organizations in each case; continued inspection should result in a gradually increasing rate of reversal. (For information on *stimulus* factors affecting rate of reversal, see Box 28, p. 167.) To some extent, however, "spontaneous" fluctuations in perceptual organization can be deliberately controlled by the perceiver. In many cases he may "force" the fluctuation by shifting his visual fixation. For example, it is well known that in the Necker cube the point of fixation on the figure will help to determine which of the alternatives will be seen. Fixating on any corner of the "front" surface in either organization will quickly bring about that organization or serve to maintain it. In fact, simply being more alert and attentive to the stimulus pattern increases the rate of fluctuation (Cesarec & Nilsson, 1963).

Such spontaneous oscillations are not confined to visual patterns. Try this experiment: Say the word "elf" aloud repeatedly and rapidly. Quite soon you will be hearing yourself say "fell," then "elf" again, and so on. Rapid repetition is important in this auditory reversible figure because it permits "elf" and "fell" to

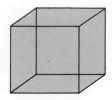

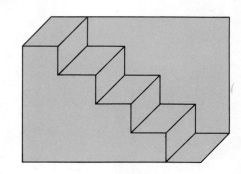

Figure 11.1. Two classical examples of reversible figures, the Necker Cube and the reversible staircase.

share their common contour, that is, the letter "f."

Satiation of Organization

It has been suggested that spontaneous or unintentional reversals reflect satiation processes. More specifically, it is assumed that, as one perceptual organization persists, there is some kind of gradual accumulation of physiological satiation from this organization. When satiation reaches a high enough level, the first form is inhibited, and the second form appears. The second form is in turn gradually satiated as the first form recovers from satiation, and eventually the first form reappears, and so on. Figure 11.2. demonstrates the way in which prior *over*satiation of one alternative can inhibit its subsequent perception. Even perceived movement shows satiation effects (see Box 29, p. 169).

The underlying mechanism of such satiation of organization is not yet understood. Perhaps the most concentrated attack on this problem has come from the study of a phenomenon known as the *figural aftereffect* (Köhler & Wallach, 1944). The general feature of this phenom-

Box 28

Which Will Be Figure—and Why?

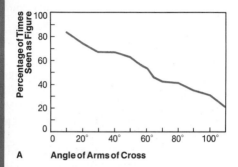

A   **Angle of Arms of Cross**

B

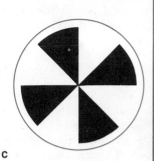

C

T. Oyama's investigations of the figure-determining factors for the Maltese cross (see Figures 5.4., p. 97, and 11.2.) are good examples of the quantitative approach to the study of such visual phenomena as reversible figures. In Oyama's work the subject continuously inspected the stimulus pattern and was instructed to report which of the two figures he was seeing at each moment. He reported by pressing one of two keys designated to represent the figures. As the keys operated separate clocks, the total time that each figure was seen during an inspection period of one minute could be recorded. The ratio of these two times is the measure of the relative dominance of the two figures in any given trial.

Oyama investigated the influence of four stimulus factors. First, by presenting different patterns varying from a stimulus pattern of two equal-angle crosses to a thin versus a fat cross, he learned that the thinner the cross, the longer it was seen as a figure. The quantitative relationship he obtained is shown in Figure A (adapted from Oyama). At 60 degrees, for example, when all angles are equal each of the two crosses is seen about half the time, as would be expected. Second, by keeping one cross constantly black (or white) and varying the brightness of the other cross, Oyama discovered that the dominance of the constant cross increased as the brightness of the variable cross approached the gray of the surrounding field. Furthermore, white tended to dominate black. Third, he found that color influences which cross will be seen as figure. Red crosses are highly likely to be seen as figure, blue crosses much less so. Colors intermediate between red and blue in the visual spectrum are intermediate in dominance. Fourth, crosses with vertical-horizontal orientation were found to be dominant over oblique crosses.

In each of these phases of the experiment only a single factor was varied; for example, in evaluating the effect of orientation, black and white equal-angled crosses were used—and only their relative tilt was changed. We therefore do not yet know whether or not these factors are *additive*— whether or not, for example, the relative dominance of a thin over a thick cross is increased if the thin cross is red and the thick cross is blue. But you can gather data on such questions yourself. Figure B should yield a striking dominance effect; that is, one of the crosses should remain as figure most of the time, with few reversals. Figure C should show frequent reversal. Can you say why?

T. OYAMA. 1960. Figure-Ground Dominance as a Function of Sector Angle, Brightness, Hue, and Orientation, *J. Exp. Psychol.*, 60, 299–305. Figures adapted by permission of American Psychological Association.

Figure 11.2. In b is reproduced the ambiguous drawing encountered earlier as Figure 5.4., p. 97. Whether the cross or the propeller tends to be seen more readily can be influenced by prior fixation of either Figure a or Figure c. Look at a for sixty seconds, carefully fixating the center. Then fixate the center of b. You will tend to see the alternative figure. The experiment can be repeated by first fixating on c, in which case the opposite version of b will be immediately favored.
E. G. Boring, *et al., Foundations of Psychology* (1948); adapted by permission of John Wiley & Sons, Inc.

enon, which has been demonstrated with numerous stimulus patterns and in various sense modalities, is that prolonged inspection of a stimulus pattern will gradually distort the initial percept as well as the perception of new patterns presented to the same receptor region (see Box 30, p. 170).

Changes With Changes in Stimulus Pattern

We now turn to perceptual changes that take place when there *are* changes in the stimulus pattern. On the basis of various studies of such changes, we can formulate a number of tentative generalizations.

First, change in perceptual organization tends to be as economical as possible, consistent with the demands made by changes in the stimulus pattern. Here is an experimental example of such economical change: In a dark room a rotating luminous rod is viewed through an opening in the form of an ellipse. When the visible part of the rod rotates, it constantly changes its length, contracting and elongating as it passes the short and long axes of the ellipse (see Figure 11.3a.). On the retina we therefore have two continuous stimulus changes, corresponding to the rotation of the rod and to the change in length of the rod. But the observer sees something else. The rod appears to remain at the same unchanging length while it rotates in a plane tilted at an angle from the frontal plane (see Figure 11.3b.). Two continuous changes in the stimulus pattern (the rotation and the contraction and elongation of length) are perceived as a single continuous change (the rotation in a tilted plane). In this way, one perceptual change encompasses two stimulus changes. Like the grouping principle of good form (Unit 10, p. 155), perception operates here to create a simpler, better economical and efficient organization (see Figure 14.5., p. 225, for another instance of this tendency).

Second, other things being equal, more strongly organized parts of the field resist change longer than weaker parts do. In general,

Box 29

Satiation of Downward Movement

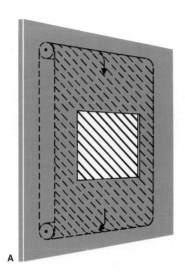

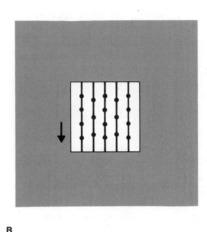

A continuous paper tape with 45-degree lines drawn on it moves constantly downward at a slow rate. It is viewed through a square aperture in a large cardboard shield in front of it (see Figure A). Under these circumstances the direction of perceived movement of the lines is *ambiguous;* they can be seen moving vertically downward or moving horizontally to the right. Subjects almost always first see the downward movement. But with continued inspection there is a shift to the horizontal direction and then an oscillation between these two directions of movement.

If we assume that these oscillations are caused by a gradual accumulation of "satiation" as the movement continues in a given direction, we should be able to change the perceptual sequence by deliberately increasing the subject's exposure to one of the alternatives. H. Wallach conducted such an experiment by requiring the subject to inspect for several minutes a moving paper tape on which were drawn lines that could *only* be seen moving downward (see Figure B). Then, when the subject was shown Figure A, he immediately tended to see the movement in the horizontal direction rather than in the usual vertical direction. Apparently the "satiation" for downward movement produced by inspection of Figure B built up resistance to seeing movement in that direction, and the alternative horizontal direction was therefore favored.

H. WALLACH. 1935. Über Visuell Wahrgenommene Bewegungsrichtung, *Psychol. Forsch.*, 20, 325–80.

Box 30

Figural Aftereffects

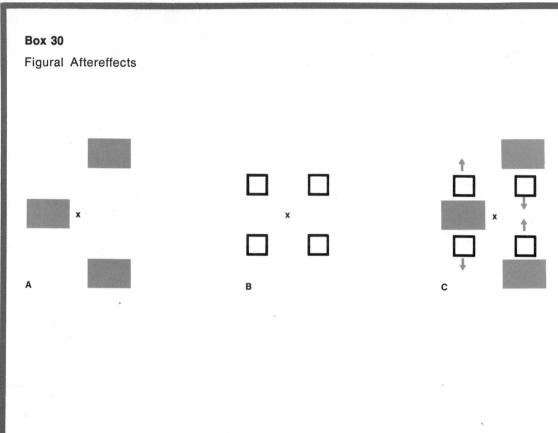

Fixate the cross in Figure A steadily without moving your eyes for about sixty seconds. Then at once shift your eyes to the cross in Figure B and, while keeping your fixation, observe the appearance of the four squares.

You will note that the distance between the two left-hand squares appears to be greater than that between the two right-hand squares. Actually, the distances are equal. The distortion of Figure B has been produced by the prior inspection of Figure A.

On the basis of many similar experiments at Swarthmore College, W. Köhler and H. Wallach have proposed that these distortions can be described in terms of a *displacement* effect caused by satiation. When a figure has been cast for a short while in a given area of the retina, there is a kind of "satiation" that causes new figures cast near that retinal area to be displaced away from it. The perceived distortion of the squares in Figure A can be understood by their displacement away from the places in which the inspection figures had been previously exposed. Figure C schematizes the relationship by showing how Figures A and B would appear if combined. The two left-hand squares are pushed apart, and the two right-hand squares are pushed together.

W. KÖHLER and H. WALLACH. 1944. Figural Aftereffects, *Proc. Amer. Phil. Soc.*, 88, 269–357.

a percept is more strongly organized when the stimuli are clearer (that is, far above threshold) and when the patterning is such that more of the grouping tendencies cooperate to produce the organization. In addition, the set, past experience, emotional state, and motivations of the perceiver—factors discussed in the next section—may influence the strength of structures in the percept. This second generalization is illustrated by the following demonstration.

We look at two identically illuminated balloons of equal size, placed side by side ten feet away from us in an otherwise completely dark room. As one of the balloons is slowly inflated to a larger size, what do we perceive? An expanding balloon? No. Characteristically, the balloon that is being inflated *appears* to move slowly toward us—*without* changing its apparent size. This particular perceptual resolution of the change in stimulus pattern is presumably favored over the accurate one because the cues for judging the distance of the two balloons are relatively weak in the dark room. It is easier to modify our notion of how far away the balloon is than to modify our notion of its size. This fact accords with our generalization. The stimuli that normally make possible our judgment of the distance of an object are poor because of the darkness; the spatial location of the balloons is therefore a weakly organized part of the percept. On the other hand,

the stimuli for judging the size of the lighted balloons are clearer, and size is thus a more strongly organized part of the percept. In line with our second generalization, the perceptual change is such as to maintain the size of the object (strongly organized) but to shift its location in space (weakly organized). If we were to repeat the experiment in a well-lighted room, we would have the opposite result; we would see the balloon remaining in place and getting larger—for now the distance cues would be stronger than the size cues.

Third, adjustment to stimulus change is often accomplished by the separation of parts of the field. A particularly strong percept in the field may often be maintained without change, through a reorganization that somehow removes or insulates that percept from its surroundings—surroundings that would tend to produce change in it. The percept thus becomes established as a more independent "subsystem" from the total "system" of the field. This so-called "separation of systems" is a fundamental characteristic of all psychological processes. We encountered it in Box 27, p. 160 (lifting the tray), and in Figure 10.3., p. 152, and we shall encounter it again in later discussion of thinking, remembering, learning, motivation, growth, and personality change.

Let us take another example. If we present a uniform green field to one eye and a uniform

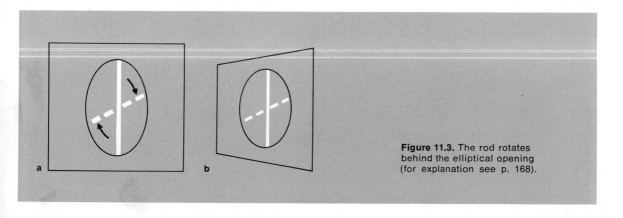

Figure 11.3. The rod rotates behind the elliptical opening (for explanation see p. 168).

red field to the other, the viewer will experience a fluctuation of the visual field. Sometimes he will see red and sometimes green but not both at the same time. We speak here of *retinal rivalry*. Apparently, if the two fields do not readily fuse into one whole by combining the stimuli from both eyes, only one field will be seen at a time. If the two tendencies are about equal, oscillation should occur; if the tendencies of one are much stronger, it will predominate most, or even all, of the time.

We have here a clear instance of how a resolution of a difficult perceptual problem is achieved. If fusion, a perceptual compromise, cannot occur, the next best thing is to "give each separate organization its chance" in turn, thus preserving the essential simplicity of the pattern yet incorporating both parts within a whole that is extended through time. "Separation of systems," therefore, can occur in the temporal as well as in the spatial dimension.

Fourth, perceptual reorganization often occurs by sudden, stepwise transformations. Perceptual changes are sometimes gradual quantitative modifications of the attributes of percepts. The object may appear to move gradually closer (as in the case of the balloon) or to grow gradually larger; the shape of the object may gradually alter; the relations among objects may gradually change. But often the changes are not of this form and are instead sudden, discontinuous "leaps" from one qualitative form to another, as in reversible figures. At one instant the organization looks this way, at the next moment that way. And the two appearances are sometimes so qualitatively unlike that it is hard to believe that the difference resulted from only a slight quantitative change in the stimulus pattern or from some other slight shift in "forces."

Throughout psychological processes of all kinds, we find manifestations of this effect. Tiny shifts in the "forces" of a situation may be sufficient to upset the balance of forces radically. This fact is true of shifts in emotional states, in motivational psychodynamics, in learning and thinking, in the crises of pathological "breakdowns" of persons under stress, and so on. The concept of the straw that breaks the camel's back has basic theoretical support.

Fifth, changes of perceptual organization often involve the creation of new forms. As we have said before, every man is a creator who makes simpler perceptual order out of stimulus complexity. This process of construction of a perceptual world is often marked by "creative" ways in which stimulus patterns are organized and reorganized (see Box 31, p. 173, for a striking demonstration).

That such perceptual reorganizations may properly be designated "creative" rests also upon the fact that the new organization was not previously in the perceiver's repertory. The new organization may appear for the first time because of the need to make sense of this stimulus situation. Furthermore, as with all essentially creative acts, the new organization accommodates the necessary data in an economical and "elegant" way. In a sense, however, this last generalization may be considered a derivative of our first one, and the dysfunction between the example of the rotating rod and the examples in Box 31 is a subtle one. Very possibly, when we have a familiar change-minimizing perceptual solution, we use it; when we do not and when we are confronted with a novel stimulus situation, we create an original solution. Put another way, only when commonplace solutions are not at hand is necessity the mother of perceptual invention.

Perceptual Set and Organization

Perceptual processes are not disembodied; they occur within an organism that is engaging in activity. Stimuli are organized not only to "fit" with one another but also to "fit" the requirements of the perceiver's ongoing activity—what he is thinking, feeling, trying to do. The perceiver has the readiness and expectations that help to govern the way he will perceive the

Box 31

Creative Perceiving

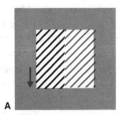 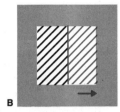 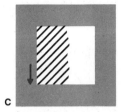 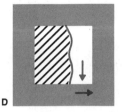

A   B   C   D

The illusion of movement described in Box 29, page 169, has been used by H. Wallach to study perceptual reorganization. A continuous paper tape moving slowly downward is viewed through an aperture. On the tape is drawn a grid of lines at a 45-degree angle. The left half of each line is black, and the right half is green, as indicated in Figure A (in Wallach's original experiment the right half was red).

The movement is first perceived as a grid of half black, half green lines moving downward. After several minutes the "satiation" produced by this downward movement builds up a strong tendency for the movement to shift to the sideways direction. But this shift is inhibited by the fact that the lines would then have to be perceived in an unlikely way as *changing color* from black to green as they move to the right past the center. The downward movement therefore continues for a much longer time than under the conditions in Box 29. Finally, however, the problem of accommodating the growing tendency to shift from the downward movement is accomplished by the perceiver through a "creative" perceptual reorganization. He suddenly sees the black lines moving sideways, and, as they reach the center, *they pass behind a transparent green surface.* This green transparency is perceptually "invented." It is clearly seen as a separate surface lying in front of the paper on which the black lines are drawn, and a vertical contour is seen in the center of the aperture defining the edge of the green transparency, as in Figure B.

An even more complex effect is obtained by showing a grid of lines that end in a scalloped edge (see Figure C). Now the difficulty of seeing sideways movement is even greater because the lines "have nowhere to go." But for many observers a remarkable perceptual solution does spontaneously occur. They see the field as separated into two parts: first, the set of lines moving sideways and, second, a white surface with a scalloped edge that *moves downward* while the lines pass behind it (see Figure D).

The restructuring occurs suddenly and without the perceiver's foresight or intention. He is surprised when it happens. It is "creative" in achieving a novel configuration that accommodates the requirements of the stimulus pattern through the separation of the total into parts and through the "invention" of new parts.

H. WALLACH. 1935. Über Visuell Wahrgenommene Bewegungsrichtung, *Psychol. Forsch.*, 20, 325–80.

stimuli "out there." In a word, he is set to perceive something; the "thing" expected may be something quite specific, or it may be quite general.

The concept of *set* refers in general to the readiness of the organism to make a particular response. There are various types of sets. In a motor set, a person is ready for a particular action of his muscles—the runner on his mark is set to sprint. A mental set is a readiness for a particular thought process. A perceptual set is a readiness for a particular organization of stimuli—after hearing the words "pork and," one is ready to hear "beans," and he may hear "beans" even though the word actually spoken is "greens."

The Determinants of Set

There are two main determinants of set: first, prior experience and, second, such central factors in the person as needs, emotions, attitudes, and values. In short, we tend to see what we saw before and what fits best with our current orientation to the world. The effect of this process is to make perception more rapid and efficient, often by permitting, through a kind of "closure," an organized percept that could not have been achieved from the "raw" stimulus alone. Usually the effect is also adaptive; but just as grouping principles occasionally prevent realistic perception, set can sometimes blind us to present reality.

Prior Experience and Perceptual Set

The sheer frequency with which the stimulus pattern has previously been perceived will help create a set. For instance, the more familiar a word, the greater the set toward its perception, as shown, for example, by experiments that find a close relationship between the frequency of word usage in the English language and the ease of recognition of the same words on brief exposure.

Box 32

Prior Experience
and Organization

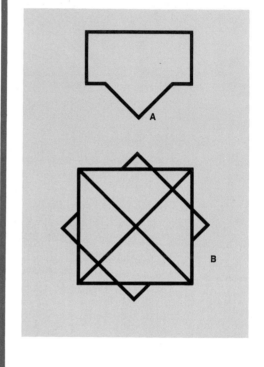

Look at the simple geometrical design in Figure A. Then look at Figure B. Do you see Figure A in Figure B? It is hard to see at once because it is embedded within the larger figure in such a way as to be deliberately camouflaged, but with a careful search you can find it.

These two figures are examples of many such figures constructed by the German psychologist K. Gottschaldt in order to study the effect of prior experience on perception. To determine whether or not a great deal of familiarity with Figure A would make it more easily recognizable in Figure B, he showed Figure A to one group of subjects 520 times (with instructions to memorize it) and showed it to another group only 3 times. When the subjects were later shown Figure B and asked to describe it, only about one person in twenty saw the simple Figure A in it, and *there was no difference between the two groups in the tendency to see it.* Gottschaldt concluded that sheer frequency of prior experience with an object does not account for the readiness to perceive it.

But later experimenters like Siao-sung Djang have shown that, when dealing with simple figures that are not so completely camouflaged within the larger figure, the amount of prior familiarity with the simple figure *does* help to determine ease of recognition. Gottschaldt had chosen a situation in which the stimulus structure of Figure B was so strong that it was unusually difficult for Figure A to be seen even under favorable conditions.

Even for the strongly organized Gottschaldt figures there is evidence that, under certain conditions, prior experience with A-type figures does indeed help somewhat in detecting them within B-type figures. C. B. Lucero, working with the identical figures, taught her subjects a "key" that attached a different color name to each A figure. Subsequently, they were shown the corresponding B figures, with the key either present or absent. Under both conditions the trained subjects noticed their presence within the B figures significantly more often than did members of a control group that had had no prior exposure to the A figures. All subjects were instructed to report the perception of an A figure by giving its color name, and, as control-group subjects were supplied with the key during the test trials, their greater difficulty in recognizing the A figures presumably resulted from lack of earlier experience with these figures.

This apparent contradiction between Gottschaldt's and Lucero's results is most probably because of the difference in the way subjects were able to report seeing the embedded A figure. Gottschaldt simply asked his subjects for a description of the B figure and considered the corresponding A figure to have been recognized only if it was spontaneously mentioned. Lucero, on the other hand, supplied her subjects with a key that not only set the subject to seek the hidden A figure but also provided him with a convenient verbal label for reporting its detection. Under such circumstances the effect of prior experience had apparently been sufficiently enhanced to overcome, at least to some extent, the camouflaging organizational factors. Perhaps most significant in Lucero's research is her discovery that the more strongly organized the B figure, the smaller the difference between the trained and the control groups in frequency of recognition of the A figure.

K. GOTTSCHALDT. 1926. Über den Einfluss der Erfahrung auf die Wahrnehmung von Figuren, *Psychol. Forsch.,* 8, 261–317. Figures adapted by permission of Springer-Verlag, Berlin.
K. GOTTSCHALDT. 1929. Über den Einfluss der Erfahrung auf die Wahrnehmung von Figuren, *Psychol. Forsch.,* 12, 1–87.
SIAO-SUNG DJANG. 1937. The Role of Past Experience in the Visual Apprehension of Masked Forms, *J. Exp. Psychol.,* 20, 29–59.
CAROL B. LUCERO. 1961. Visual Discrimination of Camouflaged Figures. Unpublished doctoral dissertation, University of California, Berkeley.

Box 33

Wife or Mother-in-Law?

Look at Figure A. What do you see?

You may see the slightly turned profile of an attractive young woman. Or you may see an old hag. (When E. G. Boring published this example of an ambiguous stimulus, he termed it the "wife and mother-in-law" picture!) With continued inspection you will be able to see alternately each of the two possible organizations. Normally about 60 per cent of subjects *first* see the young woman and about 40 per cent the old hag.

In order to test the effect of a *prior set* on how this ambiguous picture is perceived, R. W. Leeper performed the following experiment. Two groups of subjects were shown a preliminary series of pictures. Group I saw Figure B as one of the pictures in the series. Group II saw Figure C as one of the pictures in the series.

Later both groups were shown the ambiguous version (Figure A) and asked to report what they saw. The effect of the set toward "young woman" or "old hag" induced by the previous exposure of that version was conclusive: 100 per cent of group I saw the young woman in Figure A, and 95 per cent of group II saw the old hag.

You can perform a similar experiment yourself. Look at Figure D and then at Figure E.

Because you have first seen the pirate in figure D, a "pirate" set will have been induced in you, and you will most likely have seen that pirate in Figure E.

Now we will induce a different set in you: Look again at Figure E, and see a rabbit!

R. W. LEEPER. 1935. A Study of a Neglected Portion of the Field of Learning: The Development of Sensory Organization, *J. Genet. Psychol.*, 46, 41–75. Figures adapted by permission of The Journal Press.

Experiments reported by Henle (1942) demonstrate, however, that even extensive familiarity will not necessarily create a dominant perceptual set. In one experiment, she exposed letters briefly in a tachistoscope (an optical apparatus that can expose stimuli for precisely timed intervals); some letters were exposed in their normal printed form, and some were reversed. Without receiving explicit instructions about what to expect, subjects were indeed slower to recognize the reversed letters than the familiar normal letters. Then, in a second experiment, they were led to expect either normally oriented letters or reversed letters (they had been shown a preliminary series containing only one kind or the other). Under these circumstances, there was no longer a significant difference in the speed of identifying normal and reversed letters in a subsequent series, which, as in the first experiment, intermixed the two types of stimuli. Therefore, a momentary set can overcome one derived from massive prior experience (see Boxes 32, p. 174, and 33, p. 176).

Recency of Prior Experience Experiences that have just occurred are more likely to determine the set in the immediate situation than less recent, even if more frequent, experiences, as is indicated in a series of experiments by Epstein and Rock (1960). The stimuli they used are the same as those shown in Figure 10.5., p. 153, and Box 33. Subjects were first shown one of the unambiguous figures (the right or left "moon" face, the young woman or the hag) several times in succession; then the other unambiguous figure was shown only once. Immediately afterward the appropriate ambiguous pattern was exposed very briefly, and the subjects reported which of the two possible figures was seen. If frequency were more important, then the figure presented earlier and several times in succession would be seen in the ambiguous pattern; if recency were more important, the last figure presented would be seen. The last figure, which had been viewed only once, was seen in 82 per

cent of the test trials in each of which the first figure had been previously shown three times; even with twelve previous exposures of the first figure, the last one was perceived in 60 per cent of the trials. The results therefore strongly suggest that recency is far more effective than frequency in determining the perception of an ambiguous figure.

Central Factors and Perceptual Set

Perceptual organization often reflects the central factors in the perceiver, for example, his needs, emotions, attitudes, and values. The extent of this occurrence depends upon the arousal of appropriate sets by these central factors.

Needs The stronger one's state of need, the more strongly he will be set perceptually toward aspects of the field relevant to that need. Many experimental studies have been made of this apparently obvious fact. Beginning with the work of Sanford (1937), hunger has been a favored variable of need in such studies. Sanford showed that incomplete words, for example, "me - -," would be more readily completed as food words, for example, "meat," "meal" (rather than "meet"), by hungry than by nonhungry persons. Similar findings have been reported in a study by McClelland and Atkinson (1948): Hungrier subjects tended to "see" more food objects than did less hungry subjects on a screen upon which, in fact, only a smudge or diffuse light had been projected.

But there is not a simple one-to-one correspondence between the state of need and the perceptual result. What is critical is the intermediate role of set. Though in general the state of need is likely to arouse an appropriate set, it will fail to do so when the total momentary situation does not favor the emergence of that set. We must always take into consideration the interaction among factors of need, stimulus structure, and set. The very complex manner in which such interactions occur is demonstrated in the study described in Box 34.

Emotions   We all know that moods and emotions affect our view of the world. If, for whatever reason, we start the day in a "black" mood —set to perceive the worst side of everything— we shall very likely continue along, at least for a while, seeing the black aspect of any situation we encounter. One experimental demonstration of the effect of induced emotion on perception is a study by Murray (1933). Children at a summer camp judged the characteristics of faces in photographs immediately after a scary evening game of "Murder." The amounts of "maliciousness" that the children saw in the faces were appreciably greater than the amounts they had seen when judging the same faces before playing the game.

Values and Attitudes   A person is likely to be set toward perceiving in accord with his values and attitudes. Here, too, we can recognize this inclination in ourselves, and many experimental studies have confirmed the general point. Among the earliest studies is one by Postman, Bruner, and McGinnies (1948), who used the Allport-Vernon Test of Values (see p. 708) to determine each individual's basic values—for example, the relative emphasis upon religious, aesthetic, social, theoretical, and other aspects of life. They then briefly exposed words relating to such values in a tachistoscope and measured the ease with which the words were recognized. Tendencies for quicker recognition clearly occurred on words related to the individual's values; for example, the word "sacred" was more quickly recognized (at a shorter exposure) by a person scoring high on religious values than by a person having other predominant values. Furthermore, there was a tendency for distortions in perception to reflect values— the person higher on religious values might see the word "scared" as "sacred." The stimulus word becomes assimilated and is made to fit with one's system of beliefs and values.

Box 34

Hunger and Skeleton Words

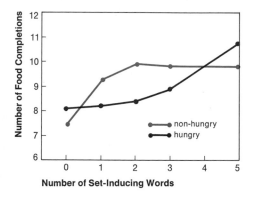

L. Postman and R. S. Crutchfield had 724 undergraduates, some hungry and some not, fill in lists of skeleton words (words with letters omitted). For each skeleton word there were possible both food-related and nonfood-related completions. (For example, "pick--" could be completed as "pickle" or "picket," "-l-k" as "milk" or as "silk.")

The experimenters varied a number of experimental conditions. Among them were the following:

INDUCED SET TOWARD FOOD WORDS To give various groups different amounts of initial set toward food completions, the lists were immediately preceded by set-inducing skeleton words that automatically *forced* food completions. That is, when the first set-inducing skeleton word was "lun - h," all subjects perceived it as "lunch," and presumably this perception provided a certain degree of food set in the solution of succeeding words.

Groups were divided into five degrees of set by varying the number of set-inducing food words from zero to five, as listed in the table.

0	*1*	*2*	*3*	*5*
				lun - h
				d - ss - rt
			lun - h	che - s -
		lun - h	d - ss - rt	b - n - na
	lun - h	d - ss - rt	che - s -	c - - kie
pick - -	pick - -	pick - -	pick - -	pick - -
etc.	etc.	etc.	etc.	etc.
(6.3)	(6.7)	(8.9)	(9.2)	(10.9)

The more initial set-inducing words, the greater the number of food completions (as shown in the table by the average number of food completions in the twenty-one-word list for each of the five groups). An induced set thus does affect the response.

DEGREE OF HUNGER Half the groups were hungry (as ascertained by their own reports at the end of the experiment and as checked by the number of hours since the last meal); the other half were not hungry.

Comparing hungry and nonhungry subjects, Postman and Crutchfield found *no* significant difference in number of food completions, the average values being 8.81 and 9.28, respectively. We see therefore that a state of hunger does not "automatically" produce food-related responses. The *degree* of hunger does, however, make a difference. The effect of hunger or nonhunger *varies depending upon the degree of set evoked.*

As the graph shows, with *zero* set-inducing words preceding the test words, hungry and nonhungry subjects did not differ significantly in number of food completions given. With *one* set-inducing word, the nonhungry subjects gave significantly *more* food completions than did the hungry subjects. For the nonhungry subjects, the effect of the addition of still more initial set-inducing words was to increase the food completions only slightly, whereas for the hungry subjects the effect was accelerated with each additional set-inducing word. With *five* such words, the hungry subjects significantly exceeded the nonhungry in food completions.

Can you account for this difference in the shape of the two curves in the chart?

L. POSTMAN and R. S. CRUTCHFIELD. 1952. The Interaction of Need, Set, and Stimulus-Structure in a Cognitive Task, *Amer. J. Psychol.*, 65, 196–217. Figure adapted by permission.

Interaction of Set Determinants

For illustrative purposes we have attempted to present "pure" examples of the effects of experiential factors and of central factors on set. Yet all these factors are highly interrelated. We can all recognize that strong needs create values and that strongly held values become needs —also that both will frequently arouse strong emotions reflecting these needs and values. Furthermore, it is obvious that we tend to experience more often and more continuously stimuli that are in accord with our needs, values, and dominant emotions, because we can largely choose where we go and therefore what experiences we are likely to encounter. At any one moment of time, therefore, such experiences are apt to be among the most frequent and most recent of experiences. This fact probably helps to account for the extraordinary persistence of attitudes and values, once acquired. Whether it is the stubborn liberal, the chronically fearful neurotic, or the unshakable bigot, we may be reasonably sure that each has maintained, and even strengthened, an attitude from earlier life by perceiving whenever possible stimuli that "fit" his initial set and serve to reinforce it. An experiment by Solomon and Howes (1951) demonstrates the need to disentangle the effects of prior experience and central factors. The experiment shows that the relation between value and recognition threshold found by Postman, Bruner, and McGinnies mostly disappears if the words for the several values are restricted to those of equal familiarity to each subject. In short, the earlier finding was primarily the result of the subjects' greater familiarity with words pertaining to their own valued areas, presumably because they had had more experience with such words.

Some have generalized from this conclusion and have argued that central factors can influence perception only through the mediation of prior experience. This generalization may lead us to a futile chicken-and-egg circularity: We tend to perceive what we have seen more often and more recently, but central factors may determine the situations to which we choose to expose ourselves. The ardent lepidopterist will spot a butterfly in a thicket at fifty yards: Because he likes butterflies? Because he has chased butterflies for years? Because he chased butterflies for years because he liked them "in the first place"? Perhaps the essential point is that perceptual organization in everyday life is rarely, if ever, solely determined by either experiential or central factors. Set, from whatever source, typically plays its part.

Attention

One important way in which perceptual set shows itself is in the perceiver's *attention*, which is a selective focusing upon certain parts or aspects of a situation. What is attended to becomes the "target" of a complex and integrated series of perceptual and motor events. When one looks at an object, for instance, his body swings in the direction of the object, the ocular mechanism turns the eyes until the image of the object falls on the fovea, the lens muscles accommodate in order to bring the image into clearest focus, and so on. In trying to hear a faint sound, one cranes forward, cups his hand behind his ear, and perhaps closes his eyes to eliminate competing visual stimuli.

Some of these actions are voluntary, some "automatic," and others quite beyond conscious control. Also, in a certain sense, we may be able to "pay attention" physiologically to a stimulus even before we become consciously aware of its existence. Tentative evidence for this possibility comes from demonstrations of bodily reactions in experimental subjects to stimuli that are not reported and are therefore presumably below the threshold of awareness. These demonstrations include instances of conditioning (see p. 288) to such apparently subliminal stimuli. Research on this question is difficult because, for one thing, it is difficult to distinguish between what a subject "really" experiences and what he is able or willing to report. Certainly we are able to react to stimulus cues of which we are unaware—the cue of eye convergence in visual distance perception is one example—but whether or not convergence constitutes "paying attention" physiologically is an open, and probably semantic, question.

In recent years extraordinary progress has been made in specifying the physiological mechanisms by which attention operates upon perception (see Unit 16, p. 255); and Russian work on the "orienting reflex," which is discussed in detail in Unit 32, p. 502, has greatly extended our understanding of the complex processes associated with the focusing of attention. For now, however, a discussion of the perceptual aspects of this phenomenon is more apt.

Focus of Attention   That part of the perceptual field that is the center (or focus) of attention is clearer, more salient, more differentiated than are other parts. It tends to stand out as figure against the rest of the field, which is ground.

A focus of attention is usually brief. Attention shifts constantly from one part to another. These shifts in visual attention, for instance, may be objectively measured by recording successive eye movements while a person looks at an object. Figure 11.4. illustrates the course of fixation while a picture is being viewed.

Attention shifts for several reasons. For one thing, there is probably in attention, as in many psychological processes, a form of "satiation" that tends to inhibit the continuation of attention in a given direction. Attention will thus tend to shift "spontaneously" after a period of focus on one part of the field. Furthermore, the shifting of attention serves an essential function in achieving total perceptual organization. With complex stimulus patterns it is impossible to organize the whole in a single glance; there must be successive steps of "exploration" of the pattern, each part or aspect being fixated in turn. In each part of Figure 11.4., rough outlines

of the picture are beginning to appear in the path that is traced by successive fixations after only a relatively brief period of exploration. Over longer periods we sometimes find that the cumulative record of fixation points essentially reproduces, in crude fashion, the essential details of the object being viewed.

Such tracing seems to be, at least in part, a learned tendency. Evidence is accumulating, so far mainly from Russian investigators (Zaporozhets, 1961, for example), that in early stages of the development of visual perception eye movements do not tend to follow the outlines of objects or to concentrate upon their more figural features. This general conclusion is

Figure 11.4 The successive fixations at various points when a picture is being viewed, as recorded by a camera that photographed eye movements of the observer. Note the differences in eye-movement patterns between a male (a) and a female (b) viewing the same painting.
Museum of Art, Carnegie Institute, Pittsburgh; by permission of *Life* Magazine.

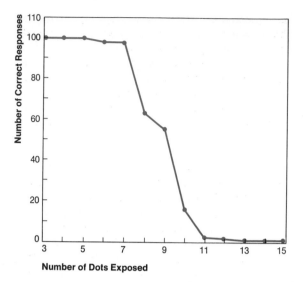

Figure 11.5. A curve giving the results of measuring the span of apprehension for one observer, who estimated the number of black dots (varying from three to fifteen) on white cards exposed for split-second intervals in a tachistoscope. Note that the number of correct responses dropped sharply beyond seven dots. Eleven dots were clearly beyond the span of apprehension.
A. D. Glanville and K. M. Dallenbach, "The Range of Attention," *American Journal of Psychology*, 41 (1929), 207–36; adapted by permission.

corded eye-movement patterns in response to the *names* of new objects and noted a tendency for these patterns to correspond to those observed when the object itself was being viewed. This correspondence seemed to be only temporary; it occurred only in the "middle stage" of the verbal learning process and disappeared when the name had been well learned. The implication, of course, is that eye movements may play some kind of mediating role in learning new words. This suggestion of so intimate a connection between the course of attention in visual—and perhaps other forms of perceptual exploration—and the acquisition of language merits further study.

drawn by several investigators from studies of children, of adults whose sight had been restored through surgery, and of individuals with brain injuries who were gradually reacquiring the ability to perceive visual patterns. What seems to come earlier in the learning process for such individuals is a tendency to trace the outlines of an object or pattern with their fingers and only later to substitute eye movements for this manual tracing. Eye-movement tracing seems to have an adaptive function; procedures especially designed to induce children and adults to trace the contours of objects visually have been found to aid visual learning and relearning.

In this context, Zaporozhets (1961) reports a fascinating observation by one of his associates, Zinchenko. Zinchenko photographically re-

Span of Apprehension Obviously the main necessity for a shift of attention is the severe limitation on the sheer amount of material that can be included within the focus of attention at one moment. One experimental approach to this problem of the maximal scope of the focus of attention is the studies on the *span of apprehension;* this term refers to the maximum number of objects that can be immediately perceived—perceived, in other words, during a time too brief to permit counting or eye movements. Scatter a small number of beans on a table. Take a very quick glimpse and try to see how many beans there are. After many tries with different numbers of beans, you will find that you will make few errors with up to five or six beans but that errors will occur when there are more beans. Figure 11.5. is a graph of the results of a careful experiment of this kind, in which a tachistoscope that exposed the stimuli for only one-fifth of a second was used.

Distribution of Attention The attention of a person at any one moment may be distributed in various ways over the whole field. It can be concentrated at one point, with little attention available for the rest. It may be diffusely spread so that no particular part is primarily in focus.

It may be divided; the person may be trying to attend to two or more things simultaneously.

There are strict limits to the extent of divided attention. The more the division, the more the loss in quality of attention devoted to each part. Evidence for this is given in several kinds of experimental studies. In one, weak pressure was applied to one finger of each hand, and the person had to say which pressure was stronger; at the same instant there was a brief visual exposure of from three to six lines, and the person had to count them. Either task when done alone was easy enough and the result was nearly perfect performance. But when the two had to be done simultaneously, with divided attention, performance on each was much poorer. Both correct answers were obtained only 12 per cent of the time; one of two correct answers was obtained only 60 per cent of the time.

Organization and Attention The limited span of apprehension and the fact that the greater the division of attention, the greater the loss in its quality, emphasize the value of perceptual organization. When parts of the field are organized into larger wholes, the attention required to perceive them effectively is less than when the parts must be attended to separately.

By grouping of objects, the span of apprehension may be extended. If nine beans fall into three clusters of three beans each, they may be correctly seen. This fact is a simple illustration of the general point that organization has the function of enabling the perceiver to cope with more material, and it helps to explain how it is possible for us to perceive complex situations with the merest glance. The necessry organizations are already available, and the stimuli "fit" into them without need for careful attention to each. The result is great efficeincy, of course; but errors may occur when certain details are wrong but go unnoticed because they "fit" well enough into the organization and cannot be picked out without careful attention. (You may

have failed to notice three printing errors in this paragraph because you were so absorbed in the meaningful organization of the content that slight errors in letters did not emerge above the attention threshold, particularly as the wrong letters did not seriously violate the proper structural appearance of the words. This phenomenon is the so-called "proofreader's illusion.")

Determinants of Attention Attention is commonly spoken of as either voluntary or involuntary. The former pertains to cases in which the individual seems to have freedom to determine his own focus of attention, freedom to choose deliberately what he will attend to. How this freedom is possible and what is really meant by "voluntary" are difficult questions, which we shall take up later, under the topic of motivation.

Involuntary attention pertains to cases in which a person seems less the agent who chooses the direction of his attention and more the pawn of "forces" that require him to attend this way or that. Some of the determinants of involuntary attention are related to the goal-directed behavior of the person. The attention of the starving man is drawn irresistibly to the food in the restaurant window. Other determinants are related to the more enduring characteristics of the stimulus objects in the environment; these objects may be such as "naturally" to attract, demand, seize, and compel his attention, despite what other activity is going on and despite what he seeks "voluntarily" to attend to.

The attention-demanding properties of stimuli have been extensively studied by the experimentalist in the laboratory and by the applied practitioner in advertising, in dress design, and in other fields. A convenient classification of these properties has been suggested by Berlyne (1966), and we shall employ his schema in organizing our partial inventory of them.

First, there are "psychophysical properties."

Among them are intensity (the bright light, the loud noise, the overwhelming odor), movement and change (the wigwag at the railroad crossing), repetition (the attention-capturing, if grating, effect of the oft-repeated slogan in a television commercial), and isolation (the startling impact of a single word occupying an otherwise totally blank page of magazine advertising). Asymmetrical and irregular stimulus patterns also draw the eye. Such properties are probably universal in their action, having little if anything to do with the individual characteristics of the perceiver; they seem just "naturally" to compel attention. A second class of attention-getting properties, in contrast, is directly dependent upon just such characteristics and is based on one's past experience and current motivational state. Here is included the undeniable attention value of the sight of a hated enemy or of a longed-for loved one, a property that seems to reside "in" the stimulus object but that emanates, of course, from one's own prior experiences with these objects. Also in this class is the immediate attention we pay to stimuli related to our momentary need states: The whiff of a broiling steak can be instantly alerting when we are hungry but can pass totally unnoticed when we are not.

A final class of attention-demanding properties is what Berlyne calls "collative variables," so named because, roughly speaking, they seem to rely for their effectiveness upon collation, or comparison, between stimuli, past or present. Novelty, one of the most reliable attractors of attention, thus depends upon the contrast between the novel stimulus, the like of which we have never before seen (or at least not for some time), and the familiar one. Closely related to novelty are such characteristics as incongruity and surprise, both of which draw our attention because the presented stimulus fails to "fit" our momentary set or expectation. The life-of-the-party male who dons his wife's hat draws our reluctant attention because he has brought two familiar items (a man's body and a woman's hat) into incongruous juxtaposition. And he can have much the same effect by suddenly appearing in a false beard. A bearded man is neither novel nor incongruous, but, in this case, the sight is unexpected.

The complexity of a stimulus pattern is yet another determinant of attention, but here the situation is somewhat complicated. With the other collative variables, an increase in degree of novelty, of incongruity, or of surprise leads to an increase in power to command attention. Not so with complexity. We are not inevitably drawn to stimuli of greater complexity; rather, it appears that individuals have a certain optimum complexity level that is most likely to attract their attention. Patterns at this complexity level are more attention-getting than those either more or less complex. We treat this question in detail in Unit 32 (see especially Box 113, p. 504) when we reconsider the problem of attention as a motivational as well as perceptual phenomenon.

Nature and Limits of Perceptual Modification

In making our case for the susceptibility of perception to "extraneous" factors, we have underplayed the characteristics of the stimulus situation that permit and even invite the selective or distorting influence of past experience and central factors. The resulting image of perception as a frail and suggestible process does not jibe with the highly accurate perceptual consensus that most people achieve in most situations. Hallucinations are exceedingly rare phenomena and even more rarely are shared with another person. We all usually see much the same thing, and the same thing is what is really "there."

The apparent contradiction is easily resolved; experimental demonstrations of perceptual modification almost always employ stimulus situations that in some way are atypical. Patterns are briefly exposed in a tachisto-scope, blanks are left in words, ambiguous pictures are used. In short, situations are contrived so that the factors that typically ensure accurate perception are quite weak. This lack of "structure" in the stimulus is the crux of the matter. This point has been implicit throughout our discussion; it merits closer examination.

Structure of Stimulus Pattern

Stimulus patterns may be arranged along a dimension of strength of structure. A stimulus pattern is said to be strongly structured when the stimuli are clear, intense, simple, and subject to strong grouping factors so that it can be perceptually organized in only one way. A stimulus pattern is said to be weakly structured when the stimuli are barely perceptible, unclear, complex, and not subject to strong grouping factors. A strongly structured stimulus pattern easily evokes a stable perception that is resistant to change—one in which the figure and ground are firmly established. A weakly structured stimulus pattern may be difficult to organize at all, or it may evoke, as in reversible figures, several alternative perceptions, each unstable and easily changed (there are even "impossibly" structured patterns, as in Figure 11.6.). It is with such ambiguous patterns that "extraneous" factors are most effective. This does not imply, however, that modifying factors like needs are most detectable when structure is at its weakest. It that were the case, a blank screen would provide the liveliest arena for the operation of set. A hungry subject is more likely to say "meat," however, when the stimulus is "me - t" than when it is "m - - t." A certain intermediate degree of structure is most sensitive to the effects of prior experience and central factors. This principle is used in projective tests of personality (see p. 719), which provide enough stimulus structure to put necessary limits on possible percepts but also enough leeway to assure a sufficient range of response among individuals, a range attributable to differing need strengths and personality styles. As in Box 35, p. 186. responses must be kept "on the point" by maintenance of a certain degree of stimulus structure, lest the variety of percepts becomes so enormous that they would defy classification and interpretation. Even in dreams, which would seem to represent zero stimulus structuring, we typically tend to employ the day's events as a fragile framework within which we weave our hopes and fears.

It should be clear why psychologists have found it essential to devise the ingenious stimulus situations that typify research on perceptual modification and change.

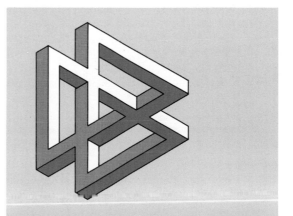

Figure 11.6. An impossible object. The lines are so connected that, as the eye systematically follows any surface, sudden perceptual "reinterpretations" of the orientation of the figure, of the relative distance of its various parts, and of other elements occur in a continuing, and necessarily futile, attempt to achieve a stable organization of an inherently unstable figure. (After Penrose & Penrose, 1958.)

Box 35

Chack = Chick or Check?

E. M. Siipola showed words in a tachistoscope for one-tenth of a second each. The subject's task was to identify and report each word. Half the 160 subjects were informed beforehand that the words would have to do with animals or birds; the other half were informed that the words would have to do with travel or transportation. Among the words were six "nonsense" words, so designed that they were *fairly close in structure to meaningful words* in the two categories, as indicated in the list.

NONSENSE WORD SHOWN IN TACHISTOSCOPE	POSSIBLE WAY PERCEPTION OF NONSENSE WORD COULD BE DISTORTED TO FIT	
	A. Animal or Bird Category	B. Travel or Transportation Category
chack	chick	check
sael	seal	sail
wharl	whale	wharf
pasrot	parrot	passport
dack	duck	deck
pengion	penguin	pension

The group instructed to expect animal or bird words responded to the nonsense words with 63 per cent A responses and 11 per cent B responses. Conversely, the other group, instructed to expect travel or transportation words, gave only 14 per cent A responses and 74 per cent B responses. The subjects perceived the nonsense words in accordance with their respective sets, and they did so by distorting each nonsense word to a meaningful form. For example, the letter "a" in "chack" was altered either to "i" or to "e" by the subject without his realizing it.

E. M. SIIPOLA. 1935. A Study of Some Effects of Preparatory Set, *Psychol. Monogr.*, 46, No. 210. Table adapted by permission of American Psychological Association.

Glossary

attention The focusing of perception involving a heightened awareness of a limited part of the perceptual field.

figural aftereffect Distorted perception, shortly after prolonged exposure to one stimulus pattern, of a new stimulus pattern falling on the same region of the receptor. Some experiments have suggested that this phenomenon is related to self-satiation.

retinal rivalry The fluctuation in the appearance of the visual field when the two eyes are separately stimulated with incompatible colors or patterns.

reversible figures Stimulus patterns that give rise to a "spontaneous" oscillation between two or more alternative perceptual organizations. The Necker cube is a classical example of a reversible figure.

set A readiness of the organism to make a particular response or class of responses. Motor sets are readiness for particular actions; mental sets, for particular thought processes; perceptual sets, for particular organizations of stimuli.

span of apprehension The maximal number of objects or items that can be immediately perceived with an exposure so brief that there is no time for counting or eye movements. The span of apprehension is increased by grouping the items.

UNIT
1

space and depth perception

overview / Various cues from the same sense or even from different senses typically give rise to a unified, though not necessarily accurate, impression of space. The perceived distance of a sound is mainly determined by its loudness, whereas both binaural cues and head movements are necessary to pinpoint the direction of its source. In the visual world, all stimuli act upon a two-dimensional retina, yet visual space is typically experienced as three-dimensional. Monocular cues or binocular cues alone can convey depth, but for a fully convincing impression a synthesis of information from both types of cues is necessary.

Does the organism have to learn how to perceive three-dimensional space? Evidence on this question has been obtained from individuals who were deprived of sensory experience from birth, tested very soon after birth, or raised in special environments designed to modify space perception. Innate spatial ability does seem to exist, but, clearly, spatial perception improves with maturation and can be significantly modified by experience.

We experience space through hearing, touching, moving, seeing. These different sensory experiences do not lead to different spaces but to a single unified space. In this same single space we can see objects localized at different places, can hear them localized, can feel them localized. The various senses provide different avenues to the perception of this unified space; it is just as appropriate to say that we hear space as to say that we see space and feel space.

The perceptual problem is one of synthesizing information from all these sources, because there is not always perfect agreement among the impressions of space that the different senses provide. There are striking cases of discrepancies between feeling space and seeing it. When we move about in complete darkness, the size and arrangement of a room may seem quite different from its size and arrangement when we can see it. At any given moment, however, the various cues are usually in harmony; the resulting single, firm impression of space is nevertheless not necessarily correct.

For example, sound effects in a play are produced offstage; the speaker at a drive-in movie is inches away at your side, not behind the screen. In neither case do conflicting impressions occur, despite the incompatible spatial information from visual and auditory stimuli. One set of cues is typically dominant. In plays and movies the visual stimuli are dominant, so that only by closing one's eyes can the locus of the sound source be detected. Recall the greater ability of the blind to judge the size, the distance, and even the texture of objects (see Box 20, p. 136). It is intriguing to realize that the blind do not show exceptional development of auditory acuity. Their advantage lies in their greater ability to employ auditory contexts. Given known and fixed sound sources, the blind can locate new sounds more accurately, apparently through a greater ability to organize a complex auditory pattern. They seem to have greater skill than do the sighted in maintaining a spatial map based on auditory landmarks and in pinpointing new auditory stimuli by reference to such a map (Fisher, 1964).

Space Through Sound

It is convenient to distinguish two aspects of a spatial organization based upon auditory cues. Precise location of the separate sound sources requires accurate perception of both the distance of the source and its direction.

Distance of Sounds

Perceived distance is determined by a number of characteristics of the sound waves. The major stimulus characteristic is the amplitude of the sound waves reaching the ear. Loud sounds tend to be heard as coming from closer objects and soft sounds as coming from more distant objects. Often, while we are listening, the intensity of the sound changes, and our perception of its distance changes correspondingly. As the sound grows louder, it seems to approach; as the sound grows softer, it seems to recede.

As a complex sound wave travels through the air, its complexity (hence its timbre) diminishes. For example, the sound waves reaching the ear from a violin at a distance have fewer overtones than do sound waves reaching the ear from a violin nearby. Timbre thus serves as another factor that determines the localization of sounds. All other things being equal, the more complex a sound, the closer to the perceiver it is likely to be localized.

These cues raise a question. Because, for example, in the natural world loud sounds usually do tend to come from nearer sources, does loudness serve as a distance cue based on what we have learned through experience? Once again the nature-nurture controversy makes its appearance. At the moment, however, we only pose the question. Later on, when we grapple with the issue, it will become clear that the origins of space perception constitute one of the most challenging problems of modern psychology.

Direction of Sounds

Under normal conditions, most of us are able to locate the direction of sound sources simply by hearing, even without the benefit of other cues. To understand the way in which this location is accomplished, we must first understand the difficulty of identifying a sound's direction with only one ear.

As we have seen, sound waves are agitations of the air that spread out in all directions from a sound source. The agitated air, when it comes in contact with the eardrums, carries, however, no "message" concerning the direction from which the agitation has traveled. If a single ear is stimulated in turn by sound waves coming from two equally loud sources at the same distance but from different directions, the effects of the two sets of sound waves on the ear are identical, and it is impossible to distinguish a directional difference.

Binaural Cues But with both ears sounds may be localized with great accuracy. The cues making possible sound localization by both ears are called *binaural cues*.

The nature of binaural cues has been systematically investigated by fixing a person's head in a sound cage and requiring him to judge the direction of sounds coming from various locations on the surface of the surrounding sphere (see Figure 12.1.).

When a sound is presented to the right or left of the median plane (the vertical plane passing through the middle of the head from front to back), the person knows which side the sound is coming from. Analysis of the physical situation immediately shows that, if the sound originates on the right side, it reaches the closer right ear a split second sooner than it reaches the more distant left ear. This slight time difference provides an essential cue to direction. Even when the time difference at the two ears is as little as 30 millionths of a second, the side from which the sound comes can be correctly identified. This time difference is far shorter than the person can consciously recognize; the effect occurs through an "automatic" integrating process in the auditory nervous system.

A simple and dramatic check on the hypothesis that the perception of direction is dependent upon the time difference at the two ears is provided by experiments with the pseudophone (see Figure 12.2.). Under these experimentally contrived artificial conditions, the sound that is actually on the right is heard as coming from the left.

There is a second important cue, an intensity difference, which arises from the stimulus difference at the two ears when a sound is to one side. A sound source on one side of the head will deliver a slightly more intense sound to the ear on that side. Though the distance difference is a factor, the effect is primarily caused

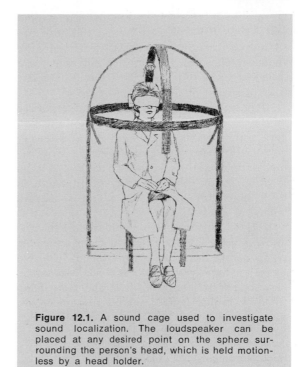

Figure 12.1. A sound cage used to investigate sound localization. The loudspeaker can be placed at any desired point on the sphere surrounding the person's head, which is held motionless by a head holder.

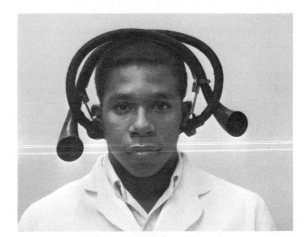

Figure 12.2. The pseudophone. A sound coming from the right side would normally first strike the right ear and then the left, but the tubes of the pseudophone divert it so that it reaches the left ear first. The effect is to reverse the perceived direction of the sound, so that it appears to come from the left side.

by the sound "shadow" cast by the head; sound waves that have to pass around the head are somewhat disrupted and their intensity slightly reduced. These slight intensity differences are sufficient to help us locate the sound correctly to left or right of the median plane.

If, however, the sound comes from anywhere in the median plane itself, it strikes the two ears simultaneously and with equal intensity and is thus heard as being somewhere in the median plane. But the person cannot tell its location in the plane; it may be in front, in back, above, or below. This plane is, then, a "plane of confusion."

The two binaural cues of differences in time and intensity are thus not sufficient to enable us to determine localization from all possible directions. And yet such localization is possible. How can it be accomplished? The main additional stimulus factor is head movement, or, more precisely, the additional stimuli to which such movement gives rise.

Head Movements Normally, when we are trying to localize sounds, we move our heads, often so slightly that the movement is not noticeable. These head movements, by alternately bringing one ear or the other closer to the source of the sound, enable us to discriminate among directions of sound that are otherwise indistinguishable. Rotating one's head from right to left enables one to tell a sound directly in front from one directly in back; for, as the head turns toward the left, a sound from in front arrives relatively sooner and more loudly at the right ear than at the left ear. Similarly, by tilting one's head from side to side, one can tell a sound directly above from one directly below. The combination of angles of head movement and of changes of stimulation pattern at the two ears "pins down" the exact location of a sound source. (The blind subjects in Box 20, p. 136, you will recall, employed this cue consistently.)

Taken together, all these facts about localization of sounds provide an excellent illustra-

tion of how perceptual organization works in the "solution" of the problem of space. Stimulus information from both ears, as well as from other receptor systems, is synthesized in an orderly, efficient, and "spontaneous" fashion to provide a compelling impression of auditory space (see Box 36, p. 193). The story will be repeated and extended in our analysis of visual space perception.

The Perception of Visual Depth

All visual stimuli act upon the retina, which is an essentially flat two-dimensional surface. Yet visual space is typically experienced as having depth, and objects are localized at some distance in a three-dimensional framework. In some way, therefore, two-dimensional information must be made to yield a three-dimensional experience. The various mechanisms contributing to this transformation can best be discussed under two main headings: monocular cues and binocular cues.

Monocular Cues for Depth

"In the world of the blind, the one-eyed man is king." For even a man with a solitary eye can achieve the marvels of seeing, and among these marvels is the ability to perceive depth. Normally, depth perception is enhanced by two eyes, just as the perception of direction of sounds is better with two ears. Useful visual depth perception can also be achieved, however, through various *monocular depth cues*, some pertaining to the visual pattern, some to the muscle adjustments of the eye, some to head movements.

Cues From the Visual Pattern To achieve the impression of depth solely from a visual pattern on a flat canvas is a problem of the artist. We all know how successfully this problem can be solved. At one point, when stress in art was on realistic representation, the "eye-fooling" (*trompe-l'oeil*) painters vied with one another

Box 36

Locating Sounds
by Head Movement

H. Wallach has conducted an experiment in which the sound source is constantly kept directly in front of the head. The sound source moves automatically as the head turns, much as in the case of the donkey with a carrot suspended from a pole attached to its head. There is a continuous buzz from the sound source, and the subject tries to locate it in space, being permitted to turn his head only to right and left. He thus receives kinesthetic cues that his head is moving, but at the same time there is no change in the auditory stimuli at the two ears.

The person hears the sound directly *overhead*—an entirely sensible "fitting together" of the two facts that there is movement of the head and that the sounds at the two ears do not change. For, as we can readily see, this stimulus situation is precisely the one that prevails when the sound is *actually* directly overhead. Here we see, then, a demonstration of the elegant workings of the perceptual system.

Another very striking fact is that the system is concerned with *phenomenal* relations, not necessarily with actual stimulus events. The figure illustrates the setup. The individual is seated on a stool inside the striped drum. His head is fixed and a sound is presented continuously and directly in front of him. The striped drum is set into motion; this motion gives the subject the impression that he is whirling about, although he is actually completely at rest. *Where does he hear the sound?*

Here again the astute reader will be able to figure out the necessary outcome. Again the sound is heard directly *overhead*—despite the fact that the head is *stationary* and the auditory stimuli at the two ears do not change, a situation that would normally lead to hearing the sound directly in *front*. What has happened, obviously, is that the *subjective impression* of movement, when combined with the fact of no auditory stimulus changes at the two ears, can make simple sense only if the sound is perceived as coming from directly overhead.

H. WALLACH. 1940. The Role of Head Movements and Vestibular and Visual Cues in Sound Localization, *J. Exp. Psychol.*, 27, 339–68.

in the use of devices to simulate depth, and one triumphed by painting velvet curtains on his picture so convincingly that his discomfited rival reached out to draw back these "curtains," thinking to see the painting beneath.

The ability to see tridimensionality from a flat picture seems to appear in life without specific training. Hochberg and Brooks (1962), a husband-and-wife team of psychologists, raised their son to the age of nineteen months with little or no exposure to *pictures* of three-dimensional objects. Nevertheless, when tested at that age, he was easily able to identify familiar objects (which he had experienced only in their three-dimensional form) from pictures of these objects.

Figure 12.3. illustrates some of the following features of a flat visual pattern, which give it the appearance of depth by making the objects appear to be at different distances from the observer. Several of these cues also help to define which area will be figure and which ground in the stimulus pattern. And it will be remembered that one characteristic of the figure is that it appears to stand out in front of the ground.

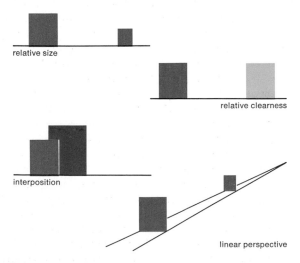

relative size

relative clearness

interposition

linear perspective

Figure 12.3. Some monocular cues for the perception of depth.

1. *Interposition:* An object that partly covers another object tends to be seen as the closer.
2. *Relative size:* The larger of two objects tends to be seen as the closer.
3. *Relative height:* The lower of two objects tends to be seen as the nearer.
4. *Relative clearness:* The clearer and more detailed the object, the closer it tends to seem visually.
5. *Linear perspective:* The greater the convergence of lines, the greater the impression of distance.
6. *Light and shadow:* Certain patterns of light and shadow favor the impression of depth. In general, areas of lighter shades of color or brighter intensities tend to be seen as nearer (see Figure 12.4.). But learning can upset this rule (see p. 202).

An ambitious attempt to subsume most or all of these cues under a single general concept —*stimulus gradient*—is described in Box 37, p. 196.

Relative Movement The listed cues from the stimulus pattern refer to what happens at a single moment in time. Another kind of cue is given by the temporal pattern of visual stimuli that occurs when the head moves from side to side. If we look at a flat picture, the relations among objects within the picture do not change, of course, when the head moves. But, in the case of objects with actual depth differences among them, head movements do make for changes in the stimulus pattern of objects viewed from successively different angles. Specifically, as the head moves to the left, nearer objects appear displaced to the right and farther objects to the left of one another. This *relative movement* (or *movement parallax*) is a powerful monocular cue for depth.

The effect can be simply demonstrated. Hold a pencil at arm's length, so that it is almost in line with any vertical object in the room, for example, a lamp. Close one eye. Though you know that the pencil is closer, it will barely appear so. Furthermore, both objects will seem to "float" in the distance, as neither is well localized by the available cues, especially if few objects and textures occupy the intervening space. Now, keeping the one eye closed, move your head horizontally. Even a very slight movement, especially if it is rapid, will convey an immediate depth impression.

Accommodation The light rays coming from an object at which we are looking are focused by the lens system of the eye in such a way as to achieve the clearest image. This *accommodation* is accomplished by the pull of the eye muscles that shape the lens into the appropriate curvature. To focus on a distant object, the lens must be flattened, and, to focus on a nearby object, it must be made rounder. When one looks at a close object, for example a book in one's hand, the amount of accommodation is thus quite different from that when one looks at a picture on a far wall.

Kinesthetic sensations from the different amounts of pull on eye muscles provide cues to the distance of the object. Because there are only minimal changes in the amount of accommodation beyond a distance of a few feet, however, such cues are effective in depth perception only for short distances. This fact can be shown by a variation on the demonstration with the pencil. Instead of moving your head, bring the pencil very slowly toward your open eye. At some point it will begin to blur, and, simultaneously, the depth difference will become clearly apparent. This illustration of the cue is exaggerated because one becomes clearly aware of a loss of sharp focus; it can be shown to operate effectively at some distance before actual blurring (and awareness) takes place.

Binocular Cues for Depth

When we look with both eyes—in binocular vision—we obtain different images of the object without head movements, because each eye looks at the object from a slightly different angle. The difference in images on the two eyes is known as *retinal disparity*.

Retinal Disparity To the maximum possible degree the perceiver seeks to harmonize and syn-

Figure 12.4. Aerial view of Ventura, California. A portion of the city is shown sprawling at the foot of mountains; roads run through ravines. But turn the page upside down. When the photograph is inverted, the usual light-shadow relationships (based on overhead lighting) are reversed. The roads now appear to wind along the *crests* of the ridge, and part of the city (at the top center) seems to hang on the edge of a deep chasm.
Pacific Air Industries.

thesize all available cues. The two different retinal images are brought together and fused whenever possible. The degree to which fusion occurs depends upon the degree of consonance of the two images. If they can be fitted together to produce a single unified field, this effect is favored. In the typical case, of course, the different views are minutely different perspectives of the same physical object or scene. But some disparity between the two stimulus patterns, however slight, does exist and must be perceptually reconciled. The almost universal solution is a percept of the simplest possible organization, a single fused three-dimensional image. Julesz (1964) has shown that retinal disparity *alone*, with all monocular cues and convergence (see the following section on convergence) eliminated, is enough to produce the impression of depth.

These facts make possible the *stereoscope*, a device for giving the impression of depth when viewing flat photographs (see Box 38, p. 198, for an explanation of how the stereoscope works).

Convergence If the two images are to fall on essentially the same retinal region, *convergence* of the two eyes must occur. The eyes swing their lines of sight so that they both are oriented directly toward the object being viewed or, more precisely—remembering the stereoscope—toward where the object appears to be. Strictly speaking, convergence as a cue for depth refers only to the kinesthetic sensations arising momentarily from muscles controlling the swing of the eyes during a change in focus.

As with accommodation, there need be no conscious awareness of muscular changes. And, as another parallel feature, convergence is also only a short-distance cue. When the objects are far away, the lines of sight become almost parallel and the amount of convergence insignificant; for distances greater than fifty or sixty feet, the convergence cue is not effective in aiding the perception of depth. When the object is too near, convergence fails, fusion is not possible, depth is lost, and "double vision" results (see p. 234).

The Synthesis of Depth Cues

We have analyzed the monocular and binocular cues for depth one at a time. But the most compelling and full-bodied experience of depth comes when many cues work simultaneously.

Situations often occur in which the cues are not harmonious; for instance when there are oddities in the spatial arrangements of objects, when the illumination is unusual, or when the stimulus pattern is poorly structured. In such situations the various cues may tend in contradictory directions, competing rather than cooperating, and the impression of depth may thereby be weakened or altered. This kind of situation can be artificially induced in the labo-

Box 37

Depth Through
Gradients

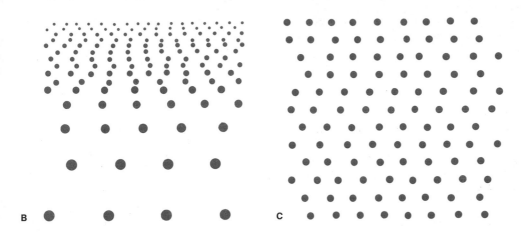

In normal viewing of the three-dimensional world, most surfaces that extend outward in depth from us have visible textures. A vivid example is a pebbly beach; thickly woven rugs, wood-paneled walls, and acoustical-tile ceilings are also typical high-textured surfaces spanning the distance from our eyes to nearby or far-off objects.

A uniform texture on the physical surface (px in Figure A) is necessarily projected on the retina (p′x′) in such a way that the density near x′ is greater than the density near p′. The greater the distance away, the greater the density of texture in the retinal pattern.

J. J. Gibson argues that such density differences, or stimulus gradients, are adequate cues for the perception of depth. Figure B, for example, is a stimulus pattern in which sizes of spots and distances between them decrease regularly from the bottom to the top. This stimulus pattern corresponds to the pattern of stimulation that is impinging on the retina in Figure A. The result is a convincing impression of a continuous receding plane, whether the pattern arises from a horizontal plane actually receding from us (as in Figure A) or from a frontal flat plane with no variation whatever in distance of points from our eyes (as in Figure B). In one case we have an accurate percept, in the other a depth illusion. One test of Gibson's hypothesis for depth perception (or anyone's hypothesis to explain any phenomenon) is whether or not it is possible to create the phenomenon "artificially" by abstracting only those aspects of the situation that are specified by the hypothesis. In this illustration the test has been passed.

Figure C has a zero gradient, that is, a perfectly regular spacing of dots. Consequently, according to Gibson's hypothesis, it gives no impression of depth. Yet such a retinal pattern might arise from an *actually* extended plane.

Gibson offers illustrations indicating that other depth cues are merely special cases of stimulus gradients on the retina. In the case of relative clearness, the light from distant objects in the environment is more diffused by the time it reaches the eye than is light from nearby objects; as a result there is a gradient of clarity among their corresponding images on the retina.

J. J. GIBSON. 1950. *The Perception of the Visual World* (Boston: Houghton Mifflin).

Box 38

The Stereoscope
and 3-D

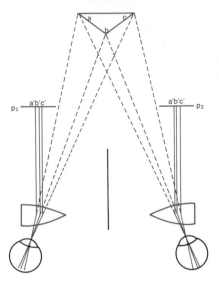

Because binocular disparity is such a powerful depth cue, it should be possible to produce an artificial impression of depth by giving each eye a slightly different picture and making the eyes converge as they would if they were looking at the real three-dimensional object.

This reasoning led the English physicist Wheatstone to invent the *stereoscope* (1838). There are several different types. The most common is the prism stereoscope shown in the figure. The two flat pictures, p_1 and p_2, are presented to the two eyes separately. The partition prevents each from seeing the picture intended for the other eye. The light rays from the pictures are bent by the prisms so that they seem to reach the eyes from a three-dimensional object, abc, on which the eyes are converged. The distances between a, b, and c differ slightly in pictures p_1 and p_2, as the retinal images would if the subject were actually looking at the real object.

The necessary photographs can be taken by moving the camera into two successive positions, or more simply with the stereocamera, now in common use, which has two lenses and takes two pictures from slightly different angles simultaneously. The lenses can be placed somewhat farther apart than the eyes actually are, and such placement accentuates the depth impression.

The so-called "3-D" movies, which had a short-lived vogue, are produced by a somewhat different stereoscopic device. Two disparate views are projected on the screen by light polarized in two different planes. The viewer wears Polaroid frames so that each eye receives only the appropriate picture. The resulting three-dimensional effect is astonishing, as viewers who have "dodged" objects thrown toward the audience and observed new depth in feminine charms will testify.

Other currently popular devices to give depth impression in the movies are based on entirely different principles, primarily those involving monocular cues. In Cinerama, for example, the depth impression is achieved by the use of a very large, curved screen on which three closely coordinated and synchronized pictures are projected from three angles. The spectator seems to be surrounded by the picture, and the various gradients of texture, movement, and so on, together with multiple sound sources (stereophonic sound), are especially effective in simulating depth.

ratory in order to study the way cues interact. For instance, by pitting the cue of interposition against the cue of relative size, we can distort the depth perception of objects. Figure 12.5. presents an interesting illustration from an experiment in which this distortion of depth was successfully achieved.

The perception of depth, therefore, cannot be thought of as a simple summation of the various cues. In general, the perceptual process seems to weigh the various cues and in this way derives a "reasonable" percept of space. But where do these cue weights come from, and why is it that their integration usually results in something "reasonable"? In Figure 12.5. the cue of interposition is dominant. Is it dominant because it can be interpreted unequivocally and thus provides a more strongly organized percept than does relative size?

Brunswik (1956) presents a convincing case for such a position. His general point is that the relative influence of a cue in perception can be almost perfectly predicted from its "ecological validity"; that is, the cues that generally prove to be more accurate in the person's environment are more heavily credited by him in depth perception.

A typical experiment by Brunswik would study the person's perception *not* in the laboratory but rather in his natural environment (ecology). The subject walks about on the street or in a park and is occasionally asked to report on the relative distances of objects in his field of view at a given moment. The experimenter then actually measures the physical distance of each object and records all the depth cues that might have been used in the situation. By relating the presence of these cues both to the subject's judgments and to the measured distances, it becomes possible to determine how much over-all importance the subject has attached to a given cue and how often its use has led to correct distance perception. For example, it has been found that interposition—perhaps the most reliable cue available for depth perception—is in fact typi-

cally assigned most weight when it is available. On the other hand, retinal size—a quite unreliable cue—is hardly used in making distance judgments even when it is available. It would be inconvenient, to say the least, if we were to attempt to touch the building across the street while despairing of any attempt to reach the aspirin close at hand.

The Origins of Space

How does it come about that the various depth cues can be integrated to yield a perception of space? This question has beset philosophers and scientists for centuries. Is this integration something gradually *learned* through the organism's adjustment to its environment—as

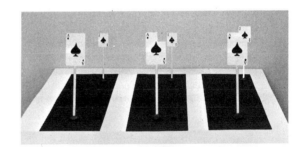

Figure 12.5. Two playing cards of the usual size are attached vertically to stands at different distances from the observer. The room is darkened so that only the cards are visible. The observer uses only one eye, and head movements are not permitted. In this situation (left panel), apart from the possible minimal contribution of relative clearness and accommodation, the effective monocular cue is *relative size*. As playing cards are familiar objects of known size, the smaller retinal image generated by the more distant card makes it seem farther away.

But then a corner is clipped from the nearer card, as in center panel, and the position of the farther stand is precisely adjusted so that in the observer's retinal image the edges of the farther card exactly fit the cutout edges of the nearer card. As shown in right panel, the more distant card now appears *in front of* the objectively closer one. The cue of *interposition* is sufficiently powerful to overcome that of known size. The result is distorted perception on two counts: Relative distance is incorrectly judged, and the objectively farther card is shrunk to an improbable miniature version of its real dimensions.

Brunswik's "ecological validity" concept suggests—or is it "given" through the inherent nature of the organism? The former is an "empiristic" and the latter a "nativistic" interpretation.

There are three main experimental strategies for evaluating this question; we shall present them in the visual sense modality, though they can apply in all senses.

1. An individual is deprived of visual experience by being raised in the dark until his spatial perception is to be tested.
2. Perceptual testing is conducted as soon as possible after birth to minimize opportunities for prior learning.
3. The individual's visual experience is carefully controlled and manipulated prior to testing to discover whether the cues for space perception are determined or modified by experience.

Experience Deprivation

Box 39, p. 201, presents the earliest systematic study of experience deprivation. The method makes possible the use of more complex perceptual situations and responses, as the subject may be relatively mature by the time testing takes place. It runs the risk, however, that relevant spatial experience has not been totally eliminated during the waiting period. The experiment in Box 39, for example, has been criticized on the grounds that the few seconds of visual experience during daily feeding, especially when combined with the experience provided during the few practice trials, might have been sufficient to permit learning of distance discrimination. Such very rapid learning does not seem so far-fetched when we consider that more mature organisms generally can become proficient in a given skill with much less practice than would be required by those at a less advanced level of maturity.

One way to minimize this problem is to employ a perceptual task that is so "natural" for the organism that such risky practice trials may be eliminated. The "visual cliff" technique of Walk and Gibson (1961) does just that. A

behavior as complicated as jumping a gap between platforms is not required; all that is needed is the ability to walk or crawl (see Figure 12.6.). Adult rats reared in the dark were found, in a number of studies, to remain consistently on the "safe" side of the visual cliff. Similar results have been found for several other species. (Further results, employing this same technique with newborn animals, are reported later.)

Deliberate deprivation of visual experience is not, however, a very popular experimental technique with human subjects. Most of what

Figure 12.6. The visual cliff. This apparatus makes possible the testing of depth perception in any animal as soon as it is able to move about in its environment. A checkerboarded surface, which drops off abruptly for a foot or so, is covered by a glass plate. The subject, animal or human, is placed on the cliff and is encouraged to cross the line over the cliff's edge. If the subject hesitates at the cliff's edge and refuses to move across it, we infer that it is capable of discriminating depth. In this illustration, the child's mother is encouraging him to cross the cliff. One crucial but well-substantiated assumption underlying this method is that animals "innately" will avoid plunging over a precipice. William Vandivert.   RUBBISH.

Box 39

A Look Before a Leap

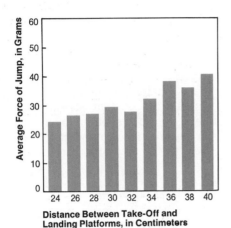

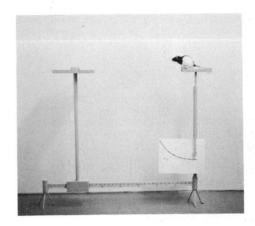

Average Force of Jump, in Grams

Distance Between Take-Off and
Landing Platforms, in Centimeters

An experiment by K. S. Lashley and J. T. Russell showed that rats, too, seem able to perceive visual space immediately without the benefit of prior experience. They raised thirteen rats in complete darkness from birth until the age of 100 days (rat adulthood). The only visual experience the rats had during that period was a few seconds of very dim illumination each day when their cages were opened for feeding.

On the critical day of the rats' first experience of full light, the experimenters tested the rats' orientation to visual space by placing each rat on a high pedestal and urging it to jump the short gap to a platform on which food was available (see photograph). After brief preliminary training at this fixed distance, to accustom the rats to jumping, the distance between the pedestal and the food platform was varied over a range of a few inches to several feet. The accuracy of each rat's perception of the changing distances was measured by the force of its leaps toward the platform; that is, it was assumed that, if the animal were perceiving the distances properly, a large gap should elicit a proportionately stronger jump than a small gap would. The force of the jump was recorded by the swing of a pointer attached to the platform and set into motion by the impetus of the leap.

Even though the rats were far from uniformly successful in hitting the platform, it was convincingly clear that they did discriminate visually among the different distances. The graph in Figure B, which plots the average force of jump against the distance to the platform, shows that the rats regulated the impetus of their leaps in fairly good accordance with the actual distance. The performance of these rats raised in darkness was virtually the same as that of rats who had been raised in the normal way.

K. S. LASHLEY and J. T. RUSSELL. 1934. The Mechanism of Vision: XI. A Preliminary Test of Innate Organization, *J. Genet. Psychol.*, 45, 136–44. Figure adapted by permission of The Journal Press.

we have learned on the human level comes from observation of patients who, because of congenital sensory defects, were accidentally deprived of normal visual experience. After their visual defects had been corrected, these patients were tested for space perception. Unfortunately, data drawn from such observations are somewhat difficult to interpret (see Box 40, p. 203, for an early example of these studies).

Spatial Abilities of the Newborn

To begin at the beginning, Wertheimer (1961) reports that a ten-minute-old infant, tested between three minutes and ten minutes of age, consistently showed eye movements in the direction of a click sounded in either ear, indicating primitive spatial perception, auditory localization, and even interaction between hearing and vision at that remarkably tender age. Infants as young as one month discriminate between solid and flat objects, even when viewed monocularly (Fantz, 1961). A ten-month-old infant, also tested monocularly, consistently avoided falling off the "visual cliff" (Walk & Dodge, 1962). The very young of several species

Figure 12.7. Test photograph for Hess study. Chicks reared with "normal" overhead lighting pecked at the grains on the left. Chicks raised with lighting from below preferred the grains on the right. The actual test photograph showed the natural colors of the grains.
E. H. Hess, "Shadows and Depth Perception," *Scientific American*, 204 (1961), 144; reprinted by permission.

(chicks, monkeys, rats, kittens, and goats, among others) also avoid the cliff. Although many studies therefore agree that at least a rudimentary ability for spatial discrimination is present at a very early age, the problem remains that perceptual testing must await the time when the newborn organism can make some kind of observable discriminating response. Depending upon the species and the technique employed, these test ages vary somewhat. Certainly, we do not have adequate data —in fact, no data at all—that have been obtained at the instant of birth; some relevant spatial experience may therefore have taken place by the time observations are made.

Experimental Control of Experience

Hess (1961) designed an experiment to determine whether the use of light-shadow patterns as depth cues (see Figure 12.4.) depends upon the organism's early experience with such patterns. He raised two groups of chicks from the time of hatching under different conditions of illumination. One group lived in a "normal" world in which all lighting was uniformly from above; the other group lived in an artificial world in which all lighting was from below (wire floors were used). At seven weeks he tested the depth perception of both groups by exposing vertical cards on which were realistic photographs of pieces of grain taken in two ways—lighted from above and lighted from below (see Figure 12.7.). The hungry chicks consistently pecked at the "grains" on the photograph that had been taken under the lighting conditions in which they had been raised. Here then is evidence that cues of depth may be learned. It is also of interest, however, that in further experiments, when chicks were tested at ages *younger* than seven weeks, the preference for "normal" (that is, overhead) lighting appeared earlier among the "normally" reared chicks than the preference for the grains lighted from below had appeared among the

Box 40 Suppose a Man Born Blind . . .

Some adults have been blind from birth because of cataracts on both eyes. This congenital blindness can be cured surgically. When the bandages are removed and the person has vision for the first time in his life, what does he see?

M. V. Senden has compiled the published reports of the visual experiences of sixty-six such cataract cases. The reported facts have not been fully substantiated, and the tests of perception were imperfect. Nevertheless there is fairly consistent agreement on the following facts:

1. On first vision, the person does not immediately experience the kind of orderly visual world seen by the normal person. He is at first greatly *confused* by the array of unfamiliar visual stimuli.
2. All is not chaos, however, for he at once sees *unitary figures* differentiated from background.
3. Furthermore, he is at once able to *fixate* the figures and scan them and to *follow* moving figures with his eyes.
4. Objects can be recognized as different, but the person can neither identify the nature of the differences between objects nor give their names, even though both are quite ordinary tasks for him in another sense modality (for example, touch). What is probably involved here is the absence of any learned association between such terms as "long" and "short" or between the conventional names of objects and the new visual patterns that will soon come to represent them.
5. Objects do seem to extend away from the person at some distance in space instead of appearing on a flat frontal plane. His judgments of distance, however, are quite poor, so that he may attempt to reach an object several yards away or reach too far when attempting to grasp a nearby object. His behavior, however, is quite unlike the groping of the blind. Again this deficit seems to be a matter of not yet having learned the correct visual-motor relationship.

I. D. London (1960) has made available a summary of a report by a Russian surgeon on similar cases; it generally agrees with Senden's generalizations, except perhaps on the fifth point. Two congenitally blind children, when their eyesight was restored, "collided with . . . objects and, in the beginning, employed the customary method of the blind, putting their hands out in front of them and touching the objects in their way." The disagreement here may be in simile rather than in fact, as both reports are rather informal accounts. One point of additional interest is that two other children, who were blinded after birth (at ages three and five), progressed toward normal vision much more rapidly than did those who had been congenitally blind.

Anecdotal evidence of this sort merits attention as long as more systematic observation of the recovery of spatial perception in the newly sighted is not undertaken. So far it has not been, possibly because postoperative difficulties render interpretation of such observations ambiguous. Take one example: For some weeks following surgery these patients experience considerable difficulty in accommodation and convergence. As both are cues for depth perception, any instance of its failure *may* arise from a "mechanical" problem and may not represent a true perceptual deficit. If the observer waits until these postoperative conditions clear up then perceptual learning may occur. Confronted by such obstacles, we may long continue to cite these two brave, if not systematic, surgeons who dare to walk where psychologists fear to tread.

M. V. SENDEN. 1932. *Raum und Gestaltauffassung bei Operierten Blindgeborenen vor und Nach Operation* (Leipzig: Barth).

I. D. LONDON. 1960. A Russian Report on the Postoperative Newly Seeing, *Amer. J. Psychol.,* 73, 478–82.

Box 41

The Upside-Down World
of Psychologists

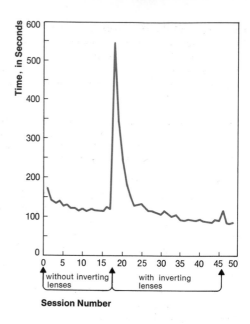

The effects of continuously wearing a lens system that inverts the visual field was first studied by George M. Stratton in 1897 at the University of California (whose psychological laboratory he founded). He wore the lenses for eight days on the right eye only; the left eye was kept blindfolded. The optical effect was to turn the whole visual field completely upside down and to reverse it from right to left.

Stratton reported severe immediate disorientation on donning the lenses. The coordination of vision and body movement was badly disrupted. He reached in the wrong direction for visually perceived objects and heard sounds coming from the side opposite from their visually perceived source A great deal of trial-and-error groping was required to accomplish such simple acts as placing a fork in food and conveying it to the mouth. After about three days the disorientation lessened, and by the end of the eight days the new visual-motor coordinations had become quite good. As the days passed, he even became less and less aware that the visual scene was upside down. Upon removal of the lenses this successful adaptation was itself destroyed, so that some degree of disorientation occurred under the restored but no longer normal circumstances. Fortunately, this second effect lasted only a brief time.

F. W. Snyder and N. H. Pronko repeated this experiment, with the subject wearing the inverting lenses for thirty days. A number of tests of visual-motor coordination were carried out before, during, and after this period. In one of the tests the subject had to sort cards rapidly into appropriate boxes. Time in seconds for completion of the task was recorded. Five trials a day were carried out for seventeen sessions before the lenses were worn, for twenty-eight sessions while they were being worn, and for four sessions after they were removed. The graph shows the average time scores for these sessions. Note the enormous slowing down in task performance after the lenses were first put on, the fairly rapid readjustment during the period of inversion, and the slight and very brief further disruption when the lenses were removed.

Toward the end of the experiment the subject was asked whether or not a scene from a tall building looked upside down to him. He replied:

"I wish you hadn't asked me. Things were all right until you popped the question at me. Now, when I recall how they *did* look *before* I put on these lenses, I must answer that they do look upside down *now*. But until the moment that you asked me I was absolutely unaware of it and hadn't given a thought to the question of whether things were right side up or upside down."

The process by which a subject wearing lenses "learns" to see the world right side up is far from clear. It is surely not learning in the usual sense of a conscious and deliberate process; subjects report no such process during the adaptation period, nor is it likely that so complex a problem could ever be solved in so rational a manner. R. Held and J. Rekosh have suggested a possible mechanism; their suggestion is based on a study of the perceptual effects of curvature-inducing lenses. Through these lenses their subjects, who had been placed in a man-sized drum, viewed a random pattern of tiny dots that completely covered the inside wall of the drum. A critical aspect of this experiment is that such a pattern looks the same with and without lenses, so that the subject is unaware of any distortion. The pattern was viewed for a half-hour by each subject under each of two conditions: first, while walking around inside the drum and, second, while being wheeled around on the same route in a specially designed cart.

After the viewing period and while still wearing the curvature-inducing lenses, the subject was required to adjust a line whose curvature he could mechanically vary until it appeared to him perfectly straight. The actual extent of curvature of the line that the subject reported as straight was taken as the measure of the degree of his adaptation to the lenses. In every instance a significant amount of adaptation was shown to have taken place following the walking-around condition. No adaptation whatever occurred while the subjects were being wheeled around.

The conclusions from these data are twofold. First, it is not necessary to be aware of a spatial distortion in order to be able to adapt to it; second, such adaptation requires *self-initiated* motor activity during the viewing period. Held and Rekosh interpret these conclusions to mean that normal spatial orientation is based upon a "learned" relationship between movement-produced stimuli and the changes in retinal patterns that accompany such changes in body position. When the nature of this relationship is changed, as by inversion or curvature-inducing lenses, the nervous system in some manner unlearns the old relationship and rapidly acquires the new one.

Lower animals may not show such rapid adaptability of space perception. In 1956, F. H. Hess hatched chicks in darkness, then hooded them with prismatic goggles that displaced objects in their visual field 7 degrees to the right (or to the left). These chicks were never able to adjust their pecks so as to compensate for this visual displacement. Instead they continued to peck 7 degrees to the right (or to the left) of the grain target.

G. M. STRATTON. 1897. Vision Without Inversion of the Retinal Image, *Psychol. Rev.*, 4, 341–60.

F. W. SNYDER and N. H. PRONKO. 1952. *Vision With Spatial Inversion* (Wichita: University of Wichita). Figure adapted by permission.

R. HELD and J. REKOSH. 1963. Motor-Sensory Feedback and the Geometry of Visual Space, *Science*, 141, 722–3.

E. H. HESS. 1956. Space Perception in the Chick, *Sci. Amer.*, 195, 71–80.

chicks reared with the artificial lighting. Taken together, these experiments suggest that there is a "natural" tendency for depth to be perceived in accord with light-shadow patterns cast by overhead lighting but that this tendency can be reversed by contrary experience after the animal has somewhat matured.

Clearly, then, spatial experience can modify spatial perception and does so, not only throughout normal development, but also under specialized training conditions. The novice driver, uncertain of the size of his automobile and its distance from others around him, will either give them an unnecessarily wide berth or err in the costly direction. Before long, his spatial judgments will be accurate to a matter of inches, and his insurance premiums will correspondingly improve. Although this adaptability seems quite limited in lower animals, the human visual system shows extraordinary responsiveness to even bizarre experiential demands (see Box 41, p. 204). But, even as the presence of innate spatial ability does not eliminate the possibility of learning effects, the malleability of spatial perception under the impact of experience does not deny the influence of innate factors. Although no definitive statement may yet be offered on the origins of spatial perception, it seems likely that the final answer will involve some intricate interplay among innate, maturational, and experiential factors.

Glossary

accommodation The readjustment in the focusing power of the eye so as to maintain a sharp image on the retina, even when the distance between the eye and the object is constantly changing.

binaural cues The stimulus cues occurring at the two ears that make sound localization possible. The identical sound waves starting at one source have different characteristics when they reach the ears. The principal binaural cues have to do with the time differences and intensity differences of the sound waves at the ears.

convergence The rotation of the eyes toward one another in looking at an object in depth. The closer the object, the greater the angle of convergence. Convergence is a cue for depth perception that becomes ineffective at distances greater than fifty to sixty feet, at which distances the lines of sight become almost parallel.

interposition A monocular depth cue in which one object is seen as partly covering another object. In this case the latter appears farther away.

monocular depth cues The stimulus characteristics that lead to an impression of visual depth with one eye. Monocular cues from the visual pattern include interposition, relative size, relative height, relative clearness, linear perspective, and light and shadow. Other monocular cues are accommodation and relative movement.

relative movement (movement parallax) The relative visual displacement of nearer objects to the right and farther objects to the left as the head moves to the left (or of nearer objects to the left and farther objects to the right as the head moves to the right).

retinal disparity The difference in retinal images on the two eyes when looking at an object in depth; this difference is produced by the slightly different angle at which each eye looks at the object.

stereoscope A device making possible the impression of depth in viewing a flat picture. The impression of depth is accomplished by presenting to each eye a separate and slightly different picture, corresponding to the retinal image that would have occurred in each eye had the actual three-dimensional scene been viewed.

stimulus gradient A variation in stimulus intensity or quality in the perceptual field. Stimulus gradients serve as important cues to perception of depth.

UNIT
1

perceptual constancies

overview / Our perception of objects is characterized by a great deal of constancy. Object constancy depends upon the maintenance of certain invariant relationships among parts of the stimulus pattern. In size constancy there is the working together of many cues; size of retinal image and apparent distance of the object are the more important ones. In shape constancy the relationship between shape of the retinal image and the apparent angle of viewing the object is most critical. In loudness constancy amplitude of the sound waves striking the ear and the apparent distance of the sound source are the relevant cues. In brightness constancy the relevant factors have to do mainly with an invariant ratio of the brightness of the object to its immediate surroundings.

Factors of set also play a significant role in governing constancy. Though the person tends naturally, in his attempt to achieve a stable view of the world, to be "object-directed," and hence likely to perceive with high constancy, he is able to adopt a "stimulus-directed" attitude, in which case constancy is greatly weakened.

Our perceptual experience is characterized by an enormous degree of constancy in the overall characteristics of objects. A man is instantly recognizable whether he is seen lying down, standing upright, or balancing on his head. A dictionary is seen as the same massive tome from every angle of observation. The adaptive value of this *object constancy* is obvious. By maintaining a stable and consistent perception of an object despite wide variations in the conditions under which we encounter it, we are able to cope more effectively with our environments.

Constancy of any property—whether it is size, shape, brightness, weight, or anything else —depends upon unchanging relationships among the relevant elements in the total stimulus pattern. Without such invariant stimulus relationships, constancy fails. Constancy can be seen therefore as another instance of transposition, which was discussed in Unit 10.

The particular stimulus relationships that are relevant differ, of course, from one property to another. Two factors in *size constancy*, for instance, are retinal size and apparent distance.

Size Constancy

The visual size of an object obviously depends, in part, on the size of the retinal image it casts. Furthermore, whenever we perceive an "object," we necessarily perceive it at a certain distance, through the operation of the depth cues discussed earlier. There are therefore at least two "facts" that determine the perception of the size of an object: the actual size of the retinal image and the apparent distance of the object. These two "facts" are integrated to yield the resultant percept—an object perceived as of a certain size and at a certain distance. Of two objects that appear to be at the same distance from the observer, the object casting the smaller retinal image usually looks smaller. Of two objects casting retinal images of the same size, the object that appears closer typically looks smaller.

A simple demonstration can be carried out by the reader. Fixate a one-inch square of white paper on a dark background about ten inches away from your eyes. After a brief inspection a good afterimage of the square will be formed.

Then look at some light surface about the same distance away, and note that the size of the afterimage, as it appears to be projected on that surface, is the size of the original square. Now look at a more distant surface, for example, the wall of the room. There you will note that the afterimage appears much larger. Careful comparisons have shown that the perceived size of the afterimage is exactly determined by the distance between the eye and the surface on which the image appears to be projected. This relationship is known technically as *Emmert's Law*. For instance, an afterimage projected on a surface ten times as far away as the original stimulus will look ten times as large as the original stimulus, even though the retinal image remains the same (see Figure 13.1.).

It is important to understand that perceived size is determined by the apparent distance of the object and not by the real physical distance. An object that is actually far away but looks as if it were close will appear smaller. Look at Figure 13.2. We see an odd sight. Is it a circus room showing side-show freaks, or are our eyes somehow deceiving us? Box 42, p. 212, gives the answer.

The earlier demonstration shows how the two cues of retinal size and apparent distance can jointly determine the perceived size of an object. Neither cue can properly be regarded as more primary than the other. We do not first detect the distance of an object and then

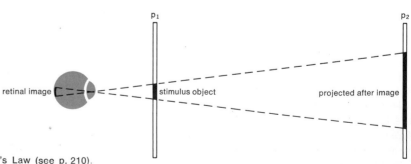

Figure 13.1. Illustration of Emmert's Law (see p. 210).

infer its size from the size of the retinal image, nor do we do the opposite. The two cues work together simultaneously as a system. The recognition of this kind of systematic relationship of cues in perception paves the way for our understanding of the phenomenon of constancy.

To a truly astonishing degree, a given object looks the same size to us whether we are near to it or far away. When the object is farther away, its retinal image is smaller, so why should we not see the object as smaller? The answer has already been given in our discussion of the working together of retinal size and distance as a single perceptual system. As an object moves away, its retinal size decreases, but its apparent distance, as determined by the distance cues, increases. To the extent that the relation between these two "facts" remains the same—that is, as retinal size decreases and a proportional increase in apparent distance results—the perceived size remains the same.

Figure 13.2. Freaks? Or illusion? See Box 42.
Reprinted with the permission of Scientific American, Inc. from the April 1959 issue of *Scientific American.* Courtesy William Vandivert.

Disturbances of Invariance

This relationship of invariance, however, does not hold under all circumstances. Over (1963) has demonstrated that, when describing an unfamiliar object with weakened cues (restriction of head movements, monocular viewing, a darkened room of uncertain dimensions), this rule breaks down. Apparently subjects in this situation judge the object's size by guessing at its nature and its distance and by guessing at the dimensions of the room. In everyday perception, however, we typically employ the same set of cues to judge both size and distance; perhaps this sharing of criteria is a necessary condition for maintaining a systematic link between apparent size and distance.

Several other investigations have shown that the relationship between size and distance is disturbed when only monocular cues are available in a restricted cue situation. This result has been obtained with both subjects who are

blind in one eye and subjects who, experimentally, have been deprived of binocular cues. Under normal (or "cue-rich") conditions, however, actual or experimentally monocular subjects do as well in judgments of size and distance of objects as do normal subjects who are allowed the full use of binocular cues (Leibowitz & Dato, 1966).

When the situation weakens the usual distance cues, known size plays an increasingly influential role. For instance, in an experiment by Ittelson (1951), playing cards of normal size, half size, and double size were placed at the same distance from the observer. He looked with one eye through a peephole at the cards and reported on their perceived sizes and distances. The perceptual process "solved" the problem by maintaining the "normal" sizes of the cards and by adjusting the perceived distances to fit. The perceiver saw all the cards as "normal" in size but at various distances; the half-size card appeared twice as far away as did the standard card, and the double-size card appeared half as far away. In other words,

Box 42

The Distorted Room

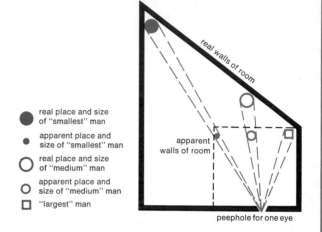

🔵 real place and size of "smallest" man

• apparent place and size of "smallest" man

◯ real place and size of "medium" man

◯ apparent place and size of "medium" man

☐ "largest" man

Figure 13.2 shows what an observer sees when he looks with one eye through a peephole into the room. It looks to him like a normal rectangular room, but the three people in it look weirdly distorted in size.

The room has been deliberately constructed so as to mislead the perceiver (see the figure). It is actually very asymmetrical; one corner is three times as far away as the other, and all dimensions are chosen so as to be exact geometrical projections of a normal rectangular room viewed from the observer's eye.

The binocular depth cues are all eliminated by requiring the subject to look through the peephole with one eye. And the cue of accommodation is ineffective at this distance. On the basis of retinal pattern alone, he cannot tell how far away the parts of the room actually are. A truly rectangular room and also any number of distorted rooms could give this same retinal pattern. His most natural assumption is that the room is a normal rectangular one of the kind with which he is most familiar, and, as the stimulus pattern is consistent with this interpretation, that is how he sees it.

But the consequence is that objects inside the room must assume perceived sizes appropriate to the perceived size and shape of the room. The nearest man therefore looks much taller than the farthest man.

Space perception involves more than a single sense modality; it involves harmonizing of information from all the senses. To what extent is there flexibility in the way the various cues are synthesized and modified in accordance with changes in the stimulus situation? Subjects were permitted to explore the distorted room with a long pointer while they continued to watch. As they did so, the room tended to lose its "illusory" symmetrical character and to assume its correct shape, with one corner much closer than the other. Here is a convincing example of how kinesthetic cues contradict and bring about change in the visual depth organization. Yet we must remember that the original stimulus situation was a highly ambiguous one, in which many alternative visual organizations were possible, and therefore it may have been relatively easy for the kinesthetic cues to overcome the visual ones.

in this situation in which distance cues were extremely impoverished, prior experience with playing cards of normal size provided the essential cue to perceived size.

Prior Experience and Constancy

The influence of prior experience with the perceived size of an object is limited by the strength of structure of the stimulus pattern (see Unit 11, p. 185). We have already noted that in the distorted-room experiment (Box 42, p. 212) human bodies take on very eccentric sizes. An even more startling perception, utterly incongruous with knowledge and past experience, is readily produced when the observer watches a person walk from one corner of the distorted room to the other. He appears to swell threefold in size. And by similar means the observer can easily be made to see water "flowing uphill." There is some evidence, however, that, if the observer assumes a particular set that emphasizes an accurate perception of the real size of the object, the effect of the distorted room may be diminished. One experimenter reports that, when the person walking across the room was the observer's wife (presumably an object whose dimensions were worth keeping stable), the illusion was markedly decreased and size constancy largely maintained.

A particularly dramatic instance of the effect of prior experience upon size constancy is provided by Turnbull (1961). Working with the BaMbuti pygmies of the Congo, he found an impressive breakdown of size constancy when these people were placed in a totally unfamiliar environment. The BaMbuti live in heavily forested country and rarely if ever can scan a view greater than one quarter of a mile. A BaMbuti taken from his forest by Turnbull, saw buffalo at a great distance and thought they were insects; he also saw a boat afar and could not believe that so tiny a boat actually held real people. The BaMbuti are apparently unable to correlate retinal image and apparent distance to achieve size constancy in a situation in which distances exceeding their usual experience are involved.

It is of course very likely that the BaMbuti would attain normal perception of size constancy if they were given prolonged experience in this new kind of environment. It is even possible that some change toward greater perception of size constancy would (or did) take place within a matter of minutes; at least that is the suggestion that might be drawn from the findings of Rock (1965). He devised an apparatus (essentially a fun-house type of distorting mirror), which made highly familiar objects (a pencil and a playing card, for example) appear smaller than their familiar sizes. This effect was quite convincing at first, but, as the subjects continued to observe these "shrunken" objects, within minutes the objects began to return to normal size. Apparently some adaptation process was at work, and we might expect it to apply in the case of the BaMbuti and their miniature buffalo.

Shape Constancy

A plate looks "round" to us even when it is tilted and the image it casts on our retina is therefore elliptical. The essential factors in such *shape constancy* are the apparent tilt of the object and the actual shape of the retinal image. The apparent tilt of the object is provided by various cues from the object and its surroundings. When we look at a tilted object, the texture of its surface appears denser toward the farther end; and, as we have seen (Box 37, p. 196), such texture gradients can provide information about tilt that is independent of the shape of the retinal image. Poor cues of tilt will, of course, tend to reduce shape constancy.

Loudness Constancy

Constancies are found not only in the visual sphere—as in size and shape—but also in all types of properties of objects. For example, we have a considerable degree of *loudness constancy*. In other words, our perception of the actual loudness of the sound source is fairly consistent whether we are close to the object or far away from it. The essential factors are two: the amplitude of the sound waves striking the ear and the apparent distance of the sound source. The apparent distance of the sound source depends upon the various factors discussed in Unit 12, p. 190. If our perception of the distance is poor, we may not be able to judge the loudness of the sound source with any accuracy.

Brightness Constancy

In most of the previous examples of constancy a factor of apparent distance from the object was involved. This is not always one of the essential factors in the invariant stimulus relationship in constancies. For example, when we turn to *brightness constancy*, the factors have to do with the intensity of the light rays emitted from the object and the intensity of the illumination of the object and its surroundings.

A common observation is that snow in deep shade looks white and that coal in sunlight looks black, even though the intensity of light striking the eye from the snow is less than that from the coal. Careful experimental analyses of the means by which this phenomenon can occur were carried out in the laboratory. The observer looks at two gray color wheels, one in full sunlight and the other in shadow. The brightness of the wheel in shadow can be altered by varying the proportions of white and black sectors. The experimenter keeps adjusting the wheel until the observer reports that it matches the brightness of the wheel in

the light. Under these conditions the match proves to be very close; the amounts of white in the two color wheels are almost identical. Yet the actual stimulus fact is that the intensity of light reaching the observer's eye from the shadowed wheel is radically less than that from the other wheel. The explanation is that the perceived brightness depends not only upon the light coming from the object, but also upon the relation of this light to the light coming from the surroundings of the object, that is, the wall against which the color wheel is viewed. Although it is true that on the lighted side the illumination of both wheel and background are higher than on the shadowed side, the ratio of illumination of the wheel to the illumination of the background is the same on both sides. It is this proportional relationship between the light from the object and the light from its background that is the major determinant of brightness constancy. This relationship is not, however, a simple one, as the following experiment shows.

Jameson and Hurvich (1961) presented their subjects illuminated squares arranged as shown in the test pattern in Figure 13.3. Square 1 was always the brightest, square 2 the next brightest, and so on through square 5. There was another square, separate from the experimenter's squares, whose illumination the subject could vary by means of a rheostat. The subject was asked to adjust the brightness of his own square until, in his estimation, it equaled the brightness of one and then another of the five squares shown by the experimenter. The experimenter then increased the illumination equally on all five of his squares and again asked the subject to adjust the brightness of his own square. This process was repeated for several levels of illumination and with many subjects.

The subjects' matchings of brightness, for all five squares and at each of several levels of illumination, were in all cases as follows when the illumination was increased: Square 1, the brightest square, showed a slight increase in perceived brightness; square 2, the second brightest, showed a very slight increase in perceived brightness; the increase in perceived brightness of square 3 was even less than that of square 2; square 4, the fourth brightest, showed no increase in perceived brightness; square 5, the least bright, showed a *decrease* in perceived brightness despite the *increased* illumination. (The reader may appreciate the results found for square 5 more easily if he performs this simple experiment: Observe an ordinary bottle of India ink under a certain illumination; then increase the illumination. The perceived brightness of the bottle will decrease.)

The results of this experiment suggest the following relation between illumination and perceived brightness: With a general increase in illumination, bright objects may become brighter, medium-bright objects may remain the same, and dark objects may become even darker.

Constancy as Achievement

Though mere knowledge of the actual situation may not be critical in the determination of constancy, we should not underrate the important role that the perceiver's learning and intention do play. We have already seen that set can influence the degree of constancy. The observer can deliberately try to minimize constancy by paying attention to the retinal-size cue and neglecting the distance cue, or by concentrating on the sheer loudness of sound at his ears without reference to the apparent distance of its source, or by judging the brightness of the light rays from the surface of the object independent of the surroundings.

Seeing the size of an object without being influenced by its distance is a neat and exceedingly difficult trick. Often the observer makes various "implicit" assumptions that affect his

perception despite his intention, as in the case of the breakdown of the size-distance proportionality. A striking example is the size-weight illusion (see Box 43, p. 216).

The conclusion is that our perception tends under natural circumstances to be "object-directed" rather than "stimulus-directed." That is, we customarily seek to achieve an accurate perception not of the isolated stimulus attribute but of the whole object. The functional value of this is obvious, inasmuch as it is with whole objects in our environment that we must cope. In order to see objects, we must necessarily take account of patterns of stimuli, not isolated stimulus attributes, and in so doing we can achieve perceptual constancy of the objects.

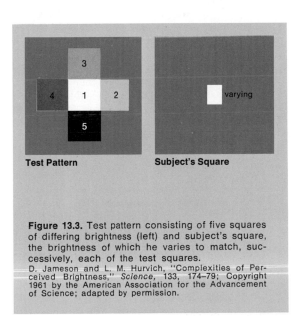

Test Pattern   **Subject's Square**

Figure 13.3. Test pattern consisting of five squares of differing brightness (left) and subject's square, the brightness of which he varies to match, successively, each of the test squares.
D. Jameson and L. M. Hurvich, "Complexities of Perceived Brightness," *Science*, 133, 174–79; Copyright 1961 by the American Association for the Advancement of Science; adapted by permission.

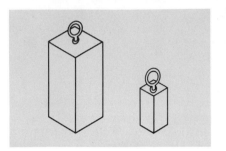

Box 43

Pound of Feathers,
Pound of Lead

A most surprising illusion can be demonstrated with two rectangular wooden blocks. One is 1 1/2″ × 1 1/2″ × 2 1/2″; the other is 3″ × 3″ × 5″, or exactly eight times the volume of the first. Concealed inside each block are pieces of lead so adjusted that the total weight of each block is exactly 300 grams. Each block can be hefted by placing the forefinger inside the metal ring on its top.

The subject is informed that the larger block weighs 300 grams. He is asked to heft the larger block and then the smaller block and to judge the latter's weight in grams. It is striking that virtually all subjects perceive the smaller block as substantially heavier than the larger block, even though the two are exactly equal in weight. For instance, in a study of 100 military officers (R. S. Crutchfield, D. G. Woodworth, and R. E. Albrecht), the average weight estimate for the smaller block was 750 grams, about 2 1/2 times the correct weight. For some of the officers the overestimate was as much as sevenfold!

This phenomenon is known as the size-weight illusion. A common explanation of the illusion is that the person "expects" the smaller block to be lighter than the larger (because of the obvious size difference), and the contrast of this prior expectation with the actual weight of the smaller when hefted makes it seem heavier. But this explanation is entirely inconsistent with the fact that the illusion persists almost as strongly after the blocks have been repeatedly hefted and even after the person weighs them on a scale. Mere "knowledge" of the objective facts is insufficient to destroy the illusion. Further results show that, even when the subject is instructed to "pay no attention" to the relative sizes of the blocks and to concentrate, in making his judgment, only on the feeling of their weights, the illusion is as great as before. And, if a subject first looks at the blocks and then closes his eyes when hefting them, the illusion is equally great.

E. Brunswik has suggested that the subject, although attempting to judge weight, is implicitly taking density (weight per cubic inch) into account. Because the small block is one-eighth the size of the large block but weighs exactly the same, the density of the small block is eight times that of the larger. The person, in judging the weight of the small block, may partly be influenced by his perception of its density. In this way the smaller and denser block is judged heavier. Brunswik has supported this explanation by finding that subjects who are carefully instructed to pay attention to the attribute of "weight" and to avoid the attribute of "density" experience less than normal amounts of the size-weight illusion.

The age-old conundrum "Which is heavier, a pound of feathers or a pound of lead?" is the mental counterpart of the perceptual size-weight illusion. The unwary person answers that a pound of lead is obviously heavier, his judgment being implictly affected by the relative densities of the objects.

R. S. CRUTCHFIELD, D. G. WOODWORTH, and R. E. ALBRECHT. 1955. *Perceptual Performance and the Effective Person* (San Antonio: Air Force Personnel and Training Research Center).

E. BRUNSWIK. 1956. *Perception and the Representative Design of Psychological Experiments* (Berkeley: University of California Press).

Glossary

brightness constancy The tendency to perceive an object as of the same brightness despite wide variations in the intensity of illumination. Brightness constancy seems to depend mainly upon an invariant relation between the intensity of light emitted from the object and the intensity of light emitted from its surroundings.

Emmert's Law The exact proportionality of the perceived size of an afterimage to the distance between the eye and the surface on which the image appears to be projected. The same afterimage projected on a wall ten times as far away as the original stimulus appears ten times as large.

loudness constancy The perception of the actual loudness of a sound source in a fairly constant way, whether the observer is close to the object or far away from it. Loudness constancy depends on the relationship between amplitude of the sound waves striking the ear and the apparent distance of the sound source.

object constancy The tendency for objects to be perceived in an established and a consistent way despite wide variations in the conditions under which they are viewed.

shape constancy The tendency for the shape of an object to be perceived correctly even though it is tilted in such a way that the retinal image it casts on the eye is of a different shape from the object itself. Shape constancy depends upon the relation of the shape of the retinal image to the apparent plane of the object.

size constancy The tendency for a given object to be perceived as the same size despite wide variations in its distance from the observer. Size constancy depends upon the relation between the retinal size and apparent distance of the object.

perception of movement and time

overview / The perception of visual movement is not explained simply by real physical movement of stimuli in the environment. Induced movement, for example, is seen when two objects are displaced in relationship to each other but the one seen moving is not necessarily the one that is actually moving. In apparent movement, a convincing impression of movement occurs when there is no real movement at all but merely a temporal succession of static stimuli, as in motion pictures. Autokinetic movement is an illusory movement occurring, for example, when a single stationary spot of light is seen in an otherwise dark room. In all these kinds of movement, "illusory" movement is not distinguishable by the observer from physically real movement.

The speed and direction of perceived movement is strongly influenced by perceptual organization of the entire field. Moving objects are often seen as having complex attributes like "causality," which are governed by specifiable features of the stimulus pattern and are subject to experimentally determined psychophysical laws. Time perception can be similarly studied, and some of the factors influencing the experienced duration of given time intervals have been specified. For example, time perception is influenced by drugs. Generally speaking, events that speed up bodily processes tend to speed up the passage of time, and psychological depressants tend to slow it down.

Time estimation for short intervals may reflect different mechanisms than those for long intervals. For short intervals, there is a tendency for unfilled periods to be underestimated in duration. For long intervals, accuracy of time estimation depends upon events in the external environment and cues within the body.

To complete our account of perception we now turn to the perception of visual movement and of time. Both involve great complexities in our understanding of perception.

Visual Movement

Perception of visual movement is one of the most fascinating topics in the study of perception. Like many basic phenomena, seeing the movement of things in our environment seems at first to present no particular problems. Question: Why do we see the object move? Answer: Simply because the object does move, and in moving it changes its location in physical space; as we note these changes, we "see" the movement. Now this "simple answer" is no answer at all. Physical movement of an object often fails to produce a perception of movement of the object, and movement is often seen where there is no physical movement at all.

Induced Movement

Recall the illusion in which the moon appears to move swiftly behind clouds. This example illustrates both that a truly moving object (the clouds) may not appear to be moving and that

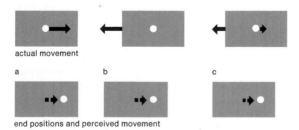

actual movement

a   b   c

end positions and perceived movement

Figure 14.1. Three experimental situations producing induced movement. The dot and rectangle can be moved independently of each other. The solid arrow indicates physical movement, and the dotted arrow indicates perceived movement. In a, only the dot physically moves; in b, only the rectangle moves; and in c, both rectangle and dot move. Yet in all cases the *perceived* movement is the *same:* The dot appears to move, and the rectangle to remain at rest. Three *different* physical movements result in *identical* perception of movement.

an object truly "at rest" (the moon) may appear to be in motion. The moving object is said to "induce" an appearance of movement in the other object, and so we refer to this phenomenon as *induced movement.*

To understand this phenomenon, let us first analyze the stimulus situation. On the retina there is an image of the moon and an image of the clouds. As the clouds approach the moon, the distance between the retinal images shortens. It is this change in distance between the two images on the retina that constitutes the stimulus for perceived movement.

If all the information we have is that the two things are displaced in relationship to one another, the situation is ambiguous from the perceiver's point of view. Either one, or both, might actually be moving. Which, then, is perceived as moving? In general, when there is a logical possibility that either object can be perceived as moving, the object that is seen as the figure, in relation to the framework provided by the other object, tends to "move."

Let us go into the darkroom, where we can demonstrate this point very simply. On the wall are a luminous outline of a rectangle and, within it, a dot of light. The rectangle and the dot are mounted separately so that they can be moved independently of each other. We shall do three experiments (see Figure 14.1.).

First, the rectangle remains fixed in place, and the dot is moved slowly to the right. The dot is seen as moving to the right and the rectangle as being at rest. Here the perception does correspond with the physical situation. Second, the dot is fixed in place and the rectangle is moved to the left. Now the perception fails to correspond with reality, for what is typically seen is exactly what was seen before —the rectangle is seen at rest and the dot as moving to the right. Third, the rectangle is moved to the left and simultaneously the dot is moved to the right. Once again, the rectangle is usually seen as at rest and the dot as moving to the right.

Here we have observed a striking instance in

which three *different* sets of physical movement result in *identical* perception of movement. The reason is clear: The changes in retinal stimulus pattern for the three situations are identical and therefore in each case permit the dot—the figural element—to "move."

When the two objects are equally figural, the one that is fixated tends to be seen as moving. Instructions, expectations, or set may determine which object will be fixated. If two dots of light are exposed in darkness, one above the other, and either is moved horizontally back and forth, we have a situation in which either the upper dot or the lower dot can be seen as moving in relationship to the other. If the person is told that he is seeing a "metronome," the upper dot appears to move. If he is told that it is a "pendulum," the lower dot appears to move (see Figure 14.2.).

Induced movement is no different for the perceiver from "real" movement. Neither is so-called *apparent movement*.

Apparent Movement

Everyone knows that a completely convincing impression of movement can be given by a rapid succession of discrete but static pictures, as in motion pictures. This apparent movement, sometimes called "stroboscopic movement," or the "phi phenomenon," can be understood as another instance of temporal fusion (see Unit 9, p. 178).

Take a simple laboratory demonstration. Two lights are mounted a few inches apart. The left one is turned on and off. A second or two later the right one is turned on and off. The observer perceives a simple succession of one light and then another light. If the time interval between flashes of the lights is gradually shortened, a point is reached at which a surprising perceptual transformation occurs. The light on the left seems to move across the intervening space to the right. Finally, as the time interval is made very short, the impression of movement disappears, and the two lights appear simultaneously, each in its own place.

By virtue of a simple change in the time interval between the two stimulus events, three qualitatively different perceptual experiences have been produced—succession, movement, and simultaneity. What is even more noteworthy is that the apparent movement is clearly seen as occurring through the empty space between the two stimulus locations.

It is natural to suppose that the apparent movement occurs because, as the eyes move from one stimulus to the other, their turning creates kinesthetic cues, which are translated into an impression of movement. This supposition is readily disproved by the fact that movement can be seen in opposite directions simultaneously (see Figure 14.3.). Furthermore, it is not even necessary that two different retinal points be successively stimulated for apparent motion to be seen. Rock and Ebenholtz (1962) devised ingenious experimental techniques that allowed their subjects to see, monocularly, two alternating and spatially separate luminous lines, although only a single retinal area was be-

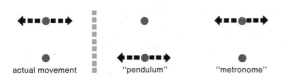

actual movement   "pendulum"   "metronome"

Figure 14.2. Meaning and movement. For explanation, see p. 221 above.

H. A. Carr and M. C. Hardy, "Some Factors in the Perception of Relative Motion," *Psychological Review*, 7 (1920), 24–39; adapted by permission of American Psychological Association.

Figure 14.3. The lights numbered 1 flash simultaneously, followed a fraction of a second later by the lights numbered 2, which also flash simultaneously. The observer sees an upward movement between the right-hand pair of lights and *at the same time* a downward movement between the left-hand pair.

ing activated. They accomplished this effect by having the subject move his eye back and forth in such a way as to ensure that each line was viewed foveally and therefore with the *same* retinal locus. A second condition was arranged in which no spatial separation was experienced between the lines, although *different* retinal areas were being stimulated. In this setup the subject moved his eye back and forth so as to see, alternately with foveal and peripheral viewing, a *single stationary* flashing line. Successive changes in retinal locus were thus achieved, and any real, or experienced, spatial separation was ruled out. Apparent movement occurred under the first condition but not at all under the second. This result suggests that it is only the appearance of distance between two points —and not their actual physical, retinal, or cortical separation—that is a necessary condition for movement to be perceived as occurring between them.

The conditions that govern the occurrence of apparent movement can be expressed in a number of generalizations dealing with the stimulus attributes and the relations among the stimuli (see Box 44, p. 223). But we are not at all clear about the specific mechanisms responsible for apparent movement, nor can we say whether the phenomenon is innate or learned. There is evidence supporting both interpretations. For example, Rock, Tauber, and Heller (1965), exploiting the fact that fish tend to swim in the direction of a rotating drum, demonstrated that newborn guppies, some tested within minutes of birth, did the same when placed inside a *stationary* drum that *appeared* to rotate. The apparent rotation was produced by illuminating vertical columns situated around the walls of the drum, successively and in sequence. The effect was that of a *single* illuminated column moving round and round, creating the illusion that the drum itself was actually rotating. When the direction of the apparent movement was reversed (by reversing the illumination sequence), the fish changed their direction. These effects occurred for all the newborn guppies on

every trial when, and only when, the columns were alternately illuminated at moderate speed. Not a single fish, however, showed any effect when the alternation rate was either very slow or very fast, which as we have seen, is characteristic of the phi phenomenon.

The implications of this result are that the newborn guppies had indeed perceived apparent movement and that, as they had no prior visual experience (they were kept in the dark between birth and testing), this perception must have an innate basis. These investigators conclude by speculating that newborn human infants also can perceive apparent movement. But to demonstrate an innate basis for a phenomenon is not to rule out its modifiability by prior experience and learning. For example, it is more difficult to perceive apparent movement between two locations when the shapes of the lights at the two points are not the same; the inference is that seeing movement in that situation simply makes much less sense (see Box 44, p. 223). Along the same lines, Toch and Ittelson (1956) conclude that the direction of apparent movement is affected by the meanings of the stimulus objects involved.

Apparent movement is also found in other senses. In touch, for instance, if very light pressures are applied successively, and at the appropriate rate, at two nearby points, there will be an impression of movement of the stimulus along the skin from one point to the other. A click in one ear followed an instant later by a click in the other ear may be heard as a single click moving through the head.

Autokinetic Movement

Under certain conditions a *single* stimulus can also produce a perception of movement in the absence of physical movement. As we look at a tiny stationary dot of light that is the only visible stimulus in a dark room, we notice an astonishing thing. The stationary light appears to move, sometimes in this direction, sometimes in that, sometimes slowly, sometimes more

Box 44

Factors in
Apparent Movement

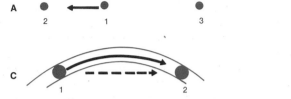
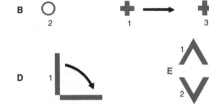

Three stimulus factors determining the *threshold* for apparent movement are the distance between the two stimuli, the time interval of the succession, and he intensity of the stimuli. A. Korte varied these factors and formulated three "laws," which state that to obtain optimal movement

1. The greater the distance between the two stimuli, the greater must be their intensity (if the time interval is constant) or the greater the time interval (if intensity is constant).
2. The greater the intensity, the greater must be the distance apart or the less the time interval.
3. The greater the time interval, the greater must be the distance apart or the less the intensity.

Grouping factors play a major role in determining the *direction* of the apparent movement. In Figure A, light 1 goes on and off, followed shortly by lights 2 and 3, which go on and off simultaneously. The movement could go from 1 to either 2 or 3. Experiments show that it tends to go to 2, which is the nearer, in accord with the principle of grouping by proximity. In Figure B, with proximity equal, the movement goes from 1 to 3, rather than to 2, because of the greater similarity of 1 and 3—the principle of grouping by similarity. In Figure C, the movement tends to take the curved path of the channeling contours, rather than to cut directly across the shortest distance from 1 to 2—the principle of good continuation.

The shape and spatial arrangements of the successive stimuli may make it difficult or impossible to see a straight linear movement from one to the other. More complex apparent movements may then result. For instance, in Figure D the line seems to *rotate* through an angle from the vertical to the horizontal, and in Figure E movement occurs in the *third dimension*; that is, the inverted V-shaped figure is seen to swing down and "flop over" into the reverse orientation.

A. KORTE. 1915. Kinematoskopische Untersuchungen *Zeitsch f Psychol*, 72, 194 296. Figures adapted by permission of Johann Ambrosius Barth, Leipzig.

rapidly. As we watch it for a considerable time, it may execute large sweeping movements or move erratically in a jerky fashion. The extent of the movement can be very great. If we point an outstretched finger at the light as it moves, we are amazed to find (when the room is sud-

denly illuminated) that the finger may be pointing as much as 30 degrees from where the dot of light actually is. Knowing that the light is really stationary does not destroy the effect. Furthermore, the movement is seen as "real" movement. A naïve observer believes that the dot actually does physically move; the informed observer finds it hard to believe that it does not.

This effect is known as *autokinetic* ("self-generated") *movement*. The essential stimulus condition for its occurrence is the absence of visual framework for the dot of light. As soon as other visual features are introduced close by into the field, for example, a line, other dots, and so on, the autokinetic movement appreciably decreases. If we structure the stimulus pattern even further by turning on the lights and revealing all the details of the room, the effect, of course, disappears altogether, and the light is seen as stationary. Pilots during night flights are susceptible to autokinetic movement of distant beacon lights and even lights on other aircraft. Many of them develop techniques to maintain a stable frame of reference, for example, lining up the distant object with an edge of the cockpit window in order to maintain correct orientation.

The complete explanation for autokinetic movement is yet to be made. Eye movements play a role. Although there is no noticeable tendency for eye movements to follow (or to lead) the direction of autokinetic movement, Matin and Mackinnon (1964) report that autokinetic movement is virtually eliminated under conditions in which eye movements are not permitted to cause movements of the retinal image (see Unit 15, p. 234, for a description of such techniques, which stabilize images on the retina). Various postures of the body also play a

role; the direction and extent of the movement can be influenced markedly by the way the eyeballs, the head, the neck, and the trunk are rotated away from the normal line of vision. We have evidence, therefore, that visual perception is affected by kinesthetic sensations from the muscles. Perceptual interaction again cuts across the various senses.

Furthermore, because the optical condition for the movement is a simple, "unstructured," or weakly structured stimulus field, we should expect that the factor of the perceiver's set would be able to exercise a strong influence, which is indeed the case. Sherif (1935) has shown that the amount of movement perceived by a subject is readily influenced by the suggestions of other persons. It is even possible, with appropriate instructions, for the stationary light to appear to trace out numerals and other meaningful designs.

Organization and Movement

The perceived direction of movement—whether induced, apparent, or real—is governed largely by organizational factors. We have already made this observation in Figure 14.1. with respect to induced movement and in Box 44 (p. 223) with respect to apparent movement (see especially demonstrations C and D). Figure 14.4. illustrates the importance of organizational factors for real movement, and Figure 14.5. illustrates another aspect by showing how a complex combination of movements in dif-

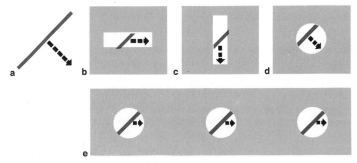

Figure 14.4. The 45-degree-angle line sweeps across the visual field (see a). When it is viewed through an aperture so that only a segment of the moving line is visible, the direction in which it appears to move (indicated by the dotted arrows) is wholly determined by the shape of the aperture. In b, it appears to move horizontally and, in c, vertically, thus conforming to the main edges of the aperture. In d, the movement is at a 45-degree angle downward toward the right. But, if a series of such circular apertures is presented in a horizontal row, as in e, and the line passes successively behind them, it appears to move in a *horizontal* direction.

ferent directions may be unified in such a way as to simplify the whole pattern.

Motion can be perceived within a very broad range of speeds. Of course, some physical movements are so slow that we cannot discern them (for example, the continuous growth of the plant's leaves), and some are so fast that we miss them altogether (for example, the rifle bullet whizzing by).

Within the discernible range, perceived speed of movement is not determined solely by actual physical speed. Here, too, organizational factors are important. Indeed visual context can some-

times produce fairly large errors in our judgment of speed. Figure 14.6. describes the stimulus conditions under which two objective speeds must be made very different before they can be *perceived* as equal. Typically, however, our perception of speed is accurate. So is our detection of any acceleration (change in speed).

Perceived Causality in Movement

Movements are perceived not only as having direction and speed but also as having "causal" power. We commented earlier on the fact that we often have the vivid perceptual impression that certain moving objects interact "causally" with other objects. A rolling billiard ball appears to set into motion another ball that it strikes; the movement of the first is perceived as somehow transferred to the second.

It should be clear that we are here concerned not with genuine physical causality but with perceived causality. In other words, the problem of perceived causality is no different

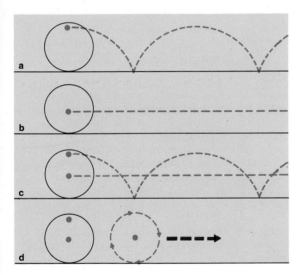

Figure 14.5. A wheel rolls slowly along a table in a table in a completely dark room. On its rim a small light is attached. The observer sees the light moving in a cycloid path, as shown in a. In b the light is attached only at the hub, and the observer sees it move along a straight horizontal path. What does he see when these two conditions are combined, with one light on the rim and one on the hub? It might be expected that he would see both the cycloid and the horizontal movements occurring together, as schematized in c. But what he sees in fact is a "simpler" and more unified pattern of move- as schematized in d. The rim light is seen as rotating around the hub light as a center while this whole "system" of rim and hub lights moves horizontally. In short, the true state of affairs—a rolling wheel—is perceived despite the minimal cues; the previous cycloid movement is entirely absent.

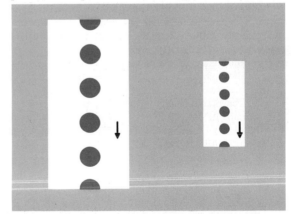

Figure 14.6. Behind each of two apertures is observed a paper tape moving endlessly downward. On the tape is printed a row of dots. The larger aperture is exactly *twice* the size of the smaller, and the dots on its tape are twice as large and twice as far apart. The observer's task is to adjust the speeds of the tapes until the dots in the two apertures *appear* to be moving at equal speeds. For equality of phenomenal speed, it turns out that the physical speed of movement of the tape behind the large aperture must be just about *twice* the speed of the smaller. (After Brown, 1931.)

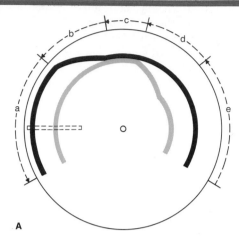

Box 45

Perception of
Causality

A

The Belgian psychologist A. Michotte has conducted a series of laboratory experiments designed to specify the stimulus conditions that give rise to different impressions of physical causality in movement.

On a cardboard disk he drew two thick curved lines, one black and one gray (see Figure A). The disk was mounted vertically on an axle so that it could be slowly rotated. In front of the disk he placed a large shield, which hid the disk except for what the observer could see through a small horizontal slot cut in the shield (the dotted slot in the diagram). In the position that the disk was shown, the observer could see only two small squares, one black and one gray.

By slowly rotating the disk counterclockwise, the experimenter could make the two squares appear to move along the slot, the pattern of movements being governed by the particular shapes of the pathways of the two lines drawn on the disk. In Figure A, the broken lines around the periphery of the disk and the letters a through e indicate the five different phases of movement of the squares as the disk turns once. Figure B shows the sequence of events as seen by the observer. At first (phase a) the two squares are at rest, the black one some distance to the left of the gray. Then (phase b) the black square appears to move toward the gray. For a fraction of a second (phase c) the two remain in contact without moving. Then (phase d) the gray square moves off to the right while the black one remains at rest. Finally (phase e), the gray square comes to rest, some distance to the right of the black.

In this basic experiment, observers reported that there was a clear impression that the movement of the black object "caused" the subsequent movement of the gray object. This impression was not experienced by them as a mere *inference* but as a direct *perception*.

Michotte then systematically varied the stimulus conditions by changing the pathways of the lines drawn on the disk. In this manner he studied the influence of variations in the speed of movement of the black square; the distance it traveled before reaching the gray; the duration of contact between the two squares; the subsequent speed of the gray square after contact was broken.

From perceptions reported by observers under these different stimulus patterns of movement, Michotte discovered that there were two distinctly different types of perceived causality. The first was "launching," in which the black object appeared to set the gray object into motion by transferring its force of motion to the gray. The second was "releasing," in which the black object appeared

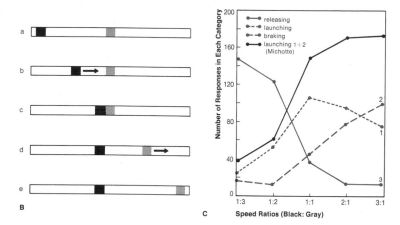

B

C

to cause the gray to move only by unleashing or "triggering" a *latent* force of motion already in the gray—there was no impression of a transfer of force of motion from the black to the gray.

The transition from "launching" to "releasing" depends primarily upon the ratio of the speeds of the two objects. When the black object strikes the gray at a considerably greater speed than is apparently imparted to the gray object, "launching" is almost invariably seen. Conversely, when the gray object takes off at a speed far greater than that of the black object, then "releasing" is seen. As the speeds approach equality, the frequencies of the two responses approach equality.

T. Natsoulas reasoned that, when the launched speed was less than the original launching speed, "braking" should be perceived, as some additional force would be inferred to explain the loss of speed at the point of contact. Michotte, whose subjects reported spontaneously, mentioned no such category; Natsoulas, however, presented his subjects with a choice among "launching," "releasing," and "braking" and found the last increasingly selected as speed ratio increased (see Figure C). It is clear that "braking" is a subcategory of Michotte's more general "launching" response, so that by combining these two responses in Natsoulas' data we can get a quantitative picture of the relative frequency of "releasing" and "launching" with changes in the speed ratio. Note that these combined results roughly confirm Michotte's original generalization and indicate that the two broad classes of responses are equally probable at a speed ratio of about 1:1.

V. Olum has extended this work to children and finds that seven-year-olds show a shift in the transition point from the "launching" to the "releasing" effect—but they still perceive "launching" and continue to do so until speed increase is substantial. As the "releasing" experience is a bit more complex than is the "launching" experience—the former brings the unleashing of a latent force into the picture—these results indicate that children are more likely to keep changes in perceptual organization to a minimum. They retain the simpler "launching" percept as long as they can.

A. MICHOTTE. 1963. *The Perception of Causality* (New York: Basic Books). Originally published in French, 1954. Figure A adapted by permission.
T. NATSOULAS. 1961. Principles of Momentum and Kinetic Energy in the Perception of Causality, *Amer. J. Psychol.*, 74, 394–402. Figure C adapted by permission.
V. OLUM. 1958. Developmental Differences in the Perception of Causality Under Conditions of Specific Instructions, *Vita Humana*, 1, 191–203.

from any other psychophysical problem like the relation of perceived color to physical attributes of light stimuli. Box 45, p. 226, illustrates how such psychophysical studies of perceived causality can be made.

The Perception of Time

There is a certain resemblance between the perception of time and the perception of causality; neither has an obvious physical stimulus. Although physical time can of course be measured, it is not a stimulus in the usual sense: It has no stimulus object emanating energies that impinge upon some time receptor. Yet physical time is certainly among the more important of many factors affecting perceived time. There must therefore be some mechanism, however indirect, that translates the physical passage of time into sensory cues.

But postulating the existence of a mechanism is a far cry from discovering one. Perhaps the most popular candidates over the years have been time-linked physiological processes; heart rate and body metabolism have been among the suggested "biological clocks." We know that time perception is influenced by certain drugs, which also affect bodily rhythms. Quinine and alcohol cause time to pass slowly. Caffeine seems to speed it up, as does high fever. Mescaline and marijuana, on the other hand, have a powerful but inconsistent effect upon time perception; they can lead to extreme errors both by speeding time up and by slowing it down. Generally events that speed up bodily processes tend to speed up the passage of time, and, conversely, physiological depressants tend to slow it down. The mediating mechanism for the perception of time, however, must still be listed as one of the unsolved psychophysiological problems.

Many investigators have suggested that time estimates may reflect the operation of two different sets of processes. Time estimation for short intervals (up to ten seconds) has been labeled "time perception" and can be regarded, like auditory perception of loudness, as a response to a (yet undiscovered) stimulus. The term "time judgment" has been applied to estimation of longer intervals (more than ten seconds), in which *remembering* the length of the interval becomes necessary, and physical time may be only one of many interacting factors that determine the time estimate.

Accuracy of perception of short time intervals is dependent upon numerous factors. For instance, there are systematic tendencies to overestimate intervals of less than about one second and to underestimate intervals of more than one second. Whether the interval seems short or long depends in part upon what goes on during the interval. If two clicks mark off the beginning and end of an interval of silence (an *unfilled* interval), it will be perceived as shorter than the same physical interval during which a continuous series of clicks is presented (a *filled* interval). And, curiously enough, a meaningful sentence will be perceived as shorter in time duration than a sequence of nonsense syllables of the same length. It might be argued that the nonsense items, which are not yet organized, present a series with many more discrete parts than does a meaningful sentence; then the interval is more filled and therefore seems longer.

Perhaps filled time seems longer because it requires more attention. Generally, from the subject's point of view, more does seem to be going on during filled intervals, and more effort seems to be demanded of him. There are instances, therefore, of apparently unfilled time being systematically overestimated, instances that are, however, effortful and even stressful. For example, time estimates made by blindfolded subjects while they are being wheeled toward a sharp precipice are longer than time estimates of the seemingly safer return journey from the brink (Langer, *et al.*, 1961).

Time Orientation

When we deal with much longer time intervals —minutes, hours, and even days—we are not concerned with a purely perceptual question but with a question of judgment. That is, we judge the duration of time in relation to specific events, for example, how many minutes have passed since the telephone rang, how long it will be before we eat. Accurate judgment of time duration depends upon two main kinds of factors: events in the external environment and events within the person himself.

External events may pertain explicitly to time—we can look at a timepiece or at the angle of the sun in the sky. Or they can be in the form of habitual cues. The remarkable ability of some individuals to awaken at a specified time in the morning has been found to depend upon cues of which the person himself may be entirely unaware, for example, the sounds of traffic, or the steps of a neighbor.

Yet it is clear that even in the complete absence of such external cues, there is considerable accuracy of time orientation. In one experiment a man spent four days in complete isolation in a soundproof room, doing what he wished. At irregular intervals he telephoned to the experimenter his estimates of the time of day. During the first day the man's "personal clock" gained more than four hours. Then it began to return to a correct pace, and by the end of the four days his guess of the time was only forty minutes in error. How was this accuracy possible in the complete absence of habitual external cues? Obviously, he was responding to certain cues from inside the body, like sleepiness, hunger, or pressure to eliminate.

There are large individual differences in the apparent speed of passage of time. Experiments have shown that a given interval of time may seem to pass as much as five times as rapidly for children of ten as for adults of sixty. And, within the individual, there are tremendous variations from situation to situation, depending upon his mental and physiological states. In depressed states of mind and during periods of frustration and failure, time slows down.

Time Perspective

Our ability to judge the duration of time permits us to develop a time dimension—a time framework within which events can be fairly accurately placed. Present events mark a particular place in the time dimension, events remembered from the past are placed earlier in this dimension, and events expected in the future are placed later. This general perception of the relations of past, present, and future is technically known as "time perspective."

Time perspective has been relatively little investigated. But casual evidence seems to suggest clearly that it varies enormously for different individuals, at different ages, and in different situations. For the soldier in the front lines under enemy attack, the time perspective is narrow; the past is not in his mind, and the only future is the next few hours of battle. The next day, lying wounded in the hospital, his time perspective expands; he may have many thoughts of his boyhood and of the years to come. In later discussions we shall see the many ways in which time perspective weaves its way into the determination of many facets of our behavior.

Glossary

apparent movement The illusory movement from one stimulus location to another as a function of temporal sequence of the stimuli. An example is motion pictures. It is also known as "stroboscopic movement"—or the "phi phenomenon."

autokinetic movement An illusion of movement as given by a stationary dot of light in an otherwise dark room. The effect is enhanced by the absence of visual framework.

induced movement The appearance of movement in a motionless object that is produced by the movement of other objects in its surroundings. For instance, moving clouds induce perceived movement of the moon.

UNIT 1

mechanisms
of the eye

overview / The optical mechanisms have the task of gathering light from objects outside the organism and focusing it upon the retina. The lens operates to maintain a sharp image on the retina for objects at different distances from the organism; the pupil controls the amount of light entering the eye. The extrinsic eye muscles produce the coordinated movements of the two eyes that make it possible to follow moving objects and to shift our gaze from object to object. They cause the two eyes to converge on the object in view, and this function is co-ordinated with the focusing of the lens to produce retinal images that give rise to a three-dimensional experience. They also cause tiny, rapid, involuntary eye movements that are essential for the maintenance of form vision.

Light-sensitive cells of the retina (rods and cones) respond to light energy with a nervous mpulse. Cones differ in their sensitivity to the various wave lengths of light and, by means of his differential sensitivity and the manner in which they are connected, make possible our experience of color. Color blindness results from defects in these cells or in their interconnec-tions.

Rods, as contrasted to cones, have larger amounts of a more sensitive photopigment and are therefore more responsive than are cones to weak lights. In the dark the quantity of active photosensitive substance in a photoreceptor reaches a maximum, and the cells become most sensitive. As they are exposed to light, the amount of photosensitive substance decreases, as does their sensitivity.

Visual acuity depends upon the optical mechanism and the distribution and connections of the photoreceptors. The fovea (a cone area) is the area of greatest acuity; the periphery (a rod area) shows the greatest sensitivity to dim lights.

We have already seen in Unit 7 how complex are the relations between the light stimulus and the visual experience. It should not come as a surprise, therefore, to find that the sequence of physiological events that occurs between the moment a light stimulus impinges on the eye and the moment we react with a visual experience is exceedingly complex.

To describe the physiological mechanisms involved in visual perception, we must first describe how the light rays from the stimulus object enter through the cornea of the eye and are focused so as to cast an image on the retina, and how these light rays then trigger a neural reaction in the retina.

Two major physiological mechanisms are involved in these events: the *optical mechanism* and the *photosensitive mechanism*. These are the mechanisms of the eye itself, the peripheral mechanisms of the visual system.

The Optical Mechanism

Virtually all living things have light-sensitive mechanisms. These mechanisms vary widely in complexity and specialization. In this unit we shall restrict ourselves to one of the most complex, the type of eye found among the higher vertebrates, including man.

Structure

A semidiagrammatic drawing of the human eye is shown in Figure 15.1. The eyeball is completely enveloped by a tough protective skin consisting of two parts. The white opaque *sclera* (white of the eye) forms a light-proof shield around most of the eye, whereas the clear transparent *cornea* functions as the entrance for light. The eye is moved by the six *extrinsic muscles* attached to the outside of each eyeball. There are two chambers of unequal size within the eyeball, both filled with almost perfectly transparent substances.

The chambers are separated from each other by the *crystalline lens* and the *ciliary muscles*.

Contraction and relaxation of the ciliary muscles change the curvature of the lens (and therefore its focusing power). Within the smaller cavity and lying on the front surface of the lens is a delicate contractile structure, the *iris* (blue, brown, gray, or some other color). Centered in the iris is a circular opening, the *pupil*, whose size is controlled by actions of the muscles of the iris.

Lining the walls of the larger (rear) chamber is the *retina*, a complex neural network consisting of light-sensitive elements and connecting cells that we shall discuss in greater detail later.

Focusing and Accommodation

When light from an outside object enters the cornea, the rays are refracted (bent) inward. As the rays continue through the crystalline lens, they are bent further, so that in a perfectly formed eye the combined action of the cornea and lens will bring a bundle of light rays from an outside point to a focus on the retina. If the object moves or if the eye turns to another object closer or farther away, the curvature of the lens changes to keep the object in focus (compare b and c in Figure 15.1.). This readjustment in focusing power, by means of which the eye can focus on objects at various distances, is called *accommodation*. The critical role of the lens in accommodation is dramatically illustrated by individuals who have no lens. If an opacity (cataract) of the lens develops, the lens may have to be removed. Without lenses and with appropriate corrective eyeglasses, clear vision is still possible—but only at the distance fixed by the focal power of the eyeglasses. Accommodation is lost, and objects nearer and farther from this fixed distance become increasingly blurred. To see clearly at different distances, different glasses or bifocal or trifocal lenses must be used.

Human eyes are not always perfectly formed. The relationship between the length of the eye-

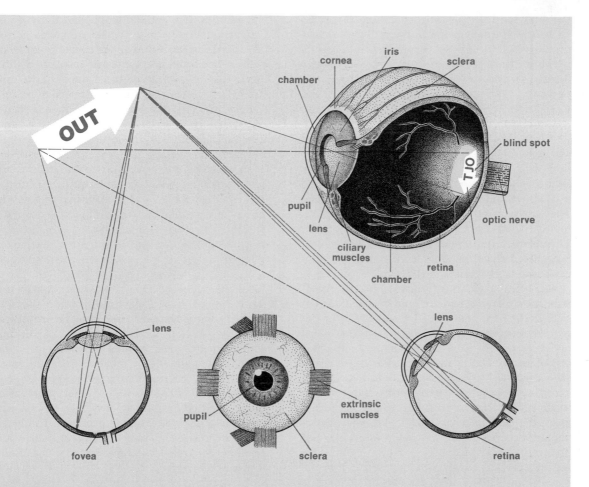

Figure 15.1. The optical mechanism. See text, p. 232, for a detailed explanation and description of the various parts of the eyeball. Note especially the following:

1. The object in the visual field when projected on the retina is reversed both horizontally and vertically: The *left* part of the object (the cuff of the sleeve) is projected on the *right* half of the retina; the *right* part of the object (the index finger) is projected on the *left* half of the retina; and the object as a whole is projected upside down.

2. The light rays from any point on the object spread out in all directions and the rays that reach the eye penetrate all the surface of the lens that is not covered by the iris. The lens (and the cornea) bends the rays so that all those that arise from a single point on the object come to a focus at a single point on the retina.

3. In the diagram the eye is focused directly on the "P" of the word "UP." Therefore part of the "U" falls on the blind spot where there are no retinal cells (see p. 237).

4. The farther the eye is from an object, the flatter the lens is. Compare the lens of the eye in the lower right corner with that in the lower left corner (see p. 232).

5. The farther the eye is from the object, the smaller is the retinal image cast by the object. Compare the retinal image on the eye in the lower right corner with that in the lower left corner.

6. The *fovea* is the section of the retina capable of greatest visual acuity (see p. 237). When the eye is looking directly at an object, the fovea will be in the center of the image cast.

erratum

ball and the focusing power of the eye may be such that the lens cannot always focus images properly (as in nearsightedness and farsightedness) or the cornea or lens may not be uniformly shaped (as in astigmatism). Then, the perceived world changes radically.

Eye Movements

The extrinsic muscles play an extremely important role in normal vision. They produce the beautifully coordinated movements of the two eyes as we shift our gaze from object to object. They also cause tiny, rapid, involuntary movements when we look at a stationary object. These involuntary eye movements have been recognized since the eighteenth century, but an experiment performed in the early 1950s (Riggs, *et al.*, 1953) dramatically disclosed the critical part they play in vision. Using an ingenious optical system for counteracting the effects of eye movements, the experimenters kept the image of an observed pattern constantly focused at one place on a subject's retina. Patterns viewed with this stabilized retinal image at first appear sharp and clear but almost immediately begin to fade, and finally they disappear completely, leaving a homogeneous gray field! The mechanisms accounting for this adaptation are not understood, but it is clear that involuntary movements, although not necessary for the perception of form, are necessary for the maintenance of form perception in normal vision.

The extrinsic muscles have, in addition, a very special function in our perception of the three-dimensional quality of space. As we have seen on page 195, vision with two eyes makes possible an accurate perception of space and distance. Each eye views an object from a slightly different direction and sees aspects of a solid object that the other eye cannot see. Therefore the images focused on the retinas of the two eyes are not identical (the phenomenon of retinal disparity; see Figure 15.2.). When two slightly different images are *appropriately* focused on the retinas, perception of a single

three-dimensional object will be the result.

Our understanding of the retinal-disparity effect will be increased if we consider the concept of *corresponding retinal points*. If one could take the retina of the right eye and simply superimpose it on that of the left eye, aligning the foveas (see Figure 15.1b.), then beneath each point on the right retina would be a "corresponding point" on the left retina. As we shall see in a later section, the neural messages from each pair of corresponding points come together to influence a single point in the visual cortex. The manner in which corresponding points are stimulated determines whether we shall perceive a two-dimensional figure, a three-dimensional figure, or two figures. When corresponding points receive identical stimulation and send the same messages to the brain, as would be the case if a two-dimensional figure were viewed on a flat, uniform wall, there is no three-dimensional perception. When, however, we view a three-dimensional scene and the images on the retinas differ slightly, the light from many points on the external objects falls not on corresponding retinal points but on points slightly displaced from them. The corresponding points of the two retinas are sending slightly different patterns of firings to the cortex, and somehow these two patterns are combined there so as to produce a single three-dimensional perception.

Now, in order for the images of the same object to fall appropriately on (or near) corresponding parts of the retinas, the two eyes must be properly directed at the object, that is, they must *converge* on the object. This convergence is produced by the extrinsic eye muscles, which control rotation of the eyes in their orbits. Occasionally these muscles are paralyzed by disease or injury. In that event, the images of the object fall on the two retinas at points considerably displaced from one another, and double vision can result. You can easily demonstrate the importance of convergence in normal vision by a simple experiment in which you give the extrinsic muscles too difficult a prob-

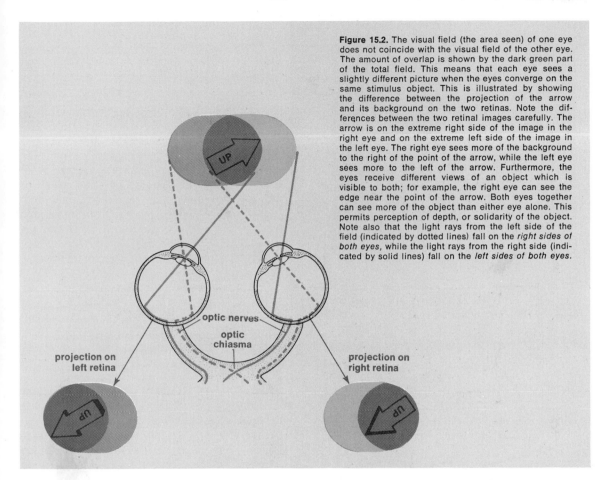

Figure 15.2. The visual field (the area seen) of one eye does not coincide with the visual field of the other eye. The amount of overlap is shown by the dark green part of the total field. This means that each eye sees a slightly different picture when the eyes converge on the same stimulus object. This is illustrated by showing the difference between the projection of the arrow and its background on the two retinas. Note the differences between the two retinal images carefully. The arrow is on the extreme right side of the image in the right eye and on the extreme left side of the image in the left eye. The right eye sees more of the background to the right of the point of the arrow, while the left eye sees more to the left of the arrow. Furthermore, the eyes receive different views of an object which is visible to both; for example, the right eye can see the edge near the point of the arrow. Both eyes together can see more of the object than either eye alone. This permits perception of depth, or solidarity of the object. Note also that the light rays from the left side of the field (indicated by dotted lines) fall on the *right sides of both eyes*, while the light rays from the right side (indicated by solid lines) fall on the *left sides of both eyes*.

lem and double vision results. Gaze at a pencil held about a foot in front of you. You see one image. Now gradually bring the pencil closer, continuing to look at it. Eventually the single image you see will break up into two images. You have passed the limits of the ability of your eyes to converge; as a result, the images of the object fall too far from corresponding parts of the retinas. The proper functioning of the extrinsic muscles, then, is vitally important for accurate vision.

The degree to which the two eyes must converge in order to achieve a single perception varies with the distance of the object from the perceiver. We have already seen that in accommodation the focusing power of the lens must vary with the distance of the object if we are to obtain a sharp image on the retina. We might very well expect convergence and accommodation to be coordinated, and indeed they are; as the curvature of the lens is changed, the eyes converge appropriately. When a stimulus for accommodation is received, *both* the ciliary muscles controlling the lens and the extrinsic muscles are activated. When you consider the use of your eyes in normal vision—as you shift your gaze constantly from place to place and to objects near and far, always perceiving a single three-dimensional scene in focus—it should be clear how delicately coordinated must be the actions of the extrinsic muscles of the two eyes with each other and with the action of the ciliary muscles of the lenses. It should also be clear that proper association between accommodation and convergence (and therefore the perception of depth) can be upset by incorrect muscular balance between the two eyes, by the presence of refractive errors induced by the cornea or lens, or by a nervous system that is not functioning properly because of injury, disease, or drugs (for example, alcohol). *Integrative* action of man's nervous system, including his brain, is of primary importance for visual perception, even at the level of the optical mechanism. We shall find again and again, as we follow this story, that we do not "see" with our eyes alone—but with our brain as well.

Pupillary Behavior

The light from a sunlit snow scene can be one billion times that in a darkened room. The amount of light that reaches the retina must be monitored so that it gets *enough* light to function under low illumination but does not get a *harmful* amount of light under high illumination. This monitoring is achieved by changes in the size of the pupillary opening. Soon after the eye is exposed to an increase or decrease in light intensity, the size of the pupil begins to decrease or increase. The speed of the change and the final size of the pupil depend upon the intensity of the light, the part of the retina stimulated, and so forth. In general, the more intense the light, the smaller the pupil becomes. As the iris opens or closes (that is, the pupil dilates or contracts), the amount of light reaching the retina is increased or decreased.

The Photosensitive Mechanism

The retina is a delicate, almost perfectly transparent membrane composed of several kinds of nerve cells, including the photoreceptors. Nerve cells, as we have seen, normally are specialized to carry messages (impulses) from one place to another. Some types have acquired special sensitivity to particular stimuli, however, and act as receptor cells, that is, as cells that convert the stimulus energy impinging on them to the kind of energy that makes up a neural impulse. The rods and cones of the eye are such cells. They are sensitive to light and are therefore called "photoreceptors."

Some animals (for example, rats) possess only one kind of photoreceptors, called *rods;* some animals (for example, turtles) have only a second kind, called *cones;* still other animals (for example, man) have both kinds. The names "rods" and "cones" suggest a true difference in the shape of these cells, but, more important, rods and cones also differ in their function, in their distribution in the retina, in the way they are interconnected, and in the way they communicate to the brain. We shall see how each of these characteristics helps us to understand some of the phenomena of visual perception.

Structure of the Retina

The retina is structurally very complex, and these structural complexities provide, at this level, the basis for some of the interaction and integration of the visual system. One very simple indication of the number of connections that must exist in this system is the fact that, although there are approximately 125 million rods and 6 million cones, only about 1 million nerve fibers leave the retina. Many rods and cones therefore have nerve fibers in common. Examples of the three major types of connections between the photoreceptors and the brain are shown in Figure 15.3. All three types include photoreceptors, connecting *bipolar cells*, and *ganglion cells* (which transmit the neural impulse directly along the optic nerve to higher centers in the brain). The most direct transmission is found only among some cones. Where it exists, a single cone is connected to a bipolar

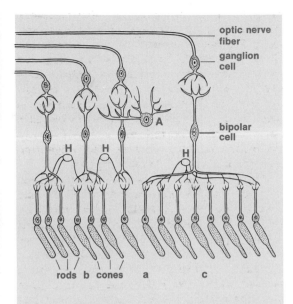

Figure 15.3. Diagrammatic representation of the three major types of connections between the rods and cones of the retina and the brain. The transmission system typical of the cones in the *fovea* is shown in a. Here each cone has its own bipolar cell, which then connects with the optic nerve, which, in turn, leads directly to the brain. What the text calls the "family party line" type of connection is shown in b. Here a group of rods *or* cones shares one bipolar cell. The mixed transmission system, typical of the periphery of the retina, is illustrated in c. A mixed group of rods *and* cones may share one bipolar cell.

The little cells labeled H and A connect one part of the retina with another, giving the anatomical basis for interaction on the retinal level.

cell, which is in turn connected to a ganglion cell. These cones are thus said to have a private line to the brain (see Figure 15.3a.). Next we have transmission systems in which several cones feed into a common bipolar cell, which in turn feeds into a ganglion cell; similar systems are to be found for the rods. These systems might be thought of as "family party lines" (see Figure 15.3b.). Finally, we have mixed rod-cone

systems, in which a number of rods and cones share a common bipolar cell. We might call this arrangement a "public party line" to the brain (see Figure 15.3c.).

In addition to the linkage involved in these transmission systems, other associations are made possible by various types of interconnecting cells. These cells permit interactions among neighboring cones, neighboring rods, and between rods and cones. Such interaction may affect even the "private lines" discussed in the previous paragraph (see Figure 15.3.). The retina, in other words, is not a relay station for isolated photosensitive elements. It is capable of extensive and complex interactions and integration.

Distribution of Rods and Cones

Rods and cones are not uniformly distributed over the entire retina. Figure 15.4. indicates their distribution in the human retina. The *fovea,* a small area at the center of the retina, consists of very thin and very closely packed cones. Each cone in the fovea has its own private line.

As we move outward from the fovea, we find a rapid decrease in the number of cones and a correspondingly rapid increase in the number of rods. As the figure shows, the absolute number of rods comes to a peak at the side of the fovea and then drops. At the periphery there are very few cones. As we move toward the periphery, another important change occurs. Each ganglion cell serves more and more photosensitive cells. In other words, there are more and more "party lines."

All the fibers of the ganglion cells meet in one bundle just to one side of the fovea. This bundle, the *optic nerve,* leaves the retina through an opening in the eyeball (see Figure 15.1.). Because there are no rods or cones at this point, light waves falling here cannot result in any neural impulses and, therefore, in any visual perception. Here you have the simple explanation of the "mysterious" *blind spot* that

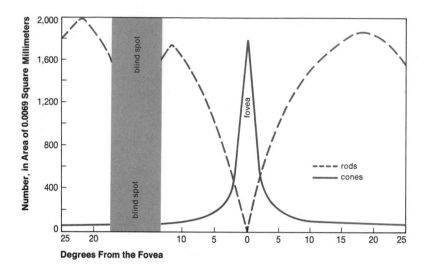

Figure 15.4. This diagram shows the numbers of rods and cones at various distances from the fovea. Note that the number of cones drops rapidly with increasing distance from the fovea, and that the number of rods increases, reaching peaks at about 20 degrees from the fovea.

S. H. Bartley, "The Psychophysiology of Vision," in S. S. Stevens, ed., *Handbook of Experimental Psychology* (1951); adapted by permission of John Wiley & Sons, Inc.

some of you discovered for the first time on p. 118.

Photochemistry of the Retina

Rods and cones contain chemicals that are very sensitive to light. When light falls on these chemicals, they begin to decompose, and while doing so they initiate activity in the rods and cones, which is the first step in getting a message to the brain. Other chemical reactions within the photoreceptors lead to restoration of the light-sensitive substances. When light is falling on the retina, both breakdown of light-sensitive substances and their restoration by chemical action are taking place simultaneously. A balance or equilibrium is reached in which the amount of light-sensitive substance present (and hence the sensitivity of the eye) depends upon the intensity of the stimulating light.

Rods and cones have different light-sensitive chemicals and differ in their sensitivity to light in two ways:

1. Cones on the average are more sensitive to longer wave lengths (that is, "reds") and rods to shorter wave lengths ("blues").
2. Light waves have to be more intense to stimulate a cone than to stimulate a rod.

In addition, the psychological consequences of stimulation of these two classes of receptors are critically different. Stimulation of the cones by different wave lengths results in the qualitatively different experiences of the various hues, whereas stimulation of the rods gives the experience only of brightness ("lighter" or "darker"). The view that rods and cones differ in their function in vision is called the *duplicity theory.*

Our knowledge of the function and distribution of rods and cones thus permits us to understand why our color vision is better at the fovea than at the periphery. Actually, as we have already noted, p. 119, everyone is color blind at the extreme periphery, where there are very few cones.

Purkinje Effect

If we keep in mind the differences between rods and cones just mentioned and add the fact that the brightness of an object will be determined by the total number of rods and cones it stimulates, we shall be in a very good position to understand the *Purkinje effect* (see p. 119).

Consider two flowers in a garden—one red (long wave length) and another blue (short wave length)—so chosen that in high illumination the red flower is brighter than the blue flower. The light from the red flower stimulates many cones and relatively few rods, and the light from the blue flower stimulates relatively few cones but many rods (see point 1 in previous section). As darkness falls in the garden, the number of cones stimulated by either flower will begin to decrease (see point 2 in previous section). Therefore the total number of retinal elements (cones plus rods) stimulated by the red flower will necessarily decrease more rapidly than will the total number of retinal elements stimulated by the blue flower. Gradually, then, as the illumination decreases, the brightness of *both* objects will fall, but that of the red flower will fall faster. Eventually a point will come when the blue flower is brighter than the red flower. This is the Purkinje effect—objects of different hues change in their comparative brightness as illumination changes. If the illumination is lowered far enough, only the rods will respond, and neither hue—blue nor red—will be seen but only objects of different intensities. In the dark all cats are gray.

Cones and Color Vision

Among the several theories that have attempted to account for the perception of color on the basis of physiological mechanisms, the two most prominently considered at present are the *triple-receptor theory* and the *opponents-process theory*. These theories both derive from rival theories of the late nineteenth century, and although in general the triple-receptor theory has had the wider acceptance, the opponents-process theory has recently found new and strong support.

The triple-receptor theory proposes that there are three types of cones, one most sensitive in the blue region, one most sensitive in the green region, and a third most sensitive to reds. The perception of any particular color, according to this theory, depends upon the extent to which the three different kinds of cones are stimulated.

The opponents-process theory suggests that somewhere within the visual system, either at the photoreceptors or at some higher level, three different pairs of biochemical or neural processes can take place in response to visual stimulation and that the members of each pair work in opposition. The proposed pairs respond to black and white, red and green, and blue and yellow. The critical idea in the opponents-process theory is that the paired "processes" compete in sending messages on the final path to the brain. A red message or a green message might thus be sent over the same nerve fiber but not both simultaneously.

For many years such color theories, based upon psychological evidence, have proposed different kinds of cones. Only recently, however, has *direct* evidence been obtained for the existence of individual cones with different photosensitive substances (Brown & Wald, 1964; Marks, *et al.*, 1964). So far, three types of cones have been identified: red, green, and blue. It is important to note that *no* theory of color vision suggests that there are as many different kinds of color receptors as there are perceived colors. *All* theories agree that our ability to perceive "all the colors of the rainbow" (and more) depends upon the particular pattern of neural firings that arrives at the cortex. To determine whether this pattern is the product of three types of receptors, an opponents-process mechanism, a combination of these, or something completely different is a major goal of current research in the psychophysiology of vision.

Color Blindness

Details of the physiological explanations for color blindness vary, of course, with the theories of color vision, but the general pattern of explanation is common to most theories. As all color theories agree that cones are essential for the perception of color, they all assume that color blindness involves some defect in these specialized sensory cells or their interconnections.

As we have observed in Unit 7, p. 119, both protanopes and deuteranopes are red-green blind, in the sense that they confuse these hues; both hues are perceived as yellow. Protanopes and deuteranopes differ, however, in their sensitivity to various wave lengths.

The protanope shows a greatly reduced sensitivity to red. He is red blind in that he simply does not see some reds. This defect is generally believed to result from the absence of the red-sensitive color substance from those cones that normally contain it. It is clear, however, because he also does not perceive green hues as green, that a further explanation of the defect is required. It is widely accepted, currently, that there is no yellow cone and that the yellow process derives from the simultaneous excitation of coupled red and green cones. Applying this view to the protanope, we can argue that his missing red substance has been replaced by the green substance, that his "red" and "green" cones are always simultaneously stimulated, and that this excitation leads to his experiencing yellow.

Most deuteranopes show normal sensitivity to all wave lengths. Their color deficiency is most easily explained by assuming a malfunction in the red-green coupling connections, so that stimulation of *either* a red or a green receptor will produce a yellow process. A second class of deuteranope shows a loss in sensitivity to green that is similar to the protanope's loss of red. These deuteranopes are green blind in the same sense that the protanope is red blind, and the explanation of their color deficiency would parallel the one given for the protanope.

Absence of a blue substance and disturbance of coupling connections have been advanced as explanations for the much rarer types of blue-yellow color blindness.

Electrophysiology of the Retina

With suitably delicate electrodes it is possible to measure neural action in single retinal cells. In this way we can study in considerable detail the response of the rods and cones to light stimulation. Among the findings from such experimentation we can list the following: First, the greater the intensity of the light, the greater the activity in most photoreceptors and the higher the firing rate of the fibers of the optic nerve. That is, an intense point of light will stimulate a single photoreceptor to initiate a large number of neural impulses per second; a weak light will result in fewer impulses. Second, rods and cones are capable of "spontaneous" discharge; that is, they initiate neural impulses from time to time, even in the absence of stimulation by light waves. Third, responses in one cell can be *inhibited* or stopped by stimulating a neighboring receptor. Fourth, under some conditions optic nerve fibers do not respond to the onset of light (on-response) but do respond when the light is turned off (off-response)! And, indeed, a fiber at times may respond to both the onset *and* the termination of a light (on-off response). That a certain fiber may show an on-response to blue light and an off-response to yellow light exemplifies one of the types of recent evidence mentioned earlier that supports an opponents-process explanation of color perception.

Sensitivity, Adaptation, and Afterimages

The amount of light necessary to stimulate the retina depends upon the state of sensitivity of the rods and cones. A primary determinant of the "state" of a photoreceptor is the amount of photosensitive substance in the cell. The more photopigment in the cell, the more likely it is to react to light. Experimental studies of retinal elements have shown that, as the eye adapts to the dark, photopigment concentrations build up. This build-up is consistent with what we have already learned about the breakdown and restoration of photopigments. We can understand, therefore, our earlier observation that the eye that is dark-adapted will be more sensitive—that is, more ready to respond to light —than the eye that is not.

Similar reasoning can lead to an understanding of negative afterimages. It will be remembered that, if we fixate the black and white figure of Box 22, p. 141, and then look at a gray wall, we experience an afterimage with the black-white relations reversed. During the initial fixation the retinal elements upon which the intense light from the white areas falls gradually become depleted of photosensitive substance. This depletion does not occur in the retinal elements upon which the weaker light from the black area falls. When the retina is stimulated by the relatively weak light from the gray wall, the already depleted retinal elements (corresponding to the original white part of the figure) will show little response, whereas the undepleted elements (corresponding to the original black part of the figure) will show relatively strong response. What had previously been seen as brighter will therefore now be seen as darker, and what had previously been seen as darker will now be seen as brighter.

The response of a photoreceptor depends not only upon the amount of photopigment present but also upon the kind of photopigment. The *visual purple* found in rods is more light sensitive than are the cone pigments. Rods also have substantially more photopigment than do cones. For these two reasons rods are much more sensitive to light stimulation than are cones.

The greater sensitivity of individual rods, as contrasted to cones, is one factor contributing to the greater *sensitivity* to light in the periphery of the eye, where the rods are numerous, than in the fovea, where cones are concentrated.

There is an additional reason for the greater sensitivity of this area, which involves the connections within the retina. To perceive light, it is not enough that receptors respond; the ganglion cells must transmit a neural message to the cortex. Although it is a fact that a single rod in its most sensitive state will respond to a single photon (the smallest possible quantity of light), it takes several such *receptor* responses to produce a response in the cortex. A

single impulse arriving at a ganglion cell is not enough to fire it, but when a *number* of rods funnel their impulses through a common "party" bipolar cell, the *sum* of the neural impulses arriving at the ganglion cell could be enough to fire that cell and send a message off to the higher centers. In some areas as many as 1,200 rods may be connected with a single ganglion cell. A rod system with such a widespread network of very sensitive elements feeding into a single ganglion cell is most likely to generate a central response to the widely scattered photons of a very weak light. Since "party line" communication is absent in the fovea, but increasingly present outside the fovea, we have here another explanation for the increased sensitivity of the periphery. This same physiological explanation may also be applied to the *summation* effect we observed on p. 142.

These facts also help us to understand a somewhat puzzling visual experience. When we observe a very faint star in the sky, it is easier to see it if we do not look directly at it, but fixate slightly to one side of it. Indeed, if the star is very faint, it will disappear when we look directly at it. Visual sensitivity (absolute threshold) is better off the fovea than at the fovea.

The difference in sensitivity of the eye to different wave lengths reflects the different sensitivities of the various photopigments. This fact is easy to see when we compare the sensitivity curve of the dark-adapted eye with the sensitivity curve of visual purple to different wave lengths of light. These curves (see Figure 15.5.) are very similar. The sensitivity of the dark-adapted eye to various wave lengths is determined by the visual purple in the rods. On the other hand, when we compare the sensitivity curve of a dark-adapted eye to that of a light-adapted eye (see Figure 7.4., p. 120), it is the difference in the pigments of the rods and cones that is reflected in the difference in these two curves.

Differential-intensity thresholds depend upon

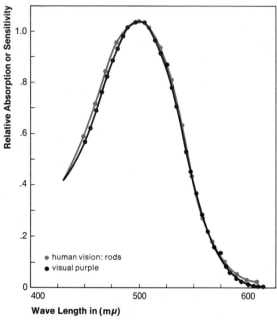

Figure 15.5. These two overlapping curves show the response of visual purple and of the human dark-adapted eye to different wave lengths of light. The visual purple curve is plotted from measures of the chemical effects of different colors of light upon test-tube samples of visual purple taken from the chicken eye. The second curve derives from absolute threshold measures of the dark-adapted, lensless (the lens filters more of some wave lengths than of others) human eye. Each point on this curve depends upon a separate threshold measure to a particular color. The extremely close fit of the two curves lends strong support to the view that the sensitivity of the dark-adapted eye (rod vision) is determined by the visual purple found in the rods.

the ability of the brain to detect differences in the rates of neural firings arriving from two sources. If the firing rates are low (as would be the case with weak lights), the brain can detect a small inequality; but if the firings are coming in at a high rate (as they would with strong lights), then the difference must be considerable before it can be detected. It can easily be demonstrated that the eye's state of dark adaptation, the retinal area stimulated, and the wave length of stimulating light will affect the firing rate from a light of fixed intensity and consequently its differential-intensity threshold.

Acuity

Visual acuity (the ability to detect small differences in object size and shape) was found in Unit 7, p. 121, to depend upon the presence or absence of defects in the ocular mechanism, the retinal position of the stimulus, light intensity, stimulus contrast, and so forth. It will help us to understand the physiological bases for some of these variables if we consider one of the standard laboratory tests of acuity. In this test the subject is presented with a series of simple patterns of light and dark lines of equal width. If the lines are too narrow, he perceives a surface of even brightness rather than a pattern. A measure of acuity is the width of the narrowest set of lines that can be perceived as a pattern. The problem can be regarded as one of differential-intensity discrimination, in that the brain will be receiving messages stimulated by the light lines and by the dark lines and must be able to tell that there are more messages coming from the former ("it's brighter") than from the latter ("it's darker").

The first limit on acuity is set by our optical mechanism. If the pattern of lines is not sharply focused on the retina, the light and dark lines will overlap substantially, and the photoreceptors cannot be expected to send different messages to the brain. Even in the "normal" eye there is a point beyond which the optical mechanism cannot resolve fine patterns. So, if we make the pattern of lines fine enough, light and dark lines will no longer be focused separately but will overlap on the retina.

A second limit on acuity is determined by the distribution and connections of our photoreceptors. The fact that the fovea contains many thin cones, tightly packed together, permits us to understand why visual acuity is best in the fovea and becomes poorer as we leave it. Two closely spaced lines of light stimulating rows of closely neighboring cones in the fovea, each with its "private lines" to the brain, can send two distinct patterns of signals to the brain. Outside the fovea the cones are interspersed with rods, their diameter is greater, and "party-line" communication with the brain is the rule. Now two closely spaced lines of light may stimulate the *same* photosensitive elements, or even if they should stimulate different elements, these elements may send neural impulses only over the *same* "party line." Therefore, visual acuity, the ability to differentiate small details, becomes poorer as we leave the fovea.

The superiority of the cones for visual acuity also helps explain why acuity is better when illumination is bright than when it is dim. The cones operate only during bright illumination.

Acuity is better when there is high contrast in the stimulus; this fact can be easily understood by again considering our pattern of lines. If the lines are black and white (high contrast), the white lines will send a large number of firings to the brain, whereas the black lines will send relatively few. The brain's task of discriminating these differences will be easy. If, however, we use a light gray instead of white, and a dark gray instead of black (low contrast), the *difference* in the numbers of firings from the two kinds of lines will be much smaller, and the task of the brain will be harder.

Interaction Effects in Vision

We can begin to understand the perceptual effects of stimuli that are in spatial or temporal proximity by remembering, first, that the retina is not built like a relay station of isolated elements but has cells *connecting* one part with another and, second, that activity in one element can *inhibit* activity in neighboring elements or *summate* with activity in neighboring elements.

Two stimulus objects may be physically isolated in the real world, but the neural responses evoked by their isolated images in the retina may be interrelated. The brain may never actually receive sets of isolated signals corresponding to the isolated stimulus objects. The photosensitive apparatus *itself* may begin the combining and organizing process. The summation and irradiation effects observed in visual perception (see p. 142) can thus be understood in terms of the interconnecting cells of the retina.

The observation that a retinal cell in action can block its neighboring cell from reacting to light suggests a possible neurological explanation for the perceptual phenomenon of simultaneous contrast (see p. 143). The explanation may run something like this: The cells stimulated by the *bright* patch of color may inhibit the action of the neighboring cells that are being stimulated by the gray patch. The result would be that the light from the gray patch would activate fewer retinal elements when the gray patch is next to a bright patch than when the gray patch is alone in the visual field. The brighter the white patch, the greater would be this inhibitory effect. Therefore, two equal gray patches surrounded by two *different* white patches would appear to be of different brightness because the *grays* would be differentially "muted." Conversely, a gray surrounded by black looks brighter than a gray surrounded by white because the first gray is less inhibited by its neighboring black.

Glossary

accommodation The change in focusing power of the crystalline lens by means of which the eye can focus on objects at various distances.

bipolar cell A neural element that carries impulses from rods and cones to the ganglion cells.

ciliary muscles Muscles attached to the lens of the eye; their contraction and relaxation produce changes in the curvature of the lens.

cones Specialized cone-shaped cells in the retina. These cells are sensitive to light waves and initiate a neural impulse when light waves impinge upon them. Cones are specially sensitive to differences in the wave length of light. Stimulation of cones gives rise to the experience of hue.

cornea A transparent covering of the front of the eye. The window of the eye.

crystalline lens A transparent structure of the eye, shaped somewhat like a convex lens and capable of change in shape by the stretching action of the ciliary muscles. The lens focuses light waves from the outside onto the retina.

duplicity theory The theory that rods and cones differ in function, that rods are primarily sensitive to intensity of light waves and cones to differences in wave length. The rods thus help us to discriminate brightness differences, the cones, hue differences.

extrinsic muscles Muscles attached to the outside of each eyeball permitting controlled rotation of the eyeball in its socket.

fovea A central part of the retina consisting of very thin and closely packed cones. Each cone in the fovea has its own bipolar cell. There are no rods in the fovea. Because of its composition, the fovea is the area of the retina capable of greatest visual acuity and of most efficient hue discrimination.

ganglion cell A neural cell that receives impulses from rods and cones via an intervening bipolar cell and transmits these impulses to the brain.

iris A delicate, colored, fibrous structure that lies on the lens and has a circular opening (the pupil) in its center. The actions of the muscles of the iris can increase or decrease the size of the pupil.

opponents-process theory A theory of color vision that proposes three pairs of visual processes: black-white, red-green, blue-yellow. The paired processes are assumed to work in opposition so that only one member of a pair can be effective at one time.

optical mechanism A general term referring to the various anatomical and physiological mechanisms involved in conducting light waves from the outside world and focusing them on the retina. Specifically, the structures and functions of the cornea, lens, ciliary muscles, iris, extrinsic muscles.

photosensitive mechanism A general term referring to the various anatomical and physiological mechanisms involved in the conversion of light waves into neural activity. Specifically, this term refers to the nature, distribution, and functions of the rods and cones.

pupil The circular opening in the center of the iris. The pupil is not a structure. It is the "hole in the doughnut."

retina A layer of light-sensitive elements (rods and cones) and nerve fibers. It lines the inner wall of the large chamber of the eyeball.

rods Specialized rodlike cells in the retina. These cells are sensitive to light waves and initiate a neural impulse when light waves impinge upon them. Rods are primarily responsive to changes in the intensity of light waves. Stimulation of the rods results in the experience of brightness but not of hue.

sclera A white opaque protective skin enveloping most of the eyeball.

triple-receptor theory A theory designed to give a physiological basis for color vision. According to this theory, there are three specialized types of cone. Some cones are assumed to be most sensitive to red, some most sensitive to green, and some most sensitive to blue.

visual purple A chemical in the rods that decomposes when light waves impinge upon them. Decomposition of this chemical is assumed to initiate nerve currents in the rods.

postretinal mechanisms of visual perception

overview / Neural impulses from the retina are transmitted through the optic nerves and optic tracts to the lateral geniculate bodies, and from there to the visual cortex on the occipital lobes of the cerebral hemispheres. At the optic chiasma half of the fibers from each eye "cross over" so as to end up on the other side of the brain. Nevertheless, the arrangement of pathways maintains a close relationship between specific areas of the retina and specific cortical areas. Impulses from the right side of the retina of each eye are sent to the right hemisphere and those from the left side of each retina to the left hemisphere.

In the lateral geniculate bodies (as in the retina) each nerve cell responds best when the retina is stimulated by a small spot of light shining in a certain part of the visual field. In the cortex there are nerve cells that respond only when the retina is stimulated by simple patterns (like lines or corners) and not when it is stimulated by points or circles of light. These findings (and their explanation in neural terms) give us a clue to the mechanisms of visual form perception.

The reticular formation is a highly interconnected network of neurons in the brain stem, which receives nervous impulses from many sensory systems and from the cortex, and which sends out impulses diffusely to various parts of the nervous system. Its activity modifies the ways in which the cortex can use incoming sensory information. It may produce an aroused, or alerted, state of the cortex, which appears to be necessary for normal perception, but it can also block or inhibit the reception of sensory information.

Our knowledge of these mechanisms and of other aspects of brain function have resulted from the use of three major research techniques: the ablation method, electrophysiological techniques, and biochemical studies of brain and behavior.

A complete description of the physiological processes of visual perception must of course include the important neural events beyond the eye: how the neural reactions in the retina are propagated within the individual's brain and how his brain reacts to and integrates these incoming signals. Even the simplest visual perception involves all these processes. We shall consider the postretinal events in two stages, involving two physiological mechanisms: the *conduction mechanism* and the *central mechanism.*

The Conduction Mechanism

The *optic nerve* consists of bundles of the nerve fibers (axons) of the ganglion cells. These fibers conduct the impulses originating in the rods and cones toward the cortex of the brain. There are three anatomical sites that we must consider along this conduction pathway—the *optic chiasma,* the *lateral geniculate bodies,* and the *occipital lobes* of the brain. The events that occur at these points have important psychological implications.

The Optic Chiasma

As we see in Figure 16.1., after the optic nerves from each eye enter the cranium, they converge and meet at the very base of the brain. This meeting place is called the optic chiasma, and here the bundles of nerve fibers making up each optic nerve are re-sorted before they continue farther into the brain. The bundles leaving the optic chiasma are called the *optic tracts.* In the re-sorting, fibers from the right sides of both retinas are bundled together and go to the right half of the brain; and fibers from the left sides of both retinas go to the left side of the brain. In the optic tracts, fibers from "corresponding parts" of the retinas are traveling together for the first time. As light from an object on the *left* side of the visual field forms an image on the right sides of both retinas, the two images from an object on the left side of the field will send signals to the same (right) side of the brain. This re-sorting also means, of course, that each retina has connections with *both* sides of the brain—the right half of each retina with the right side of the brain and the left half of each retina with the left side of the brain.

The Lateral Geniculate Bodies

These two bundles of reshuffled fibers then continue on into the brain, where they end in two masses of brain cells called the lateral geniculate bodies. These bodies serve as relay and shunting stations. The fibers that have come from the retina connect here with a new set of neurons, most of which lead directly to the cortex of the brain.

The Occipital Lobes of the Brain

These fibers from the lateral geniculate bodies end in a specific part of the cortex called the occipital lobes. The connections between specific areas on the retina and equally specific areas in the occipital lobes have been fairly well worked out and are indicated in Figure 16.1.

Our "conduction" story ends with the arrival of the impulses from the retina at the sensory area of the cortex, where the major job of integrating the impulses begins.

The Central Mechanisms

Three major research techniques have been used, on animals and on man, in the study of brain function.

First, in the *ablation* technique, different parts of the receptor organs, conduction system, or brain are destroyed, and observations are then made on the behavior of the organism.

Second, there are the two types of *electrophysiological techniques.* In one, the brain of an animal or man is exposed surgically, and specific parts of it are stimulated with a mild electrical current. Observations are then made on the resulting behavior. In this way we discover something about which part of the brain controls which behavior (see Box 46, p. 253). In the other electrophysiological technique, various parts of the lower nervous system (the receptors, or segments of the conduction system) are stimulated, and the resulting electrical responses in the brain are recorded. In this way we discover something about which parts of the retina, say, are able to instigate neural activity in which parts of the cortex.

The third, and newest, research technique for the study of brain function revolves about the analysis of biochemical activity in the brain and its relations to sensory stimulation and behavior. Work done with this technique will be discussed in Unit 29, p. 469.

The Visual Cortex

Both ablation and electrophysiological techniques played a part in establishing the general relation, shown in Figure 16.1., between parts of the retina and parts of the occipital cortex.

More recent studies with the electrophysiological approach use electrodes so small that they can record the activities of single nerve cells. We can put such a *microelectrode* into the lateral geniculate body or into the visual cortex, and we can then move a small light so that it will stimulate different points on the retina in turn, noting when the cell responds. When we attempt to find out which parts of the retina trigger a response in a certain cell, we are said to be determining the *receptive field* of that cell. Some of this work has profound significance for our understanding of visual form perception.

We might expect that the receptive field of a cell in the lateral geniculate or the visual cortex would be a small circle in the visual field. This conclusion is logical because we would expect the cell in the cortex to receive fibers coming from a small area in the lateral geniculate body, which would be relaying impulses arising originally from a small area in the retina, which would *itself* be stimulated by light from a small spot in the field.

Cells in the lateral geniculate body do have circular response fields, but in the visual cortex the typical cells are stimulated best not by a circular spot but rather by a short line (or thin rectangle) of light. To stimulate a given cell, the line of light must be at a certain place in the visual field and must be oriented in a certain direction. It is not very hard to understand how this kind of receptive field could arise.

Imagine a group of cells in the lateral geniculate, each of which is stimulated by light from one point along a certain line in the visual field. If these cells have fibers that all *come together* to stimulate one cell in the cortex, then that cortical cell will respond best when all points along the line are illuminated. Illumination of only one point on the line would have very little effect upon the cortical cell. A line in the same part of the visual field but with a different orientation would have only one point in common with the optimal line and would therefore have little effect, and a line in a different part of the visual field would have essentially *no* effect upon the cell we are discussing (see Figure 16.2.).

In this way it is possible to understand how a given cell in the cortex can come to respond to a *pattern* of response at lower neural levels. Here may be the first clue to an understanding of the mechanisms of perception of visual *forms*. The picture is even more convincing when additional results are considered. Cells have been found in the visual cortex that respond best to a line with a given orientation, regardless of where in the visual field it is located; other cells respond best to a "corner," that is, a pair of lines at right angles to each other, and still others seem to be stimulated better by moving than by stationary stimuli. All these findings can be explained by imagining that certain kinds of further convergence take place between fibers from cortical cells of the variety we first described; all these findings show that certain aspects of visual stimuli

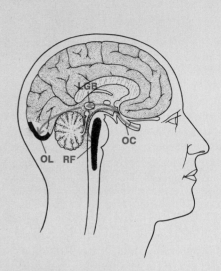

Brain Split Longitudinally

 OC optic chiasma
 RF reticular formation
LGB lateral geniculate bodies
 OL occipital lobe

erratum

Figure 16.1. The visual system. The sketch of the brain in the upper left corner outlines the route of the optic tract from the optic chiasma to the occipital lobes. Use this sketch to orient yourself on the larger drawing, which gives the details of this route. Note especially the following:

 1. The light rays from the left side of the visual field (indicated by the green stripes) fall on the right sides of both retinas, whereas the light rays from the right side of the visual field (indicated by gray stripes) fall on the left sides of both retinas. The light from the top of the field (indicated by colors of a lighter shade) falls on the bottoms of the retinas, and vice versa.

 2. The fibers from the *right side of each retina* (indicated by the dotted lines from the retinas to the occipital areas) end up on the right occipital lobe of the brain; the fibers from the *left side of each retina* (indicated by solid lines) end up on the left occipital lobe. This means that the *left visual field* is represented on the right side of the brain, the right visual field on the left side of the brain. Only half the visual world (but as seen by *both* eyes) is projected on each occipital lobe. Of course, we *experience* only one integrated whole. For example, the area striped green and white and the left half of the green and gray area are projected on the right occipital lobe; the remainder of the green and gray area as well as the gray and white area are projected on the left occipital lobe. Nevertheless we achieve one complete visual experience.

 The receptors of the fovea are more richly connected with the occipital lobes (via their "private lines") than are those of any other part of the retina. Because, in this diagram, the eyes are supposed to be fixated at the center point of the green and gray area, the inner parts of this area fall on the foveas and are given detailed representation in the lobes, whereas the rest of the picture gets less representation and is therefore shown diminished in size.

 For discussion of the other parts of the visual system pictured here (optic chiasma, lateral geniculate bodies, reticular formation), see pp. 248 and 255–6.

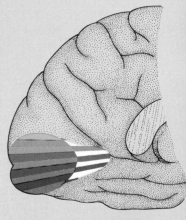

projection on left occipital lobe

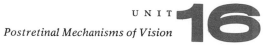
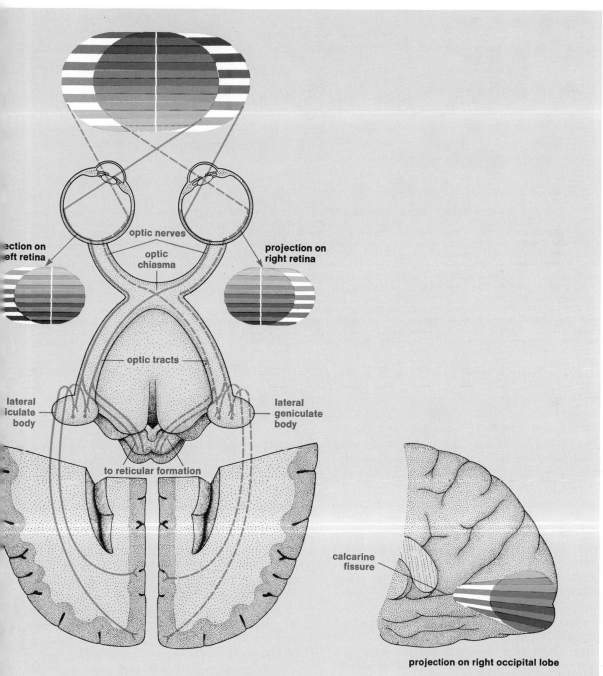

projection on
left retina

optic nerves

optic
chiasma

projection on
right retina

optic tracts

lateral
geniculate
body

lateral
geniculate
body

to reticular formation

calcarine
fissure

projection on right occipital lobe

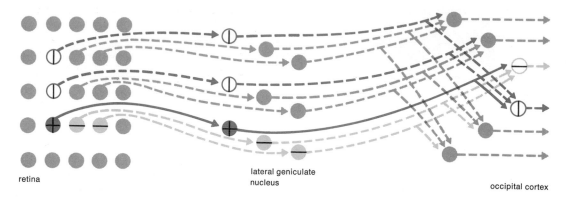

retina

lateral geniculate
nucleus

occipital cortex

Figure 16.2. Each pattern of light (that is, stimulus) hitting the retina affects many receptor cells, and the sets of cells affected by different stimuli may have some cells in common. How does the visual system manage nevertheless to develop a specific response for each stimulus? This diagram, based on the work of Hubel and Wiesel (pp. 254–5) and others, shows how it might be done. A vertical line of light would stimulate the cells in the retina, shown here with vertical stripes; a horizontal line would stimulate the horizontally striped cells. (One cell would thus be activated by *either* line.) These retinal cells are shown connected one-to-one to cells in the lateral geniculate body. It does not matter if the position of the cells in relationship to one another is different in the lateral geniculate body—the connections are important and, as there are one-to-one connections, nothing has been lost, but also nothing has been gained. At the occipital cortex, changes do take place. Each lateral geniculate cell connects with *two* cortical cells. If we assume that the cortical cells cannot be activated unless they receive three incoming impulses at once, then the only neuron activated by the horizontal stimulus will be the one that is horizontally striped, and the vertical stimulus will stimulate effectively only the vertically striped neuron. Distinctive and nonoverlapping neural responses are thus produced, responses that will activate other parts of the nervous system, producing the experience and behavior appropriate to the stimulus.

are abstracted by *coding* methods "built into" the organization of the nerve cells and suggest that perception of a given visual form depends upon stimulation of the appropriate cortical cells by means of the correct complex pathway (see Box 47, p. 254).

The experiments just discussed, taken in conjunction with certain ablation studies, lead to the conclusion that the visual system up to the cortex is *essential* for visual perception; but the next question is whether or not it is *sufficient*. Although a harder question, it may be safely answered in the negative. Activity in the visual cortical area gives rise to impulses that travel to other brain areas and is itself influenced by impulses deriving from many other parts of the brain. *The final perception is determined by the integrated pattern of activity of most of the brain.*

Retinal-Cortical Relations

A structural base for space perception is provided by the connections between retinal and cortical areas. Information from specific retinal-cortical groups of cells tells us something immediately about the spatial relations of the stimuli involved. For example, certain retinal cells are always stimulated by the top of the visual field, and the signals they send to their cortical cells are always perceived as at the top, or "up." Similarly, other retinal-cortical groups signal bottom, right, left, and so on.

A question that immediately arises is whether or not these retinal-cortical groups are innately determined units. Is the construction of the visual system predetermined, so that a specific retinal cell will be connected to a specific cortical cell and activity in this unit will

Box 46 "Mapping"
the Functions
of a Human Brain

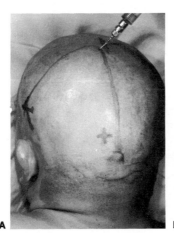

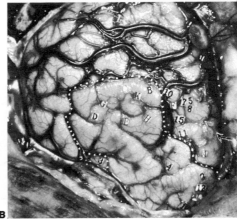

A   B

The best-known electrophysiological studies on the human brain are those of Wilder Penfield, McGill University's famous brain surgeon. He and his associates have reported on hundreds of brain operations, most of them on epileptic patients. When a patient requires surgery, a "craniotomy" is performed, that is, a bone flap is cut into the skull (see Figure A), and the brain is exposed to view. The operation is performed under local anesthesia, and the patient is conscious throughout. The surgical problem is to remove every bit of abnormal tissue with minimal interference in the functioning of the brain.

To discover how much tissue he can safely remove, the surgeon stimulates a point on the cortex with a weak electrical current. A numbered ticket is placed on the spot stimulated, and the corresponding response is recorded. The entire area is explored in this fashion, and the surgeon soon has a "map" of the functions of the brain to guide his surgery (see Figure B). Let us describe very briefly one of his cases.

"*Case C. J.* Eighteen-year-old boy suffering from epileptic seizures. Craniotomy was carried out and left occipital lobe exposed. From various diagnostic tests it appeared desirable to remove the cortex indicated by dotted white lines (see right figure). 'Mapping' of surrounding cortex was then carried out. Here are some of the responses of the boy when the various points on his cortex were stimulated: *Point 2:* 'A ball of light, all colors.' *Point 3:* 'Flashing in my eyes.' *Point 4:* 'Tiny colored lights which were moving.' *Point 8:* 'There was a short spot in the right eye.' "

Many similar investigations have led Penfield to the following conclusions: First, removal of the primary visual sensory area of the cortex results in complete blindness on that side. Second, electrical stimulation of the occipital area alone results in very elementary visual experiences—fuzzy lights, shadows, and colors—but there are no well-defined visual images of objects. Much more of the brain than the primary visual centers of the cortex is involved in the perception of objects.

The operation was carried out on C. J. Complete right blindness was produced, but C. J. no longer suffered from epileptic seizures.

W. PENFIELD and T. RASMUSSEN. 1950. *The Cerebral Cortex of Man* (New York: Macmillan). Photos courtesy W. Penfield, Montreal Neurological Institute, McGill University; reprinted by permission.

Box 47

Brain Anatomy and
Form Perception

The experiments on the receptive field of the individual cells in the visual system described on p. 249 were performed by physiologists D. H. Hubel and T. N. Wiesel of Harvard University. They found nerve cells in the cat's visual cortex that were stimulated most readily by a "line," or narrow rectangle of light. Each cell responds best to such a figure oriented in a particular direction, but there seem to be about as many cells that respond to any one direction as to any other.

A somewhat similar conclusion about the receptive fields of visual brain cells in the *octopus* was reached by J. Z. Young of the University of London on the basis of anatomical studies he did at the Naples Zoological Station. The fields for such cells also turn out to be approximately rectangular in shape. In the octopus, however, there appear to be more cells with receptive fields oriented horizontally or vertically than cells with intermediate (oblique) orientation of the field.

If the octopus does not have many cells that are "tuned" to respond to oblique orientations, then it might be expected to have trouble in learning to respond differently to figures with different oblique orientations. This difficulty was shown to exist by N. S. Sutherland (now at the University of Sussex). An octopus is trained to "attack" plastic figures, which are placed in the animal's tank. If the animal attacks a rectangularly shaped figure oriented horizontally, he is given a crab to eat; if he attacks a vertical rectangle, he receives an electric shock. Octopuses can learn to respond to the appropriate orientation in this situation, but they show almost no learning if the rectangles are oblique, that is, if one goes "up and to the right" and the other goes "up and to the left"—even though attacks on the former lead to food and attacks on the latter, lead to shock.

But what about the cat? If there are as many receptive fields with oblique orientations as there are with horizontal or vertical orientations, then this line of reasoning would suggest that cats should find it no harder to respond differently to two oblique figures than to differentiate a horizontal from a vertical figure. This fact, too, Sutherland has demonstrated. Some cats had to learn to open a door with a horizontal rectangle on it and not to open a door with a vertical rectangle. If the cat did the correct thing, he received some food as a reward. Other cats were taught to respond differently to doors with rectangles in two different, but oblique, orientations. The problem was learned equally rapidly by the animals in both groups.

The difficulty of the octopuses with the oblique rectangles reminds us that the organism cannot respond to information that it cannot handle. This illustration offers a nice example of the differences that may exist between the perceptual worlds of different species.

Why does not the octopus tilt his body or his head in attacking one of these problems and thus convert oblique to horizontal and vertical? The answer is simply that the octopus is so built that he cannot do it. The position of the eyes is controlled by receptors that are sensitive to the pull of gravity. If the head is tilted, the receptors tilt the eyes in the other direction—keeping the eyes always lined up with the horizontal plane!

D. H. HUBEL and T. N. WIESEL. 1962. Receptive Fields, Binocular Interaction and Functional Architecture in the Cat's Visual Cortex, *J. Physiol.*, 160, 106–54.

J. Z. YOUNG. 1964. *A Model of the Brain* (London: Oxford University Press).

N. S. SUTHERLAND. 1957. Visual Discrimination of Orientation by Octopus, *Brit. J. Psychol.*, 48, 55–71.

N. S. SUTHERLAND. 1963. Cat's Ability to Discriminate Oblique Rectangles, *Science*, 139, 209–10.

be perceived as at the top of the visual field? Suppose that we could disconnect an eye, invert it, and replace it. How would it function? Let us consider two possibilities. First, retinal cells could simply shift jobs. Cells that previously were stimulated by the top of the visual field, now receiving the bottom of the visual field, might connect to bottom cortical cells and signal "bottom." In this case vision would be normal. Second, if specific retinal-cortical connections are innately determined, the retinal cells might somehow establish connections with their old cortical cells. In this case cells receiving the bottom of the visual field would transmit to cortical cells that are always perceived as signaling "top," and vision would be inverted.

The experiment that these two possibilities suggest has been performed on lower animals, and the second possibility turns out to be true. In these animals space perception is innately determined. Frogs whose eyes have been inverted will jump up at a fly shown below them and jump down to one shown above them. Their perceived world is inverted, and they can never learn to correct this "false" perception.

We must be careful in extending our interpretation of these experiments. They have not been performed on higher animals, as a severed optic nerve will not reconnect in higher species. It is clear, however, that the space perception of the frog depends upon the innately determined structure of his visual system.

The Reticular Formation

The interaction within the nervous system that proves to be so important in perception is illustrated by considering the role of the *reticular formation*, a highly interconnected network of neurons in the brain stem, which has widespread influence upon other parts of the nervous system.

Part of the reticular formation can be thought of as a kind of *central station*, at which neural impulses arrive from many sensory systems. Fibers of the visual system thus carry impulses from the retina by way of subcortical nuclei to the reticular formation. Impulses *from* this formation are, in turn, diffusely conducted to various parts of the brain, including the cortex (see Figure 16.3.). These neural impulses *serve to arouse or alert the cortex*. Experiments have indicated that, if the reticular system is prevented from sending on neural impulses to the cortex (by cutting, drugging, or otherwise interfering with the pathways of the reticular system), the individual may either lose consciousness, go into a deep coma, fall into a deep sleep, or, at the very least, have great difficulty in responding to stimuli from the outside world. Even though the neural impulses from his retina, for example, do reach his occipital lobes directly from the lateral geniculate bodies, normal visual perception is difficult to sustain *unless impulses from the reticular formation are diffusely discharged into his cortex at the same time.*

This basic observation has many implications for perception. For example, an impulse from the *retina*, when it is shunted into the reticular formation, can alert the whole cortex, so that the cortex can respond more adequately to an impulse *from the ear*. Stimulation by one sensory mode (vision) can thus facilitate perception in another sensory mode (audition). Light waves from an object can act as a specific sensory stimulus and a general "alerter" at the same time. Here, perhaps, is one of the physiological bases for the "attention-demanding character" of intense stimuli.

The reticular formation also *receives* impulses from various cortical areas. The stimulation received in this way can "feed back" to the cortex, so that cortical activity can help to maintain a high level of alertness in the cortex itself! By "concentrating," we can keep more alert to incoming stimuli.

The fibers leaving the reticular formation do not all ascend to the level of the cortex. Some carry impulses that interact at various way stations in the brain with the sensory messages coming up from the receptors. That is, neural

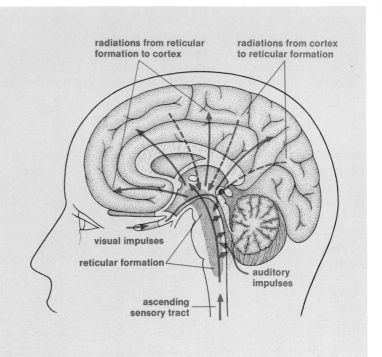

radiations from reticular formation to cortex

radiations from cortex to reticular formation

Figure 16.3. This diagram indicates some of the relationships between the reticular formation and the cerebral cortex. Note that the neural impulses from the sensory organs (ear, eye, skin, and so on) not only go directly to the cortex but also enter the ascending reticular formation through branch lines. From the ascending reticular formation impulses are sent diffusely to cover much of the cortex. Note also that impulses radiate *from* the cortex to the descending reticular formation. From the descending reticular formation these impulses are sent back to some of the lower brain centers that receive incoming sensory impulses.

visual impulses

reticular formation

auditory impulses

ascending sensory tract

signals coming down from the reticular formation and the cortex meet the signals coming up from the eyes, ears, skin, and so forth.

This descending influence can be facilitating, as shown by its participation in the *orienting response* or *orienting reaction* (see Unit 32). These terms are used to refer to the pattern of change in the organism that follows the presentation of a *new* stimulus. The response includes the turning of the head or eyes in the direction of the stimulus, as well as changes in respiration and heart beat; it also includes an enhancement of the brain response to stimuli presented to the receptors. Increase in the brain response may be measured in subcortical way stations on the sensory pathways and even in the receptors themselves and is thought to be due to facilitative impulses coming from the reticular formation.

Other impulses coming from the reticular formation may be inhibitory, decreasing the sensitivity of the organism to incoming stimuli.

Through this mechanism neural impulses originating from one sensory system of the brain can set off impulses in the reticular formation that will *block* other sensory impulses from having their usual effect upon the brain. For example, an impulse that arises in the visual centers can prevent impulses from the ear from producing the expected electrical activity in the auditory areas of the cortex. These selective inhibitory effects take place in the cortex itself and perhaps in lower centers as well. Such findings can help us to understand the very common experience of not hearing someone speak to us when our attention is completely taken up by watching an object intently. We do not hear the person because, for the moment, *we are literally deafened by our intense visual gaze!* This function of the reticular formation may also help us to understand many of the phenomena of shifts of attention and the selective effects of set on perception, which are discussed in Unit 11.

Glossary

ablation technique A research technique used in neurology and physiological psychology. Different parts of an animal's sensory receptors, neural conduction system, or brain are destroyed, and observations are then made of the animal's behavior.

central mechanism A general term referring to the various anatomical and physiological mechanisms of the entire brain.

conduction mechanism A general term referring to the various anatomical and physiological mechanisms involved in conducting neural impulses from receptor organs to the cortex.

electrophysiological technique A technique used in neurology and physiological psychology. This technique can be divided into two types. In one type, parts of the nervous system are stimulated (in various ways) and observations are made of the resulting electrical responses in the brain. In the other, specific areas of the brain are stimulated with a mild electrical current, and observations are made of the resulting experience or behavior.

lateral geniculate bodies Masses of brain cells serving as relay stations for the optic tract. The fibers from the ganglion cells of the retina connect at the lateral geniculate bodies with a new set of neurons. Some of these neurons then lead to the cerebral cortex and some to other parts of the brain.

occipital lobes The sensory areas of the cortex where fibers from the lateral geniculate bodies terminate. These areas, because they are primary receptor areas for impulses from the eyes, are called the visual projection areas or the visual sensory areas of the cortex.

optic chiasma The meeting place of the optic nerves from the two eyes, located at the base of the brain. At the optic chiasma the crossing over of the optic nerves takes place.

optic nerve; optic tract The bundle of nerve fibers of the ganglion cells carrying neural impulses from the rods and cones to the brain. This bundle leaves the retina through an opening in the eyeball called the blind spot. The portion of this conduction pathway lying between the retina and the optic chiasma is called the optic nerve; beyond the optic chiasma it is called the optic tract.

receptive field For each neuron in a sensory conducting system or in a sensory area of the cortex, the portion of the sense organ (for example, the area of the retina) that, when stimulated, will arouse activity in the cell.

reticular formation A network of neurons in the brain stem consisting of an ascending and a descending column. The ascending column receives impulses from many receptors and sends them up to the cortex in a diffuse discharge. The descending column receives impulses from the cortex, including the sensory areas, and sends them down to other structures, including the receptors and the sensory pathways.

physiological basis of auditory perception

overview / Sound waves entering through the ear canal vibrate the eardrum. These vibrations are transmitted through a system of levers in the middle ear and fluid in the inner ear and set in motion parts of the cochlea of the inner ear. The final mechanical action of the system is a distortion of the auditory hair cells, which initiate neural impulses in the auditory nerve. The total number of these impulses arriving at the *auditory cortex* determines the perceived loudness of a sound, whereas the particular nerve cells stimulated determine its pitch.

Impulses from the auditory nerve travel through a number of way stations before they arrive at the auditory cortex. Interaction of impulses from the two ears, as well as interaction with impulses from higher centers, takes place at these various levels. Localization of sounds and stereo effects depend upon a difference in stimulation of the two ears and integration of the resulting different neural patterns at the way stations and the auditory cortex.

The sequence of physiological events that takes place when we hear is no less complicated than that which occurs when we see. Here we must tell the story of how sound waves in the air become converted into vibrations of the *eardrum*, then into movements of levers in the *middle ear*, then into waves of fluid in the *inner ear*, and finally into neural impulses by the activity of the phonoreceptor elements. We must again follow the neural impulses to the brain and examine what happens there. Our story this time will be somewhat easier to tell, simply because much of what we had to say for visual perception will also hold for auditory perception.

We shall divide these physiological events into four major stages. These stages will deal with the *physical mechanism*, the *phonosensitive mechanism*, the *conduction mechanism*, and the *central mechanism*.

The Physical Mechanism

The stimulus for hearing is, of course, the sound wave (see p. 121). When a sound wave enters the *outer ear*, a series of events is started, which eventually leads to an auditory perception.

Structure of the Ear

The ear consists of three parts: the *outer ear*, the *middle ear*, and the *inner ear*. Figure 17.1. represents a somewhat schematized drawing of all three. The outer ear includes the *auricle* (which has only a minor function for man—even for those of us who can wiggle it) and the *ear canal*. Separating the ear canal from the middle ear is a thin membrane, the *eardrum*. The middle ear, the area between the eardrum and the inner ear, contains three little bones (*ossicles*), which form a chain from the eardrum to the *oval window* of the inner ear. The inner ear consists of two parts, the *vestibular apparatus* (which has nothing to do with hearing and will be discussed later) and a coiled, divided, fluid-filled tube, the *cochlea*.

The cross section of the cochlea in Figure 17.1. may give the impression that it is divided into three independent channels, but in fact the upper and lower channels are continuous at the tip of the coil, as can be seen in the extended view of the cochlea shown in Figure 17.2. The part of the cochlea nearest the middle ear thus contains both ends of a continuous tube. The third ossicle closes off one of these ends at the oval window, and the other end is closed off by a thin membrane at the *round window*. The middle partition of the cochlea is called the *cochlear duct;* it contains both the actual sensory elements that initiate the conversion of mechanical stimuli into neural impulses and the fibers of the auditory nerve that transmit the impulses to the brain.

From Sound Waves to Fluid Waves

A sound wave from the outside continues through the air in the ear canal until it reaches the eardrum, which it then causes to vibrate in accordance with its frequency. The vibrations of the eardrum are transmitted through the middle ear by the chain of ossicles, ending with in-and-out movements of the last ossicle at the oval window of the inner ear. As this ossicle moves in and out, it intermittently puts pressure on the fluid in the cochlea. Because the other end of the cochlea (the round window) is stopped with a thin membrane, the alternating pressure on the fluid in the canal causes the membrane to bulge in and out, and fluid motions are set up in the cochlea. In this way *sound waves in the outside world* are eventually transformed into corresponding *liquid waves in the inner ear*.

The Phonosensitive Mechanism

The sensory cells of audition, called the *hair cells*, are found within the cochlear duct, where they rest upon the *basilar membrane* (see Figure 17.1.). They receive their name from tiny hairlike projections, the ends of which are embedded in the *tectorial membrane*, a structure formed of a gelatinous material. As the cochlear duct is agitated by the pressure waves set up in the cochlea, the basilar membrane and the tectorial membrane move in relation to each other, and the hairs and their cells are subjected to many kinds of distortions.

These deformations produce an electrical potential, called the *cochlear microphonic*. The cochlear microphonic is thought to stimulate the production of neural impulses in the fibers of the auditory nerve, which surround the base of the hair cells.

Before describing the conduction mechanism, let us stop to indicate how the anatomical and physiological facts we have already discussed can contribute to our understanding of some of the phenomena of auditory perception. In the following discussion let us assume that the cochlear microphonic does indeed stimulate the production of neural impulses in auditory-nerve fibers.

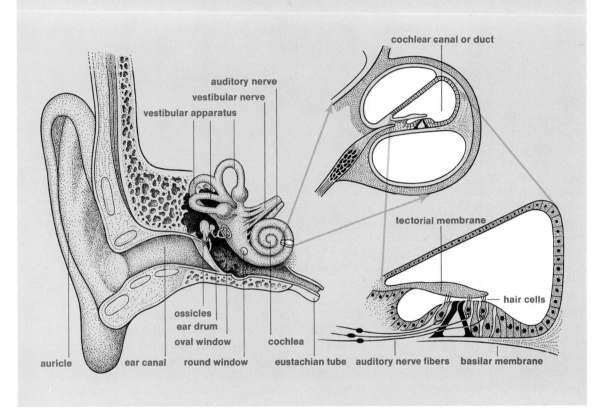

Figure 17.1. Cross section of the ear. Here we have a semidiagrammatic representation of the outer, middle, and inner ears, together with a cross-sectional view of the cochlea and an enlarged diagram of the basilar membrane. For a detailed description, see p. 260.

cochlear canal or duct

auditory nerve
vestibular nerve
vestibular apparatus

tectorial membrane

hair cells

ossicles
ear drum
oval window   cochlea

auricle   ear canal   round window   eustachian tube   auditory nerve fibers   basilar membrane

Loudness

The attribute of loudness in perception depends upon the "intensity" of neural discharges reaching the brain. Obviously an intense sound wave will set the eardrum into vibrations of greater excursion than will a less intense sound wave. For this reason, an intense sound wave will be transformed into an intense pressure wave in the liquid of the inner ear; a less intense sound wave will result in a less intense pressure wave. It is equally obvious that a more intense pressure wave will result in a greater displacement of the cochlear duct than will a less intense wave, and it is true that, the greater the displacement of the cochlear duct, the greater the intensity of the cochlear microphonic.

At this point, we must bring in an additional fact, which, at first glance, seems to make it difficult to explain how a greater cochlear mi-

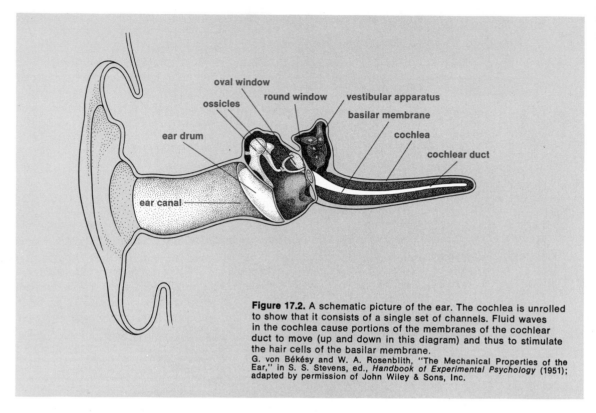

Figure 17.2. A schematic picture of the ear. The cochlea is unrolled to show that it consists of a single set of channels. Fluid waves in the cochlea cause portions of the membranes of the cochlear duct to move (up and down in this diagram) and thus to stimulate the hair cells of the basilar membrane.
G. von Békésy and W. A. Rosenblith, "The Mechanical Properties of the Ear," in S. S. Stevens, ed., *Handbook of Experimental Psychology* (1951); adapted by permission of John Wiley & Sons, Inc.

crophonic could be translated into a more "intense" neural discharge to the brain. If a cell in the auditory nerve is fired by the cochlear microphonic, an increase in the intensity of the microphonic would *not* cause a corresponding increase in the intensity of neural discharge. If the cell is stimulated enough to make it transmit an impulse, it "gives its all," in the *all-or-none* law of nerve discharge (see p. 76), which applies to all nerve cells: either they do not fire at all, or they fire with the maximum intensity possible at the time. How then could the intensity of a sound wave, which had become translated into the intensity of a cochlear microphonic, determine the "intensity" of the nerve discharge to the brain?

Actually two mechanisms are possible, and both seem to be used. First, a louder tone will stimulate a larger *number* of nerve cells. Second,

a louder tone will make each cell (that does fire) fire more often, even though, by the all-or-none law, the intensity of each single discharge will not increase. In these ways the total number of nerve impulses that reach the brain per unit time will be correspondingly large.

The relations among *intensity* of stimulus, *number* of neural impulses transmitted, and *intensity* of sensation is a general relation that holds for all modes—vision, audition, olfaction, and so forth.

Pitch

How do differences in frequencies of sound waves evoke different patterns of neural impulses in the brain and thus different perceived pitches? To answer this question, we must introduce one more fact about the pressure waves in the liquid of the cochlea. When a sound wave of a given frequency is transformed into its corresponding pressure wave, the resulting pressure wave has a characteristic effect. The amount of movement of the cochlear duct structures is not the same at all points (see Figure 17.2.). Starting from the oval window, the amount of displacement gradually increases along the length of the cochlear duct until it reaches a maximum point, after which it rapidly subsides, almost to zero. Sound waves of different frequencies will produce their *maximum* amount of movement at different points along the cochlea. For example, a pressure wave initiated by a sound wave of 300 cycles per second will produce maximum displacement at a distance of about 26 millimeters from the oval window; a sound wave of 200 c.p.s. will produce its maximum displacement at a distance of about 28 millimeters. In general, the movement in the cochlea initiated by a sound wave of very high frequency will reach its maximum, and stimulate the hair cells, near the oval window. The movement caused by a wave of a lower frequency will reach its maximum farther up the cochlea and thus will stimulate hair cells along a greater length of the cochlea. In this way differences in *frequency* of sound waves are transformed into differences in the *spatial pattern* of the sensory cells that are stimulated. The brain, in other words, will receive neural messages from one set of sensory cells when a high-frequency sound wave hits the ear and from another set of sensory cells when a low-frequency sound wave stimulates the ear. This way of sending neural messages is the major way in which the ear sorts out different frequencies and enables us to discriminate one pitch from another.

Another way that the auditory receptors might convey the message of frequency to the brain may have occurred to you. Each successive pulse of a sound wave stimulates the sensory cells into activity. Could not each burst of activity be passed along immediately to the auditory nerve fibers? After all, nerve cells fire very rapidly and are ready to fire again very soon. In this way the *frequency* of the sound would be transformed exactly into the frequency of the neural impulses going to the brain. Physiological evidence has led to the conclusion that in fact some use is made of this mechanism in pitch perception, but it is less important than the spatial patterning described above and is effective only at rather low frequencies.

Abnormal Hearing

We might first mention a rather common "abnormal" phenomenon—*tinnitus,* or ringing in the ears. Just as we have seen that there is constant activity in the retinal cells of the eye, so there is spontaneous activity in the hair cells of the inner ear. The faint ringing noise we all hear in a very quiet room is probably caused by this normal spontaneous activity. More intense ringing may occur after long exposure to a very loud sound, in certain cases of progressive deafness, and in other diseases. In the first case, the prolonged loud sound results in a mild injury to some of the hair cells, which then continue to instigate neural impulses. Usually they recover quickly, the ringing disappears, and no ill effects remain. When ringing persists, it is assumed that there is some constant irritation to the hair cells.

Another interesting abnormality in hearing is deafness for a restricted range of tones; most common is the type in which the individual cannot hear high tones. As a result of fatigue, disease, injury, or degeneration, one part of the cochlea, or one group of hair cells, may not be functioning, temporarily or permanently.

The Conduction Mechanism

The *auditory nerve* conducts nerve impulses from the hair cells in the cochlea to the brain. The fibers carrying the impulses from the ear go through several way stations before reaching the terminal area in the cortex.

The Auditory Nerve

The human auditory nerve is a bundle of about 30,000 separate nerve fibers originating around the hair cells. The separate fibers in the auditory nerve are bundled together in such a way that fibers arising from neighboring points in the cochlea stay together as they travel into the brain. This spatial organization of neural elements corresponding to different sensory cells is preserved up to the very termination of the system in the cortex.

The Lower Way Stations

Soon after leaving the internal ear the auditory nerves enter the lower brain stem and terminate at the *cochlear nuclei* (see Figure 17.3.). Here the fibers make new connections, some with fibers that go on to the next way station *on the same side* of the brain and some with fibers that *cross over* to the next way station on the other side.

This next way station is called the *olivary complex*. Here, for the first time, are opportunities for *interaction* between the fibers coming from the left ear and those coming from the right ear. As can be seen in Figure 17.3., however, *some* fibers from each ear go through the olivary complex without connecting with fibers from the other ear.

Beyond the Olivary Complex

The most direct pathway by which auditory information reaches the cortex from the olivary complex takes it through two additional neural structures, the latter of which (the *medial geniculate body*) plays a part in audition somewhat akin to that of the lateral geniculate in vision.

The various centers along the auditory pathway should not be thought of as *simple relay* stations. For one thing, at many places along the pathway fibers leave the direct route we have been describing and follow other routes, affecting other structures. For example, from the cochlear nucleus and from the olivary complex some fibers carry impulses to the reticular formation. Furthermore, a large amount of interaction results from the convergence of fibers in the auditory way stations. We have already noted the interaction of fibers from the two ears in the olivary complex; this kind of interaction occurs also in the higher way stations. Interaction also takes place between different fibers originating from the same ear.

Auditory Area of the Cortex

Most of the auditory sensory area in man's brain lies hidden in one of the major convolutions of the cortex (again see Figure 17.3.). As a result of much investigation, the specific geography of this area has been fairly well mapped. Note these two major findings: First, as was true of the auditory *nerve*, the spatial separation between the representation of tones of different frequencies is fairly well preserved in the cortex; second, the crossing over of the fibers that takes place as the two auditory pathways ascend to the brain is such that each ear is somewhat *better* represented on the other side of the brain than on its own side.

This crossing over merits further discussion. We have already seen that in vision each side of the visual *field* is represented on the opposite side of the brain: An object on the *right* side of the visual field is represented on the *left* side of the brain. We now see that a somewhat similar situation obtains in audition. A sound coming from the *right* side of the auditory field is better represented on the *left* side. Finally, as we shall soon see, the nerves that carry impulses from the skin surface show almost complete crossing over, so that a touch on the right hand results in cortical activity on the left side of the brain. Thus, a buzzing insect, alighting on the right hand, sends neural impulses from the various senses—the ear, skin, and eye—to the left side of the brain. We hear, feel, and see the insect on the right hand.

Deafness

If a cochlear duct is destroyed or if the auditory nerve leading from the cochlea is destroyed at its source, complete deafness on that side results. This result is known as *nerve deafness*. But destruction of one of the pathways after it has entered the brain does not result in *complete* deafness of either ear, because each pathway, as we have seen, carries fibers from both cochleas. Disease of the middle ear may cause what is known as *transmission deafness*

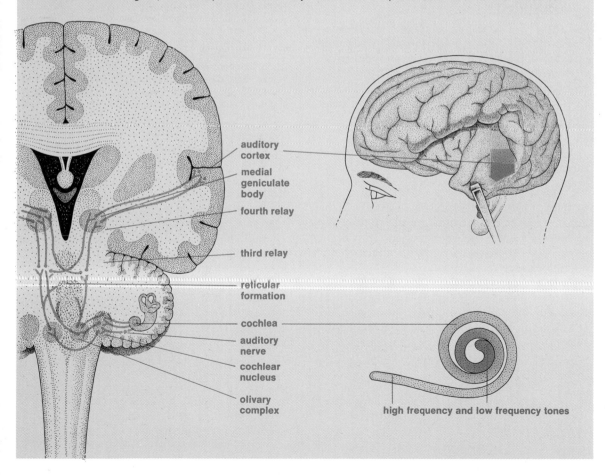

Figure 17.3. This diagram illustrates the conduction pathway of the auditory impulses from the cochlea to the cerebral cortex. Note how close the cochlea of the inner ear is to the cochlear nucleus, the first relay station within the brain. (The reader should also refer to Figure 4.6., p. 82, to locate the point of entrance into the brain of the auditory nerve.) The gradient of shading in the cochlea represents the gradient of tone localization in that organ. Lower frequency tones produce stimulation of sensory cells principally at one end of the cochlea; higher frequency tones stimulate the sensory cells at the other end. Note also the point-for-point projection of the cochlea on the cortex. That is, nerve impulses from the cochlea stimulated by high-frequency tones end deep within the fold of the cortex, and those from low-frequency tones terminate on the surface of the fold. In the diagram, the outer part of the auditory cortex has been pulled down to show this difference.

auditory cortex

medial geniculate body

fourth relay

third relay

reticular formation

cochlea

auditory nerve

cochlear nucleus

olivary complex

high frequency and low frequency tones

by interfering with the movements of the eardrum or the ossicles. In these cases, hearing may be improved by increasing the use of *bone conduction*. Even in normal hearing, vibrations of the skull may set up wave motions in the fluid of the cochleas and affect what we hear. A person who has middle-ear deafness will have difficulty in ordinary conversation, but, when he places a telephone receiver firmly against his ear, he may hear without much difficulty because the sounds are conducted through the bones of the head. Many hearing aids work on this principle. In complete nerve deafness, however, no hearing aid will help.

Central Mechanisms

As in the case of vision, much of our information about the central mechanisms in audition comes from ablation and electrophysiological studies. The latter have been especially successful in helping us to "spell out" the physiological basis of many perceptual phenomena in hearing.

Binaural Interaction

We have seen in Unit 12, p. 190, that our ability to detect whether a sound is to our right or left, in front of us or behind us, above or below us, depends upon the difference in stimulation at the two ears by sound waves coming from a a single object.

In the visual system the different images on the two retinas are integrated at the cortical levels. In the ear, however, the story is different. Several experiments using a technique developed by Rosenzweig (1954) have helped to determine where *binaural interaction*, that is, neural integration, occurs.

The experimental subject (a cat) wears a set of earphones that permits the experimenter to stimulate either ear independently, and recording electrodes are inserted into one part or another of the auditory conducting mechanism. In the experiment each ear may be stimulated with a single click of *equal* intensity, but the click in one ear may be made to occur a thousandth of a second before the other; or both ears may be stimulated *simultaneously*, but one click may be a bit more intense than the other; or only one ear may be stimulated. In this way the experimenter can reproduce the stimulus patterns that give rise to auditory localization. In every instance, of course, the electrical responses in various parts of the brain are recorded.

The results of many such experiments have led to the following conclusions:

1. No binaural interaction is detected at the cochlear nuclei (stimulating the *right* ear has no effect on the neural responses at the *left* cochlear nucleus).
2. Some binaural interaction begins as soon as the olivary complex is reached (stimulating the right ear does have an effect on the left olivary complex).
3. The degree of interaction increases at each succeeding relay station.

These findings show once again that the nervous system as a whole, not only the "higher" centers, is built for interaction. Long before the impulses from the receptors reach the cortex, they begin to create a patterned, integrated set of responses.

Another important finding is that, when stimulation at both ears is identical in time and intensity, cortical activity at the two hemispheres is identical; when stimulation is made to differ at the two ears in time or intensity, cortical activity differs between the two hemispheres. And the greater the difference in stimulation at the two ears, the greater the difference in activity at the two hemispheres. Because *perception* involves cortical activity, these different cortical patterns help us to understand how the perception of the direction of sound is dependent upon different stimulation at the two ears.

Brain Asymmetry

We have noted (see Figure 17.3.) that tones of different frequency are represented at different points within the auditory cortex. Another kind of difference within the human auditory cortex now appears to be emerging. The auditory cortex of the *left* side of the brain appears to be predominantly involved in the perception of speech, whereas the auditory cortex on the *right* side is more important in the perception of certain nonspeech sounds, for example, melodies (see Box 48).

Box 48

Meaning on the Left,
Thunder on the Right

A glance at Figure 17.3., which illustrates the connections in the auditory system, shows that sounds entering one ear instigate neural messages that will reach both sides of the cortex. It has been shown, however, that the crossed pathways (from right ear to left side of brain and vice versa) are stronger than the uncrossed pathways. If we bear this fact in mind and consider certain experiments performed at the Montreal Neurological Institute, we can conclude that different sides of the brain have different functions in audition.

A subject is provided with an earphone for each ear, and the apparatus is so wired that is is possible to deliver separate messages to the right and left ears. Using this apparatus, Doreen Kimura presented different spoken digits to the two ears at the same time. After two or three pairs of digits were presented, the subject was asked to report what he had heard. More of the digits that had entered the right ear (and thus the left brain) were reported correctly by most people than were digits that had entered the left ear! This superiority of the right ear is already present in four-year-old children.

It has been thought that this difference between the two sides of the brain is related to older findings that the left side of the brain is usually more important in language *production*. The present evidence suggests that the left brain is also especially important in verbal *perception*.

Further evidence for the difference is presented in Brenda Milner's studies of people who have had large portions of one temporal lobe or the other removed in order to provide relief from epilepsy. If the *left* temporal lobe is removed, the patients have difficulty in understanding and remembering verbal stories, as well as excessive difficulty on the conflicting-digits test discussed a moment ago. Lesions of the temporal cortex on the *right* side of the brain lead to difficulty in the perception and learning of certain nonlanguage sounds, for example, musical tones and melodies.

D. KIMURA. 1961. Cerebral Dominance and the Perception of Verbal Stimuli, *Canad. J. Psychol.*, 15, 166–71.
D. KIMURA. 1963. Speech Lateralization in Young Children as Determined by an Auditory Test, *J. Comp. Physiol. Psychol.*, 56, 899–902.
B. MILNER. 1962. Laterality Effects in Audition, in V. B. Mountcastle, ed., *Interhemispheric Relations and Cerebral Dominance* (Baltimore: Johns Hopkins Press), pp. 177–95.

Glossary

auditory cortex The area of the cortex that receives impulses from the ear via the auditory neurons. It lies just below the lateral fissure. Only a small part of this area can be seen from the surface of the brain.

auditory (cochlear) nerve A bundle of about 30,000 separate nerve fibers stemming from the hair cells in the cochlear duct. This bundle leaves the internal ear, enters the lower brain stem, and finds its first relay station in the cochlear nuclei.

auricle The projecting, external part of the outer ear. Sometimes called the *pinna*.

basilar membrane A membrane in the cochlear duct upon which the hair cells rest.

binaural interaction An effect of the neural influences coming from the fibers of one ear upon the neural activity in the fibers coming from the other ear.

cochlea A coiled, divided, fluid-filled tube containing the sensory elements involved in hearing. One end of the cochlea is closed off by the third ossicle at the cochlea's oval window; the other end is closed off by a thin membrane at the cochlea's round window.

cochlear canal (or duct) The partition or structure dividing the cochlea into two major channels. It is filled with fluid and contains the hair cells.

cochlear microphonic An electrical potential caused by deformation of the auditory hair cells. This potential probably stimulates production of neural impulses in the fibers of the auditory nerve.

cochlear nuclei The first relay centers on the route of the auditory impulses from the inner ear to the cortex. They are located in the brain stem.

ear canal The opening from the outer ear to the eardrum. Conducts sound waves from the outside to the middle ear.

eardrum A thin membrane separating the ear canal from the middle ear. Sound waves striking the eardrum cause it to vibrate.

eustachian tube A cavity connecting the middle ear with the pharynx. The eustachian tube is usually closed where it connects with the pharynx, but it opens when we swallow or yawn. When it opens, the atmospheric pressure in the middle ear is equalized with the atmospheric pressure on the outside.

hair cells (auditory) The sensory cells of audition. These cells convert the wave motion of the cochlear fluids into the cochlear microphonic. The hair cells are found in the cochlear duct and rest upon the basilar membrane.

inner ear The innermost section of the hearing apparatus. It consists of two parts: the vestibular apparatus and the cochlea.

medial geniculate bodies The final relay station on the route of the auditory fibers from the inner ear to the auditory cortex.

middle ear A cavity between the outer and inner ear. Contains the three ossicles. The middle-ear cavity opens into the eustachian tube.

nerve deafness Deafness resulting from injury to the cochlea or auditory nerve. Most elderly people suffer from some degree of nerve deafness. If the auditory nerve is completely destroyed, no hearing aid can help.

olivary complex The second relay, or synapse center, on the route of the auditory fibers from the inner ear to the cortex. Located in the brain stem.

ossicles The three bones forming a chain from the eardrum to the oval window of the cochlea. They transmit vibrations of the eardrum to the fluid in the cochlea.

outer ear The outermost and only visible part of the hearing apparatus. Includes the auricles and the ear canals.

oval window An opening in the cochlea into which is fitted the last of the three bones leading from the eardrum. It is the vibration of this ossicle in the oval window that sets the fluid in the cochlea into wavelike motion.

phonosensitive mechanism A general term referring to the various anatomical and physiological mechanisms involved in the initiation of neural impulses in the inner ear. Specifically, the operation of the hair cells in the cochlear canal and the function of the basilar membrane.

round window An opening in the cochlea across which is stretched a thin membrane. As vibrations at the oval window produce changes in the pressure on the cochlear fluid, the membrane bulges in and out, permitting the fluid in the cochlea to respond as wave motion.

tectorial membrane A mass of gelatinous matter situated above the hair cells in the cochlear duct; the hairs of these cells terminate in the tectorial membrane. When the hair cells are moved in relation to the tectorial membrane, they are temporarily squeezed out of shape. This deformation produces the cochlear microphonic.

tinnitus The condition of hearing a ringing in the ears when there is no outside source that causes the ringing sounds.

transmission deafness Deafness resulting from interference with the movements of the eardrum or of the ossicles. In these cases partial hearing may be restored through the transmission of vibrations by the skull. Many hearing aids work on this principle.

physiological basis of the chemical and somesthetic senses

overview / The taste buds of the tongue and mouth contain taste-sensitive cells that respond differentially to the stimuli for the four basic taste qualities: sweet, sour, bitter, salty. When the taste-sensitive cells are stimulated they trigger a reaction in the taste nerves which then conduct a neural impulse to the brain. Taste quality is determined physiologically by patterns of firings of the taste nerves.

The great sensitivity of our sense of smell depends upon highly specialized nerve receptor cells in the upper part of the nasal cavity and also upon amplifying action of parts of the conducting system. The conduction system, by inhibiting incoming signals, also contributes to the rapid adaptation we experience.

Simple free nerve endings serve as receptors for all four basic skin senses, touch, temperature, pressure, and pain. But there are large numbers of specialized receptors in different body areas. Of these receptors, the most common is the basket ending surrounding the skin hairs, which signals the intensity, location, and direction of arrival of touch stimuli.

The kinesthetic receptors found in the capsules that encircle the joints and in the ligaments that connect the bones at the joints make possible our perception of the position and movement of the body. Fibers from touch, pressure, and kinesthetic receptors project to the same cortical area, where a comprehensive picture of the movement, positions, and contacts of the various parts of the body is obtained.

The inner ear contains the vestibular apparatus, which is critical for our sense of balance. Disturbances of this system by inflammation or overstimulation can cause dizziness or nausea. The vestibular and kinesthetic senses are highly coordinated and give rise to the specific perceptions of limb and head movements as well as the over-all perception of our bodies in space.

The senses of vision and hearing (the primary senses for the perception of space) are probably man's most important senses. For this reason they have been described in relatively great detail. The chemical and somesthetic senses, however, also contribute considerably both to our ability to cope with our environment and to the richness of our perceptual world. A brief examination of their physiological bases will allow us to appreciate more fully the contribution of these senses. The reasons that taste and smell, as perceptions, are usually treated together have been indicated in Unit 8, p. 127, and we shall follow this grouping in discussing their physiological bases.

Taste

We shall restrict ourselves to a discussion principally of the receptor organs for taste, with only a brief discussion of the conduction mechanisms, primarily because the little that we do know about the latter would not aid directly in our understanding of taste perception.

Taste Buds

The receptors for taste are concentrated in certain areas of the tongue, but they are also found in the mucous membrane of the throat and soft palate. There are regions of the tongue that have no taste receptors and are therefore completely "taste blind." (These regions would be appropriate places for the bitter pills that many of us have occasion to swallow from time to time.) The number, kind, and efficiency of taste receptors differ from person to person and within the same person at different times. This fact helps us to understand some of the individual differences in taste sensitivity.

Studies with the electron microscope have recently given us a clear picture of the structure of the *taste bud,* a pear-shaped group of tightly packed, elongated taste-sensitive cells

(see Figure 18.1.). The life of a taste-sensitive cell is relatively short, and the taste bud contains cells in all stages of development: young, mature, and atrophied. Around the active cells are wound the endings of the *taste nerves.* Each taste-nerve fiber may go to several receptor cells, and a single receptor cell may be innervated by more than one nerve fiber. Chemical substances (in food, for example), which are usually dissolved in the saliva, reach the taste-sensitive cells through an opening in the mucous membrane called the *taste pore* and initiate a response in the cells. This response triggers a reaction in the endings of the taste nerves, which conduct a neural impulse to the brain.

We know that, in contrast to vision and

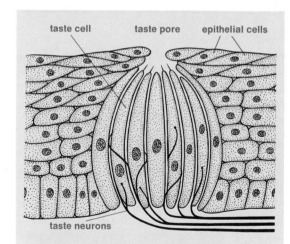

Figure 18.1. A diagrammatic representation of a taste bud. Each of these structures consists of a cluster of *taste cells,* embedded within the ordinary *epithelial cells* of the tongue. An opening to the surface of the tongue (called a *taste pore*) permits entry of the dissolved sapid substance. Stimulation of the taste cells provokes a neural impulse in the *taste neurons* that carry the information to the brain. A. J. D. De Lorenzo, "Ultrastructure and Histophysiology of Membranes," in Y. Zotterman, ed., *Wenner-Gren Center International Symposium Series* (1963); adapted by permission of Pergamon Press, Inc.

audition, in which we can distinguish many colors and many sounds, there are only four basic qualities of taste: sweet, sour, bitter, salty. We might hope to find a simple physiological system underlying these perceptual facts. For example, there might be, for each quality, a group of special receptors, which have their own distinct fibers leading directly to the cortex. What we have already learned about the taste-receptor and taste-nerve connections tells us that the system cannot be that simple; in fact, a complex coding system is used to transmit to the brain the fact that our taste receptors have encountered one or more of the basic taste qualities.

Stimulation of individual receptor cells by sapid (taste-producing) substances has demonstrated that a single cell is not limited to responding to the stimuli of a single quality. In fact, many single cells respond to the stimuli for *all* of the qualities of taste. Others may have a more limited range of sensitivity. Electrophysiological studies of single taste-nerve fibers present a similar picture. There are no fibers that fire only when the receptors are stimulated by sweet *or* salt *or* sour *or* bitter, and many fibers will fire to all of these stimuli. What, then, is unique about the message the cortex receives about a specific taste substance? A *pattern* of response emerges as the crucial factor. Different substances may produce firings in the same neurons, but they will not be firing at the same rates. We do not know how many kinds of taste receptors there are, but we do know that *many* different patterns of neural responses arrive at the cortex. There are even different patterns for different salts —and we now know that salts producing similar patterns apparently taste alike (see Box 49, p. 274).

Conductors and Central Mechanisms

The nerve fibers from the taste buds do not travel to the brain in a single fiber bundle. Those originating in the front of the tongue, the back of the tongue, and in the throat and larynx divide into several bundles and travel along in company with fibers of the various skin sensory nerves. Taste fibers from the anterior portion of the tongue cross the middle ear. It has been possible to record from this nerve in experimental animals, and recently in human subjects as well, by inserting electrodes into the middle ear. All the bundles seem to send impulses to the same general area of the cortex. Ablation studies indicate, however, that the removal of this part of the cortex does not make the individual "taste blind" but merely reduces his taste sensitivity.

Smell

There are two outstanding attributes of the sense of smell that merit particular attention: its sensitivity and its rate of adaptation. The sensitivity of the nose is remarkable. In terms of the concentration of molecules necessary to stimulate the receptor cells, it is estimated that smell is 10,000 times as sensitive as taste. This sensitivity is compensated for (frequently to our great relief) by the ease with which our sense of smell becomes adapted, so that a substance that originally provoked a very strong odor soon no longer does so.

Olfactory Receptors

The olfactory receptors are in the mucous membrane on each side of the upper part of the nasal cavity. These receptors are fairly long, column-shaped bipolar neurons, which in a sense act both as receptors and as connecting cells. From one end of these *olfactory bipolar cells* delicate "hairs" project into the fluid covering of the mucous membrane; from the other end long threads extend, which are the fibers of the olfactory nerve (see Figure

Box 49

Predicting Behavior From Neuron Firings

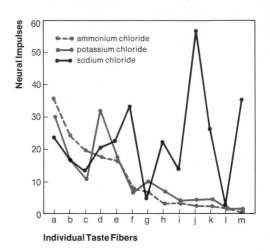

In their study of the nervous system, scientists have been able to relate neural functioning to many different kinds of behavior. By doing so they have helped us to understand the mechanisms underlying these behavior patterns. It is not often, however, that research on neural functioning leads directly to the *prediction* of complex behavior. One such instance is found in the study of taste.

As we have learned from the text, stimulation of taste receptors results in a pattern of firing across many nerve fibers. R. P. Erickson, a physiological psychologist at Duke University, studied taste mechanisms in the rat. He was able to record the firings of a number of individual taste-nerve fibers as he stimulated his animals' tongues with solutions of different salts. In the figure we see the neural activity shown by thirteen individual taste fibers when stimulated by three different salt solutions: sodium chloride, ammonium chloride, and potassium chloride. You can see that ammonium chloride and potassium chloride produce quite similar firing rates in these nerves, whereas sodium chloride yields a very different pattern of firings. If it is the pattern of neural firings that arrive at the cortex from the taste nerves that corresponds to the various taste sensations, Erickson reasoned that ammonium and potassium chlorides should taste very similar and sodium chloride should taste different from both. He put this prediction, based on neural data, to a behavioral test. He trained rats to avoid one of the salts by shocking them when they drank a solution of it. When they refused to drink the training solution, he tested their responses to the other solutions. As predicted, animals that had learned to avoid ammonium chloride avoided the potassium chloride much more than they avoided the sodium chloride, and, similarly, those trained to avoid potassium chloride showed greater avoidance of ammonium chloride than of sodium chloride. Rats trained to avoid sodium chloride showed only a little avoidance of either ammonium chloride or potassium chloride.

Erickson was indeed able to predict his rats' behavior from a knowledge of the activity of taste nerves and has lent support to the view that different patterns of firings of taste fibers correspond to different taste sensations.

R. P. ERICKSON. 1963. Sensory Neural Patterns and Gustation, in Y. Zotterman, ed., *Olfaction and Taste* (Macmillan: New York). Figure adapted by permission of Pergamon Press, Inc.

18.2.). When particles of gas reach the mucous membrane of the nose, they are dissolved by the fluid covering and, acting on the hair filaments, stimulate the olfactory cells into neural activity.

The location of the olfactory structures (see Figure 18.2.) makes it very difficult to study them in action, and we do not yet have enough well-established facts to permit us to say many things with certainty. So, when we ask how the response of the receptors to the variety of odorous substances can bring about our perception of the "spectrum" of odors, we find no undisputed answers. We do not know the details of stimulation of the receptors. We do not even know what it is about odorous substances that makes them odorous (this fact partially explains why psychologists have had so little success in their attempts to construct a helpful classificatory scheme for smell). Suggestions as to what makes a substance odorous have included such properties as the size and shape of its molecules, its chemical reactivity, and its ability to absorb infrared light.

From research on the stimulation of single receptor cells and from recordings of single olfactory fiber activity there is some evidence to support a general picture of olfactory-receptor function similar to one we have become familiar with in other senses; that is, there is evidence that there are a number of different types of receptors and that these types have overlapping sensitivities for different substances. In this view the signal for a particular odor is given by relatively nonspecific receptors sending a unique *pattern* of impulses to the cortex. Some scientists maintain, however, that the key to the perception of specific odors lies in single fibers that respond to one and only one odor. These two views are, of course, not mutually exclusive. Perhaps there are some receptor cells and fibers that are quite specific for odors and others that have a broader range of sensitivity; perhaps both kinds contribute to our perception of odor.

Conductors and Central Mechanisms

The olfactory-nerve fibers of the sensory cells ascend through tiny openings in the base of the skull and very soon reach the *olfactory bulbs* of the brain (see Figure 18.2.). In the olfactory bulb a very large number of these fibers converge on a single cell, and this cell proceeds without further interruption to the higher centers of the brain. The funneling of neural responses made possible by this arrangement is one factor contributing to the extreme sensitivity of olfaction (recall the function of the "party lines" of the rods of the eye). The system just described is in some ways the simplest we have encountered so far. Only two steps are involved: A stimulated receptor cell fires into the olfactory bulb, and a second cell relays the message to higher centers.

Transmission of impulses in this simple system is subject, however, to considerable modification and control within the bulb. Each olfactory bulb is itself a part of the brain, containing elaborate neural circuits that can exert important modifying influences. In addition, each bulb is influenced by impulses from the other bulb and from the cortical hemispheres. There are two simple ways in which a transmitted signal may be altered. First, it may be amplified. For example, if the direct action of sensory-cell fibers is enough only to produce a very slow rate of impulses in a fiber leaving the bulb, feedback circuits and other regulatory devices may result in a much more rapid rate of impulses in that fiber. Amplification of this kind is a second factor contributing to the remarkable sensitivity of the nose to very weak stimuli. Second, transmitted signals may be inhibited. Inhibition of the transmission of impulses in the bulb is the major factor accounting for olfactory adaptation. Some adaptation takes place in the receptor cells, but electrophysiological studies tell us that it is not nearly enough to account for the very rapid and complete adaptation of this sense.

The neural impulse travels directly to cortical and subcortical structures from the olfactory bulb in bundles of fibers known as *olfactory tracts* (see Figures 4.6., p. 82, and 18.2.). The locations of subsequent pathways are very complex and not completely understood, and no attempt will be made to describe them. Even the location of the cortical sensory area for olfaction is not known with certainty.

Somesthetic Senses

Sensations from the skin together with sensations of bodily position and movement are

Figure 18.2. The receptors for smell. For details of the operation of the olfactory system, see p. 273–5. Note that the olfactory nerve filaments must run only a very short distance to reach the olfactory bulb of the brain. Some of the fibers from the olfactory tract reach the olfactory bulb of the other side of the brain by way of the anterior commissure. The remaining fibers connect with other parts of the brain by way of centers in the temporal lobe.

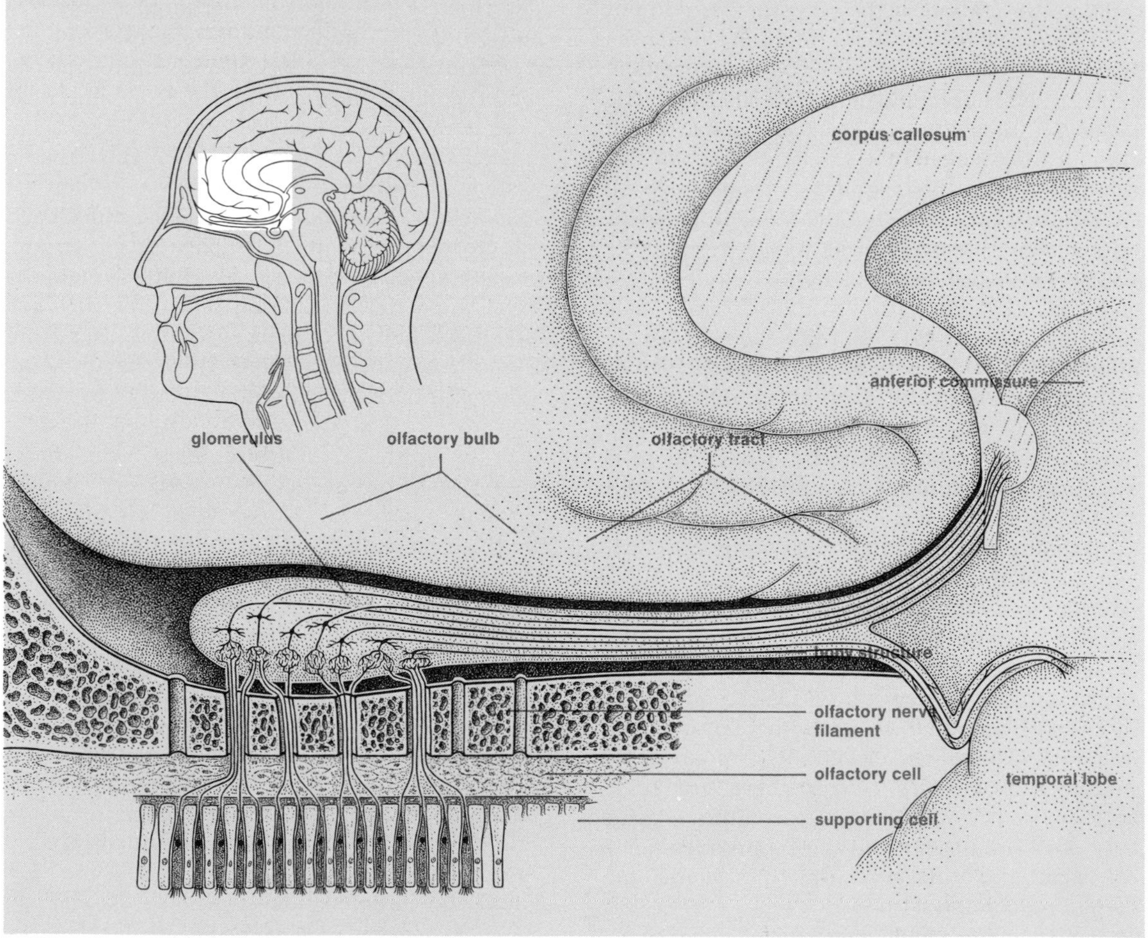

sometimes combined under the term *somesthetic* (body) sensations.

Skin Senses

The sensations of touch, temperature, pressure, and pain are thought of as originating in the skin and are therefore called *cutaneous* (skin) sensations. These closely related senses have very similar physiological mechanisms, and we shall therefore consider them together.

The Receptors

It was pointed out in the discussion of taste that, if a sense yields only a few different kinds of sensations, it is particularly tempting to look for a simple physiological system with specialized receptors for each of the qualities. And so, when structurally different receptors were found in the skin, some scientists believed that they could establish a one-to-one relationship between one kind of skin receptor and one kind of sensation, for example, the sensation of touch, pressure, temperature, or pain. We now know that this simple doctrine of specificity among the nerve endings in the skin is not accurate, although there is still considerable disagreement concerning the extent to which the classic view must be modified. The following summary presents the points about which there is most agreement and is similar in many ways to our findings for the other senses.

When considering the skin senses, it is reasonable to look first at the "hairy skin" because in man (as well as in woman) hairy skin covers more than 90 per cent of the body. Only two types of anatomically distinct receptors are found in the hairy skin, *the basket endings* of the hairs and *free nerve endings* (see Figure 18.3.). The basket endings, a complex network of nerve fibers surrounding the base of the hairs, are specific receptors for *touch*. The complexity of the basket structures and their neural connections makes it virtually

certain that, when a basket is normally stimulated (by the movement of its attached hair), it sends a *pattern* of impulses along its nerve fibers. This pattern signals not only the intensity and location of the touch stimulus but the direction of arrival as well. No matter how they are stimulated, these fibers signal *only* touch.

The free nerve endings, as the name implies, appear to be simple unspecialized endings of nerve fibers. Single nerve fibers may divide a number of times, and the endings of the divided fibers may spread over a considerable area. There is also complex interweaving of the fibers, so that a particular area of the skin may have free nerve endings from a number of fibers. This structural arrangement makes it possible for stimulation of the free nerve endings to result in complex *patterns* of neural impulses. Now, we know that the hairy skin can respond with the sensations of touch, warmth, cold, and pain, and we have just learned that the basket endings can respond only to touch; therefore the free nerve endings *must* be receptors for *warmth*, *cold*, and *pain*. There is now considerable experimental evidence to support this logic. We have additional evidence that demonstrates that they are also receptors for touch. How these seemingly identical endings can act as receptors for four different qualities of sensation is not known. One scientist has suggested that they may have relatively broad but different sensitivities to the stimuli for touch, warmth, cold, and pain and that the perception of a specific kind of sensation depends upon a specific *pattern* of impulses instigated by a number of receptors. This view, although consistent with so much we have learned about the other senses, does not yet have confirming evidence.

In the nonhairy skin there are both free nerve endings and a variety of specialized receptors. One difficulty with a simple special-receptor doctrine is that, although at first it appeared that there were a small number of structurally different receptors, it is now clear

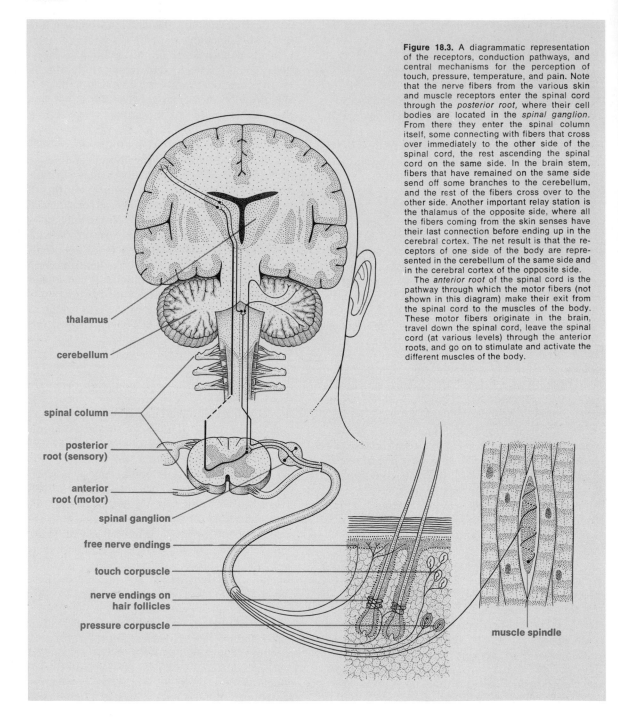

Figure 18.3. A diagrammatic representation of the receptors, conduction pathways, and central mechanisms for the perception of touch, pressure, temperature, and pain. Note that the nerve fibers from the various skin and muscle receptors enter the spinal cord through the *posterior root,* where their cell bodies are located in the *spinal ganglion.* From there they enter the spinal column itself, some connecting with fibers that cross over immediately to the other side of the spinal cord, the rest ascending the spinal cord on the same side. In the brain stem, fibers that have remained on the same side send off some branches to the cerebellum, and the rest of the fibers cross over to the other side. Another important relay station is the thalamus of the opposite side, where all the fibers coming from the skin senses have their last connection before ending up in the cerebral cortex. The net result is that the receptors of one side of the body are represented in the cerebellum of the same side and in the cerebral cortex of the opposite side.

The *anterior root* of the spinal cord is the pathway through which the motor fibers (not shown in this diagram) make their exit from the spinal cord to the muscles of the body. These motor fibers originate in the brain, travel down the spinal cord, leave the spinal cord (at various levels) through the anterior roots, and go on to stimulate and activate the different muscles of the body.

thalamus

cerebellum

spinal column

posterior root (sensory)

anterior root (motor)

spinal ganglion

free nerve endings

touch corpuscle

nerve endings on hair follicles

pressure corpuscle

muscle spindle

that there are a large number of different kinds, many of which are quite similar. There are two types of these receptors whose functions seem to be known. One serves touch in the palms of the hands and the soles of the feet, and the other, buried somewhat deeper, serves as a pressure receptor. Other special receptors very probably serve warmth, cold, and perhaps touch in the nonhairy skin, but we cannot be sure.

"Complex" Skin Perceptions

A whole set of perceptual phenomena has always bedeviled the specificity doctrine, even when it was most popular among scientists. Many of the skin perceptions (including some of the most interesting) are very much more complex than are the sensations of cold, warmth, touch, pressure, and simple pain. These perceptions include "itch," "tickle," "wetness," "roughness," and so on. Some theorists have suggested that there are specialized receptor organs for each of these complex perceptions—a "tickle receptor," an "itch receptor," and so on. But no experimental data have been found to support this hypothesis. We do know that some of these "complex" sensations are related to specific basic sensations. The simplest example is the relation between itch and pain. Increasing the intensity of a stimulus for itch will gradually shift the sensation from itch to pain, but not to touch, warmth, or cold. Does a stimulus that at full strength sends a pattern of impulses that signals "pain" send a slightly different pattern we call "itch" when it is weaker? We do not know, but it is one possibility. "Complex" skin sensations may be related in a similar way to more than one basic sensation. For example, tickle seems to involve weak stimulation of both pain *and* touch.

Conductors and Central Mechanisms

The fibers from the various skin receptors enter the spinal cord and ascend to the brain.

They show almost complete crossing over before arriving at the thalamus. Touch and pressure fibers continue on to the cortex (see Figure 18.3.). The evidence for the cortical representation of temperature and pain is not impressive, and, if these senses do project to the cortex, their representation must be rather meager.

Experiments and clinical observations clearly show that, when the fibers from the skin receptors are cut (either deliberately or by accident), sensations from areas of the skin served by these fibers disappear; we can no longer feel touch, heat, pain, itch, or tickle. This fact not only confirms the theory that the skin receptors are responsible for cutaneous perception; it also has important medical uses. Occasionally severe cases of intractable pain occur (in some of the advanced cases of cancer or in severe injuries) that cannot be alleviated by the usual methods. In such instances the surgeon will deliberately cut the skin fibers to the brain. Pain will immediately disappear, but so may many of the other skin sensations.

Perception of Our Bodies in Space

We can all perceive the position of our own bodies in space. Although we may err in varying degrees under various circumstances, in general we know whether our bodies are bent, upright, moving, or stationary.

Perception of body position and body movement is made possible by two anatomically separate but highly coordinated mechanisms, the *kinesthetic* sensory system and the *vestibular system* of the inner ear.

The Kinesthetic System

The receptors for kinesthesis are specialized sensory cells that are found in the joints between bones. Their neural impulses make possible our perception of the position and movements of the various parts of the body. Other receptors in the muscles and tendons are sensitive to the state of the muscular system and will be discussed here, even though the messages they initiate do not enter conscious awareness.

Receptors, Conductors, and Central Mechanism

Kinesthetic receptors are found in the *capsules*, which encircle the joints, and in the *ligaments*, which connect pairs of bones. These sensory elements consist of neurons that divide near their ends into several smaller branches, each of which terminates in a flattened plate. They respond when compressed and are so distributed throughout the joint that they can indicate not only the present position of a limb but also its direction and rate of movement.

The kinesthetic-nerve fibers join fibers coming from the skin and follow similar pathways into the spinal cord and up to the brain, where the information is integrated with that coming from the skin senses and the vestibular system.

Muscle Spindles

The receptors in the muscles are in the form of *muscle spindles*. A spindle consists of one or more muscle fibers, supplied with sensory nerve fibers (which carry impulses to the spinal cord) and a small motor nerve fiber (which brings impulses from the spinal cord). When the muscle is lengthened as a result of relaxation, the spindle-muscle fibers are stretched and the associated sensory fibers are stimulated, and thus the muscle spindle acts as a *stretch* receptor. The small motor fiber can function to keep the spindle-muscle fibers just taut enough so that any stretch imparted by relaxation will be sure to lead to stimulation of the sensory fibers—an example of the remarkable ways in which the organism optimizes the amount of sensory information that the receptors pass on to the central nervous system.

The nerve impulses arising from the muscle spindles and from some related receptors in the tendons (which connect muscles to bones) travel to the spinal cord and up to the cerebellum. At each place the fibers make connections through which various important reflexes are controlled, but the information they carry apparently never becomes a direct part of our conscious perceptual world.

The Vestibular System

The inner ear, it will be remembered, contains the *vestibular apparatus,* which is concerned not with hearing but with our sense of balance, or equilibrium. The vestibular apparatus of each inner ear consists of the three *semicircular canals* and the *utricle,* small liquid-filled structures that contain sensory cells equipped with hair tufts. These *vestibular hair cells* of the semicircular canals respond to wave *motions* of the fluid in the canals; the utricle is sensitive to the·*positions* of the hairs of its sensory cells and thus to the position of the head (see Figure 18.4.).

The vestibular nerve, which carries the impulses from the sensory cells of the vestibular apparatus, enters the brain stem next to the auditory nerve. In the brain stem the nerve fibers end in masses of gray matter called the *vestibular nuclei.* From here messages are relayed to muscles of the eye, to the viscera, and to the cerebellum. Although impulses also reach the cerebral cortex, the direct pathway is unknown (see Box 50, p. 282).

The familiar symptoms of seasickness seem to be caused by overstimulation of the vestibular system, which, it has just been pointed out, relays messages to the viscera. Rapid or prolonged rotation or other movements may produce dizziness, nausea, and vomiting. Much the same pattern of symptoms may also be produced by various diseases that overstimulate the vestibular system. An inflammation that affects the vestibular system of one side and results in constant stimulation on that side may thus result in dizziness or nausea.

The kinesthetic and vestibular systems, so

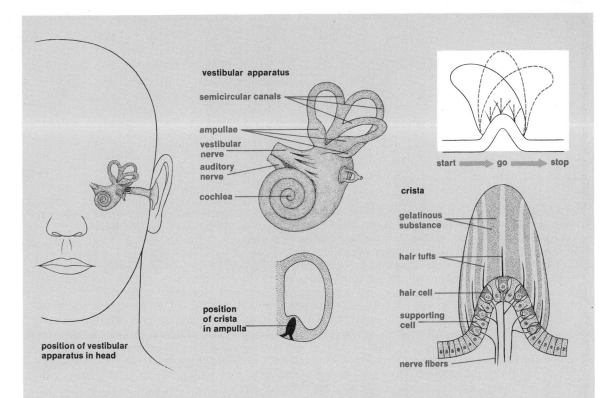

Figure 18.4. The vestibular apparatus of each inner ear consists of three small liquid-filled *semicircular canals*. These three canals correspond to the three planes of the space in which we move about: up-down, forward-backward, right-left. The base of each canal is enlarged into an *ampulla*. Each ampulla has within it the *crista*. The crista contains the *hair cells*. These hair cells lie between the supporting cells and bear on their free ends long hair tufts embedded in a gelatinous substance. The fluid in the canal, when it is moved, bends the gelatinous substance and the hair tufts. The bending of the hair tufts stimulates the hair cells, which then send neural impulses through their nerve fibers to the brain.

At the upper right of the figure is a representation of activity in the crista during various head movements. When the head starts moving or turning, the liquid at first lags behind, bending the hair tufts in the *opposite* direction. (This reaction is similar to being thrown *back* when the automobile in which you are riding suddenly starts *forward*.) As the movement of the head continues, the liquid in the canal "catches up" with the movement of the head, and the hair tufts become erect again. As long as the head is moving in a constant direction and at a constant speed, the hair tufts will remain erect. (This reaction is similar to the way in which you remain seated erect as long as the automobile is traveling smoothly, without jerks and without turning.) When the head movement *stops,* the inertia of the liquid carries it forward and the hair tufts are again bent, this time in the *forward* direction. It is for these reasons that we receive neural impulses from the vestibular apparatus only when the motion of the head is changed, as in starts, turns, sudden increases or decreases in speed, and stops. As long as we are moving at a constant rate, the brain receives no impulses from the vestibular apparatus. Frequent stops and starts or changes in direction or speed of movement (as in a "bumpy" airplane or a rocking boat) will repeatedly deform the hair tufts, stimulate the hair cells, and send a series of impulses to brain and viscera. This action may result in "seasickness"—dizziness, nausea, vomiting.

Box 50

How Serious Is Gravity?

For all but a very few humans, the force of gravity is an ever-present influence upon our bodies. It is possible to experience some of the characteristics of weightlessness by floating completely submerged in water, but prolonged exposure to true weightlessness has come only with the development of space flight. As all our movements and many of our sensations of pressure, kinesthesis, and body orientation are normally subject to the influence of gravity, it might seem that severe losses in orientation and coordination would result when gravity is removed. Surprisingly, the effects of weightlessness appear not to have been very great for most space travelers.

It is noteworthy that the normal stimulation of the semicircular canals by rotation of the head is not affected by gravity (or by its loss). Acceleration is the stimulus for these structures, and this stimulus will still be present if an astronaut turns his head to look at a passing flying saucer. Another sensory structure in each inner ear (called the "utricle") *is* stimulated by gravitational forces, however, and thus undergoes a reduction in the amount of stimulation during weightlessness. Apparently the combination of sensory information from the eyes, semicircular canals, and so on with such activation of the very sensitive utricle that does come from minor movements of the space vehicle is sufficient to prevent any feelings of disorientation in most cases. True, some American astronauts and some Russian cosmonauts have reported the "illusion" that they were flying upside down and standing on their heads. We must remember, however, that under conditions of true weightlessness it is just as illusory to feel that one is right side up.

Some other effects have been noted. Russian cosmonauts have been reported to show a very small decrease in the efficiency of finely coordinated movements like writing. Cosmonauts of the three-man Russian space ship *Voskhod* experienced some feelings of dizziness and nausea. The severity of the observed vestibular effects seemed to correspond to the cosmonauts' performance on tests of the vestibular apparatus administered on the ground. The nausea and dizziness experienced by two of the men were not felt by the third cosmonaut, who had undergone a long period of training and who proved to have the least sensitive vestibular system. Astronauts in the *Gemini 8* reported no problems with nausea, even when their capsule was tumbling end over end through space, once each second. Only when they landed in the Pacific Ocean did they feel seasick!

AMERICAN MEDICAL ASSOCIATION. 1966a. Effects of Space Vary, *A.M.A. News*, 3 (January 17), 1.
AMERICAN MEDICAL ASSOCIATION. 1966b. Space Dangers Met by Pilots, *A.M.A. News*, 13 (March 28), 1.
JAMES D. HARDY. 1964. Weightlessness and Sub-Gravity Problems, in J. D. Hardy, ed., *Physiological Problems in Space Exploration* (Springfield, Ill.: Thomas), pp. 196–208.
E. M. YUGANOV, A. I. GORSHKOV, I. I. KAS'YAN, I. I. BRYANOV, I. A. KOLOSOV, V. I. POPANEV, V. I. LEBEDEV, N. I. POPOV, and I. A. SOLODOVNIK. 1966. Vestibular Reactions of Cosmonauts During Flight in the Ship "Voskhod," *Federation Proceedings*, 25, T767–70. (Translated from *Izvestiya Akademii Nauk SSSR, Seriya Biologicheskaya*, 25, No. 6. 1965, p. 877.)

highly coordinated, not only make possible specific perceptions of limb or head movements but also contribute to the over-all general perception of our bodies. Perception of specific movements is extremely important in skilled performances (see Unit 22, p. 342).

Glossary

ampulla The enlarged base of the semicircular canal in the vestibular apparatus. There are three ampullae corresponding to the three semicircular canals. Each ampulla has within it a crista.

basket endings Receptor organs in the skin that consist of nerve endings wound around the roots of hairs. They are partially responsible for sensations of light touch.

crista The structure within the ampulla of the vestibular apparatus, containing the vestibular hair cells.

cutaneous sensations The skin sensations: touch, pain, warmth, and cold.

free nerve endings Endings of nerve fibers in the skin, unassociated with any coverings of connective tissue. They are capable of mediating all skin sensations.

kinesthetic Referring to the sensory system that provides information about the position and movements of the various parts of the body.

muscle spindles Structures found in muscles, each of which consists of one or more muscle fibers, supplied with sensory fibers and a small motor fiber. When the muscle is lengthened (stretched), the sensory fibers are stimulated, and the resulting nerve impulses are transmitted to the spinal cord and the cerebellum. The motor fiber can control the tension in the muscle fibers so that any stretch imparted to them will be sure to stimulate the sensory fibers.

olfactory bipolar cells Sensory cells for olfaction. They are fairly long, column shaped cells; from one end delicate hairs project into the fluid covering of the mucous membrane, and from the other end protrude long fibers making up the olfactory nerve. When particles of gas, dissolved by the mucus of the nose, reach these cells, neural impulses are initiated.

olfactory bulb A mass of cells and fibers resting on the base of the skull and into which the olfactory nerve fibers enter. Here the fibers connect with other fibers that form the olfactory tract leading farther into the brain.

olfactory tract Bundles of fibers going from the olfactory bulb into various cortical and subcortical regions of the brain.

semicircular canals Three small liquid-filled canals in the vestibular apparatus. Each canal is in the shape of a semicircle and is oriented in a different plane in space: up-down, left-right, forward-backward. The canals contain sensitive hair cells in a structure known as the crista.

somesthetic Pertaining to the soma or body. Hence somesthetic sensations refer to skin and kinesthetic sensations; somesthetic nerves refer to the fibers carrying neural impulses from the skin and joint receptors and the muscle and tendon spindles to the brain. The somesthetic-sensory cortical area is the area of the cortex where the impulses from the somesthetic sense organs terminate. This area lies directly behind the central fissure on the surface of the brain.

taste buds The receptors for taste, concentrated mostly in the tongue. A taste bud consists of taste-sensitive cells arranged in a pear shape and having an opening to the mucous fluid on the tongue. The opening is called a "taste pore."

taste nerves The nerves conducting neural impulses from the taste buds to the brain. The endings of the taste nerves are wound around each of the taste-sensitive cells in the taste bud. The taste nerves do not travel to the brain in a single fiber bundle but divide up into several bundles and travel along in company with fibers from various skin sensory nerves.

utricle A liquid-filled cavity, part of the vestibular apparatus. The utricle is sensitive to the position of the hairs of its sensory cells and thus to the position of the head in a gravitational field.

vestibular That part of the inner ear involved in our sense of balance. Hence, "vestibular apparatus" refers to the semicircular canals, the utricles, and their allied structures; "vestibular nerves" are the fibers that carry the impulses from the sensory cells to the brain; "vestibular nuclei" are the masses of gray matter in the brain stem where the vestibular nerve ends.

vestibular hair cells The sensory cells of the vestibular apparatus which bear on their free ends long hair tufts embedded in the gelatinous substance of the crista. When the gelatinous substance is displaced by action of the fluids in the semicircular canals, the hair tufts are bent; this bending stimulates the hair cells, which then send neural impulses through their nerve fibers to the brain and viscera.

Suggestions for Further Reading

Sensation and Perception

GIBSON, J. J. 1966. *The Senses Considered as Perceptual Systems*. Boston: Houghton Mifflin.

A highly stimulating and original treatment of many problems of visual perception, especially as related to problems of depth perception. It presents many experimental demonstrations.

GRAHAM, C. H. (ed.). 1965. *Vision and Visual Perception*. New York: Wiley.

A detailed and technical summary of the broad field of visual perception.

GREGORY, R. L. 1966. Paperback. *Eye and Brain*. New York: McGraw-Hill.

A delightful and imaginative presentation of a wide range of visual phenomena. Many excellent illustrations permit first-hand perceptual adventures.

HOCHBERG, J. E. 1964. Paperback. *Perception*. Englewood Cliffs, N.J.: Prentice-Hall.

A relatively brief yet quite comprehensive overview of the theory and data of perception.

KÖHLER, W. 1959. Paperback. *Gestalt Psychology*. New York: New American Library. Originally published 1929.

Written by one of the founders of Gestalt psychology. The book demonstrates the critical significance of the *experienced* world for the scientific study of perception and behavior.

MUELLER, C. G. 1965. *Sensory Psychology*. Englewood Cliffs, N.J.: Prentice-Hall.

A clear introduction to the study of man's senses.

Physiology of Perception

FIELD, J., H. W. MAGOUN, and V. E. HALL (eds.). 1959. *Handbook of Physiology, Section I. Neurophysiology*, Vol. I. Baltimore: Waverly.

A comprehensive and authoritative treatment of the physiology of sensation, especially Chapters 15 to 31. This work is highly technical.

THOMPSON, R. F. 1967. *Foundations of Physiological Psychology*. New York: Harper.

A first-class general textbook, thorough and up to date.

part three
**adaptive
behavior**

UNIT 1

conditioned-response learning

overview / Conditioned-response learning is achieved through conditioning trials. These trials consist of repeatedly presenting, at approximately the same moment, an unconditioned stimulus (which reliably triggers a certain unconditioned response) and a conditioned stimulus (which at first does not evoke that response). Conditioning is successful when, by continuous pairing of the two stimuli over a number of trials, the conditioned stimulus becomes able to evoke the response when presented alone. Stimuli similar to the conditioned stimulus also can evoke the response (generalization), but, with appropriate training, discrimination (restricting the range of generalization) can be achieved. The loss of the conditioned response (extinction) can be brought about by failing to reinforce the learned connection, that is, by eliminating the occasional pairings of the unconditioned and the conditioned stimulus necessary to maintain an already established conditioned response.

Reconditioning an extinguished conditioned response typically requires fewer trials than the original conditioning. One hypothesis to account for this "saving" is that the conditioned response has not truly been totally unlearned but that nonreinforcement has inhibited its appearance. Inhibition also can theoretically account for spontaneous recovery—the reappearance after extinction of a conditioned response without additional conditioning trials; in this case we assume a gradual dissipation of inhibition.

Conditioned-response learning is not necessarily restricted to only the simplest of learning phenomena. For example, through higher-order conditioning (a conditioned stimulus serving as the unconditioned stimulus for yet another stimulus), certain more complex behavior may, at least in theory, be accounted for.

The many kinds of learning that man and beast display can be grouped into categories in terms of their complexity. The simplest type of learning is usually categorized as *conditioned-response learning*. The first systematic analysis of this type of learning was made by Pavlov, the Russian physiologist, around the turn of the century.

In conditioned-response learning the individual is presented with an original stimulus (one that evokes a fairly simple response) and a neutral stimulus (one that does not evoke that response). After sufficient repetitive pairings of these two stimuli, the individual acquires the tendency to make a response to the neutral stimulus—a response that the stimulus did not formerly evoke.

This form of learning can be demonstrated at almost all levels of animal life, and, interestingly, conditioned responses are not more easily established in more advanced animals than in more primitive animals. Conditioning, therefore, not only seems to be universal, but also may involve the same mechanism in all species. Perhaps it is this promise of universality, coupled with the relatively simple experimental procedures for establishing conditioned responses, that is responsible for the continuing popularity of conditioned-response learning as a research topic for both psychologists and physiologists. The same considerations may contribute to its occupation of central positions in many general theories of learning—theories that seek to embrace all levels of animal and human adaptive behavior. The term "conditioned response" has, at one time or another, been employed in theoretical explanations of every possible type of learning, thinking, and problem solving. Such usage reflects a theory about conditioned response—the theory that conditioned responses are basic to all higher-order learning. We shall use the term in a purely descriptive sense, to refer to a training technique and a learning process that, taken together, differ in some important respects from all other kinds of learning.

The qualifier "classical" became necessary some thirty years after Pavlov's original work. During the early Pavlovian period, research on conditioned responses had remained largely within his original theoretical and experimental model. Subsequent work, discussed in Unit 20 as "instrumental conditioning," has made significant departures in method and interpretation.

Pavlov was primarily interested in the study of the digestive glands (for which he was awarded the Nobel Prize) but noted, as a laboratory curiosity, that the secretions from the salivary glands of the dog could be controlled by learning as well as by direct physiological or biochemical means. Becoming interested in what he called "psychic influences" on the salivary gland, he soon devoted most of the facilities of his laboratory to investigating them systematically, and the era of "conditioned responses" in psychology, physiology, philosophy, literature, and science fiction was initiated (see Box 51, p. 289). In Soviet Russia today, where the fields of psychology and physiology as they apply to the study of learning are so intertwined as often to be indistinguishable, Pavlovian views remain a dominant force.

Pavlov and his co-workers very early isolated and named some of the most basic phenomena of conditioned response: first, *conditioning*, that is, the acquisition of a stimulus-response relationship; second, *generalization*, that is, the tendency of the organism to transfer its acquisition to other situations; third, *discrimination*, that is, the limiting of the acquisition to a specified situation; fourth, *extinction*, that is, the loss of the conditioned response.

Conditioning

The fundamental facts of acquisition are easily described. A dog is harnessed into an experimental apparatus that permits precise administration of stimuli and measurement of responses. Then, in a typical demonstration, powdered food is placed in the dog's mouth,

Box 51

Conditioned Response
—A Russian First?

Although I. P. Pavlov and his colleagues have an unchallenged place in the history of psychology for their systematic work on the conditioned response, they did have their historical forerunners, as M. R. Rosenzweig has pointed out: As early as 1852, for example, a book on digestion by F. Bidder and C. Schmidt, German physiologists, reported the then striking observation that simply *showing* food to a dog could provoke the flow of digestive juice. The authors also stated that casual introspection demonstrates that the sight or even the mere thought of food can provoke the flow of saliva. Bidder and Schmidt's main interest was in the secretions that aid digestion, and they did not carry these behavioral observations further. The French physiologist C. Richet confirmed in 1878 the observations of Bidder and Schmidt; he reported that, when a dog with a gastric fistula (an opening from the outside into the stomach) was allowed to smell meat, the lining of the stomach became red, and gastric juice began to flow.

A colleague of Richet went further and made an artificial gastric fistula in a human subject—for therapeutic reasons, of course. The patient was a young man who had accidentally burned his esophagus so badly with a caustic solution that it closed completely, and the surgeon made a gastric fistula through which his patient could be fed. It worked perfectly, and Richet conducted experiments with this subject during the year that followed the operation. Because there was no connection between the mouth and the stomach, Richet could obtain pure gastric juice, unmixed with food. The subject had only to put tasty food in his mouth to start the gastric juice flowing. Once again, stimuli acting on sense organs at a distance from the stomach could elicit gastric secretion.

An even clearer anticipation of salivary conditioning is found somewhat later on (1872) in the work of the French physiologist Claude Bernard:

"Saliva flows abundantly when a tasty substance stimulates the nerves of the mucous membrane of the mouth, and . . . gastric juice forms when food touches the sensitive lining of the stomach. This mechanical stimulation of the peripheral sensory nerves . . . can, however, be replaced by purely psychic or cerebral stimulation. A simple experiment demonstrates this. Taking a fasting horse, you expose the duct of the parotid gland on the side of the jaw; you open the duct, and no saliva flows. If you then show the horse some oats or, even better, if you do not show him anything but make a motion which indicates to the animal that you are going to feed him, immediately a jet of saliva flows continuously from the parotid duct."

Certainly, then, the phenomena that aroused Pavlov's attention had been previously observed. It remained—and it was no small remainder—for Pavlov and his co-workers to convert a laboratory curiosity into a highly sophisticated theoretical system.

M. R. ROSENZWEIG. 1962. The Mechanisms of Hunger and Thirst, in L. Postman, ed., *Psychology in the Making* (New York: Knopf).
C. BERNARD. 1872. Des Fonctions du Cerveau, *Revue des Deux Mondes*, 98, 373–85.

which stimulates his salivary glands, and saliva flows. The flow of saliva under these circumstances is automatic and unlearned and is therefore known as an *unconditioned response,* abbreviated as "UR." The powdered food that elicits this UR is called an *unconditioned stimulus,* or "US." Suppose we now take some other stimulus—for example, a bright light—that has no influence on the action of the salivary glands and turn it on just before we place the food (US) on the dog's tongue. Each time the light is paired with the food we speak of a *reinforcement* trial. After a number of such reinforcements, the light alone will elicit the flow of saliva. The action of the glands under these circumstances is a new response and is known as a *conditioned response,* or "CR." The light that can now call forth this CR is known as the *conditioned stimulus,* or "CS." A new stimulus-response relationship has been established in the dog. Whereas formerly he had only US → UR, he now also has CS → CR. The CS has substituted for the US, but the nature of the substitution is a matter of some controversy and, as we shall note later on, has considerable relevance to learning theory. At one extreme, the CS can be considered as having completely acquired the characteristics of the US, if only temporarily, and from the "point of view" of the central nervous system is now identical with it. The contrasting position is that CS is a warning signal for the coming of the US but a signal that remains quite distinguishable from US in the subject's experience, behavior, and physiological reaction.

Put in this way, the issue would seem to be an empirical one. For one thing, we would ask, are the behavioral responses to the US and CS different, or, in other words, is the UR distinguishable from the CR? The consensus is that the two are certainly not always identical, and there is general agreement on the nature of some of the differences. The CR does not occur as promptly after the CS as does the UR after the US; that is, its latency is greater. Also, the CR is generally weaker; for example, somewhat

less salivation occurs in response to the light than in response to the food. Furthermore, even after the CR has been well established, it occasionally fails to appear; the warning message of the CS can apparently sometimes be "ignored."

In a complex act it may be difficult to identify the US-UR relationship on which the learning of the act is presumed to have been initially based. In an adult particularly, the original US for what may be a current CR is very likely lost in his long-ago early development. This gap must be bridged if conditioning is to remain a broadly applicable process. Attempts to bridge it have made use of the phenomenon of *higher-order conditioning.*

Higher-Order Conditioning

Consider our earlier examples. If, after the dog is conditioned to salivate at the light stimulus, we couple the light with a bell, the dog will salivate to the bell alone. In this case it is "as if" the light were now the US and the bell the CS. Presumably this process can go on for several more steps. We can accompany the bell with a touch on the nose, and soon the dog will salivate to a touch on the nose. This "chaining" process by which conditioned stimuli come to serve as "unconditioned" ones for new, more remote, conditioned stimuli is know as "higher-order conditioning."

Temporal Patterning

The temporal patterning of events is as important in conditioning as it is in perception. The crucial factor is the time relationship between the US and the CS. There are four major time patterns normally used in conditioned-response training: First, there is *simultaneous conditioning,* in which the CS may begin from a fraction of a second to five seconds before the US and continue along with it until the response occurs. Second, there is *delayed conditioning,* in which the CS begins from five seconds to several minutes before the US and then continues with it. Third, there is *trace conditioning*, in which the CS is given first and then removed before the US starts. (Presumably only some neural "trace" remains when the US starts; hence the name.) Fourth, there is *backward conditioning*, in which the US is given first and then removed before the CS starts.

Experiments reveal that the simultaneous technique with a CS lead of about half a second is more efficient than even the delayed or trace technique and it is almost impossible to obtain backward conditioning. These well-established facts fit well with the notion that the CS is essentially a warning signal. The individual behaves as if the CS were a signal or a warning that the US is about to take place, and his response (CR) prepares him for the oncoming US. For example, the light can be understood as a signal for "food is coming." In all techniques but backward conditioning the dog has time to react with a flow of saliva, so that, when the food actually appears, he is ready for it (see Figure 19.1.).

Generalization

Once a CS → CR relationship is established, stimuli that are similar to the original CS can evoke the CR, even though these similar stimuli have themselves never appeared in the original training. This phenomenon is called *generalization*. The dog, after conditioning, will thus salivate to the bright light that was used as a CS in the original training. But he will also tend to salivate to somewhat dimmer or somewhat brighter lights than the original CS. In general, the more similar the new stimulus is to the original CS, the more effective it will be. This phenomenon has been labeled the "gradient of generalization."

Generalization in classical conditioning situations has been demonstrated with a wide variety of conditioned stimuli, and generalization gradients have been shown for a number of dimensions along which a CS can be varied. A classic demonstration of stimulus generalization is presented in Box 52, p. 292.

Generalization has definite adaptive value, for stimulus situations are never exactly repeated in nature. If a conditioned response could be evoked only when the conditioned stimulus occurs in a form identical with that during the original training, the conditioned response would have little value in preparing the organism for an environmental change. A simple illustration will make this clear. A stoplight must be reacted to with equal vigor despite variations in its degree of "redness."

Discrimination

One way to limit the degree of generalization is by specific training. For example: Every time a light of intensity A is presented, it is reinforced with the unconditioned stimulus of food; when a light of intensity B is presented, no food is

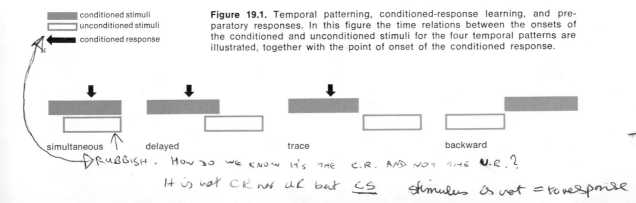

Figure 19.1. Temporal patterning, conditioned-response learning, and preparatory responses. In this figure the time relations between the onsets of the conditioned and unconditioned stimuli for the four temporal patterns are illustrated, together with the point of onset of the conditioned response.

conditioned stimuli
unconditioned stimuli
conditioned response

simultaneous   delayed   trace   backward

Box 52

Generalization of
Conditioned Responses

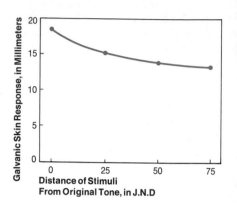

In 1937 C. I. Hovland of Yale University reported what has become one of the most quoted experiments in this field. He used the *galvanic skin response* (see p. 596) as the unconditioned response (UR). The subject has no awareness of this response, and it is beyond his voluntary control. The unconditioned stimulus (US) was a slight electric shock ("unpleasant but not painful") delivered to the wrist. The conditioned stimulus (CS) was a tone of a specified loudness. After sixteen combinations of the CS and US, the tone alone called forth a change in the galvanic skin response. The subjects (college students "paid by the hour") were then tested with three new tones 25, 50, and 75 j.n.d.s removed in frequency from the original tone (see p. 112 for the meaning of a "j.n.d.").

The galvanometer showed a deflection of 18.3 mm. to the original tone (this figure, then, is the size of the CR); 14.9 mm. to the tone 25 j.n.d.s removed from the original tone; 13.62 mm. to the tone 50 j.n.d.s removed; and 12.89 to the tone 75 j.n.d.s removed (see figure). The less similar the new and the original stimulus, the less effective is the new stimulus in evoking the conditioned response. It should be pointed out, however, that the exact shape of the generalization curve is still in dispute.

C. I. HOVLAND. 1937. The Generalization of Conditioned Responses, *J. Gen. Psychol.*, 17, 125–48. Figure adapted by permission of The Journal Press.

placed on the animal's tongue. Eventually, the animal will acquire a *conditioned discrimination* so that he will salivate to a light of intensity A and not to a light of intensity B. Just as generalization has adaptive value, so does discrimination. To return to our previous example of the traffic light, it is obvious that the ability to discriminate a red light from a green light has survival value.

Conditioned discrimination training can be a useful technique in studying perception in children and animals. For example, if an infant or a dog cannot make a differential motor response, such as moving this or that limb, to two sounds of similar pitch despite considerable conditioned discrimination training, then we may assume that this pitch difference is not perceived by the individual.

Extinction

Once a conditioned response has been established, the CS will elicit the response without the US. The presentation of the CS without the US is called *nonreinforcement*. For example, the light is presented, and no food is on the tongue; the CR (salivation) occurs. The conditioning has been successful. What will happen as such nonreinforced responses continue to be elicited? Typically, the strength of the response gradually decreases until a point is reached at which the CS fails to evoke the response at all. When this occurs, we say that *extinction* has taken place.

Rate of Extinction

The speed with which extinction takes place is determined by many of the same factors that determine the speed of acquisition of a conditioned response, for example, temporal patterning of stimuli and number of reinforcements. In general it has been found that the stronger the original conditioned response, the slower the extinction process. (Some experimenters actually use the rate of extinction as a measure of the strength of the conditioned response.) Almost invariably, no matter how complete the extinction may seem to be, some aftereffect remains. After "complete" extinction has taken place, it is thus easier to re-establish the conditioned response by further reinforcements than it was to establish it initially.

Inhibition

This "saving" in later conditioning trials—the *reconditioning* procedure—requires some mechanism to account for the lingering of some aftereffect despite the apparent disappearance of the CR. The mechanism that has been postulated for this purpose is known as *inhibition*. Briefly, it is assumed that nonreinforced trials result in an active neurological process that inhibits or blocks the conditioned response.

One class of evidence supporting this hypothesis is that extinction itself generalizes. The extinction of one CR (say, salivating to a light) will result in partial extinction of other CRs (for example, blinking to the sound of a bell). It is as if the subject during extinction acquires a generalized inhibition of conditioned stimuli. With this concept of inhibition, extinction comes about as a result of active masking of the CR by a competing process of inhibition of the CR, and not as a result of a passive weakening and fading away of the CR. We can now see that, even though a CR is extinguished, the neurological basis for it remains, and therefore a reconditioning procedure will not be starting from scratch; it can build upon what still remains in the nervous system. Although "inhibition" may therefore seem to explain the "saving" in reconditioning procedure despite the apparent disappearance of the CR, the existence of an inhibition process of this sort has not been demonstrated.

This postulated "inhibition" process can be used to explain a curious and interesting additional conditioning phenomenon—*spontaneous recovery*.

Spontaneous Recovery

After extinction has occurred, the CS → CR relationship may reappear without any additional training. For example, a dog's conditioned response to the light has been extinguished, and he has been removed from the experimental room. If we return him there at some later time, we may find that the light will elicit the flow of saliva all over again! This reappearance of an extinguished CS → CR relationship without additional training is called "spontaneous recovery."

This phenomenon might be explained if we assume that inhibition itself dissipates in the "rest" interval. When the animal is returned to the experimental room after the rest, the CR, which had been blocked by the inhibition, is no longer blocked and therefore can be evoked

Box 53

Conditioned Nausea

N. Kleitman and G. Crisler of The University of Chicago have reported the conditioning of a complexly integrated pattern of responses that was, at the same time, involuntary in nature.

Using eight dogs as subjects, the experimenters first prepared the animals by cutting a permanent opening (fistula) into each animal's salivary glands. They were able therefore to collect and measure the saliva as it was secreted. As a conditioned stimulus, the dog was harnessed into place in a stock, and a tube was tied around the lower jaw so that all the saliva secreted could be collected and measured. The animals were left in the stock for a constant period of time (from fifteen minutes to two hours for different dogs) without anything being done to them. The CS was thus "being placed in the experimental situation." The unconditioned stimulus was an injection of about 40 mg. of morphine, which was administered to the animal after the lapse of the predetermined waiting time. This procedure was repeated daily for many months.

Morphine, when injected subcutaneously, does not act upon some single localized receptor but upon many centers in the nervous system. The unconditioned response is best described as "general nausea." It includes panting, profuse salivation, shivering, vomiting, and other signs of distress.

Very soon after the experiment was started, a complex "conditioned response" began to appear. In many instances, as soon as the dog was placed in the stock—and long before the morphine was injected—the animal showed all the behavior characteristic of nausea: excessive salivation (in some dogs as much as 300 to 400 c.c. of saliva was secreted in an hour), shivering, retching, panting, and vomiting. As a consequence of conditioning, then, the dogs "learned" to become nauseated at the sight of the "hospital room."

The possibility of conditioning nausea has been used in the attempt to break "bad habits" in human beings. The alcoholic is administered a drug (Antabuse), which produces a feeling of nausea when he drinks alcohol. He may very soon reach a state in which he proclaims, "I can't stand the sight of the stuff"; the once tantalizing sight of his favorite bottle becomes a CS eliciting conditioned nausea. The heavy smoker has sometimes subjected himself to similar procedures in an effort to "break" the habit, with some success. But, as with all classical conditioning, backsliding (extinction) occurs with each unmedicated (nonreinforced) drink or smoke. For this reason, durable "cures" are rare, but reconditioning is somewhat more rapid in return engagements.

N. KLEITMAN and G. CRISLER. 1927. A Quantitative Study of a Salivary Conditioned Reflex, *Amer. J. Physiol.*, 79, 571–614.

again upon the presentation of the CS.

Successive spontaneous recoveries follow a law of diminishing returns. That is, if spontaneous recovery is tested day after day, the extent of spontaneous recovery will grow less and less.

Significance of Extinction

The facts of extinction can be understood in terms of its adaptive function. If time after time the US failed to follow the CS, it would be of little value for the organism to continue to respond. In some instances such continuation could even prove to be a handicap. On the other hand, too rapid or permanent extinction of a conditioned response that had been reinforced frequently in the past life of the individual might be premature and thus nonadaptive.

We have been stressing the adaptive value of

Box 54

Imagination Is
Conditionable

C. Leuba and R. Dunlap, psychologists at Antioch College, devised the following four-step experimental design to study the conditioning of imagery. First, the subject was put under deep hypnosis; second, he was given conditioned trials in which, for example, the sound of a bell (CS) was paired with a pinprick of the hand (US); third, while still under hypnosis, he was instructed to forget the conditioning session, and he was then awakened from the trance; fourth, once the subject was awake, the experimenter specified a number of situations that he was to imagine, and he was to report in detail what he experienced during these attempts. These situations included, among others, imagining the "sound of a doorbell."

The following protocol for subject J. J. shows the distinctive response that occurred when the sound of the doorbell was imagined. After J. J. was awakened, his responses to the various imagined situations specified by the experimenter were as follows (the imagined situation is given first, the response second):

"*Gasoline*—'Driving an automobile.'
Green light—[S closed his eyes] 'A dark room.'
Doorbell—'Feels sort of like being stuck by a pin, can't locate it particularly. Funny idea.' [S rubbed his hand; then looked at it.]
Radio hum—'Hear a record.'"

Several CS-US combinations were employed. Perhaps the most dramatic pairing was the sound of a metal snapper serving as the CS for the appearance of a geometric design (a diamond with a red letter S drawn in its center). During the posthypnotic test session the subject was asked to imagine a number of stimuli and to report if anything appeared on a *blank* white card while he was doing so. Nothing was "seen" on the card until the metal snapper sound was imagined; then the following dialogue between E (experimenter) and S (subject) ensued:

"At that point, S smiled, looked intently, and reported seeing a 'diamond.' E inquired: 'Any color?' S replied 'Yes, red; and there's a red S in the middle of the diamond.' S then turned the card over. 'It is there too. It's vague now and disappears.' After the design had disappeared, E actually snapped the snapper a number of times. S smiled, looked more intently at the card, and said, 'It's there when you snap the snapper.' He examined the card carefully and said, 'What goes on here?'"

Leuba and Dunlap report that their subjects typically seemed genuinely surprised and puzzled by the appearance of these conditioned sensations; they did not "make sense," and no explanation for such incongruous connections could be given. But is this kind of experience so unfamiliar? A feeling of fear and apprehension, sometimes even physical pain (a headache), often strikes the most normal of us in life situations in which such a reaction just doesn't "make sense." Perhaps some long-forgotten "conditioning" is at work; the analogy is in fact explicitly employed in several theories of the origin of unrealistic, or neurotic, behavior.

C. LEUBA and R. DUNLAP. 1951. Conditioning Imagery, *J. Exper. Psychol.*, 41, 352–5.

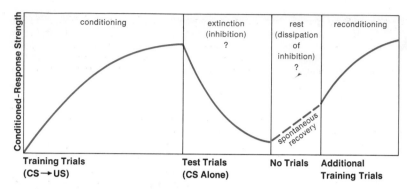

Figure 19.2. A dog's eye view of classical conditioning phenomena.
G. A. Kimble and N. Garmezy, *Principles of General Psychology*, 2nd ed.; Copyright © 1963 by The Ronald Press Company; adapted by permission.

conditioned responses. Obviously, however, not all the characteristics of their acquisition, generalization, discrimination, or extinction are perfectly adaptive. An appreciation of both the adaptive and nonadaptive features of conditioned responses must be gained if we are to understand the role of conditioning in adaptive behavior.

Conditioned Responses and Behavior

If conditioning were restricted to the acquisition of relatively simple responses to simple stimuli, conditioning would have little importance in the total adaptive economy of the individual. It appears, however, that certain complexly integrated patterns of responses—especially many cases of so-called "irrational" behavior—may also be viewed as instances of conditioning. In many forms of learned behavior conscious decisions and motives seem to play a decisive role, but in some behavior rather complex responses appear to be triggered automatically by some apparently neutral and trivial event. This phenomenon is especially true

of emotionally toned behavior. On the basis of experimental work in these fields it has been suggested that many allergy reactions, "irrepressible" outbursts, and complex visceral and glandular responses that accompany intense feelings and emotion can best be understood as acquired conditioned responses (for an illustrative experiment, see Box 53, p. 294). Perhaps the presence in emotional behavior of conditioned components not easily available to consciousness or control is exactly why we find it so difficult to change that behavior. This possibility may also be the reason that the reacting individual does not himself understand why he feels or behaves the way he does under some circumstances (see Box 54, p. 295).

Even with these extensions of classical conditioning to more complex behaviors, it remains a process with obvious limitations for the task of explaining typical learning achievements in men and animals. It is to these more typical forms of learning that we turn in the next unit, leaving the reader with a graphic review of classical conditioning in Figure 19.2.

Glossary

backward conditioning A training procedure in which the US is presented first and the CS is presented after cessation of the US. The least efficient method of conditioned-response training.

conditioned discrimination The behavior of an organism, after appropriate conditioned-response

training, in responding in two different ways to two different stimuli. For example, if after conditioned-response training a dog salivates to the tone of a bell, but not to the noise of a click, we have an instance of conditioned discrimination.

conditioned response The response that is evoked

by the conditioned stimulus after conditioning has occurred, abbreviated to "CR." The CR is usually different from the UR and normally has a longer latency.

conditioned-response learning The process of training by which a neutral stimulus is repeatedly paired with one that typically produces a certain response until the neutral stimulus alone can evoke that same response.

conditioned stimulus The stimulus to which a new response becomes related through the process of conditioning, abbreviated to "CS."

delayed conditioning Training procedure in which the CS begins from five seconds to several minutes prior to the US and continues until the response occurs. *Efficient*

extinction The training procedure of presenting the CS unaccompanied by the US. This term is also used to refer to the loss of conditioning as a result of this procedure. Sometimes called "experimental extinction."

generalization (in conditioning) The fact that a conditioned response may be elicited by stimuli that have not been used in the conditioning training. The more similar the new stimuli are to the stimulus used in the training, the greater is the probability that generalization will be evident. This phenomenon is sometimes referred to as the "gradient of generalization."

higher-order conditioning Conditioned-response learning in which what was formerly the CS serves as the US for a new CS.

inhibition A hypothetical process assumed to operate during extinction. Dissipation of inhibition is then assumed to occur during a rest period following extinction, thus accounting for the saving shown in reconditioning and for spontaneous recovery.

reconditioning training Resuming the conditioning procedure some time after the originally acquired CR has been weakened or removed through extinction.

reinforcement (in classical conditioning) When the unconditioned stimulus accompanies presentation of the conditioned stimulus.

simultaneous conditioning Training procedure in which the CS begins simultaneously with or up to five seconds before the US and continues until the response occurs. It is one of the most efficient conditioning procedures. *V. little*

spontaneous recovery The return in strength of an extinguished CR after a lapse of time and with no additional conditioning.

trace conditioning Training procedure in which the CS is presented first but is removed prior to the onset of the US. It is a fairly efficient method of conditioning.

unconditioned response The original response evoked by the unconditioned stimulus without training. It is abbreviated to "UR."

unconditioned stimulus The stimulus that evokes the unconditioned response without training. It is abbreviated to "US."

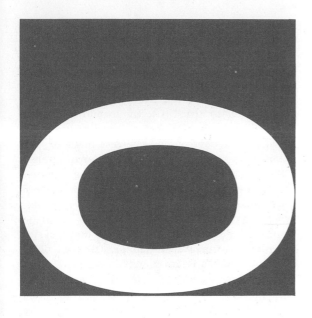

instrumental learning

overview / The primary distinction between learning through classical conditioning and learning through instrumental conditioning is that in the former the organism's response has no effect upon environmental events, whereas in the latter the learned response does have effects upon them and can be truly adaptive to the situation. The training procedures for instrumental learning may be systematic, as with instrumental conditioning procedures; or they may not, as in trial-and-error problems, in which the learner himself determines the course of his training experience.

Many of the phenomena of classical conditioning, like generalization, discrimination, and higher-order conditioning, find parallels in instrumental conditioning. A crucial element of this general procedure is reinforcement, the assignment of "good" or "bad" consequences to the organism's responses during conditioning. There are various schedules of reinforcement; they refer to various conditions under which reinforcement of desired responses is given. These different schedules lead to differences in the rate of instrumental conditioning and in the speed of extinction of the response after reinforcement is terminated.

The Law of Exercise (or frequency) and the Law of Effect (or reward) have been invoked to account for the phenomena of instrumental learning. Both can be effectively criticized, experimentally and theoretically. A "cognitive" theory like Tolman's, which makes a crucial distinction between learning and performance, presents a useful alternative conceptualization.

As we have seen, classical conditioning techniques can produce adaptive behavior. Through these procedures the conditioned stimulus comes to act as a "signal" that the US is about to occur, and the CR can be seen as a preparatory adjustment for the coming US. Thus, after Pavlov's dog is conditioned in the usual manner, the light causes the dog to salivate "in preparation" for the dry powdered food that is about to be placed in his mouth. Or when the dog has been subjected to a pairing of a buzzer (CS) and an electric shock (US), he comes to make the various cringing and other adjustive postural changes (CR) when he hears the buzzer. These conditioned responses are adaptive to the degree that they enable the dog to be "set for," and thus to be able to minimize, the effects of the painful shock that inevitably follows the buzzer.

But note that no matter what conditioned responses the dog makes, the environmental event—favorable or unfavorable—must inevitably occur. Salivating does not speed up the coming of food, nor does cringing prevent the shock. In the classical conditioning situation the organism's responses provide no control over the environment, no power to change the environmental event. And it is precisely because of this lack of control and power that the conditioned-response technique has only limited value for the study of adaptive behavior.

Most of what we call "adaptive behavior" is characterized by action that removes the organism from an undesirable environment, that carries the individual into a desirable environment, or that changes certain features of the environment—in a word, action that *controls* the environment. When the hungry dog comes into the house and runs to his food dish, his behavior is adaptive precisely because it does control his environment—he has changed a "nonfood" into a "food" environment. When he is scratched by a cat and thereafter crosses the street when he sees the cat arching his back and spitting, he is again demonstrating that he has learned to control the environment—by re-

moving himself from a dangerous environment. And, to repeat, this kind of adaptive learning cannot be studied in the classical conditioning setup—a setup in which the animal's behavior, no matter how well learned, cannot control, affect, or alter the environment.

In order to investigate the formation of complex adaptive habits that cannot be studied by the classical conditioned-response methods, psychologists have developed a number of alternative experimental techniques. These alternative techniques are frequently described as methods designed to study *instrumental learning* and *trial-and-error learning*. They are so called because the learned responses that they develop can be instrumental in changing or controlling the individual's environment in adaptive ways.

At about the time Pavlov was carrying out his earliest work on classical conditioning, the American psychologist Edward Lee Thorndike, with quite a different kind of experimental approach, was formulating the principles of what came to be known as "trial-and-error learning." Thorndike, while still working for his degree at Columbia University (having previously studied with William James at Harvard), studied the intelligence of chicks, rabbits, and cats. Confining his cats in "puzzle boxes" (from which they could escape by clawing down loops of string, pushing on levers, turning buttons), Thorndike observed what the animals did and recorded the time it took the cats to get out of the boxes on successive trials. The significant observations he made are, first, that the animal tries many things—squeezing through the bars, clawing and biting at any loose object within the box, thrusting its paw out, and so on; second, that gradually the "errors" (responses that do not release the animal from the box) are eliminated and only the successful responses remain—the animal has learned "by trial and error, and accidental success."

This pattern of behavior differs in at least two significant ways from that shown in classical conditioning. In the first place, the final to-be-learned response (for example, pushing the lever) is not inevitably or automatically elicited by an unconditioned stimulus. The animal must "discover" the appropriate response. Contrast this activity with the classical conditioning procedure in which the to-be-learned response is automatically evoked by a specific stimulus; the animal has nothing to "discover." In the second place, as we have already seen, pushing a lever actually makes the box open, whereas salivating does not make the food appear.

These differences do not preclude the possibility that a common set of principles may help us to understand the learning of all habits—whether learned under classical conditioning procedures or under instrumental learning procedures. And some psychologists, impressed with the similarities of these two forms of behavior, have tried to develop a set of learning principles based upon conditioned-response theory that will accommodate both. To further this objective, they have attempted to stretch the very terms of conditioning to cover the phenomena of instrumental learning. This attempt is indicated by their use of the phrase *instrumental conditioning*.

Instrumental Conditioning

One illustration of this approach is found in the work of the American psychologist B. F. Skinner. The procedures and terminology characteristic of Skinner's work can be conveniently illustrated in the context of his favorite experimental apparatus (commonly referred to as the "Skinner box") and his favorite experimental animal (the pigeon). The Skinner box (see Figure 20.1.) contains a small round window that can be illuminated and that, when pecked while illuminated, causes a pellet of food to be delivered to a tray. In a typical so-called "instrumental conditioning procedure" the hungry naïve bird at first wanders about the box pecking randomly at this and that. Eventually he pecks at the illuminated window, and the automatic mechanism delivers a food pellet; this

reward for the appropriate response is called a *reinforcement*. After a number of these reinforcements, the pigeon is more likely to peck at the window than at anything else. In fact, he is rather undiscriminating in that he will continue to peck vigorously no matter how the window is lit—whether by a dim light, by a bright light, or by a light of any color. In short, he shows *generalization* of the now-conditioned pecking-at-the-window response. If food is delivered only when there is a light of a specific quality (in hue or in brightness), however, then *discrimination* takes place—the pigeon learns to respond only to that particular light. If unreinforced trials now occur (that is, if food fails to appear consistently following the correct pecking response), the pigeon eventually stops

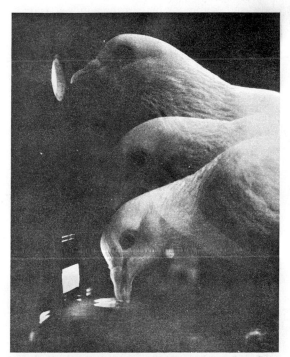

Figure 20.1. A pigeon performing in a Skinner box. This bird has been successfully conditioned and goes rapidly through the sequence of pecking at the illuminated window at the top and seeking the food pellet.
Courtesy Professor Norman Gutterman.

pecking—*extinction* takes place. Savings can also be demonstrated in that fewer reinforcement trials are necessary to re-establish the extinguished response.

Higher-Order Conditioning

Higher-order conditioning (observed in the technique of classical conditioning) is said to have its instrumental conditioning analogue in the phenomenon of *secondary reinforcement*. In higher-order conditioning the CS is successively transferred from one stimulus (for example, a bell) to another (for example, a light), the earlier conditioned stimulus (the bell) serving as the unconditioned stimulus for the new CS (the light). In secondary reinforcement, the pigeon is trained to peck at an unlighted window, and each peck causes the window to be lit briefly at the same time the food pellet is delivered. The lighted window, it is asserted, eventually comes to serve as a reinforcer in its own right, the food pellet no longer being necessary. That is, the bird will now peck at the window when the reinforcement is nothing more than a brief illumination. The reinforcement is now "secondary," in that it is assumed to derive its effectiveness from having previously been conditioned to a "primary" reinforcer, the food pellet.

Reinforcement

The most crucial and at the same time the most conceptually shaky element in the picture of instrumental conditioning is reinforcement. As we have already seen, one of the characteristics distinguishing classical from instrumental conditioning lies in the fact that in classical conditioning the animal has nothing to discover—the US automatically, accurately, and inevitably calls forth the "proper" response, the UR; in instrumental conditioning, however, the animal has to discover, of the many spontaneous responses he does make in the situation, which is

the proper or correct response, and then he must learn to select this response and drop all others. Now, how does the animal know which is the correct response? How can he recognize the correct response once he has made it? And how does he learn to prefer this response to all others? The answer given is that the correct response is the response that is reinforced, and that he learns to repeat this response *precisely because it is reinforced*. This explanation leads to the commonly accepted definition of instrumental conditioning as that form of learning in which the frequency of a spontaneously occurring response increases after the response is reinforced a certain number of times. If we now ask what "reinforcement" is, we are told that it is the pairing of *any* response with a reinforcer and that a reinforcer is an event that increases the frequency of the response. And this answer, obviously, has led us into a most embarrassing circularity in our basic definition of instrumental conditioning: Instrumental conditioning is that form of learning in which the frequency of a spontaneously occurring response increases after the response has been paired with an event that increases the frequency of that response. (!)

This circularity can be avoided by attempting to give a common-sense meaning to reinforcement: Reinforcement is *reward*. A pellet of food for the hungry pigeon is thus a reward; so is escape from a confining box to a restless cat. But, if we accept this definition, we are faced with the very tough problem of deciding what we mean by "rewarding" and how we can know, for each animal, at any given moment, what is and what is not "rewarding."

As we shall see later on (p. 308), determining how learning is related to "reward," "punishment," "drive," "motive," and so on is a most difficult and disputed problem in current theories of learning. Indeed we shall see that some theorists (notably Tolman) have held that learning has nothing to do with reinforcements, rewards, punishments, drives, and motives (however defined) but that rewards, punishments, and drives have relevance only for the performance of an already learned act, not with the acquisition of the act.

Despite the conceptual confusion and ambiguity of the concept of reinforcement, a great deal of experimental attention has been devoted to teasing out the role of "reinforcement" (even if ill-defined) in the adaptive behavior of the animal. One set of experiments that has given rise to a number of surprising findings is that which has examined the effects of different schedules of reinforcement.

Schedules of Reinforcement The term *schedules of reinforcement* refers to the probability relation between the performance of the instrumental response and the occurrence of the reinforcement. The simplest case is a schedule providing 100 per cent reinforcement, that is, reinforcement each time the response is made. This 100 per cent reinforcement is a rather limiting and artificial state of affairs; nature is not so generous and consistent. Certainly, even the most constantly hovering mother cannot possibly notice and reward each occurrence in her child of a response-in-training. The most common situation in nature is a schedule of *partial reinforcement*, that is, a situation in which reinforcement occurs less than 100 per cent of the time.

Experimental interest in partial reinforcement was sparked by early findings that, although a habit is learned more slowly under a schedule of partial reinforcement, it is actually more resistant to extinction than is a habit learned under a schedule of 100 per cent reinforcement (see Box 55, p. 304).

An almost endless variety of partial-reinforcement schedules has been experimentally employed, but essentially they involve the manipulation of three main factors—the number of responses per reinforcement, the *amount of time* elapsed between reinforcements, and the constancy or changing rate of the previous two factors.

1. A reinforcement may be given each time a certain *number of responses* has been emitted, no matter what the elapsed time between reinforcements: for the pigeon, a pellet for a fixed number of pecks; for the piece-rate worker in a factory, a specified amount of money for each batch of units completed. The payoff here is for work done, not for time put in.

2. The reinforcement may be delivered after a certain *amount of time*, regardless of the number of responses that may have been made in the interval. Here the hourly wage earner is the appropriate analogue (and clock watching an understandable corollary). As time, and not responding, is of the essence for this schedule, animals (and men) frequently learn not to respond except immediately before the end of the waiting interval when a rewarded response is imminent. In fact, the habit acquired under this reinforcement schedule may be said to involve learning to estimate the intervening time interval, as well as learning to perform the required action.

3. The number of responses (or the amount of time) required for a reinforcement may be held constant throughout an experiment, or it may be varied. It may vary randomly, or it may vary systematically, increasing or decreasing the number of responses (or seconds) required for a reinforcement. The efficacy of such a varying-reinforcement schedule in keeping a subject "at work" has lucrative results in the random-reinforcement schedule that is built into slot machines in gambling casinos. The one-armed bandit pays off the player on a randomly varying partial-reinforcement schedule.

At present there is no universally accepted theory that explains the increased resistance to extinction that follows partial reinforcement. Perhaps the most widely accepted theory is the so-called *discrimination hypothesis*. As Kimble (1961), a learning theorist, has phrased it: "The essential point in this hypothesis is that conditions which make it difficult for the organism to recognize that training has ended and extinction begun will lead to great resistance to extinction. Among the conditions leading in this direction are partial reinforcement and irregularly patterned reinforcement." In the typical instrumental-conditioning procedure, under a 100 per cent reinforcement schedule, the pigeon has learned that pecking at the window *always*

Box 55

Occasional Versus
Continuous Rewards

At Indiana University, W. O. Jenkins and M. K. Rigby measured the relative strengths of responses that were periodically or continuously reinforced.

The apparatus used (somewhat like that in the photograph, but with water, rather than food, as a reward) was a modified "Skinner box," originally designed by B. F. Skinner. Among their experimental procedures they had two groups of thirsty rats who were taught to press a lever to get a drink of water. After preliminary training the animals of group I were placed in the box for a total of 180 minutes (divided into half-hour sessions) and were permitted to press the lever as frequently as they wished, but they were rewarded with water only every two minutes, for a total of ninety rewards. Group II rats were in the box 180 minutes (in half-hour sessions) and were rewarded *every time* they pressed the lever. They piled up 2,400 reinforcements. In terms of number of reinforcements, then, the cards were heavily stacked in favor of group II.

Immediately after this training, "extinction" tests were started. The animals were allowed to press the lever—but no reward was ever given. They were tested this way for three daily one-hour periods. The table summarizes the experimental conditions and gives the results.

Group I, given *90 intermittent rewards*, pressed the bar 129 times during the extinction period—just slightly over 140 per cent of the number of previous reinforcements. Group II, given *2,400 continuous reinforcements* in the original training, yielded only 100 responses during the "extinction" period—or just slightly over 4 per cent. The less consistently you reward, the *stronger* the habit!

Group	Minutes in Box	Number and Conditions of Reinforcement	Number of Lever Pressings During Extinction Period
I	180	90; 2-min. intermittent	129
II	180	2,400; continuous	100

W. O. JENKINS and M. K. RIGBY. 1950. Partial (Periodic) Versus Continuous Reinforcement in Resistance to Extinction, *J. Comp. Physiol. Psychol.*, 43, 30–40.

B. F. SKINNER. 1938. *The Behavior of Organisms* (New York: Appleton). Photo courtesy Chas. Pfizer & Co., Inc.

results in a food reward. A few unrewarded trials are sufficient to permit him to recognize that something has changed—that the connection between response and reward no longer holds, and extinction rapidly occurs. On the other hand, under partial reinforcement, it should take longer for extinction to occur, for, in the training series itself, there was a considerable number of unreinforced trials, and therefore it takes the animal longer to make the discrimination between the training trials and the extinction series (in which the trials are unreinforced).

Classical Versus Instrumental Conditioning

The descriptive terms used in instrumental conditioning indicate clearly how some theorists have stressed the parallel between classical and instrumental conditioning. This parallelism, furthermore, cannot be dismissed as merely a verbal analogy. Indeed, despite some clear-cut differences between the two types of conditioning (see especially pp. 301–2), there are certain points at which these two types cannot be easily differentiated. Kimmel and Kimmel (1963) have shown, for example, that a classical unconditioned response—the galvanic skin response (GSR), which is a physiological reaction to stress—can be instrumentally conditioned, despite the fact that the GSR is automatic and reflexive, rather than voluntary, behavior. But the crucial issue consists not only of the formal relation of instrumental to classical conditioning but also of the adequacy of instrumental conditioning in accommodating the full range of complex and adaptive learning phenomena that make up instrumental learning. Here, too, the instrumental-conditioning experimenters and theorists can call upon supporting evidence for their assertion that instrumental conditioning is enough. For example, Fonberg (1956) reports that a conditioned-avoidance response in dogs, established in one specific situation (lifting a leg to avoid an electric shock), also appears when the animal is confronted with a totally different problem (making a difficult, stressful discrimination between two auditory tones). In other words, a response that served to avoid one kind of trouble was "remembered" and used by the animal in an attempt to cope with another kind of trouble. This is complex behavior indeed, and it is easy to see how, by recourse to the concept of generalization, even this complex behavior might be described as an instance of instrumental conditioning.

Trial-and-Error Learning

Not all psychologists are happy, however, with the attempt to seek parallels between classical and instrumental conditioning or with the attempt to explain all instrumental learning in terms of conditioning principles. A number of alternative ways of conceptualizing the data of instrumental learning have been championed. Some of these alternatives antedated the instrumental-conditioning approach and provided the basis for Skinner's concepts; other approaches differed radically. As an instance of the former type, we have Thorndike's Law of Exercise and Law of Effect; and, as an instance of the latter, Tolman's "cognitive" theory.

A comparison of how Thorndike and Tolman dealt with the data of "trial-and-error" learning (Thorndike's term, see p. 300) will clarify two things. First, it will permit us to see clearly the genesis of many of the concepts popular in current learning theory. Second, it will bring into clear relief the significant differences between the now traditional "reinforcement" concepts (whether cast in the language of Thorndike, Skinner, or "common sense") and the cognitive approach, which challenges many of the common beliefs so long taught about the learning process.

Maze Learning

The most popular device for studying trial-and-error learning in animals has been the maze. In 1901 Small at Clark University published his

Box 56

Mazes

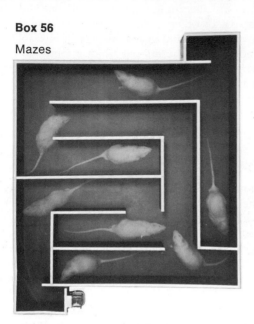

The maze cen be defined as a problem that requires for its solution the selection of the shortest route to a goal. The maze usually has walled alleys, and is called an "alley maze." The particular sequence of turnings and correct alleys varies from maze to maze. It has been estimated that more than 150 different maze patterns have been used to study learning in animals. In almost all mazes it is possible for visual, auditory, tactual, olfactory, and other stimuli emanating from the alleys, from the environment outside the maze, or from the choice point itself to serve as cues differentiating the correct pathway from the blind alley. The progression of a single rat as he blunders his way from the start (top) to the goal box (bottom) is shown in this multiple-exposure photograph.

C. H. HONZIK. 1936. The Sensory Basis of Maze Learning in Rats, *Comp. Psychol. Monogr.*, Vol. 13, No. 64. Photo Albert Fenn, Time-Life Books, *The Mind*, © 1964 Time Inc.

study of the "mental processes of the rat," in which he used a small-scale reproduction of the Hampton Court Palace hedge maze. Since then thousands of laboratory rats, hamsters, guinea pigs, mice, ants, cockroaches, cats, fish, and even college sophomores have been running, hopping, crawling, swimming, and shuffling their way through various kinds of mazes, under the worried and wearied eyes of experimental psychologists.

In essence, the maze consists of a series of points at each of which a choice must be made. At each point (see Box 56), the subject must discover which alley is the correct choice and which the wrong choice; then he must "string together" or organize these various choice-point discriminations and run them off in proper sequence.

It may be helpful if we diagram the characteristics of maze learning (see Figure 20.2.). This scheme is sufficiently general to apply to all forms of trial-and-error learning in which one of several possible responses is actually adaptive (the goal box is reached) or is selected by the experimenter as correct (a food pellet is delivered only if the lever is pressed at the appearance of a certain stimulus).

The Laws of Exercise and Effect

The Laws of Exercise and Effect comprise Thorndike's major explanation of how an animal learns to retain the "correct" response and to eliminate all others. Let us first consider the *Law of Exercise*. In its simplest formulation this law states that, when differences in *frequency* and in *recency* between R_3 and all other Rs are large enough (see Figure 20.2.), R_3 will become the response that will most probably be elicited by the stimulus situation at any future time.

There are two constraints characteristic of the usual trial-and-error learning situation. In the first place, R_3 must occur at least once on every trial, for the trial continues until R_3 is performed (the trial is terminated only when the rat reaches the goal box). In the second place, R_3 will always be the most recently performed response at the start of any new trial, for it is the last response of the previous trial. As a consequence of these two constraints, over a large series of trials R_3 will have occurred more frequently and more recently than any other response. If the Law of Exercise is valid, R_3 will therefore become the response most likely to be elicited by the stimulus situation. In this way we can account for the retention of the "correct" response and the elimination of all the others. Thorndike, however, believed that the Law of Exercise alone was not enough to account for learning. He pointed out that another important reason why R_3 is retained and the other responses are eliminated is that R_3 is usually followed by some good effect (the rat eats in the goal box), whereas the other responses are usually followed by a bad effect (the rat goes hungry). This relationship between the nature of the effect and the retention or elimination of the response he called the *Law of Effect*—a relationship that Skinner and others call "reinforcement."

The apparent simplicity of these laws and their ability to summarize many experimental results as well as "real-life" observations without recourse to "complex mental processes" appealed to many psychologists and educators. As a result these laws and their implications have permeated much of our thinking about learning and have influenced many of the educational practices in our schools. It is highly probable that the layman, if asked how his dog, his son, or his neighbor learns, would appeal to some sort of Law of Exercise (he might use the word "practice") and some sort of Law of Effect (he might use the phrase "reward and punishment").

In 1932 Edward C. Tolman published *Purposive Behavior in Animals and Men*—a book that was destined to influence learning theory greatly. The publication of this book started experimental and theoretical questioning of the Laws of Exercise and Effect. The issue is still

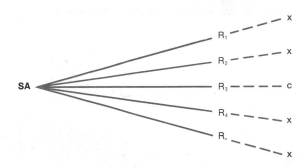

Figure 20.2. R_1, R_2, R_3, R_4, and so on represent an array of responses that the stimulus situation SA can elicit from the individual. The "x"s afer R_1, R_2, and R_4 represent "incorrect" responses, and the c after R_3 indicates that it is the "correct" response. In the case of behavior in a maze, at a choice point the c response is of course making the correct turn, whereas the "x"s include making the wrong turn, running back into the alley, scratching in perplexity, and so forth.

very much alive, and decades of experimental work have produced considerable heat—and some light. The most that can be done here is to present a very few of the relevant basic studies and point up their implications.

Tolman's Critique of the Law of Exercise There are many experiments in which the subject performs the wrong act as frequently as the correct act yet finally learns to do the correct one. Tolman's book is replete with experimental illustrations of this fact (see Box 57, p. 308, for one such experiment). The experimental evidence—from both animals and men—seems to show clearly that the sheer frequency or recency of performing the correct act in an instrumental-learning situation cannot, by itself, account for the retention of that act. Yet it seems clear from other experiments, as well as from everyday observations, that many trials and repetitions of the correct response are required before learning takes place.

Tolman's answer to this paradox is phrased in cognitive terms: During trial-and-error learning the individual is given an opportunity to

Box 57 Hidden Learning in the Rat

In 1929 H. C. Blodgett of the University of California reported his now famous experiment on "latent learning" in the rat.

Using the six-unit alley maze shown in Box 56, p. 306, he ran three groups of hungry rats, each animal being given one trial per day. Group I (*control*) always found food in the food box and was allowed to eat there for three minutes, after which it was removed to another cage for the remainder of its rations. Group II for the first six days did not find food in the box. When it arrived there, it was confined for two minutes, removed to another cage, and *one hour later* given its daily rations. From the seventh day on these animals did find food in the box and thenceforth were run under the same conditions as the control group. Group III ran the maze for the first *two* days without food and from the third day on found food.

During the no-food periods groups II and III showed no signs of learning, that is, they chose the wrong alley about as frequently as the correct alley (see figure). The control group did show a decrease in errors. But on the first day *after* food was found, groups II and III showed tremendous improvement, cutting their error scores by about 50 per cent, and on the second day they had caught up with the control group! Despite the fact that during the first period they had not been practicing the correct responses more than the wrong responses, they had been learning something about the maze, as is indicated by their performance *immediately after the introduction of food*. The evidence of their learning was "latent" or hidden until it had become "worthwhile" to show it!

H. C. BLODGETT. 1929. The Effect of the Introduction of Reward upon the Maze Performance of Rats, *Univ. Calif. Publ. Psychol.*, 4, 113–34.

discover which response leads to which consequence. The more opportunities he has for this, the quicker and more firm will be his learning. But this holds for the wrong acts as well as for the correct acts. He must learn, in other words, that R_1 leads to x as well as that R_3 leads to c. And to learn both these sets of relationships he needs many trials. It is not differential frequency or recency of R_3 over R_1 that is the deciding factor but the total frequency of $R_1 \rightarrow x$, $R_2 \rightarrow x$, $R_3 \rightarrow c$, $R_4 \rightarrow x$, and so on that is important. In the *latent-learning experiment* (see Box 57), the rat is thus given many opportunities to learn that this alley leads to a dead end and that alley leads on to other alleys, and so forth. Then, when he finds food in the food box, he will choose R_3 in preference to the other responses because he wants the food and he "knows" that R_3 leads to the food—but not because R_3 has been retained or learned while all the other responses have been eliminated. The learning process becomes one of learning the consequences of *every* response. In essence, then, trial-and-error learning for Tolman is discovery—discovery of the meaning of all the observed cues, of what leads to what. Frequent experience with the entire situation increases the probability that the necessary discovery will be made. It is essential to see clearly the difference between Tolman's and Thorndike's treatment of the role of exercise if one is to understand one of the fundamental differences between the two major contemporary theories of learning—the reinforcement and cognitive theories.

Tolman's Critique of the Law of Effect Tolman has also subjected the Law of Effect and its various reformulations to critical examination. For example, Clark L. Hull, a contemporary of Tolman, restated the Law of Effect somewhat in these terms: The strength of a response is a function of the number of times that response has resulted in some decrease in the need state of the individual. In other words, the more frequently a conditioned response has been rewarded, the more probable its occurrence. But evidence soon accumulated that suggested that the efficiency with which a response is learned, or the "strength" of a habit, does not depend merely upon the number of times R₃ has been followed by "good consequences" or the number of times an individual has been "rewarded" for performing that act. As we have seen (Box 55, p. 304), partial reinforcement can result in a more persistent habit than does 100 per cent reinforcement. Such evidence seems on the face of it to offer difficulties for a simple Law of Effect.

Tolman's book contains other experimental evidence that questions the validity of the Law of Effect. Nevertheless, it is clear that rewards and punishments and motivation in general are important in adaptive behavior. How can this apparent contradiction be resolved?

Learning and Performance One way that Tolman suggests for dealing with this problem is to distinguish between "learning" and "performance." We have already seen in the *latent-learning* experiment (Box 57, p. 308) that an animal may have learned something but may not reveal it in performance until it becomes "worthwhile" to do so. We have here an experimental demonstration that learning and performance are not the same.

Tolman has proposed that reward and punishment have different functions for learning and for performance. For learning, the function of reward and punishment is to enable the individual to discover which acts are rewarded and which acts are punished—"what leads to what." The fact that one response is rewarded and another punished does not "stamp in" one response or eliminate the other. In other words, by this view rewards—positive or negative— only convey information; they do not directly affect the probability that the response will be performed by the animal on some future occasion.

In performance, as distinguished from learn-

ing, the function of reward and punishment is to determine which response will be made and with what efficiency and speed. With a "better" reward or with a higher degree of motivation the individual will perform what he has previously learned with more efficiency or speed. Therefore, our everyday observation that with better rewards there is better "learning" really signifies that better rewards lead to better performance. In many of our studies we measure performance and not learning. The laws that relate degree of rewards and motives to learning are really, according to this view, "laws of performance."

A Perspective

It is no accident that our account of conditioning and instrumental learning has emphasized animal learning in specially devised, confining surroundings—Pavlov's dog in the harness, Thorndike's cat in the puzzle cage, Skinner's pigeon in the lever box, Tolman's rat in the maze. This emphasis reflects the desire of learning experimenters to study learning processes in the laboratory under conditions of rigorous control and experimental manipulation. And it reflects the hope of learning theorists that the principles of learning discovered in these simple laboratory conditions will prove to be general principles that can account for *all* learning —human as well as animal, complex as well as simple, higher-order as well as lower-order. As we move on now in the next units to such higher-order adaptive functioning—verbal learning and memory, skills, thought and language, problem solving—we shall begin to see how well this hope is justified. We should not have high expectations in this regard, however. Our hopes must be tempered by what we have already seen—that, even in their attempts to deal with laboratory-controlled and simple forms of learning, the theoreticians are still confronted by unsolved basic problems. The theory of learning is still in the making.

Glossary

discrimination hypothesis The hypothesis that, to the extent that extinction of an instrumentally conditioned response is slower, it is more difficult to recognize when the conditioning procedure has ceased. Partial and irregular reinforcement thus delays extinction.

instrumental conditioning A procedure in which a given response is followed by a reinforcing stimulus. Conditioning is said to have occurred if the response subsequent to reinforcement is in some way strengthened.

instrumental learning The outcome of instrumental-conditioning procedures in which the learned response is not automatically triggered by the unconditioned stimulus and in some way represents an adaptive change in behavior (for example, acquiring food or avoiding a painful stimulus).

latent learning Learning that does not display itself in performance until some later time.

Law of Effect The law that, in its simplest form, states that, when one response is followed by some good effect and other responses by bad effects, the former will become the most probable response that the stimulus situation will elicit at any future time. This law has been proposed to hold for all trial-and-error learning.

Law of Exercise The law that, in its simplest form, states that, when differences in frequency and recency between one response and all others become large enough, the former will become the most probable response that the stimulus situation will elicit at any future time. This law has been proposed to hold for all trial-and-error learning.

reinforcement (in instrumental conditioning) The operation of presenting a subject with a rewarding stimulus, or withdrawing a noxious stimulus, after the subject has made the appropriate response.

schedules of reinforcement The plan or schedule determining when and how often desired responses are reinforced in instrumental conditioning.

secondary reinforcement Analogous to higher-order conditioning in classical conditioning. The presentation of an initially nonreinforcing stimulus, which, through prior instrumental conditioning, has acquired reward value, as the reinforcing stimulus in training a new instrumental response.

trial-and-error learning Discovering and consistently performing the "correct" response in a situation that permits a number of different responses. The correct response can be verified to be correct only by actual trial. Roughly synonymous with instrumental learning.

verbal learning

overview / Man is the verbal animal, and much of our learning is of verbal materials. Verbal learning, of words or of "nonsense" materials, exemplifies the acquisition, transfer, and retention effects seen in all learning.

More meaningful material is usually learned more rapidly, but less meaningful items may be retained better simply because they are "distinct" and stand out as figure against the ground of the more usual meaningful words we already know.

The memory mechanism is not passive. When we recall a group of items previously presented to us in a random order, we impose a structure upon them, ordering them by meaningful categories and repeating the order from trial to trial.

We learn better when consciously trying to learn, for then we tend to use to an optimal degree the techniques of labeling, organizing, associating (in other words, "thinking about") the materials to be learned.

Things previously learned affect present acquisition. The amount and direction of transfer of specific information from one task to another depend upon the relations between the items in the two tasks. There is also general transfer between tasks involving quite dissimilar items, but this transfer can be shown to depend upon other relations between the tasks.

Retention is affected by interference from other things we have learned, either before or after the original learning of the material in question. We also "unlearn," when conflicting learning comes between original learning and the retention test.

The question of whether or not forgetting also includes spontaneous fading of learned material over time is partly dependent upon the unsolved problem of whether or not there are separate mechanisms in short-term and long-term memory and is related to the question of whether learning is a gradual or an all-or-none process.

Many different kinds of things can be learned. We have explored some of the general principles that have been proposed by those who have tried to understand the learning process. We were not very attentive to the nature of the material that was to be learned because we hoped that the principles might apply to a wide variety of subject matter. We must recognize the possibility, however, that some of our conclusions should be restricted to one or another kind of learning material. The necessity for this restriction may become clear as, in this unit and in Unit 22, we focus attention upon two important specific varieties of human learning—verbal learning and motor skills.

The first experimental investigations of human learning were those of Ebbinghaus, a German psychologist who undertook an investigation of his own memory processes. Using poetry and nonsense syllables (see p. 315) as materials, he demonstrated the increments in learning that resulted from repeated exposure to the material and the loss of the knowledge as time passed after the original learning. We give a name ("retention" or "memory") to the process through which a bit of learning is retained within the organism for some greater or lesser amount of time and another name ("forgetting") to the loss of knowledge that may occur with time.

This descriptive use of the words does not commit us to a decision on many other questions. Is learning a continuous process, or does it occur in discrete bits and pieces? Does just one process underlie all these changes (one that grows with learning, stays high during memory, and may then fade with forgetting), or are there two or more different processes in action? Does the loss of knowledge (that is, forgetting) that so often occurs with the passage of time come about because new (conflicting) things are being learned, or is it a consequence of a continuing process that would take place even if there were no new stimuli coming to the organism during this interval? These questions

are some of those to which we shall seek answers. For several of them, critical evidence will come when we talk about the physiological basis of adaptive behavior and memory (Unit 29). For all of them, some meaningful answers can result from examination of behavioral experiments in learning and memory.

Is Verbal Learning Unique?

Why is verbal learning singled out for special attention? Most of the reasons are fairly obvious, but some less than obvious considerations arise when we ponder the question for a while.

First, people use language all the time and are producing verbal utterances almost continually. We are always learning something new and most of it by way of language channels. Apparently verbal learning should represent a large part of human adaptive behavior.

Second, partly as a result of this fact, verbal-learning experiments are relatively easy to conduct. The experimenter can get good control of the stimulus materials, presenting them by way of the eye or the ear, and he can be sure of which response the subject is making. It is possible to control many characteristics of the situation, like time intervals, the nature of verbal materials, and the difficulty of the learning task.

Third, because language is a uniquely human attribute, one might expect studies of verbal learning to provide insights into the nature of the processes that distinguish man from other animals.

The second reason cannot be denied. It is certainly true that many experiments in verbal learning would be almost impossible with other kinds of material and that it is possible to explore many interesting questions because control of the materials and of the subjects is easier than in many other areas of investigation.

The other reasons—that language is such a common means of human learning and that language is a uniquely human process—will not provide a justification for studies of verbal learning unless we are willing to assume that studies of verbal learning do tell us something about *language* as such. Here we must be cautious. As we shall see in detail in Unit 24, there is good reason to believe that the development of language takes place according to principles that differ from those of simple learning. To the extent that this belief is true, most of our present findings will have only limited relevance to the problems of language.

Materials and Methods of Study

It may seem obvious that verbal-learning experiments will involve the use of words and possibly sentences as the materials to be learned. Many experiments are so designed—Ebbinghaus explored the learning of poems in many of his experiments. He realized, however, that words and, even more, connected sentences have an undesirable feature. Some words are more familiar to us than are others and may therefore be more easily learned. Even more important, each word is more closely related to certain words than to others. For both reasons it would be easier to learn the sequence "dog-cat-rat-cheese" than to learn "eft-alb-wen-zealot."

Now such differences among words as familiarity and interrelatedness are interesting and deserve to be studied for their own sake. But, when we are trying to discover the effect of some other experimental variable upon the development of learning—for example, the amount of time spent studying the materials—we would like all elements of the learning material to be equally familiar and equally associated with one another. For this reason, Ebbinghaus invented the *nonsense syllable*. Such syllables are commonly constructed by putting together a sequence of *consonant-vowel-consonant* ("CVC"s, as they are often called), for example, "tob," "duf," "yad." These syllables are not completely "nonsensical" and associations do exist among

them, but they are much more homogeneous than a random group of meaningful words and are widely used in verbal-learning research.

The material to be learned may be presented either to the ear or to the eye, and the subject is asked to respond either in speech or in writing. Many experiments use some version of the *memory drum*—a device that automatically presents each item for the period of time desired.

Experimental Procedures

Many procedures have been devised for structuring a verbal-learning task; some have become rather standard and should be noted briefly.

In the *serial-learning* task, the subject is given a series of words (or CVCs, and so on) one at a time; this series may contain, for example, twelve items. After the complete list has been presented, the experimenter starts a second presentation. This time, however, as the syllables are given, the subject attempts to recall the item next on the list before it appears. The list is presented over and over again until the subject can correctly *anticipate* each succeeding item.

It is common to think of each word in the serial-learning list as serving both as a response (to the preceding word) and as a stimulus evoking recall of the following word. These roles are separated in the *paired-associate* task. There the subject is presented with a series of pairs of items, for example, "xul-bef," "nac-deg," and so forth. On subsequent trials he is given only the first word of the pair (the stimulus), and he attempts to produce the second word (the response).

A *free-recall* problem involves a single list of items, but the order of their presentation is usually varied from trial to trial. The responses of the subject (the items he can remember) are collected after each complete presentation of the list, and no fixed order of recall of the items is demanded.

Measures of Learning and Retention

Obviously each of these methods would provide some evidence about the "amount" of learning that had taken place at the time of each trial. When we graph the results of such an investigation, as in Figure 21.1., we have a *learning curve*, which typically shows an increase in correct responses on successive trials.

More information is available, however, than "number correct" in the results of a verbal-learning experiment. We shall see that the answers to many interesting questions depend upon noticing *which* items are recalled on each trial rather than simply *how many*.

In all the foregoing discussion we have given examples that involve the measurement of *recall*. It is sometimes interesting to organize a problem so that we measure *recognition* instead. In such situations, the subject is not required to produce the response word himself; rather, he is given a group of words that includes the correct one and must identify the correct one.

Of necessity, either measure always reflects both *acquisition* and *retention*—the amount that was originally learned and the extent to which it has been remembered up to the time of measurement. When we are primarily interested in acquisition, we seek to minimize the role of retention by testing immediately after the learning trial; when we are primarily interested in retention, we try to start from a standard level of acquisition and vary the interval between the learning trial and the test.

Factors Affecting Acquisition

Many characteristics of the material to be acquired and the ways in which it is presented have effects upon the speed of learning. It is unnecessary to convince the reader that a *greater amount* of material (a longer list of words, for example) will take longer to learn than will a smaller amount or that many repetitions of a list will lead to better performance than will a few. Some other factors are not so obvious and lead to interesting inferences about the learning process.

Meaningfulness

It seems quite reasonable to predict that the more meaningful the material, the easier it will be to learn, but in order to test this notion we must have some clear definition or measure of *meaningfulness*. Psychologists have used several methods, most of which are based on the assumption that a more meaningful word (or CVC) is one that more readily evokes an association, or evokes more associations, when it is given to a subject in a free-association task (see p. 781) than does a less meaningful word. The number of associations elicited is the *association value*.

Using this definition of meaningfulness, the general finding has been that the more meaningful the items in a list, the more readily the list is learned (see Box 58, p. 318). Furthermore, in paired-associate lists, in which we separate the stimulus items from the response items, the evidence clearly demonstrates that whereas

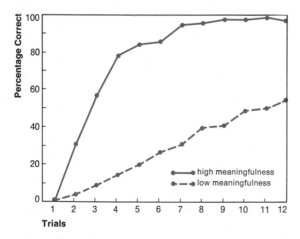

Figure 21.1. Learning curves showing improvement, over trials, in the number of correct anticipations on a paired-associate task. The average percentage correct for the group at each trial is shown. Items of high meaningfulness were learned faster than were items of low meaningfulness.

greater meaningfulness of either stimuli or response items facilitates learning, variation in response meaningfulness is the more important of the two.

Just as more meaningful items are generally more easily learned, so are they more easily retained. But there are exceptions to this rule, with respect to both learning and retention. In certain studies *less* meaningful items even appear to be learned and retained more readily. A possible explanation for these effects comes from study of the effects of the interrelations of the various items within a list.

Intralist Relations

If a list of equivalent items is presented for learning, we can study the question of which items are most readily learned *within* the list. Let us note two findings from such studies and then consider their interpretation.

First, as a serial-learning list is presented over and over again, the items toward the beginning and the end of the list are learned most readily. The items in the middle are learned more slowly; the most difficult items are those just after the middle. This phenomenon is called the *serial-position effect* (see Figure C in Box 58, p. 318).

Second, if a list contains a small number of items that differ in character from the majority of the items (for example, a few nonsense syllables in a long list of meaningful words), the "isolated" items are learned more readily and are retained better after the list is completely learned. This fact was first noted by von Restorff in 1933 and is called the "von Restorff effect," or the *isolation effect.*

Both findings can be understood from a consideration of the perceptual characteristics of the list. The application to the von Restorff effect is obvious. The isolated items "stand out," almost as a figure against the background of the other items. They are most vivid and therefore most readily learned. The serial-position effect is then explained by noting that the ends

of a list are more highly differentiated simply by virtue of being at the extremes; the items there are learned first, for any item at the extremes is "isolated."

This approach can be used to explain the occasional finding that items of low meaningfulness are more readily learned and retained than are items of high meaningfulness. For example, from a list that contained nine meaningful words and one nonsense syllable, the nonsense syllable may be learned readily because it is distinctive.

Organization

Suppose we present to a subject a list of words that fall into four categories, for example, proper names, animals, vegetables, and professions. We present the words in random order, without calling the subject's attention to the nature of the stimuli. Later the subject tries to recall as many of the words as he can. Bousfield and his associates (1944) have demonstrated that, in this form of free-recall situation, a clear pattern appears in the responses: Items that belong to the same category tend to follow one another in the recall list. Although the items have been presented in random order, they are recalled not in random order but in meaningful *clusters.* Evidently retention is not a passive process leading to an automatic recall of individual items—grouping takes place during the retention period as items from different parts of the list are grouped together to form meaningful clusters.

It may be tempting to try to explain the clustering phenomenon solely on the basis that the words forming a cluster are highly associated with one another and that the recall of one therefore stimulates the recall of the next. Experiments show, however, that the amount of clustering cannot be completely explained by word-to-word associations. This point is proved by showing that words belonging to the same category (for example, "dog-wolf") are clustered more readily than are uncate-

Box 58

An Experiment in
Verbal Learning

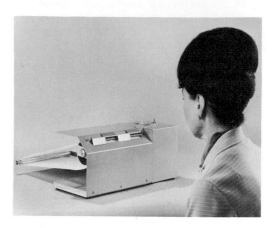

L. Postman of the University of California has reported an extensive series of experiments in verbal learning, from which the following description is taken.

In one experiment ninety students learned a twelve-item list of nonsense syllables; another ninety students learned a twelve-item list of common words. The standard "memory drum" (see photograph) and the "anticipation" method of learning were used. The items were successively exposed in the window of the drum for two seconds each. Beginning with the second time around, the subject was required to call out the *next* item on the list before it appeared in the window. The lists were repeated until the subject could "anticipate" every item during a given run.

For the nonsense syllables the fastest learner required thirteen runs of the list, the slowest learner ninety-three runs. To derive a "group" curve, the experimenters calculated the *average* number of trials required to achieve one correct anticipation, then the average to achieve two correct anticipations, and so on. From these averages a learning curve was plotted, as shown in upper chart. By this method every subject is included in every point on the curve. Note that the curve for the meaningful material has a steeper slope.

To analyze the serial-position effect, the average number of failures in anticipations was determined for each item separately and plotted as shown in lower chart. The middle items of the nonsense list (items 6, 7, 8) were much more difficult to learn than were the end items (items 1, 12). The absolute difference between the middle items and the end items was not as great for the meaningful words as for the nonsense items, but the relative difference was about the same. In each case about three times as many failures in anticipation were made for the middle items as were made for the end items.

L. POSTMAN and L. RAU. 1957. Retention as a Function of the Method of Measurement, *Univ. Calif. Publ. Psychol.*, Vol. 8, No. 3. Figures adapted by permission. Photo courtesy Lafayette Instrument Company.

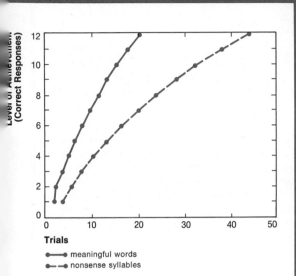

Trials

●——● meaningful words
●--● nonsense syllables

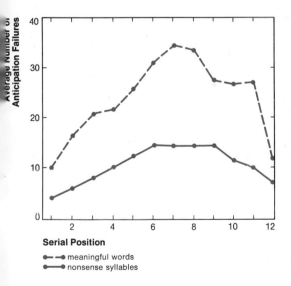

Serial Position

●--● meaningful words
●——● nonsense syllables

gorized pairs that have the same strength of association (for example, "dog-house"). It is not enough to think that the words in memory are linked together in a chain. To some extent they must be thought of as placed in bins, each of which will tend to be emptied in turn during recall.

An interesting finding is that clustering tends to increase with repeated presentations of a list and that, furthermore, recall scores are better for lists with clusters than for lists without clusters. When we take advantage of the categories or associations that underlie clustering, we are effectively reducing the number of individual things that have to be recalled; the task therefore becomes easier (see Box 59, p. 320).

Another way of demonstrating that organization takes place during retention is to present a list several times, with the items newly scrambled for each presentation. An opportunity for recall is given after each presentation, and we note whether or not a pair of words that appeared in sequence in the response after one trial will show the same consecutive order on the next trial. The words may have no obvious relation to each other, but if they appear consecutively in recall on repeated trials, they have obviously formed some relationship within the subject's memory. This form of subjective organization can be shown even when the items on the list are nonsense syllables.

Other forms of organization that depend upon the fact that we are dealing with the elements that form language can be studied with verbal material. After our discussion of the influence of meaningfulness and of clustering upon learning and retention, it should not be surprising to learn that it is easier to memorize "rapid flashes augur violent storms" than "rapid deter sudden bouquets neighbors." The first example forms a whole; the other (although made up of similar parts) remains five separate words with no apparent meaningful or grammatical relationships. Actually there

Box 59

Organization
—A Double-Edged Sword

When we face the task of learning something new, particularly if the material is low in meaning, one common technique is to try to find some reorganization of the material that will make it easier for us. An experiment by B. J. Underwood and G. Keppel at Northwestern University illustrates the usefulness of this method but reminds us that not all reorganizations will be uniformly helpful.

The subjects were required to learn a list of ten trigrams (three-letter strings like "TFA," "BSU," and so on). Each trigram was constructed so that it could be transformed into either of two three-letter words by rearranging the letters. Thus "tfa" could become "fat" or "aft." The list of trigrams was given five times, with a free-recall trial after each presentation.

Separate groups of subjects worked under different conditions. Half were "instructed"; that is, it was pointed out to them that the order of the letters in a trigram could be changed to form a common word. The others were "not instructed"; they did not receive this information.

When the subjects were told that they could recall the letters within the trigram in any order (for example, "fta," "aft," and so on—as long as all three letters were given), the instructed group showed faster learning than did the non-instructed group. More than 95 per cent of the correct responses in the instructed group were given in the form of words (for example, "aft," "fat"); these subjects clearly made use of their extra information, reorganizing each set of three letters into a new item, in order to take advantage of the increase in meaningfulness as well as what amounts to a reduction in the total number of things to be learned. Of course, these techniques are not the exclusive property of those who have received specific instructions; within the not-instructed group about half the subjects responded with words 80 per cent or more of the time. Their average performance was better than that of the remainder of the not-instructed group and approached that of the instructed group.

In another experiment some subjects learned with the requirement (more common in verbal-learning studies) that they reproduce the trigrams with the letters in the *same* order as that used in the presentation trials. Under this condition the instructed group was inferior to the not-instructed group! The authors concluded that this difference resulted because the instructed group took the hint offered by the instructions and "encoded" the meaningless trigrams into words in order to facilitate learning but made errors in "decoding." The instructed subjects *tried* to decode (none of their incorrect responses was a word) but found it difficult. Errors in which the appropriate letters are given but in an incorrect order (for example, "fta") probably indicate failures in decoding; they were more than five times more common in the instructed group than in the not-instructed group.

Presumably the instructed group would have shown superior performance if there had been available one common decoding rule that told how to get back from the word to the meaningless trigram, but there was not. The student who has had the experience of working out complex schemes for remembering course material without being able to reproduce the material on the examination now has the comfort of understanding why.

B. J. UNDERWOOD and G. KEPPEL. 1963. Coding Processes in Verbal Learning, *J. Verb. Learning Verb. Behav.*, 1, 250–7.

are two different ways in which the two strings of words differ. Consider the other alternatives: "rapid bouquets deter sudden neighbors" and "rapid augur violent flashes storms." The first maintains the grammatical form of English sentences but as a unit is low in meaningfulness; the second is an ungrammatical random rearrangement of the meaningful sentence first presented. Marks and Miller (1964) gave subjects several strings of words of these four kinds and then tested for free recall. The normal sentences were learned most rapidly, the meaningless word lists (for example, "rapid deter sudden bouquets neighbors") were learned most slowly, and the two intermediate strings were of intermediate difficulty. Analysis of the kinds of errors that were made gave further evidence that both meaningfulness and adherence to grammatical rules play a part in learning verbal material.

Intent

In most of the experiments in verbal learning (including all those already discussed in this unit) the subject is instructed to do his best to learn the material being presented. In everyday life we learn many things "incidentally" without instructions to learn. *Incidental learning* and its differences from *intentional learning* have been studied by many psychologists; let us consider how such studies are performed and the implications of the results.

A common way to compare incidental and intentional learning in the laboratory involves the use of pairs of subjects. One of each pair is told that he is to act as an "experimenter" and to present learning material of some kind to his "subject." Afterward, both "experimenter" and "subject" are tested for recall of the material. The subject will have been trying deliberately to learn and will thus provide a measure of intentional learning; the experimenter will not have known that he is to be tested, and any learning he demonstrates will presumably be "incidental." With this and

similar procedures, it has been demonstrated that incidental learning does take place and that it is generally inferior to intentional learning.

If we ask how this difference arises, we quickly come close to some very basic problems. We might say that the intentional learner, as compared to the incidental learner, is more highly "motivated." A better approach is to ask exactly what does happen to a subject under conditions of incidental and intentional learning and to examine the differences that we see. If instructed to learn, a subject will try to produce labels for the items, to put them in categories, to form associations based upon them, and so on. We all to some extent use methods similar to those taught in the Improve-Your-Memory courses that we see advertised. These activities make up a *set* to learn, which we have achieved largely but perhaps not exclusively through previous experience in learning situations. We are less likely to resort to such mnemonic devices under incidental-learning conditions.

Transfer

In the laboratory and in the outside world, how well and how rapidly we learn anything depend to a large extent upon the kinds and amount of things we have learned previously. We use the word *transfer* to describe the effects of past learning upon present acquisition. We usually think of transfer as *positive:* The veteran teacher who has learned the names and seating positions of children in many classes over the years will memorize the names more easily in a new class than will a novice teacher who is doing it for the first time. Here we have an instance in which past practice on similar tasks has resulted in positive transfer to a new task. But transfer under some circumstances may be *negative;* that is, previous learning on similar tasks may hinder learning of a new task. The veteran teacher may do worse with her later classes than with her earlier ones, for the memory of the names of children who occupied the particular seats in the previous classes may interfere with and cause confusion in her attempt to associate new names with the seats.

In a large number of experiments, psychologists have investigated almost all conceivable factors that might influence transfer. From such studies have come some general rules about kind and amount of transfer that will result under different circumstances.

Transfer of Specific Information

The most important set of conditions determining the degree of transfer concerns the relationship between the material originally learned and the new to-be-learned material. With some important exceptions, the more *similar* the two tasks, the greater the transfer. In experimental studies of this effect paired-associate lists have usually been employed, allowing us to distinguish the stimulus and response factors in transfer. The usual convention is to refer to the originally learned list as "list A" and to the to-be-learned list as "list B."

The relationship between the A and B lists of paired associates can be any one of three types, and the transfer effects differ accordingly.

In type 1, the *first* (stimulus) members of the corresponding pairs in list A differ from those of list B, but the *second* (response) members of the pairs are identical. This is similar to the situation in which there are two lists of foreign words, the English equivalents of which are to be memorized.

If in learning list A you have the *French* words before you and you cover up the English equivalents while you attempt to give them correctly—and if in the case of list B the same words are given in *German* and you attempt to respond with the correct English equivalent— you have satisfied the conditions for the type 1 situation.

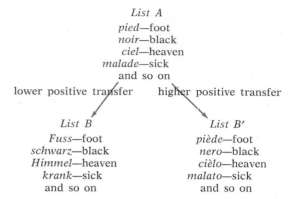

List A
pied—foot
noir—black
ciel—heaven
malade—sick
and so on

lower positive transfer   higher positive transfer

List B   List B'
Fuss—foot   *piède*—foot
schwarz—black   *nero*—black
Himmel—heaven   *cièlo*—heaven
krank—sick   *malato*—sick
and so on   and so on

For this kind of problem, the experimental evidence is clear that learning list A *facilitates* the later learning of list B. The more similar the first members of the pairs in list A are to the first members of the corresponding pairs in the second list, the greater is the facilitation, as would be the case in Italian and French— lists A and B'. We can now state a general principle: *When the stimulus members of the corresponding pairs are different, but the response members are the same, the transfer effect is positive; the less the difference between the stimulus members, the greater the magnitude of the positive transfer.*

In type 2, the situation is reversed. Here the stimulus members of the corresponding pairs are the same, but the response members differ, as in the following situations:

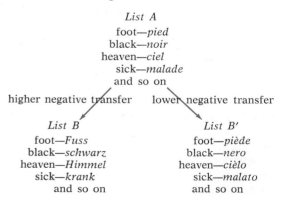

List A
foot—*pied*
black—*noir*
heaven—*ciel*
sick—*malade*
and so on

higher negative transfer   lower negative transfer

List B   List B'
foot—*Fuss*   foot—*piède*
black—*schwarz*   black—*nero*
heaven—*Himmel*   heaven—*cièlo*
sick—*krank*   sick—*malato*
and so on   and so on

If in learning list A you have the English words before you and your task is to respond with the correct French word—and if in list B you have the English word before you and your task is to respond with the German word—then learning list A will *interfere with and slow down* the subsequent learning of list B. This interference is less the more similar the second members of the corresponding pairs, as in lists A and B′. The formal statement of this relationship is *when the stimulus members of the corresponding pairs are the same, but the response members are different, the transfer effect is negative; the greater the difference between the response members, the greater the magnitude of the negative transfer.*

The significant point is that, although each corresponding pair of associates is made up of *identical elements* in both types, the *temporal patterning* of these elements differs (for example, in type 1 we have *"pied*-foot," *"Fuss-*foot"; in type 2 we have "foot-*pied*," "foot-*Fuss"*), and this difference makes for entirely different transfer effects. Here we have a dramatic illustration of the role that stimulus *patterning* can play, the importance of which we have already seen in perception and learning. (The alert student who has two language vocabularies to memorize in an evening will no doubt see the practical value of these two laws in helping him to arrange his material for study.)

In type 3, learning psychologists have been concerned with the effects on transfer of various degrees of relationship between the stimulus members of one list and the response members of the other list. In one especially important case there is *no* similarity between the stimulus members of either list and the response members of the other list. Such is the case, in short, in which the two lists are entirely different from each other, as when learning the English equivalents of French words and learning the names of various statistical symbols:

List A
pied—foot
noir—black
ciel—heaven
malade—sick
and so on

List B
σ—standard deviation
r—correlation coefficient
Σ—sum
M—average
and so on

Here the specific information learned in list A has no demonstrable effect on the learning of the specific information of list B. Stated formally, *when all the corresponding stimulus and response members of the two lists are different from each other, the transfer effect is zero.*

Transfer of General Information

Both the sign and degree of transfer effects in types 1, 2, and 3 were, as we have seen, dependent upon the relations between the corresponding items in the two lists. We must differentiate, however, between specific and *general* transfer. So far we have restricted our discussion to specific transfer. The nature of general transfer in these circumstances may be quite different from that of specific transfer.

When we learn a task, we usually acquire not only the specific components of the material (for example, the specific association of *"oui*-yes") but also many other aspects of the task that make for good performance in the learning situation. These aspects may include such varied things as learning how to fixate attention on the memory drum as well as possible, how to organize the materials into meaningful groups, how to use mnemonic devices to form associations, and so on (see Box 60, p. 324). These general skills, strategies, and study habits acquired on one set of tasks can influence later learning even of quite different

Box 60

Transfer of General Information
in Verbal Learning

H. Woodrow at the University of Minnesota posed the following question: How can training in one verbal-learning task be given so as to maximize transfer to other *kinds* of learning tasks? To answer this question, the following experiment was performed.

The *control group* (106 students) was tested in six different forms of memorizing (poetry, prose, facts, dates, Turkish-English vocabulary, and consonants) at the beginning and end of a thirty-three-day period, with no intervening practice. The *practice group* (34 students) was given the same tests, but during the interim it was given a total of 177 minutes of practice in memorizing poetry and nonsense syllables. The *training group* (42 students), also tested at the beginning and end of the period, spent 76 minutes listening to an exposition of the technique of memorizing and 101 minutes in practicing the memorizing of poetry and nonsense syllables. The rules that were taught to the training group *and that they were told were the important things to learn* included the following principles: learning by wholes, use of rhythm and groupings, attention to meaning.

First the differences in scores made by the three groups on the initial and end tests were calculated. The gains made by the *control group* were then subtracted from the gains made by the *practice* and *training groups* to discover how much the practice and training had contributed. The results are presented in the table.

PERCENTAGE GAINS IN THE END TESTS AFTER SUBTRACTION
OF PERCENTAGE GAINS OF THE CONTROL GROUP

Material	*Gains Practice Group*	*Gains Training Group*
Poetry	3.7	22.2
Prose	−3.2	22.0
Facts	8.1	17.7
Dates	8.5	58.7
Vocabulary	4.0	55.8
Consonants	−1.0	14.4

It is clear that drill on such simple things as memorizing nonsense syllables and poetry, *when the methods of memorizing are stressed*, can result in sizable amounts of transfer to *various* learning tasks and that the amounts of transfer are uniformly larger than when the methods of memorizing are not stressed.

H. WOODROW. 1927. The Effect of Type of Training upon Transference, *J. Educ. Psychol.*, 18, 159–72. Table adapted by permission of American Psychological Association.

material. When this influence occurs, we speak of "general transfer."

Some of the conditions that govern the degree to which general transfer will occur have been studied in an experiment by Postman and Schwartz (1964). Various groups of college students were required to memorize two consecutive lists. Some of them were paired-associate lists, and some were lists for serial learning; some were made up of words (adjectives) and some of nonsense syllables. Different groups were given different combinations of these types of lists. Performance on *any* list when it was given second (to one group of students) was much better than when it was given first (to another group), demonstrating the presence of general transfer. Not all combinations of lists showed the same degree of transfer, however. Both the *form* and the *material* of the lists had an effect. For example, if a subject's two lists were of the same form (both serial or both paired-associate), the amount of transfer was greater than if the two lists were of different form. Similarly, if a subject's first list was made up of the same kind of material (adjectives or nonsense syllables) as his second list, then the amount of transfer was greater than if the two lists were different in material.

These findings suggest the importance for general transfer of the ability to organize the materials in the way required by the particular method of presentation and of the ability to differentiate items of the specific kind of material used in the list.

Retention

Things that are learned are remembered over a period of time and can be recalled as required at a later date. If memory were perfect—if any material once learned were never lost—we would not have to discuss this topic separately. We would still have to study the physiological basis of memory, as will be done explicitly in Unit 29, but there would be nothing more to

say about retention at this time. On the other hand, even if memory were not always perfect but the loss of learned material proceeded at the same rate no matter what the material, the degree of original learning, or the conditions of learning, our problem would still be relatively simple.

Of course, neither of these conditions represents the true state of affairs. Material is "forgotten," and many characteristics of the learning situation, of the learned material, and of the other activities of the learning (and remembering) individual will influence the amount retained at any time. In the discussion of meaningfulness, we have already given some examples of the differences in retention as a function of the material learned; we now must consider more general problems.

Interference

A great deal of the attention of psychologists has been directed toward the causes of forgetting. Among the processes that have been suggested as major sources of retention loss is *interference*. The list that an experimenter gives a subject is only a very small part of the stimuli that the subject is exposed to, and when he is asked a day later to recall that list his performance, so it is assumed, is impeded by the tendency to make other responses he had previously learned or by the tendency to make the responses he has learned between the time of the original learning and the retention test.

These two sources of interference are given separate names. The deleterious effect of learning that preceded the original learning of the to-be-retained material is called *proactive inhibition,* or *PI;* the interference due to learning coming between original learning and the retention test is termed *retroactive inhibition,* or *RI.*

The following diagrams illustrate the experimental designs used to investigate proactive inhibition and retroactive inhibition.

Proactive Inhibition

EXPERIMENTAL GROUP

Learn B ——————→ Learn A ——————→ Recall A

CONTROL GROUP

Learn A ——————→ Recall A

Retroactive Inhibition

EXPERIMENTAL GROUP

Learn A ——————→ Learn B ——————→ Recall A

CONTROL GROUP

Learn A ——————————————→ Recall A

If an experimental group does worse on recall of A than does its control group, we assume that this decrement is caused by interference from B. In the first instance, we refer to proactive inhibition because B precedes the learning of A. In the second instance, we refer to retroactive inhibition because B follows the learning of A.

The importance of the interference mechanism is underscored by studies in which the nature of the interfering, or B, material is varied. The more different the B material is from the A material, the less deficit in performance results, for the B responses are not as likely to come into competition with the A responses when they are being recalled. The complex nature of the sources of interference is demonstrated by experiments in which the experimental group receives its interpolated learning in a different room from that used for original learning and retention. Under these circumstances RI is much less than in the usual situation, in which the same room is used throughout. The tendency to produce the responses of the interpolated material is partially tied to the simple fact that these responses are associated with the room in which they were learned.

Unlearning

When one begins learning the second of two tasks, he has some tendency to produce the responses of the first task. But those responses are now incorrect, and, as the subject realizes this fact, the responses will suffer from his direct attempt to *unlearn* them. Such unlearning will then contribute to the poorer recall of the A material in the A-B-A design. In this design at least two factors account for the loss of A: the interference effect of the B material on the recall of A and the suppression of the A material when B is initially learned. As the student can see for himself, the unlearning mechanism plays no direct role in PI.

Spontaneous Recovery

The importance of RI in the production of retention loss may seem quite obvious once it is pointed out. Obviously, if you learn B *after* A, it seems perfectly understandable that B will still be prominent and competing for influence over your behavior when you try to recall A at a later time. But it is not so obvious that PI should exist at all—that something you have learned *earlier* should interfere with the retention of a well-learned task. Underwood (1957) demonstrated the importance of PI in experimental tasks by noting that subjects who had had a great deal of practice on serial lists retained only about 25 per cent of a newly learned list twenty-four hours later, whereas subjects who had not had any previous practice retained 70 per cent of their first-learned list. The "better-trained" subjects did *worse*, because the specific things they had learned while being trained interfered in some way with their memory of the new list!

Now, if PI effects are present—if material learned earlier is going to interfere with more recently learned material—the early material must "come back" somehow, even though it is unlearned and overridden by the learning of the new task. This explanation is exactly what is proposed, that is, that the unlearned material shows a recovery much like the spontaneous recovery that follows the extinction of a conditioned response (p. 293). This recovery has been used to explain the effect of the retention interval upon the later memory for two lists learned consecutively. If retention of such lists is measured soon after acquisition, the one last learned will be much better retained; but, if retention is not measured until a day later, the two lists will be recalled equally well. The *spontaneous recovery* of the prior (first list) learning reinstates its responses, and they conflict with the second list in recall.

No mention has been made so far of any memory loss due to simple "forgetting," that is, to a completely passive loss over time of the learned material. The common-sense view of forgetting is that this sort of "fading away" is the major cause of memory loss. Psychologists, however, have come to the conclusion that it plays at most a very small part in the changes that take place with time. The apparent fading of memories that we consciously experience would then be the *result* of the processes just discussed (interference, unlearning, and spontaneous recovery). It now seems likely that, if there is any process of "pure decay" in forgetting, it takes place largely in a short period of time immediately following the presentation of the stimulus materials. This possibility is treated in connection with the *short-term* and *long-term memory* problem.

Short-Term and Long-Term Memory

The observations and experiments discussed so far have dealt with retention over long periods of time—hours or days. Is it necessary to have a separate discussion of short-term memory? Will not the same processes (interference and so on) be able to account for the forgetting observed over a period of seconds? These questions are not completely resolved as yet.

The current interest in this question among experimenters in verbal learning was stimulated principally by an experiment done by Peterson and Peterson in 1959. They gave subjects single CCCs (three-consonant strings, for example, "j-q-b") and asked for recall after a period of three, six, nine, twelve, fifteen, or eighteen seconds. During the interval the experimenters prevented the subject from silently

rehearsing the CCC items by keeping him busy with the task of counting backward by 3s from some number given to him just after the presentation of the CCC. As can be seen in Figure 21.2., there was apparently some forgetting after only three seconds and a loss of almost 90 per cent after eighteen seconds.

Can this astonishingly fast memory loss be explained in terms of the unlearning or interference processes we have outlined in our earlier discussion of forgetting? It does not seem likely, because the subjects were involved in a quite dissimilar activity, which should not have provoked conflict with learned material either during or after the interval. Can the result then be explained as a proactive effect? The most likely candidate for the source of PI is in the experiment itself; as a subject sits through the retention period for one CCC, the items that he has been exposed to earlier in the experiment might arise to conflict with the current item at the time for its recall. The Petersons pointed out, however, that this argu-

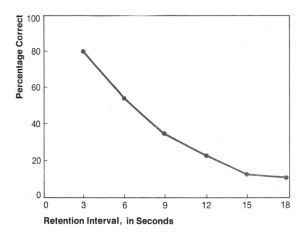

Figure 21.2. The percentage of items (three-consonant strings) correctly recalled after time intervals filled with a widely differing task. This curve is an example of a forgetting curve—one that shows a surprising amount of retention loss very soon after the learning of an item. Other experiments show that, even when a single consonant is used, there is some forgetting during the first fifteen to thirty seconds.

ment could lead one to expect that subjects would get worse and worse during the experiment; in fact, they tended to get better with practice at the task.

If we could leave the question here, we could conclude that there must be some other source of forgetting—perhaps the simple fading of the stimulus trace briefly mentioned before. There is more to say, however. Others (Keppel & Underwood, 1962) have done similar experiments and have shown that memory scores *do* worsen somewhat as the first few items of the experiment are given—evidence that PI is involved. It has also been argued that RI could take place even from counting backward, and another set of experiments has pointed to yet another source of interference—intraunit interference—which may play a part in all forgetting and may have produced the high percentage of forgetting in the Petersons' experiment. In some of the investigations (for example, Melton, 1963) of short-term memory, the number of consonants making up each item has been varied. As the size of the item is changed from one to five ("q" versus "x-m-r-p-b," for example), an enormous effect is seen upon the ability to recall the item a few seconds later. The consonants within a single item conflict with one another, and naturally more of this intraunit interference arises in the longer items. There is some forgetting of even the single-consonant items, however.

Immediate Memory

As the number of consonants in the item increases, a point is reached beyond which it cannot be "recalled" correctly even when no retention interval is imposed—an example of the fact that there is a limit even to *immediate memory*. Here we are dealing with the same phenomenon as that involved in measurement of the "digit span" in intelligence testing, in which the psychologist recites a randomly ordered string of digits (for example, 6-8-3-5-9) and the person being tested tries to repeat them immediately thereafter. The average adult can-

not perform this task well if there are more than about seven numbers in the string. How then can we learn such longer strings, as the ten or more digits that are required to make a long-distance call? If someone does learn all the digits on the first presentation of a telephone number, it is because he has grouped the digits and has thus effectively cut down on the number of elements in the string. To the practiced telephone user, 1-9-0-3-4-2-9-3-3-1-1 becomes 1 (long-distance dialing number), 903 (area code), 429 (local exchange), 3311. When someone learns such a number after a series of repetitions, it is partly because he has forced some organization of the components into larger (and thus fewer) groups, even when no obvious categories like area code are available.

If we leave the reader with the impression that all the arguments for separate mechanisms in short-term and long-term memory have been disposed of, it would be unfortunate. This field of research in verbal learning is an active one, and conclusions will have to be postponed. We *have* shown that the interference theory is sufficiently flexible to explain findings that at first glance appear to require a new mechanism. In Unit 29, as we consider the physiological basis of memory, we shall have to attack this general question once more, because we shall see some data that suggest that different chemical or physiological changes are involved in "recent" and "remote" memories. In other words, although we cannot at present differentiate between long-term and short-term memory on the basis of retention scores, we seem to be able to do so by biochemical tests. If we can in fact do so, it would be surprising if no differences were eventually found in retention during the short-term and long-term periods.

All-or-None Versus Incremental Learning

As we proceed with the learning of a list of items (a paired-associates list of nonsense syllables, for example), performance gets continuously better on subsequent presentations

Box 61

A Little Learning May Be a
Nonexistent Thing

Do we come to learn a single item by a process of gradual incremental strengthening, that is, by moving from a state of no learning through a state of little learning to a state of complete learning? Or do we learn by a single "quantum jump" from a state of no learning to a state of complete learning? Some recent experiments have cast doubt on the "little learning" interpretation—an interpretation commonly accepted by most psychologists. Irvin Rock, now at Rutgers University, presented a paired-associate list to subjects over a series of trials and measured their learning via the anticipation method. For one group of subjects there was a crucial new twist, however. At the end of each trial, Rock replaced the items that had been incorrect with new items. If the subjects really had learned a little something about these items (even though the responses were incorrect), they would suffer some retardation in learning on the following trials as a result of this switch, because they would now have to learn completely new items. Their over-all performance was as good, however, as that of the subjects who were given the same list throughout. The author concluded that learning takes place on an all-or-none basis; when a response is incorrect, learning of that item is still at a "none" level, so it does not harm the performance of the subject when he receives a new item instead.

It has been pointed out, however, that the behavior of the subjects determined which items would be discarded, and, because the discarded items were the ones missed, they would naturally be the more difficult ones, whereas the easier items would be retained. Quite conceivably it is no worse to have to master a new item of average difficulty than an old, partly learned, but difficult one. Both groups of subjects might thus perform equally without assuming the all-or-none learning hypothesis.

William Estes of Stanford University provided a control for that problem in some similar experiments. With a list of paired associates, he gave his subjects first one training trial and then two test trials on which they were not informed of the correct responses. On the first test trial his subjects were correct on 49 per cent of the items. To confirm Rock's findings, we must look at the remaining 51 per cent. If these items represent instances in which partial learning had taken place, we would expect to see evidence of it on the second test trial. Only 9 per cent were correct on the second trial, however, a value easily obtained by guessing, because digits were used as the response items in this experiment. To answer the criticism of Rock's method, we must look at some additional items used in the experiment. On these items the subjects received a second training trial between the two test trials. Now, if the items that were incorrect on the first test trial were especially difficult ones, we might expect the performance on them to be poor after the second training trial. The percentage correct for these cases on the second test trial was, however, even a little higher than the percentage correct for all items on the first test trial.

These findings and interpretations are not accepted by all psychologists, but, regardless of the outcome of this line of investigation, it is worth noting that long-established assumptions need not remain such; often they can be, and should be, re-examined in the light of new data.

I. ROCK. 1957. The Role of Repetition in Associative Learning, *Amer. J. Psychol.*, 70, 186–93.
W. K. ESTES. 1960. Learning Theory and the New "Mental Chemistry," *Psychol. Rev.*, 67, 207–23.

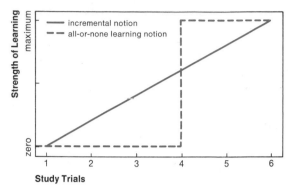

Figure 21.3. Schematic representation of the learning of a single paired associate as explained by an incremental theory and by an all-or-none theory. The response was first given correctly after the fourth trial. At that point, according to the incremental theory, the strength of the association between the two members of the pair had become great enough to control the verbal response. According to the all-or-none theory, all the learning takes place on the fourth trial. Note that the exact shape of the incremental curve may be different from the one here, which is used for illustrative purposes.
B. J. Underwood and G. Keppel, "One-Trial Learning," *Journal of Verbal Learning and Verbal Behavior*, 1, 1–13; adapted by permission of Academic Press, Inc.

because, of course, we get more pairs correct as practice continues. But what is happening to each individual pair? It has generally been assumed that the acquisition of each pair also grows by small steps, that with experience we become more and more likely to make the correct response to the stimulus word, regardless of the competing tendencies that we might feel. Of course, on any trial the response will be

either correct or incorrect, but it could still be true that there is an underlying, continuously variable process of learning that leads to a correct response when it gets above a certain level.

A simpler alternative can be suggested. It is an *all-or-none principle* applied to learning, in which the suggestion is made that each pair (item, response, and so on) is at any one time either completely "learned" or completely "unlearned." It may be forgotten, then relearned; but in any case it is always "all" or "none" in strength. Figure 21.3. shows the contrast between these two possibilities.

As is shown in Box 61, p. 329, the evidence for an all-or-none position has come from experiments that suggest that a subject who did not respond correctly on a given pair after one presentation of a paired-associate list had learned absolutely nothing about that pair. These experiments have been challenged, and others have claimed to find some effect of the first presentation upon later performance. One possible conclusion may be that there are several all-or-none processes operating in the learning of any item rather than one *incremental process;* these processes would have very similar effects upon the responses of a subject, but the "multiple all-or-none" has at least the virtue of mimicking a basic characteristic of the nervous system that underlies all this behavior. Here again we are faced with an unsolved problem.

Glossary

acquisition The process of attaining a new response, memory, knowledge, and so on.
all-or-none learning One theory, according to which each unit (item, response, and so on) is at any moment either learned completely or not learned at all. Opposed to the concept of incremental learning.
anticipation method A training procedure in verbal learning, according to which the subject is required to produce the next correct item when he is presented with the preceding item.

association value The capacity of a word or nonsense syllable to evoke associations. A nonsense syllable that reminds people of many meaningful words thus has *high* association value; one that reminds people of no or very few meaningful words has *low* association value.
clustering The tendency to reproduce items in meaningfully related groups, even though these items had originally been learned in a random order.
free recall The method in which a subject tries to recall (without regard to order) as many as possible of a series of items previously presented to him.

immediate memory Memory for events that have just occurred. The memory span is a measure of how many items may be held in immediate memory at any time.

incidental learning Acquisition that takes place when the learner has received no instructions from the experimenter to learn the material. (Compare with intentional learning.)

incremental learning According to one theory, everything is learned in small steps and thus may be partially learned at any given time, even though our method of measurement (for example, whether a response is correct or incorrect) may not precisely reflect this fact.

intentional learning Acquisition that takes place when the learner has received instructions from the experimenter to learn the material or when there is an explicit mental set to learn.

interference The presumed disruptive influence upon a response of the tendency to make other responses that were learned either before or after the "correct" response. Interference theory states that all forgetting is the result of interference.

isolation effect (von Restorff effect) In verbal learning, the observation that the perceptually differentiated item in a group of items will be more quickly acquired and better retained than items that are less perceptually differentiated. Originally demonstrated by the German psychologist von Restorff.

learning curve A graphic method of presenting the change in performance of an individual or group of individuals during the acquisition process. In a learning curve the successive time or trial intervals are usually plotted on the abscissa and the performance units on the ordinate.

long-term memory Memory for items, responses, events, and so forth, acquired long previously—usually hours, days, or more.

meaningfulness A characteristic of a word, nonsense syllable, and so forth. As a construct in theories about learning, defined in two ways: the average *number* of associations given to an item; the *percentage* of people giving any association to the item.

memory drum An apparatus used in verbal-learning experiments, designed to present one set of items at a time with a predetermined exposure time and at a predetermined interval between exposures of items.

nonsense syllable A combination of consonants and vowels presumed to be of low meaningfulness. Invented by Ebbinghaus, a German psychologist, and used extensively as items in verbal-learning experiments.

paired associates Material used in verbal learning, consisting of a list of pairs of items in which one serves as "stimulus" and the other as "response." *Paired-associate learning* is learning to respond with a *second* item of a pair when the *first* item is presented.

proactive inhibition (PI) The disruptive effect upon recall of A by the acquisition of B previous to the learning of A.

recall method A method of measuring retention by which the person is required to reproduce the items previously learned. The number of items reproduced, divided by the number of items originally learned, is his "recall score," expressed in percentage terms.

recognition method A method of measuring retention by which the person is required to identify the set of items previously learned from among a larger collection of items. The number of items identified correctly, divided by the total number of items originally learned, is taken as the person's "recognition score."

retention The process of or capacity for remembering things whereby responses or knowledge once acquired become available for use by the organism on later occasions.

retroactive inhibition (RI) The disruptive effect upon recall of A by a new acquisition, B, interpolated between the original acquisition of A and its later recall.

serial-learning list Material used in verbal learning consisting of a list of single items. In serial learning, the items are presented in the same order on every trial and must be learned in the proper order.

serial-position effect The observation that in verbal learning the items toward the beginning and end of the series to be learned are more quickly memorized than the items in the middle of the list.

short-term memory Memory for events or items recently presented; usually they are presented singly and only once.

spontaneous recovery In verbal learning, the return in strength of an item that was first learned and then unlearned.

transfer Refers to the effect upon the learning of one task, B, by the previous learning of another task, A. When the learning of A has a facilitating effect on the learning of B, we speak of *positive transfer;* when it has a deleterious effect, we speak of *negative transfer.*

unlearning The process by which the probability of occurrence of a previously correct response is reduced, if the response is made when it is incorrect.

acquisition of skills

overview / Skills consist of a number of perceptual and motor responses, modified and integrated into new patterns and sequences of performance. Possession of a specific skill enables an individual to realize a particular set of goals with precision and efficiency.

The acquisition of skills is a slow process in which the learner first develops discrete responses and then consolidates and integrates these individual responses into new patterns. These patterns of responses may, in turn, become the base for further consolidation and the emergence of higher and higher levels of integration and organization of responses. Well-developed skills may continue to show gradual improvement over several years of practice and are typically very well retained for long periods.

Two characteristics of the training conditions are particularly important in determining the rate of acquisition of skills: whether the skill is practiced in *parts* or as a *whole* and whether the training is *massed* or *spaced*. For skills in which a number of relatively independent activities exist, practicing parts of the skill may be advantageous. But, for a skill that requires simultaneous performance of its various components, practice on the skill as a whole will be a more efficient procedure. Concentrating practice into short periods of time (massed practice) tends to depress the performance of perceptual-motor skills beneath the level achieved when practice is spread out (spaced practice).

Developing kinesthetic knowledge of skilled responses and learning to react to the kinesthetic feedback of these responses are important factors in the acquisition and control of skilled behavior. Feedback from other sensory channels exerts significant control as well, and distortion or elimination of feedback channels can seriously disrupt performance.

As people muddle through their world of problems, they gradually accumulate a larger and larger collection of conditioned reactions, memorized sets of items, and selected responses; and they acquire something else. Many of these bits and pieces of adaptive behavior become integrated into patterns and sequences of performance that we call *skills*.

The Nature of Skills

Skills vary tremendously, of course, in their nature and complexity. Reading, writing, and speaking are "verbal skills." Painting, playing the piano, and arranging flowers are "artistic skills." Skiing, playing tennis, and diving are "athletic skills." Performing an appendectomy, fixing a splint, and assessing the pulse of a patient are "medical skills." Rewiring an "electronic brain," repairing a leaky faucet, and operating a lathe are "mechanical skills." There is no end to the variety of skills that we are constantly called upon to develop.

The difference between skilled and unskilled performance is easily recognized and appreciated. On the ski slopes amateurs and professionals alike can appreciate the beauty, precision, and control of movement of a slalom run by a great champion as they watch him boom down the course, skis flat and together, cutting through the gates with sure and graceful moves. A trip to the beginners' slope shows in clear contrast the awkwardness, struggles, and falls of the neophyte. The pleasure of hearing a concert violinist will be mixed with awe as he plays an intricate cadenza with incredible speed and precision. Later in the concert this same precision may appear in the delicacy of touch with which he approaches a quiet romantic passage. On the other hand, we can easily understand someone's slipping from the room or even from the house when Junior begins the scrapings and squawkings that seem the inevitable accompaniment of learning this difficult instrument. Aside from the difference in quality, one of the major adaptive differences between skilled and

unskilled performances is that the skilled performer achieves his goal more frequently than does the unskilled performer.

That skilled and unskilled performances differ is clear enough, but what is necessary for a skilled performance? Let us now consider some of the essential characteristics of skills.

Skills as Goal-Related Responses

Any one skill consists of a number of different perceptual and muscular (motor) responses. These different responses are brought into relation with one another because they subserve a common goal—the goal of the skilled behavior. When you read "ducking, bobbing, weaving, and punching," you immediately think of boxing. In boxing, these responses are seen as intrinsically related to each other, but they are related only because they have the common goal of knocking the opponent out before he knocks you out. Without that goal there is no necessary relation among them. For example, any six-footer who moves to New England quickly acquires a ducking response after bumping his head on a few of the low doorways characteristic of our early American homes. He does not, fortunately, simultaneously start weaving, bobbing, and punching. Depending upon the goal, any particular perceptual or motor response may thus be a component of quite different skills.

Skills as Integrated Wholes

Skills are much more than collections of previously acquired responses related by their common goal orientations. When a skill is developed, something new is added. Each response, when it becomes part of a skill, is *modified;* and the pattern, taken as a whole, acquires distinctive attributes of its own. Piano playing provides a good illustration of what we mean.

Anyone who has played the piano knows that piano playing does not consist of a series of discrete responses to discrete sets of stimulus patterns. When one begins to take piano lessons, the playing of each note is a response to a specific visual cue; at a later stage these specific stimulus-response sequences seem to disappear. At least in terms of perception, playing a composition on the piano does *not* consist of seeing one note on the music sheet, making the proper response to that note, seeing the next note, making the proper response to that note, and so on. The perception is more "global" (see Box 62).

This phenomenological observation is fully supported by neurophysiological considerations. It takes time for a neural pattern to travel from the retina of the eye to the brain, and from the brain to the arm, wrist, and finger muscles. It takes time for the muscles to react. And there just is not time enough for all this to happen, note after note, to make possible the playing of a swift cadenza by a skillful pianist. Lashley (1951) has made this point very clear:

"The finger strokes of a musician may reach sixteen per second in passages which call for a definite and changing order of successive finger movements. The succession of movements is too quick even for visual reaction time. In rapid sight reading it is impossible to read the individual notes of an arpeggio. The notes must be seen in groups, and it is actually easier to read chords simultaneously and to translate them into temporal sequence than to read successive notes in the arpeggio as usually written."

We must conclude that the neurophysiological control of the movements of a skillful musician is different from the control of a discrete response or even of a series of discrete responses. Both perceptual and neurological facts argue that, when a sequence of acquired responses becomes a skilled performance, *the increase in the speed and smoothness of the temporal sequence reflects some genuine reorganization.*

Skills and Precision

This reorganization results in an increased precision in a number of aspects of a skill: in the timing, choice, and execution of responses. Our champion skier knows precisely when to begin his turn, what kind of turn is most appropriate for the conditions, and how to execute it. A correlate of the precision of skilled responses is their efficiency. In the growth of skills, unnecessary and wasteful movements are eliminated, and precision in the control of strength, speed, and direction of responses develops. A skill enables an individual to achieve his goals efficiently, with no wasted movements or effort in the movements produced. It is a common observation that an expert "makes it look easy."

Box 62

The Phenomenologist
as a Piano Player

M. Bentley has described the experiences of the novice-turning-pianist in the following terms. Just about the time the piano student begins to make rapid progress in the smoothness of his performance, he finds:

"The perception shrinks. Individual notes upon the staff are no longer apprehended as individuals. They come in groups and their meanings are group-flashes. Again, the individual determination which leads from this or that note upon the score to this or that movement toward the appropriate black or white key disappears. After the group-flash comes, without intermediation, a sequence of rapid movements. Still later, the score may wholly drop out of clear perception and serve as a vague and obscure cue to a complicated series of movements. The sound itself as it flows along may be the controlling object and then we have the curious fact of an action where the perceived object is the result of the action and not its antecedent. This stage informs us that the action is becoming automatized."

M. BENTLEY. 1925. *The Field of Psychology* (New York: Appleton).

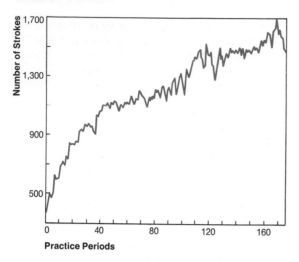

Figure 22.1. The acquisition of typing skill by subject X in a study by Book. This subject had never used a typewriter prior to the experiment. The curve represents 174 consecutive daily half-hour practice periods (with time out "owing to trouble with apparatus, sickness, and other unavoidable causes"). The measure of progress in the skill was the total number of correct strokes made on the typewriter during each practice session. Punctuation marks, carriage shifts, space shifts, and so on were all counted as strokes.

In fact, he not only makes performance of the task *look* easy but also *makes* it easy in the sense that he puts less effort into achieving his results than would be necessary for the unskilled person.

The Development of Skills

The course of the development of a skill, like that of other forms of learning, is depicted in performance curves. The typical curve obtained in the development of a skill is similar in shape to a learning curve. It is negatively accelerated and occasionally shows several periods of stalemate or lack of progress. These level portions of the curve are called *plateaus*.

In Figure 22.1. is shown a curve portraying the acquisition of typewriting skill. Three stages can be differentiated in this curve. First,

there is a continuous rise from the first practice period to about the 42nd day. Second, from about the 42nd to the 80th day there is no apparent improvement. The subject has reached a plateau. Third, from the 80th day to about the 110th day the subject's performance begins to rise again, and then at the 110th day it starts leveling off a second time. There is some indication that after about the 160th session the subject (now a skilled typist) is beginning to show additional improvement.

Acquisition and Consolidation

The first two stages, the initial rise and the leveling off in improvement, may be regarded as the acquisition and consolidation of component parts of the skill. The beginning typist must first learn to hit the correct key for the corresponding letter or symbol on the manuscript. An analysis of his performance shows that he attends to each letter as he types out each word. As time goes on, there is an improvement in performance; but this improvement soon reaches a plateau, and additional practice does not seem to result in corresponding gains. Something very important does occur during this plateau period, however.

As the discrete responses are practiced, they become more "automatic" and require less directed awareness (refer back to Bentley's description in Box 62, p. 335). When this stage is reached, the individual's attention is released, as it were, for "bigger and better things." He can now pay attention to relations among his discrete responses, to patterns, and to the more complex phases of his task. He is no longer *coping* with each letter. And it is at this point that the plateau ends and the series of discrete performances is ready to be transformed into a skill.

Just as the skilled musician reads a whole series of notes simultaneously and translates them into temporal sequence, the typist integrates the separate *letter* responses into new responses and begins to read and type *words*.

A skill is now in the making. When this progress occurs, the performance curve will leave the plateau and begin to rise again. Occasionally the typist will then achieve another plateau and another rise. What seems to happen here is that the typist begins to read and type *phrases* rather than words. After the end of the first plateau the organized nature of his responses achieves higher and higher levels of integration.

In the early stages of skill acquisition, the learner can see the gross nature of his response and the unsuccessful results of his efforts. But, as he improves, his responses are no longer so obviously wrong. When he becomes very accomplished, the discrimination between his responses and the "perfect" response becomes very difficult to make, and all his responses are in some ways successes. At this stage, improvement may become very slow and even imperceptible. In such tasks as telegraphy, typing, and industrial assembly work, however, performance continues to improve over millions of cycles of practice (Crossman, 1959). According to Fitts (1964), similar evidence is found in

". . . case studies of the conditions of practice necessary for attainment of championship performance in individual athletic competitions, such as skating, swimming, diving, and track events, in games of skill such as bowling or golf, in competitive sports such as baseball and football, and in artistic performances such as singing and playing musical instruments. It is very rare for peak performance in any of these activities to be reached short of several years of intensive, almost daily practice. And the fact that performance ever levels off at all appears to be due as much to the effects of physiological aging and/or loss of motivation as to the reaching of a true . . . limit in capacity for further improvement."

The acquisition process does not always show the neatly divided phases we have described. The new integrated responses may develop at different times so that there is a gradual shift from the discrete-response stage to a stage in which all responses are integrated. As a result many skill-acquisition curves show no plateaus. Book (1925) observed that, in learning typewriting, the beginner sometimes successfully attempted to read and type some words before the discrete letter responses were firmly learned. Furthermore, even after the curve leaves the plateau continued improvement in discrete responses can take place.

Rate of Acquisition

Most of the skills that have been studied develop very slowly. We can partially account for this fact by the amount that must be learned and by the time necessary for integration and consolidation of discrete responses. There is, however, an additional factor that contributes to the slow development of the initial stages of many skills: The individual often does not already have in his repertoire of separate responses those particular responses that form the component parts of the skill. Whereas the simple responses of hitting the keys are easily made in our examples of typewriting and piano playing, there are many skills for which the simple components must be learned. One of our earliest acquired skills, learning to walk, provides a good example. At first the infant is simply unable to make the controlled foot and leg movements that will get him across the floor. Only after he has learned these simple movements will he be able to integrate them with other responses into skilled locomotion. The problems are no smaller for the adult who tries for the first time to hit a ball with a tennis racquet or to dive from a diving board. The responses are not under control and must be learned. One characteristic of the "all around athlete" is that he either has acquired or has "built-in" unusual control over a wide variety of responses, so that he is not slowed down in this initial stage of skill acquisition.

Part-Whole Training

Some practice on the components of a skill is always essential before a series of discrete responses can become an integrated skill. An obvious question is whether *part training* (practice on the components) or *whole training* (practice on the complex task) is more effective in the development of skills. On theoretical grounds it would appear that either method may be more efficient, depending on circumstances.

The arguments favoring whole training derive from the fact that the essence of a skill lies in the *integrated* nature of its component parts. The experimental evidence is clear that in an integrated task the performance of a single component by itself is different from the performance of the same component when it is embedded in the entire task (see Box 63, p. 339, for an illustrative experiment). This difference may make it inefficient to train on the discrete response first and then to attempt a combination, because we learn to do different things with the "same" response under these two conditions.

The arguments that favor part training suggest that, when the discrete responses are novel and difficult, the part method may speed up the acquisition of the discrete responses. Furthermore, it is also possible that the more practice is given on the discrete responses, the more quickly they become "automatized" and therefore the more quickly ready for integration into a skill. These considerations suggest that in certain instances the part method, or a combination of part method and whole method, may be superior to the whole method alone (for an experimental demonstration, see Box 64, p. 340).

Although all skills involve patterning, they vary in the degree of integration involved. Some "skills" are thus actually composed of several relatively independent activities. Carpentry is a good example. The skillful carpenter can saw, nail, plane, and fit materials together. Training in sawing may be carried on independently of training in nailing without any loss caused by lack of integration. The same is true of surgery, which can also be broken down into a number of relatively independent component skills. A skill whose performance involves *simultaneous* components, however, will be more efficiently taught by the whole method. In driving an auto-

mobile, we must operate the brakes, the throttle, the clutch, and the steering wheel more or less simultaneously. Training on steering alone, shifting gears alone, and so on may not be as efficient as training on the whole complex.

The general rule would then be that whole training increases in effectiveness as the integration of the component parts of the skill increases in importance.

Distribution of Training

The relationship between training periods and rest periods has interested psychologists since the earliest days of learning studies. The use of *massed practice*, in which a large number of training trials is given in a single session, is usually contrasted with *spaced practice*, in which the same number of trials is spread across a number of sessions with rest periods between.

In Figure 22.2. are shown results typical of experiments comparing these two conditions. The motor skill that the subjects were trained to acquire involved the "pursuit rotor," an apparatus similar to a phonograph turntable, with a small circular target placed a short distance from the edge. The subject holds a stylus (a metal instrument much like a pencil) in one hand, and his task is to keep the stylus in contact with the target as the turntable and target rotate. Among the noteworthy results: First, performance under massed conditions is poorer than under spaced conditions. Within some single learning sessions performance actually deteriorates under massed conditions. Second, over the entire course of the experiments, the level of performance under massed conditions approaches the performance under spaced conditions. Third, the performance of the massed group is better at the beginning of a new session (after a rest) than at the end of the previous session. Such improvement in performance during a period of no practice is described as a *reminiscence effect*. It is most easily demonstrated after massed practice sessions as illus-

Box 63

Relation of Part to
Whole in Motor Skills

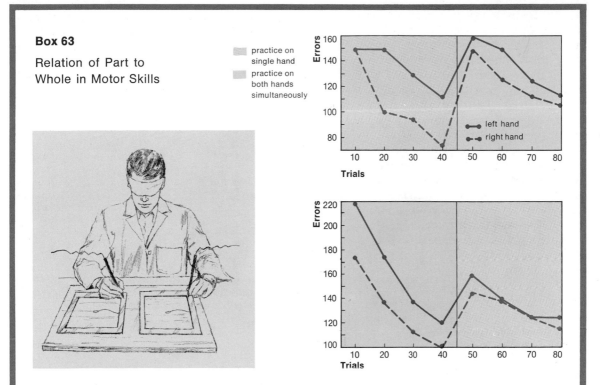

C. E. Beeby at the University of London demonstrated that, when a well-practiced simple movement is integrated into a larger act, the simple movement may show a loss in efficiency.

The task was to follow with a stylus the 1/16-inch brass strips around the squares as rapidly as possible without breaking contact between the stylus tip and the strips. Both hands were to move in a counterclockwise direction. Each slip of the stylus off the brass strip was recorded as an error. This task was to be done *blindfolded* (see illustration).

Group A started by practicing with one hand, then with the other, and was then tested on both hands simultaneously. Group B started with both hands simultaneously, then was tested on one hand alone. The results show that the transition from the simple to the complex *or from complex to simple* resulted in loss of skill. In group A the error scores for each hand increased when there was an attempt to combine the two movements in one simultaneous act. In group B the left (or right) hand did *better* when it was part of the two-handed movement than when it was shifted to a solo performance. The rise in error scores occurred when the shift was from the "easy" to the "difficult" task (group A) or from the "difficult" to the "easy" task (group B). The learning and performance of a single component task are significantly different from the learning and performance of the "same" task when it is part of a larger whole.

C. E. BEEBY. 1930. An Experimental Investigation into the Simultaneous Constituents of an Act of Skill, *Brit. J. Psychol.*, 20, 336–53. Figures adapted by permission of British Psychological Society.

Box 64

From Components to Skills

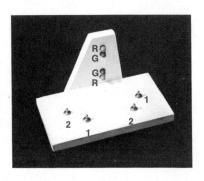

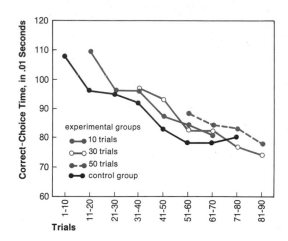

R. M. Gagné and H. Foster at Connecticut College measured transfer of training to a complex motor skill with varying amounts of practice on a component part. The task was to learn to throw the appropriate toggle switches (see photograph) *as rapidly as possible* when certain lights went on.

COMPONENT TASK	COMPLEX TASK
Only one upper and one lower light of the same color were used, and one switch on the left and one the right.	For this task all four lights and all four switches were used.

Stimulus	*Response*	*Stimulus*	*Response*
Lower red light	Left switch 1	Lower red light	Left switch 1
Upper red light	Right switch 1	Lower green light	Left switch 2
		Upper red light	Right switch 1
		Upper green light	Right switch 2

One hundred and twenty navy enlisted men were divided into three *experimental* groups, trained first on the component task and then on the complex task, and a *control* group that had only the complex task. One experimental group was given ten trials on the component task before being transferred to the complex task; the second, thirty trials; and the third, fifty trials. Performance was measured by the time it took to make a correct choice. The learning curves for all groups on the complex task (see chart) indicate that the more practice one has on the component task, the greater is the transfer to the complex skill. The control group's starting average on the complex task was 108; the starting averages for the 10-, 30-, and 50-trial practice groups were, respectively, 110, 98, 89. It will be seen, however, that the control group, which spent all its time on the complex task, learned more quickly than did any other group. Although practice on a component part helps the learning of a complex skill, the most efficient method for this particular skill is working on the complex skill from the very beginning.

R. M. GAGNÉ and H. FOSTER. 1949. Transfer of Training From Practice on Components in a Motor Skill, *Jour. Exp. Psychol.*, 39, 47–68. Figure adapted by permission of American Psychological Association.

trated here but may also occur during long rest periods. A similar improvement in performance during a long rest was referred to by William James more than seventy-five years ago when he said that we learn to swim during the winter and to skate during the summer. The generally accepted interpretation of these results is that massed training produces an inhibitory effect on *performance* but has no effect on *learning*. Diminution of the inhibitory effects during rest periods would account both for reminiscence and for the fact that performance under the two conditions gradually approaches the same level.

Retention of Skills

Most of us have tried at one time or another to return to one of our youthful skills like cycling or roller skating and have been pleasantly surprised at the speed with which our proficiency returns. Our experience agrees with the general finding that skills are retained very well. In his review of motor skills, Bilodeau (1966) points out that most studies of motor skills find so little forgetting that it is impossible to determine the variables that produce it. In one such study (Fleishman & Parker, 1962) subjects were given seven weeks' practice on a

complex perceptual-motor task. They were then tested for retention as much as two years later, and the authors found "virtually no loss in skill regardless of the retention interval." Two explanations are usually offered for the extremely good retention of skills: First, skills are in general very well learned and therefore well retained, and, second, in the retention periods very few new responses are developed that would interfere with a specific skill. After we give up our bicycles, we learn many things but few that would directly interfere with the pedaling, balancing, and steering necessary for cycling.

Knowledge and Skills

Our skilled performances depend upon several kinds of knowledge—knowledge of what to do; exteroceptive knowledge concerning the state of the world outside us; kinesthetic knowledge of the state of our muscles, joints, and tendons; and knowledge of the results of what we have done.

A medical student who has seen many operations and has memorized, letter-perfect, the full detailed procedure for removing a cataract, but has never himself held a surgical instrument in his hand, would, of course, be a menace if let

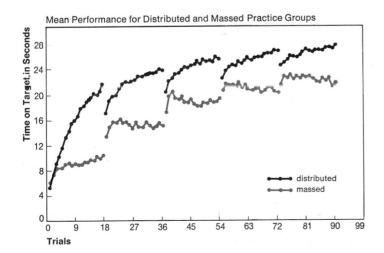

Mean Performance for Distributed and Massed Practice Groups

Figure 22.2. The acquisition of a motor skill (pursuit rotor) under massed and spaced learning conditions. Subjects were given five practice sessions of eighteen thirty-second trials each. The "spaced" group had a 1.5 minute rest between trials, and the "massed" group had two seconds. The performance measure is the time on target for a thirty-second trial.
J. M. Digman, "Growth of a Motor Skill as a Function of Distribution of Practice," *Journal of Experimental Psychology*, 57, 311; Copyright 1959 by the American Psychological Association; adapted by permission.

loose on a patient in an operating room. Why? Does not he have the knowledge of what to do? Not completely. He has the knowledge of how the operation should appear visually, for he has observed it and read about it, but he does not know how it should "feel" kinesthetically. He lacks kinesthetic knowledge of what to do, of what his kinesthetic receptors should be telling him as he places the scalpel in position, as he cuts, as he removes tissue, and so on. Kinesthetic knowledge is just as genuine a type of knowledge as is any other kind. Because *this* knowledge attribute of skills is so frequently missed, the point merits further discussion.

Most adaptive behavior depends upon knowledge gained through the visual and auditory senses. There are, of course, other senses through which knowledge can be gained. Frequently the knowledge provided by one sense may serve the same end as knowledge provided by another sense. For example, we may learn a piece of poetry by reading it or by hearing it. But each sensory system also contributes its own unique knowledge.

The knowledge provided by the kinesthetic system cannot be provided by our eyes and ears. Just as the only way of receiving visual knowledge is via patterned visual stimulation of the retina, so there is only one way of receiving kinesthetic knowledge—and that is via the kinesthetic receptors. These receptors can be stimulated only by actual movements of the body. Herein lies one of the most important functions of "action" or practice. It is not merely muscular *exercise;* it is a method of *perceiving* via the kinesthetic system. When you listen to your typing instructor and look at the diagrams he draws on the blackboard, you are not "exercising" your ears and your eyes. You are perceiving by ear and eye and thus obtaining knowledge about typing. Similarly, when you practice typing "Now is the time for all good men to come to the aid of their party," you are perceiving kinesthetically and obtaining additional knowledge about typing. Without this additional knowledge the development of

skillful typing is impossible, just as it is impossible without the visual or auditory knowledge.

The need to develop kinesthetic knowledge of the responses to be made is partially responsible for the difficulty of making new responses required by a skill and for the initial slow development of skills, as discussed earlier. It is also responsible for a shift in many skills from exteroceptive control to kinesthetic control. Piano playing is a good example of a skill in which the initial control is largely visual but in which, as the skill develops, kinesthesis becomes increasingly important; in the final stages the expert may eliminate visual control completely, playing with closed eyes. Box 65, p. 343, gives us experimental evidence on this same point.

Many skills involve, of course, the harmonious coordination of exteroceptive and interoceptive knowledge. Our expert skier uses multiple and subtle kinesthetic cues to respond to the conditions underfoot, like soft spots and bumps. He does not, however, ignore the tree looming before him or the larger rises and falls of the landscape that he can observe visually.

Feedback

Knowledge of what to do and of the state of the outside world and of our bodies is not enough; the performance of skills also requires knowledge of the *results* of what we have done. We may not recognize vagueness when we "think about" doing a thing, but this vagueness dramatically reveals itself when we begin to perform. The main reason, of course, is that the consequences of performance are immediately made clear to us. We move our muscles and our muscles report back. In short, *feedback* occurs. The execution of a skilled performance is a continuous process of behavior in which each phase is governed by what went before, by what will happen next, and by the final goal aimed at. Any interference with the feedback of such skilled performance will have serious dis-

Box 65

"Visually Minded" Versus "Kinesthetically Minded"

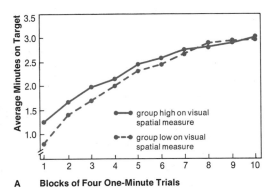

A   **Blocks of Four One-Minute Trials**

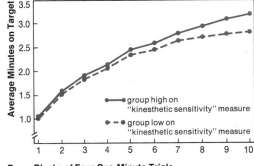

B   **Blocks of Four One-Minute Trials**

A complex skill may at first be controlled visually and then later come under kinesthetic control; this fact was demonstrated in a study by E. A. Fleishman and S. Rich of Yale University. Their subjects learned to control a "target follower" in order to track a target that moved at variable speeds on an irregular path around a circular plate. The subject controlled left-right movement of the target follower with one hand and movement toward or away from himself with the other. Coordination of the two hand movements made it possible to move the target follower in any direction.

These psychologists reasoned that, if visual cues are predominant in the early control of the task, individuals who make superior use of visual cues should do better in the early learning of the task. On the other hand, if kinesthetic cues are dominant late in the task, individuals "sensitive" to kinesthetic cues should have an advantage there. The experimenters gave a visual spatial test and a kinesthetic sensitivity test to a large group of subjects and divided them into groups high and low on visual "spatial ability" and into groups high and low on "kinesthetic sensitivity." The results for these groups on the learning of the hand-coordination skill beautifully support their reasoning. In Figure A the superior visual group (high spatial measure) clearly has an early advantage, but, as training progresses, the poorer visual group catches up. In Figure B the two kinesthetic groups begin at the same level, but, in the later stages as kinesthesis becomes important, the kinesthetically more sensitive group surpasses the less sensitive group. This shift in the sensory control of skilled behavior probably explains in part how certain skills "become automatic" as they are better acquired.

E. A. FLEISHMAN and S. RICH. 1963. Role of Kinesthetic and Spatial-Visual Abilities in Perceptual-Motor Learning, *J. Exp. Psychol.*, 66, 6–11. Figures adapted by permission of American Psychological Association.

Figure 22.3. The photograph shows how delayed auditory feedback is produced. The subject speaks into a microphone and his speech is recorded by a special tape recorder. The taped speech is then fed to another section of the recorder, where it is played to the earphones worn by the subject. The delay introduced between the recording and playback of the speech can be controlled by adjustments in the recorder.

rupting effects. Indeed, one of the active experimenters on skills defines a skill as "a response" in which "receptor-effector-feedback processes are highly organized, both spatially and temporally" (Fitts, 1964).

A classic example of the effect of disruption of feedback on a basic skill is given by the disease *tabes dorsalis*. In this disease the nerve pathways from the legs to the brain can be completely destroyed, while motor nerves from the brain to the legs remain unimpaired. The *tabes dorsalis* patient, therefore, while retaining control of his legs, will lack kinesthetic feedback from them and must depend upon vision to tell him what his legs are doing. He can walk only by constantly looking down at his feet and shuffling along. To see this shambling caricature of normal walking is to see a dramatic illustration of the importance of kinesthetic feedback to a basic skill.

The crucial importance of feedback can be seen in the performance of one of our most complex skills—speech. The marvelous coordination of glottis, neck muscles, jaw muscles, chest muscles, tongue, lips, and larynx that is required for human speech depends upon two major kinds of feedback—kinesthetic and auditory. For speech to continue smoothly, we must not only feel what our muscles are doing but also hear the sounds we produce.

The important role of auditory feedback can be shown in an unusual experiment involving "delayed auditory feedback." In this experiment the subject speaks into a microphone that is connected to a tape recorder. The tape recorder stores the speech for a fraction of a second before playing it back to the subject through earphones (see Figure 22.3.). In this way an "artificial" delay is introduced between the moment the subject speaks a word and the moment he hears it. When the auditory feedback is delayed for as little as two-tenths of a second, the subject's speech will show a variety of disruptions including faltering, stuttering, and even complete blocking (Lee, 1950). We have here a striking demonstration of how auditory feedback can play a critical role in the control of normal speech.

The recognition of the crucial importance of auditory feedback in speech has led to a number of effective remedial procedures for those with various speech defects. As an example, for the deaf, for whom auditory feedback is impossible or greatly attenuated, an attempt has been made to substitute *visual* for auditory feedback. The deaf person is helped to control his speech by watching his own "sound patterns"—visible records of the muscular movements that produce speech or visual patterns produced by the sound waves of speech. In this

Box 66

Controlling Silent Speech
by Listening to It

Subvocalization is considered one of the most difficult problems to overcome in increasing silent-reading speed. It is particularly difficult to overcome in individuals in whom the subvocal activity is limited to the vocal musculature (and does not involve movements of the lips and jaws) because such individuals are often not aware that they are subvocalizing. Apparently the kinesthetic feedback from the vocal musculature is too feeble to be effective in helping them suppress the minimal vocal muscle movements.

Three psychologists at the University of California at Berkeley—C. D. Hardyck, L. F. Petrinovich, and D. W. Ellsworth—thought they saw a way to increase the effectiveness of the feedback and thus to increase the control over the interfering subvocal muscular movements. They argued—on the basis of the delayed-auditory-feedback experiments—that, because auditory feedback is extremely effective in controlling very fine motor adjustments of the speech musculature, all that one would need to do would be to convert the ineffective kinesthetic cues of the subvocalizers into the more effective auditory cues. That is, if subvocalizers could be made to *hear* the minimal activity of their vocal muscles, they would be helped to eliminate this unwanted activity during their silent reading.

A total of fifty college students from a reading-improvement class was tested; it was found that seventeen subvocalized. All seventeen were treated in the following manner.

A brief discussion was held with the subject, informing him of his tendencies to subvocalize during "silent" reading. The subject was given earphones to wear and was asked to remain relaxed. Feedback was introduced by placing mesh electrodes over the thyroid cartilage of the neck. The output from these electrodes (which could pick up minimal muscle movements) was channeled (via various appropriate devices) to an audio amplifier and then to the earphones. When the subject was relaxed, the audio circuit was opened, and he was asked to swallow. The subject heard his swallow, for the swallow resulted in an immediate burst of static in the earphones. He was then requested to experiment with the sound to satisfy himself that he could control it (stop it and start it) by such actions as swallowing, clenching his jaw muscles, turning his head, whispering, and so on. The subject then began to read silently, with instructions to keep this auditory feedback to a minimum during his reading.

The dramatic results of this treatment are best described in the experimenters' own words:

"Originally it was planned to administer the feedback treatment over several sessions to determine the number of feedback treatments necessary to establish normal reading patterns. This was found to be unnecessary. The feedback treatment was remarkably effective. . . . In all cases one session of the feedback was sufficient to produce complete cessation of subvocalization. . . . The level of speech muscle activity was monitored at the end of 1 month, and again after 3 months. . . . None of the subjects gave any evidence of subvocalization in either of the tests."

C. D. HARDYCK, L. F. PETRINOVICH, and D. W. ELLSWORTH. 1966. Feedback of Speech Muscle Activity during Silent Reading: Rapid Extinction, *Science*, 154, 1467–8.

Box 67

2.42 Minus 0.71
Does *Not* Always Equal 1.71

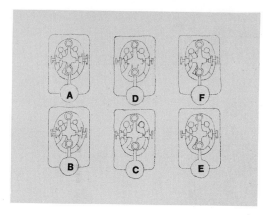

E. E. Ghiselli and C. W. Brown, at the University of California, tested the time-and-motion method of analysis with the following experiment: With telegraph keys arranged as shown, subjects learned to tap the keys in a certain sequence (for example, A, B, C, D, C, E, F, A). The time between each pair of keys was recorded automatically. After the subjects had reached their maximum speed, they were instructed to eliminate some superfluous steps in the sequence (for example, they now tapped A, B, C, E, F, A) and were permitted enough practice until they had again reached a maximum speed. Two examples of the results are given here.

procedure the deaf person is first taught what the "normal" speech pictures for various sounds and words look like. He is then shown the pictures his own speech makes. He sees what he says. This visual feedback enables him to adjust and change his own sounds until he begins to approximate the normal.

Another recent use of "feedback therapy" has been applied to the treatment of reading problems caused by subvocal activity. Subvocalization refers to such activities as inaudible articulation, lip movement, and whispering during "silent" reading. An individual who subvocalizes to any great extent is limited to a reading speed of approximately 150 words per minute. It was reasoned that, if the individual could be helped to eliminate subvocalization, his silent-reading speed should increase. And indeed it was found possible to achieve this end by converting the movements of the speech musculature during subvocalization into auditory signals and feeding them back to the individual for his use in controlling the muscle movements (for further details, see Box 66, p. 345).

Sequences and Time (in Seconds) Required to Make Each Movement

EXAMPLE 1

First Sequence			*Second Sequence*	
A-B	0.40		A-B	0.44
B-C	0.28		B-C	0.30
C-D	0.39 ⎫ 0.71		(Eliminated)	
D-C	0.32 ⎭		(Eliminated)	
C-E	0.30		C-E	0.29
E-F	0.39		E-F	0.41
F-A	0.34		F-A	0.37
Total time	2.42		Total time	1.81

EXAMPLE 2

B-C	0.23		B-C	0.21
C-D	0.30 ⎫ 0.59		(Eliminated)	
D-C	0.29 ⎭		(Eliminated)	
C-E	0.17		C-E	0.11
E-A	0.31		E-A	0.30
Total time	1.30		Total time	.62

In the first example, the seven movements required 2.42 seconds. Elimination of movements C-D and D-C should have reduced the time to 1.71 seconds ($2.42 - 0.71 = 1.71$). But it did not. Most of the movements of the second sequence required *more time* than originally. The "saving" was 0.61 seconds instead of the "predicted" 0.71 seconds.

In the second example, elimination of C-D and D-C *reduced* the individual times of the remaining movements. A saving of 0.68 seconds resulted instead of the "predicted" 0.59 seconds.

This simple experiment testifies to an important psychological principle: Human activity consists of integrated patterns, and in an integrated pattern we cannot add (or subtract) elements and expect simple additive changes.

E. E. GHISELLI and C. W. BROWN. 1955. *Personnel and Industrial Psychology.* Copyright 1929 by McGraw-Hill Book Company, Inc. Table adapted by permission of McGraw-Hill Book Company, Inc.

Time-and-Motion Studies

Although we cannot, in this book, devote much space to specific practical problems, we might indicate one important implication of the psychology of skills for certain industrial practices. The development of methods of work in industrial organizations is largely in the hands of the industrial engineer and the efficiency expert. These specialists developed a technique of speeding the performance of skilled operations which is known as *time-and-motion analysis.*

In time-and-motion analysis the industrial engineer gets a detailed picture of each movement involved in a particular task. He then identifies the movements that seem essential and those that seem superfluous. On the basis of such an analysis the industrial engineer trains the worker to change the sequence of his movements so as to eliminate the superfluous ones.

An approach like this one sometimes reflects a fallacious assumption about the nature of skilled acts. We have already seen that the individual components of a complex task cannot be considered unrelated units. Yet some efficiency engineers assume that, if one movement is eliminated from a task, the total time for completing the task should be reduced proportionately, and they expect the efficient worker to behave that way after being "properly taught." As a concrete experimental demonstration of the inadequacy of such reasoning, Ghiselli and Brown (see Box 67, p. 346) have shown

that the person performing even a simple motor task integrates all the movements into a pattern, and the elimination of any one movement, *even if such an elimination results in a simpler task,* may increase the time per unit for the remaining movements. The pattern of the whole is changed, and the "efficiency" gained is less than the time-and-motion analyst would expect. Proper training for improving a skill rests on sound psychological analysis of the skill.

Glossary

feedback A general term referring to the process by which action initiated by a subject provides an additional source of stimulation. The *consequences* of action thus become apparent to the performer and influence his succeeding acts.

plateau A portion of a learning curve showing no change in efficiency of performance. A plateau is often found in a curve depicting the acquisition of a perceptual-motor skill.

reminiscence effect Improvement in performance

during a period of no practice. It is most easily demonstrated after massed practice but may also occur during long rest periods.

skill An organized sequence of integrated responses executed with precision and efficiency.

time-and-motion analysis A method of analyzing a skilled motor performance in terms of specific movements, designed to identify "superfluous" movements in the performance.

images, language, and thought

overview / Thinking is mental activity that can take place in the absence of direct sensory input, though it is by no means unresponsive to environmental demands. Rather, thinking may be regarded as adaptive, whether it is "directed" toward solving a specific problem or even when it is "autistic," reflecting inner needs with few reality constraints. It involves the interplay of symbolic representations of things in the real world—the interplay of images and words. Usually we are well aware of our thought processes, but often we are not. Thinking can be systematically studied through observation of the thinker's behavior, however; we do not depend solely upon his introspective report.

Images and percepts share many qualities, but, with few exceptions, the two may be easily distinguished. Although images typically are the "stuff" of thinking, we cannot conclude that the substantial differences among individuals in the amount and vividness of their imagery relate to their thinking abilities.

Language plays a critical role in human adult thinking, but there is no doubt that even creative thinking can occur in the absence of language. Nevertheless, even during "silent thinking" we employ language, although, in this circumstance, our "inner speech" is somewhat primitive and simplified. Language is not a passive vehicle serving thinking, nor does it wholly mold our thought processes. Rather, the development and adult functioning of language and thinking are highly interdependent processes.

In our study of adaptive behavior so far we have considered how man's commerce with his environment leads to the development and maintenance of new behaviors. In discussing conditioning, memorizing, and the learning of skills, our focus has been upon the acquisition and retention of new information from the external world. Or, put another way, it may have seemed that without continuous sensory input we would have nothing to learn and nothing to remember. Yet our mental life does not grind to a halt the moment outside stimulation is shut off. Quite the contrary, it is just then that many of us experience our most intense and often most adaptive mental activity—in short, we have time to think.

Thought is sometimes regarded as evolution's highest achievement and, indeed, as defining the essence of human existence. The French philosopher René Descartes put it succinctly, *Cogito, ergo sum* ("I think, therefore I am"). Yet it is difficult to present a rigorous definition of thinking. Such a definition would clearly set off thinking as a form of behavior involving the transformation or reorganization of already available "old" information, as distinguished from learning in which the emphasis is upon the acquisition of new information. One could equate thinking with all mental activity that occurs in the absence of immediate sensory input from the outside world. But treating thinking in this way does not imply that it is independent of the outside world; rather, as we shall see, all forms of thinking (and there are many forms) are responsive to environmental demands.

Perhaps the distinctive feature of thinking is that it involves the interplay of symbolic representations of elements of the real world—of images and words for things rather than of the things themselves. Sometimes this interplay is active, directed, and guided, as in problem solving, and we shall discuss this type of "directed thinking" in Unit 26. At other times the interplay of images seems spontaneous, even haphazard, as we lose ourselves in seem-

ingly aimless daydreaming. The adaptiveness of the first kind of thinking is unarguable, but it is difficult to regard the latter as more than idle fantasy. Yet such meanderings of thought play an important role in creative thinking and problem solving and can serve an adaptive function. Indeed, even so-called *autistic thinking*—thinking mostly dominated by one's wishes and needs and little constrained by logic or reality —may be adaptive. Every child has elaborate fantasies of adventure and romance, triumph and adulation; and many an adult regrets that such daydreams have lost their ability to satisfy. The fact of daydreams would alone argue that such thinking is adaptive in the sense that it brings pleasure. It may be truly adaptive in the sense that it provides the individual with a substitute reaction to ease the pain of frustrating reality. Therein lies the rub, however, for fulfillment of needs through fantasy may interfere with a realistic appraisal of the situation and, therefore, may ultimately prove maladaptive. In the normal development of the individual, autistic thinking tends to give way to realistic thinking when the former fails to work, that is, when it becomes clear that neither the physical nor the social world conforms to one's fantasies.

It seems reasonable to regard thinking, in all its forms, as one broad facet of man's adaptive repertoire. From this point of view, the study of thinking is not restricted to the study of introspective reports of mental processes and images. We can also study thinking through the observation of behavior alone—as we must do with very young children and animals. Furthermore, as we shall see, much of what is properly considered thinking in human adults goes on "automatically" or unconsciously. One may never be consciously aware of some of the intervening processes contributing to the solution of a problem.

Images and Thinking

What is the content of our experience when we try to "think through" a problem? First, there

are percepts of actual objects: high fences, locked doors, empty pockets, long lists of written numbers, crying children. Second, there are images of remembered objects (*memory images*) or of objects that have not existed and do not exist except in our imagination (*created images*).

Similarities Between Images and Percepts

We can experience images in as real, rich, and varied a form as our percepts. Just as we can see, hear, smell, taste, or feel physically existing objects, so can we "see" objects that are not there; "hear" music when none is being played; "smell" foods that we have not had for years; and see, hear, and feel "the silken, sad, uncertain rustling of each purple curtain" as we read Edgar Allan Poe.

We found that individuals differ in perceptual capacity, some excelling in vision, some in hearing, some in smell. We also find important individual differences in imagery capacity and preferences. Two major findings have come out of the scientific study of such individual differences.

First, individuals appear to differ greatly in the *vividness* of their imagery. The classic study in this area is represented by Sir Francis Galton's "breakfast table" investigation in the 1880s. He asked each of his subjects to recall his breakfast table as he had sat down to it in the morning and to report what he had experienced —whether or not the imaged objects were colored naturally, whether or not they were distinct and well defined, and so on. Galton received many different reports, ranging from a report of images as vivid as the original perceptions of the real objects to a report of no images at all.

Second, individuals differ in their favored *modes* of imagery. Some people, for example, have images that are predominantly visual; others have images that are predominantly auditory. Some of us, in thinking of the sea, "see" its swelling waves; others "hear" its roar; some

tell of the "smell" of its spray. Most people, however, experience a combination of these modes. For an interesting description of such combinations, see Box 68, p. 354.

Differences Between Images and Percepts

Despite the similarities between images and ordinary perceptions, most of us can almost always tell the difference between them quite easily. On what basis can we do this? There have been several suggestions.

One is that the image is usually less vivid and less clearly experienced than the percept of a real object. This statement does not always hold, however. On occasion many of us have experienced images that were as detailed, clear, and vivid as the percept of a real object. Again it is Sir Francis Galton who tells of the astonishingly detailed and precise imagery of an eminent scientist of his time:

"Mr. Flinders Petrie . . . informs me that he habitually works out sums by aid of an imaginary slide rule, which he sets in the desired way and reads off mentally. He does not usually visualize the whole rule but only that part of it with which he is at the moment concerned." [Quoted in Humphrey, 1948.]

We do not have to depend only upon such informal reports. Careful experimental evidence is available that demonstrates the high degree of vividness and precision that is possible in images, Box 69, p. 355, for instance, presents some illustrations of a particularly detailed kind of image, the *eidetic image*.

Another suggestion is that the difference between image and percept lies in the greater lability of the image. The percept of a real object is constrained by the object's stimulus properties (size, color, shape, location, and so on). Images, on the other hand, are more labile. A visual image can be shifted from spot to spot at will; sometimes it is organized together with one group of objects, sometimes with another. (Remember Albert Einstein's reference in Box 68, p. 354, to the "combinatory play" among his images?) It can even be "seen" inside an opaque

Box 70

**The Real Becomes
the Imagined**

In 1910, C. W. Perky at Cornell University reported the following experiment: She prepared cardboard forms with their centers cut out in the shape of a book, a banana, an orange, a leaf, and a lemon. These forms could be so placed that, when a lantern was turned on, colored light would shine through the cutout forms, and the corresponding colored figure would be cast on the ground-glass window.

The subject was seated facing the window, with the lantern turned off. He was asked to fixate the screen while he "imagined" a colored object, "for instance, a tomato." He was then to describe his "image" if any image took shape. After these instructions, the lamp was turned on (without the subject's knowledge) with an intensity *below* the minimum necessary for vision. Then, very slowly, the intensity was stepped up until it was *well beyond the previously determined minimum for actual vision.* As soon as the subject began to describe his "image," the lamp was turned off, and, after he had finished his description, he was requested to "imagine" another object, "for instance, a book." The objects actually cast on the screen were a red tomato, a blue book, a deep-yellow banana, an orange orange, a green leaf, and a light-yellow lemon.

All the subjects (nineteen sophomores and eight graduate students) believed that they were imagining the objects and their appropriate colors, yet not one of them "imagined" the object until the illumination had gone well above the minimum required for normal perception. *They were seeing actual objects but believed that they were "imagining" them.* When the subject was asked whether or not he was "quite sure that he had imagined all these things," the question aroused surprise and indignation. Sophomores and graduate students in psychology alike had mistaken the perception of a real object for an image!

c. w. PERKY. 1910. An Experimental Study of Imagination, *Amer. J. Psychol.,* 21, 422–52.

self of the particular features of the image; as a result he may be unable to think about his problem in an entirely fresh way. Furthermore, much complex thought is characterized by its high degree of abstractness. Concrete images may interfere with the abstract symbolization that is required for some types of problems.

In addition to the question of whether images help or hinder thinking, there is the second problem posed by the stubborn facts of individual differences in imagery capacity. Some people, it will be remembered, are capable of experiencing many and vivid images; some people lack this capacity almost entirely. How are these individual differences in imagery related to thinking ability?

"Imageless Thought"

At the beginning of the present century many German, French, English, and American psychologists were involved in a long and often

bitterly waged controversy over the question of *imageless thought*—whether or not people could think without images. The imageless school asserted that thinking can take place without imagery and cited as evidence the introspective reports of their subjects who often failed to report any images while thinking. The imagery school insisted that people who did not report images were simply reporting inadequately and were failing to notice fleeting images. The imageless-thought battle ended with a "no decision" when psychologists turned their attention to other questions about the thinking process. Very often in science a problem is abandoned unsolved, as fads and interests in the science change.

Language and Thinking

The images most frequently used in thinking are words. The most common way of communicating the solution of a problem is with words. The achievement of a new concept often results in the coining of a new word or in giving an old word new meanings. For these and other reasons, most psychologists will agree that there is a close relationship between thinking and language, so close that some psychologists —for example, Jean Piaget—use the analysis of language of the child to study the thinking of the child.

But with language, as with the imageless-thought problem, we must distinguish between what is *necessary* for thinking and what may be *helpful* for thinking. Even if we grant that language plays a critical role in man's thinking, it is not necessary to conclude that language is *essential* for thought processes. If that were true, lower animals would certainly be "mindless," and even preverbal children would not be capable of thinking. Yet it is clear from informal observation and careful experimental work that both young children and animals are quite capable of solving problems. This problem solving has all the appearances of thinking. Indeed, rats are apparently also capable of insight in a problem-solving situation that lends itself to an insightful solution (see Box 71, p. 358).

Admittedly, the average man can solve more difficult problems than can the average animal. But some men are better problem solvers than are others, yet we do not (or should not) infer from this the existence of *qualitatively* different thought processes. Furthermore, it is to be remembered that it is man who decides what is to be called "difficult" and that, typically, animal thinking is investigated in man-relevant problem situations. We do not know, nor is the human psychologist likely to find out, how well man would fare in attempting to solve the problem of navigating accurately over long distances, given the same equipment available to salmon and migratory birds, who do such navigating extraordinarily well. Our point here is not to champion the cause of the underprivileged species but only to indicate that to lay claim to thinking as an exclusive human preserve makes little sense, logically or empirically. Although the specifics of human language no doubt influence the way we think, it is unnecessary to deny ourselves, in our study of human thought, the use of data on children's and animals' thought.

Speech in Silent and Communicative Thought

Language plays an important role both when we are thinking to ourselves (the *silent thinking* stage) and when we are formally expressing our thoughts, either through speaking or writing (the *communicative thinking* stage).

That words make up a good part of our experiences during the "silent thinking" stage seems clear from the introspective reports of many observers. Objective experimental evidence is also available that suggests the same thing. It has been shown that when a person is thinking, minimal movements of the throat and tongue can sometimes be detected by sensitive instruments. These movements are such as to permit the interpretation that the person is

Box 71

The Rat and Creative Problem Solving

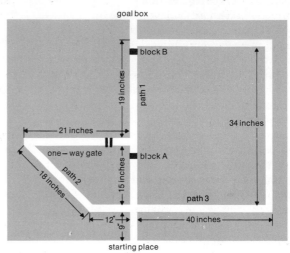

Many psychologists maintain that even the rat is capable of creative problem solving. In 1930 E. C. Tolman and C. H. Honzik at the University of California reported their classical experiment on "insight" in the rat using an elevated image (having no sidewalls and elevated from the floor of the room, see photograph).

The apparatus that they used presented three paths to the food box. Path 1 was the shortest, 2 the next shortest, and 3 the longest. Paths 1 and 2 had a common final segment that path 3 did not share. First the rats were given *preliminary training.* Animals deprived of food for twenty-four hours were placed in the starting box and permitted to find their way to the food box. They were given ten trials a day. They soon learned (after trying the various paths) to take the shortest path to the food. When the experimenters then *blocked* path 1 at point A, the rats would turn back to the choice point and would almost always (about 93 per cent of the time) take path 2.

In the *test run* the block was *for the first time* placed in the common section of paths 1 and 2 (at point B). Then when the rats backed out of path 1, they did not take path 2 but path 3—the longest path, *but the only one still open to the food box.* Of the fifteen rats in this experiment, fourteen behaved in this way.

Backing out of path 1 and taking path 3 was a relatively new and original solution—and one that seemed to the human psychologists observing the rats' behavior to show "insight" and "inference," or what we are tempted to call "creative problem solving."

E. C. TOLMAN and C. H. HONZIK. 1930. "Insight" in Rats, *Univ. Calif. Publ. Psychol.,* 4, 215–32. Figure adapted by permission.

really "talking to himself" (for one such experiment, see Box 72, p. 360).

Although language is involved in both the "silent thinking" and the "communicative" stages, detailed analysis indicates that language plays two different roles in these two stages. In the "silent thinking" stage the specific grammar and vocabulary of the language seem to play a relatively minor role in determining the nature and content of the thought.

Vigotsky (1939), a Russian psychologist, has characterized the *inner speech* that occurs in "silent thinking" in the following manner: First, it is abrupt and incomplete; second, it makes many assumptions about the "self-evident" nature of the facts and relations involved in any line of reasoning; third, it is relatively independent of the rules of grammar.

In the "communicative" stage, language serves what might be termed a "policing" and "editing" function, and here the specific structure of the language may play a more significant role. We realize that we cannot be so abrupt and elliptical. We must "spell out" our steps, we must use words more precisely, we must pay some attention to grammatical construction; else we run the risk of not communicating at all. We realize these necessities because we have learned that our private world is not shared by others.

The differences between speech in the "silent thinking" and the "communication" stages do not represent sharp breaks. The degree of difference depends, in part, upon the relationship between the speaker and the listener. In general, the more common the sympathies and context shared by the listener and speaker, the more elliptical, abrupt, unfinished, and grammatically unrestrained speech can be. At one extreme is the instance in which we are talking to ourselves; at the other extreme is the formal, written communication addressed to an unknown audience.

When we talk to ourselves, we each have a perfect friend, a completely sympathetic and understanding "audience" who shares our context completely. We use the vaguest of words without any fear that we shall be misunderstood. We use the "felt sense" of words, rather than the dictionary meanings. We are not constrained by grammatical rules. We skip steps in our reasoning, feeling that we "understand" what we have not spoken.

Conversation among good friends of like mind may be only slightly removed from talking to oneself. Such conversations may also consist of somewhat abbreviated speech. Often we find that no sooner does one friend begin to speak than the other will immediately anticipate the purport of the speech and begin his reply, only to be understood immediately and to be interrupted by the beginning of another reply. Such a conversation may well include mere beginnings of sentences, snatches of phrases, and elliptical exclamations.

Increasing formalization of speech can be illustrated in the difference between the professor's language when he lectures and when he writes. His lectures are apt to be more informal, sentences are not completed, tenses are mixed, plural nouns are coupled with singular verbs, participles are left hanging, and phrases like "the whatnot" abound. Yet this garbled and grammatically "barbarous" spoken language may be perfectly understood by most listeners, whereas the same words, read in a manuscript, may cause confusion and bewilderment. Why? One reason seems to be that in speech the audience not only hears the words but also sees the speaker's facial expressions, hears stresses and emphases, sees gestures; furthermore, all of the communication takes place in a very specific context. When reading a manuscript, however, the reader is mostly dependent upon the written words. He does not have the multitude of nonverbal cues that the listener has when he not only hears but also sees the speaker.

Speech, then, becomes more formal as we attempt to communicate with others, and it increases in formality as the "psychological distance" between the speaker and listener increases.

When we prepare to communicate our thoughts—when we attempt to "dress up" our thoughts for public display—we often find that we cannot do so. In the light of day, as it were, we find that we have assumed too much, that our thinking process has not been completed. The reason we sometimes cannot find the words for our thoughts is that we really did not have the thoughts clearly in the first place; we had only assumed that we had them. The second stage is thus not merely a stage of "expression"; it is very frequently a continuation of the stage of creation. We correct, fill in, revise, and even completely alter our "thinking" as we attempt to express it. But now we are doing our "thinking" under the constraints imposed upon us by the dictionary meaning of words and by the rules of grammar.

That the constraints of language may help the thinking process has been shown in a study by Gagné and Smith (1962). They found that training subjects to put all their thoughts into words while working on a problem—and requir-

---

Box 72

Implicit Speech in Thinking

E. Jacobson of the University of Chicago demonstrated that "During . . . thinking involving words or numbers, muscular contractions appear . . . in at least some of the muscles which participate when the same words or numbers are actually whispered or uttered out loud."

Because even the most minute muscular contractions are accompanied by electrical potential changes, Jacobson used an instrument to detect and record such changes. Two fine platinum-iridium wire electrodes were inserted about one centimeter into the tip of the tongue and the underlip of the subject. The electrodes led to an amplifier and a string galvanometer. Only well-trained subjects were used.

The subject, lying relaxed with eyes closed upon a couch in a quiet, darkened room, was instructed to *imagine* or to recall certain poems, multiply (mentally) certain numbers, think of such abstract matters as "eternity," and so on. Throughout, the vibrations of the string of the galvanometer were photographed. We quote from Jacobson's statement of results:

"When the electrodes are connected in the speech musculature of the trained subject, the string shadow is practically quiet. . . . But promptly after the signal is sounded to engage in mental activity . . . marked vibrations appear, indicating action-potentials. Soon after the subject hears the signal to relax . . . the vibrations cease. . . . The series of vibrations during mental activity occur in patterns evidently corresponding with those present during actual speech . . . but of considerably less voltage."

This experiment and many similar ones by other workers gave support to the so-called "motor theory of thinking," that is, that all thinking involves minimal speech movements. Perhaps a more conservative conclusion is that some thinking involves such implicit speech or, yet another interpretation, that some individuals characteristically show minimal speech movements while thinking.

E. JACOBSON. 1938. *Progressive Relaxation* (Chicago: University of Chicago Press).

ing them to spell out the general principle involved—resulted in a significant improvement in their subsequent problem-solving ability.

Language—Vehicle or Mold?

Most psychologists agree that there is a close relationship between language and thinking, but there is disagreement on the nature of this relationship. The major question of disagreement can be stated simply: Is language merely a reproducing instrument for voicing or clarifying ideas, or is language itself the shaper of ideas? One analysis—language as a vehicle—suggests that the nature of thinking depends very little upon the nature of language. Neither the vocabulary nor the grammar of a language determines the product of thinking. According to this position the development of thinking and language in the child go along concurrently but more or less separately. As the child learns new words, he can better communicate his thoughts and better remember his conclusions, but that is all. Language is a convenient "vehicle" for thinking.

The other analysis maintains that language

Box 73

It Houses

Benjamin Lee Whorf, a student of linguistics, argues that ". . . the background linguistic system [the grammar] of each language is not merely a reproducing instrument for voicing ideas but rather is itself the shaper of ideas." He supports his arguments, in part, by comparing the way various languages "dissect nature." He points out that we tend to differentiate between "things" and "events" in a hard and fast way because in the English language we divide most of our words into nouns and verbs.

"Our language thus gives us a bipolar division of nature. But nature herself is not bipolarized. If it be said that strike, turn, run, are verbs because they denote temporary or short-lasting events, i.e., actions, why then is fist a noun? It is also a temporary event. Why are lightning, spark, wave, eddy, pulsation, flame, storm, phase, cycle, spasm, noise, emotion, nouns? . . . It will be found that an 'event' to *us* means 'what our language classes as a verb.' . . . In the Hopi language, lightning, wave, flame, meteor, puff of smoke, pulsation, are verbs—events of necessarily brief duration cannot be anything but verbs. Cloud and storm are at about the lower limit of duration for nouns. Hopi, you see, actually has a classification of events . . . by duration type, something strange to our modes of thought . . . in Nootka, a language of Vancouver Island . . . we have as it were, a monistic view of nature that gives us only one class of words for all kinds of events. 'A house occurs' or 'it houses' is the way of saying 'house' exactly like 'a flame occurs' or 'it burns.'·

Whorf would thus maintain that because of our grammar (nouns and verbs) we divide the world into "events" and "things," whereas the Hopi use quite another basis (their grammar classifies words by "duration" type) and the Vancouver Islanders make no division at all between a "thing" and an "event." *Grammar* thus determines the perception of the world around us, and that perception will, in turn, determine the content and direction of our thinking.

B. L. WHORF. 1956. *Language, Thought and Reality.* (New York: Wiley).

inevitably molds thought. A number of linguistic studies have been cited to support this view. The studies of the language and thinking of different societies and cultural groups have thus been interpreted to show that the nature of the thinking of a group corresponds to the nature of its grammar and vocabulary (see Box 73, p. 361). Some clinical studies have indicated, for example, that the disturbance in the thinking of the schizophrenic patient corresponds to the disturbance in his language. According to this formulation, the development of language and thought must be seen as a highly interdependent process. As the child learns new words and new ways of putting words together, the very nature of his thinking is changed, and, as he achieves new concepts, the very structure of his language is affected.

Glossary

autistic thinking. Refers to thinking that is strongly influenced by personal desires and needs at the expense of regulation by objective reality.

"communicative thinking" stage Refers to the communication of one's thoughts to others—either in writing or in vocal speech.

created image An experience (visual, auditory, and so on) of an object that has never existed as a stimulus object for the person undergoing the experience. An "imagined" object.

eidetic image A particularly vivid and detailed memory image. It is found more frequently among children than among adults and may be evoked at will sometimes months after the original viewing of the stimulus object.

imageless thought Thinking that can proceed in the absence of imagery—or, in its more extreme form, thought in which imagery plays no role.

inner speech The speech used when "talking to one's self." According to Vigotsky, the "inner speech" of the adult is similar to the "egocentric speech" of the child.

memory image An experience (visual, auditory, and so on) of an object that has once existed as a stimulus object for the person but is now not present in his visual field.

"silent thinking" stage The stage in the thinking process that does not involve communicating the thoughts (either in writing or in vocal speech). Frequently characterized by "inner speech."

UNIT 2

development
and structure
of language

overview / The development of language ability can be usefully investigated by regarding children's speech as true languages in their own right, rather than as merely poor copies of adult language. Very early in life infants can produce all sounds necessary for adult language, but they only gradually evolve the ability to produce words and, later, meaningful and grammatically correct phrases and sentences. Before this evolution occurs, however, children's speech does follow systematic, though different from adult, rules.

Many processes contribute to the child's acquisition of an adult vocabulary and grammar. Imitation is certainly a factor, as is conditioning, but they are insufficient in themselves. Rather, the gradual acquisition of adult language ability can be profitably viewed as an ongoing problem-solving enterprise during which the child evolves, tests, and verifies increasingly accurate hypotheses concerning the content and structure of adult language.

Adult language involves an enormous amount of redundancy. We really repeat ourselves, informationally speaking, to an astonishing extent, but such repetition is essential for effective communication. Redundancy permits us to overcome the several sources of distortion that enter into our perception of speech, and accurate perception is, as with the child, often a problem-solving process.

The psychological study of language development is, strictly speaking, a fairly recent phenomenon; it has shown a tremendous upsurge in the 1950s and 1960s. Not that psychologists ignored the topic before that time: There were many studies, of children's speech for example, that established changes by age in vocabulary size, sentence length, and use of nouns and verbs. These investigations had in common a perhaps implicit assumption that child language is simply not-yet-correct adult language. From this vantage point, determining the speed with which child vocabulary and grammar approached adult levels seemed a proper emphasis. This approach yielded many of the basic facts of language acquisition, and this information often had practical utility. (For example, studies of vocabulary growth guided writers of children's books.)

Development of Language

The explicit objective of the more recent approach, which is generally referred to as *developmental psycholinguistics*, is to achieve understanding of the development of language processes. The guiding assumption of this approach is that child language is in fact a true language, with its own systematic rules. It is not just a poor copy of the adult tongue into which it is eventually transformed.

McNeill (1966), reviewing the field of developmental psycholinguistics, succinctly presents the challenge it faces:

"The fundamental problem to which we address ourselves is the simple fact that language acquisition occurs in a surprisingly short time. Grammatical speech does not begin before 1.5 years of age; yet, as far as we can tell, the basic process is complete by 3.5 years. Thus, a basis for the rich and intricate competence of adult grammar must emerge in the short span of 24 months."

Development of Sound Patterns

Spoken language from a "brutishly materialistic" view, as Osgood (1953) has pointed out, "is nothing more than a complexly integrated series of skilled movements of the diaphragm, vocal cords, jaws, lips, and tongue, with air being driven through the varied openings at appropriate moments and pressures." This complex is built up from a series of relatively simple and automatic muscle twitches. The very first sound produced by the speech musculature is the "birth cry"—the sound that announces the triumphant entry of an infant into the world. From this first simple noise develops the marvelous variety of sounds that make up

adult language. Let us trace briefly the development of this repertoire of sounds that is essential for speech.

One of the characteristics of infant life is undifferentiated mass activity. Almost every muscle of the infant is exercised in random fashion: muscles of the legs, arms, eyes, fingers, toes. The vocal apparatus is also a muscular system and joins in this random activity. In the course of this undirected and uncontrolled movement of the jaws, lips, tongue, and vocal cords, various sounds are produced. When the baby's general body musculature is relaxed, the muscles of its vocal apparatus are also relaxed; the sounds produced then are quite different sounds, and random combinations appear as the result of purely chance conditions of the physiological state of the infant.

Some investigations have suggested that, in the early course of development, babies are capable of making all the sounds that the human voice can produce, including French trills and German gutturals. In the beginning are the universal sounds! In other words, all normal babies, no matter what their culture or race, produce the same speech sounds (see Box 74, p. 367). Only later, as children begin to repeat the sound patterns they hear in their "native" environment, do they lose the tendency—and even the ability—to utter "foreign" sounds.

This shift toward the adult pattern is noticeable as early as the fifth or sixth month among English-speaking children (as shown in Box 74, pp. 367), although it will still be some time before the child can produce the approximately forty phonemes (essentially, the irreducible sound elements of speech) that have been distinguished in spoken English. For example, Irwin (1947) reports that the average child spontaneously vocalizes only about half of these phonemes by one year of age.

This handicap is not as large as it may seem, as Dewey (1923) has estimated that only nine sounds are required in English to pronounce half the words commonly used in speech. The

Box 74

Sound Patterns in the Infant and Young Child

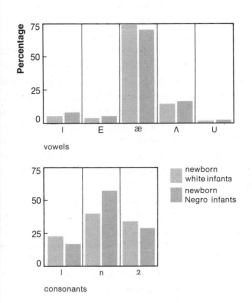

vowels

consonants

newborn
white infants

newborn
Negro infants

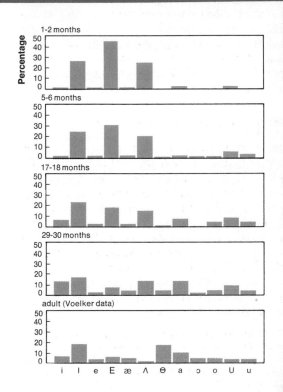

1-2 months

5-6 months

17-18 months

29-30 months

adult (Voelker data)

O. C. Irwin at the University of Iowa has long studied sound patterns among children. In one study, the sounds of ninety-five infants were sampled each month until they were thirty months old. In another, fifty newborn white infants were compared with thirty newborn Negro infants. The frequency of the more *prominent* elemental speech sounds was noted, and "sound profiles" were constructed in the following manner: A given consonant may constitute, for example, 35 per cent of the total number of consonants that a child produces. The percentages are determined for each of the consonants, and the results are then plotted as a "consonant profile." In the same way a vowel profile can be determined. From these profiles Irwin has drawn the following conclusions (among many others):

1. Racial differences are not present at birth. The vowel and consonant profiles for white and Negro infants show almost complete identity (see Figure A).

2. Starting with the fifth or sixth month of life, the newborn pattern *gradually* changes into the adult pattern, and at the age of thirty months the infant's pattern reflects his adult environment (see Figure B).

O. C. IRWIN. 1948. Infant Speech, *J. Speech Hear. Dis.*, 13, 31–4.
O. C. IRWIN. 1952. Speech Development in the Young Child, *J. Speech Hear. Dis.*, 17, 269–79.

most overworked vowel is the "i" (as in "lip"); the most used consonant sound is "n." At the other extreme, "oi" (as in "toy") and *z* (as in "has") are the least used vowel and consonant sounds.

Obviously, the beginnings of language learning depend upon the development in the child of adequate control over the production of at least a basic repertoire of frequently used speech sounds. Furthermore, because other physical characteristics of speech contribute to the quality of a spoken language (loudness and pitch, for example), the ability to manipulate these characteristics must mature before true language development can take place. Control over these features of sound begins quite early. Osgood (1953) notes that infants appear to experiment with varying the loudness of the same phoneme by the second month of life and, about a month or two later, do the same with pitch. In the first of these skills the infant is practicing control over the muscles of the diaphragm; in the other he is exercising some control over the vocal-cord muscles.

Development of Words

Generally speaking, the child is physically ready to produce words within the first year of life. He can produce a reasonable number of phonemes and can effectively vary other characteristics of the sound elements. By six months or so the infant has reached the *"syllabic babbling" stage*, and, in the course of this spontaneous "playing" with sounds, he may easily emit recognizable words. By nine months he will often imitate adult-produced sounds, and, if parents can restrain their propensity to "baby talk" and instead speak English, they may be rewarded by fair imitations of real words out of the mouths of babes. But are these "words" in the conventional sense? Do they indicate an ability for a sound to "stand for," or symbolize, some object or occurrence in the real world? At first, certainly not. Just as language is more than a collection of sounds,

so is a single word. Any adult can "read" a foreign language as long as it has the same alphabet as does his native language, but he may not understand it. Similarly, the infant can make the "right" sounds, but this ability does not imply that they convey meaning to him.

The importance in language learning of babbling and imitation cannot be denied, however. If the infant did not "choose" to babble or to imitate, he would suffer some disadvantage, at least in the earliest stages of language acquisition. Babbling, for instance, provides the practice in vocalizing that leads to acquiring control over sound production. But, as we know from studies of the congenitally deaf or dumb, the lack of either or both of these activities does not prevent full comprehension of one's native language. For such children, entry into the world of language is certainly different from that of the normal child, but their later development and ultimate level of achievement can be much the same.

To return to our initial question: When does a child begin to acquire meaningful words—and how does this come about?

First Words One reasonable basis for asserting that an infant understands the meaning of a word, at least at some rudimentary level, is that he makes some consistent and sensible response to hearing that word. Simple as this criterion may sound, it is not easily applied, for we can never determine when "hearing the word" is in fact the effective stimulus. Take the case of a mother shouting "stop!" whenever she sees her infant on the verge of some dangerous action. If the infant learns to stop whatever he is doing as a consistent response to the word "stop," it would be tempting to conclude that he now "understands" the word. But he probably does not; it is much more likely that he has learned this response to the total stimulus situation, including the abruptness and loudness of the shout, the expression on his mother's face, and so on. In fact, as anyone with a young infant can readily prove to himself, almost any word or, indeed, any syllable or sound enunciated in the same urgent way will have the same inhibitory effect. A more stringent requirement is that the infant make some selective or discriminating response to a given word before we are willing to concede him his first true word. Upon hearing the word "ball" he will look at the ball and not at his mother or at anything else nearby.

By this criterion it appears that the infant begins to understand words sometime late in his first year. Shortly after this period, at about one year of age on the average, he will be able to speak his first words—"speak" in the sense of using the words appropriately, hence meaningfully. These early words, first comprehended and later spoken, typically refer to names of objects. These nouns predominate in children's earliest speech and constitute about 50 per cent of the eighteen-month-old child's vocabulary. By age 3.5—the age by which a basic grammar has been developed—the distribution of children's parts of speech (percentages of nouns, verbs, and so on) has quickly moved from the heavier use of nouns to a close approximation of the adult distribution.

Learning First Words In early language learning, the child acquires some words in a process akin to conditioning, some in a process similar to rote learning, and some in a process that has much in common with problem solving. Allport (1924) has given the classical description of how *verbal conditioning* may play a role. The mother holds up a doll and at the same time pronounces "doll." The sound "doll" is the unconditioned stimulus that evokes from the child the unconditioned response (imitative response) "doll," or "dah." The sight of the doll is the conditioned stimulus. Upon frequent repetition the sight of the doll alone comes to evoke the word "doll." We might then assume that generalization takes place, that is, that any object visually similar to a doll will also evoke the response "doll," and that soon, perhaps, all

dolls, pictures of dolls, and small children will be called "doll."

Phrases and even sentences can be learned, presumably, via the rote-memory process. The child is not given his toy until he repeats after his mother "please" or "thank you very much." In this way he may learn "by heart" a number of little social formulas. These learned phrases, however, are rarely true sentences. Even if the child occasionally can partially grasp their meanings, we can regard his performance as indicating rote-memorizing ability, not the beginnings of grammar. Children rarely produce spontaneous sentences at this period, and, when they do, they typically consist of two words. Furthermore, as we shall see, children employ a very different grammar. Frequently, when a child does attach meaning to a phrase or sentence, his meaning may have no relation to the meanings that the adult has in mind, as when the hymnal phrase "gladly the cross I'd bear" was learned as "Gladly, the cross-eyed bear."

Opportunities for trial-and-error learning also abound. Our baby who had learned the word "doll" may have done so in the following manner. When he wanted his doll, he may have babbled any number of sounds that appeared to him to be appropriate—until he finally received his toy. Eventually he learned that such-and-such a sound would produce the toy, and the problem "How do I get a doll?" was solved by the acquisition of a specific verbal response. He has truly learned a word because, presumably, he now knows that the sound "doll" signifies a particular object.

Development of Grammar

So far we have brought the child only a little way along the road to adult language competence. At about a year and a half he has a working speech repertoire of about two dozen words, although he can understand many more. He can at times grasp the message of a sentence, but he cannot produce one that is mean-

Box 75

Animal Communication

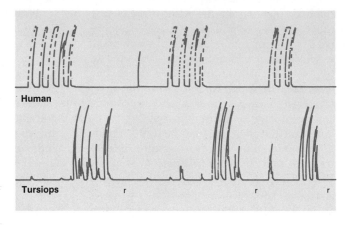

Man, in his occasional concern lest he be challenged as king of species, reserves for himself certain uniquely "human" talents. He claims the use of tools as one such exclusive talent, but this skill is not unknown in other animals (see Box 93, p. 425, and Box 96, p. 430). Man can make a stronger case for language. In the sense that man possesses a well-developed vocabulary of verbal symbols and grammar, this claim certainly brooks no challenge by even the highest primates. Inability to speak does not mean that animals are incapable of genuine communication, however.

Certain communications, like distress cries, occur in a wide variety of species, as we might expect from the obvious adaptive advantage (therefore possible evolutionary basis) such warnings have. Although distress cries differ in detail from animal to animal, they appear to share certain physiognomic characteristics that make them a nearly universal tongue. Even man has little difficulty in sensing the urgency conveyed by such a sound. Intensity, high pitch, a rapid repetitive tempo—all seem to stimulate alertness and to signal threat. But some animals are capable of considerably more complex and differentiated communication.

The honeybee has been credited as surprisingly "articulate," at least in announcing the location of food to its hive mates. We owe this conclusion to the ingenious experiments of an Austrian naturalist, K. von Frisch, who reported that an intricate dance provides a reliable means of communicating complex information. He began with the observation that a honeybee, upon finding a new food source, returned to its hive, and soon many bees flew from the same hive and arrived on the scene.

Von Frisch then found those characteristics of the scout bee's dance that seemed to be related to the actual distance and direction of the food from the hive. When the food was close by (less than fifty yards or so), the dance pattern was a circular one. For greater distances, the dance form was a "figure eight," and in general the more rapid the dance, the farther away was the food source. Even the direction of the food seemed to be conveyed by the dance; the angle of the scout's dance on the vertical face of the hive corresponded to the angular direction of the food source relative to the position of the sun at the time. Recent work by other investigators has determined that the bees may also use the dance to communicate the location of prospective nesting sites. Unfortunately, more recent research by American scientists, Dennis L. Johnson and Adrian M. Wenner of the University of California at Santa Barbara, has cast very grave doubts on those early analyses of von Frisch. As of this writing the significance of the bee's dance is very much up in the air.

A talkative species is the dolphin (*Tursiops truncatus*). Recent research, primarily by J. C. Lilly, has begun to describe the complex vocalization patterns possessed by these relatively large-brained mammals. In line with the dolphin's historic cooperativeness with man (the volume by A. Montagu and J. C. Lilly gives fascinating accounts of this cooperativeness), this animal, in addition to having his own repertoire of vocalizations, apparently has an ability (and willingness) to mimic human speech. Lilly trained his dolphins to do so in the following manner. The experimenter would shout a series of sounds (nonsense vowel-consonant combinations), and, at first, if the dolphin emitted any sounds at all in response, he would be rewarded with food. Gradually and increasingly, only the sounds resembling those made by the experimenter were rewarded. This training continued until there was a significant tendency for the dolphins to reproduce both the numbers and durations of the sounds made by the experimenter.

The figure presents one specimen record of such mimicry. Each vertical spike represents a sound burst, and distance along the horizontal time axis represents the duration of the bursts; food reward occurred at the times indicated by r, noted below the dolphin record. The record shown here is of a twenty-five-second "conversation" and clearly depicts the ability of a dolphin to mimic human "speech" on this occasion. This record is not an exceptional one but reflects on the considerable skill consistently developed in the fully trained dolphin.

We thus have examples of animals communicating with one another in their own "vocabulary" and even examples of their learning to mimic our own. Has man reciprocated? By all means. Beginning with King Solomon's legendary ability to converse with all manner of species, there has been much fable and fact supporting man's urge, if not his overwhelming success in the attempt, to learn to mimic animal "languages." K. Lorenz, a German naturalist, also well known for his work on imprinting (see p. 5), recounts some of his experiences along these lines in an appropriately titled volume, *King Solomon's Ring*. This book provides a charming introduction for those readers who would like to extend the "People to People" program down the evolutionary ladder a step or two.

K. VON FRISCH. 1953. *The Dancing Bees* (New York: Harcourt).

D. L. JOHNSON. 1967. Honey Bees: Do They Use the Direction Information Contained in Their Dance Maneuver? *Science*, 155, 844–7.

A. M. WENNER. 1967. Honey Bees: Do They Use the Distance Information Contained in Their Dance Maneuver? *Science*, 155, 847–9.

A. MONTAGU and J. C. LILLY. 1963. *The Dolphin in History* (Los Angeles: University of California Clark Memorial Library).

J. C. LILLY. 1965. Vocal Mimicry in *Tursiops:* Ability to Match Numbers and Durations of Human Vocal Bursts, *Science*, 147, 300–1. Photo reprinted by permission; copyright 1965 by the American Association for the Advancement of Science.

K. LORENZ. 1952. *King Solomon's Ring* (London: Methuen).

ingful. He has the elements of language but is ignorant of the rules for putting these elements together; in short, he has words, but no grammar. Perhaps the single most important characteristic of language is grammar. It is grammar that differentiates language from communication. Communication without grammar is possible, as we see in animals (Box 75, p. 370), but such communication is not properly called "language." And it is at this age—about eighteen months—that the child stands at the threshold of a two-year period of very rapid learning, during which he will acquire the basic grammar of his native tongue. Perhaps not accidentally, it is also the period of most rapid vocabulary growth; his two dozen words grow to almost 1,500. How does this growth come about?

Grammar acquisition, conditioning theory would assert, comes about through processes no different from those involved in the acquisition of words or of any other conditioned responses. At first the child spontaneously emits a variety of sounds, and, through systematic reinforcement by parents and others of the right (or approximately right) sound or combination of sounds, a word is gradually learned (like learning the word "doll," as we have discussed). More often he will be induced to vocalize something like the right sound by his tendency to imitate adult speech, and his more correct imitations will be rewarded. Certain combinations of words (phrases, sentences) can be learned in a similar fashion. Proper voice intonations can also be acquired in this manner. The child learns to say "give me the doll" when he wants the doll—and "no, no, doll" when he no longer wants it—by gradually building up these verbal responses, each to accompany the correct situation. Discrimination learning is the primary feature of the process, and language is increasingly "shaped" toward its adult form through selective reinforcement.

Chomsky (1959), among others, has been particularly searching in his analysis of the shortcomings of a conditioning model to explain the learning of language. We cannot review here the details of the debate, which is still raging, but perhaps we can briefly convey, by a few examples, the flavor of the criticisms that have been leveled. First, perhaps, is the puzzling fact that near-adult language competence can be acquired in so short a time. There are simply too many ways in which words can be combined to make meaningful sentences for each combination to be learned in a traditional conditioned-response manner. For example, Miller (1965) gives a conservative estimate of the number of possible twenty-word sentences in the English language: The figure is 10^{20} (a "10" followed by nineteen zeroes). It would take, he further estimates, about 1,000 times the estimated age of the earth just to *listen* to all these sentences. There are many possible rejoinders to this dramatized argument, but none can handle the essential criticism, which is that the child cannot possibly learn separately each of the sentences he becomes capable of producing.

Another fact that is awkward for traditional learning theories is that children's earliest grammatical constructions are not crude approximations of adult sentences. Recordings of young children's spontaneous speech disclose numerous instances of phrases and sentences that could not possibly represent imitations, however crude, of adult speech. A child of about two will say things like "allgone doggit" or, in a verbose moment, "me want car go." Whatever the length of the sentence produced, clearly a qualitatively different grammar is involved. Imitation of, and reinforcement by, the adult cannot account for it.

There is also evidence that language can be learned in the absence of any produced speech, spontaneous or imitative. Lenneberg (1962) reports the case of a boy who, for physical reasons, had never been able to speak yet showed quite adequate comprehension of the complexities of the English language. In short, his understanding of language could not have derived from reinforcement because he never exhibited external responses that could be selectively reinforced and shaped. Without belaboring the point, some things seem to be missing in a conditioned-response explanation of language development—an alternative explanation seems to be required.

Grammar Acquisition as Problem Solving

The essence of this alternative approach is that, at about eighteen months, the child seems to take on actively the language of his native culture as a problem to be solved. At approximately eighteen months a child's physical development (he has learned to walk pretty well) and his mental development have progressed to a point at which the ability to communicate more efficiently with the speaking world becomes essential. Just knowing the names of things no longer suffices for effective communication and adaption. He now needs to understand more.

How does he approach this problem? The story is far from complete, but the broad outlines seem clear enough. The suggested explanation for the child's (and the adult's) ability to understand and produce utterly novel sentences is that, because the child cannot possibly learn each of the sentences he seems capable of comprehending, he must develop some *general* rules that enable him to decipher novel sentences and to construct new ones.

Such rules of construction (grammar) certainly exist in any adult language, as those who have struggled with learning the grammar rules of their own or other languages will attest. But the observation that one can speak perfectly good English without consciously "knowing" its grammar suggests that linguistic rules are acquired and operate *implicitly* rather than explicitly. None of us invokes such rules each time we construct a brand-new sentence; rather, a grammatically correct sentence just "happens." The contrast between the efficiency and reliability of this typical process and the tedious construction of a correct sentence

in a newly learned foreign language is enormous. In the latter case we must consciously apply explicitly learned rules; in the former, such rules seem "instinctive."

Does the child go about learning his native language in much the same way that an adult learns a foreign language—first learning and consciously applying its grammatical rules and gradually, through practice, becoming able to apply them automatically? Apparently not. He seems to start out with grammar of his own invention. This grammar may represent his hypotheses to account for the puzzle of language. As he applies his rules in attempting to communicate with the real world, he acquires information as to their adequacy, revises his hypotheses and develops new ones, and eventually comes up with adult grammar.

We owe the discovery that these early grammars are *qualitatively* different from adult grammar to a new application of a traditional technique from the science of linguistics. This technique is to infer the grammar of a language through analysis of many examples of its sentences. By assuming that children's early speech might be a true "foreign" language, with rules of its own, rather than just an imperfect copy of adult language, psycholinguists have been able to construct systematic grammars for child language. Data for these studies are usually obtained longitudinally, that is, from the same group of children observed for short periods on a number of occasions, usually during a phase of rapid language development. Everything the child says (and that is said to him) on each occasion is tape-recorded, and transcriptions of these voluminous complete records provide the raw material from which grammatical rules—and changes in these rules over time—are inferred.

Brown and Fraser (1964) provide a fascinating and detailed account of one such expedition into the alien land of child language, and McNeill (1966) summarizes the results from several others. Only a few selective findings from this body of research can be presented here.

Early child speech contains many two-word sentences, like *make go, two car,* and *want eat*. As in a telegram, "unnecessary" words like articles and prepositions are omitted. But, in contrast with telegrams, such sentences are often (by adult standards) ungrammatical. There is a grammar, however, although a simple one. Linguistic analysis can demonstrate that these two-word sentences are not random combinations of the few words the child knows but follow certain systematic rules. McNeill (1966) discusses two such rules that have been found to operate consistently in early speech records.

The two grammatical rules for two-word sentence construction are based upon a distinction between what are known as Class I ("pivot") and Class II ("open") words. Table 24.1. presents some Class I and Class II words

Table 24.1
Speech of the Two-Year-Old

CLASS I

a   that   allgone   my   byebye   big   two   see   hi dirty   more   pretty

CLASS II

other   come   hot   shoe   baby   mommy   daddy   milk plane   dolly   pretty

Class I ("pivot") and Class II ("open") words adapted from McNeill's (1966) discussion of sentence structure in the earliest grammars. The original data were taken from speech records of two-year-old children. Generally speaking, a sentence can be formed by combining any two words, one from each list or both from Class II (see text for more detail).

found in the speech of a "typical" two-year-old child—a composite constructed from actual speech records obtained in a number of studies. As these classes do not correspond to any standard English classifications, they are best appreciated by reading over the words listed in each class and the discussion that follows. The two rules of sentence construction are as follows: First, a sentence may be constructed by combining a Class I word and a Class II word; second, a sentence may be constructed

by combining two Class II words. A child's speech consists of sentences constructed according to the first rule. Although Class II words frequently occur alone as single-word utterances, Class I words rarely do at this stage. The heterogeneity of Class I words from the point of view of adult grammar is readily apparent in Table 24.1. Articles, pronouns, verbs, adjectives, and adverbs are all represented. Class II consists primarily of nouns, but other parts of speech do occur. The adjective "pretty" is in both lists, but keep in mind that this listing does not come from a single child. In actuality, a given word for a given child is in one class or the other, not in both.

These limited examples illustrate the primitive but systematic beginnings of a grammar from which children progress quite rapidly. Much is being learned from analysis of children's speech records as to the typical course followed by the child as his early grammar evolves into adult grammar during the two-year period. We cannot present these findings in detail here, but we shall say a little about the factors contributing to this process.

For one thing, children seem to enjoy practicing their language skills, playing with words and sentences even while alone. Such play can contribute to language learning, for there is evidence that it is systematic. Weir (1962) reports in her book, *Language in the Crib*, that the monologues of her two-and-a-half-year-old son, overheard before he dropped off to sleep, often exhibited a clear pattern. In one instance, he took a single Class I word ("go") and constructed a series of sentences according to the first rule and using different Class II words: "go for glasses," "go for them," "go to the top," "go throw," and so forth.

Practice is unable by itself, of course, to account for *changes* in the child's grammar. Grammar development is facilitated by tutelage from the parent. Thus Slobin (1967) noted from speech records he had collected that parents repeat their children's utterances quite frequently (as much as 30 per cent of a child's speech is repeated). These repetitions, however, are not faithful reproductions of what the children have said. Rather, parents rephrase what the child has said, retaining the message but putting it into correct grammatical form. Slobin's point is that these "expansions" of children's speech, as they are called, may play a role in language development because the child frequently can and does imitate these expan-

sions, although by no means always correctly. Nevertheless, when the imitation is correct, it has the potential to contribute to grammatical development (for a further development of this view, see Box 76).

We shall leave our "average child" at this point in his language development and jump ahead to an analysis of the adult language to which he aspires. He is not yet four years old,

Box 76

How to Talk Small and
Influence Development

Courtney B. Cazden at Harvard (1965) compared the relative effectiveness of the "expanding" versus the "enlarging" techniques for accelerating language development. With one group of children she spent forty minutes daily for three months (starting at age 2.5) *expanding* every sentence spoken by the child during the entire period. In another group the number and duration of daily conversations were the same, but, instead of expanding upon each of the child's remarks, she replied with a comment that *enlarged* upon what the child said but did not (as in the case of expansion) repeat any part of his sentence. An example is needed to clarify the different treatment accorded these two groups: A child says, "baby hungry." Cazden, to an expansion-group child, might reply, "The baby is hungry," supplying the grammatically missing ingredients. In the second group, however, her response might be "Yes, he wants to eat." The children in both groups were given a language-ability test at the beginning and at the end of the three-month experimental period, and the degree of their improvement was compared with that shown by a control group of children of the same age who had no special treatment and whose advancement over the three months therefore reflected normal development during this period.

The results, briefly put, were that the "expanded" group did show slightly greater advancement than did the control group. The second "enlarged" group, however, improved considerably more. Apparently, expanding children's speech and thus providing them with the opportunity to imitate expansions does bring about some progress, as D. I. Slobin has suggested. But, somehow, more advantage was to be had from the greater variety and richness of the remarks accorded the second group, even though it had been denied the opportunity to profit from imitating grammatically correct adult expansions of speech. The reason for this outcome is not clear. Members of the second group may have had a greater chance to think about the meanings of what they said and had the benefit of a linguistically richer experience. And, because all children in this experiment had been drawn from culturally disadvantaged homes where conversations with adults were surprisingly rare, even this limited amount of extra verbal stimulation might have set off a general acceleration in language development.

C. B. CAZDEN. 1965. Environmental Assistance to the Child's Acquisition of Grammar. Ph.D. dissertation, Harvard University.

has already mastered the rudiments of adult grammar, and possesses a workable vocabulary. He is yet to learn many more words, his vocabulary will increase at least twentyfold by the time he is adult, and his speech will become increasingly complex in its grammatical construction. And he has still before him the task of learning to read and write. But we know that he is safely started on the road to achieving competence in adult language, and at the end of that road we shall revisit him.

The Structure of Adult Language

As we have seen, knowing the words of a language is not the same as knowing the language; we must know how the words are put together. One way of studying this problem is to analyze the grammar of the language, as grammar specifies how words are supposed to go together in any language. This approach is used by the linguist and the grammarian. Another approach is to analyze language as it naturally occurs in order to infer some regularities in its normal usage beyond those constraints imposed by its formal grammar. This latter approach characterizes much of the work of the psycholinguist.

The Frequency Count

A great deal of the psychologist's work in language and communication makes use of the statistical approach. Here the question is, What words and sequences are most frequently spoken? Once we know what words and word sequences do appear most frequently, we are in a better position to understand the functional rules of sentence construction.

The most comprehensive dictionaries of modern English reveal a total vocabulary of well over a million words. The supply of English words is so generous that we could talk away for weeks before we would *have* to use the same word a second time. But statistical counts of word usage indicate that we do repeat ourselves—and at an astonishingly great rate. On the average, we repeat a word every ten to fifteen words. The fifty most commonly used words make up about 60 per cent of all the words we speak and 45 per cent of all the words we write. This repetitious use of a very few words (arranged and rearranged in a large number of patterns) to express an infinite number of ideas is characteristic of most languages. Here we have a striking demonstration of the importance of patterning in language.

Why should we be so niggardly in our use of words? Several answers can be immediately suggested. First, a good number of the words (according to estimates, as many as three-quarters of all of our words) have very limited usefulness because they are the specialized words of the sciences, technology, and trade jargons. Second, most of us know only a very small portion of even the general words; we simply have not learned all the words of our language. The average adult is said to have a use-and-recognition vocabulary of 30,000–60,000 words, and a highly literate adult is not likely to go much beyond 100,000. But our word usage is not limited by the size of our vocabulary alone. It is also limited by *syntax* and a *verbal-context effect*. That is, once we have spoken one word, the next word is to some degree determined or restricted by the rules of grammar and by the meaning, rhythm, or sound of the previous word.

Verbal Context and Frequency Count

A fairly precise quantitative measurement of one of the constraints upon our language has been developed by analyzing the sequence of letters constituting printed English. Letters, even more than words, occur with differential frequencies; for example, the letter "e" appears much more frequently than do any of the remaining twenty-five letters of the alphabet. The letters in one part of a sequence limit the possibilities and influence the probabilities of the appearance of another letter in a later part of the sequence. For example, once we have writ-

Box 78

Long-Rang
Verbal Con

N. G. Burt
English m
into accou
entation, a
might be

They us
100 passag
10,000 lette
tinued gue

Ten gr
menters w

From t
was deter
suffice it t
of upper
imposed
about thi
predicting
to make
Because
influences
what has

N. G. BURTO
J. Psychol.

Box 77

53‡‡†305))6*;4826)4‡.)4‡);806*;48†8
¶60))85;1‡(;:‡*8†83(88)5*†;46(;88*9
6*?;8)*‡(;485);5*†2:*‡(;4956*2(5*
—4)8¶8*;4069285);)6†8)4‡‡;1(‡9;4
8081;8:8‡1;48†85;4)485†528806*8
1(‡9;48;(88;4(‡?34;48)4‡;161;:188;‡?;

Edgar Allan Poe's short story "The Gold Bug" makes romantic use of the systematic patterning of letter sequences in language.

Poe's hero, Legrand, while rummaging around Sullivan's Island, finds an old piece of parchment, which he uses to wrap up the "gold bug"—a curious beetle that has attracted his fancy. Later, in his cabin, he discovers that on this parchment, "rudely traced, in a red tint," are the characters reproduced above. For Legrand this message is an easy one to decode.

"My first step [he smugly explains to the obligingly bewildered narrator of the story] was to ascertain the predominant letters, as well as the least frequent. . . . Now in English, the letter which most frequently occurs is *e* . . . *e* predominates so remarkably, that an individual sentence of any length is rarely seen, in which it is not the prevailing character. . . . As our predominant character is 8, we will commence by assuming it as the *e*. . . . Now of all *words* in the language 'the' is most usual; let us see therefore, whether there are not repetitions of any three characters, in the same order of collocation, the last of them being 8. . . . Upon inspection, we find no less than seven such arrangements, the characters being ; 4 8. We may therefore assume that ; represents *t*, 4 represents *h*, and 8 represents *e*—the last being now well confirmed. Thus a great step has been taken."

From this first "great step," the rest follows easily, and within two more pages of Poe's story Legrand has the solution:

"A good glass in the bishop's hostel in the devil's seat—forty-one degrees and thirteen minutes —northeast and by north—main branch seventh limb east side—shoot from the left eye of the death's head—a bee-line from the tree through the shot fifty feet out."

And thus, because all who would use language must operate within the structured confines of language patterns, William Legrand could easily understand the dead Captain Kidd's message; a buried treasure chest, "filled to the brim," was the reward.

Elementary, my dear Watson, elementary!

---

ten the letter "q," it must almost invariably be followed by the letter "u"; once we have written the two letters "th," the third letter can be one of only eight or nine letters (see Box 77).

Presumably one could discover the frequencies of different letter sequences in the English language by taking large samples of printed English and tabulating all the different letter sequences. We can thus count the number of times the following (and every other conceivable sequence) occurs: "th," "tha," "the," "thi," "tho," "thr," "ah," "aha," "aho." From such a count, we could then estimate the constraining influence of, say, "th" upon the third letter.

Tha
pro
con

plex
so
"ma
skil
"kn
a l
upo
in l
cal
late
ope
kno
a s
me
fer
gue
sul
un
the
rec
deg
of
let
pei
gue
aga
dif
wo
in
let
mi
en
ele
an
"g
fle
ta

Re
fii
el
ne

Box 79

Information, Freedom of Choice,
and Perception of Speech

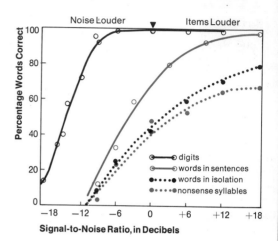

G. A. Miller, G. A. Heise, and W. Lichten at Harvard University sought an answer to the question of why a word is heard correctly in one context and incorrectly in another when perceptual conditions are difficult.

Digits, nonsense syllables, words (in random order), and sentences (consisting of the same words connected by "of"s, "the"s, and so on to make meaningful statements) were spoken against noisy backgrounds varying in intensity. Each item was heard with the background noise sometimes louder and sometimes softer than the item by 18, 12, and 6 decibels.

The results indicate that intelligibility is highest for digits and lowest for nonsense syllables and that a word is harder to understand when it is heard in isolation than when it is heard in a sentence. The experimenters explain these results as follows. All the digits, with the exception of "five" and "nine," have *different* vowels. As *the alternatives are thus limited*, the digits can be interpreted correctly on the basis of a "marginal impression" of the vowel sound alone. With nonsense syllables a listener must perceive *each* sound correctly; one sound does not give a clue to the other sounds in the same syllable. The difference between words in a sentence and scrambled words can be similarly understood. When "apples grow on ——" is heard, the range of possible continuations is sharply restricted, and again the slightest impression of the fourth word is enough to permit a good guess.

Most words consist of several sounds. Each sound can be considered as one bit of "information." The preceding data are summarized as follows: The amount of information necessary for the correct perception of a word depends upon the range of alternative possibilities (the listener's freedom of choice). As the range of alternatives increases, the amount of information necessary per word also increases, and so the noise level must be decreased to permit the correct perception of the whole word.

G. A. MILLER, G. A. HEISE, and W. LICHTEN. 1951. The Intelligibility of Speech as a Function of the Context of Test Material. *J. Exper. Psychol.*, 41, 329–35. Figure adapted by permission of American Psychological Association.

in meaningful language is that the missing word is more easily predicted when the additional "context" words *surround* the gap than when the same number of words precede it. "I am going to put some ——" is less likely to be properly completed than "to put some —— on my egg," yet both phrases have provided contexts of six words.

There is an impressive correspondence in normal speech between the lack of redundancy of a word and the tendency to hesitate and then place emphasis on that word. It is as if the speaker also had to solve a more complex problem when he has to select a less predictable word. And, because it is less predictable, by emphasizing it he may be warning the listener to pay attention. In fact, the length of the pause before words in normal speech in one group of subjects significantly correlates with the time it takes other subjects to supply those same words when they are represented as gaps to be filled in (Goldman-Eisler, 1964).

Redundancy in language is obviously of great help. Although a redundant language may be inefficient in that it uses more symbols than are absolutely necessary, it is efficient in that it decreases the probability of error in perception. Speech is almost always heard under unfavorable conditions such as noise, competing stimuli, or inattention. If there were zero redundancy in language, no amount of surrounding letters or words could tell us anything about the unperceived letter or word. In order to comprehend speech under those circumstances, we would have to perceive *every sound and every word accurately*. This necessity would make of speech a highly inadequate communication system (see experiment in Box 79, p. 380).

Perception of Speech   Almost every generalization about the production of speech also holds for the perception of speech. Just as the skillful speaker must be able to produce systematically patterned sounds, he must also be able to perceive patterns of sounds; and, just as learning

the meanings of words shares many aspects of problem solving, so does hearing words.

Much of the work on the perception of speech has been done by engineers at Bell Telephone Laboratories, who are primarily interested in determining the adequacies of their communication devices. Among their techniques is that of changing or distorting speech sounds to determine the intelligibility of speech under difficult conditions of transmission. Let us give some illustrative findings:

1. Wide changes in the intensity of speech have little effect on perception. Therefore, as the intensity is raised from about 50 decibels to 140, no significant change in intelligibility of spoken words occurs (see Figure 24.1.).

2. Wide changes in the "spectrum" of speech sounds can be tolerated without any significant loss in understanding. The *speech spectrum* refers to the range of different sound frequencies and amplitudes that are found in ordinary

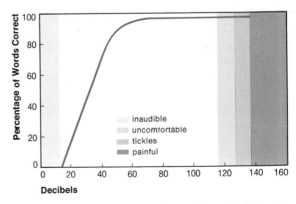

Figure 24.1. The curve shows the relationship between the percentage of English monosyllabic words that can be recorded correctly and the intensity of the speech at the listener's ear. Changes in intensity of almost 100 decibels do not change a listener's ability to hear correctly, even though the intensity may reach the stage at which it is actually painful. Over the range of 50 to 140 decibels, therefore, intensity does not seem to be a crucial determinant of intelligibility of speech.
G. A. Miller, *Language and Comunication;* Copyright 1951 by McGraw-Hill Book Company, Inc.; adapted by permission.

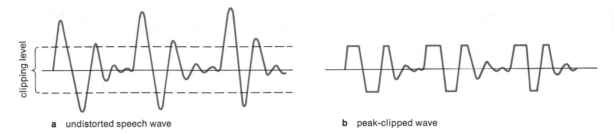

a undistorted speech wave   **b** peak-clipped wave

Figure 24.2. Distortion of speech wave by amplitude selectivity. The usual wave form (Figure a) is clipped electronically along the dotted lines so that only the center portion of each wave (Figure b) reaches the listener's ears. Such "peak clipping" has practically no effect on intelligibility. The clipped wave will be just as intelligible to the listener as will the undistorted wave.
G. A. Miller, *Language and Communication;* Copyright 1951 by McGraw-Hill Book Company, Inc.; adapted by permission.

speech sounds. Male voices, speaking at a conversational level, can range in frequency from 100 cycles per second to about 8,000 cycles and in intensity from about 20 to 120 decibels. By the use of appropriate instrumentation, the normal spectrum can be radically altered. Recorded speech may thus be passed through a transmission system that will "clip off" all the upper or all the lower frequencies and pass on only the remaining sounds. What happens when we mutilate normal speech sounds in this way? The data indicate that with meaningful words perception is still adequate, even if we hear only the frequencies above 1,900 c.p.s., or only the frequencies below 1,900 c.p.s. We not only can clip off certain frequencies but also can do the same for amplitude, so that only the loud or only the soft components of the normal spectrum are heard. Again, violent distortions have remarkably little effect on the intelligibility of such speech (see Figure 24.2.).

3. Another type of distortion of the normal speech pattern is produced by intermittent interruptions. By the use of telephonic equipment we can arrange a situation in which the recorded speech is interrupted, say, ten times every second, so that, out of a speech sequence that lasts ten minutes, the sound is actually on for only five of those minutes. Yet, under these conditions, the listener's ability to understand is not impaired (Miller & Licklider, 1950).

The significance of these experiments is this: The sound waves produced by spoken speech may undergo extensive changes in many of their characteristics—frequency, amplitude, harmonies, duration—but a careful physical analysis of what is left indicates that the essential pattern of the total sound wave remains constant. As long as a specific organization is maintained, we can understand what the sound waves are saying. This dependence upon patterning reflects in part the general biological tendency to organize discrete stimuli in perception, but in part it also reflects a long and complex skill-training process.

Perception of Speech as Problem Solving   We are bound by grammatical and sense-making rules in producing speech, and we are helped by these rules in perceiving speech. As we have seen in the experiment described in Box 79, p. 380 verbal context plays an exceedingly important role in the very perception of sounds and words. Miller (1951), in discussing such experiments, couches his description of the perception of speech almost entirely in terms of intelligent problem solving and ties together much of what we have been saying.

"If enough of the discourse is perceived to reveal the basic pattern of the sentence, the range of possible words that can be substituted into the pattern is greatly decreased. Thus the probability of a correct guess is increased. For example, in the sentence 'He threw the —— out the window,' we can immediately reject all parts of speech except nouns. Then we can reject all the nouns that are associated with unthrowable objects. Then we can give preference to certain things that people are known to throw— balls, rocks, bombs, etc. So we get down to a rather small number of possibilities. . . . Because the elimination of unlikely possibilities occurs so quickly and so automatically, it is difficult to imagine how the process takes place. The nature of the situation somehow influences what a listener expects, and from this relatively narrow range of expected events he chooses one that seems to him the most probable."

This quotation sets the stage for us to return to our discussion of thinking and problem solving. Although we have learned something of the ways in which thinking and problem solving contribute to a child's development of adult language skills, we have not yet asked how the ability to think and reason itself develops in the child.

Glossary

developmental psycholinguistics Refers to the psychological study of the development of language, treating child language as a "true" language with its own systematic rules (for example, grammar).

redundancy in language Refers to the fact that certain letters and words, occurring in certain contexts, carry varying degrees of new information. A word with 100 per cent redundancy contributes no information; a word with zero redundancy contributes completely new information.

speech spectrum The range of sound frequencies and sound amplitudes in speech.

"syllabic babbling" stage The stage in the infant's development of speech when certain combinations of sounds are typically repeated over and over again in different pitches and with different volumes.

syntax The rules of serial ordering of words in a language (sentence structure).

verbal conditioning Refers to a special instance of conditioning in which the conditioned response is a word or a combination of sounds.

verbal-context effect The effect of preceding words or letters on the probability of appearance of a given word or letter. If the preceding words or letters completely determine what the next letter will be, we speak of a large verbal-context effect.

development
of thinking

overview / Our understanding of the development of thinking owes much to the work of Piaget. His primary general developmental principles are organization (increasing integration of simple systems into more complex ones); equilibration (the driving force behind this continuous integration process); adaptation, which subsumes the processes of assimilation (taking in from the environment whatever can be effectively incorporated); and accommodation (adapting the existing internal mental organization so that hitherto unassimilable stimuli can be assimilated). These general developmental principles are used by Piaget as guides to the understanding of the progressive development of the child's knowledge of the world and his ability to deal effectively with it. And in Piaget's system, the operative or key words are "progressive development"—continuous, systematic, predictable mental growth.

For Piaget, cognitive development can be viewed as a series of sequential stages, the broadest of which are the sensorimotor stage (little more than the exercise and gradual integration of inborn reflexes and evolving the notion of a stable object), the stage of concrete operations (the beginnings of the capacity for symbolic thought and the development of language, and of such principles as conservation), and—finally—the stage of formal operations in which the adult capacity for abstract thinking finally emerges.

Broadly speaking, these stages follow one another in an invariable sequence and appear to be achieved, roughly speaking, at about the same ages in all children. Substantial individual differences in the timing of mental development occur with given societies, however, and certainly among different societies. Furthermore, explicit training can accelerate mental development, at least up to a point.

Other theories of cognitive development depart from Piaget's views in a number of ways, particularly with regard to the role of education and experience.

From the beginnings of man's recorded history philosophers have speculated on the nature of thought, or of the "mind," at birth. Some, like John Locke, have regarded the newborn's mind as totally blank, a *tabula rasa* (blank tablet) ready to be written upon by life's experiences. Others, like Plato, regarded certain "ideas" as universally given, so that thinking could be regarded as developing from innately common origins.

Jean Piaget, almost fifty years ago, undertook through careful experimentation and observation to seek understanding of a number of facets of the mental development of the child. Thinking was only one of these facets; he also studied developmental processes in perception, language, intelligence, even the emergence of children's concepts of causality and morality. Much of his early data came from observations of his own children, observations both of their spontaneous behavior and of their response to ingenious little "experiments." These data and subsequent more systematic experimentation led Piaget to the formulation of a number of principles that could apply to the broad range of developmental processes with which he was concerned.

Piaget's General Principles

At the heart of Piaget's theory of human cognitive development lies his insistence that mental growth (or cognitive development) is the inevitable outcome of the infant's interaction with his physical world. But what determines what an infant does, and why does he act at all? By what means do his actions and their effects upon the environment and upon his organism bring about a progressive development in the child's knowledge of the world and in his ability to deal effectively and intelligently with it? Piaget's general developmental principles—organization, equilibration, and adaptation—embody his attempts at answering these questions.

Organization, Equilibration, and Adaptation

Roughly speaking, *organization* refers to Piaget's belief that the elements of mental life (he calls them *schemata*) become increasingly interrelated with one another into larger systems or totalities, which themselves represent new and more complex schemata.

But what is the driving force for this process of ever more complex cognitive organization? Piaget postulates that mental structures, or schemata, are intrinsically "motivated" to function at a higher level—a tendency that he calls *equilibration.* Piaget seems to be saying that we are constantly driven to do what we can do (what we already have a schema for doing) but that, each time we act, we strive in some way to *increase* the adaptiveness and complexity of our behavior and schemata. Equilibration seems to represent Piaget's sole theory of motivation, and it goes far beyond motivational theories that regard all behavior as attributable, directly or indirectly, to the familiar bodily needs. There is a direct parallel in this view with recent reformulations of motivational theory that propose, for example, that curiosity is not a derivative of physiological survival needs but represents a motive in its own right—a need to explore, examine, manipulate—in short, a need to know.

Piaget describes the continuing exchange between organism and environment as *adaptation,* a general term implying that such exchanges result in a progressive growth in the complexity of mental structures, making them more able to cope effectively with environmental demands. He postulates two complementary concepts, which specify how adaptation occurs. These concepts are *assimilation* and *accommodation.*

The concept of assimilation proposes that any organism has a tendency to take in from the external world only those things that it can incorporate effectively. We have certain bodily structures and functions that enable us to digest certain foods, and it is these foods that are sought and assimilated. By the same token, Piaget asserts, existing structures, or schemata, take in those aspects of environmental stimulation that they are able to handle. In other words, food for thought is also selected, chosen to be digestible by the current level of development of the mental apparatus. Practically, this selection means that an infant (or child or adult) tends to perceive only that portion of the world that he can make sense of in terms of what he already knows, although some distortion may result from squeezing the new information into the not-quite-right existing mold. He will also tend to respond only to situations with which he is familiar and for which old responses are more or less adequate. Obviously, assimilation is a conservative principle that attempts to maintain a mental *status quo*. Were this the sole adaptive mechanism, existing schemata could not change and mental organization could not become more complex. Something else is clearly required.

That something else Piaget calls *accommodation*. It is the complement of assimilation in the sense that, when new stimuli are not assimilated to existing schemata yet are too insistent to be ignored, accommodation takes over. Quite simply, accommodation means that new schemata are formed, or old ones are modified or brought together, to create more complex new organizations.

All these concepts, taken together, tell us that in the development of mental life there is "a continuous creation of increasing complex forms and a progressive adaptation of these forms to the environment." In everyday terms, the theory claims to account for the indisputable fact that normal mental development, at any point along its course, represents a continual striving to grow in our understanding of the world about us. Typically, what we try to understand is not the totally new but rather the almost understood that lies at the boundaries of our present comprehension.

Given this tendency for man's mental grasp to exceed—but only ever so slightly—his mental reach, we would expect that mental development would proceed bit by bit along a smooth and continuous course. Not so, says Piaget. Instead, he suggests, there are three major stages in development, and each stage represents a discrete and qualitative step upward from the preceding one. And it is in the framework of these stages that Piaget presents theoretical descriptions of cognitive development from birth to intellectual maturity.

Piaget's Stages of Cognitive Development

Piaget's general principles apply to all three stages, although the specifics of their operation necessarily vary from stage to stage. He further asserts that the stages are invariable in the *order* of their occurrence for all children, although the ages at which they are achieved may vary considerably from individual to individual. In this respect the age range that we shall cite for each stage has been assigned by Piaget and others to serve as rough boundaries, not as absolute limits. Furthermore, the stages are said to be hierarchical; that is, each successive stage requires and incorporates the mental organization of the immediately preceding stage. We shall not debate any of these assertions now, but we shall keep them in mind throughout the discussion that follows. In our account of Piaget's three development stages, we shall not discuss the many substages (six in the first major stage alone) detectable within each

Stage 1: Sensorimotor

The first stage—the *sensorimotor stage*—extends from birth to roughly two years of age. In the beginning, according to Piaget, mental organization consists only of some inborn reflex responses. Underlying these responses are the simplest of schemata, isolated from one another. The newborn thus has a separate schema that triggers a sucking response when the bottle is put to his lips and one that sets off a grasping reflex when his hand encounters the bottle. For a time, a month or so, the exercise of these simple reflexes is apparently all there is to cognitive development. Then these separate schemata begin to come together. The infant first sees, then grasps, then sucks at the bottle. He can now orient to impinging stimuli, for example, turning toward the source of a sudden sound or bright light. There is, however, some evidence that such orienting responses may be present even at birth. Wertheimer (1961), working with what were perhaps history's youngest human subjects for a behavioral experiment, reported that an infant, only ten minutes after delivery, showed eye movements that followed a sound source varying in location.

Gradually, the infant, who at first is at the mercy of environmental stimulation, moves on to initiate his own behavior. He begins to practice responses that lead to "interesting" outcomes, batting at a rattle or kicking off his covers. The concept of a unified object or "thing" begins to emerge, as the initially separate looks, feels, sounds, and tastes of the object fuse into a single organization (see Box 80, p. 389).

When an object is first achieved, it has an ephemeral life; it ceases to exist when it is no longer perceived. A dropped toy is simply gone. But then, toward the end of the first year, the object becomes a "permanent" one, and the infant will actively search for it. Active experimentation with objects increases, and the infant delights in manipulating new things and causing things to happen in his world. The parent who has picked up the teddy bear for the seventeenth time and returned it to the crib, only to see it launched on yet another flight, will testify to the energy and persistence of such an activity. By a year and a half or so, the child appears to have acquired the capacity to think about things, even when they are not present, and to create new uses of objects—in short,

in some small sense, he seems to have become inventive, creative, and imaginative.

The amount and variety of development that take place within this first stage make it clear that infants are not simply "little people" who see the world in much the same way we do. The notion that the mental life of the infant is *qualitatively* different from ours is hard to believe because we can no longer imagine a world that is comprised, for example, not of tangible, permanent objects but of transient, disconnected experiences. The infant is incapable of many kinds of mental processes that are accessible to even the least intelligent adults. These qualitative lacks continue to persist, as we shall see, for many years, so that not until adolescence can the normal child think as does a normal adult. The implications of this general fact for theories of cognitive development and of educational technique are considerable. The implications for parenthood are equally numerous and perhaps more obvious.

Stage 2: Concrete Operations

The second stage—the stage of *concrete operations*—extends from about two to eleven years. This period is regarded by Piaget as one in which the transition is made between the extreme literalness of perception still evident in the child at the close of the sensorimotor period and a well-developed ability for abstract thinking, which characterizes the third stage.

At about the age of two the child begins to show his first symbolic activity. Whereas before objects were what they were and nothing more, now he can enjoy "make-believe" play. The crib becomes a rowboat, but woe to him who thinks that imagination implies confusion. Join the child in his game and praise the seaworthiness of his vessel. Overdo this and you will be firmly corrected. "A bed is not a boat," you may be told.

Language, a very important symbolic activity, also has its most rapid development during

Box 80

Piaget Infers
Infantile Schemata

What can be the basis of Jean Piaget's detailed hypotheses concerning the mental life of an infant, who, after all, seems to do little more than sleep and thrash around? The basis is the same as for all psychological study—the observation of behavior. The two verbatim records in this box deal with sequences of behavior from which Piaget inferred the coordination of two schemata. In the first, Piaget describes how a manual schema was assimilated into a visual one. We are shown how, within a period of twenty days, the infant progresses from a stage in which looking at his hand and moving his hand are independent to a stage in which seeing his hand enables him to control its movement.

"At age two months and four days, Laurent [Piaget's son] by chance discovers his right index finger and looks at it briefly. At two months and 11 days, he inspects for a moment his right hand, perceived by chance. At two months 14 days, he looks three times in succession at his left hand and chiefly at his raised index finger. At two months 17 days, he follows the spontaneous movement of his hand for a moment, and then he examines it several times while it searches for his nose or rubs his eye. At two months 19 days, he smiles at the same hand after having contemplated it 11 times in succession. I then put his hand in a bandage; as soon as I detach it (half an hour later) it returns to the visual field and Laurent again smiles at it. The same day he looks very attentively at his two clasped hands. At age two months and 21 days, he holds his two fists in the air and looks at the left one, after which he slowly brings it towards his face and rubs his nose with it, and then his eyes. A moment later the left hand again approaches his face, he looks at it and touches his nose. He recommences and laughs five or six times in succession while moving the left hand to his nose. He seems to laugh before the hand moves, but looking has no influence on the movement. Age two months and 24 days: at last looking acts on the orientation of the hands which tend to remain in the visual field."

In the next record, Piaget describes how his daughter progresses to the point at which a hearing schema is absorbed into a visual one.

"At age one month, Jacqueline still limits herself to interrupting her crying when she hears an agreeable voice or sound, but she does not try to mark the sound. At one month 6 days, same reaction. At one month 10 days, on the other hand, Jacqueline begins to smile at the voice. . . . At two months 12 days, Jacqueline turns her head to the side whence the sound comes. For example, on hearing my voice behind her, she turns in the right direction. At two months 26 days, she localizes the source of sound quite accurately with her glance. She searches until she finds the person who is speaking, but it is difficult to say whether she identifies the source of the sound or whether this is simply accommodation to the sound."

J. PIAGET. 1952. *The Origins of Intelligence in Children*, trans. Margaret Cook (New York: International Universities Press). Originally published 1936. Text material reprinted by permission.

the early years of this stage. Words come to stand for things, and action can sometimes be replaced by thought. But although the child is learning to "play with" his environment and to achieve considerable mastery of his world, his view of reality is highly egocentric. He stands at the hub of his experiences and can understand them only in reference to himself. For example, experiments have shown that a child of five or six is incapable of describing how a scene (say, a model of a village) would look if viewed from any other angle than his own current visual perspective. Indeed, he cannot conceive that the scene *can* look any different from what it obviously *is*.

Somewhat similar is the phenomenon that Piaget calls "centering," the tendency of the young child to center, or focus upon, only a single aspect or quality of a situation. This tendency is illustrated perhaps most clearly in the young child's failure to master the principle of invariance or *conservation*. Because the child centers upon a particular characteristic of an object, say its shape, he fails to realize that other characteristics of the same object, for example weight, can remain invariant despite highly visible but actually irrelevant changes in shape. For example, the young child does not realize that a certain mass of clay will weigh the same though it be rolled into a ball, elongated into a sausage, or squashed flat as a pancake.

Beginning at about age seven, the child begins to master the principle of conservation. That is, he comes to understand that a certain property of an object does not change despite changes in other perceivable features. Mastering the concept of conservation in its various manifestations (quantity, weight, volume, number, and so on) is, in Piaget's theory, a set of cognitive abilities to be attained within the latter part of the period of concrete operations. This notion of conservation is first grasped with regard to matter. A year or so later, conservation of weight becomes understood. Finally, conservation of volume is achieved (Box 81,

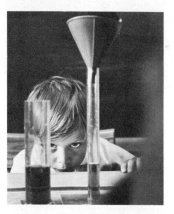

Box 81

Conservation

Each type of conservation can be tested for in a variety of ways, most of them directly attributable to the procedures originally employed by Piaget and his co-workers. We have already said something about the ways in which a fixed quantity (for example, a lump of clay) is made to "change in other perceivable features." The test material involved may be liquid rather than solid. In that case, the child is shown two identical water tumblers filled to the same level (top). One tumbler is poured into a tall, thin bottle (center); the other remains untouched. After the pouring has been completed (bottom), the child is questioned. This questioning is by no means a simple matter. One cannot ask even a bright six-year-old, "Is the quantity of liquid in the two containers the same?" The inquiry must be appropriate to the child's development level. Instead, we may ask, "Suppose you are very thirsty and want to drink the water in one of the bottles. Is there just as much water in each bottle?" The child who has not yet achieved conservation of quantity may answer that there is more in one bottle because it is bigger (taller) or more in the other because it is bigger (wider). On the other hand, he may reply that there is less in one because it is thinner or less in the other because it is shorter. In any case, he has been misled by a different, irrelevant "perceivable feature"—height or breadth—and has failed to grasp the invariance of quantity involved.

Clearly, the tests and the testers in these situations require considerable ingenuity. The physical setup must be suited to the principle under evaluation; the questioning must be understood by the child yet must not bias him toward any one response. And, with all these problems properly solved, there still remains the final and most critical task: judging whether or not the child's response indicates a grasp of conservation. Sometimes a child, when looking at the containers of water, points to the tall bottle and asserts confidently, "There's more in that bottle 'cause it's much bigger." No problem—no conservation is being shown. At the other extreme, an older child who has grasped the conservation principle patiently explains to the tester that the amount of water in the two containers "must" be the same because "the water came from the same-sized tumblers." Again, an easy judgment. But with children in the midst of the transition, responses are often ambiguous. This ambiguity accurately reflects a wavering between the prelogic of a "centered" perception (taller = more) and the logical necessity of conservation when the total situation has been understood.

And what of the child who, responding with a perfectly consistent but private logic, says, "There was a lot more water in the first bottle 'cause I drank it first, and I was much thirstier then"? You be the judge, then join the tester in his confusion.

Photos *The New York Times.*

p. 390, provides further illustrations of conservation experiments).

During this period the child also acquires a number of other kinds of cognitive abilities. For example, he can now arrange a number of sticks in serial order, say from shortest to longest. In brief, during this developmental period, the child begins to look "rational" to adults because he has become able to think and reason in much the same way as adults do. But one important distinction still remains: So far he can apply his newly developed cognitive ability only to concrete objects in his immediate environment. He cannot yet carry out the same thinking operation symbolically—for example, when words rather than objects are involved. Acquiring this ability to reason *abstractly* is the task of the next and final developmental stage.

Stage 3: Formal Operations

The last stage—the stage of *formal operations*—extends to approximately fifteen years of age. It is during this stage that the child (or, by now, the preadolescent) begins to apply concrete operations to *hypothetical* situations. With regard to serial order, for example, he becomes able to solve problems like, "If a *Glink* is taller than a *Zuv* and shorter than a *Blam*, which is the tallest of all?" It is no longer necessary to have real objects (like sticks), nor need the object names even refer to actual objects in the physical world. In addition to performing his once concrete operations in these more abstract ways, he acquires, bit by bit, the more complex logical reasoning abilities characteristic of adult thought. Getting the idea of proportionality—A is to B as C is to D—illustrates one of these newly emergent cognitive achievements. He also becomes capable of forming hypotheses designed to explain unfamiliar phenomena. In fact, many of the tasks employed to define this period of formal operations are very much like scientific experiments. The boy or girl, typically, is presented with a problem that can be solved only by systematically manipulating a number

of variables, carefully observing the effects of these variations, forming explanatory hypotheses based upon these observations, then testing these hypotheses one by one until the correct one is discovered.

This stage marks the end of the developmental road that began with the infant who had not even the notion of stable objects existing in a real world; it ends with the individual who can think logically and can do so with respect to abstract objects. By the end of this period the individual has achieved, in Piaget's theoretical model, the stage of cognitive maturity. Not, however, that he can no longer learn or grow wiser. Rather, he has finally been endowed with a full (adult) set of thinking tools with which to continue his ever more complex adaptations to his physical and social worlds. This achievement of intellectual maturity, interestingly enough, comes at about the same time as does physical and biological maturity.

Variations in Cognitive Development

We have already pointed out that there are wide variations in the ages at which the three developmental stages are attained but that Piaget argues that the orderly sequence of development is maintained despite such variations. Data from large-scale studies of children from Western nations (notably American, English, Scandinavian, and Swiss) strongly support Piaget's assertion that a fixed, stable sequence of development exists with respect to the major stages. The sequence of development *within* a stage may be upset for certain groups, however. For example, Hyde (cited in Flavell, 1963) found in an Aden (Middle Eastern) sample of children a number of instances of failure to show the expected sequences. On occasion, the notion of conservation of volume was achieved by these children before conservation of weight. Such evidence suggests the need for studying cognitive development in non-Western societies, preferably in those whose habits of training and educational methods are very unlike our own. This kind of study, combined with systematic observation of the *same* children throughout their development in longitudinal studies, rather than observation of different groups at different ages, seems necessary before a final determination can be made of the universality of Piaget's proposed sequence of stages in cognitive development.

With respect to age norms, that is, the age at which each new stage is attained, there is abundant evidence of considerable variation. First, as we might expect, more intelligent children generally show more rapid cognitive development. Feigenbaum (1963), for example, showed that, within a group of children aged four to seven years, the child's grasp of the conservation concept varied with his tested intelligence. Differences in age norms among children of different societies have frequently been demonstrated. Hyde's work, mentioned earlier, indicates that Adenese children achieve some of the stages somewhat later than do Western children. In another study, on conservation tasks, Laurendeau and Pinard (1963) found children on the French West Indian island of Martinique to be, on the average, four years behind Canadian children living in Montreal.

Such group differences may reflect true differences in the rates of cognitive development in different cultures, which may in turn be caused by factors like variations in the kind and quality of education afforded schoolchildren. Another factor may be at work, however. As the typical method of administering Piaget-type tasks involves considerable give-and-take conversation with the child (which assumes a certain language facility), it is possible that a given child's true stage of cognitive development may be masked by an inadequate vocabulary or by shyness or timidity in the experimental situation. Wallach (1963), in summarizing a number of studies in which the child could respond in a Piaget situation *nonverbally* (for example, by pointing at the one ball among several balls of clay that seemed to him to contain the same amount of clay as

an elongated piece), concludes that one or two years can be taken off the Piaget age norms when such testing techniques are employed.

Developmental Acceleration Through Training

It seems clear, then, that Piaget's age norms are very rough signposts along the road to adult thinking ability. Nevertheless, they remain as useful reminders that there may be limits, if only very broad ones, to the kind of thinking skills available to a child at a given point in his development. Therefore, certain materials may be too difficult to learn, and certain teaching techniques may be unsuitable for children before a certain age. How confining are these limits for any particular developmental task? We do not yet know, but psychologists have sought to stretch these limits and to establish the points beyond which they cannot be pushed (for an illustrative experiment, see Box 82, p. 394).

There is a kind of happy irony in the fact that Piaget's proposal of developmental stages, with its implications of limits on what a child can do mentally at a given age, should have provided a major impetus for such research. What was first regarded as a pessimistic view of the potentialities of development now serves as a springboard for studies that extend human potentials. The intent of most of this research, however, has not been the discovery of training techniques for speeding cognitive development. Rather, most of these researchers have been primarily concerned with increasing our understanding of the basic processes involved. If, for example, we can establish which of several training methods is most effective in speeding the acquisition of the principle of conservation, then we are likely to have learned something more about the emergence of this principle in the course of normal cognitive development. But, as with all scientific research and perhaps especially with research on human development, "pure" results point quickly to "practical" applications. The so-called "New

Box 82

Testing the Limits

Jan Smedslund, a Norwegian psychologist, has carried out a series of experiments designed to test the effects of special training on the age norms for various Piaget tasks. In one of these experiments, five- to seven-year-old children who had not yet attained the concept of conservation of weight were given extensive experience in weighing objects of different shapes. Time after time they had opportunities to guess at the relative weights of two objects, comparing, on a balance scale, a "standard" piece of clay with other pieces deformed in a variety of ways. Apparently, this training gradually taught these children the principles of the conservation of weight. They seemed to learn that distorting the form of a clay object—for example, from a long snake into several balls—did not affect the actual weight. At least the correctness of their responses and the kinds of explanations they gradually became able to offer after a period of such training were indistinguishable from those given by a group of children of about the same age who had already grasped the idea of conservation of weight "naturally," that is, in the course of their development. But was this achievement the same for the "speed up" and the "natural" children? Smedslund asked this question in the next phase of his study.

Both groups of children were repeatedly tested in a rigged experimental situation that, in all but one respect, was the same as a training session. A standard piece of clay and a deformed piece were compared on a balance scale. The two pieces were initially of identical weight, and this fact was pointed out to the child. The experimenter then changed the shape of one of them and while doing so removed a small bit of it. Therefore, when he replaced the two pieces on the scales, the manipulated piece of course weighed less.

When confronted with this situation, the two groups responded in dramatically different ways. Every one of the children who had "learned" conservation of weight through Smedslund's training procedures showed what amounted to a cognitive relapse. Sooner or later, each abandoned the newly learned principle and reverted to nonconservation explanations, the kind he had given before being trained. Again the children asserted that the round ball of clay was heavier because it was fatter, or they gave other reasons. They rarely showed any surprise at the failure of conservation, indicating that perhaps they had never really believed it. The "natural" group, by contrast, was more resistant. Almost half these children invented explanations that were at least possible for the rigged situation, yet they preserved the notion of conservation. One of them, for instance, assumed that the deformed object, which weighed less, must have lost a piece of clay somewhere along the way. Perhaps, he suggested, it had fallen off, or the tester had taken some away—plausible hypotheses, even accurate ones. Most important, the hypotheses are consistent with the conservation principle.

We see from such experiments that training procedures can speed up the age at which a particular cognitive task can be mastered but that the pace of cognitive development cannot be stretched beyond certain limits. We have a lot more to learn about how to stretch, how far to stretch, and what methods work best for what children.

J. SMEDSLUND. 1961. The Acquisition of Conservation of Substance and Weight in Children: III. Extinction of Conservation of Weight Acquired "Normally" and by Means of Empirical Controls on a Balance, *Scand. J. Psychol.*, 2, 85–7.

Math," which is rapidly supplanting traditional teaching techniques for this subject matter, owes a good deal to a Piaget-type analysis of the learning processes involved. The assessment of intelligence may soon show a similar influence as current work on new mental tests that embody a developmental-stage concept of the growth of cognitive abilities begins to bear fruit. Without going into the merits of individual efforts of this sort, it seems safe to conclude that "practical" effects will result mainly in educational practice and evaluation and that some of these effects will tend to accelerate cognitive development in broad segments of the population.

Is such acceleration a good thing? If we can for a moment forget that in our culture speed and efficiency are confounded with quality and ultimate worth, we may recognize a legitimate concern. Some investigators (and Piaget seems to be among them) have questioned the advisability of such tampering with normal (that is, unmanipulated) development. Would it, after all, be a good thing if eight-year-olds could reason like adults? Might not such an imbalance between intellectual "powers" and worldly experience cause trouble? We do not know. The few relevant data come almost wholly from studies of gifted children, too atypical a source upon which to base general statements. Most of this evidence, if we can credit it, is reassuring with regard to the effects of acceleration. But some of it suggests that personality development and social adjustment may be adversely affected. So, although numerous studies find, for example, that intellectually more mature children tend to be more self-accepting, more popular, better adjusted, and so on, reports like those of Fowler (1962), which record his success in teaching his two-year-old daughter to read, also suggest that we keep a wary eye for possible undesirable "side effects" of such training. In the case of his daughter and in other studies involving cognitive stimulation of bright young children, Fowler notes some evidence that emotional adjustment may suffer somewhat in the course of such training. Whether or not such effects are a necessary accompaniment of accelerative procedures remains a very open question.

A related yet independent question is whether or not accelerating the rate of cognitive development necessarily leads eventually to higher adult ability. Again, we do not know, for there are not yet adequate data on the adult abilities of individuals systematically accelerated during development. Each person may have a built-in ceiling beyond which he cannot go, no matter how quickly he progresses toward that ceiling. Recent attempts at what has been called "compensatory education" are just that—*compensatory*. As such, their objective is not to raise the ultimate ceiling but rather to bring the individual closer to the adult level of cognitive ability, which, had he not come from a disadvantaged group, he would have achieved without the intervention of special training.

Do these compensatory education procedures work, even in the short run? So far, the results seem promising. Stendler (1967) conducted a summer program for culturally disadvantaged preschool children and specifically provided training on Piaget-type tasks. Her training procedure was based on the rationale that gaining competence in such logical operations would help the children to overcome some of the learning difficulties they characteristically encountered when first exposed to formal schooling. During the course of the training program, considerable acceleration was noted, and the carryover of such progress to the school years is currently being assessed. Another study along these lines, and with a similar sample of children, was conducted by Gray and Klaus (1965). It also provided cognitive training but placed greater emphasis upon changing attitudes toward learning in the child and in his family. Also explicit attempts were made to establish close personal relationships with the children. Some of the encouraging results of this study, comparing the per-

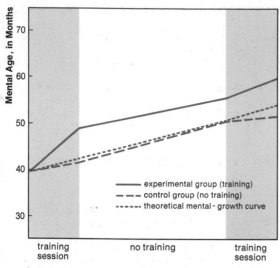

Figure 25.1. Preschool-training effects on intelligence. The dotted line represents *expected* normal growth in mental age from about age four on for a child whose IQ is 87 (Stanford-Binet) at that age. (This was the average IQ of the children in both groups at the start of the study.) Relative to this theoretical base line, the children receiving two ten-week training sessions not only showed greater than normal growth during the sessions but also maintained their advantage over the period of almost ten months between sessions. The control groups, by contrast, actually lost some ground during this period (their rate of mental development begins to fall below the theoretical curve), indicating that culturally disadvantaged children may be subject to a *progressive decline* in IQ relative to normally developing children with the same intelligence range. S. Gray and R. A. Klaus, "An Experimental Preschool Program for Culturally Deprived Children," *Child Development*, 36, 887–98; © 1965 by The Society for Research in Child Development, Inc.; adapted by permission.

formance of one group of children who had two ten-week training sessions in consecutive summers with the performance of a control group of equal intelligence, can be seen in Figure 25.1.

In such future work, the theoretical framework proposed by Piaget will probably continue to be one of the leading guides. But there are other theoretical analyses of the development of thinking, some perhaps as comprehensive and as influential as Piaget's, and we turn now to a brief account of them.

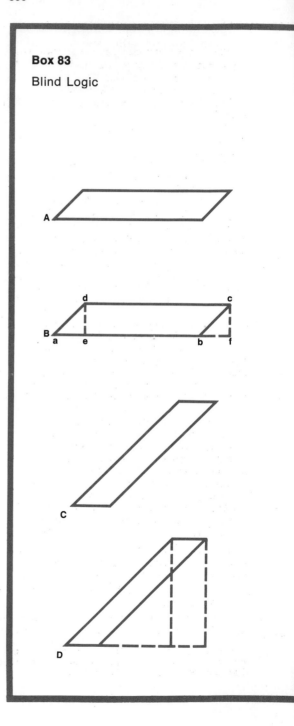

Box 83

Blind Logic

M. Wertheimer bemoaned the ease with which teachers seemed to assume that a logical analysis of a problem is the only or best instructional approach. Let him explain:

"I am visiting a classroom. The teacher: 'During the last lesson we learned how to find the area of a rectangle. Do you all know it?'

The class: 'Yes.' One pupil calls out: 'The area of a rectangle is equal to the product of the two sides.'

'Now,' says the teacher, 'we shall go on.' He draws a parallelogram on the blackboard (Figure A). 'This is called a parallelogram. A parallelogram is a plane quadrilateral the opposite sides of which are equal and parallel.'

He labels the corners a, b, c, d.

'I drop one perpendicular from the upper left corner and another perpendicular from the upper right corner.

'I extend the base line to the right.

'I label the two new points e and f' (Figure B).

With the help of this figure he then proceeds to the usual proof of the theorem that the area of a parallelogram is equal to the product of the base by the altitude, establishing the equality of certain lines and angles and the congruence of the pair of triangles.

The teacher now gives a number of problems all of which require finding the areas of parallelograms of different sizes, sides and angles. Before the end of the hour the teacher assigns ten more problems of this kind for homework.

At the next meeting of the class, one day later, I am there again.

The lesson begins with the teacher calling on a pupil to demonstrate how the area of a parallelogram is found. The pupil does it exactly. . . . A written quiz brings good results.

Most people would say, 'This is an excellent class; the teaching goal has been reached.' But observing the class I feel uneasy, I am troubled. 'What have they learned?' I ask myself. 'Have they done any thinking at all? Have they grasped the issue? Maybe all that they have done is little more than blind repetition. How can I clarify it? What can I *do*?'

I ask the teacher whether he will allow me to put a question to the class. 'With pleasure,' he answers, clearly proud of his class.

I go to the board and draw this (Figure C).

Some are obviously taken aback.

One pupil raises his hand: 'Teacher, we haven't had that yet.'

Others are busy. They have copied the figure on paper, they draw the auxiliary lines as they were taught, dropping perpendiculars from the two upper corners and extending the base line (Figure D). Then they look bewildered, perplexed.

Some do not look at all unhappy; they write firmly below their drawing: 'The area is equal to the base times the altitude'—a correct subsumption, but perhaps an entirely blind one. When asked whether they can show it to be true in this case, they too become perplexed.

With still others, it is entirely different. Their faces brighten, they smile, they turn their papers through 45°. . . .

Wertheimer's Figure D is of course the teacher's Figure A turned around. Clearly, for many of the students, there had been a mastery of a narrow exercise but no understanding. Wertheimer's point is that it is possible and necessary to teach problem-solving skills in ways that do promote understanding and that such teaching techniques follow from a *psychological* analysis of processes involved, not a *logical* one.

Wertheimer's book presents lucid analyses and specific teaching techniques for a variety of problems. For a starter, the reader should approach Figure A scissors in hand.

M. WERTHEIMER. 1945. *Productive Thinking* (New York: Harper). Excerpts reproduced by permission of Harper and Brothers. Copyright 1945 by Harper and Brothers. Figures adapted and text material reprinted by permission; copyright 1945, 1959 by Valentin Wertheimer.

Other Theories of Cognitive Development

Many of the leading figures in the development of Gestalt psychology explicitly concerned themselves with cognitive processes. Koffka (1928), in a book entitled *The Growth of the Mind*, presented a detailed theoretical analysis attempting to account for cognitive development in the child. Köhler (1925) applied these principles to understanding the problem-solving behavior of apes (see Box 93, p. 425, for an illustration of this work). Max Wertheimer, the main founder of Gestalt psychology, increasingly turned his attention from perception to the analysis of creative thinking and, in his *Productive Thinking* (Wertheimer, 1945), offered a detailed analysis of effective and ineffective techniques of classroom teaching and learning, following directly from Gestalt principles of organization (see Box 83, p. 396).

Sharing this Gestaltist origin but moving beyond it in his *Comparative Psychology of Mental Development*, Werner (1948, originally published in German in 1926) set forth a theory of cognitive development that, in many ways, parallels Piaget's. Werner proposed that mental organization becomes increasingly differentiated, with higher-order structures being formed from more primitive ones, and that totally novel structures arise, as the child passes successively through sensorimotor, perceptual-imaginal, and conceptual-symbolic stages of mental development. Even without further details on Werner's theoretical position, the reader will easily recognize here striking similarities with Piaget's formulations.

We conclude with yet another theory of mental development, currently put forth by Bruner (1964). He too proposes three major stages of development (enactive, iconic, and symbolic), which also show strong parallels with Piaget's and Werner's stages in that there is a progression, in the stuff of mental life, from actions and percepts through images to a final stage in which thought is predominantly the complex and flexible manipulation of such symbols as words. The important distinction between Bruner and Piaget seems to lie in their relative emphasis upon the effects of specific and teachable skills, like language training, upon the pace of mental growth. Bruner states his position:

"I shall take the view . . . that the development of human intellectual functioning from infancy to such perfection as it may reach is shaped by a series of technological advances in the use of the mind. Growth depends upon the mastery of [information-processing] techniques and cannot be understood without reference to such mastery. These techniques are not, in the main, inventions of individuals who are 'growing up'; they are, rather, skills transmitted with varying efficiency and success by the culture—language being a prime example. Cognitive growth, then, is in a major way from the outside in, as well as from the inside out."

Glossary

accommodation For Piaget, the type of adaptation in which old schemata are modified or new ones formed in order to absorb environmental stimulation that can be neither ignored nor made, by assimilation, to fit into the existing organization.

adaptation For Piaget, the process of continuous interaction between existing schemata and environmental stimulation. Assimilation and accommodation are the two complementary types of adaptation.

assimilation For Piaget, the type of adaptation in which existing schemata select for incorporation into mental life only those aspects of environmental stimulation that fit or that can be forced to fit into the existing organization.

conservation An aspect of mental development, in

Piaget's theory, in which the child comes to understand that certain properties of an object (weight, for example) do not change, despite changes in other perceivable features of the object.

equilibration For Piaget, the intrinsic process or tendency for schemata to function continuously at higher and more complex levels. Essentially, the "motivational" basis for cognitive growth.

organization For Piaget, the view that mental life is built up by the increasing interrelation of simple elements or schemata combining to form new and ever more complex schemata.

schemata The basic elements of mental life (or cognitive organization in Piaget's theoretical system). Sensorimotor reflexes present at birth are examples of the simplest schemata.

creative problem solving: characteristics and process

overview / "Creative problem solving," or "productive thinking," refers to achieving solutions that are new and original for the individual and is a form of "directed thinking." Although such thinking is not wholly free of influence from emotional factors, it is more closely tied to the external environment and can be appropriately analyzed in perceptual terms. Perception in a problem-solving situation is ever changing and involves apparent discontinuities in the stream of awareness. Changes in how an object is perceived can lead to a solution sometimes quite abruptly, as in the sudden insight of an "aha!" experience. It should be clear, however, that some insights—no matter how abruptly they may appear, and no matter how blinding the accompanying "aha!" experiences—simply turn out to be erroneous "solutions." That is, the term "insight," as used by the psychologist, describes an *experience* that sometimes occurs in the process of problem solving; "insight" is not used as an *explanation* of creative thinking.

The process of creative problem solving can be subdivided into four stages: preparation, incubation, illumination, and verification. Or, by another classificatory scheme, i can start by setting the general range within which the solution is expected to fall, then move to a narrower functional solution, and then try out a number of specific solutions. The problem solver can move forward and backward through these three levels until a satisfactory specific solution is achieved.

Problems may be grouped into three major categories: explanation, prediction, and invention. Explanation involves a fairly well-structured stimulus situation in which most of the information necessary to answer "why" is present. Prediction involves a less structured situation and invention the least structured. Past learning and experience play an important role in all types of problem solving, but, as in the phenomenon of functional fixity, such experience can interfere with problem solution.

In earlier units we have had a good deal to say about the nature of thought processes and the role of images and language in thinking. We have also dealt with the development of thinking from its primitive forms in infancy into the complex cognitive skills that constitute adult thinking. We have not yet examined, in detail, what specifically goes on when an individual confronts and solves a problem.

Many of the problems we face in our daily environment require nothing more than reproducing what we have learned to do in the past in similar situations. This type of *reproductive problem solving* we have already discussed in preceding units when considering the processes of learning and memory.

In this section we shall turn our attention to *productive thinking,* often referred to as *creative problem solving.* Such creative problem solving requires that the individual produce new and original solutions. Problem solving can properly be considered creative, regardless of whether or not the particular solution has previously been produced by someone else. What matters is whether or not it is novel *for the individual.*

In turning to an analysis of creative problem solving, we remind the reader, first of all, of a distinction briefly made earlier (Unit 23) between apparently spontaneous thought processes (for example, daydreaming, autistic thinking) and the kinds of thinking processes to be discussed here. Problem solving is a form of what has been called *directed, guided,* or *controlled thinking.* This distinction seems to be largely based upon a dichotomy between emotional and rational thought; daydreaming is seen as "wishful thinking," whereas problem solving is presumably a rational activity involving only accurate perceptions and realistic adaptation to an environmental challenge.

Although such a separation has merit—an imaginative daydream does seem very different from concentration on getting a correct solution to a problem in biochemistry—too much may be made of the apparent difference. One risk is that we may attribute total rationality to the scientist wrestling with his problem and, therefore, assign total objectivity to his method of search and to the ultimate validity of his findings. This is not the case. Typically, the scientist's pursuit of truth is (and should be) a passionate undertaking—it is an intellectual adventure beset by human hopes and fears and, most certainly, is not free from emotion and powerful motivational pressures. The difference between wishful thinking and scientific problem solving—and it is a real difference— is that the latter must "check" the validity of his thinking with the rules of scientific bookkeeping, rules whose primary function is to help the investigator draw valid conclusions from his data. In a sense, the very need for such systematic rules (for example, having adequate control groups in an experiment) confesses to the "emotional" element in scientific problem solving, as they prevent (although not always) the investigator from being "carried away by his emotions." The term "scientific" problem solving is not meant, of course, to restrict problem solving to scientists or to problems of science. Nor is problem solving restricted to the kinds of highly structured problems of rigorous logic characteristic, for example, of mathematics. Problem solving occurs in all domains of human activity. In that sense every individual is a scientific problem solver.

The distinction between emotional and rational thinking and, correspondingly, between spontaneous and directed thinking is at most a matter of degree. The rational support of an important belief about business matters, for example, is not immune from the urges of fantasy and wish fulfillment. Daydreaming and problem solving perhaps differ more clearly in the extent to which thought is tied to the immediate stimulus situation. In daydreaming, what we perceive in the world "out there" has little constraint on our thought processes. In problem solving, on the other hand, there is a continuous interplay between our perceptions and our thinking—so much so that submitting problem solving to analysis in perceptual terms seems a useful initial task.

A Perceptual Account of Problem Solving

Some perceptions seem intrinsically to compel thought. Often we begin to think about a problem and try to solve it simply because, like the unconquered peak, "it is there." It may take no more than merely the appearance in our field of vision of a "problem"—one that in reality need not concern us at all—to start us working on it "just for fun."

Now stop! Before continuing, turn to Figure 26.1. and follow the directions given with it.

When you first looked at the figure, you may have seen a problem: How was the girl to straighten out the painting hanging askew on the wall? If, in addition, you realized that the girl could stand on the chair in order to reach the picture, you had gone ahead and solved the problem. All this mental activity was performed without instructions and without personal involvement or frustration. In such an instance, in which one's personal needs play a very small part, we speak of "task-oriented" thinking and problem solving.

Changing Perceptions of the Problem

As we work away at a problem, our perceptions undergo continuous change. When bodily movement or manipulation of physical objects is involved (as in finding a certain house on a street, painting a picture, repairing a typewriter), the relations among the physical objects change, and so do our perceptions. But, even when we remain seated at a desk as we try to recall the name of an acquaintance, try to come up with a good ending to the story we are writing, or attempt to solve mentally a mathematical problem, we experience a stream of ever shifting perceptions of the attributes and objects of the problem.

Figure 26.1.
Look at the figure carefully. What is going on there? As you keep looking at it, try to remember your stream of thought. Spend as long as you wish at it. After you have finished with it, return to the text. As you continue reading, you will soon find out what this figure is all about.

Box 84

Can You Solve This?

• • •

• • •

• • •

Starting anywhere you wish, draw four *straight* lines that will pass through every one of the nine dots, without lifting your pencil from the paper.

Do not read the rest of this box until you have attempted to solve the problem. If after two minutes you have not solved it, read the following "hints."

The nine dots tend to be perceived as a square. But there are no boundary lines to prevent your drawing a line *extending beyond* the "perceived" edge of the "square." Nothing was ever said about staying within the "perceived confines" of the nine dots, yet the organizing nature of perception is such as to lead you to see a block to the movements of your pencil, where no block exists in fact.

Discontinuities in Perception

This "stream of perceptions" is a very curious stream. There are discontinuities in it; it seems to disappear and go underground for short or long stretches. Even the most complete account of a person's experiences in solving a problem will often indicate that there are "conscious lapses," large time intervals during which he does not seem to be "thinking" or "working" on the problem at all, yet substantial progress seems to be made. Occasionally, progress seems to be made even while he is asleep. After such a "silent" period the solution may suddenly appear, or substantial progress may be made. These lapses in the stream of the perceptions of the problem have been labeled "incubation periods"—times of ripening and maturing of ideas.

The moment the problem solver makes a significant advance toward the solution, whether following an incubation period or not, he has vivid experiences. With certain problems the striking changes in perception *are* the advances. The problem solver suddenly "sees" a solution—or a partial solution.

The Quickly Solved Problem The course of the stream differs tremendously from problem to problem. With an easy problem we may find that, very soon after we have perceived it, we perceive the solution. It is as if the stream of problem perception could be described as a short straight line with only two easily identifiable points.

The Difficult Problem Quite the contrary seems to be true of very difficult problem solving. With difficult problems, for which the solutions come only after a great deal of work, we can often distinguish (scattered among the "silent" periods) several major changes after the initial perceptions—one or more "turning-point" percepts and, finally, the solution percepts. The turning-point percepts accompany sudden significant advances toward the final solutions. To continue our analogy, it is as if the stream of our perceptions of a problem had several major bends to be rounded before we finally sail home.

Changes in Perceptual Content

As we make progress toward a solution, we find that objects begin to mean different things. A limb of a tree, initially perceived with the meaning of "a limb of a tree," may now be seen as "a long rake if broken from the tree"; a penny, initially perceived as a relatively worthless coin, may now be perceived as an efficient conductor of electricity; a piece of ice, initially perceived as cold and wet, may now be perceived as something that can be molded into the shape of a lens and used to focus the sun's rays to start a fire. Indeed, the perceived meanings of the same objects that make up the initial and later perceptions may be so different that it sometimes seems as if entirely different objects are involved.

As we work on a problem, we may suddenly see that what we had perceived as a block to the goal is not a block at all. Sometimes the barrier to solution has been a creation of our own perceptual processes (for an illustration of this point, see Box 84).

Perceiving the Solution

As we approach the solution of a difficult problem or of a problem whose solution has been unaccountably evading us, we may experience a characteristic pattern of changes in perception, feelings, and even emotional excitement. One such pattern of experience occurs just before the solution. This experience can perhaps best be described as the "almost there" feeling. We "see" and yet do not see the solution. It is an "on the tip of our tongue" feeling. We feel, rather than precisely know, what should be done, but somehow we cannot phrase it or make it concrete. It is the sort of feeling in which William James has said the solution "tingles, it trembles on the verge, but does not come" (see Box 85, p. 405, in which a poet and a psychologist describe the "almost there").

The most easily recognized pattern of changes in perception, feelings, and emotional excitement is the one that occurs at the very moment of solution. When it occurs, it is unmistakably different from most of our other experiences. It is sudden, complete, intense. When we attempt to communicate our experiences at such a moment, we make liberal use of such a descriptive phrase as "like a flash." We often cry out with an explosive, "That's it!" "Of course!" "Oh sure!" If we had happened to be a Greek mathematician named Archimedes, who had just found the solution to King Hiero's problem of assaying the gold content of his crown, we would (or so goes the ancient story) have leaped from the tub in a rush of joy and run through the streets shouting loudly to the world (in classical Greek, of course), "I have found it, I have found it!" We are referring to the "insight" experience.

Even the psychologist's more technical descriptions of this "insight" experience often use the vivid phrase *"aha!" experience,* first introduced by the Viennese psychologist Bühler (see Box 86, p. 407).

Not all learning and problem solving ends with this sudden and intense experience. Memorizing a list of history dates or working out an arithmetic problem by well-known methods seems devoid of this exhilarating sensation. But even when the "aha!" experience does occur, it is no guarantee of success. We may feel all the excitement of an insight and yet discover in the next moment, or on the next day or month or year, that our solution will not work. This possibility emphasizes the point that we are using the word "insight" as a description of an experience, not as an explanation of how solutions are arrived at.

Process Description of Problem Solving

Not only the psychologist but all creative workers have been interested in the description of the problem-solving process. Each one brings somewhat different testimony, but one descriptive schema appears again and again. This schema is the classical four stages of creative thought: *preparation, incubation, illumination,* and *verification.* Though this neat schema occasionally does violence to the actual sequence of events, it will do as a general framework, and we shall briefly describe these four phases.

The Four Stages

The first stage, preparation, can be briefly described as the period when the problem solver becomes acquainted with the various features of the problem and begins to "play" with ideas. The stimulus pattern evokes first this and then that association. Often these associations seem to be random and "free" in nature, directed by the demands of the problem, but not completely restricted by these demands. Gradually a more disciplined attitude is taken. Certain suggestions and ideas are discarded, others are examined more carefully, and problem solving in earnest gets under way. Frequently this stage merges rapidly and without any noticeable "break" into the illumination and verification stages, and the problem is solved.

The second stage, incubation, varies greatly in its nature and its duration. It may last a few minutes, several days, weeks, months, or even years. It is a stage in which the problem is laid aside and no "conscious" work is done upon it but after which renewed attention to the problem results in prompt solution or at least in a prompt advance beyond the previous point of progress. The testimony of creative thinkers is filled with accounts of the incubation period. Mathematicians, inventors, poets, scientists, and artists have testified that this or that solution unaccountably occurred while they were

Box 85

The Shape of the
"Almost There"

In the following passages we have two descriptions of the "almost there" experience. Both come from highly creative people: Paul Valéry, the French poet, and William James, the founder of American psychology.

Paul Valéry: "There is that one where the man whose business is writing experiences a kind of flash —for this intellectual life, anything but passive, is really made of fragments; it is in a way composed of elements very brief, yet felt to be rich in possibilities, which do not illuminate the whole mind, which indicate to the mind, rather, that there are forms completely new which it is sure to be able to possess after a certain amount of work. Sometimes I have observed this moment when a sensation arrives at the mind; it is a gleam of light, not so much illuminating as dazzling. This arrival calls attention, points, rather than illuminates, and in fine, is itself an enigma which carries with it the assurance that it can be postponed. You say, 'I see, and then tomorrow I shall see more.' There is an activity, a special sensitization; soon you will go into the dark-room and the picture will be seen to emerge." (Quoted in Hadamard, 1949)

William James: "Suppose we try to recall a forgotten name. The state of our consciousness is peculiar. There is a gap therein; but no mere gap. It is a gap that is intensely active. A sort of wraith of the name is in it, beckoning us in a given direction, making us at moments tingle with the sense of our closeness, and then letting us sink back without the longed-for term. If wrong names are proposed to us, this singularly definite gap acts immediately so as to negate them. They do not fit into its mould. And the gap of one word does not feel like the gap of another, all empty of content as both might seem necessarily to be when described as gaps. . . . But the feeling of an absence is *toto coelo* other than the absence of a feeling. It is an intense feeling. The rhythm of a lost word may be there without a sound to clothe it; or the evanescent sense of something which is the initial vowel or consonant may mock us fitfully, without growing more distinct. Every one must know the tantalizing effect of the blank rhythm of some forgotten verse, restlessly dancing in one's mind, striving to be filled out with words."

shaving, bathing, listening to a concert, or rounding a pond on Hampstead Heath. There can be no doubt of its reality.

This possibility points to an important consideration. An analysis of creative problem solving that restricts itself to the person's reports of "what he is thinking about" may not be adequate. Much may occur without any conscious experience. We must supplement the person's reports with other kinds of observations and analyses.

Illumination was described in our earlier discussion of "insight." Often the person, as soon as he feels he has hit upon the general solution, will assume that the problem has been solved and will do no further work on it. As a result he may have ended his problem solving prematurely. His "general idea" may not work.

Verification is the last stage. The proposed solution may be worked out in more specific detail, and it may be applied and tested. If it meets the test, the problem is solved.

Harvard psychologists R. W. Brown and D. McNeill have subjected William James' "tip of the tongue" phenomenon to an ingenious experimental investigation. Noting that tip-of-the-tongue (or, as they abbreviate it, TOT) states occur too rarely in nature to permit systematic study, they hit upon a device that was extraordinarily successful in generating an abundant supply of them. They presented definitions of infrequently used words and then asked their subjects to discover the words being defined. They felt that these words, forty-nine in all, although not common, were likely to be within the "passive" vocabulary of their subjects (Harvard and Radcliffe undergraduates) yet not so familiar as to be promptly identified. (Examples are "nepotism," "ambergris," and "sampan."

Sometimes a word was immediately recognized, and sometimes it drew a complete blank, but often enough (about six times per subject in a two-hour session) a TOT state was induced. The states were apparently convincing to the observer as well as to the subject. The authors describe the behavior of one subject: "The signs of it were unmistakable; he would appear to be in mild torment, something like the brink of a sneeze, and if he found the word his relief was considerable." Once "seized" by such a state, the subject was asked to provide, as far as he could, the following information about the word that was on the tip of his tongue: its first letter and number of syllables, any words that sounded like the missing word, and words similar in meaning. When this information had been provided, the subject was told the word, and he then noted whether or not it was indeed the one he had had in mind.

The subjects' guesses of the number of syllables in the missing words were impressively accurate. In 57 per cent of the cases the guess was exactly right. (Both the actual and guessed numbers ranged from one to five syllables.) When there was an error, it was rarely greater than one syllable. Even the words that had been listed as sounding like the missing word showed a strong tendency to resemble it in number of syllables, having exactly the same number in 47 per cent of the instances. Almost identical results were obtained for guesses of the first letter; they were correct 57 per cent of the time, and 49 per cent of the "sounds like" words started with the same letter.

Several other ways of analyzing these data confirmed the impression that, while in the TOT state, subjects had quite a lot of information about the missing word. Whatever details are still to be discovered about the tip-of-the-tongue phenomenon, it is already clear that the gap in this "almost there" experience is very far from "contentless."

J. HADAMARD. 1949. *Psychology of Invention in the Mathematical Field* (Princeton: Princeton University Press).
W. JAMES. 1950. *Principles of Psychology* (New York: Dover). Originally published 1890.
R. W. BROWN and D. MCNEILL. 1966. The "Tip of the Tongue" Phenomenon, *J. Verb. Learn. Verb. Behav.*, 5, 325–37.

Developmental History of a Solution

This four-stage description can be supplemented by Duncker's fairly detailed account of how specific solutions are developed within the problem-solving process. Duncker's description is based on careful observation of what people actually do and say as they go about solving a problem in a laboratory situation.

The analysis is couched in perceptual terms. Duncker speaks of the creative problem-solving process as consisting of a related series of organizations, each influenced by what preceded it. This series, his analysis shows, can be grouped into three major levels.

When a person first tackles a problem, the initial organization that he achieves can be described as a *general range*, which is a very general restatement of the original problem that indicates the direction of a possible solution. This initial organization may emphasize some general property of the sought-after solu-

Box 86

The "Aha!" Experience—as Seen by a
Psychologist and Her Subject

The "aha!" phenomenon, as seen by the psychologist looking on and as reported by one person undergoing the experience, is found in an experiment by Helen Durkin at Columbia University.

Each subject was given a puzzle, with the instructions:

"As you solve, please think aloud. Express every idea as it comes to you as you work even if it seems irrelevant. Try to tell me also how you feel about it as you go along. My chief interest is to find out as fully as possible just what goes on in your mind as you work."

Here is Durkin's description of her subjects' behavior at the moment of sudden reorganization of their perceptions—usually just before they solved the puzzle:

"A short pause of peculiarly quiet intentness which sometimes involved an appearance of great tension, and at others seemed to be merely a cessation of all visible activity. The tension seemed to be one of suspense rather than of effort.

This pause ending either in an explosively expressed elation, or in relieved relaxation.

There was a tendency to jump to the conclusion, with considerable certainty that the solution had been arrived at, even when the subject was not at all sure of the details."

The following brief excerpt is taken from the "thinking out loud" of one of Durkin's subjects:

"Oh, I saw it before I moved it. It came suddenly upon me as from the outside and I felt absolutely sure. Just like a flash and I knew I was right. Wasn't conscious of it . . . didn't reason about it—it came to me from the outside."

H. DURKIN. 1937. Trial-and-Error, Gradual Analysis, and Sudden Re-organization, *Arch. Psychol.*, Vol. 30, No. 210.

tion or some general method that might bring about the solution. The general range is followed by the *functional solution*, which reformulates and narrows the general range. Functional solutions have the typical form "If such and such could be achieved, the problem would be solved."

The next step, *specific solution*, can be described as a reformulation and a further specification of the functional solution. If a given specific solution is found unsatisfactory, the subject may revert to the stage of the preceding functional solution and seek some other specific solution. Failing in that, he may revert to the general range and start out on other functional solutions and go on from there. He may even, of course, try out different general ranges.

Duncker's description can be clarified through specific illustrations from his classic study of problem solving. In one of his experiments he presented his subjects (University of

Berlin students) with the schematic sketch shown in Figure 26.2. and the following problem: "Given, a human being with an inoperable stomach tumor. We know that if we apply certain rays, with sufficient intensity, the tumor can be destroyed. The problem is: how can these rays, at the required high intensity, be applied to the tumor without at the same time destroying the healthy tissue which surrounds the tumor?"

Duncker asked his subjects to "think out loud" while they worked at this problem. Figure 26.3. presents a diagrammatic summary of the thinking of one subject as he attempted to solve the problem. It will be seen that his

problem-solving process consisted of several general ranges, functional solutions, and specific solutions.

The first general range adopted by this student was "I must find some way of avoiding contact between the rays and the healthy tissue." This general range could and did lead to several more specific restatements of the problem (functional solutions): Use a free path to the stomach; remove healthy tissue from path of rays; insert a protecting wall between rays and healthy tissue; displace tumor toward the surface. From each of these functional solutions a specific solution suggested itself to the subject. These solutions in

Figure 26.2. This schematic diagram, used by Duncker in his cancer problem, is intended to represent a cross-section of the body, with the tumor in the middle and the radiation apparatus on the left. The line with the arrow represents the course of the rays.

Read the problem as presented in the text and see if you can solve it.

K. Duncker, "On Problem Solving," *Psychological Monographs,* 58 (1945), No. 5; adapted by permission.

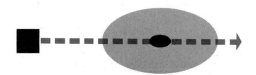

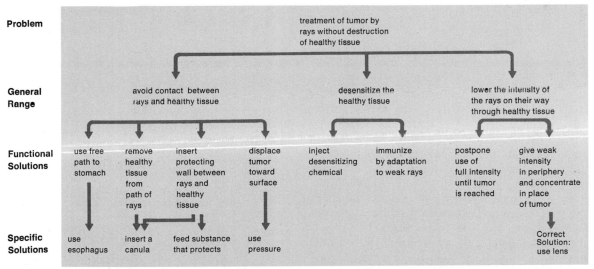

Figure 26.3. A "family tree" of attempted solutions evolved by one subject working on Duncker's cancer problem.
K. Duncker, "On Problem Solving," *Psychological Monographs,* 58 (1945), No. 5; adapted by permission.

Box 87

Computer Simulation
of Thinking

The very notion of machines that can "think" and exhibit "intelligent behavior" is too often enveloped by an aura of mystery, which, although it triggers entertaining fantasies, clouds understanding. The basic principle involved in computer simulation of thinking—or, for that matter, the simulation of any psychological process—is, in fact, a very simple one: If we can program (that is, give operating instructions to) a computer so that it "behaves" like a man, then the specific assumptions about a particular psychological process embodied in the program may be on the right track. The computer, used in this way, is truly a model of man, if only for a limited portion of his behavior. The computer program that simulates problem-solving behavior allows us to "build a man" in our theoretical image of the problem-solving process, and from study of the responses of such a "man" we may learn whether or not our theoretical assumptions have been correct and, if not, in what respects they have been wrong.

"Right" and "wrong," in this context, mean only that the computer response has succeeded or failed to correspond with the typical human response. And "response" means not only the directly observable behavior but also the thought processes. If the human being typically makes mistakes in a given situation, the computer must also, if the theory's assumptions are to be supported.

From this set of facts it should be clear that one must know a good deal about the psychological process one wishes to simulate before there is even an attempt at programming. A. J. Newell and H. A. Simon developed a series of programs to simulate problem solving. They intensively observed human subjects at work on the problems that the program was intended to handle, record-

turn were either rejected by the experimenter as inadequate or were recognized as inadequate by the subject himself. As each specific solution was rejected, the subject would go on to a different functional solution and to different general ranges, until he finally adopted this one: "Lower the intensity of the rays on their way through healthy tissue." This third general range finally did lead to the correct solution. Let us quote the student as he approached this last lap and went through the functional solution into the specific: "Somehow divert . . . diffuse rays . . . disperse . . . stop! Send a broad and weak bundle of rays through a lens in such a way that the tumor lies at the focal point and thus receives intensive radiation." (This solution is closely related to the best solutions: Send several weak bundles of rays from various points outside the body, all these weak bundles to meet at the tumor; thus the intensity of the rays necessary for destruction is attained only at the tumor. Or stick to a single ray source but rotate the body so that only the tumor is constantly exposed to the rays. The rays, incidentally, cannot be focused by ordinary lenses, as suggested by the student,

ing not only the subjects' actions but also their verbal reports on their thinking during the entire process. The plan for this program for problem solving was that it duplicate as far as possible the complete sequence of reasoning and decisions typically followed by the human subjects. This duplication, however, is no mere copying process because it is precisely here that the creative, theoretical aspects of this type of simulation program clearly appear. From the mass of observations of the problem-solving behavior of many human subjects—and no two persons attack the same problem in precisely the same way—it was necessary to abstract the principles of reasoning and choice that seemed most general in accounting for the course of the subjects' behavior. The adequacy of the experimenters' analysis of observation and their theoretical synthesis of general principles are directly tested by the ability of the computer to reproduce typical human behavior. To the extent that any simulation program *predicts* human problem-solving behavior in *new* situations, the theoretical propositions embodied therein remain promising.

The computer serves essentially as an experimental tool and is a "thinking machine" only in that, if the psychologist is clever enough to provide it with the principles that in reality guide human thought, it too can "think" like a man. Some people are concerned about the implications of the "artificial intelligence" embodied in computer approaches to thinking. U. Neisser expresses well one note of concern, on which we shall conclude:

"The deep difference between the thinking of men and machines has been intuitively recognized by those who fear that machines may somehow come to regulate our society. If machines really thought as men do, there would be no more reason to fear them than to fear men. But computer intelligence is indeed 'inhuman': it does not grow, has no emotional basis, and is shallowly motivated. These defects do not matter in technical applications, where the criteria of successful problem solving are relatively simple. They become extremely important if the computer is used to make social decisions, for there our criteria of adequacy are as subtle and as multiply motivated as human thinking itself."

A. J. NEWELL and H. A. SIMON. 1961. Computer Simulation of Human Thinking, *Science*, 134, 2011–7.
U. NEISSER. 1963. The Imitation of Man by Machine, *Science*, 139, 193–7.

but nevertheless the experimenter accepted this as a solution.) The total duration of this problem-solving attempt was about half an hour.

This description is generalized from many observations. Not every problem solver goes through the three levels of general range, functional solution, specific solution, in that order. Almost every conceivable "exception to the rule" is found if a large enough group of subjects is examined. Nevertheless, Duncker's scheme, insofar as it does represent an accurate picture of the typical or modal problem-solving

process, helps to fill out the more global four-stage analysis. These two models, together with the perceptual account of problem-solving experiences, provides us with a description of the problem-solving process (for another strategy for studying this process, see Box 87).

Types of Problems

Our description of the problem-solving process is, as we have pointed out, a generalized one. The "natural history" of one creative problem-solving event differs from that of almost every other one, and these differences reflect differences in types of creative problems. In order to understand these differences we shall divide the types of problems into three major categories: *explanation, prediction,* and *invention.*

These three types can be distinguished by the different goals involved in each. In explanation, the goal is *to seek an understanding of why a specified event has occurred.* In prediction, certain conditions are given, and the goal is *to anticipate an event that has not yet happened.* In invention, the goal is *to create a novel set of conditions that will result in a specified event.*

Note: Before continuing, follow the instructions in Box 88.

Explanation

Problems in explanation have given rise to some of the most inspiring creative achievements of the human mind. The work of Galileo, Copernicus, Newton, and Einstein, for example, belongs to this category. But even in our everyday lives, explanation problems are probably those most commonly experienced. They most readily give rise to erroneous solutions and, paradoxically, are often the easiest to solve of all three types. (You saw one instance if you followed the instructions in Boxes 88, 89, and 90.) Because we are all so familiar with explanation (who has not tried to explain an event after it has happened?), we shall first examine explanation and then point out how it differs from prediction and invention. We shall find that all three types involve the same general psychological processes.

Causal Relations The most elemental form of explanation is almost a pure perceptual act. We know from Unit 14, however, that the perception of "cause" is a fairly compelling one and that it can be viewed as an instance of the grouping phenomenon in perception. The

Box 88

Invention

The photograph illustrates one of L. Székely's experiments performed at the University of Stockholm. In his experiment actual objects similar to those pictured here were placed on a table in front of the subject, and he was given instructions somewhat like the following: "Using *only* these objects, see whether or not you can balance the wooden plank on the edge of the prism in such a way that after a few minutes one of the ends of the plank will tip down *automatically,* that is, without being touched, or blown upon, or the table shaken, and so on." Székely reports that the vast majority of his subjects required several minutes and "considerable mental effort" to solve this problem. Pretend that you are one of his subjects and that you actually have these objects before you. Can you solve the problem in *two minutes?* Time yourself. *After two minutes, whether you have solved it or not, please turn to Box 89, p. 415, and follow the instructions there.*

L. SZÉKELY. 1950. Knowledge and Thinking, *Acta Psychologica,* 7, 1–24. Photo courtesy L. Székely, University of Stockholm.

"cause" will often be immediately perceived in the event itself. Frequently we do not feel that we have done any *thinking;* we just *see* the "cause" out there.

Very often, of course, these primitive explanations are completely wrong. Many are even judged wrong by the person himself and sometimes at the very moment he is "perceiving the cause." As has been pointed out:

"Someone comes home of an evening. A gust of wind slams the door shut behind him. At the same moment at the other end of the corridor, the light goes on in a room whose door is ajar. Although one knew ever so well that no causal connection exists between the door's blowing shut and the light's going on, that rather someone in the room has turned on the light, by chance at exactly the same moment—still he would be unable to escape the compelling impression of causal relationship." (Duncker, 1945)

Explanations and the Stimulus Pattern   To understand why the perception of cause is so basic and why these primitive explanations frequently go wrong, we must first remind ourselves of the stimulus factors that influence our causal perceptions. Among these factors are those of similarity and proximity (see Unit 10). Events A and B have a tendency to be perceived as causally related if they occur simultaneously or within a very brief period of time, if they are close to each other in space, or if they resemble each other in shape or form. In Duncker's illustration the simultaneous occurrence of the door's blowing shut and the light's going on results in a "compelling causal relationship" in perception. We have been "trapped" into a wrong explanation by the operation of simple perceptual law. The experiments of Michotte (discussed in Box 45, p. 226) provide other illustrations of how the perception of cause is determined by certain features of the stimulus pattern. Very frequently, when we observe two events in close spatial or temporal proximity, we "jump" to the conclusion that the events are causally connected.

The history of science is filled with illustra-

tions of just this tendency to jump to conclusions. In medicine it leads frequently to the treatment of symptoms rather than of real causes. A variant is seen in the error (common to some scientists as well as to laymen) of arguing cause-and-effect from the observation of "correlation." We may observe that, whenever juvenile delinquency becomes common, the divorce rate also increases; and, whenever juvenile delinquency decreases, so does the divorce rate (meaning that there is a "correlation" between juvenile delinquency and divorce rates); and from this correlation we might argue that juvenile delinquency must be caused by broken homes. Actually, of course, this causal relationship may not be true at all. Both juvenile delinquency and divorce may be caused by some third factor like economic or social upheaval.

In our efforts to explain an event we may be victimized in another way by the stimulus situation. Often the event we are trying to explain contains *too few* of the objects or facts that are essential for the explanation. Because, however, the event is such a dominant stimulus that we tend to limit our attention to it, we are at a disadvantage in our effort to discover the explanation. For example, the explanation of a child's temper tantrum may involve factors that are far removed in time and space from the tantrum itself. The explanation may involve not only the events immediately preceding the tantrum but also the history of the parents' relationship with each other and with the child.

On the other hand, the event may contain *too many* objects or facts, many of them irrelevant to the problem. The professional magician typically makes use of this principle. For example, he traditionally has a shapely lady "assistant," a perceptual prop whose eye-catching assets mask other aspects of the stimulus situation that are essential to seeing through his trick. Recall his sweeping movements and magnificent gestures, which create the perceptual diversion he needs to permit him to carry out the trick "before our very

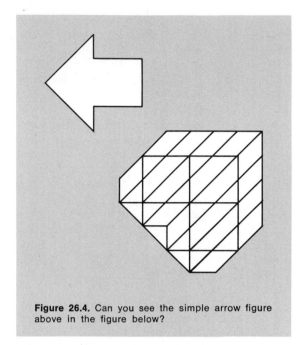

Figure 26.4. Can you see the simple arrow figure above in the figure below?

the time to do addition, and by 12 per cent! Apparently, adding one irrelevant or unfamiliar feature to as simple and familiar a task as addition or subtraction is enough to produce what Katz called *mental dazzle*.

"Mental dazzle," concludes Katz, "appears particularly well suited to emphasize the contrast between logic, which deals with the formal connections between the objects of thinking, and the defective manner in which those objects actually are comprehended."

Explanations and Past Learning The same object can be perceived with many different meanings; and frequently, of course, it is only by seeing a particular attribute of an object that we can achieve the explanation. For example, in Székely's experiment (Box 89, p. 415), the explanation lies in the candle. We can, however, see a candle with the meaning either of "a solid physical object with constant weight" or of "a source of light." Neither meaning will help us at all in our explanation. Only when we see that loss of weight is a characteristic of a burning candle can we achieve the proper explanation.

Paradoxically, many of the very same factors that make explanations so difficult to arrive at may under other circumstances make the explanations easy to achieve. For a specific example, let us return to Box 90, p. 416. Note how the very perception of the event to be explained almost "forces" the correct clue upon us. As we focus on the dominant feature of the situation, here is what we see: As the candle burns, the short end of the board on which it rests gradually rises. Almost by the principle of proximity alone we are directed to the real source of the effect—the burning candle. The final step is the simple one of recalling the fact that a burning object loses weight.

The significance of this illustration lies in the fact that very often in "real life" an event does provide most of the material necessary to achieve an adequate explanation. The elements of a causal relationship are frequently

eyes" (see Figure 26.4. for an instance of this effect operating in simple perception).

The disturbing effects that "excess stimuli" can have on problem solving were investigated in 1950 by David Katz, a German psychologist. He presented groups of schoolchildren with simple arithmetic calculations to perform—addition and subtraction. Some groups worked with undenominated numbers (for example, 10.50 plus 13.25 plus 6.89 . . .); other groups worked with numbers preceded by a familiar denomination (for example, $10.50 plus $13.25 plus $6.89 . . .); and still others, with numbers carrying an unfamiliar designation (for example, Kr. 10.50 plus Kr. 13.25 plus Kr. 6.89 . . .). He found that, first, the addition of a monetary designation increased the difficulty of calculation and, second, this difficulty became still greater when a foreign denomination was used. Katz repeated parts of this experiment with adults and found that even then denominated numbers increased

Box 89

Prediction

The photograph shows another problem that Székely used in his experiment. This time we have a problem in "prediction." When the objects had been arranged as illustrated, the experimenter asked the subject: "What will happen if the candle were to be lighted?" Different subjects, of course, were used for this problem than for the "invention" problem of Box 88. Székely found that this problem was somewhat easier to solve than the preceding one was, but it still took some doing. Of course you have an advantage over Székely's subjects because you have already attempted to solve the invention problem. If you have not solved the preceding problem, however, see what you can do with this one. Pretend that you actually have the pictured setup before you. Can you predict what will happen when the candle is lighted? *Can you say why?* Time yourself. You have only *one* minute.

After one minute, whether you have solved this problem or not, please turn to Box 90, p. 416, and follow the instructions there.

Photo courtesy L. Székely, University of Stockholm.

found close to each other in space or time, or similar to each other in certain characteristics. In other words, there is some degree of correspondence between cause and effect in the outside world and what happens in our perceptions.

Prediction

The goal of prediction is to understand a *future* event. This fact immediately suggests that the stimulus pattern confronting the problem solver in a prediction problem is not as highly structured as that in a problem of explanation in which the event is already complete.

As we have seen in Unit 11, perception is typically quite accurate because stimulus patterns in everyday life are usually quite well structured. When stimulus structure is relatively weak, however, mental sets can play a larger role in determining, and sometimes distorting, the perception. Thus, in prediction, the objects and the relations among them are so relatively few and undefined that the stimulus conditions will not, with the same degree of probability as in explanation, "direct" the correct organization. Székely's experiment gives us an experimental illustration. The subjects who attempted to explain an event did much better than the subjects who attempted to predict *the very same event.*

Paradoxically, the relative lack of stimulus structure in the prediction problem may sometimes help us to solve it. Because the explanation problem presents us with a fairly well-specified stimulus pattern, it may be relatively difficult to break away from the first solution we attempt, even if this solution is wrong. The first solution, it must be remembered, is the one most clearly determined by the stimulus pattern. We are, as it were, "bound" by the stimulus pattern. On the other hand, the prediction problem, by presenting relatively few stimuli, may make it easier for us to break away from any solution that does not work.

Box 90

Explanation

This photograph shows still another of Székely's experimental problems. This time we have a problem in "explanation." In his experiment the pictured arrangement was set up and the experimenter lit the candle. After a few minutes the plank tipped over as shown. Székely's subjects, after having seen it occur, were asked to *explain why it occurred*. This problem was relatively easy for Székely's subjects—but not a "cinch" for all of them. Again you have a considerable advantage over them because you have wrestled with the two previous problems. If you have not solved the preceding problems, however, try this one. Pretend that you have actually seen the event described. Can you explain *why* the lever tipped down after the candle had burned for a few minutes?

Photo courtesy L. Székely, University of Stockholm.

There are not enough stimuli to make us "stimulus-bound."

Experiments have supported this analysis. For instance, experiments on *functional fixity* show that, when a person actually sees an object functioning in one way, it becomes more difficult to perceive other possible uses for that object. The consequence is that problem solving is interfered with (see Box 91, p. 417). Furthermore, it appears that the degree of functional fixity depends on the importance of the function served by the object when it was initially perceived; the more functional an object's earlier or ongoing use, the more difficult it is to "see" another use for it (see Figure 26.5.).

Invention

We have defined the invention problem as one in which the goal of the problem solver is to arrange a novel set of conditions that will result in some desired event. Defined thus, invention encompasses a wide range of problems. Combining colors and forms into an oil painting; arranging wheels, gears, and spouts to make a new catsup-bottle filler; devising a new system of mathematics; writing a novel, a symphony, or a slogan—these are all inventions. What distinguishes an invention from an explanation or a prediction is the fact that, for invention, there are even fewer guides from the stimulus situation and that it makes heavier demands upon one's resources (see Box 92, p. 419).

No inventor sets out just to "create"—he always sets out to create a specific *something*. But this "specific something" has not yet happened, and therein lies much of the inventor's difficulty.

If the problem is to invent "sensies" (movies that will transmit to the audience not only what the actors do and say but also what they feel, taste, and smell), then it is "sensies" that will determine the materials and devices the inventor must work with. But our inventor's

Box 91

Functional Fixity—
A Barrier to
Creative Problem Solving

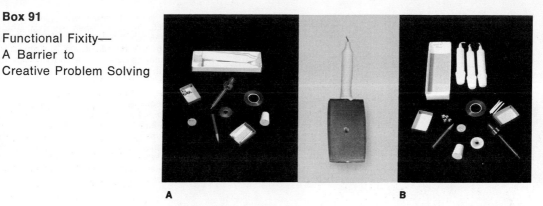

A   B

The German psychologist Karl Duncker first proposed the concept of "functional fixity" about 1930, and he illustrated it with a few simple experiments. Because these experiments were done with so few subjects, several American psychologists repeated them, and they obtained results similar to Duncker's. R. E. Adamson at Stanford University did one such experiment.

The task: Mount three candles vertically on a soft wooden board, using any object on the table. Among the objects are three cardboard boxes and a number of matches and thumbtacks. *The solution:* Mount one candle on each box by melting wax on the box and sticking the candle to it, then tack the boxes to the screen (see central portion of figure).

For one group (twenty-nine college students), the candles, matches, and tacks were placed *in* the three boxes before they were presented to the subjects (Figure A). *The boxes were thus seen functioning as containers*, whereas in the solution of the problem the boxes would have to be seen as "supports" or "shelves." For the second group (twenty-eight subjects), the boxes were empty and placed among the other objects (Figure B). There the boxes were not seen functioning as containers. Twenty minutes were allowed for the solution.

Of the first group, only twelve of the subjects (or 41 per cent) were able to solve the problem—apparently the remaining subjects in this group could not perceive the boxes with the meaning of "platform" or "shelf." Of the second group, twenty-four (or 86 per cent) were able to solve the problem.

These results give striking evidence that functional fixity may be an important barrier in creative problem solving. Note also the "mental dazzle" operating here.

R. E. ADAMSON. 1952. Functional Fixedness as Related to Problem-Solving, *J. Exper. Psychol.*, 44, 288–91.

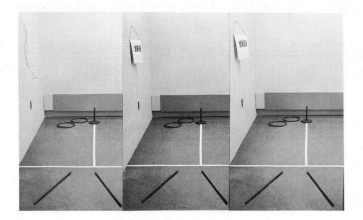

Figure 26.5. A ring-and-peg problem. The task here was to put the two rings on the peg while standing behind the chalk line. Any object in the room could be used. The problem could be solved with a piece of string with which to tie the two sticks together. The only string in the room hung on a nail on the wall. When it hung there alone without any apparent function (as in left panel), no subject failed to solve the problem. When the string was made somewhat functional by being used to suspend an old calendar (as in central panel), a number of subjects failed the problem. When the string was highly functional in that it supported a current calendar (as in right panel), more than half failed.

"sensies" do not exist. "Sensies" never have existed. "Sensies" therefore do not constitute a "stimulus pattern" that can give much guidance to the inventor.

To be sure, sometimes the specific thing that the inventor seeks to achieve may not be as foreign as "sensies" to his experience. Something similar to it may have occurred in the past. For example: The feeling of strength through delicate beauty has already been expressed in stone in Michelangelo's *David*, and the sculptor may have this in mind as he attacks his own block of stone. But *David* can have only limited value as a guide for the sculptor, because his problem is to create something new and original.

Nevertheless, originality must build upon a solid base of past learning and experiences. Creative inventions cannot spring full-blown from an empty mind or from a man devoid of specific skills. The painter must be aware of the tremendous range of colors, shapes, and materials that can be manipulated and arranged; the writer must be aware of the infinite variety and subtlety of human experience; the creative engineer must know a great deal about electronics. Furthermore, even the most novel solution very probably has borrowed from one's earlier solutions of perhaps simpler problems. Even observation of child behavior suggests that invention is greatly aided by prior solution of problems that are part of a new and more complex problem. Take a preschool child who astonishes his parents by producing an "artistic masterpiece" with his ten-cent box of crayons. They would perhaps be a bit less astonished had they observed, over the years, the child's fumbling attempts to grasp a crayon, his first wavering lines, the time (through accident) he "discovered" that a blue crayon over yellow produced green, and his "invention" of shading when he chanced to push an unwrapped crayon when it was lying on its side. We are not trying to downgrade our child artist but merely to point out that he, like his fellow inventors through time, had first to master many relevant skills and serve a kind of apprenticeship. During this apprenticeship they achieved many "part solutions" that could in some way contribute to the inventive solution of later and more complex problems (more about this topic in our discussion in Unit 27 of knowledge as a determinant of problem-solving effectiveness).

Box 92

The Inventor's Difficulty
—An Ambiguous Stimulus Pattern

W. S. Battersby. H. L. Teuber, and M. B. Bender at New York University tested the problem solving of men under three specified stimulus conditions. Although they were primarily interested in comparing brain-injured people with normal people, we shall consider here their results only on the uninjured men.

The Maier "string problem" was used. Each subject entered a room in which were a desk, a table, and two strings hanging from the ceiling. His task was to tie the strings together, although they were too far apart to reach one while grasping the other. The solution: Attach a weight to one string, give it a swing, run over to the other, catch the first string when it swings close, and then tie them together.

The "restricted" group was told that it could use only the objects provided by the experimenter. Upon completion of instructions the experimenter placed scissors on the desk. At successive two-minute intervals a clothespin, a small pulley, a yo-yo, and a fish-line sinker were similarly placed. Any one of these objects could serve as a weight.

The "less restricted" group was told that it could use any object in the room, *including* objects that the experimenter would place on the desk. Again at two-minute intervals the experimenter provided the five objects.

For the "unrestricted" group the five objects were on the *table* when the subject entered the room, but his attention was not drawn to them. The subjects were instructed to use any object *in the room.*

For the "restricted" group the experimenter pointed to the specific objects relevant to the solution; for the "less restricted," this pointing was more ambiguous ("use *any* object including . . ."); for the "unrestricted," there was no pointing.

The "restricted" group solved the problem in 2.4 minutes (average), the "less restricted" in 7.5 minutes, and the "unrestricted" in 15.2 minutes.

The analogy to the situation facing the inventor is clear. The inventor's goal does not specify the objects that will help him to achieve it, and, to the degree that it does not, his problem is magnified.

W. S. BATTERSBY, H. L. TEUBER, and M. B. BENDER. 1953. Problem-Solving Behavior in Men With Frontal or Occipital Brain Injuries, *J. Psychol.*, 35, 329–51.

Glossary

"aha!" experience An intense experience occasionally accompanying the sudden realization of how a problem can be solved. This experience may accompany false solutions as well as valid ones. The term "insight" is sometimes used for this experience.

creative problem solving (productive thinking) Achieving a solution to a problem that is new and original *to the individual.* Previously acquired knowledge enters into the process but must be transformed to fit the novel demands of the problem.

directed thinking Guided or controlled thinking. Thinking directed toward achieving a certain goal that, in a problem-solving situation, is the solution to the particular problem.

explanation A category of creative problem solving. Refers to those problems in which the person seeks to understand why a certain event has occurred.

functional solution A term proposed by Karl Duncker, a German psychologist, to refer to the second step in problem solving. The functional solution is characterized by a narrowing of the "general range," and thus specifies the nature of the final, but not-yet-achieved, "specific solution." (See also "general range" and "specific solution.")

general range A term referring to the step that occurs first in problem solving. It is a very general restatement of the original problem. This restatement indicates the direction of the to-be-sought-for solution.

illumination The third stage of problem solving. Identical with the "aha!" experience and refers to the sudden recognition of how a problem is to be solved.

incubation The second stage that may occur in the problem-solving process. During this stage no "conscious" work is done on the problem, but, when one returns to it, a prompt advance beyond the previous point of progress is noted. It has been suggested that during the "silent" or incubation period creative problem solving goes on despite the lack of conscious effort.

invention A category of creative problem solving. Refers to problems in which the person seeks to discover and arrange the objects that will be necessary to bring about a desired end. He must also understand why these objects will bring about the desired end.

prediction A category of creative problem solving. Refers to problems in which the person seeks to anticipate what will happen, given certain conditions. He must also understand why these specified conditions will bring about the anticipated event.

preparation The first stage of the problem-solving process. This is the period when the person becomes acquainted with the problem and "plays" with ideas for its solution.

reproductive problem solving Applying previously acquired knowledge, directly and without change, to solve a problem.

specific solution A term that pertains to the final step in problem solving. This step involves a further specification of the "functional solution" and, if successful, is the final, correct solution. (See also "general range" and "functional solution.")

verification The fourth stage of problem solving. At this stage the proposed general solution may be specified or it may be applied and tested.

determinants
of creative
problem solving

overview / Determinants of creative problem-solving effectiveness can, with some forcing, be categorized as situational or personal. Situational factors are transient and typically subject to experimental manipulation. Included in this category are spatial and temporal aspects of the presented problem stimulus pattern (including sets induced by prior activity), as well as relatively short-term emotional and motivational states. Problem-solving efficiency can suffer when such states reach high intensity, so that success, as well as failure, can inhibit performance. Because situational factors are modifiable factors, certain practical suggestions for improving problem-solving proficiency follow from an analysis of them. A number of psychologists have done considerable work on the practical question of how one can improve one's thinking. Indeed some of the more recent work has even led to a program of instruction for school children which has been shown to have positive effects on their creative problem solving.

Personal factors are relatively enduring determinants of problem-solving behavior and include knowledge and information relevant to the problem, general intelligence, and diverse personality factors. These personal factors typically interact with situational factors, as when the chronically insecure person is most affected by experimentally induced failure.

Persons who show creativity—by no means a simple and unitary talent—seem to possess, in addition to usually high intelligence, a combination of "childlike" traits (imagination, awe and wonder, sometimes tactless honesty) and "mature" traits (independence, responsibility, an accurate appraisal of reality). Perhaps creativity hinges on just these seemingly incompatible traits: the creative person—whether artist, scientist, or revolutionary—is able to merge the wonder, imagination, and honesty of a child with the cognitive skills of a mature and realistic adult.

In our analysis of the nature of problem solving in Unit 26 we discussed the roles played by stimulus structure and by knowledge and past experience in working at different types of problems. We shall now examine in some detail the operation of these factors, and others, as they influence the process of creative problem solving—a process that usually involves rather complex chains of reasoning and requires some considerable amount of time for solution.

We shall make a distinction between *situational factors* and *personal factors*, though no doubt the reader is by now wary of such separations and will anticipate our familiar assertion that the various factors are interactive rather than separate in their effects.

Situational Determinants

Here we shall be concerned, not only with the part played by the stimulus pattern that the problem presents, but also with the transitory mental sets and motivational and emotional states that are induced in the problem solver by the particular problem situation. Although these latter factors are unquestionably linked to the more enduring personality make-up of the subject (for example, the chronically anxious student will be more easily flustered when faced with a tension-inducing problem than will a characteristically placid student), we shall reserve a discussion of this interaction for the latter part of this unit.

Stimulus Pattern

If we can specify how the stimulus pattern facilitates or inhibits creative problem solving, we can use this information to improve our problem solving. The major interest in a scientific analysis is the understanding it gives us, but a scientific understanding also has practical implications, and we shall examine some possible practical uses of this analysis presently. As Lewin, a theoretician in psychology, used to point out, there is nothing as practical as a good theory.

The Gestalt psychologists, who have been interested in studying the influence of stimulus patterning on perceptual organization, have sought to demonstrate that the problem-solving process is in general analogous to the perceptual process and that the concepts of perceptual reorganization can be applied profitably to an analysis of the problem-solving process.

Some experimentation has been done on the effect of specific stimulus patterns on problem solving, and with encouraging results. On the basis of experiments that are available, we can state as a reasonable hypothesis that the spatial arrangement of the objects and events of a problem situation can facilitate or hinder the achievement of a solution in much the same way that it facilitates or hinders the achievement of a perceptual organization.

When the objects relevant to the solution of a problem are in the visual field of the perceiver, the problem will be solved more readily than when they cannot be perceived simultaneously (see Box 93, p. 425 for an experimental demonstration).

Another factor concerns the spatial subgrouping of the elements of the problem material. If the solution requires that object A be seen as a part of object X, and A is placed so that it can be seen as a part of object Y, the solution may be impeded (see the demonstration problem in Figure 27.1.). This effect can be accentuated by familiarity with the objects. Frequently the solution to a problem requires us to interpret a familiar object in a novel manner. When the object is located among other objects that have been seen together in the past (for example, a hammer is shown with nails and boards), it will tend to inhibit the novel interpretation (for example, it will be more difficult to see that the hammer might also be used as a measuring stick). In other words, proximity can enhance the likelihood that functional fixity will interfere with problem solution, and, by the same token, spatial separation of functionally

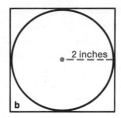

Figure 27.1. A square is drawn so that it just encloses a circle. The *circle* has a radius of 2 inches. What is the area of the *square*? Both a and b give the same information, but b is easier to solve. Why?

In a, the radius is so placed as to make it difficult to perceive it as "part of" the square. In b the radius can more easily be seen as "part of" the square.

Just prior to the outbreak of World War I, Wolfgang Köhler, one of the founders of Gestalt psychology, had gone from the University of Berlin to do some field studies at the Anthropoid Station on the island of Tenerife. With the outbreak of the war Köhler, as a German national, was interned at Tenerife by the Spanish government, and he was forced to remain there from 1913 to 1917. Out of his internment came his famous book, *The Mentality of Apes*. Among other things, Köhler studied the chimpanzee's use of implements in solving problems. One of the observations from this group of studies follows.

Tschego, an adult female chimpanzee, was tested for her ability to use sticks as rakes to pull in food from outside her cage. One simple factor that determined whether or not she could do so was the *spatial location* of the implement in relation to the food. Even a stick that she had *often* used as a rake lost all "instrumental value" if it was not visible to Tschego when she was gazing directly at the food!

Köhler summarizes:

"I have used every means at my disposal to attract Tschego's attention to the sticks in the back of her cage and she did look straight at them; but in doing so she turned her back on the objective, and so the sticks remained meaningless to her ... at the same time, *sticks*—and other substitutes—*which she beheld in the direction of her objective, were made use of without any hesitation*, and she devoured what food she could reach with relish."

w. KÖHLER. 1925. *The Mentality of Apes* (New York: Harcourt).

---

related objects should make it easier to "see" new uses for familiar objects. In any event, it seems a reasonable hypothesis at this time that the spatial arrangement of the objects and events of a problem situation can facilitate or hinder the achievement of a solution in the same way that it facilitates or hinders the achievement of a perceptual organization.

Temporal Organization and Set

Some problems present us with temporally as well as spatially patterned objects—some parts of the problem situation precede other parts. How does the temporal organization of such problems affect the ease or difficulty of solution?

We have seen that temporal patterning of stimuli can affect simple sensation and perception, as shown by the phenomena of adaptation, fusion, temporal summation, and so on (see Unit 9). In addition, we discussed set—another important perceptual effect of temporal patterning significant for our present discussion. In Unit 11, we saw that, if we are presented with several objects in succession, the perceptual attributes of the later objects reflect the influence of the earlier objects. This effect is sometimes referred to as the *Einstellung* (German word for "set") effect because the initial work on this phenomenon was done in Germany.

The influence of sets on problem solving has been studied extensively, and a classic experiment in this field is one by Luchins (see Box 94, p. 427). His results indicate that solving a number of problems by one method of attack tends to trap the person into using the same method of attack on later problems, even though the method is now inefficient.

Some have argued that being caught by this *Einstellung* effect is simply a tribute to the usual efficiency of one's problem-solving strategy. If we have a general solution that "works," it is appropriate to continue to apply it in a series of very similar problems. Along the same lines, others attribute the effect to the typical and usually highly adaptive tendency for the problem solver to behave more and more automatically as an initially difficult problem, requiring some thought, is followed by additional problems that are solvable by the same principle. He gradually narrows his perception of the situation, eventually confining it to the single principle. Usually this is a quite sensible procedure, and one which speeds his solution.

An interesting extension of this sort of explanation is provided by Knight (1963). Using a somewhat modified version of the *Einstellung* test (this time with five jars rather than three), two groups of subjects (college students in a classroom situation) were required to solve a series of twenty-one water jar problems. The two groups differed in only one respect: One group (High Effort) on its very first trial was presented with a problem that was rather difficult to solve. The jar capacities were (A) 1,000, (B) 0, (C) 371, (D) 247, (E) 25; target—199 quarts. The Low Effort group was confronted with an easier problem: (A) 1,000, (B) 0, (C) 300, (D) 10, (E) 1; target—293 quarts. Both problems were solvable by the same principle: (C) − (D) + 3(E). Not surprisingly, the High Effort group took considerably longer to solve its first problem. On subsequent trials it showed, in comparison with the Low Effort group, a sub-

stantially greater *Einstellung* effect, persisting in the use of the initial, more complex principle when a far simpler one was feasible. Furthermore, the High Effort group, when confronted with a problem for which the initial principle would not work at all, continued to demonstrate the *Einstellung* effect by evolving overly complicated principles similar to the initial principle. Perhaps most startling is the finding that on the last problem (jar capacities—1,000, 0, 680, 640, 320; target—1,000) only seven of twenty-two subjects in the High Effort group saw the obvious solution, whereas eighteen of twenty-four did so in the Low Effort group!

The lesson of this experiment seems quite straightforward: The more we invest initially in deriving a certain problem-solving principle, the more likely we are to stick to it. Whether this "investment" is cognitive, motivational, or emotional, we cannot say—it is probably a bit of each—but the practical implications of this finding, which we shall soon spell out, are not difficult to see.

Emotional and Motivational States

As we have pointed out, a problem situation can induce various emotional and motivational states in the problem solver. These states can, in turn, influence the effectiveness of problem solving. There are many experimental ways to create stress and emotional pressure in a problem-solving situation, and psychologists have used them in problem-solving studies. In one of them, Ray (1965) devised a problem in which the subject had to discover the principle governing the designation as "correct" of only one of the digits in a series of numbers. (The principle was to select the last digit in numbers composed of three consecutive digits only.) Half of his subjects, however, were first presented with a "similar" problem in which there was in fact no "correct" principle that could be discovered. This "failure" group worked for twelve minutes on this frustrating task before attacking the true and solvable problem. The

Box 94

Practice Makes Blindness

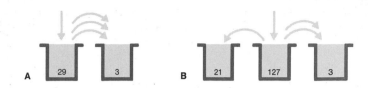

A. S. Luchins, while at New York University, investigated the following question: "Several problems, all solvable by one somewhat complex procedure, are presented in succession. If afterwards a similar task is given which can be solved by a more direct and simple method, will the individual be blinded to this direct possibility?" Adapting a technique previously used at the University of Berlin, Luchins carried out a series of *Einstellung* (mental set) experiments to answer the question.

The task: Obtain a required volume of water, using certain empty jars for measures. The table presents the basic eight problems used.

Problem	Given Empty Jars Holding Number of Quarts as Listed			Obtain the Following Number of Quarts of Water
1	29	3		20
2	21	127	3	100
3	14	163	25	99
4	18	43	10	5
5	9	42	6	21
6	20	59	4	31
7	23	49	3	20
8	15	39	3	18

Problem 1 was an illustrative problem; problems 2 through 6 were "training problems"; problems 7 and 8 were "critical test problems." Problem 1 is presented and the solution shown diagrammatically (Figure A). Problem 2 is next shown, and the answer is again diagrammed (Figure B) and explained: "One fills the 127-quart jar and from it fills the 21-quart jar once and the 3-quart jar twice. In the 127-quart jar there then remains 100 quarts of water." The method that solves problems 2 through 6 may also be used in 7 and 8. *But* problem 7 may be solved *more directly* by subtracting 3 from 23 and problem 8 by adding 3 to 15.

An experimental group was given problems 1 through 8 in succession (at intervals of about 2 1/2 minutes). A control group went from problem 1 to problems 7 and 8, skipping problems 2 through 6.

In the following table are shown results on the critical test problems (7 and 8) from one experiment done with college students. The experimental subjects gave far fewer direct solutions. Previous success with one technique can thus blind a person to simpler solutions.

Group	Number of Subjects	Percentage Indirect Solutions	Percentage Direct Solutions	Percentage Other Solutions or Complete Failures
Control	57	0	100	0
Experimental	79	81	17	2

A. S. LUCHINS. 1942. Mechanization in Problem-Solving, *Psychol. Monogr.*, Vol. 54, No. 6. Table and figures adapted by permission of American Psychological Association.

"control" group—the other half of the subjects —went directly at the true problem. Of the control subjects, 49 per cent solved the true problem within allotted time limit, and only 32 per cent of the "failure" group did so—a significant difference. (A similar technique of inducing failure and frustration produces similar results with rats—see Box 95, p. 429.)

This finding probably comes as no surprise. There is abundant evidence that intellectual ability in general suffers from failure. Such evidence ranges from experimental situations in which tested intelligence actually drops, following a short-term induced-failure situation, to the increasingly depressed IQ scores of minority-group children as they grow older—in part a function of frequent school failure caused by inadequate intellectual preparation and stimulation. The effects of frustration can also be quite pervasive. Later on (Box 161, p. 762) we describe how a minor frustrating experience decreases the constructiveness of children's play.

Perhaps less expected is Levitt's (1956) suggestion that success can sometimes "spoil" creative problem solving. In his review of experimental results with the water-jar *Einstellung* task, he notes that in experiments by Cowen (1952a, 1952b) both a "praise" group and a "severe stress" group persisted longer in using the initial and no longer best solution in later trials than did a "mild stress" group. Perhaps a feeling of success, if sufficiently powerful, can, like frustration and failure, be a source of stress and hence of reduced problem-solving efficiency.

Too strong motivation, insofar as it leads to stress, may also lead to a decrease in problem-solving efficiency. Box 96, p. 430, provides experimental evidence on the effects of degree of motivation on problem solving in the chimpanzee and points to a general result consistent with observations of human beings.

This general result is depicted in Figure 27.2.; the relationship between problem solving and intensity of motivation can be described as an inverted "U curve." That is, as the intensity of the problem solver's motivation increases, his problem-solving effectiveness also increases *up to an optimal point*. Beyond that point any increase in intensity of motivation will result in a decrease in problem-solving efficiency. This curve is to be taken merely as an abstract representation of the shape of the motivation-efficiency relationship. Psychological science is not yet in a position to provide precise quantitative specifications for the curve. In fact, there can be little doubt that the optimal point on the curve will vary tremendously from one person to another. This variation is in part attributable to enduring personality factors within the individual, some of which we shall discuss later in this unit.

Some Practical Suggestions

From each of the foregoing analyses of the situational determinants of problem solving—spatial patterning, temporal patterning, set, and emotional and motivational states—we can derive some practical suggestions for improving problem-solving effectiveness.

Remembering that the spatial arrangement of the objects and events of a problem situation

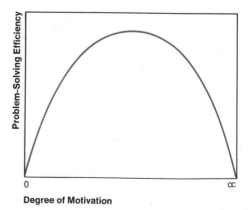

Figure 27.2. A hypothetical curve representing the suggestion that the relationship between degree of motivation and problem-solving efficiency is curvilinear. As the degree of motivation increases from zero, the problem-solving efficiency first increases and then decreases.

Box 95

Frustration and Fixation

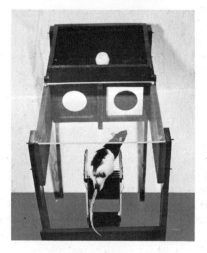

The effect of frustration coupled with punishment on problem-solving behavior in the rat has been experimentally studied by N. R. F. Maier, N. M. Glaser, and J. B. Klee. Rats were placed on a pedestal in a jumping stand facing two doors, one locked and the other unlocked. If the animal jumped against the locked door, it bumped its nose and fell into a net below; if it jumped against the unlocked door, it was able to get through to food. A black card with a white circle on it was affixed to one door and a white card with a black circle to the other door.

In the usual learning problems one card always marks the unlocked door, which is randomly switched between left and right. The rat's task is to learn to jump to the "correct" card.

In the present experiment, however, the investigators deliberately frustrated the rat by making the problem *insoluble*. They did so by arranging it so that each card brought rewards 50 per cent of the time and punishment 50 per cent of the time, regardless of whether it was on the right or on the left. Furthermore, they forced the rat to jump from the pedestal by giving it an electric shock.

Under these circumstances most animals soon developed a fixed habit of jumping either always to the left or always to the right. This pattern of jumping is just as "good" as any other, inasmuch as the animal will in any case receive 50 per cent rewards and 50 per cent punishment.

That the stereotyped habit became inflexible and maladaptive to changes in the situation was clearly shown when the experimenters made the problem actually soluble by regularly meting out punishment for jumps at the side on which the rat was fixated and unlocking the door on the opposite side. Under these circumstances, the rat persisted in jumping to the same side on which it was fixated, even though it was punished every time. This stereotyped behavior lasted for hundreds of successive trials. It persisted *even after the door on the other side was entirely removed so that the rat could plainly see that jumping to that side would give access to the food.*

Here on the rat level we seem to have rigidly stereotyped behavior, experimentally induced through prolonged frustration, that looks remarkably like the fixated habits, ineradicable through usual means, that are often observed in human beings.

N. R. F. MAIER, N. M. GLASER, and J. B. KLEE. 1940. Studies of Abnormal Behavior in the Rat: III. The Development of Behavior Fixations through Frustration, *J. Exper. Psychol.*, 26, 521–46.

Box 96

Intensity of Motives and Problem Solving in the Chimpanzee

In 1945 H. G. Birch investigated the relationship between motivation and problem solving in young chimpanzees. He used the "stick problems," which require the animal to rake in food with a stick. The problems differ in spatial patterning and complexity (see figure). In problem 1 the stick is next to the food; in 4 the stick is *behind* the animal as he faces the food; in 7 the animal has to take the *short* stick behind him, with it pull the string attached to the *long* stick into reach, pull in the long stick by the string, and finally sweep in the food with the long stick. Motivation was varied by depriving the animals of food for two, six, twelve, twenty-four, thirty-six, and forty-eight hours before testing.

The results are best described in Birch's own summary:
"When motivation is very low the animals are easily diverted from the problem by extraneous factors and behavior tends to deteriorate into a series of non-goal-directed acts. Under conditions of very intense motivation, the animals concentrated upon the goal to the exclusion of other features of the situation which were essential to the solution of the problem. Also, the frequent occurrence of frustration responses, such as tantrums and screaming, when a given stereotyped pattern of response proved to be inadequate, hindered the animals in their problem-solving efforts. Those animals who worked . . . under intermediate conditions of motivational intensity . . . were not so dominated by the desire to obtain the food that they were incapable of responding to other relevant features of the problem situation. Their behavior was characterized by both direction and flexibility in response."

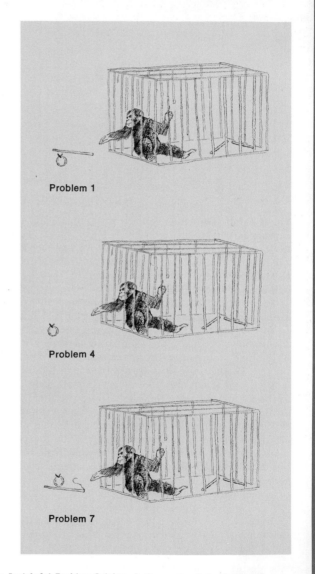

Problem 1

Problem 4

Problem 7

H. G. BIRCH. 1945. The Role of Motivational Factors in Insightful Problem-Solving, *J. Comp. Psychol.*, 38, 295–317.

can facilitate or hinder a solution, apparently we should be able, by proper spatial arrangement of objects, to change a difficult problem into an easy one. This reasoning points to a very simple practical suggestion for improving problem-solving efficiency for certain types of problems: The problem solver does not usually face an immovable array of materials and objects. He is allowed to manipulate and rearrange them. (When this setup is not possible physically, he can imagine rearrangements.) By deliberately trying out various spatial arrangements and not remaining fixated on the original one, he increases the probability of arriving, by chance alone, at an arrangement facilitating the solution. We shall see later that the general principle implicit in this "hint to the problem solver" has been experimentally tested with encouraging results.

There is another way of dealing with the problem of the stimulus pattern. As we pointed out earlier, certain features of the problem can be so dominating that they draw all or most of our attention to them at the expense of the less obvious but crucial features. To deal with this possibility, it is reasonable (even if paradoxical) to *reduce* the attention you pay to the problem you wish to solve. One way to do so is to take a break. Forget the problem for a while, and do something else. When you return to it, your excess attention to the previously dominant objects may be weakened.

Frequently, the crucial objects for a solution may not even be present in the immediate situation. To encourage seeking elsewhere for the missing link, it is sometimes helpful to work on related problems. The stimulus pattern of a related problem may include the objects that are necessary to solve the original problem. Perhaps "reasoning by analogy" is often fruitful for this reason (see Box 97, p. 432).

Just as the spatial organization of objects and events of a problem situation may facilitate or hinder a solution, so can their temporal sequence. Many problems require the solution of a series of subproblems. Sometimes the prob-

lem solver finds it difficult to realize that this sequence is not rigidly fixed once and for all. Another practical suggestion stems from the recognition that this temporal sequence can be varied in several ways.

We may have a choice between starting with where we wish to end and starting with where we are at the moment. In the first instance we start by analyzing the goal. We ask, "Suppose we did achieve the goal, how would things be different—what subproblems would we have solved, and so on?" This analysis in turn would determine the sequence of problems, and we would work back to the beginning. In the second instance we start by analyzing the present situation, see the implications of the given conditions and layout, and attack the various subproblems in a "forward direction." In some instances it may even be preferable to start in the middle; that is, we can say: "Let us assume I can solve the first four subproblems involved, and I now have arrived at such-and-such a point. Where can I go from here?" (This leaves for some later time the solution of the first four subproblems.) For different kinds of problems, certain temporal sequences may prove more efficient than others. The advice of the backwoods Vermonter who said, in response to the tourist who asked how to get to St. Johnsbury, "If I were you, I wouldn't start from here!" may be sound advice for the problem solver. Unlike the bewildered tourist, we do not always have to start from "here."

Sometimes our temporal sequence may be the most efficient, but the time intervals between the solution of one set of subproblems and the start of another may be too short or too long. Here it may help to vary the tempo of our work on any one problem. In some cases it may be preferable to work away at the various subproblems until we have solved them all; in other cases we may want to take frequent breaks. Again, our knowledge about the effects of temporal ordering is not specific enough to permit us to say which we should do for any specific problem, but it is clear that the timing

Box 97

**If at First You Don't Succeed
—Don't Try Again; Try Another Problem**

In his book *How to Solve It* the mathematician G. Polya of Stanford University gives many valuable hints to college students on how to deal with mathematical problems. Among other suggestions he stresses the importance of analogies, "auxiliary problems," and "related" problems:

"People often use vague, ambitious, incomplete, or incompletely clarified analogies, but analogy may reach the level of mathematical precision. All sorts of analogy may play a role in the discovery of the solution and so we should not neglect any sort. . . . We may consider ourselves lucky when, trying to solve a problem, we succeed in discovering a *simpler analogous problem.*

Auxiliary problem is a problem which we consider, not for its own sake, but because we hope that its consideration may help us to solve another problem, our original problem. . . . The auxiliary problem may appear more accessible than the original problem; or it may appear instructive; or it may have some sort of aesthetic appeal. Sometimes the only advantage of the auxiliary problem is that it is new and offers unexplored possibilities; we choose it because we are tired of the original problem all approaches to which seem to be exhausted.

We can scarcely imagine a problem absolutely new, unlike and unrelated to any formerly solved problem. . . . In fact, when solving a problem, we always profit from previously solved problems. . . . Hence the question: *Do you know a related problem?* . . . The intention of using a certain formerly solved problem influences our conception of the present problem. Trying to link up the two problems, the new and the old, we introduce into the new problem elements corresponding to certain important elements of the old problem."

All these practical suggestions from a teacher of mathematics add up to methods of enlarging the range of stimuli that play upon us as we go about the business of trying to solve problems. Perhaps this idea lies behind the Inventor's Paradox, that is, "the more ambitious plan may have more chances of success than the more limited one." As Polya points out:

". . . when passing from one problem to another, we may often observe that the new, more ambitious problem is easier to handle than the original problem. More questions may be easier to answer than just one question. . . . The more ambitious plan may have more chances of success provided it is not based on mere pretension but on some vision of the things beyond those immediately present."

G. POLYA. 1946. *How to Solve It* (Princeton: Princeton University Press). Text material reprinted by permission.

between subproblems can be important, and therefore, whenever we do get "stuck," that varying our timing may help.

In our analysis of the *Einstellung* effect we saw that one of the hazards to problem solving comes from too much attachment to a method of attack that has proved effective in the past for solving problems similar to the new one. One suggestion that can help "break" such a mental set is to turn away from the problem for a while. On returning to it after the lapse of some time, we must begin with "fresh" attention instead of responding blindly and inattentively.

Another approach is that of Maier (1933), who sought to overcome the stereotyping effects of set by attempting directly to make salient for the problem solver the necessity of varying his attacks on the problem. In demonstrating this technique, Maier performed several experiments at The University of Michigan; among them was the following.

In an introductory course in psychology 384 students were divided into a control group (206 students) and an experimental group (178 students). Three problems were presented to each group. The experimental group also received a twenty-minute lecture followed by general hints on "how to reason" (see Box 98, p. 434) before it was given the problems. The three problems included the "string" problem, which we have already described (see Box 92, p. 419), and two similar "reasoning" problems.

Within the hour allowed for solution of the problems, the experimental group earned a total correct-solution score of 49.2 per cent, whereas the control group earned only 39.7 per cent. These results indicate that a twenty-minute general lecture improved the problem-solving ability of the experimental group. A second experiment on different students (testing their reasoning ability before and after the lecture) gave similar results, and Maier concluded, in part:

"The results of both experiments indicate that when subjects are carefully instructed to guard against habitual activities and persistent directions, but to be alert for new points of view, there is a decided increase in reasoning ability as measured by the increase in solutions found to difficult problems. . . . One cannot equip a person with the ability to form solution-patterns, but one can train him to clear the ground so that the solution-pattern is not prevented from appearing."

We must avoid overgeneralizing from the results of Maier's experiment, however. In the first place, as Maier himself specifically points out, his experiments do not prove that we can "equip a person with the ability to form solution-patterns." In part this ability is dependent upon the person's basic intelligence, and no amount of well-designed lectures or "how-to-think" books can do very much to change that. In the second place, "clearing the ground so that the solution-pattern is not prevented from appearing" may sometimes make very little difference. Successful problem solving necessitates a store of previously acquired knowledge, as we have noted earlier in Unit 26. If the store of knowledge is not there or if the knowledge was acquired in ways that make it unavailable for novel and creative problems, no amount of "ground clearing" can help. Finally, Maier's findings do not imply that all we need do to get rid of "habitual activities and persistent directions" is to listen to a general lecture. Personality factors may effectively inhibit the development of "new points of view." We cannot say to a person who gets emotionally upset by ambiguous stimulus patterns, "Be alert to new points of view, guard against habitual directions," and expect any more success than we can from saying to a neurotically anxious person, "Stop worrying!" More fundamental difficulties are present—as we have seen in our discussion of emotional and motivational factors —than general lectures and admonitions can remedy.

Certainly we have not been arguing that our

Box 98

A Psychologist's Lecture
Notes on How to Reason

N. R. F. Maier's lecture that was successful in improving the problem-solving scores for 178 students covered the following points:

1. The solution of a problem, when it is the product of reasoning, consists of a pattern that is made up of parts of different past experiences.
2. The pattern forms suddenly, as does the hidden face in a picture puzzle.
3. Meanings of elements depend on the pattern of which they are a part. The sudden formation of a pattern therefore results in sudden changes of meaning.
4. The solution pattern overcomes a difficulty.
5. The difficulty is what one sees it to be. It is not in the problem. (Illustrations were given that show how the same problem can be solved in different ways, each solution being the conquering of a different difficulty.)
6. The particular difficulty one sees determines what one will do about it, that is, what direction one will take (for example, one doctor will seek a serum to immunize man to certain germs; another will seek a means of preventing the germ from traveling).
7. All difficulties cannot be overcome. Therefore one must find a difficulty that can be overcome.
8. Most people see the same difficulty.
9. The difficulties we see are often determined by our past contact with problems (for example, other diseases have been conquered by the discovery of serums). Such difficulties are habitual difficulties and give rise to habitual directions.
10. Habitual directions do not solve difficult problems. Problems are difficult when a successful direction is not obvious.

Maier then summarized his lecture with the following "Hints on How to Reason":

"Locate a difficulty, and try to overcome it. If you fail, get it completely out of your mind and seek an entirely different difficulty.

Do not be a creature of habit and stay in a rut. Keep your mind open for new meanings.

The solution pattern appears suddenly. You cannot force it. Keep your mind open for new combinations, and do not waste time on unsuccessful attempts."

N. R. F. MAIER. 1933. An Aspect of Human Reasoning, *Brit. J. Psychol.*, 24, 144–55. Text material reprinted by permission.

"helpful hints" are really to no avail, for such factors as personality, store of knowledge, and even general intelligence—all personal factors— are powerful enough to override whatever problem-solving tactics we may employ in a given situation. By no means. These "hints" do work, and, what is more, highly systematic training in "productive thinking" has recently been shown to have positive effects on creative problem-solving ability (see Box 99, p. 437). But the more enduring personal factors are determinants of considerable importance to understanding individual differences in problem-solving ability, and we shall now turn to these factors.

Personal Factors

As we have mentioned, people vary in the extent to which they are susceptible to such situational influences as stimulus pattern, set, and optimal level of motivational arousal. These individual differences reflect the interaction between the situational determinants we have listed and such enduring characteristics of the individual as knowledge, intelligence, and personality traits. There are many examples of such interactions.

Among the situational determinants, it will be remembered, are the perceptual characteristics of the specific objects presented in the problem situation. But the way in which an object is perceived is in part determined by one's knowledge about the object. For example, the physiognomic properties of an object often suggest all kinds of novel uses, but with increased knowledge about an object the physiognomic properties play a minor role. The knowledgeable astronomer who has learned that the moon is a dead mass of matter that can only reflect light from the sun and has no interior source of radiant energy will rarely see in the moon the "ignorant" child's perception of "a hot bird flying through the night sky." Yet this is the stuff of creative poetry.

We have also seen that the specific temporal patterning of a problem can induce a mental set

that inhibits creative problem solving. But the evidence seems clear that the strength of the *Einstellung* effect is also influenced by the individual's intelligence. Many experiments indicate that lower intelligence is associated with greater susceptibility to the *Einstellung* effect.

Finally, we know that the amount of stress induced in the individual by the problem situation can influence problem solving. But the degree of stress that even the best efforts of the experimenter can induce very clearly reflects differing personality traits of the different individuals. Thus Ray (1965) reports the following experiment. The problem was to transfer a stack of doughnut-shaped rings of varying diameters from one peg to another, moving one ring at a time without placing a larger ring on top of a smaller and using a third peg as a "way station." One group was instructed to work as quickly as possible; another was permitted to work at its own speed. Among his many results Ray found that the "speed" group showed a much greater range in the number of moves made than did the "no-pressure" group. The instruction to "work as fast as possible" was heeded—at least in terms of number of moves made—by some subjects *and not by others*. Situationally induced pressure, therefore, seemed to be controlled by differences among individuals, differences that very probably reflected variation among the subjects in enduring personal characteristics: a finding of several other studies. The reader will probably recognize among his friends some who "blow up" under the pressure of timed examinations and others who "keep their heads," solving problems with efficiency under these circumstances.

Always keeping in mind, therefore, that the situational and the enduring personality factors interact, we can now consider these latter factors in some detail.

Knowledge

Every discussion of creative problem solving— whether by the practical inventor who generalizes from his own experiences or by the psychologist who theorizes on the basis of laboratory experiments—stresses the intimate relationship between knowledge and creativity. This relationship can be summarized in two contradictory statements: First, the more knowledge an individual has acquired in the past, the greater the possibility that he will be creative with new problems; second, the less knowledge an individual has acquired in the past, the greater his creativity. The reason for this apparent contradiction is that both statements are valid—when properly specified as to meaning.

On the one hand, it is clear that in order to solve a difficult problem a person must have the specific knowledge required for that solution. The more numerous the meanings we have learned to attach to an object, the more flexible we can be; that is, we can use the object in more varied ways in attempting to solve a new problem.

On the other hand, facts can be restrictive. In many instances the very well-informed individual is overly trained upon certain traditional or stereotyped meanings of an object. This functional fixedness, as we have seen earlier (Unit 26), may prevent a person from achieving the novel and even bizarre meanings essential to a creative solution. Knowing less, he may be freer to come up with unusual ideas. Furthermore, the "facts" he has learned may be positively misleading.

Much of the "knowledge" we acquire—whether through experience or formal education—is simply wrong. Insofar as this statement is true, the ability to do creative problem solving is damaged by the acquisition of this "knowledge." Probably Charles Kettering, the famous inventor, had this thought in mind when he said, "The inventor is a fellow who doesn't take his education too seriously." In this respect the many instances in which creative scientists have moved from their initial fields of study and flourished in new fields can be evidence for the "fresh approach," particularly when it is taken by a generally able prob-

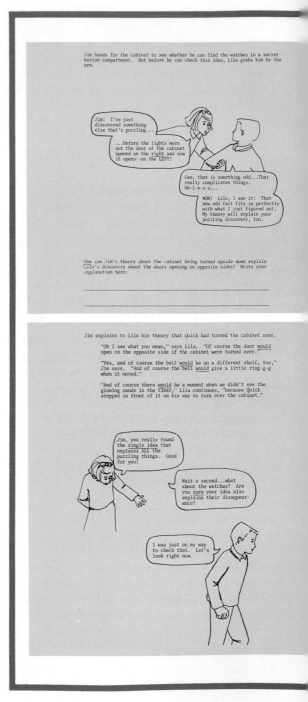

Box 99

From the Catalogue
at Utopia University

"Psychology 101—*Productive Thinking.* This course is intended to develop the student's ability to use various skills and strategies that favor originality and effective problem solving. It attempts to enhance understanding of the student's own thought processes, increase his readiness for independent thought, and seeks to foster a sense of enjoyment in the use of the mind."

You will probably not find a course like this one listed in your college catalogue, but several thousand fifth-grade and sixth-grade children in schools throughout the United States have been learning how to think productively in this way by using materials developed by psychologists M. V. Covington, R. S. Crutchfield, and L. B. Davies at the University of California, Berkeley. Specifically, the children work through a series of sixteen cartoon-text booklets, each featuring mysterious and baffling situations to be explained. The basic idea is to teach the children to use their minds by having them learn to solve problems in the manner of imaginative scientists, scholars, and detectives.

As a problem develops, the student is led through successive steps of the lesson, which require him to learn about and to practice a variety of thinking skills and strategies. For instance, at various points the student is asked to write down ideas for solving the problem. On subsequent pages he compares his own ideas with a range of illustrative examples of relevant, fruitful, and original ideas that he might have thought of. Each lesson is so designed that the student gradually works toward the solution and is eventually brought to make the discovery for himself. The "discovery" experience is intended to foster a sense of competence in coping with difficult and complex thinking tasks.

To provide a thread of continuity among the problems, each lesson features two elementary-school children, Jim and Lila Cannon, and recounts an adventure in which the reader participates (and identifies) with these fictional and appealing children (see the two sample pages from one of these booklets).

These investigators believe that virtually everyone, regardless of his intelligence or his initial level of thinking competence, can profit substantially from direct instruction in the skills basic to all productive thinking.

Extensive research has indicated that school children who are taught by this method show considerable superiority to control children in terms of problem-solving performance on a broad range of thinking tasks, some of which are quite dissimilar to those used in the training program. Additionally, there are marked increases in the *willingness* of the instructed children to engage in complex thinking activities, as well as noteworthy changes in their general work habits, including persistence in the face of obstacles and difficulties.

M. V. COVINGTON, R. S. CRUTCHFIELD, and L. B. DAVIES. 1966. *The Productive Thinking Program.* Berkeley: Educational Innovation. Augmented edition in press. Columbus, O.: Merrill.
M. V. COVINGTON and R. S. CRUTCHFIELD. 1965. Experiments in the Use of Programmed Instruction for the Facilitation of Creative Problem Solving, *Programmed Instruction.* 4.

lem solver. Perhaps, as has been suggested with some seriousness, scientific problem solvers of proven ability should be turned loose on the "sticky" questions in fields other than their own. This version of "musical chairs" would allow scientists to employ their generally applicable skills of observation and reasoning while taking a "new look" at old and difficult problems. Such scientists, equipped with a little (but not too much) knowledge, may ask penetrating and profound questions that open up new avenues to solution.

Availability of Knowledge Useful knowledge that has been forgotten is useless. Sheer memory is a very important determinant of creative prob-

lem-solving ability, because only knowledge about the object that is remembered can be used in problem solving. As we have seen, however, memory is not an all-or-nothing affair. Some attributes of knowledge may be easily recalled, some recalled with difficulty, and some completely forgotten. To put it another way, various attributes of objects that we have learned are differentially available (see Box 100 for an experimental illustration of the relationship between different degrees of availability of meanings of common objects and problem solving).

The Uses of Knowledge The availability of knowledge, then, is of crucial importance in

---

Box 100

"Availability" of Meanings and Problem Solving

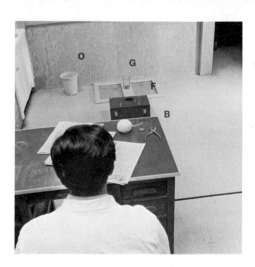

P. Saugstad and K. Raaheim at the University of Oslo tested the hypothesis that problem solving may depend on the general availability of specific meanings for certain objects.

Among the subjects tested were ninety-five Oslo high-school boys. *The task:* Using anything on the table, transfer the balls from the glass G to the container O without stepping beyond the black line (see photograph). *Solution:* With the pliers the nail is bent into a hook, tied to the string, and thrown so as to catch the wooden frame F, which is then pulled around the obstruction B to within reach of the subject. The newspapers are then rolled into tubes and with the aid of the rubber bands are made into one continuous tubing. The balls can now be rolled through this long paper tube into the container O.

problem solving. Once available, the knowledge may be used in three different ways when we are engaged in creative problem solving: First, we may reproduce a bit of knowledge in a new situation directly and without change. For example, in Figure 27.1. we apply directly to the new problem, without any change, our previously learned knowledge that the area of a square is equal to the square of one of its sides. Second, we may transform an experience so that it becomes applicable to the solution of a problem (see Box 101, p. 440). Third, we may combine many specific experiences into one abstraction. This generalized knowledge is now applicable to the solution of a problem in which the specific knowledge (which was derivable from or included in the generalization) is not helpful in solving the problem (see Box 102, p. 441).

Any specific piece of knowledge can, of course, appear in any one of these three forms. Thus the knowledge that "wood floats," when stated in this way, is a reproduction. When stated in the form "A wooden pellet when released at the bottom of a container of water will shoot up to the surface," it is a transformation. When stated in terms of the Hydrostatic Principle, it is an abstraction. Obviously any specific piece of knowledge that is available in all three forms will be more useful than the same piece of knowledge available in only one form.

At a previous time the subjects had been given a "functional availability" test. For example, they had been told that a nail could be used to fasten, catch, stick, and hang things. They had then been asked to write down three illustrations for each function. The same was done for the other objects to be used in the later problem.

To solve the problem, two "unusual" meanings are involved: the nail as a "hook" and the newspapers as "tube." Particular attention was therefore paid to mentions of "hook" and "tube" (or "funnel") in the subjects' illustrations of the functions of a nail and a newspaper, respectively. Three groups were thus distinguished: subjects who had mentioned both "hook" and "tube," those who had mentioned one *or* the other, and those who had mentioned neither. On the Saugstad problem the three groups performed as shown in the table.

Function Available	Number of Subjects	Percentage of Solutions
Hook *and* tube	18	89
Hook *or* tube	40	42
Neither	37	19

Success in problem solving may sometimes be determined by the availability of a specific meaning for a specific object. On the basis of later research, however, Raaheim warns that we must not fail to distinguish between two quite separate aspects of problem solving of this sort. First, the subject must discover what it is that is "missing" in the situation. In the present example, he must recognize that he needs some way of bringing the glass G to his table, then some way of getting the balls in that glass into container O. Second, only after he achieves this "part solution" can the subject discover how to employ the available objects in order to fill the "missing" functions discovered in the first phase of his problem-solving activity.

P. SAUGSTAD and K. RAAHEIM. 1956. *Problem-Solving as Dependent on Availability of Functions.* Table adapted by permission of Universitets forlaget, Oslo. Manuscript.

K. RAAHEIM. 1965. Problem Solving and Past Experience, in P. H. Mussen, ed., *European Research in Cognitive Development. Monogr. Soc. Res. Child. Develpm.*, Vol. 30, No. 2.

Box 101

Simple Knowledge
Creatively Transformed

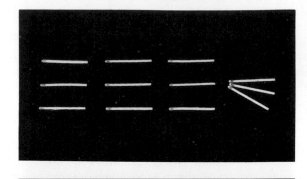

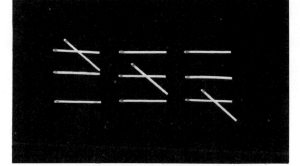

L. Székely demonstrated how a very simply acquired experience may be used in creative problem solving. The subject was given three columns of match sticks, with three sticks in each column, and three more sticks with which to work (top photo). His task was to distribute the three extra sticks among the three columns in such a way that every vertical and horizontal row would have four sticks in it. Few subjects solved the problem.

One day later the subjects were asked to participate in an entirely separate experiment. In this new experiment a horizontal row of lines was shown, and the subject was *instructed* to draw a perpendicular through every third line (see drawing).

Some subjects, while carrying out these instructions, suddenly asked for some match sticks, saying that they wanted to try out an idea. They then solved yesterday's problem as shown in bottom photo.

Two things should be noted: The subjects returned to yesterday's unsolved problem "of their own accord," and the newly acquired experience was transformed a bit before it was applied to a new problem.

Try this experiment on your friends.

L. SZÉKELY. 1945. Zur Psychologie des Geistigen Schaffens, *Schweitzer Zeitsch. Psychol.*, 4, 110–24.

Box 102

Specific Knowledge
Versus Abstraction

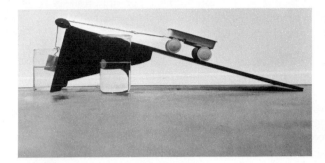

An abstract principle is often more useful in solving problems than are concrete statements of specific knowledge. We shall try to demonstrate this thought, with you as a subject. If you are too sophisticated for this experiment, try it on your less sophisticated friends.

On an inclined plane stands a cart attached to a string. The string runs over a pulley to a block of wood that is just barely touching the surface of water in a container. The whole arrangement is so balanced that the cart remains stationary. Standing on the table is a beaker of water. Nothing else is available (see figure). Your task is to set the cart in motion so that it will move *down* the inclined plane. You are not permitted to touch the cart or put anything into it; nor may you lift the wooden block with your hands. Here is a bit of knowledge that helps to solve the problem: *Wood floats.*

Second problem. Everything remains as before, *except* that in place of the wooden block you now have a small lead weight. Again the arrangement is so balanced that the cart is at rest (the same figure will do). Same problem: Cause the cart to move *down.* Here is a bit of knowledge that helps to solve the problem: *Lead sinks.*

If you don't understand the solution to this second problem, let us review your freshman physics a bit. Take the two bits of specific knowledge, "wood floats" and "lead sinks" and see them as specific instances of an abstract generalization: *Whether a body floats or sinks depends upon the ratio between the body's weight and the weight of the displaced quantity of water.* If this Hydrostatic Principle doesn't seem to help you, let us state it in still another manner—in terms of Archimedes' Principle: All bodies, when immersed in water, appear to lose a certain part of their weight. The "lost weight" corresponds to the quantity of water displaced.

Now can you solve the second problem—and *understand* its solution? (This "experiment" is a revision of one performed by Székely.)

We see how an abstract principle may help when specific knowledge fails.

L. SZÉKELY. 1950. Knowledge and Thinking, *Acta Psychologica*, 7, 1–24.

Intelligence

Roughly speaking, intelligence is a relatively stable "given" of the individual, a personal ability he brings, in much the same measure, to every new problem-solving situation.

But there is more direct empirical evidence of the relation of intelligence to problem solving. The importance of these studies lies not in demonstrating the common-sense point that brighter people are better problem solvers but in giving a fuller experimental and theoretical account of the precise role of intelligence in the problem-solving process. We have already mentioned the greater susceptibility of less intelligent subjects to the *Einstellung* effect—a susceptibility hindering effective performance in this problem situation. Klausmeier and Loughlin (1961), in testing the problem-solving performance of eleven-year-olds, found that one distinguishing difference between high- and low-IQ children was that the former showed greater skill in verifying their tentatively proposed solutions and therefore finally submitted fewer incorrect solutions. Osler and Trautman (1961) found that children of superior intelligence—particularly on more complex problems—typically went about seeking a solution by developing and testing hypotheses as to the correct principle and therefore were more likely to achieve sudden "aha!"-type solutions. Children of normal intelligence, by contrast, developed fewer hypotheses and seemed to approach solutions by trial and error, therefore gradually.

Personality

It is difficult to disentangle the effects of what are usually regarded as "personality" determinants from those of other factors with which they typically interact in a problem-solving situation. If a subject is so tense that he fails to solve a relatively simple problem, is it because he is generally a tense individual (personality), because he regards the problem as a test of his general adequacy as a person (excess motivation in the situation arising from a personality trait), or because he is not very bright and therefore sees problem solving as an area of weakness and becomes tense (intelligence × personality × motivation)?

Another difficulty is the confusing variety of personality factors that seem to be related to problem solving. Studies have shown that such factors as flexibility, initiative, and confidence are characteristic of good problem solvers. In addition, there is fairly convincing evidence that a tendency to conform to social pressure is associated with poor problem-solving performance. For example, Nakamura (1958) found that conforming college students did worse on a variety of problems than did those who showed independence of judgment, even when intelligence differences between conformers and nonconformers were taken into account. Quite a different kind of correlate of problem-solving ability is reported for nursery-school children by Maccoby, Dowley, Hagen, and Degerman (1965). The ability to inhibit motor movement, measured by such tasks as the ability to draw lines and to walk "very slowly," was found to go with superior performance in solving hidden-figure perceptual problems. It was not that the better problem solvers were less active children —measurement of general activity level at play showed no such relationship—but rather that the ability to control and restrain motor activity when required to do so was a trait directly associated with ability to solve certain problems. Is this finding "just" owing to the ability to follow instructions carefully—both in the motor tests and in the problem-solving situation—or is some personality factor of "impulse control" involved? The investigators raise this question and propose further research to answer it.

These examples of research on personality determinants of problem-solving ability highlight some of the complexities of the issue. Instead of studying the relations of various personality traits to the process of problem solving, we can study the personality characteristics of people who have clearly manifested creativity in their work or professions.

Creativity and Personality The psychological study of creative persons has an honorable past and a highly active present. The picture it has provided of creative individuals of all kinds is reasonably consistent. Much of the recent work on this question has come from the Institute of Personality Assessment and Research (University of California), where intensive studies have been made of a variety of creative groups—like architects, writers, artists, mathematicians, business innovators, and scientists.

In these groups of individuals, all of whom were at least moderately high in intelligence, it was found that the more creative individuals were not necessarily the more intelligent. Nor had these more creative individuals necessarily shown superior scholastic performance. When they are compared with not highly creative persons of the same intelligence level, many striking personality differences emerge. Perhaps the most provocative of these differences is that creative persons often present a curious mixture of personal maturity and "childlike" traits. The creative person tends to be self-confident, dominant in his dealing with others, and quick to take the initiative and to persevere. Yet he tends to be nonconformist, even irresponsible at times, and his independence of judgment sometimes borders on the militantly unconventional. He is open to experience and does not suppress the unpleasant; he is thus able to be devastatingly accurate in his perception of himself and others. Perhaps his creativity hinges on just this point: He is able to merge the wonder, imagination, and honesty of the child with the cognitive skills of a mature and realistic adult.

This portrait seems to hold generally for creative individuals of various sorts. That it is indeed applicable to research scientists—who might be expected to be a bit more "responsible" and "hard-headed"—is supported by the following conclusion from a study that compares creative research chemists and psychologists with scientists who have had the same professional opportunity but who have not shown great creativity (Chambers, 1964):

"The creative scientist thus emerges as a strongly motivated, dominant person who is not overly concerned with other persons' views or with obtaining approval for the work he is doing. He is not the type of person who waits for someone else to tell him what to do, but rather thinks things through and then takes action on his own, with little regard to convention or current 'fashion.' He then is prepared to face the consequences of making unpopular decisions or of pursuing unconventional paths in his search for evidence relating to nature's laws."

When speaking of creativity in terms of achieving eminence in a lifelong career, it is easy—too easy—to assume that creativity is a single unitary trait. But a moment's reflection will demonstrate how varied are the abilities and skills required to make up even a single creative act. Research on this question clearly supports one's reflection; for example, Guilford and his associates, employing the technique of factor analysis, have reported the existence of over two dozen relatively independent abilities associated with creative problem solving and thinking in general (Merrifield, *et al.*, 1962). Faced with such diversity, the appeal of using a global criterion for creativity—a creative lifetime—is evident.

Glossary

Einstellung The German word for "mental set." The common use of this German word reflects the fact that the mental-set experiments originated in German psychological laboratories.

personal factors (in problem solving) Refers to such relatively enduring determinants of problem solving as pertinent knowledge, general intelligence, and personality characteristics. These determinants interact strongly with situational factors.

situational factors (in problem solving) Refers to such transient and manipulable determinants of problem-solving behavior as spatial and temporal aspects of the stimulus pattern and experimentally induced motivational and emotional states. These determinants interact strongly with personal factors.

locus of learning

overview / Learning and memory must be correlated with changes in some parts of the nervous system. In this unit we consider which parts of the nervous system participate in these changes; in the following unit we discuss *what* the changes are, biochemically and physiologically.

There is some evidence that learning can take place in the spinal cord when it is separated from the brain, and it has been established that an animal deprived of cerebral cortex can learn and remember. Nevertheless, all the complex behavior of higher animals depends upon the presence of the cerebral cortex, working in conjunction with many other parts of the nervous system.

Some investigators have believed that all parts of the cerebral cortex contribute equally to the ability to learn. The preponderance of modern evidence has favored another view, however: the belief that different parts of the cerebral cortex contribute in different ways to adaptive behavior. Portions of the posterior association area of the cortex are each related to a specific sensory system; each appears to receive input from a given cortical sensory area and is essential to normal learning and memory based upon stimuli from that modality. Damage to the frontal association area produces changes that are less easily characterized; they may, however, be summarized as disruptions in the ability to integrate correctly stimuli that are currently coming to the organism with plans for motor activity formed on the basis of previous experience. Conclusions such as the foregoing are based upon experiments with various kinds of animals and upon the study of people with localized damage to the brain. In a human being, damage to the cerebrum (particularly the left side) can produce a unique change—aphasia, the loss of language ability.

In earlier units (Units 15–18) we have considered the question of the physiological basis of sensation and perception. We described the nature of the activity of various parts of the nervous system when a stimulus is presented to the individual, and we discovered that certain parts of the brain are essential if perceptual experience is to be normal and complete. In all behavior one or more of these perceptual mechanisms must be involved, for, although stimuli are not always necessary to "excite" us into activity, they *are* always present as a background, affecting the ongoing activity of the nervous system and thus "steering" the behavior.

A given stimulus pattern does not always produce or facilitate the same response. When, as a result of experience, there is a consistent change in the response to any stimulus pattern, we usually say that learning has taken place. This "learning" is of course correlated with some change in the nervous system, and our interest now is in studying the location and nature of such changes.

Most of the experiments in this field (indeed until quite recently almost all of them) have used the ablation method (see p. 248), a method first employed systematically by the French physiologist Pierre Flourens (1824). Flourens' work is important for several reasons. To begin with, it was the first *experimental* study relating behavior to the brain, standing in contrast to the uncontrolled observations upon which the phrenologists had based their claims (see Box 103, p. 447). Flourens' work is also important because his conclusions exemplify the patterns of thought and research that characterized this field of investigation for many years and that still influence us today. For one thing, Flourens noted that the brain is composed of several organs, each with its own functions. He considered the cerebellum the "seat of the principle which coordinates locomotor motion" and the cerebrum the "seat of intelligence." This distinction is still regarded as relatively sound. Second, he thought that the cerebrum is functionally indivisible. "Sensations, perception, and volition . . . occupy the same seat in these organs, [and] constitute therefore essentially one factor." This conclusion stands in contrast to the view taken by many scientists that different intellectual functions are controlled by different parts of the cerebrum. The further developments in this controversy we shall later discuss at length. We should note at this time, however, another aspect of Flourens' conclusion: that the various intellectual faculties are all one *because* they share a common structure in the brain.

The long line of research that began with Flourens and is still continuing has attempted to specify the locus of learning: *Where* in the nervous system does learning take place?

Learning Without the Cortex

Spinal-Cord Learning

Can any learning take place without the participation of the brain; in other words, can learning take place in the spinal cord? Experimentation on this topic has been restricted to animals, as we must have a subject whose brain has been surgically "disconnected" from the part of the body that is to be trained, although human paraplegic patients (in whom the lower half of the body has been "disconnected" from the brain by a spinal injury) could also be studied.

The basic technique in these studies is fairly simple. Under surgical anesthesia the spinal cord of the animal is cut completely through, thus severing all the neural connections between the lower part of his body and the brain. An animal with the cord cut is called a *spinal animal* and with proper care can be kept alive for years. During the postoperative period conditioned-response training is instituted. Both the stimuli and the responses for the conditioning training must be chosen so as to involve only the lower part of the body. (Visual and auditory stimuli cannot, of course, be used in such training because they would involve the

Box 103

Phrenology

Although P. Flourens' book marks the beginning of experimental work on the brain-mind problem, the general question had been dramatically raised fourteen years earlier by two German physicians, F. J. Gall and G. Spurzheim. In their six-volume *Anatomy and Physiology of the Nervous System* they laid the basis for phrenology by asserting that first, the brain is the organ of the mind, second, different kinds of behavior are controlled by separate parts of the brain (see figure), and, third, the external shape of the skull reflects the shape of the brain underneath. (Protuberances and dips on the skull presumably reflected over- or underdevelopment of the brain underneath.)

Science has treated Gall and Spurzheim with ridicule. Yet their anatomy and neurology were sound, and their general theoretical position was a reasonable one for the time. Why, then, did their contemporaries and history treat them so meanly? One might venture two explanations: First, phrenology seemed to be an easy way of "finding out about people"—just feel the bumps on their heads! In the hands of the uncritical and the charlatans, phrenology became a morass of pseudoscientific nonsense. Second, the supporting *data* Gall and Spurzheim used fell far short of scientific standards. Here is how Spurzheim relates the "discovery" that physical love is controlled by the cerebellum:

"Being physician to a widow who was subject to very strong hysterical fits, during which she drew her head backward with great violence, Gall sometimes supported her head with his hand, and, in doing so, observed that her neck was very large and hot. He was acquainted with her character [Gall's case history of this patient makes it clear why she is sometimes referred to as "Gall's passionate widow"] . . . and he accordingly considered in connection with her passion, this magnitude of the neck, and the consequent development of the cerebellum."

When a reasonable theory is wildly overstated, the good in an idea is thrown out with the bad. Nevertheless, as E. G. Boring reminds us, phrenology accomplished two things:

". . . it forced the problem of correlation of mind and brain to the fore . . . [and] by going to extremes, Gall made a radical but less extreme view actually seem conservative. Without a Gall, Flourens might never have conceived the problem of finding different functions for the cerebrum, the cerebellum, the medulla and the cord."

F. J. GALL and G. S. SPURZHEIM. 1810. *Anatomie et Physiologie du Système Nerveux* (Paris: Schoell).

E. G. BORING. 1950. *A History of Experimental Psychology*, 2nd ed. (New York: Appleton).

brain.) If the spinal animal, under these circumstances, is able to acquire a conditioned response, we have evidence that simple acquisition is possible without the help of the brain. In this case, presumably, the integration of the incoming sensory stimuli and the outgoing motor impulses is wholly under the control of the spinal cord.

The results from such experiments are somewhat ambiguous. Using electric shocks to a spinal dog's two hind legs as the conditioned and unconditioned stimuli, some experimenters have failed to find any evidence of hind-leg movement. Others have reported more positive results. In one experiment isolated muscles in the dog's leg were conditioned to "twitch" when the tail was shocked or pinched (see Figure 28.1.). The same group of workers has also reported that animals whose spinal cords are severed in early infancy will in many cases eventually develop nearly normal walking behavior. It may be argued, however, that the acquisition of walking is principally owing to maturational processes and that we should not consider it evidence for spinal learning.

In any event, it seems clear that if the spinal cord can learn, it is restricted to very simple conditioning. For acquisition of the complex responses involved in the adaptive behavior of man and beast, the spinal cord is not enough. We must look higher up for the locus of most learning.

Subcortical Learning

The levels next above the spinal cord where we might find the locus of the control of learning are the subcortical structures of the brain. Can learning take place there, without the help of the cerebral cortex? The obvious method of approach is to examine the behavior of *decorticate animals,* that is, animals whose entire cortexes have been removed or destroyed.

Decorticate animals can show some signs of learning in simple problem situations. One experimenter (Bromiley, 1948) was able to train a completely decorticate dog to avoid a shock to its leg by flexing it when a whistle was sounded. He was also then able to extinguish this response and retrain the dog to flex its leg to the onset of a light. The dog survived thirty-three months without a cerebral cortex, but its behavior remained at a very low level of complexity. For the first twenty postoperative days the dog had to be given water by means of a stomach tube, before it could learn to lap the water from a pan held under its nose. It was able to swallow pieces of meat placed on the

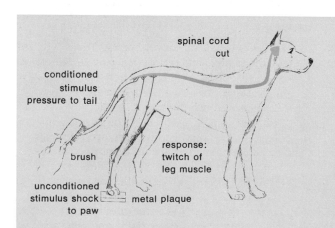

spinal cord
cut

conditioned
stimulus
pressure to tail

brush

response:
twitch of
leg muscle

unconditioned
stimulus shock
to paw

metal plaque

Figure 28.1. Can the spinal cord learn? This picture illustrates the procedure used by the investigators who reached an affirmative answer. A cut is made across a dog's spinal cord, and then conditioning trials are begun. On training trials the tail is stimulated with a brush (conditioned stimulus), and the paw is given an electric shock (unconditioned stimulus). The shock causes a response: a contraction of a muscle dissected free from the upper leg. After sufficient training the muscle responds to the conditioned stimulus alone. The brain cannot have been involved in this change in behavior because the nerve pathway between it and the leg had been cut.

back of its tongue, but it took the dog more than four months to relearn to eat food from a pan.

It would appear then that, at least among animals like the dog, the cortex is not needed for the acquisition of the most primitive kinds of problem solving—very simple conditioned responses and sensory discriminations. For these kinds of problems, the subcortical mechanisms alone may be sufficient. But by themselves they do not seem sufficient for the acquisition, retention, and control of the more complex patterns of behavior that characterize the dog, let alone even higher animals.

Cortical Learning

It appears obvious that we shall, in the cerebral cortex, find the major locus of complex adaptive behavior. For we are at the end of the road; there is no place else to go. The very complexity of the cortex suggests that we have found the right spot. The number of neural cells in the cerebral cortex has been estimated at more than 9 billion. These 9 billion cells can fire in an astronomical number of different groupings and sequences. We have here all the complexity needed for integrative action. It would seem that the cerebral cortex *must* be the locus of learning and problem solving.

But not necessarily. All that we have demonstrated is that the centers below the cerebral cortex cannot *alone* provide the neurological basis for acquisition. It is still possible that even the most complex forms of learning and problem solving depend upon these lower centers *in conjunction with the cerebral cortex.*

Actually this possibility is the one favored by many contemporary workers in the field. The long search for the "place" where learning occurs is no longer directed toward finding a specific, sharply delimited "point locus." Any acquisition may involve simultaneous changes in the cerebral cortex, subcortical structures, spinal cord, and perhaps even peripheral nerve

endings in the sensory organs and muscles. What the experimenter does when he studies the relationship between the cerebral cortex and learning is to "tap" *one point of a complex circuit.*

The Problem of Cortical Localization

Are different kinds of learning and problem solving dependent upon different areas of the cortex? In a sense we are asking the same question that the phrenologists-anatomists Gall and Spurzheim asked (and answered affirmatively) in 1810.

Experimental work in the last 150 years has led to various suggestions concerning cortical localization of intellectual functions. These suggestions have ranged from specificity hypotheses (in the tradition of Gall and Spurzheim) to complete nonspecificity ones (in the tradition of Flourens).

An American psychologist, Karl S. Lashley, provided perhaps the strongest case for "nonspecificity" in the cortical control of learning. He performed an extensive series of experiments involving cortical ablation in the rat. Working mostly with mazes, he found that the *specific part* of the cortex that was destroyed was of little consequence in determining an animal's learning score. A lesion of one part of the cortex had the same effect as a lesion of the same size in another region. It is for this reason that Lashley spoke of the *equipotentiality* of the regions of the cortex. The important consideration was not *which part* of the cortex was destroyed but *how much* was destroyed. A large lesion anywhere had a more profound deteriorating effect than a smaller one. Lashley referred to this finding as the *mass action* effect. He recognized that there are areas within the cortex with specific sensory and motor functions, but he believed that these regions (as well as all other parts of the cortex) shared in the control of learning and problem solving.

Others were quick to offer alternative explanations of Lashley's data, and many subsequent experiments seem to have demonstrated some limitations to his conclusions. One argument stresses the complexity of learning (particularly of maze learning) and of the brain. If the task we call "maze learning" really depends upon *many* different sensory and motor abilities and if each of these abilities is localized in one specific part of the cortex, then lesions of different sizes in different parts of the cortex would be expected to produce just the results Lashley obtained: A small lesion almost anywhere would disrupt some one "ability" and make maze learning a little difficult; a larger lesion almost anywhere would probably disrupt several "abilities" and produce a more profound effect upon maze learning. Those who argued in this fashion could suggest that there were *no* cortical areas for "learning" as such, whereas Lashley felt that *all* of the cortex shared in the control of learning.

A third major view about cortical functions in learning must be discussed at some length. This view does not fit well with Lashley's data but appears to be bolstered by many recent experiments, particularly with more complex animals like monkeys and men.

Learning Areas

Because there are special areas that seem to be related to certain sensory and motor functions, could not there be areas of cortex particularly designed to operate in learning and problem solving? There are, for example, areas of cortex whose destruction does not seem to produce sensory or motor changes, and, the higher the animal is in the phylogenetic scale, the larger these areas are. These facts have led to the belief that such areas are primarily involved in learning, and they have even been named the *association areas* of the cortex. In a typical mammal there are two such areas, the frontal and the posterior association areas, each of which can be divided into various subareas (see Figure 28.2.).

Evidence that they play a special role in

learning would be provided if we could show that destruction of these areas is correlated with a loss in learning ability. We get an "extra dividend" of evidence if we can show that different parts of the association cortex are important to different *kinds* of adaptive behavior. Both kinds of evidence are now available.

Posterior Association Area

Although many kinds of animals have been used in studies of the role of the association areas, our knowledge is perhaps most complete for the popular zoo animal, the rhesus monkey. In the monkey we have an animal whose association areas are rather highly developed, and we gain the advantage of working with an animal that is rather similar to humans.

The posterior association area, as can be seen in Figure 28.2., is surrounded by the various primary sensory areas, and lesions of this area produce *deficits* in learned behavior involving sensory discriminations (see Box 104, p. 452).

Furthermore, subareas of this posterior association cortex play different roles. There seem to be separate regions within the posterior association area that are particularly important for learning discrimination tasks based upon each of the various kinds of sensory input.

But why should different parts of the association area be related to learning in different sensory modalities? What features of the anatomy of the brain can explain these relationships? In exploring these questions, let us consider the visual system and the *inferotemporal cortex;* lesions of this area cause a profound deficit in the learning of visual problems. Earlier we traced the principal visual pathway from the eye via optic nerves and tracts to the lateral geniculate body and thence to the cortex of the occipital lobe (see p. 248). The inferotemporal area may receive its important inflow through fibers that begin in the occipital cortex and that relay across the cortex to terminate in this association area.

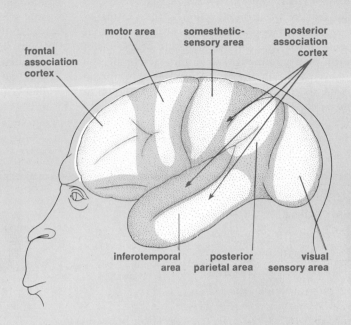

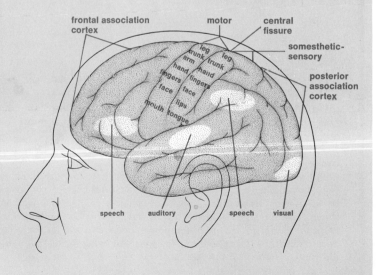

Figure 28.2. The functional map of the cortex. Represented here are the more definitely established functional areas of the human and the monkey cortex. Note the sensory areas that receive impulses fairly directly from the sense organs (via the thalamus) and the motor areas that send impulses that reach the musculature. Note the relatively large extent of the motor area in man that is given over to control of the movements of fingers and hands—the organs capable of the finest manipulation. The control of motor activity is not entirely restricted to the motor areas shown here. Motor activity can be produced by stimulation of other parts of the cortex as well, and the cerebellum and various subcortical structures are also important in the initiation and organization of movement.

Also indicated are the association areas and the regions of cortex that are particularly important to the comprehension and production of human speech.

It might be of interest to compare the figure with the Gall and Spurzheim map of the brain shown in Box 103, p. 447.

Some evidence for this explanation comes from a consideration of animals that have been subjected to a *split-brain* operation. The essential feature of this operation is the cutting of the major commissures, the fiber tracts that connect cortical cells of one side of the brain with neurons in corresponding parts of the other half of the cortex. If, in addition, in the same animal, we make a cut through the optic chiasma from front to back, the activity aroused by light entering one eye will affect the cortex only on the same side of the brain.

This statement is true because the excitation will go to the lateral geniculate *only* on the same side (crossing over at the chiasma is impossible), and the excitation will not be transmitted to the corresponding parts on the other side of the brain at the cortical level (because the commissures are cut). We end with an animal that has two almost completely independent half-brains! This technique has been a very useful addition to the methods of study of brain function, and some of the results and their implications are presented in

Box 104

Cortical Localization
in the Monkey

What does the association cortex "do"? Is it really the place where learning takes place? Is it a sensory area? Is it a higher-level perceptual region? Or what? These questions are unresolved, debated questions. It is clear, however, that the posterior association cortex does not play the same role as does the primary sensory cortex of the brain, although subregions of the posterior association area are somehow related to different sensory systems.

When a lesion is made in the inferotemporal areas of the monkey's brain (see Figure 28.2.), he becomes "visually stupid," that is, he is much slower in learning a visual problem than is an unoperated animal. This fact however, does not prove that the inferotemporal area is a "learning region." For example, if we destroy part of the occipital cortex (the visual *sensory* area), an animal may also become "visually stupid"—simply because he can't *see* as well as before. William A. Wilson and Mortimer Mishkin, psychologists then at the Institute of Living, Hartford, Connecticut, compared the effects of lesions of the inferotemporal cortex and the lateral portion of the occipital cortex. Although both operations changed the visually guided behavior of the monkeys, the *pattern* of change was quite different for the two operations.

Box 105. p. 456. For our present purposes, it is useful to consider the effects of adding the split-brain operation to certain lesions of the cerebral cortex.

Let us return to the inferotemporal cortex. Those effects of lesions in this area that were described earlier occur only if the lesion is produced bilaterally (on both sides); with a lesion of only one side, there is little or no change in behavior. Furthermore, if to a unilateral inferotemporal lesion we add a unilateral lesion of the occipital visual cortex *on either side*,

we still get no profound disruption in visual learning (see Figure 28.3., p. 454). Let us perform the split-brain procedure on an animal. If this operation is performed on a monkey with his intact occipital and inferotemporal areas on the same side of the brain, he still remains essentially normal. If, however, we cut the commissures in a monkey who has his normal occipital and inferotemporal areas on different sides of the brain, he immediately displays the learning difficulty we have been studying. The conclusion is that normal visual behavior de-

This difference is clearly shown when the operated monkeys are tested on the *patterned-string* problem and the *learning-set* problem. In the patterned-string problem the ends of two strings are placed within reach of the caged monkey; a bit of food is attached to the far end of one string. The strings may cross each other one or more times, but the full length of both strings is exposed. The monkey is allowed to pull in only one of the strings. In this problem there is very little new to learn. Lesions of the occipital cortex produce errors on this kind of problem; lesions of the inferotemporal cortex do not. A learning-set problem is a series of visual discrimination problems (see figure). A tray containing two objects (for example, an ashtray and a toy horn) is presented to the monkey, and he is allowed to lift one; he receives the same pair of objects for several trials and can learn that food is always to be found under only one of them, the ashtray, let us say. We then repeat the procedure with two new, completely different objects. As this testing is done over and over, normal monkeys and monkeys with occipital lesions learn each new problem faster and faster. Monkeys with inferotemporal lesions, however, show much less of this "development of a learning set." The patterned-string test seems to be more a measure of sensory function and the learning-set problem a measure of learning ability; these two problems thus provide evidence for somewhat different functions of the cortical regions under consideration.

The inferotemporal area is essential to normal *visual* learning; the *posterior parietal* cortex plays a part in learning based on touch and kinesthetic cues. Martha Wilson, a psychologist now at the University of Connecticut, demonstrated this difference by comparing the performances of monkeys that had these two lesions—performance on visual problems like those discussed and performance on learning problems that could be solved only by using tactual information. The inferotemporal lesion caused a deficit only on the appropriate kinds of visual problems; the posterior parietal lesion only on the tactual problems.

Further refinement of the lesions and the tests used, and evidence based upon other experimental procedures, will help us to clarify the exact contribution of association cortex to the adaptive behavior of the organism, but we already know the broad limits within which the answers will be found.

W. A. WILSON, JR., and M. MISHKIN. 1959. Comparison of the Effects of Inferotemporal and Lateral Occipital Lesions on Visually Guided Behavior in Monkeys, *J. Comp. Physiol. Psychol.*, 52, 10–7.
M. WILSON. 1957. Effects of Circumscribed Cortical Lesions upon Somesthetic and Visual Discrimination in the Monkey, *J. Comp. Physiol. Psychol.*, 50, 630–5.

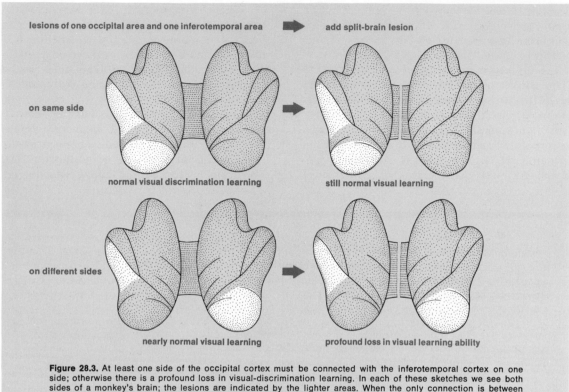

Figure 28.3. At least one side of the occipital cortex must be connected with the inferotemporal cortex on one side; otherwise there is a profound loss in visual-discrimination learning. In each of these sketches we see both sides of a monkey's brain; the lesions are indicated by the lighter areas. When the only connection is between the two different areas on different sides of the brain and thus by way of the corpus callosum, behavior may be slightly poorer than normal (lower left). When the corpus callosum is cut, learning ability is greatly impaired (lower right).

pends upon the existence of at least one intact occipital area plus one intact inferotemporal area, that these two areas must be able to interact, and that this interaction normally takes place via cortico-cortical connections, including the interhemispheric commissures. It therefore appears that a direct path for the visual information that plays a part in adaptive behavior is from the eye to the occipital cortex via the lateral geniculate body and from the occipital area to the inferotemporal area by cross-cortical fibers. Thus we see that for learning (as opposed to perception) additional areas of the cortex appear to be essential.

Frontal Association Area

Lesions of the frontal association cortex have very little, if any, effect upon the ability of a monkey to learn individual discrimination problems but will produce profound effects upon the animal's ability to *use* sensory information in certain forms of adaptive behavior.

We have a most striking demonstration of this effect in the *delayed-response problem*. In this problem the monkey watches the experimenter place food in one of two identical containers. The monkey is not allowed to approach either container until after a *delay* of several

seconds. When he then makes his choice, he gets the reward if he indeed chooses the baited container. One can give the monkey many such trials, randomly placing the food in one container or the other.

In these circumstances, normal monkeys can learn to respond correctly after delays of several hours or more. If, however, an animal's frontal association area is destroyed, he will inevitably fail at such a problem even with a delay of only a few seconds. The animal will watch the experimenter hide a piece of food and then, only five seconds later, may go, apparently at random, to either of the two containers.

Another problem that "frontal" animals fail to solve is the alternation problem. In this situation the monkey sees two closed containers on each trial—if he wants to get the food reward on any trial, he must alternate, that is, go to the container *other* than the one he chose on the previous trial. Here, too, the frontal animal may find impossible a problem that normal monkeys will learn rather rapidly.

If we attempt to analyze these problems, we note that they are not simply related to sensory learning functions. In the first place, they are not peculiarly dependent upon one or the other sensory modality. It is true that the monkey (like man) is a visual animal and would usually depend principally upon vision in orienting himself to either of these problems and in guiding his choice. Normal monkeys *can* learn the alternation problem in the dark, however, and *can* solve an auditory version of the delayed-response problem, whereas frontal monkeys cannot. In the second place, one can show that the frontal animal is capable of the basic sensory and motor adjustments necessary to a problem, even though he cannot perform quite like a normal, unoperated monkey. For example, a frontal operate may perform well on a "zero-second" delayed-response problem (in which the animal is allowed to get the food immediately after the container is baited), even though he appears to be completely lost when

the delay is extended to five seconds.

The most common interpretation of these results focuses upon the apparent importance of the delay interval—the delay within the delayed-response problem and the delay period between trials in the alternation problem. The suggestion is made therefore that these areas of the frontal association cortex are essential to some aspect of memory; when they are destroyed, the animal can see where the experimenter puts the food and, in the delayed-response situation, will go there if permitted to do so immediately; but he cannot hold in memory even for five seconds the information concerning which container is baited.

A proponent of this view must find some way to account for the fact that the animal without functioning frontal areas can learn many kinds of problems as rapidly as can a normal animal, for example, a difficult visual discrimination. Certainly learning to choose the container with a plus sign on the cover involves memory—memory of the outcome of the previous trial, for example. A full answer to this paradox would require a complete understanding of the nature of learning and memory and of their interrelation. An adequate temporary answer lies in the suggestion that the frontal cortex is concerned only with *short-term* memory; discrimination tasks involve long-term memory. And this answer suggests, of course, that short- and long-term memories are quite different from each other. We shall discuss this possibility at some length later on (p. 474).

There are alternative hypotheses about the role of the frontal cortex in behavior, however. One suggestion is that it plays some essential role in "attention." Upon destruction of the frontal cortex, the animal is therefore more subject to interference by extraneous events that take its attention from the important stimuli, present or past, that are essential to adaptive behavior. This point of view gains some support from the fact that a frontal animal improves on delayed-response problems if he is kept in the dark during the delay period—a procedure that minimizes possible interference.

A third hypothesis has proposed that the frontal deficit be considered an enhancement of the tendency to *perseverate*—the tendency to make the same response even though it would be more adaptive to change to a new form of behavior.

These three hypotheses do not exhaust all those that have been put forth, but they are quite enough to exhaust the student who is interested of course in the one, correct answer. It is useful to consider two possible resolutions of the problem. First, we must realize that the theories are not as different as they may seem at first glance. An interference with ability to maintain "attention" may be what we mean by "a lack of short-term memory," and "enhanced perseveration" may result if the animal is not sufficiently "attentive" to changing conditions. In other words, our understanding of the behavioral processes of memory, attention, and perseveration may not yet be sufficient.

Second, we must remember that throughout this discussion we have been dealing with a large cortical area that may very well have many different subregions with different functions. If it has, then we would not be surprised to find that lesions of the total area will produce many different changes. In other words, our understanding of the anatomical substrate, the frontal association cortex, may not yet be sufficient.

We should not, however, overemphasize the apparent uncertainties of frontal-lobe function. We do know that these association areas are essential to normal performance of many kinds of adaptive behavior. The functions deranged are relatively complex—they are not limited to simple sensory learning but involve higher-order organization of past and present input toward an adaptive outcome in behavior.

Cortical Functions in Human Beings

In the preceding sections we have dealt at some length with the results of studies in which

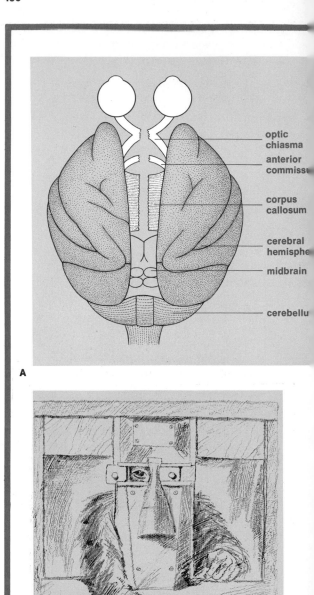

optic
chiasma

anterior
commissu

corpus
callosum

cerebral
hemisphe

midbrain

cerebellu

A

B

Box 105

The Monkey With
Two Brains

The central nervous system is one great *unified* structure, controlling experience and behavior by the *integrating* interaction of its many, many neurons. The great truth of this statement for the normal animal is underlined by the remarkable findings that come from studies of instances in which this unity is destroyed.

The standard split-brain procedure of Roger Sperry of the California Institute of Technology involves cutting the optic chiasma and the corpus callosum (see Figure A). When this operation has been performed, the visual information entering one eye of the animal reaches directly only one side of the brain, and, unless subcortical connections are used, it cannot reach the other side. The effects of this operation on learning and memory are striking but understandable.

The basic fact is that there are now two mostly separate brains. If the animal is taught a visually guided problem (for example, to choose a cube and ignore a sphere that is presented at the same time), with input restricted to only one eye, and if it is then tested with the other eye, no memory of the task is demonstrated at all (see Figure B). In fact, the other eye can be used to teach the animal to follow a response pattern exactly the opposite of that guided by input to the first eye (for example, to choose the sphere and not the cube). If you are accustomed to imagining the "conscious" experience of each animal you read about, try the split-brain monkey. It may throw you into confusion to try to achieve the state of mind in which your "knowledge" of the appropriate response varies inexplicably from time to time (as the experimenter changes the seeing eye). The problem may be cleared up by considering how foolish it would be to try to introspect for the (single) monkey if the brain were completely cut in half; it would be quite necessary to introspect separately for the "two brains" thus established! The split-brain preparation approaches that condition.

When a monkey whose two brain halves have learned opposite things is permitted to look with *both* eyes open simultaneously, no evidence of strong conflict appears within the animal or in his responses. He seems to be dominated for a while by one half the brain and then the other, but we never see evidence that the two halves of the brain are having a tug of war—over the control of an individual limb, for example. Even when total unity is denied the brain, it controls activity in such a way that either one pattern of activity or the other wins out; there is never a confused compromise.

R. W. SPERRY. 1961. Cerebral Organization and Behavior, *Science*, 133, 1749–57. Figure B adapted by permission from the cover of the January 1964 issue of *Scientific American*.

animals were used to explore the role of the cerebral cortex in adaptive behavior, and we may seem to have lost sight of our principal interest in human behavior and experience. The most important reason for this emphasis upon studies with animals is that we simply cannot do many of the experiments that would be necessary to obtain the desired information about people. There are some sources of direct information concerning cortical functions in human beings, and it is comforting that they appear to lead to conclusions compatible with those that come from the study of other species.

Perhaps the best evidence we have from the study of human beings comes from investigations of people who have suffered accidental brain injuries. In addition, there are observations of patients who have had portions of their brains destroyed by disease and of patients who have had portions of their brains surgically removed or incised in attempts to control disease. It is sometimes possible to gain information from study of the exposed brain during an operation.

At the outset, we should recall that these investigations confirm the existence of the primary sensory areas in the posterior portion of the cortex—areas essential to sensory function of one modality or another. As we saw in Box 46, p. 253, electrical stimulation of these areas will lead to experiences that are appropriate to the known sensory connections of the region, and their destruction causes profound disturbance in the related sensory functions.

It appears also that there may well be areas comparable to the subareas of the posterior association cortex of monkeys. Injury to these areas could then explain the fact that human brain damage may be followed by *agnosia*, the inability to recognize formerly familiar objects. Presumably there are many different kinds of agnosia, corresponding to the various sense modalities and each resulting from damage to one of the subareas of the association cortex.

As usually stated, the concept of agnosia implies that the disorder in recognition occurs

Box 106

Cortical Localization
in Man

Usually when the brain is damaged by disease or by accidental injury, the victim is not studied carefully unless the damage produces some noticeable change in behavior. As a result, only those who have serious symptoms are seen; only those brain-damaged people who become *patients* contribute to our ideas about the role of neural structures in human behavior.

It is possible to approach more closely the experimental methods used with animal subjects by studying people with known brain injuries, whether or not they demonstrate obvious effects. Such a method may turn up more subtle results and expose the full range of the effects of a given lesion.

This method has been used extensively by Hans-Lukas Teuber, a psychologist at the Massachusetts Institute of Technology, and his several collaborators. Teuber has studied war veterans known to have received penetrating head injuries with presumed brain damage; he enlisted the cooperation of these men, most of whom were active, effective members of society, and compared them with control subjects on a series of psychological tests. Some of the results may be taken as evidence that both the specificity hypothesis and the nonspecificity hypothesis about cortical localization are incorrect when stated in extreme terms.

From what we know about the visual sensory system, we should expect partial lesions of the occipital cortex to produce visual *scotomata* (abnormal blind spots), and they do. The subject is seated, with his eyes focused upon a spot directly in front of him. The experimenter then moves a small target spot to different parts of the visual field. The man with damage to his occipital cortex is not able to see the target when it moves into the blind part of his visual field, the part corresponding to his lesion (see drawing).

Less expected findings appear. An individual with a scotoma can be given tests that call upon the use of the remainder of the visual field. Changes are seen then also. People with scotomata somewhere in the visual field have, for example, a slower average rate of dark adaptation than do controls, even though the blind areas are not involved in the dark-adaptation test.

Finally, there are some visual tests that seem dependent upon wide areas of the cerebrum. The hidden-figure test that is illustrated here (diagrams) is an example. People with damage anywhere in the brain are on the average slower than normal in discovering where in each of the five complex figures the simple one can be found embedded.

We see, then, three levels of complexity of visual tasks, related to different amounts of specificity of localization. Some abilities are related to a highly specific region, a given subarea of the occipital sensory cortex. Other visual tasks are affected by a lesion anywhere in the visual area and others by damage in any portion of the cerebrum. There is some specificity of neural systems, but the cortex is not arranged in a simple mosaic of independent areas.

H.-L. TEUBER. 1959. Some Alterations in Behavior after Cerebral Lesions in Man, in E. Bass, ed., *Evolution of Nervous Control From Primitive Organisms to Man* (Washington: American Association for the Advancement of Science), pp. 157–94.

H.-L. TEUBER and S. WEINSTEIN. 1956. Ability to Discover Hidden Figures after Cerebral Lesion, *Arch. Neurol. Psychiat.*, 76, 369–79. Figure B adapted by permission of American Medical Association.

without any loss of simple sensory function. There is not complete agreement on this point, however. Some investigators believe that any disturbance in recognition must be based upon simpler sensory losses, which should be demonstrable as increases in sensory thresholds and so on. Certainly many studies show that lesions of the cerebral cortex produce losses on behavior tests of different levels of complexity. The studies of Teuber and his associates (see Box 106, p. 458) demonstrate what may be considered three levels of visual tasks, all of which may be affected by lesions in the "visual areas" of the brain.

In any event, we can assign a major role in simple *and* complex functions dependent upon each sensory modality to the regions of the cortex centered around the sensory areas we have previously discussed.

Frontal Cortex

There are many descriptions of the behavior of people with damage to the frontal region of the brain. Unfortunately, there are almost as many differing descriptions as there are people studied. The descriptions of what happens to people after frontal damage often are couched in general terms, such as inability to think abstractly, lack of concern for consequences, and inability to plan ahead. It seems almost certain that each of the descriptions contains some grains of truth, but, when one looks at studies that have used adequate objective testing with proper controls, one sees very little that is definite. One thing is certain; people with frontal injury do *not* show the great difficulty on the delayed-response problem that is so easily obtained with monkeys and other animals. Some success has been achieved, however, in showing that the effects of frontal damage on people and monkeys may have common underlying bases, even though the behavior may be superficially different.

An example comes from studies in which people with frontal damage are asked to sort

cards (similar to playing cards). If a man with frontal damage starts out sorting according to suit, for example, he may perform quite as efficiently as a normal subject. But, if the "rules of the game" are changed abruptly, and if sorting according to number is called for, he may persist in working as before, not showing the required adaptability to changing situations. It has been thought that this kind of effect can be explained by assuming an enhanced tendency to perseverate, the same process that has been cited as one explanation of the disturbances shown in monkeys with lesions of the frontal cortex.

The tests on which people with frontal-lobe damage do not perform as well as normal people do often involve some dependence on proper orientation or motor control. For example, frontal damage produces difficulty in the simple task of touching parts of the body that are indicated on a diagram and difficulty in following a path through a maze. Such findings and the "perseverative" difficulties mentioned previously—as well as the common report that an individual patient "can't plan ahead" or "ignores the consequences of his actions"—have evoked the suggestion that the frontal lobe is involved in a system that prepares, or organizes, responses (even before the stimulus that triggers activity is given), taking into account other present and planned actions of the individual. According to such a summary (Pribram, 1962) the frontal cortex is involved in the control of behavior by our "intentions"; its role in motor control is considered to be most evident in responses we think of as "voluntary" rather than reflexive in nature.

Speech Areas

One of the most striking changes that can occur after brain damage is *aphasia*, a loss or disturbance of speech. Aphasia is observable only in human beings, obviously, for *Homo sapiens* is the only species now living that produces and understands speech.

The kinds of speech disorders that follow brain damage are usually separated into two major varieties. In *sensory aphasia*, the patient is unable to understand or recognize spoken language, although he knows that he is being spoken to and suffers no loss in his ability to discriminate among nonspeech sounds. In *motor aphasia*, the problem is with the production of speech, usually in finding a word. The word may be lost completely for the moment or other words that are somehow related to it may be substituted. Other kinds of expressive (motor) disorders include changes in fluency, the occasional production of meaningless or ungrammatical speech, and disruptions of the ability to control the speech organs so as to produce the sounds of the language.

A striking feature about the relationship between the brain and language is that a cerebral lesion that produces aphasia is almost always found to be on the left side of the brain. This evidence that the left side has a special importance in controlling language can be verified in normal subjects. If an anesthetic drug like sodium amytal is injected into a blood vessel that carries blood principally to the left side of the brain, it produces a group of temporary changes in behavior, including aphasia; the same drug distributed to the right side of the brain does not usually have this effect. Some people, however, do appear to be "right-brained" as far as control of speech is concerned; this arrangement is more prevalent among left-handed people.

We may now ask whether more precise localization of areas important to speech is possible. The evidence demonstrates a certain degree of relationship between the kind of aphasia and the location of the damage. Sensory aphasia tends to occur with damage to an area near the junction between the parietal, occipital, and temporal lobes; motor aphasia tends to occur with damage to an area in the lower part of the frontal lobe (see Figure 28.2.). These relationships are not perfect, however; in fact, a lesion almost anywhere on the left side of the cerebrum may cause at least a temporary aphasia of almost any kind.

It is intriguing to wonder "why" the control of language depends so strongly upon one side of the brain, considering that many other abilities are related to both halves of the cerebral cortex. One way to answer this question is to point out that many of the functions that we assume to be dependent upon both sides of the brain turn out to have unilateral representation when we analyze the situation a little more closely. For example, although "visual sensation" is represented on both sides of the occipital cortex, the sensation from a certain point of the visual field will be projected to only one small area on one occipital lobe. Another way of looking at what we know suggests another explanation. Speech is uniquely human—other evidences of strong unilateral control of behavior come from studies of human beings, whereas animals show bilateral control of all but simple sensory and motor functions. Is it possible that the human brain has relinquished the insurance —the safety—that comes from having two systems, each able to carry out a certain function, in order to "release" more cells for the expanded number of jobs that the brain must do?

Locus of Learning

We embarked upon a study of the cerebral cortex because it was evident that an animal deprived of cortex could do very little interesting learning. We have discovered that even the loss of small subregions of cortex can profoundly affect the ability of the subject to show various forms of adaptive behavior. It has been stated repeatedly, however, that the manifestation of any behavior depends upon the integrity of a *complex* system of cells and that the fact that destruction of a certain cortical area is followed by a decrease in learning ability does not mean that learning takes place in that area alone. Indeed, the fact that a certain kind of learning "requires" the cortex does not preclude the possibility that it also "requires" participation by some subcortical structure that we glossed over in our trip up the nervous system.

It would be extremely difficult or impossible to prove, by using the lesion method, that *certain* subcortical structures play a special role in learning and memory, because if we destroyed these structures we would, essentially, destroy the animal. A large lesion of the ascending reticular formation, for example, may produce an animal that sleeps continuously; with such a subject, it is difficult to find out whether or not the area that was removed included some cells that were especially involved in the physiological changes in learning, because we cannot keep the animal awake long enough to study its performance on most learning tasks.

Other kinds of experiments can be done, however, and several studies have been performed in which EEG records (see p. 567) were taken from electrodes in various parts of the brain while the animal was exposed to a learning problem. The experimenter observes the records to discover whether or not the wave forms that arise from a given region of the brain change in relation to changes in behavior. Studies of this kind have led some scientists to suggest that the reticular formation is in-

deed important to learning and that it may be here that an early phase of learning actually "takes place."

The most striking evidence suggesting a role in learning for subcortical structures comes from a lesion study, however. Some people have had large portions of the limbic area—including the amygdala and the hippocampus (see p. 592)—removed surgically. The patients who underwent such procedures turned out to have extreme learning and memory difficulties. They could remember quite well things that they had experienced and learned *before* the operation. They could also learn new information, but retention of this new material was exceedingly fragile and short-lived. They could not remember from day to day the name of the psychologist who came to examine them after the operation.

Even this brief survey makes it clear that there is now a large amount of knowledge about the importance of different neural structures to the systems underlying learning, although we cannot specify exactly *where* in the nervous system this learning takes place. Maybe we should not expect to be able to reach this level of explanation until we know *what* happens in the nervous system when learning takes place—the topic to which we turn in the next unit.

Glossary

agnosia The inability to recognize a formerly familiar object; this inability may result from cortical injury.

aphasia Language disturbance following cortical injury. *Sensory aphasia* refers to the inability to understand spoken language. *Motor aphasia* is the inability to find the appropriate word and produce it correctly.

association area Cortex that is not primarily sensory or motor in nature. The frontal association area is in the frontal lobes; the posterior association area contains cortex at the junction of the temporal, parietal, and occipital lobes.

decorticate animal An animal whose entire cerebral cortex has been destroyed or removed.

delayed-response problem A problem in which the subject has to respond in terms of a stimulus that is no longer present—for example, the problem of choosing the one of two identical closed containers in which he previously saw a reward placed.

equipotentiality A principle, asserted by Lashley, that for certain specific functions one part of the cerebral cortex can do whatever any other part can do.

inferotemporal cortex An area on the bottom edge

of the temporal lobe in monkeys that performs an important function in visual learning.

learning set The improvement in the speed of learning a new problem that results when a subject learns many different problems in turn; "learning to learn."

mass action The principle proposed by Lashley that the capacity for learning and retention of a brain-injured animal is determined by the total amount of cerebral cortex still remaining.

perseveration The tendency to continue doing, or to repeat doing, whatever one has just been doing. An enhanced tendency to perseverate is proposed as one of the effects of lesions of the frontal association area.

phrenology A doctrine originally advanced in 1810, relating a person's skull formations to his personality and behavior. The doctrine rests on three assumptions: First, different traits are controlled by different areas of the cortex; second, the larger a certain area of the cortex, the more pronounced the associated trait in the individual; third, the external shape of the skull reflects the shape of the brain underneath.

posterior parietal area An area just in front of the occipital lobe, which is important in learning based on tactual and kinesthetic stimuli.

scotoma A blind spot in the visual field, often caused by destruction of part of the visual sensory cortex.

spinal animal An animal whose spinal cord has been cut through, thus severing the neural connections between the lower part of his body and his brain.

split-brain animal An animal that has received a cut along the midline of his brain, dividing the two sides so as to provide the animal to some extent with two separate brains. A typical operation involves the corpus callosum and other forebrain commissures, along with the optic chiasma.

physiological mechanisms of learning

overview / Studies of the nature of the physiological changes accompanying learning and memory were very rare until quite recently, and definite conclusions are still rare.

The psychophysiological evidence suggests that there are at least two stages of memory: a short-term memory that soon fades and a long-term memory, the establishment of which may depend upon whether the short-term process is allowed to run without disruption.

The short-term memory may consist of reverberating, self-exciting neuron circuits. Other explanations of memory, particularly long-term memory, have involved changes in the structure of complex chemicals within the neuron, variations in the substances that control synaptic transmission, and the physical growth of axon endings.

In the preceding unit we addressed ourselves to the question of the locus of learning: *Where* in the nervous system does learning take place? We saw that this question has attracted the attention of many research workers for over 150 years and that much has been learned. Their studies tell us where we must look for an answer to the next question: What happens in the nervous system when something new is learned? This is the question of the physiological dynamics or *mechanisms of learning.*

In the discussion of the physiological proc-

esses in perception (Units 15–18), we found that the basic neurophysiological events of nervous transmission appear to be sufficient to understand what happens in the nervous system when we see, hear, smell, touch, and so on. As we speak of learning, however, we enter a realm in which we do not even know for certain which physiological mechanisms are at work in the nervous system.

The crucial thing that we seek in hunting for the physiological basis of learning is some mechanism for *permanent change* in the nervous system—else how can we account for memory? Until recently very little could even be conjectured about the answer to this question. But research in this area is now rapidly increasing, and this whole question has rapidly become one of the most active and most exciting research areas in biochemistry, physiology, and psychology.

Reverberating Circuits

One possible answer can be provided without invoking any new physiological or chemical mechanisms beyond the basic phenomena of neuron activity that are already familiar to us. It is proposed that a new *pattern of activity* is set up in the brain as a result of each new experience and thus that "learning" consists primarily of the organized activity patterns displayed by the neural elements. For example, suppose that we want to train a rat to push a lever in a Skinner box (see p. 301). It is not unreasonable to assume that a neural pathway can be traced from the cells in his retina activated by the visual stimuli from the bar, through a complex sequence of neurons in the brain, to the neurons that control the muscles involved in lever pressing. Before training, the rat does not press the lever, because it is assumed that *at least* one of the neurons along the pathway cannot be excited by the preceding neuron in the chain. The synaptic gap has not been "jumped," and the neural impulse thus comes to an end at that synapse. When we provide the rat with the learning trials, the hypothesis states, the effect of the training (the sight of the bar *plus* the events following an "accidental" pressing of the bar) is to produce continuing activity in an auxiliary neuron, whose axon also enters into that crucial synapse. This new neuron, like the neuron on the original path, although unable by itself to activate the succeeding neuron, can, together with the original neuron, provide enough total excitation so that activity can be transmitted to the next neuron and on down the chain to provoke

the response (see Figure 29.1.).

But how can we expect neural activity produced by a training trial to last for any appreciable length of time after the trial is over? The immediate neural response runs its course and dies out well before one second elapses. And sometimes, of course, minutes and hours can elapse between one trial and another. A partial answer is provided by the concept of *reverberating circuits*. It has been hypothesized that closed loops of neurons are present within the brain and specifically within the cerebral cortex. If neural activity were started in such a loop, it might continue to reverberate indefinitely, transmitting the excitatory message around and around, and thus providing a permanent new aspect to the brain's pattern of electrical activity. This reverberating circuit would be the neural basis of the memory (see Figure 29.1.).

There are serious objections to this theory, unfortunately. Many treatments and conditions that would be expected to disrupt severely any ongoing reverberating neural activity in the brain do not cause the complete loss of memory that would be expected—if memory depends upon a persisting pattern of neural activity. For example, abnormal conditions like convulsions and anesthesia and normal states like sleep may be accompanied by extreme changes in the amount and regularity of neural activity in the brain; yet these conditions do not result in any appreciable loss of long-standing memories. As a result of such evidence, the role that reverberating circuits are thought to play in learning and memory has been drastically reduced. These circuits are now assumed to play a role only in short-term memory. As usually expressed, this revised theory states that immediately after a trial in a learning experiment a short-lasting reverberating circuit of activity is formed and that this circuit serves as the neural basis for a "short-term memory."

Before the reverberating activity dies out (and with it, the short-term memory), the reverberating neural activity will have led to a

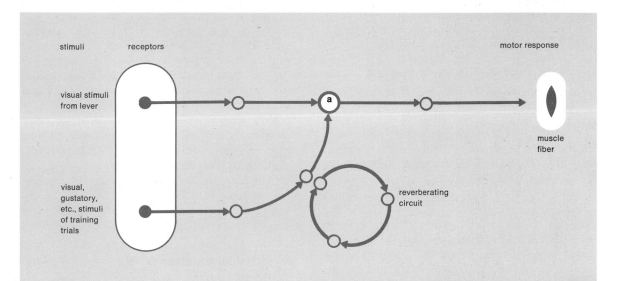

Figure 29.1. A neuronal model of learning. Let us assume that each neuron schematically pictured here can be stimulated into discharge by any one impulse delivered to it from a neuron that precedes it in the chain, *except* for the neuron with the large cell body (a). This neuron has a bigger threshold; it requires *two* impulses presented simultaneously to provoke it into activity.

Without training there would be no response, for the activity initiated by the sight of the lever could not get past the large-threshold barrier presented by neuron a. When activity is started in the lower group of neurons by the gustatory and other stimuli and *maintained* along with impulses entering the upper chain, the response at the muscle fiber will occur. The activity coming in from the receptors along the lower neurons will not continue long after a training trial is over, unless some such special mechanism as a reverberating circuit is provided.

permanent change in the brain. This permanent change will be the neurological mechanism for a "long-term memory." These two stages of memory are thus presumed to have different structural bases (Hebb, 1949). We will consider later the physiological evidence for the existence of two stages of memory. At present it will suffice to say that, if there *are* two different kinds of memory, a reverberating-circuit mechanism might underlie the short-term stage. There is, however, no direct proof either that reverberating circuits exist or that, if they do, they underlie short-term memory. But what mechanisms might underlie long-term memory?

Synaptic Changes

For a long period of time the only mechanisms that received any serious consideration as candidates for the neurological basis of long-term memory were purely structural ones. Basic to all the structural hypotheses was the assumption that the ease with which activity in an axon can excite activity in an adjoining neuron depends upon the facility with which the appropriate synapse can be traversed. It was therefore suggested that learning might consist of the development of more or larger axon terminals from many neurons converging on synapses; another suggestion was that learning involved a narrowing of the relevant synaptic clefts. Either would facilitate transmission across the synapse (see Figure 29.2.).

These structural hypotheses are still reasonable and widely believed, but it is extremely hard to produce direct evidence to support them. In the first place, there would be many difficulties in obtaining appropriate measures of the exceedingly small differences in size that might be involved. Second, even though we have some ideas about where learning takes place, it would still be very unlikely that we would chance upon the specific synapses (among the millions in the brain) involved in any specific bit of learning. Finally, we must note that other complications would be added to our experiment by the fact that one cannot take out a synapse, measure it, and then put it back in the brain, to examine it later for changes.

Although there is no direct evidence for this explanation of learning, there are some observations that allow interesting speculations closely allied to the theory. Altman and Das (1965) have shown that many neurons in the brains of rats are developed after birth. The hippocampus, which has often been proposed as a crucial structure in learning and memory, includes a large number of these late-maturing cells. These small nerve cells may act as crucial middle links in neuron chains that control behavior, forming connections between fibers bringing excitation into the hippocampus and neurons leaving it. As these cells are fully formed only after birth, their connections and thus the exact nature of the neuron systems that are established might be determined in part by the learning and experience of the individual. In this way, the pattern of synaptic connections would be fashioned by learning and, once having been fashioned, would form the physiological basis of the learned act.

Environment and Brain Growth

It may also be pertinent to mention here the evidence that environmental stimulation can change the size and weight of the cerebral cortex. Krech, Rosenzweig, and Bennett have demonstrated this fact by discovering that rats reared in an enriched psychological environment (full of objects to manipulate, varied paths to explore, and problems to solve) developed a thicker and heavier cortex than did

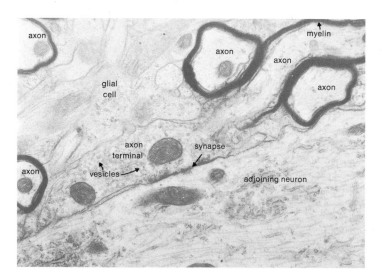

Figure 29.2. The photograph (taken from a rat spinal cord) was taken with an electron microscope, and what we see is magnified about 23,000 times. (This true picture is not as simple as our diagrams of neurons running freely through empty space and nicely connected with one another!) At the upper right a segment of axon is seen, ending in a terminal that has a synapse with the neuron that fills the bottom of the picture. Other axons are seen in cross section. One possible mechanism of learning would involve an increase in the number of axon terminals, their growth in size, or closer approach to the dendritic surface. (Glial cells, which differ from neurons, exist throughout the nervous system. Their functions are not completely understood.)
Courtesy Sanford L. Palay, M.D.

their brothers—rats that had lived out their lives in an impoverished environment (see Figure 29.3.). There is even some evidence that in the "psychologically enriched" rats the dendrites of the cortical neurons have more branches than do the dendrites in the "psychologically impoverished" animals. The greater number of dendritic branches would make possible, of course, better synaptic connections among the neurons—and so these data also support the structural theories of learning.

Transmitter Substances

The same investigators, however, found data that also implicated *biochemical* as well as structural mechanisms in learning. If a neuron is going to influence activity in a neuron with which it makes synaptic contact, the first neuron must release into the synaptic space the appropriate transmitter substance, which will move across the space and help to stimulate the next neuron (see p. 77). If a synaptic connection is then going to be returned to a resting state so that it can be used again, the transmitter substance must be destroyed, once it has done its job, by the appropriate enzyme. For efficient synaptic transmission, there must then be appropriate amounts of both transmitter and enzyme. Krech and his colleagues have explored many aspects of the general hypothesis that the greater the efficiency of synaptic transmission, so defined, the greater will be the learning ability. This hypothesis, it will be readily seen, suggests a "biochemical" mechanism of learning to *supplement* the structural mechanisms. In these studies they have measured the level of *acetylcholine* (*ACh*), which is believed to be the transmitter at some brain synapses, and the amount of *acetylcholinesterase* (*AChE*), the enzyme that eventually breaks down the ACh. Their experiments confirmed the general hypothesis (see Box 107, p. 470).

Several other experiments have been done with drugs that modify the level of ACh or

Figure 29.3. Rats in an "enriched environment." The stimulation and challenge of these surroundings lead to changes in brain size and brain chemistry.
E. L. Bennett, *et al.*, "Chemical and Anatomical Plasticity of the Brain," *Science*, 146, 610–19; Copyright 1964 by the American Association for the Advancement of Science; reprinted by permission.

AChE and produce changes in learning and memory consistent with the Krech, *et al.*, hypothesis. An interesting example of these experiments is the study by Deutsch, Hamburg, and Dahl (1966), who used a drug called DFP. This chemical is an *anti*cholinester*ase*—that is, it prevents AChE from destroying ACh; it thus increases the amount of active ACh. The experiment seems to show that a certain amount of ACh is *optimal* for memory of the simple maze habit that these experimenters taught their rats. If DFP is given when rats have not learned a problem well, it facilitates their performance on the problem by making more ACh available. When a habit has been well learned and an opportunity given for a complete buildup of ACh, however, the DFP injections cause a loss in memory. In this case presumably an excess of ACh results from the injection; the neurons are continually under a state of stimulation, so that the synapse cannot effectively transmit the incoming information.

Box 107

Learning ⇌ Chemistry

If neuron activity depends upon synaptic transmission and if synaptic transmission requires the chemicals called "transmitters," then the efficiency of neuron activity as seen in adaptive behavior should be related to the activity level of the transmitter substance in the brain. This hypothesis was put forward in 1953 by David Krech and Mark Rosenzweig, psychologists, and Edward Bennett, a biochemist, at the University of California, Berkeley. Their subsequent investigations have shown that, although the chemical mechanisms involved are rather complex, the general hypothesis has some validity.

In their studies, these scientists have measured the adaptive behavior of rats in several situations such as solvable and unsolvable mazes. Originally they looked for a relationship between these measures and a measure of the amount of acetylcholinesterase (AChE) activity in the brain. AChE is the enzyme that controls the chemical reaction by means of which the transmitter substance acetylcholine (ACh) is destroyed. The assumption was that AChE activity would be an indicator that a great deal of synaptic transmission was going on. Correlations were found between adaptive behavior and AChE activity, but some of the correlations were negative—the *more* AChE activity, the *poorer* the adaptive behavior.

This outcome might be explained in the following way. If there is too much AChE activity at a synapse, the ACh may be broken down too rapidly and have no chance to have its effect. The problem is analogous to that involved in measuring the amount of crime in a community by counting the number of policemen. A greater number of policemen may indicate a higher crime rate, but, if there are enough policemen, the crime rate will be low. A better measure would be obtained by considering the number of criminals as well—the more criminals relative to policemen, the more crime. This kind of reasoning required that the investigations of synaptic efficiency take into account the ACh itself, as well as the amount of the enzyme (AChE) that destroys it.

The new hypothesis, that the efficiency of synaptic transmission will correlate with the amount of ACh relative to the amount of AChE (the acetylcholinesterase that destroys the ACh), has been borne out. Strains of rats with higher ratios of ACh to AChE are superior in learning behavior.

There is more. In other experiments, these scientists have demonstrated that the individual's experience affects its brain chemistry. Some rats were raised in a quiet, dimly lit room without a chance to see or touch other animals. Other rats were raised in groups of ten to twelve with "toys" in their cages and each day were put in an open "play area" with barriers and detours (see Figure 29.3.); they also received some training on various mazes and discrimination problems. When the brains of the animals were examined, the group that had been given the enriched environment was found to have had a higher AChE activity in the cortex than did the isolated rats and even greater superiority in the weight of the cortex. We have always assumed, of course, that the brain *must* be influenced by experience, and we are now beginning to see some of the ways that this takes place.

M. R. ROSENZWEIG, D. KRECH, and E. L. BENNETT. 1960. A Search for Relations between Brain Chemistry and Behavior, *Psychol. Bull.*, 57, 476–92.

D. KRECH, M. R. ROSENZWEIG, E. L. BENNETT, and B. KRUECKEL. 1954. Enzyme Concentrations in the Brain and Adjustive Behavior Patterns, *Science*, 120, 994–6.

E. L. BENNETT, M. C. DIAMOND, D. KRECH, and M. R. ROSENZWEIG. 1964. Chemical and Anatomical Plasticity of the Brain, *Science*, 146, 610–9.

Chemical Changes Inside the Neuron

So far we have emphasized changes in the synapse—either structural or chemical changes —in our search for the crucial physiological mechanism in learning. Now we must consider the possibility that changes take place during the learning process *within*, rather than between, neurons. These *intra*neural changes would then direct the new activity of the organism. This possibility does not necessarily conflict with those described above, because changes at the synaptic region may well be caused by internal chemical changes of the cell. The intraneural hypothesis does invite our attention to the biochemical events inside the neuron; and, by suggesting that the "memory" *storage* mechanism of the brain may be found within the chemical nature of its individual neurons, it presents the first major primarily *biochemical* theory of learning—as opposed to a primarily structural theory.

In Unit 1 we discussed two important substances, ribose nucleic acid (RNA) and deoxyribose nucleic acid (DNA), which are found within each living cell. Neither is a single chemical; the names refer instead to classes of compounds, each of which can occur in an infinite number of forms. The structure of DNA determines the exact kinds of RNA that will be produced by the cell; RNA in turn controls the production of proteins, including the structural components of the cell and the enzymes that govern its activity. In this way the activity of each cell of the body (and thus eventually of the whole organism) is determined largely by the varieties of DNA and RNA within it. Genes are made of DNA and are transmitted—in all their infinite variety of chemical composition— from parents to child. And through their specific chemical composition the DNA molecules (genes) determine the child's characteristics of structure and behavior. The evolutionary history of the species and the genetic background of any individual within the species are thus mirrored in that organism's DNA; the DNA carries the "evolutionary memory" (the determinants of the structure and function of the *species*) into every cell of the body of the newborn.

The major hypothesis concerning intraneuronal chemical changes states that "individual memory" (the consequences of learning within a single lifetime of one *individual*) is carried by the structure of the RNA within the neurons. This hypothesis assumes that neural activity (accompanying a learning experience) can *change* the detailed chemical structure of the RNA within the neurons involved in a given learning experience. Experience of the individual would thus be laid down in the details of the chemistry of the RNA in his neurons, much as the "experience" of his ancestors is reflected in the details of the chemistry of the DNA. Because RNA controls protein synthesis within the neuronal cell body, a change in RNA could, for example, determine how much transmitter substance the neuron would release at synapses with other cells. The result would then be "learning" (see Figure 29.4.).

Several kinds of evidence support this hypothesis. Let us list three: First, it has been reported that administration of RNA (or of a drug that increases its manufacture in the brain) produces better learning or memory in experimental animals or in old people; second, Hydén (1962) has demonstrated that rats taught a balancing task show changes in the proportions of different kinds of RNA in parts of the brain that receive fibers from the semicircular canals; and, third, exposure of the brain to the enzyme that *breaks down* RNA causes memory *losses* in cats, fish, rats, and flatworms.

Such studies do not support directly the most important part of the RNA theory, that is, the assertion that the *structure* of RNA is specifically related to learning. In other words, they are all explicable on the proposition that RNA is essential to the general well-being and functioning of the cell; and, on the assumption that "if a little is good, a lot is better," a *generally* better functioning neuron will "learn"

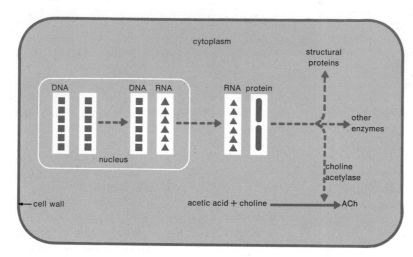

Figure 29.4. The control of cellular activity by nucleic acids. When cells divide in the developing organism, each DNA molecule reproduces itself so that each cell carries the genetically determined "evolutionary memory" (represented in the left half of the nucleus). RNA is produced in the nucleus; its exact nature is determined by the specific nature of the DNA. RNA moves out of the nucleus and stimulates the production of protein: The specific kind of protein is dictated by the nature of the RNA. Many of these proteins are enzymes and thus control other chemical reactions. The enzyme that assists in the *formation* of the transmitter substance acetylcholine is specified in the diagram.

more quickly than one that does not function as well. There have been some claims that specific memories can be transferred from one animal into another by taking RNA from the brain of a trained animal and injecting it into an untrained animal; the untrained animal now shows a "memory" for what the first animal had learned. These results, if substantiated, could prove that the exact nature of a memory is "coded" as a specific RNA. Unfortunately, these latter findings have not been well substantiated to date.

Even if the details of the RNA theory are incorrect, it is still probable that activities within the neuron that depend upon its ability to construct proteins are necessary to learning, memory, thinking, and the consequent adaptive behavior. Many of the RNA studies support this conclusion, as does the fact that memory losses have been reported to follow the injection *into the brain* of puromycin, a substance that directly inhibits the synthesis of proteins.

Two Stages of Memory?

We now return to the question that was briefly raised earlier in this unit and that was discussed from a different point of view in Unit 21: Is there only one mechanism underlying memory, or are there two or more different stages in memory, each with its own physiological basis?

The Consolidation Hypothesis

The two-stage view is supported by the currently popular consolidation hypothesis. According to this hypothesis, a process that will be the mechanism of "short-term memory" begins within the nervous system immediately after a learning trial. This process is short-lived and fades away, but it is instrumental in producing a second change in the nervous system, one that will be more permanent and that will serve as the basis for "long-term memory." But in order for the short-term process to produce the long-term process, the short-term process must be allowed to run its course without disruption or interference. The short-term memory, in other words, must be given an opportunity to be *consolidated* into a long-term memory.

One approach, therefore, to testing the consolidation theory would be to provide the subject with something to learn, then interrupt the short-term process *after the learning trial but before the long-term process has had an opportunity to become established*. The subject should not develop a long-term memory.

An experimental procedure often used in

these studies—with rats—is the *"step-down"* procedure, devised by Jarvik and Essman (1960). This procedure can be used because it happens to be "natural" for a rat placed on a small platform a few inches above the floor to step down to the floor within a few seconds. The rat will do so rather consistently day after day. Now suppose that on one day the floor is electrified and that stepping onto it produces a painful shock to the foot. When the rat is afterward put back on the platform, even twenty-four hours later, it will remain on the platform—for several minutes or longer, if necessary. The rat has learned from the earlier experience that stepping onto the floor is punished, and it remembers it the next day. In this situation, memory is demonstrated by the rat's *not* stepping down onto the floor.

If now we *interfere* with the rat's "short-term memory" immediately after his first experience of "step-down → foot shock" *before this short-term memory has had an opportunity to become consolidated into a long-term memory,* then the rat should show no evidence of remembering the shock experience when tested the next day—and should blithely step down again! The method used most often to interrupt the rat's consolidation of his short-term memory consists of passing an electric current across the brain of the animal. This current results in a very high level of activation of neurons all over the brain. One effect is to produce a convulsion; another effect is to disrupt any patterned neural circuits (for example, reverberating circuits) that may be active. When *electroconvulsive shock (ECS)* follows "step-down—foot shock" pairing quickly enough and we test the rat a day later, it does indeed act as if it had no memory of the event; the rat steps down promptly from the platform with no apparent expectation of shock!

When there is a longer interval between the shock and the ECS, the rat *does* remember the shock, and it remains on the platform when tested the next day. We conclude therefore that this longer interval has allowed consolidation

to run its course and has allowed the memory of the shock to be recorded in the relatively invulnerable long-term memory. The length of interval necessary to produce the more permanent memory varies widely, depending upon the nature of the task and of the disrupting agent. For example, when anesthetics have been used to disrupt the physiological activity of the brain, the effect appears to be stronger than with ECS; that is, anesthetics can be administered at a greater interval after the trial and still disrupt the memory.

Some long-known facts about the effects of accidental head injury in human beings seem to parallel the findings of these animal experiments. We refer to injuries that produce a temporary loss of consciousness but that are not severe enough to cause permanent damage to brain tissue. A common finding in such cases is that the patient awakens with a "gap" in his memory for the events just preceding the accident. This *retrograde amnesia*—a forgetting going backward in time from the point of its production—is what one would expect on the basis of the consolidation hypothesis. It is as if the events that had just taken place were still in short-term memory at the time of the injury and the disruption of ongoing neural activity produced by the incident were sufficient to destroy the short-term memory—whether carried by reverberating circuits or some other mechanism—before consolidation could take place. The patient says "Where am I?" not only because he doesn't recognize the hospital, but also because he can't remember how he came to be injured.

It is also possible to *facilitate* learning or memory in animals by procedures that are designed to *enhance* consolidation. Injections of stimulants like strychnine or picrotoxin into the central nervous system seem to *improve* learning. The injection is given after each trial on a learning problem when consolidation is presumably taking place. The drug consolidates the long-term memory of the just experienced learning trial more quickly or more firmly (see

Box 108, p. 475).

What chemical events go on during the consolidation process? Several suggestions have been offered, and considerable experimental evidence is being accumulated.

The experiments of Agranoff and his colleagues (1965) support the hypothesis that, during the consolidation process, new proteins are developed in the neurons and that these proteins play an essential role in long-term memory. Much of this work has been done with goldfish. A fish is placed in a small rectangular tank, which is divided into two halves by a barrier that comes from the bottom almost to the surface of the water. When a signal light is turned on, the fish must swim across the shallow barrier region into the other end of the tank within twenty seconds; otherwise he receives an unpleasant electric shock. This training is continued for several trials until the animal learns very well how to avoid the shock. Immediately before training—and in some experiments immediately after—Agranoff injected the antibiotic puromycin into the goldfish's brain. Puromycin is a protein inhibitor and would thus prevent the formation of new protein in the neuron. The animals (even those injected prior to training) did *not* show impairment in their rate of *acquisition* of this shock-avoidance task. This result is interpreted to mean that the *short-term* memory process is *not* dependent upon the formation of new proteins. But, when these same fish were tested several days later, they showed poor retention for the task. This result is interpreted to mean that the consolidation of short-term memories into long-term memories *is* dependent on the production of new proteins. If the injection came more than an hour after learning, it had no effect on later memory—consolidation had already taken place, presumably, and inhibition of protein synthesis could not affect the memory.

The process of memory that we have just outlined—a short-term storage process that then feeds into a long-term memory (see Figure 29.5b.) may seem complex enough, but other and possibly more complex suggestions have on occasion been made. For example, there may be two or more processes that are separate and independent; the long-term process takes time to reach its full effectiveness, but it develops whether or not the short-term process is interrupted (see Figure 29.5c.). Or there may be three or more processes, developing independently, sequentially, or both, as illustrated in Figure 29.5d. In any event, it seems quite unlikely that there is only one simple process underlying "learning and memory."

Anatomy, Chemistry, Physiology, and Learning

In Unit 28 we discovered that certain portions of the nervous system are essential to normal learning and adaptive behavior, and in the present unit we have considered several different theories about the chemical and physiological events that may be related to the processes of learning. Just as adaptive behavior depends upon a series of complex systems of neurons (in the periphery, spinal cord, subcortex, and cortex), so must it depend upon many complex biochemical systems. Ribose nucleic acid structure, the synthesis of protein, the growth of axon terminals, and the production and release of transmitters—all are closely related, all may be influenced by experience and by one another, and all may play a role in the control of new patterns of behavior.

An important aspect of the current interest in the chemical mechanisms of learning must be emphasized. Discoveries in the field have an excellent chance of leading to practical applications, applications that could produce enormous changes in our learning ability and thus in every aspect of our lives. At the very least it may become possible to provide treatment for mental retardates and senile people; at the most it may become possible, instead of reading this book, to substitute for it the swallowing of an RNA pill labeled "Introductory Psychology" (but see Box 109, p. 476).

Box 108

Chemistry → Learning

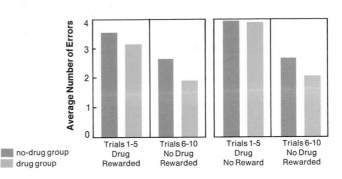

no-drug group
drug group

Experiments in which administration of certain drugs has caused animals to perform better on laboratory learning tasks have opened new fields for understanding and application, but their results have had to undergo careful scrutiny. Scientists find it easier to believe that learning can be *damaged* by some added outside influence (as by a drug injection or an operation) than that it can be *enhanced* by such "abnormal" influences.

Even when it can be clearly established that subjects receiving a certain drug perform better than do controls (subjects who do not receive the drug), various explanations have to be weighed. They may perform better not because of enhancement of *learning* but because of a change in motivation or reward or because of some other condition that affects performance.

An experiment done in James McGaugh's laboratory at the University of California, Irvine, shows one way to overcome such objections. The special feature of this experiment was the use of one kind of "latent learning" design (see p. 308). Rats ran through a six-unit maze once each day for ten days. *Half the animals* were rewarded with food each day. Half of this half received an injection of 1757 I.S. (a central-nervous-system stimulant) after each of the first five trials. The left panel of the figure shows that the injected rats made fewer errors than did the controls on the first five days and that this difference *continued* even when they were treated exactly alike.

Even stronger evidence that the drug-induced difference results from something more permanent than a motivating or activating effect comes from the *remaining half of the rats.* During the first five days, none of the latter group was rewarded in the maze; half of these rats got 1757 I.S. during this period. For the last five days, rewards were provided for all rats, but no drug injections were given. Note, in the right panel of the figure, that the drug and nondrug groups were practically identical in performance before reward, even though the drug was being administered. When reward was added, the groups became different, even though they were now being treated exactly the same. This result strongly suggests that a great deal of (latent) learning was going on during the first five days, even though it did not show up in performance. But, more important, the drug-injected animals were learning much more than the controls were during the first five days of the experiment. If the difference in performance on trials 6–10 was the result of a motivational or rewarding effect of the drug, we should have seen this difference during trials 1–5 *while* the drug was being given.

The learning ability of rats *can* be increased by chemical treatment. Do we believe that this has no implications for the human species?

W. H. WESTBROOK and J. L. MCGAUGH. 1964. Drug Facilitation of Latent Learning, *Psychopharmacologia*, 3, 440–6.

Box 109

Brave New Worlds

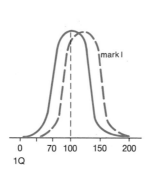

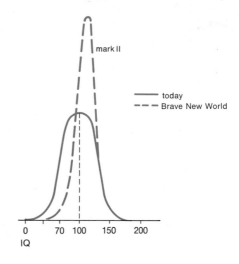

Our knowledge of the biochemistry of learning may foretell a glorious future in which daily doses of smartness syrup will develop a race of intellectual giants; but sober reflection brings to mind grievous problems that will arise.

The enhancement of learning ability through chemistry takes place in a living organism, and we cannot ignore other influences. The California group (see Box 107, p. 470) has shown that opportunities for learning will affect brain size and chemistry. Chemicals improve learning ability, but learning experience influences chemical activity. It is by the interaction of the best environment *and* the best chemicals that the Brave New World will be fashioned.

But what will this enhancement of human abilities be like? David Krech has speculated on the following probabilities: The simplest possibility is that the appropriate treatment will improve the general intelligence of all people (Brave New World, mark I). Each individual and thus the average will be shifted toward the brighter end of the scale of intellectual functioning. Another definite possibility (Brave New World, mark II) is suggested by some of the experiments that have already been done with animals and human beings. Here we see that those that are already high in ability do not improve; the effect of psychological and chemical treatment is to improve only those on the lower end of the scale. Finally, we must consider the high probability that psychochemical treatments will change *specific abilities* rather than general "intellectual functioning." For example, we might be able to develop at will in different persons proficiency in arithmetic reasoning, verbal intelligence, or musical ability.

Suppose we do learn how to develop each individual to his maximum potential by chemical and environmental stimulation. The question of who will receive the important psychochemical treatment will certainly arise, particularly if it cannot immediately be made widely available; social controversy over who will control the drugs seems possible and even probable. Perhaps we need an elixir of goodness to take along with our syrup of smartness.

D. KRECH. 1967. Psychochemical Manipulation and Social Policy, *Ann. Internal. Med.*, 67 (Part II), 19–24, 61–7.

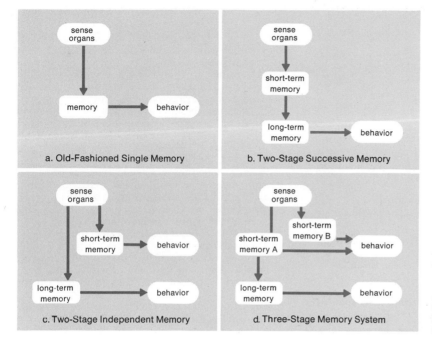

Figure 29.5. Schematic representations of some of the ways in which memory might be organized. The different boxes may be different neural systems or simply different biochemical processes. A lesion or other disruption may interfere with any of the stages or may interrupt their connections with the receptor systems, the motor systems, or one another.

Glossary

acetylcholine (ACh) A chemical that acts as a transmitter substance at some synapses in the nervous system. Specific enzymes are required in its formation and in its destruction.

acetylcholinesterase (AChE) The enzyme that breaks down acetylcholine at the synapse. This action is necessary so that the synaptic mechanisms can return to a resting state, to be used once again.

consolidation A process that is hypothesized to take place after exposure to a learning trial or to an experience. Consolidation is presumed necessary if the effect of the experience is to become permanent.

electroconvulsive shock (ECS) An electric current passed through the brain that is intense enough to cause a convulsion, that is, an involuntary series of generalized contractions of the muscles of the body. Electroconvulsive shock is sometimes used as therapy for mental disorders.

reverberating circuit A series of neurons so arranged that they form a continuous, potentially self-exciting, unending circuit of connections. It is presumed to exist and is offered as a possible explanation of memory.

step-down procedure A shock-avoidance problem in which an animal learns that stepping down from a small raised platform onto a grid floor will give an unpleasant electric shock to its feet.

Suggestions for Further Reading

Learning

EBBINGHAUS, H. 1964. Paperback. *Memory: A Contribution to Experimental Psychology.* New York: Dover. Originally published 1885.

A first-hand account of the work of the pioneer experimenter in human verbal learning and memory.

DEESE, J. E., and S. HULSE. 1967. *Psychology of Learning.* 3rd ed. New York: McGraw-Hill.

An excellent and detailed treatment of the theory and data of the core topics of the field of learning, both human and animal.

HILGARD, E. R., and G. BOWER. 1966. *Theories of Learning.* 3rd ed. New York: Appleton.

An excellent, up-to-date summary of current theories of learning.

SKINNER, B. F. 1953. Paperback. *Science and Human Behavior.* New York: Macmillan.

One of the most influential of American learning theorists presents a broad overview of his approach to the understanding of behavior.

TOLMAN, E. C. 1967. Paperback. *Purposive Behavior in Animals and Men.* New York: Appleton. Originally published 1932.

The book that has been described as marking the coming of age of "behaviorism." It contains an account of many important experiments in animal learning, as well as a presentation of Tolman's system of behavior.

Language

BROWN, R. 1959. *Words and Things.* New York: Free Press.

An unusually engrossing account of language learning by one of the main figures in the field of psycholinguistics.

CARROLL, J. B. 1964. Paperback. *Language and Thought.* Englewood Cliffs, N.J.: Prentice-Hall.

A brief but highly informative introduction to the development of language and thought, beginning with a useful formal linguistic analysis.

Thinking and Problem Solving

DUNCKER, K. 1945. "On Problem-Solving," *Psychol. Monogr.,* 58, No. 5. Trans. L. S. Lees.

A series of experiments on creative thinking, together with a searching analysis of the psychological processes involved; not easy reading but rewarding.

FLAVELL, J. H. 1963. *The Developmental Psychology of Jean Piaget.* Princeton: Van Nostrand.

A thorough summary of the theoretical position and research achievements of Jean Piaget and his many followers.

HUMPHREY, G. 1963. Paperback. *Thinking.* New York: Wiley. Originally published 1951.

By a long-time worker in the area of human thinking and problem solving; traces the history of experimental and theoretical attacks on these problems from their beginnings in the late nineteenth century to present times.

POLYA, G. 1946. *How to Solve It.* Princeton: Princeton University Press.

A little book, widely reprinted, that contains many helpful suggestions on how to solve problems. It is written by a distinguished mathematician.

TAYLOR, C. W., and F. BARRON (eds.). 1963. *Scientific Creativity: Progress and Potential.* New York: Wiley.

Selected papers from a series of annual conferences on the criteria, measurement, and determinants of creative work, especially in the sciences.

WERTHEIMER, M. 1959. *Productive Thinking.* Rev. ed. New York: Harper.

Essays and demonstration experiments in creative thinking. Of special interest is Wertheimer's account of what constitutes good and bad teaching in the field of mathematics.

Physiology of Adaptive Behavior

DEUTSCH, J. A., and D. DEUTSCH. 1966. *Physiological Psychology.* Homewood, Ill.: Dorsey.

A general textbook with a good presentation of the physiological processes involved in adaptive behavior.

THOMPSON, R. F. 1967. *Foundations of Physiological Psychology.* New York: Harper.

A first-class general textbook, thorough and up-to-date.

part four

motivation
and emotion

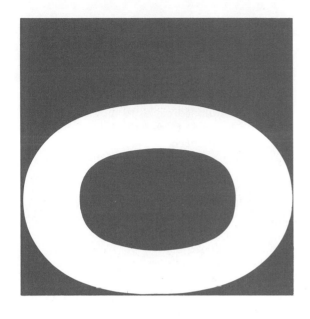

views of
human motivation

overview / Even the most cursory examination of the behavior of man leads one to the assertion that man is not a passive victim of circumstances. Instead we all easily assert that man seems to decide which stimuli to react to, which to ignore, and which information to learn, which to neglect. These observations form the basis for ascribing to man some sort of an inner "directing drive" or "inner spring." This inner directing force is what most of us mean by "motivation."

When we attempt to delineate this inner force more clearly, we find ourselves faced with some of psychology's most difficult questions. Does man have but one overriding motive—or many? Do all human motives directly serve biological tissue needs (such as food, shelter, sex) or are some motives not tied to tissue needs? At present, the answer seems to be the latter—but not all psychologists would agree. Around all of these questions have raged many theoretical battles in psychology, and many "systems" of psychology are characterized by their answers to these questions. Psychologists, however, are not the only ones who have wrestled with the problem of motivation. Biologists, philosophers, theologians, statesmen, and almost all thoughtful people have also wondered and worried about the inner wellsprings of man's behavior.

There have been many ways of conceptualizing human motivation, each coherent and appropriate in its historical context, each allied to prior conceptions, each incomplete yet with undeniable kernels of truth. These views reflect differing emphases on a number of factors, among them the extent to which man is automaton or a free agent, the extent of social and cultural influences, and the role of consciousness in directing behavior.

So far we have been concerned with how man grows, what he perceives, and how he behaves. Our emphasis has been upon specifying and understanding the influences of the external environment upon actions and experiences. How loud must a sound be for it to be heard? Under what stimulus conditions is movement perceived? What sequence of experimental training is most effective for the acquisition of a certain behavior? How is memory affected by subsequent environmental events? The individual may have seemed at times to be pushed into the background, playing the role of the innocent bystander, the target of environmental stimuli to which he automatically responds. This view has been serviceable so far, in the sense that orderly and lawful relationships have been found to exist between stimulus and response.

In most instances, however, some hedging has been necessary. We have often alluded to the effects of "set" and "central factors" upon perceptual and learning phenomena. People are more likely to see what they expect to see, learn best what is important to them, remember most what they find most interesting. To this extent our innocent bystander has been regarded not as a completely passive victim of external circumstance but as having some say in the nature of his response to the impinging environment. And, of course, that man attends and responds at all to external events presupposes some kind of directing force that maintains him as an active and responsive participant in constant interaction with the environment. So far we have dealt with this active aspect of behavior by making use of the rather catch-all notion that man is continually motivated to adapt.

But is this formulation too narrow? To act in order to obtain food is an indisputable requirement for survival—it is adaptive. To act in the satisfaction of curiosity, however, serves no immediate adaptive purpose, and failure to do so has no obvious biological consequence. Consider a child assembling a jigsaw puzzle for

a candy reward and his friend solving the same puzzle simply because he wants to see what will appear. Yet, as we shall see, both hunger and curiosity are reliable human motives. The apparent biological urging of a *motive* does not even inevitably ensure its priority; the pangs of unfulfilled curiosity may take precedence, up to a point, over the hunger pangs of the unfilled stomach.

The point is that not all human motives serve the satisfaction of immediate biological tissue needs. As a first definition, we can think of motives as consciously experienced urges to action. These urges to action do not necessarily imply that we know the ultimate purposes, goals, and consequences of such action, nor do they seem to require some known physiological deficiency. The same is true even of the so-called "tissue-need motives." We eat because we feel hungry, not in order to gain nourishment so that we may survive. Nevertheless, the biological determinants of behavior are important here as elsewhere, and therefore one avenue to an understanding of the motives of man is an understanding of his physiological involvements.

Man has had an ageless preoccupation with his own motives and with the motives of others. This search is an expression of a need to make sense of the events in one's world. A complicated series of behaviors of another organism can be "understood" by ascribing to the organism a motive. And by "motive" in this sense one means what the organism is trying to do, is trying to bring about.

The answers given in the search for man's motives have differed widely from time to time, from culture to culture. The "explanations" have been a function of the then prevailing conception of man's nature and of his place in the universe. The various conceptions are not to be regarded merely as "antique curiosities." We shall discover that, however inadequate each was in accounting for the full complexity of human motivation, it nonetheless contained an essential germ of truth and that the modern account of human motivation really reflects, though in altered form, each of the prior conceptions.

Man, the Pawn of Fate

Man has often been regarded as a passive instrument of supernatural forces outside himself. These supernatural forces have assumed many forms and guises, but they are similar in that they have been viewed as the real determinants of man's action. The gods of Olympus join in rivalry and conflict with one another, using man as a pawn in their own designs. In some conceptions, the forces of good and evil grapple for his soul; in others, inscrutable forces lay out a predetermined track that man fatalistically trudges, unable to deviate from it.

Motivation in this conception is outside the person, and in this perspective the problem of motivation is not really a scientific problem, for there is no way the scientist can measure or control the supernatural forces that motivate man.

Man, the Rational Master

Quite opposed to the notion of man as a pawn of fate is the view of man as the rational master. By this view, we behave as we do because we take account of our situation, calculate and weigh consequences, and finally act in accord with a rational analysis. The locus of motivation is now in the mind, and the laws of motivation are laws of rational process; we choose what we do, and we do what we choose. Motives are therefore reasonable, and the "reason" for an action is synonymous with its motive.

Man, the Machine

But rational approach was not satisfactory to those who conceived of man as a machine, a more complex apparatus than other physical machines, but a machine nonetheless.

The problem of motivation became, in a way, superfluous, for one does not ask what motivates a simple machine. We do not ask about the motivation of the doorbell. We are satisfied to account for its behavior in terms of the pushed switch, the flow of electric current through the wires, the vibration of the clapper caused by magnets, and the sound of the clapper on the bell ringer.

Man, too, has been included in such a "push-button" model. Certain features of the behavior of organisms do indeed seem to lend themselves to this simple-machine conception, especially *reflexes* and *tropisms*.

Reflexes

We are all familiar with the knee-jerk reflex, which is tested routinely by the doctor to determine whether or not the nervous system is functioning properly. This simple, involuntary, and apparently "automatic" muscle movement is an example of mechanical or machine-like behavior. The "button" is pushed (the knee is tapped), the impulse is sent from the knee through the spinal cord and back to the leg muscles, and the "machine operates" (the leg jerks). Questions about mind, purpose, goal seem entirely superfluous.

Of course, behavior is usually much more complex than the knee jerk, but more complex behavior can be explained by assuming a very large number of simple reflex mechanisms, interconnected to provide the final response of the organic "machine." One reflex response can be conceptualized as the stimulus for the next reflex response, and a long chain of reflexes can be assumed to account for a whole behavioral sequence.

However plausible such an account might seem when applied to innate behavior, it is inadequate to explain complex behavior, behavior that reflects learning and involves much more than running through a built-in sequence

positive phototropism

negative phototropism

Figure 30.1. A representation of positive and negative phototropism in a hypothetical fish. Light falling on the eye results in stimulation to the fins by way of the nerves, indicated by the lines connecting eyes and fins. In the case of a *positive* phototropism the nerves are crossed so that a greater intensity of light on the right eye activates the left fin and the animal is swung toward the light; then, with both eyes equally stimulated, the fish is propelled toward the light. In *negative* phototropism, the nerve connections are not crossed, and a greater intensity of light on the right eye activates the right fin so that the animal is swung away from the light; then, with both eyes equally stimulated, it is propelled away from the light.

of simple reflexes. This embarrassment was removed with the conception of the "conditioned reflex" (see p. 288), according to which by simple association *new* stimulus-response connections could be established in the "organic machine."

Tropisms

A somewhat similar approach to the mechanistic view of man arose from the study of so-called "tropisms," observed in insects and lower animals. Tropisms are coordinated "forced movements" that occur in response to the stimulus situation (the cockroach scuttling from the light is one example). They serve a biological survival function in that through them the organism is brought into effective orientation with its physical environment. The mechanisms underlying tropisms may be conceptualized in very simplified terms without involving foreknowledge, purpose, or goal (see Figure 30.1.).

Man, the Social Product

At first glance, this view appears to be at the opposite pole from a machine conception of motivation. The essence of this view is that man responds to the requirements of his particular social group as they are expressed in his society's values, ideals, and sanctions. Presumably, these social purposes serve the adaptive demands of environment occupied by the specific culture. Because these demands may change, so may a society's values; its members' motives are therefore not fixed in a machine-like fashion. The social group that suddenly finds itself in competition with another group for the scarce assets of their region may begin to elevate courage and combativeness in its scale of values. A new cultural value is not simply announced; it gradually makes its way into the spirit of a culture in a variety of ways, not the least of which are changes in the manner in which children are reared. But this development does not happen quickly; there is a *cultural lag*. The process of modifying a socially induced motive may take time, several generations or even longer. One of the blocks to social change is that the very values and motives that would speed it along are discouraged by other practices of the society. For example, cultural lag may someday come to haunt industrial societies that have succeeded in inculcating motives of initiative and ambition. The "work ethic" confronts the increasing availability of leisure, a situation in which the motivations of an "easy-going nature" would be the most adaptive.

Cultural Relativism

Man, as a social product, not only undergoes motivational changes in response to environmental changes but also, by the same token, displays quite different motives and values in different social situations. The notion of *cultural relativism*, as evolved by anthropologists, rejects any assumption of a universal "human nature" and holds instead that the behavior of any individual can be understood only in relation to the dominant motives of his particular culture.

One's culture is the frame of reference within which his motives, purposes, goals, and values are induced; they can "make sense" only if we can construct and share, for the moment, his psychological situation, that is, the world as he perceives it.

Social Determinism

The conception of man as a social product is often closely associated with stress on *social determinism*. This doctrine asserts that there are laws of societies, of social organizations, and of historical trends that transcend individual "human nature." That is, the individual is considered as merely a unit, or part, of the larger social system, taking his direction and fulfilling his narrow roles as dictated by the requirements of the system as a whole. He is the cork bobbing powerlessly on the surging stream of history, the cog in the machine, the mere tool through which inexorable forces of economic determinism express themselves.

The notion of social determinism leads us back again to the conception of man as prey to motivational forces over which he has little control. To the extent that the "requirements of the system" and the forces of "economic determinism" arise from social situations over which man can exert no control, such influences upon human motivation are indeed inexorable. But this powerlessness is often illusory, a by-product of a society's frequent unawareness of the social forces to which it is subject, not of its inability to change them. A sustained program of economic development cannot directly (or immediately) change the dominant values of an underdeveloped nation's people, but it can generate environmental changes that, through social determinism, will inevitably have this effect. Legislation affecting political rights and educational and economic opportunities cannot directly (or immediately) modify a nation's prevailing attitude toward its underprivileged minority groups. Such legislation can and does, however, have very real effects on the social contexts in which these groups live and in the long run must help to change the values of the society.

Social determinism, whatever its limitations as a complete theory of human motivation, need not be a fatalistic view of "human nature." Admittedly, the behavior of a given individual at a particular point in time is in large part socially determined. But man can exert control over the forces from which these motivational influences stem.

Man, the Unconscious Being

Allied to the conception just discussed is the notion of *unconscious motivation*. Man, in this view, is often unaware of the real reasons for much of his behavior. The real reasons, in this instance, are deep-seated "instinctual" tendencies, which are manifested in complex and often devious ways. His choices and actions are not the outcome of rational analysis of a situation, of deliberate weighing of consequences. In this sense, his actions are "irrational." As in the case of the conception of the rational man, the motives of the unconscious man are all in himself, but the manner in which they govern his behavior and experience is entirely different. He really neither chooses what he does nor does what he chooses.

Not that he fails to make "sense" of his behavior. He experiences needs and desires, goals and intentions, and he tends to see most of his behavior as meaningfully related to them. But the "motives" he consciously experiences are often elaborate false fronts for the real "unconscious motives," and his "understanding" of his motivation is merely rationalization.

Although there have been many historical forerunners of such views, it is through Sigmund Freud and his theory of psychoanalysis that the conception has come to fullest flower. His theories aim not only at an explanation of human motivation but at the wider problems of understanding the total personality. We shall postpone a detailed description of his theories until later. Now we need note only that the impact of Freud's views of unconscious motivation has been and continues to be immense, spreading to the outermost reaches of our conceptions of man, as expressed in current literature, art, theology, education, and medicine.

Man, the Animal

In its broadest sense, the "biological" view of man's motives is one of the most influential views in contemporary theories of motivation. In a way, it is an extension of the "man, the machine" approach with the important elaborations that the evolutionary origins of the "machine" and the details of its inner operations become important foci of speculation and investigation.

Darwin was by no means the first to conceive of man as an animal. But his theory of biological evolution caused a re-examination of man's concept of himself and of the universe that reached to the widest borders of thought and whose effects reverberated in controversy for many years.

One of the effects of Darwinism was the search for common qualities in the behavior of man and that of lower animals. Simpler explanations of man's behavior were sought in the model of animal behavior, and this greater attention to animal behavior led to a much broader view of the complexity of that behavior itself. Thus, evolution involved not only the "descent of man" but also an "ascent" of lower animals. It was observed that many "lower" animals, too, engage in goal-directed action, express emotions, prefer monogamous sexual relationships, show maternal tenderness for their young, become frustrated and "neurotic," "reason," and so on. The effect of such observations was to throw doubt on the need for peculiarly "human" explanations of man's behavior.

Innate Drives

What was considered really basic about motivation (human or other) was a set of simple biological *drives* that set the organism into action. These drives were intimately related to physiological requirements for food, water, oxygen, avoidance of painful stimuli, and the like. Presumably, these innate drives came into being through evolutionary processes of natural selection, and in this manner they came to serve the necessary functions of survival of the organism. The explanation of motivated action was largely reduced to an explanation of just how the drives are brought into play, their effects on behavior, and their disappearance, once satisfied. For instance, the depletion of food substances in the body leads to a state of unrest in the animal; he engages in activity and finds and eats food; his body is replenished and his drive reduced. Any individual organism failing to respond in this manner would soon be dead, his progeny never born; hence his species would therefore be somewhat more likely to become extinct.

The initial doctrine of innate drives has given way to a more sophisticated modern conception in which the routines and complexity of the biological bases of motivations have been greatly extended. But what remains unchanged in this view of "man, the animal" is that the sources of motives are to be found in the biological nature of man.

Glossary

cultural lag The preservation of many elements of a culture for some time after environmental changes have caused these elements to be no longer adaptive.

cultural relativism The doctrine that asserts that human motives, values, and actions are entirely relative to the particular culture in which they occur. Thus, the "human nature" of one culture is alleged to be different from the "human nature" of another.

drives Aroused states of the organism, related to physiological requirements of the body, which set the organism into action. In one view of motivation, drives are considered to be innate biological tendencies, on the basis of which all complex motivation is developed through learning, taking the form of derived or acquired drives. In other views of motivation, drives are regarded as only a limited segment of the whole of the motivational energies of the organism.

motive A need or desire coupled with the intention to attain an appropriate goal. In accounting for behavior, motive is not synonymous with "cause."

reflex A simple, involuntary, and unlearned response of a particular part of the body to a particular stimulus, like the knee-jerk response to a blow on the knee or the contraction of the pupil of the eye when exposed to light.

social determinism The doctrine that asserts that there are laws of societies transcending laws of individual "human nature." The individual's behavior is considered to be dictated mainly by the requirements and characteristics of the social system as a whole.

tropisms Unlearned movements of an organism, serving to orient it in such a way that a certain distribution of stimuli is achieved. Tropisms (from the Greek word for "turning") are of many types; for instance, the negative phototropism of the cockroach running from the light or the positive phototropism of a moth being drawn toward it. Tropistic behavior occurs to a variety of stimuli; for example, "geotropism" refers to response to the pull of gravity. Baby rats "automatically" climb an inclined plane, thus showing negative geotropism.

unconscious motivation Pertaining to a form of motivated behavior in which the person is unaware of his needs and desires, intentions, and goals; that is, he engages in unconscious coping—solving problems, adaptively circumventing barriers, and the like—in order to achieve unconscious ends.

attributes
of motives

overview / Instincts, although clearly biologically rooted, are nevertheless responsive and adaptive to the environmental contexts in which they are expressed. For this reason it has appeared possible to some psychologists to regard all human needs as biologically based, perhaps not directly but ultimately. The individual thus acquires new needs through learning that the pursuit of certain goals will indirectly serve to satisfy one biological need or another. This "deficiency" view of motivation regards all behavior as set off by some sort of physiological imbalance, and, when automatic "homeostatic" bodily mechanisms fail to restore a balance, voluntary action directed toward the same end is triggered. Viewed in this way, a biological need, which is essentially a body tissue deficiency, is quite distinct from a felt need; therefore conscious awareness is by no means a necessary accompaniment of a motivated state of the organism.

Needs and motives, however defined, are substantially influenced by learned cues from the external environment, but the individual may still experience motivated states even when there is no external input, and even when there are no biological deficiencies. For example, it seems clear that men and animals have a need to be active and to explore new environments. Although such needs, which may be called "abundancy motives," no doubt have some basis in the physical organism, they can hardly be regarded as serving to restore some physiological imbalance.

One way of reconciling and integrating these different views of human motivation is to assume a hierarchy of needs, with physiological deficits earning first priority. By this conception "higher" needs do not influence behavior until more crucial (for sheer survival) "lower" biological needs are satisfied. The former are not merely derivatives of the latter, however, but are needs in their own right, despite their apparent independence of any biological deficiency.

Innate patterns of behavior, sometimes termed *instincts*, provide the clearest illustrations of biologically rooted motives. A wasp paralyzes and brings a caterpillar to her nest, with the result that her young when hatched are supplied with meat. Such behavior abounds and provides impressive demonstrations of quite complex acts attributable to inborn patterns of the nervous system. Once triggered by the appropriate stimulus, a complex chain of behavior unfolds. But this chain of behavior does not unfold "blindly"; rather, it adapts to the environment in which it occurs. Nest building by birds, for example, is sufficiently flexible to permit a wide variety of materials to be sought and used. When the appropriate inner and environmental events initiate nest building, whatever material is at hand and suitable is woven into the fabric of the nest. As Box 110, p. 493 illustrates, it is possible experimentally to analyze the determinants of an "instinct" into physiological and environmental factors. This interaction of innate behavior patterns with environment is an important source of encouragement for attempts to derive all motivation from a relatively simplified biological base.

According to this view, all behavior serves to satisfy basic tissue needs, either directly or indirectly. Because most behavior does not involve a *direct* response to a biological drive, it has been necessary, for those who hold this view, to regard all other drives as "acquired" or "derived," and in this sense they become "second-order" drives in contrast to "first-order" biological needs. For example, we may learn that social prestige is a valuable asset in seeking to satisfy the sex drive. The motive of seeking social prestige is thus regarded as a "second-order" drive that is gradually acquired and that is to be understood as serving the "first-order" sex drive.

This analysis is by now a familiar one. We encountered it in Unit 20 when "secondary reinforcement" was invoked to account for learning that occurred in the absence of rewards that di-

rectly satisfied primary or "first-order" biological drives. It is also an extraordinarily flexible explanation because theoretically the motive can move farther and farther away from its biological base. If wealth enhances social prestige, then the need to acquire wealth becomes a higher-order acquired motive twice removed from its distant primary sex drive. Not surprisingly, this approach permits the assumption that almost any of countless human motives depends upon one or more of a small number of physiological needs.

The very flexibility of this view of human motivation suggests some of its possible weaknesses. The attempt to trace all motives to some tissue need runs certain risks and is vulnerable to a number of telling criticisms.

Motivation as Biological Deficiency

Historically, the biological view of motivation has maintained a restricted focus. "Biological" has been interpreted as referring only to certain well-recognized tissue needs, for example, needs for water, nutritional elements, oxygen, and so on (for a discussion of the physiological nature of tissue needs, see Unit 36). Inherent in this approach is what has been called a *deficiency motivation* conception, the notion that the organism is impelled to action only when it lacks some important ingredient. In other words, a motive is no more than a physiological imbalance. Behavior ceases when this balance is restored: It ceases when there occurs what is called "need reduction." A detailed consideration of one of the influential ancestors of this deficiency view should provide perspective.

Homeostasis

In 1932 Walter Cannon wrote *The Wisdom of the Body,* in which he described the remarkable manner in which the physiological system functions as a whole in order to maintain equilibrium of conditions necessary to keep the or-

Box 110

Maternal Behavior
in the Rat

Among the many interrelated maternal behaviors of the mother rat, like nursing, cleaning, and defending her young, is the interesting phenomenon of *retrieving*. If the baby rats (called "pups") are placed a few feet outside the nest, the mother rat will rush forth and drag them back to the nest.

B. P. Wiesner and N. M. Sheard at the University of Edinburgh have made careful experimental studies of this retrieving behavior. As a measure of retrieving strength they used the number of pups that the mother would retrieve successively in a five-minute interval. (The retrieving response is apparently not weakened by its consummation. Retrieving will continue almost indefinitely, as rapidly as the pups are placed in the test situation. For instance, in one case a mother rat retrieved fifty-eight pups in seven minutes.)

The investigators studied the change in the retrieving score under different experimental conditions. For instance, they found that retrieving was very high during the days immediately following birth of the young but that, as the days went by, the retrieving score steadily decreased. Careful analysis demonstrated that the relevant factor accounting for this gradual decline in retrieving response did not have to do simply with the length of time since the mother had given birth. Rather, the critical factor was the gradual change in the *appearance* of the pups as they grew older. After retrieving had declined—because the "matured" pups no longer were adequate retrieving stimuli for the mother—newborn pups of other mothers were placed in the test situation; the maternal rat vigorously retrieved them, even though they were not her own. When these pups grew up, retrieving again diminished. By periodically providing the mother with newborn young, the experimenters were able to maintain the retrieving response at a high level for an indefinite period (429 days in one of the rats). We see, therefore, that a continual stimulus can maintain the aroused motive state even after the conditions that first aroused it have long disappeared.

It was also discovered that, if the decline in retrieving has gone too far, the introduction of newborn young will not be an adequate stimulus to restore the original high level of retrieving response.

Wiesner and Sheard then tested the effects of injecting various gonadotropic hormones (see Unit 36) under various conditions. Note the following significant facts:

1. The hormones greatly increase the mother rat's sensitivity to the arousal of retrieving.

2. Virgin females, which normally do not retrieve, retrieve actively when injected.

3. Even *male* rats will retrieve when injected with the maternal hormones, though they never exhibit this behavior under other circumstances.

4. The range in types of objects that the maternal rats will retrieve is greatly widened with injection. For instance, guinea pigs and mice will be actively retrieved. So will rabbits considerably larger than the mother rat herself. And, indeed, a small bundle of rags moved in a jerky fashion will be readily retrieved.

We see in these results a remarkable demonstration of the interaction between internal and external instigators of motivational states. It is also of interest to see that what we may take to be simply an "instinct" can be experimentally analyzed in terms of its systematic determinants.

B. P. WIESNER and N. M. SHEARD. 1933. *Maternal Behavior in the Rat* (London: Oliver Boyd).

ganism alive. This self-regulating process he called *homeostasis.*

He described the "automatic" physiological mechanisms by which the volume of blood and the concentrations in it of sugar, salt, oxygen, and carbon dioxide are kept constant; by which the temperature of the body is maintained within narrow limits; and by which foreign particles and invading organisms are removed from the blood stream. These mechanisms are "automatic" in that they occur without the awareness and voluntary action of the organism as a whole. For example, the needs for food and water can be temporarily met by the body's reservoirs of fat and water in body tissues. Amazingly wide variations in temperature of the external environment can be tolerated, at least temporarily, through the automatic body adjustments of sweating, shivering, panting, and other heat-regulating mechanisms.

Sooner or later, however, the automatic homeostatic mechanisms can no longer maintain the necessary "steady states" in the body. At this critical juncture the organism as a whole must be aroused to take "voluntary" action to correct the body deficits and disturbances. By this view, needs as bodily deficits become conscious.

There is a tremendous variety of body needs, for there are many specific ways in which essential homeostasis can be disrupted. In each case, with sufficient imbalance, there may be an incitement of motivated action by the whole organism to correct the condition. Some imbalances lead to the emergence of unusual and "unnatural" or "artificial" needs. For example, calcium deficiency in rare cases may lead to a bizarre "calcium hunger." The drug addict alters his physiological functioning so that the body comes to require a certain amount of the drug. Withholding the drug may result in the most acute and distressing states of need. Box 111, p. 495, describes the creation of such an "artificial" or induced motive.

Not every form of severe physiological imbalance arouses a specific need. A person may simply feel vaguely sick or "queer," or he may feel nothing out of the way, even though vital functions are being fatally impaired, as in certain kinds of cancer.

Obviously, the functions most likely to require periodic voluntary action, such as supplying food or adjusting temperature, are those that, through biological development, have come to be connected with readily aroused and explicit needs.

Tissue Needs and Conscious Needs

The homeostatic conception of motivation encounters frequent disparities between *tissue needs*, physiologically defined, and *conscious needs*. On the one hand, we may remain unaware of even an urgent physiological deficiency, for example, a vitamin deficiency. On the other hand, we may experience what is usually regarded as a tissue need, for example, hunger, in the absence of any nutritional deficiency whatever (see Box 112, p. 496, for an experimental demonstration). In short, the relationship between tissue need and conscious need is far from perfect.

Influences from the External Environment

Part of the lack of correspondence between tissue needs and conscious needs can be ascribed to the fact that stimuli arising from various objects and events in the external environment serve as important instigators of motive states. In some cases, objects or events are such as to arouse needs that did not exist the moment before. These objects and events may have pronounced effects in directing behavior even when there is complete satiety of inner bodily needs (Box 112, p. 496, also demonstrates this point, but any party nibbler can provide his own evidence). In other cases objects and events heighten or prolong a motivational state already aroused, for example, the effect of the smell of food on a hungry man. The human being is particularly susceptible to such instiga-

Box 111

Morphine Addiction
in Chimpanzees

At the Yale Laboratories of Primate Biology, S. D. S. Spragg experimentally induced morphine addiction in four young chimpanzees. Injections with a hypodermic syringe were made in an injection room near the living cages twice daily at 9 A.M. and 5 P.M. The period during which the injections were regularly given varied among the chimpanzees from six weeks to thirteen months.

From three to seven weeks after injections began, the first signs of *physiological* dependence on the drug appeared. As the hour for injections approached, the animals would show a pattern of symptoms commonly found when the drug is withheld from human addicts: yawning, restlessness, excess salivation, lethargy, crying, and irritability.

After a further period clear evidence of *need* for the drug began to appear. Genuine addiction began to manifest itself. Behavioral evidence for the existence of the need was convincing. For example, as the regular hour for injection approached, the animal would show signs of excitement and eagerness, would struggle to get out of its cage, would lead the experimenter down the corridor and into the injection room, would sometimes voluntarily get on the table and assume the usual posture for receiving the hypodermic needle. Furthermore, if the animal were led away from the injection room by the experimenter without having received the drug, it showed obvious signs of distress and frustration. All these signs of desire completely disappeared after the injection was given and did not reappear until the animal had again been without the drug for some time.

As another step, Spragg placed the animals in a situation in which they could freely choose between a black box containing food or a white box containing the hypodermic syringe. When the animals had been recently injected, the choice of the food box predominated, but when the animals had been deprived of *both* food and morphine for approximately eighteen hours, the choice of the white box containing the hypodermic syringe predominated. When they were deliberately frustrated in getting at the two kinds of reward boxes, the animals spent more time trying to get at the syringe box. Further experiments showed that the white box served as a more effective reward object for inducing the animal to solve problems than did the food box.

It is clear that a strong drive was induced in these animals through the upsetting of their normal physiological functioning by repeated injections of the drug. We see that "artificial" needs may thus take on all the characteristics of primary survival drives.

S. D. S. SPRAGG. 1940. "Morphine Addiction in Chimpanzees," *Comp. Psychol. Monogr.*, Vol. 15, No. 7.

tors. He has learned a vast repertory of "cues," "symbols," or "signals" that arouse the motivational state, which before learning would have been powerless to do so. The dinner gong can excite one need; the word "naked" another.

Even when the individual sits quiescent, unaffected by tissue needs or outer stimuli, he is still subject to arousal by motive states. The reason is that he has a constant flow of ideas, thoughts, and images that are somehow produced and directed by "autonomous" processes of the nervous system. Observed from without, the quiescent man may suddenly and inexplicably go into action. We are all familiar with this

Box 112

Social Eating in Hens

The German psychologist E. Bayer carried out experimental studies of the influence of social and physical stimulus factors on the eating behavior of chickens. In one set of studies a hen is allowed to eat from a large heap of grain until she stops. Then a second hungry hen is brought and begins to peck from the heap. The first hen then resumes pecking at once even though she has already eaten to full satisfaction; she may eat an additional 60 per cent or more under the social influence of the second hen. The hunger motive increases even more if *three* hungry hens are introduced after the hen has stopped eating. Conversely, if the experiment is reversed so that three hungry hens together eat from the heap of grain to full satisfaction and a fourth hungry hen is then brought into the group and starts pecking, there is not a sufficient stimulus to induce the three hens to eat more.

Other experiments of Bayer demonstrate that the persistence of eating depends upon the physical stimulus characteristics of the pile of grain. In one experiment, for example, the hen is placed before a heap of 100 grains of wheat of which she eats 50, leaving the rest untouched. If the same hen with the same degree of hunger is confronted with a larger original heap, she will eat a larger absolute amount of the wheat.

In a further experiment a hen ate to full satisfaction from a heap of grain. Then the remaining food was removed with a brush and immediately replaced. When this was done, the hen invariably resumed eating. With some hens this procedure could be repeated eight times or more, and the net result was to increase the total amount eaten in the session by as much as 67 per cent.

E. BAYER. 1929. Beiträge zur Zweikomponotentheorie des Hungers, *Zeitsch Psychol.*, 112, 1–54.

phenomenon in ourselves. As we sit "wrapped in thought," ideas occur to us that may trigger a rather lively motive state.

The homeostatic assumption that the need depends upon some kind of tissue deficiency and will cease only when the deficiency is removed has been extended to broader conceptions of motivation. In this looser sense, all motivation springs from a disturbance or imbalance of the "normal" state of physiological or psychological equilibrium. In other words, the basis of motivation need not be a tissue need but may be any state of disequilibrium. And the function of all motivated behavior is to restore equilibrium. By this view, man bestirs himself only when something is wrong or lacking. He may be hungry, uncomfortable, faced with danger, or just generally anxious. In brief, motivation is initially tension arousal and ceases with tension reduction.

This view will be recognized from our earlier discussion (Unit 20) of reinforcement-based theories of learning. The notion that a response can be learned only when it leads to a reduction in a need is a logical, if not altogether necessary, counterpart of the belief that for any behavior to occur there must be some deficiency, some homeostatic imbalance.

Critiques of Deficiency Theories of Motivation

The deficiency theory of motivation has been attacked from various directions. The play of children, human and animal, provided the data for the earliest challenges. Bühler's (1928) observations of young children focused attention upon the fact that play was as common and without apparent purpose as it was (by tension-reduction theory) "unnecessary." Nissen (1930) called attention to much the same phenomenon by his demonstration that rats will leave their safe and familiar nests "just" to explore mazes that contained novel objects. They would do so even if they had to undergo electric shock in order to effect this exploration. In short, homeostasis did not adequately account for such behavior.

Recognition of such data called for some theoretical overhaul. It has come from many quarters. Hendrick (1943), a psychoanalyst, proposed an "urge to mastery" as an innate drive in man's biological repertoire. White (1959) suggested a motive of "effectance," which he defines as the tendency to explore and influence the environment. Both views speak of a motive in terms of its ultimate effect.

One way in which a biological, need-reduction approach can accommodate these data is to postulate play, exploration, and curiosity as biological drives in themselves. This postulation has been offered but, as White (1959) has pointed out, at considerable cost to the integrity of the biological approach. For one thing, there has been an embarrassing proliferation of new "biological" drives, one for each variety of unexplained but apparently motivated behavior (an activity drive, an exploratory drive, and so on). For another thing, the postulation prejudges a scientific question. Play, curiosity, and exploration must have a physiological basis in the sense that *all* behavior is determined by what goes on in the physical organism. But whether or not this physiological basis will, upon discovery, resemble in any useful way, say, the

tissue deficiencies underlying thirst, we do not know. Because we are ignorant in this respect, it seems scientifically foolhardy to foreclose debate and speculation concerning the nature of all motivation by requiring allegiance to some kind of tension-reduction model.

Abundancy Motivation

Behavior as a response to biological deficiency can be viewed as behavior under the influence of survival and security motives. Sexual activity, eating, running from danger or pain, building nests or houses to avoid extremes in temperature—all these activities clearly increase the probability of the survival or security of the individual or its species. And it makes good sense to say that survival or security motives are tension-reductive: They seek to *remove* deficiencies or discomforts and to *avoid* anxiety or danger.

Opposed to these survival and security motives is another type, which might be called "satisfaction and stimulation motives." The yearning to explore or to understand, to create or to achieve, to love or to feel self-respect—all these desires are clearly not in the service of removing discomfort or danger. Their source does not seem to be biological deficiency, and their aim does not seem to be tension reduction. Rather, they appear to involve tension *increase* and a state of abundancy beyond the needs for immediate survival and security.

Table 31.1., p. 498, presents the principal human motives classified under the two main types: survival and security (deficiency motives) and satisfaction and stimulation (abundancy motives). The table shows that both deficiency and abundancy motives may pertain to the *same* object. The body is thus the object of both survival motives (as in avoidance of hunger) and satisfaction motives (as in seeking sensory pleasure). Any useful theoretical treatment of motives would do well to integrate both types within a single scheme.

Table 31.1.
The Human Motives

	Survival and Security (deficiency motives)	*Satisfaction and Stimulation* (abundancy motives)
Pertaining to the body	Avoiding of hunger, thirst, oxygen lack, excess heat and cold, pain, overfull bladder and colon, fatigue, overtense muscles, illness and other disagreeable bodily states, etc.	Attaining pleasurable sensory experiences of tastes, smells, sounds, etc.; sexual pleasure; bodily comfort; exercise of muscles, rhythmical body movements, etc.
Pertaining to relations with environment	Avoiding of dangerous objects and horrible, ugly, and disgusting objects; seeking objects necessary to future survival and security; maintaining a stable, clear, certain environment, etc.	Attaining enjoyable possessions; constructing and inventing objects; understanding the environment; solving problems; playing games; seeking environmental novelty and change, etc.
Pertaining to relations with other people	Avoiding interpersonal conflict and hostility; maintaining group membership, prestige, and status; being taken care of by others; conforming to group standards and values; gaining power and dominance over others, etc.	Attaining love and positive identifications with people and groups; enjoying other people's company; helping and understanding other people; being independent, etc.
Pertaining to the self	Avoiding feelings of inferiority and failure in comparing the self with others or with the ideal self; avoiding loss of identity; avoiding feelings of shame, guilt, fear, anxiety, sadness, etc.	Attaining feelings of self-respect and self-confidence; expressing oneself; feeling sense of achievement; feeling challenged; establishing moral and other values; discovering meaningful place of self in the universe.

Maslow and Self-Actualization

A reflection of this view is found in Maslow's (1954) treatment of motivation. In his treatment, all motives, those involving tension reduction as well as the others, are combined in one interrelated scheme, without prejudging the question of the tissue-need basis of all motives. Basic to Maslow's scheme is the view that a fundamental motive of man is to express his potentialities in their most effective and complete form, a need for *self-actualization*. This view Maslow adapted from Goldstein (1939).

Specifically, Maslow conceptualizes the following five levels of needs, arranged in a ladder from "lower needs" at the top to "higher needs" at the bottom:

1. physiological needs, for example, hunger, thirst
2. safety needs, for example, security, stability
3. belongingness and love needs, for example, affection, identification
4. esteem needs, for example, prestige, self-respect
5. need for self-actualization

The terms "lower" and "higher" merely indicate that certain needs appear earlier in the developmental process, are more closely linked to biological necessities, and are narrower in scope. Most important of all, according to Maslow, who wished to stress the *developmental* nature of motivation, a "lower" need must be adequately satisfied before the next "higher" need can fully emerge in a person's development. One cannot devote himself to ensuring his safety until his insistent physiological requirements are met. Only after a basic sense of security is attained can relationships of love and belongingness with people reach their full power. And an adequate degree of satisfaction of one's need for love permits full-fledged striving for esteem and self-respect. Finally, only when all the preceding levels have been successively achieved can the tendency toward self-actualization reach its height.

Development of the individual's motivational structure is not, of course, a matter of sharp,

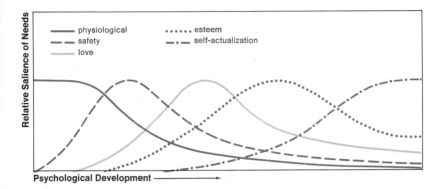

Figure 31.1. A schematic portrayal of the progressive changes in relative saliency of the five main classes of needs, as described by A. H. Maslow. Note that the peak of an earlier main class of needs must be passed before the next "higher" need can begin to assume a dominant role.

discontinuous steps—each "lower" need need not be completely gratified before the next "higher" need emerges. It is more in the nature of a succession of waves, in which predominance among the different needs gradually shifts from one to another (see Figure 31.1.).

This "natural" course of development can go wrong when there is insufficient gratification of needs at any given level. The next higher needs are thereby prevented from full emergence, and the highest may never appear. The man whose lifelong environment provides the barest essentials for physical survival is not likely to develop pressing needs for achievement, prestige, beauty. The chronically hungry man will never seek to build a brave new world. He is much too concerned with satisfying his immediate and pressing hunger needs. Only the person freed of the domination of his "lower" needs can become motivated by other than deficiency-based drives. The ideal physical and social environment is therefore one that makes possible the gratification of each level of needs as it reaches its crest in the individual.

Glossary

abundancy motivation Motivation characterized by *desires* to experience enjoyment, to obtain gratification, to understand and discover, to seek novelty, to achieve and create. It includes the general aims of satisfaction and stimulation. In contrast to deficiency motivation, it may often involve seeking tension *increase* rather than tension reduction.

conscious need A need of which one is explicitly aware. A conscious or felt need may or may not be accompanied by some physiological deficiency or tissue need.

deficiency motivation Characterized by needs to remove deficits and disruptions and to avoid or escape danger and threat. It includes the general aims of survival and security. Deficiency motivation is tension-reductive in its aim.

homeostasis The maintenance of steady physiological states of the body through self-regulating mechanisms, for example, the maintenance of uniform body temperature or of specific concentrations of substances in the blood. The mechanisms function without the awareness or voluntary action of the person.

instinct An innate pattern of behavior, elicited by certain stimuli and fulfilling certain basic biological functions for the organism. The term refers both to the drive and to the activity appropriate to satisfy the drive.

self-actualization The notion, embodied in various theories of personality, of a basic human tendency toward making actual what is potential in the self, that is, toward maximal realization of one's potentialities.

tissue need A need based upon a specific physiological lack or deficiency in some aspect of biological functioning. A tissue need may or may not be accompanied by awareness.

motivational arousal and interaction

overview / Intensity of motivational arousal can be observed on both behavioral and physiological levels and is also directly experienced by the individual as degree of alertness and excitement. The nature of a particular state of arousal is a function of both internal states of imbalance and external stimulus conditions. A first response to external stimulus change is the orienting reaction that, depending upon the specific nature of the change (for example, its intensity), is often followed by an adaptive or a defensive reaction. These responses are not direct responses to stimulus change per se, however, but instead are a function of the relation between the physical change and the cognitive state (uncertainty, expectation) of the individual. When there is an extreme reduction of amount and frequency of stimulus change over a prolonged period, the resultant sensory deprivation brings about a number of behavioral and physiological changes. Men and animals apparently have a pervasive need to maintain, most of the time at least, a moderate level of sensory stimulation.

Motives, in their interactions, often come into conflict. These conflicts can be categorized in three general situations: approach-approach, avoidance-avoidance, and approach-avoidance. Experimental studies of behavior in such situations, however simplified they may be, help us to understand the dynamics of motivated behavior.

Motivation, as is obvious by now, is a complex affair, involving many diverse questions. For example, what are the most useful ways to classify motives? What are their bases in tissue needs and psychological imbalances? How do motives emerge and develop in the individual?

Quite apart from questions about the nature and origins of motives, which we have already discussed, there are general considerations having to do with the ways that any given motive is *aroused* and how, once aroused, it interacts with other motives.

Motivational Arousal

On a *behavioral* level, motivational arousal is associated with the vigor, intensity, and persistence of action. *Physiologically*—and this aspect is treated in detail in Unit 36—arousal is reflected in a gamut of bodily responses: heart rate, muscle tension, and brain-wave pattern, to mention only a few. In terms of *conscious states,* arousal relates to the degree of alertness, concentration of attention, or level of anticipation or excitement. This dimension of arousal can be applied to a wide variety of motives—those clearly involving tissue needs as well as those not so obviously physiological. Thus both hunger and curiosity can range in intensity of arousal from lackadaisical interest to passionate pursuit.

Conditions of Arousal

Motivational arousal depends both upon internal states of bodily imbalance and upon the external stimulus conditions. In this unit we shall restrict ourselves to the external stimulus conditions that shape and control motivational arousal.

The most general statement that can be made about a stimulus situation leading to motivational arousal is that such arousal is elicited by a *change* in the stimulus field. This change can be an increase or a decrease in intensity or a change in quality. Take a light stimulus, for example: The light is turned on or off, is made more or less bright, or changes color; any of these stimulus changes can initiate the first stage of motivational arousal by orienting the individual toward that changing part of his stimulus field.

Orienting Reactions

The laboratory study of the role of such external stimulus factors in arousal, under the name of *orienting reaction* or *orienting response,* has received a great deal of attention in Russian psychological and physiological laboratories—especially in those that follow in the Pavlovian tradition, for it was Pavlov (1927) who first pointed out that this reaction could be investigated under strict laboratory controls.

Berlyne (1960) cites an eloquent comment by Pavlov on the importance of the orienting reaction, or, as Pavlov called it, the "what-is-it?" reflex:

"It is this reflex which brings about the immediate response in man and animals to the slightest changes in the world around them, so that they immediately orientate their appropriate receptor organ in accordance with the perceptible quality in the agent bringing about the change, making full investigation of it. The biological significance of this reflex is obvious. If the animal were not provided with such a reflex its life would hang at every moment by a thread. In man this reflex has been greatly developed with far-reaching results, being represented in its highest form by inquisitiveness—the parent of that scientific method through which we hope one day to come to a true orientation in knowledge of the world around us."

The orienting reaction itself involves a number of different bodily reactions, but in general these reactions fulfill two functions: They increase the flow of information that the individual can receive from his environment, and they prepare for some appropriate action on the basis of this information. To return to our previous illustration, when the intensity or color of a light undergoes a sudden change, a person may turn to face the light, the pupils of his eyes may momentarily dilate and permit more light to flood his retinal field, and photochemical changes may occur in the retinal elements and thus lower various sensory thresholds. In addition to these reactions—which can be viewed as increasing the information the person can receive from the light—a whole host of other bodily changes occur. These changes may include an increase in muscle tonus and changes in heart rate and in respiration, all of which obviously relate to a state of heightened attention and readiness to respond quickly. In short, the action pattern that characterizes the initial motivational arousal is a complex and pervasive one, involving many body systems, and its effect is to clear the psychological and physiological decks for immediate and effective action.

Orienting Reactions and Uncertainty Let us return to a more detailed consideration of the stimulus conditions that initiate this complex set of events. In our example, we pointed out that a change in the objective stimulus alone (for example, the brightness of the light) facilitated initiation of the orienting reaction. But sheer change alone is not enough. Typically, initiation of the orienting reaction is determined by the interaction between a stimulus *change* and the *cognitive* state of the person. Or, as Hunt (1965) has put it, the arousal potential of a situation seems to depend upon the degree of disparity "between the incoming information of the moment and that information already . . . stored within the brain." Paraphrasing this statement, we can say that the degree of motivational arousal is a function of "uncertainty." It is the uncertainty about what has just happened "out there" among the external stimuli that draws our attention, not stimulus change per se.

Optimal Uncertainty This approach leads immediately to speculation concerning the relation between degree of uncertainty in a situation and its motivating value. At first sight it might appear obvious that the greater the uncertainty, the greater the motivational arousal. True, a situation that is completely certain (no novelty, no surprise, no challenge) rarely initiates or sustains interest. But, on the other hand, when a situation is excessively complex, new, and uncertain, the individual may well wish to escape to less confused, albeit less challenging realms.

Some empirical evidence does seem to indicate that *moderate* uncertainty is the optimal condition for eliciting interest and maintaining an optimal motivational state. But the question is difficult to ask experimentally, partly because

uncertainty is an internal state rather than a direct and universal characteristic of a stimulus pattern. Some notion of the complications to which this state of affairs can lead, in the study of the orienting reaction to patterns of differing physically defined complexity, can be gleaned from Box 113, p. 505.

Adaptive Reactions

What follows the orienting reaction? In many situations it is the *adaptive reaction*. To return to our light example: If we increase the brightness of the light, then, quite rapidly, certain aspects of the initial orienting reaction are replaced by responses more adaptive to the specific situation. Some of these replacements involve a reversal of former orienting responses; the pupils now contract, and the light threshold is raised. In a sense, the adaptive reaction is opposite to the orientation reaction in that its function is to restore matters to their "normal" state, to desensitize the individual by appropriate adjustments. This function contrasts with the alerting and sensitizing functions of the orientation reaction. There are other differences; the adaptive reaction is much less pervasive and involves only behavioral and physiological reactions specifically relevant to the situation being adapted to. If the stimulation is visual, adaptation involves only those reactions that serve to restore a comfortable visual situation. In addition to the changes noted in response to a brightening light, the individual may also close his eyes, avert his face, or switch off the light. Furthermore, such adaptive responses do not extinguish with repetition as do orienting responses.

Defensive Reactions

But what if the stimulus is too intense to be handled adequately by the organism's stock of adaptive responses? The effect is the *defensive reaction*, which resembles the orientation reaction in that it too is highly pervasive in its operation. The individual gasps, blinks, "freezes" into immobility; blood vessels contract, and various hormonal changes take place. The defensive reaction is adaptive, however, because it serves to counteract painful stimulation and, like the adaptive reaction, persists until the job is done. People in the limelight may eventually cease to give orienting reactions when faced with the glare of publicity but always will, in defense, blink at the photographer's flashbulb. If the stimulus is sufficiently intense, as is probably the case with the flashbulb, the orienting reaction is entirely bypassed, even on the very first occasion. Sokolov, a Russian psychophysiologist who is responsible for developing the classification of reactions we are discussing (and for much of their empirical elaboration), depicts this relation clearly (see Figure 32.1., p. 506). On first presentation, a stimulus will evoke an orienting reaction unless it is exceptionally weak, in which case no reaction will occur, or very strong, in which case a defensive reaction will be evoked. If the stimulus is repeated often enough, the orienting reaction will drop out, and, depending upon the intensity of the stimulation, either a defensive reaction or no reaction at all will result.

The tendency for defensive reactions to replace adaptive reactions when stimulation becomes too intense also argues that some intermediate level of stimulation is preferred. Further data on this point come from the considerable body of research on "sensory deprivation," a phenomenon that deals with the effects on experience, behavior, and physiological functioning of prolonged exposure to stimulation-deficient environments.

Sensory Deprivation

For a research problem born in the 1950s, the volume of experimental attacks is impressive and exhibits an extraordinary variety of techniques whereby psychologists have managed to

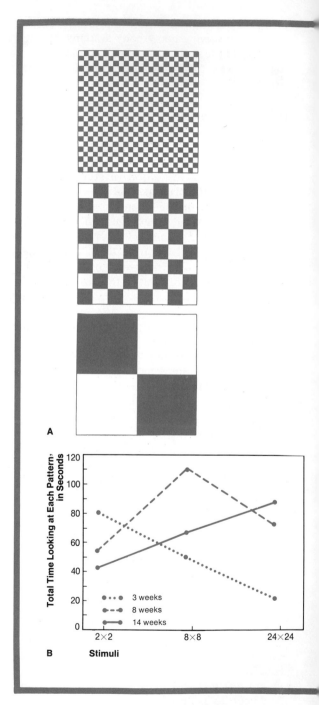

Box 113

To Each His Own . . .

Until recently, studies of the attention-eliciting properties of visual patterns of varying complexity resulted in agreement that the more complex the pattern, the more likely it was to capture the subject's interest. This consensus was challenged by M. Hershenson, a psychologist at the University of Wisconsin, who found that newborn infants preferred to look at the *least* complex of three checkerboard patterns and, in fact, looked least of all at the most complex pattern. In short, these results were the precise opposite of those obtained by previous investigators.

Noting that Hershenson was the first to test these visual preferences on newborns and that the youngest subjects in earlier studies had been at least two months old, three Canadian investigators (W. M. Brennan, E. W. Ames, and R. W. Moore) speculated that this apparent inconsistency was a direct result of the age differences in the subjects. They reasoned that the ability to assimilate visual information develops at a very rapid rate between birth and two months, so that newborns can best comprehend patterns of quite low complexity, whereas older infants have already reached a stage at which they can handle the more complex patterns and are thus more likely to orient toward and attend to such patterns. It followed from this analysis that it should be possible to select infants at three different ages so that the youngest group would prefer the simplest pattern, the "middle-aged" group would prefer a stimulus of intermediate complexity, and the oldest group would prefer the most complex pattern.

They chose as their three age levels three weeks, eight weeks, and fourteen weeks and tested ten infants at each of these ages. The visual patterns used are shown in Figure A and were exposed one at a time in a specially designed apparatus. This apparatus was mounted atop the infant's crib or cradle and included a peephole through which the experimenter could observe when the infant's eyes (his head was restrained from movement) were fixed on the particular pattern exposed during each of twelve trials. (Each of the three checkerboards was thus shown a total of four times, the order of presentation being varied randomly.) The amount of time the infant spent looking directly at the pattern during each trial was recorded and summed for each of the three checkerboards.

Figure B depicts the quite unmistakable results of this experiment. As had been predicted by erboard (as Hershenson had found) and that infants of three months of age preferred the most complex one (as other studies have shown), but also—and most dramatically—that the "middle-aged" infants indeed chose to look longer at the pattern of intermediate complexity.

It does then seem that some sort of capacity to absorb or "make sense" of information may underlie what we prefer to attend to and that each of us has an optimal level of complexity determined by his particular capacity in this respect. Increases in mental ability generally, or perhaps increases only in certain facets of intelligence, appear to provide likely bases for this developmental change in preferred complexity level. Could it be that, as a child grows older and comes to prefer increasingly complex patterns, his *experienced* degree of uncertainty, through it all, remains unchanged at some self-selected optimum level?

M. HERSHENSON. 1964. Visual Discrimination in the Human Newborn, *J. Comp. Physiol. Psychol.*, 58, 270–6.
WENDY M. BRENNAN, ELINOR W. AMES, and R. W. MOORE. 1965. Age Differences in Infants' Attention to Patterns of Different Complexities, *Science*, 151, 354–6. Figure A adapted by permission; copyright 1966 by the American Association for the Advancement of Science.

erratum

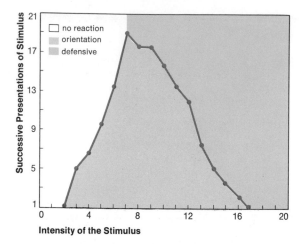

Figure 32.1. Occurrence and nonoccurrence of orienting and defensive reactions as a function of stimulus intensity and number of stimulus presentations. Thus, after five presentations of a stimulus with intensity of 12, the orientation reactions occurs, whereas after seventeen presentations of a stimulus with intensity of 12, the defensive reaction occurs. On the other hand, with seventeen presentations of a stimulus with intensity of 4, no reaction occurs.
D. E. Berlyne, *Conflict, Arousal, and Curiosity* (McGraw-Hill, 1960); adapted by permission of E. N. Sokolov.

deprive their subjects of their usual diet of environmental stimulation. More accurately, subjects have usually been deprived of any *variation* in stimulation (see Box 114, p. 507).

What are the effects of this radical restriction of normal stimulation maintained for hours, days, and even longer? Not the peaceful *nirvana* of homeostasis but some kind of discomfort and deficit instead. Experienced boredom and motor restlessness were the least of the reactions. Thought processes were noticeably disturbed, and performance on intelligence tests was substantially worsened. Daydreaming (an attempt at self-stimulation?) was a frequent result and active hallucinations a logical, if less prevalent, successor. Physiological effects were legion, including those upon brain-wave activity. In short, sensory deprivation often results in severe disturbances in the gamut of human

functioning and is sufficiently disturbing for subjects to signal for immediate release (via a "panic button" that is always present), despite the resulting cost in pride and wages (subjects for these experiments are typically paid at a respectable hourly rate). Some subjects are not so affected, however, and it remains for further research to discover the sources of substantial individual differences in reaction to sensory deprivation.

Very often sensory-deprivation experiments have gone all the way, in the sense of attempting to eliminate internal as well as external stimuli. Specifically, by restriction of motor activity, proprioceptive and kinesthetic sensations were markedly reduced. Such restriction generally increased the deprivation-induced effects, so much so that Zubek (1963) was encouraged to test the effects of *heightened* motor activity in counteracting the effects of prolonged deprivation of external stimulation. One group of subjects were subjected to a week-long deprivation of "outside" stimuli but were permitted to move about as they pleased and were even required to perform calisthenic exercises for six five-minute periods each day. A second group experienced identical external deprivation but, in addition, were required to remain in bed and, of course, did not perform the exercises. A variety of intellectual and perceptual tests were administered to both groups throughout the experiment; on most of these tests the "exercise" group, as predicted, showed significantly less impairment of function.

Taking a walk to "clear the cobwebs" induced by sustained attention to a monotonous task is therefore something more than a flimsy pretext to escape the unpleasant. Prison routine characteristically includes regular exercise periods. The effectiveness of the "coffee break" in improving employee performance as well as morale may owe as much to movement-produced stimulation as to caffeine. The implications for the highly confined inhabitants of nuclear submarines and orbiting spacecraft are clear. We have placed emphasis upon the need

Box 114

The Distress of
Reduced Stimulation

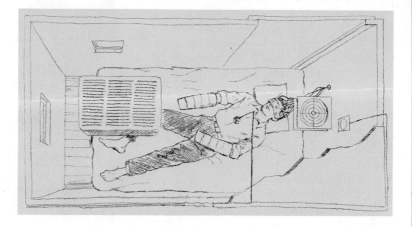

The disturbing effects of severely reducing even simple sensory stimulation, like lights or sounds, have been studied by J. C. Lilly. Naked except for a blacked-out head mask for breathing, he immersed himself in a floating position in a tank of tepid water. Variation in sensory stimulation was thus minimal. At first he felt relaxed, but soon he developed an intense need for "stimulus-action." Despite his intention to remain motionless, "hidden methods" of self-stimulation developed: twitching muscles, stroking one finger with another, and so on. When all bodily movements were inhibited, his attention concentrated on the very few remaining stimuli that "became the whole content of consciousness to an almost unbearable degree."

In a series of experiments at McGill University, W. Heron, B. K. Doane, and T. H. Scott confined themselves (and others) to severely reduced stimulation for several days at a time. The subject lay on a bed in a small soundproof cubicle, twenty-four hours a day, sitting up to eat meals and being released only to go to the toilet. The room was always lighted. He wore plastic goggles that prevented pattern vision. Touch stimulation was limited by his wearing cotton gloves and cardboard cuffs. Auditory stimuli were restricted by a foam-rubber pillow covering his ears. Wires were attached to his scalp to permit the experimenter to record his brain waves (see p. 567).

Most of the subjects went to sleep soon after entering the cubicle. After waking, they gradually became restless, with spells of acute unpleasant feeling. They appeared eager for stimulation, and talked and reminisced.

The reduced stimulation produced vivid and weird hallucinations, irritability, and childish and disorganized thoughts. There was also a change in the subject's brain waves profound enough to lead the experimenters to conclude that a sharp reduction in sensory stimulation "can cause disorganization of brain function similar to, and in some respects as great as, that produced by drugs or lesions."

Varied stimulation is necessary for the normal working of the human brain.

J. C. LILLY. 1956. Mental Effects of Reduction of Ordinary Levels of Physical Stimuli on Intact Healthy Persons, *Psychiat. Resch. Repts.*, 5, 1–9.

W. HERON, B. K. DOANE, and T. H. SCOTT. 1956. Visual Disturbances After Prolonged Perceptual Isolation, *Canad. J. Psychol.*, 10, 13–8.

Figure courtesy *Scientific American*.

for stimulation, in part, because these phenomena promise a radical revision of our traditional conceptions of motivation. Recognition of stimulation needs may also permit a toehold on certain vexing, if familiar, motivational dilemmas. Take the situation in which we are strangely attracted by experiences we should sensibly shun—sensibly, that is, if the avoidance of pain and the pursuit of pleasure told the whole story. The hurtling roller-coaster ride or the horror movie frightens but fascinates. Animals often investigate most persistently what they most fear. Berlyne (1960) has shown this experimentally, reporting that shocking rats at a certain region of the apparatus caused them to *increase* the time spent in exploring that region. This behavior may make evolutionary sense if it is regarded as an attempt to "understand" potentially harmful situations, but, in any case, on some occasions there is a seeking after a normally too high and unpleasant level of arousal.

Motivational Interaction

Once motivationally aroused, the organism typically engages in directed action that reduces or abolishes the aroused state. The specific patterns of directed action vary widely depending upon the particular motive, the particular individual, and the particular situation. Despite this considerable specificity, certain useful categorizations can be applied to the general nature of such directed action. The simplest is the categorization into <u>approach</u> and <u>avoidance</u> behavior.

Regardless of the specific nature of any given motive, its effect is to move the individual either closer to or farther away from the focal object in the stimulus situation—he approaches, or he avoids. The rat races down the maze alley toward the food in the goal box; it backs away from the threatening cat. The infant stretches out his hand toward the brightly colored rattle; he averts his head from the proffered spoonful of puréed spinach. Not all approach and

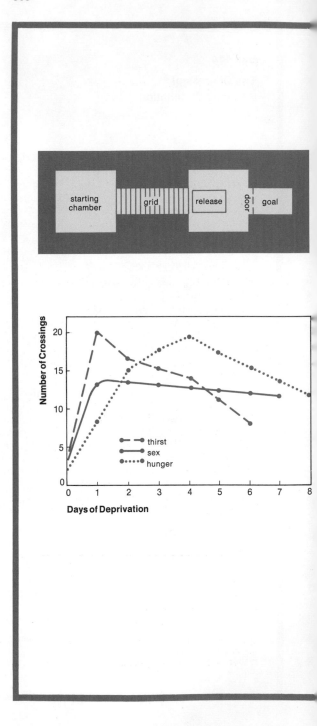

Box 115

Ordeal by Electric Shock

C. J. Warden at Columbia University, following earlier work by F. A. Moss, developed the obstruction-box technique for measuring the strength of animal drives. The floor plan of the apparatus shows the starting chamber, where the rat is placed; the passage, which has an electrified grid on the floor; and the compartment that contains the goal object.

For measuring the strength of a particular drive, for instance sex, an incentive object—in this case a female rat in heat—is placed in the goal compartment. The male rat is placed in the entrance compartment and permitted to run across the electric grid. As he steps on the release plate, the door to the female in the goal box opens. The moment the male comes in contact with the female he is picked up and returned to the entrance compartment. This testing procedure is continued for a period of twenty minutes. The strength of the motive is measured by the number of crossings in the standard twenty-minute period.

Warden and other investigators have used this standardized technique to compare the strength of various motives of the rat. For example, it has been found that the number of crossings in a twenty-minute period increases as a function of number of hours without food, water, or a female in heat (for the male). The maximum number of crossings occurs after fewer days of deprivation for thirst than for hunger. With very prolonged deprivation the number of crossings decreases, presumably because of the animal's weakened bodily state. There is little drop, however, in the case of the sex drive (see chart).

Taking maximal values for each, it appears that thirst is slightly stronger than hunger and that the sexual drive is somewhat less strong than thirst and hunger. But it is perhaps most striking that maternal drive, as measured by the number of crossings of the electric grid made by the mother rat to reach her litter in the goal box, is stronger than all the others.

The exploratory drive of rats was also measured by counting the frequency of crossings of the electric grid to reach an unfamiliar maze, attached to the goal box and containing sawdust and other objects calculated to elicit exploratory activity.

Taking maximal values from several different studies, we can show the comparative strengths of the several drives by the following number of crossings:

maternal 22.5   thirst 20.5   hunger 18.0   sex 13.5   exploratory 6.0

It should be noted that this method of measuring drives places the animal in a conflict situation. It is therefore highly likely that the figures are not fully reliable as indicators of relative strength of animal drives. Very possibly the electric shock itself has a different frustrating effect on the different motives. Furthermore, it has been pointed out that if one uses other intervals of time to count crossings, for example five minutes or ten minutes rather than the standard twenty minutes, the relative ordering of the drives may change somewhat.

C. J. WARDEN. 1931. *Animal Motivation Studies: The Albino Rat;* copyright, 1931 Columbia University Press. Figures adapted by permission.

F. A. MOSS. 1924. Study of Animal Drives, *J. Exper. Psychol.,* 7, 165–85.

Box 116

To Pop or
Not to Pop

Somewhere at the intersection of motivational and personality research lies the realm of *experimental psychodynamics,* which involves setting up standard (and, presumably, lifelike) social environments in which motivational conflict can be systematically observed.

A large-scale study making extensive use of standard situations was carried out by L. Murphy and her associates in the nursery school conducted by Sarah Lawrence College. Among the situations employed in this investigation of personality in very young children was one designed to study aggression and destruction it was called "balloons."

A child is brought into a room containing about ten balloons of various shapes and sizes. First, he is given an opportunity to break the balloons spontaneously; if he does not, he is, in sequence, invited to break them, then urged to do so, and finally offered the willing services of the experimenter to do the breaking for him. Some children enthusiastically break all the balloons; others break only one and hastily attempt to dispose of the "evidence." For the particularly restrained child who continues to resist temptation, a last-ditch device is employed in order to elicit a reaction to destruction; the experimenter "accidentally" steps on a balloon, breaking it.

The point of this procedure is to permit the psychologist to observe how the child resolves two opposing forces: the "approach" impulse to destroy and the "avoidance" inhibition against doing so. This approach-avoidance formulation proved applicable for most of the children, but for a few some qualification was necessary. Some children, for example, resisted the balloon-breaking impulse not from some moral scruple against destruction (or, more primitively, from fear of consequences) but from a reluctance to do away with entertaining toys.

avoidance involve overt bodily action. In thought we can feel drawn toward the object of our desires and feel repelled by the painful and unpleasant.

In these illustrations the outcome is not difficult to predict. The individual will simply approach until he achieves the goal, or he will simply move away until the negative object is completely avoided. But this pattern is not life. It is the rare situation that presents us with the simple problem of responding to either a single positive or a single negative motive. Typically there are two or more motives aroused within us at any one moment. At times these multiple motives are compatible. They may even facilitate one another; we eat with added zest when the food before us is at the same time our sensory favorite and "good for us." Each motive—to enjoy or to be nourished—is somewhat heightened by the presence of the other. Multiple motives usually, however, conflict in some degree with one another. Perhaps

With most of the children the problem was to infer the separate intensities of the approach and avoidance forces. And different children whose behavior *seemed* the same might have been responding to approach and avoidance forces of quite different strengths. For example, of two children who quickly proceeded to the business of balloon breaking, one might have been displaying powerful destructive impulses that overwhelmed his merely moderate degree of inhibition, and the other might have been only moderately destructive but even less inhibited. These two patterns are illustrated in the behavior of two children, Camille and Kene.

"I. *Camille:* Powerful destructive impulses, moderate inhibition or avoidance of destructiveness. [Camille enters and inspects the balloons, holding her hand to her head somewhat coyly. Sits down on the floor, still coy.] *Experimenter says:* You can play with them. What would you like to do with them? *Camille:* I'm not going to tell you. I'm afraid I'll bust it. [Looks up archly] Put my foot on it and it'll go smash! You can blow it right up again, won't it? [Two minutes] [She inspects and examines them. Decides which are hers and which are experimenter's.] *Experimenter:* Do you want to break one? *Camille:* Yes. Try to shoot it: step on it! [Inside one minute she has stamped on and broken every balloon, shrieking and giggling; very tense, almost ferocious expression, especially around mouth. Is very concerned and tense when experimenter asks:] Is it naughty? [Looks at experimenter anxiously:] Will you cry?

II. *Kene:* Moderate destructive impulses, quite low inhibition of destructiveness. [Kene picks up a balloon as soon as he enters the room; friendly but unconcerned with experimenter.] Balloons! [He plays with them freely, tossing them in the air, shouting. Tells experimenter to catch the ones he throws.] . . . [One minute] *Experimenter:* Would you like to break some? *Kene:* No, coz I like balloons. [Continues to play as before.] . . . [Two minutes] *Experimenter:* You can break them if you want to. *Kene:* Uh huh . . . I'll break that one. [He steps on it boldly.] Bang! [He is pleased and excited by the noise. Grins, jumps up and down. Proceeds to break several more in the same way.] *Experimenter:* Is it fun? *Kene:* Uh huh! [eyes shining; grinning broadly] *Experimenter:* Is it naughty? *Kene:* Uh huh! [perfunctory; engrossed in trying to break a long balloon. Later he denies it is naughty.] Makes an awful noise! [He says this smiling in a tone of approval.] [Breaks all but two. Is bored; asks for other toys.]"

L. B. MURPHY. 1956. *Personality in Young Children,* Vol. 1 (New York: Basic Books). Text material reprinted by permission.

the simplest case of motivational conflict involves the confrontation of a single approach motive by a single avoidance motive. This situation translates easily into an experimental procedure, particularly in research with animals. For example, some kind of noxious barrier can be interposed in an alley between the animal and a desired object in the goal box. This procedure not only permits us to examine how the animal attempts to solve the approach-avoidance but also provides us with a way to measure the relative strengths of various approach motives (see Box 115, p. 508). But for the study of confrontation of approach and avoidance in people it is often not necessary to provide an external barrier, because so many of the things we desire to have or do are already surrounded by social taboos, the breaking of which we have been taught to avoid. Box 116, p. 510, provides an example of this conflict in young children.

Not all cases of motivational conflict are of the approach-avoidance type. The conflict may be among alternative goal objects or among alternative means to the goal or away from an undesirable situation. The essence of conflict is simply that the person cannot go in two different directions at once.

Patterns of Conflict

Conflict situations, as analyzed by the psychologist Lewin (1935), fall into one of three basic patterns: approach-approach, avoidance-avoidance, and approach-avoidance.

The *approach-approach* conflict is that between two positive goal objects. It is likely to be the least painful of conflict situations, for the person can choose between two desirable things. It is also true that choosing one necessitates losing the other, however, and this necessity can be a source of quite intense conflict. The man trying to decide which of two girls to propose to, or which of two jobs to take, can get himself into a state of prolonged and tortured indecision. The more nearly equal the two goals, the greater the conflict will be, and the person may remain poised indecisively halfway between the two. But it is an unstable equilibrium because the attractiveness of a goal object increases as it is approached (see Box 117). As soon as the person makes a tentative move toward one goal object, its compelling force thus increases slightly while the other goal object loses attractiveness slightly. The result is that the pulls on the person are now unbalanced, and he will move ever more energetically to the nearer goal (see Figure 32.2.).

The *avoidance-avoidance* conflict occurs when the person is confronted by two negative things, one of which he must choose. It is a case of choosing the lesser of two evils, a choice between the devil and the deep blue sea. For example, a man is required by his employer to choose between the unwelcome alternatives of being transferred to a branch office in a city he dislikes or resigning from the firm. In this situa-

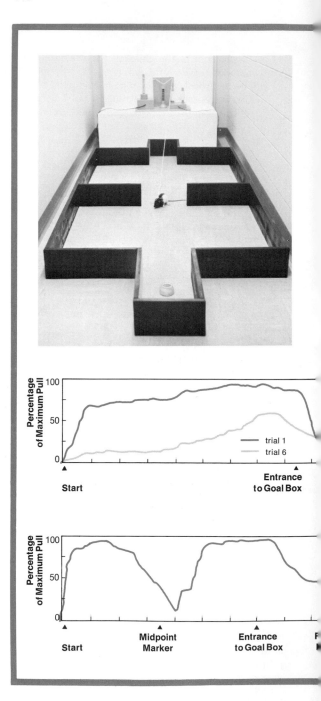

Box 117

Goal Gradient
in the Rat

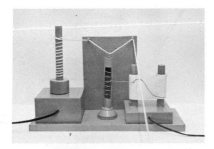

In 1935 at the University of Chicago, D. Krech developed a method for measuring the strength of the rat's goal-directed motivation.

The rat, wearing a harness to which a restraining string was attached, ran from the starting chamber to the food box (see photo on the left). The string was played out at a slow constant rate as it unwound from a cylinder rotated by an electrically driven motor. The rat could not proceed through the box faster than the motor played out the string, no matter how much force he exerted. The string passed through a hook mechanism attached to a fixed spring in such a manner that, when the animal strained against the string, the spring was stretched. This stretching in turn moved a stylus that made a continuous record on a moving roll of waxed paper of the amount of force exerted at each moment by the rat in tugging against the harness toward the goal. The rat thus, as shown in the photograph on the right, "wrote" its own record of its striving toward the goal.

A typical record for one rat is shown in the upper graph. Two points are noteworthy:

1. There appears to be evidence of lessening tension as the rat enters the "goal region" (food box) even before the actual goal object (food) is obtained.

2. The dip in strength of pull in the middle is determined by the side partitions, which do not in any way provide an obstacle for the animal. Apparently they serve as a kind of perceptual "landmark" and function somewhat as a "subgoal." Arrival at this subgoal is accompanied by a temporary lessening in the pull, which is resumed in its full vigor once past this point. When the side partitions are removed, animals no longer give any sign of lessening pull at that point.

The lower graph illustrates the effect of progressive satiation of hunger drive on the *gradient* of pull toward the goal. Six consecutive trials were given with three minutes of feeding in the food box after each trial. The graph shows a record of trials 1 and 6. Note that on trial 1 the animal pulled strongly almost from the very beginning, whereas by trial 6, when he had had fifteen minutes of eating, he began at a low level and only gradually reached a fairly high level as the goal was closely approached. The attractiveness of food, even for a satiated animal, increases as he comes closer to it.

D. KRECH. 1935. Measurement of Tension. Paper read at Symposium on Topological Psychology, Bryn Mawr, Pa.

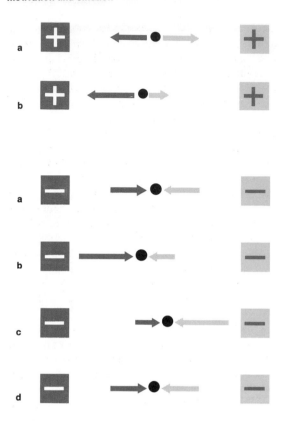

Figure 32.2. The approach-approach conflict situation is characterized by an unstable equilibrium (a), in which a step toward either goal (b) is sufficient to resolve the conflict by further enhancing the attractiveness of that goal in preference to the other.

Figure 32.3. The avoidance-avoidance conflict situation. Here we have a stable equilibrium (a) in which a step away from one object is immediately redressed by the increased negativity of the object toward which the step is taken (note the difference in the arrow lengths in b). This results in bringing the person closer to the other object (c). But this, in turn, increases the negativity of the second object, and, after some fluctuations, the individual is brought back to the point of equilibrium (d) from which he started (a).

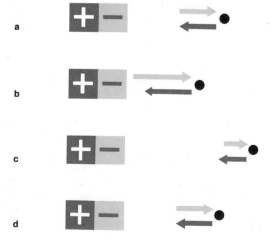

Figure 32.4. The approach-avoidance conflict situation. Here we have a stable equilibrium (a) in which a step toward (or away from) the goal produces compensating changes in the relative strengths of the positive and negative forces (as in b, where the negative force is increased more than is the positive). The consequence of the change in relative strengths of the positive and negative forces is to shift the person's locus further away from the goal, which now results in a reversal of the relative strengths of the positive and negative forces (c). The final consequence is that the person is returned to the original point of equilibrium (d).

tion the equilibrium tends to be a stable one, that is, the person stays balanced as long as possible between the two negatives. The reason is that the repulsion by a negative object grows less, the greater its distance. As he takes a step away from one of the two negative objects, its repellent force thus becomes less; yet this move brings him a step nearer the other object, whose negative force becomes greater, and he is pushed back again (see Figure 32.3.). Usually there is a third force in the situation, which requires him to make a decision between the two. For instance, the employer may insist that he decide on his job move by a certain date.

The *approach-avoidance* conflict, as we noted earlier, is a familiar one. In a way, it is the "truest" conflict; it is certainly the most agitating. Here the person is both attracted and repelled in the same direction. This situation may arise because the goal object *itself* has both positive and negative features, as in the case of a job that pays well but involves living in an undesirable city. Or it may be because the path to the positive goal necessitates going through a negative region; for instance, the rat must run across the electric grid to obtain the reward (as in Box 115, p. 508). The alcoholic must go through the distress of going "on the wagon" in order to win back his self-respect. There is also the case in which the positive goal comes first but is inevitably followed by something negative: The stolen jam means a spanking; the binge means a hangover; the forbidden pleasure means the subsequent loss of self-respect.

The approach-avoidance conflict also results in a kind of stable equilibrium, in that at a certain distance from the goal the positive and negative forces balance, and a step closer or away tends to make the individual return to the point of equilibrium (see Figure 32.4.). Experimental attempts have been made to determine the point of equilibrium in such situations (see Box 118, p. 516).

These analyses of conflict situations are overly simplified, as they fail to reflect all the dynamics of the motivational processes. In many situations the simple goal gradient does not hold. In approach-approach conflicts, for example, what often happens, as we all know, is that as we move toward one positive goal, the idea of the incipient loss of the other makes it appear more desirable than before, and we are then swung back to it. This vacillation can go on for some time. For instance, a man goes on his way to propose to one girl, but as he walks he thinks of all the to-be-lost charms of the other, and this thinking halts him in his tracks. The real point is that, when there is a case of mutual exclusion of positive things, there is more to the matter than which goal is more attractive. For if, by having one, the other is irretrievably lost, each alternative takes on a certain negative character in addition to its positive character, and the equilibrium is not as unstable as before.

Most conflicts are likely to include more than two goals, more than two possible directions of action. The man choosing between the two jobs sees positive and negative features in each and may indeed see other possibilities that involve taking neither job. Furthermore, situations are not usually as "neat" as our examples. It is not necessarily certain that taking this job or this wife will forever preclude the alternative. Often the more realistic case is that there has to be a postponement of one goal in favor of the other or a putting off of an immediate gratification in favor of a later one.

By no means, however, are we underrating the importance of conflicts in which a person sees a situation as starkly a case of this choice or that. People frequently find themselves in situations that have, in their perception, no more options than this one—particularly when unconscious motives enter the picture. Reactions to conflict take many forms and differ from person to person, but discussion of these reactions is best reserved for later consideration. We discuss the nature and range of conflict reactions in Unit 46.

Box 118

Gradients of Approach
and Avoidance

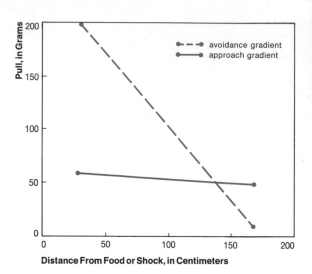

Using a method somewhat similar to that described in Box 117, p. 512, J. S. Brown measured the strength of a rat's pull toward a food goal and also the strength of pull away from a point at which it had received an electric shock. By recording the strength of pull at two distances—30 and 170 centimeters from the food (or shock)—the experimenter could determine the *gradient* of force of pull for both the approach and the avoidance tendencies.

The graph shows the gradients. Note that the approach gradient is very flat, indicating that the attractiveness of the goal is only slightly less at the distant point than at the nearer point. On the other hand, the avoidance gradient is very steep, so that, though there is strenuous pull away from the region of the electric shock when the rat is close to it, the amount of pull is almost zero when it is at a distance of 170 centimeters. At the point where the two gradients cross (roughly 130 centimeters from the goal), the tendencies to approach and to avoid are presumably about equal.

An earlier finding by N. E. Miller confirms this assumption. First he trained rats to run along an alley to a food box and then gave them an electric shock while they were eating there. The next time the animals were placed in the alley, they ran toward the goal but slowed up and stopped at a point short of the goal. Presumably this point was the one at which the approach and avoidance tendencies were equal. By varying the intensity of hunger or of shock, Miller found that the distance from the goal where the animal would stop could be appropriately manipulated. When the rat was hungrier, the point of equilibrium was closer to the goal; when the rat had suffered a more painful electric shock, the point of equilibrium was more distant.

J. S. BROWN. 1948. Gradients of Approach and Avoidance Responses and Their Relation to Motivation, *J. Comp. Physiol. Psychol.*, 41, 450–65. Figure adapted by permission of American Psychological Association.

N. E. MILLER. 1944. Experimental Studies of Conflict, in J. M. Hunt, ed., *Personality and the Behavior Disorders* (New York: Ronald), 431–65.

Glossary

adaptive reactions A general response, usually to change in the external environment, that tends to diminish the impact of the change by desensitizing the organism in a number of ways. It often follows the orienting reaction and is in many ways opposite to it.

defensive reactions A general response to intense stimulation, involving both behavioral and physiological reactions, that serves to counteract such stimulation when it becomes painful to the organism. In this sense, it is adaptive but differs from the adaptive reaction in a number of ways. For example, the adaptive reaction involves a lowering of sensory thresholds, whereas the defensive reaction almost always involves a heightening of them.

orienting reaction, orienting response A general response, usually to a change in the external environment, consisting of various behavioral and physiological reactions that tend to increase the information reaching the organism from the new situation and to ready it for prompt action.

dimensions and description of emotional experience

overview / The study of emotions has long been outside the mainstream of psychological research, and many psychologists have come to see it as an almost extraneous phenomenon, interfering with scientifically "lawful" behavior. For that very reason, attempts to organize systematically the range of human emotions, or even to catalogue and describe them fully, are few and rarely complete.

One schema that may be used to characterize specific emotions and to differentiate among them includes these four general dimensions: intensity of feeling, level of tension (or impulse to action), hedonic tone (degree of pleasantness or unpleasantness), and degree of complexity. This schema may be imposed upon the inventory of emotional states, which itself can be subdivided into several main types. They include, among others, the primary (or directly goal-oriented) emotions, emotions triggered by sensory stimulation, those pertaining to self-appraisal, and those related to other people.

Descriptions of specific emotions illustrating these types, if they are to convey the richness and subtlety of human feelings, must at the moment be more literary than formal and rigorous in their focus. A blending of these two orientations to provide a scientifically precise yet comprehensive conceptualization of human emotion must await further research and theoretical developments.

Most laymen and even many psychologists regard the study of man's feelings and *emotions* as the main business of psychology. Certainly, they may reason, perception and learning and problem solving are fundamental human activities that account for man's success at mastering his environment, and motives may be seen as providing the force that drives and directs these activities. But, the argument continues, is not each of these functions one step removed from the most immediately and clearly experienced stuff of human existence—the emotional life?

Despite the undebatable importance of emotions in the life of man, psychological research and theory frequently skirt detailed treatment of this subject. Most often this relative neglect of emotion reflects the experimental psychologist's concern with other phenomena. The very success of this almost inadvertent quarantine of emotion as a research problem has at times been used as the very evidence for its lack of true importance. In this way a preference by psychologists for working on one problem rather than on another—an inevitable and universal occurrence in scientific research—has brought about some distortion of the proper role and status of the psychology of emotion. As one example, many psychologists have come to see the study of emotions as interfering with the orderly unfolding of a psychological process in accordance with behavioral laws, an observation that is in fact quite true but only because the behavioral laws themselves make no provision for the influence of emotional factors. From this point of view it is but a small step to regarding emotions as introducing random and uncontrolled factors into the study of man's behavior; as a result emotions come to be regarded as a source of "error" in psychological research, rather than as a subject that presents a host of questions requiring scientific answers.

Because of this general neglect it is not surprising that present-day psychology can yield few formal attempts to organize and categorize the vast world of emotional experience, and it even lacks a thorough inventory and set of descriptions for the full range of emotions. We must turn to the poets, the playwrights, and the novelists, who have made the bravest attempts at concrete descriptions of emotional experience. It is to their artistic creations that we usually go for accounts of feelings of jealousy, terror, remorse, guilt, ecstasy.

Dimensions of Emotional Experience

One of the difficulties with any attempt to describe emotions in the abstract is that emotions are thereby taken out of the immediate context in which they occur. Emotions occur as essential and inseparable aspects of all experiences. It is not the feeling of fear in general that we should seek to describe but a particular experience of fear as it occurs in a specific situation—what the individual perceives, feels, and thinks about. In just this way, by describing emotions in recognizable, "real-life" contexts, writers have most effectively contributed.

In view of the infinite variety of situations that exist for any one person, however, his emotional experiences would seem to defy classification. Yet our language does have terms for specific emotions, and these terms do point in a useful way to certain general "types" of emotional experience that we readily distinguish. Although each experience of "anger," for example, is in some degree different from every other experience of "anger," something does seem common to all "anger" experiences. If so, then we may be encouraged to attempt to classify and thus to distinguish each recognizable emotion by means of a set of general dimensions.

This attempt is no small task. First, of course, we must propose the dimensions themselves, which will serve as the basis for classifying the bewildering array of emotional experiences. One way to approach this search is to derive such dimensions and classification schemata through wholly empirical means, as is illustrated in Box 119, p. 522. For present purposes, however, we prefer a schema based upon a blending of both empirical and theoretical considerations. Specifically, we suggest as a useful schema one made up of four general dimensions: intensity of feeling, level of tension, hedonic tone, and degree of complexity.

Intensity of Feeling

Emotional experiences range in intensity of

feeling all the way from the barely noticed tinge of a momentary mood to the most powerful of passions. Anger may vary from a faint vexation to a violent rage; joy, from a mild contentment to a sweeping ecstasy. The greater the intensity, the greater the tendency for the entire self to be involved, to be in the "grip" of the emotion.

Level of Tension

Although we tend to think of all emotions in terms of feelings of agitation and upset, it is clear that emotional experiences vary widely in level of tension. Tension refers to the impulse toward action. The person feels impelled to attack the frustrating barrier, to flee from the threatening object, to dance with delight. Here we have the "active" emotions. The more "passive" or "quiet" emotions may not involve such impulses to action; the sad person may sit without desiring to move; the contented person does not feel driven to act. "Active" and "passive" emotions are equally central to the person, equally involve the self. The difference between them lies in the degree of associated excitement and the strength of the impulse to action.

Intensity of feeling and level of tension are often correlated. A high degree of tension is very likely to mean a more intense feeling. But acute intensity may also be found in emotions with little tension as, for instance, in a profound depression.

Hedonic Tone

Emotional experiences vary widely in their pleasantness or unpleasantness, that is, in what is technically called their *hedonic tone*. Feelings of grief, shame, fear, and remorse are clearly unpleasant, whereas feelings of joy, pride, contentment, and reverence are as clearly pleasant. Some emotions are less clearly placed on a hedonic continuum. A feeling of pity, wonder, or surprise may be neither clearly pleasant nor clearly unpleasant.

The intensity of the feeling will, of course,

affect the hedonic tone. A faint anger may not be particularly unpleasant, but a state of fierce rage is. And there are interesting paradoxes in which a usually pleasant emotion may become so intense as to be unpleasant, for example hunger, or in which a mild negative emotion may feel pleasurable, for example, a satisfying sorrow, a titillating fear ("You frighten me, Sir," said the maiden to her masterful suitor, "but that is not enough for marriage!").

Degree of Complexity

These paradoxes point to the important fact that emotional experiences, being patterns of diverse feelings, are often highly complex. We often feel in an "indescribable" state of emotion, and it is this very complexity of elements that makes it impossible for us to say just how an emotional experience "feels" or whether it is pleasant or unpleasant. In contrast, a great many of our emotional experiences are simple and uncomplicated; we feel a pure fright at the earthquake, a pure elation in sudden good fortune, a pure grief in the death of our beloved dog.

Classification and Description of Emotions

The four-dimensional schema can be used to characterize any specific emotional state. In order to categorize specific emotions into more general types, we employ the following six main classes, starting with the most primary and goal-directed. Only some of them will be discussed.

1. primary emotions, for example, joy, fear, anger, grief
2. emotions pertaining to sensory stimulation, for example, pain, disgust, horror, delight
3. emotions pertaining to self-appraisal, for example, shame, pride, guilt
4. emotions pertaining to other people, for example, love, hate, pity
5. appreciative emotions, for example, humor, beauty, wonder
6. moods, for example, sadness, anxiety, elation

Primary Emotions

Joy, anger, fear, and grief are often referred to as the most basic or *primary emotions*. The situations that evoke them are usually basically simple. Also they are intimately involved with aroused, goal-striving activity and therefore likely to have high degrees of associated tension.

Joy The essential situational condition for joy is that the person is striving toward a goal and attains it. The intensity of the joy depends upon the level of tension that had built up in the course of the motivated act. When the goal is unimportant, the emotion may be no more than mild satisfaction; for an extremely important goal, the result may be transports of joy.

Joy is the emotional counterpart of the release of tension with goal attainment. The suddenness with which the goal is achieved and tension released thus affects the intensity of the joy, a kind of emotional "aha!" phenomenon (see p. 408). When a game is won easily, the winner may feel only mild elation, but winning a game at the last instant, when all seemed lost, may evoke an ecstatic feeling.

There are, of course, qualitative differences in experienced joy, related largely to mixture with other emotions. The savage joy of the person who sees his enemy struck down is not the same as the ecstatic joy of the religious experience.

But our concern here is not with the nuances of joyous feeling. The main point is to see that it is goal attainment and tension release that are the essential situational determinants.

Anger The essential condition for arousing anger is the blocking of goal attainment, especially when there is persistent frustration of goal attainment, with the gradual accumulation of tension. At first there may be nothing more than a slight feeling of exasperation or vexation; with prolonged frustration the person may become truly angry and eventually may reach a state of rage or fury.

Box 119

Dimensions of Emotion

H. Schlosberg reasoned that, in order to detect the dimensions along which emotions vary (and, therefore, by which they can be described efficiently), it would be best to study emotion in a situation that provides a wide variety of distinguishable emotional states.

As a starting point for his investigation, Schlosberg turned to some earlier work on facial expression of emotions by R. S. Woodworth, who had developed a scale of emotions that appeared to fit the empirical data of several other investigators. Woodworth constructed his scale on the ingeniously simple principle that some emotions are very easily distinguished from one another, whereas others are frequently mistaken for one another. His point, now an obvious one, was that clearly distinguishable emotions must lie far apart on any scale, whereas those that are confused with one another must fall at about the same points on the scale. First he proposed a scale running as follows: love, happiness, mirth, surprise, fear, anger, suffering, determination, disgust, and contempt. Some of these emotional states, those close to one another on the scale, proved hard to tell apart reliably; love, happiness, and mirth, for example, were frequently confused. Therefore, they were lumped to define a single region of the scale rather than treated as adjacent but separate points.

Schlosberg had subjects apply Woodworth's scale to judgments of emotions from both posed and unposed photographs. His initial results suggested that the scale might better be expanded into two relatively independent scales, or dimensions: pleasantness-unpleasantness and attention-rejection. With these two dimensions at right angles to each other (the way to portray graphically "independent" dimensions) Schlosberg was able to generate a roughly circular surface (see figure) within which later experiments showed that subjects could reliably locate a variety of separate emotions. (The surface is actually oval, rather than circular, indicating that subjects could make finer distinctions along the pleasant-unpleasant axis than along the attention-rejection axis.)

Schlosberg added a third dimension, perpendicular to the oval surface, which is essentially an intensity dimension and which he called "level of activation." By thus adding depth to his schema, he made it possible to distinguish among individual emotions that lay at about the same point on the oval plane. Grief and suffering were cases in point: "On the surface" they were very much alike, but grief was characteristically rated considerably below suffering on the intensity axis.

A totally different approach to establishing the dimensions of emotion was taken by J. Block, whose work is described in Box 125, p. 548. He factor-analyzed the data from his American sample and, with this technique, found that three factors, or dimensions, could "explain" the relationships among the fifteen emotions judged in his study. Two were immediately identifiable with two of Schlosberg's emotions: Block found a factor ranging from contentment to worry (pleasantness-unpleasantness) and another ranging from such intense emotions as anger and elation on one end to boredom and nostalgia on the other (intensity or activation level). The third factor, on which sympathy, nostalgia, grief, and love were high on the scale, Block called "interpersonal relatedness," and he did not regard it as similar to Schlosberg's remaining dimension of attention-rejection. With some stretch of the imagination, however, we might view all four of Block's third-factor emotions as being "attentive," at least to other people; certainly they are not "rejecting" emotions.

H. SCHLOSBERG. 1954. Three Dimensions of Emotion, *Psychol. Rev.*, 61, 81–8. Figure adapted by permission of American Psychological Association.
J. BLOCK. 1957. Studies in the Phenomenology of Emotion, *J. Abnorm. Soc. Psychol.*, 54, 358–63.

Not all such thwarting will lead to anger. As we shall see in Unit 46, thwarting has many different possible consequences, of which anger is but one. A great deal seems to depend upon the extent to which there is an identifiable barrier to goal achievement. If the person simply cannot see what is preventing his goal achievement, anger is not so likely to occur; but if he sees (rightly or wrongly) an obstacle that is causing the trouble, and particularly if the thwarting seems to him somehow "unreasonable" or "deliberate" or "malicious," anger is more likely to occur and to be expressed in aggressive action against the thwarting object.

Fear Joy and anger are, in a sense, emotions of "approach," that is, they involve striving for goals. Fear, on the other hand, is an emotion of "avoidance," involving an escape from danger. And, because the world is full of potential dangers, fear is a very commonly experienced emotion. Some observers of human nature even consider it the core of human behavior; in their view, "it is fear that makes the world go round."

The essential situation for the onset of fear is perception of a dangerous object or condition that threatens. The key fact in the situation seems to be lack of power or capability to handle the threat. If a person does not know how to ward it off, especially if he sees his escape route blocked, fear is induced by his feeling of powerlessness in the grip of overwhelming forces, an earthquake or some other natural cataclysm, for example, or—as an example on a more modest scale—a father's harsh threats as they appear to a child.

In time we may become habituated to dangerous objects and live close to them without alarm; we can do so because we have learned how to cope with them. But if the immediate situation changes, so that our well-established means for handling them are disrupted, fear emerges.

It is especially noteworthy that unexpected alterations in our usual surroundings can induce fear. It is as if we had organized our worlds in such a way as to protect ourselves, and any disruption in the order may cause immediate apprehension. It is commonplace that a young child is often made anxious and apprehensive by changes in his customary surroundings. The "terror of the unknown" is not merely a literary expression, for, universally, the strange and the unfamiliar may cause dread. This reaction is a very primitive one, which we also note in animals (see Box 120, p. 525).

Fear, perhaps more than any other emotion, is acutely contagious. Seeing and hearing others in a state of terror will often induce panic in the onlooker, even when there is nothing else in his situation to account for it. A scream of terror is "heard" in the "guts" of the listener, as well as of the screamer. Noting this phenomenon of emotional contagion, we begin to suspect that emotional states can transmit unmistakable information, a notion important to Tomkins' theory of emotion which we shall discuss later (p. 559).

The so-called *startle response* bears an uncertain relation to fear. Working with this response in young infants, many years ago, Watson (1924) concluded that sudden loss of body support and sudden loud sounds were the critical stimuli. Since his day, laboratory psychologists have experimented extensively with the effects of these stimuli. They have been especially interested in the pattern of physiological upsets and bodily expressions during startle, on the assumption that studying the startle pattern is a simple way to study the effect of fear. It is obvious that, when suddenly startled, we often feel momentary fright. Yet we cannot equate startle with fear; there are many instances in which the startle fails to arouse fear, perhaps arousing a quite different response, such as laughter.

The sudden stimulus may "trigger" the emotion of fear when the rest of the situation predisposes toward it. Note the difference in emotional effects of a loud automobile backfire

Box 120

The Fear of the Strange
in the Chimpanzee

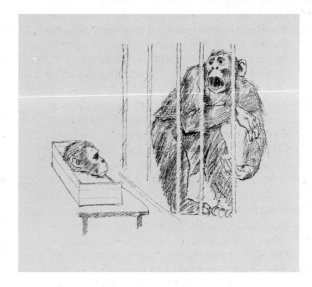

In a series of experiments at the Yerkes Laboratories of Primate Biology, D. O. Hebb tested the fear responses of thirty chimpanzees when confronted with strange and unfamiliar objects.

Among the objects were an ape head, a skull, a human head (from a window-display dummy), anesthetized chimpanzees, pictures, toy animals. These test objects were presented to the chimpanzee while he was in his home cage. The animal was lured to the front of his cage by an offer of a small amount of food. The hinged top of a box was then lifted, exposing one of the test objects. "Fear" was ascribed to the chimpanzee if definite signs of withdrawal from the object were observed. Accompanying such withdrawal were signs of unusual excitement such as erection of hair, screaming, threatening gestures, and so on.

From the data it is clear that *either* a lack of responsiveness in a whole animal (the anesthetized chimps) *or* the lack of a body when the head is seen is the most effective determiner of fear.

Hebb's explanation runs somewhat along these lines: First, through past learning the chimpanzee comes to expect certain events when stimulated by an object (for example, when seeing a head, he "expects" to see the rest of the body). Second, neurologically, this reaction means that, as a result of stimulation by such an object, a *coordinated sequence of neural events* is started in the animal's brain. Third, the immediate source of fear is a *disruption* of this patterned sequence. Fear is thus seen as a direct result of *profound disorganization of cerebral processes.* Fourth, strange, dead, or mutilated bodies arouse perceptual and intellectual processes that are *incompatible* with an already ongoing pattern of activities, and the result is *fear*.

The fear reaction—withdrawal or flight—tends to restore "cerebral equilibrium" by removing the animal from the whole complex of disrupting and incompatible stimuli.

D. O. HEBB. 1946. On the Nature of Fear, *Psychol. Rev.*, 53, 259–76.

on a person when he is reading a suspense thriller at night and when he is sitting in a stadium watching a football game. In the former situation the backfire may well lead to fear; in the latter it is more likely to lead to surprise, annoyance, or nothing whatever.

Grief Joy, anger, and fear have to do with seeking goals or escaping from dangers. Grief is concerned with the loss of something sought or valued. The intensity depends upon the value; usually the most profound grief comes from the loss of loved persons, and deep feelings of grief may come also from the loss of prized possessions. These cases are examples of intense and enduring grief; there are all shades of grief, down to the merest feeling of disappointment or regret.

Joy, anger, and fear are typically "active" emotions, involving great tension. Grief is typically regarded as "quiet," less characterized by tension and activity. Yet we are all aware of a wide range of expressions of grief, varying not only in level of tension and activity but also along other dimensions. Parkes (1965) has reviewed the evidence on the range of grief reactions to bereavement and describes the typical reaction to loss of a loved one as running a quite consistent course. After an immediate reaction of emotional numbness there is a period during which deep depression and despair (quiet) alternates with attacks of anxiety and yearning over the loss (tense and active). During this time other reactions are common: Among them are insomnia, loss of appetite, irritability, and social withdrawal. Both the fluctuation in mood and the side reactions gradually decline in intensity but flare up occasionally when outside events, for example anniversaries, reactivate the sense of loss. Less typical grief reactions found by Parkes (more often found among bereaved psychiatric patients) include "chronic grief," an abnormal prolongation of the period of mourning (often accompanied by self-blame); "inhibited grief," in which the loss is consciously denied and such "substitute" reactions as emotional clinging and extreme irritability occur; and "delayed grief," in which any direct emotional reaction does not appear for weeks or even years.

As with all emotions, simply the essential loss of something valued is far from the entire story. For we are told of many cases in which the loss of something valued is not accompanied by grief. In some cultures the death of a loved one is said to be an occasion for quiet joy; the loved one has joined "his fathers," has gone to the "happy hunting ground." It would thus appear that what is critical is how the loss is perceived and in what context. The immediacy of the personal loss may be dwarfed by wider perspectives: The dead one is now happier, is "waiting for me to join him after the grave."

Emotions Pertaining to Sensory Stimulation

Emotions pertaining to sensory stimulation are those that more clearly pertain to pleasant and unpleasant sensory stimulation by objects. The stimulation may be mild or intense. The resulting emotion tends to be directed toward the positive or negative object.

Pain Physical pain is the most important cause of intense physical stimulation leading to emotional arousal. At low intensities the pain sensation may be perceived as peripheral to the self, and it may evoke neither an emotional feeling nor an avoidant action. At higher intensities an unpleasant emotional state is aroused, and with extreme pain may come the most acute emotional agitation.

One's understanding of the "pain situation" has much to do with the intensity of emotional arousal. The physician warns, "This will hurt a bit," and usually it does hurt a little less because we know the cause of the pain. The painful emotion has parallels with the emotion of fear, in that both are minimized if one feels capable of dealing with the conditions that arouse them. A report (Cohen, 1964) of a tragic reaction to the hallucinogenic drug LSD illustrates this point. As a practical joke, co-workers of a woman placed some of this drug, which induces a feeling of unreality, hallucinations, and so on, in her cup during a morning coffee break. Soon after, the woman left work, complaining of a headache. That evening she was found dead, a suicide. Cohen surmises that, had the woman known that her psychotic-like fears had been induced by LSD, the experience would have been not nearly as terrifying as it apparently had been. Because she could not understand its cause, her fear became unendurable and death preferable. (Box 129, p. 560, illustrates the complex links that exist between such physiological events and our perception of them.)

Disgust   There are various kinds of objects that, when seen, smelled, tasted, or touched, arouse disgust—acute unpleasant feelings that involve strong avoidance tendencies and marked sensations of bodily upset like nausea and vomiting. Again it is the closeness of contact with the self that is all-important. In our culture slimy objects like slugs tend to evoke strong disgust. The feeling is much stronger when the object is not merely seen but is also placed in contact with the skin.

Note that by "disgust" we mean only this primary emotion that includes the essential bodily sensations of nausea and related upsets. In popular parlance the term is used more generally to refer to any kind of aversive feeling: "She is a disgusting person," or "I'm disgusted with myself." But these emotions are more complex and will be considered later under classes of emotions pertaining to self and to other people. It is true, of course, that authentic feelings of disgust are sometimes aroused by other people as stimulus objects. In some cultures, merely the touch of a person of lower or "unclean" caste might evoke genuine disgust and even nausea. Obviously, cultural standards and specific past experience of the individual play a major role in determining what objects will evoke genuine disgust.

Pain and disgust tend to incorporate feelings of bodily upset as essential parts of the emotional experience. Beyond these two more explicit negative emotions there is a large and ill-defined class of unpleasant emotional experiences that pertain to a tremendous array of negative stimulus objects. They include feelings of aversion, dislike, discomfort, and distress, which are directed mainly at the negative stimulus object.

They range in intensity from minor irritations and annoyances (see Box 121, p. 528) to extreme horror, which is induced by witnessing profoundly affecting events, particularly events involving terrible accidents, maiming of bodies, destruction of objects. Fortunately or not, man can defend himself against horror by failing to see the event or, once having seen it, by "forgetting" it. Though this process leads to greater comfort, it prevents adaptation. So the veteran of combat may too soon praise the glories of war.

Delights   A vast array of objects and events have the power to evoke pleasurable feelings. We may call these emotional experiences delights; they vary in intensity from minor enjoyments, satisfactions, and likings to the utmost ecstasy. The sources of delights are well-nigh inexhaustible. Some are the pleasant sensations in the body as it is touched, stroked, or caressed. Some come from perceptions of body movement and functioning (delights in muscular activity, rhythmical dancing, singing) and from the feelings associated with mild degrees of body need (pleasant hunger, pleasant weariness).

Other sensory delights pertain to external objects, their textures, colors, and shapes, their sounds, tastes, and smells. There are limitless varieties of activities surrounding and engaging us that give enjoyment—playing games, reading, thinking, sports, pleasant work, the ballet, the burlesque, the ball game.

Box 121

How to Be Annoyed
507 Ways

In 1928 H. Cason studied common annoyances as experienced in a sample of more than a thousand people of both sexes, varying in age from ten to ninety years, and representing wide ranges of intelligence, wealth, physical characteristics, race, religion, and locality (all American). The subjects rated 507 common annoyances on a rating scale varying from "extremely annoying" to "not annoying." These 507 represented a careful distillation from 21,000 collected from large groups of people.

It was Cason's belief that in the ordinary affairs of civilized man the simple and often trivial annoyances and irritations have far greater significance for people's adjustment than do the more violent forms of emotion that have been more widely studied. He concerned himself with annoyances that were concrete and objective, especially those with irrational aspects. Reactions to some of the annoyances were strong enough to be classed as cases of anger; others were matters of disgust; still others included an element of fear.

These 507 annoyances were classified into five groupings, with most of them falling into the category "human behavior." The five categories and the percentage of annoyances in each category were as follows:

	Percentage
human behavior	59.0
nonhuman things and activities, exclusive of clothes	18.8
clothes and manner of dress	12.5
alterable physical characteristics of people	5.3
persisting physical characteristics of people	4.4
	100.0

Emotions Pertaining to Self-Appraisal

Feelings of success and failure, of shame, pride, guilt, and remorse are emotions in which the essential determinants have to do with a person's perception of his own behavior in relation to various standards of behavior.

Feelings of Success and Failure   Attainment of goals and the attendant release of tension result, as we have seen, in joyful emotion. But beyond this situation is the more complicated one in which there is perception of the quality of our performance compared with our intentions. Feelings of success and satisfaction do not necessarily accompany accomplishment of a task. These feelings occur only to the extent that the person's attention is centered on his achievement, and they are determined by his level of aspiration. If he perceives that he has reached or exceeded his level of aspiration, an emotion of satisfaction is engendered. If he feels that he has fallen short of it, a sense of failure and a feeling of dejection is aroused.

Some of the 507 annoyances are listed in the table. In each case the average annoyance score is shown for both males and females. The possible range is from 0 to 30.

Average Scores for Some Specific Annoyances

Annoyance	Male	Female
A person coughing in my face	28.5	29.3
To see or hear an animal being cruelly treated by a person	28.0	28.3
The odor of garbage	24.0	25.5
A person in automobile I am driving telling me how to drive	23.0	18.5
To have to get off the sidewalk to pass people who are taking up all the room	21.3	19.0
To see a person picking his (or her) teeth	15.3	21.3
To see a woman smoking a cigarette in public	16.5	18.3
To be held very close by my dancing partner	6.8	19.3
A beggar asking me for some money in a public place	14.0	10.8
To find a newspaper disarranged when I begin to read it	11.8	9.5
To see bobbed hair on a woman over forty	10.5	8.3

It will be seen that a great many of the annoyances are probably not unique to the year 1928 but persist even today. On the other hand, certain ones clearly indicate changes of custom and standards even in the short period.

Norman Livson administered this same list to several hundred students over a period of several years in the 1950s, or about twenty-five years after Cason's work. Most of the items in the list maintained their level of annoyance; "a person coughing in my face" remained highly irritating, to cite one example. Some items, however, dropped sharply: to see women smoking, predictably, was hardly a bother any more, nor was the odor of garbage. The latter finding is somewhat surprising; technological breakthroughs eliminating odors are probably the explanation, more so, at any rate, than any greater cultural tolerance for bad smells. Bobbed hair, for obvious reasons never a hair-raising problem, vanished from the annoyance list. But what irritations does the future hold in store?

H. CASON. 1930. Common Annoyances: A Psychological Study of Every-Day Aversions and Irritations, *Psychol. Monog.,* 40, No. 2, 1–218.

Success and failure must be defined in terms of the person's own perceptions, his own level of aspiration. He may feel that he has succeeded when others would judge he has not; and he may feel that he has failed when others would judge him successful. As we have already seen in discussing level of aspiration, he may come to perceive that he has set his aimed-at level too low, so that even when he achieves it, he will feel despondent. Outward success may taste like "ashes in the mouth" (an interesting link to sensory-stimulation emotions), and this feeling will be intensified by the contrast he perceives between the praises accorded him by others and his own inner judgment of failure.

Not, of course, that whenever he perceives his performance as falling short of his standard he will feel the dejection of failure. As we shall see in Unit 46, p. 761, there are many resources of self-defense against the feelings of failure (as there are against the perception of horror), and his emotions may be quite different—resentment of others who succeed, anger at self, and so on.

Although it is the inner-personal rather than the external-social standards of performance that directly determine what is failure and what is success for him, social factors clearly play an enormous role in shaping these inner standards. The person comes to set and adjust his standards in some degree of meaningful relationship with those of other people; for one thing, he is often competing with others, and the common evaluation of performance is strongly pressed upon him. Furthermore, the very nature of social living makes him especially conscious of the judgments that others are constantly making about him. The very perception of one's self is highly dependent upon one's perception of the social world.

Pride and Shame   When successes or failures in goal achievement are perceived as signifying basic accomplishments or defects of the self, deeper and more central emotions of pride or shame may be engendered. In general, the feeling of pride results from the person's perception that his behavior is in accord with what is called for by his ideal-self conception. Conversely, the feeling of shame results from his perception that his behavior falls short of what is required by his ideal picture of self.

Merely perceiving that there is a discrepancy between self and ideal self is not always, however, a sufficient condition for emotions of shame. Individuals may come to have a realistic acceptance of the gap between self and ideal self, just as in level-of-aspiration experiments some subjects feel no sense of failure in falling short of their level of aspiration. They apparently are able to recognize the reasonableness of performance short of the ideal, coupled with a persistent effort toward the ideal; in short, they exhibit a common-sense acceptance of the fallibility of human nature, in themselves as well as in others.

On the other hand, there are strong forces in society designed to make the individual continuously evaluate his behavior and conduct with respect to the dictates of ideal self, and thus the emotions of pride and shame are especially likely to be aroused in a social setting, as in a group. For example, as part of the social training of children, parents and others deliberately try to induce such self-evaluative attitudes in them. They may say to the errant child, "Aren't you ashamed of yourself?" "Do you think you have behaved the way you know is right?" Or they may call his attention to the "model" behavior of another child in the situation: "Why can't you act the way Johnny does?" There is abundant evidence from empirical research that such "psychological" discipline is far more effective in lasting conscience-building than is the rod and that it is most effective when the family atmosphere is a warm one so that the child has a greater stake in living up to parental standards.

These examples are obvious and direct applications of external social standards of self-appraisal and conduct. To a very considerable extent external standards eventually become internalized. Standards that a person originally perceived as outside himself are now perceived as his own; that is, they form an enduring part of the person's self and are no longer dependent upon the application of actual social forces.

There are, of course, all degrees and varieties of such "internalization." For some people and some cultures, standards of conduct are not highly "internalized"; the external signs of approval or disapproval of the group continue to be the main determinants. The person feels shame when the group expresses its disapproval of his conduct and pride when it expresses approval.

For other individuals and cultures the ideal self is thoroughly "internalized." The person carries his code as part of himself and is affected by it regardless of the immediate presence or absence of outer social evaluations. He need not rely on others to ask if he feels ashamed of his conduct, for he asks himself; he needs no one to look askance, for he sees himself as if through the perspective of others.

Most people live somewhere between these two extremes and experience both sets of forces. In privacy the individual does not always revert to an asocial outlook, nor in public is he by any means subject exclusively to the evaluations of those around him. Furthermore, his behavior may be regulated by unconscious factors to an important degree. Guilt may thus be a realistic reaction to breaking one's own consciously held code, or it may be a neurotic reaction to an "imagined" transgression.

Guilt and Remorse Emotions of guilt and of shame are not the same, though they are often closely linked. Guilt is a feeling of wrongdoing, of violation, which is generally experienced as distressing or painful. The essential circumstances evoking the emotion involve the perception of one's action in a situation as divergent from the "right" or "moral" or "ethical" action required by the situation.

The emotion of guilt may be slight and fleeting, a mere "twinge of conscience." At the other extreme, it may be a prolonged torture of "agonizing appraisal." The milder degrees of guilt feeling may at times even be somewhat pleasant and exhilarative in tone. This is not surprising in light of the fact that, when a person violates what he perceives as "right," it is often simply because of the more powerful force of positive pleasures to be gained. As anthropologists and others have pointed out, moral prohibition tends to be created by society just because there is social necessity for restraint of certain activities that are themselves desirable. But there is much more to the story. The very imposition of the prohibition may have the paradoxical effect of making what is prohibited appear attractive: "Forbidden fruits are sweetest." Furthermore, the very act of violation is often in itself satisfying because it is experienced as a successful defiance of outer authority, an expression of autonomy and power of self.

The basic source of the individual's belief in the "rightness" or "wrongness" of certain acts, as we noted earlier, may or may not be conscious. But, given the fact that he does perceive acts in this way, the emotion of guilt flows directly from his perceived transgression of the morality.

It is important here to understand that there are wide differences in the way a person perceives the guilt-inducing situation. He may see quite specifically just what is "required" of him and recognize quite clearly how he has violated this requirement. His consequent feeling of guilt is likely to be directly and explicitly attached to the action: "I feel guilty because I allowed the store clerk to give me too much change." But other situations may be far more complex, and his perceptions of exactly what is required and how his actions relate to it may be unclear. The resulting guilt feeling may not be so explicitly connected with a given act or given feature of the situation and may contain "unconscious" elements—elements of which he is partially or wholly unaware. We may all feel a vague and perhaps even intense guilt when the world is thrown into war. There is a kind of "free-floating" anxiety. Indeed, one of the marked features of such ill-defined and "irrational-appearing" guilt feelings is their anxiety component; the person feels an anxious guilt but is not quite clear about just why the feelings of fear or dread or distress appear or in what connection; nor is he clear about how he can modify his behavior to prevent the guilt feeling. Like the prisoner of Kafka's novel *The Trial*, he knows not what crime he is charged with.

Especially in cases of ill-defined guilt feelings a person tends to perceive the guilt as deep within himself; it is not so much that any of his acts is bad but that he is a bad person. The most profound and agitating guilt emotions—like those found in the fanatically self-punishing or in the insane—are of this sort; the self is seen as the focal point and basic source of the guilty action. Here, of course, we have crossed into the realm of personality disorders, which we treat in detail in Part Five, particularly in Unit 47. At the other extreme, the fact that guilt can be experienced as "objectified" and not basically related to one's real self-conception helps to explain the distinction between guilt and shame.

There can be feelings of shame without associated feelings of guilt; indeed this condition is perhaps the more common. A man may feel shame when caught using the wrong fork at an elegant dinner party but not guilt. His shame stems from a sense of having made a fool of himself in the eyes of others or of having failed to live up to his ideal self-picture of the "sophisticate." But there is no cause for feelings of guilt, for there has been no violation of moral standards. For the young child such standards do not yet exist. A child only gradually "learns" to experience guilt; his first reaction to being caught at the cookie jar is one of shame—or even, more primitively, fear.

Emotions Pertaining to Other People

Much of our emotional experience pertains to the relations of self to other people as objects in our surroundings; the feelings are directed toward them. Such *emotions pertaining to other people* (and other external objects) often become crystallized over time in the form of enduring emotional predispositions or attitudes. The variety of such interpersonal emotions seems endless, but many fall along our familiar dimensions of positive-to-negative emotions. We shall deal only with the extremes.

Love   Perhaps only psychologists would feel a definition is required—and would attempt to provide one. Nevertheless, by the word *love* we refer both to an enduring emotional disposition toward another person and to the immediate feeling of strong emotion in the presence of that person.

Feelings of love take many forms, depending upon the particular nature of the perceived relationship of object and self. The tender and protective feelings central to maternal love clearly flow from the perception of the child as weaker and needing help. The excitement and elation of "romantic love" come from the desire

and anticipation of being together, the idealized imagining of shared delights. The strong element of sexual excitement, found in some emotions of love, obviously derives from the person's perception of the sexual adequacy of the other person to his own sexual desires. The love of the child for his mother may include basic elements of feelings of need for protection and help. Conversely, the love of the mother for her child seems to involve the need to protect (Box 122, p. 534, tells us that the two are intimately connected). And there may even be in the emotion of love pronounced elements of submissiveness and fear, like those aroused in a child by a powerful father.

Emotions of love may vary in all these and many other forms; the intensities of experience may range from mild to profound, the degree of tension from the most serene affection to the most violent agitated passion. What, then, is common to all that makes us call them love? The core of the feeling in love seems to be the feeling of being drawn to the other, desiring to be drawn. Clearly too, the self is apprehended as closely identified with him. Furthermore, there is an essential feeling of devotion of self to the other. As seen from the point of view of the person, his love is always and necessarily "unselfish," for otherwise it is not the stuff of love. Whether it is really unselfish, as judged by an impartial observer, is quite another matter. We have all seen cases that we would call selfish, for instance the "love" of a demanding and possessive mother for her daughter.

Furthermore, the intensity of the arousal depends upon such other factors as the accessibility or inaccessibility of the loved object. ("Absence makes the heart grow fonder," but only as long as it is not a case of "Out of sight, out of mind"!) The unattained loved one is loved the more fiercely; the thwarting of one's heart's desire, to be in contact with the loved person, leads to increased tension and intensified feeling. Indeed, this element may be the critical requirement for "romantic love."

Such feelings are quite pervasive, giving rise

to a variety of responses, some quite involuntary. Hess and Polt (1960), for example, investigated the effects of various "love"-inducing stimuli on pupil size of the eye, an indication of interest arousal not under conscious control. The subjects, half of them male and half of them female, were placed in a room with constant illumination. A camera recorded each subject's pupil size every ten seconds. First a measurement of pupil size under experimental conditions was obtained while the subjects looked at meaningless test patterns. Then the subjects were presented with meaningful pictures associated normally with love or sexual excitement and instructed to attend to them. The presentations of the meaningful pictures were interspersed with presentations of the meaningless test patterns, so that the subject's pupil size might return to "normal" after each potentially arousing presentation. The male subjects showed only a slight increase in pupil size when shown pictures of a baby, a woman holding a baby, a nude male, and (to provide a presumably mild and "sexless" comparison stimulus) a serene landscape. When the male subjects were shown a picture of a nude female, however, their pupil sizes increased sharply. The female subjects, by comparison, showed a distinct increase in pupil size when shown the baby, the woman holding the baby, and the nude male, and they recorded a slight increase when shown the nude female. When the landscape was shown, their pupil sizes actually decreased. If we can accept "eyes widening with excitement" as a measure of intensity of feeling and for level of tension, then these results point to a distinction by no means obvious between the sexes in their response to love and sexual stimuli.

Hate Hate, like love, involves the two characteristics of an enduring disposition and a periodically aroused intense emotional feeling. The obvious conditions for arousal of the hate experience have to do with the exposure of self to the hated person or object. The feeling of

hate is accentuated in situations that tend to arouse other negative emotions as well. Being blocked in one's goal striving, being threatened, being made jealous or envious intensify the emotion of hate. What seems to happen is that all these negative emotions are readily concentrated on a single target in the situation. Almost any person who is already endowed with some negative properties will readily become the target of this emotion.

The essential core of the emotion of hate is the desire to destroy the hated object. Hate is not simply a feeling of dislike, aversion, or loathing, for these feelings would simply lead to an avoidance tendency. We do not seek to destroy what we dislike; we merely avoid it. But hate is essentially an emotion involving approach. We seek out the hated object, cannot rid ourselves of obsessive thoughts about it, and do not rest satisfied until we have destroyed it.

The hated person must necessarily be perceived as playing a central role in our world. Just as we can be jealous only of a person psychologically close to us, so we can hate only a person psychologically close to us.

In some cases, such as traditional family feuds or pathological fixations, persistent hate may take on some of the attributes of a positive feature of the person's world. He "nurses" his hate, savors it, channels much attention and effort toward it. And if his aim is finally achieved and the hated object destroyed, he may feel a sense of loss. The hated object has actually become a central and needed object, giving meaning to the person's world. It had enabled him to organize a stable set of beliefs and attitudes around this negative value. "Love thy enemy" may have more than one meaning!

Hate can be turned inward, and we can observe this fact in the person who, through accident of birth or upbringing, is forced to identify with a group he dislikes, for example, a religious or racial minority group or a particular economic class. He may dislike the

Box 122

Motherless Mothers

The maternal "instinct" indeed appears instinctive, particularly if we base our judgment on its apparent universality. In all human societies the arrival of a new baby seems to trigger a variety of emotional reactions in women. A general air of excitement prevails, and pleas to see the infant, to hold it, and to play with it are heard from all sides. Of course, such behavior may be socially learned and, indeed, it would be an unfortunate (and depopulated) society that failed to instill in its women the urge to care for their children. The fact that this same response can be clearly seen in other species begins to argue for some innate determination of the so-called "maternal drive." Almost certainly, however, both innate and social-learning factors play a part and, what is more, those factors may interact with one another in rather complex ways.

G. D. Jensen and C. W. Tolman present evidence that maternal impulses are probably intensified by the physiological changes in the mother associated with birth and nursing. They observed that monkey mothers are all-embracing for the first few days after they have given birth; that is, they accept and mother strange infants and even older babies. Within a few months, however, they begin to confine maternal attention exclusively to their own offspring. Somehow—and the mechanism is far from understood—for a female whose physiology is in a "maternal" state the sight of an infant sets off intense mothering responses, as we have seen in Box 110, p. 493. These responses can be quite undiscriminating, as when the mother rat retrieves baby rabbits many times her own size.

University of Wisconsin psychologists Harry and Margaret Harlow have studied extensively an even more complex aspect of maternal behavior. Their general question was a simple one: What kinds of mothers do "motherless" mothers make? Or, translated, what are the effects on the later maternal behavior of female monkeys who, in their own childhood, have not been adequately mothered? There have been a number of experiments designed to answer this question. In one (by B. Seay, B. K. Alexander, and H. Harlow), observations were made of the behavior of nine monkey mothers who had been permitted no contact with their own mothers from birth. These mothers

group because he accepts the standards of the majority. Self-hate may be intensified if he becomes able to divorce himself from the despised group. The *nouveaux riches* can become most contemptuous of their former fellows in poverty, and the individual who has been able to conceal his "inferior" ethnic, racial, or social class origin often rails most against these groups. Such self-hate may involve an extremely delicate balance. A person who has managed to "pass" is, in a sense, afforded the

opportunity to become especially virulent in his hate of his former group. Because he now believes himself no longer a member of the group, whatever self-protective defenses he may once have had against its disparagement are now removed. He runs the risk that he may at any moment become again identified as a member of the group, however, and, if it were to happen, he would have to face his own hate, now enlarged. The case of the highly anti-Semitic Ku Klux Klan leader who took his

were about four years old at the birth of their own babies; in each case it was the mother's first baby.

The results were dramatic. Seven of the nine mothers were totally inadequate by any criterion of reasonable maternal care. At best, they were indifferent; each consistently avoided her child and refused to nurse it. Often the mother was abusive to the point of endangering the infant's life. One mother "sometimes bit the infant," "occasionally crushed the infant's face and body to the floor," and "responded to emotional disturbance on the part of the infant by somersaulting, violently, causing the experimenters to fear for the life of the infant." This infant did not make contact with the mother's nipple until the fifth week of its life. Obviously, these infants could not survive under such "care," and, in fact, intensive care by the experimenters was required to keep them alive. Despite this kind of treatment by the mother, however, each infant persisted in attempting to cling to her, sometimes hanging on to her back where it would be safe from attacks (see photograph), rather than clinging in front, as is normal for infant monkeys.

A convincing demonstration that only mothered monkeys can make good mothers? Perhaps. But what about the other two "motherless" mothers who did not show such behavior and who, instead, reared their infants in an adequate manner? Both of them, it turned out, had had some limited contact with other baby monkeys as they were growing up; the seven "bad" mothers had had none—they had not only been unmothered but also without playmates. From this and several other experiments, Harlow and Harlow have shown that social experience with age mates goes a very long way toward undoing the effects of "motherlessness."

This suggestion was supported by some additional findings. First of all, even the "bad" mothers began to "let up" on their children after having socially interacted with them for three or four months, however abnormally. At least active rejection had reached normal levels, compared to the behavior of normal mothers with babies of the same age. More impressive, perhaps, is the tentative finding that "bad" mothers can reform; the three who had had second babies by the time that this study was reported all showed adequate maternal care toward their second children. Two were even overprotective! Apparently even "bad" mothers can learn to love.

G. D. JENSEN and C. W. TOLMAN. 1962. Mother-Infant Relationship in the Monkey, *Macaca Nemestrina:* The Effect of Brief Separation and Mother-Infant Specificity, *J. Comp. Physiol. Psychol.*, 55, 131–6.

H. F. HARLOW and M. K. HARLOW. 1966. Learning to Love, *Amer. Scientist*, 54, 244–72.

B. SEAY, B. K. ALEXANDER, and H. F. HARLOW. 1964. Maternal Behavior of Socially Deprived Rhesus Monkeys, *J. Abnorm. Soc. Psychol.*, 69, 345–54.

life when his Jewish origins were "exposed" in the press makes the point perfectly. Having been thus involuntarily "returned" to the group he swore to destroy, quite logically (and madness, accepting the madman's perception of the situation, is by no means illogical) he had to destroy himself as well.

This inventory of emotions could go on, for we have far from exhausted the repertoire of human feelings and reactions. No explicit treatment has been given to what might be called the *appreciative emotions*—the emotions of wonder and awe, of the whole gamut of aesthetic feelings. What of religious emotions (see Box 123, p. 536)? Neither have we yet spoken of the world of humor, but do so a little in Box 124, p. 537. And what of *moods*, those pervasive and transitory emotional states that are difficult to link to concrete aspects of the immediate situation? And what of the more general question of the determinants of such shifts in emotional experience? Why, for example, do

Box 123

Religious Emotions

The "religious sentiment" was described by William James in the following passage:

"In the psychologies and in the philosophies of religion, we find the authors attempting to specify just what entity it [the 'religious sentiment'] is. One man allies it to the feeling of dependence; one makes it a derivative from fear; others connect it with the sexual life; others still identify it with the feeling of the infinite; and so on. Such different ways of conceiving it ought of themselves to arouse doubt as to whether it possibly can be one specific thing; and the moment we are willing to treat the term 'religious sentiment' as a collective name for the many sentiments which religious objects may arouse in alternation, we see that it probably contains nothing whatever of a psychologically specific nature. There is religious fear, religious love, religious awe, religious joy, and so forth. But religious love is only man's natural emotion of love directed to a religious object; religious fear is only the ordinary fear of commerce, so to speak, the common quaking of the human breast, in so far as the notion of divine retribution may arouse it; religious awe is the same organic thrill which we feel in a forest at twilight, or in a mountain gorge; only this time it comes over us at the thought of our supernatural relations; and similarly of all the varied sentiments which may be called into play in the lives of religious persons. As concrete states of mind, made up of a feeling *plus* a specific sort of object, religious emotions are of course psychic entities distinguishable from other concrete emotions; but there is no ground for assuming a simple abstract 'religious emotion' to exist as a distinct elementary mental affection by itself, present in every religious experience without exception. . . . There thus seems to be no one elementary religious emotion, but only a common storehouse of emotions upon which religious objects may draw."

One indication that religious experience fits within the framework of emotional phenomena is given in an experiment by Walter Pahnke, a Harvard psychologist. Divinity students, just prior to attendance at chapel on an occasion of great religious significance, were administered either psilocybin (see p. 545) or a placebo. The students were not told whether they had received the placebo or the "real thing." The religious experience during the service, as reported immediately afterward by each subject, was markedly greater for those who had received the drug. Of the ten students who had taken psilocybin, nine reported having had mystical experiences; of the ten subjects in the placebo group, only one did so. The content of these experiences varied widely. Drugs do lead to amplification and elaboration of experience but by no means induce a uniform emotion. *What* we feel remains a function of what we expect or intend to feel.

Aelfrida Tillyard many years ago anticipated this conclusion. On that occasion individuals were asked to report their emotional experiences during meditational exercises. Some of the subjects approached the situation with the purpose of obtaining deeper religious experience. Such experience was what they generally achieved. Others had no such expectation and religious experiences did not result for them.

W. JAMES. 1902. *The Varieties of Religious Experience* (New York: Longmans).

W. N. PAHNKE. 1963. Drugs and Mysticism: An Analysis of the Relationship Between Psychedelic Drugs and Mystical Consciousness. Unpublished doctoral dissertation, Harvard University.

A. C. W. TILLYARD. 1927. *Spiritual Exercises and Their Results: An Essay in Psychology and Comparative Religion* (New York: Macmillan).

Box 124

Death, Sex, and Humor

Much of the psychological speculation on the bases of humor has been summed up by J. C. Flugel, who discusses, among others, the following motivational functions served by humor:

1. *Expression of superiority.* Many instances of humor express the person's attitudes of superiority toward others. Thomas Hobbes long ago stated it when he characterized laughter as "sudden glory arising from some eminency in ourselves by comparison with the infirmity of others." A great many jokes have this readily recognizable element of implied contempt or derision with respect to minority groups, for instance, jokes aimed at the "drunken Irish," the "dumb farmer," or the "uneducated Negro."

2. *Expression of aggression.* Humor is, of course, a highly convenient vehicle for expressing aggressions in a safe, socially acceptable, and somewhat indirect manner. (Note the parallel with the facial expressions involved in smiling and sneering and in smiling and baring the teeth!) Sometimes humor lies in aggressions toward those of superior status or manifest self-importance. The pompous person who slips on a banana peel may evoke hilarity; a cripple in the same situation may not.

The aggression is usually directed outwardly, as in frequent anti-Semitic jokes. But it may also be directed at oneself, as in anti-Semitic jokes told by Jews themselves. And the outward and inward directions of aggression may sometimes be neatly combined. A Jewish card player abuses his partner: "What sort of fellow are you to sit down to play cards with the sort of fellow who sits down to play cards with a fellow like you?"

3. *Expression of sexuality.* The obvious elements of sexuality and obscenity contained in many jokes suggest that humor offers a ready avenue for the expression of such socially tabooed thoughts. Flugel comments that the sex joke is often in the nature of a "seduction" of the listener, that is, he is invited, as it were, to "participate" in the sexual transgression.

4. *Defense against reality.* There is always an essential aspect of "playfulness" and unreality in humor. The point is that the humor may serve the person as a way to protect himself against the pains and threats of reality. We may laugh to prevent ourselves from feeling personally humiliated or from being too painfully touched by the tragic misfortunes of others. And there is so-called "gallows humor," in which the person in desperate straits jokes as a way of fending off the grim reality. The condemned criminal, being asked, "Isn't there anything you'd like to say before they pull the rope?" replies, "Yes, tell the judge maybe he done a good thing after all; this is gonna be a mighty good lesson to me."

Humor, we see, is all things to all men.

J. C. FLUGEL. 1954. Humor and Laughter, in G. Lindzey, ed., *Handbook of Social Psychology* (Cambridge, Mass.: Addison-Wesley).

emotional states seem to "wear out"? Even the most sparkling flow of wit begins to bore, and the seemingly inexhaustible well of tears soon runs dry. Is this "wearing out" in some sense a satiation phenomenon akin to that which we have seen in perception, in which prolonged exposure to an unchanging stimulus pattern results in its "rejection"?

Again, as so often before, we have many more questions than answers. In certain respects, we are not very much beyond the descriptive stage in our understanding of emotions. True, empirical investigations guided by emerging theories of emotion (to be discussed in Unit 35) are beginning to yield at least partial explanations. Another avenue of approach to understanding emotional phenomena is through the study of their development.

Glossary

appreciative emotions A class of emotions (for example, humor, beauty, wonder) characterized by the person's appreciative orientation toward objects and events in his world and toward his own place in the "cosmic scheme of things."

emotion A stirred-up state of the organism, reflected variously in emotional experience (the *feeling* of the emotion), in emotional behavior, and in certain patterns of physiological change.

emotions pertaining to other people A class of emotions arising mainly in connection with the person's perceived relations with other people (for example, love, envy, pity). Such feelings often become crystallized in the form of enduring emotional predispositions, or attitudes.

emotions pertaining to self-appraisal A class of emotions (for example, shame, pride, guilt) in which the essential determinants have to do with a person's perception of his own behavior in relation to various standards of behavior and conduct, both external and internal.

emotions pertaining to sensory stimulation A class of emotions (for example, pain, disgust, delight) that most clearly pertain to pleasant or unpleasant sensory stimulation by objects.

hedonic tone That aspect of emotional experience having to do with the degree of pleasantness or unpleasantness of the emotional feeling.

moods Pervasive and transitory emotional states (for example, sadness, anxiety, elation) that tend to give an affective coloring to the entire momentary experience of the person.

primary emotions The class of emotions (for example, joy, anger, fear, grief) usually regarded as most basic, simple, and primitive and typically associated with goal striving and high degrees of tension.

startle response The pattern of bodily reactions typically occurring as a result of sudden, intense stimulation—like a loud and unexpected sound. The startle response is not identical with a fear reaction.

UNIT 3

development, determinants, and discrimination of emotions

overview / Starting with a single, generalized emotional response of excitement in infancy, human beings gradually evolve increasingly differentiated patterns of emotional expression over the course of development. By early childhood most of the common emotions are already discernible, but complexity and subtlety of expression continue to increase. Intensity of expression, or "emotionality," appears to decrease with age, from the earliest years through to old age. What is not clear, however, is whether this observed decrease in emotionality with age represents a genuine decrease or whether it merely indicates that the intense emotionality of childhood is still present, but is "clamped down" and can quickly surface under appropriate circumstances. Superficially, at least, it does appear that life becomes emotionally easier as we grow older.

"Emotionality" is to an important extent determined by hereditary factors, but, for emotions in general, early experience is a crucial factor, as it is in the closely related question of determinants of personality characteristics. Much remains to be done on this question, but, whatever the direction of future research, the inescapable influence of the immediate social situation in which the given emotion is expressed must be emphasized.

One source of difficulty in research on emotions is that they are neither easily defined nor discriminated. Questions of whether emotions are to be defined and judged on the basis of experienced feeling, observed behavior, or measurable physiological events continue to arise. Generally speaking, these three sources of data agree, but even experienced judges are still only moderately accurate in their assessments. Furthermore, some emotions are "out there" and easily judged; others, less overtly expressed, are much more difficult to discriminate reliably. As a rule, single cues are of minimal help, but, when patterns of multiple cues are the basis of judgment, accuracy is improved.

Our cataloguing and classifying of emotions in Unit 33 dealt with the full range of human emotions. This presentation conveniently put aside a number of questions to which we now turn. Briefly, in this unit we shall be asking three questions: First, do we find in children the same complexity and richness of emotional experience and expression as in adults? Second, are these various emotions unlearned attributes of human behavior, emerging universally and unaffected by specific earlier experiences? Third, are the distinctions we drew among different emotional states reliably discerned as we observe the emotional behavior of persons? The answer to all three questions is an unqualified "no!" We shall now see why.

The Development of Emotions

One thing is clear about the development of emotions: The course runs from lesser to greater differentiation as the child grows into man. At first there is perhaps only one emotion in the repertoire of the newborn. Only after some years do we begin to detect the variety of emotional states—and the sometimes highly subtle shades of difference between them—that mark adult emotional life. This fact of increasing differentiation with age makes possible the widely different patterns of emotional behavior that do in fact exist among individuals, even among those from the same social setting.

Differentiation of Emotions

Whether the stimulus is a loud noise, sudden loss of support, pain, wet diaper, hunger, or tickle, the newborn responds with a fairly diffuse emotional outburst that can best be labeled "general excitement"; it is close kin to the "arousal" that we have dealt with at length. In the course of development, this generalized excitement becomes more and more differentiated until by the end of the first two years the baby's emotional life has become a more discriminating and a "richer" one. He has fewer outbursts, but the kinds of situations that lead to emotional episodes increase in variety, and the nature of his responses becomes more specifically adapted for those situations (see Figure 34.1.).

According to Bridges (1932), there is a definite temporal pattern in the differentiation of the emotions. The generalized response of excitement first becomes differentiated into a general negative response and a general positive response called "distress" and "delight" respectively. As time goes on, these still quite general responses split into more and more specific ones. Distress comes to find expression in a variety of emotions: anger, disgust, fear, or jealousy. Delight also becomes differentiated and can express itself as appreciation and joy in numerous pursuits. The rate at which these emotions become differentiated varies from infant to infant, and the exact ages at which the various emotions appear are difficult to determine. Figure 34.2. presents one developmental history based on Bridges' observations of sixty-two infants in the Montreal Foundling Hospital. The emotional development of children brought up in normal family surroundings with more, and more varied, interaction with parents and other family members would probably result in more rapid differentiation.

There is no direct evidence for the course of the later emotional differentiation through childhood into adulthood. But there is some indirect evidence that children become increasingly more accurate in judging emotions as they approach adulthood; this evidence might be taken to indicate that they are, at the same time, becoming increasingly able to experience the full gamut of adult emotions. This view and the common observation that children become emotionally more "complex" as they mature appear to support the hypothesis of a continuing process of emotional differentiation.

Age Changes in Emotional Expression

Accompanying the tendency toward increased emotional differentiation are developmental

Figure 34.1. Chart indicating the change in frequency of emotional outbursts in children and the nature of the exciting situation. It is based on data collected by W. E. Blatz and D. A. Millichamp (1935) in observations of the behavior of five children. Over a two-year period 2,095 emotional outbursts were observed and recorded in these infants. It will be noted that the *number* of emotional episodes drops from a total of 500, during the period from one to four months, to 170 during the period from twenty to twenty-four months. At first most of the episodes (more than 60 per cent) were initiated by physical discomfort—wet diapers, pins sticking in skin, illness, and so on or by the cessation of adult attention. As time went on, other situations called forth emotional responses. "Social thwarting" refers to such stimuli as teasing a child, laughing at him, refusing him a request. "Inadequacy" includes such situations as a child's inability to reach for desired objects or inability to do something. "Environmental change" includes being placed in an unfamiliar physical or social environment and being exposed to loud and sudden noises.

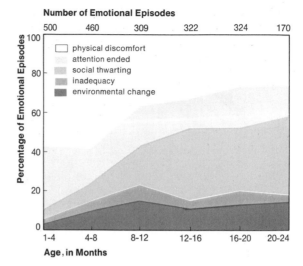

Number of Emotional Episodes

Figure 34.2. A diagrammatic representation of the progressive differentiation of emotions in the child during his first two years.
K. M. B. Bridges, "Emotional Development in Early Infancy," *Child Development*, 3, 324–41; © 1932 by The Society for Research in Child Development; adapted by permission.

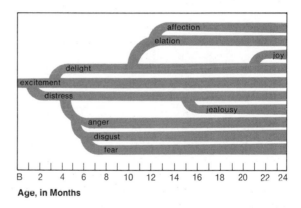

Age, in Months

changes in the nature of emotional expression. For example, it is clear that children do become less "emotional" with age, in the sense that they exhibit violent outbursts less frequently. Macfarlane, Allen, and Honzik (1954) report that, in a group of normal children, temper tantrums declined steadily from age three onward for both boys and girls. Whereas about 60 per cent of all children at age three had tantrums with at least moderate frequency, at age fourteen only about 15 per cent on the average had them. Whether this age trend represents a lessened urge to "blow up" or a greater ability to con-

trol one's temper or both is a moot point.

Chown and Heron (1965), in their review of changes in "emotionality" in later adulthood and old age, are confronted with the same dilemma. They summarize evidence that points to increasingly less frequent and intense emotional outbursts as one grows old but conclude that "it looks as though emotion is present but clamped down rather than nonexistent, and can be strongly aroused by unexpected disasters." Indik, Seashore, and Slesinger (1964), however, do find from their study of psychological strain from young adulthood to old age that a major source of emotional upset—"job-related strain" —decreases steadily throughout this period. Furthermore, psychosomatic symptoms (see p. 733), which might be regarded as an indication of "clamping down" on emotions, also decrease with age. The best but still very tentative resolution we can draw from these data and from a number of recent studies of adjustment to aging and retirement is that life does become emotionally easier as we grow older. At least, it seems to do so for those who survive. The relative contributions to this age trend of biological aging processes, of changes in social roles, and of such personal factors as "coming to terms" with oneself have still to be evaluated.

Some Determinants of Emotions

The fact that some general "average" trends in the emotional development can be detected in no way implies, of course, that this course is uniform for all individuals. The enormous variety of emotional styles is one of the most obvious features of the human species. Some people are quietly cheerful, some boisterously happy, some explosive, others brooding. Although each of us is probably capable of exhibiting any given emotion at one time or another, we each seem to have a characteristic emotional tone, at least in our normal life circumstances. These emotional "orientations" are frequently so pervasive as to be undistinguishable from personality traits. Is a tendency to quick anger an emotional characteristic or a trait of personality? Because of this fuzzy distinction, much of what we know of the determinants of personality (see Unit 44), particularly regarding the so-called "traits of temperament," applies as well to an understanding of individual differences in emotion.

Hereditary Determinants

There are decided differences among infants in "emotional" kinds of behavior, for example, frequency and loudness of crying, restlessness, and general activity level. Some of these "emotional" traits appear to persist into later development. (Yarrow and Yarrow, 1964, review some of the evidence on the developmental consistency of such traits.)

The existence of such differences at birth and even their persistence into later life are not firm demonstrations of hereditary determination, however. Instead, these differences may be the effects of intrauterine influences prior to birth or may reflect certain complications of pregnancy and delivery (see Box 8, p. 32). Studies of twins, a method that will be encountered frequently throughout the text whenever we attempt to detect hereditary influences, go more directly to the point. A number of studies of twins, assessing the relative importance to emotional behavior of hereditary and environmental factors, use the general rationale that, to the extent that identical twins are more like one another than are fraternal twins, the trait in question is hereditary. Vandenberg (1962) and Gottesman (1963) report findings with this method for large numbers of emotional and personality characteristics and are in substantial agreement with one another. For our present purposes, perhaps the most pertinent finding is that the general trait of "emotionality" is substantially determined in human beings by hereditary factors. Loehlin (1965), working with Vandenberg's data, appears to have refined the original conclusion. His analysis suggests that some aspects of "emotionality" are hereditary whereas others are not. Examples of the hereditary facets are ability to control one's impulses and to be adventurous and fast-acting. Very little influenced by heredity, on the other hand, are such characteristics as nervousness, jumpiness, and feeling restricted by rules. With a little stretch of the imagination we may be led to look for direct physiological bases for "hereditary emotionality," whereas "nonhereditary emotionality," which seems more interpersonal or social in its character, would turn our sights to childhood upbringing and experiences.

Early Experience Determinants

We have already noted that experiences during pregnancy and delivery may affect a child's later emotional behavior. Also, we saw in Box 122, p. 534, that an absence of "mothering" exerts profound effects on a child's later ability to behave appropriately to her own offspring. Many lines of evidence support the importance of social stimulation for normal progress in several areas of development. For example, adequate early stimulation is critical for intellectual development (see p. 468). More to the point is our detailed treatment of the effects of early experience on later personality, of which emotions are a part (see p. 735). Even more relevant is a study of infants (Ourth & Brown, 1961), which reports that, even in the first few days of life, "mothered" babies (those who were frequently held and rocked) cried less than those who were given only routine care.

Hallucinogenic Drugs

There has been considerable research interest in the effects of *hallucinogenic drugs*—LSD, psilocybin, and mescaline are examples—on emotional experiences. The gist of informal and formal experimentation with these drugs, as it concerns us here, is that they apparently induce an openness to emotion and feeling that is rarely accessible to the ordinary person in his workaday life. How do these drugs work? What accounts for their apparently very different effects on different individuals or even on the same person on different occasions? In his overview of the data on the three drugs, Unger (1963) concludes that they have very similar effects but that the enormous variation in their impact is largely a function of the situation, very broadly and very psychologically defined, in which they are ingested.

In short, as we have observed earlier, the social context in which it takes place must be assigned uppermost importance if emotional behavior is to be understood. Without doubt, we still have a long way to go to arrive at a full understanding of the sources of man's feelings, passions, and emotions.

Discrimination of Emotions

It would be difficult to convince a dedicated mother that her newborn's emotional reactions are in reality as diffuse as we have described. Folklore, ancient and modern, tells us that a mother can indeed judge from the tone of her baby's cry whether it is hungry, wet, or in need of company. There is some evidence to the contrary. Sherman and Sherman (1929) found that college students, who were shown motion pictures, were unable to distinguish reliably among the emotional reactions of newborn infants to situations that were designed to induce "rage" (restraint of infant's head), "fear" (sudden loss of support), "pain" (needle prick), and "hunger" (feeding overdue). Admittedly this experimental design stacks the cards in a number of ways, as all four emotions are rather similar and motion pictures are not quite the same as "life." Most important, mothers have strong involvement and intensive experience with their own children, a probable advantage in judging that was denied the college students. Berlyne (1960) cites Russian data that indicate that a mother shows distinctive physiological responses to the cry of her infant and not to others, even when she is not consciously aware that it is her own child. Although this detection ability is something other than the ability to discriminate among emotions, it does suggest an extraordinary potential in mothers to respond quite sensitively to cues from their babies; this potential, in turn, makes it somewhat more likely that they can distinguish among the very few and rather blatantly expressed emotions of which their offspring are capable. But, as we shall now see, the situation is quite different for the expression and discrimination of adult emotional states.

Problems of Definition and Measurement

Before turning to the evidence on this question, we must first consider how emotions are to be defined and what concrete procedures are to be used in measuring them. And the problem of definition and measurement in the scientific study of emotion is a particularly thorny one. For any given emotion there can be many sensible definitions, allowing for a variety of quite different measurement operations.

Take "anger" as an example. Does it refer to how a person feels, to how he is behaving, or to such physiological events as changes in heart rate and blood pressure? They are all reasonable ways to define anger, but they point to very different procedures: Shall we ask the individual to report on his emotional state? Shall we simply observe his behavior in the situation? Or shall we carry out certain measurements on his organism? We can, of course, do all three, but, as we shall soon see, the different sets of measurements may lead to different conclusions as to whether the person is "really" angry or not.

Even if we can agree upon which facet of emotion is being discussed, the well-established fact still remains that emotional responses, however defined and measured, are highly unpredictable. Do the same situations lead to anger in all persons? Is there a "standard" behavioral response to anger? Do all people show the same facial expressions when they feel angry? Is there high consistency among individuals in the bodily events accompanying the experience of anger? The answer to each of these questions is a strong "no." Nor is the situation much better within the world of a single individual: Each of us gets angry at different things at different times, expresses this emotion differently depending upon the occasion, and perhaps even feels anger differently "inside." Despite

this complexity, the different ways in which emotion may be expressed do show certain systematic, if intricate, interrelationships. For example, Funkenstein, King, and Drolette (1957) have reported that individuals who directly *express* either anger or anxiety showed an increase in adrenaline in the blood; those who apparently became angry but kept it "bottled up" showed, instead, an increase in a different substance, noradrenaline. These two hormones, though both involved in the body's response to emotional stress, each produce different somatic response patterns (see p. 580).

Evidence indicating a link between the behavioral expression of an emotion and its physiological manifestations does not, however, tell us how or whether we can discriminate *among* different emotions. And this question is the critical one in the issue of definition and measurement. A verbal definition, no matter how carefully framed, is useless to the scientist if he cannot through *observation* actually make the distinction it requires. In short, if the scientific observer has no way of telling whether a person is angry or frightened, in love or lustful, then these traditional emotional categories are, for the time being, scientifically inaccessible. But let us examine the evidence for and against this statement.

Emotions and Self-Report

Can we tell what we are feeling? "Of course," we answer. "If we can't, then who can?" But this claim to special privilege and authority for the "feeler" exposes a major flaw in this source of evidence. Any phenomenon that, by its very definition, is observable only by a single individual (and never to an "outside observer") poses great difficulties for scientific inquiry. Admittedly, we can and do agree upon definitions of various emotional states, but this consensus remains only verbal unless it can be shown, for example, that, when ten people say that they are happy, they are in fact feeling the "same thing." But how can we be certain that self-reports of the "same" emotional state, even if they sound alike, indicate true consensus in what is experienced? One piece of evidence that is encouraging in this respect, indicating substantial agreement among persons in how they seem to experience different emotions, is presented in Box 125, p. 548.

One important source of indirect evidence on this issue is the usual presence of a behavioral consensus. When someone tells us he feels frightened, he almost always is behaving in the way we have seen other people behave when they said they were frightened. Furthermore, if our informant tells us that a moment before he was only apprehensive and not yet really frightened, we accept the distinction because it jibes with our observations of his just previous behavior. The point at issue comes to be whether or not we can reliably discriminate another person's emotions on the basis of his behavior.

Emotions and Expressive Cues

We all judge others' emotional states primarily by noting their facial expressions and bodily movements and postures. A considerable body of research has been devoted to determining the validity of judgments based on such *expressive cues*. The results are not entirely consistent, as Box 126, p. 550, demonstrates. Emotions differ in the ease with which they can be judged. The emotions that adults judge most accurately (from photographs of posed emotional expressions) are surprise, anger, fear, contempt, and happiness. Suspicion and pity, which we would probably regard as more subtle emotions, prove to be the most difficult to judge accurately (Feleky, 1922; Kanner, 1931). Children present a somewhat different picture. Although they too can judge happiness quite accurately, they do most poorly on judgments of contempt, an emotion that is quite easy for adults to identify (Gates, 1923). The average three-year-old can identify laughter, but surprise—easily judged by

adults—cannot be judged accurately until the child is eleven. The inference is that children have to learn the cues for each emotion and that emotions differ in the ease with which their cues may be learned.

Adults can also learn to use new cues for judging emotions, but apparently their ability to do so varies with their attitudes and past experience. Dittman, Parloff, and Boomer (1965) asked psychotherapists and professional dancers to judge the pleasantness of a woman's emotional state from motion pictures of her behavior. Both groups based their evaluations almost entirely on facial-expression cues, with minimal attention to such nonfacial cues as posture, movement, and muscular tension. When facial cues were blotted out in subsequent trials, both groups demonstrated an ability to make consistent judgments based on these usually neglected nonfacial cues. In a final set of trials, when all cues were again made available, however, only the professional dancers showed an increased reliance on nonfacial cues; psychotherapists reverted to their former almost exclusive reliance on facial cues. Both groups thus found that they *could* use a "new" category of cues for judging emotion, but only the dancers, who are presumably more aware of whole-body movement, showed some lasting effect from this learning experience.

All findings reported so far in this section are based upon judgments of emotions in which both the judges and the judged share the same culture. Could we do as well in judging the emotions of persons from cultures other than our own? We already know that young children who, in a sense, can be regarded as "immigrants" to our adult culture, cannot do so. We also know of the difficulties in communication experienced by newcomers to a community, even when they are well versed in the local language. In part, these difficulties may arise from their deficiency in another language, one in which dictionaries are of no help—the language of gestures. For the Japanese a smile may convey regret and apology; for the Chinese a hand-

Box 125

"Red" Envy,
"Green" Grief

Is *fear* "rough" or "smooth," "wet" or "dry," "angular" or "rounded," "soft" or "loud," "empty" or "full," "green" or "red"? In a study by J. Block, subjects were asked such questions about a list of fifteen emotions: love, anger, envy, humiliation, nostalgia, pride, fear, boredom, contentment, sympathy, grief, worry, elation, guilt, anticipation. His aim was to investigate the ways that different emotions appear to people through the use of physiognomic terms not normally applied to the description of emotions. It was assumed that this procedure would result in a more valid phenomenology of emotions than could be achieved through usual descriptions, as they are likely to be colored by mere verbal conventions and stereotypes.

Forty male and forty-eight female college students were asked to characterize each of the fifteen emotions with respect to a set of twenty pairs of physiognomic terms. In general, rather high agreement was found in the way the subjects characterized each of the different emotions. Men and women were analyzed separately, and it turned out that, with the exception of *grief*, the correspondence of descriptions between men and women was very high. In the case of grief, aside from the many terms on which men and women agreed, women used such terms as "low," "green," "weak," "smooth," and "rounded," whereas men characterized it as "high," "red," "strong," "rough," and "angular."

The degree of similarity or dissimilarity of descriptions of each emotion with every other one was computed statistically. Wide differences in similarity were found among the emotions. For instance, guilt and worry were described in highly similar physiognomic terms, as were envy and fear, elation and love. Conversely, there was extreme dissimiliarity among certain other pairs, such as guilt and contentment, boredom and love, nostalgia and anger. And for still other pairs the relationship was about zero; that is, the emotions seemed neither similar to one another in their physiognomic connotations nor dissimilar. Examples were fear and boredom, sympathy and pride, guilt and nostalgia.

It should be stressed that mere conventional verbal usage in the description of emotions would probably not account for the findings. For one thing, we do not have well-established verbal conventions for referring to most emotional feelings. And the few conventions we do have may not coincide with the physiognomic terms we actually use in making phenomenological descriptions of emotions. For example, *envy* turned out to be characterized more frequently as "red" than as "green."

A preliminary *cross-cultural comparison* was made by following the same procedures with a sample of male and female subjects in Norway. In general the descriptions of emotions by the American and Norwegian subjects were highly similar. There were, however, certain striking differences between the two cultural groups in degree of relationship among pairs of emotions. For example, among Americans, *grief* and *guilt* were described in highly similar terms, whereas among Norwegians the two were seen as unrelated. This finding may illustrate an effective approach to the cross-cultural study of values and attitudes.

J. BLOCK. 1957. Studies in the Phenomenology of Emotion, *J. Abnorm. Soc. Psychol.*, 54, 358–63.

clap may denote concern. Not only do the specific meanings of particular gestures vary among human societies, but also cultures differ in general gestural style. Efron and Foley (1937) showed this difference in a comparative study of the gestures of immigrant Italians and Russian Jews living in the same American community. From observations of the behavior of these two groups in conversation, with the focus on hand and arm gestures, they concluded that immigrant Italians characteristically employed relatively simple, short, and smooth movements, usually performed at the side of the body. For the Jews the movements were quite complex, often jerky and irregular, and were carried out in the plane of the body with considerable movement outward and toward the listener. Even when members of these two groups expressed surprise in a conventional American manner, say, by raising both hands, the pattern of movement thus reflected their differing gestural "accents."

The fact that, despite these cultural differences, there remain a number of behavioral expressions of emotional states common to all mankind—for example, a downturned mouth to express grief—indicates that some of this behavior may be biologically rooted. Charles Darwin argued for this position in 1872, in his book *Expression of the Emotions in Man and Animals*. His general point was that emotional expressions are vestiges of movements that, in their original forms, were adaptive for the organism. For example, the characteristic expression for grief—the downturned mouth—may derive from the facial pattern involved in crying, whose function is to call for help when in distress. The corners of the mouth are necessarily turned down when the mouth is open during crying, and, he held, this single feature survives as the "natural" and universal expression of the general state of unhappiness. If this view is correct, then the behavioral vocabulary of emotional expression is at least in part universal and serves us all in judging others' emotions.

Emotions and Bodily Processes

A vast number of somatic cues have been associated with emotional experience. Although the details of their operation are reserved for later discussion, let us now enumerate some that are relatively easy to measure: respiration, heart rate, galvanic skin response (related to sweating), skin temperature, dilation of the pupils and eye blinks, salivary secretion, and gastrointestinal movements. Others, like turning pale or blushing, although undoubtedly related to emotional states, are more difficult to assess quantitatively. Some somatic cues, like trembling or rapid eye blinks, are easily visible to the naked eye; others, like the galvanic skin response, are "visible" only through the use of special instruments. The layman thus infers an emotional state from normally visible cues, the expert from these cues and also from his instrument readings. Neither is always correct. A blushing bride may be merely warm rather than excited or embarrassed; the suspect whose elevated blood pressure is indicated on a polygraph ("lie detector") may be frightened rather than guilty. The point to underline is that single, isolated somatic cues are by themselves unreliable indicators of specific emotional states.

Attempts to identify specific emotions from *patterns* of physiological cues have met with more success (see Box 127, p. 552). Just as the layman can better establish the condition of the bride if he also notices whether or not she is trembling, so the polygraph expert can be more confident in his evaluation if he heeds a variety of different indicators (see Unit 37).

More subtle and complex emotions seem impossible to judge from somatic cues alone.

Generally speaking, the broader the scope of physiological observation, the more valid the judgment. There are some emotions, however, that are hard to tell apart on a physiological basis. As we noted earlier, fear and anger, when openly expressed, both increase the secretion of adrenaline. Ax (1953) reports other physiological indicators shared by these two emotions;

Box 126

Recognizing Emotional
Expression

Common human experience over the ages seems to give undeniable proof that people are generally able to recognize the emotions that other people are experiencing simply by observing expressions of the face, gestures, and so on. On the other hand, there is also ample evidence of failure to identify emotional expressions. The grin reflecting nervous fear may be mistaken for expression of pleasure; a set face and pallor may indicate anger rather than pain or determination.

There have been numerous experiments designed to ascertain just how accurately observers can judge the emotions of others on the basis of outward expression alone. Here are some of the main findings:

1. The pattern of facial expression of a given emotion tends to be highly variable among different individuals. In one of the earlier studies C. Landis photographed each subject's face while he engaged in the following types of genuine emotion-evoking situations: smelling ammonia, hearing a loud noise, viewing pornographic pictures, listening to music, writing out an account of an embarrassing event, decapitating a rat with a dull knife, getting an electric shock, and so on. On the basis of detailed mapping of the movements of the facial musculature during each of the induced emotions, he concluded that for none of the emotions was there a common expressive pattern among his subjects. On the basis of facial expression alone, the different emotions could presumably not be distinguished by an observer.

Part of the reason for this surprising finding may be that Landis included few if any really pleasant emotions in his study; other evidence shows that the most reliable discrimination among emotional expressions is found in expressions of the pleasant contrasted with the unpleasant. Furthermore, of course, Landis restricted himself to facial expression alone and to an analytical study of the details of the expression, rather than making judgments based upon the total perceptual impression of the face.

2. The latter approach was used by several investigators who asked observers to name the emotion expressed in each of a number of still photographs of faces. The photographs were obtained by

among them are an increase in heart rate and in systolic blood pressure. Certain indicators, however, do discriminate the two: Anger is accompanied by muscular tension and fear by an increase in respiration rate.

The conclusions from studies using each of the three levels of cues converge on much this same point: It is relatively simple to detect a state of generalized and undifferentiated arousal, but detection becomes increasingly difficult as we attempt to discriminate more and more finely among distinct emotions. In our own experience, feeling "excited" is a clearly recognizable, if diffuse, condition. With equal confidence, we can characterize another's behavior as generally "wound up." Experiential, behavioral, and somatic cues often agree that a state of general arousal exists, at the same

having professional actors *pose* and intentionally portray the designated emotions. The results showed that observers, though able to some extent to identify the posed emotions correctly, tended to make large errors. Some pairs of emotions were rarely confused, for example, love and contempt; other pairs were very frequently confused, for example, fear and anger. It is important to note that with such *posed* photographs the role of deliberate social communication is large. Success in recognizing facial expressions of emotion under this circumstance may tell us something about the *social* perception of emotions but little about the distinguishing expression of emotion when the individual is alone and not seeking to communicate his emotional state to others.

Incidentally, certain facial features prove to be more expressive of emotions than do others. K. Dunlap cut photographs in half, so that the eyes and the mouth could be judged separately. He found that the *mouth* provides far more informative cues about emotion than the *eyes* do—despite conventional belief to the contrary. R. Plutchik confirmed and extended this conclusion with his finding that the mouth, this time in comparison with several other facial features, exerted the most consistent influence upon judgment of emotion.

3. As greater numbers of expressive cues are added to those of facial expression, accuracy in identifying emotions increases. Body posture is a useful cue; so are gestures. Motion pictures allow more accurate judgments than do still pictures, and observations made in "live" situations lead to even better performance, particularly if they permit the judge to see the social context in which the behavior is occurring.

4. Different types of cues may convey information about different aspects of an emotional experience. P. Ekman studied the relative effectiveness of head and body-posture cues for judging still photographs on Schlosberg's three dimensions of emotion (see Box 119, p. 522). His conclusion, in his own words:

"Head cues carry information primarily about what particular affect is being experienced, and relatively little about intensity of affect or level of arousal. Body cues reverse this pattern, communicating information primarily about level of arousal or degree of intensity of an affective experience, but relatively little about what particular affect is being experienced."

C. LANDIS. 1924. Studies of Emotional Reactions: II. General Behavior and Facial Expression, *J. Comp. Psychol.*, 4, 447–501.

K. DUNLAP. 1927. The Role of Eye-Muscles and Mouth-Muscles in the Expression of the Emotions, *Genet. Psychol. Monogr.*, 2, No. 3.

R. PLUTCHIK. 1962. *The Emotions: Facts, Theories and a New Model* (New York: Random House).

P. EKMAN. 1965. Differential Communication of Affect by Head and Body Cues, *J. Soc. Psychol.*, 2, 726–35.

time disagreeing on the specific emotion involved. For example, a person who is observed to be, and reports himself to be, in an agitated state almost always also reflects this state physiologically in his galvanic skin response. This link can even be observed in newborn infants. Weller and Bell (1965), working with sixty neonates between two and five days of age, found a highly significant correlation between variations in the infant's galvanic skin response and his degree of arousal, as assessed from a number of behavioral indexes like crying and various bodily movements. The impact of this line of evidence has suggested to many investigators that emotion can be considered as "nothing but" arousal, a view we shall consider as we turn to a consideration of some of the current theories of emotion.

Box 127

The Similarity—and Difference —of Opposites

J. R. Averill, a psychologist at the University of California, Los Angeles, undertook to contrast the automatic response patterns triggered by two quite different, even opposite, emotions—mirth and sadness. Employing a large number of different physiological indicators of emotional states, he measured the responses of college students (eighteen in each group) to motion pictures selected to elicit either mirth or sadness. Each film lasted about fifteen minutes. The mirth group viewed a slapstick comedy, which was presumably effective because it set off audible laughter in more than half the subjects. The sadness group also appeared appropriately affected by a presentation of the life and death of President John F. Kennedy. A third group of eighteen subjects, the control group, was intended to provide data on reactivity to a relatively unemotional stimulus, and it viewed a nature film.

Each subject in all three groups had been measured on all physiological indicators for six minutes preceding the emotion-inducing stimuli, so that "base line" scores indicating normal and ongoing reactivity levels were available. The difference between these scores and those obtained in response to the emotion-inducing motion pictures provided the basic data for this experiment.

From among Averill's numerous findings, several are most relevant for our purposes. Both the mirth and sadness groups became generally more aroused (as measured by such indicators as the galvanic skin response, or GSR); neither group was aroused more than the other was, but both groups were aroused more than the control group was. Apparently sadness—which seems so "quiet" an emotion—does involve considerable arousal or excitement, at least when elicited under the particular conditions of this experiment. But, beyond a common element of arousal, the two emotions could be clearly differentiated by their *patterns* of response on other physiological measures. Cardiovascular changes (for example, increased blood pressure) were more marked for the sadness group than for the mirth group. Physiological arousal per se was thus insufficient to discriminate the two quite different emotions. In order to discriminate, it was necessary to make use of response patterns based on a number of separate indicators of reactivity in the autonomic nervous system.

J. R. AVERILL. 1966. Autonomic Response Patterns during Sadness and Mirth. Unpublished doctoral dissertation, University of California (Los Angeles) Library.

Glossary

expressive cues   Those bits of behavior that convey, usually without conscious intention, information about an individual's emotional state. Facial expressions and postural changes are examples.

hallucinogenic drugs, "psychedelic" drugs   A class of substances, some synthetic (as is LSD), some occurring in nature (for example, peyote), which may lead to hallucinations and other "mind altering" effects. Such a drug's influence on a given individual is very much a function of the psychological context in which it is taken as well as his physiological status.

current theories of emotion

overview / Current theories of emotion may conveniently be classified into "nothing but" and "something more" views. The former orientation tends to regard emotions as by-products of certain physiological disturbances and as disruptive of orderly behavior. As experiences in their own right, they are not of true scientific interest. The latter orientation takes the opposite tack: Emotions are regarded as phenomena that are highly influential in psychological functioning, even to the point of dominating the directions of experience and behavior.

Theories of both kinds are still quite primitive, as they are highly general "points of view" more than outcomes of detailed and comprehensive analyses of emotional phenomena.

When we discussed theories of learning, we dealt primarily with differing hypotheses to account for the modification of behavior by experience. When we deal later with theories of personality, we shall be similarly concerned almost exclusively with the processes that might account for its development. Theories of emotion, by contrast, place heavy stress upon definitional issues as much as upon the issue of how emotions arise. In fact, most theories of emotion may more properly be regarded as "points of view," in the sense that none attempts a fully detailed and comprehensive analysis of emotional behavior. Rather, they are sets of propositions that attempt to tell us what emotion "really" is.

One of these points of view, stated with some oversimplification, asserts that the *feeling* or awareness of emotion is nothing but an incidental occurrence without significant adaptive value. For psychologists holding this view, emotion is "nothing but" a pattern of bodily processes that are triggered by environmental stimuli.

"Nothing But" Views

The general theme here is that emotions are by-products of more fundamental events. The specifics of these views vary, but there is consensus on the point that an experienced emotional state is indeed nothing but an incidental occurrence. Adopting this vantage point, a psychologist may consider how feelings come about but need not regard emotions *as primary motives* of human behavior.

Emotion and Bodily State

The conception of emotion as nothing but a reflection of bodily states is embodied in one of the earliest of modern theories of emotion, the James-Lange theory, which will be discussed later, p. 606. In this theory the experiencing of a somatic event *is* the emotion.

There are a number of objections to this point of view. It is clear from our earlier discussion in Unit 34 that different emotions cannot reliably be discriminated from one another by changes in bodily processes alone. We can therefore question whether or not emotions are "nothing but" sets of somatic events and the accompanying cognitive events of little significance. Empirical evidence on this point can be obtained by inducing directly in the person's body a specified pattern of bodily states corresponding to a specific emotion. Under such conditions, quite aside from his immediately prior mental state, he should experience the emotion—whether it be fear, anger, or grief. In other words, the *feeling* of the emotion would be completely determined by the artificially induced bodily states. Such experiments have been attempted (see Box 128, p. 557), but we must realize that not all the bodily correlates of any specific emotion are yet known and therefore the conclusions based on such experiments must be regarded with great caution.

Emotion as Disruptive

Although it has been expressed in a variety of ways, another central view has been that emo-tion is disruptive—that it interferes with the orderly operation of "normal" factors influencing behavior. Young (1961), an experimenter in the field of emotion, presents one clear version of *emotion as disruptive: "When an individual is affectively* [that is, emotionally] *disturbed by the environmental situation to such an extent that his cerebral control is weakened or lost . . . that individual is emotional"* (italics in original).

This statement highlights two assumptions of this position: First, only intense emotion is implicitly dealt with. Mild emotional states, by contrast, not only do not lead to being "disturbed by the environmental situation" but may even be helpful accompaniments to successful adaptation. A quiet sense of competence is a usual experience when one's behavior is effectively accomplishing something. Such a mild emotional state, it can be argued, even helps to maintain a high level of performance and is by no means disruptive. Second, it assumes that emotional behavior is the opposite of rational behavior. When a person is behaving irrationally, we say he is being "emotional"; on the other hand, when he is mastering the situation, we say that he has kept his emotions "under control." Leeper (1965) traces this view of emotion to the fact that emotion is, in truth, most *visible* precisely when it interferes with "normal" patterns of behavior. Certainly, an emotional state that leads to a disruption in expected behavior is more likely to be noticed. And interference is most likely to occur in the presence of very intense emotion.

Taken in its extreme form, the view that emotions are disruptive is, in an important sense, "unscientific." To argue that emotion involves the breakdown of orderly laws of behavior is to imply that emotional behavior is itself not orderly, that is, that it does not exhibit any systematic relationships to other psychological phenomena. Furthermore, emotion is denied any function or purpose, thus placing it beyond the pale of modern psychological theory, which regards, with minor exceptions, behavior

Box 128

"Cold" Emotion

The critical role of the perceived situation in governing the experience of emotion is shown in an ingenious way by the following experiment by G. Marañon. Adrenaline was injected into the blood stream of human subjects in a neutral laboratory situation. As we shall see in Unit 37, the effect of adrenaline is to produce some of the kinds of physiological upset that are normally found in cases of strong emotion. What would be the effect of producing such upsets by adrenaline injections when there is no external situation appropriate to evoke an emotion?

The subjects reported palpitations and trembling, but no emotional experience. It was "cold" emotion. They described their feelings as "I feel as if afraid," "I feel as if I had a great fright, yet am calm."

Here we have a simple case in which the situation was not of such a nature psychologically as to evoke a true emotion; though an artificially induced bodily upset was highly similar to the physiological changes in real emotional states, it was not *by itself* sufficient to evoke a genuine feeling of emotion.

The reader might speculate on the results of a hypothetical experiment in which adrenaline would be injected while the person was in a situation not entirely neutral in emotion-evoking power. That is, the situation, though not quite adequate to arouse an emotional response, would, with a little intensification, be capable of doing so. What, under these circumstances, would be the effect of the adrenaline? Might the threshold for arousal of the emotion be lowered?

G. MARAÑON. 1924. In *Revue Française d'Endocrinologie*, 2, 301.

---

as adaptive—and emotion is not a minor class of behavior.

Emotion as Arousal

In a certain sense, *emotion as arousal* is a "cleaned up" version of the previous theory. Arousal, as commonly understood, implies at least a certain degree of excitement, but it allows us to speak of a continuum of emotional reactivity (from mild to intense). Also, this view carries no implication of irrationality or of disruption in normal patterns of behavior. We have earlier reviewed some of the evidence for emotional arousal as an easily identifiable state, quickly recognizable whether by behavioral, experiential, or physiological cues. Furthermore, these cues generally seem to agree; that is, when we feel aroused, we usually appear so to others, and our bodily processes also manifest the condition.

By its very definition, however, arousal is a highly diffuse state. In fact, arousal is so general a characteristic that we have applied the concept to both motivational and emotional states. Some psychologists argue that the resulting blurring of the traditional distinction between emotional and motivational aspects of experience and behavior would be a welcome side effect of the arousal concept. Duffy (1962) argues in just this way; she maintains that "emotion" is a scientifically meaningless term because it cannot be reliably distinguished from other behavioral events. She suggests, as we noted in Unit 32, that both emotion and motivation be incorporated within the concept of "activation," essentially another term for arousal. This kind of schema is tempting in its apparent simplicity, and its adoption might yield as a by-product the dissolution of the barrier between emotional and motivational events. But are we willing to write off emotion as an extraneous and outdated concept? To do so might seem reasonable if we had to describe only the "dumb" behavior of experimental animals. But the data of experience raise a problem of another order. Our language is immensely rich in terms for communicating emotional experience, so much so that one may wonder whether emotion can be dispensed with if a full account of human behavior is to remain the challenge of psychological theory.

Our hypothetical champion of emotion as an independent and theoretically useful entity might argue: "When I feel hopeful, suspicious, or amused, something very real is happening to me. What does it matter if I exhibit these emotions, through my outward behavior and inner physiology, in ways different from other people? What if the psychologist, with all his objective measurements, is unable to tell whether, at a given moment, I am feeling haughty or merely bored? I can tell the difference, so it's his job to understand how come I can." Some psychologists have attempted to reply to this challenge while holding firm in their claim that arousal remains the key to the problem (see Box 129, p. 560). Others find the data of human experience so convincing as to require a more primary and respectable role for emotion within psychological theory. For these people, emotion is "something more" than an incidental phenomenon accompanying more fundamental processes.

"Something More" Views

The essential theme of this general position is that emotions are not secondary and derivative occurrences but require consideration in their own right. There are many approaches that could fall within this rubric. We shall deal with only two of them. Both of these views agree that emotions have an adaptive function. Both argue that emotions represent "first order" forces in human behavior, forces that not only require explanation but that cannot be ignored if human behavior is to be fully comprehended. They differ—and the difference may not be a large one—in the manner in which they put emotion into the theoretical picture.

Emotion as a Representational Process

Behind the formidable title of *emotion as a representational process* lies a highly coherent and deceptively simple formulation. The chief proponent of this view is Leeper, and much of what follows is taken from the most recent statement of his position (Leeper, 1965). He maintains that the traditional and still honored distinctions among various kinds of psychological events create artificial barriers and generate needless controversy. Although separate categories for perception, learning, motivation, and emotions have been and remain useful, they obscure the possible advantages of viewing them all as aspects of a common "representational process." Most important, for our purposes, a representational process can be regarded as varying along a number of dimensions. Perceptions thus vary along a motivational dimension; they can range from motivationally neutral to motivationally intense. For example, perceiving the numerical sequence "38–22–36" is probably a universally bland experience, yet, if identified as anatomical data, it may become (for about half our readers) at least somewhat tinged by a motivational brush. Moving one step further, motivational processes themselves may be seen to range along an emotional continuum from emotionally neutral to emotionally highly charged. The urge to scratch at a perceived itch is unmistakably a motive, but hardly an intense emotional experience. The sight of a mortal enemy, however, not only motivates aggressive action but, additionally, arouses a feeling of emotional fury.

Leeper's essential point is not that motives influence our perceptions and that emotions have modifying effects upon the expression of motives. If this effect were all, the point would be an obvious and well-accepted one. What must be emphasized, instead, is that emotions *are* motives in their own right. Emotions, according to Leeper, are intrinsically directional; they are not merely general and indiscriminate physiological arousers. Furthermore, such "emotional motives" can be as effective in directing behavior as can physiologically based motives but are independent of tissue needs and can be triggered by more subtle and complex "social" cues. They are influenced by the meanings (past and present) of stimuli. For this reason, an *absent* stimulus can evoke an "emotional motive" as readily as can one that is stridently present. For example, the failure of a friend to show up for an important appointment (literally, the perception of his *not* being where he is supposed to be) can be an adequate stimulus for disappointment or anger. The representational process, at this moment, is a synthesis of the perception of "no friend where expected," of a complex fabric of interwoven motivational and emotional states, and even of cortical events underlying these perceptions, motives, and feelings.

Leeper suggests that "emotional motives" are a distinguishing feature of higher species and may hold the key to understanding their superior adaptive abilities. If a man's momentary perception of a new situation instantly embodies not only the external stimuli but also the emotional motivation that, in terms of his past learning and present physiological state, is most appropriate to the environmental situation, he is thereby highly likely to respond quickly and effectively. The representational process can therefore be seen as providing a speculative arena in which all kinds of psychological forces can have influence. By allowance for so highly efficient an integration of all "information" from the situation, the odds for successful adaptation to environmental challenges are improved.

Emotions as Primary Motives

As a cardinal assumption of his comprehensive theory of personality and behavior, Tomkins (1962) treats *emotions as primary motives*. He asserts that "the primary motivational system is the affective [emotional] system, and the bio-

logical drives have motivational impact only when amplified by the affective system." We can here touch only on a few facets of Tomkins' position as it pertains to our present discussion. His main thesis is that psychology has been stymied in its attempts to understand human behavior more fully by its almost total exclusion of the data of consciousness. Foremost among the exiled psychological phenomena has been man's conscious experience of feelings and emotions. The inevitable result of this exclusion has been, according to Tomkins, "a continuing fruitless search in the guts and bowels of man for distinctive emotional responses [that has] been sufficient to reinforce the belief that affect is a hopeless will-o'-the-wisp, essentially recalcitrant to scientific psychological investigations."

Tomkins intends to end the quarantine on conscious feelings as psychological data. First of all, he argues, emotions are really not as private as some believe. Rather, they are easily apprehended by others and can communicate information in a reliable manner. (The reader may wish to evaluate this claim against the data given in Unit 34.) Most of this communication of emotion, he claims, takes place in the facial musculature, and facial responses help to make both the outside observer *and the individual himself* aware of his continuing emotional state. Box 130, p. 562, presents some of the evidence on the role of facial cues in the judgment of emotions. Assuming for the moment that emotional states can be accurately recognized by the person himself and by the outside observer, how does emotion come to have the decisive influence that Tomkins claims for it? He proposes that emotions are the basic "targets" of man, that they define the inborn "wants" and "don't wants" that dominate the behavior of infants, and that, in elaborated form, they do the same for adults. They do so, Tomkins suggests, in the following manner: The neonate is endowed with certain "given" positive and negative affects. Joy or excitement, for example, is innately positive; fear and pain

Box 129

Mad, Glad—or Just Excited?

S. Schachter and J. E. Singer proposed to test whether or not "emotional states may be considered a function of a state of physiological arousal and of a cognition appropriate to this state of arousal." Let us look at their argument closely, then at their data in support of it. In brief, they suggest that the intensity of an emotional experience is determined by how generally excited or aroused the person is and that its quality (or direction) is determined by the nature of the situation in which the arousal occurs.

The experiment takes its lead directly from G. Marañon's demonstration that physiological arousal alone does not bring about a convincing emotional experience (see Box 128, p. 557). Schachter and Singer go a step further in their interpretation of these earlier results; they argue that, as Marañon's subjects probably knew that they were being injected with a stimulant, their experience of "cold" or "as if" emotions was consistent with the fact of physiological arousal *and* their understanding that the excitement they were feeling was *supposed* to be "nonemotional."

What would happen then if the subject were kept unaware of the expected effect of the physiological stimulus and, at the same time, were placed into situations that differed in the kinds of emotions that they could be expected to arouse? This general question was the basis of the first set of experiments.

Subjects were volunteer college students, whose health records had been checked to ensure no risk of harmful effects from the experimental procedure. Each subject was told that he would receive an injection of a new drug "Suproxin" and that the point of the investigation was to determine the effect of this drug upon vision. Beyond this common experience the circumstances for each group of subjects varied—and therein lies the tale.

Some subjects were informed that the drug would cause an increase in the heart rate, hand tremors, and a feeling of warmth and flushing in the face. The drug was in fact epinephrine, a stimulant of the sympathetic nervous system, and this description was a quite accurate account of usual reactions to the drug. This group was called the "informed group." A "misinformed group" was told that

are innately negative. At first, the newborn infant "automatically" smiles in pleasure at being well fed or stimulated by a fascinating rattle. A loud, explosive sound or an open safety pin in his diaper inevitably sets off negative affects. As he develops, the child first learns to wish for positive emotional states and not for negative ones. Later on, as his abilities for adaptive behavior mature, he learns to act in ways that will maximize states of positive affect and minimize states of negative affect. Although he thus "knows" from birth that eating is "good" and pain is "bad," only through further maturation and learning does he become able to go to the market or restaurant as soon as he starts getting hungry and become able to avoid situations that are bound to cause him pain and distress.

Tomkins believes that these innate positive and negative affects derive from three basic

it would experience numbness and itching, with no suggestion that there might be excitement or agitation. A third group—the "uninformed group"—was told nothing of expected reactions to the drug. Members of each of these three groups were then observed during "intermissions," whose purpose was ostensibly to allow the drug to act, so that its effects upon visual perception could be studied. These intermissions took one of two forms for each subject.

In the first of these intermission conditions another "subject," a confederate of the experimenters, undertook to play the clown. He indulged in a series of rather wild antics designed to create a mood of euphoria in the true subject. In the second condition the confederate "subject" joined with the true one in answering a questionnaire whose contents were designed to justify irritation even in the most tolerant and even-tempered subject; one question, for example, was about the frequency of his parents' extramarital sexual relations. In this situation the confederate expressed increasing anger, finally ripping the questionnaire to shreds and stomping out of the room. The confederate in both the euphoria and anger conditions did not know whether the subject was in the informed, misinformed, or uninformed group. He was kept ignorant in order to ensure that his provocative behavior would, on the average, be the same for all groups.

This experimental design—three "explanation" conditions and two emotion-inducing conditions—yielded six groups in all. The data, from direct observation of the subjects' behavior and from their responses to a variety of self-report inventories, are quite complex, and we can touch on them only very briefly. Subjects exposed to the euphoric confederate, for example, behaved more euphorically (joining in his manic activity and so on) and reported that they felt more elated *the more misinformed they were.* That is, informed subjects were least euphoric, uninformed ones somewhat more euphoric, and the misinformed group consistently most euphoric.

The experimenters infer from these results that an individual, given a certain degree of general arousal, tends to "label" his emotional state in accordance with his environmental situation. The misinformed subject had not been led to expect the physiological arousal that was indeed induced by the injection; therefore he "explained" his bodily excitation by adopting the emotional mood of the confederate. He becomes no longer simply mysteriously agitated; he is simply very happy. The anger condition shows the same general results—more misinformation, more anger.

The major conclusion—that, given the same state of physiological arousal, the nature of the expressed emotion can be manipulated by manipulations of the social situation—seems supported.

S. SCHACHTER and J. E. SINGER. 1962. Cognitive, Social, and Physiological Determinants of Emotional State, *Psychol. Rev.* 69, 379–399.

affects that have been built into the organism through natural selection in the evolutionary process. They are first, an affect for the preservation of life, or, put more directly, an innate fear response to a life threat; second, an affect for people that is shown, for example, in responding to another's smile both by an experience of joy and by returning the smile; third, an affect for novelty—the pleasurable excitement induced by a new situation.

This view of course evokes once again the troubling distinction between motive and emotion. Tomkins is not troubled; he accepts that physiologically based motives can by themselves direct behavior. Such motives are characteristically *amplified* by emotional states, however. A sharp bodily pain is certainly biologically negative, but, once defined as possibly signifying cancer, it becomes immensely magnified to intense anxiety. Similarly, we normally

Box 130

The Eyes Have It

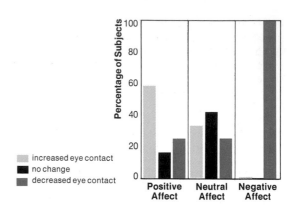

Everyday language abounds in testimonials to the active participation of the face in emotional communication and experience. Individuals and nations often go to absurd and even self-defeating extremes to "save face," and "losing face" can be among the most painful of experiences. "Face up to it" counsels our conscience (or an external critic), exhorting us to confront an emotionally disagreeable event. More specifically, the eyes come in for particular mention. The judge of character confidently asserts, "Only an honest man can look you in the eye." The starlet confesses, "I just *love* dark glasses because people can't tell what I'm really feeling." And, of course, the "evil eye" is a thing of terror in human societies throughout the world.

Such folklore is suggestive. But, as we have seen (Box 126, p. 550), only the grossest judgments of emotional state can be made with any reliability from facial cues. S. S. Tomkins suggests a number of reasons why man cannot make better use of such information. For one thing, there seems to be a widespread taboo on looking at another's face, especially directly into his eyes. Not only is it impolite to stare, but, in some cultures, it is an insult triggering the most serious consequences. Consider also that, in many societies, veils are worn, and glances must be "stolen." When eyes chance to meet, it may be an occasion for embarrassment for both parties. Quite often, standing face to face and looking directly into another person's eyes may signify insolence or intimacy, pride or passion. Whatever the emotion conveyed, the action is not one to be taken lightly.

That this taboo on staring may even have an innate basis is suggested by its presence in some animal species. Many primates, for example, convey a challenge to a rival by a direct stare; the rival, if

eat when hungry, but, were a catastrophe to make future food supplies highly uncertain, our usually mild biological hunger drive would become transformed into a desperate search for provisions. Biologically speaking, such knowledge should thus not cause us to hurt more or to feel more hungry, but, experientially, it arouses emotions that in turn immensely amplify the sense of urgency.

Where does all this theorizing leave us? When we are angry or in love, are we experiencing an emotion or responding to a biological motive? Are we exhibiting a transient mood or an enduring personality trait? Or are we merely assigning a situationally reasonable label to a diffuse state of bodily excitement? The eventual answer will likely involve a blend of all these elements.

he wishes to avoid combat, indicates his surrender by averting his face and not looking back at his opponent. From all these facts we may well infer that we use facial cues rather poorly in judging emotions simply because we find it difficult to look directly at the faces of other people. Some of these points are solidly based in experimental evidence; others still await formal demonstration. One study tested the effect of inducing different moods on the incidence of eye-to-eye contact. Working with male college students, R. V. Exline and L. C. Winters set up a situation that permitted both the experimenter and a second observer (behind a one-way mirror) to observe the direction of gaze of the subject. At the outset the subject was interviewed for five minutes, ostensibly about his leisure-time activities. Immediately afterward the experimenter "confessed" that, in reality, he had been evaluating the subject's intelligence and maturity. At this point the subject was treated to one of three conditions, intended to induce different emotional states: first, *positive affect*—subject was told that he had made an excellent impression; second, *negative affect*—the experimenter expressed surprise at the subject's disappointing performance and told him that he had been rated very low; third, *neutral*—no evaluative information of any kind was offered.

All three groups then continued in their interviews (the topic this time was "travel interests") for five additional minutes. Throughout both interview sessions—both before and after the differing emotional states had been induced—the experimenter had been looking directly at the subject's eyes. The amount of time the subject returned the glance, that is, looked directly at the experimenter's eyes, was recorded both by the experimenter and by the second observer.

The results were evaluated in a number of ways. The figure presents one particularly interesting comparison of the *change* in the tendency to look directly at the experimenter as a function of the intervening treatment. The findings were clear-cut. Subjects who had been flattered and presumably made to feel quite favorably disposed to the experimenter (obviously a good judge of character!) were most likely to increase eye contact with him in the second interview. Insulted subjects *all* met the experimenter's eye less often following the "evaluation" remarks. As expected, the neutral group showed no systematic change, but, *within* the group, those who liked the experimenter (as had been determined from a specially designed attitude scale) looked directly at him more during the second interview; those who did not like him looked at him less. In each case, then, the quality of the induced effect had influenced, probably quite involuntarily and without the subject's knowledge, his visual orientation toward the object of his emotion. And such orientation seems likely to provide a useful cue to emotional state.

S. S. TOMPKINS. 1962. *Affect, Imagery, and Consciousness: Vol. 1. The Positive Affects* (New York: Springer).
R. V. EXLINE and L. C. WINTERS. 1965. Affective Relations and Mutual Glances in Dyads, in S S Tomkins and C. E. Izard, eds., *Affect, Cognition and Personality* (New York: Springer). Figure reprinted by permission.

Glossary

emotion as a representational process The view that emotion joins with perception, learning, and motivation as an integral part of a single unified process, rather than that the functions are separate, even if interacting, entities.

emotion as arousal The view that identifies all emotion (as well as all motivation) as involving a generalized state of arousal. According to this theory, emotion is one end of a continuum of activation, with the inertia of sleep at the other end.

emotion as disruptive The view that emotions are to be regarded as nothing more than causes of breakdowns in the normal and orderly processes of physiological functioning and behavior.

emotions as primary motives The view that biological drives derive their motivational effectiveness primarily from being accompanied and amplified by emotional states, states that are largely innate in their origins.

physiology
and motives

overview / The general state of arousal of the organism characterizing all motives can be studied with the EEG, or electroencephalogram, which measures brain activity. Novel stimuli evoke an orienting response involving changes in the pattern of firing of the brain, overt movements, and internal adjustments, all designed to help maximize the organism's information about the new stimulus.

Primary control of the mechanisms involved in seeking and eating food (the hunger motive) is centered in the hypothalamus. This small subcortical structure has extensive connections with the cortex, other subcortical structures, and the viscera, which give it an important integrative role in the internal states of the organism. Two areas of the hypothalamus are critical for the hunger motive; the lateral area, which produces the onset of hunger, and the ventromedial nucleus, which acts to terminate eating. Stomach contractions, blood-sugar level, body temperature—all act to inform the hypothalamus of the current body demands; taste and smell can also provide motivating stimuli.

The hypothalamus contains thirst centers as well. Cellular dehydration and loss of body fluids give the primary information about the body's water needs, but dryness of the mouth may also provide a cue.

The autonomic nervous system controls the smooth muscles of the viscera and blood vessels, the cardiac muscle, and the glands. Autonomic responses form a major and critical part of the mechanisms of the sex motive, and control of these responses is centered in the hypothalamus. The sex hormones of the gonads, although relatively unimportant in the sex motive of the adult human, can completely control the motive in lower organisms. Sex hormones have the critical role in the very early life of the individual of determining the "sex," structurally and behaviorally, that the adult will become.

In earlier units we have discussed the physiological bases of perception and of learning; now, in this and the next unit, we shall consider the physiological processes that underlie motivation and emotion. The physiological mechanisms we have studied will make it easier for us to understand motivation and emotion, for they depend upon both our perceptions and what we have learned. We shall find it necessary, however, to explore the functions of several other bodily structures and systems in addition to those whose primary influence is upon perception and learning.

It is often simplest to think of perceptual and learning processes as inaugurated by activities (stimuli) *outside* the body. Motivation and emotion, too, are clearly influenced by external stimuli, but here we shall see that activities *within* the organism are relatively more important in the instigation and control of these psychological processes. For this reason, in studying the physiological basis for motives and emotions, we shall focus attention on certain "regulatory systems" within the organism and consider the *autonomic nervous system* and the *endocrine system*, as well as the cerebrospinal nervous system discussed in Unit 4.

The living organism is in a state of constant activity. Chemical balances are continuously being upset, and momentary chemical instabilities are being continuously adjusted. At any given time some gland or other is pouring its *hormones* into the blood stream; these hormones are carried to various bodily organs, muscles, and other glands, which respond by contracting, relaxing, and secreting bodily fluids or other hormones. And the nervous system is constantly firing and conducting impulses.

A large part of this activity is "silent"—it is never consciously experienced by the individual. No conscious effort is required to direct and coordinate this myriad of reactions that maintain our bodies in an extremely high degree of homeostasis (see p. 492). Many of the mechanisms that maintain this high degree of constancy work exclusively within the organism.

Nerve cells thus draw glucose for their normal energy requirements from the blood stream, and the blood stream in turn replaces this glucose by drawing from the store of glycogen in the liver. We are also unaware of the chemical interchanges going on in our bodies to maintain a stable level of acidity in the blood. Yet a very slight shift toward acidity greater than the appropriate level would result in coma and death; a shift toward greater alkalinity would cause convulsive fits.

Other mechanisms responsible for bodily homeostasis activate the gross muscular "responses" of the body. These responses are necessary in order to provide the body with supplies from the outside, or to eliminate toxic elements from within the body, or to remove the organism from external injury. And we are, of course, quite aware of most of this behavior.

Normally we reserve the term "motive" for bodily processes that involve the latter class of responses and are reflected in awareness. It should be clear, however, that the observable behavior in motivation and emotion represents but a *part* of all the physiological events involved. What we observe when we see a man fighting for his life is only a small segment, overwhelming as it may appear, of the thousands of chemical, hormonal, and neural reactions going on within him. We see the eruption of the volcano; most of the activity is hidden from view. To understand the physiology of motivation and emotions, we must examine many of the "hidden" and "silent" events. And, when we examine the internal and external events, we find a beautifully integrated complex of processes.

Most of the research on the physiology of motivation has been concerned with such "basic" motives as hunger, thirst, and sex. Relatively little that is reliable is yet known about the physiological aspects of the more complex motives, for example, curiosity and gregariousness. Most of our discussion, therefore, will necessarily center on hunger, thirst, and sex. But, before we take up these motives, we must consider the physiological nature of the general state of arousal that characterizes *every* motive.

Arousal and the Brain

A necessary condition for the expression of motivation is an alert, active organism. Although sleep itself, as we shall see, may be a motive, the sleeping animal displays none of the patterns of integrated activity that we associate with motivated behavior. For this reason we begin our discussion of the physiology of motivation with an account of some of the activities of the cortex that are related to the level of arousal of the organism.

The EEG

In 1929, the psychiatrist Hans Berger first demonstrated conclusively that the electrical activity of the human brain could be recorded through the unopened skull, and he thus gave us a way to "look at" the activity of the brain. The electrical waves that are recorded from the cerebral cortex in this way are called "brain waves"; the record is called an *electroencephalogram (EEG)*.

The EEG is usually picked up by electrodes that are pasted to the scalp at various points. The wires lead to an amplifier, the electrical output of which controls the position of an inked pen on a continuously moving paper chart. In this way the brain waves write the record of their own activity.

When an organism is resting quietly, not paying close attention to any stimulus, a fairly rhythmical EEG can be recorded. This pattern is called the "alpha wave," and in human beings it has a rate of eight to twelve waves per second (see Figure 36.1.). Changes, in either direction, of the state of arousal produce characteristic alterations in the EEG.

When a novel, attention-getting stimulus is presented, the alpha wave abruptly disappears. The EEG waves become smaller in size and much more irregular in form. This result does not mean necessarily that the nervous system is responding less actively or in a more random way. Indeed, it may mean that the individual neurons have become much *more* active but active in complex patterns of excitation that tend to be canceled out in the relatively gross record we see in the EEG. At any rate, this blocking of the alpha rhythm is typically associated with an alert organism—as observable in behavior. If the same stimulus is presented several times, it evokes less and less alerting behavior in the subject, and a comparable change is seen in his EEG—the alpha wave begins to reappear.

This last point indicates that the blocking of the alpha wave is not a necessary consequence of the presentation of any given stimulus; it depends upon both the state of the brain and the importance or novelty of the stimulus. It is especially interesting that a novel stimulus of a low intensity will produce a greater arousal response than will a familiar, expected stimulus of much higher intensity—just what we would expect if this "electrical arousal" is an accurate measure of the psychological arousal of the individual.

The Orienting Response

EEG arousal is but one part of a sequence of reponses, visible and internal, that are produced by a novel stimulus. An animal will turn its head and eyes, will prick up its ears, and may move to investigate the source of the stimulus. This behavior reflects the "orienting response" we discussed in Unit 32 (see p. 502). Various other changes occur as well, including changes in the size of the pupil, in general blood pressure, and in the activity of the sweat glands. Apparently the major function of the orienting response is to maximize the organism's information about a new stimulus and its readiness to cope with it. If the stimulus proves to be important, appropriate responses can be made or new ones learned. If, however, the stimulus does not prove to be of any consequence, the

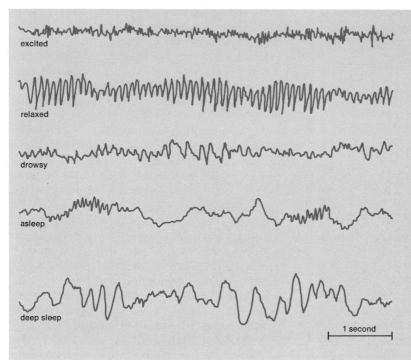

excited

relaxed

drowsy

asleep

deep sleep

1 second

Figure 36.1. Brain waves typical of various states of alertness. Note the change in shape and frequency of the brain waves as the relaxed individual becomes excited or falls asleep. The frequency can be judged with the help of the one-second marker. H. H. Jasper, "Electroencephalography," in W. Penfield and T. Erickson, eds., *Epilepsy and Cerebral Localization* (1941); adapted by permission of Charles C. Thomas Company.

organism "habituates" and ignores it on presentations that follow.

The orienting response may be one of the basic physiological mechanisms behind the curiosity motive in animals as well as in people. A child investigating a novel toy or a rat exploring an unfamiliar maze is each demonstrating the effects of the orienting, or "what-is-it?," reflex. Either may find himself in trouble on some occasions as a consequence of this response, but the experience of each species has proven that the risk is worth the resulting better acquaintance with the environment.

The Hunger Motive

Our knowledge about some of the facts of hunger as we experience them in daily life gives us a starting point for asking questions about the mechanisms of the hunger motive. If we miss breakfast, we normally do not suffer extreme hunger pangs, but, if we are then forced to go without lunch, we soon find it highly important to seek and eat food. As the nutrient content of the body is depleted, the various organs (for example, the liver) that have stored up surpluses (of glycogen, for example) replenish the blood stream. With this replenishment we can survive even if we miss several meals. We cannot do so indefinitely, however, because the stored supply itself becomes depleted. At some point the autonomous homeostatic processes prove inadequate, and a larger segment of the body becomes involved. The organism must seek and ingest food from the outside. The orienting response and the adaptive behavior of

the animal are called into play so that the autonomous homeostatic mechanisms can take over again. We can ask, "What crucial signal resulting from food deprivation in the body (that is, what 'internal stimulus') tells the brain that food-getting activities are now indicated?"

First, however, we must realize that there are stimuli other than those originating within the body that produce or influence the feeling of hunger and food-seeking or eating behavior. The odor or sight of foods can arouse hunger and eating, even when there is no physiological deprivation. Furthermore, habits and custom can influence hunger: Setting the table or noticing that the clock says that it is dinner time can arouse our hunger, even if we have recently had a healthy snack. Finally, other environmental conditions, apparently quite unrelated, may have an effect: We "don't feel like eating" during hot weather, and we are "starving" after a walk in the snow.

Whatever the stimuli that initiate eating, recent research has indicated that the area of the brain most sensitive to these stimuli is the hypothalamus.

The Hypothalamus

The hypothalamus is located deep at the base of the brain. It is so small (constituting only about 1 per cent of the total brain weight) that it was easily ignored for many years. It now appears that this tiny collection of nuclei serves the most central role in the control of motivation and emotion.

This structure is well placed and well connected for its integrative role (see Figure 36.2.). It receives impulses from all the senses and has two-way communication with the cerebral cortex, the thalamus, the limbic system, the reticular formation, and the viscera. Perhaps equally important is the fact that the hypothalamus has a greater density of blood vessels than has any other part of the central nervous system,

and thus through the blood stream the hypothalamus may be easily influenced by the overall chemical state of the body.

It has now been fairly well established that two specific regions of the hypothalamus are important in the control of hunger and eating. Much of the evidence suggests that activity in the *lateral nucleus* of the hypothalamus produces the onset of hunger, and the *ventromedial nucleus* of the hypothalamus acts to terminate eating. These structures have therefore been called the "feeding center" and the "satiety center," respectively. When the lateral nucleus is stimulated electrically, a well-fed animal will immediately start eating, and, when this area is removed, the animal does not eat at all and dies of starvation. When the ventromedial nucleus is stimulated, a hungry animal that is eating will stop, and, if this area is destroyed, the animal will overeat until it is grossly overweight (see Figure 36.3.). If both the lateral and the ventromedial regions are destroyed, the animal refuses to eat, just as he does after the lateral lesion alone. This fact suggests that the lateral area alone has direct control over the feeding responses and that the ventromedial works by inhibiting ("putting a brake on") the lateral area when the organism has had enough to eat.

Signaling Mechanisms

The demonstration that the hypothalamus contains organizing systems that will initiate and terminate eating does not answer our earlier question concerning the bodily changes that produce the signal that triggers these hypothalamic nuclei into action.

We saw earlier that food deprivation can lead to a decrease in the concentration of blood sugar. Experimental evidence seems to indicate that chemical change—the fall in blood sugar —serves as an internal stimulus that instigates hypothalamic action. If we inject *insulin* into

Figure 36.2. The *hypothalamus* consists of the collection of nuclei (the white areas) at the base of the brain. The nuclei to which frequent reference will be made in the discussion are labeled "dorsomedial," "lateral," and "ventromedial."

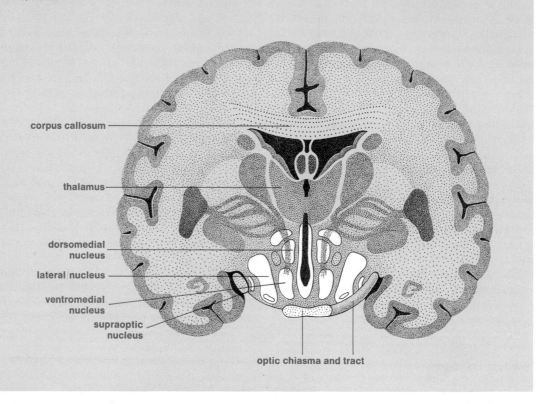

corpus callosum

thalamus

dorsomedial nucleus

lateral nucleus

ventromedial nucleus

supraoptic nucleus

optic chiasma and tract

Figure 36.3. Hypothalamic hyperphagia. The gross obesity of the rat (whose weight has spun the indicator completely around the dial & beyond for a total of 1080 grams) is the result of voracious overeating (hyperphagia). The hyperphagia was caused by experimental destruction of the ventromedial hypothalamus, the "satiety center," which normally acts to terminate eating. A normal rat is shown for comparison.
Courtesy Neal E. Miller, Rockefeller University.

an animal, it produces a fall in blood-sugar level, and the animal increases its food intake. Daily injections of insulin will cause an increase in eating sufficient to render an animal obese. A number of studies suggest that blood-sugar changes affect the hypothalamus directly. For example, when blood-sugar level is increased, the neural activity of the ventromedial nucleus (the satiety center) is increased, and the activity of the lateral nucleus (the feeding center) is decreased (see Box 131, p. 572, for discussion of another relevant phenomenon).

The observation that changes in environmental temperature influence food intake suggests another possible internal stimulus for the normal hypothalamic control of eating. It has been suggested that, because eating has an influence upon body temperature, animals eat to keep warm and stop eating when they are warm enough. In light of this suggestion it is of interest to note that changes in temperature of the hypothalamus have an effect on eating. Cooling of an area of the hypothalamus causes goats to begin eating, and warming of this same area makes them stop.

It would be possible to report observations and experiments that put in question the efficacy of any one of these internal stimuli. Furthermore, we have already noted the effect of external stimuli, habit, and social factors upon hunger and eating—influences that we assume reach the hypothalamus by way of the cerebral cortex (see Box 112, p. 496). The safest conclusion, then, would seem to be that all these factors, together with blood-sugar level and temperature, inform the hypothalamus of the current demands of the body and the current state of the external world with respect to food and hunger. The hypothalamic centers "strike a balance" and provide control over the responses of the individual (see Box 132, p. 573, for a study of the control of eating in human beings).

The hypothalamic centers are not as all-powerful as this conclusion would imply, however. In the first place, animals made to eat excessively by lesions of the ventromedial nucleus do not lose complete control of their ability to stop eating. They eat voraciously at first, but finally, when they reach a new level (one of extreme obesity, to be sure), they taper off and maintain this new level. If they are put on a diet and are forced to lose weight, they will return to their new fat level when given the opportunity. If animals are artificially fattened by insulin injections *before* the ventromedial nucleus is destroyed, the effect of the subsequent operation is to bring them up to the same fat level as that of animals having the operation but not artificially fattened beforehand (see Figure 36.4.). So what appears to be true is that the destruction of the ventromedial hypothalamus has not destroyed "the" center for inhibiting eating but that its destruction has seriously interfered with this function. Furthermore, in animals with ventromedial lesions, taste and other factors become very important. Adding a little quinine to a normal diet or changing its texture by adding bulk to it, neither of which would affect the eating of a normal animal, will cause these animals to stop eating completely. They are voracious but very "finicky" eaters.

Related findings emerge from further study of animals with lateral hypothalamic lesions. If they are given a normal diet of dry food and water, they will starve to death. But, if they are force-fed particularly palatable foods, they will gradually recover and can eventually be brought around to eating a normal diet. These "recovered laterals" will starve to death, however, if a little quinine is put into their food. Once again a particular sensitivity to taste factors is found. Apparently then, the lateral hypothalamus, important though it is, is not "the" center for controlling the onset of eating.

Finally, we might mention that there is ample evidence that stimulation or destruction of portions of the cerebral cortex and the limbic structures (see p. 592) can produce changes in food intake in human beings and other animals.

Box 131

Jack Sprat and
His Brother Rat

Normal animals are able to maintain a rather precise control over their weights. For example, P. Teitelbaum, a University of Pennsylvania psychologist, demonstrated that rats artificially fattened by insulin injections will rapidly return to their normal weights as soon as the injections are discontinued. This fact suggests that there must be some long-range factor related to the animals' weights that exerts control over amounts eaten. G. C. Kennedy, of the London National Institute for Medical Research, proposed precisely this view in suggesting the existence of a substance (a metabolite) circulating in the blood that remains in equilibrium with stored fat and acts on a hypothalamic satiety center.

G. R. Hervey, working at the University of Cambridge, found strong experimental support for the view in a very ingeniously designed experiment. He created artificial "Siamese twins" by surgically uniting pairs of rats early in life. These animals ("parabiotic animals") exchanged blood throughout postsurgical life. When the animals were grown, he destroyed the ventromedial nucleus of the hypothalamus ("the satiety center") in one member of each pair. These animals showed the gluttonous overeating to be expected from the operation and rapidly grew obese. The startling finding was that their untreated "twins" gradually became thinner and thinner and thinner as their partners grew fat.

Interchange of blood between the animals is relatively small and it is clear that the unoperated animal is not able to profit from the food-rich blood of his brother. But why then does he become thin? Hervey suggests that destruction of the ventromedial nucleus disturbs the satiety center and makes the operated rat relatively insensitive to the postulated fat-related substance. Only when this animal is very fat is there enough of the metabolite to control its eating. As the metabolite builds up toward this high level in the *operated* rat, the amount that enters the *normal* twin's blood is sufficient to act on *his* satiety center and *prevent him* from eating.

P. TEITELBAUM. 1962. Motivational Correlates of Hypothalamic Activity, *Excerpta Medica, Int. Congr. Ser.*, 47, 697–704.
G. C. KENNEDY. 1953. The Role of Depot Fat in Hypothalamic Control of Food Intake in the Rat, *Proc. Roy. Soc.* Ser. B., 140, 578–92. Photos courtesy G. R. Hervey, University of Aberdeen; reprinted by permission.
G. R. HERVEY. 1959. The Effects of Lesions in the Hypothalamus in Parabiotic Rats, *J. Physiol.*, 145, 336–52.

Box 132

The Pushbutton Cafeteria

A number of experiments that have helped us assess the cues important for the control of eating and drinking in the rat have used an interesting technique. Tubes fitted into the animal's mouth and digestive tract are connected to supply reservoirs so that, when the animal presses a lever, food or water is injected directly into its stomach, its mouth, or both, as the experimenter wishes.

A clever adaptation of this technique was recently developed by H. A. Jordan, S. P. Zebley, and E. Stellar, research scientists at the University of Pennsylvania, in order to study the control of food intake in man. The college-student subjects could obtain food (Metrecal) by pressing a button that resulted in the delivery of a shot of food either into the mouth through a straw (oral intake), into the stomach through a swallowed tube (intragastric intake), or both. The students "ate" their Metrecal breakfast in the apparatus daily, throughout the course of the experiment. Although they were unable to identify the cues they used to regulate their diet, they were able to control the amounts eaten in the intragastric-intake condition as well as they could in the oral condition. In other words, without the normal cues of chewing, tasting, smelling, and swallowing the food and without knowing how they did it, subjects controlled their food intake as well as if they had been eating in the normal manner! This new technique promises to be a valuable tool in studying the control of eating and drinking in the human, as it has been in the rat.

H. A. JORDAN, S. P. ZEBLEY, and E. STELLAR. 1967. A Comparison of Voluntary Oral and Intragastric Food Intake in Man, Paper read at the Eastern Psychological Association Annual Meeting, Boston.
H. A. JORDAN, W. F. WIELAND, S. P. ZEBLEY, E. STELLAR, and A. J. STUNKARD. 1966. Direct Measurement of Food Intake in Man: A Method for the Objective Study of Eating Behavior, *Psychosom. Med.*, 28, 836–42.

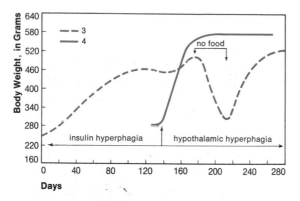

Figure 36.4. Rate of weight gain in hypothalamic hyperphagia, after destruction of the ventromedial nucleus of the hypothalamus in two rats. Before the operation animal no. 3 was made to overeat and become obese by protamin zinc insulin injections; animal no. 4 was at its normal weight at the time of operation. These rates are compared with animal no. 3's rate of weight gain after the animal had been starved back to its normal weight. P. Teitelbaum, "Disturbances in Feeding and Drinking Behavior After Hypothalamic Lesion," in M. R. Jones, ed., *Nebraska Symposium on Motivation* (1961); adapted by permission of the University of Nebraska Press.

These effects are neither as clear-cut nor as well understood as are those that follow hypothalamic manipulations, but they provide ample support for the conclusion that what we call "hunger" depends upon many influences from the environment and the rest of the body, acting upon fairly complicated neural mechanisms in the brain (see Box 133, p. 575, for other motivational effects produced by direct action on the brain).

The Thirst Motive

Having considered some of the physiological bases of hunger, we are in a better position to study thirst, for we shall find here parallel and interrelated problems.

The body is approximately four-fifths water, of which we lose one to two quarts every day. Normally we replenish this water and maintain a constant internal state of hydration. The question of what constitutes thirst is another of those important questions that seem simple at first glance. If you ask the "man on the street" how he controls his water drinking, he would probably tell you he drinks when he is dry and stops when he has had enough. But the real question, of course, is how he knows he is dry and how he knows he's had enough. If pressed a little, he would probably point out that he is dry when his throat is dry but would also agree that he continues drinking long after he has wet his throat. Let us see if we can find support for this commonsense knowledge and learn more about the thirst motive.

Our layman's dry-mouth theory is precisely the one suggested by the physiologist Cannon (1932). He suggested that when the body needs water an adequate flow of saliva is prevented, and a dry mouth or dry throat results. The dryness serves as the stimulus for the sensation of thirst and initiates drinking.

At first glance this theory appears to run into serious difficulties. When dogs are given atropine (which stops the normal production of saliva) or have their salivary glands removed, they do not drink excessively even though their mouths are constantly dry; people who are born without salivary glands do not drink more than normal people do. Furthermore, injections of pilocarpine, a drug that causes a large increase in saliva flow and thus keeps the throat and mouth constantly wet, fails to lessen the desire for water. These objections are serious, but we shall see later that this theory may yet be partially correct.

Now, however, let us consider other possible mechanisms. As the body loses water, individual cells lose water and become dehydrated. This fact has led to the theory that *cellular dehydration* is the crucial fact in thirst. Injection into the body of substances that draw fluid from the cells has been shown to produce thirst in experimental animals.

Yet another mechanism appears to be operating, the total *blood volume*. A great loss of blood produces thirst, even though the cells of the body have not lost fluid. An equivalent

Box 133

"Rewarding" Brain Centers

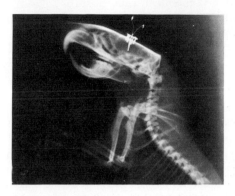

The crucial role of brain activity in "motivated behavior" is dramatically illustrated by the "self-stimulation" experiment pioneered by J. Olds and P. Milner at McGill University in 1954.

In this experiment fine wire electrodes are permanently implanted through the skull into various lower brain centers of experimental animals. The accompanying figure is an X-ray photograph showing electrodes in place in an intact rat. During experimental sessions the electrodes are connected to wires going to a lever and to an electrical current source, so that when the lever is depressed a brief, weak electrical pulse is delivered to the brain. Rats placed in a box with the lever available to them quickly learn to press it to receive the brain stimulation, and, if the experimenter turns off the current at its source, they soon stop pressing the lever.

The results of some of the extensive research with self-stimulation by Olds and his associates show what a powerful and important effect it is. Rats will press the lever at rates as high as 5,000 times per hour, or more than once per second, to receive this electrical stimulation. They will press for fifteen to twenty hours until they drop exhausted, will sleep, and will then return to press again. Animals will cross an electrically charged grid to reach their "brain lever" and in doing so will withstand stronger foot shock than they will to obtain food when hungry for twenty-four hours. They will also learn to run through a complex maze for stimulation at least as well as for food.

Reports on the use of the self-stimulation technique with human patients give us a hint about the nature of the effects. C. W. Sem-Jacobsen and A. Torkildsen of Gausted Mental Hospital, Oslo, report that patients seem to like the brain stimulation, they appear pleased and smile when stimulated, and they will press a lever for self-stimulation just as the rats do. Their descriptions of their feelings during stimulation give the impression of a "good feeling" but not one that can be identified with any particular rewards or experiences.

The initiation of purposive behavior is indeed a complex affair. Even the rat is impelled by more than an empty stomach, a depleted water supply, or hormonal pressures. There seem to be specific brain centers whose stimulation is alone enough to result in a "primary rewarding effect."

J. OLDS and P. MILNER. 1954. Positive Reinforcement Produced by Electrical Stimulation of Septal Area and Other Regions of Rat Brain, *J. Comp. Physiol. Psychol.* 47, 419–27.

J. OLDS. 1961. Differential Effects of Drives and Drugs on Self-Stimulation at Different Brain Sites, in D. E. Sheer, ed., *Electrical Stimulation of the Brain* (Austin: University of Texas Press).

C. W. SEM-JACOBSEN and A. TORKILDSEN. 1960. *Depth Recording and Electrical Stimulation in the Human Brain.* In E. R. Ramey and D. S. O'Doherty, eds., *Electrical Studies on the Unanesthetized Brain* (New York: Hoeber). Photo courtesy J. Olds, The University of Michigan; reprinted by permission of *Scientific American.*

effect can be produced by injecting into the body a chemical that absorbs blood serum without disturbing the individual cells of the organism.

When we wonder how these changes in the organism could influence behavior and experience, our attention turns once again to the hypothalamus. Destruction of certain regions of the hypothalamus is followed by a complete cessation in voluntary water intake, whereas electrical stimulation of the hypothalamus can elicit "compulsive drinking" in experimental animals. It also appears that the cellular dehydration theory of thirst and the suggestion that control of thirst is in the hypothalamus may support one another. When a microscopic amount of a concentrated salt solution is injected into the appropriate part of an animal's hypothalamus, the animal immediately begins drinking. Presumably the hypothalamus contains *osmoreceptors*, specialized cells that signal their state of hydration to other parts of the nervous system; the injected salt is taken up by the cells, produces a state of relative dehydration in them, and thus produces thirst in the organism as a whole.

Curiously, the hunger and the thirst systems in the brain appear to overlap, at least in the rat. The lesion of the lateral area that makes rats stop eating also makes them stop drinking. That these systems do not involve exactly the same cells can be demonstrated by chemical tests. It we inject into this area a minute amount of an acetylcholine-type drug, we produce drinking, whereas injection of other substances produces eating (Grossman, 1960). These results suggest that the cells that initiate drinking are cholinergic, that is, that they use acetylcholine as their transmitter substance at the synapses (see p. 469), whereas the cells involved in eating use other transmitter substances. If the rat is carefully nursed after a lesion of the lateral area, the animal once again eats ordinary food and drinks water. Just as the recovery in eating was fragile and easily disturbed by taste changes, the recovery in

drinking is incomplete. Careful studies show that these rats cannot adjust their drinking to balance their bodies' needs for water. The "recovered" animals drink only in order to wet their mouths when eating dry food. The dry-mouth theory of Cannon appears, then, to be at least partially true.

The Sex Motive

Earlier in this unit we mentioned the autonomic nervous system. Now we shall have to consider this system in some detail, for it plays a major role in the physiological mechanisms of the sex motive.

The Autonomic Nervous System

In the early years of the nineteenth century a French physiologist, Bichat, became the first to suggest that the controlling activities of the entire nervous system could be divided into a "voluntary" part and an "involuntary" part. By about 1920 (primarily as the result of the work of an American physiologist, Langley) the existence of two specialized, yet interrelated, nervous systems was well established. The "voluntary system," now called the cerebrospinal nervous system, was described in detail in Unit 4. What Bichat had called the "involuntary" nervous system was further subdivided. One part of the involuntary system was named the *sympathetic nervous system* and another part the *parasympathetic nervous system*. Both systems together Langley called the *autonomic nervous system*. Langley's terminology has been widely adopted and is in common use today.

The autonomic nervous system serves three classes of effector organs. First, it serves the *smooth muscles*, the muscles of the viscera, blood vessels, and so on, which differ structurally from the skeletal muscles of the limbs and trunk. The smooth muscles do not have the horizontal striations across the fibers that characterize the skeletal muscles (which are therefore also called *striated,* or striped, *muscles*). Second, it serves the *cardiac* muscle. Cardiac or heart muscle is specialized muscle that is continuously in action throughout the life of the organism. Third, it serves the *glands.* The glands secrete various chemical products. Some glands have *ducts,* or outlets, which direct these products into specific localized areas of the body. Examples are the tear glands, which secrete tears into the eyes, and the salivary glands, which secrete saliva into the mouth. Other glands have no ducts; they secrete their products directly into the blood stream, which carries these chemical products, called *hormones,* throughout the system. These glands are called *ductless glands* or *endocrine glands.*

The *sympathetic nervous system* centers about two chains of ganglia running along the sides of the spinal cord. Figure 36.5. shows one of these chains. The ganglion cells are supplied by nerve fibers from the spinal cord, which are called "preganglionic neurons." A single preganglionic neuron makes contact with many sympathetic ganglia. The ganglion cells of the sympathetic system are thus built to facilitate *widespread discharge.* Because the ganglia of the sympathetic system are connected with the visceral organs, many visceral organs can be thrown into coordinated activity when any one part of the sympathetic system is stimulated. For example, when a nervous impulse comes down the spinal cord from the hypothalamus and travels across a preganglionic neuron to the ganglia of the sympathetic system, the following *pattern* of visceral responses occurs simultaneously: dilation of the pupil, increase in heart rate, rise in blood pressure, rerouting of the blood from the skin and stomach to the muscles of the limbs, inhibition of the peristaltic movements of the stomach, and so forth. All these reactions, taken as a whole, prepare the organism for *emergency action*—for flight or fight. This automatic, unconscious, and uncontrollable series of visceral reactions has been *initiated* by signals from the hypothala-

mus but has been *patterned* and put into execution by the structure of the sympathetic nervous system.

Fibers of the *parasympathetic nervous system* supply the same visceral organs as do those of the sympathetic nervous system. But, as can be seen in Figure 36.5., there is one important difference in their structures. The parasympathetic system is more specific and discriminating in its connections with the visceral organs than is the sympathetic. For example, the stimulation of the parasympathetic nerve that supplies the tear glands results in stimulation of the tear glands *only*, not of many other visceral organs as well.

The effects of stimulation by the two systems are usually *opposite in direction.* For example, stimulation of the heart by the sympathetic system accelerates the heart; stimulation by the parasympathetic system slows it down. Most visceral organs are thus supplied by two nervous systems, each having an effect opposite from the other. This functioning in opposite directions is called *reciprocal innervation.* Reciprocal innervation gives us a built-in neurological mechanism for homeostatic control. As one nerve accelerates the heart beyond normal, the stimulation of another can slow it down again to the normal rate.

As we have already seen, the sympathetic and parasympathetic systems are triggered by the preganglionic neurons that come from the spinal cord. These preganglionic neurons, in turn, receive impulses from the cerebrospinal system by way of the hypothalamus.

The hypothalamus is involved in almost all patterned visceral reactions. Injury to the hypothalamus can result in disturbances in stomach reactions, metabolic functions, temperature regulation, and so on. As a result, the hypothalamus has sometimes been called the "head ganglion" of the autonomic system. When we remember that the hypothalamus, in turn, is connected with the cortex as well as with other centers of the brain, we can see that the brain controls the viscera.

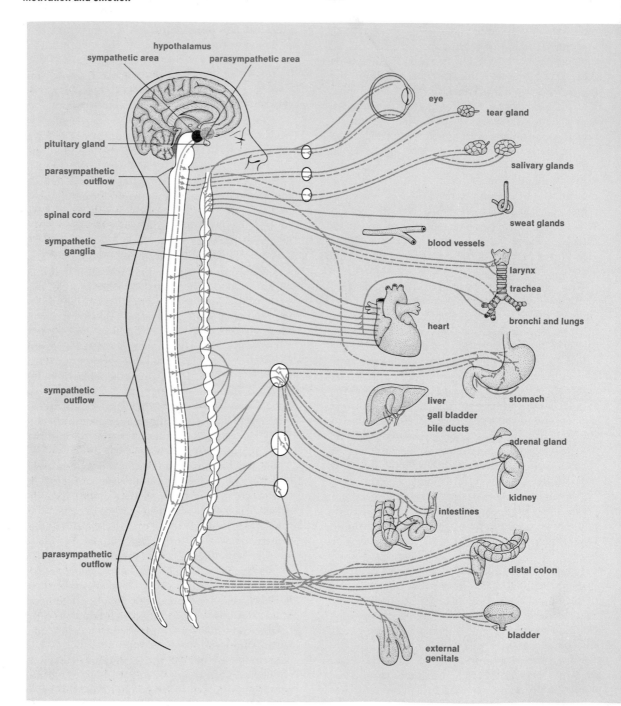

Sexual Stimulation and Response

In considering the sexual motive in the normally developed adult human we must recognize that external stimuli—visual, auditory, and olfactory—play a major role in the onset of the motive. It still depends upon the time, the place, and the right girl (or boy). Learning is crucial in determining the importance of these stimuli. The pale, delicate skin that arouses one man may appear merely unhealthy and unappealing to another. Because learning, and presumably cortical activity, play an important role in sexual behavior, it is not surprising that with increased cortical destruction there is found, at least among some animals, a decreasing inclination or even a decreasing ability to perform the sex act (see Figure 36.6.).

In addition to the influence of learned stimuli on the onset of the sex motive, there are other stimuli that control "built-in" responses and are little influenced by learning. Tactual stimuli (touching, rubbing, stroking) elicit such responses from both primary and secondary sex areas.

If, then, visual, auditory, olfactory, and tactual stimuli initiate sexual desire, what physiological processes do they initiate? The major mechanisms are autonomic. A study of human sexual response (Masters & Johnson, 1966) has detailed these responses. Initially we find a widespread congestion of the blood vessels (vasocongestion), which affects the genitalia and the secondary sex areas (for example, the breasts) and which may appear on the skin surface as a flush. In addition, we find an increase in heart rate and in blood pressure. As the sex urge increases in intensity, there is massive autonomic involvement, including widespread and deep vasocongestion, deeper breathing, heart-rate increases from normal values of about 72 to as high as 180 beats a minute, marked elevation of blood pressure, a well-developed and widespread generalized body flush, and extensive bodily perspiration unrelated to physical activity. Masters and

Figure 36.5. Here we have a semidiagrammatic representation of the hypothalamus, the spinal cord, the sympathetic nervous system, and the parasympathetic nervous system. The solid lines represent the sympathetic system, the dotted lines the parasympathetic system.

Consider first the sympathetic system. A nervous impulse originates in the lower part of the hypothalamus. From there it descends the spinal cord, and at some point about halfway down the cord (at the area labeled "sympathetic outflow") it connects with *preganglionic neurons* and leaves the cord (indicated by small arrows). The preganglionic neuron then enters one of the sympathtic ganglia, where it makes several connections. The nervous impulse then travels up and down the chain of ganglia, making contact with many sympathetic ganglia. When one preganglionic neuron is thrown into action, many ganglia are thus excited. From these ganglia, post-ganglionic neurons extend to the various visceral organs—sweat glands, blood vessels, heart, external genitals.

Now consider the parasympathetic system. There, too, the nervous impulse originates in the hypothalamus, but in its upper part. From there it descends the spinal cord and leaves the cord at one of two levels (the areas labeled "parasympathetic outflow"). From there the impulse is conducted to the same visceral organs supplied by the sympathetic system. Note, however, that for the most part any single fiber of the parasympathetic system serves relatively fewer visceral organs than does any single fiber of the sympathetic system.

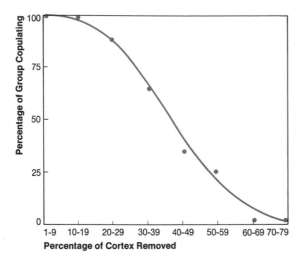

Figure 36.6. The effects of cortical injury on the mating behavior of male rats. Each point represents a separate group of animals and indicates the percentage of that group that continued to copulate after cortical destruction. Destruction of less than 20 per cent of the cortex affected very few animals. Destruction of 50 to 59 per cent of the cortex completely eliminated mating in 75 per cent of the rats. No rat with 60 per cent or more of his cortex destroyed was observed to copulate. (It is of interest to note that female rats continue to mate despite *total* decortication.)
F. A. Beach, "Instinctive Behavior," in S. S. Stevens, ed., *Handbook of Experimental Psychology* (1951); adapted by permission of John Wiley & Sons, Inc.

Johnson emphasize a point about which there has not always been agreement. They say: "The parallels in reaction to effective sexual stimulation emphasize the physiologic similarities in male and female responses rather than the differences. Aside from obvious anatomic variants, men and women are homogeneous in their physiologic responses to sexual stimuli."

Our knowledge of the hypothalamus and its broad control of autonomic responses should lead us to expect it to be important in the sex motive, and we find that it is. Electrical stimulation of a part of the lateral hypothalamus has induced the complete sex pattern, including ejaculation, in the male rat (Vaughn & Fisher, 1962). Injection of male hormone into a differ-

ent hypothalamic nucleus can produce male sex responses in both male and female rats. In addition, electrical stimulation of several other subcortical areas important in emotion and pleasure has yielded sex responses in monkeys.

The Endocrine System

The first point to note in our discussion of the effects of hormones on sexual behavior is that hormones are critical for the *development* of both sexual structures and normal sexual behavior. In human beings, once this development takes place, sex hormones play a relatively unimportant role. The loss of sex hormones by the female after *menopause* need not interfere with the sex urge. In adult men, removal of the testes sometimes causes marked reduction in sex drive, but very frequently no change is experienced in sexual behavior for as long as twenty years after the operation. It appears that in some men testicular hormone is not necessary for normal sexual activity. For other species, however, hormones produced by the endocrine system play a critical role not only in the development of sexual behavior but also in maintaining it.

Among the endocrine glands important for behavior are the *gonads*, the *pituitary*, the *thyroid*, and the *adrenals* (see Figure 36.7.). In general we can distinguish two systems of control of the endocrine, or ductless, glands: First, some of the glands (for example, the posterior part of the pituitary gland and the adrenal medulla) are dependent upon their connections with the autonomic nervous system for stimulation and control. Second, some of the glands (including part of the pituitary gland and the gonads, or sex glands) form a self-regulating and coordinated system.

The hormonal secretions of the endocrine glands, as they are carried through the body by the blood stream, evoke many different kinds of reactions from the visceral organs into which they diffuse. As far as behavior is concerned, these reactions are of three general types.

First, hormones acting directly on the nervous system during development can produce major and permanent changes in the structural and physiological bases of behavior. We shall elaborate on this point later. Second, hormones may have a temporary effect upon immediate behavior. For example, adrenaline (a secretion of the adrenal glands) has the same emergency and energizing effect during fear as does the autonomic nervous system. Third, the constant and regular secretions of the endocrine glands have long-lasting effects, helping to determine the general level of energy, the general level of the sex drive, and so on. They are the biochemical mechanisms that help to determine our *continuing* motivational and emotional states.

Central to our interest in the sex motive are the gonads and their hormones. The gonads (the *testes* in the male, the *ovaries* in the female) have both glandular and nonglandular functions. Their nonglandular function is the production of germ cells (spermatozoa in the male and ova, or eggs, in the female). Their hormonal function is the secretion of the so-called "sex hormones."

The testes produce several hormones, among them *testosterone*, the male sex hormone. It should be noted that the normal testes also produce *estrogen*, the female sex hormone. Testosterone and *androsterone* (another male sex hormone) are both called *androgens*.

The ovaries produce two types of hormones: estrogen and *progesterone*. Estrogen has female functions similar to those of testosterone in the male. (See Box 134, p. 582, for important studies of the effects of these hormones on behavior.)

The production of these hormones is regulated by hormones from the anterior pituitary gland called *gonadotropic hormones*. There is a reciprocal relation between the activity of the anterior pituitary and the gonads. In the male, for example, the production of testosterone depends upon the presence of a gonadotropic hormone (see Figure 36.8.). If insufficient testosterone is present the amount of the gonadotropin secreted will be increased; when enough testosterone is present, it halts the secretion of gonadotropin. These mechanisms ensure a stable amount of testosterone in the body.

Let us now return to a consideration of how

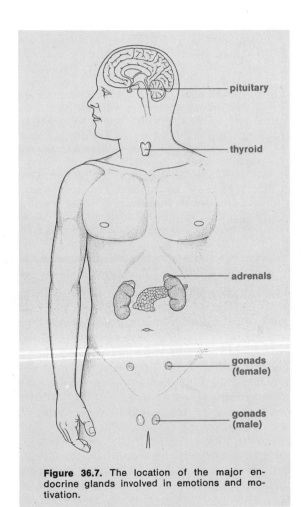

Figure 36.7. The location of the major endocrine glands involved in emotions and motivation.

pituitary

thyroid

adrenals

gonads (female)

gonads (male)

Box 134

The Ring Dove and
the Bow-Coo

D. S. Lehrman, a psychologist at Rutgers University, has developed an unusually broad and interesting program of research in his studies of the cycle of reproductive behavior of the ring dove. His work gives a clear picture of the relations between the changing behavior of the birds and changes in their anatomy, hormone production, and other physiological functions.

The behavior of the ring dove during its reproductive cycle, as detailed by Lehrman, is not unlike that of many other birds. The male courts the female; they choose a nest site and spend about a week building a nest. Copulation takes place during this period. In the second week the female lays her eggs, and the two birds share the work of incubating. When the young are hatched, both parents feed them until they are ready to fend for themselves, after which the male starts courting, and the whole cycle begins again.

In Lehrman's experimental setting the cycle begins when a male and a female ring dove are placed in a cage, together with nesting material and a potential nest site, a small glass bowl. Soon after they meet, the male begins bowing to the female and making cooing sounds (the bow-coo). An understanding of the details and significance of the bow-coo is important because of its critical and widespread effects on the subsequent behavior and internal states of both birds during the reproductive cycle.

The bow-coo is triggered by the sight of the female bird but depends upon the presence of the male hormones of the testes. Females and castrated males do not perform the bow-coo. The bow-coo leads the female to enter into and to continue her part of the reproductive cycle, and directly and indirectly it induces the anatomical and physiological changes underlying these behavior patterns. A female alone will not build a nest, lay eggs, or incubate them, nor will one caged with a castrated

sex hormones play a critical role in the development of the neural basis of sexual behavior. Most of the research in this area has been done with animals. In the very early life of the animal (before birth in the monkey and guinea pig and within the first ten days after birth in the rat), the administration of male sex hormones produces male characteristics. Normally these androgens are supplied by the testes of the male fetus. But, for example, if a monkey pregnant with a *female* fetus is injected with male hormones, the fetus will develop a penis and scrotum. In addition, these females show male patterns of play and social behavior as they grow older (Young, *et al.*, 1964). The ab-

sence of androgens prepares the animal for the female role. Castration of newborn male rats before they begin producing testosterone leads to atrophy of their reproductive systems. Such an animal in the adult state responds to injections of female hormones with the complete pattern of female sexual behavior. Male rats, when castrated as adults, never respond in this fashion.

It appears that initially both sexes are basically female in terms of the nervous system; that is, the nervous system is organized so as to produce a pattern of female sexual behavior. Only in the presence of male sex hormones do the male structure and potential for male

male. But if a female is separated from a normal male only by a plate of glass, so that she can see and hear him, he will bow and coo, and she will make a nest, lay eggs, and incubate them.

These behavior patterns are under the direct influence of the female hormones, as Lehrman shows in a series of experiments. If a pair of birds are given a ready-made nest with eggs when they first meet, they do not incubate the eggs but begin the usual cycle of courting and nest building, even covering the eggs in their nest-building activity! If a pair of birds are injected with estrogen, they immediately begin nest-building and are ready to incubate in three or four days, rather than the normal seven or eight days. But, when birds are injected with progesterone, they will incubate almost immediately, if eggs are provided by the experimenter. Estrogen influences nest building, and progesterone controls incubation. In normal birds visual and auditory stimuli from the courting male act through the female nervous system to start the production of pituitary gonadotropic hormones. These hormones in turn start the ovarian secretion of estrogen and later progesterone. The female hormones not only influence behavior as we have shown but also lead to major changes in the ovaries, which grow in weight from about 800 mg. to 4,000 mg. by the time the eggs are ready to be laid.

It should be recognized that, important as the bow-coo is, other behavior influences the cycle as well. We find, for example, that a female will produce a level of progesterone high enough to make her ready for incubation simply by being exposed to a courting male but that she will produce the same amount of progesterone and be ready to incubate sooner if, in addition to the courting male nesting material is available and she participates in nest building.

The male, of course, does not see the bow-coo, but it is his courting and participation in nest building that stimulate his progesterone production and prepare him for incubating.

Lehrman has performed similar analyses of parental feeding behavior, showing its relation to nest building, incubating the eggs, and the production of the pituitary hormone prolactin.

It is easy to agree with Lehrman that the reproductive behavior cycle of the ring dove is not a series of responses to changing stimuli but rather a "psychobiological" cycle in which external stimuli, behavior, and internal states all interact.

D. S. LEHRMAN. 1964. Control of Behavior Cycles in Reproduction, in W. Etkin, ed., *Social Behavior and Organization among Vertebrates* (Chicago: University of Chicago Press).

sex patterns develop. Once developed, these patterns cannot be reversed by a subsequent change in hormonal balance.

Under certain circumstances similar results can occur in the human. If a woman pregnant with a female child is given extensive treatment with testosterone, the child may develop external male genitalia. On the other hand, a male fetus that fails to produce testosterone will not develop normal male organs.

In normally maturing organisms testosterone in the male and estrogen in the female are responsible for the growth of the sex organs and the development of *secondary sex characteristics*. Among secondary sex characteristics controlled by testosterone are the following: growth and distribution of hair on the body, enlargement of the larynx (Adam's apple) and the consequent development of the typical masculine bass voice, skeletal proportions of the body, and the thickness and texture of the skin. These and similar changes occur very rapidly during adolescence, when there is a great increase of testosterone secretion. An indication of the role of testosterone in these bodily changes is seen in castration effects. If the male sex glands are removed prior to maturity, the secondary sex characteristics will not develop in the male. But if testosterone is administered in time, normal male development does take

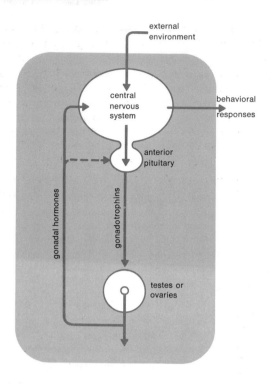

external
environment

central
nervous
system

behavioral
responses

anterior
pituitary

gonadal hormones

gonadotrophins

testes or
ovaries

Figure 36.8. The diagram illustrates the reciprocal relations among the central nervous system, the pituitary gland, and the gonads. The central nervous system mediates the effects of environmental changes and exerts a regulatory influence over the anterior pituitary gland, which in turn controls the ovaries and testes through the production of the gonadotropic hormones. The hormones from the latter glands in turn "feed back" to the central nervous system and pituitary gland to influence both behavior of the animal and the level of anterior pituitary activity.
G. W. Harris, "Central Control of Pituitary Secretion," in John Field, ed., *Handbook of Physiology* (1960); adapted by permission of the American Physiological Society.

place. Estrogen, in contrast, controls the development of the breasts and the deposits of fat on the thighs and causes the broadened hips characteristic of the feminine figure and soft, smooth feminine skin.

The level of sex hormones, although apparently not necessarily important in determining the intensity of the sex drive in man, is critical in lower mammals. Removal of the

sex glands during adulthood results in a gradual loss of sexual activity in the male rat and an immediate loss of sexual responsiveness in the female. Normal responsiveness can be recovered through hormone treatment. Experimenters who need sexually receptive female rats make regular use of these effects by removing the ovaries from female rats and then treating them with female hormones. Figure 36.9. shows the recovery of sexual behavior, effected by hormone treatment, in castrated male rats.

An interaction between sex hormones and experience in initiating sexual behavior has been shown in the cat (Rosenblatt & Aronson, 1958). Adult male cats castrated before puberty show no sexual responses to receptive females. Androgen treatment induces sexual responsiveness, and animals given androgen and sex experience continue to show sexual behavior even after the withdrawal of the sex hormones. Alternatively, treatment by sex hormones without accompanying sex experience produces an animal that shows no sexual responses upon removal of the hormones.

The two examples that we have chosen to illustrate the effects of sex hormones on sexual responses suggest a general principle. As we go up the evolutionary scale from the lower mammals to the human being, there is a progressive relaxation of hormonal control over sexuality and a progressive increase of cortical control.

The cortex comes to play an increasing role not only in initiating the sexual response but also in *inhibiting* it. Schreiner and Kling (1953) found that destruction in the cat of parts of the brain resulted in an extreme state of *continuous hypersexuality*. Their interpretation of these results suggests that destruction of these brain areas removes the controlling mechanism in the brain that regulates sexual behavior.

Sexual motivation, perhaps more than any other kind, is dependent upon every integrating mechanism in the body—the brain and central nervous system, the autonomic nervous system, and the hormonal system. Both physiological and psychological evidence testifies to the complex interrelations involved in the sex motive.

Sleep

Why we sleep no physiologist knows. But that the need for sleep is an important motive no one can deny. We do know that a normal person deprived of sleep suffers disastrous effects upon perceptual processes, intellectual ability, and personality.

It is generally believed that sleep is produced by chemical changes in the body. Presumably certain chemicals are produced while one is awake that are somehow poisonous to the body, and the sleeping state allows these chemicals to be destroyed. Among the chemicals that have been implicated are serotonin and norepinephrine (see p. 601). There is very little definite knowledge on this question, however.

We know that certain brain systems are critically involved in sleep and wakefulness. As a person becomes drowsy and eventually falls asleep, we see definite changes in the EEG. At first, in light sleep, the alpha rhythm becomes smaller in size and less regular. When he is definitely asleep, this irregular alpha is interspersed with periods in which sleep spindles, groups of very rapid waves, appear in the EEG. In deep sleep the alpha wave disappears entirely, and large slow waves appear (see Figure 36.1.). These stages of the EEG are related to other changes in the body of the sleeper. His body temperature and blood pressure decline, and his rate of breathing becomes more regular; he becomes harder to awaken by a sound or a touch.

We have seen (p. 255) that the reticular formation acts as an arousal system; we are not now surprised to learn that part of the reticular formation acts as a wakefulness system. External stimuli help to keep us awake, and the amount of such stimulation affects the amount of activity in the reticular formation. Furthermore, electrical stimulation of the reticular for-

mation can awaken a sleeping animal, and destruction of this region can make an animal comatose.

There appear to be structures that act as sleeping centers. Stimulation of certain parts of the thalamus can induce sleep; a limited destruction in the hypothalamus has been reported to prevent sleep in the cat. One experimenter (Jouvet, 1967) has presented some evidence that suggests that the nerve cells at the midline of the brain stem initiate sleep. These cells, according to Jouvet, produce

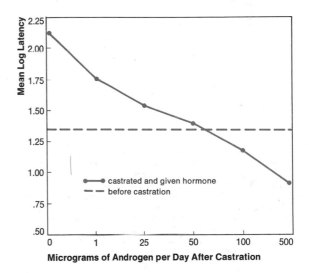

Micrograms of Androgen per Day After Castration

Figure 36.9. The effect of hormonal treatment on copulatory behavior of castrated male rats. "Mean log latency" refers to the interval of time that elapses between the introduction of a receptive female and the occurrence of the first copulation. The dotted line shows the average latency for normal rats. After castration and with no treatment (0 on the horizontal scale), the mean log latency rose from about 1.30 to well over 2.00 (after castration). With 1 microgram of androgen per day, the latency of the castrated animal dropped to 1.72. In general, the speed with which coitus is initiated by the castrated male depends upon the amount of the male hormone given. With 500 micrograms per day the castrate's mean log latency drops below that of the normal rat.
F. A. Beach, "Instinctive Behavior," in S. S. Stevens, ed., *Handbook of Experimental Psychology*, (1951); adapted by permission of John Wiley & Sons, Inc.

serotonin, which counteracts the alerting effect of the reticular formation. This counteraction in turn produces the first stages of light sleep.

Let us return to our sleeping man. After he has been asleep for about an hour, the EEG pattern changes. It comes to look much like that of the earliest stages of sleep, or even that of a waking, alert person! For some time, investigators assumed that this simply indicated that the individual was indeed almost waking up. It was discovered, however, that during the period in which this EEG is produced, the subject is more deeply asleep than ever. He is harder to awaken than at any other period of the night, the muscles of his body become extremely relaxed, and reflexes are very hard to elicit. This period of sleep is thus called "paradoxical sleep" because the EEG looks like that of an alert person, whereas the other signs show that it is the deepest phase of sleep. Paradoxical sleep makes up approximately 25 per cent of the total night's sleep for the normal adult.

Another feature of this stage of sleep that can be determined by electrical recording or by simple observation is the occurrence of *rapid eye movements* (*REM*). It has been discovered that, if a person is awakened during the time that he is displaying REMs, he will almost invariably report that he has just been dreaming.

The content of an individual's dream is related to physiological and behavioral responses measured during the REM period. More REMs are found during dreams in which the subject reports that he watched rapidly moving scenes than for dreams in which he was staring at stationary objects. The direction of REMs (up and down, or sideways) even correlates with the direction of movement of objects (a bouncing ball or passing automobile) in the dream.

When stimuli are presented to a person in REM sleep, he will often incorporate them into his dream; for example, a humming tone may be heard in the dream as an airplane. When two such stimuli are made part of the dream, their effects are about as far apart in time in the report of the dream as the stimuli actually were in real life.

Why does this kind of sleep occur and occupy so much of our sleeping life? Even though we can give no definite answer we can point out, as we did for sleep in general, that deprivation of REM sleep can produce behavioral and physiological changes and that definite neural structures are involved in its production. If people or animals are deprived of REM sleep for several nights by being awakened each time their EEG shows the characteristic signs of REM, they show a large rise in amounts of REM sleep as soon as they have opportunities for uninterrupted sleep.

Some hints about the possible role of REM sleep have come from noting that it is much more frequent in infants than in adults. In the newborn it occupies 50 per cent of the sleeping period (and thus about 33 per cent of the total twenty-four-hour period). The percentage decreases steadily throughout development and continues to decrease slowly until old age. The conclusion has been reached that REM sleep serves its most important functions in early development.

The fact that the brain functions as intensively during REM sleep as during the waking state may be the crucial point in a final understanding of its function. It has been suggested that this stage of brain activity is important because it provides for a high level of activity that is *not* dependent upon external stimulation. The developing brain needs excitation, but in the very young such excitation is not available from outside sources. The REM sleep provides this essential activity. The continuing need for REM sleep in the adult is accounted for by a slight addition to this view. We may presume that regular non-REM sleep, though necessary perhaps to overcome some biochemical imbalance produced in the *waking state*, itself has deleterious effects if continued too long. The REM stage provides for reactivation of the sleeping brain, disrupting the sleep without disturbing the sleeper.

Glossary

adrenal gland Consists of two distinct parts. The adrenal cortex secretes several hormones, including hormones important for response to stress. The adrenal medulla, comprising the core of the gland, secretes epinephrine and norepinephrine and plays an important role in controlling the visceral accompaniments of emotion.

androgens The general name for male sex hormones. Androgens include testosterone and androsterone.

androsterone A male sex hormone whose production site is not definitely established. It seems to have the same effects as does testosterone.

autonomic nervous system The nervous system that supplies the visceral organs and is mainly responsible for the automatic responses of the body. The autonomic system is comprised of two subsystems—the sympathetic and the parasympathetic.

electroencephalogram (EEG) A record of the electrical activity of the cerebral cortex (brain waves) recorded from the outside surface of the skull. The EEG gives a measure of the organism's state of arousal or state of sleep.

endocrine system A term referring to the *ductless* glands of the body and their reactions. Ductless glands are organs of the body that manufacture chemical compounds called "hormones" and secrete them directly into the blood stream. Another name for the endocrine system is the "hormonal system."

estrogen The female sex hormone manufactured and secreted by the ovaries. It seems to be partly responsible for the growth of the female sex organs, for development of the female secondary sex characteristics, and for control of the sex drive.

gonadotropic hormone A hormone of the pituitary gland that controls, in part, the manufacture and secretion of the sex hormones of the testes and ovaries.

gonads The sex glands. In the male they are known as the "testes," in the female as the "ovaries."

hormones Chemical compounds manufactured by the endocrine glands and secreted into the blood stream. The hormones, carried by the blood stream to the visceral organs of the body, can stimulate these organs into activity or can inhibit their activity.

lateral nucleus A hypothalamic nucleus whose destruction inhibits eating.

menopause A condition occurring in women normally at about the age of fifty, at which time there is a diminution in rate of secretion of ovarian hormone, cessation of menstruation, and the beginning of the atrophy of the ovaries, uterus, mammary glands, and vagina.

osmoreceptors Postulated specialized cells in the hypothalamus presumed to be responsible for the initiation of sensory impulses evoking the sensation of thirst. The osmoreceptors are supposed to be stimulated into action when they shrink as a consequence of absolute or relative dehydration.

ovaries Female sex glands, having both glandular and nonglandular functions. Their nonglandular function is the production of ova, or eggs. Their glandular function is the manufacture and secretion of the sex hormones, among them estrogen and progesterone.

parasympathetic nervous system Part of the autonomic nervous system. The parasympathetic system supplies the visceral organs via nerve fibers from the spinal cord and is somewhat more specific in its discharge to these organs than is the sympathetic system.

pituitary gland Consists of two distinct glands. The posterior pituitary seems to be completely controlled by the hypothalamus, and its major hormone is the antidiuretic hormone. The anterior pituitary is controlled partly by the hypothalamus and partly by the other endocrine glands. It secretes six different hormones, which control, among other things, general bodily growth, secretions of the adrenal cortex, sex glands, and thyroid. It is sometimes referred to as "the master gland."

progesterone A female sex hormone produced by the ovaries. It is primarily concerned with the preparation of the uterus for pregnancy and of the breasts for lactation.

rapid eye movements (REM) Eye movements characteristic of the period of deep sleep during which dreaming takes place. It has been shown that REMs are related to dream content.

reciprocal innervation Refers to the fact that most of the visceral organs of the body are supplied by two nervous systems—the sympathetic and the parasympathetic—whose effects on any one organ are *opposite* in direction. That is, when the sympathetic accelerates action, the parasympathetic decelerates action.

secondary sex charateristics The appearance and other nonreproductive distinctive characteristics of the male and female (for example, distribution of hair, sound of voice, skeletal proportions of body, thickness of skin).

smooth muscles The muscles of the body control-ling the visceral organs.

striated muscles The skeletal muscles of the body responsible for movement of limbs, trunk, and so on. They are so called because under the mi-croscope the muscles appear to have horizontal lines running across the fibers; they are some-times also called the "skeletal muscles."

sympathetic nervous system Part of the autonomic nervous system. The sympathetic nervous sys-tem consists of two chains of ganglions running along the side of the spinal cord, and the fibers coming to and leaving these ganglia. The gan-glion cells are supplied by nerve fibers from the spinal cord, called "preganglionic" neurons; they supply, in turn, various visceral organs, through connections with the postganglionic neurons. The sympathetic nervous system is built for wide-spread discharge.

testes Male sex glands, having both glandular and nonglandular functions. Their nonglandular func-tion is the production of spermatozoa. Their glandular function is the manufacture and se-cretion of the sex hormones, among them *testosterone* (the male sex hormone) and estro-gen (the female sex hormone).

testosterone The male sex hormone, produced by the testes. It seems to be important in speeding up growth of the male sex organs, controls de-velopment of secondary sex characteristics, and helps to determine the sexual activity of the in-dividual.

thyroid gland A ductless gland whose hormone has general and specific effects. They increase metabolic action of almost all body cells, raise blood pressure, speed up heart rate, and so on. The rate of production of thyroid hormone is in part controlled by a pituitary hormone called the thyrotropic hormone.

ventromedial nucleus A hypothalamic nucleus that is involved in eating and emotional behavior. Destruction of the ventromedial nucleus results in voracious eating; it turns tame animals into savage and vicious ones.

physiology and emotion

overview / The primary centers for the physiological control of emotional behavior are in the cerebral cortex, the limbic system, the hypothalamus, and the reticular formation. The hypothalamus can initiate extremes of emotional behavior, but the cerebral cortex and the limbic system modify and inhibit its action to produce normal emotional responses.

Emotional responses are an integration of skeletal, autonomic, and glandular responses. The prominence of visceral responses in aroused emotional states has led to widespread use of such visceral measures as blood pressure, heart rate, sweat-gland response, and respiration as indexes of emotional behavior. The fact that these autonomically controlled responses are involuntary has made possible such practical applications as the use of the lie detector.

The hormones of the adrenal glands, the thyroid gland, and the pituitary gland are of special importance for emotional response. The adrenal medulla provides hormones that complement and support the action of the sympathetic nervous system in emotions. Hormones of the adrenal cortex have a critical function in the response of the organism to stressful situations. Early emotional experiences have important modifying effects on the adult response of the adrenal cortex and the adequacy of adult response to stress. Thyroid hormone controls metabolism, and its increased production during emotion produces a generally "speeded-up" organism. The pituitary or "master" gland exerts widespread influence over the endocrine system; it is particularly important in emotion because it interacts with the adrenal cortex and the thyroid gland and secretes hormones that control their functioning.

The two most prominent early physiological theories of emotion were in disagreement over the temporal sequence of bodily emotional reactions and experienced emotion. The James-Lange theory maintained that bodily reactions precede emotional experience. The Cannon-

Bard theory proposed a mechanism that argued simultaneous occurrence. The Papez-MacLean theory gives the structures of the limbic system a critical place in the mechanisms of emotion. Lindsley's activation theory stresses the role of the reticular formation in emotional response and argues for a close relationship between arousal and emotional states.

In Unit 33 we were able to describe a wide variety of emotions that man experiences—joy, fear, rage, shame, pride, love, humor, and so forth. But it will also be recalled that we found a paucity of psychological research directed at the whole gamut of the emotions. In this unit, in which our concern is with the physiological processes underlying emotions, we shall find that appropriate research has been even more limited, being restricted almost entirely to the primary emotions of fear and rage. Our first look, then, will be at the physiological mechanisms that initiate and organize these two emotions.

The Instigation and Control of Emotion

The prominence of "gut" responses in intense emotional behavior has traditionally led to an emphasis upon the viscera in discussions of emotion. As we see later in this unit, the visceral organs are indeed very much involved in emotional behavior. Evidence from brain ablation and stimulation studies indicates, however, that the initiation and control of emotional behavior occur primarily within such brain structures as the cerebral cortex, the limbic system, the hypothalamus, and the reticular formation.

Cerebral Cortex and Limbic System

In 1892, Goltz, a German physiologist, noted that dogs whose cerebral cortex had been removed surgically ("decorticate dogs") were quick to display anger and rage. This research was the starting point of a series of extirpation studies that have contributed significantly to our knowledge of the relation among the cortex, other parts of the brain, and emotion. In 1925, Cannon made similar but more extensive observations with decorticate cats, and he as well as many other investigators have confirmed Goltz's original findings. Cannon described the behavior displayed by his decorticate cats as *sham rage* and pointed out that it differed in many ways from the rage of a normal animal. Sham rage occurs in response to almost any stimulus—the gentlest of handling, even merely touching the animal's cage can provoke it. The decorticate animal will attack, but his attack is undirected; he may even bite himself! The rage is usually short-lived and ceases almost as soon as the "irritating" stimulus is removed. While it lasts, however, it seems very much like the real thing: dogs bark, growl, and bite; in cats there is erection of hair, and they hiss, spit, bite, and strike with unsheathed claws.

These findings suggest that the intact cortex inhibits a lower brain center that produces emotional responses. When the cortex is removed, all inhibitions are also removed and the lower brain center takes over. Other work, as we shall see shortly, indicates that this center is within the hypothalamus. In this view, a normal animal, although capable of exhibiting extreme emotional behavior, ordinarily inhibits these responses through the action of the cortex. A decorticate animal, released from the restraints of the cortex, will, with minimal stimulation, show an uninhibited hypothalamic emotional display. This simple interpretation was upset by a number of studies designed to test a mechanism of emotion proposed by Papez (1937). He suggested that a ring of interconnecting cortical and subcortical structures surrounding the brain stem, the *limbic system* (see Figure 37.1.), was involved in the initiation of emotional behavior.

To test whether or not the limbic system had a special involvement in emotional response,

Bard and Mountcastle (1948) removed all the cortex *except* the limbic cortex from a group of cats. These animals not only failed to show sham rage but were, in fact, extremely unresponsive to rage-provoking stimuli. They paid no attention to the hair pulling and tail pinching used in attempts to arouse them, and even very strong electric shocks evoked no signs of anger other than vocalizations and spitting. The removal of limbic structures in a second operation on these same animals turned them from placid, friendly pussies into ferocious beasts. It appears, from these data, that limbic structures inhibit the hypothalamus and that the nonlimbic cortex in turn modifies the inhibiting effects of the limbic system. This interpretation is strengthened by the fact that removal of only limbic structures or combinations of limbic structures can produce a ferocious animal.

Although our discussion shows that we have developed considerable knowledge about the interrelations of the cortex, the limbic system, and emotion, we should not think that our knowledge is complete. It is an annoying fact

for any theory that removal of the amygdala, one of the limbic structures, can produce *either* a placid *or* a ferocious animal. The conditions that lead to these opposite results are still unknown. There always seems to be one more puzzle to go for the scientist!

The Hypothalamus

In Unit 36 we described the influence of the hypothalamus upon a wide range of behaviors. Prominent among them is the action of the hypothalamus as a center for organized emotional responses. The evidence that the hypothalamus acts as a center controlling integrated emotional behavior comes from a number of sources; this evidence is abundant and convincing.

Bard and his associates, as part of an extensive program to investigate the neurophysiological basis of emotion, performed a number of experiments in which they removed from the brain different areas and combinations of areas. They found that the posterior part of the hypo-

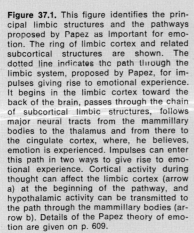
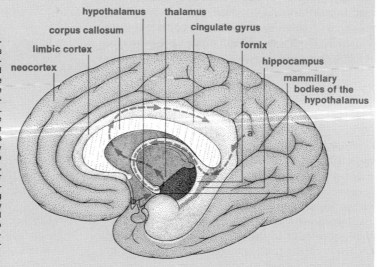

Figure 37.1. This figure identifies the principal limbic structures and the pathways proposed by Papez as important for emotion. The ring of limbic cortex and related subcortical structures are shown. The dotted line indicates the path through the limbic cortex, proposed by Papez, for impulses giving rise to emotional experience. It begins in the limbic cortex toward the back of the brain, passes through the chain of subcortical limbic structures, follows major neural tracts from the mammillary bodies to the thalamus and from there to the cingulate cortex, where, he believes, emotion is experienced. Impulses can enter this path in two ways to give rise to emotional experience. Cortical activity during thought can affect the limbic cortex (arrow a) at the beginning of the pathway, and hypothalamic activity can be transmitted to the path through the mammillary bodies (arrow b). Details of the Papez theory of emotion are given on p. 609.

hypothalamus — thalamus — cingulate gyrus — corpus callosum — fornix — limbic cortex — hippocampus — neocortex — mammillary bodies of the hypothalamus

thalamus was the critical area for integrated emotional expression. As long as this area remains, no matter how much of the brain in front of it is removed, an animal is capable of organized emotional behavior. But, if, in addition to the areas in front of it, the complete hypothalamus is removed, integration is lost. An animal in this condition will make emotional responses, but they are only partial or incomplete. Even a spinal animal can show bits and pieces of autonomic and skeletal emotional responses, but only when the hypothalamus is present does organized emotional behavior occur (see Figure 37.2.).

Complementing the findings of these ablation studies are the results of experiments using electrical stimulation of the hypothalamus in otherwise normal animals. A number of emotional responses may be evoked by stimulating the hypothalamus, but the most dramatic is the development of a completely coordinated and *directed* rage response (see Figure 37.3.). The difference between the rage shown by decorticate animals and animals whose hypothalamus is electrically stimulated is striking. One can with complete safety pull the hair or pinch the tail of a decorticate animal, for while, as we have said, he will show a complete rage response, it will not be directed at the source of annoyance, the experimenter. Usually the biting, hissing, and striking will be directed at the air in front of him. In contrast, an animal that does have an intact cortex and whose hypothalamus is electrically stimulated shows rage responses upon little or no provocation, and he will viciously and accurately attack his annoyer and continue the attack as long as stimulation is continued. The difference is not difficult to understand if one recalls the importance of the cortex to perception (see Part Two). Without the cortex an animal is not able to use the information from his sense organs to identify or to localize the experimenter as a source of annoyance or as a target for attack.

In addition to rage responses, hypothalamic stimulation produces two different patterns of *fear* responses, which can be described as flight and alarm reactions.

The effects of lesions within the hypothalamus confirm its importance to organized emotional behavior. Studies using this technique have identified a center for the inhibition of rage in addition to confirming a center for the initiation of rage. Destruction of the posterior hypothalamus, the area we found to be critical for the expression of organized emotional responses, produces an emotionally unresponsive animal, as we would expect. Destruction of the ventromedial nucleus creates a permanently vicious animal. Here we seem to have a "rage inhibitory center" (see Figure 37.3.).

Rage, then, is clearly more than a "gut reaction." A good part of the instigation, control, and coordination of intense rage responses is to be found within the brain, primarily in the cerebral cortex, the limbic system, and the hypothalamus.

Emotional Response

The familiar overworked descriptions of emotions—"screaming with rage," "frozen in terror," "fighting for life"—make clear our recognition of the overt, or skeletal, signs of emotional responses. Some autonomic emotional responses are equally familiar. Increased heart rate, rapid breathing, and a hollow feeling in the pit of the stomach have been experienced by most of us when frightened in the dark by a strange sound. Less obvious are changes in blood pressure, sweating, changes in pupil size, and flushing or paling of the skin. The autonomic responses are caused in part by the activities of the endocrine glands, which pour epinephrine and thyroid hormone (see pp. 601, 605) into the blood stream—and we are usually not aware of these activities.

So impressive are the activities of the heart, blood vessels, respiratory muscles, and secretory glands in aroused emotional states that many experimenters have attempted to measure emotion in terms of them alone. It is well,

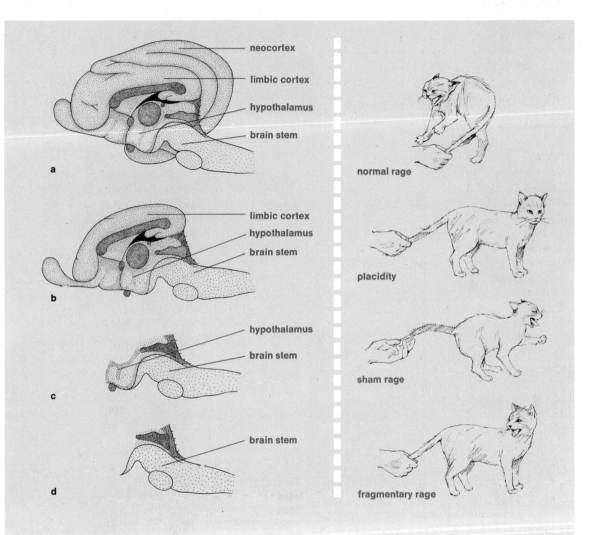

Figure 37.2. We have here a summary of the results of a number of ablation experiments on the cat. The experiments show the relationships between various brain structures and the emotional expression of rage. Cat A, a cat with an intact brain, is attacking the pinching hand with a normal rage response. Cat B has had all the neocortex removed, leaving the limbic cortex and all the subcortical structures; it shows the placid response to an annoying stimulus that is characteristic of this preparation. The only brain structures remaining in cat C are the hypothalamus and the lower structures of the brain stem. It is demonstrating a typical undirected sham rage response to a mere touch of the tail. Cat D, lacking the hypothalamus, as well as all structures above it, gives only a partial rage response to tail pinching.

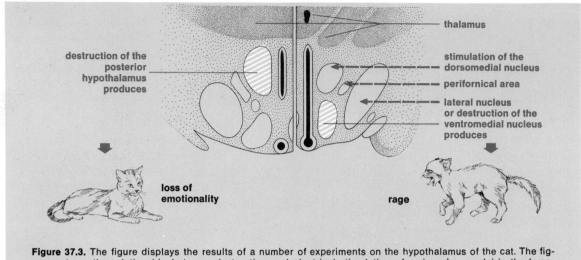

Figure 37.3. The figure displays the results of a number of experiments on the hypothalamus of the cat. The figure portrays the relationship between destruction and electrical stimulation of various key nuclei in the hypothalamus and rage.

because of this emphasis, to keep in mind the importance of skeletal responses in emotions. Emotional responses are an integration of skeletal, autonomic, and glandular responses. That many of these skeletal emotional responses differ from ordinary voluntary responses is nicely illustrated by an interesting clinical finding. One fairly common effect of brain damage is a partial paralysis that interferes with the normal *voluntary* movement of some part of the body —an arm, a foot, a hand, the face, and so on. Among the victims of this kind of paralysis are some who are quite capable of making *emotional* responses that require the use of these same "paralyzed" parts. One can, for example, find individuals who have partial paralysis of the muscles on one side of the face. These individuals have a rather peculiar lopsided look, one side of the face visibly sagging; they have difficulty speaking, lacking complete control of the muscles around the mouth. Yet, when they frown or smile, they may appear perfectly normal. The lopsided look, the muscular sag, completely disappear. Obviously the control of these

emotional responses is different from the control of voluntary responses of the same area.

Many of the visceral reactions accompanying emotional states are unobservable to the naked eye. The development of ingenious measurement instruments has made possible the detection and precise recording of many of these visceral events (see Box 135, p. 598, for some of these modern measuring devices). The study of bodily changes during emotion has many theoretical, medical, and other practical applications. Perhaps the two most commonly used (and most sensitive) measures of bodily effects of emotion are changes in the electrical characteristics of the skin and variations in blood pressure.

Galvanic Skin Response

It was early discovered that under emotional stress the electrical properties of the skin undergo change. If a very weak electrical current (one that cannot be felt) is passed through the skin and the resistance of the skin to the passage of this current is measured with a galvanometer, it is found that *under emotional stress the resistance drops*. In other words, when one is in an emotional state, the skin becomes a better conductor of electricity.

It was later found that the change in the electrical properties of the skin could be measured without passing an outside current through the skin. Stress or excitement alone can lead to a change in the *electrical potential* of the skin.

The change in skin resistance, or in electrical potential, has been known by many names, some of them still in use. Among the more common are *galvanic skin response* (abbreviated to "GSR") and psychogalvanic reflex ("PGR").

In one way or another these changes are related to sweating. As is true of most electrical conductors, the skin, when moist—when it sweats—becomes a better electrical conductor. If at such a time a current is passed through the skin, it will show lowered resistance. In the case of skin potential (in which no outside current is used) two theories have been proposed. One is that secretion of sweat brings about an electrochemical effect in the skin that produces a change in electrical potential. The other theory considers the change in electrical potential a muscular effect. As we know that every time a muscle contracts a small electrical current is created, we should find, according to this theory, that, when the smooth muscles of the sweat glands contract, the "skin" potential also changes. In other words, what we record when we measure skin potentials is really the potentials created by the contraction of the smooth muscles of the sweat glands. Whichever theory is correct (or even if both theories are sound), the action of the sweat glands is obviously involved in the GSR.

Physiological and anatomical evidence indicates that the sweat glands are supplied exclusively by the sympathetic nervous system. Therefore, any time there is a change in the GSR, there must have been activity in the sympathetic nervous system. Because the sympathetic nervous system is thrown into action

when the individual is under stress, a change in the GSR indicates emotional arousal. It is for this reason that the GSR has become such a popular measure of emotionality. It is especially valuable because the subject is not conscious of the changes in his skin, cannot do anything to inhibit them, and for this reason would find it difficult to deceive the instrument.

A major difficulty with the GSR as a measure of emotionality stems from the firm interrelations between the cerebrospinal and autonomic nervous systems. Almost any sensory stimulus (for example, flashing a light in the eye) or concentrated mental activity may also be accompanied by changes in GSR. The activity of the autonomic nervous system and changes in the GSR are not, then, restricted to "emotional states." Whether we are experiencing the emotions of love or rage or showing mental alertness on a high intellectual plane, our brain and sweat glands are involved.

Blood Pressure

The heart contracts and expands as its muscles contract and expand rhythmically. As the blood leaves the heart, it is pumped out in spurts into the constraining arteries. The pressure of the blood as it courses through the circulatory system can change, and with astonishing rapidity, when a person becomes emotional. The simplest device for measuring the pressure of the blood flow is called a *sphygmomanometer*.

The regulation of blood flow and blood pressure is partially controlled through various hormonal elements secreted from the adrenals and partially through the movements of the skeletal muscles that help to force blood through some of the peripheral vessels (for example, stamping our feet to keep warm). The major controlling mechanism, however, is the autonomic nervous system.

Most of the blood vessels of the body are supplied mainly by the sympathetic nerves, although a few are supplied by both the sympathetic and the parasympathetic nerves. The

Box 135

Bioelectric Measurement

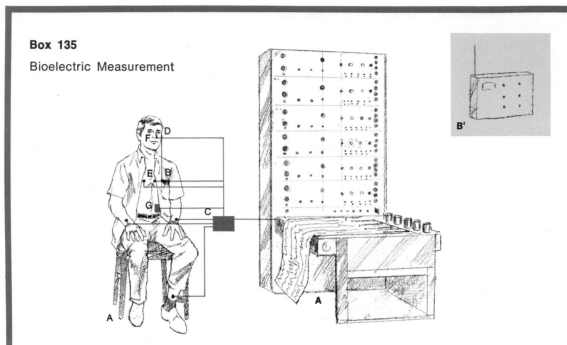

Early physiological measuring instruments depended largely upon relatively simple mechanical systems. A good example is the stethoscope, which detects the sound of the heart beat with a diaphragm and transmits it to the ears through two air-filled tubes. The development of sensitive and powerful amplifiers, the miniaturization of components, and the appearance of radiotelemetry capable of transmitting signals both from within and from outside the body have revolutionized much of modern biophysical measurement. Although the family physician still uses the stethoscope, most modern physiological measurement depends upon the detection of changes in electrical potentials. These potentials may be produced within the body, or an instrument may make use of a physiological effect (for example, a movement) to produce or modify an electrical potential. In either case the signals are sent to an amplifier, and the amplified signal can then be used to make a temporary or a permanent record of the events. In the figure, the polygraph A illustrates a standard amplifier-recorder combination. It is connected directly to the subject by wires and amplifies the signals coming over these wires. The implified signals control marker pens that make a permanent record on a moving roll of paper. The same end is achieved somewhat differently by the radiotelemetry system B-B'. The subject carries a small radio transmitter B, which transmits signals to a

autonomic nerves can do two things. They can change the diameter of the arteries (relaxing or constricting the smooth muscles that surround them) and they can alter the force and rate of the heart stroke. Both effects will change the blood pressure and control the supply of blood

to various parts of the body. By constricting the blood vessels in some parts of the body (say, in the stomach walls) and dilating the blood vessels in other parts (say, in the limbs), they can cause the blood to flow rapidly and in large quantities from the constricted parts of

receiver B'. Here they are amplified and can be used to control any kind of recorder. In our illustration a permanent record is being made on a magnetic tape.

Our subject is "wearing" a number of instruments in order to illustrate various kinds of devices used in bioelectric measurement. The three electrodes from C pick up the electrocardiogram or EKG. This widely used device detects electric potentials originating in the heart and gives not only the heart rate but also a detailed picture of each heart beat. The EKG has many uses both in research and in medical practice. In hospitals, for example, it is an extremely important tool for diagnosing faulty heart functioning; it also can be connected to an alarm system so that, if a patient's heart behaves abnormally or stops, an alarm will sound calling a nurse or physician.

Another measure of heart rate is given by the photoplethysmograph D worn on the subject's left ear. This consists of a very small infrared light bulb on one side of the ear lobe and an equally small photodetector on the other. Light must pass through the flesh and the blood vessels of the ear lobe to activate the photodetector. When a pulse beat reaches the ear lobe, more blood goes through the vessels, expanding them, and as a result less light reaches the detector. The instrument is sensitive enough to detect the differences in light transmission during the waxing and waning of the pulse, and the photodetector sends corresponding electric signals. We have arbitrarily connected the photoplethysmograph to the radiotelemeter. It is understood, of course, that the signals from any of the "detectors" could be sent either by radiotelemetry or over wires.

Instruments E and F measure respiration. The impedance pneumograph E is probably the method more frequently used. It consists of two electrodes, one attached to each side of the rib cage. A very small alternating current is sent between the electrodes. As the chest expands and contracts, the resistance to the alternating current (impedance) changes, causing changes in the electrical signal.

F is a thermistor clipped to the inside of the nostril. A thermistor is simply a small resistor made of a material that changes electrical resistance over a very wide range as its temperature changes. A standard current is passed through the thermistor, and temperature changes are reflected in changes in current flow. It can be used to measure respiration rate because, as the subject inhales, he cools the thermistor, and, as he exhales, he warms it. Thermistors have been used in many other applications to measure both internal and external body temperature.

The device we see near the subject's stomach, G, is the *receiver* of another radiotelemetry system. We cannot see the transmitter because the subject has swallowed it! It is now possible to make radio transmitters the size of a large pill, and they are, in fact, called "radio pills." Each radio pill has a special sensitivity; our subject could thus have swallowed a pill to measure the amount of acid in his stomach, one to measure the temperature, or a third to measure the pressure in the stomach. Radio pills obviously simplify the problem of measurement in the human digestive tract, as well as in the relatively inaccessible body cavities of experimental animals.

P. H. VENABLES and I. MARTIN, eds. 1967. *Manual of Psycho-physiological Methods* (New York: Wiley).

the system to the dilated parts. In this way the most active tissues (the muscles of the limbs when one is frightened and turns to run away from a threatening situation) receive a quickly mobilized and plentiful supply of blood—just when they need it most.

It is precisely because of these effects that changes in blood pressure and blood flow are considered the best bodily indicators of the preparatory or *emergency* functions performed by the autonomic nervous system. Many other autonomic effects of emotion can also be inter-

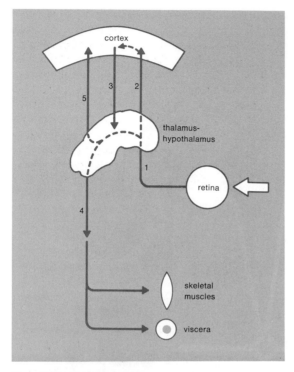

Figure 37.6. Diagrammatic representation of the Cannon-Bard theory. For explanation see pp. 608–9.
W. B. Cannon, "Again the James-Lange and the Thalamic Theories of Emotion," *Psychological Review*, 38, (1931), 281–95; adapted by permission of the American Psychological Association.

generally accepted view that, when we perceive an emotional stimulus, we first experience the emotion and that this experience is followed by our bodily reactions. James describes this "incorrect" view for us: "Common-sense says, we lose our fortune, are sorry and weep; we meet a bear, are frightened and run; we are insulted by a rival, are angry and strike."

In contrast to the "common-sense" view, the James-Lange theory asserts that when we perceive an emotional stimulus we immediately respond with the muscular and glandular responses characteristic of emotion and appropriate to the situation. It is when the feedback from these emotional responses arrives at the cortex that we *experience* the emotion. James' presentation has become classic.

"My theory . . . is that *the bodily changes follow directly the perception of the exciting fact, and that our feeling of the same changes as they occur is the emotion*. . . . We feel sorry because we cry, angry because we strike, afraid because we tremble, and not that we cry, strike or tremble, because we are sorry, angry, or fearful, as the case may be."

The James-Lange theory, then, gives the bodily changes (skeletal and smooth-muscle effects) priority over conscious awareness as far as temporal sequence is concerned.

The Cannon-Bard Theory

In 1927, Cannon suggested an alternative theory. Cannon's theory was taken up by another physiologist, Bard, who revised Cannon's formulation and then did much experimental work in support of it. This theory, known as the *Cannon-Bard theory,* differs from the James-Lange theory in two important ways: First, it proposes a different time order for the emotional experience and the bodily responses, and, second, it introduces the thalamic-hypothalamic area as important to emotion.

We can learn the essential features of the theory by following the effects of an emotion-producing stimulus as the theory describes them (see Figure 37.6.). Emotional stimuli, like all stimuli, produce sensory neural impulses that follow the normal sensory routes to the thalamus (path 1) and through the thalamus to the cortex (path 2). But, as the emotional impulses pass through the thalamus, they stimulate fibers going to the hypothalamus, and the whole thalamic-hypothalamic area is thrown into a *state of readiness* to initiate an emotional pattern of skeletal and visceral responses. The cortex responds to the incoming "emotional" impulses by releasing its normal inhibition of the lower centers (path 3) (see p. 592). The thalamic-hypothalamic area, having been "primed" to respond and now released from inhibitory influences, simultaneously sends out two sets of neural messages. A pattern of neural firings goes to the skeletal muscles and viscera to produce the bodily expression of the emotion (path 4). Another set of impulses, reflecting this same pattern, goes to the cortex (path 5). When these latter impulses combine with the original sensory input, the emotion is experienced. According to this theory, the emotional feeling and bodily reactions occur *simultaneously,* and both are initiated by lower brain centers.

The Papez-MacLean Theory

The theory of emotion Papez presented in 1937 focused a new and strong interest on the place of the *limbic system* in emotions (see Figure 37.1.). Papez accepted the hypothalamus as a center for the integration and initiation of the *bodily* expression of emotion, but he argued for the limbic system as the site of emotional *experience*. He described the specific path that neural impulses of emotional stimuli would follow from the hypothalamus to the limbic cortex (cingulate gyrus), where the emotional experience arises. He considered the cingulate gyrus to be the reception center for emotional responses from the hypothalamus in the same way that the occipital lobe of the cortex is the reception area for visual impulses. The theory was developed from anatomical and clinical data, some of which have been considered quite questionable, and it has not received wide acceptance among psychologists. It has generated a great deal of important research, however, and, despite the fact that we now know that some of the details of the theory are wrong, it has gained a permanent place for the limbic system in all serious discussions of the problems of emotions.

MacLean strengthened the case for implicating the limbic system in emotion by emphasizing that the only cortical representation of visceral processes is in the limbic cortex. Heart, respiratory, circulatory, and sweat responses are unaffected by stimulation or ablation of the nonlimbic cortex. These same visceral responses *are* affected by stimulation or by destruction of considerable portions of the limbic cortex. He revised Papez's picture of the structures to be included in the limbic system on the basis of more recent knowledge and argued for the amygdala and the hippocampus as more central to emotional experience than the cingulate gyrus: Thus the *Papez-MacLean theory* arose (see Figure 37.7.). Although the importance of the limbic system for emotions is now unquestioned (the use of MacLean's term "visceral brain" for the system is now widely used), the details of its functioning are still far from clear.

The Lindsley Activation Theory

In 1951, Lindsley, one of the early workers in the area of the reticular formation (see p. 255) and arousal presented an "activation" theory that he felt could apply to emotional behavior, sleep-wakefulness, and certain problems of abnormal behavior (see Figure 37.8.). In applying his theory to emotions he stresses two points. First, when the anterior end of the brain-stem reticular formation is destroyed, eliminating reticular stimulation of the brain, the behavioral picture is, as he says, "the antithesis of emotional excitement or arousal, namely, apathy, lethargy, somnolence, catalepsy, etc." Second, stimulation of the lower brain-stem reticular formation causes overt skeletal and visceral emotional responses. To strengthen the case that the same processes cause arousal and emotion he argues for a continuum of parallel arousal and emotional states. For example, when one first awakes, the quiet drowsy state is one of little arousal and is completely unemotional. At the other extreme, rage represents a highly emotional state and one of high arousal. Although the extreme cases cited seem clear, it is not clear that the proposed continuum exists. In emotional behavior the implication of the reticular formation with its intimate connection to the hypothalamus, its importance in controlling the state of arousal

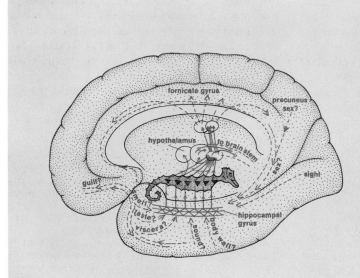

Figure 37.7. This diagram by MacLean presents a rather light view of part of his theory, but does have serious aspects. The many arrows going to the hippocampal gyrus are designed to emphasize that this limbic cortex may be the receptor area for all kinds of emotional stimuli. The little sea horse represents the hippocampus (the Latin word for sea horse), and MacLean suggests that it may be a motor area for emotional responses. The hippocampal gyrus and the hippocampus are thus assumed to have primary responsibility for the reception of emotion producing stimuli and the initiation of emotional responses. The remaining pathways are as given by Papez (see Figure 37.1.).

P. D. MacLean, "Psychosomatic Disease and the Visceral Brain, Recent Developments Bearing on the Papez Theory of Emotion," *Psychosomatic Medicine*, 11 (1949), 338–53; adapted by permission of Paul B. Hoeber, Inc.

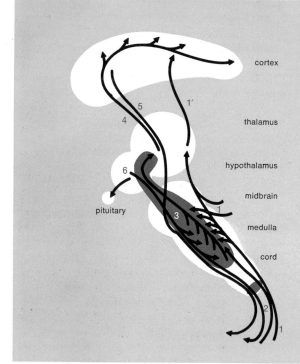

Figure 37.8. The diagram presents some of the principal nervous structures and probable pathways involved in emotional behavior, as given by Lindsley. Since the reticular formation (r.f.) arouses the cortex, it necessarily occupies a central position in Lindsley's "activation" theory of emotion. The diagram portrays the close connections among the reticular formation and sensory input, bodily and visceral responses, and hypothalamic activity. The primary route for sensory information from the body is over path (1) to the thalamus, where it is relayed to the cortex via the thalamic cortical projections (1'). Major sensory input to the r.f. (the dark green area) is indicated by the many collaterals running to it from the primary path. A separate path (2) is provided for sensations from the viscera to affect the r.f. The arousal effect of the r.f. upon the cortex depends upon upward pathways within the r.f. (3) and a path making possible the diffuse projection of r.f. impulses from the thalamus to the cortex (4). Another path (5) represents the major route for impulses from the cortex to the striped muscles. Influence of the r.f. on emotional bodily responses can occur where this path travels through the r.f. Hypothalamic activity feeds into the r.f. over still another route (6) to affect r.f. functioning, and at the same time the r.f. can affect hypothalamically controlled visceral emotional responses by acting on this path.

D. B. Lindsley, "Emotion," in S. S. Stevens, ed., *Handbook of Experimental Psychology* (1951); adapted by permission of John Wiley & Sons, Inc.

of the organism, and its broad sensory input is logical, but widespread acceptance of the *Lindsley activation theory* waits upon further experimental support.

The research laboratory has provided us with many "facts" about the physiology of emo-tions, but in physiology as in psychology (see Unit 35, p. 255) we are far from a useful set of integrating concepts that can be called a "the-ory." And this lack is true even when we restrict ourselves (as we have in this unit) to the emotions of fear and rage.

Glossary

adrenocorticotropic hormone (ACTH)—A hormone of the pituitary gland that controls the manufac-ture and secretion of the hormones (steroids) of the adrenal cortex.

antidiuretic hormone A hormone secreted by the posterior pituitary gland. It functions primarily to control the rate and volume of urination. Emo-tional upset may inhibit secretion of the hor-mone, resulting in frequent and excessive urina-tion.

Cannon-Bard theory A theory proposed by Cannon and modified somewhat by Bard to the effect that the emotional feeling and the body reaction occur simultaneously and that both are initiated by the lower brain centers of the thalamus and hypothalamus. This theory is to be contrasted with the James-Lange theory.

cretinism A pathological condition caused by ex-treme and chronic hypothyroidism during early life. The individual is dwarfed, and mental growth is retarded. Very early thyroid treatment of the cretin child usually results in normal phys-cal and mental growth.

emergency theory of emotions The theory that states that the evolutionary role of the emotions, with their accompanying visceral reactions, is facilitation of emergency action in times of dan-ger.

epinephrine, norepinephrine Two chemically simi-lar hormones secreted by the adrenal medulla. These hormones have somewhat different effects on the visceral organs, but in general their com-bined effect is the same as the effect of stimu-lating the visceral organs via the sympathetic nervous system; they are therefore said to "mimic" the sympathetic nervous system.

galvanic skin response Change in the electrical potential of the skin. This change often occurs during emotional excitement. It is known by many other names, among them the "psycho-galvanic reflex" (PGR).

hyperthyroidism A condition of continuous exces-sive thyroid hormone production.

hypothyroidism A condition of chronic insufficient thyroid hormone production. Extreme hypothy-roidism before birth and during infancy and childhood results in a pathological condition called cretinism.

James-Lange theory A theory independently pro-posed by William James of America and Carl Lange of Denmark to the effect that bodily changes precede the feeling of emotion and that it is the perception of bodily changes that is the emotional feeling. This theory is to be contrasted with the Cannon-Bard theory.

limbic system A ring of interconnecting cortical and subcortical structures surrounding the brain stem. This system contains the only cortical rep-resentation of visceral processes and is a central feature of the Papez-MacLean theory.

Lindsley activation theory A theory that stresses the function of the reticular formation in emo-tion and the close relationship between states of arousal and emotion.

Papez-MacLean theory A theory proposed by Papez, who emphasized the limbic system as the site of emotional experience. Its modification by Mac-Lean revised the structures to be included in the system and focused on different structures within the system.

sham rage The "anger" or "rage" responses shown by decorticate animals when touched or handled. These responses are so called because they are not evoked by the usual situational determinants of rage, are not directed against any specific target, and cease almost as soon as stimulation of the animal is withdrawn.

sphygmomanometer A device for measuring the systolic and diastolic pressure of blood flow in a major artery. Systolic pressure is the maximum pressure shown by the blood during the contrac-tion phase of the heart; diastolic is the minimum pressure during the expansion phase.

thyrotropic hormone A hormone of the pituitary gland that controls, in part, the manufacture and secretion of thyroid hormones.

Suggestions for Further Reading

Motivation and Emotion

COFER, C. H., and M. H. APPLEY. 1964. *Motivation: Theory and Research.* New York: Wiley.

A thorough and critical review of the broad field of motivation and one of the standard references for this complex and variegated topic.

DARWIN, C. 1965. Paperback. *Expression of the Emotions in Man and Animals.* Chicago: University of Chicago Press. Originally published 1872.

A classic discussion of the problem, significant in the development of the study of animal behavior.

LORENZ, K. 1966. *On Aggression.* New York: Harcourt.

A fascinating essay on the instinctual roots of one of the primary drives by an eminent naturalist and ethologist.

MASLOW, A. H. 1962. *Toward a Psychology of Being.* Princeton: Van Nostrand.

One of the earlier and more eloquent exponents of the view that human motivations are "something more" than biological deficiencies. This work in fact contains the outlines of a theory of personality based upon Maslow's rather novel motivational views.

Physiology of Motivation and Emotion

DEUTSCH, J. A., and D. DEUTSCH. 1966. *Physiological Psychology.* Homewood, Ill.: Dorsey.

Contains a good presentation of the physiology of motivational and emotional processes.

THOMPSON, R. F. 1967. *Foundations of Physiological Psychology.* New York: Harper.

A first-class general textbook, thorough and up to date.

WILLIAMS, R. J. 1956. *Biochemical Individuality.* New York: Wiley.

A comprehensive summary of individual differences in the hormonal composition of man, written by a biochemist who has pioneered in this study and who has initiated the concept of "chemical anthropology."

part five
the individual

UNIT 3

psychological
measurement

overview / Statistical treatment of data obtained from psychological measurement procedures serves a number of essential purposes. Frequency distributions and various measures of central tendency and dispersion provide informative descriptive summaries of individual differences in psychological characteristics as they occur in the population. Psychological measurement, like all measurement, depends of course upon available scales for quantifying individual differences, and the nature of psychological characteristics almost always prevents the use of scales with absolute zero points and equal units. Typically, our statements about individual differences must be couched in terms of relative values; that is, rather than determining absolute amounts of the given quantity, we can rank individuals only along a given psychological dimension. Even with such measurement, however, it remains possible to evaluate the extent of the relationship between any pair of variables, and we do so by means of correlation. Correlations tell us the extent to which a change in one characteristic is associated with a change in another, but, by themselves, they cannot specify which is cause and which is effect. That relationship is a matter of interpretation; it is a logical or psychological task, not a statistical one.

All measurement involves some degree of error. There is the error resulting from inconsistency with repeated measures, either in the instrument or in the characteristic being measured. Here we have a matter of the reliability of measurement. Validity, by comparison, refers to the extent to which the instrument measures what we intend it to measure; if it falls short in this respect, we have an error in validity. A third form of error is sampling error, by which we mean the imperfection arising from the hard fact that we can measure only samples from a population, not all individuals composing it. By assuring that these samples are drawn from the population in an unbiased manner, and through the application of various principles of mathematical probability, it is possible to estimate the extent of sampling error. From this point we can go on to make statements about the confidence that can be placed in whatever conclusions we reach from the statistical analysis of psychological measurement data.

The scientific study, analysis, and understanding of many of the problems generated by the fact of ubiquitous individual differences cannot be undertaken unless we first have some way of *measuring* these individual differences—whether differences of intelligence, abilities, personality, or attitudes. And the scientific usefulness of any measurement hinges upon its reliability and its validity. With reliable and valid measurement techniques we can discuss rationally some of the bitterly fought social questions of the day. Without these statistical tools we cannot understand the scientific evidence on these problems, and we can only revert to the same dreary prejudices and arguments that have held sway for so long.

The word *statistics* is often taken to mean simple enumeration. The number of people killed on our highways annually or the number of births per year are the kinds of things that are usually called "statistics." But enumeration of events makes up only a very small part of statistics. The major part is made up of carefully worked-out *methods of analyzing numerical data.* Statistical methods permit us to summarize such data, to assess their reliability and validity, to generalize from observed events to new events. Statistical methods, properly used, are among the most powerful analytical tools of physics, astronomy, medicine, genetics, psychology, economics, sociology, political science, business, and almost every other human enterprise whose data can be stated in numbers. An understanding of simple statistics is almost as necessary for modern man as is the ability to read and write. And for the study of individual differences among men it is, of course, of absolute importance.

Quantifying Individual Differences

Our first task is to quantify the degree of individual differences. We need measurement techniques that will give us *numerical* answers to the questions we shall ask about individual differences. The statistical operations that we must perform in order to obtain numerical answers are very much the same whether we are concerned with individual differences in personality or individual differences in height and weight. Let us therefore start our discussion of statistical procedures with the measurement of individual differences in height and weight. This problem is relatively simple because our units of measurement (inches, pounds) are already familiar to us. We can then apply what we learn here to the more complex problems involved in the measurement of intelligence, personality, and attitudes.

Frequency Distribution

Entering the University of Washington in 1923–1924 were 629 freshmen, and in due course they were weighed and measured. Their weights were recorded to the nearest full pound, and their heights to the nearest half-inch. The shortest freshman was 60.5 inches tall; the tallest, 76 inches. The lightest weighed 100 pounds; the heavyweight tipped the scales at 216 pounds. Here, then, are 1,258 numbers—inches and pounds—telling us a story of individual differences. If we are to read and understand this story, we must arrange these numbers in a simple and orderly way. The first step is to arrange them in *frequency tables.*

A *frequency table* is just what its name im-

Table 38.1.
Frequency Distribution of Heights of Entering
Freshmen, University of Washington, 1923–24

INCHES	NUMBER
76.0–75.0	3
74.5–73.5	5
73.0–72.0	43
71.5–70.5	64
70.0–69.0	148
68.5–67.5	156
67.0–66.0	115
65.5–64.5	51
64.0–63.0	33
62.5–61.5	8
61.0–60.0	3
	$N = \overline{629}$

Tables 38.1.–38.11 adapted by permission from G. I. Gavett, *A First Course in Statistical Method;* Copyright 1925 by McGraw-Hill Book Company, Inc.

Table 38.2.
Frequency Distribution of Weights of En
Freshmen, University of Washington, 1923

POUNDS	N
220–210	
209–199	3
198–188	5
187–177	16
176–166	35
165–155	82
154–144	129
143–133	162
132–122	138
121–111	44
110–100	14
	$N = \overline{629}$

(Gavett, 1925)

plies—a table that tells us how frequently certail values occur. When dealing with large numbers of measurements, it is usually desirable to *group* the individual values into equal *class intervals* and to specify the number of cases that fall within each given class interval. For example, from the array of data in Table 38.1., we can see that heights between 71.5 and 70.5 inches occurred 64 times among the 629 freshmen, whereas heights between 68.5 and 67.5 occurred 156 times.

A graph has many perceptual advantages over a table. We can transform frequency tables into frequency graphs. There are two commonly used types of frequency graphs: *histograms* and *frequency curves.*

Figures 38.1. and 38.2. show how Tables 38.1. and 38.2. look when made into histograms. Here the measurements are indicated along the horizontal base lines, and frequencies are indicated along the vertical axes. Figures 38.3. and 38.4. show the same data as frequency curves (or, more technically, "frequency polygons"). The only difference between histograms and frequency curves is that, in constructing a frequency curve, instead of representing the data

with a bar we place a point in the middle of each interval at the appropriate frequency value; then we connect these points.

We now have a useful tool for describing the distribution of individual differences. Human traits, capacities, and behavior are distributed in many different ways. The *shape* of the frequency curve can tell us several interesting things about the nature of the individual differences portrayed. Sometimes the curve looks like an L, sometimes it looks like a rectangle, and sometimes it is so irregular that it defies simple description (see Figure 38.5.). The shape most commonly found, however looks somewhat like Figures 38.3. and 38.4.

The curves in Figures 38.3. and 38.4. can be described as more or less symmetrical: high toward the middle and tapering off gradually at each end. The curve for freshmen heights, however, is more symmetrical than that for their weights. A curve that departs from the symmetrical shape is called a "skewed curve." Because curves can depart from perfect symmetry to a greater or lesser degree, we can speak of "degree of *skewness*" of a curve. The symmetry, or the degree of skewness of a fre-

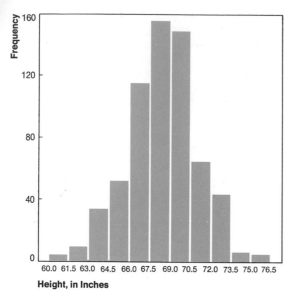

Figure 38.1. Histogram of the distribution of heights among the 629 freshman entering the University of Washington in 1923–1924.

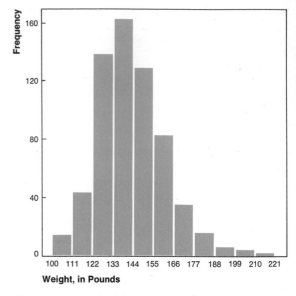

Figure 38.2. Histogram of the distribution of weights among the 629 freshmen entering the University of Washington, 1923–1924.

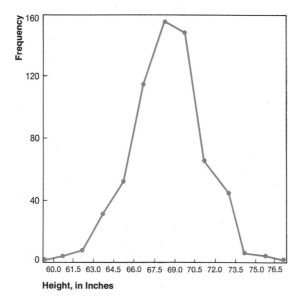

Figure 38.3. Frequency curve for the data of Table 38.1. Each point is placed in the *middle* of the interval.

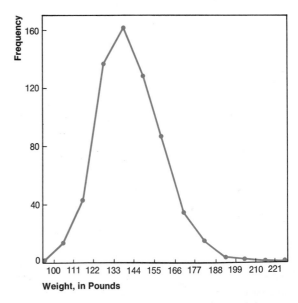

Figure 38.4. Frequency curve for the data of Table 38.2. As in Figure 38.3., each point is placed in the middle of the interval.

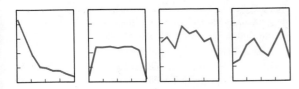

Figure 38.5. Four infrequently found shapes of distribution curves.

quency distribution curve, plays a very important part in statistical analysis of data.

Almost all measurements of behavior, learning performance, memory, intelligence, or sensory capacity give skewed frequency distribution curves. This basic fact has significant implications for our understanding of the nature of individual differences among men. For one thing, as we shall soon see, it emphasizes the caution with which we should use such concepts as "the average man" or "average intelligence."

Measures of Central Tendency

The word "average" is used by many of us as a synonym for "typical," "most frequent," or "representative." All these words refer to some kind of *central tendency*—a middle value between two extremes. When we attempt to give these words exact mathematical meaning, however, we find that they are synonymous only when the distribution curve is symmetrical. These "averages" can mean quite different things when the distribution curve is skewed—and we have just pointed out that almost all measurements of behavior yield skewed curves.

Mean, Mode, Median There are three frequently used mathematical measures of central tendency. First, there is the familiar arithmetical *mean*. It is the arithmetical sum of all the values in a distribution divided by the number of cases. Put as a formula, it is written

$$M = \frac{\Sigma X}{N}.$$

M stands for the arithmetical mean, the Greek capital letter Σ for "sum of," X for the individual values, and N for the number of cases. The 629 freshmen thus weighed, all told, 89,475 pounds. The ΣX is therefore 89,475; N is 629; and M, the arithmetical mean, is found by dividing ΣX by N, which gives us 142.25 pounds. Rounding this figure off to the nearest pound, we get 142 pounds. The same kind of calculation for freshman heights gives us an arithmetical mean of 68.0 inches.

The second measure of central tendency is the *mode*. When we say that Jim McGraw is a freshman of "average height," we may mean that Jim's height is that which occurs most frequently among freshmen. This meaning of "average" (the typical) is quite common. We can get a good estimate of the modes for the freshmen's heights and weights from either the histograms or the frequency curves. The histograms (Figures 38.1. and 38.2.) suggest that the mode for height will fall somewhere in the class interval between 67.5 and 68.5 inches (as can also be seen from Table 38.1. and as is represented in Figure 38.1. by the bar on the 67.5–69.0 position) and that the mode for weight will be between 133 and 143 pounds. But we can obtain a closer approximation of the modes. We assume that they will fall halfway along their respective modal class intervals. This will give us 68.0 inches for height (halfway between 67.5 and 68.5 inches) and 138 pounds for weight (halfway between 133 and 143 pounds).

The third measure is called the *median*. When we say that Tony Morales is of "average" height, we may mean that he is neither short nor tall but exactly in the middle. For example, if the 629 freshmen were lined up in order of height, with the shortest man at one end and the tallest at the other, Morales would be the 315th man—314 are shorter and 314 taller. His height would be called the "median height." It is a simple matter to array, count up, and find the median of a distribution. Doing so, with our material, we find the median for weight (rounded off) to be 141 pounds, for

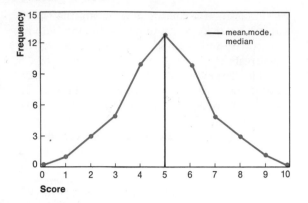

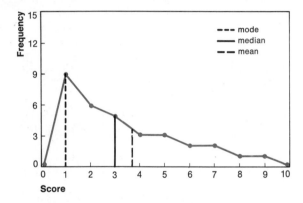

Figure 38.6. These two curves, one symmetrical and one skewed, indicate the different locations of the three measures of central tendency. Note that in the symmetrical curve the mean, mode, and median must be at the same point (value 5), whereas in the skewed curve they occupy three different points: The mode has a value of 1, the median of 3, and the mean of about 3.8.

Table 38.3.
The "Average Freshman" as a Function of the Central-Tendency Measure Used

MEASURE USED	HEIGHT	WEIGHT
Arithmetic Mean	68.0 inches	142 pounds
Mode	68.0 inches	138 pounds
Median	68.0 inches	141 pounds

(Gavett, 1925)

close to a symmetrical shape, whereas for weight the curve is definitely skewed. Figure 38.6. makes it clear why the shapes of the distribution curves result in these differences.

The meaning of "average man" or "average intelligence," therefore, may refer to any one of three different measures of central tendency, each with a different value and each mathematically correct. Each measure has certain advantages and certain disadvantages. The arithmetical mean is strongly influenced by the values of the extreme items, whereas the mode and the median are not. And sometimes the extreme values are "unnatural," and their full influence should not be allowed play. For example, suppose four students earn scores of 75, 80, 80, and 85 on an examination. The mean, mode, and median for this group are each 80. Now suppose a fifth student joins the group— a student who had overslept and comes late to the examination—and suppose he earns only 15 points. The mean of this group of five is now 67; the mode and median, however, remain at 80. To say that this group of five "averaged" 67 seems a bit misleading. This low average is caused by the accidental fault of one man. If we wish to get an average that will reflect every score including the extremes, we use the arithmetic mean; if we wish one that will not be influenced by extreme scores, we use either the mode or the median.

If all we know about a group is its average, our best guess of what the group is like would have to be stated in terms of the average. But doing so can sometimes lead to serious errors. for example, suppose we have two sets of scores made by two groups of contestants in a dart-

height (rounded off) the median is 68.0 inches.

We now have three different "average freshmen" entering the University of Washington in 1923, as indicated in Table 38.3. Notice that the "average" weight varies with the measure used, whereas for height all three measures give the same value. The reason for this difference between weight and height stems from the fact that the distribution curve for height is fairly

throwing game: 8, 8, 9, 9, 9, 9, 10, 10 and 3, 5, 7, 9, 9, 11, 13, 15. Both distributions are symmetrical, and for both groups the average is 9, whether measured by the mean, the mode, or the median. It is clear, however, that the two groups are quite dissimilar in one very important respect. In the first group the scores cluster closely together; in the second, the individual scores are widely scattered or dispersed. An average is not enough; we must also have information on the degree of dispersion of the scores in the group. Measures of dispersion give us information about extent of individual differences.

Measures of Dispersion

For a quick, qualitative impression of the degree of *dispersion,* a look at the frequency-distribution curves is usually enough. For example, in Figure 38.7. are two distributions with the same averages but different dispersions. It is obvious that distribution *a* has a smaller dispersion about the average than does distribution *b* and that therefore the average is more representative of *a* than of *b*.

If we wish to state the degree of dispersion more precisely in *numerical* terms, we must use one of the many available quantitative measures of dispersion. Let us consider some of the more common ones.

Range The *range,* or the distance between the highest and lowest scores, is the simplest numerical measure of dispersion. To return to our dart-throwing scores, the range for the first set of scores is thus 2 (that is, 10 minus 8); for the second set it is 12 (15 minus 3). These ranges suggest that the degree of individual differences is greater for the second group than for the first.

For many purposes, and with many distributions, the range is an adequate measure of dispersion and tells us what we wish to know. It is too easily influenced by a single extreme value, however. For example, let us suppose

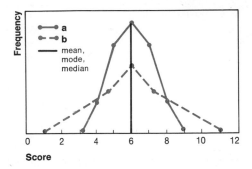

Figure 38.7. Two distribution curves, both symmetrical, both having the same mean, median, and mode but differing in dispersion. The scores of curve b are obviously more scattered (have greater dispersion) than are those of curve a.

that in 1923 a basketball star, who was seven feet one inch tall, had decided to enter the University of Washington. Because he would have been only one freshman among 630, he would have affected the mean height very little —in fact, when it was rounded to the nearest inch, not at all. He would, however, have changed the range considerably, as shown in Table 38.4.

Clearly, a measure of dispersion so unstable that it can be seriously changed (from 15.5 to 24.5) by one score out of 630 cannot be a very good measure of the degree of dispersion of scores or individual differences for the entire group. Because of this and other considerations, slightly more complicated but more stable measures of dispersion have been developed.

Table 38.4.
Freshmen Heights With and Without Hypothetical Basketball Star

MEASURES	WITH THE STAR	WITHOUT THE STAR
N (Number of students)	630	629
M (Arithmetic mean)	68.0 inches	68.0 inches
Tallest man	85.0 "	76.0 "
Shortest man	60.5 "	60.5 "
Range	24.5 "	15.5 "

(Gavett, 1925)

Average Deviation We can minimize the influence of a single extreme score by calculating a dispersion measure that takes account of every score in the distribution, not just the two extremes. To do this we first determine by how much *each* score differs from the group average, and then we can calculate the *average* of these differences to get a simple measure of dispersion. Let us return to our dart-throwing example.

There are eight scores in each group. The arithmetic mean of each distribution is 9. Now let us see how much each individual's score differs from the arithmetic mean of his group *without* regard to sign, that is, whether below or above the mean. The values for these individual deviations are listed in the *d* columns of Table 38.5.

In group II we find the score of 3 deviates from the group mean by 6 points, the score of 5 by 4 points, and so on. If we sum the individual deviations, we get a total of 4 for the first group and 24 for the second group. Therefore the *average deviation* for the eight scores in group I is .50 (4 divided by 8). For group II, the average deviation is 3.00. The scores of the second group have a larger average deviation (are more widely dispersed) than the scores of the first group.

The formula for the average deviation is simply

$$A.D. = \frac{\Sigma d}{N}.$$

A.D. stands for "average deviation," Σd for the sum of the individual deviations from the group mean, and *N* for the total number of cases.

Standard Deviation A more useful measure of dispersion is the *standard deviation*. The logic of the standard deviation is similar to that of the average deviation. Again we obtain the individual deviations from the mean. But this time we square each of the deviations, sum the squared deviations, and divide by the number of cases. The reason for squaring the deviations before getting their average lies in certain mathematical considerations that need not concern us here. Because we squared the individual deviations, however, we end with a dispersion measure expressed in squared units instead of in the original units (for example, in "inches squared" instead of in "inches"). If we wish to express the dispersion measure in terms of the original units, all we need to do is take the square root of the result.

This final result, the standard deviation, is usually symbolized by the letters *S.D.* or by the Greek letter sigma (σ), and its formula is

$$\sigma = \sqrt{\frac{d^2}{N}}. \quad \text{erratum}$$

Returning again to our dart-throwing example, we would calculate the σ as shown in Table 38.6.

The statistics we have learned here can be applied to the measurement of many things—the heights and weights of people, intelligence-test scores, reading-ability tests, or personality measurements. Some of these things create special problems, however, and it is to these special problems that we now turn.

Table 38.5.
Two Sets of Hypothetical Individual Scores
and Deviations From the Mean

	GROUP I		GROUP II	
	Scores	d	Scores	d
	8	1	3	6
	8	1	5	4
	9	0	7	2
	9	0	9	0
	9	0	9	0.
	9	0	11	2
	10	1	13	4
	10	1	15	6
Σ (Sum)	72	4	72	24
M (Mean)	9		9	

$$A.D. = \frac{\Sigma d}{N} = \frac{4}{8} = .50 \qquad A.D. = \frac{\Sigma d}{N} = \frac{24}{8} = 3.00$$

(Gavett, 1925)

Table 38.6.
Calculation of Standard Deviation for Two Sets of Hypothetical Scores

SCORE	d	d^2	SCORE	d	d^2
8	1	1	3	6	36
8	1	1	5	4	16
9	0	0	7	2	4
9	0	0	9	0	0
9	0	0	9	0	0
9	0	0	11	2	4
10	1	1	13	4	16
11	1	1	15	6	36
$\Sigma = 72$		4	$\Sigma = 72$		112
$M = 9$			$M = 9$		
$N = 8$	$\Sigma d^2 = 4$		$N = 8$	$\Sigma d^2 = 112$	

$$\sigma = \sqrt{\frac{\Sigma d^2}{N}} = \sqrt{\frac{4}{8}} = \sqrt{.50} = .07$$

$$\sigma = \sqrt{\frac{\Sigma d^2}{N}} = \sqrt{\frac{112}{8}} = \sqrt{14} = 3.74$$

(Gavett, 1925)

Units of Measurement

If Shirley Cohen weighs 120 pounds, Tony Morales 150 pounds, and Jim McGraw 180 pounds, we can make several simple comparisons. We can rank the three and say that Jim is the heaviest, Tony next, and Shirley the lightest. We can make quantitative comparisons and say that Jim weighs 50 per cent more than Shirley or that the difference in weight between Jim and Tony is equal to the difference in weight between Tony and Shirley. All this information seems quite obvious. But now let us take a second set of measurements and see what happens.

Suppose that we give intelligence tests to the same three people and find that Shirley has a score of 100, Tony 110, and Jim 120. Again we can rank the three and say that Jim is the most intelligent, Tony next, and Shirley the least intelligent. We can also make a quantitative statement to the effect that Jim has scored 10 points more than Tony and Tony 10 points more than Shirley. But we cannot conclude that Tony is 10 per cent more intelligent than

Shirley, that Jim is 20 per cent more intelligent, or that the amount of difference in intelligence between Jim and Tony is the same as that between Tony and Shirley! To understand why we cannot make these conclusions we must consider various problems of measurement.

Absolute Zero

Length is measured with a calibrated ruler of some sort. The numbers on the ruler start, of course, at zero. Suppose we measure the length of three bars and find that one bar extends from 0 to 10 inches along the ruler, another from 0 to 20 inches, and the third from 0 to 40 inches. As the ruler, in each case, starts at the zero point, the second bar must be twice as long as the first, and the third must be twice as long as the second (Figure 38.8.).

Let us suppose, however, that we had a ruler whose numbered units did not start at the zero point but at some unspecified distance from the zero point, as in Figure 38.8. Furthermore, let us suppose that we again measured three bars (different ones, this time) and again found that the first bar ended at the 10-inch mark, the second at the 20-inch mark, and the third at the 40-inch mark. Even with this very queer measuring stick we could still rank the three bars with

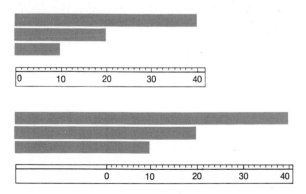

Figure 38.8. A pictorial representation of the difficulties that exist when we use a measuring instrument that does not have an absolute-zero point of origin (lower figure).

complete accuracy and say that the second bar was longer than the first and that the third was the longest of all. We could not say, however, that the second bar was twice as long as the first or that the third was twice as long as the second. A little reflection will make it clear that in order to make quantitative comparative statements (for example, "This is twice as long . . ." or "He is 10 per cent brighter than . . ."), we must have measuring instruments that have a real zero starting point.

Most measurement instruments with which we are familiar do have a real zero (absolute zero) starting point. A reading of zero on a reliable weighing scale thus literally means "no weight." Not all of our physical measurement instruments are of this kind. For example, on the familiar Fahrenheit or centigrade temperature scale the zero on the thermometer is not at the absolute zero of heat, and a temperature of 80° F. is not twice that of 40° F. When we turn to psychological measurement instruments, we find that very few of our tests have a real zero starting point. We have no tests in which a score of zero means that the person has absolutely no intelligence or absolutely no honesty, cowardice, shyness, or neuroticism. It is even difficult to conceive what zero intelligence or honesty could mean.

Because our mental and personality tests have no absolute zeros, we cannot make ratios of our scores and say that Tony is 10 per cent more intelligent than Shirley is. Direct comparisons of this sort are not justified. As a result, many problems of psychological measurement arise. But, before turning to some of the suggested solutions to these problems, let us consider a second difficulty with many psychological measuring instruments.

Equal Units

Another important characteristic of the usual physical measuring instrument is that all units are equal in magnitude—an inch is the same length whether it is the first inch on the ruler or the last. This equality permits us to say that the difference in length between 20 inches and 30 inches is the same as that between 10 and 20.

Suppose, however, that we had a measuring instrument on which there were not *equal units* of measurement—the "inches" becoming progressively longer. Now the distance between 20 and 30 "inches" would be greater than the distance between 10 and 20 "inches."

For no intelligence or personality tests do we know whether the units of measurement are of equal magnitude. For example, in most tests it is essential to add scores from many subtests to arrive at one total score. A "reasoning ability" test may consist of "verbal reasoning" problems and "arithmetic reasoning" problems. We do not know, however, whether or not each arithmetic problem is equal in difficulty to each verbal problem. That is, we do not know whether or not a score of 10 points on the arithmetic problem is equal to a score of 10 points on the verbal problem. Let us assume that Shirley Cohen and Tony Morales have earned the scores shown in Table 38.7.

From these scores it appears that Shirley's general reasoning ability is higher than Tony's is (120 versus 115). But, because these two tests almost certainly do not have units equal to each other, this conclusion does not necessarily follow. Quite possibly a difference of 3 points on the arithmetic-reasoning subtest is much more significant than is a difference of 8 points on the verbal-reasoning subtest. Therefore Tony's total score may actually indicate a higher reasoning ability than does Shirley's score.

Table 38.7.
Hypothetical Scores on Two Subtests

	VERBAL PROBLEMS	ARITHMETIC PROBLEMS	TOTAL
Shirley Cohen	98	22	120
Tony Morales	90	25	115

(Gavett, 1925)

In order to meet this and similar problems, several statistical devices have been developed that, within limits, do permit numerical comparisons among scores obtained on different subtests. Almost all these devices require that the original scores (sometimes called *raw scores*) first be changed into *converted scores*. The simplest kind of converted score, the one most commonly used, is the percentile score.

Percentile Score

A *percentile score* tells us a person's standing in relationship to the rest of the group. The percentile points divide the total distribution of scores into 100 parts, each containing 1 per cent of all the cases. For example: Suppose that 1,500 people took the verbal-reasoning subtest. To convert their raw scores into percentile scores, we first determine how many scores would be placed in each percentile (or each 100th part). We do so by dividing 1,500 by 100, which gives us 15. We now take the lowest fifteen scores—they constitute the first percentile. The top value of these fifteen cases is the point above which lie 99 per cent of the cases and below which lie 1 per cent. We do the same for the second percentile, the third, and so on until we have 100 percentile points. We can then easily transform any raw score into its percentile equivalent by reference to these points. A score with a percentile value of 50 would mean that 50 per cent of the 1,500 people who took the test scored above that point and 50 per cent scored below that point. A percentile value of 90 would mean that only 10 per cent scored above that point and 90 per cent scored below it.

Percentile scores vary from 0 to 100 *no matter what the range of the raw scores.* As a result, it is possible to compare the performances of different people on quite diverse tests having quite different "raw" units of measurement.

Despite the undoubted value of percentile scores and other kinds of converted scores

(like "standard scores"), we must remember that all comparisons of scores made on psychological tests must be treated with caution. At best the comparisons are only relative (for example, relative to the particular group that took the test). When we have neither absolute zero nor equal units of measurement, we cannot make comparisons in absolute terms.

Correlation

The description of individual differences not only involves comparing one person with his fellows but also involves comparing two aspects of the same person. For example, what relation exists between being good in arithmetic and being good in music? Can there be an all-around able person, or are most of us good in some things, average in others, and poor in still others? To answer these and other questions, we must have some way of expressing the degree of co-relation of, say, ability in arithmetic with ability in music.

A *correlation plot* is a simple graphic device picturing the relation between two sets of scores.

Let us start with some hypothetical data. Suppose we give ten students three tests—a

Table 38.8.
Hypothetical Scores on 4 Sets of Measures for 10 Students

STUDENT	NO. CORRECT VERBAL-REASONING TEST	NO. CORRECT ARITHMETICAL REASONING TEST	NO. ERRORS MAZE TEST	WEIGHT (IN POUNDS)
A	98	24	40	135
B	82	21	46	130
C	90	20	48	160
D	95	26	36	125
E	85	23	42	145
F	100	27	34	165
G	80	22	44	143
H	78	19	50	157
J	102	28	32	140
K	91	25	38	150

(Gavett, 1925)

verbal-reasoning test, an arithmetical-reasoning test, and a maze-learning test—and we record the students' weights to the nearest pound. Suppose that for the first two tests the score for each student is determined by the number of problems correctly solved, whereas the score for the third test is recorded in terms of the number of errors made before one perfect run through the maze is completed. These hypothetical results are shown in Table 38.8.

Positive Correlation

A *positive correlation* refers to two sets of measures whose values go together. Let us start by taking two sets of the scores from Table 38.8.: the verbal-reasoning scores and the arithmetical-reasoning scores. To make a "picture" of the relationship between these two sets of scores, we construct a graph with the verbal-reasoning scores on the horizontal axis, the arithmetical-reasoning scores on the vertical axis. (It does not matter which axis we use for

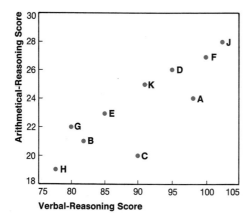

Figure 38.9. The correlation plot based on the data in Table 38.8 and indicating a positive correlation between test scores on arithmetical reasoning ability and verbal reasoning ability. Each point represents the scores of the subject on each of the two tests. For purposes of clarity, the subject's "name" (A, B, C, and so forth) has been placed next to the point. Ordinarily the names of the subjects are not indicated, but only the score points.

which test.) In this graph (see Figure 38.9.) a student's score on each test is represented by one point. For example, the point representing student A's performance tells us that he scored 98 on the verbal-reasoning test and 24 on the arithmetical-reasoning test.

An inspection of Figure 38.9. shows a clear trend among the ten subjects. The higher the person's verbal-reasoning score, the higher his arithmetical-reasoning score tends to be. We have here a positive correlation. *Whenever the correlation plot shows a trend from the lower left corner to the upper right corner, a positive correlation exists.* But it will also be noted that there are some exceptions to this trend. Subject C, for example, is definitely out of line. Although he did better than subjects G, B, and E on the verbal test, he did worse than they did on the arithmetic test. We can conclude therefore that, although there is a positive correlation, it is not a perfect positive correlation.

Negative Correlation

In Figure 38.10. data are plotted for the verbal-reasoning test and the maze test. Now we find that the higher the score on the verbal test, the fewer the errors on the maze. We have here a *negative correlation* between the two sets of scores. *Whenever the correlation plot shows a trend from the upper left corner to the lower right corner, a negative correlation exists.* But again, we do not have a perfect negative correlation; note, for instance, the scores made by subjects A and C.

This negative correlation, however, signifies a positive relation. In our reasoning test we have recorded the number of solutions achieved, whereas in our maze test we have recorded the number of errors made. Obviously, the more errors made, the poorer the performance. Therefore this negative correlation between scores really means that a good performance on the maze test is associated with a good performance on the reasoning test. The sign of a correlation (whether positive or

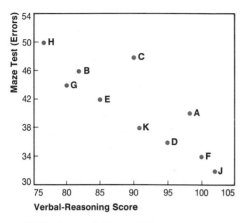

Figure 38.10. A correlation plot based on the data in Table 38.8. and indicating a negative correlation between maze test errors and verbal reasoning scores.

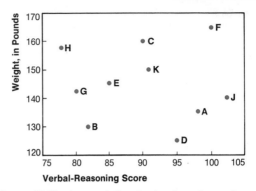

Figure 38.11. A correlational plot based on data in Table 38.8. (indicating a zero correlation between the weight of the subjects and their performance on the verbal-reasoning test). Note that the points do not arrange themselves in any special form but are scattered all over the correlational plot. This graph therefore represents a *zero* correlation.

negative) merely tells us the relationship between the *scores* on the two tests. The *meaning* of the correlation depends upon the meaning of the scores.

Zero Correlation

In Figure 38.11. we have constructed the correlation plot for the verbal-reasoning test and the body weights of the subjects. The correlation between body weight and verbal-reasoning scores is very close to zero. When the points on the correlation plot do not fall in any specific trend but are found scattered haphazardly, a *zero correlation* exists.

It is clear from the examples we have given that a positive or negative correlation can be something less than perfectly positive or perfectly negative. In many instances we need to know how *much* less than perfect is the correlation. This requirement has been satisfied by the development of the *correlation coefficient*— a single index that gives us both the sign and magnitude of the correlation.

By general agreement, it has been decided to call a perfect positive correlation +1.00 and a perfect negative correlation −1.00. The correlation coefficient can thus range from +1.00 to −1.00. For example, a correlation coefficient of +0.14 is low positive; a correlation coefficient of −0.90 is high negative. The size of the correlation refers to the distance from zero (whether positive or negative), not to its positiveness or negativeness. Thus a −0.90 correlation would be considered higher than a +0.14.

Rank-Order Correlation

There are several ways of determining the magnitude of a correlation coefficient. The simplest is the *rank-order correlation coefficient*, the symbol for which is ρ (the Greek letter rho).

The basic logic behind the formula for ρ is readily grasped, and we shall sketch it here through an example.

The first step in obtaining ρ is to rank the subjects in terms of their performances on each of the two tests being analyzed. We then compare the ranks and from that derive the value of ρ. Table 38.9. presents the necessary steps for getting a ρ for our illustrative data from the verbal and arithmetic tests of Table 38.8.

In column 4 we have ranked the performance of the ten subjects on the verbal-reasoning test. The highest score, 102, was earned by subject J, and he is given the top rank of 1;

Table 38.9.
Rank-Order Correlation Between VR and AR Tests

1	2	3	4	5	6	7
	NO.	NO.	RANK	RANK		
	CORRECT	CORRECT	ON	ON		
SUBJECT	VR TEST	AR TEST	VR TEST	AR TEST	D	D²
A	98	24	3	5	2	4
B	82	21	8	8	0	0
C	90	20	6	9	3	9
D	95	26	4	3	1	1
E	85	23	7	6	1	1
F	100	27	2	2	0	0
G	80	22	9	7	2	4
H	78	19	10	10	0	0
J	102	28	1	1	0	0
K	91	25	5	4	1	1

$$\Sigma D^2 = 20$$

$$\rho = 1 - \frac{6\Sigma D^2}{N(N^2-1)} = 1 - \frac{120}{10(99)} = 1 - \frac{120}{990} = 1 - .12 = +.88$$

(Gavett, 1925)

the next best score was 100, earned by F, and he receives the rank of 2; A ·is ranked 3; and so on. In column 5 we have ranked the ten subjects according to their scores on the arithmetic-reasoning test.

If there were a perfect positive correlation, there would be no difference between the two sets of ranks. For example, subject J, who received rank 1 in the verbal test, would also receive rank 1 in the arithmetic test. The man who received rank 2 in the verbal test would also receive rank 2 in the arithmetic test, and so on down to the man who would be ranked tenth in both lists. If in this case we obtained the differences between the scores of column 5 and those of column 4, we would get a column of zeros.

If the correlation were something less than perfect, however, the differences between the ranks (column 5 minus column 4) would not all be zero. A man receiving the third rank in one test could get the fifth rank in the second test and so on. The greater the disparities in ranks, the lower would be the positive relationship between the two sets of scores. Therefore the average of the rank differences obviously pro-

vides a way of measuring the degree of correlation—the larger the average, the lower the positive correlation.

Again, for various mathematical reasons, we do not deal with the differences among the ranks, but with the squares of these differences. In other words, we square each value in column 6 to give us the values in column 7.

Since a +1.00 is the highest positive correlation possible, to obtain the correlation coefficient we should *subtract* from 1.00 the average of the differences between the ranks. The higher the average of the differences between the ranks, the lower will be the correlation coefficient.

We arrive finally at the following formula: The size of the correlation should be 1.00 minus the average of the differences between the ranks, or

$$\rho = 1 - \frac{\Sigma D^2}{N}.$$

And this "logically" derived formula is similar in structure to the mathematically derived formula. For various mathematical reasons that need not concern us now, the actual formula is

$$\rho = 1 - \frac{6\Sigma D^2}{N(N^2 - 1)}.$$

Applying this formula, we get a ρ of +0.88 for the correlation coefficient between verbal- and arithmetical-reasoning scores among our ten hypothetical subjects. We have now expressed in numerical terms the positive correlation indicated in Figure 38.9.

The same reasoning is involved in the negative rank-order correlation. In a perfect negative correlation the top man in one test would be the worst man in the second test; the subject who received a rank of 2 in the first test would receive a rank of 9 in the second and so on. In this case the differences between the two sets of ranks would be at their maximum. If we subtracted the average of the differences between the ranks from 1.00, we would end up as far away from a +1.00 as we could get, that is, at −1.00. For an illustration of a negative correlation, the student is urged to work through the rank-order correlation between the verbal-reasoning test and the maze test, using the data in Table 38.8.

Product-Moment Correlation

The correlation coefficient that is most commonly used is the *product-moment correlation coefficient*. The formula for this correlation coefficient (which is symbolized by the letter *r*) is

$$r = \frac{\Sigma xy}{N\sigma_x\sigma_y};$$

x and *y* are the deviations of the individual scores from the group means, σ_x is the standard deviation of the scores on test X, and σ_y is the standard deviation of the scores on test Y. An example of how a product-moment correlation coefficient is calculated is given in Box 138, p. 630.

As a general rule, the rank-order correlation coefficient is preferred when the number of cases is small (about fifteen to twenty) and when there are few ties in ranks. In other cases the product-moment correlation coefficient is a more desirable measure.

A logical error that is frequently made in the interpretation of the correlation coefficient is the cause-and-effect argument. It is often assumed that, if two variables are highly correlated, one is the *cause* of the other. A high correlation between two events may, however, mean merely that both events are caused by some *third* factor, not that one event causes or influences the other. In statistical work the correlation coefficient is often used in problems in which we know there is no causal relationship between the two sets of measurements we are correlating. We shall see some examples in the following pages.

Errors of Measurement

Whenever we measure anything—the length of a table or the personality of a patient in a mental hospital—our measure suffers from some degree of error. The error may be due to an imperfect measuring instrument, to an imperfect method of applying the instrument, to our careless reading of the instrument or recording, or to any one of a number of other factors.

Because so much of reasoning in science depends upon the results of measurement, a great deal of concern has been shown for errors of measurement, and we have learned much about their nature, source, and control. For cases in which we have been unable to eliminate them, we have developed techniques that enable us to estimate the degree of error. Knowing the magnitude of our error, we can state the degree of our confidence in any conclusions based on measurements. The study of errors of measurement is one of the basic studies in statistics.

We shall concern ourselves here with two types of error problems: the reliability and the validity of our instruments.

Reliability

No absolutely perfect measuring instrument exists. Even the simplest kind of measuring instrument, the ruler, is not without built-in error. We all know that some measuring instruments give us larger errors than do others, however. A metal ruler, for example, may give us larger errors than does a wooden ruler because metal expands or shrinks as the room temperature rises or falls. Obviously, a ruler that expands and shrinks would be "unreliable," for, if we used it to measure the same object twice, it might give us two different readings, depending upon the temperature of the room. A "reliable" ruler would give us the same answer no matter how many times we measured the same object.

Box 138

$$r = \frac{\Sigma xy}{N\sigma_x\sigma_y}$$

The product-moment correlation coefficient was developed by the English mathematician Karl Pearson and is sometimes referred to as "Pearson's coefficient of correlation." Seven steps are involved. Using the hypothetical data of the table, we can demonstrate them:

Subject	Score on X	Score on Y
A	126	120
B	123	100
C	122	60
D	100	50
E	80	25
F	67	23

1. We obtain the group means for test X and test Y, which are 103.0 and 63.0 respectively.

2. Then we determine for each subject the amount by which his score deviates from the group mean. We do this separately for each test. Subject A, with 126 points, is thus 23 points away from the group mean on the X test. Subject A therefore has an x score of 23. (When the letters are in lower-case type, they refer to deviations from the average.) He is 57 points away from the group mean on the Y test, which gives him a y score of 57.0. In the same manner we obtain the x and y scores for each subject.

3. We then multiply each person's x score by his y score. For example, for subject A we multiply 23 by 57; the product is 1,311.0. We do the same for each of the other five subjects.

4. We then sum all six products, which total 4,347.0. This is the value for Σxy.

5. We then obtain the σs of the x scores and the y scores. They turn out to be 22.8 for the x scores and 36.1 for the y scores.

6. We now multiply the σ of the x scores by the σ of the y scores and by the number of subjects, which gives us a product of 4,938.48. This is the value for $N\sigma_x\sigma_y$.

7. Finally, we divide this last product into the sum of the xy products (step 4). This gives us the product-moment correlation coefficient, which, in this illustration, is +.88.

This simple consideration gives us the definition of reliable and unreliable measuring instruments. Reliability of a measurement device (including its method of application) can be defined as *the degree to which repeated measurement of the same quantity with the instrument will give the same readings.*

Reliability Measured by Correlation Let us suppose that we want to determine the degree of reliability of a new intelligence test. We could administer the test to a group of children and record their scores. One week later we could give them the same test and again record their scores. We would now have two sets of scores for the same group of children on the same test. If the test and its method of application are reliable, the children should receive the same, or very similar, scores on both occasions. This statement would be true, of course, only if the children's intelligence had not changed during the one-week interval. If the test is not reliable, the children would receive widely different scores at the two testing periods. Let us assume, in an illustrative case, that we have obtained the data shown in Table 38.10.

How reliable is this test? On the first testing child K was tops; on the second testing he was tops again. On the first testing J was second, as he was also on the second testing. But not every child achieved the same rank on both occasions. For example, child G was fourth on the first testing but came out fifth the second time around. The test is not perfectly reliable. If it were, we would get a correlation of +1.00 between the first and second testing. The actual correlation (rank-order) is +.98. (The reader is invited to work out this rank-order correlation coefficient for himself.) Obviously, if the test had been a very unreliable one, the correlation would have been very low. The correlation coefficient, therefore, gives us *a numerical index expressing the degree of reliability of a test.* When a correlation coefficient is used for this purpose, it is called a *reliability coefficient.*

It is not always desirable, however, to repeat the same test at two different times. It is always possible, for example, that the child may re-

member what he did the previous week and merely repeat his performance on the basis of memory. In that event, the correlation between the first set of scores and the second would give us a measure of the child's memory rather than of the test's reliability. Or there is the possibility that the child's intelligence itself may actually have changed during the interval, and we would therefore have no way of knowing whether a low correlation between the first and second testing was a result of the change in intelligence or of a lack of testing reliability. Or the child may be bored with the test the second time, and the low test-retest correlation may be caused by lack of motivation rather than by any unreliability of the test or the testing procedure.

Several techniques have been developed in an attempt to avoid these problems in determining the reliability of a test. Among these techniques is one known as *comparable-forms reliability.*

Comparable-Forms Reliability   Most psychological tests consist of large numbers of items, problems, and questions. Let us assume an arithmetic-reasoning test made up of fifty different arithmetic-reasoning problems. We then proceed to construct another fifty-item test of arithmetic reasoning. The correlation between the two comparable forms would give us the reliability of either form. We can therefore give a group of subjects the first fifty items at one time and, at a later time, the other fifty items. What we have are two comparable forms of the same test.

The comparable-forms method avoids the "memory" problem and perhaps the "boredom" problem discussed earlier, but it still leaves the problem of timing. The two forms are given at different times. Many things can happen during the interval to make it difficult to interpret the correlation between the two comparable forms. Partly to meet this problem, the *split-half reliability* method has been developed.

Table 38.10.
Hypothetical Scores for 10 Children
on Test X Taken Twice

CHILDREN	SCORES ON TEST X FIRST WEEK	SCORES ON TEST X SECOND WEEK	RANK ON 1ST TESTING	RANK ON 2ND TESTING
A	100	110	7	6
B	110	100	6	7
C	90	90	8	8
D	120	130	5	4
E	140	140	3	3
F	80	80	9	9
G	130	120	4	5
H	70	70	10	10
J	150	150	2	2
K	160	160	1	1

(Gavett, 1925)

Split-Half Reliability The reasoning behind the split-half reliability method is identical with that behind the comparable-forms method. Let us return to our arithmetical-reasoning test. Instead of constructing two comparable forms and giving each form at a different time, we can give our subjects a 100-item test at one sitting and then ourselves split the 100-item test into two 50-item tests. For example, for each subject we have a record of his performance on 100 items. Suppose we now take these 100 items and split them so that the performance on the odd-numbered items (1, 3, 5, 7, and so on) makes up one subscore for each subject and the performance on the even-numbered items (2, 4, 6, 8, and so on) makes up another subscore for each subject. For all practical purposes we have scores on two comparable forms of the test for each subject. Next we correlate the subject's score on all the odd-numbered items with his score on all the even-numbered items; in this way we determine the reliability coefficient of either half and, from this estimate, the reliability of the whole. That is why this method is sometimes called the "odd-even reliability coefficient."

This method has the following advantages over the comparable-forms method: First, both subtests (even and odd) are taken at the same time, under the same conditions of motivation, the same conditions of testing, and the same state of alertness. Second, because we have split the test by the odd-even method, we have ensured comparability of forms—not only in content but also in manner of administration. That is, each subtest contains items that come both early and late in the total sitting so that such factors as fatigue and lagging interest are presumably equated for both subtests.

These and other methods can give us valuable information on the adequacy of a test as a measurement instrument. However, knowing that a test is reliable is not enough to enable us to assess its value as a measurement instrument. It may be highly reliable and still a very poor measurement instrument because it lacks validity.

Validity

The terms "reliability" and "validity" are used fairly interchangeably in everyday speech. In measurement theory, however, these terms have different meanings. The statistician, concerned with the question of the reliability of an instrument, asks how consistently the instrument measures whatever it measures. When he is concerned with the question of validity, he asks whether the instrument is measuring what he wants it to measure. An instrument may give consistent measurements (have high reliability), but it may not be measuring what we think it measures (it may have low validity). For example, weekly quizzes in your psychology course may give consistent results in the sense that week after week you earn a 75. The quizzes are reliable indicators. But indicators of what? If your psychology instructor intends them as measures of your understanding of the principles of psychology, he may be wrong. They may be measuring mainly rote memory. Thus, they would have low validity as indicators of psychological understanding.

For many measurement instruments, of course, there are no serious problems of validity. A quiz designed to determine whether you can give the textbook's definitions of specific psychological terms is, by definition, a valid test of whether you can do so. Such a test is said to have *face validity*—it is valid on the face of it!

But most tests that seek to measure more complex phenomena are not that easily "validated." For one thing, validity, like reliability, is not an all-or-nothing affair. A test may have degrees of validity. Your quiz grades may be influenced *only* by your understanding of psychological principles. In that case we would say that the quiz has perfect validity as a measure of understanding of psychological principles. But more probably your score on it is the resultant of your psychological understanding *plus* rote-memory ability. The test still has some validity for psychological understanding and some validity for rote-memory capacity, but it is no longer a "pure" test of either. As with reliability, we must have some way of expressing the *degree* of the validity of a measuring instrument. And again, as with reliability, the correlation coefficient provides us with just such a way.

Validity Measured by Correlation It is clear that a test is valid to the degree that its measurements correlate with the actual thing it is supposed to measure. For example, suppose we wish to determine the validity of a test designed to measure the ability of students to get high grades in school work. We would give the test to a large number of students and see whether the scores they made on the test correlated highly with the actual grades they received in their school work. Their school grades would, of course, be the final criteria of the validity of the test. If the correlation between the test scores and the criterion scores is high, the test obviously measures what it is intended to measure and it has high validity. If the correlation is low, the test has low validity. When the correlation coefficient is used in this way, it is called a *validity coefficient*.

The general principle is simple enough: To determine the validity of a test, we correlate the scores of the test with the criterion. The difficulty is that frequently we cannot find a criterion with which to correlate the test scores. Suppose we want to measure the validity of an intelligence test. We can get the scores of the test easily enough, but what will serve as our criterion of "intelligence"? Grades in school? Money earned in "real life"? Originality and creativity? Leadership in social affairs? Different people might suggest different criteria, and some of the criteria would themselves pose problems of measurement. For example, even if we all agreed that "intelligence" refers to originality and creativity, we would still have the problem of finding generally acceptable and quantifiable measures of originality and of creativity to correlate with our intelligence test.

There have been many attempts to solve the criterion problem. Among the more common techniques is the so-called *"known-group" method* of validity determination.

Known Groups and Validity There are no easily available criterion scores for originality and creativity. There are, however, certain well-known people whom most of us would regard as "highly original and creative." Thus, a group of inventors, scientists, and artists might be picked who exemplify originality and creativity. These people could then be considered as a "known group" of creative people.

Presumably this known group is more creative than is the average run of men. We would give our test to this known group and also to a large, randomly selected group of people and compare the results. If the test has any validity as a measure of "originality and creativity," the average member of the "creative" group should score higher than the average member of the control group, and the greater the difference between scores, the more valid the test.

Sometimes it is easy to choose the proper known group; sometimes it is quite difficult. Nevertheless, in many instances we have no better way of determining the validity of tests than by the known-group method. But, whether we use face validity, correlation with criterion scores, or the known-group method, we must have some information on the validity of a test before we can interpret its results sensibly.

A test may have high reliability but low validity, in the sense that it turns out not to measure what we intended it to measure. A test of low reliability cannot have high validity, however; if a test is capricious in its measurement, now giving a high reading, now a low one, for the same unchanging object, its measurements are being determined by "chance" factors—in other words, it has low reliability. Unreliable tests cannot consistently correlate highly with any set of criterion scores because what the tests measure is largely error; therefore they must have low validity.

Reliability and validity pertain to errors of measurement and of conceptualization; therefore they arise from an inadequacy in the measurement instrument. But quite aside from this, there is still another major source of error in any investigation that uses measurement. We may make a *sampling error*.

Sampling the "Average" Man

Whenever we measure a group of people, we have one of two reasons for choosing them. We may be interested in these particular people themselves, or we may be interested in a specific category of people of which the particular group is supposed to be a sample.

In the former instance there are no measurement problems aside from those we have already considered—reliability and validity. If we wish to know what Berkeley freshmen will score on our scholastic-aptitude test, we measure all the freshmen at Berkeley, and that is all there is to it.

If we want to know what the "American freshman" will score on our test, however, we immediately run into a whole set of measurement problems. We cannot, or do not wish to, test every American freshman. We therefore test a *sample* of freshmen, and from the results we generalize to the all-American freshman. But how do we know that the results of our sample freshmen correctly portray the American freshman? Perhaps our sample freshmen are brighter than the average American freshman—or duller. As soon as we measure a sample of a group instead of the entire group, we introduce the possibility of sampling errors. In scientific investigations we are not primarily interested in the specific individuals we are measuring. For example, when the psychologist studies how quickly a group of sophomores can learn a list of nonsense syllables using the recitation method, he is not interested in that specific group of sophomores. He is not even interested in sophomores in general. He is interested in how people—all people, of all

colors, of all educational levels, of all cultures —respond to active versus passive learning methods. Most scientific investigations are in theory concerned with infinitely large *populations*.

In most studies it would be literally impossible to test and measure every member of the population. We are therefore forced to use a sampling technique. Usually, however, we are being "forced" to do what is good for us. Even if we had the facilities to test and measure every member of the population in which we are interested, it would be a wasteful and foolish thing to do. In many instances we can obtain almost as precise an estimate of the population score by measuring a sample as we can by measuring the total population. It is therefore more sensible and economical to study samples. And a sample need not be very large to be a "good" sample. A group of 3,000 carefully chosen Americans, for example, can be a better sample of the total population of more than 200 million Americans than can 1 million that are poorly chosen.

Biased and Unbiased Samples

Although the technique of obtaining a good sample is highly refined, the guiding principle is simple. Ideally, in drawing a sample from a large population, we must use a procedure that permits every member of the entire population *an equal opportunity to be included in the sample*. In other words, our technique must not be systematically biased in favor of any kind of person. For example, suppose we want to determine the average body weight of all the residents of New York City. To do so, we must first obtain a representative sample of New York residents.

One method, used in the past, was to take the city telephone directory and draw, say, every 500th name. But this method inevitably results in a *systematically biased sample* for it has systematically drawn only those New Yorkers who have telephones and has systematically excluded all those who do not. For our purpose, this group is obviously not a good sample of New Yorkers. It may be, for instance, that New Yorkers who have telephones are in the higher-income brackets, eat more, and therefore weigh more than do New Yorkers who have no telephones.

Once we have a systematically biased sample, there is very little we can do to correct the sample mathematically. Whatever measurements we make on telephone-subscribing New Yorkers cannot safely be generalized to all New Yorkers.

One way to avoid systematic bias would be to write the name of each New Yorker on standard-sized slips of paper, place all the papers in a huge bin, shake the bin vigorously, and then blindly pick out, say, 3,000 names at random. We would have chosen what is called a *random sample*.

Frequently, of course, it is not feasible to use such an ideal "random" method, so we attempt to approximate the ideal method. We might, for example, take every third city block and choose every tenth family in each block for our sample. This method would give us an approximation to a random sample.

Although we may thus avoid systematic bias or error in our sample, the possibility still remains that our sample would deviate from the population because of unsystematic or "chance" events. For example, perhaps *just by sheer chance* we might include, say, many more names of women or of older people, proportionally, than there are in New York City. However, unlike the situation in which there are systematic biases, we can do something about "chance" errors. We can predict their magnitude. To understand how this prediction is possible, it is necessary to make a rather long detour and discuss the question of *probability*.

Probability

One of the most important mathematical achievements in the field of probability theory was the discovery that "chance events" behave lawfully. That is, if we record all our observations of recurring chance events and make a distribution curve of these observations, the distribution curve will take the shape of what is called a *normal curve*.

The phrase *chance event* is used in the mathematical sense and means an event that has so many completely interrelated causes that it is impossible to predict (at the time) the exact nature of the occurrences. "Chance" does not mean uncaused. For example, suppose we toss ten dimes into the air. What determines how many heads and how many tails will fall? Many things: the force of the toss, the weight of the dimes, their position in the hand when tossed, the spin given to the coins, and so on. It is impossible to predict whether a particular dime will fall heads or tails, and therefore we say that it is a chance event.

Although we do not know, for any single series of throws of the ten dimes, how many heads will show, we can calculate, from the mathematical theory of probability, the approximate number of times we will get 10, 9, 8, 7, 6, 5, 4, 3, 2, 1, and 0 heads in, say, 10,000 throws.

Mutually Exclusive Events Let us toss one dime. Knowing nothing about the forces that determine how this particular dime will fall at this particular moment, we can say that the probability that we will get a head is 1 out of 2, or, as it is usually written, $h = 1/2$ (where h stands for the probability of a head). The same is true, of course, for a tail, that is, $t = 1/2$. Because the dime can fall so that only heads *or* tails show, the two possible occurrences are *mutually exclusive events*. The probability that the coin will fall so that *either* a head or a tail comes up is 1, that is, $1/2 h + 1/2 t = 1$. (Certainty, in probability nomenclature, is represented by the value of 1.) This simple operation is an illustration of an important general probability rule: *The probability of occurrence of two or more mutually exclusive* *events is obtained by adding the probabilities of the individual events.*

Independent Events. Now let us throw two dimes at a time. The probability that one dime will fall heads is 1/2; the probability that the other dime will fall heads is also 1/2. What is the probability that both dimes will fall heads? When we have two dimes, the events are *not* mutually exclusive. That is, one dime can show a head, but this does not mean that the other dime cannot also show a head. The falls of the two dimes are *independent events*.

For independent events the following rule holds: *The probability of the occurrence of independent events is obtained by multiplying the probabilities of the individual events.* For example, with two coins the probability of getting two heads is found by multiplying 1/2 (that is, the probability that one dime will show a head) by 1/2 (the probability that the other dime will show a head). Expressed mathematically it is $1/2\,h \times 1/2\,h$, or $1/4\,h$. The same is, of course, true for two tails $(1/2\,t \times 1/2\,t$, or $1/4\,t)$.

We can now make a probability prediction. If we were to throw two dimes 10,000 times, we would expect to find that two heads would come up about 1/4 of the time, or 2,500 times, and that two tails would come up about 1/4 of the time, or 2,500 times. For the remaining 5,000 throws we would expect one head and one tail. The predicted distribution is shown in Figure 38.12. as a frequency histogram. From this figure it will be seen that the most probable event is one head and one tail, but in 25 per cent of the throws we would get two heads and in 25 per cent of the throws, two tails.

By similar reasoning we can determine the probabilities for three, four, five, or any number of coins. In Table 38.11. and Figure 38.13. we present the data for ten coins. The most probable event—the one we would expect to occur 24.6 per cent of the time (in 2,460 throws out of 10,000; see Table 38.11.)—is five heads and five tails. But also by chance we would occasionally expect to find all ten heads showing up, which

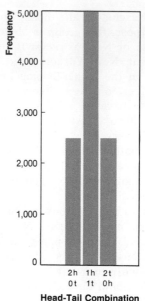

Figure 38.12. A frequency histogram of the theoretically derived distribution of head-tail combinations that we might expect to find if we flipped two coins 10,000 times.

Table 38.11.

Theoretical Expectations of Head-Tail Combinations for 10 Coins Tossed 10,000 Times

COMBINATIONS OF H(EADS) AND T(AILS)	FREQUENCY
10h and 0t	10
9h and 1t	98
8h and 2t	439
7h and 3t	1,172
6h and 4t	2,051
5h and 5t	2,460
4h and 6t	2,051
3h and 7t	1,172
2h and 8t	439
1h and 9t	98
0h and 10t	10
	10,000

(Gavett, 1925)

would occur 0.1 per cent of the time (or in 10 out of 10,000 throws). In other words, the chances are 1 in 1,000 that we shall get ten heads showing at one throw.

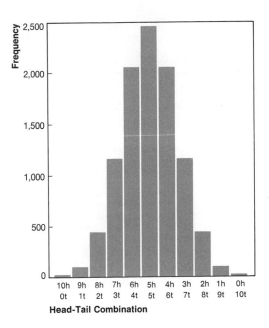

Figure 38.13. A frequency histogram of the theoretically derived distribution of head-tail combinations that we might expect to find if we flipped ten coins 10,000 times.

The Normal Curve Note one very important characteristic of the two histograms shown in Figures 38.12. and 38.13. They are perfectly symmetrical around the most probable event. As the number of coins is increased, the histograms maintain their perfect symmetry, but their shapes gradually change from the sharp, angular shape of the two-coin histogram to the somewhat bell-shaped appearance of the ten-coin histogram. As the number of coins increases, the number of head-tail combinations to be plotted necessarily increases, and the histogram becomes smoother and smoother, ultimately approaching in form the normal distribution curve. This eventuality is what we meant by saying that chance events behave lawfully—they give a beautifully smoothed bell-shaped distribution curve.

Because the normal curve was constructed through the application of mathematical theory (some of the basic aspects of which we have just worked through), a great deal is known about its mathematical properties. It is these properties that make the normal curve of such great value in estimating sampling errors. The most important of these properties, and the one immediately relevant to our problem, is the fixed relation that the standard deviation bears to the curve. The relation is such that *the standard deviation measures off constant proportions of the curve from the mean.* An example will make this point clear.

First, let us calculate the standard deviation for the theoretically derived distribution shown in Table 38.11. and Figure 38.13. Using the formula we have already developed on page 622,

$$\sigma = \sqrt{\frac{\Sigma d^2}{N}},$$

we find that the standard deviation is 1.58. The most probable outcome of a throw of ten dimes will be five heads and five tails, which is the mean of the distribution. Let us therefore start at 5.0 on the base line of Figure 38.14. (which portrays the data of Figure 38.13. as a smooth curve rather than as a histogram) and measure off a distance of 1σ on either side. We arrive at a score of 3.42 on one side and 6.58 on the other. In a perfectly normal curve, exactly 34.13 per cent of all cases will be found between the mean value and the value 1σ away from the mean, or—put another way—more than 68 per cent of scores fall in the range from -1σ to $+1\sigma$.

Let us now mark off another σ distance. We arrive at 1.84 and 8.16. Between 3.42 and 1.84 will be found approximately 13.59 per cent of the cases, and the same is true for the interval between 6.58 and 8.16. *These relations between the standard deviation and the distribution of cases in a normal distribution are always present, no matter what the absolute size of the mean or the size of the standard deviation.*

Standard Error

We have now completed our detour and are ready to return to New York City, the weights

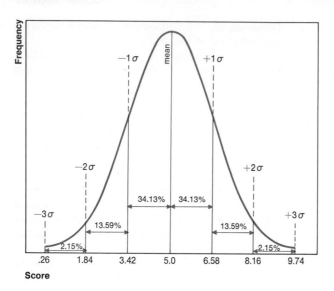

Figure 38.14. Here the data of the histogram in Figure 38.13. are portrayed as a ''smooth curve'' with the mean at 5. The percentage values shown are characteristic of every normal distribution curve; thus within the area marked off by $+1\sigma$ and -1σ will be found 68.26 per cent of all the scores in the distribution; within the area marked off by $+2\sigma$ and -2σ will be found 95.44 per cent of all the scores in the distribution; and between the area marked off by $+3\sigma$ and -3σ will be found about 99.75 per cent of all the scores in the distribution. The theoretical normal distribution curve will never hit the base line, although it will continue to approach it. Therefore, no matter how many sigma distances we go from the mean (on both sides), we shall never encompass 100 per cent of the cases. Of course, a curve representing actual data does hit the base line on either end because it reflects a limited number of cases.

of its residents, and sampling errors.

Suppose we wish to estimate the mean weight of all New Yorkers from a random sample of only 100 New Yorkers. We have the name and weight of each New Yorker on a separate slip of paper. From this total set of slips we draw 100 at random, and we then calculate the mean weight of the sample of 100. Let us assume that this value is 120 pounds. We then calculate the σ of this distribution of 100 cases. Let us assume that σ equals 19.5 pounds. With only this information we can now determine how reliable an estimate of the true mean weight of all New Yorkers our sample mean of 120 pounds is.

In order to understand how we can do so, let us perform a hypothetical experiment. To do it we must first obtain 10,000 different random samples of the New York population, each sample consisting of 100 cases, and calculate for each sample its mean. We shall thus obtain 10,000 means.

Our first mean, based on our first random sample of 100, we found to be 120 pounds. We now throw the 100 slips of paper back into the huge bin that is New York, shake it up again, and draw a new sample of 100 names. Calculat-

ing the mean of this new sample, we may find it to be 122 pounds. Again we throw the 100 names back, and again we draw a new sample. In this way we build up our total of 10,000 means.

For each draw of 100 names it is a matter of pure chance which 100 names we get. It is therefore a matter of pure chance (within the limits of all New Yorkers' weights) what the mean weight of each sample will be. It will be recalled that, when we record repeated chance events and throw these observations into a distribution curve, we obtain a normal distribution curve with the most probable value in the center and with the values of the deviant sample means falling on either side of the curve. Therefore we know in advance that, if we were actually to calculate the 10,000 means, they would distribute themselves in a normal curve.

The standard deviation of such a curve is called the *standard error of the mean* and is symbolized by σ_m. The formula for σ_m (the derivation of which can be found in any book of mathematical statistics) is

$$\sigma_m = \frac{\sigma}{\sqrt{N-1}};$$

in this equation σ is the standard deviation of our sample, and N is the number of cases in our sample. To return to our illustration: As the σ of our sample was 19.5 and the N was 100, the $\sigma_m = 1.97$ (see Figure 38.15.).

This standard error of the mean enables us to make probability statements about the distance between our sample mean of 120 and the true mean of all New Yorkers. Let it be recalled that the curve in Figure 38.15. encompasses *all possible* averages obtainable from groups of 100 New Yorkers and is a normal distribution curve. As the sigma of this normal distribution curve is 1.97, there are about 68 chances out of 100 (twice 34 per cent) that our sample mean is not more than plus or minus 1.97 pounds away from the true mean. In statistical language this statement is written as follows: "The mean is 120 ± 1.97."

We can state the probabilities with even more confidence. Because we know that 99.74 per cent of all the cases fall within plus and minus 3σ of the mean, we can say that there are over 99 chances out of 100 that our sample mean is not more than plus or minus 5.91 pounds away from the true mean.

Precision and Size of Sample   The level of confidence in the previous example is high (one that any betting man would be willing to risk all on), but the range of ± 5.91 pounds is pretty wide. Can we reduce this range and still maintain the same level of confidence? There is a relatively simple way to try to do so. When we recall that the standard of the mean is determined by the formula

$$\sigma_m = \frac{\sigma}{\sqrt{N-1}},$$

it is clear that by increasing the N (number of cases in our single sample) the σ_m is reduced. For instance, if our sample had 200 cases, rather than 100, we would have obtained a standard error of the mean of about 1.30 pounds, rather than 1.97 pounds. With a sample of 200 cases we

can state our conclusions with the same degree of confidence but with more precision; that is, there are more than 99 chances out of 100 that our sample mean is not more than plus or minus 3.90 pounds (three times the new standard error of the mean) away from the true mean.

While every increase in sample size decreases the standard error of the mean, this increase follows the law of diminishing returns because the N in the σ_m formula is under the square-root sign. That is, an increase in N from 100 to 200 may show a sizable drop in the standard error; an increase of another 100 will show a smaller decrease in the standard error; an increase of another 100 will show a still smaller decrease; and soon the point will be reached at which an additional number of cases will show very little decrease in the size of the standard error of the mean. The determination of what size sample we should use rests mainly upon two considerations: the desired precision of the results and the available time, money, and energy. For some measures we wish a highly precise result, and in such cases we must have a large N; for some measures, however, a less highly precise estimate of the true mean is sufficient.

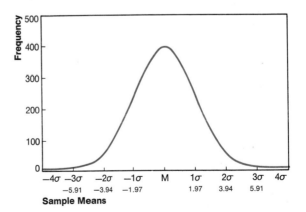

Figure 38.15. A normal distribution curve representing the theoretically expected distribution of the means of 10,000 random samples of 100 cases each taken from the same population. The standard deviation of one obtained sample is 19.5 and the σ_M is 1.97.

Everything we have said about the mean of a sample is equally true for other measurements we obtain from samples. We can never be certain that our obtained means are the true means, that our obtained correlation coefficients are the true correlation coefficients, or that our obtained differences between groups are the real differences. With the use of the standard-error statistic we can state the probabilities that our obtained measurements are within a specified distance from the true values. Sometimes the probabilities are high enough so that we are willing to go ahead as if we really did know the truth. Most scientists will not accept confidence limits of anything less than 95 chances out of 100 before they "go ahead." But even when we demand such high odds, we are still betting on probabilities. The scientist is a gambling man. He has no choice.

Glossary

absolute zero A measuring instrument whose units are numbered from a "real" zero is said to have an absolute zero as its starting point. Such an instrument is contrasted with a measurement instrument whose numbered units start at some unspecified distance from the zero point. The Fahrenheit and centigrade thermometers and most intelligence and personality scales are illustrations of the latter type of measurement instruments. When a measurement instrument does not have an absolute zero as its starting point, we cannot make direct ratio comparisons of scores; that is, we cannot say that a score of 50 on such an instrument is twice the value of a score of 25 and so on.

average deviation (A.D.) A measure of dispersion based on the average of the deviations of every score in the distribution from the mean of all the scores of the distribution. The formula for the average deviation is

$$A.D. = \frac{\Sigma d}{N}.$$

The average deviation is less influenced by extreme scores than is the range or the standard deviation.

biased sample The result of a sampling procedure that systematically excludes certain kinds of subject or systematically underrepresents certain kinds of subject that should be included. It is contrasted with a "random sample."

central tendency A middle value between the extremes of a set of measures. There are many different kinds of central-tendency measures. Among the more common are the mean, median, and mode. These three measures of central tendency, even when based on the same scores, need not yield identical values. They will do so only in a perfectly symmetrical frequency curve. Each measure of central tendency has a somewhat different meaning.

chance event An event that has so many complexly interrelated causes that it is impossible (at the time) to predict the exact nature of the occurrences.

class interval The range of values treated within one group. For example, if we were to treat all values from 10 to 20 as one group and from 21 to 30 as another group, these ranges would be called "class intervals."

comparable-forms reliability A method of determining the reliability coefficient for a measuring instrument by obtaining the correlation coefficient between two comparable forms of the same test, administered to the same group of subjects.

converted scores When a raw score is changed into another kind of score, it is referred to as a converted score. The simplest, and the most commonly used, converted score is the *percentile* score.

correlation coefficient A single index that gives both the sign and magnitude of a correlation. A correlation coefficient can vary from +1.00 (a perfect positive correlation) to −1.00 (a perfect negative correlation). Two common correlation coefficients are the rank-order correlation coefficient (ρ) and the product-moment correlation coefficient (r).

correlation plot A graphic device picturing the relationship between two sets of scores. In such a graph a person's scores on two different tests are represented by one point. When the scores of a number of people are thus plotted on the graph, we can determine, by inspection, the *sign* of the correlation. When the points on a correlation plot show a trend from the lower left corner to the upper right corner, a *positive correlation* exists; when the trend is from the upper left corner to the lower right corner, a *negative correlation* exists; and when no specific trend is apparent, a *zero correlation* exists.

dispersion The degree of scatter among the individual scores of a set of scores. If the scores all cluster closely around some measure of central tendency, we speak of a low degree of dispersion; if the scores are widely scattered around the central tendency, we speak of a high degree of dispersion. There are a number of quantitative measures of degree of dispersion, among them the range, the average deviation, and the standard deviation.

equal units An important characteristic of the usual physical measuring instrument. All units are equal in magnitude; for example, the distance from four inches to seven inches is equal to the distance from ten inches to thirteen inches. This characteristic is to be contrasted with that of many psychological tests (intelligence, personality) in which we do not know whether or not the units of measurement (scores) are of equal magnitude; that is, the difference between a score of 100 and 110 IQ points may *not* be equal to the difference between a score of 110 and 120 IQ points.

face validity Tests that are assumed to be valid simply by definition. For example, a ruler is a valid measuring instrument of length, by definition of what constitutes length.

frequency curve A graphic representation of the data from a frequency table. The measurement values are represented along the horizontal base line of the graph; the number of cases for each value, along the vertical axis. For each class interval a point, in the middle of the interval, is placed at the appropriate height to indicate the frequency of occurrence of cases in that interval. The points are then connected by lines to form a frequency "curve." The more technical name for this kind of frequency graph is "frequency polygon."

frequency table An orderly arrangement of discrete values in terms of the frequency of occurrence of the different values. Usually the different values are grouped together into class intervals, and the frequency table presents the number of cases falling into each class interval.

histogram A bar diagram that presents the data from a frequency table. Each class interval is represented by a separate bar, and the height of each bar indicates the number of cases falling within that class interval. The bars are usually arranged so that the bar representing the class

interval with the lowest measurement value is at the extreme left of the diagram and the one with the highest measurement value at the extreme right. The histogram is sometimes referred to as a "frequency graph."

independent events Two events are said to be "independent" when the occurrence of one does not influence, in any degree, the probability of the other's occurrence. For example, when two coins are flipped, the fact that one may fall heads does not influence at all the probability that the other will also fall heads—or tails. The probability of the occurrence of independent events is obtained by multiplying the probabilities of the individual events.

"known-group" method A method for determining the validity of a test by comparing the scores made on the test by a group previously "known" to be high on a certain trait with the scores of a group "known" to be lower on that trait.

mean (M) The arithmetical mean, frequently called the "arithmetical average," is the most commonly used measure of central tendency. It is the arithmetical sum of all the values in a set of data divided by the number of cases. The formula for the mean is written

$$M = \frac{\Sigma X}{N}.$$

The value of the mean can be strongly influenced by a few extreme values found in the set.

median A measure of central tendency. It refers to that value in an array of values arranged from the lowest to the highest that occupies the middle point. In such an array the median value would thus have as many cases below it as above it. The value of the median is not very strongly influenced by extreme items in the set of values.

mode A measure of central tendency. It refers to the *most frequent* value occurring in a set of values. The terms "most popular" and "most frequent" can be regarded as synonymous. The value of the mode is not at all influenced by a few extreme items in the set of values.

mutually exclusive events Two events, one of which, when it occurs, makes impossible the simultaneous occurrence of the other. For example, when a coin is flipped, the showing of a head makes impossible the simultaneous showing of a tail. The showing of head and the showing of tail are thus mutually exclusive events. The probability of occurrence of two or more mutually exclusive events is obtained by adding the probabilities of the individual events.

negative correlation Inverse relationship of the

values of two sets of measures. For example, if we found that children who are good in arithmetic are *poor* in reading and that those who are poor in arithmetic are *good* in reading, we would have a negative correlation.

normal curve A perfectly symmetrical, bell-shaped frequency curve having certain well-defined mathematical characteristics. Among these are the following: Within the area of the curve marked off by $\pm 1\sigma$ (from the mean) will be found 68.26 per cent of all the scores in the distribution; within the area marked off by $\pm 2\sigma$ will be found 95.44 per cent; and within the area marked off by $\pm 3\sigma$ will be found 99.75 per cent. A distribution curve made up of many chance events will approximate a normal distribution curve.

percentile score One type of a converted score expressing a person's score relative to his group in percentile points. A percentile point divides the total distribution of scores into 100 parts, each containing 1 per cent of all the cases. A percentile score of 90 thus means that 10 per cent of the people in the group scored above that point and 90 per cent scored below. Percentile scores vary from 0 to 100, no matter what the range of the raw scores. Percentile scores make it possible to compare the performance of people on diverse tests having quite different raw units of measurement.

population *All* the objects or people of a given class. For example, a population of vocabulary items would refer to all the words in a given language.

positive correlation Direct relationship of the values of two sets of measures. For example, if we found that children who are good in arithmetic are also good in reading and that those who are poor in one are poor in the other, we would have a positive correlation.

probability A mathematical theory dealing with the lawful and therefore predictable relations among truly chance events.

product-moment correlation coefficient (*r*) The product-moment correlation coefficient, symbolized by the small letter *r*, is based on the values of the individual deviations and the standard deviations of the two sets of scores. The formula for the product-moment correlation coefficient is

$$r = \frac{\Sigma xy}{N\sigma_x \sigma_y}.$$

The product-moment correlation coefficient is sometimes called "Pearson's coefficient of corre-

lation" after its inventor, Karl Pearson, an English mathematician. This coefficient is commonly used where *N* is relatively large.

random sample The result of a sampling procedure permitting every member of the population an equal opportunity to be included. Contrasted with a "biased sample."

range The simplest numerical measure of dispersion. It is calculated by obtaining the difference between the two extreme (or end) values of a distribution; thus the value of the range is greatly influenced by one extreme score.

rank-order correlation coefficient (*ρ*) A correlation coefficient symbolized by the Greek letter *ρ* (rho) based on a comparison of the ranks of people on two sets of scores. The formula for the rank-order correlation coefficient is

$$\rho = 1 - \frac{6\Sigma D^2}{N(N^2 - 1)}.$$

The rank-order correlation coefficient is usually employed where the number of cases (*N*) is relatively small (about fifteen to twenty cases).

raw scores The original scores obtained from a measuring instrument, contrasted with *converted scores*.

reliability coefficient Refers to the degree to which repeated measurement of an instrument will give the same or similar readings. This degree is determined by getting the correlation coefficient between two sets of measurements of the same object by the same measuring instrument. The higher the correlation, the more *reliable* the instrument.

sample A portion of a *population*, taken as representative of the whole population. If the sample is truly *random*, conclusions based on it can be taken as valid for the whole population.

sampling error An error contributing to lack of representativeness of a *sample*. When we measure a sample of subjects and attempt to generalize to the total population, we may make wrong generalizations because our sample was not perfectly representative of the population.

skewness Refers to deviation of the shape of a frequency curve from a normal curve. A skewed curve, therefore, is a frequency curve that departs from the symmetrical normal curve either by having more cases on the right of the mean than on the left, or vice versa. In a skewed curve the values for the mean, median, and mode are not identical.

split-half reliability A method for determining the reliability coefficient for a measuring instrument by obtaining the correlation coefficient between two equal halves of the same test. By splitting a test into two halves, the scores on the odd-numbered items are grouped together to form one subscore and the scores on the even-numbered items to form the second subscore. For this reason the split-half reliability method is sometimes referred to as the "odd-even method."

standard deviation (S.D., σ) A measure of dispersion based on the average of the deviations *squared* of every score in the distribution, from the mean of all the scores of the distribution. The formula for the standard deviation is

$$\sigma = \sqrt{\frac{\Sigma d^2}{N}}.$$

The standard deviation is the most commonly used measure of dispersion.

standard error of the mean (σ_m) The standard deviation of a theoretical frequency curve made up of many sample means. Called the "standard error" because it is useful in estimating the degree to which the obtained sample mean deviates from the true mean of the population.

statistics The mathematical discipline relating to the analysis of numerical data. Statistical methods are designed to summarize such data, to assess their reliability and validity, to determine the nature and magnitude of relationships among sets of data, and to guide us in our attempts to generalize from observed events to new events.

validity coefficient The degree to which the measurements obtained with an instrument correlate with the criterion measures. When we ask whether or not an instrument is *valid*, we ask whether or not it measures what we think it measures. The higher the correlation coefficient between the scores on a test and the criterion scores, the more valid the test.

zero correlation The absence of a relationship between two sets of scores. For example, if we found that some children who are good in arithmetic are poor in reading, whereas other children who are good in arithmetic are also good in reading, we would tend toward a zero correlation.

intelligence and its measurement

overview / The practical usefulness of intelligence tests has long overshadowed the theoretical need that intelligence be adequately defined as a psychological entity. Even utilitarian considerations demand a definition, however, if only to decide whether intelligence is a unitary ability or a composite of a number of relatively independent abilities. Nevertheless, psychologists have largely resisted this demand and have instead pursued a pragmatic course, developing intelligence tests of diverse sorts that appear to "work," notwithstanding the vagueness of the human ability (or abilities) they intend to measure. These tests employ a number of criteria for acceptable test items that are sufficiently general to apply to tests developed from different theoretical views of the nature of intelligence.

Perhaps the fundamental criterion for an intelligence-test item is that it become easier to pass as the child grows older. This principle leads to the concept of mental age; the well-known intelligence quotient (IQ) is simply the ratio of mental age to chronological age. This ratio works until adolescence, at which time mental growth (as measured by intelligence tests) seems to reach a plateau, so that revised definitions of the IQ become necessary.

Intelligence tests are valid to the extent that they show sensible relationships with generally understood indexes of mental ability. Their validity is thus supported by their correlation with measures of school success and occupational achievement. These social attainments are, however, also related to such other characteristics of the individual as his aptitudes, abilities, and interests. Tests designed to measure these characteristics are generally of low validity, so that they typically are used only in conjunction with a number of other indicators to arrive at recommendations concerning an individual's educational program or career choice.

About the year 1900, at the request of the school authorities of Paris, the French psychologist Alfred Binet undertook to develop a set of tests that would identify mentally deficient school children, so that they could be placed in schools in which they would not be held to the standard curriculum. From that time on, intelligence tests have been used primarily to help predict the capacity of children and students to profit from "intellectual" training. The extension of intelligence testing to adults followed immediately. During World War I nearly 2 million men were screened for intellectual fitness and assigned to various specialties on the basis of intelligence tests; in World War II the number rose to several million, as the variety of intelligence and special-aptitude tests also multiplied. Today virtually no individual of the Western world can escape one or more such tests during his lifetime.

Intelligence and Intelligence Tests

Amid this enormous activity the question "What *is* intelligence?" has never received a completely satisfactory answer. The theoretical issue has been subordinated to the utilitarian emphasis of such massive testing programs. The chief requirement for intelligence tests has been that they "work," that they do a usefully accurate job of classifying individuals into ability categories. If we are, however, to understand whether or not and how intelligence can be modified, the role that it plays in the total functioning of the individual, and its biological (genetic and physiological) and social determinants, we must have some understanding of its nature.

Intelligence is a concept variously used and variously defined. Some people define it as the ability to adapt to new circumstances, others as the ability to learn, and still others as the capacity to deal with complex and abstract material.

Different psychologists have championed these (and other) definitions, and much research has been addressed to these issues. None of this research, however, has resulted in a clear definition of intelligence. For this reason many psychologists reached the point at which they no longer asked, "*What* is intelligence?" They decided instead that they could do a useful job of measuring intelligence without defining it. In this respect they were doing what the early physicists did when they studied heat. Long before the physicists could agree on a sound definition of heat, they had invented reliable thermometers to measure changes in temperature, and with these instruments they were able to discover many important physical laws.

The need to confront the problems of the definition and meaning of intelligence is not easily evaded, of course, for the reasons we have already discussed. Even for those whose main concern is practical prediction from intelligence tests, the issue of understanding what it is that such tests are measuring is of immediate importance. If nothing else, such understanding could lead to different and perhaps better tests. Consider, for example, the following basic question: Can we regard intelligence as a unitary ability, or are there instead many relatively independent abilities that, for convenience or through ignorance, we lump into a single trait? The answer to this question could determine whether or not we should abandon our search for a better test of "general" intelligence and seek to devise instead separate tests for separate intellectual abilities.

Rather than undertake the unrewarding semantic exercise of a formal definition of intelligence, we shall attempt to develop the concept of intelligence gradually, as we now examine the process of making intelligence tests and the research findings from them.

The Making of an Intelligence Test

There are many different kinds of intelligence tests. There are *individual tests* (which test one person at a time) and *group tests* (which test a number of people at a time); *speed tests* (whose scores are determined by the number of correct responses made within restricted time limits) and *power tests* (in which the difficulty of the tasks successfully completed determines the score); *verbal tests* (requiring verbal responses to questions) and *performance tests* (involving such nonverbal responses as stringing variously colored beads in a specified order).

But, whatever the type, intelligence tests usually consist of relatively large collections of different test items, or tasks, and an intelligence-test score is based on the total number of those tasks completed successfully. In constructing a test, various kinds of items are tried out, for example, word definitions, arithmetic problems, perceptual tasks, following complex directions. In the initial construction of the test the psychologist is guided by the following simple principle: As an intelligence test is designed to measure the "intellect" rather than, say, temperament or motor skills, it seems clear that the items in the test should be of an "intellectual" nature. When an item is being considered for inclusion in an intelligence test, its content is examined with a common-sense definition of "intellectual" in mind. If the psychologist is satisfied that an item offers an intellectual task, it is included for trial. A test made up of such items is, by the test maker's own definition, an "intelligence test." But the test must meet several other validating criteria before it can be accepted as useful.

Criteria for Test Items Beside being "intellectual" in content, prospective test items must satisfy several rather specific criteria.

1. The behavior required by the item must be within the repertoire of the individuals to whom the test will be given. Infants cannot speak, and only nonverbal responses are therefore called for in infant mental tests; for illiterate or preliterate people the tester cannot use items that require reading or writing.

2. The item should be interesting to the person in order to reduce unwanted variations in performance resulting from poor motivation or flagging attention.

3. In line with the second criterion, the item should neither favor an individual nor put him at a disadvantage because of the particular group to which he belongs. For example, a certain item may appeal more immediately to boys or be more familiar to them than to girls; this is usually true of items involving mechanical problems. Because sexually neutral test items are hard to come by, the alternative solution is to balance the bias by awarding each sex an equal number of its favorites. Although this problem is difficult in the case of sex, it is more difficult when we attempt to be fair to a cultural minority. In any society, psychologists usually come from the dominant social group; as a result, they tend, perhaps unintentionally, to pick items meaningful and familiar to their own group. For example, in our society most psychologists come from the white, middle-class, urban culture, and therefore the chosen items reflect their culture rather than those of lower classes, Negroes, or rural people. As we shall see on p. 689, psychologists have recognized this problem, and they have put a great deal of effort into the construction of "culture-fair" tests.

4. The fourth criterion reflects the common-sense assumption that people grow "brighter" as they grow older, at least through the childhood years. According to this criterion, the item should effectively discriminate among children of different ages, in such a way that an increasing number of children are able to pass it at each higher age level. For example, in preparing the 1937 revision of the Stanford-Binet Intelligence Test, Terman and Merrill (1937) tested the ability of children of various ages to define such words as "connection" and "carrying." They found that almost no eight- or nine-year-olds could pass this item. About 10 per cent of the ten-year-olds were successful. Beyond that age the percentage of children able

to handle the item increased rather regularly. Thirty per cent of the eleven-year-olds, 50 per cent of the twelve-year-olds, more than 60 per cent of the thirteen-year-olds, and 70 per cent of the fourteen-year-olds were able to handle the item successfully. At the age of seventeen more than 90 per cent of the subjects could handle it. This item, therefore, was considered a good one because an increasing number of children were able to pass it with each higher age level.

5. The final criterion we shall discuss is that the item show a positive relation to the total intelligence-test score. Specifically, individuals who pass the item should earn a higher score on the over-all test than those who fail it. The rationale for this criterion implies a particular view of the nature of intelligence, that it is at least a somewhat unitary, generalized ability of the individual. To pass any given item should make it more probable that other items would be passed if, indeed, it is meaningful to speak of people as *generally* more or less intelligent. To reverse the perspective, it would seem to be absurd to permit success on a particular mental-test item to add a point to the total test score if those able to pass the item were shown, by this same total score, to be *less* intelligent than those who failed it.

Standardization of Test Items In order to apply these criteria for test items, we must first collect responses to them from a large and adequate sample of persons. For example, to say that the "average" ten-year-old can pass a particular item and that the "average" eight-year-old cannot implies, of course, that we have previously tested the item on a representative sample of the entire population of ten-year-old children and of eight-year-old children. To assert that passing a given item is positively related to the total intelligence-test score implies that we have obtained responses on this item, and on the total test, from a representative sample of the population of persons for whom the test is intended. This procedure for es-

tablishing the "standard" quantitative test performance by a representative sample of the kinds of persons to be tested is called *standardization* of the test items.

The problem of obtaining a sample truly representative of the entire desired population is beset with obvious difficulties. Yet if the sample used in standardizing an intelligence test is unrepresentative of the entire population of individuals, the test will be limited in its usefulness. If the test is given to individuals from groups not properly included in the standardization sample, it may yield biased results, which can give rise to dangerously misleading interpretations.

Once we have arrived at a collection of items that, through the process of standardization, have been demonstrated to meet the criteria we have discussed, we are well on the way to having a usable intelligence test. A crucial question remains. Does this test give a *valid* measure of intelligence? In order to comprehend fully the considerable body of research that has been devoted to the question of validity, we must first become familiar with the two major quantitative measures in terms of which performance on intelligence tests is stated— mental age and IQ.

Mental Age

It will be remembered that the Terman-Merrill task of defining words was passed by about 60 per cent of thirteen-year-old children. Such an item, because it can be passed by a majority of thirteen-year-olds, is therefore placed at year 13 on the intelligence-test scale. Similarly, every item in an intelligence test can be given its appropriate age-level value. When a child is tested, his score, based on the number of items passed, can then be described in terms of age.

For example, suppose that a child passes all the items that were passed by at least 60 per cent of all the ten-year-olds taking this test, as well as some of the items for eleven- and twelve-year-olds. He then is credited with all

the items up to and including those for ten-year-olds, plus those he passes above the ten-year age level. If he passes half the items for year 11 and one-fourth the items for year 12, he receives an additional six months' credit for the items for eleven-year-olds and three months' credit for the items for twelve-year-olds. Totaling these credits gives him a total *mental age*, or *MA*, of ten years and nine months. This method of scoring is illustrated in the following listing, which gives some of the tests for the years 6 and 14 in the 1937 Stanford-Binet revision, together with the scoring credits:

Year 6 (six items, two months' credit for each item passed)

1. Giving meanings of such words as "orange," "envelope," "puddle"
2. Stringing a chain of seven differently shaped beads in a specified order
3. Discovering missing details or absurdities in pictures
4. Counting up to nine blocks
5. Pointing out similarities and differences in pictured objects
6. Tracing the correct path through a pictured maze

Year 14 (six items, two months' credit for each item passed)

1. Vocabulary of more difficult words
2. Discovering the rule followed in a series of paper foldings
3. Telling how to measure out three pints, using a four-pint and a nine-pint can
4. Pointing out absurdities in pictures
5. Directional orientation: "Suppose you were going west, then turn to your right, then . . . ," and so on
6. Giving the meaning of abstract words

Intelligence Quotient As we have seen, to say that a child has a mental age of ten years and nine months means that he has passed the same items as the average child ten years and nine months old. But suppose that, although he has a mental age of ten years and nine months, he has a *chronological age* (*CA*) of nine years and six months. Obviously he is somewhat brighter than the average child of nine and a half. We can, if we wish, indicate

this fact by a score that will express his *mental age as related to his chronological age*. This score is called the *intelligence quotient*, or the *IQ*.

On the Binet test the IQ is obtained by taking the ratio of mental age (MA) to chronological age (CA) and multiplying it by 100 in order to remove decimal points. We thus arrive at the formula:

$$IQ = \frac{MA}{CA} \times 100.$$

Our child with a mental age of 10.75 and a chronological age of 9.5 would then have an IQ of 113:

$$IQ = \frac{10.75}{9.50} \times 100 = 113.2$$

(the decimal fraction is usually dropped). Another child with a chronological age of ten years and nine months who also obtained a mental age of exactly ten years nine months would have an IQ of 100:

$$IQ = \frac{10.75}{10.75} \times 100 = 100.$$

It can be seen that an IQ of 100 will be characteristic of the *average* child of any age, an IQ greater than 100 will indicate an intelligence somewhat superior to the average, and an IQ lower than 100 will indicate a somewhat less than average brightness. It should be clear that this convenient outcome (average *IQ* = 100) is not the result of a magical collusion between some Great Psychologist and Nature but necessarily results from the arbitrary arithmetic convention we have adopted to express the IQ. (See Box 139, p. 650, for a further discussion of the meanings of IQ scores.)

One feature of this method of determining the IQ promises trouble—the assumption that mental age continues to increase with chronological age. If, instead, there is a certain chronological age beyond which mental age no longer increases but remains stationary, then an individual who has once reached his peak will earn

Box 139

The Genius and the Moron

The Child Whose IQ Is	Is Equaled or Excelled by (Children out of 10,000)
160	1
152	8
140	70
130	300
120	1,100
110	2,700
100	5,000
90	7,300
80	8,900
70	9,700
60	9,900

We all have a strong urge to translate IQ scores into such descriptive and colorful terms as "genius," "moron," and "idiot." For the most part, however, psychologists have shied away from such translations, primarily because the IQ scores for large populations show a normal distribution curve. That is, there is no sharp break between an IQ of, say, 50 or 70 (the IQ scores that are conventionally taken as the limits defining the moron) and lower or higher IQs. Furthermore, we know full well that whether or not an individual's performance justifies the honorific term "genius" depends as much upon other factors as it does upon IQ—upon *special* skills, abilities, motivation, and other personality factors.

As IQs are relative scores, the most helpful guide to understanding the meaning of an IQ score is in terms of the number of children in the total population who equal or exceed such a score. The values in the table are based on such estimates made by R. Pintner, A. Dragositz, and R. Kushner for the revised Stanford-Binet Intelligence Test.

The data tell the important story of individual differences in intelligence-test scores. A test of 2,904 children shows a range of about 140 IQ points, from a low of 34 to a high of 174, with a standard deviation of 16.4. In intelligence, as among the other abilities of man, pronounced individual differences are the striking fact.

R. PINTNER, A. DRAGOSITZ, and R. KUSHNER. 1944. *Supplementary Guide for the Revised Stanford-Binet Scale* (Stanford: Stanford University Press).

lower IQ scores the older he grows, despite the fact that his intellectual abilities have not faltered. And there is good reason to believe that the growth in mental age does reach a relatively stationary level after a certain chronological age. Because of this "built-in" limitation of the IQ measure, it is necessary to modify the formula

$$IQ = \frac{MA}{CA}$$

for ages at which apparent gain in mental ability (as measured by the MA) fails to keep pace with chronological age. When does this transition point occur?

Mental-Growth Curve It is not surprising that mental age, at least among the young, does show a growth curve. Most tests are so constructed as to guarantee a growth curve because, as we have seen, one criterion for any item to be included in an intelligence test is that it show such an age trend (see criterion 4, p. 647). The growth curve of mental age is not, however, wholly of our own creation—a statistical artifact. The significant thing is that we have been able to find reasonable intellectual tasks that *do* give us such growth curves over a certain age range. Presumably if intelligence did not grow with age, we would not be able to discover such test items. And as Figure 39.1. illustrates, the same children studied throughout their development show a regular increase in MA as they grow older, through the age of fourteen.

Such findings certainly support the conventional formula for computing children's IQs. But what of older age groups? Until recently a simplifying assumption was made in computing the IQ from the Stanford-Binet test for older children and adults. As mental age no longer seemed to keep pace with chronological age by age fifteen, "final" chronological age was set at fifteen years. The formula for everyone older than fifteen became

$$IQ = \frac{MA}{15} \times 100.$$

This rather arbitrary and not wholly satisfactory solution has been replaced in a recent revision of the Stanford-Binet test (Terman & Merrill, 1960) by a different method of determining the intelligence quotient. In this method, initially developed for the Wechsler intelligence tests, the IQ simply represents the relative standing of the individual within his specific age group. For example, for two adults of different ages, of whom one scores higher than the average for his age group and the other scores lower than the average for his age group, we can say that the former has a higher IQ than does the latter. But now the IQ is no longer a quotient.

Wechsler Adult Intelligence Scale An approach to intelligence testing that was developed shortly after World War II departs from the

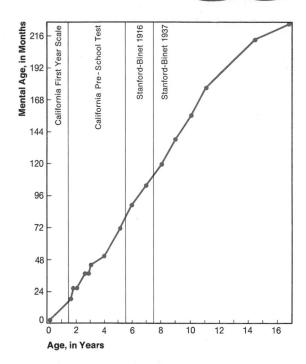

Figure 39.1. This curve represents the average mental ages of children studied in the Berkeley Growth Study, in which the same children were measured regularly over a period of many years for various characteristics, among them intelligence. Four different forms of intelligence tests (appropriate for each age range) were used: The California First Year Scale, The California Pre-School Test, the 1916 form of the Stanford-Binet Intelligence Test, and the 1937 revision of the Stanford-Binet Test. It will be noted that there is a diminished rate of growth in mental age after fourteen years.
N. Bayley, "Development and Maturation," in H. Helson, ed., *Theoretical Foundations of Psychology;* Copyright 1951 by D. Van Nostrand Company, Inc.; adapted by permission.

Binet strategy, with its dependence upon the mental-growth curve and the consequent link between mental and chronological age. The Stanford-Binet was initially developed for children and, as we have just seen, ran into difficulties when applied to adults. In addition to the IQ-computation problem, the items for the Stanford-Binet did not sample (and did not intend or claim to do so) the intellectual abilities of adults. The Wechsler Adult Intelligence Scale (Wechsler, 1958) does do so and, furthermore, arranges its items in two broad subscales: *verbal* and *performance*. Within these subscales, there are several subtests, each of which contains only items of a certain type. The verbal subscale includes subtests for information, comprehension, vocabulary, memory span for digits forward and backward, arithmetical reasoning, and recognizing verbal similarities. The performance subscale includes subtests involving object assembly (putting together cutout parts to complete a figure, like a human profile—very much as with a jigsaw puzzle), picture completion, arrangement of pictures in meaningful sequence, construction of certain designs from blocks, and learning to pair numbers with symbols.

Because this Wechsler test is designed for adults (there is another version suitable for testing children), the standardization samples were of course composed of adults. The criterion of selecting items that become less difficult with age was thus necessarily eliminated; the other criteria we have mentioned still applied. Furthermore, in computing the IQ from performance on this test, the mental-age concept could be abandoned. Instead, the IQ simply indicates, as we have already pointed out, the place of the individual in the distribution of scores for his age group.

The Validity of Intelligence Tests

The Wechsler and Stanford-Binet tests are commonly used to assess intelligence in the United States, and they have been adapted for use in other countries. These tests seem to measure very much the same thing—whatever that thing may be. A number of studies have found a correlation of about .80 between the two. One or the other, and sometimes both, is used as a standard against which to validate other mental tests. Correlations between a new test and the standard are interpreted as indicating the degree to which the new instrument is a valid measure of intelligence. Correlations of .60 or .70 are considered "acceptable." This approach to assessing validity is limited, as it is essentially a question-begging operation because it assumes that the "standard" is a valid measure of intelligence, and this assumption is yet to be proved.

If we are not content to validate intelligence tests against one another, then we must glance again at our emerging definition of intelligence for a clue to new validating criteria. So far we have made the assumption that this capacity we call "intelligence" develops with age, at least up to a point. Also, we have generally treated it as if it were a more or less unitary ability, despite attempts, like Wechsler's, to measure some of its possible separate facets as well. We can safely make yet another assumption: Intelligence is an adaptive ability and will reveal itself through more effective performance in the common tasks of social life. For the child as he grows up, these tasks are to be found in school; for the adult, they include his later educational attainment and, most important, his occupational choice and success.

Intelligence and School Success Two kinds of measures of school success have been correlated with intelligence-test scores—grades earned in school and subject-matter achievement tests. In the first case, subjective factors are involved, for the determination of a student's grades can obviously reflect a teacher's judgment of and attitude toward the student. In the second case, such possibly biasing factors play no role, for achievement tests are usually objectively scored, comprising the familiar true-false, multiple-choice, matching, and completion items, and are designed to measure how much of the subject matter of the course the student has mastered.

In both cases the correlations are positive. Correlations between intelligence tests and school grades average about .50, with some school subjects typically showing higher, and some lower, correlation coefficients.

Cronbach (1960) reviews studies of the relationship between intelligence and ultimate educational attainment. For those awarded the Ph.D. degree, IQ averages about 130. The mean IQ for all college graduates is 120. High-school graduates average 110. These values, of course, are for groups and have little to say about the individual case. Educational attainment is the result of an enormous variety of factors. But, for the purpose of assuring us that these tests do measure socially relevant intellectual abilities, these differences among IQ scores seem to make the point.

Intelligence and Occupational Aptitude When psychological testing was first tried in industry, intelligence tests were used almost exclusively in selecting workers for various occupations. This procedure was based on the belief that intelligence is a general factor important in the performance of all types of work. Later research cast some doubt on this assumption, and specialized *aptitude* tests were designed for each major occupational category. Nevertheless, intelligence-test scores do correlate highly with most kinds of work proficiency.

Two kinds of occupational-proficiency measures have commonly been used. One is the proficiency shown by an employee during the *training* period for his job. This measure of his performance is apt to be fairly objective and reliable, for he is being rated by skilled teachers and training personnel under standard conditions. The second measure is the worker's actual *performance* on the job after he has completed his training period. Here such measures as productivity or ratings by supervisors can be used. Two major conclusions can be drawn from a comprehensive survey by Ghiselli (1955)

of the validity coefficients of almost every conceivable aptitude test:

1. There is a wide range in the degree to which intelligence-test scores correlate with occupational proficiency. With training performance, the correlations range from −.03 for "gross manual workers" to .61 for "personal service occupations." With actual work on the job, the correlations range from −.10 for sales clerks to .47 for electrical workers (see Table 39.1. for some further illustrative findings).

2. For all the jobs examined, the over-all correlation between intelligence-test scores and job proficiency is almost as high as in any other *single* kind of aptitude test. The average correlation for *all* the tests with training performance on all the jobs was .27, whereas for intelligence tests with all the jobs it was .38. With actual work on the job, the average correlation for *all* the tests was .16; for the intelligence tests it was .19.

Not only do brighter persons do somewhat better than duller persons on the same job, but also some jobs seem to require or attract people of higher intelligence than do other jobs. According to data gathered from World War II enlisted men (Harrell & Harrell, 1945), such professions as teaching, law, engineering, and accounting average at least 120 in IQ. Clerical and sales personnel are somewhat

Table 39.1.

Correlation Coefficients Between Intelligence Tests and Various Occupations

OCCUPATION	TRAINING PERFORMANCE	JOB PERFORMANCE
Managerial work	.46	.28
Mechanical repairmen	.38	.18
Complex-machine operators	.34	.28
Computing clerks	.23	.18
Vehicle operators	.18	.14
Agricultural workers	.05	.00
Bench workers and assemblers	.02	.22
Salesmen	(no data)	.31

Data from E. E. Ghiselli, "The Measurement of Occupational Attitude," *U. Calif. Publ. Psychol.*, 8 (1955).

lower but still well above the mean. Various groups of manual workers fall, on the average, below an IQ of 100. These mean differences again accord with a functional view of intelligence and attest to the validity of the instruments we use to measure it. Perhaps the most interesting aspect of these findings, however, is the truly remarkable range of IQ scores found within any occupation. For example, some farm hands score above 140, whereas some lawyers fall below 100. Again the caution: Intelligence has something, but far from everything, to do with which occupations we select (or are selected by) and how well we do in them.

These kinds of data are an impressive testimonial to the pervasiveness of intelligence throughout man's behavior. Man's diverse abilities, whether expressed in school or in work, are reflected to some degree in "intelligence" as measured by intelligence tests.

Abilities, Aptitudes, and Interests

We have seen that, although intelligence has something to do with various measures of ability and achievement, it tells far from the whole story. Clearly, other factors contribute to an individual's pattern of abilities, aptitudes, and interests. The recognition that a highly intelligent individual may turn out to be a good musician but a poor scientist, a mediocre streetcar conductor but an excellent electrician, has led to the development of aptitude tests. *Aptitude* refers to the potential ability of a person to perform a specific kind of activity. Such ability is to be distinguished from proficiency achievement, which refers to the person's present performance. An aptitude test, therefore, is designed to detect some dormant or undeveloped ability within a person and to predict how well he will perform after he has had proper training in that activity.

Such tests, it was believed, would be of great value to many people. For industry, aptitude tests could be helpful in selecting people for various kinds of jobs; for the individual, they could be helpful in selecting the type of education, training, or work that would be proper for him. The usefulness of aptitude tests rests on the assumption, then, that different occupations require different abilities and that people differ in their ability patterns.

Occupational Ability Patterns

The evidence seems clear that different occupations require different proficiencies. The office clerk must be more proficient at number work than must the garage mechanic. But experience during two world wars has shown that people from various walks of life can learn highly specialized military duties with about the same efficiency. Retail tradesmen, for example, learned to be engine-room mechanics about as easily as did civilian machinists. This experience, together with continued research (recall the fact that intelligence tests correlate positively with almost every occupation), has suggested a revision of the original belief that for each person there exists a specialized type of work that is ideally suited to his specialized aptitudes. It appears, rather, that we can divide people into three broad groups in this respect.

Some people have no special aptitude that stands out above the rest, and the general level of all their aptitudes is so low that they can carry on only relatively unskilled or semiskilled work. Aptitude tests could be of no help in directing them into specific occupations. For other people, the general level of all of their aptitudes is so high that they can be successful in almost any occupation or profession. Aptitude tests can be of no great help to them either. But most people have an intermediate level of general ability. For them it is important to know which aptitudes stand out above the rest, so that they will be able to capitalize on their strongest points. For these people aptitude tests might make the difference between success and failure.

Psychologists have thus been spurred on to devise a multitude of aptitude tests. These many kinds of tests have been used for many different objectives and with varying degrees of success.

Varieties of Aptitude Tests

Some aptitude tests are designed to measure general aptitudes. There are tests of general mechanical aptitude and tests of general scientific aptitude that are supposed to predict future success in any kind of job involving mechanical ability or in any scientific field. There are also tests of specific aptitudes, designed to predict an individual's success as, for example, a garage mechanic, a lathe operator, a physicist, or a geologist.

In designing aptitude tests, a purely practical and common-sense approach was first attempted. Test items were selected primarily on the basis of the nature of the performance to be predicted and ranged from intellectual items to measures of quickness of muscular response. The various aptitude tests thus designed can be classified into four broad categories.

Intellectual Tests We have already seen that intelligence tests have been used with some success in predicting proficiency in the various trades and crafts and in the more "scholarly" occupations. In addition to the usual items found in general intelligence tests, aptitude tests occasionally have "tailor-made" items for the specific occupations involved. For example, an arithmetic item in a test for cashiers may take the form of a series of transactions that involve making change.

Spatial-Perceptual Tests Tests of this type are designed to measure speed and accuracy in perceiving spatial relations. Frequently these spatial relations are presented in the context of mechanical problems, and their solution requires the application of mechanical principles

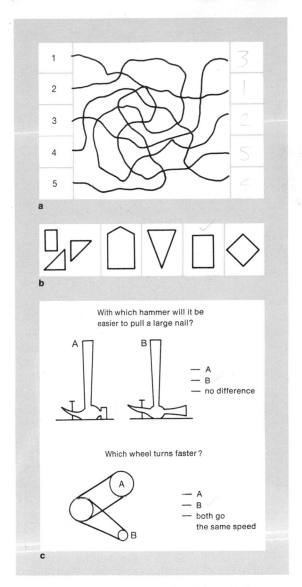

Figure 39.2. Examples of items found in spatial-perceptual aptitude tests. In a ("pursuit test") the subject is required, by eye alone, to follow the winding path from each of the five points of departure and to indicate where the path terminates. In b (spatial relations) the several smaller forms in the square on the left can be assembled to make one of the four forms on the right. Item c is self-explanatory.
E. E. Ghiselli and C. W. Brown, *Personnel and Industrial Psychology, 2nd ed.;* Copyright 1955 by McGraw-Hill Book Company, Inc.; adapted by permission.

Figure 39.3. Examples of items found in motor-aptitude tests. In a ("dotting"), the individual is required to make a single dot in each of the series of irregularly placed small circles. Speed and precision of movement are important here. In b ("tapping"), the squares, which the person must tap with his pencil, are relatively large, so that precision of movement is relatively less important than in the dotting test. Speed is emphasized here.
E. E. Ghiselli and C. W. Brown, *Personnel and Industrial Psychology*, 2nd ed.; Copyright 1955 by McGraw-Hill Book Company, Inc.; adapted by permission.

as well as accurate perception of spatial relations (see Figure 39.2.).

Motor Tests   Motor tests are designed to measure speed and dexterity of simple movements. Included as items in these tests are dotting and tapping tasks measuring speed and accuracy (see Figure 39.3.); dexterity tasks, in which the individual is required, for example, to pick up very small pegs and insert them into holes (finger dexterity) or to pick up a block in each hand, turn the blocks over, and replace them in their original location (hand dexterity); and reaction-time tasks in which quickness of response is measured. In simple reaction-time tasks the subject is required to depress a telegraph key with his finger as soon as a signal light goes on, and the time between the appearance of the stimulus and the onset of the response is measured. In complex reaction-time tasks, several different stimuli are presented serially, and the subject is required to make a different response to each. Sometimes the score is determined by the speed of his reaction, sometimes by the number of errors made.

Talent Tests   A number of tests have been designed to measure such special aptitudes as

musical or artistic talent. One of the oldest is the Seashore test for musical talent, designed in 1919. It makes use of a number of phonograph records that present musical notes or patterns of notes differing in pitch, intensity, time, rhythm, and timbre. On each record the subject has to make a number of comparisons between the patterns of notes. With pitch, for example, pairs of notes that differ from each other in frequency from twenty-four vibrations per second to one half vibration per second are sounded. The person has to choose which of the pair has the higher pitch.

Validity of Aptitude Tests

All these aptitude tests yield disappointingly low validity coefficients. When used in industry, the spatial-perceptual tests show the highest correlation with proficiency at work, the intellectual tests next, and the motor tests last (see Table 39.2.). For all tests investigated and for many different jobs, the highest average validity coefficient is found with the perceptual speed test, a correlation of .27.

The rather low validity of aptitude tests may

Table 39.2.

Average Validity Coefficients for Various Types of Aptitude Tests for Various Jobs

TYPE OF TEST	CORRELATION
Intellectual	.19
Spatial-Perceptual	
Spatial relations	.14
Pursuit	.19
Perceptual speed	.27
Mechanical principles	.26
Motor	
Dotting	.15
Tapping	.14
Finger dexterity	.19
Hand dexterity	.14
Arm dexterity	.17

(Data from Ghiselli, 1955)

have more serious consequences when they are used to counsel a person about his future career than when they are used to assign employees to certain kinds of jobs. In the latter instance, even a test with low validity might still be better than no test at all. The fact that an employment office on the basis of aptitude tests makes errors in, say, 20 per cent of the people allocated to jobs may be of minor importance to the industry and perhaps even to the individual. Changes can be made. But the situation is quite different in the counseling office. If an aptitude test for nursing has a very low validity coefficient and if the counselor misdirects even one student into taking the nursing course—in which she may fail miserably after a year or two of trying—a fairly grave error has been committed. Counseling offices are fully aware of the low validity of most aptitude tests and are therefore reluctant to let final decisions about what people should do with their lives rest upon these test results alone.

The low validities of most aptitude tests (including the so-called "talent" tests) has led to a reorientation in aptitude-test construction. Instead of depending solely upon common-sense appraisals of the requirements for any specific occupation, factor-analysis methods are now being used in an attempt to determine which abilities are important for which occupations. Instead of testing for distinctive "vocational aptitudes," more general and perhaps more basic aptitudes are being investigated: First, rather than single specialized tests, batteries of tests are now used for each occupation; second, other general factors like the individual's personality and interests are being measured in an attempt to help determine his vocational aptitudes. This development is a reflection, again, of the basic principle we have observed at work throughout this book: A person's behavior is determined by many factors—perceptual, intellectual, and motivational—operating simultaneously.

The Strong Vocational Interest Blank

It is instructive to note that it was the applied psychologists who were concerned with the occupational abilities of men and who made the first attempts to study and measure the interests of men. Only recently has their work been incorporated into the general body of psychological knowledge.

The initial work on measuring occupational interests was done by Strong of Stanford University, who in 1927 published for the first time the Strong Vocational Interest Blank. Since then the interests of thousands of people, in various professions and occupations, have been measured and tabulated by psychologists.

The method of constructing this interest test was purely empirical. Strong collected several hundred items of many kinds—statements about occupations, school subjects, recreational activities, personality characteristics—and then asked his subjects to indicate the degrees of their interest in each item on a three-point scale. For example, one occupational item was "actor," and the respondent was asked to indicate whether he liked, was indifferent to, or disliked actors. A recreational item was "collecting postage stamps," and again the respondent was asked to signify whether he liked, was indifferent to, or disliked stamp collecting. Strong then gave these tests to hundreds of people from various professions and occupations. He found that people from certain occupations tended to respond to certain items in similar ways. For example, 60 per cent of successful engineers said they disliked actors, whereas only 47 per cent of men in general said they disliked actors.

On the basis of such an analysis Strong was able to determine various patterns of likes, dislikes, and indifferences, which characterized forty-five different occupational groups for men and twenty-five for women. It is clear that this determination represents a purely empirical, descriptive analysis. It does not tell us why morticians, for example, have the interests they do, nor does it even tell us that they are interested in being morticians. All it tells us is that the average successful mortician likes certain things, dislikes others, and is indifferent to still others.

Validity of Interests Inventories

The mere fact that people of one occupational group have different interests than people of other groups has some practical value for vocational counseling. A test based on such preference patterns has face validity. When any individual receives a high "engineering" score on an interest inventory, we can, by definition, say that such a person has an interest pattern similar to that of most engineers. We have, therefore, one more bit of information about him that will enable us to advise him on his vocational choice. If, for example, his pattern of interests is similar to that of real-estate salesmen and if other tests are consistent with this finding, he may be well advised to become a real-estate salesman.

Our confidence in the usefulnes of interests inventories does not rest only upon this point. A consistent research finding has been that the patterns of likes and dislikes that characterize a person as a member of a given occupational group remain constant over the years. By now there are a number of groups of people who were first tested on the Strong test during their high-school and college days and have been retested many years later. The correlations between their test and retest scores are consistently high (see Table 39.3.). The pattern of interests seems to be a rather permanent characteristic of an individual.

Another line of corroborative evidence comes from studies showing that occupational experience seems unimportant in the development of interest patterns. That is, it appears that a person's interest pattern develops before he selects an occupation and that this pattern

Table 39.3.

Permanence of Interest Scores

NUMBER OF SUBJECTS	EDUCATIONAL LEVEL	AGE AT TIME OF TEST	AGE AT TIME OF RETEST	MEDIAN CORRELATION
50	College Freshmen	19	20	.88
50	College Freshmen	19	38	.72
50	College Seniors	22	27	.84
228	College Seniors	22	44	.75

(Data from Strong, 1951)

remains relatively constant thereafter. For example, undergraduates who show high interest scores characteristic of physicians tend to remain in the medical profession for longer periods of time than do undergraduates who do not show such high interest scores. The latter tend to drift away from medicine even after they have completed their medical training. The same is true of people in engineering and other professions.

It should be remembered, of course, that, though these studies indicate that most people change very little in their interest patterns, all people are not necessarily stable in their preferences. As a matter of fact there are great individual differences in stability of interests, even among adults. Some people show radical changes in their interests as measured by any of the available interest tests.

One point merits a great deal of thought and concern. The interest test is used in counseling centers and in employment offices to help recruit new members for the various occupations and professions. Such use of the interest test can be negative as well as positive. For example, the college student whose interest pattern is not similar to that of the typical "successful engineer" may be discouraged from entering the profession. But this discouragement may have unfortunate consequences for society and the welfare of the profession. Some professions may very well need different kinds of people with patterns of interest different

from those of the present practitioners. This possibility is especially likely in a changing world in which new demands are being made on all professions and occupations. But there seems to be a "freezing" of the status quo. We are recruiting only conformers.

As we learn more about the abilities of man, we learn to predict better. In this instance, our ability to predict is put to use in selecting, and by selecting we eventually control. But, because we are selecting on the basis of our past experience, we may be "controlling out" possibilities for change. If so, grave questions of social policy must arise.

Glossary

aptitude The potential ability of a person to perform a specific kind of activity. The term is to be distinguished from "proficiency" or "achievement," which refers to the person's present performance capacity.

group tests Tests, designed to measure the general intelligence or specialized aptitudes of people, administered to large groups simultaneously. The Army General Classification Test (AGCT), used in World War II to measure the mental capacity of the American soldier, is an example.

individual tests Tests designed to measure the general intelligence or specialized aptitudes of people and administered to one person at a time. The Stanford-Binet test is an example.

intelligence quotient (IQ) A converted score based on performance on an intelligence test that expresses the individual's mental age (MA) in relation to his chronological age (CA). The formula for this relationship is

$$IQ = \frac{MA}{CA} \times 100.$$

The average IQ is therefore necessarily 100, because the average ten-year-old will receive an MA of 10 and so on. For persons older than fifteen years, the formula is revised to

$$IQ = \frac{MA}{15} \times 100.$$

mental age (MA) A converted score, based on performance on a mental test and determined by the level of difficulty of the test items passed. If a child, no matter how old he is, can pass only those items passed by the average ten-year-old, he will be given a mental-age score of 10. This unit was first proposed by Binet and is fairly widely used today. Because of the nature of the developmental curve, the MA unit is difficult to apply after the age of fifteen. See also *intelligence quotient*.

performance tests Tests designed to measure the general intelligence or specialized aptitudes of people and consisting primarily of motor- or perceptual-test items in which verbal facility plays a minimal role. The term is to be contrasted with "verbal tests."

power tests Tests designed to measure the general intelligence or specialized aptitudes of people in which the difficulty of the tasks that are successfully completed determines the score. To be contrasted with "speed tests."

speed tests Tests designed to measure the general intelligence or specialized aptitudes of people in which the scores are determined primarily by the rapidity with which correct answers can be given.

standardization When used in connection with tests, the procedure of administering a new test to a representative sample of people in order to determine the scale values for the scores. For instance, before we can assign a test item to a given age level (in the Binet test), we must give this item to a large number of children to determine its age level.

verbal tests Tests designed to measure the general intelligence or specialized aptitudes of people and consisting primarily of verbal-test items. The term is to be contrasted with "performance tests."

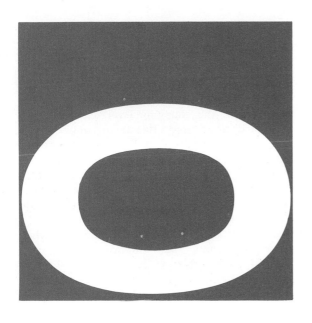

development
and structure
of intelligence

overview / Axiomatic to a reasonable definition of intelligence is that, at least through childhood, it increases with age. Research evidence generally supports this expectation. A quite independent question, however, is the extent to which one's IQ (a measure of an individual's intelligence *relative* to others of the same age) remains constant. Data on this issue from longitudinal studies (testing the *same* individuals over time) indicate that the IQ is far from constant and that predictions of later intelligence from tests in the preschool years especially are of low validity.

The structure of intelligence is quite a separate issue. The various theories can be categorized into three broad points of view: First, intelligence is a unitary ability, so that an intelligent individual tends to show superior ability in all intellectual tasks; second, intelligence is composed of a limited number of broad, relatively independent abilities; third, there is no general intelligence, nor are there broad types of mental abilities, but rather each specific intellectual task draws upon one or more specific and discrete abilities.

Research data do not permit an easy decision on the relative validity of these three conceptions of the structure of intelligence, partly because the principal method of such research (factor analysis) does not yield unequivocal results. The issue is further complicated by the suggestion in the evidence that the structure of intelligence changes with age.

The major question that may be asked about the development of intelligence is "How stable is intelligence over time?" Although it is clear that mental age increases with chronological age (at least up to adolescence), there is the question of whether or not the IQ (mental ability *relative* to chronological age) remains the same for a given individual throughout his life. The basic question of stability of intelligence thus comprises two issues: first, the average trend of mental ability from birth to death; second, the constancy of the IQ over time. These issues have different theoretical and practical implications.

Age and Intelligence

We have already seen in the previous unit (see Figure 39.1., p. 651) that *absolute* mental ability increases up to adolescence. Not that the rate of increase is the same for all children, or even that mental growth is always regular; it is not, and we shall present shortly some of the factors known to influence the course of mental development. This general intellectual growth with age conforms to the undebatable notion that older children are, on the average, intellectually more capable than younger ones. Beyond adolescence, however, it is by no means obvious what, if any, age trend is to be expected. True, we hope to grow wiser as we grow older, but we have no assurance that mental tests measure wisdom. What then is known of the fate of intelligence with aging through the adult years?

Cross-Sectional Studies

The general picture from cross-sectional studies (different age groups of people measured at a single point in time) is that intelligence reaches its peak at about age thirty and then begins to fall off ever more rapidly as we approach old age. This observation is true (in Wechsler's terms) of both "verbal" and "performance" intelligence, although the former reaches its peak, for the average person, a few years earlier. In a pioneer report of cross-sectional data of age differences in IQ, Jones and Conrad (1933) anticipated what has proved to be a reliable generalization. They found that performance on tasks involving general information declines very little, if at all, with age but that tasks in which rapid, "insightful" responses are critical do show a considerable drop. Because sheer speed of response seems

to figure in many mental-test tasks, however, some of the age-related decline may be attributable to a "nonintellectual" slowing down of the general pace of response as we grow older. Furthermore, the cross-sectional method is susceptible to confounding factors. One has to do with the changing level in educational standards over time. This factor might be especially important for studies conducted before the advent of universal minimum-education standards in the United States. For example, it is known that less-educated people do score somewhat lower on intelligence tests than do better-educated people. And if persons now aged sixty had received less education when they were young than did present-day thirty-year-olds when they were young, the difference in tested intelligence between these age groups *might* have reflected a historical trend in educational standards, rather than age changes per se.

A study by Tuddenham (1948) supports the reasonableness of this argument. He found that World War I and World War II soldiers (the latter with a higher average education) differed considerably in intelligence *when tested at the same age*. The World War II men scored higher, indicating that generational differences in educational standards may account for age differences in intelligence-test scores in cross-sectional studies.

Longitudinal Studies

Longitudinal studies bypass this difficulty. If we test the intelligence of the *same* individuals at two or more points in time, there is, of course, no effect of differing educational levels. The results from the few such longitudinal investigations we have present a picture of the age-intelligence relationship that runs counter to the assumption that intelligence declines in older people. Owens (1953) retested 127 men thirty years after they had taken the Army Alpha Intelligence Examination at the time of their entrance to college and found that these men scored significantly *higher* on the second testing than they had on the first. Bayley and Oden (1955) make the same general point and, furthermore, indicate that this result occurs in both sexes and over a considerable age range (see Figure 40.1.).

These results cannot be easily explained. One hypothesis that has been suggested is that intelligence does drop for the average person as he grows older but not for those who were mentally superior to begin with. (Both the Owens and the Bayley-Oden studies involved samples of above-average intelligence.) This contrast may indicate some biological difference between the mentally superior and the less superior, or it may reflect different life experiences of the two groups. The superior younger man may lead a more stimulating life than does his duller fellow citizen, and this continued stimulation may reflect itself in his higher score in later age. It may not be fruitful at this date, however, to speculate on the relative merits of these hypotheses because there is a major difficulty with data supporting the conclusion that people of superior intelligence continue to grow brighter with age whereas people of inferior intelligence do not. Mentally superior people have been tested by the longitudinal method, whereas the "average person" has so far been adequately studied only by the cross-sectional method. Obviously, more longitudinal studies must be made before we can settle this question.

Stability and Predictability of Intelligence

Investigation of stability and predictability of intelligence is the exclusive preserve of longitudinal studies because such questions require repeated measurement of the same persons over time. Not only do the data from such studies promise eventual understanding of adult changes in intelligence with age, but they also cast into a different light the apparent regularity of intellectual development implied by

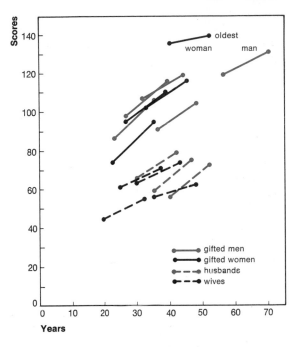

Figure 40.1. Average scores earned on a Concept Mastery Test by 422 "gifted men," 346 "gifted women," and their spouses. The Concept Mastery Test was designed by Terman. It consists of difficult vocabulary items and analogy items dealing chiefly with abstract ideas. The subjects have been grouped according to age at first testing. For example, in the lower left corner we have the scores of a group of wives who were first tested when they were about twenty years old and then retested when they were about thirty-two years old. The first and second tests for each group (twelve years apart) are connected. Note that all groups show similar tendencies to increase in scores over the twelve year period. "Gifted," as used here, refers to men and women who, while still children, were shown to have IQs ranging from 140 to 200. Note also the increase in scores made by the oldest woman (forty years at first testing, fifty-two at second) and the oldest man (fifty-six years at first testing and about seventy at the second).
N. Bayley and M. Oden, "The Maintenance of Intellectual Ability in Gifted Adults," *Journal of Gerontology*, 10 (1955), 91–107; adapted by permission.

the average mental-growth curves. The fact that the *average* curve is smooth up through adolescence does not require the inference that all, or even most, children show the same regular progression in intellectual development.

Quite the contrary is true; this regularity masks quite substantial changes in tested intelligence for many children during this period.

Honzik, Macfarlane, and Allen (1948) found from a longitudinal study of over 200 children that, during the school-age interval from six to eighteen years, 85 per cent of the group varied ten or more IQ points. Within that same period almost 10 per cent of the children fluctuated at least thirty points, a variability of about two standard deviations. (Stability of the IQ was greater for the less-bright child, a finding since substantiated in a number of investigations of the intelligence of infants, children, and adults.) The general picture of IQ predictability, as reported by these same investigators, is that mental tests are more predictive, over any given number of years, the older the individual is at the time of the tests. For example, over a three-year span, IQ at age two predicts IQ at age five only minimally (a correlation of .30); scores earned at ages seven and ten, however, correlate almost .80. This same study found practically a zero correlation (.07) between IQ at twenty-one months and at age eighteen. One clear conclusion that these data on instability directly suggest is that a single IQ score obtained relatively early in one's school career is utterly undependable for predicting later intelligence or scholastic and occupational achievement.

The possibility remains, however, that certain *items* or *groups of items* from very early mental tests *can* predict later intelligence. A report by Cameron, Livson, and Bayley (1967) lends some support to this speculation. They find, for example, that a tendency to vocalize, in infant girls only, substantially predicts later IQ (as late as age thirty-six), whereas the *total* score on infant-intelligence tests has *no* predictive value. This outcome confronts us with a challenge to the common view that intelligence is a unitary trait. The additional fact that IQ fluctuates arouses the suspicion that intelligence may be a heterogeneous assortment of separate abilities. We now turn to a direct examination of the evidence on the structure of intelligence.

The Structure of Intelligence

Seemingly endless controversy, and almost as much research, has focused on the issue of the structure of intelligence. Briefly put, the main argument revolves about how many separate and distinguishable aspects of intelligence exist. A secondary question has been—and remains—whether or not, and if so in what way, the structure of intelligence changes with age. On the first point, there are proponents for the views that intelligence, first, is a general and unitary capacity; second, is composed of a small group of broad and moderately independent factors; or, third, is a collection of discrete and separate abilities. On the second point—changes in structure with age—the main battle has been drawn between two camps. One claims that intelligence becomes increasingly differentiated with age, involving more relatively independent factors as we move through childhood into adulthood; the other claims that no systematic changes in structure take place over time.

Generality of Intelligence

The main case for any view of the structure of intelligence is based upon intercorrelations among mental abilities and upon how these intercorrelations are interpreted. It is clear that if every measure of intelligence correlated perfectly with every other measure, the unitary hypothesis would be strongly supported. If, on the other hand, all intercorrelations were zero, then the third view—that intelligence is a collection of discrete abilities—would be inevitable. Of course, as reality will always have it, the outcome is somewhere in between: Most measures of intelligence correlate positively, but only moderately, with one another. To help us interpret the meaning of any given set of intercorrelations among intelligence measures, the methods of *factor analysis* are employed. Without going into the details of this statistical technique, offering an example of how it is applied to studying the structure of intelligence may be of help.

Suppose we give a group of subjects two tests, an arithmetic-reasoning test and a vocabulary test, and we find that the two tests correlate positively. This single correlation, no matter how high, does not permit us to decide whether the two tests are measuring a general capacity related to "intelligence" or a specific capacity related to "verbal comprehension"—as even an arithmetic-reasoning test must be read and the words understood to be solved. We need more information. Suppose we now give the same subjects another test—a performance intelligence test that requires no reading—and then examine the resulting correlations obtained among all three tests. If we now find that the performance test correlates more highly with the arithmetic-reasoning test than with the vocabulary test, it might be argued that there are at least two abilities involved—one that is reflected in both the arithmetic-reasoning test and the performance test and another that is reflected in the vocabulary and the arithmetic-ability test. If all the correlations among the three tests are about the same size, then some over-all general ability seems to be involved.

By adding more and more different kinds of tests to our battery and studying the resulting correlations, we may eventually be able to discover the minimum number of different abilities we have to postulate in order to account for all the mental capacities of man. When we add many tests to our battery, however, we run into a major difficulty. The study of the interrelations of even a small number of tests involves a large number of correlations. Between two tests there is only one correlation; among three tests, there are three different correlations; among four tests, there are six correlations; among twenty tests, there are 190 correlations; and among fifty tests, there are 1,225 correlations. To deal with so many correlations simultaneously and to see which tests tap the same abilities require some method of arranging the many correlations into groups, so that the correlations within any one group have about the same interrelationships. The mathematical technique of factor analysis is designed to do just that. It should be pointed out, however, that there are different forms of factor analysis, based upon different mathematical assumptions. These different forms permit *alternate* interpretations of the structure of intelligence, even from the same set of intercorrelations.

The Two-Factor Theory At about the time that Binet was developing the first modern-style intelligence test (the early 1900s), Charles Spearman, a British psychologist and statistician, proposed that only a single "general intelligence" factor existed; he called this factor *g*, and said that it accounted completely for correlations among measures of mental ability. Certainly, he admitted, performance on any given task was not entirely a function of *g* (which at times he equated with "mental energy") but involved an additional factor specific to each task. These specific factors he labeled the *s* factors. Performance on an arithmetic-reasoning test would thus be determined by $g + s_1$, and performance on a vocabulary test would be determined by $g + s_2$. The fact that the two tests correlate positively would be accounted for by their common sharing of *g;* that the correlation is not perfect is accounted for by the fact that different and unrelated *s* factors are involved in each. Spearman "proved" his *two-factor theory* of intelligence (*g* and *s*) by application of a form of factor analysis (which he invented) to various sets of mental-test data that were then becoming available.

The Spearman view came under attack from the moment of its birth. To this day, however, it remains one of the many reasonable and useful ways of regarding intellectual performance. And it has to its credit the stimulation of considerable research and of other equally reasonable and useful conceptions of intelligence.

The Group-Factor Theory A major response to the two-factor theory is found in the work of L. L. Thurstone at The University of Chicago. Using a different method of factor analysis (which he invented), Thurstone came to the conclusion that most of the mental capacity of man could be accounted for by postulating seven primary mental abilities (Thurstone, 1938). They are

1. *Number*—the ability to add, subtract, multiply, and divide. This ability is not the same as arithmetic-reasoning ability because it involves only the four fundamental arithmetic processes.
2. *Word fluency*—the ability to write and speak with ease. This ability is not the same as verbal meaning (the next primary ability) because a person who knows very few words may be able to use them fluently, whereas a person who knows many words may be halting in his speech.
3. *Verbal meaning*—the understanding of ideas in word form.
4. *Memory*—the ability to retain and revive impressions or to recall and recognize past experiences.
5. *Reasoning*—the ability to solve complex problems, profit from experience, and plan new activities based on past experience.
6. *Spatial perception*—the ability to perceive size and spatial relationships correctly.
7. *Perceptual speed*—the ability to identify stimulus objects quickly. In developing reading skill, for example, it is necessary to identify entire words without carefully examining each letter in the word.

Tests were devised for each of these factors. These tests are known as the "Thurstone Primary Mental Abilities" tests ("PMA"). Thurstone did not, however, find that these primary mental abilities were independent. Each, in fact, correlates positively with each of the others. For example, *number* correlates .46 with *word fluency*, .38 with *verbal meaning*, .18 with *memory*, and so on; *verbal meaning* correlates .51 with *word fluency*, .39 with *memory*, and .54 with *reasoning*.

These findings imply that a general factor

could also be detected among the primary mental abilities. Thurstone recognized this implication. The point at issue is perhaps no issue at all. The two-factor theory accounts for the fact that mental tests generally show positive intercorrelations with one another; Thurstone's *group-factor theory* accounts for the fact that these correlations are somewhat higher among tests that, on their face, seem to measure a particular facet of intelligence. Of course, the more comprehensive we are in our definition of intelligence and the more diligently we work at finding new tasks to represent each facet, the more group factors we might find. Guilford has, also through factor analysis, found at least forty (Guilford, 1956) and has proposed a theoretical schema for intellectual ability (Guilford, 1959, 1967) that predicts that eventually 120 factors will be found.

The practical test of the validity of this proliferation of factors, and of tests to measure them, lies in their ability to predict behavior better than is possible by a single test score. So far the evidence is not conclusive. Whether or not this group-factor theory leads to a better theoretical understanding of intelligence also has not been determined. Some work has suggested, however, that the genetic determinants may follow a "group-factor" pattern. Box 140, p. 667, presents some of the relevant data.

The Sampling Theory The third view of the structure of intelligence is, in the words of one of its major proponents, that "our ability to solve [an intellectual task] depends upon a large number of things—genes we have inherited, pieces of information we have acquired, skills we have practiced, little habits of thought we have formed, all and sundry influences from past and present" (Thomson, 1952). According to this *sampling theory* of mental ability, tests correlate with one another *not* because of a common *g* or of common group factors but because the tests overlap in the particular discrete mental skills they sample from the vast total pool of specific abilities. One test, for ex-

Box 140

Patterns of Intellectual Inheritance

If intelligence can be differentiated into somewhat independent aspects, we might expect that the relative contributions of heredity and environment might vary with different aspects of intelligence. Put another way, any evidence that the balance of nature and nurture varies among different aspects of intelligence would be an impressive argument against considering intelligence as a single, unitary ability. To date, there is substantial support for this argument, and there is some agreement upon the particular facet of mental ability most influenced by genetic factors.

Thelma G. Thurstone, L. L. Thurstone, H. H. Strandskov, and, later on, D. B. Blewett compared identical twins (from single fertilized eggs and therefore genetically identical) with fraternal twins (from different eggs and therefore genetically related but different) on the Thurstone Primary Mental Abilities (PMA) tests. Both studies found that the correlations among scores of identical twins were generally higher, particularly on the tests that measured verbal and spatial abilities. The verbal-ability finding is particularly provocative, for it is in this aspect of intelligence that educational and other environmental factors are expected to be of greatest importance.

S .G. Vandenberg, also employing the identical-versus-fraternal-twin design, offered some possibly clarifying data from an extensive study at the University of Louisville, in which more than 100 psychological characteristics were measured. He also found that PMA verbal and spatial abilities (as well as, for the first time, numerical ability) have a significant hereditary component. Now the PMA verbal-ability test consists of six subtests. Vandenberg calculated separate determinations of the relative contributions made by heredity for each of the subtests. And he found that one of these subtests —a vocabulary test—showed no evidence whatever of a genetic contribution. This unexpected result became even more surprising when it was discovered that the vocabulary test from the Wechsler Intelligence Scale for Children, which was also included in the Vandenberg study, shows a very substantial hereditary component. One possible explanation for this contradiction, suggested by Vandenberg, is that the method used to assess vocabulary level may be critical; the PMA vocabulary test is of multiple-choice design, whereas the Wechsler test calls for spontaneous definitions of words by the subject. This same tendency for "free" as opposed to "restricted" measurement methods to yield higher heritability estimates was found in tests of other verbal abilities. This finding implies that the degree of heritability of intelligence varies, not only in verbal, spatial, and numerical abilities and the like, but also in particular manners or "styles" of cognitive functioning.

At this stage in the scientific game it must be considered a good thing to find such data, which prevent us from coming to too firm a set of conclusions about the structure of intelligence.

THELMA G. THURSTONE, L. L. THURSTONE, and H. H. STRANDSKOV. 1953. *A Psychological Study of Twins* (Chapel Hill: University of North Carolina Psychometric Laboratory Report No. 4).

D. B. BLEWETT. 1954. Experimental Study of the Inheritance of Intelligence, *J. Ment. Sci.*, 100, 922–33.

S. G. VANDENBERG. 1962. The Hereditary Abilities Study: Hereditary Components in a Psychological Test Battery, *Amer. J. Hum. Genet.*, 14, 220–37.

Box 141

Idiot Savant

From time to time there arise in the human population so-called "idiot savants"—feeble-minded persons with one or several highly developed specialities. The most intensively studied case is that of L, reported by M. Scheerer, E. Rothmann and K. Goldstein. L was first brought in by his mother, for psychological and neuropsychiatric examination, when he was eleven years old. His case was studied from 1937 to 1943.

Medical examination throughout the six-year period showed him to be healthy and physically well developed with no signs of neurological disturbance. His EEG was normal. But his mental examination revealed a world of paradoxes.

He could tell the day of the week for any given date between 1880 and 1950. He could add up correctly the totals of ten to twelve two-place numbers just as quickly as the examiner could call them out. He could spell correctly many words *forward* and *backward* and never forgot the spelling of a word once he was told how to spell it. He could play *by ear only* such musical compositions as the *Largo* by Dvořák and could sing, from beginning to end, the "Credo," "Si Ciel," and "Adagio Pathé-tique" from the opera *Otello*.

On the other hand, he was unable to follow the regular school curriculum. His general information was extremely substandard. He knew the meanings of very few words. He was almost com-

ample, may require abilities s_1, s_3, s_4, s_9, s_{21}, and s_{33}; another test may require s_1, s_2, s_5, s_9, s_{26}, and s_{33}. Therefore, the two tests will show some positive correlation because they have the specific abilities s_1, s_9, and s_{33} in common. Clearly, the data in support of the sampling conception of intelligence would be equally compatible with the data presented in support of either of the other two theories. As Thomson puts it, if one were to assume the validity of the sampling theory, then:

"The correlation coefficients between performances in tests will show exactly the same relationships with one another as they would have done had our ability depended on our possession of a small number of common 'factors.' But it does show that perhaps we haven't, that perhaps they are fictions."

If group factors are indeed fictions, Thomson's theory would anticipate that the search for new group factors must logically be endless because there are an infinite number of ways in which tests may overlap in their sampling of innumerable specific abilities. Guilford's 120 factors, then, may be only the beginning. See Box 141 for an extreme example of the complexities that the structure of intelligence can exhibit in an individual.

Age Changes in the Structure of Intelligence

That the structure of intelligence may change with age is another possibility that work with the problem has suggested. For example, Garrett (1946) has proposed that there is a progres-

pletely deficient in logical reasoning and was at a total loss in any problem involving abstractions. His IQ on the Binet was 50!

L seems to bear dramatic testimony against the notion that intellectual activities are determined by a unitary quality or capacity. But his case does not permit us to assume that intellectual activities are determined by a host of separate and independent capacities, one for each type of performance.

In the first place, as Scheerer, Rothmann, and Goldstein point out, L's superiority in a few narrowly specialized activities does not necessarily indicate special *endowment* in those capacities. Rather, what L seems to demonstrate is the effect of special motivation and practice in a very narrow field of activities. Any normal child *could* do what L did—and much more. These writers suggest the following analysis of the idiot savant.

There are both general and specific intellectual capacities. Abstract capacity and intelligence are essential for the normal functioning of *all* intellectual activities. When abstract intelligence is impaired, the person may be driven, to an abnormal degree, to exercise and develop those specific functions that are less impaired. But, because there is a close *interdependence* among all functions of the person, this interdependence can result only in atypical forms of expression in his relatively intact capacities. He therefore develops "queer" performance patterns. He can add two-place numbers but cannot understand the logic and rules of arithmetic. He can spell, but he cannot understand the meanings of words.

The performance of the idiot savant, no less than that of the normal person, is determined by the interaction of special capacities and general capacities.

M. SCHEERER, E. ROTHMANN, and K. GOLDSTEIN. 1945. A Case of "Idiot Savant": An Experimental Study of Personality Organization, *Psychol. Monogr.*, 58. No. 4.

sive differentiation in mental ability throughout the period of mental growth. Put another way, children should show more influence from *g*, adults more and clearer group factors. It is as if the structure of intelligence changes from a Spearman-like plan to a Thurstone-like plan as the child grows older.

The previous section should warn us, however, that detecting such changes in the kind, number, and interrelations of intelligence factors will be a difficult task indeed. One first precaution is obvious: Any talk of changes with age should involve data from the same mental test, factor-analyzed by the same method, and preferably based on the same individuals (longitudinal study). Few studies satisfy these requirements, but research and discussion on this

question nevertheless flourish. The consensus, to date, tends to support Garrett's hypothesis. As a recent example, we can point to the study of Osborne and Jackson (1964), which did satisfy the basic requirements listed. Employing a battery composed largely of subtests from Wechsler's Intelligence Scale for Children, they reported eight factors for six-year-old children tested immediately before entering the first grade. One year later these *same* children on the *same* test required ten factors to account for the intercorrelations among the various subtest scores.

One qualification to the acceptance of the differentiation hypothesis must be entered. Whatever evidence is offered in its support is also consistent with the more mundane hypothesis that the results arise from differences in the adequacy of test batteries employed at different ages *even* when the same tests are used for the different age groups. Any one test battery may be more appropriate for older children than for younger children. Conceivably, test constructors have been more thorough in their coverage of the intellectual domain of older subjects. Psychologists quite possibly may be less differentiated in their conception of the very young child's mental world and, therefore,

may measure it less comprehensively. If so, then the lesser differentiation of the young child may be in the mind and instrument of the tester, not in the child's intellectual abilities. At the very least, this consideration suggests the prudence of withholding final judgment on the differentiation hypothesis, as well as all other aspects of the structure of intelligence, until such time as we become more adept at thorough and systematic sampling of the ever-changing domains of man's intelligence.

Glossary

factor analysis A statistical technique applied to intercorrelations among mental tests (or any other set of measurable quantities) that detects the number of separate factors mathematically necessary to account for the obtained intercorrelations. Different factor-analytic methods can yield somewhat different results, but all typically find considerably fewer factors than the original number of tests.

group-factor theory A theory of the structure of intelligence that considers it to be divisible into a relatively limited number of group factors, each encompassing a number of highly related intellectual abilities.

sampling theory A theory of the structure of intelligence that considers it to be divisible into an essentially limitless number of discrete mental skills and accounts for the typical positive correlation among mental tests by assuming that some overlap usually exists in the samples of discrete skills measured by any given pair of mental-ability tests.

two-factor theory A theory of the structure of intelligence that considers it to be divisible into a single general factor (g), which enters into all intellectual performance, and a host of independent specific factors (s), related only to performance on a particular mental task.

variations
in intelligence

overview / The considerable variation among individuals and groups in intelligence can be attributed to a variety of sources. Genetic factors are of substantial importance, as shown by studies of the intellectual abilities of genetically related individuals, primarily studies that compare parents with their children and those that compare twins. Environmental factors also play a significant role in individual differences in intelligence, of course, and research on both man and animals indicates the intelligence-stimulating effects of rich environmental experiences, particularly when they occur in the earlier years of life.

Although intelligence, at least after early childhood, remains relatively stable throughout development, there is still room for important change. The determinants of change are often personality factors, but the nature and direction of the influence of such factors often depend upon the sex of the individual.

Racial, national, and class differences in intelligence-test performance exist, but their true causes are difficult to find. First of all, these factors interact so that at times it is impossible to identify which factor, if any, is the single cause of variation. Furthermore, when making group comparisons of this sort, we must attend to the crucial distinction between true intellectual ability and its estimate, as obtained through standard intelligence tests. Both the test content itself and, equally important, the nature of the total psychological situation in which the test is administered are rarely equivalent for groups living in a society in which equality of opportunity has not yet been assured. It is currently impossible, therefore, to determine how much, if any, of the difference in intelligence found in any group comparison reflects a real difference in mental ability. "Culture-fair" tests are of some help in making this determination, but the ultimate answer must await a world in which every individual is afforded the opportunity to express fully his intellectual potential.

Individuals and groups vary enormously in intelligence and abilities, and determining the origins of these differences is a central issue in psychological research. The issue, phrased in its broadest sense, comes to this question: To what extent can these variations in intelligence be attributed to genetic factors and to what extent to environmental factors?

In considering this issue we must, for the moment, suspend the awareness we have just developed that intelligence has many facets, for the bulk of research on nature and nurture in mental ability has employed some form of over-all IQ as its critical measure. The relevant evidence, although gathered by a variety of methods, points to an impressive regularity when taken together.

Perhaps the most general view of the findings is provided by Erlenmeyer-Kimling and Jarvik (1963), who have summarized the results from fifty-two studies, reported in the past half-century, on the problem of the heritability of human intelligence (see Figure 41.1.). Despite enormous differences among these studies in a number of important characteristics, for example, socioeconomic composition and nationality of the sample (data from eight countries were included) and types of tests used, the general picture that emerges is strikingly consistent and clear: *The closer the genetic relationship*

among people, the more alike they are in intelligence. These correlations probably represent minimal values because the studies have dealt with childhood data rather than with adult data and have not separated boys and girls. There is reason to believe that both these considerations make for an underestimate of the degree of heredity influence (see Box 142, p. 676). In fact, the median values shown in Figure 41.1. come very close to what would be predicted if heredity were the *sole* determinant of intelligence-test scores. The unmistakable influence of the environment can, however, be seen in the higher correlations for related individuals reared together than for individuals reared apart, even though the degree of blood relationship is the same for both groups. Also note the difference between unrelated persons reared together and apart.

Figure 41.1. gives us a quick, generalized, over-all view of the roles of heredity and environment in determining intelligence-test scores. Let us now make a more detailed examination of this major area of research.

Twin Studies of Genetic Influence

Logically and traditionally, twin studies fall into two classes: first, comparisons between identical twins reared together and identical twins reared apart and, second, comparisons

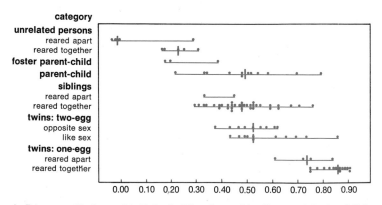

Figure 41.1. Correlation coefficients for intelligence-test scores from ninety-nine groups. The categories are arranged so that genetic closeness increases, reading down the column. The groups were unequal in size, age, ethnic compositions, and socioeconomic stratification; also many different intelligence tests were used. The individual correlation coefficients for each group are indicated by a green dot; median values are shown by vertical lines. Parent-child correlations are based upon the average intelligence estimate of both parents when possible; otherwise, only mothers' intelligence was included.

between identical twins reared together and fraternal twins reared together.

Identical Twins Reared Apart

A classic study of identical twins reared apart is based on nineteen pairs of such twins analyzed by Newman, Freeman, and Holzinger (1937). Table 41.1. presents a summary of some of the data from that study. It shows, for one thing, that a difference in educational opportunity, even among genetically identical people, can make for a difference in IQ and that the more marked the difference in educational advantages, the bigger the difference in IQ. The largest difference shown in Table 41.1. (case 11) was found between two sisters who had been separated when they were eighteen months old. One of the girls was reared in the backwoods and had been given only two years of formal schooling, whereas her sister was brought up in a good farming community and had gone through college. When these twins were tested at the age of thirty-five, the girl who had gone to college received an IQ score twenty-four points higher than her sister.

However the data of Table 41.1. make it also perfectly clear that hereditary factors play a significant role in determining IQ. On the average the difference found between identical twins reared apart is only eight IQ points.

The correlation for the IQs between the identical twins reared apart was .77. The same authors found a correlation of .88 for identical twins reared together. The former figure thus gives a rough indication of the relative contribution of heredity to intelligence, and the difference between the two figures gives a rough indication of the relative contribution of environment. (The reader, however, should be cautioned that these correlation coefficients cannot be directly interpreted as simple estimates of the percentages of fractions of relative contribution of heredity and environment. There are compelling mathematical reasons why.)

Table 41.1.
Identical Twins Reared Apart

CASE NUMBER	SEX	AGE AT SEPARATION	AGE AT TESTING	DIFFERENCES IN EDUCATIONAL ADVANTAGES *	DIFFERENCES IN IQ BETWEEN TWINS†
11	f	18 mo.	35	37	24
2	f	18 mo.	27	32	12
18	m	1 yr.	27	28	19
4	f	5 mo.	29	22	17
12	f	18 mo.	29	19	7
1	f	18 mo.	19	15	12
17	m	2 yr.	14	15	10
8	f	3 mo.	15	14	15
3	m	2 mo.	23	12	−2
14	f	6 mo.	39	12	−1
5	f	14 mo.	38	11	4
13	m	1 mo.	19	11	1
10	f	1 yr.	12	10	5
15	m	1 yr.	26	9	1
7	m	1 mo.	13	9	−1
19	f	6 yr.	41	9	−9
16	f	2 yr.	11	8	2
6	f	3 yr.	59	7	8
9	m	1 mo.	19	7	6

* The differences in educational advantages were obtained in the following way: From the case material each of five judges rated the educational advantages of every twin on a scale of ten points, and then these five ratings were summed. Therefore the highest score any one twin could get would be 50. The difference between any two twins is the value given in the table. Thus, in case 11, one sister was rated as having thirty-seven-point better educational advantages than her twin.

† A minus sign before the IQ difference means that the twin who received the higher rating for educational advantages obtained a lower IQ score. Thus, in case 19 one sister was rated as having a nine-point educational advantage over her twin, yet she scored nine points *less* in her IQ test.

(Data from Newman, Freeman, & Holzinger, 1937)

Twins Reared Together

The importance of hereditary factors is further emphasized by comparing the correlations, from the same study, in IQ scores between identical twins with the correlations between fraternal twins, both reared together. The IQs of identical twins, as we have just seen, correlated .88. A correlation of .63 was found for

Box 142

Age, Sex,
and Inheritance

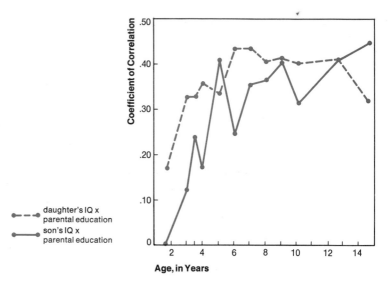

That heredity plays an important role in intelligence has been well established, particularly in studies of parent-child resemblances in intelligence. The *extent* of these parent-child relationships has appeared quite variable, however, with different studies reporting different values. One suggested reason for this variation in findings is that parent-child resemblances in intelligence-test scores may increase as the child grows older. Related to this explanation is the possibility that the rate of growth

fraternal twins (who are no more genetically alike than are any pair of siblings). This figure may be similarly compared to the rough estimate of .40 for siblings reared apart, which may be read from Figure 41.1., and we also have the earlier correlation between identical twins reared apart. If we now take these four correlations and arrange them as in Table 41.2., we can see two things. First, identical twins are more alike in intelligence, whether reared together or apart, than are other siblings (that is, .88 and .77 for identical twins versus the cor-

Table 41.2.

Correlations in Intelligence Among Identical Twins and Nonidentical Siblings Reared Together and Apart

Environmental Variable	*Genetic Variable*	
	IDENTICAL TWINS	NONIDENTICAL SIBLINGS
Reared Together	.88	.63
Reared Apart	.77	.40

responding correlations of .63 and .40 for the other siblings). Second, either identical or non-

of parent-child resemblance may differ with the sex of the child. Inasmuch as the various studies dealt with groups differing in age and sex, we might then expect the observed difference in findings.

At least two considerations support the reasonableness of the first hypothesis. For one, the tests used to measure intelligence are quite different at different ages; therefore, an increasing parent-child correlation might arise from increasing similarity in the measures applied to parent and child. That is to say, the older child is evaluated by tests more like the ones used to assess his parents' intelligence. But, this factor aside, it would be reasonable to assume that any genetic factor would express itself best when both parent and child were in comparable stages of development. A parent's IQ at age six would thus be the best predictor of the child's IQ at age six. To test this assumption would require data from a *two-generation* longitudinal study, a requirement that will soon be fulfilled by ongoing longitudinal studies. By the same reasoning we would expect that the adult IQ of a parent would predict the adult IQ of the offspring better than would the offspring's IQ at some earlier age. And on this matter we have the following data.

Marjorie Honzik of the University of California, Berkeley, presents data on the increasing correlation between estimates of parental intelligence and the IQ of children over the age range twenty-one months through fifteen years. Additionally, she presents data on the rate of growth of parent-child resemblance for boys and girls separately. These findings are based upon a longitudinal investigation of more than 100 children of each sex. Estimating parental intelligence from their education, Honzik presents correlations of these estimates for mothers and fathers with children's IQs from childhood into adolescence (see figure).

Two clear conclusions may be drawn from the results in this figure: First, parental education does not relate to children's intelligence initially but does so after a certain age; second, girls reach this age of significant correlation earlier than boys do. The implication to be drawn from these data is that a genetically based sex difference exists in rate of mental development, paralleling the well-established earlier physical maturation of girls. That is, girls come into their adult inheritance— intellectual as well as physical—earlier than boys do.

M. P. HONZIK. 1963. A Sex Difference in the Age of Onset of the Parent-Child Resemblance in Intelligence, *J. Educ. Psychol.*, 54, 231–7.

identical siblings, when reared together, are more similar in mental ability than when reared apart (that is, .88 and .63 for those reared together versus the corresponding correlations of .77 and .40 for those reared apart).

The "twin" method is clearly a powerful tool for determining the relative influence of heredity and environment on the development of intelligence, and we have previously seen evidence for this statement in Box 140, p. 667. Logically, one would expect it to be suited to the study of nature-nurture contributions for other charac-teristics as well, and such is indeed the case. For a particularly impressive report of the "twin" method applied to personality characteristics, see Shields' work in Unit 44, p. 731.

Parent-Child Resemblance in Intelligence

Parents and their children eventually show an average correlation in intelligence of about .50. This fact, standing alone, has an equivocal bearing upon the nature-nurture issue because, after all, parents and children typically share environments as well as genes. Again the reared-apart–reared-together contrast proves useful. This time the comparison is made between children reared with their biological parents and children reared apart from their biological parents. In one longitudinal study, Skodak and Skeels (1949) found that adopted children's intelligence, tested repeatedly between the ages of two and fourteen years, showed an increasing relation to the IQ and education of their *biological* mothers. In contrast, at no age was there a significant correlation with the educational level of their *foster* mothers, who had reared the children from earliest infancy, although the IQs of these adopted children did show a substantial average increase, most probably because of richer intellectual environment in the adoptive homes. Nor was there even a tendency for the correlation to increase systematically with age, despite the accumulation of shared experience between foster mother and child. This finding is the more surprising when we consider that social agencies attempt to place children for adoption with foster parents whose educational level is roughly in line with the intelligence and education of the true parents, so that this selective placement alone should have led to some correlation.

These Skodak-Skeels data on adopted children have been systematically compared with the developmental trend in parent-child intelligence correlation found in another longitudinal study of children who were raised with their biological parents (Honzik, 1957). The results from the two studies are compared in Figure 41.2. The similarity in curves from the two studies for both mother and father, in developmental trend as well as in eventual level, gives ample support to Honzik's conclusion that the relationship is largely genetic. Furthermore, the foster-parent results suggest that parental educational level is not, by itself, an important environmental factor contributing to individual differences in children's intelligence.

To say that parental education is not an important factor in influencing the child's IQ is not, of course, to say that there are no environmental factors within the family that contribute to the child's IQ score. There are a number of such factors, and we now turn to a consideration of some of them.

Environmental Influences on Intelligence

To begin with, let us take another look at some of the data we have just reviewed. In the Skodak-Skeels study the average IQ of the true mothers was 86; of their children 106. It can reasonably be assumed that one of the factors that contributed to this substantial difference was the fact that the foster home provided an intelligence-stimulating family environment and thus raised the child's IQ. That early experience can influence basic intelligence is a position that psychologists have increasingly come to adopt. This view has been furthered by many kinds of evidence from research studies with animals (Krech, 1968). These studies have demonstrated that, when greater opportunity for "intellectual" stimulation is given to young rats —for example, by devising living cages that permit and encourage a wide range of sensory experiences and problem-solving activities—not only are the adult animals more "intelligent" but also there are changes in brain structure and in brain chemistry that may be related to increased mental ability. (This evidence is reviewed in Unit 29.)

Another line of evidence has come from the observation that children who spend their earliest years, from birth onward, in institutions that provide little stimulation beyond that necessary for physical care tend to be stunted in their mental, as well as in their emotional, development. R. A. Spitz, a psychiatrist and the first to call attention to this phenomenon (Spitz, 1949), attributed these effects to the absence of the normal mother-child interaction. Despite cogent criticisms that have been leveled at the details of his research, his general finding has been receiving confirmation from more recent research. For example, working with infants raised in their own homes, Yarrow (1963) found that the amount and quality of mothers' stimulation of their children showed substantial relations to the children's development, assessed as early as age six months. To cite a specific result: A correlation of .65 was found between the child's IQ at six months and a rating (based upon direct observation) of the

amount of time spent by a mother in social interaction with her child.

The animal studies we have cited and other investigations with people indicate that the effect of early environmental experience upon mental development may be long-lived. Perhaps the most dramatic and persuasive finding has been reported by Skeels (1966). He compared the adult status of two groups of subjects who, as young children, had been classified as "mentally retarded." One group, with an average IQ

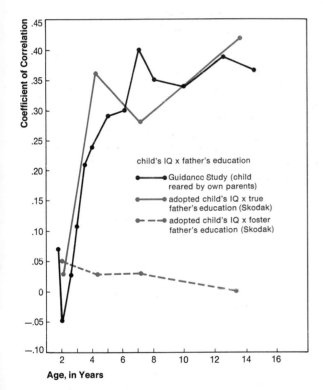
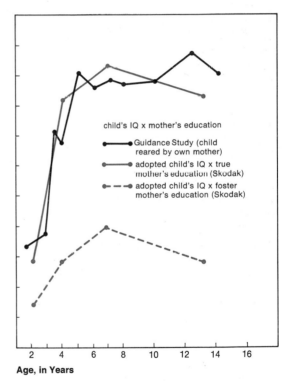

Figure 41.2. Trends in parent-child intelligence correlations for children reared together with biological parents and children reared apart from biological parents. The two upper curves in each half of the figure directly compare the relative influence of biological parents upon their children's intelligence—in the one case when the children are reared by their own parents (from the Guidance Study at the University of California reported by Honzik), in the other when reared by foster parents (Skodak and Skeels). The two curves are essentially identical in both instances. By contrast, the foster parents' intelligence has a negligible correlation with the intelligence of their adopted children.
M. P. Honzik, "Developmental Studies of Parent-Child Resemblance in Intelligence," *Child Development*, 28, 215–28; © 1957 by The Society for Research in Child Development, Inc.; adapted by permission.

of 64 at about age two, had participated in an experimental program that involved a radical change from the usual institutional environment. Each child in this "experimental" group was assigned to the daily care of an older girl, herself mentally retarded, for about two years and remained in her charge until later adoption. This arrangement guaranteed a considerable degree of social stimulation for the child of the "experimental" group. The other ("contrast") group consisted of somewhat brighter children (average IQ of 87), who remained in the usual institutional setting—a setting that provided much less social stimulation for the young children. Skeels found some startling differences between the experimental and contrast groups in their adult achievements, all favoring the group that had experienced greater social stimulation during their early years. For one thing, all members of the experimental group were found to be self-supporting, whereas 40 per cent of the contrast group were still cared for in institutions. The average number of years of schooling for the experimental group was over twelve years (high-school graduation level), whereas only one member of the contrast group had completed high school. These findings certainly point to a substantial increase in mental ability for the experimental group from their initial "mentally retarded" level.

Although these results certainly raise questions about the accuracy of early diagnosis of mental retardation and the validity of early-age intelligence tests, the fact remains that children provided with a socially enriched environment experienced radical shifts in their mental development. Aside from the obvious and profound implications for public policy on the care of retarded children, these data tell us not only that intelligence is clearly modifiable but also something about the environmental conditions contributing to change in intelligence.

But we need to know much more. For example, not all individuals are likely to profit equally from environmental stimulation. Whether or not and to what degree a person undergoes changes in mental ability may be a function of the individual's sex, personality characteristics, or the age at which the stimulation occurs.

Sex and Personality in Intelligence Change

Sontag, Baker, and Nelson (1958) compared children who showed substantial increases in intelligence from age six to age ten with those who showed decreases in IQ during the same interval. One general finding was that boys were more likely to gain in intelligence and that girls were more likely to lose. A number of personality traits were associated with intelligence gains: competitiveness, independence, verbal aggressiveness, and persistence in efforts to master difficult and challenging problems. Furthermore—and this seems consistent with this trait picture—highly feminine girls were least likely to increase in IQ. The over-all portrait can be fairly summarized as indicating that highly achievement-motivated children may be able to increase their tested intelligence during the elementary-school years and that this motivation appears somewhat incompatible with what we regard as high femininity.

Haan (1963) partially confirms but qualifies this latter finding in her own study of correlates of intelligence change in men and women over the age range of twelve to thirty-seven years. Here again, men more often than women increased their IQs during this period. The women who did show gains in intelligence, however, showed differential changes that clearly reflected their changes in personality. Women who were tomboys as adolescents but who, in adulthood, had become more feminine were most likely to increase in verbal intelligence. Women showing the reverse trend—highly feminine in adolescence but less so when adult—tended to show gains on a measure of intelligence involving arithmetical ability.

A common thread running through the Sontag, *et al.*, and the Haan studies involves the masculinity-femininity dimension. Males more often than females show increases in IQ; traits usually regarded as "masculine" appear to be associated with increases either in males or in females.

Another common theme of the two investigations seems to fall somewhere in the motivational area. Haan, like Sontag, *et al.*, found that the direction of IQ change was associated with particular styles of motivational functioning. For both sexes, persons most likely to gain in IQ were those who as adults characteristically employed "coping" mechanisms (realistic and flexible approaches to problem situations) rather than "defense" mechanisms (inappropriate and maladaptive forms of behavior to be discussed later on in Unit 46). It is probably inferring too much from the Sontag, *et al.*, and Haan data to claim that they plainly demonstrate the importance, in IQ gain, of a strong and realistically applied drive to learn and master environmental challenges. But such a formulation clearly fits their data and is in line with other evidence that the subject's motivation to succeed on an intelligence test, whatever the source of the motivation, contributes to his more effective performance.

The general point that motivation may affect performance on an intelligence test has wide and significant social implications. It suggests that situational factors—extrinsic to the individual's intelligence—may help to determine the IQ score by raising or lowering his motivation. Particularly important are such situational social factors as the degree of rapport between the tester and the person tested and the type of social setting in which the testing takes place. All these factors, as we shall see, make for some major difficulties in interpreting racial, national, and class differences in intelligence-test performance, and even sex enters the picture.

In this discussion of the correlates of intelligence change, we encountered a reference to differences between the sexes. These specific findings, however, must be put in the context of the general finding that sex makes very little difference in over-all intelligence. This finding is in part the result of efforts (as in the Stanford-Binet test) to select items of equal difficulty for both sexes in the initial construction of the tests. Also, the direction of any sex difference is heavily dependent upon the kinds of abilities most heavily sampled by a particular test, as the sexes do differ in their patterning of mental abilities. In general, women excel in verbal abilities, including vocabulary; men usually do better on spatial and numerical tests. Characteristic patterns of abilities are also found among groups, as we shall see in the following discussion.

Racial, National, and Class Differences

Closely tied in with the study of individual differences in ability as a function of heredity is the analysis of *group* differences in abilities. Are the people of certain nations more capable than those of others? Does higher socioeconomic status within a given society go along with, or is it even attributable to, higher intelligence? Perhaps the most loaded of these questions, at least in recent times, is that of possible racial differences in intellectual endowment. This issue continues to stimulate controversy and research, despite the fact that modern genetic theory has radically revised our traditional notion of "races" as distinct, genetically different populations of human beings. The modern view denies any sharp discontinuities and focuses instead on making tentative distinctions among certain geographical groupings of peoples based on different patterns of the *average* levels of certain hereditary characteristics.

Social-Class Differences

It is in the area of socioeconomic differences in intelligence that the evidence for group differences is most solid and least subject to distorting interpretations. Perhaps the absurdity of postulating specific genes for social class and, at the same time, affirming the American ideal of an "open society" in which the more capable can move up the social ladder can account for the relative rationality of discourse on this topic.

What are the facts? First, while we may be an "open society," we are certainly not a "classless" one. Various communities in this country have been carefully studied by a number of social scientists, and all investigators seem to agree that our society is definitely "class-structured" as far as sociological measures and behavior of people are concerned. For example, in "Yankee City," the name given to a New England community studied by Warner and Lunt (1941), and "Oldtown," the name used by Davis, Gardner, and Gardner (1941) for their Southern community, six distinct classes seem to exist: the upper-upper, the lower-upper, the upper-middle, the lower-middle, the upper-lower, and the lower-lower. People in each of these classes have parties together, marry into each other's families, differ from the other classes in education and occupation.

Social classes exist, and the differences among them are defined in terms of differences in wealth, influence, educational level, occupation, and social behavior. Considerable research has involved a comparison of the IQs of people from different socioeconomic levels. Tyler (1956), after reviewing the many studies in this field, concludes that "the relationship of IQ to socioeconomic level is one of the best documented facts in mental test history." It seems quite clear that higher IQs are found among the families of the upper socioeconomic levels than among the lower levels (see Box 143, p. 683).

One quite substantial source of evidence for social-class differences in intelligence has, in a sense, already been given in our earlier discussion of the validity of intelligence tests (Unit 39). There we presented data (for example, from Harrell & Harrell, 1945) indicating large differences among various occupational groups in their test scores. In that context the existence of IQ differences among occupations that varied in their intellectual demands seemed so obvious and unarguable that, rather than interpret those data as evidence for variation in intelligence associated with social class (which, in turn, is in large measure determined by occupation), we treated the IQ differences as supporting the validity of the intelligence tests themselves.

Origins of Class Differences Do people tend to become members of certain socioeconomic groups because of native differences in capacity, or are their IQ scores determined by their socioeconomic levels?

Different occupations clearly require different levels of general intelligence. This fact means that people, given equal opportunities, will eventually find the occupational level suited for their intellectual level. Although a condition of completely equal opportunity does not exist, nevertheless there is "enough" equal opportunity to lead us to expect a trend in that direction. We have also seen that intelligence-test scores are determined by hereditary factors to a considerable degree. It therefore seems highly probable that, to some extent at least, the differences in average IQs of the different occupational groups reflect native biological differences in capacity.

On the other hand, we must remember that IQ scores also reflect educational opportunities. Because the educational facilities of the lower socioeconomic groups tend to be inferior to those of the upper groups and because (perhaps as a result) their attitudes toward education tend to be less favorable, a part of the difference in IQ scores is undoubtedly the result of environmental differences.

These facts have very important implications for the functioning of a democratic society. Some of these implications apply to group differences in general and are best reserved for our concluding discussion. But there is a specific point that needs to be made concerning

Box 143

Occupational Level and Intelligence—
United States, England, U.S.S.R.

D. M. Johnson at the University of Illinois has examined a number of studies of children and adults from various occupational groups. The data of these studies, using different intelligence tests and carried out in three different countries, were made comparable by converting all the scores into standard scores. The results of this analysis tell a convincing story of a high relationship between occupational level and intelligence. In comparing England and the United States, Johnson obtained the results shown in the table.

OCCUPATIONAL LEVEL	CHILDREN		ADULTS	
	U.S.	*England*	*U.S.*	*England*
Professional	116	115	120	132
Semiprofessional and managerial	112	113	113	117
Clerical, skilled trades, retail business	107	106	108	109
Rural owners, farmers	95	97	94	(no data)
Semiskilled, minor clerical, minor business	105	102	104	105
Slightly skilled	98	97	96	84
Day laborers, rural and urban	96	95	95	96

For the Russian comparison he used data published in 1929 by a member of the Labor Institute at Kharkov. The intelligence-test scores for more than 2,300 children in a large Ukrainian city were presented in that report. The children had been classified in six occupational groups; the highest was composed of "children of officials having university education," and the lowest of "workmen's children of whom one or both parents were illiterate." The categories were not otherwise described, and Johnson could therefore not place them in the same table with the data for the American and English children. But the range of occupational levels is apparently the same among the three studies. After converting the scores into standard IQ scores, Johnson found that the Russian children from the six different occupational levels earned average IQs of 117, 109, 105, 101, 97, and 92.

Apparently, then, the hierarchy of intelligence of children in Russia, in the United States, and in England is remarkably similar. The day laborer and his child—no matter under what flag and in what society they live—have lower IQs than do the professional man and his child.

But one word of caution: These results are based on *average* figures. Again the variability within each group and the overlap among the groups were large and significant.

D. M. JOHNSON. 1948. Application of the Standard-Score I.Q. to Social Statistics, *J. Soc. Psychol.*, 27, 217–27. Table adapted by permission.

social-class differences in particular: Heredity means differences as well as similarities between offspring and parents. This point is especially true for any trait like "intelligence" that is undoubtedly determined by a large number of genes or hereditary factors. As a result we must expect to find children who are brighter than their parents and children who are duller. This expectation, based on genetic grounds, is amply confirmed by research findings. The differences in IQ among the children of parents from various occupational groups are based on *average* figures. We also find wide individual differences within each group and considerable overlap among the groups. One of the most important implications of this genetically determined variability is that, if we wish to maximize the human resources of our society, it becomes essential to create conditions in which each individual, no matter what his socioeconomic background, will be given an opportunity to achieve up to the limit of his potentialities. The son of the lawyer or the professor may be limited in his capacity, and the son of the day laborer may have the capacity to become our most brilliant scientist. We cannot classify in advance. Genetic theory (see Unit 1.) and actual experience both affirm that the highly capable person may come from almost any socioeconomic group.

Racial and National Differences in Intelligence

Most of the studies of racial and national differences in intelligence that we shall encounter in this section have been of ethnic and racial groups in the United States. Not that there have been no studies of the comparative intelligence of peoples of different nations, each in its own land; however, such studies are extremely difficult to interpret. It is almost impossible to devise intelligence tests that are the "same" for different national and ethnic groups living in different cultures. Even if a standard American intelligence test is translated into various foreign languages—which has been done for many languages—we can by no means then argue that the tests are now comparable. They are not the same, psychologically speaking, because different cultures deal with different concepts, objects, and tasks.

What, then, are the alternatives if we wish to assess national and racial intelligence differences in different lands? We can seek to devise intelligence tests composed of items that would be equally applicable to all groups—the "culture-fair" test that we shall discuss later on. Or we can attempt to construct tests that are psychologically equivalent for the groups being compared, although the actual test items are therefore necessarily different. A mental-test item designed to assess "practical" information—a sensible component of intelligence—might then, for one group, ask for an enumeration of the uses of electricity and might, for another, ask about the various ways in which an animal that has strayed from a herd may be located. Such attempts have been made, and they probably lead to more meaningful results than do "translated" tests, but still it would be the foolhardy psychologist who would insist that he has thus been able to achieve full psychological equivalence. But even if such an ideal could be attained, and a universal intelligence test derived, one that was psychologically equivalent for all peoples and all races in all lands, what then? We would expect to find that some differences do indeed exist. There is some evidence that this is the case. For example, recall our earlier discussion of cultural and national differences on Piaget-type tasks that seem to approach psychological equivalence (see p. 392).

Even if this finding were general, the problem of making statements on intelligence would persist, to the extent that we define intelligence as native endowment, rather than as current level of intellectual achievement. The trouble is that nations and cultures vary in the emphasis that they place on what we would call "intellectual achievement," and they certainly vary enormously in the extent and effectiveness of the formal educational opportunities afforded their members. And all these factors influence performance on intelligence tests.

For these reasons we shall restrict our study to intelligence differences among different groups in the United States. After all, we all speak the same language and are exposed to a common social environment, educational system, and a value for intellectual achievement. The problem certainly should be simpler. Is it?

National Differences Because the United States has been a "melting pot" for so long, there has been a great deal of interest in comparing the intellectual levels of the different national groups who have emigrated to this country. A number of studies seem to agree that Americans of Jewish, Scandinavian, German, and English origin earn higher IQs than do those of Southern European origin.

These studies are difficult to interpret because, among other things, they were done on immigrant groups and their children. This fact immediately raises the added difficulties of the influence of bilingualism and of social status. Children born to newly arrived immigrant groups, in comparison with children of native-born parents, are obviously much more likely to be exposed to a language other than English in their home environments. The immigrant groups vary considerably in the extent to which they continue to speak their native languages and in the speed with which they acquire proficiency in English and use it in talking to their children. The sources of this variation are many. Certain national groups, more than others, are forced by social and economic pressure to dwell in ghetto surroundings and are therefore far more likely to continue to favor their native languages. Other groups may do so as much, or more, from pride as from pressure; they choose to preserve and transmit their heritage to their children, and language is one means of doing so.

What is the effect on the child of his exposure to another language in the home? At one extreme, when only a foreign language is spoken by his parents and even by most other adults and children in his everyday environment, he is under an obvious handicap. His performance in school as well as his performance on English-language intelligence tests may suffer. Thus, a substantial portion of the findings of national differences among *children* may be attributable to a language factor. Furthermore, it is not unlikely that this factor may still be reflected in adult intelligence scores, for early handicaps of this sort may lead to persisting motivational, emotional, and even cognitive barriers to the achievement of one's intellectual potential. When the home is bilingual, that is, when both the native tongue and English are spoken, the effect is not so obvious. The general finding has been that bilingualism may interfere with at least early intellectual performance, but there are exceptions. For example, Peal and Lambert (1962) compared the performance on various intelligence tests of Canadian children from Montreal who spoke both French and English with the performance of children who spoke only English. Their surprising finding was that bilingual children scored higher on both verbal and nonverbal tests. Perhaps even more surprising was that these children also had more favorable attitudes than did their monolingual peers toward English-Canadians and less favorable attitudes toward French-Canadians. The possibility therefore exists that, at least in certain circumstances, bilingualism may be associated with greater cognitive flexibility or competence.

The picture is further complicated when we consider that nationality rarely can act alone, for in the United States there is a clear confounding of ethnic origin with social class. Quite simply, ethnic groups (and here we can include racial groups) are not similarly distributed along the full range of social classes, so that it becomes difficult to decide whether a given intelligence difference arises from nationality or race on one hand or from social class on the other. Most likely, it is a "bit of both" affair, as certain recent research findings suggest.

The recent report by Lesser, Fifer, and Clark (1965) underlines the complexity of the situation. They studied four aspects of mental ability (verbal, reasoning, facility with numbers, and spatial concepts) in six- and seven-year-old children from both middle- and lower-class families drawn from four ethnic groups (Chinese, Jewish, Negro, and Puerto Rican). They took great care to create *"culture-fair" tests* (of which more later) and tried very hard to make sure that children from all eight groups were motivated to perform at their best on the battery of mental tests. Their results, to say the very least, give little comfort to the seeker after simplicity. We can mention only a few of their findings here, and even these findings must be condensed. For one thing, there was more similarity among middle-class children from the four ethnic groups than among lower-class children, and this similarity was present on each of the mental-ability tests. Apparently, membership in the middle class has some kind of a homogenizing effect, as we might expect, because the distinctive cultural features of different ethnic groups are known to begin to fade as families move up the socioeconomic ladder. Nevertheless, certain abilities are better developed in certain groups: For example, Chinese children in general ranked first on reasoning and spatial abilities, whereas Jewish children ranked first on verbal and numerical abilities. Negro children did relatively best on verbal ability, attaining second rank, and relatively poorest on numerical and spatial abilities. Of special interest for the discussion of racial differences in intelligence that follows is the finding that social class was a more important influence on the performance of Negro children, on all four abilities, than on the performance of the other three groups. In other words, middle-class Negro children showed a greater advantage over lower-class Negro children than was the case when the middle-versus-lower comparison was made for the other three groups. Such results raise more questions than they answer, but they do provide certain proof against glib generalizations. Social class, ethnic origin, racial factors—all apparently have something to do with intellectual functioning. But what these differences are—and the more interesting question of how such differences come about—remains a continuing challenge to psychological investigators.

Racial Differences As we have just seen, it seems almost foolhardy to attempt to sort out the separate effects of any single factor like race. Yet, social myths and social realities being what they are in the United States, the issue of racial differences in intelligence, particularly with regard to Negro-white comparisons, has long been and continues to be one upon which much research and even more debate have been lavished. The attempt to measure and explain these assumed racial differences in abilities faces two major difficulties. In the first place, it is almost impossible to study *pure* races. Wherever people of originally different racial stock live together, considerable race mixing occurs. It has been estimated, for example, that in the United States about 20 per cent of the people classified as "whites" have Negro parentage in their family lines.

One might accept this estimate as fact and still argue that the members of the so-called "Negro group" would have a different average racial composition than those of the so-called "white group." But then we run into the second difficulty. Negroes and whites are not subjected to the same environmental influences. In the United States the average Negro obviously does not have the same educational advantages as does the average white person. Any differences in test scores that we might find would therefore be difficult to interpret.

Despite these difficulties, a great many of useful data on this question of Negro-white differences have been accumulated. In these studies no attempt was made to define these groupings biologically; "common sense" or social definitions have been used. Their findings may be summarized as follows.

1. Negro children, on the average, earn lower intelligence-test scores than do white children. One of the most carefully controlled early studies was that of Tanser (1939). His study of the Negroes in Kent County (Ontario, Canada) took advantage of what seemed to be an unusually favorable research opportuniy. Kent County (on the north shore of Lake Erie near Detroit) was one of the few parts of Canada in which extensive attempts had been made to establish Negro settlements. The ancestors of the Negro population had moved to Kent County before the Civil War, during the days of the underground railroad. According to Tanser, most of the schools there were integrated, racial discrimination was at a minimum, and the socioeconomic status of the Negro and white groups were more nearly comparable in Kent County than anywhere else in North America.

In Tanser's study, carefully chosen samples of 386 whites and 103 Negro pupils were tested with four different intelligence tests, both verbal and nonverbal. On all tests the average white child surpassed the average Negro child. For instance, on the National Intelligence Test, the mean IQ for the white children was 103.6, for the Negro children, 89.2. This difference held whether rural Negro and rural white children or urban Negro and urban white children were compared.

This study, however, has been subjected to cogent criticism. Regarding the presumed equivalence of environmental factors for Negroes and whites in Kent County, we have the comments of a long-time and observant resident of that community, who details the very many social and cultural disadvantages still experienced by Negroes living there (see Box 144). Although such a demurrer by no means negates Tanser's

Box 144

A Dissenting Opinion

Mollie Stevens Smart, a psychologist at the University of Rhode Island, has commented on H. A. Tanser's claim that Kent County was a region of true racial equality. Describing herself as "probably the only member of the American Psychological Association who was born and grew up in Kent County," she gives her impression of the community as it was in the 1920s and 1930s:

"The Negroes lived in the East End, and in a few spots on the outskirts of town. Nearly all of their houses were small wood buildings, often lacking paint and tending towards dilapidation. The theaters had a policy of seating Negroes in certain areas. The all-Negro school had been abandoned by my day. My elementary school classes always included Negro children, but I remember none during the last 3 years of high school. My Negro classmates were usually poorly clothed and badly groomed. Negroes held the low-status jobs. They were servants, garbage collectors, and odd-job men. People called them 'Nigger' more often than 'Negro.' I did not know until I grew up that a Negro could be a doctor, lawyer, teacher, member of Parliament, or even a clerk in a store. The only Negro boy of my acquaintance who went to college became an M.D. and went to a larger city to practice. It was often said that ambitious Negroes should go to Detroit where they would have opportunities for advancement.

"I cannot conceive of any social advantages which Negroes enjoyed in Kent County at the time of the Tanser study. They did have the political equality contained in the right to vote."

MOLLIE S. SMART. 1963. Confirming Klineberg's Suspicion, *Amer. Psychol.*, 18, 621.

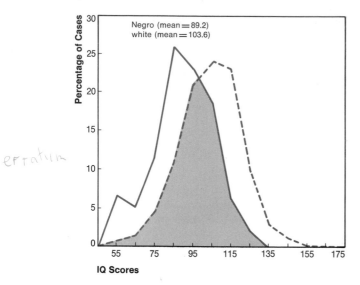

erratum

Figure 41.3. Distribution of IQ scores for 386 white children and 103 Negro children of Kent County, Ontario, Canada.

is inescapable: Any decision to use differences in the average IQ scores of the two "racial" groups as a basis for classifying in advance any individual child, Negro or white, is scientifically unjustified.

3. The Negro child's IQ score shows a consistent rise when his educational opportunities are improved. A number of studies have demonstrated that Negro children who leave the South and enter Northern schools (where presumably they have better educational opportunities) show an increase in IQ. Table 41.3. shows

Table 41.3.
Mean IQs on Philadelphia Tests of Mental and Verbal Ability

Grade Entered	Number of Children	Grade in Which Test Was Taken			
		1A	2B	4B	6B
1A	182	86.5	89.3	91.8	93.3
1B–2B	109		86.7	88.8	90.9
3A–4B	199			86.3	87.2
5A–6B	221				88.2

(Data from Lee, 1951)

findings, it does emphasize once again the enormous difficulties in any attempt to rule out "other" factors when making Negro-white comparisons.

2. IQ scores for Negro and white children overlap to a large degree. The difference between the average Negro child and the average white child clearly does not adequately describe the difference between the mental capacities of the two groups: To return to Tanser's study, Figure 41.3. presents the distribution curves of IQ scores for the Negro and white children. About 18 per cent of the white children earned lower IQs than did the average Negro child, and about 22 per cent of the Negro children earned higher IQs than did the average white child. The shaded area of the two curves represents the degree of overlap between the two groups. With this high degree of overlap (a finding that is characteristic of most studies on this question) and with the recognition that Negro children in the public schools of this country have earned IQ scores as high as 200, one conclusion

the results of one such study performed in the city of Philadelphia. Here one sees that the longer the Southern-born Negro children remained in the Philadelphia schools, the more their IQ scores increased. The children whose IQs averaged 86.5 when they entered the first grade thus earned 89.3 in the second grade, 91.8 in the fourth grade, and 93.3 in the sixth grade. The children who entered later never did catch up with the children who had moved to the North earlier. Add to this information the evidence reported earlier in this unit, and add the Gray and Klaus data (p. 395) on the increase in intelligence associated with an enriched environment, and we may conclude that at least some, if not all, of the observable differences between the Negro and white children may be adequately explained in terms of environmental factors.

Although the three conclusions we have listed

are amply supported by scientific evidence, no unequivocal answer can be given to the question of whether or not the remaining differences in the IQ scores between the Negro and white children can be explained by biological or environmental factors. Because it is impossible to find sizable groups of Negro and white children who have equally good home environments, equally good schooling, equally good social and occupational opportunities, no definitive study has yet been made on this question. The only valid conclusion we can draw is a negative one: There is no scientific proof that the differences in the IQ scores between Negro and white children are caused by inherited biological factors, nor is there any scientific proof that these differences are caused solely by environmental influences.

Because of these difficulties in making group comparisons of intelligence, psychologists devote considerable effort to creating testing instruments—and techniques of administering these instruments—that will be "fair" to all groups. Should this "fairness" be achieved, one source of apparent group variations in intelligence would be removed. This is the aim of *"culture-fair" intelligence testing.*

"Culture-Fair" Intelligence Testing

Some notion of the number of nonintellectual factors likely to affect performance on intelligence can be gained by returning to the study of Lesser, Fifer, and Clark (1965), which compared the scores on four mental tests of middle- and lower-class children from Chinese, Jewish, Negro, and Puerto Rican backgrounds. Let the authors speak for themselves concerning some of the precautions they imposed in order to provide psychologically comparable testing situations:

"(1) All tests were administered individually; reading and writing were not required of the children. (2) Directions were stated in the simplest possible terms. (3) Psychological testers who spoke one primary language of the cultural groups (Spanish, Yiddish, several Chinese dialects) administered the tests so that the instructions and test questions could be given in English, in the primary language of the child's cultural group, or (more often) in the most effective combination of the two languages for the particular child. (4) Extensive practice materials were provided in introducing each subtest to insure comprehension of the directions and to allow each child to become familiar with the test materials and the requirements of the task; it was only after the tester was convinced that the child understood what was being asked of him that the scored test items were presented. (5) The pressures of testing were controlled by allowing long periods of acclimation to the testing situation and to the examiner. (6) Testers were recruited from the same cultural group as the child being tested; considerable evidence . . . indicates the importance of matching the general cultural backgrounds of tester and testee. (7) Since each child was tested in his own public-school building, a degree of familiarity with the physical surroundings was insured."

Furthermore, all children who had chronic health problems were eliminated from the samples. If a child appeared temporarily ill or visibly fatigued, testing was postponed to a later occasion. If signs of distress were observed during a testing session, the session was curtailed and resumed at a later date. An especially important precaution was the design of special tests for each mental ability, in consultation with school personnel from each cultural group, in order to ensure that the tests were potentially of high and equal interest to children of all groups. Additionally, the tests were not "speed" tests, that is, each child had more than enough time to do as well as he could on each test item so that cultural differences in a "do things as quickly as possible" attitude and tendencies of individual children to panic when rushed were largely prevented from influencing test performance.

This listing of precautions taken to ensure that intelligence (and not a mélange of intelligence and numerous nonintellectual factors) was in fact being evaluated in the study is only a partial one; the investigators attended to, and attempted to control, many other possible influences upon performance. When we consider that this study is by no means typical but, rather, represents extraordinary care in assuring psychological equivalence in the testing situation, we can only wonder how much of the data that have been reported as indicating intelligence differences among groups can be wholly credited. By and large, published reports on this topic involve "standard" intelligence tests given in "standard" school situations and, as such, must involve built-in "loading" of the situation in favor of the cultural majority group.

Many investigators have attempted to construct what have been called "culture-free" or *"culture-fair" intelligence tests*. The basic principle underlying these attempts is to avoid test items in which the differential experience of different cultural groups would give one group an advantage over another. Standard tests frequently show higher scores for urban over rural children (though this difference is fast decreasing because television and other mass-communication media are both extending and homogenizing the range of experiences available to the growing child), and urban children very probably get higher scores because the standardization samples upon which the tests were developed were preponderantly composed of the more accessible urban school population. If the shoe were on the other foot and a typical test item read, "Which of the following objects is different from the others: *plow, spreader, tractor, harrow,*" the advantage of a rural upbringing would be immediately evident. The farm child would be more likely than the city child to spot the correct response (*tractor*).

It is difficult, if not impossible, to devise a "culture-free" test because, insofar as items refer to objects and events in the real world, one's cultural background and experience will affect one's ability to respond directly. Instead, the more usual goal has been the "culture-fair"

test, in which items refer to objects and events with which practically everyone would have had considerable and approximately equal experience. Another approach to making a test fair is to seek to balance items in such a way that each group's special experiences will be equally sampled.

Regardless of the approach, efforts at developing "fair" tests have been, at best, only moderately successful. They never have eliminated and never can eliminate biasing factors that are in the culture, not in the test (see Box 145, p. 691). But "culture-fair" tests are useful instruments· and should continue to be developed. Why? In what sense are such tests truly better and less biased? In the sense that intelligence can profitably be viewed as a measure of *ability* rather than as a measure of achievement. If, for certain purposes, we define the purpose of an intelligence test as measuring an individual's ability to learn—to profit from experience, to master new skills, to adapt effectively to new situations—then we require an instrument that does not confuse potential with achievement. A minority-group child who earns a low score on a conventional intelligence test is often assigned to a "slow learners" class, a practice that frequently serves to perpetuate his educational disadvantage. As Katz (1964) comments, in his intensive review of the effects of desegregation on the intellectual performance of Negroes:

"The widely accepted practice of assigning children to homogeneous ability groups (the 'track' system) should either be abandoned entirely or modified to afford maximum opportunity for periodic re-evaluation of potentiality. Ability grouping tends inevitably to freeze teachers' expectations as well as children's own self-images, hence it is particularly dangerous to intellectual development in the early grades."

In the final analysis, any truly unbiased testing of potential intellectual ability must move beyond the "culture-fair" test to the culture-fair school and, ultimately, to the

Box 145

Whose Standards?

Almost without exception intelligence tests are standardized on samples drawn from the national population. The intent of test developers is to set up a yardstick that will make possible the comparison of any individual's performance with that of people in general. What follows from this practice is that individuals who are tested regard their scores as indicating where they stand in relation to others in the larger society.

Psychologists I. Katz, E. G. Epps, and L. J. Axelson of New York University proposed that the Negro tends to view ability tests as measuring him against the standards of the white majority and that his performance on such tests might be affected by this attitudinal factor. To test this hypothesis, 116 undergraduate males from an all-Negro Florida college were administered a form of a digit-symbol substitution task of the sort commonly found in intelligence tests. The test was administered to three groups of students, each with its special instructions: First, the test was defined as nonevaluative and was said to be given only to elicit students' general interest in that kind of task; second, the test was said to be administered only at that college and would be used to evaluate each student in comparison with his classmates; third, the test "will be used to evaluate your intellectual ability by comparing you with students at other colleges and universities throughout the United States."

Not surprisingly, the nonevaluative condition (instructions 1) called forth the poorest performance. A digit-symbol substitution test is a rather dull activity, and, given the absence of any external motivating factors, the students apparently did not work very hard at it. What is less obvious, although predicted by the experimenters, was the finding that performance was consistently poorer under the national norm (instructions 3) than under the college norm (instructions 2). Furthermore, students in the national-norm group rated themselves higher on a "cared about doing well on the task" scale. We are thus confronted with the apparent paradox of poorer performance under presumably more highly motivated conditions, a paradox easily resolved if we regard the higher motivation as generating either overanxiety to succeed or too much concern and fear of failure.

The same test with the same three sets of instructions was given to groups of students from an all-white college in the same community, and no differences in performance between the college-norm group and the national-norm group were found. A simple but very important moral can be drawn from these data: When the person being tested is a member of a minority group, much of the relevant "psychological situation" is beyond the control of the best-trained and best-intentioned tester. Results from ability testing of minority groups in an unfair world should always be interpreted with caution.

I. KATZ, E. G. EPPS, and L. J. AXELSON. 1964. Effect Upon Negro Digit-Symbol Performance of Anticipated Comparison With Whites and With Other Negroes, *J. Abnorm. Soc. Psychol.*, 69, 77–83.

culture-fair society, for built into our society are forces that engender in certain minority groups attitudes that penalize them in intellectual performance. "Culture-fair" tests are helpful, and our society is ready, if not indeed uncritical, in accepting them (see Box 146, p. 692). But the fundamental problem is a societal one.

Box 146

**There's Many a Slip Twixt
Psychology and the Press**

Leon Rosenberg, a psychologist at the Johns Hopkins University School of Medicine, had an interesting and meaningful collision with the press. He had been working at developing an intelligence test stressing perceptual abilities, a test intended to provide more valid assessments of the intelligence of young handicapped children (and in this sense a form of "culture-fair" test). The test was still in the experimental stage, by no means yet validated for the special group for which it was intended, and certainly not a finished instrument suitable for use as a general intelligence test capable of eliminating the effects of cultural influences in the testing of all types of disadvantaged groups.

These are the basic facts; let the psychologist speak for himself as he recounts his collision with the press, and even with professional colleagues sensitized to the admittedly important issue of racial and cultural differences in intelligence and the possible dependence of such differences on the nature of the testing instrument used.

The scene opens on a conversation between the psychologist and a local newsman. The newsman has already been told about the true purpose of the new test and has reacted indifferently. He then asks:

" 'What about culturally deprived children and your test?' 'Well,' I explained, 'we have some promising data [on this].' The data suggested that our test did not penalize disadvantaged children in the way that certain other instruments did. As I described this data the reporter noted that we had included an accidental racial comparison. Now his interest was really aroused. We talked about the many statements made in the past regarding 'Negro intelligence.' I proceeded to attack racist views of the intelligence of Negroes and the reporter wrote furiously in his notebook. We ended the interview with my reminding him that the Johns Hopkins Perceptual Test was a research instrument; it was very new and it would take several years of research before we could ascertain its actual value as a diagnostic tool.

A short time later the article appeared [in the local newspaper] with the following captions: 'Hopkins I.Q. Test Attempts to Void Cultural Influences'; 'Hopkins I.Q. Test Airs Race Issue.' The reporter had written: 'A Hopkins psychologist has developed an I.Q. test designed to elimi-

Glossary

"culture-fair" intelligence testing A determination of intelligence made in such a way as to ensure that all individuals are afforded the opportunity to express their true ability, regardless of the culture subgroup to which they belong. In order to achieve this goal, many psychological factors must be equated. Among them are language familiarity, prior practice, rapport with the tester, and motivational aspects in the testing situation. Also, the items in the intelligence test must be equally appropriate for all groups.

"culture-fair" intelligence tests Tests of mental ability that attempt to ensure that the test items are equally difficult for all groups, regardless of race, nationality, and social class—or any other nonintellectual factor. "Culture-fair" tests are only one of the many requirements which must be met before we can make meaningful comparisons between groups differing in cultural backgrounds.

nate cultural influences in measuring intelligence—a test which could scientifically discredit racist claims that Negroes are inferior.' "

Another newspaper requested an interview with the psychologist, was granted it, obtained the same factual report, and published the following:

"The Johns Hopkins Perceptual Test designed by Dr. Leon Rosenberg should assure him a place in history. His new test is something that the world has been crying for over the years and could prove the key to many of the locked doors that result in the recurring cycles of poverty and misery in the United States."

A few weeks later, perhaps the most august of American newspapers chose to honor the psychologist and to do so without even interviewing him. Essentially, it reprinted the original newspaper report, but, with its circulation, the message was amplified and read worldwide. Other newspapers and magazines reprinted the report and editorialized on it. Let us return to our about-to-be beleaguered psychologist:

"Educational magazines began to make excited reports. No one made an effort to verify their information with me. The mail began to flood my office. We finally mimeographed a statement explaining why the Johns Hopkins Perceptual Test was not for sale and mailed out some 300 copies. The most amazing thing was the frequency with which people simply sent in orders for copies of the test. These requests came mainly from educators and school counselors, with a sprinkling of school psychologists, probation officers, industrial psychologists, personnel selection people, and teachers in a variety of special schools.

These requests asked nothing about norms, validity and reliability studies, or even the price of the instrument. They were careful, however, to note whether our invoice should be in duplicate or triplicate. . . . [There is an] amazing number of people in our own and allied professions who are willing to spend money on anything that someone suggests might be a 'better' intelligence test for disadvantaged children."

Despite these pressures, the psychologist understandably and necessarily did not release the test for use to any of these eager and uncritical applicants. In this case the public was protected by the professional integrity of the psychologist. We can only hope that such ethical restraint is and will continue to be the rule among all those involved with the development of unbiased tests of intelligence and other psychological characteristics.

L. A. ROSENBERG. 1967. On Talking to a Newspaper Reporter: A Study of Selective Perception, Distortion Through Rumor, Professional Gullibility, or How to Ride the *Zeitgeist* for All It Is Worth, *Amer. Psychol.*, 22, 239–40. Text material reprinted by permission of American Psychological Association.

UNIT 4

personality:
definition
and description

overview / A generally acceptable definition of personality is difficult to arrive at, but agreement can be reached on certain criteria for an eventual definition. These criteria include comprehensiveness (all aspects of the individual must be considered), modifiability (despite hereditary influences, personality is an ever-adapting phenomenon), pattern and organization (the personality is *not* an agglomeration of isolated and easily separable characteristics), and uniqueness (no man can be exactly like another).

Psychology must, however, ignore, at least to some extent, this last criterion and seek certain general characteristics in personality organization. These general characteristics can be broadly classified into traits and typologies. A trait is an enduring characteristic of a person that can be observed in a wide variety of situations and can be used to describe the behavior of most individuals. For example, people are more or less warm, reserved, irritable, and so on. Traits can be observed at a number of levels, and it is sometimes useful to distinguish between such levels, like, for example, "surface" warmth and "real" warmth.

As we sketch a portrait of an individual personality by describing his standing on a number of traits, we draw a trait profile. When people resemble one another in their trait profiles, we begin to speak of personality types. There are a wide variety of typological systems, and each permits us to make useful distinctions among persons. These distinctions are only relative, however, and do not point to abrupt discontinuities with the world of personalities.

Typologies have been subjected to much criticism because of their apparent implication of discontinuity, yet this criticism is rarely merited since at least modern typologies by no means speak of such abrupt distinctions among discrete types. Instead, they postulate dimensions along which individuals can vary, choosing to focus on certain points along these dimensions.

The study of personality is one of psychology's most intriguing puzzles and most difficult challenges. All psychological knowledge should ultimately contribute to the understanding of personality—what shapes it, why it differs from individual to individual, how it develops and changes throughout the course of life. The fact that most areas of psychology have been only minimally integrated into the body of modern personality theory is sufficient proof that a comprehensive theory of personality has not yet been achieved. As a result, we may expect that complete agreement among psychologists on even a definition of personality has not yet been reached. In this expectation we shall not be disappointed. Allport (1937) lists fifty definitions, drawn from philosophy, theology, law, and sociology and psychology.

Among the earliest definitions of personality is one that was most likely the source of the term and that regards personality as the *outward* aspect of the individual—how the person is perceived by and how he affects other people. (In the Roman theater an actor's mask was called a *persona*—the face he presented to the audience.) As we shall see later on, an influential modern derivative of such a view holds that personality is in large part molded by others' reactions to an individual. In this view, some members of minority groups may in fact become avaricious or indolent, not because of some inherent trait in that group, but because the majority in the world about them perceives them in this way and expects them to act in this way. We tend to become what others say we are. This intriguing definition of personality, which emphasizes the "social stimulus value" of the individual, does not, however, do justice to the effects of the multitude of other determinants of personality that must be included in a comprehensive definition.

Toward a Definition of Personality

Most psychologists can agree upon a number of general characteristics of an ideally broad definition of personality. Nevertheless, the working definitions that guide their own efforts may underplay or totally ignore one or more of these characteristics. We shall attempt not to present an ideal definition of personality but instead to provide a useful framework for discussion. Such a framework might be phrased as follows: *Personality is the integration of all of an individual's characteristics into a unique organization that determines, and is modified by, his attempts at adaptation to his continually changing environment.*

Comprehensiveness

Nothing that is Human is Alien to the Compleat Psychologist. Our generalized formulation of personality includes the individual's traits, abilities, beliefs, attitudes, values, motives, habitual modes of adjustment. It includes what we call "temperament"—the typical emotional reactions, mood states, and energetic attributes of the person—as well as what in older terminology was called "character," that is, the moral outlook and conduct of the person. But it must include much more. The general framework must permit us to study the many different kinds of factors that influence the development of personality. Genetic influences upon personality, as we shall see, are of substantial importance, even though their effects may be indirect, subtle, and difficult to detect. Differences in nutrition, disease, and even climatic conditions can affect bodily functioning and hence behavior. These factors also play their part in forming personality. Different cultures, from the national down to the neighborhood level, exert their special influences. And, of course, the "culture" represented by the individual family is of primary importance, particularly if we are to account for personality variation *within* a given broader culture. Finally, there is the influence of specific critical events of various sorts—a crippling accident, a death in the family, a moment of supreme horror or extraordinary good fortune. Our conception of personality must be sufficiently broad to make a place for all of these factors.

Another dimension of complexity is added by the *modifiability* of personality. If we are sufficiently skillful and our theory sufficiently powerful, we can see in most persons a thread of consistency and predictability. Some personality characteristics are enduring; the mother who insists that her child was stubborn from his first day on earth may often speak the truth. Other personality characteristics appear early only as potentials, finding expression gradually and taking their particular final forms from the interplay of endowment with environment. The infant born with a heightened reactivity to external stimuli may become the explosive adult, triggered into irritability with every new crisis. Or he may become unusually responsive to new situations, greeting them with an alert curiosity.

When development is indeed smooth and continuous, all well and good; we may safely focus upon stable traits and gradually expressed potentials. But the discontinuities also fall within the province of personality study. The unusual mood of the moment, the single errant behavior that just doesn't "fit" our conception of a person—they too challenge a comprehensive theory of personality.

Then there is the question of *levels* of personality. We can describe personality on the level of overt behavior—the man is as he seems —or we can speak of underlying characteristics that, not being directly observable, must be inferred. A new neighbor exhibits special friendliness. Is he "really" warm and gregarious, or does the extremeness of his friendly behavior mean that underneath he is "really" anxious and socially ill at ease in this new neighborhood? In any particular case there may be a specific answer; in the general case— the study of personality—the only answer is that we must be able to treat all levels of behavior and understand the intricate interactions among them.

Organization, Pattern, and Uniqueness

The ingredients of personality study, then, are individual differences in all manner of traits, genetic and environmental determinants, and behaviors on various levels. Their blending into a "whole" man is the final, essential task. But whether the "whole" man exists in actuality has occasioned considerable research and discussion among psychologists. Although it is true that man often gives integrated responses to his total situation, it is equally true that he sometimes responds with only an isolated portion of himself. The man who continues to vote the "straight ticket" of his parents throughout a lifetime of elections, despite important changes in his social values and economic interests, may not be performing on the political scene as a "whole" individual. Although it is possible to investigate such "part-processes" in personality, many psychologists maintain stoutly that such an approach is doomed to failure and that the essence of personality is the patterning of characteristics and their organization within a unique, whole person. The most eloquent spokesman for this position has been Allport, who, from his earliest writings to his recent ones (for example, Allport, 1961), has insisted that no number of "general" laws for the "average" man's response to this or that situation can ever lead to an adequate understanding of personality. His central theme is the uniqueness of the individual. His alternative to the "general" law is the use of "idiographic" methods, which preserve the distinct pattern or "style" of the individual. Numerous studies by Allport and others have shown this approach to be practicable, demonstrating, for example, that the "style" of an individual's behavior—something that cannot be described by a traditional enumeration of general characteristics—is maintained over a variety of forms of expression. Voice, posture, gait, handwriting, even artistic productions bear the stamp of uniqueness, as evinced by the ability of judges to match these characteristics correctly. In the pioneer work on this problem (Allport & Vernon, 1933), college students were able to match with above-chance accuracy brief personality sketches of persons unknown to them with specimens of the handwriting of these individuals. (Professional graphologists, whose business it is to do just that, in fact proved to be more accurate judges than did students in this study.) Such demonstrations indeed support the claim that persons show identifiable unique characteristics.

More recent studies have extended Allport's notion of "style" into the cognitive realm. The concept of "cognitive style" suggests that, just as an individual's voice, posture, gait, and handwriting bear the stamp of uniqueness, so do his methods of perceiving, judging, thinking, and remembering (see Box 147, p. 700).

Description of Personality

No matter how unique and how whole we regard personality, a scientific approach requires that we describe and analyze this uniqueness and wholeness of the individual. There are two main approaches to personality description —in terms of *traits* and in terms of *types*. If, when asked to describe someone, you enumerate several characteristics—"he's rebellious, intelligent, talkative, dedicated, and so on"— you have defined a number of distinct traits that you feel exist in a marked degree for that person. Your implicit assumption is that each person may have a different set of such traits. If, however, you reply, "he's the intellectual type," or "he's the authoritarian type," then you have adopted a typological approach to personality description. Your assumption is that people can be categorized according to the *fixed pattern* of traits that characterize them. These two approaches are, of course, intimately related, but they merit separate discussion.

Traits

A *trait* is an enduring characteristic of the individual's behavior in a wide variety of situa-

tions. To ascribe the trait of "punctuality" to an individual's behavior implies that he tends regularly to arrive on time—at work, at parties, in meeting trains. A trait characterizes an individual's behavior to a lesser or greater degree. The man was presumably called "punctual" not because he is perfectly punctual in all possible circumstances but because he is highly punctual as compared with other people. When we talk about a personality trait, therefore, we mean to signify a dimension along which people's behavior varies in the amount of the trait exhibited, from those showing a great deal of the trait to those showing very little.

As we compare people and seek to specify what differentiates their personalities, we naturally focus attention on those behaviors in which differences among individuals are most marked. But to do so may lead to neglect of other trait dimensions in regard to which people of a given population do not differ appreciably in amount. The traits that most people of a given group share may, however, often be as important for our understanding of their personalities as the traits in which they differ. For example, the native Dobu psychologist among his own Dobu people might never think to ascribe to them the trait of "suspiciousness," for everyone in that culture is excessively suspicious. A visiting psychologist may at once pick out this trait as the most noteworthy component of Dobu personality, even though individual Dobuans do not differ much in the amount of suspicion they exhibit. The visiting psychologist notices the trait because he views it in a larger frame of reference, comparing it with the lesser degrees of suspicion found in other cultures.

One reason why we may be blind to certain basic traits of personality that play a vital role in the whole "meaning" of personality structure is that we tend to view man within the fairly narrow milieu of our own society or culture. In principle, a full-fledged personality description should include all the identifiable traits that exist in an individual.

Levels of Traits Traits are of many different kinds or classes. Some pertain to temperamental characteristics; some to typical ways of adjusting; some to abilities, interests, values; some to social relations. But the fundamental distinction is one of levels. Some traits are easily observable, and therefore easily measured, because they refer to "surface" characteristics of the individuals. If an acquaintance smiles frequently, laughs easily, and generally has a rosy view of things, we say he is cheerful. Each of us would use many of the same cues in making this judgment, and the cues would have much the same meaning for all of us. Therefore, the trait "cheerfulness" would be assessed with high agreement among observers, and probably with high validity. Other traits are defined as "deep-seated," and underlying "surface" traits. Our friend may thus "seem" cheerful, but "underneath" he may "really" be depressed.

This sudden shower of quotation marks denotes, as usual, an area of current controversy in personality description and measurement. It is meaningful to say that someone "seems" cheerful but is "really" depressed only if our theory is such as to conceive that personality has at its core characteristics that are not themselves directly observable. Such a central system of characteristics must therefore be inferred, and the rules of inference are usually complex; furthermore, these rules are never uniform because they are tied to particular theories of personality. For example, our friend is said to be "really" depressed because our *theory* leads us to *infer* that when a man is too cheerful considering the actual mess he has made of his life, his cheerfulness must betray an unconscious satisfaction that he is failing, because his failure relieves unconscious guilt over some transgression that is no longer remembered. If our theory is different from this one, then we would infer a different real underlying trait for our consistently smiling friend, or we might even ascribe to him only the trait of "cheerfulness" that he manifests.

Irrespective of the level used, the array of possible descriptive attributes of behavior is so vast that some method for reducing these attributes to manageable proportions must be used. One such method is factor analysis.

Factor-Analytic Description of Traits Through an assiduous search of the English language Allport and Odbert (1936) complied a list of 17,953 adjectives used to describe distinctive and personal forms of people's behavior. About 4,500 of these terms clearly designate consistent and stable modes of an individual's adjustment to his environment; each of these words, in a sense, represents a potential trait to be measured and analyzed. Cattell (1946) undertook to reduce this list to manageable proportions, employing as his primary tool the statistical method of factor analysis (see p. 664). He first pruned the list down to 171 terms by eliminating synonyms, rare words, and the like. The 171 trait names were further reduced to thirty-five main "trait clusters" through combination of all the traits that correlated fairly highly with one another. These "trait clusters" are Cattell's *surface traits*, characteristics that are easily defined and readily observable. The thirty-five trait clusters were used as the basis for constructing thirty-five rating scales. About 200 men (soldiers, professional and business men, artists, skilled workers, and so on), divided into a number of small groups of intimate acquaintances, served as subjects. Two members from each group first were trained in the rating technique and then rated their fellows independently. The two ratings were averaged to obtain the final rating for each man.

The ratings were then subjected to factor analysis. It was found that twelve factors were adequate to account for most of the individual differences among the men in the rated traits. Cattell has continued to refine and extend this list of traits in a number of directions. A recent count has expanded the twelve factors to twenty (see Table 42.1.).

Box 147

Cognitive Styles

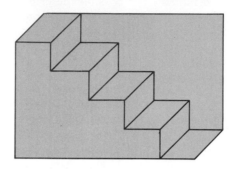 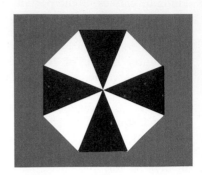

In recent years the notion of "cognitive style" has been enjoying considerable popularity, in part because it promises an avenue for understanding how personality factors can influence perceiving, learning, thinking, and remembering. That such influences exist cannot be seriously doubted; casual observation demonstrates the influence of a personal style in even the most impersonal experimental situation. A very cautious individual, serving as a subject, will, for example, attend meticulously to the details of a new stimulus situation, perhaps taking more time to learn its every detail but thereby becoming able to recall the material more accurately. Traditionally, studies of perception and learning have paid little heed to such differences among subjects.

G. S. Klein, R. W. Gardner, and H. J. Schlesinger, psychologists at New York University, provide a demonstration of how far-reaching a cognitive style can be. Thirty subjects were classified as *tolerant* or *intolerant* of "unrealistic" experiences on the basis of the *range* of stimulus conditions in which they perceived apparent movement (see p. 221). All subjects were explicitly informed that no real movement would take place and were even shown the apparatus and given an explanation of how two lights, separated by some distance and alternately flashing on and off, could give rise to the illusion of a moving light between them. The subject who continued to see such apparent movement over a wide range of conditions was regarded by the experimenter as more tolerant of an "unrealistic" experience than the subject who saw the movement only over a narrower range.

Evidence that this difference between tolerant and intolerant subjects was a pervasive cognitive

Table 42.1.
Some Examples of Cattell's Source Traits

Reserved-Outgoing	Practical-Imaginative
Emotional-Stable	Forthright-Shrewd
Humble-Assertive	Placid-Apprehensive
Sober-Happy-go-lucky	Conservative-Experi-
Expedient-Conscientious	menting
Shy-Venturesome	Relaxed-Tense
Trusting-Suspicious	

Popular rather than technical names are used to identify the traits.

These factors are presumably *source traits*, which through complex dynamics come to determine the more familiar *surface traits*. The precise names given by Cattell to these factors are merely convenient identifying labels. Their actual nature must be discovered by further study.

Considerable research has dealt with the generality of these source traits. Do they appear in children as well as in adults? Can they be found in different behavior domains, for

style came from their behavior on a number of quite different perceptual tasks. Tolerant subjects also reported more reversals in viewing both the Maltese cross and the staircase figure. As both these reversible figures do not "really" reverse—the stimulus itself does not change, just as there was really no moving light—seeing more reversals was regarded as another instance of tolerance of "unrealistic" experiences.

In another task, subjects wore *anisiekonic lenses,* which distort the visual field; for example, apparent sizes and shapes of objects change, and the floor beneath the subject's feet appears to slant downward and away. Individuals differ in their susceptibility to this effect, and, as predicted, tolerant subjects experienced this distortion more quickly than did intolerant subjects. On still another type of task, the Rorschach ink blots (see p. 719), tolerant subjects responded easily when required to describe what each blot "looks like"; intolerant subjects were quite uncomfortable with the task, frequently apologized that the blot didn't "really" look like what they said it was, and felt called upon to justify their responses by presenting supporting evidence in some detail.

In an earlier experiment, J. M. Kaplan, a Harvard doctoral candidate working under Klein's direction, had presented data that could be interpreted to extend the scope of this cognitive style even further. He found that subjects who more readily experienced anisiekonic-lens distortion were also better at recalling contradictory elements of a story that they had learned previously. The subjects who experienced such distortion less readily found it difficult to remember such conflicting material, indicating a relative inability to handle this kind of "unrealistic" situation.

"Tolerance for unrealistic experience" is but one of many cognitive styles that have been proposed in recent years. Two of the best known are "sharpening versus leveling" (the degree to which an individual emphasizes or minimizes differences among stimuli) and "field dependence versus field independence" (the degree to which perception is influenced by external frames of reference). There is some evidence of consistency in the personality traits accompanying given cognitive styles, which, in turn, encourages the view that a cognitive style may represent a rather firmly based and stable characteristic of the individual. As such, it may be reliably measured, and the result will be improved predictive accuracy and greater understanding of individual behavior.

G. S. KLEIN, R. W. GARDNER, and H. J. SCHLESINGER. 1962. Tolerance for Unrealistic Experiences: A Study of the Generality of Cognitive Control, *Brit. J. Psychol.,* 53, 41–55.

J. M. KAPLAN. 1952. Predicting Memory Behavior From Cognitive Attitudes Toward Instability, *Amer. Psychol.,* 7, 322. Abstract.

Figure A adapted by permission of John Wiley & Sons, Inc.

example, with data obtained by self-report questionnaires, as well as with behavior ratings? Other work has moved beyond the original descriptive task and is concerned with the extent of the genetic determination of each source trait.

Such factor-analysis methods in personality research are of utmost importance in simplifying the study of traits. But these methods are tools, not solutions to the problem of understanding personality organization. The primary trait factors that result from a factor analysis depend greatly upon the trait dimensions originally included in the test battery. A factor analysis of test results cannot, of course, come up with trait factors that summarize personality characteristics not included in the original pool of traits. And, of course, the selection of the original dimensions to be tested inevitably reflects the beliefs of the investigator concerning the basic nature of personality and what aspects are central. Cattell's source traits, despite their exhaustive and representative base in the Allport-Odbert adjective list, almost necessarily have been influenced somewhere in the long line between 17,953 adjectives and twelve factors by their author's assumptions. It is not surprising, therefore, that different factor-analysis studies do not entirely agree on the "primary" trait factors they "discover."

Trait Profiles Once a set of basic trait dimensions has been established, through factor analysis or other means, we wish to be able to summarize the description of each individual with respect to all these dimensions. One convenient way is to plot a *trait profile*. This plotting requires that, on each dimension, the person's standing relative to that of the general population be ascertained. Figure 42.1. gives profiles for three individuals on eight traits.

The trait profile facilitates our inspection of the pattern of an individual's traits. It permits us to see how that pattern, as a whole and in detail, compares and contrasts with the trait patterns of other people. By computing an "index of profile similarity"—one of a number of possible measures of the distance between any pair of profiles—we are able to state in quantitative terms the degree of similarity or dissimilarity in the personalities of two individuals as measured on these traits. And, when similarity is quite high, we begin to speak of persons belonging to the same "type."

Personality Types

Confronted with the bewildering complexity and diversity of the different traits ascribed to man, philosophers, educators, and psychologists from the beginning of recorded history have "solved" the problem of personality description by using the notion of *personality types*. The universal popularity of type theory may be regarded as yet another testimonial to man's need and ability to impose order upon a chaotic stimulus situation. A type provides a shorthand for talking about a set of separate traits by

making the assumption that generally recognizable *patterns* of personality characteristics do in fact exist.

Many and varied *typologies* (systems of individual types intended to embrace the full range of personality) have been proposed. Some typologies stress the role of a single dominant trait that organizes all other characteristics around it; some have no such central theme but focus on particular combinations of traits. Some arise from theoretical conceptions of personality; others are empirical, arising from intensive observation of representative samples of individuals from particular cultures. Biological bases underlie some typologies; others focus upon the influence of early experience.

Despite these differing emphases, typologies share certain features. First, they intend to provide a framework within which every individual, no matter how idiosyncratic, may find a place. If a person is not a "pure" example of any of the types within the typology, then he may be described by the degree to which he resembles one of these types; for example, he may be intermediate between the "authoritarian" and the "democratic" types. Second, types always consist of a distinctive pattern of separate personality traits, even when the type relies upon a single dominant trait for its organizing principle. For example, the "authoritarian" personality type has at its core an exaggerated respect for, and obedience to, authority. Box 148, p. 704, illustrates how this single trait extends into many facets of personality and defines a pattern of many characteristics. Third, typologies must possess a certain hardiness, an ability to survive despite dramatic changes in individual life situations or radical differences in cultural context (see Box 149, p. 705). For example, the typology that includes "introvert" and "extrovert" types, which we shall soon discuss, assumes their universal occurrence and makes the assumption that introverts will remain introverts come rain or shine. Although this restriction is not a

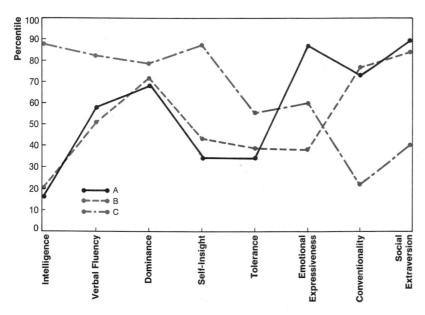

Figure 42.1. Comparative profiles for three individuals on a set of eight traits. The vertical scale indicates the amount of each trait exhibited by the individual in terms of his percentile standing relative to the entire population of people measured on the trait. The profiles of A and B are obviously very similar except for a difference in *emotional expressiveness.* C's profile differs markedly from those of the other two.
After Arbuthnot, 1948; adapted by permission.

necessary one, typologies characteristically attempt to describe universal and enduring behavior patterns, just as traits and trait factors intend to refer to universal and enduring single dimensions of personality.

Some "Classical" Typologies

Historical accounts of type theories begin with Hippocrates (*c.* 400 B.C.), who postulated that there are four types of temperament, associated with four main kinds of fluids, or "humors," of the body:

Body "Humor"	Temperament
Blood (Latin: *sanguis*)	Sanguine: optimistic, hopeful
Black Bile (Greek: *me-lan coln*)	Melancholic: sad, depressed
Bile (Greek: *coln*)	Choleric: irascible
Phlegm (Greek: *flegma*)	Phlegmatic: apathetic

Needless to say, the specific "humors" postulated by Hippocrates are not consistent with our modern knowledge of physiology, but his

temperamental types still flourish in our thinking, and our modern personality vocabulary perpetuates the ancient words used for the humors of the ancient physiology. His theory was the classical forerunner of modern theories correlating temperament with glandular secretions (see pp. 601). And it was the beginning of a long line of type theories in which personality make-up was conceived to be intimately related to body constitution and physique.

Asthenic Versus Pyknic One of the earliest of modern theories relating physique and personality was that of Kretschmer (1936). He presented evidence that there is a characteristic body type for each of the two main kinds of mental illness—schizophrenia and manic-depressive psychosis. The schizophrenic tends to have a thin, long-limbed, narrow-chested body, which Kretschmer called the *asthenic type;* the manic-depressive tends to have a short, fattish, barrel-chested body, called

Box 148   The Authoritarian Personality

Authoritarianism has always been one of the most basic problems of human society. It appears in its most spectacular form in political dictatorships, but it can be found in less dramatic and often more insidious forms in almost every type of interpersonal relationship and social organization. One of its aspects that has especially interested psychologists is the role of personality in authoritarian behavior.

For instance, an extensive study by T. W. Adorno and his associates provides evidence that a syndrome of "authoritarian" traits can be identified as a central and enduring part of some people's personalities. The main traits making up the syndrome appear to be the following:

1. great concern with authority relationships with people; extreme deference to superior authority and exercise of one's authority over those in subordinate positions;
2. heavy stress on conventional behavior, values, and morality; close conformity to group norms;
3. overcontrol and denial of one's own "immoral" impulses and feelings and projection of them onto the outgroup; exaggerated sense of one's own moral "rightness"; lack of self-insight;
4. depersonalization of social relations; tendency to manipulate and exploit people as objects rather than to treat them as human beings and expectation of being exploited in turn; sadistic tendencies (enjoyment in hurting other people) together with masochistic tendencies (enjoyment in being hurt);
5. rigidity of thought processes; excessive stereotyped thinking; prejudice and intolerance toward minority groups.

The Adorno study suggests that the development of this syndrome comes from severe disciplinary treatment of the child, typically involving excessive stress on the rightness of parental rules and values, with insistence on complete obedience to them reinforced by punishment. Often such severe discipline is accompanied by a parental attitude of emotional rejection of the child and by exploitative manipulation of the child.

The consequences are that the child develops extreme submissiveness to parental authority, which later extends to all authority figures. This submissiveness is accompanied by an unquestioning acceptance of the rightness of the values of the authorities. But there is also a strong hostility toward the parents or other authorities. This hostility cannot be readily expressed in direct aggression against the authority figure; for one thing, there is fear of punishment by the all-powerful authority and, for another, such aggression would be incompatible with belief in the complete rightness of the authority. The hostility is thus repressed (see p. 763) and the aggression displaced toward safer targets like minority groups, those in positions of inferior status, and sometimes the self.

Evidence for this general picture is found by Adorno and his associates—and by numerous other investigators—through studies of many groups of subjects, using many kinds of techniques, like psychiatric interviews, attitude questionnaires, laboratory tests, sociological surveys.

It should be emphasized that the "authoritarian" syndrome is not the exclusive characteristic of any single ideological movement, social class, or occupation. "Authoritarian personalities" can be found everywhere—in the labor union as well as in industrial management, in social clubs as well as in governmental bureaucracy; and they are by no means unknown in the church and even in the classroom.

T. W. ADORNO, E. FRENKEL-BRUNSWIK, D. J. LEVINSON, and R. N. SANFORD. 1950. *The Authoritarian Personality* (New York: Harper).

Box 149

The Self-Conceited Man

What is your immediate picture of "The Self-Conceited Man"? Perhaps you can jot down a list of specific characteristic behavior and compare your impressions of this personality type with excerpts from the sketch written under the same title by John Earle, an Englishman, in 1628.

"A self-conceited man is one that knows himself so well that he does not know himself. . . . He is now become his own book, which he pores on continually, yet like a truant reader skips over the harsh places, and surveys only that which is pleasant. In the speculation of his own good parts, his eyes, like a drunkard's see all double, and his fancy, like an old man's spectacles, makes a great letter in a small print. He imagines every place where he comes his theatre, and not a look stirring but his spectator; and conceives men's thoughts to be very idle, that is, only busy about him. . . . If he has done anything that has passed with applause, he is always reacting it alone, and conceits the ecstacy his hearers were in at every period. His discourse is all positions and definitive decrees with *thus it must be* and *thus it is*, and he will not humble his authority to prove it. . . . A flatterer is a dunce to him, for he can tell him nothing but what he knows before: and yet he loves him too, because he is like himself. . . . In sum he is a bladder blown up with wind, which the least flaw crushes to nothing."

This personality type is recognizable even now—a tribute to the durability of human character types. "The Self-Conceited Man" has withstood the cultural upheavals of the last three centuries of man's history, and it is difficult to envisage a future society that would find him alien and incomprehensible.

R. ALDINGTON. 1924. *A Book of Characters* (New York: Dutton).

the *pyknic type*. Kretschmer generalized this typology to the normal population, asserting that there are distinctly different patterns of personality traits biologically linked with these two body types. The asthenic-type person was said to be shy, sensitive, aloof, and withdrawn. The pyknic type was said to be jovial, lively, outgoing, and inclined to mood fluctuations.

This typology, though perhaps overstated, had its kernel of truth and has served as an effective springboard for ongoing attempts to establish physique-personality relations. Its most articulate descendant is the one proposed by Sheldon, which we shall examine in our later discussion of constitutional determinants of personality (see Box 157, p. 736).

Introvert Versus Extrovert Probably the most widely known typology is that of introversion-extroversion advanced by Jung (1923). This typology was just one aspect of an elaborate theory of personality. The introvert was described as subjective in orientation—as primarily interested in ideas, imagination, and inner life—as tender-minded and idealistic. The extrovert was described as having an orientation directed outward to the objective world of things and events—as primarily interested in social activities and practical affairs—as tough-minded and realistic.

The simple introvert-extrovert dichotomy has become solidly entrenched in our popular thinking; but, at least in its overly simplified form, the evidence does not support such a dichotomy. Attempts to measure people along the introversion-extroversion dimension have shown that, rather than falling into two distinct types, people are distributed all along the dimension with most around the center (see Figure 42.2.).

Actually, Jung's conception was far more complex than has been represented here, and he did not regard the introversion-extroversion variable as a simple one. That it is not a simple affair has been confirmed by factor-analytic studies that identify as many as five separate

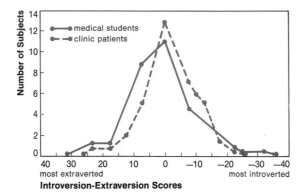

Figure 42.2. Distribution of scores of senior medical students and patients on the Neymann-Kohlstedt Introversion-Extroversion Test. Despite the differences in age, educational level, and so on between the two groups, there is no difference in score distributions. Most scores are not concentrated at the two extremes, as would be implied by a simple type theory that would categorize people as either extroverted or introverted.
C. A. Neymann and G. K. Yacorzynski, "Studies of Introversion-Extroversion and Conflict Motives in the Psychoses," *Journal of General Psychology*, 27 (1942), 241–55; adapted by permission of The Journal Press.

introversion-extroversion factors: social introversion, thinking introversion, depression, tendency to mood swings, and happy-go-lucky disposition (Guilford, 1940).

Eidetic Types Quite a different typology was proposed by Jaensch (1930) on the basis of study of eidetic imagery (see Box 69, p. 355). He concluded that people fall into several distinctly different types, on the basis of the forms of eidetic imagery they experience. These differences in experience were related, he thought, to basic differences in styles of perceptual and cognitive functioning and thus to differences in over-all personality patterns. Jaensch's theory, though not confirmed by experimental evidence, played a part in the initiation of modern research that seeks to find relationships between personality variables and habitual modes of perceiving. Our earlier discussion of "cognitive styles" (see p. 698) is in this broad tradition.

Value Types Numerous typologies have been built around the notion that people can be classified into discrete value types. Here the conception is that each person has some sort of unifying philosophy of life—a dominant value—that shapes and structures his entire personality. One such theory was that of Spranger (1928), who sought to classify all people into six "ideal" value types:

1. *The Theoretical.* Dominant interest in discovery of truth; seeks to observe and to reason; chief aim in life is to order and systematize his knowledge.
2. *The Economic.* Dominant interest in what is useful; concerned with the production of wealth; believes in practice rather than theory, utility rather than aesthetics.
3. *The Aesthetic.* Dominant interest in form and harmony; believes beauty is the greatest truth and judges each experience on its aesthetic merits.
4. *The Social.* Dominant interest in love of people; concerned with other people's affairs and with their welfare; a warm and humane outlook.
5. *The Political.* Dominant interest in power; whether in politics or in other activities, the aim is to gain influence and control over people and events, to become a leader.
6. *The Religious.* Dominant interest in comprehending the unity of the universe; concern with mystical experiences and with what is divine in every phenomenon.

Very few people completely fit these "ideal" value types. Most people have a mixture of these values, with some primary and some secondary. This fact is demonstrated in the results of personality tests that were designed to measure people on these six value dimensions (see Box 150, p. 707).

Empirical Typologies The preceding section presented a number of theoretical typologies, theoretical in the special sense that each was proposing a universal scheme intended to encompass all mankind. Standing in contrast to theoretical typologies are those based upon the personality groupings that are actually found to exist in a particular sample of individuals. The essence of such empirical typologies is their intent to reflect "what goes with what," free from the theoretical predilections of the

Box 150

Measuring Personal Values

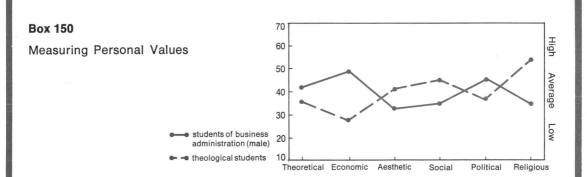

The notion of six "ideal" value types proposed by E. Spranger later led to the development of an inventory designed to measure the relative importance of each of these six values to the individual. This inventory, called the Study of Values, was constructed by G. W. Allport and P. E. Vernon at Harvard University and later revised with the help of G. Lindzey. It consists of forty-five items pertaining to the subject's attitudes and preferences. The items were selected on the basis of their apparent relevance to one or more of the six value areas—theoretical, economic, aesthetic, social, political, religious.

An example of one type of item is the following statement, to which the person is to answer "yes" or "no."

"Are our modern industrial and scientific developments signs of a greater degree of civilization than those attained by any previous society, the Greeks, for example?

A "yes" answer gives a point toward the economic value, a "no" answer a point toward the aesthetic value.

Another type of item is a multiple-choice question like the following:

"If you could influence the educational policies of the public schools of some city, would you undertake—

a. to promote the study and participation in music and fine arts;
b. to stimulate the study of social problems;
c. to provide additional laboratory facilities;
d. to increase the practical value of courses."

Can you figure out which of the six values each of the four possible answers is meant to reveal?

Total scores are computed for the subject on each of the six values, and a profile is plotted with the midpoint of each scale at 40. This profile provides a quick picture of the pattern of his values.

The graph shows two "averaged" profiles for a group of male students of business administration and a group of theological students. Note the differences.

G. W. ALLPORT, P. E. VERNON, and G. LINDZEY. 1951. *A Study of Values: A Scale for Measuring the Dominant Interests in Personality.* Rev. ed. (Boston: Houghton Mifflin). Figure adapted by permission.

Box 151

An Empirical Typology

A research study, now being conducted by Norman Livson at the Institute of Human Development at the University of California, Berkeley, is attempting to establish a typology to describe the kinds of personality organizations to be found in children during their developmental years. The raw data for this study are the complete case records of more than fifty children of each sex whose physical, intellectual, and personality development were studied from birth through adolescence in an ongoing longitudinal investigation directed by Jean Macfarlane of the Institute. It proved possible for judges to summarize the salient characteristics of each child's personality by means of a Q-sort, a technique that requires the judge to rank-order a large number of descriptive items as they apply to a particular individual. Employing the 100 items of Block's California Q-set, each child was described in terms of which items were extremely characteristic of him, which somewhat less so, and so on.

The resultant Q-sorts for each child were correlated with the Q-sorts of all other children of the same sex; the correlation coefficient between any two children measured their similarity in personality profile and therefore indicated the degree of personality resemblance between them. The higher the correlation, the more similar the personalities of the two children were; the lower the correlation, the less similar. These correlations were subjected to a cluster analysis (a statistical method similar to factor analysis) in order to discover groups of children who resembled one another highly. These groups, within which all children have high correlations with one another, constitute empirical types.

The cluster analysis detected five types among the boys, four among the girls. Although, of course, not all children were "pure" examples of given types, it was possible to assign more than 80 per cent of them to one type or another. Some children, however, were stubborn "residuals"—they simply could not be forced into the mold of any of the types. For example, the boy least like any of the types was judged to be self-defeating, giving up easily when confronted with problems, and quite excitable. He also had few friends and limited interests. In social situations he was withdrawn and ill at ease. This same boy, now in his early thirties, remains a "residual." He has never married and still lives with his parents, expressing satisfaction with a sheltered but rather solitary life.

"Residuals" (some of whom may be residuals because of their extraordinary adaptability or capacities) serve as a continual reminder that any classification scheme must be an approximation. And

investigator. Box 151, p. 708, illustrates how a typology of nine types can be derived from a purely empirical examination of the personality traits in a sample of 100 children. The gulf between the theoretical and the empirical typology, however, is not so wide as each would claim; predilection is never fully nullified, nor does theory proceed unchecked by the realities of empirical data. In short, Kretschmer's ty-

pology could not have arisen in the absence of intensive observation, and the empirical typology presented in Box 151, p. 708, is probably not entirely innocent of theoretical persuasion.

Evaluation of the Typological Approach Types have been subjected to severe criticism. For example, Allport (1937) argues:

"Every typology is based on the abstraction of some

what should induce even greater caution is that the "residual" of one society may be a common type in another.

As we cannot present here a full description of each of the nine types in terms of the 100 Q-sort items, a summary portrait of only one type for each sex is presented. We have selected type 5 for boys and type 4 for girls because they are interesting types, although infrequently found.

A TYPE 5 BOY

Characteristically

Is a genuinely dependable and responsible person.
Appears to have a high degree of intellectual capacity.
Is productive; gets things done.
Has high aspiration level for self.

Uncharacteristically

Has a wide range of interests.
Favors conservative values in a variety of areas.
Is gregarious.
Tends to be rebellious and nonconforming.
Sees what he can get away with.

A TYPE 4 GIRL

Characteristically

Is a talkative individual.
Is unable to delay gratification.
Is self-indulgent.
Expresses hostile feelings directly.

Uncharacteristically

Has a wide range of interests.
Behaves in a sympathetic or considerate manner.
Is calm, relaxed in manner.
Has warmth and is compassionate.

Empirically derived types of this kind reflect no claim to universality; the particular types found in this study are anchored to a sample of children from a specific community, Q-sorted by certain judges employing a particular set of personality-descriptive items and having certain information available to them. But, even with these restrictions, empirical typologies like this one can help our research quest for understanding of personality. For example, rather than seeking determinants of the 100 separate personality traits for each of the boys and girls, it is now possible to look for differences among the nine types of children in their early family atmosphere as well as in their later educational careers and vocational (and marital) fates. Such a study is now under way.

JEAN W. MACFARLANE. 1938. Studies in Child Guidance: I. Methodology of Data Collection and Organization, *Monogr. Soc. Res. Child Develpm.*, 3, No. 6.
J. BLOCK. 1961. *The Q-Sort Method in Personality Assessment and Psychiatric Research* (Springfield, Ill.: Thomas).

segment of the total personality, and the forcing of this segment to unnatural prominence. All typologies place boundaries where boundaries do not belong. They are artificial categories.

This harsh judgment is unavoidable in the face of the conflicting claims of various typologies. Many of them pretend to embrace the total personality, and to follow the cleavages that occur in nature. But the very typologies that have proclaimed themselves 'basic,' contradict one another. Compare, for example, the supposedly foundational types of Kretschmer, Spranger and Jaensch. Certainly not one of these typologies, so diverse in conception and scope, can be considered final, for none of them overlaps any other. Each theorist slices nature in any way he chooses, and finds only his own cuttings worthy of admiration."

Most proponents of typologies—and particularly modern advocates—would be in full agreement with this last point, but, as for the criticism that most people are "mixed," for example, falling somewhere between the "pure" extrovert and the "pure" introvert, its target is largely a straw man. Not only do modern typologies define their types by a profile of several characteristics (the Jungian schema has three dimensions in addition to introversion-extroversion), but these dimensions are also considered continuous, not all-or-none dichotomies. The hard core of current conceptions of typologies is simply that certain trait profiles are more frequent than are others, so that they serve as convenient reference points for classification of all individuals. The universality that has been claimed by many typologies, especially theoretical ones, is less easily defended. What these typologists overlook is that any given personality type is but a particularly stable organization of biological and cultural forces at a particular time and place.

The attraction of types and typologies for psychologists—and a powerful attraction it must be to have survived continual criticism—may in part depend upon the ability of this approach to preserve something of the flavor of the unique individual and to do so without wholly sacrificing the generality necessary for the usual methods of scientific investigation. As Kluckhohn and Murray (1948) have observed, "Every man is in certain respects like all other men, like some other men, [and] like no other man."

Glossary

asthenic type The type of physique characterized by a thin, long-limbed, narrow-chested body, which was asserted by Kretschmer to be associated with shy, sensitive, aloof, and withdrawn characteristics, and—in cases of mental disease—with schizophrenia. This type is contrasted with the pyknic type.

personality types The qualitatively different categories into which personalities may allegedly be divided. There are simple type theories, which postulate a very limited number of categories, and complex type theories, involving classification of persons on a large number of dimensions.

pyknic type The type of physique characterized by a short, fattish, barrel-chested body, which was asserted by Kretschmer to be associated with jovial, lively, outgoing characteristics, with an inclination to mood fluctuations, and—in cases of mental disease—with manic-depressive psychosis. Contrasted with the asthenic type.

source traits In Cattell's system, the more fundamental and less directly observable traits that underlie and "account for" the surface traits.

surface traits In Cattell's system, clusters of traits that are easily defined and typically observed to go with one another.

trait An enduring characteristic of the individual that is manifested in a consistent way of behaving in a wide variety of situations. Traits are of many varieties; some are broad in scope, some narrow, some on the surface, and others deep-seated.

trait profile The composite of an individual's standing on each of a set of trait dimensions, relative to the population.

the measurement of personality

overview / The choice of methods for personality measurement and the adequacy of these methods are necessarily considered in the contexts of the particular view of personality one has adopted and the particular purposes that one's measurements are intended to serve. There is no unequivocal "best" method for measuring "true" characteristics of the personality.

There is therefore enormous diversity in the methods and goals of personality measurement. One broad category is that of ratings, within which many significant variants may be found. Another is situational tests, which provide opportunities for observing what are hopefully "natural" samples of an individual's behavior. Personality inventories and projective techniques both involve self-report by the person being studied but differ in the manner in which the information thus gathered is analyzed and interpreted.

Personality assessment refers to programs designed to provide a comprehensive evaluation of personality, using many methods and many situations. Such programs are at times employed to arrive at detailed descriptions of certain selected groups of individuals, for example, creative persons. The general issue of the best means through which personality-descriptive data can lead to effective prediction of behavior remains a complex and controversial one.

In the previous unit we saw that types are defined by trait profiles, trait profiles by individual traits, and individual traits by their measurement. Just as we have seen that it is meaningful to ascribe a "deeper level" trait to an individual only if we are ready to accept a particular theory of personality, so it is of little use to ask what kind of personality measurement is "better" unless we append to our question the qualifications "according to what theory?" or "for what purpose?" It may be difficult to accept such a relativistic criterion of goodness, in part because in our everyday thinking we regard someone's personality as composed of attributes that the person really "has." This tendency to reify personality traits—to regard them as *entities* that a person has just so much of, rather than as characteristics of his behavior—is aggravated when we speak of personality measurement. The term "measurement" unfortunately reinforces this impression. Because a person's height and weight can be accurately determined, we may be misled to expect that the assessment of his warmth or his anxiety can be accomplished by one, and only one, measurement by some suitable instrument.

This physical analogy is the villain in the story of personality measurement, suggesting, as it does, a crippling oversimplification of the nature of personality. A moment's reflection, and it is clear that "warmth" is not a characteristic whose degree may be read on some psychological thermometer. "Warm on what level?"—in innermost feeling or in social expression? "Warm in what manner?"—through quiet support or obtrusive demonstrativeness? "Warm in what situations?"—with intimates, with casual acquaintances, or even with strangers? Each of these manifestations is a legitimate aspect of the trait "warmth"; each can be measured, and each may yield different scores in the same individual.

For this and other reasons, although it is meaningful to speak of a "warm" person, it is necessary to consider a variety of conceptions and to apply a number of appropriate quantification methods. The synthesis of the various results from such a strategy provides perhaps the best avenue to understanding a trait and its place in the organization of personality.

Personality research has taken this mandate for diversity to heart. In principle, any item of behavior is fair game. A child's story to her doll, a letter to a friend, the tape-recorded conversation of a couple on their honeymoon—all have served as raw data in the study of personality. Spontaneous behavior is observed, interviews are conducted, personality inventories are constructed, test situations are set

up, even physiological responses are recorded. For any instance of personality measurement to be useful, it need meet only the two criteria that apply to any measurement in any branch of science: reliability and validity. The measurement method must yield consistent results, and it must accurately reflect some relevant aspect of the attribute in question.

Reliability and validity, which were discussed in Unit 38, are not the only considerations that have influenced the development of methods for the measurement of personality. As we review some of the more widely used approaches, it will become apparent that convenience and efficiency have been relevant factors. Instruments and techniques must work, but they must also be workable.

Measurement Techniques

One of the many distinctions that may be made among personality-measurement techniques is that between measurements made from observation of the person's natural behavior in realistic social situations and measurements based on required performances in test situations. Ratings, perhaps the most frequently used personality-measurement method, typically are made of behavior observed in relatively natural settings.

Ratings

A personality *rating* is nothing more than assignment of a numerical score to an observed subject in terms of a rating scale (see Table 43.1.).

Table 43.1.
An Illustrative Rating Scale for the Measurement of the Trait of Dominance-Submission

Instructions: Place a check mark before the category that best describes the behavior of the individual.

————1. Takes the lead in all his relations with other people; is always dominant and assertive.

————2. Usually takes the ascendant role in his relations with others, but occasionally may follow rather than lead.

————3. Is about equally likely to take the dominant role or the submissive role in his relations with others.

————4. Usually takes the submissive role, but occasionally is ascendant over others.

————5. Takes the submissive role in all his relations with other people; is always led and dominated.

The Q-sort of Box 151, p. 708, is another example of a rating method. When we comment that a friend is argumentative, we have made a rating on a two-point scale: yes or no. In fact, an *adjective checklist* is a formal instance of this rating procedure; the task of the rater is simply to check off which of a very large number of trait adjectives describe a subject's behavior (see, for example, Gough, 1961).

Usually, however, there is an attempt to make finer discriminations; five-point scales are common, and even eleven-point scales are not infrequent. Quite apart from the validity of such ratings, the degree of precision that can be attempted, that is, the number of points in the scale, depends largely upon the adequacy of the information upon which the rating will be based. The more observational data available, the greater the discrimination that should be possible. In addition, the more clearly the scale points are specified, the more likely it is that the discriminations will be reliable ones. Imagine, for example, that you have been asked to rate a number of acquaintances on the trait "competitiveness" and have been instructed only to use a five-point scale: very competitive, above average, average, below average, and very uncompetitive. Under these conditions it is unlikely that your ratings would agree highly with those made by others, even if all raters had had the same opportunity to observe the same subjects. On the other hand, and at the other extreme, if each of the five scale points

were clearly specified by a number of behavioral cues (as in Table 43.2.), agreement would certainly be enhanced. To specify would not only ensure that you shared a common definition of "competitiveness" with the other raters, but the meanings of such ambiguous terms as "very" and "above average" would have been sharpened.

Ratings may be made on the basis of direct observations of a person's behavior, either in a limited setting (for example, ratings of chil-

Table 43.2.
An Illustrative Rating Scale for the Measurement of the Trait of Competitiveness, With Detailed Criteria for Each Scale Point

————1. Extreme or hectic drive to excel competitors; either won't play if he can't win, or always picks inferior opponents, or cheats to win. Beating his competitors practically his only satisfaction in a play or work situation. Competitive drives dominate major part of his activities—a diffused set extending to many people and to all sorts of situations that to most individuals would not be competitive.

————2. Enjoys excelling competitor to the point of being upset when he loses; takes his failure to win very hard, or can't restrain an overt expression of satisfaction when he wins. Not so extreme as (1) but characteristic and noticeable by anyone with whom he comes in contact. Either several fields in which competitive drive is very pronounced but not so extreme as (1) or has one field in which it is terribly important to excel others.

————3. Is stimulated by competitive situations and enjoys excelling but can accept defeat without much strain. Periodic competitive sprees but not persistent and pervasive nor extreme.

————4. No real competitive relationship; enjoys games for the fun of playing them but relatively unimportant who wins.

————5. Sensitive to competitive situations but gets disorganized, is let down, unproductive, or flees from them. Resistive in negative way. Extremely discouraged about his abilities, or appears to seek defeat compulsively.

(Data from Macfarlane, Allen, and Honzik, 1954)

dren's traits from their behavior on the school playground), or in much broader settings (for example, ratings of workers by their supervisors on the basis of behavior occurring in many diverse situations, formal and informal). Ratings may also be made on the basis of personal interviews with the individual or on the basis of a study of various sources of information about him—life-history documents, work records, test scores, and so on—from all of which the rater seeks to gain an over-all impression of the individual's traits.

Ratings have been made on a great many different personality attributes, and they have proved indispensable for much of the research on personality. But they are fraught with dangers. Some traits cannot be rated in a reliable and valid fashion, no matter how well designed their rating scales. It is the general rule that, wherever possible, ratings should be made by several different raters, so that the degree of agreement of their judgments can be checked. When it is not feasible for more than one rater to observe the subject in action, then other raters may make their judgments from detailed descriptions (not evaluations) provided by the lone observer. In this case, apparent agreement would be artificially inflated because, however objective the observer attempted to make his description, it would probably reflect the opinion he had already implicitly made at the time. Despite his best intentions he would be less likely to perceive and to record data not consistent with his impression of the person.

Validity is, of course, an elusive notion in personality ratings. What can be the criterion against which the accuracy of a rating is to be evaluated? No single objective criterion exists, and the validity of a personality rating scale is checked, when it is at all, by its ability to predict an assortment of separate criteria. A set of "warmth" ratings by observers is valid to the extent that it correlates with the judgment of family members and close friends, for example, or with the degree of the subject's participation in humanitarian activities. Each separate criterion is highly fallible; collectively, they may be adequate. In most cases, the consensus of the ratings is the criterion; the subject *is* as warm as the average of several ratings says he is.

Self-Ratings   The person may also rate himself on various traits. There are obvious pitfalls in the use of self-ratings, in that they are susceptible to distortions caused by lack of frankness, limitation of perspective, and self-deception. The self-rating may thus disagree markedly with ratings made by objective observers.

But it should be recognized that the most important use of self-ratings is to provide measures of how an individual views himself. And the *self* is an organized and enduring perception in the individual's experience: It is unique to him and constitutes a central part of his *personality structure.* Assuming that the person reports frankly, his self-ratings are presumably the best evidence we can obtain on what the person believes about himself. And the fact that self-ratings may often deviate from the objective appraisals of observers is itself a fertile source of information about degrees of self-deception and self-insight. For example, in one procedure, the person checks which in a long list of adjectives he regards as true of himself. A team of expert observers uses the same list to check him. The degree of agreement between his description and the average of theirs is then computed. High agreement presumably indicates high self-insight; low agreement, low self-insight. In this case, clearly, consensus defines truth. But this "truth" may ignore a more basic truth. The self is often seen by the person as consisting of more central layers (the "real me") and the more peripheral layers (the unimportant part of "me"). This basic characteristic of the self (rather than low self-insight) may often be responsible for the discrepancies between the results of self-ratings and ratings by others.

Situational Tests

Another valuable approach to personality measurement in a "natural" social context is to place the person in a standard test situation that is an approximate replica of a "real life" situation and to record data on his behavior. The assumption is that his behavior in the test situation may fairly closely reflect his general behavioral traits. This reflection is likely to be closer the more "real" the test situation is. Sometimes, indeed, the subject may not realize that it is a test at all. For instance, MacKinnon (1938), in a classic forerunner to his later use of *situational tests* during World War II to assess OSS personnel, measured "honesty" in a sample of subjects by placing each one alone in a standard test situation in which he was to solve a series of numerical problems. An answer booklet was available, but he was instructed not to look. The experimenter observed him through a one-way screen, recording whether or not he violated the prohibition. (Box 116, p. 510, presented a similar, if more explosive, illustration.)

The situational test may often involve interpersonal behavior among several subjects who are being observed. For example, a group of five subjects may be assigned a topic to discuss, being left free to choose their own leader, set their own rules, and proceed as they see fit. The behavior of each person as he interacts with the others is recorded by observers and scored on one or more personality variables, such as dominance, poise, leadership, negativism, tolerance, originality. The scores may be objectively derived through the counting of behavior items (for example, the number of times the person initiated suggestions during the discussion), or they may be obtained through ratings.

Some situational tests are deliberately contrived to confront the individual with conditions of stress or with conflicts to be overcome in the assigned task. Milgram (1963), for example, placed his subjects in an extraordinarily stressful and conflicted situation by having them administer increasingly painful electric shocks to other subjects. In reality, in each case, the other "subject" was a confederate of the experiment and feigned painful reactions to an actually nonexistent shock. The performance in this situation of the true subject provided a measure of his ability to engage in antisocial acts (inflicting pain) when under social pressure, that is, the experimenter's stated expectation that he do so. In another kind of situation the subject may be required to work on a problem in cooperation with another person who is actually the experimenter and who deliberately causes well-timed interferences in the subject's attack on the problem. The distinctive manner in which he reacts to the stress and handles the interpersonal conflict provides data for measuring various dimensions of personality.

In life's normal course there are many common stress situations, which provide invaluable personality data. Adjustment to military service, to a new job, to marriage—each provides opportunities to observe personality in action under stress. Such outcomes in these situations as psychiatric breakdown, being fired, and divorce are thus highly relevant as objective behavioral indexes of reactions to stress situations.

Personality Inventories

A principal approach to personality measurement is through *personality inventories*, which are aimed at a great variety of traits. Some have to do with interests (for example, the Strong Vocational Interest Blank; see p. 657). Others have to do with emotional adjustment, social relations, attitudes, and values.

An inventory consists of a large number of statements or questions, each to be answered in one of several specified categories like "agree" or "disagree," "like" or "dislike." The score on a particular trait dimension is not based on the answer to a single item but on answers to several items that, taken together, constitute the scale intended to measure the trait in question. One inventory may provide measures of a dozen or more traits at the same time.

There are two quite different methods of establishing the direction in which the answers to an item are to be scored. In the *a priori* method the test constructor designs an item whose meaning, on the very face of it, clearly indicates how the item is to be scored. This method is used in the Allport-Vernon-Lindzey Study of Values (see Box 150, p. 707). In the *empirical* method the direction in which the item is to be scored is established by pretesting a large collection of items on criterion groups known to be high and low on the trait in question. The items on which the answers of the two groups differ significantly are included in the final inventory scale. An example of the empirical method is the Minnesota Multiphasic Personality Inventory (abbreviated MMPI). It consists of 550 simple statements, to each of which the person is to answer "true," "false," or "cannot say." The items refer to such diverse topics as bodily complaints ("I am troubled by discomfort in the pit of my stomach every few days or oftener"), fears and anxieties ("I am afraid when I look down from a high place"), behavior characteristics ("Often I cross the street in order not to meet someone I see"), social and moral attitudes ("I do not blame a person for taking advantage of someone who lays himself open to it").

This inventory was developed by administering a very large number of initial items (considerably more than the final 550 items) to groups of persons known to be high or low on the various personality characteristics to be measured. For example, items on which a group of persons known to be high on paranoia (institutionalized psychotics diagnosed as paranoid) responded significantly differently from normal persons were retained to make up the "paranoia" scale of the final inventory. An individual's score on the scale is then determined by the number of items on which he responds in the way in which the criterion group of paranoiac persons had responded.

The test is scored on a number of scales. The scales are measures of traits that, if possessed in extreme degree, are likely to be symptomatic of disturbances of personality, for example, "depression," "hysteria," "paranoia." The MMPI is one of the devices most widely used by clinicians for the diagnosis of personality disorders.

Another inventory, constructed in somewhat the same manner but aimed at the measurement of more favorable and positive traits having significance for social living and behavior in general, is the California Psychological Inventory (Gough, 1957). It includes eighteen scales grouped under four broad categories: first, measures of poise, ascendancy, and self-assurance; second, measures of socialization, maturity, and responsibility; third, measures of achievement potential and intellectual efficiency; and, fourth, measures of style of thinking and orientation to life.

Gough, in his CPI, has placed special emphasis on developing a personality inventory that would be applicable in a variety of cultures. His scales intend to measure "traits of character which arise directly and necessarily from interpersonal life, and which should therefore be relevant to the understanding and prediction of social behavior in any and all situations and in any culture." The statements that define his scales refer to situations common to most cultures; for example, in his Socialization scale, the subject responds to such items as "Before I do something I try to consider how my friends will react to it." The strategy has apparently worked well; numerous studies attest to the validity of many of the CPI scales in a number of countries. To take one instance, Gough and Sandhu (1964) report that the Socialization scale (in which a *low* score indicates delinquency) discriminated with great effectiveness between college students and imprisoned delinquents of comparable age in India.

Personality inventories have come under fire because of evidence that *response sets* substantially affect their scores; for example, subjects tend to agree with socially desirable items, almost apart from their content. Methods for correcting these biasing tendencies, and thus for improving validity, are being devised, and some more recent personality inventories attempt to rule out those factors in selecting their items.

One of the reasons that such response sets tend to operate in the taking of personality inventories is that the individual is aware that he is being tested and is often aware of the obviously intended diagnostic meaning of a particular item. For this reason it is of value to have less direct measures of personality traits, measures in which the intention of the test is less obvious to the individual. This thought brings us to the so-called "projective techniques."

Projective Techniques

Projective techniques are mainly used to reach the deeper and subtler aspects of personality. The essence of these techniques is the presentation of weakly structured or ambiguous stimulus materials to which the person responds. In this connection we should recall that mental set has a greater influence on the perception of a weakly structured stimulus than on that of a well-structured stimulus (see p. 185). It is therefore assumed that weakly structured or ambiguous stimulus materials will encourage a greater degree of "projection" of the subject's deep-lying tendencies than will more direct methods; as he perceives and interprets the stimuli, he is unaware of what he is revealing. Among the more commonly used projective tests are the Rorschach Ink Blot Test and the Thematic Apperception Test.

Rorschach Ink Blot Test This widely used projective technique, designed in 1911 by the Swiss psychiatrist Hermann Rorschach, consists in the presentation of ten standard ink blots, some black and white, some colored. The subject is asked to describe the various things he sees in the blots, and his responses are scored in a number of categories, pertaining to, first, the location in the blot of the thing seen; second, the kind of stimulus characteristic emphasized, for example, form, color, shading, texture, movement; third, the content of the percept, for example, animal, human being, inanimate object, and so forth; and, fourth, the originality of the response.

These various scores are taken to be "indicators" of specific tendencies. For instance, seeing the blot as a whole is regarded as an indication of tendencies toward abstract and theoretical orientations, whereas concentration on many small details of the blots indicates compulsive attention to trivial things; "color" responses are considered to be related to emotional expression; "human movement" responses to richness of inner life. Ratios of the separate scores are also considered highly diagnostic. A high ratio of color to form responses is thus interpreted as signifying a tendency to exhibit uncontrolled emotional behavior; a high ratio of human movement to color responses is taken to mean a withdrawn, introversive tendency; and so on.

Although the scoring of the Rorschach is more or less standard, the interpretation is decidedly not. It requires a highly skilled tester to synthesize the information from the entire pattern of test scores and to arrive at the conception of the structure of the personality. Such conceptions are "intuitive," and the same test scores may be quite differently interpreted by different experts. In addition, as the data of Box 152, p. 720, indicate, the responses may have different significance for people of different cultures. This possibility raises doubts concerning the basic validity of the technique, and, although studies directed at the question of validation show inconsistent results, the test continues in wide use.

Thematic Apperception Test This test is another widely used projective technique. Known as the

Box 152

**How Ink Blots Are Described
in Different Cultures**

The Rorschach Ink Blot Test (see p. 719) is used to study the individual's personality through analysis of his reports of what he sees in a set of standard ink blots. Striking cultural differences in perceptual responses to the blots have been reported.

For example, one study showed that primitive desert Moroccans emphasize tiny *details* of the blots to a much greater degree than do Europeans (Bleuler & Bleuler). Shown here is one of the standard blots, of which a typical description given by European subjects is "two women quarreling." A typical Moroccan response was to identify the tiny, scarcely perceptible marks on the small protrusions at the top of the figure (see arrows) as an alignment of Arab riflemen opposed by a row of Christian warriors.

At the other extreme we find the Samoans, who tend to give relatively few fine-detail responses and a large number of "whole" responses; that is, they perceive the entire blot as a map or an animal (Cook). Furthermore, the Samoans differ markedly from typical Europeans and other samples of subjects in giving numerous responses to the *white spaces* in the blots, which they perceive as objects rather than as holes. For instance, in the blot shown here, the middle white area might be seen as an island.

These differences in perceptual emphasis, which can be multiplied in numerous other studies, may reflect the operation of cultural factors in a quite direct way. Moroccan art and religion give great importance to fine details; for the Samoans, white is a symbolic and highly valued color.

Not that Moroccans cannot see "wholes" or Samoans "details." The point is that, given these ink blots, which are susceptible to many different perceptual organizations, people of different cultures tend to look at them in different ways.

Nor does this range of perceptions "prove" that the "Moroccan personality" is different from the "Samoan personality" and from the "European personality." The problem of designing measures of personality that are equally valid for different cultures is full of pitfalls.

M. BLEULER and R. BLEULER. 1935. Rorschach's Ink-Blot Tests and Racial Psychology, *Charact. Pers.* 4, 97–114. Figure reprinted by permission of Hans Huber, Berne.
T. H. COOK. 1942. The Application of the Rorschach Test to a Samoan Group, *Rorsch. Res. Exch.*, 6, 51–60.

"TAT," it was designed by Morgan and Murray (1935) especially for the purpose of measuring the various "psychological needs" postulated in Murray's theory of personality. This theory assumes that some twenty "needs" are to be found in some degree in every person (see Table 43.3.). Murray further assumes that it is the relative amounts of each need and the manner in which the needs become organized during the individual's development that characterize his personality. The TAT consists of a standard set of twenty test pictures, each depicting a simple scene of ambiguous meaning, for example, an old woman looking past the averted face of a younger woman, a man standing with head bowed beside a bed on which a partially undressed woman is lying. (A sample TAT picture is shown in Figure 43.1.) The subject is asked to tell a story about each picture, indicating what is happening, how it came about, what will happen next. The stories are then analyzed by a TAT expert, who looks for certain consistencies and recurrent themes in the natures of the plots, in the types of heroes, or in the kinds of outcomes. Such characteristics in the stories are taken to reveal important aspects of

Table 43.3.
Murray's Tentative List of Psychological Needs

NEED	BRIEF DEFINITION
Abasement	To submit passively to external force. To accept injury, blame, criticism, punishment. To become resigned to fate.
Achievement	To accomplish something difficult. To rival and surpass others.
Affiliation	To seek out and enjoy close and cooperative relationships with other people. To adhere and remain loyal to a friend.
Aggression	To overcome opposition forcefully. To attack, injure, or punish another.
Autonomy	To get free, shake off restraint, break out of confinement. To be independent and free to act according to impulse. To defy convention.
Counteraction	To master or make up for a failure by renewed striving. To overcome weaknesses. To maintain self-respect and pride on a high level.
Defendance	To defend the self against assault, criticism, and blame. To conceal or justify a misdeed, failure, or humiliation.
Deference	To admire and support a superior. To yield readily to the influence of others. To conform to custom.
Dominance	To control one's human environment. To influence or direct the behavior of others by suggestion, seduction, persuasion, or command.
Exhibition	To make an impression. To be seen and heard. To excite, entertain, shock, or entice others.
Harmavoidance	To avoid pain, physical injury, illness, and death.
Infavoidance	To avoid humiliation. To refrain from action because of fear of failure.
Nurturance	To give sympathy to and gratify the needs of weak and helpless persons. To feed, help, support, console, protect, nurse.
Order	To put things in order. To achieve cleanliness, arrangement, balance, neatness, and precision.
Play	To act for "fun" without further purpose. To like to laugh and make jokes. To seek enjoyable relaxation of stress.
Rejection	To separate oneself from a disliked object. To exclude, abandon, or remain indifferent to an inferior person.
Sentience	To seek and enjoy sensuous impressions.
Sex	To form and further an erotic relationship. To have sexual intercourse.
Succorance	To have one's needs gratified by the sympathetic aid of another person. To be nursed, supported, protected, loved, guided, forgiven, consoled.
Understanding	To ask or answer general questions. To be interested in theory. To speculate, formulate, analyze, and generalize.

(Adapted from Murray, 1938.)

Figure 43.1. A TAT picture. Many different stories can be told to each TAT picture.
H. A. Murray, *Thematic Apperception Test;* Copyright 1943 by the President and Fellows of Harvard College; adapted by permission.

the person's needs, attitudes, conflicts, identifications, aspirations, and self-conception.

The use of the TAT has been extended to problems beyond those of the measurement of the Murray needs. Box 153, p. 724, presents an interesting use of the TAT for an issue in the interaction of culture and personality.

The TAT—indeed any *single* technique for measurement of personality—does not have adequate validity for useful predictive purposes. This lack is one very real factor contributing to the recent attacks in the popular press on the evils of "testing," personality testing as well as ability testing. These exposés draw their most dramatic examples from claims of the flagrant misclassification of individuals based upon the

results of single tests. To a large extent the target of these attacks is a "straw man" as well as a "dead horse." Even in the past it was the rare psychologist who attempted to characterize an individual on the basis of his performance on a single test. Today, the typical procedure is an approach called *personality assessment*, which relies upon a large *battery* of diverse measuring techniques rather than upon any single test for the appraisal and prediction of personality.

Personality Assessment and Prediction

"Personality assessment" is a rather loose term, covering any situation in which a number of different kinds of personality measurements are carried out on the same individuals and are later combined to yield a comprehensive personality description or a prediction of a specific performance.

Personality inventories, projective techniques, situational tests, and ratings—all contribute to this end. And, typically, each main dimension of personality is measured through not one but a combination of different techniques. Intensive assessment also includes the collection of numerous data concerning the person's body characteristics, physiological functioning, life history, work history, social background, and the like. There is no standard design for carrying out a personality assessment, no standard inventory of measurement techniques to be employed in all studies. Certain of the more widely used personality inventories and projective tests, however, appear in most personality assessments.

Assessment of Creativity

Assessment studies often focus upon the prediction of some specific future performance, frequently success in a particular occupation. In these cases situational and other tests are devised that are specifically tailored to the prediction goal. For example, in a large-scale assessment program conducted at the Institute of Personality Assessment and Research, University of California, Berkeley, to ascertain the personality characteristics of creative architects, some forty distinguished and creative American architects were intensively studied (MacKinnon, 1963). In groups of ten, they spent three days in residence at the Institute taking a variety of standard personality inventories, projective tests, achievement tests, and certain tests that called upon original thinking about architectural problems. There was also opportunity for the assessment staff to observe and to rate the behavior of the architects in such relatively natural situations as mealtimes and evening social gatherings. It was found that the personality characteristics of the more highly creative architects could be significantly differentiated from a control group of about forty of the less creative, on the basis of the total assessment battery (see Table 43.4. for some differentiating characteristics based upon the architects' self-descriptions). Such intensive assessment procedures are of course not feasible for very large groups. Therefore, if psychologists are to extend their understanding of creativity and its determinants to its full range in the normal population, it becomes necessary to devise tests of creative ability that can be administered quickly and reliably to large samples of subjects. Such tests have been devised (for example, Guilford, *et al.*, 1951), with full recognition of the risks inherent in employing specific tasks to measure objectively so sweeping and complex a construct as creativity. (For an illustration of some of Guilford's tests and a highly creative if irreverent set of responses, see Box 154, p. 726.) Tests of this kind do and will serve many purposes, among them increasing our ability to determine eventually whether or not what we know about the personality characteristics of highly creative persons applies to variations in degree of creativity throughout its full range.

But how can we handle such masses of data, whether from assessment batteries or individ-

Table 43.4.

Gough Adjective-Checklist (1961)
Items Differentiating the Self-Reports of 40 Highly Creative Architects from 41 Less Creative Architects (Matched for Age and Geographical Location)

CHECKED BY 80% OF HIGHLY CREATIVE GROUP BUT LESS THAN 80% OF UNCREATIVE GROUP	CHECKED BY 80% OF UNCREATIVE GROUP BUT LESS THAN 80% OF CREATIVE GROUP
Inventive	Responsible
Determined	Sincere
Independent	Reliable
Individualistic	Dependable
Enthusiastic	Clear-thinking
Industrious	Tolerant
Artistic	Understanding
Progressive	Peaceable
Appreciative	Good-natured
	Moderate
	Steady
	Practical
	Logical

D. W. MacKinnon, "Creativity and Images of Self," in R. W. White, ed., *The Study of Lives;* copyright © Atherton Press; adapted by permission; all rights reserved.

ual tests, in order to maximize their predictive value?

Intuitive Versus Statistical Prediction

There are two major strategies for translating data into explicit predictions about individual personalities. On the one hand, the psychologist may array before him the full record of any individual—ratings, test scores, interview material, and so on—and, from a more or less conscious application of his implicit and explicit theories of personality and from his more or less precise understanding of what makes for (let's say) a good architect, arrive intuitively at a prediction. At the other extreme, this clinical insight is replaced by the computer. Statistical analyses assign the weights to be attached to each measurement, and the weighted score leads to a totally "objective" prediction. The distinction here is not on the kind of data used; the intuitive prediction can make use of quantitative test scores, whereas the statistical one can make use of highly subjective ratings. The issue revolves about how the data are combined, not how they are gathered.

Box 153

A Tale of Two Tongues

Personality differences certainly exist, on the average, between members of different cultures, and projective techniques have been shown to be sensitive to such differences, as in Box 152. But what of an individual whose life experience spans two cultures? Will his current way of life predominate in the picture of his personality provided by a projective test? Or, instead, does the culture of his childhood maintain its organizing influence upon his personality? Perhaps the two "personalities" may live side by side; we shall see.

Susan Ervin at the University of California, Berkeley, administered the Thematic Apperception Test (TAT) on two occasions to each of sixty-four men and women who had been raised in France but who had lived in the United States for some time (an average of twelve years). All subjects spoke French and English fluently, so that on one test occasion the entire procedure—the experimenter's instructions and the subject's stories—was conducted in French and on the other in English. For half the group, the French TAT came first and, for half, the English. All subjects therefore told stories relating to the same TAT pictures in both languages, some six weeks elapsing between the first and second test sessions. Nine pictures were used on each occasion, and stories were requested by standard TAT instructions. In Ervin's words, the subjects were asked "to tell what was happening, what had happened in the past, what would happen in the future, and what the characters were thinking and feeling. In addition, at the second session, they were instructed to tell a different story if they recalled the first."

TAT stories can be scored in a variety of ways for a variety of themes. Ervin chose to score only those eight themes for which comparative studies of French and American cultures indicated a likelihood of personality differences. The scoring scheme employed in this study is rather complex, but the essential point is that the more frequently a given theme occurs in the course of a subject's set of nine stories in a given language, the higher this score is on that theme *as expressed in that language*.

If the language used for the TAT made no difference, then the subjects would give the same themes to the same degree on the two occasions. But Ervin's main result is that there were statistically significant differences for three of the nine themes. These French bilinguals in their French-

The issue, at first glance, would seem to be an empirical one. Numerous studies have pitted the intuitive skills of experienced psychologists against statistical methods, each employing the same information to predict the same outcome. Gough (1962), reviewing the evidence, believes that it points to the superiority of the statistical approach. As he points out, however, the two approaches have not been evaluated under entirely comparable conditions.

The essential point in this controversy is, or should be, not "who wins" but how prediction

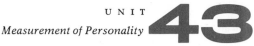
language stories expressed more verbal aggression toward peers and were much more likely to make loved ones suffer by rejecting them or by doing something immoral. Also, for women only, achievement themes showed a difference depending upon the language; the Frenchwoman (or her heroine in the story) showed greater ambition and aspiration for herself or loved ones when the tale was told in English.

An illustration of the contrasts that occurred in stories by the same person about the same picture is furnished by the following excerpts from the test protocols of a twenty-seven-year-old Frenchwoman married to an American. In her first session she responded in *French* to the TAT picture that depicts a young man, face averted, turning away from a young woman who is holding him. In her second session she responded in *English* to the same picture.

French Response	*English Response*

French Response

"She seems to beg him, to plead with him. . . . I think he wants to leave her because he's found another woman he loves more, and that he really wants to go, or maybe it's because . . . she's deceived him with another man. I don't know whose fault it is but they certainly seem angry. Unless it's in his work, and he wants to go see someone and he wants to get in a fight with someone, and she holds him back and doesn't like him to get angry. I don't know, it could be many things."

English Response

". . . Well I think it was a married couple, average. . . . He's decided to get a good education and maybe after he would have a better job and be able to support his wife much better. . . . He keeps on working and going to college at night some of the time. . . . He finally decided that was too much. He found he was too tired, he was discouraged . . . and his wife tries to cheer him up . . . eventually he'll probably keep on working his way through and finally get his diploma and get a better job and they will be much happier."

The conclusion drawn by Ervin from all of her data is that her subjects have "two personalities." She points out that this view is no more remarkable than the fact that each of us behaves somewhat differently in different social contexts. The adult who acts and feels a little more like his childhood self when he is "back home" amid scenes and figures of his youth than when he is in his usual surroundings should be a familiar example.

An early self and a contemporary self do in fact appear to coexist, and the TAT can detect each of them. In this respect, the results are a tribute to the sensitivity of a projective test in measuring subtle shifts in personality. The results may be embarrassing when the test intends to evaluate *only* the enduring central core of personality, which is presumably immune to influence from the social setting in which the test is administered and from the mood of the moment. But perhaps the task itself, so defined, is not a possible one.

S. M. ERVIN. 1964. Language and TAT Content in Bilinguals, *J. Abnorm. Soc. Psychol.*, 68, 500–7.

can be improved. Prediction contests do not reflect the psychologist's typical approach to prediction. He may often employ statistical methods to achieve gross classifications and then rely upon his intuition to refine them further. For example, an applicant to a school of architecture who scores low on a test of proven predictive validity might be ruled out of consideration by a statistical prediction equation, but an intuitive judgment might come into play to reverse the decision. Perhaps the candidate's obvious high motivation for further education

Box 154

Creativity:

An Exercised Exercise

Russell Baker, a *New York Times* columnist, was stirred to the following moving response to a few of J. P. Guilford's tasks designed to assess creativity. We quote only his more restrained creative comments:

"Think of eight to twelve uses for each one of the following objects: (a) A rubber ball. (b) A brick. (c) A wire clothes hanger. (d) A one foot ruler.
(A)—Uses for rubber ball: (1) Games. (2) Plug up rainspouts. (3) Throw at neighbors' dogs when they start sniffing around your boxwood.
(B)—Uses for a brick: (1) Construction. (2) Destruction. (3) Place under short movie actors during love scenes to put them in kissing range of leading ladies. (4) Hold in hand when greeting encyclopedia salesmen at front door.
(C)—Uses for a wire clothes hanger: (1) Hang clothes on. (2) Unbend and use curled end to jab ineffectually at rubber ball plugging up rainspout. (3) When visiting an enemy, place wire hanger in one of his closets containing other wire hangers, thus triggering wire hangers' well-known propensity to tangle with other wire hangers and inducing nervous breakdown in enemy when he goes to closet.
(D)—Uses for a one foot ruler: (1) Prop windows open. (2) Snap in two to relieve nervous tension. For this purpose, keep one foot ruler in closet containing wire hangers.
Make a sentence out of these ten words in one minute: chap, night, the, stories, clever, one, late, me, told, interesting.
You want me to write, 'The clever chap told me interesting stories late one night,' and then mark me off as uncreative. Nobody creative has written a phrase as ridiculous as 'the clever chap' since 1909.
The only conceivable sentence a creative man could make of this puzzle is: 'Interesting—the clever stories told late one night chap me.'
Try to think of four to eight things that might happen if we suddenly had three arms.
1. When asked by their wives to bring home a case of milk, a wheel of cheese, five gallons of paint, etc., men would say, 'I've only got three hands.'
2. The millions of people unable to afford new three-armed wardrobes—dresses, shirts, suits, etc. —would have to wear their extra arms under their clothing. Thus, eventually, everybody would become ashamed of having a third arm and women would be arrested for showing them on the beach.
3. The price of manicures would rise fifty per cent.
4. Some embittered failure whose future was destroyed because he failed to do well on a psychological test would immediately start eliminating America's leading research psychologists, always carrying the murder weapon in the new third hand which the F.B.I. would have had no time to fingerprint."

RUSSELL BAKER. Observer: Three Arms and a Wire Hanger, *The New York Times*, December 12, 1965, p. D10. © The New York Times Company. Reprinted by permission.

and his intense identification with a grandfather who achieved eminence in this field would influence the final decision.

There is no assurance that, in instances in which intuition seems the only recourse, the result is improved accuracy of prediction. Nor is the statistical method, as current research is demonstrating, totally incapable of taking account of such rare and "qualitative" factors. What is certain is that there is room for improvement and that, in the primary quest for a greater understanding of personality, psychological research and theory will necessarily serve the secondary goal of prediction of human behavior.

Glossary

adjective checklist A personality-descriptive instrument consisting of a large number of trait adjectives (for example, "warm," "irritable," "responsible"). The observer simply indicates which are true of the person being described.

personality assessment A procedure for the comprehensive appraisal of personality and the prediction of individual behavior that employs a large number of different measurement instruments and techniques.

personality inventory A method for the measurement of traits of personality like those reflecting interests, attitudes, emotional adjustment, social relations. An inventory consists of a large number of simple statements or questions, each to be answered in terms of specified categories. A given trait is measured by the total score on a large number of items.

personality structure The particular manner in which the individual's traits, abilities, motives, values, and so on are dynamically organized to form his unique personality.

projective technique A method intended for the measurement of deeper-lying tendencies in a person, tendencies not readily ascertainable through more direct methods. It consists in the presentation of weakly structured or ambiguous stimulus materials (for example, ink blots) into the perception and interpretation of which the perceiver is said to "project" tendencies of which he may be unaware.

ratings Perhaps the most widely used method of measuring personality traits. The person's score on a given trait dimension is determined by his placement on a rating scale by a rater. There may also be self-ratings.

response sets Attitudinal factors tending to introduce bias into self-report personality inventories. One such factor is "social desirability," in which a person tends to agree with an item that is generally considered to express a "good" characteristic and tends to disagree with "bad" items.

self The "I" or "me" of which the person is aware in his thoughts, feelings, and actions. The self, like any other perceived object, has a structure with various properties and is subject to development and change. The term "self" is to be distinguished from the terms "ego," "personality," and "organism." The self is but one part of the total personality of the individual.

situational test A method for measuring personality traits in which the subject is observed in a standard test situation that is an approximate replica of a "real life" situation. The test situation often involves interpersonal behavior among several subjects being tested.

sources of the determinants of personality

overview / The development of personality may be regarded as a never completed process, for constant change in response to a variety of influences is the rule. Among the factors affecting the course of personality are hereditary and somatic determinants, the former necessarily expressing themselves through the latter. In addition, however, somatic factors reflect, through changes in bodily make-up and functioning, the enduring influence of environmental factors, beginning with prenatal environment. Often there is an interaction between a somatic susceptibility and a particular life stress, as we find in psychosomatic disorders.

How the child has been reared in the home and the experiences he confronts in his outside environment have decided effects on the course of his personality development, although the nature, mediation, and duration of such effects are still very much in question. Furthermore, we must include in the picture various social and cultural factors that, aside from affecting child-rearing practices, impinge directly upon the individual throughout his lifetime.

Such direct influences are difficult to pin down, particularly since the psychological impact of a given action can only be assessed properly in the context of the larger culture within which it takes place. What may increase an individual's self-esteem in one society may be an act of humiliation in another. Furthermore, particularly within a diverse society such as our own, the meaning of a social act may vary importantly from person to person. Also, considerable influences on personality development stem from social-class differences. Aside from quite distinctive patterns of child rearing, different social classes expose their members to varying value milieu throughout development.

In sum, the multiplicity of personality determinants and the infinite nuances in the ways they may interact make the prediction and understanding of personality characteristics one of the most difficult tasks within the province of psychology.

In the preceding units our treatment of personality was essentially a static one because personality description, like a still photograph, freezes its subject at a point in time. Furthermore, the implicit focus was upon the adult personality. But, an individual personality is always a growing and changing result of many factors—from childhood through adulthood. In fact, in the philosophy and psychology of some cultures it is impossible to speak of *the* personality because of this constant flux (see Box 155, p. 730).

Box 155

An Indian View of Personality

The historian Arnold Toynbee has suggested that the Indian world of the sixth century B.C. saw the individual human personality as a complicated network of relations among innumerable psychic events, rather than as a single stable enduring structure. He writes:

". . . Buddha made the discovery that the supposed indivisibility of an 'individual' personality was an illusion. With the discerning eye of intuition, He diagnosed a personality as being a fleeting series of innumerable successive psychological states. . . . [Each] was discontinuous with both its predecessors and its successors. Two forces, and two only, held them together: the wind of desire, which drove them along in company like a herd of hurrying cloud-racks, and the load of *karma*—the cumulative balance of the self-recording moral profit-and-loss account to which desire gives rise in its vain attempt to satisfy itself."

A. TOYNBEE. 1961. *A Study of History, Vol. 12: Reconsiderations* (New York: Oxford University Press).

As we now consider the many factors that determine personality at the different stages of the individual's life, it will become clear that we are confronted with the most complex, and least completed, of psychology's tasks. There is research evidence that personality is influenced by factors that arise from hereditary and somatic sources, as well as from early childhood experiences. But we shall also soon see that theoretical explanations of such influences are, at best, incomplete and imprecise.

Hereditary Factors

As we have seen in Unit 41, p. 674, there is convincing evidence of the role of genetic constitution in determining individual differences in intelligence. The data on genetic determination of the nonintellective aspects of personality are not as clear. For one thing, the available measures of intelligence are better validated and more widely accepted than are the measures of most personality attributes, and in general less work has been done on the inheritance of personality. Nevertheless, the available evidence does seem to indicate that heredity plays a powerful role in influencing the temperamental aspects of personality. Animal breeders have long been aware, for example, of the marked difference in temperamental characteristics of animals of various breeds and strains. Some breeds of dogs are placid, others skittish and easily upset. Carefully controlled studies in behavioral genetics, reported in Unit 1, p. 34, confirm this picture.

Studies of Kin Resemblance

Similar studies with human beings are understandably lacking, so that we must have recourse to less direct lines of evidence. Foremost among them are studies of kin resemblance, that is, studies of the degree to which blood relatives show similar personality characteristics. The major limitation here is that genetic similarity usually goes along with environmental similarity. Children of the same parents are exposed to the same family atmosphere, so that any resemblance in personality among them may not be regarded as exclusively reflecting hereditary factors. We all know children who "take after" their parents, but this fact alone, when it is indeed a fact rather than a family myth, can by itself confirm nothing about the extent of genetic influence. Comparisons of fraternal and identical twins do provide some useful clues, however. For example, Gottesman (1963) finds that identical twins are more alike on several scales of the MMPI personality inventory than are fraternal twins. But to interpret these findings as evidence for a hereditary factor requires the assumption that the environments of identical twins are no more similar than are those of fraternal twins. When we consider such facts as the custom of dressing identical twins alike and the difficulty that even friends have in telling them apart (being therefore less able to treat them differentially), the assumption of no-more-similar environments is not easily supported.

Of course, if children are raised by other than their own parents, hereditary and environmental factors are separated. If, furthermore, the children are identical twins reared in different families, the experimental situation for evaluating genetic influence is ideal. The reader will recognize this situation as one version of the twin-study technique that has proved so valuable in studies of the heritability of intelligence. Fortunately, an effective study employing this design for personality traits has been carried out by Shields (1962), who, through an appeal on a BBC television program, was able to locate forty-four pairs of identical twins who had been reared apart for a substantial period of time. Most had been separated by the age of six months, and the separation had endured for a minimum of five years. Primarily from this same source, Shields also located the same number of identical twins whose homes had been the same throughout their childhoods. At the time the twins in both groups were assessed

—through interviews, intelligence tests, questionnaires, and physical examinations—they ranged in age from eight to fifty-nine, although most were in their thirties and forties. Great care was taken to assure that the twins were indeed identical, and such techniques as comparison of blood groupings, fingerprints, tendency to color blindness, and physical characteristics were employed.

The outcome of this investigation strongly supports the possibility of influence of hereditary factors in the determination of a number of characteristics. Identical twins, whether raised apart or together, when compared to a third group of thirty-two pairs of fraternal twins, were very much alike in almost all characteristics measured. For example, identical twins reared apart had an average weight difference of 10.5 pounds, whereas those raised together differed by 10.4 pounds. Contrast this similarity with an average weight difference between fraternal twins of 17.3 pounds. Similar results, that is, minimal differences between both sets of identical twins and substantial ones for fraternal twins, were also found for intelligence and for questionnaire measures of extroversion and neuroticism. Even smoking habits showed this same kind of result: 78 per cent of the separated twins were both either smokers or non-smokers; 71 per cent of the reared-together twins showed this similarity in smoking habits, but only 50 per cent of fraternal twins were thus similar. What is perhaps most impressive among the findings of this study—and we have cited only a few of them—is not the expected greater resemblance of identical over fraternal twins but that the reared-apart twins were, as often as not, *more* alike than those who had been reared together.

Heredity-Environment Interaction What can we make of these findings? That environment is of no relevance to physical, intellectual, and personality development? Certainly not. A recent review of the contributions of "twin research" to psychology (Vandenberg, 1966) stresses the critical importance of understanding the interaction of hereditary influences with physiological, psychological, and even sociological forces. Furthermore, there is an understandable and perhaps laudable tendency to seek for hereditary influence in characteristics where its existence is already known or suspected. Such was the case in Shields' study. But, still more, we must remember that environment does not, in a certain sense, have its fair turn at bat in such studies. Even when identical twins are adopted into different homes, there is the strong likelihood that, for a number of reasons, the homes will be relatively similar: for example, in regard to social class and certainly in regard to the general national culture. A fair conclusion is the one provided by Shields himself: "Family environments can vary quite a lot without obscuring basic similarity in a pair of genetically identical twins [but] even monozygotic twins brought up together can differ quite widely."

An ingenious way to skirt the problem of possible environmental differences in the rearing of identical and fraternal twins has been taken by Freedman and Keller (1963), who made monthly assessments of various physical, mental, and emotional characteristics of twins during the first year of life. The critical point in this study was that during the first year of life it was not at all obvious whether a given pair of twins was identical or fraternal. The parents of identical twins could not therefore have treated them more alike than could the parents of fraternal twins. Nor was it possible for the investigators to introduce bias into their observations that might make identical twins appear spuriously more alike than fraternal ones. Only when the year of observation was completed was the identical-fraternal diagnosis made (by means of blood-group determinations) and the average degree of resemblance on various traits calculated separately for the now-known sets of identical and fraternal twins. The major finding of this study was that for *every* characteristic measured identical twins

showed greater similarity than did fraternal twins, indicating at least some degree of hereditary influence throughout a broad sampling of traits.

Cattell has carried out a number of studies in which kin resemblance has been employed to arrive at "nature-nurture ratios" for various of his source traits. Among these studies is one that finds, as did Shields, a strong hereditary component in an introversion-extroversion dimension (Cattell & Scheier, 1960). This result is supported by another line of evidence in which the stability of a trait throughout development is regarded as some indication that the trait is partly genetic. Honzik (1964) has noted that several long-term studies of the same persons measured repeatedly over time have agreed in the finding that introversion-extroversion is a highly stable dimension of personality from early childhood through adolescence. Activity level is another trait that, by this criterion, also appears to have a substantial hereditary component.

Somatic Factors

In terms of mechanisms, hereditary influences express themselves, of course, through *somatic factors*. "Somatic factors" refer to the physiological make-up of the individual, such as his characteristic hormonal activity, neurological status, acuity of sense organs, and bodily build. It is obvious, however, that such somatic factors are not solely genetic in origin; they are always to some extent determined also by environmental influences, and indeed what we sometimes think of as a genetically based somatic characteristic turns out to be primarily environmentally based. We must remember that the environment begins its influence on the child not at birth, but at conception. Prenatal influences upon the developing organs and functions of the fetus are thus one example of an environmental (*in utero*) origin of a somatic characteristic. Ader and Conklin (1963) have found, for example, that pregnant rats that the experimenters handled and played with during pregnancy produced litters that were significantly less emotional, even when fully grown, than were litters from mothers who had not been so treated. One possible mechanism for this effect is that the manipulation, which is apparently anxiety-provoking for rats, caused hormonal changes in the mothers that in turn were transmitted to the fetuses via the mother-fetus blood exchange and affected their postnatal "personalities." This effect is a far cry from the myth that the mother can create a musical genuis *in utero* by assiduous concert going during pregnancy, but, as with many myths of mankind, this one may well contain its kernel of truth. The general principle that the experiences of the mother during pregnancy, by altering the uterine environment of her developing offspring, may somewhat influence the child's somatic make-up and thus his personality and intelligence is very probably sound.

Whatever the determinants of somatic factors may be, there is no doubt that differences among people in bodily constitution and physiological functioning can have effects upon personality. For instance, we have noted on p. 605 that unusual glandular conditions may markedly affect the individual's development—as in the case of cretinism resulting from undersecretion of thyroid hormone. Serious diseases occurring at crucial stages of development, or chronic ill health in general, may often be associated with personality changes.

Psychosomatic Disorders

The causal connections between somatic factors and personality functioning are difficult to disentangle. Not only may somatic factors influence behavior and personality, but the reverse may also be true. For instance, there are many kinds of bodily or somatic disturbances that may be caused by behavioral or psychological factors—they are referred to as *psychoso-*

matic disorders. One of the common psychosomatic disorders is stomach ulcers, which are assumed by many to be caused by chronic anxiety. It is unlikely, of course, that psychological factors are the exclusive determinants of any disease or somatic process. It is possible that, for some individuals, ulcers may be primarily attributable to anxiety, whereas for others some constitutional susceptibility may be the major cause (see Box 156, p. 734). Most often, however, one may suspect an *interaction* between a constitutional predisposition and personality factors. Some individuals with high degrees of constitutional susceptibility may thus develop ulcers under relatively mild stress; others with low degrees of susceptibility may develop ulcers only when stress is severe; and still others may never develop ulcers, regardless of the emotional burdens they may bear.

Block, *et al.* (1964, 1968), tested just this kind of formulation with regard to childhood asthma, a condition long suspected of having psychological origins. Asthma is a somatic allergic reaction, and these investigators classified each of a number of asthmatic children as high or low on the Allergic Potential Scale, which included such items as skin reactivity to certain allergens, total number of different allergies, and a family history of allergy. Then for these children the experimenter obtained measures of various psychological factors that have been proposed as contributing to the development of childhood asthma. The major finding was that, of these asthmatic children, those who were low on the Allergic Potential Scale had experienced more of these deleterious psychological factors than had the children who were high on the scale. For example, mothers of low allergic-potential children, in comparison to mothers of equally asthmatic but high allergic-potential children, were more poorly adjusted, had more marital conflict, and generally felt more ambivalent toward their children. In brief, then, childhood asthma was primarily a psychologically determined disorder for some children and a somatically based disorder for

Box 156

**Psychological Factors and
Gastric Ulcers in the Rat**

Bodily changes that accompany emotional states may cause permanent damage to the body. It has long been believed that stomach ulcers may be caused, at least in part, by the constant irritation and stimulation of the gastrointestinal tract consequent upon emotional stress. In 1956 W. L. Sawrey and J. D. Weisz, at the University of Colorado Medical School, succeeded in inducing experimental gastric ulcers in rats by placing the rats in a "conflict situation."

The apparatus consisted of three large rectangular boxes with brass-rod grid floors. Each box contained a food platform at one end and a water bottle at the other. The grid floor was divided electrically into three equal sections. The two sections next to the food and water were kept continuously charged; the center portion was uncharged.

Nine animals (three in each box) were placed in the uncharged section and left to live in the box for thirty days. During every forty-eighth hour the shock was turned off, and the rats were allowed to eat and drink at will. During the other forty-seven hours the animals had to cross one of the charged sections of the floor to get food or water. In this way a strong approach-avoidance conflict was produced: The rats sought to *approach* the goals but at the same time held back because of the fear of shock.

A control group of five rats was kept on a forty-seven-hour hunger-and-thirst schedule for thirty days in their home cages in order to observe the effects of food and water deprivation alone. Both the control and "conflict" rats were sacrificed and autopsied at the end of the thirty-day period.

No evidence of gastric ulcers was found among the five control animals. Among six of the nine "conflict" animals numerous ulcers were found in the lower region of the stomach. Actually, two of these six rats died before the experiment was over because of extensive stomach hemorrhages.

Another experiment, by Sawrey, J. J. Conger, and E. S. Turrel, indicated that shock plus hunger (but without conflict) could account for some *but not all* of these results. The psychological conflict per se did make a direct and significant contribution to the formation of an ulcer.

More recently, Sawrey and D. H. Long repeated the original experiment, employing the same "conflict situation" apparatus, but on this occasion they employed four different genetic strains of rats. Not only did they find significant differences in susceptibility to ulcer formation among the strains (primarily because of the much greater ulcer resistance in one strain), but they also discovered a rather general tendency for male rats to develop ulcers more frequently than female rats.

The evidence from animal experimentation thus indicates both sex and other genetic differences in proneness to develop ulcers, a result not incompatible with what is known about ulcers in man (and woman). Certainly, if rats' stomachs are so clearly and differentially sensitive to bodily expressions of emotion, we may easily suspect that the same is true of our own.

W. L. SAWREY and J. D. WEISZ. 1956. An Experimental Method of Producing Gastric Ulcers, *J. Comp. Physiol. Psychol.*, 49, 269–70.

W. L. SAWREY, J. J. CONGER, and E. S. TURREL. 1956. An Experimental Investigation of the Role of Psychological Factors in the Production of Gastric Ulcers in Rats, *J. Comp. Physiol. Psychol.*, 49, 457–61.

W. L. SAWREY and D. H. LONG. 1962. Strain and Sex Differences in Ulceration in the Rat, *J. Comp. Physiol. Psychol.*, 55, 603–5.

others. Put another way, some of these children might never have developed asthma if they had not had particularly stressful psychological pressures, whereas others, without any psychological pressures, would have developed asthma anyway. The caution sounded here is that it is misleading to assign a blanket designation to any physical disorder as psychosomatic, or as reflecting the influence of personality.

Not every somatic factor that affects personality does so *directly*, that is, by providing a structural or physiological mechanism that determines the individual's functioning. The effect may be indirect, mediated by others' reactions to the person. A physically crippled person, if regarded with obvious pity by others, may develop inferiority feelings and excessive shyness simply because of this pitying reaction, not because of any real handicap produced by his crippled state. This factor of social appraisal and reaction also immensely complicates the problem of interpreting correlations found between personality traits and types of body physique. If it is true that fat men are jolly, is this because of a direct effect of physical constitution on temperament, or simply because the fat man seeks to accommodate himself to society's stereotype that all fat men are jolly? That there is a relationship between personality traits and types of body physique (regardless of which is cause and which is effect) has been supported by considerable research (see Box 157, p. 736).

A particularly clear example of the difficulties encountered in separating the direct and indirect effects of somatic factors is provided by research on personality correlates of adolescent maturation rate. As we saw in Unit 3, puberty is characterized by very highly visible changes in body size and build, as well as by numerous hormonal changes. Because boys, for example, can differ by five or more years in the ages at which they begin and complete this metamorphosis into adulthood, two men who have near-identical physiques may,

for several years during their youth, have presented quite different appearances. One may have been several inches taller than the other and appeared considerably older and more masculine. Therefore the first question that arises is whether or not any personality differences were induced by these temporary physical differences. If so, a second question may be raised: whether such differences are attributable to differences in reactions to them by their families and friends or, rather, to the direct effects of the hormonal differences that led to the differing maturational rates in the first place. Jones (1965) summarizes the results of several studies on these points in reporting that the early-maturing boy, in adolescence *and* adulthood, tends to be a rather poised, responsible individual who lives up to society's standards and expectations and generally makes a "good impression." The late-maturer, in contrast, is often restless and highly expressive, and relatively unsuccessful socially during his adolescent years. In adulthood, however, he tends to become more self-reliant and tolerant than the early-maturer and tends to show greater intellectual interests. Jones attributes these enduring differences primarily to differences between the boys in their "social stimulus value"; for example, early-maturing boys are more likely to be treated as adults at an earlier age and to adopt adult roles, possibly in somewhat inflexible form. Peskin (1967), working with boys from another longitudinal personality study, finds many of the same personality differences but places greater explanatory emphasis on "invisible" factors; for example, the late-maturing boy has had more time to become psychologically better prepared for the hormonal upheaval accompanying puberty. This factor may have made it possible for him to "grow up" into a more adaptable adult at a slower rate. In both studies the magnitudes of the personality differences attributable to maturational rate, whatever the means by which they may be mediated, are quite small.

Box 157

Physique and
Temperament

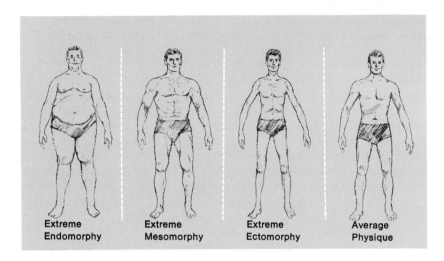

Extreme
Endomorphy
Extreme
Mesomorphy
Extreme
Ectomorphy
Average
Physique

A particularly interesting attempt to show relationships between physique and temperament has been made by W. H. Sheldon and his colleagues at Harvard University. In his original study he examined and measured thousands of photographs of nude male bodies and concluded that every physique can be identified in terms of the respective amounts of three components: *endomorphy*, the fatty, visceral component; *mesomorphy*, the muscular component; *ectomorphy*, the "skinny" component. A person's somatotype, that is, his over-all body build, is described by a three-digit number indicating the amount of each component. For each component the figure originally ranged from seven at maximum to one at minimum. The scale has since been extended upward to account for deviant cases, and the entire scheme has also been applied to the classification of body types in women.

The figure illustrates persons extreme in a given component, with minimum amounts of the other two components. It also shows a person of average physique, that is, approaching the middle value on all three components.

As a second step, Sheldon, from studying correlations among personality traits among children, isolated three main clusters that he considered adequate to account for all the important individual differences in temperament. These clusters, which could also be rated on a seven-point scale, were

Viscerotonia. Relaxed posture, love of physical comfort, slow reaction, indiscriminate amiability, deep sleep, need of people when troubled, and so on.

Somatotonia. Assertiveness of posture and movement, love of physical adventure, competitive aggressiveness, general noisiness, need of action when troubled, and so on.

Cerebrotonia. Restraint and tightness in posture and movement, overly fast reactions, inhibited social response, poor sleep habits, chronic fatigue, need of solitude when troubled, and so on.

Sheldon hypothesized that a given physique and a given temperament are different expressions of the same genetic factor. He predicted that endomorphy would go along with viscerotonia, mesomorphy with somatotonia, and ectomorphy with cerebrotonia.

In order to check these predictions, Sheldon somatotyped 200 college men and then rated each of them on the three temperamental components, on the basis of prolonged observation of their behavior. The correlations between somatotype and temperament proved to be astonishingly high in the direction predicted by Sheldon. The correlation between endomorphy and viscerotonia was .79, that between mesomorphy and somatotonia .82, and that between ectomorphy and cerebrotonia .83.

Unfortunately, as critics have pointed out, these correlations are simply too good to be true; sources of measurement error and complexity of personality determinants being what they are, we cannot expect to find simple relationships of this magnitude. Sheldon had failed to ensure that the two classes of measurements were made independently of one another. Because he himself had rated both physique and temperament, it is probable that, without his intending it, his knowledge of the subjects' body builds influenced his ratings of temperamental traits.

Although it is true that no subsequent investigation, using greater experimental precautions, has been able to reproduce correlations as high as Sheldon's and that some have found no significant relationships between physique and temperament, the consensus after more than twenty years of sporadic investigation supports the main outlines of Sheldon's formulations. One of these studies, by psychologists J. B. Cortés and F. H. Gatti at Georgetown University, employed a highly objective method to assess somatotype and, for temperamental ratings, depended upon self-descriptions by subjects, who checked off adjectives they felt characterized their personalities. Temperament scores were then obtained by summing the checks of appropriate clusters of adjectives. For a sample of 100 college women the physique-temperament correlations (in the same order as reported earlier) were .36, .47, and .49—statistically all highly significant.

The design of this study seems to ensure that physique and temperament were measured independently. Furthermore, the authors argue, because people tend to describe themselves in flattering terms, the temperamental ratings, being to that extent in error, should show lower relationships with physique than might be found with more objective personality assessments. But it is also possible that these correlations merely represent the fact that self-ratings reflect acceptance by the individual himself of cultural stereotypes attached to his own body build. As we have suggested, the fat man learns to satisfy society's expectation that all fat men show "indiscriminate amiability."

Research with children may help to settle this question, for, presumably, the child's behavior has been less molded by cultural expectations than has the adult's. M. Davidson, R. McInnes, and R. Parnell find support for the predicted physique-temperament relationships in seven-year-olds. And N. Livson, in a study in progress at Berkeley, finds that males who are somatotyped in adulthood as ectomorphs were, in early childhood, rated as shy and reserved and were also observed to sleep restlessly, experiencing frequent bad dreams—a description compatible with cerebrotonia, the temperamental component that Sheldon associates with ectomorphy.

Another kernel of truth seems to be lurking here. If and when the existence of a physique-temperament relationship is firmly established, the next challenge will be to determine the roles of genetic and cultural factors in such a link.

W. H. SHELDON, S. S. STEVENS, and W. B. TUCKER. 1940. *The Varieties of Human Physique* (New York: Harper).

W. H. SHELDON and S. S. STEVENS. 1942. *The Varieties of Temperament* (New York: Harper).

J. B. CORTÉS and F. H. GATTI. 1964. Physique and Self-Description of Temperament, *Amer. Psychol.*, 19, 572. Abstract.

M. DAVIDSON, R. MCINNES, and R. PARNELL. 1957. The Distribution of Personality Traits in Seven Year Old Children: A Combined Psychological, Psychiatric and Somatotype Study, *Brit. J. Educ. Psychol.*, 27, 48–61.

Childhood Experiences

Most personality theories, as we shall soon see, place heavy stress on the role of childhood experiences, and this stress has led to voluminous research on the effects of various childhood experiences upon personality. But there are sharp contradictions in the findings and interpretations of this research.

Perhaps the greatest interest and most heated controversies have centered on the "proper" and "improper" methods of feeding, weaning, and toilet training and on their alleged consequences for personality formation. There have been shifting fads and fashions in these and other child-training practices, often governed by ill-tested assumptions. Stendler (1950) presents an unnerving review of the enormous vacillations in child-training practices that have been recommended by experts in women's magazines since 1890. In that first decade love and affection were panaceas for every childhood emotional problem; later on (1910–1920) the reverse was "true," and mothers were cautioned against the dangers of cuddling babies and urged to adhere to strict feeding schedules and uncompromising discipline. The pendulum has continued to swing in this fashion; Sigmund Freud, the psychoanalyst, brought it back for a time to the love-and-affection pole; J. B. Watson, the behaviorist, stressing conditioning principles in child training, returned it to the "no pampering" pole.

Research continues, fortunately, regarding the relative merits of such practices as bottle feeding or breast feeding, late or early weaning, fixed or flexible feeding schedules, early or late toilet training. Heinstein (1963), for example, explored the general hypothesis that, with respect to early feeding regimes, it is not the precise *form* of the practice that is significant, but the particular *meaning* it has for the infant. The "same" practice can be quite different psychologically, depending upon the manner in which the parent carries it out. Heinstein explored the later incidence of emotional difficulties and behavior problems as related to different patterns of nursing. His conclusion gives no comfort to seekers after simple guidelines for "proper" maternal behavior, because he found that the "best" pattern of nursing (breast versus bottle, long versus short duration) depended upon the personality characteristics of the mother, as well as the child's sex:

". . . neither breast nor formula [bottle] feeding appears to be preferable, given either a favorable or an unfavorable environment for boys. Girls with a warm mother did much better with breast feeding rather than with formula feeding, whereas girls with a cold mother showed less disturbance if formula fed rather than breast fed. For boys, short nursing was to be preferred with an unfavorable environment, but long nursing was the regime of choice if the boy's personal-social environment was favorable. For girls, the reverse was true. Short nursing resulted in fewer problems when the mother was stable, while long nursing was associated with less maladjustment if the mother was unstable."

A similarly complex picture emerged from Moore's (1964) study of the effects on personality development of various forms of separation from the mother. Previous research by a number of investigators had demonstrated that prolonged and extreme maternal deprivation, as is sometimes the fate of orphans or of young children from broken homes, interfered with normal emotional and intellectual development. Moore found, however, that breaks in a continuous mother-child relationship are not necessarily injurious. Working with children (aged six to eight) from an English longitudinal study of personality development, among whom many different patterns of maternal separation could be found, he offers the following generalizations: Children whose mothers continuously cared for them became more conforming and self-controlled with a somewhat greater tendency toward guilt reactions. Stable substitute care, in either sex, resulted in greater self-confidence and less inhibition. When the child was often separated from the mother, however, but with frequently changing arrangements for substitute care, insecurity, anxiety, and dependence was a common resultant. It seems likely, even unavoidable, that the eventual answers to what constitutes the "best" practice in other child-training aspects will be equally complex.

This fragmented sampling of research findings indicates a little of what psychologists are coming to know about the influences of early environment on personality development. An important qualification should be borne in mind regarding such influences. It is easy, but incorrect, to regard them as somehow bridging time and acting upon personality directly at some later date. Even in the case of extreme traumatic experiences in childhood, like the death of a parent, there is no raw wound whose pain continues to interfere directly with later human relations. Rather, if an effect in adult life is apparent, it is necessarily traced through a long, unbroken chain of emotional-choice points from the original experience to the current personality difficulty. Initially the separation may have caused the child to become frightened and to withdraw in mistrust, which, in turn, may have angered others in his family, which, in turn, may have made him the more fearful, and so on and so on. The possible number of paths is theoretically infinite, so that any given long-term effect is by no means inevitable. When viewed in this perspective, no childhood experience can be regarded as irrevocably damaging and no maladaptive adjustment to such an experience is forever irreversible. Furthermore, there is the recent suggestion that childhood *traits* are not all predictive of adult adjustment and that, rather, the personality characteristics evident in early adolescence only are predictive of adult psychological health (Livson and Peskin, 1967).

Social and Cultural Influences

The range of possible long-term effects of any given childhood practice or experience becomes staggering when we bring into the picture the broader social context in which the event occurs. Once we apply the criterion of cultural

relativism—simply, the notion that a given event must be interpreted within the values and norms of the particular culture and the larger society in which the child is being reared—it seems foolhardy to assert the existence of any "law" that systematically links a given childhood experience to a particular adult personality outcome. To take a particularly clear-cut example, in one society the act of circumcision at puberty heralds the boy's entrance into manhood and is perceived by the newly made man as an experience of pride as well as of pain. In another group, in which this practice is not common and is not imbued with this critical psychosocial meaning, circumcision would necessarily exert a very different effect upon personality development. The boy and/or his social group might see it or even define it as an act of punishment, or they might see it as only a casual medical procedure, presumably neutral with respect to personality meanings and effects.

Such social and cultural influences are by no means uniform *within* a given society. We are all well aware of the persistence of the values and practices accompanying social and cultural differences within communities in the United States that, to a greater or lesser extent, preserve their ethnic identities, even over many generations of residence in this country. Some such subgroups are praised for this allegiance to their native cultures, whereas others are criticized for their lack of adaptability—but we shall save this material for our later discussion of social attitudes. What concerns us here is that different groups within this nation do raise their children according to differing sets of values and hold their adult members to differing standards of conduct. To some—but only to some—extent this variation reflects differences in "national character," and much has been written by social psychologists, anthropologists, and sociologists on such questions as why the Chinese are industrious, the Germans efficient, the Latins loving. Such material is beyond the scope of the present section, and we shall comment only upon the obvious fact that we must add social and cultural influences to those genetic, somatic, and childhood-rearing factors we have already discussed in some detail. There is, however, a social influence that seems to cut across ethnic-group lines—social class, particularly as it affects child-rearing practices.

Social-Class Determinants

The man on the street will have much to say about, for example, how the "rich" and "poor" differ in the ways they bring up their children. In one respect he will be right—socioeconomic class membership does relate systematically to differences in the values and practices of parents within these groups as they raise their children. Bronfenbrenner's (1958) summary of social-class differences over the past three decades does point to certain generalizations: For one thing, working-class parents are more likely to employ "physical" disciplinary techniques; middle-class parents are more prone to "psychological" means like reasoning, "disappointment," and withdrawal of affection. More recently, a comprehensive study of differences in professed values and practices of 400 Washington, D.C., families (half working-class, half middle-class) underlined some of the distinctive differences in the social contexts for fifth-grade children in these homes. In one report Kohn (1959a) notes that, whereas parents of both groups valued the trait "honesty" highest in a list of seventeen traits that they considered it desirable to instill in their children, working-class mothers chose obedience, neatness, and cleanliness as next most important. By contrast, middle-class mothers selected self-control, curiosity, and consideration for others as valued traits. The implication here of a difference on a dimension from external conformity to inner control is certainly not in line with the common bias that working-class parents are unconcerned with imparting values for "good" behavior to their children. These findings grow in interest when viewed with the finding of another of

Kohn's reports (1959b) on these families, in which (as reported by Bronfenbrenner, 1958) more working-class parents frequently employ physical punishment in order to make sure that their children achieve the general characteristic of respectability represented by the specific traits they most highly value. Middle-class parents, on the other hand, are found to eschew physical methods but are quite likely to apply verbal methods like shaming and even sarcasm. Perhaps the intent and/or effect of the *socialization* methods employed by working-class parents is to train their children to "stay out of trouble," and, indeed, they risk more retaliation from the larger community for any delinquent acts than do middle-class children. In contrast, middle-class parents seem to place greater emphasis upon self-control and inner standards, that, in the long run, may be expected to be more effective but, conceivably, may also represent a "luxury" in child-rearing practices not so available to the working-class parent.

There is of course much more we can say about social and cultural influences upon personality development, even as they pertain to social-class differences alone. Such class differences are reflected in the schools and in the peer groups whose values become so dominant in the life of the child while he is growing into adolescence. But we must pause, hopefully secure in the belief that we have conveyed something of the complexity of determinants of personality development. Perhaps a fitting conclusion to this discussion of the intricately intertwined determinants of personality and of our present inadequate theoretical understanding of their relations is the following quotation. It summarizes the impressions of the director of a forty-year study of the personalities of almost 200 individuals whose development had been examined intensively since early childhood.

"We have found from a review of life histories that certain deficits of constitution and/or environment, and certain unsolvable interpersonal conflicts have long-term effects upon the individual, up to age 30. We have also found that much of personality theory based on pathological samples is not useful for prediction for the larger number of persons. Many of our most mature and competent adults had severely troubled and confusing childhoods and adolescences. Many of our highly successful children and adolescents have failed to achieve their predicted potential. It is clear that we need more sophisticated theory that will help us weigh the relevant components—the types of stress, the compensating supports, in various types of organisms, at the various developmental periods—if we are to predict which combinations of factors forestall and which combinations facilitate maturity and strength." (Macfarlane, 1964)

Glossary

psychosomatic disorders Bodily disorders caused by psychological factors; for example, stomach ulcers caused by chronic anxiety.

socialization The process by which socially determined factors become influential in controlling a person's behavior.

somatic factors (in personality) Physical characteristics of the organism, such as hormonal levels, sensory acuity, body build, and so on, that can influence the rate and direction of the individual's personality development and functioning.

theories of personality

overview / Personality theory has as its self-assigned mandate the comprehension of the functioning of the "whole man," with reference both to general laws of behavior and to variation among individuals. As such, it aspires to the solution of the most difficult of problems and denies itself the convenient exclusion of the currently inexplicable phenomena. There are many coherent theories of personality; our discussion focuses on those that presently appear to be most influential with respect to personality research and psychotherapeutic practice.

On this basis a selected few theories are briefly discussed—Freud's primarily, but also those of Adler, Horney, Sullivan, Erikson, and Fromm. There are such other theories as that of Rogers that are significant for techniques of psychotherapy but do not aspire to be "theories of man" in the sense just defined. The theories that are presented are substantially interrelated—they all draw upon the Freudian or psychoanalytic premises—but they vary not only in details but also largely in their degree of emphasis upon the relative importance of universal biological determinants, on one hand, and upon the influence of the familial and social context, on the other. Freud tended to stress the former, whereas more recent theorists tend to place greater emphasis upon the latter.

There are many instances of Freud's commitment to a biological foundation for personality development, perhaps the clearest of which is the important role assigned to instinctual urges which are regarded as wholly biological. Among these are oral, sexual, and aggressive impulses. Even the Freudian psychosexual stages are ultimately biological in the sense that those stages are defined as the encounters between the physiologically based impulses and the psychosocial environment in which they seek expression. As we move beyond Freud, in point of time and theoretical development— from Adler, through Horney and Sullivan, Erikson and Fromm— more scope and influence is assigned to familial factors and to the broader social context.

Personality theorists may be suspected of delusions of grandeur because their task is to explain all human behavior and individual differences therein! Their mandate encompasses that of all other psychological theorists and a bit more. A learning theorist may choose, occasionally at his peril, to rule out certain broad areas of psychological phenomena in his construction of an explanatory schema. For example, conditioning theory flourished for several decades with almost total disregard for motivational factors. Personality theory, however, is denied this simplification not only by definition but also by necessity. Its assignment is to comprehend the functioning of the "whole man," and, in its attempts to do so, it dare not rule out any kind of determinant or any form of behavior lest, because of the interactive and integrated nature of personality, the entire enterprise be seriously threatened. Any theory of personality, therefore, even if it chooses for the time being to neglect a particular factor, must nevertheless provide room within its general framework for ultimate handling of what it has neglected. A psychoanalytic theory, for example, may have nothing to say concerning the effects of physiological differences among individuals, but it must remain possible at least to think about such effects in the language and within the context of the theory.

Small wonder, then, that general theories of personality frequently are open to the charge of indulging in generalities. Very often not enough is known to justify anything more than a tentative formulation for some regions of the uncharted wilderness called personality; any premature assertions may shut off certain areas to further exploration and foreclose later, and necessary, modification and elaboration. But an insufficiently articulated personality theory may prevent effective formulation of research problems and may thus be denied the fruits of testing that are indispensable for its further development. Despite this difficulty, theory-guided research on personality continues and makes its contribution to such develop-

ment. Personality theory as a whole, however, takes its current form less from the results of empirical research than from the sifted experiences, insights, and speculations of those, like psychotherapists, who observe and ponder the human condition in its everyday, experimentally uncontrolled functioning. In the discussion that follows, therefore, we shall emphasize those theories that currently most stimulate personality research and those that most influence psychotherapeutic practice.

Freud and Psychoanalysis

Sigmund Freud, a Viennese physician born in 1856, moved from a promising career in physiological research into the treatment of mental disorders. Starting about 1890 and continuing to his death in 1939, Freud evolved, at first alone and later with the aid of an ever-growing circle of colleagues, what is today known as "psychoanalysis." Although Freudian theory certainly had roots in earlier speculations, it represents so profound a revolution in thinking about personality development that the history of modern theories may, in all justice, be considered to begin with Freud.

Psychoanalysis is many things—a theory of personality, a method of psychotherapy, and, for many, a philosophical view of life. Its effects on man's thought during the first half of this century have been incalculable, and its force continues in its many modern variants. Our concern here is only with the psychoanalytic theory of personality.

Id, Ego, Superego

Freud conceived of man as a dynamic system of energies. The personality is constructed of three main systems—the *id*, the *ego*, and the *superego*. These three systems of psychological forces, dynamically interacting with one another, produce the individual's behavior.

The *id* is the primitive system, out of which gradually evolve the other two. The *id* is the sole source of all psychic energy (libido). The energy takes the form of *unconscious* instincts that drive the organism. The instincts derive from the inherited, biological nature of the organism. The two main classes of instincts are those concerned with survival—hunger, thirst, and especially sex—and those concerned with destructive impulses, which take the form of aggression. The *id* impulses are "primitive, blind, irrational, brutish" demands for immediate gratification (the "pleasure principle").

But the *id* is, by definition, blind, that is, it has no access to the outside world, to objective reality. Whereas the *id* can conjure up an image of food, it is by itself incapable of initiating behavior appropriate for actually acquiring food. In short, it cannot satisfy the biological instincts it harbors. As a consequence, there emerges the *ego*, a system of forces operating according to the "reality principle," that is, having the function of *conscious* control and redirection of the *id* impulses in such a way that gratifications can be achieved. The *ego* is thus the system of cognitive processes—perceiving, thinking, planning, deciding—that serves as the intermediary with the external world.

In expressing basic impulses, the individual may run afoul of the rules and values of his society. These rules and values are made clear to the child by his parents' rewards and punishments for his conduct. As a consequence, there gradually evolves in the child the *superego*. The *superego* is a system of restraining and inhibiting forces upon those basic impulses—especially sex and aggression—that are regarded as dangerous or detrimental by society if they are directly expressed in their raw and primitive forms. The *superego* in time becomes the internal substitute for the external forces of parental and societal control. It becomes, in short, the child's conscience and moral sense. A well-developed *superego* tends to result in automatic and *unconscious* control of *id* impulses.

When the *id* impulses are blocked from immediate and direct gratifications by the environment, by parental or societal restrictions, or by the *superego*, the libidinal energies are displaced toward substitute forms of satisfaction—forms that are attainable or permissible. A person whose raw aggressive impulses are thus blocked from direct expression may become a biting drama critic or a punitive judge. This displacement is not, of course, deliberate but is, according to Freud, unconscious. The flexibility in the directions of such displacements accounts for the rich diversity in people's patterns of specific interests, motives, attitudes, and habits. The critical point, however, is that such displacements do not imply new motivational energies but only the channeling and modification of the original ones. In classical psychoanalysis, *all* motivation traces its source to the biological *id* instincts. As we shall see, this Freudian axiom is one that later theory has most diligently and effectively challenged.

The *id, ego,* and *superego,* should not be thought of as entities, as "little men" who run the human psyche. Rather, they are convenient shorthand terms for different kinds of psychological processes serving different functions. The forces of *id, ego,* and *superego* are often in conflict, and this conflict leads to arousal of anxiety. Each person develops his characteristic way of reducing these anxieties, and these characteristic ways (called "defense mechanisms," which we will discuss on p. 761) constitute a distinctive aspect of the personality structure of the individual.

Psychosexual Stages

Freud conceived of the process of personality development as consisting of stages, which blend into each other. Individual differences in adult personality, he assumed, are mainly traceable to the specific manner in which the person experiences and handles the conflicts aroused in the three psychosexual stages through which the child passes during the first five years of life.

In the *oral stage*, the first year, the infant's attention is centered mainly on the erogenous zones of the mouth. He is pleasure-bent on sucking. If there is inadequate gratification or anxiety and insecurity surrounding the nursing situation, there may be a permanent fixation of some libidinal energy on oral activities. This fixation may give rise, in the adult personality, to the so-called "oral character," a syndrome of traits including dependence, passivity, greediness, and excessive tendencies toward oral activities, as in smoking, chewing, or garrulous speech.

In the *anal stage*, the second and third years, the infant's concern centers mainly on anal activity. Here again, as a result of parental emphasis on toilet training and taboos on anal eroticism, enduring anal fixations may occur. The anal character associated with such fixation embodies such traits as stubbornness, stinginess, punctuality, and a tendency to inflict pain upon others.

In the *phallic stage* the child's interest turns to the sexual organs and to the pleasures associated with their manipulation. (Freud scandalized Victorian society by the assertion that childhood sexuality, with its sexual fantasies and masturbation, is universal, a view that is now more generally accepted.) At this stage there typically occurs what Freud called the "Oedipus complex" (after the classical myth of King Oedipus, who unwittingly killed his father and married his mother). During this stage the boy normally directs his erotic feelings toward his mother and the girl toward her father. By thus placing themselves in the fantasied roles of father and mother, respectively, the boy and the girl come to establish the primary *identifications*, out of which later derive all the complex male and female social identifications that constitute a great part of the adult personality. But complications in the usual course of the Oedipus complex may lead to such aberrations of later personality development as homosexuality, authority problems, and rejection of appropriate masculine and feminine roles.

Following this stage and characterizing the relatively quiescent period from about age five to the first stirrings of adolescence, is what Freud called the *latency period*. Within the strict framework of psychoanalytic theory no important personality changes can be expected because no new instinctual impulses appear. Society, presumably temporarily satisfied with the accomplishment of its primary civilizing, or socialization, requirements, is content to permit the child to develop along an already determined direction and within already prescribed limits. Conflicts are therefore minimized, anxiety little aroused, and fundamental personality change made unnecessary and therefore unlikely.

But this truce between instinctual demands and the constraints of reality shatters with the emergence at puberty of adult sexual drives. Now the final challenge of personality development takes place—the *genital stage*. If too much libidinal energy has already been tied up through fixation at the three pregenital stages, the individual will fail to meet the challenge of the final stage of development. He will fail to shift his focus away from his own body, from his own parents, and from his own immediate needs to that of adult heterosexuality and to a sense of larger responsibility, which includes the needs of others. In a word, he will remain immature. Or, put another way, if he accomplishes all these developmental tasks, he has achieved psychological maturity—the hallmark of the genital stage. (Another way of organizing personality within the Freudian framework is outlined in Box 158, p. 748.)

A Perspective

This cursory glimpse of Freudian theory is scarcely adequate for an understanding of its dominant influence upon subsequent theorizing about personality development. Furthermore, the very pervasiveness of the psychoanalytic outlook makes an appreciation of its contributions the more difficult today. By now we all "know" that early experiences and the ways in which childhood conflicts are resolved profoundly affect the course of personality development and the nature of adult character. We also "know" that a good part of human motivation is unconscious. But, in large measure, what we now regard as axiomatic, even obvious, is the result of a gradual filtering through of these psychoanalytic notions into popular literature, and finally into "common sense."

The original Freudian postulates are of course open to question. Is all motivation basically of the same unchanging instinctual "stuff," or may it not change in essential nature? Are the first five years of life so fatefully crucial for permanent personality make-up, or may not later childhood and adult experiences play even more decisive roles? Are social influences given a sufficiently heavy emphasis? Are sex and aggression really the main motives? Are the Oedipus complex and the oral, anal, phallic, and genital stages really universal, or are they found only in some cultures? Is unconscious motivation so all-important? Almost every one of these questions has been answered in the negative by some personality theorists, researchers, and therapists.

In raising and trying to answer such questions, however, most other personality theorists show—either in their building upon Freud's theories or in developing alternative views—a clear debt to the original Freudian conception. Perhaps the most impressive evidence for the viability of psychoanalytic theory is that it has managed to preserve its essential outlines in the context of the various theories that have grown out of it.

Offshoots from this main psychoanalytic trunk have grown in a number of widely different directions and with varying success. Some flowered briefly, then died. Others, most notably the theory of Carl Jung, developed along original lines and continue to flourish but outside the main area of current theoretical development. Perhaps the most fruitful branch theory was initiated by one of Freud's students, Alfred Adler, who emphasized the importance of social factors. It is this branch—the so-called "neo-Freudian" movement—whose growth we shall attempt to trace in the discussions that follow.

Adler and Striving for Superiority

The central characteristics of Adler's theory lie in his stress on the social rather than on the biological determinants of personality and in his conception of the eternally upward drive of the self.

In his view, the prime source of man's motivation is the innate striving for superiority. That is, the main aim of life is to perfect oneself; all other motives are expressions of this aim. As Adler put it in 1930:

"I began to see clearly in every psychological phenomenon the striving for superiority. It runs parallel to physical growth and is an intrinsic necessity of life itself. It lies at the root of all solutions of life's problems and is manifested in the way in which we meet these problems. All our functions follow its direction. They strive for conquest, security, increase, either in the right or in the wrong direction. The impetus from minus to plus never ends. The urge from below to above never ceases. Whatever premises all our philosophers and psychologists dream of—self-preservation, pleasure principle, equalization—all these are but vague representations, attempts to express the great upward drive."

Compensation

The directions taken in the strivings for superiority are in the nature of what he called *compensation*. According to Adler each one of us, very early in life, becomes aware of some weakness or deficiency within himself. At the very least, the inescapable inferiority of every child, relative to any adult, assures the universality of such an experience. The perception of such a deficiency or inferiority calls into play strivings to overcome, or compensate for, the imperfection. Paradoxically, but predictably, the person may ultimately distinguish himself in the very area in which he was most deficient—

Box 158

Freudian Character Types

A fundamental psychoanalytic axiom is that character reflects the relative dominance within a given individual of *id*, *superego*, and *ego*. When one of the three is clearly dominant or, in Freudian terminology, claims the lion's share of the "libido," one of the following three "pure" character types may be seen.

The "erotic" type is, in Freud's words, "governed by the dread of loss of love, and this makes them peculiarly dependent on those who may withhold their love from them." The "obsessional" type is "governed by anxiety of conscience." The "narcissistic" type "is focused on self-preservation." The id, the superego, and the ego, respectively, dominate these styles of life.

Freud was well aware that any typology was not an ultimate one but, rather, served a particular theory. His qualification is much like the one we sounded in our discussion of types in Unit 42: "Let it be admitted at once that there is no need to suppose that . . . these libidinal types are the only possible ones; if we take other characteristics as our basis of classification we might be able to distinguish a whole series of other psychological types."

But what of the usefulness of this typology? Its first test is that it can be translated into behavioral terms and, further, that the translations made by different persons conversant with psychoanalytic theory agree. H. Peskin approached these questions by having several individuals familiar with the theoretical bases for these character types describe "pure" examples of each type in terms of the 100 items of the California Q-set (see Box 151, p. 708). The personality sketches obtained in this way for each type agreed quite highly among different experts. The items listed below as very characteristic or very uncharacteristic of "erotic," "obsessional," and "narcissistic" types are some of those that fell at either extreme in the average Q-sorts computed for each type. They represent an expert consensus on the psychological meanings of the Freudian typology.

the painfully stuttering child works hard at overcoming his defect and ends by becoming the fluent orator Demosthenes. The compensatory strivings may also take indirect forms—the bodily handicapped child may devote himself to the pursuit of ideas; the homely girl may become a business tycoon.

The course of personality development, according to this view, is a continuous process of reactions to inferiority—real or fancied—or, in other words, an *inferiority complex*. And, inasmuch as inferiority can occur in so many

spheres and certainly in some form in every person's experiences, there is endless fuel for striving. Adler sees the stage of childhood as especially important, not as in Freud's theory because of the pressures of childhood sexuality, but because, as noted earlier, the intrinsic weakness of the child in the world of adults inevitably makes for strivings to overcome these deficits. Inferiority feelings are thus essential requirements of psychological growth. It is only when excessive stress is laid upon the inferiority or when the strivings repeatedly

An "Erotic" Type

CHARACTERISTICALLY

Emphasizes being with others; is gregarious.

Judges self and others in conventional terms like "popularity," "the correct thing to do," "social pressures," and so on.

Is self-dramatizing, histrionic.

UNCHARACTERISTICALLY

Tends to be rebellious and nonconforming.

Is bothered by anything that can be construed as a demand.

Values own independence and autonomy.

An "Obsessional" Type

CHARACTERISTICALLY

Is critical, skeptical, not easily impressed.

Prides self on being "objective" and rational.

Interprets basically simple and clear-cut situations in complicated ways.

UNCHARACTERISTICALLY

Tends to transfer or project blame.

Engages in personal fantasy and daydreams, fictional speculations.

Is self-dramatizing, histrionic.

A "Narcissistic" Type

CHARACTERISTICALLY

Tends to transfer or project blame.

Shows condescending behavior in relations with others.

Is consciously unaware of self-concern; feels satisfied with self.

UNCHARACTERISTICALLY

Is protective of those close to him.

Tends toward overcontrol of needs and impulses; delays gratification unnecessarily.

Tends to feel guilty.

Freud regarded these types as representing normal modes of adjustment but went on to predict qualities of the neuroses and psychoses to which each would be most prone when adaptation failed. In this and other respects, Freud's typology provided him with a convenient set of reference points for elaborating his views of personality organization.

s. FREUD. 1931. Libidinal Types, in J. Strachey, ed., *Sigmund Freud: Collected Papers*, Vol. 5 (New York: Basic Books).

H. PESKIN. 1963. Characterological Description of Person Cluster Analyses of Case-Record Q-Sorts, *Institute of Human Development Report* (mimeographed), Institute of Human Development, University of California, Berkeley.

fail that an inferiority complex may develop, with all its detrimental consequences for further adjustment.

Uniqueness of Personality

Adler stresses the uniqueness of each personality, reflecting the particular direction of strivings for superiority that the individual has taken. This basic direction tends to be established in childhood as a consequence of the particular inferiorities perceived by the child and the particular methods of coping with them. And this basic direction serves to guide all his behavior and to engender the distinctive goals, interests, and values that uniquely characterize him.

The paths to perfection vary widely among people. For one man, perfection may be sought in the complete knowledge of a certain field of science; for another, in religious revelation. Or it may mean perfection in artistic creation, or in athletic prowess, or in raising a family. What is for one individual the goal of perfection may for other people be anything but "perfect" —a Hitler striving for mastery of the "master race," a psychotic obsessed with the goal of committing the "perfect murder." But despite examples of socially detrimental aims, Adler thought that, under optimal circumstances of development, strivings for superiority take socially constructive forms having to do with cooperative relationships with people, identifications with the group, and efforts to bring about the ideal society.

Adler's emphasis on social factors and on the conscious functioning of the self in adjusting to these factors is carried a step further by Horney.

Horney and "Basic Anxiety"

In her descriptions of the "neurotic personality of our time" Karen Horney (1937) makes *basic anxiety* the primary concept. It is the arousal and fate of this anxiety, rather than of the sexual and aggressive impulses à la Freud, that are central for our understanding of the individual personality.

Basic anxiety stems from anything that causes insecurity in the child, especially in relation to his parents: being dominated by parents, being inconsistently treated, being given too much or too little responsibility, being treated with coldness or indifference, being involved in parental conflicts, and so on. The child tries to cope with the feelings of anxiety by various adjustive and largely irrational acts; if the anxieties are intense and prolonged, these adjustment methods become crystallized into enduring motivational patterns, in the form of "neurotic needs."

By "neurotic needs" Horney means those needs that are excessive, insatiable, and unrealistic. She lists neurotic needs for affection and approval, for someone to depend on, to restrict one's life within narrow borders, for power, to exploit others, for prestige, for personal admiration, for personal achievement, for self-sufficiency and independence, and for perfection and unassailability. These needs may appear in everyone, and many of the needs are "desirable." But they are called "neurotic" to the extent that they come to dominate the person.

Neurotic needs interfere with life adjustments inasmuch as many of them are inherently incompatible—some require a person to seek love and close relationships with other people; others require him to aggress against people. Conflict is the inevitable result.

The basic anxiety, the "neurotic needs," and the conflicts to which they ultimately lead are not, according to Horney, biological or instinctual in origin. They are social; they arise from culturally induced disturbances in the child's developmental experiences.

Sullivan and Interpersonal Relations

An even bigger stride toward stress on social determinants of personality is taken in the theories of Harry Stack Sullivan (1953). Indeed, for him, personality is "the relatively enduring pattern of recurrent interpersonal situations which characterize a human life." There is no personality apart from its relations with other people; all that is distinctly human is a product of social interactions from birth onward—and the fundamental motivating force is the continuing need for interpersonal security. The study of personality is thus really the study of the whole interpersonal situation, not of an isolated individual.

The regular stages of personality development do not result from gradual unfolding of instinctual tendencies, as implied by Freud and some others, but from the fact that there is a fairly regular sequence of interpersonal events that are likely to occur, at least in our society. The first important interpersonal event is the infant's feeding by the mother, an event that may be productive of either security or anxiety in the infant. This experience determines how the individual will later tend to approach and perceive other interpersonal situations that have similar elements, and in turn these experiences modify what comes after.

In preadolescence the earlier forms of interpersonal relationships—dependence upon people—give way to relationships of equality, reciprocity, and intimacy with people. Adolescence confronts the person with the special problems of developing patterns of heterosexual relationships and of somehow integrating the simultaneous demands for sexual gratification, security, and intimacy. Later adolescence involves the development and refinement of all the complex interpersonal relationships that encompass the duties and responsibilities of social living. We see therefore that Sullivan provides a framework for viewing personality development as a continuously evolving process and for viewing personality, at any given point in time, as a sensitive and adaptive adjustment to interpersonal situations.

Erikson and Psychosocial Crises

As we have seen, this increasing recognition of the continuing growth of the personality within a context of changing social forces—from Adler through Horney to Sullivan—was accompanied by an increasing rejection of Freud's emphasis on the role of instinctual drives. This neo-Freudian development was essentially revolutionary in character. On the other hand, Erik Erikson has accomplished much the same "socialization" process for traditional psychoanalytic theory while remaining within its Freudian framework. Erikson's work falls into the area of psychoanalytic theory known as "ego psychology"—an area concerned with such issues as the role of cognitive processes in the individual's adaptation to physical and social reality.

According to Erikson, the individual, as he progresses through his developmental stages, meets with a "psychosocial crisis" peculiar to each stage. It is psycho*social* because society

has developed social institutions specific to each stage in the attempt to mold and socialize the individual as he progresses through these stages. For example, in the first stage the child is completely dependent on the "social institution." The oral stage thus presents a psychosocial crisis in which the child is confronted with the issue of trust versus mistrust, particularly in regard to his mother. In resolving this issue, enduring attitudes are developed with respect to such matters as feeling that the world is a safe and nurturant place, being able to offer affection freely to others, and so on.

In Erikson's scheme there are eight psychosocial crises extending through the life span into old age (Erikson, 1959). Of these crises, most interest has been stirred by his proposal that *identity formation* is the task, and the crisis, of adolescence. It is at this time that the various, and often incompatible, self-perceptions and aspirations that the adolescent has acquired throughout his development must be integrated if an effective adult personality is to evolve. A boy, for example, can identify with his cheerful and emotionally accessible mother; with his man-of-few-words, rather withdrawn father; and with a happy-go-lucky uncle who at one time played an important part in his life. If the boy, during the course of adolescence, is unable to fashion some coherent self-image from these clashing elements—by dropping one or more or by taking compatible aspects of each—he will suffer what Erikson has called *identify diffusion*. In more familiar terms, he will not have succeeded in "finding himself," and it is this "search for identity" that the reader may recognize as a recurrent theme in modern drama and literature.

A certain degree of identity diffusion is an almost inevitable, even a desirable experience of adolescence. One can "find himself" too early, and premature identity formation may prove, at some later point in life, to be as disruptive as excessive delay. If the individual, for whatever reason, "decides" (although it is by no means a wholly conscious process) who and what he is without the wisdom and perspective gained from experimenting with a number of roles, then his chosen identity may fail to meet later crises or to bring him enduring personal fulfillment. The boy who has always known that he would become a physician or the girl who has always known she would marry the boy next door upon high-school graduation runs the risk of having foreclosed too soon on life's potentialities.

It is perhaps no accident that the neo-Freudian movement and such theorists as Erikson have had the most profound influence upon American conceptions of personality. The two lines of development agree on redefining personality as a reality-oriented, continually learning, and always adapting system. Such a conception is indeed more in line with other aspects of the American ethos, with its emphasis upon productivity and adjusting to the immediate situation, than is the classical version of psychoanalytic theory. The latter, with its instinctual anchorings and stress on early experience, seems to place cramping bonds about man's potential to change and to adapt. As we shall see later on, the implications of this revolution—or evolution—for psychotherapy have been equally profound.

Fromm and "Escape From Freedom"

All theorists we have discussed until now have more or less heeded the impact of culture upon personality development. But none has gone as far in this respect as has Erich Fromm. Fromm, in his classical 1941 essay, considers personality a product of the manner in which social conditions provide or fail to provide what the growing person needs. But Fromm considers social conditions that reach far beyond family influences. In his view, the individual's personality is shaped by his relation to the whole society of which he is a part. To understand personality, therefore, it is essential to study the nature of the particular society in which the person develops.

Fromm's main thesis is that, as the child develops, he gradually gains freedom from the control of parents and other primary groups and that this newly-won independence may, by separating him emotionally from others, result in loneliness and fear. The child is then driven to "escape from freedom" and attempt to restore his security by seeking new and productive relationships with other people and groups. On the other hand, he may attempt to regain feelings of security through submission to authority and through excessive conformity to the dictates of society.

Whether the constructive or the detrimental effects occur depends upon the nature of the particular society and its adequacy or inadequacy in meeting man's basic needs. The innate human needs, distinguishing man from animals, are to achieve a sense of personal identity, to create, to attain a stable and consistent way of perceiving and understanding the world, and to establish in it a secure position. The individual's personality is the product of these basic human needs and the specific constraints and opportunities of his society.

Fromm undertakes to show how each different type of society—communist, fascist, feudal, socialist, capitalist—may be expected to lead to the formation of a particular kind of personality. The "sane society" is one in which the basic human needs are optimally met, so that feelings of loneliness, isolation, and despair are avoided.

From these all-too-brief descriptions of some currently influential personality theories it should be clear that their self-assigned task is hardly less than the comprehension of man's total functioning. Recognizing this mandate, we can understand why a complete theory of personality may be psychology's greatest challenge and perhaps—in some distant future—will represent its final and ultimate achievement.

Glossary

anal stage (Freud) That stage in personality development, some time in the second and third years of life, during which control of defecation is emphasized by the parents. Certain personality traits are held to be associated with problems occurring during that period.

basic anxiety (Horney) Feelings, originating in childhood, of loneliness, helplessness, and counterhostility in the face of the environment, which is regarded as threatening.

compensation (Adler) An aspect of the effort to overcome the inferiority complex through exaggeration of behavior in areas in which the person may be especially competent and that may win social rewards.

ego (Freud) That aspect of personality that is in contact with the external world and constitutes what is usually defined as "the self." Both the *id* and the *superego* affect the *ego* but are theoretically separate concepts.

genital stage (Freud) The culminating phase of development in respect to sex, in which the person has a genuinely affectionate relationship with the sex partner.

id (Freud) That division of the psyche from which come blind, impersonal, instinctual impulses that demand immediate gratification of primitive needs.

identification (Freud) A process of learning in which the child "feels like" (identifies himself with) important persons in his world, primarily members of his family.

identity diffusion (Erikson) Prior to the successful achievement of an adult identity, there is a period or stage during which the individual experiences role diffusion, a set of disconnected part-identities.

identity formation (Erikson) The process whereby earlier part-identifications and other experiences result in the achievement of a coherent and integrated adult identity or sense of self.

inferiority complex (Adler) A repressed fear and resentment of being inferior, especially in some bodily feature or organ, leading to a variety of distorted behaviors, and to compensation.

latency period (Freud) A period of personality development, extending roughly from age five to early adolescence, during which sexual forces are subordinated and anxiety and personality change are in theory minimized.

oral stage (Freud) That stage of personality development—the earliest one, during infancy—in which the desire for nourishment of the senses (hunger, sensual stimulation, and so forth) is dominant.

phallic stage (Freud) That stage in personality development in which interest is focused upon pleasure attainable through and associated with the genital organs (about ages three to five).

superego (Freud) A system within the total personality developed by incorporating the parental standards as perceived by the *ego*, or, somewhat more broadly, by incorporating the moral standards of society as perceived by the *ego*.

UNIT 4

frustration, conflict, and defense

overview / Frustration can arise from an environmental thwarting of one's desires, or it may result from an internal motivational conflict. In any case, the result is one of a large number of possible reactions to frustration and conflict. Some are constructive in their effects, as when the individual redoubles his efforts or realistically redefines the conflict situation. Others are disruptive; inappropriate aggression or even general behavioral disturbance are examples of this. Additionally, there may be indirect effects of frustration and conflict, foremost among which is anxiety.

Defense mechanisms represent attempts by the individual to reduce, at least for the moment, such feelings of anxiety. These mechanisms, if they are to serve their function, must be unconscious, that is, the person is not aware of using them; and, by definition, these mechanisms involve a certain degree of distortion or denial of one's true self or of external reality. As such, they ultimately cannot be fully adaptive. The various commonly employed mechanisms—repression, reaction-formation, rationalization, insulation, and projection, which are here selected for discussion—are very likely learned in childhood, and an individual's choice of a preferred mechanism (or mechanisms) tends to reflect what was "suggested" and what "worked" in his family environment throughout development.

Defense mechanisms do serve to protect the self against anxiety—that is their "purpose." As they necessarily involve a certain degree of maladaptiveness vis-à-vis self and external reality, they inevitably represent something less than ideal adjustments to conflict situations. But in so far as they perform their primary function—to guard the *ego* against too-painful threats—they tend to endure through their too-frequent and effective operation. Since they do "work," the individual is unlikely to expose himself to the reality he so fears, and thereby risks no challenge to his "preferred" defense mechanisms.

Inherent in the structure of all human societies is the inevitability of a sense of personal frustration. In the simplest case, the individual desires something, and circumstance denies it to him. Circumstance, of course, can be "objective"—a man is thirsty, and no water is to be had. More often, when men live together, frustration derives from a conflict between personal wants and society's restraints and prohibitions, for at the very heart of human social groups lies the necessity to balance individual needs against the collective needs of the group. Because societal standards become internalized as we mature, that is, become "part of ourselves," the arena of this conflict often shifts to "inside" the person. Probably the most common ground for the occurrence of conflict and the experience of frustration is within the individual, and it is best to look there also to understand their effects and the psychological processes that are developed to cope with them.

In approaching these problems, one useful distinction is to be made between immediate and transient effects of short-term motivational conflicts (as were discussed in detail in Unit 32) and the more pervasive and enduring effects that characterize personality conflicts and that, under certain circumstances, lead to the "defense mechanisms" that shape so much of normal and abnormal behavior. Another classification scheme is based upon the "direction" of their effects—constructive, disruptive, or indirect.

Constructive Effects of Frustration and Conflict

Frustration and conflict are commonly regarded as "bad" for the person. The destructive effects of frustration tend to occupy the attention of psychologists and laymen alike. There has been less stress on the fact that, as frustration or conflict begins to build tension, the changes occurring in the psychological situation may facilitate goal attainment.

The increased tension has the effect of focus-ing the organism's attention more firmly on the particular motive state. It becomes more salient and other concurrent motive states may diminish in potency. Irrelevant and distracting features of the whole field may drop out. The attractiveness of the goal may be enhanced by the frustration ("The grass is greener on the other side of the fence").

Intensified Striving

All these effects lead to direct attempts to reach the goal by intensified striving. Within limits, the greater the blockage, the greater the mobilization of effort to overcome it. We are all well acquainted with the manner in which the "challenge" offered by the thwarting of our goal-directed efforts produces a more intense "response." Indeed, it is probably only when there is some blocking of goal attainment that motive strength reaches its fullest height. Without blockage, the activity is more or less "habitual" and only peripherally motivated. Intensified striving may take the form of compensation, a mechanism we discussed earlier (Unit 45, p. 747). A Teddy Roosevelt, physically puny as a youth, may thus devote a major part of his life activities to building up his physical strength.

Such intensified striving will often result in breaking through the barrier or overcoming the conflict. But if the barrier is too strong and the compensatory action fails, other types of adjustive action may follow.

Changing the Means to Goals

The person may take a new look at the whole situation and reconsider whether or not his previous goal-directed action was the most appropriate one for attaining the goal. The enhanced tension may highlight features of the situation that he had not seen, particularly as he is forced to search more widely for alternate pathways to the goal. As we have seen (p. 428), however, a moderate increase in tension often does result in finding a new path to the goal and in overcoming the frustration—but the level of tension must not be too high.

Substitution of Goals

Just as the person may find an alternative path to the goal, so he may find an alternative goal that will satisfy the need or desire. The effect of the increased tension is to make him search more widely and thus to increase the likelihood that he will perceive an available substitute. Furthermore, the increased tension will make the alternatives appear more attractive.

Rarely, however, will the substitute goal have the identical properties of the original goal or be exactly equal in desirability. Probably some sacrifice will be involved in taking the substitute, and some of the initial tension may remain unresolved (see Box 159, p. 758).

Redefining the Situation

If intensified striving, changing of means, and substitution of goals do not succeed in resolving the frustration or conflict, more fundamental changes in the situation may occur.

One obvious way of removing conflict, its consequent frustration, and increased tension is to make choices among the alternatives. As we have seen, sometimes the choice is an absolute one; in other cases the person decides to attain this goal first, and later that one. In either case the increased tension helps to force a choice—and choice in conflict situations is adaptive behavior. The tension has brought about a redefining of the situation, so that the conflict is eliminated.

The redefining of the situation may be such that things that were separate and opposing are now consolidated and harmonious. For instance, man's separate and conflicting desires to be self-assertive and to retain the love of the group are synthesized in an effort to be elected to the leadership of the group, which will satisfy both initial desires.

In general, such redefining of a situation involving frustration means that the person introduces new elements into the situation or that he broadens the perceived context of the specific situation. This redefinition may occur in a sudden "insightful" way, or it may be a more gradual alteration when frustration is chronic.

Disruptive Effects of Frustration and Conflict

If the constructive effects of frustration and conflict fail to bring about goal attainment, the tension continues to increase. Eventually it will reach levels at which its effects are no longer facilitative but are disruptive of the goal-directed activity.

The reasons for this result are several. For one thing, the increased mobilization of energy may become so great as to exceed what is appropriate for the task; the person may try too hard and may thus disrupt the fine coordination of effort. For another thing, the extreme tension may result in *cognitive narrowing;* the person focuses his attention so completely on the blocked pathways or the inaccessible goal that he is blinded to the existence of alternative pathways or substitute goals. And, finally, the increased tension is often accompanied by emotional agitation, which interferes with the rational processes of deliberation and choice: He gets "rattled" and panicky and loses control.

Frustration Tolerance

It is clear that there is a kind of threshold level beyond which the tension results in qualitatively different kinds of effect on behavior. We may call this threshold the *frustration tolerance.* An individual may experience a considerable degree and persistence of frustration and conflict without exhibiting signs of disorganization or disruption. He may continue to strive toward the goal, look for new paths or substitute goals, and seek to make realistic and rational choices. But with still further increase in tension, he may become overly agitated, emotionally upset, and no longer able to cope in constructive ways with the problem situation. We would say that he has exceeded his frustration tolerance.

Frustration tolerance is clearly not a fixed quantity of tension but a variable quantity, depending upon the person and the situation. In one situation the individual may be able to withstand a great deal more tension than in another. In part this tolerance will depend upon what he has been experiencing in just previous situations and what he anticipates will happen next. Two different individuals in the same frustrating situation may exhibit quite different frustration tolerances.

Once the level of arousal approaches and exceeds one's frustration tolerance, several major disruptive effects of the frustration appear. We shall discuss two of them: aggression and escape.

Aggression

Aggression can be viewed in its simplest form as a kind of direct attack upon the obstacle or barrier, and in this sense it is really adaptive behavior. Yet aggression may be deleterious in that it prevents the person from coping effectively with the barrier. Aggression sometimes gets too intense and out of control, and the barrier may require a more subtle approach than a frontal attack induced by anger. Furthermore, the frustration may not stem from an identifiable barrier at all but may be an experience of lack or loss or a conflict with another motive. Under these circumstances there is no "logical" object to attack, and the aggression may be diffused over many objects, some quite unconnected with the frustration. This generalization of aggression becomes greater when the frustration becomes more intense and the sources of the frustration become less clear and available. The person may strike out wildly, attacking anything within reach.

Box 159

What Is an Effective Substitute?

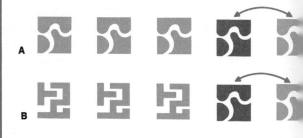

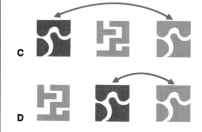

A number of investigators, primarily stimulated by the theorizing of Kurt Lewin, have studied experimentally the question of what kind of activity will serve as an effective substitute for an activity that has been blocked. The basic experimental technique rests upon the phenomenon of voluntary resumption of an interrupted activity: If the subject undertakes a task and is interrupted before he completes it, he will tend voluntarily to resume working at the task when he is later given the opportunity; another task that follows the interrupted task and is completed may, to some extent and under some circumstances, serve as a substitute for the interrupted task. The *substitute value* of a task is measured by the tendency to resume the interrupted task when given an opportunity. A high resumption rate means that the intervening task has little substitute value; a low resumption rate means that it has much substitute value.

Using this design, Mary Henle was able to show that the manner in which the substitute task is *perceptually organized* with the interrupted task helps to determine its degree of substitute value. In one experiment she varied the extent to which the interrupted and substitute tasks were perceived as connected by varying the degrees of their *isolation* from other tasks in the whole series. There were two groups of subjects. For the first group, the five tasks in the series were all of the same type, jigsaw puzzles (see Figure A). The fourth puzzle was interrupted, and the tendency to resume work on the fourth after completion of the fifth was recorded. The resumption rate proved to be high, that is, the substitute value of the fifth task for the interrupted task was low.

The second group of subjects also had five tasks (see Figure B). The last two were identical with the last two in the other group, but the first three tasks were of a different type, paper-and-pencil mazes. Again the fourth task was interrupted and its later resumption recorded.

According to principles of perceptual isolation, tasks four and five should be experienced as more closely connected in the second condition than in the first, inasmuch as they tend to stand out against the "background" of the initial three dissimilar tasks. The substitute value of task five should thus be greater in the second condition than in the first, and this greater value is just what the results showed: The resumption of the interrupted task was appreciably less in the second condition than in the first.

In another variation, Henle showed that substitute value is greater when the interrupted and substitute tasks are in immediate temporal *proximity* than when they are separated from each other in time. Three tasks were presented, two completed and one interrupted (see Figure C). For one group of fourteen subjects, the interrupted task (a jigsaw puzzle) came first, followed by a dissimilar task (a maze), which was completed, and then by a similar task (another jigsaw puzzle), which was intended as the substitute for the interrupted task. For another group of sixteen subjects the same tasks were given, but the order was changed, so that the interrupted task came second, just before the substitute task. The design is schematized in Figure D.

In the first group 64 per cent of the subjects resumed the interrupted task, whereas in the second group only 25 per cent did so. The substitute value of a task is thus clearly greater when it is in close proximity to the task for which it is to serve as a substitute.

K. LEWIN. 1935. *A Dynamic Theory of Personality* (New York: McGraw-Hill).
M. HENLE. 1942. An Experimental Investigation of Dynamic and Structural Determinants of Substitution, *Contrib. Psychol. Theory*, 2, No. 3.

There may be reasons why the person cannot express aggression directly at the source of frustration. The source may itself be dangerous; for instance, the child does not dare attack the father who has frustrated him. Or there may be various social standards concerning the proper objects for aggression.

In such cases the aggression may be handled by *displacement* to other objects. That is, the aggression, instead of being directed at the perceived source of frustration, is directed elsewhere, often toward entirely innocent objects or people, "scapegoats" (see Box 160, p. 761). Displacement can also be a chronic reaction to frustration and conflict; when it is, it belongs among the defense mechanisms discussed later in this unit.

Escape

A second major disruptive effect of frustration and conflict is the tendency to escape from the frustrating situation. The man caught in the dilemma of deciding which of two attractive girls to marry may finally "leave the field" altogether, escaping into an unhappy permanent bachelordom.

Though such *escape reactions* may provide relief from the excessive tension, the escape is a disruptive act in that it prevents attainment of the goal. It should be clear that this escape reaction is not the same as a fear-induced flight from dangerous objects. The escape may, of course, be only temporary. For, as we have already seen in the earlier discussion of approach-avoidance conflict (Unit 32, p. 515), the organism may vacillate at a point of uneasy equilibrium, not entirely removed from the positive goal and yet not too close to the negative object. When such reactions become chronic, it becomes reasonable to speak of personality defense mechanisms, which we discuss later in this unit. One of them—regression —is illustrated in Box 161, p. 762.

Indirect Effects of Frustration and Conflict

Up to this point we have been concerned only with the direct constructive and disruptive effects of frustration and conflict on the aroused motives that are being frustrated. But the motivational dynamics are far more complex than these effects alone. The organism is a unified system in which effects have their effects in turn, and so on, and in due course feed back on, and further influence, the original state of affairs. This circular character of processes helps to make motivation, especially human motivation, such a fascinating puzzle.

It is when we study the indirect results of frustration and conflict that we become most conscious of these all-important feedback consequences. The indirect results come about because the effects of frustration tend to diffuse and generalize, affecting all of the person's perception and behavior.

The indirect effects may themselves be constructive. The man who has experienced many frustrations and conflicts may come to perceive that the world is really full of difficult problems and difficult decisions. If he has successfully coped with his past frustrations, he may generalize these experiences into the confident belief that he will be able to handle future problems. It is partly through such repeated mastering of frustrations that the person's frustration tolerance is gradually built up to a higher level.

The diffused effects of frustration are also often destructive. The man enraged by frustration on one problem is not likely to approach other problems coolly, calmly, and effectively. The original disruption frustrates other motives, and this frustration in turn produces an even greater state of tension. This process also helps to account for the interaction of tensions accompanying different aroused motive states. A series of unrelated and minor frustrating experiences can result in a final powerful outburst. That is why we often observe someone

Box 160

Frustration and Aggression

N. E. Miller and R. Bugelski at Yale University studied the effects of frustration in a real-life setting. Boys at a summer camp were required to take part in a long and uninteresting testing session that was deliberately made to run overtime so that the boys would miss their weekly trip to the local theater, considered by them a high point of the week. By the end of the session the situation had turned into a genuinely frustrating one.

All the boys were given brief attitude scales before and after the testing session. Half of them rated their attitudes toward Mexicans before and toward Japanese after the session, the other half toward Japanese before and toward Mexicans after the session.

It was found that after the frustrating testing session the attitudes toward Mexicans and Japanese were much more unfavorable than they had been before the session. Here we see a clear instance of frustration leading to an aggressive reaction, but an aggressive reaction of a quite indirect sort. The boys did not express direct aggression toward the real source of their frustration, those administering the long examination. Instead, their aggressions were expressed in hostile attitudes toward remote objects (Mexicans and Japanese) and through the channel of mere verbal expression, not through overt action. This expression constituted a kind of scapegoating as a function of aggression.

N. E. MILLER and R. BUGELSKI. 1948. *Minor Studies of Aggression: II. The Influence of Frustrations Imposed by the In-Group on Attitudes Expressed Toward Out-Groups, J. Psychol.*, 25, 437–52.

showing an upset far out of proportion to the minor frustration of his immediate situation ("the last straw").

Frustration and Anxiety

The very existence of a frustration or conflict and the particular way a man responds to it may subject him to the punishment or threats of society, to painful feelings of guilt, or to the threats of loss of self-esteem. All these threats or punishments arouse in him feelings of *anxiety*.

The crucial significance of the relationship between frustration and anxiety is that anxiety leads the person to exhibit various defensive effects of frustration and conflict. These effects are to be distinguished from the more immediate constructive and disruptive effects already discussed. They are reactions to the anxiety produced by the hard-to-resolve conflict rather than reactions to the initial frustration itself. They can be described as ways in which the person behaves in order to reduce or to avoid the anxiety. For this reason they are often referred to as "mechanisms of self-defense" or *defense mechanisms*.

Defense Mechanisms and Conflict

Defense mechanisms, as used in personality theory, are highly pervasive characteristics of the individual. Not only do they reflect his general personality, but also, in an important sense, they may influence the course of its development. Not only does the failure of these mechanisms to fulfill their defensive functions contribute to mental disorders, but also the quality of the disorder may mirror the person's characteristic defense mechanisms.

The sources of the conflicts from which anxiety is said to arise vary widely among different personality theories: opposing forces among *id, ego,* and *superego* (Freud); inferiority feelings versus striving for perfection (Ad-

Box 161

Frustration and
Regression in Children

At the University of Iowa, R. Barker, T. Dembo, and K. Lewin studied the effects of frustration on the deterioration in constructiveness of children's play. Thirty children between two and five years of age were observed individually while playing with a standardized set of toys. Observers rated the level of constructiveness of each child's play. By "constructiveness" was meant the extent to which the play showed imagination, elaboration, and well-structured activities. For example, sitting on the floor while connecting and disconnecting a truck and trailer was rated low in constructiveness, whereas carrying out an extensive "trip" in which the truck and trailer take part in a series of events was rated high in constructiveness.

It was found that there was a close relationship between the constructiveness of play and the mental age of the child. It was therefore possible to score constructiveness of play in terms of "mental-age units," that is, in terms of the constructiveness appropriate to children of a given mental age.

Frustration was experimentally created by permitting the children to play briefly with fascinating new toys available in a part of the experimental room normally closed off and then bringing the child back into the regular play area and locking a wire screen that was interposed between the child and the fascinating toys.

The effect of the frustration was studied by comparing the constructiveness of the child's play with the original standardized toys before and after the frustration.

In general, there was a marked decrease in constructiveness of play. On the average, the constructiveness regressed by an amount equivalent to 17.3 months of mental age. In other words, following frustration, the child played at a constructiveness level characteristic of a child about one and a half years younger.

In addition, "barrier" behavior and "escape" behavior were observed. Some children would approach the barrier and reach through the meshes of the screen or would make efforts to leave the room altogether. The children who showed a great deal of "barrier" or "escape" behavior also showed much greater regression (on the average, about twenty-four months) when they *did* play with the standard toys again. The children who showed very little "barrier" or "escape" behavior regressed only four months on the average. Indeed, in some of the latter cases, there was even an *increase* in subsequent constructiveness of play.

As the experimenters remark, "the lowering of constructiveness of play is similar to the change in behavior occurring under conditions of high emotionality in which restless movements, stereotyped repetition of sentences, and stuttering are frequent. Both changes involve reduction in degree of differentiation and level of hierarchical organization within a unit of activity, and a certain lack of realism."

R. BARKER, T. DEMBO, and K. LEWIN. 1941. Frustration and Regression: An Experiment With Young Children, *U. Iowa Stud. Child Welf.*, 18, No. 1.

ler); incompatible "neurotic needs" simultaneously driving the person to seek to be with others, to aggress against them, and to be independent of them (Horney); conflicting requirements of complex interpersonal relations (Sullivan); psychosocial crises in the process of identity formation (Erikson). Despite this diversity in assumed sources of anxiety, personality theorists seem to agree on the presence of a large number of defense mechanisms that can to some extent protect the individual against anxiety—but at the price of a certain degree of denial or distortion of reality. Many of the items in this repertoire of defense mechanisms are by now familiar to us all, another illustration of the diffusion of psychoanalytic concepts in our everyday language. We shall present a selected few of these items for discussion here.

Repression

Repression has been termed "motivated forgetting." This mechanism was first proposed by Sigmund Freud and, for some time, occupied a special place in psychoanalytic theorizing, perhaps because it involves the most direct approach to avoiding the experience of anxiety. As a result of repression, the person is not aware of his own anxiety-producing impulses or does not remember deeply emotional and traumatic past events. A person with homosexual impulses (his recognition of which would produce anxiety in him) may thus, through repression, become completely unaware of such impulses; a person who has suffered a mortifying personal failure may, through repression, become unable to recall the experience.

The deliberate suppression of painful feelings or recollections is very commonplace, but it is not repression. Repression is not deliberate but somehow occurs "automatically" as a reaction in certain situations of conflict, as a defense of the ego against anxiety.

Repression is assumed to be more than forgetting. In support of this view is the observation that some experiences seem to be so deeply repressed that intensive psychotherapy, hypnosis, or treatment by drugs may be required to recover the "lost" material. Furthermore, not only may there be difficulty in reinstating memory of the painful events themselves; the repression may also extend to neutral events that were associated with the traumatic event. In cases of amnesia, for example, a person suffering an emotional crisis may not only "forget" the conflict but also everything that reminds him of it, including his own name and identity. And, when the amnesia attack begins to wear off, the memories that first return are those most remote from the precipitating emotional crisis. It is for all these reasons that repression has been termed "motivated forgetting."

The principal evidence that some such process as repression exists rests upon a large body of clinical observation made in the course of psychotherapy. The precise nature of the processes underlying repression, if it does exist, is still unknown. Laboratory experiments on the phenomenon are understandably rare (but see Box 162, p. 764).

If repression were a simple matter of "blotting out" the conflict and all its attendant anxieties, it would, of course, be the ideal defensive reaction. But this blotting out does not seem to happen. The relief from anxiety "bought" by repression is "paid for" in other ways—for example, in reaction-formation.

Reaction-Formation

Repression of strong anxiety-provoking impulses is often accompanied by a counteracting tendency that is exactly opposed to the repressed tendencies. It is known as *reaction-formation*. For example, a fanatical crusader against vice may have become "that way" because, attracted toward these "sinful" activities, he repressed his impulses and ended by denouncing the very vices he yearns for. In like manner, a mother's excessive manifestations of concern for her child may mask an actual (repressed) hostility toward the child; extreme politeness toward a person may really mean concealed disdain; bravado may mean hidden fear.

Reaction-formation can prevent the individual from behaving in a way that would most basically create anxiety and frequently can prevent him from behaving in an antisocial manner. On the other hand, reaction-formation is also likely to have dangerous social consequences because of the irrational intensity of the reaction.

Knowing only a little about the phenomenon

of reaction-formation makes it all too easy to develop a thoroughly skeptical attitude toward people's motives. If things can sometimes mean just the opposite of what they seem on the surface, how can one distinguish the real motivation in any given case? The answer is that reaction-formation, like every defense mechanism, occurs only under fairly special circumstances. Most zealous reformers are not secret sinners; most highly maternal mothers are not hiding hatred of their children. One difference is likely to be found in the degree of obvious exaggeration of the behavior. But, despite Shakespeare ("The lady doth protest too much,

---

Box 162

The Dream Forgetters

For Sigmund Freud, dreams were the "royal road to the unconscious," and their interpretation remains today an important aspect of psychotherapy. But what of persons who say they do not dream? Freudian theory asserts that these so-called "nondreamers" actually *do* have dreams but that they do not remember them—their dreams are repressed. At first blush—and a blush that endured for decades—this Freudian explanation was empirically unstable because dreams could be known only if they were reported; when they were not reported, there was no means of detecting whether they had or had not been experienced. And explanations that cannot be empirically tested in principle are scientifically irrelevant. But research within the last fifteen years has made this explanation scientifically testable and therefore relevant because methods have been found for detecting dreams independently of the reports of the dreamer. Nathaniel Kleitman, Eugene Aserinsky, and William C. Dement, physiologists at The University of Chicago, found that a number of purely objective physiological indexes accompany dreaming. It was found that certain brain-wave (EEG) patterns, irregular respiration, and rapid eye movements (REMs) in the sleeping human subject indicated that the subject was dreaming. If the sleeping subjects were awakened when these indexes were observed by the experimenter, the subjects reported much more frequently that they had been interrupted in dreams than if they were awakened when these physiological indicators were not present.

methinks"), the intensity of the behavior is not a certain proof of reaction-formation. We must know a great deal about the person and all the attendant circumstances before we can safely interpret an intense feeling or behavior as indicating a reaction-formation.

Rationalization

Our earlier discussions of processes of perception and thinking stressed the individual's constant striving to make "sense" of his world of experience. He seeks an explanation not only of external phenomena but also of his own behavior, his own feelings. The cognitive processes involved in achieving such explanations are subject to the distorting influences of emotional and motivational factors. The individual may thus come to "explain" his behavior and feelings in conflict situations in such a way that self-esteem is maintained and anxiety avoided. Such cognitive accommodation to conflict is called *rationalization*.

Rationalization takes many forms. In cases of personal failure or of violation of moral principles, the individual may find false but "good reasons" to justify his conduct. He failed the quiz "because the questions were unfair";

This objective approach to dream measurement has made it possible to show that all individuals dream very frequently, perhaps four or five times a night. Furthermore, it has been found that most of this dreaming is not remembered. When subjects are awakened as soon as ten minutes after REMs stop, very few of the dreams are reported.

To throw light on the question of whether those who report fewer dreams are "repressing" them or actually are dreaming less, an investigation was carried out by J. S. Antrobus, W. Dement, and C. Fisher. These investigators recruited two groups of subjects—those who recalled very many dreams and those who recalled almost none. These groupings not only were based upon a self-report as a "dreamer" or "nondreamer" but also were further checked by requiring the candidates for these groups to keep "dream diaries" in which, each morning, any recalled dreams were recorded. The final groups of eleven subjects each were therefore clearly quite extreme, representing the two poles of a recalled-dream dimension.

Records of the frequency of REMs were then obtained for each subject. The findings were that the "dream forgetters" spent virtually as much of their sleep time in dreaming as did the "dream recallers"—19 per cent versus 23 per cent. The dream forgetters had, on the average, 3.9 dreams a night, compared with 4.0 for the dream recallers. The percentages in dream time differed because the dream recallers had longer, but not more frequent, dreams.

A portion—but only a tiny one—of the difference in dream recall between the two groups may thus have to do with the fact that the dream recallers had slightly more dream material to recall. But most of the discrepancy in dream recall must be attributed to some sort of forgetting mechanism that operates sometime between the occurrence of the dream and the opportunity to report it. Repression may be one such mechanism. In any event, the data are not inconsistent with the Freudian explanation of the failure to report dreams.

E. ASERINSKY and N. KLEITMAN. 1955. Two Types of Ocular Motility Occurring in Sleep, *J. Appl. Physiol.*, 18, 1–10.
W. DEMENT and N. KLEITMAN. 1957. The Relation of Eye Movements During Sleep to Dream Activity: An Objective Method for the Study of Dreaming, *J. Exper. Psychol.*, 53, 339–46.
J. S. ANTROBUS, W. DEMENT, and C. FISHER. 1964. Patterns of Dreaming and Dream Recall, *J. Abnorm. Soc. Psychol.*, 69, 341–4.

part five

the individual

he need not feel guilty about cheating on his income tax "because the government is an inefficient bureaucracy that would misuse his hard-earned money" and besides "everybody does it."

The frustrated fox in the "sour grapes" parable finds many human counterparts: the man who says the job from which he was fired was not a desirable one anyway, that the girl who turned him down was not really attractive, and so on. Serving the same function as the "sour grapes" reaction is the "sweet lemon" phenomenon—the person forced into a distasteful situation rationalizes that it is really desirable.

Rationalizations usually involve a complex web of "explanations" rather than a single one, and this complex web helps make them less pervious to attack. The person has defenses "in depth," so that, if one rationalization breaks down, others are in reserve. The man accused of returning a borrowed pot in a damaged condition asserts that he never borrowed the pot, that he returned it in perfect condition, and that, besides, it already had the hole in it when he borrowed it.

In mild form, rationalization may have the beneficial function of protecting the individual against anxiety while permitting him to remain in the anxiety-producing situation and eventually to achieve an adaptive solution. In extreme forms, however, rationalization is likely to lead to worse failures of adjustment in that the person becomes so enmeshed in a web of deluded self-justification that he is hindered from realistic attack on his problems.

Insulation

The human mind seems capable, under some circumstances, of entertaining two logically incompatible concepts side by side, without awareness of the obvious discrepancy. This phenomenon has been dubbed "logic-tight compartments" and is one form of *insulation*. This mechanism insulates one set of mental contents from other sets in such a way that the normal interactions among the sets are reduced and therefore conflicts may be resolved. We saw earlier that such "separation of systems" is a general phenomenon and can be found even in simple perception.

A bizarre example of a logic-tight mind is found in the denunciatory letter of an outraged antivivisectionist to a psychiatrist who had described his experiments with animals involving electric shocks:

"I am surprised that anyone as well educated as you must be . . . would stoop to such a depth as to torture helpless little cats in the pursuit of a cure for alcoholics. . . . Instead . . . why not torture the drunks . . . if such people are weaklings the world is better off without them. . . . My greatest wish is that you have brought home to you a torture that will be a thousand fold greater than what you are doing to the little animals. . . . I'm glad I am just an ordinary human being . . . with a clear conscience, knowing I have not hurt any living creature." (Masserman, 1946)

The insulation between denunciation of torture and its advocacy helps prevent inner conflict in this antivivisectionist.

A common form of insulation is the excessive "intellectualization" some people indulge in as they approach all kinds of life problems. By attending only to the "intellectual" aspects of a problem, the person may protect himself against the anxieties that might stem from the emotional aspects of the problem. For example, a chemist who helps to solve the problem of developing a more effective fire bomb may refuse to think about the death and suffering that will result from the bomb.

Projection

One obvious way to defend against anxiety arising from failure or guilt is by *projection* of the blame onto someone else. The tennis player who muffs a stroke and looks critically at his raquet is engaging in a primitive projection. On a more profound scale, the person who is unaware of his own hostile impulses but

sees them in *other* people who hate and persecute *him* is also projecting.

Typically, the projection occurs to the extent that the person is unaware of the undesirable trait in himself. This is clearly brought out in an experiment by Sears (1936) in which ninety-seven members of a college fraternity rated one another and themselves on a number of undesirable traits, for example, stinginess, obstinacy, disorderliness. Some of the men who were rated very high on the undesirable traits by the consensus of their fellows showed little self-insight, rating themselves low on the traits, and they exhibited a significant amount of projection of these same traits, rating their fraternity fellows as especially high on them.

The direction of projection is not haphazard; rather it tends toward objects whose perceptual properties are already best suited to "fit" the displaced material. Frenkel-Brunswik and Sanford (1945) found, for instance, that extremely rigid and conventionally moralistic college girls, unable to acknowledge their own "unworthy" sexual impulses, tended to project them onto certain "inferior" minority groups. That is, they perceived these "others" as indulging in loose, rampant, and perhaps enviable sexuality. This projection served to maintain the girls' self-conception of superior "purity."

We have reviewed only a few of the more familiar defense mechanisms. There are many others, but all share certain characteristics and permit a number of general observations.

Some Comments on Defense Mechanisms

Man develops defense mechanisms, we have said, in order to protect the self from anxiety. By "develop" we do not imply a conscious adoption of these mechanisms because, were the person to be fully aware of the operation of, say, projection, this mechanism could no longer serve to protect him from feelings of threat, insecurity, and loss of self-esteem. To put the matter crudely, to be effective a defense mechanism must above all "fool" the person

himself. It is irrelevant whether or not other people are also "fooled." The politician who intentionally accuses his opponent of graft and corruption as a device to forestall the discovery of his own illegal practices may thus save his skin but not his self-esteem. Projection as a defense mechanism guards the *ego*, not the political office, for defense mechanisms are mechanisms of *self*-defense.

The relationship between defense mechanisms and the self is intimate and reciprocal. Not only do these mechanisms defend the self, but also the nature of the self helps to determine the mechanisms that will be used. No one uses equally the various defense mechanisms that we have described. We all evolve characteristic modes of protecting our self-esteem, and each person's distinctive pattern seems to appear fairly early in life. The origin and development of the individual's pattern of defense mechanisms are but little understood. It has been suggested that the mechanisms that we come to prefer represent consolidations from earlier experiences in which particular techniques, perhaps at first consciously employed, were usually successful in warding off pain. Take some simple examples: The small boy may impulsively blame his infant brother if a vase is broken because of his own carelessness. If wrongful blaming of this kind proves to be a consistently effective solution, it may gradually become an automatic, internalized, and unconscious defense mechanism—projection. And, insofar as it "works," the child has neither the need nor the opportunity to learn other ways of coping with such situations. Projection thus becomes a preferred and characteristic defense mechanism for him. As is true of all aspects of personality, however, the development of the individual's distinctive pattern of defense mechanisms doubtless reflects heredity and somatic factors as well as experiential ones.

Defense mechanisms not only defend one's self-esteem but also can help one to cope with the environment. They frequently offer solutions to, and needed respite and protection from, threatening situations against which the person actually has no realistic defense. Defense mechanisms can be regarded as attempts at adaptation. They are "bad" only in the sense that they involve a considerable degree of denial of reality. As few of us can afford to ignore the facts of our environment, such distortion is very likely to eventuate in some painful consequence. If we shirk political responsibility by rationalizing that we cannot afford to spend time in precinct work, then social reality—as evinced by the election of an incompetent government—may present us with the painful fact of an economic depression. In this example the mechanism served to circumvent the anxiety that otherwise would have arisen from the conflict between the desire to serve society and the desire to serve Mammon. Rationalization was thus adaptive in that it successfully prevented a guilty social con-

science yet was maladaptive when evaluated in terms of its realistic consequence.

The paradox may be easily resolved if we realize that the adaptive value of a given behavior can be evaluated in two independent frames of reference: Does it protect the self from anxiety? Does it represent an effective response to external reality? From the first point of view it follows—and, indeed, this conclusion has been seriously drawn—that even psychoses are adaptive in that they often permit the individual to avoid pain (witness the person who develops the delusion that his dead spouse still lives, a psychotic but effective means to avoid awareness of a devastating loss). If we keep in mind that a psychosis is an attempt at self-defense (however maladaptive it may be by a reality criterion), much of the apparently aimless and bizarre behavior of the psychotic may seem a little less incomprehensible and "unnatural."

Glossary

anxiety　A state of apprehension felt by a person, in which the source is usually not as specifically perceived as it is in fear. It often pertains to anticipations of such future danger as punishment or threats to self-esteem. Anxiety typically leads to defensive reactions.

cognitive narrowing　A narrowing of perception attention to limited parts of a situation, often as a consequence of extreme tension. It tends to be accompanied by poorer adaptability in solving problems and attaining goals.

defense mechanisms　Various forms of reaction to the anxiety aroused by conflict that serve to protect and enhance the self-picture. The mechanisms are not deliberately chosen by the person. They are common to everyone and raise serious problems for adjustment only when they occur excessively and thus prevent the person from coping realistically with his difficulties.

displacement　A defense mechanism in which a drive or feeling is shifted upon a substitute object, one that is psychologically more available.

For example, aggressive impulses may be displaced, as in "scapegoating," upon people (or even inanimate objects) who are not sources of frustration but are safer to attack.

escape reaction　The tendency to leave a frustrating situation when the frustration tolerance has been exceeded. Such escape reactions are generally regarded as disruptive, in that the failure to cope directly with the problem situation may itself lead to further adjustment difficulties.

frustration tolerance　The threshold for the maximal amount of frustration that the individual can accommodate without developing disruptive or disorganized patterns of behavior. Frustration tolerance is a variable rather than a fixed quantity, its level depending upon the characteristics of the person and the nature of the situation.

insulation　A defense mechanism involving a "separation of systems"—either cognitive or emotional—such that protective rationalizations can be preserved and disturbing thoughts and feelings can be cut off.

projection A defense mechanism involving the attribution to other people of impulses and traits that the person has but cannot accept. It is especially likely to occur when the person lacks insight into his own impulses and traits.

rationalization A defense mechanism in which the person, through cognitive distortion, finds false but "good" reasons to justify his questionable acts, failures, or unpleasant situations.

reaction-formation A defense mechanism characterized by exaggerated expression of behavioral tendencies exactly opposed to underlying "repressed" impulses.

repression The inability to recall strongly emotional and anxiety-arousing experiences. It serves as a defensive protection against the anxiety.

mental disorders and the psychotherapies

overview / When a person's psychological defenses fail to do their job, he is said to have some form of mental disorder. Mental disorders are broadly divided into the functional and the organic, depending on whether there is a known physiological basis for the condition. The more severe functional disorders are the psychoses; the milder are the psychoneuroses. The most common form of psychosis is schizophrenia. Examples of the psychoneuroses are anxiety reactions, phobic disorders, obsessive-compulsive reactions, and conversion reactions. Character disorders differ from both psychoneuroses and psychoses and refer to various kinds of long-standing socially deviant behavior.

The causes of mental disorders are highly complex and difficult to pin down. It is particularly hard to separate the physiological from the psychological causes of mental illness; probably both contribute to most disorders. A great deal of research effort has focused on the origins of schizophrenia. The evidence suggests that, in this disorder at least, a genetic predisposition is probably involved, though heredity is by no means a sole or sufficient cause of schizophrenia.

Psychotherapy refers to any form of treatment of mental illness that attempts to change an individual's behavior and outlook by psychological means instead of by medication or other physiological methods. Psychotherapy may be conducted individually or in groups. Among the techniques for the individual, the most common approaches are psychoanalysis, the behavior therapies, and client-centered therapy. Among the group psychotherapies, a method that has excited recent interest is family therapy, in which family members meet simultaneously with a therapist to work out their mutual problems. Psychotherapy—individual or group—is sometimes supplemented by other methods, sometimes called "adjunct therapies," examples of which are play therapy, psychodrama, hypnotherapy, and various kinds of "physical therapy."

What we call "mental disorder" or "mental illness" occurs when an individual's ability to cope realistically and effectively with the challenges and tasks of daily life is no longer adequate. A mental illness can thus be viewed as a failure of a person's psychological defenses to do their job—to protect him from crippling anxiety arising from psychological conflict. Or perhaps the defenses have worked "too well," in the sense that a particular defense so dominates his everyday behavior that it persistently and seriously distorts his everyday perceptions and behavior and makes him function inadequately.

The forms that mental disorders can take are varied and, as we shall see, very likely differ in the extent to which purely psychological factors cause them. Whatever their origins, however, they are exceedingly common, although for a number of reasons it is quite difficult to present more than very rough estimates of the incidence of different types of mental illness. The main reason is that making reliable distinctions among the various types presents formidable diagnostic problems; furthermore, the gross distinction between mental health and mental illness is itself by no means obvious. For better or worse, therefore, most estimates of the prevalence of mental disorders are based upon the number identified as mentally ill by the fact of psychiatric hospitalization or the active seeking of psychiatric assistance. Hospitalizations are of course a matter of formal record, but the frequency of seeking psychotherapy on an outpatient basis has by no means been ascertained. What is more, it is very likely that only a fraction of those suffering significant behavioral impairment arising from mental illness ever seek any form of assistance; thus they are not easily counted.

One approach to arriving at reasonable estimates of the incidence of psychological disturbance is through intensive surveys of representative samples of a given community; a representative sample of the total population is interviewed and the over-all figures for the

community estimated from this sample. In one such study, conducted in one area of New York City (Srole, *et al.*, 1962), it was found that fully 30 per cent of the population suffered from psychological problems judged sufficiently severe to interfere with their everyday lives—a truly startling figure and certainly one that would not even be approached if we were to rely only upon the more formal and public records of mental disturbance. Lower, but hardly reassuring, is the estimate from one national survey that 10 per cent of school children are in need of treatment for psychological disorders.

The 30 per cent estimate for the adult population includes all forms and all degrees of mental disorder, from psychiatric hospitalization to outpatient psychiatric treatment to untreated disturbance. This last category is of course most difficult to define and to count. Most reliable are the figures on hospitalization, and most recent data indicate that approximately half of all hospital beds are today occupied by psychiatric patients, totaling at any given time about three quarters of a million people. The number of patients in mental hospitals in proportion to the total population has been increasing over the past several decades (probably because of better diagnostic procedures and greater availability of hospital facilities), but, in recent years, the widespread use of intensive inpatient care and drugs has checked, and perhaps begun to reverse, this upward trend (Pugh & MacMahon, 1962). Nevertheless, an estimate, based on statistical trends (Goldhamer & Marshall, 1953), that one out of every ten people born in the United States today will at some time during his life be hospitalized for mental illness remains substantially correct.

With all this evidence in mind it is safe, if disturbing and challenging, to conclude that mental illness is a major public-health problem —and perhaps a sign of the frailty of the human condition in today's world.

Classes of Mental Disorders

The most comprehensive of current classification schemes is that proposed by the American Psychiatric Association (1952), which includes under the rubric *functional disorders* the major portion of emotional disturbances, and the ones that are most familiar to the layman. The term "functional" refers to a disorder for which no specific organic basis has yet been discovered and in the etiology of which the patient's past experience has played an important part. This statement is not meant to imply that functional disorders have no physical reflections in the nervous system—we know that they do. Nor does it imply that genetic influences are absent —we know that they are not. But because these disorders are generally not yet known to have organic causes, attempts to understand and cure them focus mainly on "psychological" procedures.

In the category of functional disorders there are two major classes. The milder is called *psychoneurosis*, the more severe *psychosis*. It is not entirely clear whether these two classes are qualitatively different, as are two entirely different physical diseases, or whether they merely differ in degree of deviation from normality, with psychoneurosis shading into psychosis.

In comparing the two, it may be said that the psychoneurotic person shows less severe cognitive, emotional, and behavioral disturbances; remains more or less in contact with reality; has some insight into the nature of his behavior; is unlikely to behave in ways actually dangerous to himself or to others; and only rarely requires hospitalization. The psychotic person, on the other hand, tends to show far more severe cognitive, emotional, and behavioral disturbances; may suffer hallucinations and delusions; tends to lack insight into his behavior; may be completely disoriented in his environment and out of touch with reality; may engage in extremely deviant and sometimes dangerous actions; and may be so incapacitated

in social functioning as to require at least temporary hospitalization.

Not, however, that psychotic persons necessarily show disturbances of function in every respect. Friedman (1964), for example, found that severely depressed psychotic patients, when compared with a group of normal persons, perform as well on a wide variety of cognitive, perceptual, and psychomotor tasks. Of a total of eighty-two measures obtained from these tasks, depressed patients showed poorer performance on only nine, and this inferior performance generally resulted from a loss of efficiency toward the end of tasks that required sustained concentration.

Psychoneuroses

In general, the various psychoneuroses (often called "neuroses") are assumed to arise when the person's conflicts are not adequately handled by the various defense mechanisms. As White (1964) has put it, "the core of the neurosis lies at the point where anxiety has blocked or distorted the learning process so that new learning essential to adjustment cannot take place."

The neurotic person's symptoms may shift from time to time, but among his shifting symptoms a dominant pattern can usually be detected. This dominant pattern probably tells us something about the nature of the individual and of his problems, just as the characteristic pattern of defense mechanisms in the individual tells us something about his personality. Some of the generally recognized forms of psychoneurotic reactions are the following.

Anxiety Reactions Anxiety reactions are characterized by generalized and persistent feelings of intense anxiety, often diffused and not identified with a realistic source. Such anxiety feelings are usually accompanied by such bodily effects as tension, palpitation of the heart, sweating, or nausea. For an example of how an anxiety reaction may develop and recur at

---

Box 163

An Anxiety Reaction

Robert W. White, a psychologist at Harvard University, presents the following summary and interpretation of a case of anxiety reaction, originally reported by H. V. Dicks.

"A man of forty came for treatment on account of severe anxiety attacks characterized especially by fear of enclosed places, difficulty in breathing (especially at night), and a most unpleasant sense of impending disaster. He had always been contemptuous of psychology and sought the aid of a psychiatrist only as a desperate last resort. He had just resigned after a distinguished career in the Government service. Considering the Government's policy too liberal, he made his resignation a matter of principle. He was living at home and considering starting out as a novice in a new profession when the anxiety attacks began to overwhelm him.

Working back through his career it was discovered that he had had some earlier bouts with anxiety. The most recent occasion was at the time of demobilization following World War I, in which he served as battalion commander and was decorated at a very early age. This circumstance well illustrates the lack of relation between neurotic anxiety and real danger: it was when demobilized and safe that the patient had attacks of anxiety. Previous to these attacks he had had another round of trouble when he entered college as a freshman. For a while he could not sit in lectures; if he went at all he took a seat next to the door so that he could leave at any time. Before this there was one attack at the age of seven when he had to sit through a church service under dimly lighted Gothic arches. Various anxieties connected with the Oedipus situation were uncovered, but they showed few links with the contents of his anxiety attacks. Finally the chain of incidents was completed by the patient's recalling a scene that took place in infancy when he had an attack of bronchial pneumonia. He was lying in a cot, coughing and nearly suffocating, in acute panic but at the same time furiously angry with his mother, who stood by unable to relieve his distress. The images included a tent over his cot and various other details. From outside sources it was

---

specific points in a man's career, see Box 163, p. 774.

Phobic Reactions Phobic reactions are characterized by excessive and groundless fears of external objects and conditions. The specific form may vary widely—fear of closed places, fear of heights, fear of animals, fear of darkness, fear of contamination by germs. Some of these specific phobias occur so commonly among people of various cultures that technical names have been given to them, for example, "claustrophobia," fear of closed places.

Obsessive-Compulsive Reactions Obsessive-compulsive reactions are characterized by obsessive and unavoidable thoughts, often unpleasant and unwelcome to the person, and by compulsive irrational acts, which follow from irresistible urges. The person's obsessive thoughts may have to do with fear that he is "losing his mind," that his child is "going to have an accident," that he is "going to strike someone," or they may have to do with insistent thoughts of an erotic nature. The compulsive acts frequently take the form of repetitive ritualistic behavior, such as highly routinized ways of moving, dressing, or eating. The compulsive

possible to verify that he had had bronchial pneumonia at the age of eighteen months, and that a tent over the bed was one of the measures used for treatment.

The form of the patient's anxiety attacks—the breathing difficulty and fear of enclosures—was apparently set by this . . . panic. His attack in church would seem to have been stimulated by the heavy arches (reminding him of the tent) and the necessity to sit still (helpless restraint). But we can understand his later attacks, especially the ones that sent him for treatment, only if we know something about the development of his personality. The patient was the eldest son and also the eldest of his circle of cousins. His parents encouraged him strongly to take the role of a big boy. He successfully assumed this role, becoming proud and markedly independent. Identifying himself with authority and the moral code, he emerged as the leader and disciplinarian of his younger relatives. This pattern was continued in school, won again in college, given much scope when he served as an army officer, and carried on while he was in the Government service. He became an energetic and successful man with a strong need for superiority. One can discern, however, that his career had something of the overdriven quality that characterizes a neurotic protective organization. It was when activity, success, and superiority were blocked that he gave way to anxiety attacks: when he lost his school distinction and became a "nobody" at college; when he lost his military distinction and became a "nobody" at demobilization; when he lost his distinction as a Government official and became a "nobody" without a vocation.

This case illustrates the early establishment of a neurotic nucleus as the result of one tremendously frightening experience. . . . As the patient's personality developed, it was encouraged to take a form that happened to serve admirably as a means of counteracting his neurotic liability. His pattern emphasized independence (rejecting the useless dependent longings), activity (preventing a passive state of helplessness), and power (the opposite of being unable to influence his mother). These strivings were effective, yielded gratification, and led to a constructive life. There was only one flaw: when they were all blocked, so that he was reduced to the status of a "nobody," he developed not just the frustration that anyone might feel under such circumstances, but more than that—acute anxiety attacks."

H. V. DICKS. 1939. *Clinical Studies in Psychopathology* (Baltimore: Wood).

R. W. WHITE. 1964. *The Abnormal Personality* (New York: Ronald). Text material reprinted by permission; copyright © 1964 The Ronald Press Company, New York.

act often appears to be a "magic" way of warding off the unpleasant obsessive thought. An adolescent boy, for example, was characterized by a neurotic compulsion to wash himself repeatedly during the day, spending a great deal of his time in a series of acts relating to body cleanliness. Investigation indicated that he suffered obsessive guilt feelings from acts of masturbation, which he regarded as "unclean."

Conversion Reactions Conversion reactions are characterized by symptoms that mimic incapacitating body ailments like blindness, loss of sensitivity in parts of the body, and paralysis of the limbs. The symptoms tend to protect the individual from having to face his anxiety-inducing conflicts. The assumption is that the individual "converts" his conflict into the form of physical symptoms that allow him to avoid or reduce the anxiety. For example, a battle-shocked soldier suffering acute anxiety finds that his arm is paralyzed and that he cannot hold a rifle. He is removed from the front lines and hospitalized. It is not a case of malingering; the soldier is actually unable to move his arm. Yet the disorder will disappear completely when his anxiety is allayed.

Psychoses

The three main classes of functional psychoses are the *affective reactions*, the *schizophrenic reactions*, and the *paranoid reactions*.

Affective Reactions Affective disorders are characterized by exaggerations of mood states, often but not necessarily involving fluctuation between extremes. For example, the person may shift from normal moods to excessive elation, become manic, and, if he goes too far, explode into violent and unrestrained behavior, sometimes dangerous to others or to himself (thus the common term "maniac"). Conversely, the person may shift from normal mood states to extreme depression, sometimes of suicidal intensity, sometimes so deep that he is thrown into a condition of bodily immobility. Some psychotic persons show alternations of extreme elation and depression (hence the term "manic-depressive"); others may have only periodic depressions or only periodic manic states.

Schizophrenic Reactions The most prevalent of all psychoses is schizophrenia, accounting currently for 25 per cent of first admissions to mental hospitals. This condition is characterized by a wide variety of symptoms, not all found in any one person. In general, there appears to be a peculiar distortion of the emotions and feelings; the person may seem completely insensitive to things that would normally be expected to evoke emotional response, for example, news of the death of a member of the family. His standards of conduct, dress, personal hygiene, and social relations may show severe deterioration. He may become excessively withdrawn, out of all touch with the external world, even to the point at which he may sit completely immobile for hours, during which time his limbs can be moved about by someone else and will remain in the positions in which they are placed. He may often be subject to hallucinations in which he "hears voices" or "sees visions." He may exhibit bi-zarre behavior, confused thought processes, chaotic speech.

Paranoid Reactions This form of psychosis is characterized by serious delusions (that is, false beliefs). The delusions are often organized into "logical" systems, which are impervious to disproof by reason or contradictory evidence.

The delusions may take many specific forms. Most common are <u>delusions of persecution and delusions of grandeur.</u> In the former the paranoid person constructs an elaborate delusional edifice "proving" that people are "out to get him," that his enemies are everywhere, that his food is poisoned, that invisible deadly "rays" are being showered on him by people who pass innocently by. "Proof"—based on overinterpretation of actual facts—is an essential feature of paranoia: A touch of indigestion "proves" that people have poisoned his food. And the paranoid person's reasoning shows logic and consistency. For example, take the connection made by a paranoid person between persecution and grandeur: "Why," he may ask himself, "are they persecuting me? It must be that I am a very important and powerful person, whom they fear! Therefore, I am the Messiah!" The paranoid reaction is thus a clear illustration of an important point: Accepting the inaccurate view of reality held by the patient—accepting his frame of reference—makes his behavior and thought processes more understandable and less irrational. His facts are awry, not his intellectual functions. This view redefines but does not solve the problem posed by mental illness. Box 164, p. 777, shows the gradual development of paranoid symptoms in an adolescent boy.

In line with this stress on "logic," the paranoid person shows little if any impairment of tested intelligence, and some individuals with pronounced paranoid tendencies do maintain good contact with reality—except for the limited areas of their delusions. The paranoid person also shows much less general behavioral deterioration than do persons with other psy-

Box 164

A Paranoid Reaction

Robert W. White also provides a description of a young man who used increasingly exaggerated paranoid defenses to cope with painful events in his life situation.

"A boy in high school was considered by his friends to be sensitive, solitary, and a little eccentric. They knew that he was an orphan and lived with an elderly, somewhat peculiar foster mother. The boy was good in his studies, especially in history and literature. His English teacher, who constantly read his literary productions, noted distinct talent but many eccentricities of content. . . . Although the boy spent a good deal of time alone, he had several friends among the students who were preparing for college. At graduation he was separated from his chums, he himself being unable to go to college. Occasionally he visited them, but it was clear that he resented his inferior position and the interruption of his own education. His friends now began to suspect that he was building up fictions about himself. He showed them an application blank that he had received from an art school. They believed that he had prepared it on his own typewriter. He also discoursed at length on his distinguished French ancestry, a theme which he was able to fill out convincingly from his knowledge of history. He repeatedly mentioned that his real mother, a countess, was now living in the city, and that he was in frequent communication with her. The friends began to feel that he was a liar, and they laid plans to expose him. One day they confronted him with numerous fatal inconsistencies in his stories and accused him of fabrication. He thereupon admitted that his stories were not true, but explained that he had been forced to disguise himself in this way in order to elude a hostile power known as the Third Element. He now claimed that he and his mother, the countess, had collaborated in preparing a set of disguising fictions to keep the Third Element off their trail. He told his accusers that the situation was growing increasingly serious. Most of his friends had turned against him, and only three remained on his side.

It is clear that this boy's [development had taken a pathological direction] before he graduated from high school. That event, with separation from his circle of friends, gave his adjustment a downward jolt and sharply increased his symptoms. He now began to lose track of the line between fantasy and fact, speaking of his fantasies of noble lineage as if they were true. The motive behind these fabrications was pathetically clear: if he could not go to college, he would at least have some form of distinction to keep him on a footing with his friends, and while he was at it he provided himself with a mother. Unfortunately his attempts at compensation only irritated his friends, and their unsympathetic action constituted a second, more direct, and more personal rejection. This event threw him into deeper psychosis. His delusions about hostile friends and a hostile Third Element reflected the real feeling of hostility that he sensed in his accusers. Unfortunately the delusions now began to assume a generalized form which made him more and more inaccessible to friendly advances from others."

R. W. WHITE. 1964. *The Abnormal Personality* (New York: Ronald). Text material reprinted by permission; copyright © 1964 The Ronald Press Company, New York.

choses. He is often perfectly able to carry on his affairs successfully at home and in business and to avoid hospitalization. He may, of course, be succeeding at the expense of damage to his family and associates. The behavior of the extreme paranoiac may exceed the bounds of tolerance of society, however; he may attack or even murder his "persecutors."

Organic Psychoses A great deal of the psychotic behavior that we have described here also frequently accompanies deterioration of the brain and nervous system as a result of accident, disease, or toxic agents. Some of the more important factors responsible for such deterioration are syphilitic invasion of brain tissue, brain tumors, degeneration of nerve tissue in senility, and, perhaps less directly, excessive use of alcohol and certain drugs. Because there are *known* organic factors underlying these psychotic behaviors, these disorders are often called *organic psychoses.*

Just as functional psychoses are presumed to reflect in part some as yet unspecified physiological disturbances, so organic psychoses are presumed to be partly determined by the past experiences of the individual. For example, the particular psychotic symptoms shown by a patient suffering from a brain tumor will in part reflect the conflicts and the ways of coping with them that characterized his "premorbid" personality. But, because the physiological bases of these psychoses are so obvious, attempts to cure them are usually restricted to some form of direct physiological intervention, for example, surgical removal of the tumor or chemotherapy.

Character Disorders

There is another category of functional disorders that are not properly classed with either the psychoneuroses or the psychoses. They are the so-called "character disorders"—a rather broad classification that is used as a kind of catchall for several types of long-standing social maladjustment like sexual deviations, alcoholism, drug addiction, and antisocial or delinquent behavior. Obviously, these behaviors may have diverse causes and may occur in persons with different kinds of personalities. There is little in common, for example, between a criminal who acts against society impulsively and one who acts in the same way out of conformity with a stable and organized subculture like a delinquent gang. What these two people have in common is some kind of socially deviant behavior.

One of the most interesting groups in this category is the *antisocial reaction* (formerly called "psychopathic personality"). This category refers to persons who show diffuse and chronic incapacity for persistent, ordered living of any kind. The individual behaves impulsively to obtain immediate gratification of his needs. He seems unable to anticipate the consequences of his actions and so fails to learn from experience, to plan ahead, or to follow long-range goals. He acts before he thinks. Similarly, he is insensitive to the needs of others. Unable to tolerate frustration, he lives from moment to moment, his actions appearing erratic, irresponsible, and unpredictable.

In appearance, the psychopath is apt to make a startlingly pleasing impression at first. His intelligence is unimpaired. He is often charming and articulate, glibly using words, flattery, fabrication to manipulate situations to his own ends. Though he appears friendly, he is usually isolated because of his incapacity to form lasting relationships.

The antisocial personality seems to suffer from a failure to have developed moral standards or conscience; it is as if in childhood he had never learned to postpone his desires in consideration of his parents' wishes or values and so failed to internalize the standards of society. In line with this make-up, he seems to have surprisingly little guilt or anxiety. Indeed, the antisocial personality tends to be comfortable in situations in which most people would feel uneasy. Not only anxiety but also other emotions seem to be lacking or shallow. As noted, he shows little capacity for real love or attachment.

Causes of Mental Disorders

The psychological processes involved in mental illness are extremely complex, and their physiological counterparts are but dimly understood. The origins of the disorders may lie in remote and relatively inaccessible life experiences of the patient and in subtle biochemical and neural disturbances. Most likely, in most cases, both contribute. To carry out controlled study on the genesis, development, and change of mental illness presents the most formidable of research problems.

The problem is placed in perspective, if not simplified, if we view the origins of mental disorders as falling within the broader issue of the origins of personality characteristics or types. Viewed in this way, much of our previous discussion (Unit 44) of the determinants of personality has relevance here.

Most of the research on causes of mental disorder has focused on schizophrenia. We shall review some of the suggestions about causation that have derived from this research on hereditary determinants, physiological and organic determinants, and life-history determinants.

On the Origins of Schizophrenia

The notion that "insanity is inherited" has long been popular. But the belief has been based on uncritical acceptance of "evidence" that several members of the same family have mental illness. The actual incidence of schizophrenia in families is very difficult to ascertain retrospectively, and even when there are clear indications of multiple cases in a family group, there is usually no way to disentangle the effects of similar environment from those of similar heredity.

The "twin study" approach, which we encountered earlier, is applicable here if we are willing to accept the assumption that the family environments of identical twins are no more similar than are those of fraternal twins. Kallman (1959) reports that, when one twin is schizophrenic, the other is six times more likely to be schizophrenic if they are identical, rather than fraternal, twins. Kallman's general thesis—the closer the blood tie to the schizophrenic relative, the greater the risk of developing schizophrenia oneself—is further supported by his finding that, with one schizophrenic parent (as compared to none), one's chances of becoming schizophrenic are sixteen times greater. With two such parents, the odds become eighty times greater.

Granting that this evidence argues for a genetic factor in schizophrenia, it by no means can be taken to indicate a one-to-one relationship. Kallman himself, among many others, has insisted that all that may be properly inferred from the evidence is that heredity determines some predisposition, or increased susceptibility, to the disorder.

A dominant view today, therefore, is that a genetic predisposition toward schizophrenia exists among some individuals that renders them particularly vulnerable to certain environmental stresses. Most such individuals are not exposed to stresses of this kind, so that, although they may exhibit certain *schizophrenic-like* characteristics, they never develop the disorder. Some are exposed, and do. In short, a genetic predisposition is a necessary, but not sufficient, condition for the development of schizophrenia.

But through what mechanisms is this genetic influence expressed? Genes affect behavior by modifying in some way the physical structure of the organism. The central nervous system, by available evidence, is the most probable locus of this effect. Russian research on the origins of schizophrenia, conducted within a Pavlovian framework, has concentrated on this facet of the problem. The findings, as reviewed by Lynn (1963), can be briefly summarized.

Consistent differences between schizophrenics and normal subjects have been demonstrated in the reactivity of the sympathetic nervous system, in electroencephalographic patterns, and in ease of acquiring conditioned responses. Such differences may provide clues for discovering the physical basis behind differential behavioral reactions to environmental stress. As for the particular nature of the environmental stress that may be involved in the etiology of schizophrenia, it has been found that marital discord and broken homes occur more frequently in the childhoods of schizophrenics. But it is always possible, of course, that marital discord is itself a symptom of undetected schizophrenia in one or both parents. In this case the psychological factor would be the manifestation of a genetic factor.

Psychological determinants are undoubtedly important, however. Our best guess at the moment is that gross factors, like an "unhappy home," will miss the mark, whereas more specific constellations of family characteristics—perhaps differing for different types of schizophrenia—will prove relevant. One such hypothesized factor, currently the stimulus for considerable research, is the tendency for a schizophrenic's parent, or his family as a whole, to exhibit striking inconsistencies between, on the one hand, values and goals they openly express to the child and, on the other, subtly "leaked" disdain and disapproval for these same valued modes of behavior. For example, a child may be urged, even coerced, into showing physical affection, but, when he does so, his behavior is met by unverbalized, but recognizable, disgust. Such a situation would put stress on any child, and, perhaps, it is this kind of continuing, unresolvable stress that, for a genetically schizophrenic-prone child, may become intolerable and lead to a schizophrenic reaction.

The general form of the approach just described is important here, not the specific formulation. The latter must await further evidence, but the approach, if it proves even roughly correct, has substantial implications.

For one thing, the fatalism of an all-or-none genetic view is dispelled, and psychotherapy becomes a possible course. And if this interactional view can be maintained for schizophrenia, for which a genetic basis is most probable, it should certainly hold for other functional disorders. In any event, functional disorders—both neuroses and psychoses—represent failures to deal adequately with the stresses of everyday life, whatever the ultimate cause or causes for the breakdown in the individual's ability to cope effectively with his world. Psychological functioning has been impaired, and psychological techniques are employed, together with other methods, to rebuild the personality.

Psychotherapy

If neurotic (or psychotic) behavior can be described as reaction to an unrealistic and inaccurate conception of one's life situation, it follows that psychological therapy that contributes toward a truer picture of the situation will be helpful. From this view one can see a place for many forms of therapy. Let us take an isolated (hence atypical) symptom. A woman, at the birth of her first child, develops a phobic reaction. She is suddenly unable to leave her home because of a dread and nameless fear that, if she does, something will prevent her from ever returning to care for her infant. Now the simple fact of the situation is that, statistically, mothers who step outside practically always return safely. Only very rarely are they killed by a bolt of lightning, an automobile, or a sudden heart attack; very few develop amnesia, are kidnapped, or simply desert their families.

What can be done for this woman? She would be perfectly right not to venture outside if danger threatened, yet she is wrong—therefore neurotic—in her gross exaggeration of the danger. We can argue and reason with her, pointing out how rarely mothers vanish on their doorsteps. We can assert, and even present documentary evidence, that not one person has been struck by lightning or kidnapped in her community for the past twenty-five years and that women of her age practically never suffer heart attacks and certainly not from stepping outside their homes. This kind of "common sense" therapy can be of some help and is probably what she has received from her friends and family before coming to professional treatment.

Counseling stresses this kind of approach. In the hands of the professional counselor, through skilled interviewing and with informed and authoritative advice given in an atmosphere of acceptance and objectivity, this procedure alone will frequently help the individual to clarify the problem and work out a solution for it.

But such problems may have "deeper" origins; the woman has been assured—and "believes"—that physical danger does not really threaten, yet her phobia persists and will continue to do so until she becomes aware of more hidden fears and conflicts that, for some reason, are presently inaccessible to her conscious search.

Psychoanalytic Therapies

To bring unconscious conflicts into awareness where they may be analyzed and become manageable is a central theme of the many varieties of psychoanalytic approaches to therapy that are based upon personality theories developed by Freud and his followers (see Unit 45). The traditional psychoanalyst devotes his main efforts to uncovering such unconscious conflicts and tracing them back to their presumed origins in the person's childhood.

The main method of classical *psychoanalysis* is that of *free association*. The patient is urged to talk freely about whatever comes into his mind, regardless of how trivial, stupid, or shameful it seems, and to let this flow of thoughts take whatever course it will. The patient's dreams, in which thoughts presumably take an even less structured and controlled form than in waking life, are also subjected to analysis. Through these techniques of free association and dream analysis the analyst seeks to discover and to interpret material of which the person has been unaware and to bring him to a deeper understanding of his problems. The analyst will assist the patient in recognizing and retaining whatever self-knowledge he has gained through these techniques—techniques that are aimed at reducing one's conscious control and censorship of the flow of thought.

Probably most widely practiced today are various forms of so-called *psychoanalytically oriented psychotherapy*, in which the classical approach is modified and adapted in a number of ways. Free association, for example, is usually replaced by more focused interviewing. The patient may be asked to associate to specific feelings or key problems. The therapist is, in general, more active than in traditional psychoanalysis, and he may combine several methods in the course of treatment—for example, re-education and reassurance to supplement the more traditional interpretation of unconscious conflicts. The couch of psychoanalysis is usually replaced by face-to-face interviewing. The goals of treatment may be more specific than those of psychoanalysis and the over-all length of treatment and the number of sessions per week reduced (see Box 165, p. 782, for an excerpt from a psychoanalytically oriented interview, in which the therapist "instructs" the patient as to the "rules of the game").

In both psychoanalysis and psychoanalytic therapy, it is assumed that important changes in interpersonal relations with the psychoanalyst may gradually take place as therapy continues. Particularly significant is the phenomenon of *transference*, in which the person is said to transfer his unconscious emotional feelings, positive and negative, from other objects or people (particularly his parents and other important figures from his childhood) to the psychoanalyst himself. Such transference is

Box 165

A Psychoanalytic Therapy Interview

The following excerpt from a therapy session between a psychoanalytically oriented therapist, Lewis Wolberg, and a relatively new patient illustrates the need to clarify the way in which one goes about communicating in this kind of therapeutic situation.

"PT. (Patient) I just don't know what's causing these feelings. I get so frightened and upset, and I don't know why.

TH. (Therapist) That's why you are coming here, to find out the reasons, so you can do something about your trouble.

PT. But why is it that I can't sleep and concentrate?

TH. That's what we'll begin to explore.

PT. But why?

TH. What comes to your mind? What do you think?

PT. I don't know.

TH. You know, there are reasons for troubles like yours, and one must patiently explore them. It may take a little time. I know you'd like to get rid of this trouble right away, but the only way one can do this is by careful exploring.

PT. Yes.

TH. And to take your anxiety feelings, for example, you may not be aware of the reasons for them now, but as we talk about you, your ideas, your troubles and your feelings, you should be able to find out what they are.

PT. How do I do this?

TH. When I ask you to talk about your feelings and thrash things around in your mind, you won't be able to put your finger on what bothers you immediately, but at least you will have started thinking about the sources of the problem. Right now, the only thing you're concerned with is escaping from the emotion. That's why you're just going around in a circle. While you're operating to seal off anxiety, you're doing nothing about finding out what's producing this anxiety.

PT. It sounds sort of clear when you say it. (laughs)

TH. Well, do you think you understand what I mean?

PT. What you're explaining now?

TH. Yes.

PT. Yes. (pause) The point is that I keep thinking about myself too much. It's that I feel inferior to everyone. I must win at rummy. When I play golf, I practically beat myself red if I don't get the low score. And this is silly.

TH. What happens when someone beats you at golf?

PT. I get upset and these feelings come.

TH. Now there seems to be some kind of connection here; let's talk some more about that."

L. R. WOLBERG. 1954. *The Technique of Psychotherapy* (New York: Grune & Stratton). Copyright 1954 by Grune and Stratton, Inc. Reprinted by permission.

facilitated by the therapist's noncommittal and neutral role, as well as by the classical "couch" arrangement, in which the patient lies on a couch with the psychoanalyst seated out of direct sight. Even the more active psychoanalytic therapies, however, allow transference to develop, though the process may be less overwhelming and less pervasive (that is, it may not call into play as many aspects of the patient's personality).

This transference process is regarded as the very core of psychoanalytic therapy and makes possible the emotional re-education of the person:

"The pathological effect of earlier emotional experiences is corrected by exposing the patient to the same type of emotional conflicts in the therapeutic situation. The therapist, however, reacts differently, not as the parents, teachers, relatives, or friends in the past. This difference between the therapist's reaction and the original parental reactions is the most fundamental therapeutic factor." (Alexander, 1946)

If in the course of such psychoanalytic therapy the woman who suffers the irrational fear of going out is brought to recall that she was always warned as a child of the dangers of the outside world and cautioned to remain at home; if she dreams of yowling and terrifying tomcats surrounding her house, these experiences are also of interest and use to therapy because they suggest the way to possible explanations of the phobia. For example —to suggest a somewhat fanciful explanation for our hypothetical patient—she may become aware that she was warned in her youth against men, that she has come to regard men as cruelly lustful "tomcats," and that, in giving birth, she has exposed her sexuality and is therefore vulnerable to their attack. But, whatever explanations may be arrived at, her present maladaptive behavior may be helped if, and only if, she can use such information or "explanations" to correct her distorted perception of the outside world as a dangerous place. The point here is not that such an explanation

delves into the past or that it invokes powerful "Freudian" drives; the "explanation" may even be incorrect in part or in whole. But if the woman can employ these explanations to unlearn her present distorted view of the world and gradually develop a correct one, then her self-imposed confinement will, *in her own eyes*, become less necessary and a brief excursion something to be dared.

She now understands and actually feels that her fears are unrealistic. They no longer make sense *to her*. Does the phobic reaction vanish? Behavioral change, unfortunately, is not automatically triggered by comprehension. She may now be able to don her coat, stride purposefully to the front door with a clear awareness of the safety of what lies beyond—and panic on the threshold.

Some psychologists have sought to explain the inflexibility of such "irrational" behavior in terms of the conditioning process. In our present example, it might be assumed that the sight of the outside world is a conditioned stimulus evoking the conditioned response of fear and panic. Regardless of how the conditioned connection began, such a conditioned fear response repeated over half a lifetime would strongly resist unlearning, or extinction —especially because the response would have been essentially self-reinforcing: Every trip on the outside, embarked upon with apprehension, was almost certain to reinforce the phobic reaction by such mechanisms as the distorted perception of a stranger's casual smile as a leer.

Such a formulation would seem to have a direct implication for a conditioning technique of therapy by which the maladaptive conditioned response could be systematically extinguished. The woman could thus be repeatedly urged to go outside, and on each occasion the absence of danger could be pointed out to her and pleasant experiences provided. Gradually the phobic response might diminish and disappear. This technique would be an example of what are called *behavior therapies*.

Behavior Therapies

Behavior therapies, although all are based on a conditioning conception of behavior, by no means constitute a homogeneous set of techniques. Included are such different procedures as inflicting a painful stimulus at each occurrence of an undesirable symptom, having the symptom practiced intentionally in order to bring it under voluntary control, or gradually desensitizing a feared stimulus by systematic relaxation procedures. Although such techniques are by no means new (the earliest date back to the 1920s), behavior therapy has undergone a recent revival. And, because it has chosen psychoanalytic therapy as its explicit opponent, heated controversy between the two is common. Breger and McGaugh (1965), for example, in a thorough review of the theoretical bases and supportive evidence for the behavior therapies, question both the supposed relevance of learning theory to these methods and the adequacy of the occasional empirical "proofs" of their adequacy. They also find that the behavior therapies tend to hold to a narrow conception of personality disorders, typically confining them to discrete behavior symptoms. Perhaps not incidentally, it is such symptoms that seem most amenable to behavior therapy. For example, Grossberg (1964) finds from his review of the various behavior therapies that they "have been most successful with disorders involving specific maladaptive behaviors. Conditioning procedures were highly effective with phobic reactions, anxiety reactions, enuresis, stuttering."

But such specific maladaptive behaviors unfortunately do not even begin to exhaust the diverse repertoire of human neuroses and psychoses. Most often the disorder is diffuse and pervades almost every aspect of a person's functioning. The need to be able to treat this wide range of functional disorders has led to various innovations in psychotherapeutic technique. They are to be considered innovations, not in the sense of necessarily being recent, but because they introduce significant departures from earlier, primarily psychoanalytic approaches. One of the foremost of these techniques is known as *client-centered therapy*.

Client-Centered Therapy

This relatively recent movement in psychotherapy, a movement parallel with, but largely independent of, the psychoanalytic approach, had its beginnings in the 1940s at The University of Chicago; it was primarily under the guidance of Carl Rogers, a psychologist. Also called "nondirective therapy," or, simply, "Rogerian therapy," this approach has gained adherents so rapidly that today it exerts a substantial influence on the practice of psychotherapy and counseling in the United States and abroad. Most client-centered therapists are psychologists, trained in university settings where teaching and research in this technique go hand in hand.

Perhaps the central feature of Rogerian therapy is its insistence that the client's internal focus of reference should guide the course of treatment, not the therapist's theoretical predilections. The therapist attempts to understand in detail the client's perceptions of his world. He helps the client to clarify for himself the nature of his problems; one technique is to summarize in more clear-cut fashion what the client, by word or gesture, has himself expressed but has not yet fully recognized. One facet of this technique is known as "reflection of feeling," a subtle act in which the therapist attempts to "bounce back" to the client, in selective and focused form, aspects of the client's expressed feelings and emotions that he, the attuned therapist, can detect but that may have so far escaped the client's awareness. Box 166, p. 785, illustrates such an exchange between a client-centered therapist and a young woman.

A guiding premise of this method is that each person has within himself the ability to find his own solutions for his problems. The

Box 166

A Client-Centered
Therapy Interview

In her fourth interview, Mrs. Teral, a 23-year-old married schoolteacher, has just told her therapist, John Shlien of The University of Chicago Counseling Center, that she is upset. The therapist notices that the client looks pained and stricken, and says:

"T (Therapist): What . . . what's hitting you now?

c (Client): I don't know.

T: Something upsetting, something that makes you feel like crying?

c: [Pause; crying softly; words lost.] I could use a little more self control, too.

T: You don't like to have to cry.

c: No, I don't. [Pause.] And I don't know why, either. I just got very upset. [Still crying.]

T: Um-hm. Something just came over you and you really don't know what started it.

c: [Long pause; still crying.] I must have been getting a little too close to something—I didn't want to talk about, or something.

T: You really don't know what made this happen. [Client looks for clock.] You've still got about fifteen minutes.

c: [Pause; still crying.] Something hit me [laughs].

T: Hm?

c: Something hit me.

T: Something hurts.

c: [Long pause.] Here I go again. [Pause.] I don't know what it was. I just . . . I'm completely gone now. My knees are shaking all over me.

T: Um-hm. [Pause.] You don't know what started this but it's really taken hold of you. [Pause; client crying.] Your whole . . . your whole body is in a turmoil.

c: I really can't concentrate on what I'm doing. All I can concentrate on is the feeling that I'm not going to smoke, I'm not going to smoke [laughs].

T: I don't know exactly what you mean there.

c: I can't even try to think what it is because I want a cigarette so bad I just have [laughs] to keep myself going. I'm not going to smoke, I'm not going to smoke [laughs].

T: All your energy is just bent toward that one thing, just . . . to keep yourself from having a cigarette, huh?

c: Yes. [Long pause.] I'm not very . . . I'm upset 'cause I said something about being dependent on [husband]. Maybe I just didn't want to start talking about that. That could be it.

T: Maybe that's kind of a tender spot."

Thus the client, with the therapist's subtle assistance, has herself come to an awareness of a "tender spot."

M. K. LEWIS, C. R. ROGERS, and J. M. SHLIEN. 1959. Time-Limited, Client-Centered Psychotherapy: Two Cases, in A. Burton, ed., *Case Studies in Counseling and Psychotherapy* (Englewood Cliffs, N.J.: Prentice-Hall). © 1959 by Prentice-Hall, Inc., Englewood Cliffs, New Jersey. Reprinted by permission.

therapist's responsibility, therefore, is to assist his client in coming up with answers that the client himself devises, answers that express the individual's unique potential for personality growth and change. The therapist's job is *not* to propose theoretical explanations of problems or to offer authoritative advice on how to go about solving them.

Given only these bare outlines, the client-centered approach may appear deceptively simple. This apparent simplicity is for some the source of this method's attractiveness and promise; for others, it is its fatal flaw and intrinsic limitation. It does not even require an explicit theory of personality. It feels no compulsion to deal with unconscious factors, in the psychoanalytic sense, although it does strive to bring the not-yet-aware into full awareness. Depth interpretation of dreams is thus not a tool of client-centered therapy, though exploration of feelings evoked by dreams is frequently undertaken.

Client-centered therapy ranks first in the diligence and sophistication of research designed to evaluate empirically the nature and extent of its therapeutic effectiveness. A fundamental tenet of client-centered therapy is that improvement in adjustment, and personality change generally, is first reflected by modifications of the person's self-perception and that such modifications in turn lead to behavioral change. Rogers and Dymond (1954) present considerable evidence for this view of personality change through psychotherapy and for the effectiveness of their therapeutic approach in bringing about such change.

Group and Family Therapy

Both *group therapy* and *family therapy* radically alter the traditional psychoanalytic therapy setting. The private (some would say "secret") nature of the classical therapist-patient relationship is replaced, in both these methods, by a heavy dose of social reality. The

influence of neo-Freudian personality theories, particularly the theory of Harry Stack Sullivan (see p. 750) will be easy to discern as we sketch the details of these newer and increasingly employed psychotherapeutic techniques.

At first glance group therapy may appear to be an economy measure; a single therapist works with several patients simultaneously. In an important sense, patients participating in group therapy become one another's therapists, exposing their problems and fears to one another, commenting upon changes in others' behavior during the course of treatment, developing transference to fellow patients as well as to the therapist. The therapist encourages this process, remaining psychologically and even physically in the background of the group and intervening primarily to make an occasional clarifying observation or interpretation. Aside from whatever benefits may accrue to the individual patient from a feeling of group belongingness, he is also afforded an ongoing opportunity for "reality testing," particularly in the realm of interpersonal relations. When he has developed a way of coping with a problem in his therapy group—a microcosm of the social world—the probability that he can carry this change over to everyday life is increased. As with all forms of psychotherapy, some persons are unwilling—or, if willing, unable—to participate usefully in a therapy group. But for many it has brought improvements apparently not attainable through individual psychotherapy.

In this instance the group is one's own family and the patient is often not a single person but, instead, the family unit. Here, the therapist serves a role that lies between those he fulfills in group and in individual psychotherapy. He cannot as easily remain in the background as in group therapy because his intervention is more often required and because family members not infrequently embroil him actively in the very conflicts that make them function poorly as a social unit. The main efforts of this form of psychotherapy are directed toward increasing the adaptability of the family as a whole, not toward treating particular individuals. The therapist cannot, as in individual psychotherapy, learn to see the world through the eyes of the individual patient and conduct his treatment within that framework because the harsh or benevolent realities of other family members are in the picture. When the misperceptions held by each of the others become clear to the therapist, his task is to help each of them to a more realistic view of the others' needs, lacks, and strengths, and thus to a more viable family relationship.

Group therapy or family therapy often accompanies individual psychotherapy, usually with a different therapist for each situation. Or individual treatment may follow group or family therapy in order to consolidate the psychological gains from these earlier therapeutic experiences. In this light, group and family therapy may be viewed as aids, or adjuncts, to individual therapy, although by no means (either in theory or in practice) is its role necessarily subsidiary. Other forms of treatment, however, are recognized as primarily adjuncts to other therapeutic procedures.

Adjunct Therapies

Although partisans of each of the following adjunct methods claim that it is sufficient treatment in itself—and such is indeed the case for certain kinds of patients with certain kinds of problems—the usual function of these procedures is to make the patient more accessible to further "conventional" psychotherapy. Among psychological adjunct methods is *play therapy*—commonly used with young children but also with uncommunicative psychotic patients—in which toys, dolls, clay, paints, and so on are used essentially as projective techniques. Pictures may be drawn, doll "families" set up—in short, channels are provided through play for conveying to the therapist information that, for

whatever reason, cannot yet be directly or verbally communicated. In the course of this procedure, trust in the therapist is often developed, and further and different psychotherapeutic procedures become wise and feasible. *Psychodrama*, in which patients enact roles in spontaneous and revealing playlets, is another such technique for facilitating communication, this time in a group setting. Box 167, p. 788, presents a third.

The so-called "physical therapies" have come increasingly to be seen as primarily adjunct procedures. For a long time, severely disturbed hospitalized patients have been given *shock therapy*. This therapy includes the administering of enough insulin or electric current to cause brief convulsive seizures and subsequent periods of lucidity. The purpose is to bring the patient for a short while into a state of mental clarity and greater contact with reality, so that the therapist can communicate with him. Shock therapies are fast being supplanted, however, by recently developed drugs, the best known of which are the *tranquilizers*.

Tranquilizers include several different types of chemical compounds. We know something—but far from all—about the physiological mechanisms by which tranquilizers affect emotional states (see p. 602), but they qualify as adjunct therapy chiefly because of their ability to reduce anxiety. Their function with psychotics, mainly with agitated schizophrenics, is essentially a calming one, so that, at the very least, custodial problems in mental hospitals have been greatly reduced and many patients, even long-term patients, can be returned to their homes. Unless the drug treatment is maintained in the home, however, relapse and return to the hospital are a likely result. Nor is the tranquilizing effect always demonstrated. Carefully conducted studies on chlorpromazine (a tranquilizer frequently used with schizophrenics) suggest that only a third of patients improve (Glick & Margolis, 1962).

The mental-hospital caseload has thus been

substantially eased, but in no sense can we conclude that in tranquilizers a cure for schizophrenia (or for any mental illness) has been found. Again, the most salutary effect of tranquilizer treatment is that it occasionally creates the conditions—lessened anxiety, an end of violent behavior, somewhat greater contact with reality—in which effective psychotherapy can be initiated and carried on. Ironically, tranquilizers may interfere with psychotherapy by reducing to placidity a patient whose anxiety level was "just right" for treatment. Considering the enormous enthusiasm for these drugs among neurotic patients, this may be a common effect today.

Research continues on a broad front, however, to discover biochemical and chemical compounds that can treat various forms of mental disorder, not as anxiety-relieving adjuncts but through *direct* intervention in the physiological basis of the disorder. As evidence mounts on the likelihood that at least some disorders have substantial constitutional underpinnings, the search for such chemotherapeutic agents is encouraged.

Goals and Effectiveness of Psychotherapy

Tens of thousands of people annually initiate (usually voluntarily) some kind of psychotherapy, often at great personal expense—financial and otherwise. Society, through growing numbers of public agencies from the local community to the Federal level, encourages and supports such treatment. Many of these people (but by no means all) conclude treatment with some sense of benefit. Presumably, then, many individuals achieve the goals they seek in psychotherapy.

To speak of the goals of psychotherapy is no narrower a task than to speak of the goals of

---

Box 167

Hypnosis and Hypnotherapy

The phenomena of *hypnosis*—a topic of considerable popular interest, and often misconception—have been the subject of a great deal of theoretical speculation and controversy. Briefly stated, the main facts as determined by psychological investigation are as follows:

1. Induction of a hypnotic state, or trance, requires the assent and cooperation of the person. Generally speaking, he cannot be hypnotized "against his will."

2. Almost everyone can be hypnotized under some circumstances. But there are great individual differences in susceptibility.

3. The effects produced in a hypnotic state do not flow from the "power" of the hypnotist; they are the result of operation of psychological processes in the person himself. The hypnotist may, of course, play a crucial role in giving various suggestions with which the person seeks to comply.

4. Various pronounced changes in behavior can be produced by such hypnotic suggestion. For instance, the person can be induced to withstand extremely painful stimulation without apparent signs of feeling the pain, as witness the successful use of hypnosis in difficult childbirth and in surgery without anesthetics. And numerous demonstrations and experiments show that the hypnotized person will follow instructions and convincingly act out roles suggested to him.

life. The goals of therapy may be as numerous as are the patients. Some patients seek to alleviate crippling emotional paralyses, others to improve endurable but unsatisfying personal relationships, still others to remove hindrances to occupational goals. Some wish to become more popular, some to become more fulfilled, some to become more successful, and some only to become more human—to cope better with the realities of their lives and to gain a modicum of happiness from them.

Precisely because the goals of psychotherapy are so varied, it is difficult to assess its effectiveness. For example, has psychotherapy been effective for a particular individual when he reports that he is considerably happier despite no improvement in his social adjustment? There are many other factors complicating the question. Many mentally ill persons may show recovery without any psychotherapy. There is the difficult problem of finding comparable groups of treated and untreated among the mentally ill. The fact that some people do seek and get treatment and others do not probably in itself reflects some psychological differences between them. Though there may be temporary improvement after psychotherapy, for some persons much of it may be lost after a short time.

An even more difficult task is to compare the relative merits of several different types of psychotherapy. The exact method used by one therapist may not be identical with that of another who is presumably using the "same" method, and the samples of patients treated by the various therapies may be different. Another difficulty in comparing different therapeutic approaches is that the skilled therapist may shift approaches with a patient during the course of treatment, either because his initial

---

5. Yet there are definite limits to what he will do under suggestion. He may, for example, "stab" a friend with a rubber knife after being instructed that the other person is an "enemy." But, if given a steel knife, he will balk at the suggestion. Though the evidence is not absolutely clear on this point, the expert consensus is that a person cannot be brought by hypnotic suggestion to commit a crime or other act that he regards as immoral or repugnant (unless perhaps his own "normal" inclinations really predispose him that way to begin with).

In general, then, it appears that hypnotic behavior is a kind of "as if" behavior. The person really knows that the situation is not what the hypnotist suggests it to be, but he is highly susceptible to behaving "as if" it were.

Inasmuch as the hypnotized person does show this far greater readiness to cooperate with the hypnotist's suggestions, it is obvious how the phenomenon may contribute to psychotherapy. In cases in which there is severe emotional blockage of the recall of deeply "repressed" material, the recall may sometimes be facilitated by placing the patient in a hypnotic state and instructing him to talk about the problem. This method was indeed that with which Freud began his work, but he soon abandoned it in favor of the free-association technique.

Such *hypnotherapy* has had success in some cases. For example, in cases of breakdown through combat exhaustion during World War II, hypnosis was sometimes effectively used to help amnesic patients recall the details of their traumatic battle experiences, thus paving the way for treatment.

But hypnotherapy is not a method of therapy in itself. It is merely a therapeutic aid, which, by inducing a particularly receptive attitude and emotional state in the patient, may facilitate the progress of the actual psychotherapy that is being conducted.

Box 168

**An Experiment with Nonprofessionals
as "Companion Therapists"**

The Interpersonal Relations Project, directed by Dr. Gerald Goodman at the University of California's Berkeley campus, is an experimental program based on the assumption that untutored therapeutic talent can be scientifically discovered and put to use in ways different from the traditional therapy enterprise. The "therapists" in the project were male college students, and their "clients" were fifth- and sixth-grade boys referred by parents who said the boys had emotional problems. They met twice or three times a week, according to convenience and inclination, and meetings lasted from one to five hours. The relationships were limited to the span of a school year. The "office" was the community. The "method" was companionship.

Here is how one student described his thirty-fifth meeting with a troubled boy:

"As we carved our soap figures Tim talked about his family. I just listened. He was much more open than he had been in the past about his dead sister. He said that he didn't like his sister and only realized his affection for her when she died. We were quiet for a while. Then Tim said 'how great' this session was. Then he said 'I love you, Walt, I really like you, I really like you a lot.' I said that I thought he was right the first time in saying 'love' although it was a little embarrassing for me as well as for him to use the term—I said that I felt that way about him too. He nodded and said 'yes, love.' . . . We both felt completely at ease talking as we felt like it and working on our carvings. I felt that Tim was happy to be able to express his feelings openly towards me, and it made me feel good for him to be able to do so."

The program starts each year by collecting systematic observations on all 1,500 of Berkeley's fifth- and sixth-grade public-school boys. Next, an announcement is sent to all parents and their boys describing the project and inviting applications for boys who are having distinct problems getting along with people. When the combined descriptions of parents, teachers, and classmates indicate that a boy is having problems, he is placed in a pool of potential participants. The pool is searched for fifty highly matched pairs of boys. Twenty-five of the matched pairs have problems with isolation, withdrawal, depression, and so forth (the "quiets"). The remaining twenty-five are designated "outgoings" and have problems with aggression, hostility, and so forth. One of each pair is randomly selected to participate and the other to serve in a nonparticipating control group. The result is fifty

---

tack worked poorly or because different tacks are more appropriate at different stages of treatment. Highly experienced therapists frequently employ this flexible strategy, probably to the benefit of the patient but certainly to the confusion of the professional therapy evaluator.

In general, we must conclude that we do not yet know how much good psychotherapy does

or how it works. But, because of the urgency of the problem, this hopefully temporary state of ignorance is not likely to impede the immense and growing use of psychotherapy. If the trend toward an increasing awareness of the importance of the social context continues, future psychotherapeutic developments may borrow heavily from social psychology.

Fortunately, psychotherapy today is a sub-

participating boys and their fifty individually matched controls—both groups evenly divided in evincing "quiet" and "outgoing" problems.

The counselors are obtained by inviting applications from students through campus-wide advertisement at the University of California at Berkeley. The job offers a modest salary. Applicants describe themselves on various psychological instruments. After that, students are scheduled to attend group-assessment sessions aimed at measuring such interpersonal traits as openness, warmth, and ability to understand others' feelings. Many applicants screen themselves out before getting to this point. The number eventually hired is probably less than 50 per cent of those students asking for applications.

After counselors are selected, they are divided into a "quiet" group and an "outgoing" group on the basis of the group-assessment ratings. Half the "quiet" counselors are then paired with boys evincing "quiet" problems, and the other half are paired with boys with "outgoing" problems. The same procedure is followed for the group of "outgoing" counselors. This pairing system produces four types of counselor-boy relationships. Half the counselors from each of the four types are then selected for group training.

Before the actual companion relationship begins, all the counselors attend two half-day experimental workshops on "helping relationships." Half the counselors also receive additional training in weekly small discussion groups throughout the year. The training is essentially self-exploration, with professional leaders functioning primarily as facilitators of communication. The most common thing discussed and demonstrated in the groups is emotional self-disclosure—being psychologically honest with oneself and with others. At the end of each group session, counselors describe one another on warmth, understanding, and disclosure scales.

Tentative findings suggest that boys with "quiet" problems gain the most from participating in the program and that boys with group-trained counselors gain more than do boys with untrained counselors. It also appears that aggressive boys improved significantly only when they have been paired with group-trained counselors. The counselors show dramatically heightened interest in the behavior of children, in working with troubled people, and in the ways they interact with friends. Counselors feel that they have begun to relate to friends better as a result of participation. Group-trained counselors change a bit more than do untrained counselors, and many give convincing details on how the training has created important changes in their lives.

These findings suggest a double payoff: Working with troubled boys not only may help the boys but also may change the students themselves.

G. GOODMAN. 1968. Companionship as Therapy: The Use of Nonprofessional Talent, in J. T. Hart and T. M. Tomlinson, eds., *New Directions in Client-Centered Psychotherapy* (Boston: Houghton Mifflin).

ject of intensive scrutiny and experiment. After several decades marking a fairly stable period in the practice of psychotherapy, influenced mainly by the psychoanalytic approaches, new methods and, indeed, revolutionary philosophies of treatment are springing up on a broad front. One indication of the current innovative climate in the psychotherapies is the rapidly increasing movement for the training and employment of nonprofessionals in mental-health work. Housewives, high-school students, even drug addicts have joined training programs and have gone on to work with emotionally troubled people. This movement, of course, opens up the possibility of greatly augmented personnel for a seriously undermanned field. But, as important or more important, it signals an easing of traditional barriers and a promising re-evaluation of conventional views of the therapist-patient relationship. Because they are nonprofessionals, these new recruits to the mental-health field may trigger fresh approaches and may even prove to be especially effective, perhaps the more so because they work with persons from similar backgrounds with whom they have shared certain common experiences. At the very least, this new trend deserves serious research to evaluate its effectiveness, and it is getting it (see Box 168, p. 790).

In this continuously developing and changing field, we can say with assurance that it is best to tackle the problem of mental illness before it starts. Preventive therapy is more likely to help than any amount of attempted cure. And the more we learn about the basic processes of personality development, the more effective we can be in our preventive therapy. For mental illness, no matter how defined and whatever its "ultimate" cause, reflects a disturbance in personality development.

Glossary

affective reaction A category of psychotic reaction marked by exaggerated emotional states ranging from euphoria and elation to profound depression and immobility. When both extremes occur alternately in the same person, the reaction is called "manic-depressive."

antisocial reaction ("psychopathic personality") A form of "character disorder" in which the individual shows a chronic and socially incapacitating tendency to seek immediate need gratification. He is a poor judge of the consequences of his social actions and fails to learn from social experience.

behavior therapy A group of techniques of psychotherapy deriving from certain "reinforcement" theories of learning.

client-centered therapy One of the main methods of psychotherapy, involving a nondirective approach by the therapist, who provides sympathetic "reflection" of the patient's expressed feelings rather than direct interpretation and evaluation of them. The patient is thus encouraged to arrive at his own insights concerning his problems and at the proper course of remedial action. Associated with the name of Carl Rogers.

counseling A form of psychotherapy dealing with the milder maladjustments in marriage, vocation, school, and so on. Counseling is generally more directive than are deeper forms of psychotherapy; the counselor is cast more in the role of the expert guide and "information" giver.

family therapy A technique of psychotherapy in which the therapist works simultaneously with all or several members of the family. The family is being treated as a psychological unit, and "family neuroses" are encountered.

free association The method employed in psychoanalysis in which the person is encouraged to report freely everything that comes into his mind.

functional disorders The general class of mental illness, including both the neuroses and psychoses, that are primarily psychological in origin and that are not caused by any known pathological changes in organic structure.

group therapy A technique of psychotherapy in which groups of patients are treated simultaneously in group discussions in the presence of the therapist. Quite often the patients are one another's "therapists," the professional therapist remaining in the background.

organic psychosis A psychotic state for which there is a well-established basis in the structure or physiological functioning of the organism. It is distinguished from functional psychosis.

paranoid reaction A form of psychosis characterized by a pervasive and often organized set of delusions, most commonly delusions of persecution or of grandeur.

play therapy A technique of psychotherapy with children in which the therapist works with the child as he plays with toys and other materials, permitting him freely and nonverbally to express emotions and conflicts.

psychoanalysis A principal method of psychotherapy first developed by Freud. It involves long and intensive exploration of the person's conflicts, repressed memories, childhood experiences, and so on. The main technique is free association, and an essential part of the psychotherapy is the process of transference, in which the patient's emotional attitudes toward parents and other people become temporarily transferred to the psychoanalyst. Through this technique, self-understanding and emotional re-education of the person are achieved.

psychoanalytically oriented therapy A modification of psychoanalysis that maintains the same theoretical orientation but is typically less intensive and often of shorter duration. More focused interviewing techniques are also employed, and the therapist is usually more active.

psychodrama A technique of psychotherapy in which the patients—alone or in groups—play roles that represent their emotional problems and in so doing come to gain emotional release and insight.

psychoneurosis The class of the milder forms of mental illness, usually not requiring hospitalization. The psychoneurotic person retains his orientation to the environment and considerable contact with reality but suffers enough disruption of cognitive and emotional processes to interfere with his effective life adjustments.

psychosis The class of the more severe mental diseases, like schizophrenic reaction, manic-depressive reaction, and paranoid reaction. It involves serious disruptions of cognitive and emotional processes, often necessitating at least temporary hospitalization.

schizophrenic reaction The most prevalent of all psychotic reactions, marked by extreme emotional withdrawal and diminished contact with reality, by a general deterioration in social behavior, and, often, by hallucinations. Frequently there is a striking incompatibility, or split, between emotion and behavior; hence the popular term "split personality."

shock therapy A psychotherapeutic aid involving the induction of a convulsive seizure in the psychotic patient, through the administration of insulin or electric shock. One result, particularly in very depressed patients, is a temporary period of lucidity during which the therapist can communicate with him.

tranquilizers A class of drugs used to modify a mental patient's mood, usually to reduce anxiety. This effect makes the patient socially more manageable and can make him accessible to psychotherapy.

transference The process, especially important in psychoanalysis and psychoanalytically oriented therapy, through which the patient transfers his disturbed emotional attitudes toward parents and other important persons in his life to his perception of the psychotherapist. This transference provides an opportunity for these basic emotional attitudes to be re-educated with the aid of the therapist.

social perception

overview / All perception is in some sense "social," and, by the same token, general principles of perceptual organization are applicable to such social-perceptual phenomena as forming impressions of other persons. Man invariably forms such impressions, even though only partial data are typically available to serve as a basis. He fills in the missing information, reconciling contradictory data or excluding it entirely if it cannot be made to fit into a unified and coherent description. The order in which information is received by the perceiver is of considerable importance, with earlier (and, especially, initial) information tending to dominate in the process of impression formation.

There are a number of sources for the content added by the perceiver as he rounds out his impression. In part his implicit theory of personality—his ideas as to which psychological traits go with one another—determines which additional characteristics he attributes to the perceived person. Stereotypes also are quite influential; once the person is tagged as belonging to a specific group possessing certain well-defined (though not necessarily accurately defined) characteristics, a complete personality portrait—the group stereotype—can be made to unfold.

In addition to these stimulus-pattern and context effects, there is a variety of social and interpersonal factors that operate in impression formation. One's formal role in the situation, one's relationships and interactions with the other persons, one's personal attitudes toward them—all these factors enter into the process of molding an impression of another human being, although the accuracy of such impressions raises still other questions.

Social psychology is the study of man with special emphasis on the influence of his social environment upon his behavior. In a certain sense, all psychology may be regarded as "social psychology," as it is difficult to imagine a situation, even within the confines of the psychological laboratory, that is not "social" in character. The isolated individual is a fiction; whatever he perceives and whatever he does are influenced by his earlier perception and learning, colored by his present needs and feelings, and stamped with his unique abilities and personality. In short, all human behavior tends to be social behavior, and all human perception tends to be (and this point is the special concern of this unit) social perception. To the extent that this statement is true, we may expect that the general psychological principles from the experimental perception laboratory will remain applicable. For example, similar principles of perceptual grouping are probably involved whether we are looking at a stimulus pattern composed of black dots on a white cardboard background or composed of persons scattered throughout a room. In any case we have the same perceiver and the same nervous system, and it is reasonable to expect a similar perceptual result. This generality of perceptual principles will become increasingly apparent as we seek to understand the processes involved in social perception. For, in order to understand social behavior, we begin by trying (as we do in studying "individual" behavior) to comprehend the psychological processes by which man perceives and organizes social stimuli. In doing so we shall confine our attention to the act of perceiving persons; here the social aspect of perception is highlighted. Also we shall in the process be treating "perception" in its most general sense—including in it judgmental processes.

Stimulus Pattern and Person Perception

Nowhere is the social character of perception more apparent, and therefore more exposed to the social psychologist's investigation, than in the act of perceiving another human being. In perceiving people all aspects of our "self" are likely to be brought into play, and the resulting experiences reflect a complex blend of our own characteristics and those of the other person, who is the "social stimulus." In forming an impression of another, we more or less consciously take note of his physical appearance (including various indications of his social role and class like dress and "hairdo"), his actions, his voice, his expressive movements, and all other cues that may be psychologically informative or meaningful. From such evidence, we formulate (not necessarily on a clearly conscious level) a fairly detailed percept (or "concept," rather) of what he is like—his thoughts, his needs, his feelings, his personality. This percept by no means consists of a hodgepodge of discrete and unrelated inferences put together from many separate impressions and observations. On the contrary. A social percept typically represents an *integration* of all available cues, and there is a strong tendency for it to embody a portrait of a "complete" person, not just a few features of his personality.

What is our motive for forming coherent impressions of other persons? This question can be answered in a number of ways, each complementary to the others. For one thing, when we must actively cope with the other person, we are necessarily driven to "make sense" of his behavior, and to do so we must come up with an over-all impression that "hangs together" and that then permits us to *predict* his actions and to adapt accordingly. For another thing, the very fact of another person's complexity defines him as a challenging "problem" to be solved, triggering our need to explore and to understand the new and the unknown. And then there is man's highly general tendency—the urge to organize perceptually any stimulus field, particularly one as complex and attention-demanding as another human being.

Organizational Factors in the Stimulus Pattern

Whatever the reasons underlying man's tendency to form unified impressions of other persons, it is clear that such impressions are almost always based on inadequate and incomplete data; or—in perceptual terms—the social stimulus is an "ambiguous figure" (see p. 185) that can be organized in a number of ways. Quite often, in order to achieve a "whole" picture, the perceiver must invent attributes that

serve to fill in the gaps in what he sees and hears. This invention of attributes seems to operate very much in accordance with the "closure" principle in simple perceptual grouping. Box 169 illustrates the operation of this tendency when the available data are exceedingly sparse. As evidence accumulates about the true nature of the other person, the task of creating a complete portrait may become simplified. What is more, this new evidence renders the other person less ambiguous; as a result,

---

Box 169

**Forming Impressions
of Personality**

Here are some terms descriptive of a certain person: "energetic," "assured," "talkative," "cold," "ironical," "inquisitive," "persuasive." What is your impression of this person?

S. E. Asch at Brooklyn College posed this question to a large number of college students. He found that the students were readily able to write down a full-bodied impression of the unknown person, with nothing but this series of trait words to go on. For instance, one student wrote the following description:

"He impresses people as being more capable than he really is. He is popular and never ill at ease. Easily becomes the center of attraction at any gathering. He is likely to be a jack-of-all-trades. Although his interests are varied, he is not necessarily well versed in any of them. He possesses a sense of humor. His presence stimulates enthusiasm and very often he does arrive at a position of importance."

Not only are the given trait terms organized to produce a unified picture of the person, but additional traits are also created in order to give the picture its full character. The person is thus described as possessing a "sense of humor" or as being "not necessarily well versed" in his varied interests. These traits seem to follow from the over-all impression that the original list produced in this particular perceiver, and so they are ascribed to the unknown person.

As Asch summarizes it:

"When a task of this kind is given, a normal adult is capable of responding to the instruction by forming a unified impression. Though he hears a sequence of discrete terms, his resulting impression is not discrete. All subjects . . . of whom there were over 1,000 fulfilled the task in the manner described. . . . Starting from the bare terms, the final account is completed and rounded."

s. e. asch. 1946. Forming Impressions of Personality, *J. Abnorm. Soc. Psychol.*, 41, 258–90.

our impressions will increasingly agree, being thereby less influenced by the idiosyncratic personal factor to be discussed later.

Sometimes, however, additional evidence can complicate rather than simplify the problem. Frequently, as we learn more about a person, our impression can no longer be a simplified one but must incorporate new and complex data while preserving a unified picture. Under certain circumstances, unity is no longer possible unless we simply ignore evidence that is incompatible with the main impression, which is precisely what many of us do. A simple experimental demonstration of this fact is presented by Gollin (1954).

Gollin presented college students with a motion picture depicting a young woman in a number of situations that might evoke contradictory impressions of her "true" personality. Their task was to create a personality sketch of the woman after viewing the picture. In two enacted scenes, the woman displayed behavior that was easily interpretable as sexually promiscuous; in two other scenes she was shown behaving in a kindly and considerate manner (helping another woman who had accidentally fallen, giving money to a beggar). These two general characteristics—promiscuity and helpfulness—quite intentionally did not represent irreconcilable opposites; neither did they immediately and obviously "hang together." The reader must remember that this study was done prior to the "Love" generation of the 1960s. Actually, a situation was created in which the student could form an impression that integrated the two into a single, unified impression, of a woman, say, who was "generous" to a fault. This type of solution was achieved by only 23 per cent of Gollin's subjects. More than twice as many students (48 per cent), however, took what seemed the easier-to-achieve solution in which only one of the two major characteristics was retained, and the other was simply totally ignored. Both of these groups, in different ways, thus managed a coherent description; the remaining subjects

(29 per cent) failed to achieve integration. Instead, their impressions faithfully reflected *both* major qualities but showed no attempt to blend the two. Whether it was because they were incapable of doing so, were insufficiently motivated to try, or were simply not aware of any "discrepancy" is not known. Whatever the reason, this study suggests that impressions are not always unified and that we are quite capable of organizing our perception of a person into two (or more) separate and not necessarily compatible parts.

To a considerable degree, our ability to arrive at an integrated impression of another person depends on how we acquire the bits and pieces of information that we must unify. This outcome was demonstrated by Asch (in another phase of the work reported in Box 169, p. 797) and later repeated by Kastenbaum (1951). Their general finding was that, when subjects were first required to form two impressions (ostensibly of two different persons), each based upon internally consistent information, and when they were then asked to combine the two into a single coherent impression, their efforts were not nearly as successful as were those of subjects who *initially* formed a single impression based on *all* the information. Dailey (1952) reports a similar finding. In his study, the first group of subjects were asked for their impression of a stimulus person after being given an array of autobiographical information concerning him. A second group of subjects were required to form two impressions: first, when they were halfway through the presentation of the information and, second, when all the information was in. The concluding impression of the single-impression group, when compared with that of the two-stage group, was found to be not only more coherent but also more accurate.

Temporal Organization Factors The experiments just discussed touch upon an additional factor of considerable importance in the process of forming impressions of persons—the factor of temporal order or sequence. All three experiments pointed to the influence that an earlier impression can have upon a later one. A wealth of additional evidence supports this observation, some of it indicating that first impressions can be so powerful that they can dominate completely all future perceptions. Certainly this view of the critical role of "first impressions" is a common one in everyday life; the new student, the job applicant, and the "blind date" are all cautioned to be on their best behavior lest they "get off on the wrong foot" and forever damage their cause.

The first impression, or *primacy effect*, apparently can be detected even over short time intervals. A typical study design is to prepare two descriptions of a hypothetical person that are mutually contradictory but not hopelessly irreconcilable. Two groups of subjects read *both* descriptions, *but in a different order*, and then describe what the person is like. They all receive the "same" information but in different sequence. The usual result is that the first description overpowers the second and dominates the final impression. Box 170, p. 800, clearly illustrates this outcome. The remarkable immediacy of this sort of primacy effect is further driven home by experiments that show that the effect can be obtained even when the stimulus material is a short list of descriptive adjectives read in a relatively rapid series. In one such experiment, Anderson and Barrios (1961) asked subjects to give their over-all impressions of stimulus persons described only by series of six adjectives, adjectives that theoretically had been provided by six different persons who were well acquainted with that person. When the stimulus person was described as "smart, artistic, sentimental, cool, awkward, and faultfinding," he typically received distinctly more positive evaluations than when the "same" description was presented in reverse order: "faultfinding, awkward, cool, sentimental, artistic, and smart." Supposedly, in the first instance, we regard an intelligent and artistically gifted person as having the right to be

critical, but, in the second case, we are initially put off by a faultfinding individual and may view his being "smart and artistic" as a trivial asset or perhaps even a pretense. This primacy effect can easily be seen as an instance of the influence of set (created by the first impression) upon all later perceptions (see p. 174).

Though the primacy effect is strong, it is by no means inescapable. In the Luchins study described in Box 170, p. 800, further experiments demonstrated that the effect could be destroyed, and even reversed so that the second paragraph was dominant, simply by cautioning the subjects not to make "snap" judgments and even by requiring them to solve some arithmetic problems in the interval between the first and second paragraphs. These findings, which betray a surprising delicacy in the usually sturdy primacy effect, suggest another factor that can help to account for the effect itself. Let us assume that what we first hear or read about a person conveys an instant first impression, so that we tend to pay less attention to subsequent information. If so, then we can regard Luchins' warning to his subjects as the equivalent of saying "keep paying attention" and his introduction of *extraneous* arithmetic problems as a way of increasing the attention value of the second paragraph when it is presented later after the "interruption." In further support of this general explanation is the study by Anderson and Hubert (1963). They found that the primacy effect is greatly reduced if the subjects, after being exposed to a set of person-descriptive adjectives, are required to recall all of them before going on to report their impression of the person. This requirement would ostensibly force the subjects to attend about equally to each descriptive item; therefore—if the attention explanation holds—the obtained reduction in the primacy effect would have been expected.

Context Effects in Impression Formation

It is one thing to account for the fact that we easily and promptly form impressions of oth-

Box 170

First Come, First Served

A number of studies of the effects of primacy and recency upon the process of forming impressions of persons has been reported by A. S. Luchins, a social psychologist. In one of these studies, a group of judges (the E-I group) was first given a description of a hypothetical young man who was rather extroverted (the E description); then some additional material indicated an introverted side to the same person (the I description). A second group, the I-E group, was given the identical descriptive material, but in reverse order: first the I description, then the E description.

E Description

"Jim left the house to get some stationery. He walked out into the sun-filled street with two of his friends, basking in the sun as he walked. Jim entered the stationery store, which was full of people. Jim talked with an acquaintance while he waited for the clerk to catch his eye. On his way out, he stopped to chat with a school friend who was just coming into the store. Leaving the store, he walked toward school. On his way out he met the girl to whom he had been introduced the night before. They talked for a short while, and then Jim left for school."

I Description

"After school Jim left the classroom alone. Leaving the school, he started on his long walk home. The street was brilliantly filled with sunshine. Jim walked down the street on the shady side. Coming down the street toward him, he saw the pretty girl whom he had met on the previous evening. Jim crossed the street and entered a candy store. The store was crowded with students, and he noticed a few familiar faces. Jim waited quietly until the counterman caught his eye and then gave his order. Taking a drink, he sat down at a side table. When he had finished the drink he went home."

Following their exposure to this information about Jim, members of each of the groups wrote personality sketches giving their impressions of Jim and predicting his behavior in a variety of social situations. These paragraphs were examined for the number of extroverted and introverted characteristics attributed to Jim by each judge, then scored as predominantly extroverted, predominantly introverted, or approximately balanced. The table clearly indicates a primacy effect, that is, the greater influence of the description first presented upon the impressions formed.

PERSONALITY SKETCH PREDOMINANTLY	PERCENTAGES OF GROUPS	
	Group E-I	*Group I-E*
Extroverted	52	34
Introverted	36	56

The E-I group typically characterized Jim as sociable, friendly, outgoing, popular, likable, and happy; the I-E group typically described him as shy, reserved, quiet, lonely, unpopular, and unfriendly. The E-I group tended to predict that he would display outgoing social behavior, that he would accept an invitation to a party, that he would stop and talk with acquaintances. The I-E group tended to predict that Jim would be withdrawn in these situations.

The two groups seem to be describing two different persons, yet they had been presented with identical descriptive material, except for the sequence. First impressions do seem to carry greater weight, at least under these experimental conditions.

A. S. LUCHINS. 1957. Primacy-Recency in Impression Formation, in C. I. Hovland, *et al.*, eds., *The Order of Presentation in Persuasion*, Vol. I (New Haven: Yale University Press).

ers, often unified ones, on the basis of sparse stimuli, and that these impressions reflect the sequence in which the informational stimuli have been supplied. It is quite another matter—and, at first glance, a more difficult one—to account for the *content* of the material that we invent to fill in the skeletal stimulus pattern in order to obtain a rounded impression. To some extent, the nature of the invented content is determined by the perceiver's personality needs and traits and by the social role of the stimulus person—at least, as it is perceived by the one who judges. These influences we shall treat later on. We shall here consider another important factor in this process: the contexts of judgment in which impressions are formed. These contexts constitute larger and quite stable systems within which person perceptions take place and therefore necessarily affect the resulting impression. (The part-whole principle of perceptual organization [p. 160] is in evidence here.)

Implicit Personality Theory One factor that determines the content we tend to select (in order to fill in a sketchy impression) is our general notion of "what goes with what" in people. This notion in fact constitutes a private theory of personality that each of us has and that determines, to a considerable extent, how we judge others. This private theory is almost never stated or examined and is therefore referred to by psychologists as an "implicit theory of personality." When we know something (but not everything) about another person and attempt to come up with a full and rounded impression of him, we draw the "missing" material from our own implicit theory of personality. For example, if we are told that the stimulus person is physically attractive, warm, and socially at ease, some of us are very likely to infer such "missing" characteristics as "well-liked" and "popular." In short, our implicit personality theory may tell us that "all people who are physically attractive, warm, and socially at ease are also well liked and popular."

Box 171, p. 802, demonstrates that only a single word is sometimes sufficient to evoke a "theory of personality," affecting both the judges' perception and behavior.

To a considerable extent, many of us hold pretty much the same implicit theory of personality, a fact especially true of people who share the same general culture, and largely because certain traits do, in fact, almost always go along with certain other traits in the real world, at least for members of the society with which we are familiar. Our implicit theories therefore tend to portray the actual state of affairs in personality organization *among the kind of people we know*. But, when we are confronted with persons who are not—or who we believe are not—part of our own, known group, we find ourselves in a circumstance in which our customary notions as to "what goes with what" are not applicable. Under these circumstances we fall back on a set of *stereotypes*.

Stereotyping Persons People are almost never perceived as isolated individuals. We perceive them as members of this or that aggregate—as "our kind" or as "not our kind," as Protestants or Catholics, as Republicans or Democrats, as Russians or Englishmen, as "straight" or "hippie." And, when we see a person as a member of a group, our perception of his personality is influenced by what we believe about his group. In the extreme case we really fail to perceive the person; we see only his group label, then proceed to reel off our well-practiced judgment of the group. For not only do we have implicit *personality* theories; we also have well-formulated, implicit *group-personality* theories. We have, in other words, *group stereotypes*. As long as we fail to perceive the true characteristics of the person and in some way distort or eliminate evidence that would challenge our stereotyped image of him, there is no need to modify our implicit group-personality theories. To illustrate: Suppose you believe that the leaders of a certain foreign

Box 171

First Impressions
Make a Difference

To study the effect of a single initial piece of information about a person on the manner in which the later impressions of him to develop, H. H. Kelley performed the following experiment at the Massachusetts Institute of Technology.

Appearing before three sections comprising fifty-five students of a course entitled Economics 70, Kelley announced:

"Your regular instructor is out of town today, and since we of Economics 70 are interested in the general problem of how various classes react to different instructors, we're going to have an instructor today you've never had before. . . . Then, at the end of the period, I want you to fill out some forms about him. In order to give you some idea of what he's like, we've had a person who knows him write up a little biographical note about him."

He then passed out mimeographed sheets. One half of the students in each section received a description that included the following sentence: "People who know him consider him to be a rather cold person, industrious, critical, practical and determined." The other half of the students found the following sentence: "People who know him consider him to be a rather warm person, industrious, critical, practical and determined."

The "guest lecturer" then entered the room and led a twenty-minute discussion. Records were kept of which students participated in the discussion. After the "guest lecturer" left, the students were asked to write a description of him, and to rate him on fifteen different attributes. The ratings given by the two halves of the class differed significantly on a number of dimensions, despite the fact that they had all observed the very same man in the very same performance. Among the differences were the following: The students who had received the "warm" description tended to rate the lecturer as considerate of others, informal, sociable, popular, humorous. The students who had received the "cold" description rated him as self-centered, formal, unsociable, unpopular, humorless. It was also found that 56 per cent of the students receiving the "warm" description participated in the class discussion, whereas only 32 per cent of students who received the "cold" description participated.

It seems clear that initially perceiving the instructor as "warm" or as "cold" called into play an implicit theory in each judge as to what traits are usually associated with one or the other of these characteristics. This process, in turn, had a marked effect on the subsequent organization of the whole impression of the instructor and even tended to influence the behavior of the perceiver toward him.

Of course, not every initial piece of information can exercise such a strong directive force on the developing impression of a person—as shown by Asch's studies of the impressions of fictitious persons formed on the basis of lists of adjectives read to the subjects. He found that, though "warm" versus "cold" produced large differences in total impressions, adjectives like "polite" and "blunt" produced much smaller differential effects. The explanation may be that the latter terms refer to a less central dimension of personality.

H. H. KELLEY. 1950. The Warm-Cold Variable in First Impressions of Persons, *J. Personal.*, 18, 431–9.
S. E. ASCH. 1952. *Social Psychology* (Englewood Cliffs, N.J.: Prentice-Hall).

nation have aggressive and warlike designs against the world, and suppose that you listen to one of their diplomats on the podium of the United Nations, appealing for peace and good will. Under these conditions you will probably "perceive" all kinds of indications of insincerity in his speech, like "cynical smiles" and "sneering tones." You will interpret what you hear as "diplomatic doubletalk," and your original perception of him as an aggressive, warlike person will thus remain unchanged. An external stimulus pattern (his appeal for peace and good will) that is inconsistent with a well-established stereotype has thus been absorbed so as to permit a constant perception of the diplomat to remain. Our success in maintaining our stereotype seems to illustrate (at least by analogy) the law of perceptual constancy (see Box 172, p. 804).

Sometimes, when we cannot "reinterpret away" data that are inconsistent with our stereotype, we adopt a different strategy—one that is reminiscent of another perceptual principle: Changes in the external stimulus pattern may bring about a perceptual separation of the parts of the field into isolated fragments rather than a change in the attributes of the major structure (see p. 171). Suppose that you firmly believe that Englishmen are insufferable snobs, and suppose that you meet an Englishman who is as democratic and "homespun" as one might wish. It is highly probable that you will set this Englishman apart as an "exception" —an "exception that proves the rule"—and your very strong percept of Englishmen in general will remain unaltered. By reorganizing your perceptual field so as to "break off" into an isolated fragment the subsystem of this particular Englishman, you will have absorbed a change in the stimulus field so as to bring about minimal change to the structured whole.

The phenomena of assimilation and contrast (p. 151) present yet other analogies for the distortion of our perception of an individual in such a way as to preserve our stereotypes. For example, many Americans believe that the Chinese are "inscrutable." When meeting a shy

and somewhat bewildered Chinese, we may therefore perceive *him* as "mysterious and inscrutable." Here we have an instance of the perceived attributes of the individual being affected by his group membership in the direction of *assimilation*—shyness becomes "inscrutability." In another example, some Americans believe that Negroes are unintelligent. When such Americans meet a Negro of obvious intellectual achievement, they may tend to *overestimate* his intellectual capacity and see him as an exceptionally bright person. Here we have an instance of the perceived attributes of the individual being affected by his group membership in the direction of *contrast*.

Because these various principles work so well to "protect" and conserve our stereotypes, a direct confrontation between our stereotyped view of a group and our view of individual human personality is rare. In fact, as we have seen, these two views work well together as long as misperception is possible. "Shyness" thus becomes "inscrutability," but, once this distortion has taken place, the characteristic of "mystery" is added quite in line with our usual assumptions about which traits are associated with one another. In short, our implicit theory of personality helps to "fill in" the quite skeletal impressions that go along with common group stereotypes, impressions that we usually find adequate until we come face to face with a flesh-and-blood member of the group. Then we are seized with the need to round out our impression in order to cope with the fact that a "whole" person is before us and must be perceptually organized.

Halo Effect

The so-called *halo effect* in person perception generally refers to the fact that the favorableness (or unfavorableness) of one's first impression of another very often leads us to attribute to him all manner of good (or bad) traits. It is as if we tended to make first a broad *evaluative* judgment about a social object and then a

Box 172

How Not to See a Factory Worker as Intelligent

The various ways in which a pre-existing stereotype in the perception of a person can be maintained despite contradictory information is well demonstrated in a study performed by M. Haire and W. F. Grunes at the University of California. They presented two groups of subjects (179 students in the introductory psychology course) with the following terms descriptive of "a certain working-man":

Group I Works in a factory; reads a newspaper; goes to movies; average height; cracks jokes; strong; active.

Group II Works in a factory; reads a newspaper; goes to movies; average height; cracks jokes; intelligent; strong; active.

The subjects were then asked to write a paragraph describing the sort of person they thought this worker was. Subjects in Group II experienced greater difficulty than did those in Group I in forming a unified impression of the person because of the term "intelligent." This term was, for many of the students, inconsistent with their stereotype of factory workers. Most of them, however, through various forms of cognitive suppression and distortion, were able to maintain their stereotype unimpaired. Among these forms were the following:

1. *Denial of the existence of the disturbing element.* "He is intelligent, but not too much so, since he works in a factory."
2. *Placing the disturbing element in a context so as to render it harmless to the original stereotype.* "He is intelligent, but doesn't possess the initiative to rise above his group."
3. *Recognizing the incongruity, but maintaining the original stereotype anyway.* "The traits seem to be conflicting . . . most factory workers I have heard about aren't too intelligent."

M. HAIRE and W. F. GRUNES. 1950. Perceptual Defenses: Processes Protecting an Original Perception of Another Personality, *Hum. Relat.*, 3, 403–12.

"halo" of specific traits compatible with that single, organizing judgment around it. (The data reported in Box 169, p. 797, to some extent illustrate this phenomenon; the warm-cold dimension is a highly evaluative one and probably for that very reason proved to be so dominant a factor.) The halo effect is quite common in our everyday social perception, extending to groups, institutions, and even abstract concepts. The term "communist" generates a whole host of evaluative adjectives, whether it is applied to a person, to a political party, or to an ideology. In a sense, the halo effect can be regarded as an instance of stereotyping because it involves a simplification of the world into two groups, the "good guys"

and the "bad guys." Once that assignment is made, our implicit theories take over—in this case our notions as to what are good and bad characteristics—and thus a full and rounded impression of a paragon or of a devil is easily generated.

Social Factors and Person Perception

So far we have spoken of influences inherent in the organizational properties of the social stimulus pattern, like sequence of information, and of broad context effects arising from implicit personality theories and stereotyping. There is, however, an additional set of factors, arising from social and interpersonal factors operating in the impression-forming situation, that are also quite powerful influences. We shall consider a few instances of this type.

Effect of Social Function

Part of what determines how we go about organizing an impression based upon only partial information is what we intend to do with that impression. A study by Cohen (1961) illustrates this point. Working with college students, he presented a list of contradictory traits—for example, both "ruthless" and "generous" were included—from which they were to form an impression of a person. Half the subjects were told that they were later to communicate their impressions based on these traits to other people. The other half were requested to attend to the facts but were informed that later they would be receiving further information from other people. The first group had thus been assigned the social function of transmitting information, the second of receiving it. Under these circumstances, the "communicators" tended to form impressions that conveyed either a *consistently good* or a *consistently bad* picture of the person. The "receivers," on the other hand, formed impressions that attempted to integrate the contradictory traits into a more complex portrait.

These results may be interpreted as indicating that the "communicators" were faced with the need to make up their minds about the social object being described and to do so in a way that would make for efficient transmission of their impressions to others. A clear-cut, even if biased, message satisfied that function best. The "receivers" were under no such pressure, and in fact were implicitly invited to defer final judgment until all the data were in. They could afford the "luxury" of complex and comprehensive impressions, and, what is more, this kind of organization was best suited to accommodating new and still unknown information because it cast the widest net.

Effect of Interpersonal Attitude

We tend to form favorable impressions of people who we believe like us. There is abundant evidence to support this understandable conclusion, but the story can become more complex. Although flattery, particularly if it is subtle, works on most of us, it is by no means a sure-fire social technique. For example, Dickoff (1961) has shown that favorable evaluations from persons who we know expect favors from us are not very effective in leading us to like them. Furthermore, we even tend to prefer accuracy to flattery. Newcomb (1956) found that subjects tended to believe that people whom they liked, more than other acquaintances, perceived their "bad side," specifically those undesirable traits they admitted having.

A further qualification is introduced in an experiment by Aronson and Linder (1965). They arranged for female subjects to overhear "accidentally" evaluative remarks made about them by another girl (actually, an accomplice of the experimenter) on seven different occasions in the course of an experiment that ostensibly dealt with a problem in verbal learning. At the conclusion of the experiment, the subjects reported their impressions of the accomplice, whom they still assumed to be "just another subject." Aronson and Linder predicted that, although the favorableness of the overheard remarks would affect the favorableness of the reported impression, any *change* in the accomplice's evaluation over the seven occasions would also be a significant factor. Specifically, they expected that girls who had overheard remarks indicating increasingly favorable attitudes toward them during the course of the experiment would be more positively inclined toward the "other subject" than would those who had had the opportunity to hear consistently complimentary remarks. Conversely, overhearing increasingly unfavorable remarks would cause the subjects to like the other person even less than if the comments

Box 173

The Perceptive Psychologist

The ability to judge others accurately is a satisfying and certainly an adaptive skill. Most of us would like to possess more of it than our experiences show us that we do, and some people turn to the study of psychology at least partially in order to "understand people" better. Does this type of training work? This is the question asked by Johan Kremers, a Dutch psychologist at the University of Nijmegen.

Six groups of undergraduate and graduate students majoring in psychology, classics, and the natural sciences were used as judges. These judges predicted how a stimulus person would act in twenty-five different situations on the sole basis of observing him present his views in a ten-minute speech on "the place of labor in life." An accuracy score was computed for each judge by counting the number of his predictions that agreed with the "true" responses.

The stimulus person and the twenty-five to-be-judged situations had been selected through earlier intensive work. Six individuals who had volunteered to serve as the stimulus person filled out a questionnaire (the same one on several different occasions one month apart) that required them to describe their typical behavior in a large number of real-life situations. For example:

1. You are attending a lecture; the audience consists of more than 30 people. You do not agree with the speaker:
   a. Do you stand up and tell him so?
   b. Do you remain silent during the lecture and communicate your objections to your neighbors afterward?

The volunteer who showed greatest consistency over time in his questionnaire replies was chosen to serve as the stimulus person, and only those situations in which his replies were *unanimously* confirmed by a number of close acquaintances were later submitted to the student judges.

The "true" responses were thus indeed impressively documented, so that the students' accuracy scores can confidently be regarded as a measure of their ability to predict at least one other person's behavior. The average numbers of correct predictions for the six groups were as follows:

	Psychology	*Classics*	*Natural Science*
Undergraduates	14.7	13.3	14.7
Graduates	15.7	14.6	14.1

There are no significant differences among these values, and the very slight superiority of psychology students, over all, can best be regarded as a chance fluctuation. Studying psychology does not offer a royal road to a greater understanding of people, at least not in the terms of this experiment. It is too much to ask, however, for a successful prediction of specific bits of behavior from the highly limited and probably very atypical data afforded by a ten-minute public oration on a rather abstract topic. Perhaps when psychologists learn much more about human behavior, their tutelage may provide an advantage in even this kind of task, but it is doubtful. This pessimism should be no cause for despair or alarm, however, because prediction of this sort is more parlor trick than science. What psychology as a scientific pursuit does intend is the discovery of general laws relating man's experience and behavior to his biological endowments, his past learning, and his social environments. In this search, hopefully, the psychologist—and his students—are a bit ahead.

J. KREMERS. 1960. *Scientific Psychology and Naïve Psychology* (Nijmegen: Janssen). Table adapted by permission.

had been consistently uncomplimentary. The results tend to confirm all predictions. The groups and their average ratings of liking the "other subjects" (a higher value denotes greater liking) are increasingly favorable 7.7, consistently favorable 6.4, consistently unfavorable 2.5, increasingly unfavorable 0.9. Hell hath no fury like a woman once loved, then scorned.

Actual social interaction thus clearly influences person perception. So does only *anticipated* interpersonal contact. Darley and Berscheid (1967) found that college students, when asked to evaluate two unknown persons on the basis of equally favorable partial information, formed distinctly more positive impressions of the one whom they were told they would soon meet and work with in a later experimental session.

There are many more interpersonal influences upon social perception, but the few we have discussed should carry the message: The impressions we form of other persons are often highly complex resultants of interpersonal forces interacting with one another. Add to this observation the easily realized fact that the kinds of people we are—with our enduring individual needs, feelings, and desires—also must join in this interaction. The total effect is one of a vastly complicated problem, one well deserving of the research interest that it continues to attract.

But to seek understanding of how we form impressions of persons and other social stimuli is but one facet of a much broader problem. The question of accuracy alone in social perception raises many questions. How accurate are our impressions? What characteristics make for good judges—and for easily judgeable social stimuli? Do traits differ in how accurately they can be assessed at first impression? Can we be trained to be more accurate judges (see Box 173, p. 806)? These and many more questions have interested and will continue to interest the student of human behavior.

Glossary

halo effect The tendency, in impression formation, to be influenced by one's general evaluation of the other person and therefore to attribute to him additional characteristics arising from that evaluation.

primacy effect The tendency, in impression formation, for the first-received information about another person to dominate the judge's subsequent handling of additional information and thus his resulting organized impression. Under certain circumstances this tendency can be overcome so that the most recently received information becomes predominant.

stereotype The social perception of an individual in terms of his group membership rather than of his actual personal attributes. Such perceptions are rarely accurate for the individual, and they may or may not be valid for the group as a whole. Once formed, stereotyped impressions are extremely resistant to change.

social attitudes

overview / Attitudes are fundamental determinants of our perception of and action toward all aspects of our social environment. Attitudes, which can be quantified by attitude scales, involve a complex organization of evaluative beliefs, feelings, and tendencies toward certain actions. There are two main classes of contributors to the formation of attitudes: influences from the social group of which one is a member and a variety of personality factors. Among the latter is the tendency of a person to feel favorably toward rewarding social objects and negatively toward frustrating or punishing ones. Attitudes also serve to defend and enhance one's self-esteem and, in general, to make sense of and help adjust to the social environment.

Attitudes are quite persistent, tending to ensure their stability in many ways. They can, however, be modified—even abandoned or reversed—under the impact of a number of factors. The characteristics of the communicator attempting to induce attitude change is important, as is the nature of his argument in relation to the currently held attitude. Also effective is a change in the individual's group affiliation, a factor sufficiently powerful to bring about major attitudinal revisions. Enforced exposure to the social object of a given negative attitude, however, is not so influential and may even backfire; the attitude may be not only maintained but also reinforced.

Several psychological factors contribute to the persistence of attitudes and their resistance to change. The major sources of this resistance are the lack of everyday relevance of many attitudes, the pressures from one's social group to maintain a given attitude, and an attitude's frequently central role in the maintenance of personal equilibrium. All these influences lead the person to avoid new and contrary information and to ignore and forget it if it is imposed.

For the social psychologist, the concept of *attitude* is of sovereign importance. Our attitudes shape our perceptions and judgments of other persons; they influence what we learn and remember; they help to govern our political, economic, religious, and other social actions.

A study by Lambert, *et al.* (1960), illustrates the influence of attitude on judgments of other persons. This study was carried out in Montreal, a community marked by a French-English schism as deep as the North-South schism in the United States. The subjects listened to recorded French and English readings of the same prose passage. They were told to disregard language and to concentrate on voice and personality in making their personality judgments of the speakers. The subjects were not told that the recordings were made by bilingual speakers, each of whom read both the French and English versions.

Both the English-Canadian and the French-Canadian subjects evaluated the "English speakers" more favorably than the "French speakers" on such traits as height, good looks, intelligence, dependability, ambition, and character. Apparently the French-Canadians had taken over the attitudes of the English-Canadians in regarding the Englishmen as superior. This attitude then influenced their judgment of the speakers' personalities.

Attitudes influence judgments. Do they also influence learning and memory? Jones and Kohler (1958) examined "the proposition that subjects who hold to one set of beliefs learn plausible statements in favor of those beliefs and implausible statements opposing them better than they learn implausible-favoring or plausible-opposing statements."

The subjects were white college students classified as prosegregationists, antisegregationists, and neutrals on the basis of their scores on an attitude scale. All subjects were given twelve statements, printed on individual cards, to read aloud. Three of the statements were plausible prosegregation arguments. For ex-ample, "Southerners will have to pay the price of lowered scholastic standards if they yield to the pressures to integrate their schools." Three were implausible prosegregation arguments. For example, "If Negroes and whites were meant to live together, they never would have been separated at the beginning of history." Three of the statements were plausible antisegregationist arguments. For example, "The present inferior condition of the Negro is the result of long and effective suppression by the Southern whites." Three of the statements were implausible antisegregation arguments. For example, "The real reason why most Southern whites oppose integration is the realization that the Negro is more capable than they are." After all twelve statements had been read, the subject was asked to reproduce as many as he could. This procedure was repeated five times.

The results are given in Figure 49.1. The hypothesis of the study is convincingly supported. Both the antisegregationists and the prosegregationists showed better learning for plausible statements compatible with their attitudes and for implausible statements opposing their attitudes. These findings suggest that we defend our attitudes by bolstering them with sound supporting arguments and by making the opposing point of view appear weak and irrational.

Campbell and his associates (1960) have studied the role of attitudes in determining political action. Six attitudes were identified that seemed most clearly relevant to the issues in the election of 1956. A representative sample of American adults was interviewed before the election to secure measures of the six attitudes. In addition, the subjects were asked to indicate how they intended to vote in the forthcoming election. After the election, a second interview was conducted to ascertain how the subjects had actually voted.

The most compelling evidence of the power of political attitudes to determine the vote is furnished by comparing the predictive capacity of the six attitudes with the subjects' own pre-

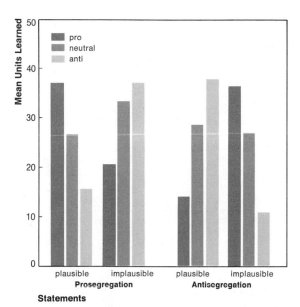

Figure 49.1. Differences in learning plausible and implausible statements of attitudes toward segregation, by groups differing in initial attitudes. Persons holding definite attitudes on the subject, either pro or con, best learn plausible statements supporting and implausible statements that favor the opposing points of view.
E. E. Jones and R. Köhler, "The Effects of Plausibility on the Learning of Controversial Statements," *Journal of Abnormal Social Psychology*, 57, 315–20; Copyright 1958 by the American Psychological Association, Inc.; adapted by permission.

election predictions of their voting intentions. The set of six partisan attitudes correctly predicted a larger percentage of the actual votes than the voters themselves were able to predict correctly.

The Nature and Measurement of Attitudes

In order to make use of the concept of attitude in understanding and predicting behavior, we must have a way of *measuring* attitudes, that is, of assigning to each individual a numerical score that indicates where he falls on the particular attitude dimension. One of the most widely used measuring devices is the *attitude scale*.

To facilitate and make concrete our discussion of attitudes and their measurement, it will be helpful if you first take the following attitude scale—a classical scale constructed many years ago by Thurstone and Chave (1929).

"Check (√) every statement below that expresses your attitude toward the church, that is, if you agree with the statement place a check mark in front of it:

1. I think the teaching of the church is altogether too superficial to have much social significance. (8.3)
2. I feel the church services give me inspiration and help me live up to my best during the following week. (1.7)
3. I think the church keeps business and politics up to a higher standard than they would otherwise tend to maintain. (2.6)
4. I find the services of the church both restful and inspiring. (2.3)
5. When I go to church I enjoy a fine ritual service with good music. (4.0)
6. I believe in what the church teaches but with mental reservations. (4.5)
7. I do not receive any benefit from attending church services, but I think it helps some people. (5.7)
8. I believe in religion but I seldom go to church. (5.4)
9. I am careless about religion and church relationships but I would not like to see my attitude become general. (4.7)
10. I regard the church as a static, crystallized institution and as such it is unwholesome and detrimental to society. (10.5)
11. I believe church membership is almost essential to living life at its best. (1.5)
12. I do not understand the dogmas or creeds of the church, but I find that the church helps me to be more honest and creditable. (3.1)
13. The paternal and benevolent attitude of the church is quite distasteful to me. (8.2)
14. I feel that church attendance is a fair index of the nation's morality. (2.6)
15. Sometimes I feel that the church and religion are necessary and sometimes I doubt it. (5.6)
16. I believe the church is fundamentally sound but some of its adherents have given it a bad name. (3.9)
17. I think the church is a parasite on society. (11.0)
18. I feel the need for religion but do not find what I want in any one church. (6.1)

19. I think too much money is being spent on the church for the benefit that is being derived. (7.5)
20. I believe in the church and its teachings because I have been accustomed to them since I was a child. (4.0)
21. I think the church is hundreds of years behind the times and cannot make a dent on modern life. (9.5)
22. I believe the church has grown up with the primary purpose of perpetuating the spirit and teachings of Jesus and deserves loyal support. (1.0)
23. I feel the church perpetuates the values which man puts highest in his philosophy of life. (0.8)
24. I feel I can worship God better out of doors than in the church and I get more inspiration there. (6.9)
25. My experience is that the church is hopelessly out of date. (9.1)
26. I feel the church is petty, always quarreling over matters that have no interest or importance. (8.6)
27. I do not believe in any brand of religion or in any particular church but I have never given the subject serious thought. (5.9)
28. I respect any church-member's beliefs but I think it is all "bunk." (8.8)
29. I enjoy my church because there is a spirit of friendliness there. (3.3)
30. I think the country would be better off if the churches were closed and the ministers set to some useful work. (10.5)
31. I believe the church is the greatest institution in America today. (0.2)
32. I believe in sincerity and goodness without any church ceremonies. (6.7)
33. I believe the church is the greatest influence for good government and right living. (0.4)
34. I think the organized church is an enemy of science and truth. (10.7)
35. I believe the church is losing ground as education advances. (7.4)
36. The churches may be doing good and useful work but they do not interest me. (5.9)
37. I think the church is a hindrance to religion for it still depends upon magic, superstition, and myth. (9.6)
38. The church is needed to develop religion, which has always been concerned with man's deepest feelings and greatest values. (1.4)
39. I believe the churches are too much divided by factions and denominations to be a strong force for righteousness. (7.2)
40. The church represents shallowness, hypocrisy, and prejudice. (10.4)

41. I think the church seeks to impose a lot of worn-out dogmas and medieval superstitions. (9.2)
42. I think the church allows denominational differences to appear larger than true religion. (7.2)
43. I like the ceremonies of my church but do not miss them much when I stay away. (5.1)
44. I believe the church is a powerful agency for promoting both individual and social righteousness. (1.2)
45. I like to go to church for I get something worthwhile to think about and it keeps my mind filled with right thoughts. (2.2)"

Reprinted from *The Measurement of Attitude* by L. Thurstone and E. Chave by permission of the University of Chicago Press; copyright 1929 by the University of Chicago.

You will notice that each statement is followed by a numerical value in parentheses. It is the *scale value* of that statement. The scale value was originally determined by having a large group of judges decide where on an eleven-point continuum the statement falls. For example, a scale value of 10.5 would mean that the consensus of the judges was that agreement with this statement would indicate an extreme antichurch attitude; a scale value of 1.2 would indicate an extreme prochurch attitude. You can now obtain your attitude score. First, arrange in rank order of their scale values those statements with which you agree. Your final score is the scale value of the middle statement, the statement below which one-half the statements lie and above which one-half the statements lie. For example, if you agreed with five statements with scale values of 1.5, 2.6, 4.0, 5.4, and 6.7, your score is the scale value of the middle statement, or 4.0. If you agreed with an even number of statements, your score is the midpoint of the scale distance between the two statements that bracket the median. For example, if you agreed with four statements with scale values of 1.5, 2.6, 4.0, and 5.4, your score is

$$\frac{4.0 + 2.6}{2} = 3.3.$$

You may interpret your score on the Thurstone and Chave attitude scale by determining where is falls on an eleven-point continuum. A score of 1 means extremely favorable; a score of 11 means extremely unfavorable. A score of 4 defines an attitude somewhat on the favorable side of neutrality; a score of 8 defines an attitude somewhat on the unfavorable side of neutrality. Your score thus represents the central tendency of your disposition to favor or oppose the church.

Note how we derived a measure of your attitude toward the church. Our raw data consist of a sample of your agreements and disagreements with certain statements about it. From this pattern we *inferred* an underlying disposition that we call "attitude." An attitude is not itself directly observable.

Note that every statement in the scale refers to the church. The church is the *social object* of the attitude. An attitude is always organized around an object; it always has a focus. The object may be anything that has psychological reality for the individual—the individual himself, a person, a group, a nation, or a political issue, a scientific theory, a commercial product.

Let us examine the content of some of the statements in the scale. Statement 34 reads, "I think the organized church is an enemy of science and truth," and statement 44 reads, I believe the church is a powerful agency for promoting both individual and social righteousness." In these illustrations the operative phrases are "I think," "I believe." Many of the items in the scale are intended, clearly, to provide indicators of the individual's evaluative *belief* about the church.

Statement 5 reads, "When I go to church I enjoy a fine ritual service with good music." Statement 43 reads, "I like the ceremonies of my church but do not miss them much when I stay away." The responses of the individual to these two statements enables us to say something about how he *feels* about the church. Assent would indicate liking, dissent disliking.

Finally, if a person agrees with statement 30, we would infer that he favors a specific form of restrictive *action* toward the church.

From this content analysis, we conclude that the concept of attitude refers to a complex inner disposition that consists of three components: an evaluative belief component, an affective (or feeling) component, and an action-orientation component. We can now summarize our discussion of the concept of attitude in a formal definition. An attitude is a complex organization of evaluative beliefs, emotional feelings, and action orientations focused upon an object, predisposing the individual to respond to the object in certain ways.

The Formation of Attitudes

Among the many determinants of the formation of attitudes two stand out as all-important: the group affiliations of the individual and the personality of the individual. An understanding of how attitudes are formed will set the stage for an examination of how attitudes, once formed, can be changed.

Group Influences in Attitude Formation

There is nothing as social as an individual's personal attitudes. Both the groups in which the individual holds membership and the groups to which he aspires to belong are important in shaping his attitudes.

In 1944, the Research Branch of the Information and Education Division of the United States Army carried out an investigation focused on the attitudes of new troops, some of whom were assigned to veteran divisions as replacements and others of whom were assigned to new, inexperienced divisions. Questionnaire surveys were conducted to measure attitude toward combat. Table 49.1. summarizes the results. Note that, in willingness for combat, the inexperienced replacements in veteran Division A are midway between troops in inexperienced divisions and the combat veterans of Division A. Green replacements seeking to affiliate themselves with the combat veterans of Division A adopted the veterans' negative attitude toward combat. Group influences have been at work.

Table 49.1.
Attitude of World War II Soldiers Toward Combat

	N	PER CENT INDICATING WILLINGNESS FOR COMBAT
Division A veterans	605	15
Division A replacements	427	28
Members of inexperienced divisions	9,850	48

S. A. Stouffer, *et al.*, *American Soldier: Combat and Its Aftermath;* copyright 1949 by Princeton University Press; adapted by permission.

The homogeneity of political attitudes and behavior among members of primary groups also suggests the operation of group influences in attitude formation. A postelection survey by Campbell, Gurin, and Miller (1954) revealed a remarkably high degree of uniformity in Presidential voting behavior, and presumably in political attitudes, among the members of primary groups. The data are given in Table 49.2. For example, when the respondents' friends voted for the Democratic candidate, 83 per cent of the respondents also voted Democratic; when the respondents' friends voted Republican, 84 per cent of the respondents also voted Republican. These results are similar to those found in other studies of group influences upon political attitudes and behavior.

Our discussion of the role of the group in attitude formation does *not* mean that the individual is passively molded by the group. For one thing, every individual affiliates with many groups, and among these groups there may be incongruent attitudes. Group influences are effective only insofar as the individual interprets them as useful to further his own ends. The influence of the group rests upon the utility of the group to the individual.

Personality Factors in Attitude Formation

The effect of group influences upon attitude development is to produce a relatively high uniformity of attitudes among the members of the

Table 49.2.
Relation Between 1952 Voting Behavior of the Individual and Members of His Primary Groups

Vote of Primary Group	How Respondent Voted (Per Cent)		
	REPUBLICANS	DEMOCRATS	OTHER
Spouses of married respondents			
Democratic	11	88	1
Republican	93	7	0
Families of unmarried respondents			
Democratic	20	79	1
Republican	91	8	1
Split	41	54	5
Friends of respondents			
Democratic	17	83	0
Republican	84	15	1
Split	47	50	3
Work associates of respondents			
Democratic	20	78	2
Republican	36	24	0
Split	55	43	2

A. Campbell, G. Gurin, and W. E. Miller, *The Voter Decides* (1954); adapted by permission of Harper & Row, Inc.

group. But in the midst of uniformity we also find diversity. A major factor making for diversity in attitudes, even within the tightest-knit groups, is the existence of personality differences among the individual members. The major functions that attitudes perform for the individual personality can be grouped into five categories according to their motivational basis.

The Instrumental Function In seeking to satisfy his needs, the individual develops favorable attitudes toward objects that satisfy his needs, or are seen as doing so, and unfavorable attitudes toward objects that thwart or punish him.

In a study by Lott and Lott (1960) children played an individual game in the company of fellow group members who were nonfriends. Each group was randomly assigned to conditions in which none, one, two, or all members were rewarded by winning the game and receiving the prize. At the end of the day, each child was asked to indicate his "best friends." The rewarded children chose as friends a significantly greater number of their fellow play-group members than did the unrewarded subjects. This immediate development of "friendship" attitudes toward the children with whom they happened to be associated in the satisfaction of winning the game is remarkable in view of the fact that their choices of "best friends" tested before the game session were based on prolonged interaction with classmates and had been found to be highly stable.

Self-Defensive Function As we have seen in Unit 46, self-defensive mechanisms operate by externalizing impulses unacceptable to the self, thus minimizing emotional conflict and anxiety. These mechanisms give rise to self-defensive attitudes. The formation of these self-defensive attitudes proceeds from within the individual; the objects to which they become attached are simply convenient targets for their expression.

The now classic study *The Authoritarian Personality*, by Adorno, Frenkel-Brunswik, Levinson, and Sanford (1950), was concerned with the over-all hypothesis that many of the political, economic, and social attitudes of an individual often form a broad and coherent pattern that expresses deep-lying self-defensive trends in his personality. Adorno and his colleagues concluded from their work that persons who hold prejudiced attitudes toward ethnic groups are characterized by a syndrome of personality traits that distinguishes them from unprejudiced persons. (Box 148, p. 704, describes the distinguishing traits in detail.)

The great volume of studies generated by this study has generally supported the concept of an authoritarian personality for whom prejudice serves important functions. We cite one supporting study. Williams (1964) and his associates carried out a field study of ethnic relations in a number of American communities during the years between 1948 and 1956. In one of the communities, "Hometown" (Elmira, New York), the sample of 529 white gentiles was separated

into an extreme group of bigots, an opposite group of tolerants, and an intermediate group. The bigots were those who reported they would find it *personally distasteful* to associate with Jews, Negroes, and Italian-Americans; who *disliked* these ethnic groups; and who endorsed *negative stereotypes* concerning foreigners, Roman Catholics, Negroes, and Jews. The tolerants did none of these things.

An authoritarian score was constructed for each person in the sample by counting the number of agreements with the following three items:

1. The most important thing to teach children is to obey every order their parents give without question, even if they think the parents are wrong. (This item presumably measures the authoritarian emphasis on adherence to discipline.)
2. Prison is too good for sex criminals: They should be publicly whipped or worse. (This item presumably measures extreme moral punitiveness coupled with anxiety about sexual impulses that characterize the authoritarian.)
3. I have to struggle for everything I get in life. (This item presumably measures the authoritarian tendency to view the world as threatening and constraining.)

The scores of the subjects on this three-item measure of authoritarianism can range from 0 (no agreements) to 3. The relationship between bigotry and authoritarianism is shown in Table 49.3. Note the remarkably large concentration of high scores among the bigots (59 per cent received scores of 3 or 2 and the almost complete

Table 49.3.
Relation Between Bigotry and Authoritarianism: Elmira, New York, Sample

AUTHORITARIAN SCORE		BIGOTS (N = 53)	INTERMEDIATE (N = 364)	TOLERANTS (N = 51)
High:	3	28%	7%	0%
	2	31	27	1
	1	26	36	63
Low:	0	15	30	36
		100%	100%	100%

R. M. Williams, Jr., *Strangers Next Door;* copyright © 1964; adapted by permission of Prentice-Hall.

absence of high scores among the tolerants (only 1 per cent received scores of 3 or 2).

Self-Expressive Function Many of the attitudes of the individual serve not to protect the self but to proclaim the self. These self-expressive attitudes express and define the sort of person the individual considers himself to be or aspires to be. The college student who conceives of himself as a political activist may develop a whole syndrome of attitudes—attitudes toward the university administration, the local city government, the faculty, the university curriculum, fraternity members, mode of dress, style of haircut, and so on—which serves to express his central values and confirm his self-identity as a political activist.

The Knowing Function People have a need to know and understand their worlds, and many of the attitudes of the individual serve the important function of helping him to comprehend his universe. Even prejudiced attitudes operate in the search for meaning. For example, the virulent anti-Semitism of Nazi Germany may be seen, in part, as an "understandable explanation" for Nazi Germans of the plight of post-World War I Germany. "Devil theories" have flourished throughout the ages as man flounders in his search for an understanding of his problems.

The Social-Adjustment Function Our attitudes can serve as "social entrance tickets" or "social exit passes." Our attitudes may facilitate and maintain our relationships with members of positively valued groups: They may increase our feelings of oneness with persons who are significant to us. Other attitudes—"rebel attitudes"—may be formed in response to our need to dissociate ourselves from or oppose still other groups or individuals. For example, the "hippie" son of a middle-class family who aspires to acceptance in the hippie community will tend to adopt values and attitudes toward material success, dress, and love that, on the

one hand, will serve as an entrance ticket to the hippie community and, on the other hand, will serve to emphasize his rejection of his middle-class background.

The Changing of Attitudes

Typically, attitude change comes about through receiving new information about the object that induces a change in the evaluative belief component. The change in the belief component, in turn, tends to bring about corresponding changes in the feeling and action-orientation components.

The individual may receive new information in various ways. He may read or listen to persuasive communications, he may observe the behavior of other people, he may talk with other people, he may undergo new, direct experiences with an object. Through any of these channels, he may gain new information that may change his beliefs about an object.

Persuasion and Attitude Change

Studies of the factors influencing the effectiveness of persuasive messages in bringing about attitude change can all be subsumed under Lasswell's classic formula of *"who* says *what* in which *channel* to *whom* with what *effect"* (Smith, *et. al.,* 1946).

The most thoroughly studied factors determining the effectiveness of persuasive communications are those connected with the identity of the communicator ("who") and with the nature of the message ("what"). We can summarize the results of many of these studies in a series of propositions.

The Communicator

1. *Communicators regarded by the audience as credible are more effective in inducing immediate change than are untrustworthy communicators* (Hovland & Weiss, 1951).

2. *The advantage of communicators high in credibility over untrustworthy communicators*

tends to disappear over time. In the Hovland and Weiss study it was found that the time trends were in an opposite direction for the high and low credibility communicators. In the group exposed to the trustworthy communicator, there was a decrease in agreement of about 50 per cent; in the group exposed to the untrustworthy communicator, acceptance of the position advocated tended to increase. This phenomenon has been called the "sleeper effect." This effect may result from the dissociation, with the passage of time, of source from content. People tend to remember what was said without spontaneously thinking about who said it.

3. *Communicators who are perceived as similar in their attitudes to the audience are more effective than communicators who are seen as dissimilar.* Anything that the communicator can do to lessen his audience's sense of dissimilarity from him will enhance his effectiveness. Weiss (1957) has shown, for example, that a persuasive attempt preceded by the expression of attitudes (irrelevant to the issue of persuasion) that are known to be similar to those of the audience increases the amount of change in positive attitudes toward the issue of persuasion. Every politician presents himself as a "man of the people" who shares with all Americans love of God and family.

The Message

1. *The acceptance of attitudes opposed by the audience will be promoted if the message is so designed that it evokes minimal counterargument in the audience.* Allyn and Festinger (1961) report a study in which a communicator recommended to an audience of teen-agers assembled for a school program that the minimum age for receiving a driver's license should be raised. Before hearing the message, half the subjects were told that the purpose of the program was to study the personality of the speaker. The remaining half of the subjects were told that the speaker "has stated his very strong opinion that teen-agers are a menace

on the roads and should be strictly controlled by effective new laws." The first group thus did not expect to hear a disagreeing persuasive communication. The results showed that the second group saw the speaker as more biased and were less influenced than the subjects who were not forewarned.

2. *The acceptance of attitudes opposed by the audience will be promoted if arguments containing material desirable to the audience are presented before the undesirable material.* McGuire (1957), who has reported a study that supports this proposition, suggests the following interpretation:

"It would seem that after receiving the earlier undesirable messages, the subject can be thought of as saying to himself, 'What this man says appears to be true, but I find it unpleasant and so I am not going to listen to him anymore.' The subject . . . who receives earlier desirable messages can be thought of as saying to himself, 'This man's comments are pleasant and worth listening to and so I shall pay close attention to him.' Thus he receives more of the source's later arguments and as a result is influenced by them . . . even with a presumably 'captive' audience, the device of selective self-exposure to information can operate."

3. *When the audience is opposed to the position advocated by the communicator, a communication that presents opposing arguments as well as arguments supporting the position at issue is generally more effective than a communication that presents supporting arguments only* (Hovland, *et al.*, 1949).

4. *If the audience, regardless of its initial position, will be exposed to later counterpropaganda (which presents opposing arguments), a two-sided presentation will be more effective than a one-sided presentation in creating sustained attitude change.* In a study by Lumsdaine and Janis (1953) subjects who were exposed to a two-sided communication were much more resistant to later counterpropaganda than were those who received a one-sided communication. The authors speculate that a person who has received a two-sided presentation "has been given an advance basis for ignoring or discount-

ing the opposing communication and, thus 'inoculated,' he will tend to retain the positive conclusion."

As every watcher of television knows all too uncomfortably, many propaganda messages threaten the individual with unfavorable or dangerous consequences unless he adapts and follows recommendations advocated by the propagandist to avert the danger. A trivial example: You will become a social isolate unless you use brand X mouthwash. The use of such threats or fear-arousing appeals raises the question of how much fear to arouse to secure maximum acceptance of the propagandist's recommendations. The experimental evidence does not permit an unequivocal answer to this question.

Janis and Terwilliger (1962) gave subjects an antismoking message that supported the conclusion that heavy smoking causes cancer and recommended that everyone should either stop smoking or cut down on it. One-half the subjects were given a low-threat version; the other half a high-threat version. The subjects were asked to express their thoughts and feelings after reading each paragraph in the communication. The main results: First, the mild-threat version produced more attitude change than did the strong-threat version; second, the high-threat group made many more statements explicitly rejecting arguments about the harmful effects of smoking, for example, "I don't believe that." The subjects in the high-threat group thus ran away, presumably to die another day.

Contradictory findings have been reported in two studies. Leventhal and Niles (1964) found that smokers who reported more fear of lung cancer showed greater agreement with the recommendations of a persuasive message. Berkowitz and Cottingham (1960) worked with the issue of the safety features of automobile seat belts. They found that a stronger fear appeal was more effective than a weaker fear appeal.

McGuire (1966) argues that these seemingly discrepant findings may be reconciled by taking into account the effect of the individual's initial level of concern with a problem upon his response to a fear appeal. He proposes that an individual with a high pre-existing level of concern may be rendered so anxious by a fear appeal that its effectiveness is reduced. Optimally, the strong fear appeal would be most effective for those persons with a low level of initial concern.

New Group Affiliations and Attitude Change

Attitude change may come with new group membership. The impact of new group memberships upon the attitudes of the individual is, of course, a resultant of both the nature of the groups and the nature of the individual. This point is convincingly brought out in Newcomb's classic Bennington College study (1943).

At the time of the study (1935–1939) Bennington College was new and geographically isolated. The students, for the most part, came from economically privileged, conservative families. The members of the faculty were predominantly liberal; they were deeply involved in the social issues of the period and felt that their sheltered students ought to face up to the realities of a "depression-torn America and a war-threatened world."

The general trend of attitude change in this college community was from conservatism as freshmen toward liberalism as upperclassmen. To illustrate: A straw vote of the students during the 1936 Presidential campaign revealed a substantial difference between the political preferences of the freshman and senior students. As Table 49.4. shows, 62 per cent of the freshmen and only 15 per cent of the upperclassmen voted for Landon, the Republican candidate. Roosevelt, the New Deal Democratic candidate, received only 29 per cent of the freshman vote but captured 54 per cent of the votes of the upperclassmen. The votes for the candidates of the American Socialist and Communist parties increased from 9 per cent among the freshmen to 30 per cent among the seniors. Table 49.4. reveals that the freshmen voted much as their

Table 49.4.
Preferences of Students and Parents for
Presidential Candidates in 1936 Campaign

	Freshmen		Sophomores		Juniors & Seniors	
	STU-DENTS	PAR-ENTS	STU-DENTS	PAR-ENTS	STU-DENTS	PAR-ENTS
Landon (*Republican*)	62	66	43	69	15	60
Roosevelt (*Democratic*)	29	26	42	22	54	35
Thomas, Browder (*Socialist, Communist*)	9	7	15	8	30	4

T. M. Newcomb, *Personality and Social Change;* copyright 1943; adapted by permission of Holt, Rinehart and Winston, Inc.

parents did, whereas the upperclassmen differed remarkably from their parents. Other data also showed a trend from freshman conservatism to senior liberalism. Attitudes toward nine specific social and economic issues were measured yearly during the four years of the study. The seniors were less conservative than the freshmen on all nine issues.

Such was the attitudinal trend in the Bennington College community, expressed in terms of average scores. This trend was not found in all students, however. Some students displayed the trend in heightened form; other students changed not at all; still others reversed the trend. Why did the observed changes occur in some students and fail to occur in others? In seeking an answer, Newcomb studied intensively nineteen conservative and twenty-four liberal seniors.

The liberal seniors were found to be strongly motivated to achieve independence from their families and to achieve status in the college community (at Bennington prestige was accorded liberal students). For these students liberal attitudes served the social-adjustment function. The following interview excerpt is illustrative:

"Of course, there's social pressure here to give up your conservatism. I'm glad of it, because for me this became the vehicle for achieving independence from my family. So changing my attitudes has gone

hand in hand with two very important things: establishing my own independence and at the same time becoming a part of the college organism."

The conservative seniors tended to reject the college community or to isolate themselves from it because of fear of disrupting their relationships with their families. The following interview excerpt shows that resistance to change among these students was a self-defensive process.

"I wanted to disagree with all the noisy liberals, but I was afraid and I couldn't. So I built up a wall inside me against what they said. I found I couldn't compete, so I decided to stick to my father's ideas. For at least two years I've been insulated against all college influences."

This excerpt points to one of the most potent sources of resistance to attitude change. Inability to sever a deep, established relationship with an early group makes it necessary for the individual to close himself off from new information.

Enforced Contact and Attitude Change

The pattern of racial segregation in America is gradually, painfully breaking down in both the South and the North. What may result from enforced contact between Negroes and whites on the job, in the school, in the neighborhood, in places of public accommodation?

One answer is supplied by Deutsch and Collins (1951) in their study of changes in attitudes toward Negroes among white housewives who lived in biracial housing projects. Two of these projects were integrated: Families were assigned apartments without regard to race. Negro and white families thus lived in relatively close physical proximity in the same apartment buildings. Two of the housing projects were segregated: Negro and white families were assigned to different buildings or to different areas in the projects.

After a period of residence in the biracial housing projects, a sample of white housewives drawn from the two integrated and the two

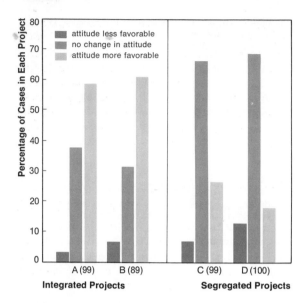

Figure 49.2. Attitude change among white housewives toward Negroes after residence in two types of biracial housing projects. The parentheses give the number of respondents in each of the four projects.
M. Deutsch and M. E. Collins, *Interracial Housing: A Psychological Evaluation of a Social Experiment* (1951); adapted by permission of the University of Minnesota Press.

segregated projects were interviewed to learn their attitudes toward Negroes. Figure 49.2. gives the results. Positive attitude change was far more frequent in the two integrated projects than in the two segregated ones (for further details on this study see Box 174, p. 821).

But enforced contact does not necessarily produce positive change in attitude toward the object. Enforced contact may sometimes produce negative change or leave the pre-existing attitude unaltered. Deutsch and Collins sum up their work and the related work of other investigators as follows:

"Prejudices are likely to be diminished when prejudiced persons are brought into situations which compel contacts between them and the objects of prejudice, provided:

1. that the behavior of the objects of prejudice is such as not to conform with the beliefs of the prejudiced. That is, the Negroes with whom the prejudiced person has contact are not 'lazy,' 'ignorant,' 'delinquent,' etc.

2. that the intimacy and amount of contact with objects of prejudice not conforming to the stereotypes of the prejudiced are such as to result in experiences which are sufficiently compelling to resist marked perceptual and memorial distortion.

3. that the contact takes place under conditions which make the nonconforming behavior seem relevant to the basis on which the objects of prejudice are grouped together. Thus, if a Negro attendant is seen to be clean and honest, there may be little effect on stereotypes if the perception of cleanliness and honesty is connected primarily with the requirements of the situation, with the classification of the individual as an attendant rather than as a Negro or Negro attendant.

4. that the prejudiced person has values or is exposed to social influences (e.g., democratic values or the social influences emanating from a policy of an official, public body) which would strongly conflict with the unabashed retention of unrationalized prejudices."

Personality and Enforced Contact The response of the individual to enforced contact will be influenced by the kind of person he is. A study by Mussen (1950) illustrates this point. He studied the effect of attendance in a racially integrated summer camp upon the attitudes of white boys toward the Negro. Measures of the boys' attitudes toward Negroes were taken before and after attendance. In addition, personality measures and data on adjustment to camp life were obtained.

Comparison of the before-and-after attitude scores revealed striking individual differences in attitude change. Twenty-four of the 106 white boys showed a significant drop in prejudice, but twenty-seven showed an increase.

Why? Mussen's data suggest that acceptance or rejection of the standards of the camp was a function of a boy's identification with the camp group. In turn, identification with the group was found to be related to enduring personality patterns.

Among the boys who increased in prejudice,

[handwritten in left margin: accepts them :: they have nice apartments not : they are human]

Box 174

Proximity and Prejudice

In a study of attitude change in biracial housing projects, psychologists M. Deutsch and M. E. Collins report the following excerpts from interviews with white housewives whose attitudes toward Negroes shifted in a favorable direction:

"I thought I was moving into the heart of Africa. . . . I had always heard a lot about how they were . . . they were dirty, drink a lot . . . were like savages. Living with them, my ideas have changed altogether. They're just people. . . . They're not any different.

I started to cry when my husband told me we were coming to live here. . . . I didn't want to come and live where there were so many colored people. I didn't want to bring my children up with colored people, but we had to come. . . . Well all that's changed. I've really come to like it. I see they're just as <u>human</u> as we are. <u>They have nice apartments</u>, they keep their children clean, and they're very friendly. I've come to like them a great deal. . . . I'd just as soon live near a colored person as a white, it makes no difference to me."

These excerpts illustrate the processes of attitude change that tended to take place. The intimate and frequent contact between white and Negro housewives in the integrated projects provided the white housewives with new information about Negroes that became incorporated in the belief component of their attitude toward Negroes. Corresponding shifts in the affective component followed.

M. DEUTSCH and M. E. COLLINS. 1951. *Interracial Housing: A Psychological Evaluation of a Social Experiment* (Minneapolis: University of Minnesota Press). Text material reprinted by permission.

Mussen found "great needs to defy authority, and strong aggressive feelings. However, they felt that the expression of aggression led to punishment, retaliation, restraint, and prohibition." A different personality pattern was found among the boys who decreased in prejudice. They "had relatively few aggressive needs and less feeling that punishment and retaliation follow the expression of aggression."

Resistance to Attitude Change

From our discussion of attitude change, the reader may have come to think that attitudes are highly labile, changing with docility as new and relevant information is presented. But, alas for the struggling educator or propagandist, the attitudes of men seem to be remarkably obdurate and refractory—at least as far as attitudes toward those large public issues that are of special interest to the social scientist are concerned.

Anchorage in Group Affiliations

Many persons reject new information or resist "thinking for themselves" because they cherish their groups and seek the approval of persons who are significant in their lives. Then, too, the anticipation of punishment for heterodoxy forces many a doubter to adhere to the "group line." Taking on attitudes that run counter to the group norms inevitably leads to the painful disruption of long-established and comfortable patterns of social relations. If the various groups with which the individual affiliates consistently support a particular position on an issue, the attitude of the individual toward that issue is highly unlikely to change even in the face of contradictory information. Indeed, the group affiliations of the individual may serve to stabilize his attitudes by providing him with informational and social support for them (see Box 175, p. 822).

Box 175

Husbands and Persistence
of Attitudes

In 1960 and 1961, Theodore M. Newcomb examined the political and economic attitudes of 139 of the 141 Bennington College students whom he had studied as undergraduates between 1935 and 1939. It will be recalled that Newcomb found that at Bennington College, during the period from 1935–1936 through 1938–1939, juniors and seniors were markedly less conservative than were freshmen in their attitudes toward many public issues of the time. Newcomb's interest in doing the follow-up study was to determine whether his students had maintained their relatively nonconservative attitudes twenty-odd years later or whether they had "regressed" to relatively conservative attitudes.

As the table shows, the degree of stability of attitudes over the interval of twenty-odd years is startling. Those individuals who upon graduation were in the least conservative quartile of the total group preferred John F. Kennedy to Richard M. Nixon by frequencies of 30 to 3; those in the next quartile, by 25 to 8. Twenty years after graduation, 83 per cent of the initially less conservative half of the group preferred Kennedy, whereas only 37 per cent of the initially more conservative half preferred him.

These findings suggest that the group as a whole is far less conservative twenty years after graduation from college than was to be expected in view of its socioeconomic status. Sixty per cent of the group expressed a preference for Kennedy. The percentage of Protestant women college students of the same socioeconomic status who in 1960 expresed a preference for Kennedy was only 28 per cent.

Why this remarkable persistence of nonconservative political attitudes? Newcomb concludes:

"If, therefore, I were to select a single factor that contributed most to these women's maintenance of nonconservative attitudes between the late 1930s and early 1960s, I think it would be the fact of selecting husbands of generally nonconservative stripe who helped to maintain for them an environment that was supportive of their existing attitudes."

T. M. NEWCOMB. 1963. Persistence and Regression of Changed Attitudes: Long Range Studies, *J. Soc. Issues*, 19, 3–14.

Political and Economic Progressivism Quartile	Nixon Preferred	Kennedy Preferred	Total
1. (least conservative)	3	30	33
2.	8	25	33
3.	18	13	31
4. (most conservative)	22	11	33
Total	51	79	130

Anchorage in Personality Structure

An attitude will tend to be resistant to change in direct proportion to the number and importance of the personality functions that it serves. If an attitude is perceived as directly serving important ends, it will be difficult to change that attitude—the individual's investment in it is simply too large to allow him to "liquidate" it. And the more important the functions an attitude serves, the more extreme it becomes and the more resistant to change. Tannenbaum (1956) found that the mean amount of attitude change induced by communications opposing the initial attitudes of his subjects was inversely proportional to the degree of extremeness of the initial attitude (see Figure 49.3.). Clearly, those subjects whose original attitudes were either extremely unfavorable (a score of 6) or extremely favorable (a score of 42) experienced the least amount of attitude change. As we move from both the extremely unfavorable and the extremely favorable ends of the valence continuum to the less extreme attitudes in the middle, the amount of attitude change is substantially greater.

Finally, attitudes that are self-protective are peculiarly obdurate to persuasion. If an individual uses an attitude to externalize unacceptable inner impulses or to allay his anxiety, he

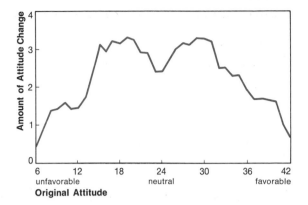

Figure 49.3. Amounts of attitude change produced by persuasive communications in subjects varying in favorableness of original attitude. Both favorable and unfavorable communications were used. Attitude changes in either direction were regarded as equivalent.
P. H. Tannenbaum, "Initial Attitudes Toward Source and Concept as Factors in Attitude Change Through Communication," *Public Opinion Quarterly*, 20 (1956), 412–25, adapted by permission of Princeton University Press.

will not readily give it up. Newcomb's "non-changers" were those subjects who were self-defensive in their personality structure. And Katz and Stotland (1959) have found that anti-Negro attitudes in highly self-defensive white college girls resist all influences designed to change these attitudes. These girls *need* the prop of prejudice.

Glossary

attitude An enduring system of positive or negative evaluations, feelings, and tendencies toward action with respect to a social object.

attitude scale A special case of the more general class of scales used in the measurement of personality. It consists of a large number of items, each designed to elicit an answer indicating a favorable or unfavorable disposition toward a specific object.

scale value A measure of the degree of favorableness of a statement in a Thurstone equal-appearing-interval scale. The scale value of a statement is the median of the frequency distribution of separate judgments of the item.

social object The target of a social attitude, upon which all its aspects are focused. The social object may be a single individual, a group of persons, a social institution, or even an abstract social concept (e.g., honesty or integration).

the experimental study of the individual and the group

overview / Human behavior almost inevitably takes place in a social context, so that other persons, directly or indirectly, influence most of our experiences and actions. Immediate group effects upon cognition are usually facilitating, that is, they stimulate thinking and enhance performance. They do so when the other persons present are merely passive spectators (the "audience effect"), as well as when they actively participate in a common task (the "coaction effect"). When engaged in such a group task, the individual tends to work for the group goal only if he will personally benefit from its attainment. Experimentally, this requirement is met in cooperatively organized groups in which the individual's reward depends solely upon the group's effectiveness. Individuals in such groups, in comparison with those working in competitively organized groups, typically develop higher morale and show greater productivity. However, comparisons of the problem-solving performance of groups working *as a unit* (as in "brainstorming") with individuals working alone have shown no consistent advantage for either strategy.

Group pressure generally exerts a powerful effect upon individual judgment, sufficient to influence the person to deny the evidence of his own senses. Individuals vary in their susceptibility to such pressure, however; the more intelligent, original, and psychologically mature subjects best withstand its effect. Individuals manifest their reaction to social pressure both by conforming to the positive expectations of others ("normative group influence") and by accepting information from them as reliable evidence about reality. In either case, conforming behavior may be uncritical and betrays a human tendency with disturbing ethical implications. Man's recent history attests to this danger.

It is a truism that the individual is born into a going society and lives out his life as a member of many groups. He is born into a family; he is educated in classes; he plays and fights in neighborhood "bunches," gangs, clubs, and teams; he worships in a congregation; he works with others. These groups make up the immediate social environment of the individual, and it is difficult to conceive of any human behavior that is not importantly influenced by one's social environment. In this sense, all behavior is "social" behavior, and, in turn, one's social groups become primary determinants of all our psychological functioning.

Group Influences

Viewed developmentally, group influences are fundamental in the transformation of the infant, who is socially a tiny barbarian, into a socialized (that is, civilized) adult. In this process, the family is of course the most relevant and powerful social group. Through his groups, the individual becomes able to cope with the myriad problems of living in a complex society. Finally, the group has certain important and unique effects on the behavior of the individual.

Effects of the Group on Cognition

We begin our examination of the effects of the group upon thinking by considering the oldest experimental problem in social psychology: *social facilitation*. Studies of social facilitation have been concerned with two problems: *audience effects* and *coaction effects*. The first problem concerns the effects of the presence of passive spectators upon the behavior of the individual. The second problem involves the effects upon the behavior of the individual of other persons actively and simultaneously engaged in the same activity.

Zajonc (1965) has recently reviewed the work on these problems, much of which was carried out in the 1930s. He proposes that the presence of others—either as passive spectators or as coactors—facilitates the performance of well-learned responses but impairs the learning of new responses. Zajonc is able to show how this proposition interprets and organizes a large number of separate studies of audience and coaction effects. One of these studies on audience effect, made during this period of early interest, found that subjects showed considerable improvement on such tasks as simple multiplication and association to familiar words—well-learned cognitive skills—when an audience was present (Dashiell, 1930). When required, however, to learn wholly new material—lists of nonsense syllables—subjects performing in the presence of several spectators, as compared to working alone, required more learning trials to master the lists and made many more errors in the course of the learning process.

Coaction experiments support the same general proposition. For example, F. H. Allport's (1920) pioneer experiment contrasted the performance on a variety of cognitive tasks of subjects who worked either in separate, isolated cubicles or around a common table. Those working alone did better than those working together in groups on a problem-solving test that required that they logically disprove certain classical philosophical arguments. This task called for a "new" response for the subjects, to say the least, and—as Zajonc suggests—is most effective in solitary conditions. On the other hand, the "working-in-group" subjects excelled in a number of tasks, again including multiplication and word association, both familiar to the subjects.

Zajonc draws a droll moral, advising the student:

". . . to study all alone, preferably in an isolated cubicle, and to arrange to take his examination in the company of many other students on stage, and in the presence of a large audience. The results of his examination would be beyond his wildest expectations, provided of course he had learned his material quite thoroughly."

Effects of the Group on Motivation

One very important question about the effects of the group upon the individual is, What are the circumstances in which the individual adopts the goal of the group as his own and voluntarily works with other members to achieve it?

It is apparent that an individual will work for a group goal only if he believes that its achievement promotes his own purposes. Deutsch (1949) approximated this condition in a well-known study. Ten experimental groups were formed, each made up of five college students who were participating in the group as a substitute for part of the regular class work in a course in introductory psychology. The groups met for one three-hour period each week for six consecutive weeks to work on puzzles and human-relations problems. In five of the groups the students were told that their individual course grades would depend upon how well the group as a whole did in comparison with four other similar groups. In these *cooperatively organized* groups, the individual purpose of each member (attaining a high course grade) was thus linked to the group goal. In the remaining five groups the subjects were told that they would receive different course grades depending upon the quality of their individual contributions to the group's solutions of the problems. In these *competitively organized* groups, one student could achieve his individual purpose only at the expense of the other students.

As compared with the competitively organized groups, the cooperative group showed the following characteristics:

1. Stronger individual motivation to complete the task of the group.
2. Greater division of labor and greater coordination of effort.
3. More effective communication among members.
4. More friendliness and greater satisfaction with the work of the group.
5. Greater productivity: The cooperative groups solved the puzzle more rapidly and produced longer and better solutions of the human-relations problems.

Deutsch's work contains one source of possible ambiguity. In his study, the cooperatively organized groups were competing with other groups for high course grades. Cooperation within these groups may then have been affected by the competition between groups.

Julian and Perry (1965) have examined the effects of "pure cooperation," "group competition," and "individual competition" upon productivity and member satisfaction. These investigators compared four-member groups of students formed to work out a laboratory exercise in experimental psychology. In the pure-cooperation conditions, the students were informed that individual grades would be assigned on the basis of the number of team points: Each member of those teams that received 90 per cent of the possible points would get an "A," 80 per cent a "B," and so on. In the group-competition conditions, the students were told that individual grades would be determined by the relative standings of the groups; each member of the team producing the best exercise would receive an "A," the next best team a "B," and so on. In the individual-competition condition, grades were assigned on an individual basis, the best paper receiving an "A," the next best a "B," and so on.

The quantity of output was measured by the number of words used in developing a research design and in presenting the exploratory material. Quality was judged in terms of the logical orderliness of the hypotheses and research design. Individual and group competition both produced a high quantity and a high quality of performance. The pure-cooperation condition resulted in the lowest level of group performance. In the pure-cooperation condition, however, the students were most satisfied with their relationships with other group members.

A caution: It may be that American students have "learned to learn" in individual- or group-competition situations. In a purely cooperative Utopia, if there ever is one, students in a pure-cooperation condition might be more productive than students in either individual- or group-competition conditions. The cooperative motive, no less than the competitive motive, may be learned.

Individual Versus Group Problem Solving

We have been concerned with the question of whether or not the *individual's* own performance changes when he works in a group. Now we turn to the question of the relative efficiency of individual versus group problem solving; group achievement—*not* the separate achievements of individuals working in a group setting —is pitted against the achievement of individuals working alone. The performances of groups —teams, assemblies, committees, commissions, councils, juries—are often assumed to be better than the *sum* of the achievements of isolated individuals of the same number. Certainly, they are expected to be better than those of a single individual. Two heads are better than one, we are told. But are they?

The comparison of the relative effectiveness of individual *versus* group problem solving is one of the few problems in social psychology in which there has been sustained interest. Work on this problem dates back to 1895 and continues unabated today.

Despite the long history—long in the short history of experimental social psychology—the problem remains confused. On one hand, a number of studies suggest that groups are superior to individuals; on the other hand, there are studies that suggest that groups are inferior to individuals. For example, in a study by Barnlund (1959), the superiority of a group solution versus pooled individual solutions was clearly established. The task was to choose among several possible conclusions in a series of logical syllogisms. Two parallel forms of a thirty-item syllogism test were constructed. Each subject first worked out his own solutions to all of the syllogisms on one form of the test. Eight or nine weeks later he was placed in a group with other subjects who had secured similar scores on the test. Each group was thus formed of individuals with similar ability. The groups were then given the task of solving through group discussion the thirty syllogisms in the second form of the test. The group solutions were compared with, first, the average individual scores of the members on the first form and, second, a computed majority score arrived at by treating the individual solutions as individual votes in determining the majority decision.

The group solutions were found to be clearly superior in both comparisons. A control group of subjects took the two forms of the test as individuals at two different times. They showed no significant change. The superiority of the discussion group is not then due to practice or familiarity with syllogisms.

Along the same lines, in 1938 Osborn, a prominent advertising executive, developed and promoted a technique of group problem solving that he called "brainstorming" (see Osborn, 1957). The essence of the technique is an absolute moratorium on all criticism by others on any ideas presented. Osborn claimed that "the average person can think up twice as many ideas when working with a group than when working alone" (but see Box 176, p. 830).

The question we raised is seemingly simple and straightforward: What is the relative efficiency of individual versus group problem solving? The evidence suggests that the question is a vastly complex one. There is no one answer. It now appears that the answer will depend upon such contingent factors as the nature of the task, the distribution of ability among group members, the arrangements for dividing and coordinating the activities of group members, the scheme for combining individual efforts into a group solution, and so on.

Conformity to Group Pressure

What happens when an individual, in trying to make a judgment on a matter, is confronted with strong pressure from the group in a contradictory direction? And, especially, what happens when he feels that his perceptions are valid, his judgment correct, his solution the right one, and yet there is a unanimous consensus of his fellows against him?

Asch (1956) has carried out a series of experimental studies on this question. His technique was to make up groups consisting of one genuine subject and various numbers (from three to ten) of other "subjects" who were actually confederates of the experimenter. These confederates were instructed beforehand to give unanimously wrong judgments at certain points during a series of visual judgments as to which one of three lines projected on a screen before the group was equal in length to a standard line. The purpose was to see how the one genuine subject (who gave his judgment as the last one in the group) would respond—whether or not he would yield to the group pressure. Would he give an answer contradictory to his own judgment, or would he remain independent of the group pressure and call them as he saw them?

The effects of group pressure proved to be very strong. About one-third of all the genuine subjects gave judgments markedly distorted in the direction of the false group consensus. And they did so even though the difference between the correct line and the line picked by the confederates was so large that anyone free from the group pressure would never have made a mistake. Furthermore, experimental variations showed that the size of the unanimous group consensus was a significant factor. When the group consisted of only one confederate and a genuine subject, the subject remained completely independent. With two against him, there was appreciable conformity; and, with three against him, the conformity reached a high level. Beyond that point—even with fifteen confederates—there was no increase in conformity. If a "partner" were introduced who consistently gave the correct answer, this virtually abolished conformity in the subject. Having the social support of just one other group member was apparently sufficient to strengthen resistance to an otherwise overpowering group pressure. Strength of stimulus structure was also a factor. As the perceptual difference between the correct and "false" lines was diminished, the amount of conformity greatly increased.

Personality Factors in Conformity Studies by Crutchfield (1955) show that there are large and consistent individual differences in tendency to conform or to remain independent under such group pressure. The experimental technique he used to measure conformity behavior is described in Box 177, p. 832.

More than 450 persons, varying in age, education, social background, intelligence, and personality characteristics, have been tested in Crutchfield's "standard group pressure" procedure. Included have been samples of military officers, college undergraduates, medical students, and middle-aged alumnae of a women's college. In all these samples the range of individual differences in total conformity scores has been enormous, extending from virtually complete independence on all items exhibited by some persons to virtually complete conformity on all items in other persons.

Many of these persons were tested as part of a larger intensive assessment of their personalities. Analysis of those personality variables found to correlate significantly with conformity scores revealed the following main characteristics of the male individual who is able to withstand the group pressure and remain independent:

1. Intelligence, as measured by standard mental tests;
2. Originality, as manifested in thought processes and problem solving;
3. "Ego strength," that is, the ability to cope effectively despite stressful circumstances;
4. Self-confidence and absence of anxiety and inferiority feelings;
5. Optimal social attitudes and behavior like tolerance, responsibility, dominance, and freedom from disturbed and dependent relationships with other people.

Box 176

Brainstorming

D. W. Taylor, P. C. Berry, and C. H. Block conducted an experiment to test the effectiveness of brainstorming. These investigators compared the problem-solving effectiveness of four-person brainstorming groups with that of so-called "nominal" groups composed of the same number of individuals who worked independently. The performance of the nominal groups controlled for the influence of group size per se, and it would equal the level of effectiveness of brainstorming groups if *participation* in fact neither hinders nor facilitates problem solving. The task of the subjects—Yale University students in an undergraduate course—was to suggest as many solutions as possible to each of three problems, with twelve minutes allowed to work on each. One of the problems was the "education problem":

"Because of the rapidly increasing birthrate beginning in the 1940's, it is now clear that by 1970 public school enrollment will be very much greater than it is today. In fact, it has been estimated that if the student-teacher ratio were to be maintained at what it is today, fifty per cent of all individuals graduating from college would have to be induced to enter teaching. What different steps might be taken to insure that schools will continue to provide instruction at least equal in effectiveness to that now provided?"

The rather startling finding—startling in view of Osborn's claims for group brainstorming—was that for each of the three problems, the nominal groups produced an average of twice as many solutions as the real groups. Furthermore, the number of original and qualitatively superior solutions produced by the nominal groups was also found to be greater than the number produced by the real groups. These results mean that brainstorming was far better when conducted individually than when conducted in a group.

This study has been criticized on the grounds that the subjects were college students who were not accustomed to working together in brainstorming sessions. The relative ineffectiveness of such ad hoc groups does not necessarily mean that stable, functioning groups are inferior to individuals.

It is also found that, on the average, females are more conforming than males. And there are indications that the basis for conforming or for remaining independent of group pressure in the females lies not mainly in the types of factors listed for the males but in their acceptance or rejection of the culturally stereotyped feminine role of passivity, dependence, and compliance.

The data also clearly reveal that there are different kinds of conforming behavior. Some persons conform in the group-pressure situation in an "expedient" way. They express outward agreement with the false group consensus though inwardly they do not believe it to be correct. That they do so is shown by the fact that, when they are tested privately on the attitude items after the group session, they revert completely to their own initial personal opinions, showing no aftereffects of their compliance to the group consensus. Other subjects, on the other hand, seem to conform mainly out of the doubts about their own judgments engendered in them by the contrary group opinion. Thus, they continue to show some of the aftereffects of the group pressure when

To meet this objection, M. D. Dunnette, J. Campbell, and K. Jaastad repeated the Taylor study with industrial employees as subjects. These men were research scientists and advertising personnel employed by a large corporation. Furthermore, Dunnette and his colleagues modified the design of the previous study in order to allow the subjects to participate in both individual and group brainstorming sessions. The problems were the same as those used by Taylor, *et al.*, with the addition of a fourth problem, the "people problem":

"Suppose that discoveries in physiology and nutrition have so affected the diet of American children over a period of twenty years that the average height of Americans at age 20 has increased to 80 inches and the average weight has about doubled. Comparative studies of the growth of children during the last five years indicate that the phenomenal change in stature is stabilized so that further increase is not expected. What would be the consequences? What adjustments would this situation require?"

The table presents the mean total number of different solutions produced by the various groups. These data indicate that individual brainstorming produced more different ideas and solutions than did group brainstorming. Nominal groups of four persons, brainstorming as individuals, produced about one-third more different solutions than did the same persons brainstorming in a group situation. And the quality of the solutions achieved by the individual brainstormers was equal to or greater than that of the group brainstormers.

	RESEARCH PERSONNEL		ADVERTISING PERSONNEL	
	Nominal Groups	*Real Groups*	*Nominal Groups*	*Real Groups*
Total (both problems of each set)	140	110	141	97
Thumbs and people problems	78	61	83	60
Education and tourist problems	62	49	58	37

D. W. TAYLOR, P. C. BERRY, and C. H. BLOCK. 1958. Does Group Participation When Using Brainstorming Facilitate or Inhibit Creative Thinking? *Admin. Sci. Quart.*, 3, 23–47.

M. D. DUNNETTE, J. CAMPBELL, and K. JAASTAD. 1963. The Effects of Group Participation on Brainstorming Effectiveness for Two Industrial Samples, *J. Appl. Psychol.*, 47, 30–7. Table adapted by permission of American Psychological Association.

tested privately even some weeks after the group session.

Those persons who remain independent of the group pressure may also be divided into several types. Some of them seem to resist the group pressure because they are rebellious and hostile toward other people; they may even move away from their own initial opinion in the direction opposite to the group consensus. They are, in a word, deliberate nonconformists. Some other independent subjects may be regarded as "true" independents. That is, they are able to resist the group pressure toward a

false answer apparently because of their intelligence, self-confidence, and "ego strength."

A cautionary epilogue to this conclusion: The demonstration of relationships between personality characteristics and conformity in one situation does not establish their existence in different situations. There appears to be only a limited tendency for persons to conform consistently over a variety of situations. The conformity behavior of the individual is determined by more than personality factors alone. Whether or not the individual conforms and how much he conforms seem to be more im-

Box 177

The Measurement of
Conformity

In work at the University of California's Institute of Personality Assessment and Research, R. S. Crutchfield has developed a technique that reproduces the essential conditions of the Asch group-pressure procedure (see p. 829) but avoids the necessity of confederates and makes all subjects in the group situation genuine subjects. An electrical communication network is used.

Five persons engage in a task in which they express their individual judgments of various kinds of stimuli, for example, determining the relative lengths of lines, choosing the answers to simple arithmetic problems, stating opinions on social issues. The stimuli are presented by slides projected on the wall in front of the group. Each person is seated in his own open cubicle, facing a switchboard. The group members are not permitted to talk directly with one another; they are permitted to communicate only indirectly through these switchboards. Each person indicates his judgment by closing one of the numbered switches on his board, and in so doing turns on certain signal lights on the switchboards of the other members. Each person in the group can thus see what judgments his fellows make on each item.

The five subjects are instructed by the experimenter to respond in a pre-established order; that is, one person is designated to give his judgment first, another second, and so on. This order of responding is rotated throughout the session, so that each person responds in each of the five serial positions.

But the subjects are being grossly deceived by the experimenter. Actually, there is *no* electrical connection among their switchboards; all the signals that allegedly show the judgments of their

portantly determined by such factors as the nature of the items being judged, the individual's perception of the particular group situation, his expectations of the consequences of conforming or failing to conform, and the strength of conviction he feels.

The Sources of Conformity

The studies of group pressure leave little doubt that the individual is powerfully influenced by the group. But why? What are the sources of conformity? We turn now to this question.

Deutsch and Gerard (1955) distinguish between two types of group influence, which they term "normative" and "informational." They define *normative group influence* as an influence to conform with the positive expectations of others. By "positive expectations" they mean those expectations whose fulfillment by persons leads to positive feelings, for example, feelings of solidarity, self-esteem, and so on. *Informational social influence* they define as an influence to accept information obtained from other persons as evidence about reality.

Informational Social Influence

As we have often suggested throughout this text, all cognitive activity—imagining, thinking, and reasoning—is an attempt to find meaning

fellow members are really being "fed" to them by the experimenter. All five subjects always receive the same information; for instance, at a given point each is falsely told that he is answering second, and each is told the same (nonexistent) answer of his (nonexistent) predecessor.

Through this deception, the experimenter can confront the subjects at certain points in the session with deliberately contrived conflicts. He does so by making it appear that all the other four members agree on a false answer. The individual's conformity tendency can thus be measured by determining the number of items on which he expresses agreement with this false group consensus and the number on which he gives the correct answer, or the judgment that he privately believes.

The amount of conformity behavior elicited by this technique is remarkably high. On easy perceptual comparisons and simple arithmetical problems, as many as 30 per cent of the subjects will conform to the false group consensus. When the arithmetical problem is made highly ambiguous (it is actually insoluble), as many as 80 per cent of the subjects can be induced to accept the clearly illogical answer allegedly agreed upon by the rest of the group. And the conformity tendencies on social issues are equally striking. For example, an expression of agreement or disagreement was called for on the following statement: "Free speech being a privilege rather than a right, it is proper for a society to suspend free speech whenever it feels itself threatened." Among control subjects answering outside the group-pressure situation, only 19 per cent expressed agreement. But, among the experimental subjects confronted with a unanimous group consensus purporting to agree with the statement, *58 per cent* expressed agreement.

As many as fifty different items on which there is such group pressure may be included in a single session. It is easily possible therefore to determine a total conformity score for each individual. These scores can then be used to study the relation of individual differences in conformity behavior to personality factors (see p. 829).

R. S. CRUTCHFIELD. 1955. Conformity and Character, *Amer. Psychol.*, 10, 191–8.

and read sense into the information continually impinging upon us from the outside world. Each of us lives in a complex, constantly changing social environment that places demands upon him to behave correctly—a social environment that provides him with no objective, logical, or empirical tests of correctness. What is the right way to worship God? Which is the best political party? What are the proper standards of sexual behavior? When we face such questions, we tend to seek answers through accepting agreement by others. Consensual validation—what many people agree on as true—provides the individual with evidence that he is behaving in a logical, correct manner.

An experiment by Hood and Sherif (1962) illustrates the operation of informational social influence. They used the autokinetic effect, which, as we have seen on p. 222, is a phenomenon in which a stationary pinpoint light, exposed in an otherwise completely dark room, will seem to move. The purpose of the experiment was presented to the subjects as a test of visual ability under conditions of low illumination.

Before he made any judgments of the extent of movement of the light, the subject was instructed to wait in the laboratory to allow time for dark adaptation to occur. While waiting he overheard another "subject," whom he had never seen, make eighteen judgments of the extent of autokinetic movement. This "subject" was a confederate of the experimenters. After making his judgments, he left the laboratory and did not return. The subject thus never committed himself in the presence of the confederate.

The experimenter encouraged the subject to make his judgments as he saw the situation. For one-half the subjects, the judgments of the previously overheard confederate had fallen within a range of one to five inches, most frequently at three inches; for the remaining half, the judgments of the confederate had been distributed between six and ten inches, most of them eight inches. The median judgment of the subjects who overheard the smaller estimates was found to be 4.0 inches; the median judgment of the subjects who overheard the longer estimates was 6.8 inches. Eighty-one per cent of the first group's judgments fell below five inches (the most they had overheard), and 70 per cent of the second group's values were above six inches (the lowest estimate overheard). The "correct" amount of movement to see was apparently determined by a tendency to agree with the information—or misinformation—provided by another person.

Normative Social Influence

A study by Milgram (1964) illustrates the operation of normative social influence. The purpose of the experiment was explained to the subjects as a study of the effects of punishment upon learning in the context of a "collective teaching" situation. The basic experimental situation was one in which a team of three "teachers" (two of whom were confederates of the experimenter) tested a fourth person, the "learner" (also a confederate of the experimenter), on a verbal-learning task. The teachers were told that the learner must be shocked each time he made an error, the amount of shock being determined by the teachers themselves. In his instructions, the experimenter emphasized that the teachers could stick to one level of shock or raise or lower the level as they wished, the shock administered on any trial being the *lowest* level suggested by *any* of the three teachers on that trial. Teachers 1 and 2 (the confederates of the experimenter), according to prearrangement, called for a 15-volt increase each time the learner erred. The naïve subject, teacher 3, was always the last person asked to indicate the level of shock to be administered for an error on any trial. On any trial, he could thus effectively control the maximum shock administered to the learner. Under the rules of the experiment, he could hold the shock level down to the initial 15-volt level throughout the entire session, or he could go along with the choices of the two confederates. The naïve subject, as teacher 3, administered the shock by depressing the appropriate level on a shock generator. The shock generator was a seemingly authentic instrument, bearing the fictitious label "Shock Generator, Type ZLB, Dyson Instrument Company, Waltham, Mass. Output 15 volts—450 volts." No subject suspected that the instrument was merely a simulated shock generator, actually incapable of delivering shocks. (For some considerations regarding the problem of misleading subjects, see Box 178, p. 835.)

The learner was strapped in an "electric-chair apparatus" in a room adjoining the room in which his teachers were seated before the shock generator. His responses were relayed to the teachers through a communication system. According to a prearranged schedule, he made thirty errors in the total series of forty trials. In addition, as the shocks administered to him in these error or "critical" trials became stronger and stronger, he grunted, protested, and demanded to be let out of the experiment. Each complaint of the learner had been prerecorded on tape, coordinated to a specific shock level. The learner indicated no discomfort until the 75-volt shock was administered, to which he responded with a slight grunt. Similar responses followed shocks of 90 and 105 volts.

Box 178

Ethics and Psychological Research

It may have impressed (and depressed) the reader that deception seems to be a major tactic in the experimental social psychologist's research. In almost every experiment reviewed in this unit, for example, the dignity or the integrity of either subject or experimenter has been threatened. In the views of many, the experimenter who deceives a subject about the purpose of an experiment (whether explicitly or implicitly) or about the conditions under which the subject is working is thereby demeaning both the subject (who has entered into the experiment in good faith) and himself (insofar as the subject will now have to reassess his evaluation of the experimenter's trustworthiness and of scientists in general). This matter has become of increasing concern to psychologists for two major reasons. First, of course, there is the question of ethics and simple individual dignity or self-regard. By what authority, it is asked, does the experimental psychologist take it upon himself to deceive any person—child, student, volunteer, or paid subject? Second, there is the purely "scientific" cost of deception. If the deception "works" and the subject really is "had," it is obvious that experimentation can work but once; the word will soon get around, and the "credibility gap" between subject and psychologist will widen. This practice risks a long-time erosion of a relationship of trust between experimenters and their subjects—an outcome that would ultimately be fatal to progress in research in human behavior.

Psychologists know all these things and worry much about them. An "easy" answer might be that one should employ deception *only* when there are no other means for accomplishing the conditions necessary for the experiment and when the experiment is an important one. But who is to say that the experiment is an important one—the experimenter, who is deeply involved, or the subject, who might be very little concerned? And who is to say that this experiment is worth the indignity of being deceived—the subject who is being fooled, or the experimenter who is doing unto others?

Some psychologists have suggested that, when the researcher faces a situation in which it appears he must use deception, he should reconsider his experimental design and seek another solution. This can frequently be done. As Herbert C. Kelman, a social psychologist at The University of Michigan, observes:

"There *are* alternative procedures that, for many purposes, may be as effective or more effective than procedures built on deception. These approaches often involve a radically different set of assumptions about the role of the subject in the experiment: they require us to *use* the subject's motivation to cooperate rather than to bypass it; they may even call for increasing the sophistication of potential subjects."

Kelman concludes with the plea that psychologists devote some of their energies to active exploration of these alternative approaches. Such explorations, however, are not certain to succeed. Alternatives to deception *may simply not exist for certain psychological questions*. In this event, should psychologists accept the fact that those questions must remain "nonresearchable"? Should they place a self-imposed limit on their scientific activity—in the name of human values and dignity? This is a most difficult question to answer and, it may be pointed out, is faced not only by the psychologist. Many kinds of medical researchers also face the same dilemma, often in exacerbated forms. It is indeed an ancient and grievous question for anyone who would experiment with his fellow man.

H. C. KELMAN. 1967. Human Use of Human Subjects: The Problem of Deception in Social Psychological Experiments, *Psychol. Bull.*, 67, 1–11.

At 120 volts, the learner shouted to the experimenter that the shocks were becoming painful. On the administration of the 135-volt shock, the learner cried out that he wanted to be released from the experiment, complaining of a heart disturbance (while being strapped into the electric chair in the presence of the three teachers, he had "incidentally" mentioned that he suffered from a mild heart condition). Cries of this sort continued with rising intensity until, at 180 volts, the learner cried out, "I can't stand the pain." At 285 volts his response to the shock was an agonized scream. At 300 volts, he shouted in desperation that he would no longer give answers to the learning task. Thereafter he remained mute.

A second group of subjects was tested in a control condition in which one naïve subject was the sole teacher. He was instructed to administer the shock each time the learner committed an error and was told that, as teacher, he was free to choose any shock level on any of the trials. In all other respects the control experimental conditions were identical.

The results are shown in Figure 50.1. Inspection of the figure indicates that the experimental subjects were mightily influenced by the two confederates, whose suggested shock levels are shown in the "stooge group" curve. Milgram comments:

"Subjects are induced by the group to inflict pain on another person at a level that goes well beyond levels chosen in the absence of social pressures. Hurting a man is an action that for most people carries considerable psychological significance; it is closely tied to questions of conscience and ethical judgment. It might have been thought that the protests of the victim and inner prohibitions against hurting others would have operated effectively to curtail the subjects' compliance."

So it might have been thought. Twenty-seven of the forty experimental subjects continued, however, to administer shocks of increasing intensity after the learner had cried out, at 150 volts, that he wanted to be let out of the

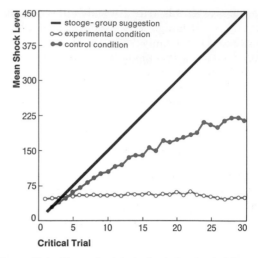

Figure 50.1. Mean simulated shock level administered by forty subjects experiencing "stooge group"-suggested levels and by forty subjects not exposed to suggestion.

experiment, complaining of a heart disturbance. Seven of the experimental subjects never stopped yielding, going along with the "stooge group" to the maximum shock level of 450 volts. Among the forty control subjects, only two administered shocks greater than 150 volts.

This experiment shows normative group influence in action, when the group supports cruel treatment of another human being. But group pressure can also have a salutary effect.

A second study by Milgram (1965) illustrates that normative group influence can lead to humane behavior. In this study, both teachers 1 and 2 (again confederates of the experimenter) defied the experimenter, refusing to continue to administer any shock at all to the learner. In these disobedient groups of forty subjects, thirty-six joined in defying the experimenter.

This result, although indicating that normative social influence can also further good, supports the general conclusion of Milgram's earlier experiment. In both instances, the individual goes along with the group, apparently irrespective of his true (though unknown) inclinations. Although benign effects of group pressure are certainly less unsettling than are malignant ones, it is difficult to draw encouragement from either phenomenon. Serious doubts as to human susceptibility linger, no matter what the direction in which the individual bows to the group.

The Crisis of Conscience

Milgram's first study demonstrates that man will treat his fellow man in a brutal and inhumane manner in response to malevolent group authority, and this result is in no way softened by the later finding.

In commenting on the implications of his work, Milgram quotes from Harold J. Laski's (1929) essay, "The Dangers of Obedience":

". . . [C]ivilization means, above all, an unwillingness to inflict unnecessary pain. Within the ambit of that definition, those of us who heedlessly accept the commands of authority cannot yet claim to be civilized men. . . . our business, if we desire to live a life not utterly devoid of meaning and significance, is to accept nothing which contradicts our basic experience merely because it comes to us from tradition or convention or authority. It may well be that we shall be wrong; but our self-expression is thwarted at the root unless the certainties we are asked to accept coincide with the certainties we experience. That is why the condition of freedom in any state is always a widespread and consistent skepticism of the canons upon which power insists."

Glossary

audience effect An instance of social facilitation in which the other persons who are present during the individual's performance are only passive spectators.

coaction effect An instance of social facilitation in which the other persons present are actively and simultaneously engaged in the same performance.

informational social influence When an individual's behavior in a group situation reflects a tendency to accept information from other persons as evidence about reality. This influence can even overwhelm evidence from one's own senses.

normative group influence When an individual's behavior in a group situation is modified to conform with what he believes the group expects of him and for which it will reward him.

social facilitation A general term, including audience and coaction effects, for the enhancement of individual performance brought about by the social presence of other persons.

Suggestions for Further Reading

Statistics and Psychological Measurement

CRONBACH, L. J. 1960. *Essentials of Psychological Testing.* 2nd ed. New York: Harper.

An elementary textbook on the construction and application of psychological tests, a highly readable account.

HAMMOND, K. R., and J. E. HOUSEHOLDER. 1962. *Introduction to Statistics.* New York: Knopf.

Presents a clear account of elementary statistical methods in psychology, with particular emphasis on the underlying logic of the methods. The book is written jointly by a psychologist and a mathematician.

HAYS, W. L. 1963. *Statistics for Psychologists.* New York: Holt.

A sound, well-presented treatment of the statistical techniques commonly employed in psychological research.

WALLIS, W. A., and H. V. ROBERTS. 1962. Paperback. *The Nature of Statistics.* New York: Collier.

An easy-to-understand presentation of the basic ideas and methods of statistics, requiring no more background than high-school mathematics.

Intelligence and Abilities

ANASTASI, A., and J. P. FOLEY. 1958. *Differential Psychology.* 3rd ed. New York: Macmillan.

A standard text in the field of psychological differences, containing considerable discussion of racial and socioeconomic differences in abilities.

GALTON, F. 1964. Paperback. *Hereditary Genius.* New York: Harcourt. Originally published 1869.

An early view, by a highly versatile scientist of the nineteenth century, of the importance of genetic factors in human intelligence. The family pedigrees of artists and oarsmen (and people with many other talents) are traced.

GUILFORD, J. P. 1967. *Nature of Human Intelligence.* New York: McGraw-Hill.

A survey by one of the most productive researchers in this field, who favors the factor-analytic approach, presenting his unifying theory of the "structure of the intellect."

HUNT, J. M. 1961. *Intelligence and Experience.* New York: Ronald.

A clear review of the course of intellectual development, with particular attention to its modifiability by experience.

TUDDENHAM, R. D. 1962. The Nature and Measurement of Intelligence. In L. Postman (ed.). *Psychology in the Making.* New York: Knopf.

An unusually lucid and entertaining account of the historical development of intelligence testing and some continuing theoretical controversies.

Personality

ALLPORT, G. W. 1965. Paperback. *Letters From Jenny.* New York: Harcourt.

An imaginative psychological analysis of an actual person, from several different theoretical points of view.

ANSBACHER, H. L., and R. R. ANSBACHER (eds.). 1964. Paperback. *Individual Psychology of Alfred Adler: A Systematic Presentation in Selection From His Writings.* New York: Harper. Originally published 1956.

As the title says, a representative look at the work of the founder of one of the first psychoanalytic schools to depart from Freud's views.

BABLADELIS, G., and S. ADAMS. 1967. Paperback. *The Shaping of Personality.* Englewood Cliffs, N.J.: Prentice-Hall.

Text and readings on the development of individuality from the point of view of social-learning theory. This approach contrasts sharply with the general psychoanalytic view.

FREUD, S. 1963. Paperback. *Outline of Psychoanalysis.* New York: Norton. Originally published 1940.

Freud's final and succinct overview of psychoanalytic theory, completed shortly before his death.

HALL, C. S., and G. LINDZEY. 1957. *Theories of Personality.* New York: Wiley.

An extremely valuable description and critique of a dozen major theories of personality, including all those discussed in this chapter.

LEWIN, K. 1935. *Dynamic Theory of Personality.* New York: McGraw-Hill.

Contains Lewin's classic discussion of the varieties of psychological conflict and their theoretical implications.

MAY, R. (ed.). 1961. Paperback. *Existential Psychology.* New York: Random House.

A collection of papers on existential psychology ranging from its development in America to its place in, and impact upon, general psychology. The purpose of the book, in the editor's words, is "to show how and why some of us who are interested in existential psychology 'got' that way."

WAELDER, R. 1964. Paperback. *Basic Theory of Psychoanalysis.* New York: Schocken. Originally published 1960.

A penetrating survey and clarification of the fundamentals of psychoanalytic theory, presented in readable form by a leading contemporary psychoanalyst.

WHITE, R. W. 1966. *Lives in Progress: A Study of the Natural Growth of Personality.* Rev. ed. New York: Dryden.

Detailed studies of the personality development of normal individuals—from their college years until later adulthood.

Mental Disorders and Psychotherapy

Psychoanalysis and psychoanalytic theory are discussed in several books in the Personality section. Waelder is particularly relevant in this respect.

KAPLAN, B. 1964. Paperback. *The Inner World of Mental Illness.* New York: Harper.

A fascinating series of first-person accounts of the experience of being seriously mentally ill.

ROGERS, C. R. 1961. *On Becoming a Person: A Therapist's View of Psychotherapy.* Boston: Houghton Mifflin.

The founder of client-centered therapy presents his special view of the role of psychotherapy in the unfolding of personal potential.

WHITE, R. W. 1964. *The Abnormal Personality.* 3rd ed. New York: Ronald.

A thoughtful and well-written textbook of abnormal psychology, rich in illustrative case material.

WOLPE, J., A. SALTER, and L. J. REYNA (eds.). 1964. *The Conditioning Therapies.* New York: Holt.

Presentations by experts in a variety of behavior therapies of the main outlines of their respective approaches.

Social Psychology

CARTWRIGHT, D., and A. F. ZANDER (eds.). 1960. *Group Dynamics: Research and Theory.* 2nd ed. Evanston, Ill.: Row, Peterson.

A collection of forty-one papers in the field of group dynamics, written by some of the outstanding experimenters and theoreticians in the field.

HYMAN, H. H. 1955. *Survey Design and Analysis.* New York: Free Press.

One of the most thorough textbooks in the field of public-opinion surveys. It deals with both theoretical and practical problems of such research.

JONES, E. E., and H. B. GERARD. 1967. *Foundations of Social Psychology.* New York: Wiley.

Comprehensive coverage of selected areas in social psychology, with emphasis on its various methodologies.

KRECH, D., R. S. CRUTCHFIELD, and E. L. BALLACHEY. 1962. *Individual and Society.* New York: McGraw-Hill.

A systematic treatment of the main areas of individual and group social psychology.

LINDZEY, G., and E. ARONSON (eds.). 1968. *Handbook of Social Psychology.* Reading, Mass.: Addison-Wesley.

A multivolume handbook, written by many authorities from the major fields of social psychology, that provides detailed coverage of both experimental facts and theoretical positions.

general glossary

ADAMSON, R. E. 1952. Functional Fixedness as Related to Problem-Solving, *J. Exper. Psychol.*, 44, 288–91. **417**

ADER, R. & P. M. CONKLIN. 1963. Handling of Pregnant Rats: Effects on Emotionality of Their Offspring, *Science*, 142, 411–2. **732**

ADLER, A. 1930. Individual Psychology, in C. Murchison (ed.). *Psychologies of 1930*. Worcester, Mass.: Clark University Press. **749**

ADORNO, T. W., E. FRENKEL-BRUNSWIK, D. J. LEVINSON & R. N. SANFORD. 1950. *The Authoritarian Personality*. New York: Harper. **704, 815**

AGRANOFF, B. W., B. E. DAVIS & J. J. BRINK. 1965. Memory Fixation in the Goldfish, *Proc. Nat. Acad. Sci. US*, 54, 788–93. **474**

ALDINGTON, R. 1924. *A Book of Characters*. New York: Dutton. **705**

ALDRICH, C. A. & M. A. NORVAL. 1946. A Developmental Graph for the First Year of Life, *J. Pediat.*, 29, 304–8. **64**

ALEXANDER, F. 1946. Individual Psychotherapy, *Psychosom. Med.*, 8, 110–5. **783**

ALLPORT, F. H. 1920. The Influence of the Group Upon Association and Thought, *J. Exper. Psychol.*, 3, 159–82. **826**

——. 1924. *Social Psychology*. Boston: Houghton Mifflin. **369**

ALLPORT, G. W. 1937. *Personality*. New York: Holt. **696, 707**

——. 1961. *Pattern and Growth in Personality*. New York: Holt. **697**

——. 1965. *Letters From Jenny*. New York: Harcourt. **838**

ALLPORT, G. W. & H. S. ODBERT. 1936. Trait-Names: A Psycho-Lexical Study, *Psychol. Monogr.*, Vol. 47, Series No. 211. **699**

ALLPORT, G. W. & P. E. VERNON. 1933. *Studies in Expressive Movement*. New York: Macmillan. **698**

ALLPORT, G. W., P. E. VERNON & G. LINDZEY. 1951. *A Study of Values: A Scale for Measuring the Dominant Interests in Personality*. Rev. ed. Boston: Houghton Mifflin. **708**

ALLYN, J. & L. FESTINGER. 1961. The Effectiveness of Unanticipated Persuasive Communications, *J. Abnorm. Soc. Psychol.*, 62, 35–40. **817**

ALTMAN, J. & G. D. DAS. 1965. Autoradiographic and Histological Evidence of Postnatal Hippocampal Neurogenesis in Rats, *J. Comp. Neurol.*, 124, 319–36. **468**

AMERICAN MEDICAL ASSOCIATION. 1966a. Effects of Space Vary, *A. M. A. News*, 3 (January 17), 1. **282**

——. 1966b. Space Dangers Met by Pilots. *A. M. A. News*, 13 (March 28), 1. **282**

AMERICAN PSYCHIATRIC ASSOCIATION. 1952. *Diagnostic and Statistical Manual of Mental Disorders*. Washington, D. C.: American Psychiatric Association. **773**

ANASTASI, A. & J. P. FOLEY. 1958. *Differential Psychology*. 3rd ed. New York: Macmillan. **838**

ERIKSON, E. H. 1959. Identity and the Life Cycle, *Psychol. Issues*, 1, No. 1. **751**

ERLENMEYER-KIMLING, L. & L. F. JARVIK. 1963. Genetics and Intelligence: A Review, *Science*, 142, 1477–8. **674**

ERVIN, S. M. 1964. Language and TAT Content in Bilinguals, *J. Abnorm. Soc. Psychol.*, 68, 500–7. **723–4**

ERVIN-TRIPP, S. & D. I. SLOBIN. 1966. Psycholinguistics, in P. R. Farnsworth (ed.). *Annual Review of Psychology*, Vol. 17. Palo Alto, Calif.: Annual Reviews. **378**

ESCALONA, S. & G. HEIDER. 1959. *Prediction and Outcome.* New York: Basic Books. **66**

ESSMAN, W. B. & M. E. JARVIK. 1960. The Retrograde Effect of Ether Anesthesia on a Conditioned Avoidance Response in Mice, *Amer. Psychol.*, 15, 498. **473**

ESTES, W. K. 1960. Learning Theory and the New "Mental Chemistry," *Psychol. Rev.*, 67, 207–23. **329**

EXLINE, R. V. & L. C. WINTERS. 1965. Affective Relations and Mutual Glances in Dyads, in S. S. Tomkins & C. E. Izard (eds.). *Affect, Cognition and Personality.* New York: Springer. **562–3**

FANTZ, R. C. 1961. A Method for Studying Depth Perception in Infants, *Psychol. Record*, 11, 21–32. **202**

FARBEROW, N. L. (ed.). 1966. *Taboo Topics.* New York: Atherton. **4**

FEDER, B. H., J. GARCIA, N. A. BUCHWALD & R. A. KOELLING. 1964. Detection of Minute Doses of Ionizing Radiation, Paper read at VII Symposium Neuroradiologicum, New York, (September). **10–11**

FEIGENBAUM, K. D. 1963. Task Complexity and IQ as Variables in Piaget's Task of Conservation, *Child Develpm.*, 34, 423–32. **393**

FELEKY, A. 1922. *Feelings and Emotions.* New York: Pioneer. **547**

FIELD, J., H. W. MAGOUN & V. E. HALL (eds.). 1959. *Handbook of Physiology, Section I. Neurophysiology*, Vol. I. Baltimore: Waverly. **284**

FISHER, G. H. 1964. Spatial Localization by the Blind, *Amer. J. Psychol.*, 77, 2–14. **190**

FITTS, P. M. 1964. Perceptual-Motor Skill Learning, in A. W. Melton (ed.). *Categories of Human Learning.* New York: Academic Press. **337, 344**

FLAVELL, J. H. 1963. *The Developmental Psychology of Jean Piaget.* Princeton: Van Nostrand. **392, 478**

FLEISHMAN, E. A. & J. F. PARKER. 1962. Factors in the Retention and Relearning of Perceptual-Motor Skill, *J. Exper. Psychol.*, 64, 215–26. **341**

FLEISHMAN, E. A. & S. RICH. 1963. Role of Kinesthetic and Spatial-Visual Abilities in Perceptual-Motor Learning, *J. Exper. Psychol.*, 66, 6–11. **343**

FLOURENS, P. 1824. *Recherches Expérimentales sur les Propriétés et les Fonctions du Système Nerveux dans les Animaux Vertèbres.* Paris: Librairie de l'Académie Royale de Médecine. **446**

FLUGEL, J. C. 1954. Humor and Laughter, in G. Lindzey (ed.). *Handbook of Social Psychology.* Reading, Mass.: Addison-Wesley. **537–8**

FONBERG, E. 1956. On the Manifestation of Conditioned Defensive Reactions in Stress, *Bull. Soc. des Sciences et des Lettres de Lodz*, 1, 1–8. **305**

FORD, C. E., K. W. JONES, C. J. MILLER, U. MITTWOCH, L. S. PENROSE, M. RIDLER & A. SHAPIRO. 1959. The Chromosome in a Patient Showing Both Mongolism and the Klinefelter Syndrome, *Lancet*, 1, 709–10. **30**

FOWLER, W. 1962. Teaching a Two-Year-Old to Read: An Experiment in Early Childhood Learning, *Genet. Psychol. Monogr.*, 66, 181–283. **395**

FREEDMAN, D. G. & B. KELLER. 1963. Inheritance of Behavior in Infants, *Science*, 140, 196–8. **732**

FRENKEL-BRUNSWIK, E. & R. N. SANFORD. 1945. Some Personality Factors in Anti-Semitism, *J. Psychol.*, 20, 271–91. **767**

FREUD, S. 1931. Libidinal Types, in J. Strachey (ed.). 1959. *Sigmund Freud: Collected Papers*, Vol. 5. New York: Basic Books. **747–8**

———. 1963. Paperback. *Outline of Psychoanalysis.* New York: Norton. Originally published 1940. **838**

FREY, M. VON & A. GOLDMAN. 1915. Der Zeitliche Verlauf der Einstellung bei den Druckempfindungen, *Zeitsch. Biol.*, 65, 183–202. **140**

FRIEDENBERG, E. Z. 1959. *The Vanishing Adolescent.* New York: Dell. **87**

FRIEDMAN, A. S. 1964. Minimal Effects of Severe Depression on Cognitive Functioning, *J. Abnorm. Soc. Psychol.*, 69, 237–43. **773**

FRISCH, K. VON. 1955. *The Dancing Bees.* New York: Harcourt. **370–1**

FROMM, E. 1941. *Escape From Freedom.* New York: Holt. **752**

FUNKENSTEIN, D. H., S. H. KING & M. E. DROLETTE. 1957. *Mastery of Stress.* Cambridge, Mass.: Harvard University Press. **546**

GAGNÉ, R. M. & H. FOSTER. 1949. Transfer of Training From Practice on Components in a Motor Skill, *J. Exper. Psychol.*, 39, 47–68. **340**

GAGNÉ, R. M. & E. C. SMITH. 1962. A Study of the Effects of Verbalization on Problem-Solving, *J. Exper. Psychol.*, 63, 12–8. **360–1**

GALL, F. J. & G. SPURZHEIM. 1810. *Anatomie et Physiologie du Système Nerveux.* Paris: Schoell. **447**

GALTON, F. 1964. *Hereditary Genius.* New York: Harcourt. Originally published 1869. **838**

GARCIA, J., N. A. BUCHWALD, B. H. FEDER, R. A. KOELLING

& L. TEDROW. 1964. Sensitivity of the Head to X-Ray, *Science*, 144, 1470–2. **10–11**

GARDNER, W. J., J. C. R. LICKLIDER & A. Z. WEISZ. 1960. Suppression of Pain by Sound, *Science*, 132, 32–3. **145**

GARRETT, H. E. 1946. A Developmental Theory of Intelligence, *Amer. Psychol.*, 1, 372–8. **668**

GATES, G. S. 1923. An Experimental Study of the Growth of Social Perception, *J. Educ. Psychol.*, 14, 449–61. **547**

GAVETT, G. I. 1925. *A First Course in Statistical Method*. New York: McGraw-Hill. **617**

GESELL, A. & C. S. AMATRUDA. 1947. *Developmental Diagnosis: Normal and Abnormal Child Development*. New York: Hoeber. **58**

GHISELLI, E. E. 1955. The Measurement of Occupational Aptitude, *U. Calif. Publ. Psychol.*, 8, 101–216. **653**

GHISELLI, E. E. & C. W. BROWN. 1955. *Personnel and Industrial Psychology*. New York: McGraw-Hill. **347–8, 653, 655, 656**

GIBSON, J. J. 1950. *The Perception of the Visual World*. Boston: Houghton Mifflin. **196–7**

———. 1963. The Useful Dimensions of Sensitivity, *Amer. Psychol.*, 18, 1–15. **147**

———. 1966. *The Senses Considered as Perceptual Systems*. Boston: Houghton Mifflin. **284**

GLANVILLE, A. D. & K. M. DALLENBACH. 1929. The Range of Attention, *Amer. J. Psychol.*, 41, 207–36. **182**

GLICK, B. S. & R. MARGOLIS. 1962. A Study of the Influence of Experimental Design on Clinical Outcome in Drug Research, *Amer. J. Psychiat.*, 118, 1087–96. **787**

GOLDHAMER, H. & A. W. MARSHALL. 1953. *Psychosis and Civilization*. New York: Free Press. **772**

GOLDMAN-EISLER, F. 1964. Hesitation and Information in Speech, in A. U. S. de Reuck & N. O'Connor (eds.). *CIBA Foundation Symposium: Disorders of Language*. Boston: Little, Brown. **381**

GOLDSTEIN, K. 1939. *The Organism: A Holistic Approach to Biology Derived From Pathological Data on Man*. New York: American Book. **498**

GOLLIN, E. S. 1954. Forming Impressions of Personality, *J. Pers.*, 23, 65–76. **798**

GOLTZ, F. 1892. Der Hund Ohne Grosshirn, *Arch. Ges. Physiol.*, 51, 570–614. **592**

GOODMAN, G. 1968. Companionship as Therapy: The Use of Nonprofessional Talent, in J. T. Hart & T. M. Tomlinson (eds.). *New Directions in Client-Centered Psychotherapy*. Boston: Houghton Mifflin. **790–1**

GOTTESMAN, I. 1963. Heritability of Personality: A Demonstration, *Psychol. Monogr.*, 77, No. 9. **544, 730–1**

GOTTSCHALDT, K. 1926. Über den Einfluss der Erfahrung auf die Wahrnehmung von Figuren, *Psy-*

chol. Forsch., 8, 261–317. **174–5**

———. 1929. Über den Einfluss der Erfahrung auf die Wahrnehmung von Figuren, *Psychol. Forsch.*, 12, 1–87. **174–5**

GOUGH, H. G. 1957. *Manual for the California Psychological Inventory*. Palo Alto, Calif.: Consulting Psychologists Press. **718**

———. 1961. *The Adjective Checklist*. Palo Alto, Calif.: Consulting Psychologists Press. **715, 725**

———. 1962. Clinical Versus Statistical Prediction in Psychology, in L. Postman (ed.). *Psychology in the Making*. New York: Knopf. **725**

GOUGH, H. G. & H. S. SANDHU. 1964. Validation of the CPI Socialization Scale in India, *J. Abnorm. Soc. Psychol.*, 68, 544–6. **718**

GRAHAM, C. H. (ed.). 1965. *Vision and Visual Perception*. New York: Wiley. **284**

GRAY, S. & R. A. KLAUS. 1965. An Experimental Preschool Program for Culturally Deprived Children, *Child Develpm.*, 36, 887–98. **395, 396**

GREGORY, B. L. 1966. *Eye and Brain*. New York: McGraw-Hill. **284**

GRIER, J. B., S. A. COUNTER & W. M. SHEARER. 1967. Prenatal Auditory Imprinting in Chickens, *Science*, 155, 1692–3. **62–3**

GROSSBERG, J. M. 1964. Behavior Therapy: A Review, *Psychol. Bull.*, 62, 73–85. **784**

GROSSMAN, S. P. 1960. Eating or Drinking Elicited by Direct Adrenergic or Cholinergic Stimulation of Hypothalamus, *Science*, 132, 872–82. **576**

GUILFORD, J. P. 1940. *An Inventory of Factors STDCR*. Beverly Hills, Calif.: Sheridan Supply. **706**

———. 1956. The Structure of Intellect, *Psychol. Bull.*, 53, 267–93. **666**

———. 1959. Three Faces of Intellect, *Amer. Psychol.*, 14, 469–79. **666**

———. 1967. *Nature of Human Intelligence*. New York: McGraw-Hill. **666, 838**

GUILFORD, J. P., R. C. WILSON, P. R. CHRISTIANSEN & D. J. LEWIS. 1951. *A Factor-Analytic Study of Creative Thinking: I. Hypotheses and Descriptions of Tests*. Los Angeles: University of Southern California Report from the Psychology Laboratory No. 3. **724**

HAAN, N. 1963. Proposed Model of Ego Functioning: Coping and Defense Mechanisms in Relationship to IQ Change, *Psychol. Monogr.*, 77, No. 8. **680**

HADAMARD, J. 1949. *Psychology of Invention in the Mathematical Field*. Princeton: Princeton University Press. **354, 406–7**

HADLER, N. M. 1964. Heritability and Phototaxis in *Drosophila melanogaster*, *Genetics*, 50, 1269–77. **35**

HAIRE, M. & W. F. GRUNES. 1950. Perceptual Defenses: Processes Protecting an Original Perception of Another Personality, *Hum. Relat.*, 3, 403–12. **804**

HALL, C. S. & G. LINDZEY. 1957. *Theories of Personality.* New York: Wiley. **838**

HAMMOND, K. R. & J. E. HOUSEHOLDER. 1962. *Introduction to Statistics.* New York: Knopf. **838**

HANES, R. M. & M. V. RHOADES. 1959. Color Identification as a Function of Extended Practice, *J. Opt. Soc. Amer.*, 49, 1060–4. **138**

HARDY, J. D. 1964. Weightlessness and Sub-Gravity Problems, in J. D. Hardy (ed.). *Physiological Problems in Space Exploration.* Springfield, Ill.: Thomas. **282**

HARDYCK, C. D., L. F. PETRINOVICH, and D. W. ELLSWORTH. 1966. Feedback of Speech Muscle Activity during Silent Reading: Rapid Extinction, *Science*, 154, 1467–8. **395**

HARLOW, H. F. 1950. Learning Motivated by a Manipulation Drive, *J. Exper. Psychol.*, 40, 228–34. **14**

HARLOW, H. F. & M. K. HARLOW. 1966. Learning to Love, *Amer. Scientist*, 54, 244–72. **534–5**

HARRELL, T. W. & M. S. HARRELL. 1945. Army General Classification Test Scores for Civilian Occupations, *Educ. Psychol. Meas.*, 5, 229–39. **653, 682**

HARRIS, G. W. 1960. Central Control of Pituitary Secretion, in J. Field, H. W. Magoun & V. E. Hall (eds.). *Handbook of Physiology Section I. Neurophysiology*, Vol. II. Baltimore: Waverly. **584**

HAYS, W. L. 1963. *Statistics for Psychologists.* New York: Holt. **838**

HEBB, D. O. 1946. On the Nature of Fear, *Psychol. Rev.*, 53, 259–76. **525**

———. 1949. *The Organization of Behavior.* New York: Wiley. **467**

HEINSTEIN, M. 1963. Behavior Correlates of Breast-Bottle Regimes Under Varying Parent-Infant Relationships, *Monogr. Soc. Res. Child Develpm.*, 28 (Series No. 88). **738**

HELD, R. & J. REKOSH. 1963. Motor-Sensory Feedback and the Geometry of Visual Space, *Science*, 141, 722–3. **204–5**

HELSON, H. 1947. Adaptation-Level as a Frame of Reference for Prediction of Psychophysical Data, *Amer. J. Psychol.*, 60, 1–29. **162–3**

———. 1964. *Adaptation-Level Theory.* New York: Harper. **162–3**

HELSON, H. & F. H. ROHLES. 1959. A Quantitative Study of Reversal of Classical Lightness-Contrast, *Amer. J. Psychol.*, 72, 530–8. **144**

HENDRICK, I. 1943. The Discussion of the "Instinct To Master," *Psychoanal. Quart.*, 12, 561–5. **497**

HENLE, M. 1942a. An Experimental Investigation of Dynamic and Structural Determinants of Substitution, *Contrib. Psychol. Theory*, 2, No. 3. **758–9**

———. 1942b. An Experimental Investigation of Past Experience as a Determinant of Visual Form Perception, *J. Exper. Psychol.*, 36, 1–21. **177**

HERON, W., B. K. DOANE & T. H. SCOTT. 1956. Visual Disturbances After Prolonged Perceptual Isolation, *Canad. J. Psychol.*, 10, 13–8. **507**

HERSHENSON, M. 1964. Visual Discrimination in the Human Newborn, *J. Comp. Physiol. Psychol.*, 58, 270–6. **504–5**

HERVEY, G. R. 1959. The Effects of Lesions in the Hypothalamus in Parabiotic Rats, *J. Physiol.*, 145, 336–52. **572**

HESS, E. H. 1956. Space Perception in the Chick, *Sci. Amer.*, 195, 71–80. **204–5**

———. 1961. Shadows and Depth Perception, *Sci. Amer.*, 204, 138–48. **202**

———. 1964. Imprinting in Birds, *Science*, 146, 1128–39. **5–6**

HESS, E. H. & J. M. POLT. 1960. Pupil Size as Related to Interest Value of Visual Stimuli, *Science*, 132, 349–50. **533**

HILGARD, E. R. & G. BOWER. 1966. *Theories of Learning.* 3rd ed. New York: Appleton. **478**

HILGARD, J. R. 1932. Learning and Maturation in Preschool Children, *J. Genet. Psychol.*, 41, 36–56. **65**

HIRSCH, J. 1963. Behavior Genetics and Individuality Understood, *Science*, 142, 1436–42. **35**

———. 1967. *Behavior Genetic Analysis.* New York: McGraw-Hill. **87**

HIRSCH, J. & J. C. BOUDREAU. 1958. Studies in Experimental Behavior Genetics: I. The Heritability of Phototaxis in a Population of *Drosophila melanogaster*, *J. Comp. Physiol. Psychol.*, 51, 647–51. **35**

HOCHBERG, J. E. 1962. Nativism and Empiricism in Perception, in L. Postman (ed.). *Psychology in the Making.* New York: Knopf. **156**

———. 1964. *Perception.* Englewood Cliffs, N.J.: Prentice-Hall. **284**

HOCHBERG, J. E. & V. BROOKS. 1962. Pictorial Recognition as an Unlearned Ability: A Study of One Child's Performance, *Amer. J. Psychol.*, 75, 624–8. **194**

HOCHBERG, J. E. & E. MCALISTER. 1953. A Quantitative Approach to Figural Goodness, *J. Exper. Psychol.*, 46, 361–4. **158–9**

HOFFMAN, M. L. & L. W. HOFFMAN (eds.). 1964. *Review of Child Development Research.* New York: Russell Sage. **87**

HONZIK, C. H. 1936. The Sensory Basis of Maze Learning in Rats, *Comp. Psychol. Monogr.*, Vol. 13, No. 64. **306**

HONZIK, M. P. 1957. Developmental Studies of Parent-Children Resemblance in Intelligence, *Child Develpm.*, 28, 215–28. **678, 679**

———. 1963. A Sex Difference in the Age of Onset of the Parent-Child Resemblance in Intelligence, *J. Educ. Psychol.*, 54, 231–7. **43, 676–7**

———. 1964. Personality Consistency and Change: Some Comments on Papers by Bayley, Macfarlane, Moss and Kagan, and Murphy, *Vita Humana*, 7, 139–42. **732**

HONZIK, M. P., J. W. MACFARLANE & L. ALLEN. 1948. The Stability of Mental Test Performance Between Two and Eighteen Years, *J. Exper. Educ.*, 18, 309–24. **664**

HOOD, W. R. & M. SHERIF. 1962. Verbal Report and Judgment of an Unstructured Stimulus, *J. Psychol.*, 54, 121–30. **833**

HORN, J. L. & R. B. CATTELL. 1966. Age Differences in Primary Mental Ability Factors, *J. Gerontol.*, 21, 210–20. **46**

HORNEY, KAREN. 1937. *The Neurotic Personality of Our Time*. New York: Norton. **750**

HOVLAND, C. I. 1937. The Generalization of Conditioned Responses, *J. Gen. Psychol.*, 17, 125–48. **292**

HOVLAND, C. I., A. A. LUMSDAINE & F. D. SHEFFIELD. 1949. *Experiments on Mass Communication*. Princeton: Princeton University Press. **817**

HOVLAND, C. I. & W. WEISS. 1951. The Influence of Source Credibility on Communication Effectiveness, *Pub. Opin. Quart.*, 15, 635–50. **816**

HOWELLS, T. H. 1944. The Experimental Development of Color-Tone Synesthesia, *J. Exper. Psychol.*, 34, 87–103. **146**

HUBEL, D. H. & T. N. WIESEL. 1962. Receptive Fields, Binocular Interaction and Functional Architecture in the Cat's Visual Cortex, *J. Physiol.*, 160, 106–54. **254–5**

HUMPHREY, G. 1948. *Directed Thinking*. New York: Dodd, Mead. **353**

———. 1963. *Thinking*. New York: Wiley. Originally published 1951. **478**

———. 1961. *Intelligence and Experience*. New York: Ronald. **838**

———. 1965. Traditional Personality Theory in the Light of Recent Evidence, *Amer. Scientist*, 53, 80–96. **503**

HYDEN, H. & E. EGYHAZI. 1962. Nuclear RNA Changes of Nerve Cells During a Learning Experiment in Rats, *Proc. Nat. Acad. Sci.*, 48, 1366–73. **471**

HYMAN, H. H. 1955. *Survey Design and Analysis*. New York: Free Press. **839**

HYMAN, R. 1964. *Nature of Psychological Inquiry*. Englewood Cliffs, N.J.: Prentice-Hall. **18**

INDIK, B., S. E. SEASHORE & J. SLESINGER. 1964. Demographic Correlates of Psychological Strain, *J. Abnorm. Soc. Psychol.*, 69, 26–38. **543**

IRWIN, O. C. 1947. Development of Speech During Infancy: Curve of Phonemic Frequencies, *J. Exper. Psychol.*, 37, 187–93. **366**

———. 1948. Infant Speech, *J. Speech Hear. Dis.*, 13, 31–4. **367**

———. 1952. Speech Development in the Young Child, *J. Speech Hear. Dis.*, 17, 269–79. **367**

ITTELSON, W. H. 1951. Size as a Cue to Distance, *Amer. J. Psychol.*, 64, 54–67, 188–202. **211**

JACOBSON, E. 1938. *Progressive Relaxation*. Chicago: University of Chicago Press. **360**

JAENSCH, E. R. 1930. *Eidetic Imagery and Typological Methods of Investigation*. New York: Harcourt. **706**

JAMES, W. 1902. *The Varieties of Religious Experience*. New York: Longmans. **536–7**

———. 1950. *Principles of Psychology*. New York: Dover. Originally published 1890. **18, 405–6**

JAMESON, D. & L. M. HURVICH. 1961. Complexities of Perceived Brightness, *Science*, 133, 174–9. **214–5**

JANIS, I. L. & R. F. TERWILLIGER. 1962. An Experimental Study of Psychological Resistances to Fear-Arousing Communications, *J. Abnorm. Soc. Psychol.*, 65, 403–10. **818**

JARVIK, M. E. & W. B. ESSMAN. 1960. A Simple One-Trial Learning Situation for Mice, *Psychol. Rep.*, 6, 290. **473**

JASPER, H. H. 1941. Electroencephalography, in W. Pentfield & T. Erickson (eds.) *Epilepsy and Cerebral Localization*. Springfield, Ill.: Charles C. Thomas. **568**

JEFFRESS, L. A. 1951. *Cerebral Mechanisms in Behavior*. New York: Wiley. **61**

JENKINS, W. O. & M. K. RIGBY. 1950. Partial (Periodic) Versus Continuous Reinforcement in Resistance to Extinction, *J. Comp. Physiol. Psychol.*, 43, 30–40. **304**

JENSEN, G. D. & C. W. TOLMAN. 1962. Mother-Infant Relationship in the Monkey, *Macaca Nemestrina*: The Effect of Brief Separation and Mother-Infant Specificity, *J. Comp. Physiol. Psychol.*, 55, 131–6. **534–5**

JOHNSON, D. L. 1967. Honey Bees: Do They Use the Direction Information Contained in Their Dance Maneuver? *Science*, 155, 844–7. **370–1**

JOHNSON, D. M. 1948. Applications of the Standard-Score I.Q. to Social Statistics, *J. Soc. Psychol.*, 27, 217–27. **683**

JONES, E. E. & H. B. GERARD. 1967. *Foundations of Social Psychology*. New York: Wiley. **839**

JONES, E. E. & R. KOHLER. 1958. The Effects of Plausibility on the Learning of Controversial Statements, *J. Abnorm. Soc. Psychol.*, 57, 315–30. **810–1**

JONES, H. E. & H. S. CONRAD. 1933. The Growth and Decline of Intelligence, *Genet. Psychol. Monogr.*, 13, No. 3. **46, 662**

JONES, M. C. 1965. Psychological Correlates of Somatic Development, *Child Develpm.*, 36, 899–912. **735**

JORDAN, H. A., S. P. ZEBLEY & E. STELLAR. 1967. A Comparison of Voluntary Oral and Intragastric Food Intake in Man. Paper read at Eastern Psychological Association Annual Meeting, Boston. **573**

JORDAN, H. A., W. F. WIELAND, S. P. ZEBLEY, E. STELLAR & A. J. STUNKARD. 1966. Direct Measurement of Food Intake in Man: A Method for the Objective Study of Eating Behavior, *Psychosom. Med.*, 28, 836–42. **573**

JOUVET, M. 1967. The States of Sleep, *Sci. Amer.*, 216, 62–72. **585**

JULESZ, B. 1964. Binocular Depth Perception Without Familiarity Cues, *Science*, 145, 356–62. **195**

JULIAN, J. W. & F. A. PERRY. 1965. Cooperation Contrasted With Intra-Group and Inter-Group Competition. Paper read at the Midwest Psychological Association Annual Meeting, Chicago. **827**

JUNG, C. G. 1923. *Psychological Types.* New York: Harcourt. **706**

KAGAN, J. 1964. American Longitudinal Research on Psychological Development, *Child Develpm.*, 35, 1–32. **49**

KAGAN, J. & H. A. MOSS. 1962. *Birth to Maturity.* New York: Wiley. **66**

KALLMAN, F. J. 1959. The Genetics of Mental Illness, in S. Arieti (ed.). *American Handbook of Psychology.* New York: Basic Books. **779**

KAMIYA, J. 1967. Conditioned Introspection. Paper read at Institute of Personality Assessment and Research, University of California, Berkeley. **12–3**

KANNER, L. 1931. Judging Emotions From Facial Expressions, *Psychol. Monogr.*, 41, Series No. 186. **547**

KAPLAN, B. 1964. *The Inner World of Mental Illness.* New York: Harper. **839**

KAPLAN, J. M. 1952. Predicting Memory Behavior From Cognitive Attitudes Toward Instability, *Amer. Psychol.*, 7, 322. Abstract. **700–1**

KARPINOS, B. D. 1961. Current Height and Weight in Youths of Military Age, *Human Biol.*, 33, 335–54. **47**

KASTENBAUM, A. 1951. An Experimental Study of the Formation of Impressions of Personality. Unpublished master's thesis, New School for Social Research. **798**

KATZ, D. 1950. *Gestalt Psychology.* New York: Ronald. **108–9**

KATZ, D. & E. STOTLAND. 1959. A Preliminary Statement to a Theory of Attitude Structure and Change, in S. Koch (ed.). *Psychology: A Study of Science,* Vol. 3. New York: McGraw-Hill. **823**

KATZ, I. 1964. Review of Evidence Relating Effects of Desegregation on the Intellectual Performance of Negroes, *Amer. Psychol.*, 19, 381–99. **690**

KATZ, I., E. G. EPPS & L. J. AXELSON. 1964. Effect Upon Negro Digit-Symbol Performance of Anticipated Comparison With Whites and With Other Negroes, *J. Abnorm. Soc. Psychol.*, 69, 77–83. **691**

KELLEY, H. H. 1950. The Warm-Cold Variable in First Impressions of Persons, *J. Pers.*, 18, 431–9. **802**

KELLOGG, W. N. 1962. Sonar System of the Blind, *Science*, 137, 399–404. **136–7**

KELMAN, H. C. 1967. Human Use of Human Subjects: The Problem of Deception in Social Psychological Experiments, *Psychol. Bull.*, 67, 1–11. **835**

KENNEDY, G. C. 1953. The Role of Depot Fat in Hypothalamic Control of Food Intake in the Rat, *Proc. Roy. Soc.*, Ser. B, 140, 578–92. **572**

KEPPEL, G. & B. J. UNDERWOOD. 1962. Proactive Inhibition in Short-Term Retention of Single Items, *J. Verb. Learn. Verb. Behav.*, 1, 153–61. **328**

KESSEN, W., E. J. WILLIAMS & J. P. WILLIAMS. 1961. Selection and Test of Response Measures in the Study of the Human Newborn, *Child Develpm.*, 32, 7–24. **66**

KILPATRICK, F. P. 1952. *Human Behavior From the Transactional Point of View.* Hanover, N. H.: Institute for Associated Research. **107**

KIMBLE, G. A. 1961. *Hilgard and Marquis' Conditioning and Learning.* 2nd ed. New York: Appleton. **303**

KIMBLE, G. A. & N. GARMEZY. 1963. *Principles of General Psychology.* 2nd ed. New York: Ronald. **294**

KIMMEL, E. & H. O. KIMMEL. 1963. A Replication of Operant Conditioning of the GSR, *J. Exper. Psychol.*, 65, 212–3. **305**

KIMURA, D. 1961. Cerebral Dominance and the Perception of Verbal Stimuli, *Canad. J. Psychol.*, 15, 166–71. **267**

———. 1963. Speech Lateralization in Young Children as Determined by an Auditory Test, *J. Comp. Physiol. Psychol.*, 56, 899–902. **267**

KLAUSMEIER, H. J. & L. J. LOUGHLIN. 1961. Behaviors During Problem Solving Among Children of Low, Average, and High Intelligence, *J. Educ. Psychol.*, 52, 148–52. **442**

KLEIN, G. S., R. W. GARDNER & H. J. SCHLESINGER. 1962. Tolerance for Unrealistic Experiences: A Study of the Generality of Cognitive Control, *Brit. J. Psychol.*, 53, 41–55. **700–1**

KLEITMAN, N. & G. CRISLER. 1927. A Quantitative Study of a Salivary Conditioned Reflex, *Amer. J. Physiol.*, 79, 571–614. **295**

KLOPFER, P. H. & J. P. HAILMAN. 1964. Perceptual Preferences and Imprinting in Chicks, *Science*, 145, 1333–4. **5–6**

KLUCKHOHN, C. & H. A. MURRAY. 1948. *Personality in Nature, Society, and Culture.* New York: Knopf. **707**

KLÜVER, H. 1926. An Experimental Study of the Eidetic Type, *Genet. Psychol. Monogr.*, 1, 71–230. **355**

KLÜVER, H. & P. C. BUCY. 1939. Preliminary Analysis of Functions of the Temporal Lobes in Monkeys,

Arch. Neurol. Psychiat., 42, 979–1000.

KNIGHT, K. E. 1963. Effect of Effort on Behavioral Rigidity in a Luchins Water Jar Task, *J. Abnorm. Soc. Psychol.*, 66, 190–2. **426**

KODLIN, D. & D. J. THOMPSON. 1958. An Appraisal of the Longitudinal Approach to Studies of Growth and Development, *Monogr. Soc. Res. Child Develpm.*, 23, No. 1. **49**

KOFFKA, K. 1928. *The Growth of the Mind.* Translated by R. M. Ogden. New York: Harcourt. **396**

KÖHLER, W. 1925. *The Mentality of Apes.* New York: Harcourt. **396, 425**

———. 1959. *Gestalt Psychology.* New York: New American Library. Originally published 1929. Hardcover, 1947; paperback, 1959. **100, 284**

KÖHLER, W. & H. WALLACH. 1944. Figural Aftereffects, *Proc. Amer. Phil. Soc.*, 88, 269–357. **166, 170**

KOHN, M. L. 1959a. Social Class and Parental Values, *Amer. J. Sociol.*, 64, 337–51. **740**

———. 1959b. Social Class and the Exercise of Parental Authority, *Amer. Sociol. Rev.*, 24, 352–66. **740**

KORTE, A. 1915. Kinematoskopische Untersuchungen, *Zeitsch. Psychol.*, 72, 194–296. **223**

KRECH, D. 1935. Measurement of Tension. Paper read at Symposium on Topological Psychology, Bryn Mawr, Pennsylvania. **512–3**

KRECH, D. 1967. Psychochemicals and Social Policy, *Ann. Internal. Med.*, 67 (Part II), 19–24; 61–7. **476**

———. 1968. Brain Chemistry and Anatomy: Implications for Behavior Therapy, in C. Rupp (ed.). *Mind as Tissue.* New York: Harper. **678**

KRECH, D., R. S. CRUTCHFIELD & E. L. BALLACHEY. 1962. *Individual and Society.* New York: McGraw-Hill. **839**

KRECH, D., M. R. ROSENZWEIG, E. L. BENNETT & B. KRUECKEL. 1954. Enzyme Concentrations in the Brain and Adjustive Behavior Patterns, *Science*, 120, 994–6. **470**

KREMERS, J. 1960. *Scientific Psychology and Naïve Psychology.* Nijmegen: Janssen. **806**

KRETSCHMER, E. 1936. *Physique and Character.* New York: Harcourt. Originally published in German 1921. **705**

KRUGMAN, H. E. 1947. Flicker Fusion Frequency as a Function of Anxiety Reaction: An Exploratory Study, *Psychosom. Med.*, 9, 269–72. **139**

LAMBERT, W. E., R. C. HODGSON, R. C. GARDNER & S. FILLENBAUM. 1960. Evaluational Reactions to Spoken Languages, *J. Abnorm. Soc. Psychol.*, 60, 44–51. **810**

LANDIS, C. 1924. Studies of Emotional Reactions: II. General Behavior and Facial Expression, *J. Comp. Psychol.*, 4, 447–501. **550–1**

LANDRETH, C. 1967. *Early Childhood.* New York: Knopf. **87**

LANGER, J., S. WAPNER & H. WERNER. 1961. The Effect of Danger Upon the Experience of Time, *Amer. J. Psychol.*, 74, 94–7. **226**

LANGFELD, H. S. 1914. Note on a Case of Chromaesthesia, *Psychol. Bull.*, 11, 113–4. **146**

LASHLEY, K. S. 1951. The Problem of Serial Order in Behavior, in L. A. Jeffress (ed.). *Cerebral Mechanisms in Behavior.* New York: Wiley. **335**

LASHLEY, K. S. & J. T. RUSSELL. 1934. The Mechanism of Vision. XI. A Preliminary Test of Innate Organization, *J. Genet. Psychol.*, 45, 136–44. **201**

LASKI, H. J. 1929. The Dangers of Obedience, *Harper's Monthly Magazine*, 159, 1–10. **837**

LAURENDEAU, M. & A. PINARD. 1963. *Causal Thinking in the Child: A Genetic and Experimental Approach.* New York: International Universities Press. **393**

LEE, B. S. 1950. Effects of Delayed Speech Feedback, *J. Acoust. Soc. Amer.*, 22, 824–6. **344**

LEE, E. S. 1951. Negro Intelligence and Selective Migration, *Amer. Sociol. Rev.*, 16, 227–33. **688**

LEEPER, R. W. 1935. A Study of a Neglected Portion of the Field of Learning: The Development of Sensory Organization, *J. Genet. Psychol.*, 46, 41–75. **176**

———. 1965. Some Needed Developments in the Motivational Theory of Emotions, in M. R. Jones (ed.). *Nebraska Symposium on Motivation.* Lincoln: University of Nebraska Press. **556, 558**

LEHRMAN, D. S. 1964. Control of Behavior Cycles in Reproduction, in W. Etkin (ed.). *Social Behavior and Organization Among Vertebrates.* Chicago: University of Chicago Press. **582–3**

LEIBOWITZ, H. W. & R. A. DATO. 1966. Visual Size Constancy as a Function of Distance for Temporarily and Permanently Monocular Observers, *Amer. J. Psychol.*, 79, 279–84. **211**

LENNEBERG, E. H. 1962. Understanding Language Without Ability to Speak: A Case Report, *J. Abnorm. Soc. Psychol.*, 65, 419–25. **372**

LESSER, G. H., G. FIFER & D. H. CLARK. 1965. Mental Abilities of Children From Different Social-Class and Cultural Groups, *Monogr. Soc. Res. Child Develpm.*, 30, No. 4. **686, 689**

LEUBA, C. & R. DUNLAP. 1951. Conditioning Imagery, *J. Exper. Psychol.*, 41, 352–5. **296–7**

LEVENTHAL, H. & P. NILES. 1964. A Field Experiment on Fear-Arousal With Data on the Validity of Questionnaire Measures, *J. Pers.*, 32, 459–79. **818**

LEVINE, S. & R. F. MULLINS, JR. 1966. Hormonal Influences on Brain Organization in Infant Rats, *Science*, 152, 1585–91. **603–4**

LEVITT, E. E. 1956. The Water Jar Einstellung Test as a Measure of Rigidity, *Psychol. Bull.*, 53, 347–70. **428**

LEWIN, K. 1935. *A Dynamic Theory of Personality.* New York: McGraw-Hill. **512, 758–9, 838**

LEWIS, M. K., C. R. ROGERS & J. M. SHLIEN. 1959. Time-Limited, Client-Centered Psychotherapy: Two Cases, in A. Burton (ed.). *Case Studies in Counseling and Psychotherapy.* Englewood Cliffs, N.J.: Prentice-Hall. **785**

LILLY, J. C. 1956. Mental Effects of Reduction of Ordinary Levels of Physical Stimuli on Intact Healthy Persons, *Psychiat. Res. Repts.*, 5, 1–9. **507**

———. 1965. Vocal Mimicry in *Tursiops:* Ability to Match Numbers and Durations of Human Vocal Bursts, *Science*, 147, 300–1. **370–1**

LINDSLEY, D. B. 1951a. Discussion, in L. A. Jeffress (ed.). *Cerebral Mechanisms in Behavior.* New York: Wiley. **61**

———. 1951b. Emotions, in S. S. Stevens (ed.). *Handbook of Experimental Psychology.* New York: Wiley. **609–11**

LINDZEY, G. & E. ARONSON (eds.). 1968 (Vols. I and II); Vols. III, IV, and V in press. *Handbook of Social Psychology.* 2nd ed. Reading, Mass.: Addison-Wesley. **839**

LIPSITT, L. P. & N. LEVY. 1959. Electrotactual Threshold in the Neonate, *Child Develpm.*, 30, 547–54. **131**

LIVSON, N. 1962. Developmental Changes in the Perception of Incomplete Pictures. Paper read at Institute of Human Development, University of California, Berkeley. **46, 152**

LIVSON, N., D. MCNEILL & K. THOMAS. 1962. Pooled Estimates of Parent-Child Correlation in Stature From Birth to Maturity, *Science*, 138, 818-20. **43**

LIVSON, N. & PESKIN, H. 1967. Prediction of Adult Psychological Health in a Longitudinal Study, *J. Abnorm. Psychol.*, 72, 509–18. **739**

LOEHLIN, J. C. 1965. A Heredity-Environment Analysis of Personality Inventory Data, in S. G. Vandenberg (ed.). *Methods and Goals in Human Behavior Genetics.* New York: Academic Press. **544**

LOEVINGER, J. 1966. Models and Measures of Developmental Variation, *Ann. N. Y. Acad. Sci.*, 134, 585–90. **45**

LONDON, I. D. 1960. A Russian Report on the Post-operative Newly Seeing, *Amer. J. Psychol.*, 73, 478–82. **203**

LORENZ, K. 1952. *King Solomon's Ring.* London: Methuen. **370–1**

———. 1966. *On Aggression.* New York: Harcourt. **612**

LORENZO, A. J. D. DE. 1963. Studies on the Ultrastructure and Histophysiology of Cell Membranes, Nerve Fibers and Synaptic Junctions in Chemoreceptors, in Y. Zotterman (ed.). *Olfaction and Taste.* New York: Macmillan. **272**

LOTT, B. E. & A. J. LOTT. 1960. The Formation of Positive Attitude Toward Group Members, *J. Abnorm. Soc. Psychol.*, 61, 297–300. **814**

LUCERO, C. B. 1961. Visual Discrimination of Camouflaged Figures. Unpublished doctoral dissertation, University of California, Berkeley. **174–5**

LUCHINS, A. S. 1942. Mechanization in Problem-Solving, *Psychol. Monogr.*, Vol. 54, No. 6. **427**

———. 1957. Primacy-Recency in Impression Formation, in C. I. Hovland, *et al.* (eds.). *The Order of Presentation in Persuasion.* New Haven: Yale University Press. **800**

LUMSDAINE, A. A. & I. L. JANIS. 1953. Resistance to Counter-Propaganda Produced by One-Sided and Two-Sided Propaganda Presentations, *Pub. Opin. Quart.*, 17, 311–8. **817**

LYNN, R. 1963. Russian Theory and Research on Schizophrenia, *Psychol. Bull.*, 60, 486–98. **779**

MCCLELLAND, D. C. & J. W. ATKINSON. 1948. The Projective Expression of Needs: I. The Effect of Different Intensities of Hunger Drive on Perception, *J. Psychol.*, 25, 205–22. **177**

MACCOBY, E. E., E. M. DOWLEY, J. W. HAGEN & R. DEGERMAN. 1965. Activity Level and Intellectual Functioning in Normal Preschool Children, *Child Develpm.*, 36, 761–70. **442**

MACFARLANE, J. W. 1938. Studies in Child Guidance: I. Methodology of Data Collection and Organization, *Monogr. Soc. Res. Child Develpm.*, Vol. 3, No. 6. **709–10**

———. 1964. Perspectives on Personality Consistency and Change From the Guidance Study, *Vita Humana*, 7, 115–26. **740**

MACFARLANE, J. W., L. ALLEN & M. P. HONZIK. 1954. A Developmental Study of the Behavior Problems of Normal Children Between 21 Months and 14 Years. *U. Calif. Publ. Child Develpm.*, Vol. 2. **543, 715**

MCGUIRE, W. J. 1957. Order of Presentation as a Factor in Conditioning: Persuasiveness, in C. I. Hovland, *et al.* (eds.). *The Order of Presentation in Persuasion.* New Haven: Yale University Press. **817**

———. 1966. Attitudes and Opinions, in P. R. Farnsworth (ed.). *Annual Review of Psychology*, Vol. 17. Palo Alto, Calif.: Annual Reviews. **818**

MACKINNON, D. W. 1938. Violation of Prohibitions, in H. A. Murray (ed.). *Explorations in Personality.* New York: Oxford. **717**

———. 1963. Creativity and Images of the Self, in R. W. White (ed.). *The Study of Lives.* New York: Atherton. **724**

MACLEAN, P. D. 1949. Psychosomatic Disease and the Visceral Brain: Recent Developments Bearing on the Papez Theory of Emotion, *Psychosom. Med.*, 11, 338–53. **609**

MCNEILL, D. 1966. Developmental Psycholinguistics, in F. Smith & G. A. Miller (eds.). *The Genesis of Language: A Psycholinguistic Approach.* Cambridge, Mass.: M.I.T. Press. **366, 374**

MAIER, N. R. F. 1933. An Aspect of Human Reasoning, *Brit. J. Psychol.*, 24, 144–55. **433, 434**

MAIER, N. R. F., N. M. GLASER & J. B. KLEE. 1940. Studies of Abnormal Behavior in the Rat: III. The Development of Behavior Fixations Through Frustration, *J. Exper. Psychol.*, 26, 521–46. **429**

MARAÑON, G. 1924. In *Revue Française d'Endocrinologie*, 2, 301. **557**

MARKS, L. E. & G. A. MILLER. 1964. The Role of Semantic and Syntactic Constraints in the Memorization of English Sentences, *J. Verb. Learn. Verb. Behav.*, 3, 1–5. **321**

MARKS, W. B., W. H. DOBELLE & E. F. MACNICHOL. 1964. Visual Pigments of Single Primate Cones, *Science*, 143, 1181–2. **239**

MARQUIS, D. P. 1931. Can Conditioned Responses Be Established in the Newborn Infant? *J. Genet. Psychol.*, 39, 479–92. **60**

MASLOW, A. H. 1954. *Motivation and Personality*. New York: Harper. **498**

———. 1962. *Toward a Psychology of Being*. Princeton: Van Nostrand. **612**

MASSERMAN, J. H. 1946. *Principles of Dynamic Psychiatry*. Philadelphia: Saunders. **766**

MASTERS, W. H. & V. E. JOHNSON. 1966. *Human Sexual Response*. Boston: Little, Brown. **579**

MATIN, L. & G. E. MACKINNON. 1964. Autokinetic Movement: Selective Manipulation of Directioned Components by Image Stabilization, *Science*, 143, 147–8. **224**

MAY, R. (ed.). 1961. *Existential Psychology*. New York: Random House. **838**

MELTON, A. W. 1963. Implications of Short-Term Memory for a General Theory of Memory, *J. Verb. Learn. Verb. Behav.*, 2, 1–21. **328**

MERRIFIELD, P. R., J. P. GUILFORD, P. R. CHRISTIANSEN & J. W. FRICK. 1962. The Role of Intellectual Factors in Problem Solving, *Psychol. Monogr.*, Vol. 76, No. 10. **443**

METZGER, W. 1953. *Gesetze des Sehens*. Frankfurt/Mainz Kramer. **154**

MICHOTTE, A. 1963. *The Perception of Causality*. New York: Basic Books. Originally published in French 1954. **228–9**

MILGRAM, S. 1963. Behavioral Study of Obedience, *J. Abnorm. Soc. Psychol.*, 67, 371–8. **717**

———. 1964. Group Pressure and Action Against a Person, *J. Abnorm. Soc. Psychol.*, 69, 137–43. **834**

———. 1965. Liberating Effects of Group Pressure, *J. Pers. Soc. Psychol.*, 1, 127–34. **836**

MILLER, G. A. 1951. *Language and Communication*. New York: McGraw-Hill. **381, 382**

———. 1964. *The Science of Mental Life*. New York: Harper. **18**

———. 1965. Some Preliminaries to Psycholinguistics, *Amer. Psychol.*, 20, 15–20. **372**

MILLER, G. A., G. A. HEISE & W. LICHTEN. 1951. The Intelligibility of Speech as a Function of the Context of Test Material, *J. Exper. Psychol.*, 41, 329–35. **380**

MILLER, G. A. & J. C. R. LICKLIDER. 1950. The Intelligibility of Interrupted Speech, *J. Acoust. Soc. Amer.*, 22, 167–73. **382**

MILLER, N. E. 1944. Experimental Studies of Conflict, in J. M. Hunt (ed.). *Personality and the Behavior Disorders*. New York: Ronald. **516**

MILLER, N. E. & R. BUGELSKI. 1948. Minor Studies of Aggression: II. The Influence of Frustrations Imposed by the In-Group on Attitudes Expressed Toward Out-Groups, *J. Psychol.*, 25, 437–52. **761**

MILNER, B. 1962. Laterality Effects in Audition, in V. B. Mountcastle (ed.). *Interhemispheric Relations and Cerebral Dominance*. Baltimore: Johns Hopkins Press. **267**

MISHKIN, M. 1962. A Possible Link Between Interhemispheric Integration in Monkeys and Cerebral Dominance in Man, in V. B. Mountcastle (ed.). *Interhemispheric Relations and Cerebral Dominance*. Baltimore: Johns Hopkins Press.

———. 1966. Visual Mechanisms Beyond the Striate Cortex, in R. W. Russell (ed.). *Frontiers in Physiological Psychology*. N.Y.: Academic Press. **454**

MISIAK, H. & V. S. SEXTON. 1967. *History of Psychology: An Overview*. New York: Grune & Stratton. **18**

MONTAGU, A. & J. C. LILLY. 1963. *The Dolphin in History*. Los Angeles: University of California Clark Memorial Library. **370–1**

MOORE, T. W. 1964. Children of Full-Time and Part-Time Mothers, *Int. J. Soc. Psychiat.*, 2, 1–10. **738**

MORGAN, C. D. & H. A. MURRAY. 1935. A Method for Investigating Fantasies: The Thematic Apperception Test, *Arch. Neurol. Psychiat.*, 34, 289–306. **721**

MOSS, F. A. 1924. Study of Animal Drives, *J. Exper. Psychol.*, 7, 165–85. **508–9**

MUELLER, C. G. 1965. *Sensory Psychology*. Englewood Cliffs, N.J.: Prentice-Hall. **284**

MÜLLER, J. 1948. The Doctrine of the Specific Energies of Nerves, in W. Dennis (ed.). *Readings in the History of Psychology*. Translated by W. Brady from *Handbuch der Physiologie*. New York: Appleton. Originally published in German 1838. **81**

MURPHY, G. 1966. Parapsychology, in N. L. Farberow (ed.). *Taboo Topics*. New York: Atherton. **7–8**

MURPHY, L. B. 1956. *Personality in Young Children*, Vol. 1. New York: Basic Books. **510–1**

MURRAY, H. A. 1933. The Effect of Fear Upon Estimates of the Maliciousness of Other Personalities, *J. Soc. Psychol.*, 4, 310–29. **178**

——. 1938. *Explorations in Personality.* New York: Oxford. **721**

MUSSEN, P. H. 1950. Some Personality and Social Factors Related to Changes in Children's Attitudes Toward Negroes, *J. Abnorm. Soc. Psychol.*, 45, 423–41. **820**

——. (ed.). 1969. *Carmichael's Manual of Child Psychology.* 3rd ed. New York: Wiley. **87**

NAKAMURA, C. Y. 1958. Conformity and Problem Solving, *J. Abnorm. Soc. Psychol.*, 56, 315–20. **442**

NATSOULAS, T. 1961. Principles of Momentum and Kinetic Energy in the Perception of Causality, *Amer. J. Psychol.*, 74, 394–402. **228–9**

NEISSER, U. 1963. The Imitation of Man by Machine, *Science*, 139, 193–7. **410–1**

NETTER, F. H. 1953. *The CIBA Collection of Medical Illustrations, Vol. I: Nervous System.* Summit, N.J.: CIBA Pharmaceutical Products. **87**

NEUGARTEN, B. L. & ASSOCIATES. 1964. *Personality in Middle and Later Life.* New York: Atherton. **69**

NEWCOMB, T. M. 1943. *Personality and Social Change: Attitude Formation in a Student Community.* New York: Dryden. **818**

——. 1956. The Prediction of Interpersonal Attraction, *Amer. Psychol.*, 11, 575–86. **805**

——. 1963. Persistence and Regression of Changed Attitudes: Long Range Studies, *J. Soc. Issues.*, 19, 3–14. **822**

NEWELL, A. J. & H. A. SIMON. 1961. Computer Simulation of Human Thinking, *Science*, 134, 2011–7. **410–1**

NEWMAN, H. H., F. N. FREEMAN & K. J. HOLZINGER. 1937. *Twins: A Study of Heredity and Environment.* Chicago: University of Chicago Press. **675**

NEYMANN, C. A. & G. K. YACORZYNSKI. 1942. Studies of Introversion-Extroversion and Conflict Motives in the Psychoses, *J. Gen. Psychol.*, 27, 241–55. **706**

NICOLSON, A. B. & C. HANLEY. 1953. Indices of Physiological Maturity: Derivation and Interrelationships, *Child Develpm.*, 24, 3–38. **49**

NISSEN, H. W. 1930. A Study of Exploratory Behavior in the White Rat by Means of the Obstruction Method, *J. Genet. Psychol.*, 37, 361–76. **497**

OLDS, J. 1961. Differential Effects of Drives and Drugs on Self-Stimulation at Different Brain Sites, in D. E. Sheer (ed.). *Electrical Stimulation of the Brain.* Austin: University of Texas Press. **575**

OLDS, J. & P. MILNER. 1954. Positive Reinforcement Produced by Electrical Stimulation of Septal Area and Other Regions of Rat Brain, *J. Comp. Physiol. Psychol.*, 47, 419–27. **575**

OLUM, V. 1958. Developmental Differences in the Perception of Causality Under Conditions of Specific Instructions, *Vita Humana*, 1, 191–203. **228–9**

OSBORN, A. F. 1957. *Applied Imagination.* Rev. ed. New York: Scribner. **828**

OSBORNE, R. T. & C. L. JACKSON. 1964. Factor Structure of the Wechsler Intelligence Scale for Children at Pre-School Level and After First Grade: A Longitudinal Analysis. Paper read at Annual Meeting of American Psychological Association, Los Angeles. **669**

OSGOOD, C. E. 1953. *Method and Theory in Experimental Psychology.* New York: Oxford. **366, 368**

OSLER, S. E. & G. E. TRAUTMAN. 1961. Concept Attainment: II. Effect of Stimulus Complexity Upon Concept Attainment at Two Levels of Intelligence, *J. Exper. Psychol.*, 62, 9–13. **442**

OSTERBERG, G. 1935. Topography of the Layer of Rods and Cones in the Human Retina, *Acta Ophthal. Suppl.*, 61, 1–102. **238**

OURTH, L. & K. B. BROWN. 1961. Inadequate Mothering and Disturbance in the Neonatal Period, *Child Develpm.*, 32, 287–95. **545**

OVER, R. 1963. Size- and Distance-Estimates of a Single Stimulus Under Different Viewing Conditions, *Amer. J. Psychol.*, 76, 452–7. **211**

OWENS, W. A. 1953. Age and Mental Abilities: A Longitudinal Study, *Genet. Psychol. Monogr.*, 48, 3–54. **662**

OYAMA, T. 1960. Figure-Ground Dominance as a Function of Sector Angle, Brightness, Hue, and Orientation, *J. Exper. Psychol.*, 60, 299–305. **167**

PAHNKE, W. N. 1963. Drugs and Mysticism: An Analysis of the Relationship Between Psychedelic Drugs and Mystical Consciousness. Unpublished doctoral dissertation, Harvard University. **536–7**

PALAY, S. L. 1958. The Morphology of Synapses in the Central Nervous System, *Exper. Cell. Res.*, Suppl. 5, 275–93. **468**

PAPEZ, J. W. 1937. A Proposed Mechanism of Emotion, *Arch. Neurol. Psychiat. Chicago*, 38, 725–43. **592**

PARKES, C. M. 1965. Bereavement and Mental Illness: Part 2. A Classification of Bereavement Reactions, *Brit. J. Med. Psychol.*, 38, 13–26. **526**

PAVLOV, I. P. 1927. *Conditioned Reflexes.* Translated by G. V. Anrep. London: Oxford. Originally published in Russian. **502**

PEAL, E. & W. E. LAMBERT. 1962. The Relation of Bilingualism to Intelligence, *Psychol. Monogr.*, Vol. 76, Series No. 27. **685**

PEARSON, K. & A. LEE. 1903. On the Laws of Inheritance in Man, *Biometrika*, 2, 357–462. **55**

PENFIELD, W. & T. RASMUSSEN. 1950. *The Cerebral Cortex of Man.* New York: Macmillan. **253**

PENROSE, L. S. & R. PENROSE. 1958. Impossible Objects: A Special Type of Visual Illusion, *Brit. J. Psychol.*, 49, 31–3. **185**

PERKY, C. W. 1910. An Experimental Study of Imagination, *Amer. J. Psychol.*, 21, 422–52. **356**

PESKIN, H. 1963. Characterological Description of Person Cluster Analyses of Case-Record Q-Sorts.

Berkeley: *Institute of Human Development Report* (mimeographed). **747–8**

———. 1967. Pubertal Onset and Ego-Functioning: A Psychoanalytical Approach, *J. Abnorm. Soc. Psychol.*, 72, 1–15. **735**

PETERSON, L. B. & M. J. PETERSON. 1959. Short-Term Retention of Individual Verbal Items, *J. Exper. Psychol.*, 58, 193–8. **327**

PFAFFENBERGER, C. J. 1963. *The New Knowledge of Dog Behavior*. New York: Howell. **36**

PIAGET, J. 1952. *The Origins of Intelligence in Children*. Translated by Margaret Cook. New York: International Universities Press. Originally published in French, 1936. **389**

PINTNER, R., A. DRAGOSITZ & R. KUSHNER. 1944. *Supplementary Guide for Revised Stanford-Binet Scale*. Stanford: Stanford University Press. **650**

PLUTCHIK, R. 1962. *The Emotions: Facts, Theories and a New Model*. New York: Random House. **550–1**

POLYA, G. 1946. *How to Solve It*. Princeton: Princeton University Press. **432, 478**

POSTMAN, L. (ed.). 1962. *Psychology in the Making*. New York: Knopf. **18**

POSTMAN, L., J. S. BRUNER & E. MCGINNIES. 1948. Personal Values as Selective Factors in Perception, *J. Abnorm. Soc. Psychol.*, 43, 142–54. **178**

POSTMAN, L. & R. S. CRUTCHFIELD. 1952. The Interaction of Need, Set, and Stimulus-Structure in a Cognitive Task, *Amer. J. Psychol.*, 65, 196–217. **178–9**

POSTMAN, L. & J. P. EGAN. 1949. *Experimental Psychology*. New York: Harper. **140**

POSTMAN, L. & L. RAU. 1957. Retention as a Function of the Method of Measurement, *U. Calif. Publ. Psychol.*, 8, No. 3. **318–9**

POSTMAN, L. & M. SCHWARTZ. 1964. Studies of Learning to Learn: I. Transfer as a Function of Method of Practice and Class of Verbal Materials, *J. Verb. Learn. Verb. Behav.*, 3, 37–49. **325**

PRATT, K. C. 1937. The Organization of Behavior in the Newborn Infant, *Psychol. Rev.*, 44, 470–90. **66**

PRIBRAM, K. H. 1962. Interrelations of Psychology and the Neurological Disciplines, in S. Koch (ed.). *Psychology: A Study of Science*, Vol. 4. New York: McGraw-Hill. **460**

PUGH, T. F. & B. MACMAHON. 1962. *Epidemiologic Findings in the United States Mental Hospital Data*. Boston: Little, Brown. **772**

PYLES, M. K., H. R. STOLZ & J. W. MACFARLANE. 1935. The Accuracy of Mothers: Reports on Birth and Developmental Data, *Child Develpm.*, 6, 165–76. **47**

RAAHEIM, K. 1965. Problem Solving and Past Experience, in P. H. Mussen (ed.). *European Research in Cognitive Development. Monogr. Soc. Res. Child Develpm.*, 30, No. 2. **439**

RAY, W. S. 1965. Mild Stress and Problem-Solving, *Amer. J. Psychol.*, 78, 227–34. **426, 435**

REICHARD, S., F. LIVSON & P. G. PETERSEN. 1962. *Aging and Personality: A Study of Eighty-Seven Older Men*. New York: Wiley. **70**

RESTORFF, H. VON. 1933. Uber die Wirkung von Bereichsbildung im Spurenfeld, *Psychol. Forsch.*, 18, 299–342. **317**

RETHLINGSHAFER, D. & E. D. HINCKLEY. 1963. Influence of Judges' Characteristics Upon the Adaptation Level, *Amer. J. Psychol.*, 76, 116–23. **162–3**

RICE, C. E. & S. H. FEINSTEIN. 1965. Sonar System in the Blind: Size Discrimination, *Science*, 148, 1107–8. **136–7**

RICHARDS, T. W. & H. NEWBERG. 1938. Studies in Fetal Behavior, *Child Develpm.*, 9, 79–86. **67**

RICHTER, C. P. 1959. Rats, Man, and the Welfare State, *Amer. Psychol.*, 14, 18–28. **603**

RIGGS, L. A., R. RATLIFF, J. C. CORNSWEET & T. N. CORNSWEET. 1953. Disappearance of Steadily Fixated Visual Test Objects, *J. Opt. Soc. Amer.*, 43, 495–501. **234**

ROBBINS, L. C. 1963. The Accuracy of Parental Recall of Aspects of Child Development and of Child Rearing Practices, *J. Abnorm. Soc. Psychol.*, 66, 261–70. **48**

ROBBINS, W. J., S. BRODY, A. G. HOGAN, C. M. JACKSON & C. W. GREENE. 1928. *Growth*. New Haven: Yale University Press. **56, 57**

ROCK, I. 1957. The Role of Repetition in Associative Learning, *Amer. J. Psychol.*, 70, 186–93. **329**

———. 1965. Adaptation to a Minified Image, *Psychonom. Sci.*, 2, 105–6. **213**

ROCK, I. & L. BROSGOLE. 1964. Grouping Based on Phenomenal Proximity, *J. Exper. Psychol.*, 67, 531–8. **155**

ROCK, I. & S. EBENHOLTZ. 1962. Stroboscopic Movement Based on Change of Phenomenal Rather Than Retinal Location, *Amer. J. Psychol.*, 75, 193–207. **221**

ROCK, I., E. S. TAUBER & D. P. HELLER. 1965. Perception of Stroboscopic Movement: Evidence for Its Innate Basis, *Science*, 147, 1050–2. **222**

———. 1961. *On Becoming a Person: A Therapist's View of Psychotherapy*. Boston: Houghton Mifflin. **839**

ROGERS, C. R. & R. F. DYMOND (eds.). 1954. *Psychotherapy and Personality Change*. Chicago: University of Chicago Press. **786**

ROSENBERG, L. A. 1967. On Talking to a Newspaper Reporter: A Study of Selective Perception, Distortion Through Rumor, Professional Gullibility, or How to Ride the *Zeitgeist* for All It Is Worth, *Amer. Psychol.*, 22, 239–40. **692–3**

ROSENBLATT, J. S. & L. R. ARONSON. 1958. The Influence of Experience on the Behavioral Effects of

Androgen in Prepuberally Castrated Male Cats, *Animal Behav.*, 6, 171–2. **584**

ROSENZWEIG, M. R. 1954. Cortical Correlates of Auditory Localization and of Related Perceptual Phenomena, *J. Comp. Physiol. Psychol.*, 47, 269–76. **266**

———. 1962. The Mechanisms of Hunger and Thirst, in L. Postman (ed.). *Psychology in the Making.* New York: Knopf. **289**

ROSENZWEIG, M. R., D. KRECH & E. L. BENNETT. 1960. A Search for Relations Between Brain Chemistry and Behavior, *Psychol. Bull.*, 57, 476–92. **470**

RUSH, G. P. 1937. Visual Grouping in Relation to Age, *Arch. Psychol. N.Y.*, 37, No. 217. **156**

SANFORD, R. N. 1937. The Effects of Abstinence From Food Upon Imaginal Processes: A Further Experiment, *J. Psychol.*, 3, 145–59. **177**

SAUGSTAD, P. & K. RAAHEIM. 1956. *Problem-Solving as Dependent on Availability of Functions.* Oslo: University of Oslo Library. **439**

SAWREY, W. L., J. J. CONGER & E. S. TURREL. 1956. An Experimental Investigation of the Role of Psychological Factors in the Production of Gastric Ulcers in Rats, *J. Comp. Physiol. Psychol.*, 49, 457–61. **734**

SAWREY, W. L. & D. H. LONG. 1962. Strain and Sex Differences in Ulceration in the Rat, *J. Comp. Physiol. Psychol.*, 55, 603–5. **734**

SAWREY, W. L. & J. D. WEISZ. 1956. An Experimental Method of Producing Gastric Ulcers, *J. Comp. Physiol. Psychol.*, 49, 269–70. **734**

SCAMMON, R. E. 0000. The Measurement of the Body in Childhood, in Harris, *et al.* (eds.). *The Measurement of Man.* Minneapolis: University of Minnesota Press. **59**

SCHACHTER, S. & J. E. SINGER. 1962. Cognitive, Social, and Physiological Determinants of Emotional State, *Psychol. Rev.*, 69, 379–99. **560–1**

SCHAFER, R. & G. MURPHY. 1943. The Role of Autism in a Visual Figure-Ground Relationship, *J. Exper. Psychol.*, 32, 335–43. **153**

SCHAFFER, H. R. 1966. Activity Level as a Constitutional Determinant of Infantile Reaction to Deprivation, *Child Develpm.*, 37, 595–602. **66**

SCHEERER, M. 1963. Problem-Solving, *Sci. Amer.*, 208, 118–28.

SCHEERER, M., E. ROTHMANN & K. GOLDSTEIN. 1945. A Case of "Idiot Savant": An Experimental Study of Personality Organization, *Psychol. Monogr.*, Vol. 58, No. 4. **668–9**

SCHILDKRAUT, J. J. 1965. The Catecholamine Hypothesis of Affective Disorders: A Review of Supporting Evidence, *Amer. J. Psychiat.*, 122, 509–22. **602**

SCHILDKRAUT, J. J. & S. S. KETY. 1967. Biogenic Amines and Emotion, *Science*, 156, 21–9. **602**

SCHLOSBERG, H. 1954. Three Dimensions of Emotion, *Psychol. Rev.*, 61, 81–8. **522–3**

SCHREINER, L. & A. KLING. 1953. Behavioral Changes Following Rhinencephalic Injury in the Cat, *J. Neurophysiol.*, 16, 643–59. **584**

SCHUTZ, F. 1965. Sexuelle Prägung bei Anatiden, *Zeitsch. Tierpsychol.*, 22, 50–103. **5–6**

SCOTT, J. P. & J. L. FULLER. 1965. *Genetics and the Social Behavior of the Dog.* Chicago: University of Chicago Press. **35**

SEARLE, L. V. 1949. The Organization of Hereditary Maze-Brightness and Maze-Dullness, *Genet. Psychol. Monogr.*, 39, 279–325. **36–7**

SEARS, R. R. 1936. Experimental Studies of Projection: I. Attribution of Traits, *J. Soc. Psychol.*, 7, 151–63. **737**

SEAY, B., B. K. ALEXANDER & H. F. HARLOW. 1964. Maternal Behavior of Socially Deprived Rhesus Monkeys, *J. Abnorm. Soc. Psychol.*, 69, 345–54. **534–5**

SEM-JACOBSEN, C. W. & A. TORKILDSEN. Depth Recording and Electrical Stimulation in the Human Brain. 1960. In Ramey, E. R. & D. S. O'Doherty (eds.). *Electrical Studies on the Unanesthetized Brain.* New York: Hoeber. **575**

SENDEN, M. V. 1932. *Raum und Gestaltauffassung bei Operierten Blindgeborenen vor und Nach Operation.* Leipzig: Barth. **203**

SHANNON, C. E. 1951. Prediction and Entropy in Printed English, *Bell Syst. Tech. J.*, 30, 50–64. **378**

SHELDON, W. H. & S. S. STEVENS. 1942. *The Varieties of Temperament.* New York: Harper. **736–7**

SHELDON, W. H., S. S. STEVENS & W. B. TUCKER. 1940. *The Varieties of Human Physique.* New York: Harper. **736–7**

SHERIF, M. 1935. A Study of Some Social Factors in Perception, *Arch. Psychol. N.Y.*, No. 187. **224**

SHERMAN, M. C. & I. C. SHERMAN. 1929. *The Process of Human Behavior.* New York: Norton. **545**

SHIELDS, J. 1962. *Monozygotic Twins Brought Up Apart and Brought Up Together: An Investigation Into the Genetic and Environmental Causes of Variation in Personality.* London: Oxford. **731**

SHURRAGER, P. S. & E. CULLER. 1940. Conditioning in the Spinal Dog, *J. Exper. Psychol.*, 26, 133–59. **448**

SIIPOLA, E. M. 1935. A Study of Some Effects of Preparatory Set, *Psychol. Monogr.*, Vol. 46, Series No. 210. **186**

SIMMEL, M. L. 1966. Developmental Aspects of the Body Schema, *Child Develpm.*, 37, 83–95. **108–9**

SIMPSON, G. G. 1966. The Biological Nature of Man, *Science*, 152, 472–8. **26–7**

SKEELS, H. M. 1966. Adult Status of Children With Contrasting Early Life Experiences, *Monogr.*

Soc. Res. Child Develpm., Vol. 31, No. 3. **679**

SKINNER, B. F. 1938. *The Behavior of Organisms.* New York: Appleton. **304**

——. 1953. Paperback. *Science and Human Behavior.* New York: Macmillan. **478**

SKODAK, M. & H. M. SKEELS. 1949. A Final Followup Study of One Hundred Adopted Children, *J. Genet. Psychol.*, 75, 65–125. **678**

SLOBIN, D. I. 1967. The Role of Imitation in Early Language Learning, in N. S. Endler, L. R. Boulter & H. Osser (eds.). *Contemporary Issues in Developmental Psychology.* New York: Holt. **374**

SMALL, W. S. 1901. An Experimental Study of the Mental Processes of the Rat, *Amer. J. Psychol.*, 12, 206–39. **305**

SMART, M. S. 1963. Confirming Klineberg's Suspicion, *Amer. Psychol.*, 18, 621. **687**

SMEDSLUND, J. 1961. The Acquisition of Conservation of Substance and Weight in Children: III. Extinction of Conservation of Weight Acquired "Normally" and by Means of Empirical Controls on a Balance, *Scand. J. Psychol.*, 2, 85–7. **314**

SMITH, B. L., H. D. LASSWELL & R. D. CASEY. 1946. *Propaganda Communication and Public Opinion.* Princeton: Princeton University Press. **816**

SNYDER, F. W. & N. H. PRONKO. 1952. *Vision With Spatial Inversion.* Wichita: University of Wichita Press. **204–5**

SOKOLOV, E. N. 1958. *Vospriiate i Uslovny Refleks (Perception and the Conditioned Reflex).* Moscow: University of Moscow Press. **504**

SOLOMON, R. L. & D. H. HOWES. 1951. Word Frequency, Personal Values, and Visual Duration Thresholds, *Psychol. Rev.*, 58, 256–70. **180**

SONTAG, L. W., C. T. BAKER & V. L. NELSON. 1958. Mental Growth and Personality Development: A Longitudinal Study, *Monogr. Soc. Res. Child Develpm.*, 23, No. 2. **680**

SPERLING, G. 1960. Negative Afterimage Without Prior Positive Image, *Science*, 131, 1613–4. **141**

SPERRY, R. W. 1961. Cerebral Organization and Behavior, *Science*, 133, 1749–57. **457**

SPITZ, R. A. 1949. The Role of Ecological Factors in Emotional Development in Infancy, *Child Develpm.*, 20, 145–56. **678**

SPRAGG, S. D. S. 1940. Morphine Addiction in Chimpanzees, *Comp. Psychol. Monogr.*, Vol. 15, No. 7. **495**

SPRANGER, E. 1928. *Types of Men.* New York: Stechert. **706**

SROLE, L., T. S. LANGNER, S. T. MICHAEL, M. K. OPLER & T. A. C. RENNIE. 1962. *Mental Health in the Metropolis: The Midtown Manhattan Study.* New York: McGraw-Hill. **772**

STENDLER, C. B. 1950. Sixty Years of Child Training Practices, *J. Pediat.*, 36, 122–34. **738**

——. 1967. Environmental Intervention in Infancy and Early Childhood, in M. Deutsch, A. R. Jensen & I. Katz (eds.). *Race, Social Class and Psychological Development.* New York: Holt. **395**

STERN, C. 1960. *Principles of Human Genetics.* 2nd ed. San Francisco: Freeman. **87**

STOUFFER, S. A., A. A. LUNSDAINE, M. H. LUNSDAINE, R. M. WILLIAMS, JR., M. B. SMITH, I. L. JANIS, S. A. STAR & L. S. COTTRELL, JR. 1949. *The American Soldier, Vol. 2.: Combat and Its Aftermath.* Princeton: Princeton University Press. **814**

STOYVA, J. & J. KAMIYA. 1968. Electrophysiological Studies of Dreaming as the Prototype of a New Strategy in the Study of Consciousness. *Psychol. Rev.*, 75, 192–205. **12–3**

STRATTON, G. M. 1897. Vision Without Inversion of the Retinal Image, *Psychol. Rev.*, 4, 341–60. **204–5**

STRAYER, L. C. 1930. Language and Growth, *Genet. Psychol. Monogr.*, Vol. 8, No. 3. **65**

STRONG, E. K., JR. 1951. Permanence of Interest Scores Over 22 Years, *J. Appl. Psychol.*, 35, 89–91. **658**

SULLIVAN, H. S. 1953. *The Interpersonal Theory of Psychiatry.* New York: Norton. **750**

SUPA, M., M. COTZIN & K. M. DALLENBACH. 1944. Facial Vision: The Perception of Obstacles by the Blind, *Amer. J. Psychol.*, 57, 133–83. **136–7**

SUTHERLAND, N. S. 1957. Visual Discrimination of Orientation by Octopus, *Brit. J. Psychol.*, 48, 55–71. **254–5**

——. 1963. Cat's Ability to Discriminate Oblique Rectangles, *Science*, 139, 209–10. **254–5**

SZÉKELY, L. 1945. Zur Psychologie des Geistigen Schaffens, *Schweitzer Zeitsch. Psychol.*, 4, 110–24, 332–47. **440**

——. 1950. Knowledge and Thinking, *Acta Psychologica*, 7, 1–24. **412, 441**

TANNENBAUM, P. H. 1956. Initial Attitudes Toward Source and Concept as Factors in Attitude Change Through Communication, *Pub. Opin. Quart.*, 20, 413–25. **823**

TANNER, J. M. 1962. *Growth at Adolescence.* 2nd ed. Oxford: Blackwell. **56, 87**

TANSER, H. A. 1939. *The Settlement of Negroes in Kent County, Ontario.* Chatham, Ont.: Shephard. **687**

TAYLOR, C. W. & F. BARRON (eds.). 1963. *Scientific Creativity: Progress and Potential.* New York: Wiley. **478**

TAYLOR, D. W., P. C. BERRY & C. H. BLOCK. 1958. Does Group Participation When Using Brainstorming Facilitate or Inhibit Creative Thinking? *Admin. Sci. Quart.*, 3, 23–47. **830–1**

TEITELBAUM, P. 1961. Disturbances in Feeding and Drinking Behavior After Hypothalamic Lesions, in M. R. Jones (ed.). *Nebraska Symposium on Motivation.* Lincoln: University of Nebraska Press. **574**

———. 1962. Motivational Correlates of Hypothalamic Activity, *Excerpta Medica, Int. Cong. Ser.,* 47, 697–704. **572**

TERMAN, L. M. & M. A. MERRILL. 1937. *Measuring Intelligence.* Boston: Houghton Mifflin. **647**

———. 1960. *The Stanford Binet Intelligence Scale: Manual for the Third Revision.* Boston: Houghton Mifflin. **651**

TEUBER, H. L. 1959. Some Alterations in Behavior After Cerebral Lesions in Man, in E. Bass (ed.). *Evolution of Nervous Control From Primitive Organisms to Man.* Washington: American Association for the Advancement of Science. **458–9**

TEUBER, H. L. & S. WEINSTEIN. 1956. Ability to Discover Hidden Figures After Cerebral Lesion, *Arch. Neurol. Psychiat.,* 76, 369–79. **458–9**

THOMAS, A., S. CHESS, H. G. BIRCH, M. E. HERTZIG & S. KORN. 1964. *Behavioral Individuality in Early Childhood.* New York: International Universities Press. **66**

THOMPSON, R. F. 1967. *Foundations of Physiological Psychology.* New York: Harper. **87, 284, 478, 612**

THOMPSON, W. R. 1957. Influence of Prenatal Maternal Anxiety on Emotionality in Young Rats, *Science,* 125, 698–9. **32–3**

THOMSON, G. H. 1952. Chapter in C. Murchison (ed.). *A History of Psychology in Autobiography,* Vol. 4. Worcester, Mass.: Clark University Press. **666**

THORNDIKE, E. L. 1898. Animal Intelligence, *Psychol. Monogr.,* 1, No. 8. **300**

THURSTONE, L. L. 1938. *Primary Mental Abilities.* Chicago: University of Chicago Press. **666**

———. 1944. *A Factorial Study of Perception.* Chicago: University of Chicago Press. **153**

THURSTONE, L. L. & E. J. CHAVE. 1929. *The Measurement of Attitude.* Chicago: University of Chicago Press. **811**

THURSTONE, T. G., L. L. THURSTONE & H. H. STRANDSKOV. 1953. *A Psychological Study of Twins.* Chapel Hill: University of North Carolina Psychometric Laboratory Report No. 4. **667**

TILLYARD, A. C. W. 1927. *Spiritual Exercises and Their Results: An Essay in Psychology and Comparative Religion.* New York: Macmillan. **536–7**

TOCH, H. E. & W. H. ITTELSON. 1956. The Role of Past Experience in Apparent Movement: A Revaluation, *Brit. J. Psychol.,* 47, 195–207. **222**

TOLMAN, E. C. 1967. *Purposive Behavior in Animals and Men.* New York: Appleton. Originally published 1932. **478**

TOLMAN, E. C. & C. H. HONZIK. 1930. "Insight" in Rats, *U. Calif. Publ. Psychol.,* 4, 215–32. **358**

TOMKINS, S. S. 1962. *Affect, Imagery, Consciousness: Vol. 1. The Positive Affects.* New York: Springer. **559, 562–3**

TOYNBEE, A. 1961. *A Study of History, Vol. 12: Reconsiderations.* New York: Oxford. **730**

TRYON, R. C. 1940. Genetic Differences in Maze Learning in Rats, in National Society for the Study of Education. *The Thirty-ninth Yearbook.* Bloomington, Ill.: Public School Publications. **36–7**

TUDDENHAM, R. D. 1948. Soldier Intelligence in World Wars I and II, *Amer. Psychol.,* 3, 54–6. **662**

———. 1962. The Nature and Measurement of Intelligence, in L. Postman (ed.). *Psychology in the Making.* New York: Knopf. **838**

TURNBULL, C. M. 1961. Some Observations Regarding the Experiences and Behavior of the BaMbuti Pygmies, *Amer. J. Psychol.,* 74, 304–8. **213**

TYLER, L. E. 1956. *The Psychology of Human Differences.* New York: Appleton. **682**

UNDERWOOD, B. J. 1957. Interference and Forgetting, *Psychol. Rev.,* 64, 49–60. **326**

———. 1962. One-Trial Learning, *J. Verb. Learn. Verb. Behav.,* 1, 1–13. **330**

UNDERWOOD, B. J. & G. KEPPEL. 1963. Coding Processes in Verbal Learning, *J. Verb. Learn. Verb. Behav.,* 1, 250–7. **320**

UNGER, S. M. 1963. Mescaline, LSD, Psilocybin, and Personality Change, *Psychiatry,* 26, 111–25. **545**

VANDENBERG, S. G. 1962. The Hereditary Abilities Study: Hereditary Components in a Psychological Test Battery, *Amer. J. Hum. Genet.,* 14, 220–37. **544, 667**

———. 1966. Contributions of Twin Research to Psychology, *Psychol. Bull.,* 66, 327–52. **731**

VAUGHN, E. & A. E. FISHER. 1962. Male Sexual Behavior Induced by Intracranial Electrical Stimulation, *Science,* 137, 758–60. **580**

VENABLES, P. H. & I. MARTIN (eds.). 1967. *Manual of Psychophysiological Methods.* New York: Wiley. **598–9**

VIGOTSKY, L. S. 1939. Thought and Speech, *Psychiatry,* 2, 29–52. **359**

WAELDER, R. 1964. *Basic Theory of Psychoanalysis.* New York: Schocken. Originally published 1960. **838**

WALD, G. 1964. The Receptors of Human Color Vision, *Science,* 145, 1007–16. **119**

WALD, G. & P. K. BROWN. 1958. Human Rhodopsin, *Science,* 127, 222. **242**

WALK, R. D. & S. H. DODGE. 1962. Visual Depth Perception of a 10-Month-Old Monocular Human Infant, *Science,* 137, 529–30. **202**

WALK, R. D. & E. J. GIBSON. 1961. A Comparative and Analytical Study of Visual Depth Perception,

Psychol. Monogr., Vol. 75, Series No. 519. **200**

WALLACH, H. 1935. Über Visuell Wahrgenommene Bewegungsrichtung, *Psychol. Forsch.*, 20, 325–80. **169, 173**

———. 1940. The Role of Head Movements and Vestibular and Visual Cues in Sound Localization, *J. Exper. Psychol.*, 27, 339–68. **193**

WALLACH, M. A. 1963. Research on Children's Thinking, in *Child Psychology: 62nd Yearbook of the National Society for the Study of Education.* Chicago: University of Chicago Press. **393**

WALLIS, W. A. & H. V. ROBERTS. 1956. *The Nature of Statistics.* New York: Macmillan. **838**

WARDEN, C. J. 1931. *Animal Motivation Studies: The Albino Rat.* (New York: Columbia University Press) **508–9**

WARNER, W. L. & P. S. LUNT. 1941. *The Social Life of the Modern Community.* New Haven: Yale University Press. **682**

WATSON, J. B. 1924. *Psychology From the Standpoint of a Behaviorist.* 2nd ed. Philadelphia: Lippincott. **524**

WECHSLER, D. 1958. *The Measurement and Appraisal of Intelligence.* Baltimore: Williams & Wilkins. **652**

WECKROTH, J. 1960. *Dimensions of Color Sensation.* Stockholm: University of Stockholm Psychology Laboratory Report No. 88. **116**

WEIR, R. 1962. *Language in the Crib.* The Hague: Mouton. **374**

WEISS, W. 1957. Opinion Congruence With a Negative Source on One Issue as a Factor Influencing Agreement on Another Issue, *J. Abnorm. Soc. Psychol.*, 54, 180–6. **817**

WELLER, G. M. & R. Q. BELL. 1965. Basal Skin Conductance and Neonatal State, *Child Develpm.*, 36, 647–57. **551**

WENNER, A. M. 1967. Honey Bees: Do They Use the Distance Information Contained in Their Dance Maneuver? *Science*, 155, 847–9. **370–1**

WERNER, H. 1948. *Comparative Psychology of Mental Development.* Chicago: Follett. Originally published 1926. **396**

WERTHEIMER, M. 1923. Untersuchungen zur Lehre von der Gestalt, *Psychol. Forsch.*, 4, 301–50. **157**

———. 1959. *Productive Thinking.* Rev. ed. New York: Harper. 1st ed. published 1945. **396, 397–8, 478**

———. 1961. Psychomotor Coordination of Auditory and Visual Space at Birth, *Science*, 134, 1692. **202, 388**

WESTBROOK, W. H. & J. L. MCGAUGH. 1964. Drug Facilitation of Latent Learning, *Psychopharmacologia*, 3, 440–6. **475**

WHITE, R. W. 1959. Motivation Reconsidered: The Concept of Competence, *Psychol. Rev.*, 66, 297–333. **497**

———. 1964. *The Abnormal Personality.* 3rd ed. New York: Ronald. **773, 774–5, 777, 839**

———. 1966. *Lives in Progress: A Study of the Natural Growth of Personality.* Rev. ed. New York: Dryden. **839**

WHORF, B. L. 1956. *Language, Thought and Reality.* New York: Wiley. **361**

WICKENS, D. D. & C. WICKENS. 1940. A Study of Conditioning in the Neonate, *J. Exper. Psychol.*, 26, 94–102. **60**

WIESNER, B. P. & N. M. SHEARD. 1933. *Maternal Behavior in the Rat.* London: Oliver & Boyd. **493**

WILLIAMS, R. J. 1956. *Biochemical Individuality.* New York: Wiley. **612**

WILLIAMS, R. M., JR. 1964. *Strangers Next Door.* Englewood Cliffs, N.J.: Prentice-Hall. **815**

WILSON, M. 1957. Effects of Circumscribed Cortical Lesions Upon Somesthetic and Visual Discrimination in the Monkey, *J. Comp. Physiol. Psychol.*, 50, 630–5. **452–3**

WILSON, W. A., JR. & M. MISHKIN. 1959. Comparison of the Effects of Inferotemporal and Lateral Occipital Lesions on Visually Guided Behavior in Monkeys, *J. Comp. Physiol. Psychol.*, 52, 10–7. **452–3**

WOLBERG, L. R. 1954. *The Technique of Psychotherapy.* New York: Grune & Stratton. **782**

WOLPE, J., A. SALTER & L. J. REYNA (eds.). 1964. *The Conditioning Therapies.* New York: Holt. **839**

WOODROW, H. 1927. The Effect of Type of Training Upon Transference, *J. Educ. Psychol.*, 18, 159–72. **324**

WORCHEL, P. & K. M. DALLENBACH. 1947. Facial Vision, Perception of Obstacles by the Deaf-Blind, *Amer. J. Psychol.*, 60, 502–53. **136–7**

YAI, H. 1959–1960. The Formation of Pressure Sense Pattern, *Japan. J. Psychol.*, 30, 32–3. **142**

YARROW, L. J. 1963. Research in Dimensions of Early Maternal Care, *Merrill-Palmer Quart.*, 9, 101–14. **679**

YARROW, L. J. & M. R. YARROW. 1964. Personality Continuity and Change in the Family Context, in R. Worchel & D. Byrne (eds.). *Personality Change.* New York: Wiley. **544**

YOUNG, J. Z. 1964. *A Model of the Brain.* London: Oxford. **254–5**

YOUNG, P. T. 1961. *Motivation and Emotion.* New York: Wiley. **556**

YOUNG, W. C., R. W. GAY & C. H. PHOENIX. 1964. Hormones and Sexual Behavior, *Science*, 143, 212–8. **583**

YUGANOV, E. M., A. I. GORSHKOV, I. I. KAS'YAN, I. I. BRYANOV, I. A. KOLOSOV, V. I. POPANEV, V. I. LEBEDEV, N. I. POPOV & I. A. SOLODOVNIK. 1966. Vestibular

Reactions of Cosmonauts During Flight in the Ship "Voskhod," *Federation Proceedings*, 25, T767–70. Translated from *Izvestiya Akademii Nauk SSSR, Seriya Biologicheskaya*, 25, No. 6 (1965), 877. **282**

ZAJONC, R. B. 1965. Social Facilitation, *Science*, 149, 260–74. **826**

ZAPOROZHETS, A. V. 1961. The Origin and Development of the Conscious Control of Movements in Man, in N. O'Connor (ed.). *Recent Soviet Psychology*. New York: Liveright. **181, 182**

ZUBEK, J. P. 1963. Counteracting Effects of Physical Exercises Performed During Prolonged Perceptual Deprivation, *Science*, 142, 504–6. **506**

index